Competition Law

Competition Law

Fourth Edition

Richard Whish BA BCL (OXON)
Professor of Law at King's College London

Butterworths
A Member of the LexisNexis Group

Members of the LexisNexis Group worldwide

United Kingdom	Butterworths Tolley, a Division of Reed Elsevier (UK) Ltd, Halsbury House, 35 Chancery Lane, LONDON, WC2A 1EL, and 4 Hill Street, EDINBURGH EH2 3JZ
Argentina	Abeledo Perrot, Jurisprudencia Argentina and Depalma, BUENOS AIRES
Australia	Butterworths, a Division of Reed International Books Australia Pty Ltd, CHATSWOOD, New South Wales
Austria	ARD Betriebsdienst and Verlag Orac, VIENNA
Canada	Butterworths Canada Ltd, MARKHAM, Ontario
Chile	Publitecsa and Conosur Ltda, SANTIAGO DE CHILE
Czech Republic	Orac sro, PRAGUE
France	Editions du Juris-Classeur SA, PARIS
Hong Kong	Butterworths Asia (Hong Kong), HONG KONG
Hungary	Hvg Orac, BUDAPEST
India	Butterworths India, NEW DELHI
Ireland	Butterworths (Ireland) Ltd, DUBLIN
Italy	Giuffré, MILAN
Malaysia	Malayan Law Journal Sdn Bhd, KUALA LUMPUR
New Zealand	Butterworths of New Zealand, WELLINGTON
Poland	Wydawnictwa Prawnicze PWN, WARSAW
Singapore	Butterworths Asia, SINGAPORE
South Africa	Butterworths Publishers (Pty) Ltd, DURBAN
Switzerland	Stämpfli Verlag AG, BERNE
USA	LexisNexis, DAYTON, Ohio

© Reed Elsevier (UK) Ltd 2001

A CIP Catalogue record for this book is available from the British Library.

1st edition   1985
2nd edition   1989
3rd edition   1993

ISBN 0 406 00266 5

Printed and bound in Great Britain by The Bath Press, Bath

Visit Butterworths LexisNexis *direct* at www.butterworths.com

Preface

This is really the first edition of a new book rather than the fourth edition of an old one. Enormous changes have occurred since the third edition was published in 1993, both in the EC and the UK. In EC law the Commission has adopted several new block exemptions; most notable of these is Regulation 2790/99, with the accompanying *Guidelines on Vertical Restraints*, which have substantially changed the way in which vertical agreements are analysed under Article 81 of the EC Treaty. The Commission has been pursuing cartels under Article 81 with great determination, and has adopted the *'Whistleblowers' Notice'* to encourage participants in cartels to provide it with information in return for leniency. The case law on Article 82 has developed considerably since 1993, in particular in relation to pricing practices, so-called 'essential facilities' and collective dominance. The EC Merger Regulation was amended in various ways by Regulation 1310/97, and a substantial decisional practice has developed; there have also been important judgments of the CFI and the ECJ on the ECMR, most notably in *France v Commission* and in *Gencor v Commission*. Most radically of all, the Commission's *White Paper on Modernisation* has proposed major changes to the way in which Article 81 is applied in practice; in particular it is intended that the Commission's monopoly over decision-making under Article 81(3) should be abandoned and that the system of notifying agreements to it for individual exemption should be abolished.

The changes to UK law have, if anything, been more fundamental than those in the EC. The second and third editions of this book discussed at length the need for, and the Government's proposals for, modernisation of the domestic law of the UK. This was finally achieved in 1998 when the Competition Act received the Royal Assent, modelling the domestic law of the UK on Articles 81 and 82. In this edition the chapters on the Restrictive Trade Practices Act 1976, the Resale Prices Act 1976 and the Competition Act 1980 have been dropped, and new chapters on the 1998 Act have been inserted in their place. The chapter on the monopoly provisions in the Fair Trading Act 1973 has been retained, and there is a specific chapter dealing with UK merger control. It became clear in June 2001 that the reform of UK competition law is by no means complete: an Enterprise Bill will be introduced into Parliament in the Spring of 2002 to introduce criminal penalties for participation in cartels, to reform fundamentally the domestic system of merger control, and to amend the law on monopoly investigations.

Competition law has never had a higher profile than it does today. Competition cases regularly feature on the front pages of newspapers and at the beginning of news bulletins: this preface is being written on the day after the European Commission prohibited the merger between GE and Honeywell, and a week after the judgment of the appeal court in the US in the *Microsoft* case. Each of these events was given considerable coverage in the media. Competition law is a key component in the economic policy of more than 80 countries in the world today. There are many differences in the substantive provisions of competition law from one country to another, but in essence these laws are concerned with one thing: preventing the abuse of market power to the detriment of consumers. The phenomena discussed in this book – cartels, tacit collusion, vertical agreements, abusive pricing practices, mergers and so on – are universal. I have attempted to place each of them in their economic context, and to explain how the law should be applied to them. I hope that the book can provide useful insights even in those jurisdictions where the substantive rules differ from those in the EC and the UK.

I have had the benefit of assistance from many friends in the world of competition law and policy in preparing this edition, too numerous to name individually here. However I would like to mention in particular the staff of the Office of Fair Trading and the Merger Task Force, Charles Dhanowa, Chris Swift, Dorte Hoeg-Nielsen, Jonas Koponen, Simon Bishop, Zoltan Biro and Cristina Caffara, all of whom provided valuable comments. I have had the great benefit of research assistance at King's College from Manish Das, Kit Brown, David Bailey, Dipesh Santilale and Sonia Jassal, each of them a great credit to the Law School here. I acknowledge with thanks the financial support of the Centre of European Law at King's College that made their assistance possible. I am very grateful to the staff at Butterworths for their endless patience; this edition was originally due to be published in 1997, and I could hardly have been more indulged. My special thanks are due to Dr Anil Sinanan, for always being there to remind me that there are other things in life than competition law.

I have been able to include developments in the law up until the end of July 2001.

Richard Whish
King's College London

Contents

CHAPTER 1
Competition policy and economics   1

CHAPTER 2
Overview of EC and UK competition law 45

CHAPTER 3
Article 81(1) 65

CHAPTER 16
Vertical agreements 535

CHAPTER 17
Abuse of dominance (1): non-pricing practices 601

CHAPTER 18
Abuse of dominance (2): pricing practices 633

CHAPTER 23
Particular sectors 853

Table of statutes

References in this Table to *Statutes* are to Halsbury's Statutes of England (Fourth Edition) showing the volume and page at which the annotated text of the Act may be found.

References in the right-hand column are to page numbers.

FOREIGN ENACTMENTS

Table of statutory instruments

References in the right-hand column are to page numbers.

Table of EC legislation

References in the right-hand column are to page numbers.

Table of MMC reports

References in the right-hand column are to page numbers.

PAGE

Table of OFT reports

References in the right-hand column are to page numbers.

Table of cases

O

PAGE

P

V

Decisions of the European Court of Justice are listed below numerically. These
decisions are also included in the preceding alphabetical list.

PAGE

List of abbreviations

ATC	Average Total Cost
AVC	Average Variable Cost
CFI	Court of First Instance
CWP	Concurrency Working Party
DG COMP	Directorate of Commission responsible for Competition Policy
DGFT	Director General of Fair Trading
DTI	Department of Trade and Industry
ECJ	European Court of Justice
ECMR	European Community Merger Regulation
ECOSOC	Economic and Social Committee
ECSC	European Coal and Steel Community
EEA	European Economic Area
EEIG	European Economic Interest Grouping
EFTA	European Free Trade Association
ESA	European Free Trade Association Surveillance Authority
ETSI	European Telecommunication Standards Institute
FETTCSA	Far East Trade Tariff Charges and Surcharges Agreement
FSA	Financial Services Authority
FTA	Fair Trading Act
FTC	Federal Trade Commission
GISC	General Insurance Standards Council
ICPAC	International Competition Policy Advisory Committee
MTF	Merger Task Force
NCAs	Natural Competition Authorities
OECD	Organisation For Economic Cooperation and Development
OFT	Office of Fair Trading
PRS	Performing Rights Society
ROCE	Return on Capital Employed
RPI	Retail Price Index
SMEs	Small and Medium-sized Enterprises
SSNIP	Small but Significant Non-transitory Increase in Price
SWIFT	Society for Worldwide International Financial Telecommunications
UNCTAD	United Nations Conference on Trade and Development
WTO	World Trade Organisation

CHAPTER I

Competition policy and economics

Competition law has grown at a phenomenal rate in recent years in response to the enormous changes in economic behaviour that have taken place around the world. The expansion of the law has been geographic: there are now at least 80 systems of competition law in the world, in all continents and in all types of economies; many others are in contemplation. Competition law has been applied to economic activities that once were regarded as natural monopolies or the preserve of the state: telecommunications, energy, transport, broadcasting and postal services, to name a few examples, have become the subject of competition law scrutiny. The liberal professions, sport and the media are also within the scope of the subject. This exponential growth in competition law will, if anything, increase in the years ahead. In this chapter an attempt will be made to explain why competition law is considered to be so vital to modern economies based on the market mechanism. It will explore first the theory of competition itself and then the various functions that a system of competition law might fulfil. The chapter will conclude with a discussion of one of the key economic concepts of fundamental importance to understanding competition law, namely market definition and its rôle in determining whether a firm or firms have market power.

Competition law is about economics and economic behaviour, and it is essential for anyone involved in the subject – whether as a lawyer, regulator, civil servant or in any other capacity – to have some knowledge of the economic concepts concerned. As Brandeis J once said 'A lawyer who has not studied economics ... is very apt to become a public enemy'[1]. In the early days of competition law in the European Community the rôle of economics was insufficiently recognised, at a time when the politics of market integration were in the ascendant; however the position has changed substantially, and competition lawyers now regularly work together in complex cases with economists who specialise in matters such as market definition, the determination of market power and the analysis of particular types of business behaviour.

---

1 For interesting discussions of the relationship between competition law and economics, see Jenny 'Enforcement: Is Economic Expertise Necessary?' [1998] Fordham Corporate Law Institute (ed Hawk), ch 11; Nicolaides 'An Essay on Economics and the Competition Law of the European Community' (2000) 27 Legal Issues of European Integration 7.

1. THE THEORY OF COMPETITION

Competition means a struggle or contention for superiority, and in the commercial world this means a striving for the custom and business of people in the market place. The ideological struggle between capitalism and communism was a dominant feature of the twentieth century. Many countries had the greatest suspicion of competitive markets and saw, instead, benefits in state planning and management of the economy. However enormous changes took place as the millennium approached, leading to widespread demonopolisation, liberalisation and privatisation. These phenomena, coupled with rapid technological changes and the opening up of international trade, have unleashed unprecedentedly powerful economic forces. The consequences of these changes impact upon individuals and societies in different ways, and sometimes the effects can be uncomfortable. Underlying them, however, is a growing consensus that, on the whole, markets deliver better outcomes than state planning; and central to the idea of a market is the process of competition.

The important issue therefore is to determine the effect which competition can have on economic performance. To understand this one must first turn to economic theory and consider what would happen in conditions of perfect competition and compare the outcome with what happens under monopoly, recognising as one does so that a theoretical analysis of perfect competition does not adequately explain business behaviour in the 'real' world.

(A) The benefits of perfect competition

At its simplest – and it is sensible in considering competition law and policy not to lose sight of the simple propositions – the benefits of competition are lower prices, better products, wider choice and greater efficiency than would obtain under conditions of monopoly. According to neo-classical economic theory, consumer welfare is maximised in conditions of perfect competition[2]. For this purpose 'consumer welfare' is not a vague generalised concept, but instead has a more specific meaning: that allocative and productive efficiency will be achieved; the combined effect of allocative and productive efficiency is that society's wealth overall is maximised. A further benefit claimed for competition is that it will have a dynamic effect by stimulating innovation as competitors strive to produce new and better products for consumers.

---

2   See Asch *Industrial Organization and Antitrust Policy* (Wiley, revised ed, 1983) ch 1; Scherer and Ross *Industrial Market Structure and Economic Performance* (Houghton Mifflin, 3rd ed, 1990) chs 1 and 2; Lipsey and Chrystal *Principles of Economics* (Oxford University Press, 9th ed, 1999) ch 9; on industrial economics and competition generally, see also Tirole *The Theory of Industrial Organization* (MIT Press, 1988); Hay and Morris *Industrial Economics: Theory and Evidence* (Oxford University Press, 1991); Peeperkorn and Mehta 'The Economics of Competition', ch 1 in Faull and Nikpay *The EC Law of Competition* (Oxford University Press, 1999); Bishop and Walker *The Economics of EC Competition* (Sweet & Maxwell, 1999) ch 2; on the psychology of competition from the business manager's perspective, see Porter *Competitive Strategy: Techniques for Analyzing Industries and Competitors* (Macmillan, 1998). Readers may find helpful, in coping with the terminology of the economics of competition law, the *Glossary of Industrial Organisation, Economics and Competition Law* (OECD, 1993) and Black *Oxford Dictionary of Economics* (Oxford University Press, 1997).

(i) Allocative efficiency

Under perfect competition economic resources are allocated between different goods and services in such a way that it is not possible to make anyone better off without making someone else worse off; consumer surplus – the net gain to a consumer when buying a product – is at its largest. Goods and services are allocated between consumers according to the price they are prepared to pay, and price never rises above the marginal cost[3] of production (cost for this purpose including a sufficient profit margin to have encouraged the producer to invest his capital in the industry in the first place, but no more).

The achievement of allocative efficiency, as this phenomenon is known[4], can be shown analytically on the economist's model[5]. Allocative efficiency is achieved under perfect competition because the producer, assuming he is acting rationally and has a desire to maximise his profits, will expand his production for as long as it is privately profitable to do so. As long as he can earn more by producing one extra unit of whatever he produces than it costs to make it, he will presumably do so. Only when the cost of a further unit (the 'marginal cost') exceeds the price he would obtain for it (the 'marginal revenue') will he cease to expand production. Where competition is perfect, a reduction in a producer's own output cannot affect the market price and so there is no reason to limit it; the producer will therefore increase output to the point at which marginal cost and marginal revenue (the net addition to revenue of selling the last unit) coincide. This means that allocative efficiency is achieved, as consumers can obtain the amounts of goods or services they require at the price they are prepared to pay: resources are allocated precisely according to their wishes. A monopolist however can restrict output and increase his own marginal revenue as a consequence of doing so[6].

(ii) Productive efficiency

Apart from allocative efficiency many economists consider that under perfect competition goods and services will be produced at the lowest cost possible, which means that as little of society's wealth is expended in the production process as necessary. Monopolists, free from the constraints of competition, may be high cost producers. Thus competition is said to be conducive to productive efficiency. Productive efficiency is achieved because a producer is unable to sell above cost (if he did his customers would immediately desert him) and he will not of course sell below it (because then he would make no profit). If a producer were to charge above cost, other competitors would move into the market in the hope of profitable activity. They would attempt to produce on a more efficient basis so that they could earn a greater profit. In the long-run the tendency will be to force producers to incur the lowest cost possible in order to be able to earn any profit at all. Eventually an equilibrium will be reached where price and the average cost of producing goods necessarily coincide. This in turn means that price will never rise above cost. If on the other hand price were to fall below cost, there would be an exit of capital from the industry and, as output would therefore decrease, price would be restored to the competitive level.

3   That is to say, the cost of producing an additional unit of output.
4   Allocative efficiency is also sometimes referred to as 'Pareto efficiency'.
5   *Scherer and Ross* p 19 et seq; *Lipsey and Chrystal* p 139 et seq.
6   See pp 4-5 below.

(iii)   Dynamic efficiency

A further benefit of competition, which cannot be proved scientifically, is that producers will constantly innovate and develop new products as part of the continual battle of striving for consumers' business. Thus competition may have the desirable dynamic effect of stimulating important technological research and development. This assumption has been questioned. Some argue that only monopolists enjoy the wealth to innovate and carry out expensive research[7]. Schumpeter was a champion of the notion that the motivation to innovate was the prospect of monopoly profits and that, even if existing monopolists earned such profits in the short term, outsiders would in due course enter the market and displace them[8]. A 'perennial gale of creative destruction' would be sufficient to protect the public interest, so that short-term monopoly power need not cause concern. Empirical research tends to suggest that neither monopolists nor fierce competitors have a superior track-record in this respect, but it would seem clear that the assertion that only monopolists can innovate is incorrect[9].

The theoretical model just outlined suggests that in perfect competition any producer will be able to sell his product on the market only at the price which the market is prepared to bear. The producer is a price-taker, with no capacity to affect the price by his own unilateral action. The consumer is sovereign. The reason why the producer cannot affect the price is that any change in his own individual output will have only a negligible effect on the aggregate output on the market as a whole, and it is aggregate output that determines price through the 'law' of supply and demand.

(B)   The harmful effects of monopoly

Under conditions of monopoly the position is very different[10]. The monopolist is in a position to affect the market price. Since he is responsible for all the output, and since it is aggregate output that determines price through the relationship of supply to demand, he will be able to increase price by reducing the volume of his own production. Furthermore, again assuming a motive to maximise profits, the monopolist will see that he will be able to earn the largest profit if he refrains from expanding his production to the maximum possible. The result will be that output is lower than would be the case under perfect competition and that therefore consumers will be deprived of goods and services that they would have been prepared to pay for at the market price. There is therefore allocative inefficiency in this situation: society's resources are not distributed in the most efficient way possible. The inefficiency is accentuated by the fact that consumers, deprived of the monopolised product they would have bought, will spend their money on products which they wanted less. The economy to this extent is performing below its potential. The extent of this allocative inefficiency is sometimes referred to as the 'deadweight loss' attributable to monopoly; the loss itself is known as the 'welfare cost of monopoly'.

---

7   Galbraith *American Capitalism: The Concept of Countervailing Power* (Houghton Mifflin, 1952).
8   *Capitalism, Socialism and Democracy* (Taylor & Francis Books, 1976).
9   *Scherer and Ross* ch 17.
10 See *Scherer and Ross* ch 2; *Lipsey and Chrystal* ch 10.

The objection to monopoly does not stop there. There is also the problem that productive efficiency may be lower because the monopolist is not constrained by competitive forces to reduce costs to the lowest possible level. Instead the firm becomes 'X-inefficient'. This term, first used by Liebenstein[11], refers to a situation in which resources are used to make the right product, but less productively than they might be: management spends too much time on the golf-course, outdated industrial processes are maintained and a general slackness pervades the organisation of the firm. Furthermore the monopolist may not feel the need to innovate, because he does not experience the constant pressure to go on attracting custom by offering better, more advanced, products. Thus it has been said that the greatest benefit of being a monopolist is the quiet life he is able to enjoy. However it is important to bear in mind that inefficient managers of a business may be affected by pressures other than those of competition. In particular their position may be undermined by uninvited takeover bids on stock exchanges from investors who consider that more efficient use could be made of the firm's assets[12]. Competition may be felt in capital as well as product markets.

A final objection to the monopolist is that, since he can charge a higher price than in conditions of competition (he is a price-maker), wealth is transferred from the hapless consumer to him. This may be particularly true where he is able to discriminate between customers, charging some more than others[13]. While it is not the function of competition authorities themselves to determine how society's wealth should be distributed, it is manifestly a legitimate matter for Governments to take an interest in economic equity, and it may be that one of the ways in which policy is expressed on this issue is through competition law[14]. A further point is that the very prospect of earning large monopoly profits can encourage firms to misallocate resources, as this induces wasteful expenditure on attempts to acquire a monopoly position which is a loss to society at large[15].

Thus runs the theory of perfect competition and monopoly. It indicates that there is much to be said for the 'invisible hand' of competition which magically and surreptitiously orders society's resources in an optimal way, as opposed to the lumbering inefficiency of monopoly. However, we must now turn from the models used in the economist's laboratory to the more haphazard ways of commercial life before rendering a final verdict on the desirability of competition.

(C) Questioning the theory of perfect competition

(i) The model of perfect competition is based on assumptions unlikely to be observed in practice

The first point which must be made about the theory of perfect competition is that it is only a theory; the conditions necessary for perfect competition are extremely unlikely to be observed in practice. Perfect competition requires that on any particular market there is a very large number of buyers and sellers, all producing identical (or 'homogeneous') products; consumers have perfect

---

11 'Allocative Efficiency vs X-Efficiency' (1966) 56 Am Ec Rev 392–415.
12 See eg Hall 'Control Type and the Market for Corporate Control in Large US Corporations' (1977) 25 J Ind Ec 259–273; this issue is discussed further in ch 20, p 726.
13 See *Lipsey and Chrystal* pp 161–170; on abusive pricing by dominant firms generally see ch 18.
14 See pp 15-21 below on the various functions of competition law.
15 Posner 'The Social Costs of Monopoly and Regulation' (1975) 83 J Pol Ec 807.

information about market conditions; resources can flow freely from one area of economic activity to another: there are no 'barriers to entry' which might prevent the emergence of new competition, and there are no 'barriers to exit' which might hinder firms wishing to leave the industry[16]. Of course a market structure satisfying all these conditions is unlikely, if not impossible: we are simply at this stage considering theory, and the theory is based upon a number of assumptions.

Between the polar market structures, of perfect competition on the one hand and monopoly on the other, there are many intermediate positions. Many firms will sell products which are slightly differentiated from those of their rivals or will command some degree of consumer loyalty, so that there will not be the homogeneity required for perfect competition. This may mean that an increase in price will not necessarily result in a substantial loss of business. It is unlikely that a customer will have such complete information of the market that he will immediately know that a lower price is available elsewhere for the product he requires, yet the theory depends on perfect information being available to consumers. This is why legislation sometimes requires that adequate information must be made available to consumers about prices, terms and conditions[17]. There are often some barriers to entry and exit to and from markets; this is particularly so where a firm that enters a market incurs 'sunk costs', that is to say costs that cannot be recovered when it ceases to operate in the future.

Just as perfect competition is unlikely to be experienced in practice, monopoly in its purest form is also rare. There are few products where one firm is responsible for the entire output: normally this happens only where the state confers a monopoly, for example to deliver letters[18]. Most economic operators have some competitors; and even a true monopolist may hoist prices so high that customers cease to buy: demand is not infinitely elastic[19]. In practice, most cases involve not a monopolist, in the etymological sense of one firm selling all the products on a particular market. Rather, competition law concerns itself with firms that have 'market power', and to determine this it is necessary to consider to what extent purchasers consider that alternative products might be a suitable substitute for those they acquire from their existing supplier. One firm may produce all the 'widgets' on the market, but purchasers may consider that, if 'widgets' are too expensive, 'blodgets' would be a reasonable substitute. In other words, market power does not exist in relation to a product, but in relation to a *relevant product market*, and the definition of this market must meet two criteria: it must be sufficiently narrowly drawn to exclude non-substitutes and it must be sufficiently broadly drawn to include all substitutes[20]. In practice defining the market can give rise to formidable difficulties. The problems associated with establishing the relevant product market and market power are discussed further in the final section of this chapter.

---

16 See pp 39-41 below for further discussion of barriers to entry and exit.
17 The Competition Commission in the UK has quite often considered that the provision to consumers of information on matters such as price was an important remedy; see ch 18, pp 668-669.
18 See ch 23, p 872 on the 'reserved area' permitted under EC law in the postal sector.
19 Demand is inelastic when an increase in price does not produce a large change in the level of demand; it is elastic when demand falls swiftly if prices are raised.
20 Asch *Economic Theory and the Antitrust Dilemma* (Wiley, revised ed, 1983) p 146.

(ii) Other problems with the theory of perfect competition

Apart from the fact that perfect competition and pure monopoly are inherently unlikely, there are other problems with the theory itself. It depends on the notion that all businessmen are rational and that they always attempt to maximise profits, but this is not necessarily the case. Directors of a company may not think that earning large profits for the shareholder is the most important consideration they face: they may be more interested to see the size of their business empire grow or to indulge themselves in the quiet life that monopolists may enjoy[1].

A further problem with the theory of perfect competition is that its assertion that costs are kept to an absolute minimum is not necessarily correct. It is true that the private costs of the producer will be kept low, but that says nothing about the social costs or 'externalities' which arise for society at large from, for example, the air pollution that a factory causes, or the severed limbs that must be paid for because cheap machinery is used which does not include satisfactory safeguards against injury. It has been argued that competition law should not concern itself with these social costs[2], and perhaps it is true that this is a matter best left to specific legislation on issues such as conservation, the environment and health and safety at work; also it would be wrong to suppose that monopolists do not themselves produce social costs. However it is reasonable to be at least sceptical of the argument that in perfect competition the costs of society overall will inevitably be kept at a minimal level. Lastly, there is the difficulty with the theory of perfect competition that it is based on a static model of economic behaviour which may fail to account for the dynamic nature of markets and the way in which they operate over a period of time. Firms such as Xerox and IBM, that may have dominated their industries at a particular time in history, nevertheless have found themselves to be engulfed subsequently by competitive forces in the market; it remains to be seen whether the same fate might befall Microsoft. Schumpeter's gale of perennial destruction may affect even the most powerful economic operators.

Given these doubts it might be wondered whether pursuit of an unattainable ideal of perfect competition is worthwhile at all. Indeed some theoreticians have asserted that it might be positively harmful to aspire to a 'second-best solution' in which something similar to, but falling short of, perfect competition is achieved[3]. A second-best solution may actually compound allocative inefficiency and harm consumer welfare, as one distortion in the market inevitably affects performance in other parts of the economy. Where competition is imperfect and monopoly exists, attacking individual vulnerable monopolies while leaving other ones intact might simply exacerbate the pre-existing allocative inefficiency. One should guard against the assumption that tinkering with individual sectors of the economy will necessarily improve performance in the economy as a whole.

Apart from the issue of 'second-best', there is the further problem that if perfect competition cannot be attained, some alternative model is needed to explain how imperfect markets work or should work. In particular it will be necessary to decide how monopolists or dominant firms should be treated, and an adequate theory will be needed to deal with oligopoly, a common industrial phenomenon which exists where a few firms between them supply most of the products within

1   *Scherer and Ross* pp 44–46; see also *Bishop and Walker* p 16, n 13.
2   Bork *The Antitrust Paradox* (Basic Books, 1995) pp 114–115.
3   Lipsey and Lancaster 'The General Theory of Second Best' (1956–57) 24 Rev Ec Stud 11–32; also *Scherer and Ross* pp 33–38 and *Asch* pp 97–100.

the relevant market without any of them having a clear ascendancy over the others. Some economists would argue that, as the most common market form is oligopoly, competition policy ought to be designed around an analytical model of this phenomenon rather than the theory of perfect competition[4].

(D) Questioning competition itself

The comments just made question various aspects of the theory of perfect competition itself. A second line of enquiry considers whether competition is so obviously beneficial anyway. There are some arguments that can be deployed to suggest that competition may not yield the best outcome for society.

(i)   Economies of scale and scope and natural monopolies

The first relates to economies of scale, scope and the phenomenon of 'natural monopoly'[5]. In some industries products can be produced very cheaply and the market for them may be large, so that there is no difficulty in each producer expanding output to the point at which marginal cost and marginal revenue intersect and disposing of the entire amount. In reality this is often not the case. In some markets there may be economies of scale to be achieved, meaning that the average cost per unit of output decreases with the increase in the scale of the outputs produced; economies of scope occur where it is cheaper to produce two products together than to produce them separately. In some markets a profit can be made only by a firm supplying at least one quarter or one third of total output; it may even be that the 'minimum efficient scale' of operation is achieved only by a firm with a market share exceeding 50%, so that monopoly may be seen to be a natural market condition[6]. Similarly, economies of scope may be essential to profitable behaviour. Natural monopoly means a situation in which any amount of output is always produced more cheaply by a single firm: the cost of production is lowest when one firm serves the entire market. Natural monopoly is an economic phenomenon, to be contrasted with statutory monopoly, where the right to exclude rivals from the market is derived from law. Where natural monopoly exists, it is inappropriate to attempt to achieve a level of competition which would destroy the efficiency that this entails. This problem may be exacerbated where the 'natural monopolist' is also required to perform a 'universal service obligation', such as the daily delivery of letters to all postal addresses at a uniform price; performance of such an obligation may not be profitable in normal market conditions, so that the state may confer a statutory monopoly on the undertaking entrusted with the task in question. The lawfulness under EC and UK competition law of 'special or exclusive rights' conferred by the state is one of the more complex issues to be considered in this book[7].

Where the minimum efficient scale is very large in relation to total output, a separate question arises as to how that industry can be made to operate in a way that is beneficial to society as a whole. It may be that public ownership is a solution, or that bureaucratic regulation should be introduced while leaving the

4   On tacit collusion, oligopoly and parallel behaviour see ch 14.
5   *Lipsey and Chrystal* p 153; *Scherer and Ross* pp 97–141.
6   See Schmalensee *The Control of Natural Monopolies* (Lexington, 1979); Sharkey *The Theory of Natural Monopoly* (Cambridge University Press, 1982).
7   See pp 189–210 and ch 9, p 304.

producer or producers in the private sector[8]. A further possibility is that firms should be allowed to bid for a franchise to run the industry in question for a set period of time, at the end of which there will be a further round of bidding. In other words there will be periodic competition to run the industry, although no actual competition within it during the period of the franchise[9]: this happens in the UK, for example, when companies bid for television or rail franchises or to run the national lottery. The 100% share of the market that a firm might have after it has won the bid does not accurately reflect its market power if it was subject to effective competition when making its bid.

(ii) Particular sectors

As well as the complexity of introducing competition into markets that might be regarded as natural monopolies, it might be that social or political value-judgments lead to the conclusion that competition is inappropriate in particular economic sectors. Agriculture is an obvious example. Legislatures have tended to the view that agriculture possesses special features entitling it to protection from the potentially ruthless effects of the competitive system. An obvious illustration of this is the Common Agricultural Policy of the EC[10]. Similarly it might be thought inappropriate (or politically impossible) to expose the labour market to the full discipline of the competitive process; this point is demonstrated by the judgment of the European Court of Justice in *Albany International BV v Stichting Begrijfspensioenfonds Textielindustrie*[11] which concluded that collective bargaining between organisations representing employers and employees is outside Article 81 EC. Systems of competition law have often shown a tendency to refrain from insisting that the liberal professions should have to sully their hands with anything as offensive as price competition or advertising, although the European Commission has taken a stricter line in recent years[12]; a special régime exists for the regulatory rules of the liberal professions under the UK Competition Act 1998[13]. The European Commission has been developing its policy in recent years on the application of the competition rules to sport[14].

(iii) Beneficial restrictions of competition

Another line of argument is that in some circumstances restrictions of competition can have positively beneficial results. This may manifest itself in various ways. One example is the suggestion that firms which are forced to pare costs to the minimum because of the pressures of competition will skimp on safety checks. This argument is particularly pertinent in the transport sector, where fears are sometimes expressed that safety considerations may be subordinated to the profit motive: an example would be where airlines compete fiercely on price. It may

---

8   See ch 23, pp 866-868.
9   See Demsetz 'Why Regulate Utilities?' (1968) 11 J L Ec 55–66; for criticism of the idea of franchise bidding see Williamson 'Franchise Bidding for Natural Monopolies in General and with respect to CATV' (1976) 7 Bell J Ec 73–104.
10 On the (non-)application of EC competition law to the agricultural sector, see ch 23, pp 855-858; leading texts on the common agricultural policy are cited at p 855.
11 Case C-67/96 [1999] ECR I-5751, [2000] 4 CMLR 446; see ch 3 p 70.
12 See ch 3, p 69 .
13 See ch 9, pp 306-307 .
14 XXIXth *Report on Competition Policy* (1999), points 139-142.

be that specific safety legislation can be used to overcome this anxiety; and monopolists seeking to enlarge their profits may show the same disregard for safety considerations as competing firms, a charge levelled against Railtrack in the UK following a series of serious rail accidents in the late 1990s and 2000. Safety was an important issue in the debate in the UK as to whether National Traffic Control Services, responsible for the control of air navigation, should be privatised, provision for which was made in sections 41 to 65 of the Transport Act 2000. Another possibly beneficial restriction of competition could arise where two or more firms, by acting in concert and restricting competition between themselves, are able to develop new products or to produce goods or services on a more efficient scale: the benefit to the public at large may be considerable; both Article 81(3) EC and sections 4 to 11 of the UK Competition Act 1998 recognise that, in some cases, agreements may be tolerated which, though restrictive of competition, produce certain beneficial effects[15]. A further example of the same point is that a producer might impose restrictions on his distributors in order to ensure that they promote his products in the most effective way possible; although this might diminish competition in his own goods (intra-brand competition), the net effect may be to enhance the competitive edge of them as against those produced by his competitors (inter-brand competition)[16]. These examples suggest that a blanket prohibition of agreements that restrict competition may deprive the public of substantial advantages.

(iv)   Ethical and other objections

A more fundamental objection to competition might be that it is considered in some sense to be inherently objectionable. The very notion of striving for superiority may be considered ethically unsound. One argument (now largely discredited) is that 'cut-throat' competition means that firms are forced to charge ever lower prices until in the end the vicious cycle leads them to charge below marginal cost in order to keep custom at all; the inevitable effect of this will be insolvency. The prevailing attitude in much of UK industry during the first half of the twentieth century was that competition was 'harmful' and even destructive and it was this entrenched feeling that led to the adoption of a pragmatic and non-doctrinaire system of control in 1948[17]. It was not until the Competition Act 1998 – 50 years later – that the UK finally adopted legislation that gave the Director General of Fair Trading effective powers to unearth and penalise pernicious cartels[18]. Economically the argument that competition is a cut-throat business that leads to insolvency is implausible, but industrialists do use it. Another argument is that competition should be arrested where industries enter cyclical recessions – or even long-term decline – in order that they do not disappear altogether[19]. Again competition might be thought undesirable because of its wasteful effects. The consumer may be incapable of purchasing a tin of baked beans in one supermarket because of the agonising fear that at the other end of town a competitor is offering them more cheaply. He will waste his time (a social cost) and money 'shopping around': such an argument once commended

15   On horizontal cooperation agreements generally see ch 15.
16   On vertical agreements generally see ch 16.
17   See Allen *Monopoly and Restrictive Practices* (George Allen & Unwin, 1968); on the reform of UK law see ch 9, pp 285-288.
18   On these powers see ch 10, pp 335-342 and 348-356.
19   *Scherer and Ross* pp 294–306; see also ch 15, pp 528-529 on restructuring agreements.

itself to the Restrictive Practices Court in the UK[20]. Meanwhile competitors will be wasting their own money by paying advertising agencies to think up more expensive and elaborate campaigns to promote their products[1]. A commentator on the petrochemicals industry has argued that conventional competition leads to chronic waste in which everyone loses, and that attention should be focused not on the supposed evils of cartelisation but rather on the freedom for firms to *exit* from an industry if and when they see the opportunity to operate more profitably on another market[2].

(v)   Industrial policy

One practical objection to promoting competition is that it may be considered to be inimical to the general thrust of industrial policy. Admittedly the suggestion has been made that, in conditions of perfect competition, firms will innovate in order to keep or attract new custom. However Governments often encourage firms to collaborate where this would lead to economies of scale or to more effective research and development; and they may adopt a policy of promoting 'national champions' which will be effective as competitors in international markets[3]. There are certainly circumstances in which the innovator, the entrepreneur and the risk-taker may require some immunity from competition if they are to indulge in expensive technological projects. This is recognised in the law of intellectual property rights which provides an incentive to firms to innovate by preventing the appropriation of commercial ideas which they have developed[4]. A patentee in the UK is given the exclusive right for 20 years to exploit the subject-matter of his patent[5]. A similar incentive and/or reward is given to the owners of copyright, registered designs and analogous rights[6]. This is a recognition of the fact that in some circumstances competition suppresses innovation and an indication of the vacuity of relentlessly pursuing the ideal of perfect competition. The relationship between competition law and the law of intellectual property is a fascinating one, in particular the tension between on the one hand the desire to keep markets open and free from monopoly and on the other the need to encourage innovation precisely by granting monopoly rights. These issues will be considered in chapter 19.

(vi)   Competitions are there to be won

The last point which should be made in this brief survey of objections to competition is that the competitive process contains an inevitable paradox. Some competitors win. By being the most innovative, the most responsive to customers' wishes, and by producing goods or services in the most efficient way possible, one firm may succeed in seeing off its rivals. It would be strange, and indeed harmful, if

20   See *Re Black Bolt and Nut Association of Great Britain's Agreement* (1960) LR 2 RP 50, [1960] 3 All ER 122.
1   *Scherer and Ross* pp 404–407.
2   Bower *When Markets Quake* (Harvard Business School, 1986).
3   This can be an important issue in some merger cases: see ch 20, p 725.
4   See generally Cornish *Intellectual Property: Patents Copyright Trade Marks and Allied Rights* (Sweet & Maxwell, 4th ed, 1999).
5   Patents Act 1977, s 25.
6   See the Copyright, Designs and Patents Act 1988, ss 12-15, 191, 216, 269.

that firm could then be condemned for being a monopolist. As Judge Learned Hand opined in *US v Aluminum Co of America*[7]:

> '[A] single producer may be the survivor out of a group of active companies, merely by virtue of his superior skill, foresight and industry... The successful competitor, having been urged to compete, must not be turned upon when he wins.'

(E)   Empirical evidence

A separate issue is whether there is any empirical evidence to support, or indeed to contradict, the case for competition and, if so, what the evidence can tell us. It is notoriously difficult to measure such things as allocative efficiency or the extent to which innovation is attributable to the pressure of competition upon individual firms. Economists have often suggested that there is some direct causal relationship between industrial structure, the conduct of firms on the market and the quality of their economic performance[8]: this is often referred to as the 'structure-conduct-performance paradigm'. A monopolistic structure can be expected to lead to a restriction of output and a loss of economic efficiency: a natural consequence of this view would be that competition law should be watchful for any acts or omissions that could be harmful to the structure of the market, and in particular for conduct that could foreclose access to it and mergers that lead to fewer players. Others argue that this schematic presentation is too simplistic. In particular it is said to be unsound because it is uni-directional and fails to indicate the extent to which performance itself can influence structure and conduct[9]. Good performance, for example, may in itself affect structure by attracting new entrants into an industry. Other economists have attempted to measure the extent to which monopoly results in allocative inefficiency and leads to a deadweight loss to society[10]. There are of course formidable difficulties associated with this type of exercise, and many of the studies that have been published have been criticised for their methodology. Scherer and Ross devote a chapter of their book to this problem[11] and point out that there has been a dramatic expansion in the range and intensity of empirical research into industrial organisation in recent years. Their conclusion is that, despite the theoretical problems of such research, important relationships do exist between market structure and performance, and that the research should continue[12]. More prosaically it might be added that, even if there are difficulties in measuring scientifically the harmful effects of monopoly in liberalised market economies, the economic performance of the Soviet Union and its neighbours in the second half of the twentieth century suggests that its effects can be pernicious.

7   377 US 271 (1964).
8   This schematic model of industrial behaviour was first suggested by Mason 'Price and Production Policies of Large-Scale Enterprise' (1939) 29 Am Ec Rev Supplement 61–74; see *Scherer and Ross* chs 3 and 4.
9   Phillips 'Structure, Conduct and Performance – and Performance, Conduct and Structure' in Markham and Papanek (eds) *Industrial Organization and Economic Development* (1970).
10   Weiss 'Concentration-Profit Relationship' in *Industrial Concentration: the New Learning* (eds Goldschmid and others, 1974); Gribbin *Postwar Revival of Competition as Industrial Policy*; Cowling and Mueller 'The Social Costs of Monopoly Power' (1978) 88 Ec J 724–748, criticised by Littlechild at (1981) 91 Ec J 348–363.
11   *Industrial Market Structure and Economic Performance*, ch 11.
12   Ibid, p 447.

A separate issue which has been little explored by industrial economists is the impact that competition law itself has upon economic behaviour. The tendency has been for the law to react to economics; little attention has been paid to the reaction of economic behaviour to the law.

(F) Workable competition

The discussion so far has presented a model of perfect competition, but has acknowledged that it is based upon a set of assumptions that are unlikely to be observed in practice; it has also been pointed out that there are some arguments that can be made against competition, although some of them are less convincing than others. If perfect competition is unattainable, the question arises whether there is an alternative economic model to which it would be reasonable to aspire. Some economists have been prepared to settle for a more prosaic theory of 'workable competition'[13]. They recognise the limitations of the theory of perfect competition, but nonetheless consider that it is worthwhile seeking the best competitive arrangement that is practically attainable. Quite what workable competition should consist of has caused theoretical difficulties[14]; however a workably competitive structure might be expected to have a beneficial effect on conduct and performance, and therefore be worth striving for and maintaining.

(G) Contestable markets

In recent years some economists have advanced a theory of 'contestable markets' upon which competition law might be based[15]. According to this theory, firms will be forced to ensure an optimal allocation of resources provided that the market on which they operate is 'contestable', that is to say provided that it is possible for firms to enter the market without incurring sunk costs[16] and to leave it without loss. While this theory aims to have general applicability, it has been particularly significant in discussion of the deregulation of industries in the US. In a perfectly contestable market, entry into an industry is free and exit is costless. The emphasis on exit is important as firms should be able to leave an industry without incurring a loss if and when opportunities to profit within it disappear. A perfectly *contestable* market need not be perfectly *competitive*: perfect competition requires an infinite number of sellers on a market; in a perfectly contestable market an economically efficient outcome can be achieved even where there are only a few competitors, since there is always the possibility of 'hit and run' entry into the market. Even an industry in which only one or two firms are operating may be perfectly contestable where there are no impediments to entry or exit, so that intervention by the competition authorities is unnecessary. The theory shifts the focus of competition policy, as it is more sanguine about markets on which

13 Clark 'Toward a Concept of Workable Competition' (1940) 30 Am Ec Rev 241–256; Sosnick 'A Critique of Concepts of Workable Competition' (1958) 72 Qu J Ec 380–423 (a general review of the literature); see also *Scherer and Ross* pp 52–55.
14 See Asch *Industrial Organization and Antitrust Policy* (Wiley, revised ed, 1983) pp 100–104.
15 See Baumol, Panzar and Willig *Contestable Markets and the Theory of Industry Structure* (Harcourt Brace Jovanovich, revised ed, 1988); Bailey 'Contestability and the Design of Regulatory and Antitrust Policy' (1981) 71 Am Ec Rev 178–183.
16 See p 6 above.

few firms operate than the 'traditional' model of perfect competition; having said this, it is questionable whether the theory of contestability really adds a great deal to traditional thinking on industrial economics or whether it simply involves a difference of emphasis.

As far as the specific issue of deregulation is concerned, the theory of contestability suggests, for example, that the existence within the air transport sector of only a few airlines need not have adverse economic effects provided that the conditions for entry and exit to and from the market are not disadvantageous. It is not clear how significant the theory of contestable markets is likely to be in the formulation of EC and UK competition policy, other than in the particular area of deregulation. In the UK Competition Commission's investigation of *CHC Helicopter Corpn/Helicopter Services Group ASA*[17] the Commission cleared a merger that would create a duopoly in helicopter services where the market was found to be contestable. The European Commission was less impressed by contestable market theory in *Far East Trade Tariff Charges and Surcharges Agreement (FETTCSA)*[18].

(H)   Effective competition

On some occasions, legal provisions and regulators use the expression 'effective competition'. For example it is found in Article 2(3) of the European Community Merger Regulation ('the ECMR'), as part of the test for determining when a merger is incompatible with the common market: 'effective competition' must not be significantly impeded. In the UK, OFTEL published a strategy statement in January 2000, one of the objectives of which would be to achieve 'effective competition in all main UK telecoms markets'[19]. The UK Utilities Act 2000 provides that the Gas and Electricity Markets Authority should have, as one of its tasks, the promotion of effective competition in the gas and electricity sectors[20]. The idea of effective competition does not appear to be the product of any particular theory or model of competition – perfect, workable, contestable or any other. Indeed, given the number of theories and assumptions already discussed in this chapter, and the many others not discussed, the idea of effective competition, free from theoretical baggage, may have much to commend it. Effective competition does connote the idea, however, that firms should be subject to a reasonable degree of competitive constraint, from actual and potential competitors and from customers, and that the rôle of a competition authority is to see that such constraints are present on the market[1].

17 Cm 4556 (2000); for comment, see Oldale 'Contestability: The Competition Commission Decision on North Sea Helicopter Services' (2000) 21 ECLR 345.
18 OJ [2000] L 268/1, [2000] 5 CMLR 1011, para 119; this case is on appeal to the CFI, Case T-213/00 *CMA v Commission* (judgment pending).
19 OFTEL, January 2000; this document can be found on OFTEL's website at http://www.oftel.gov/about/strat100.htm.
20 Utilities Act 2000, ss 9 and 13, amending the Gas Act 1986 and the Electricity Act 1989 respectively.
1   For further discussion see *Bishop and Walker* ch 2, 'Effective Competition and Market Power'.

(I) Conclusion

What can perhaps be concluded at the end of this discussion is that, despite the range of different theories and the difficulties associated with them, competition does seem to possess sufficient properties to lead to a policy choice in its favour. Competitive markets seem, on the whole, to deliver better outcomes than monopolistic ones. This is why competition policy has been so widely embraced in recent years; there is probably a greater global consensus on the desirability of competition and free markets today than at any time in the history of human economic behaviour. In particular monopoly does seem to lead to a restriction in output and higher prices; there is a greater incentive to achieve productive efficiency in a competitive market; the suggestion that only monopolists can innovate is unsound; and competition provides the consumer with a greater degree of choice. Furthermore, in markets such as telecommunications, energy and transport competition has been introduced where once there was little, if any, and this seems to have produced significant benefits for consumers.

A system of competition law intended to protect the process of competition will be likely to deal with at least the following four issues, although the needs of any particular economy or state will vary. The first is the need to prevent firms from entering into agreements which have the effect of restricting competition, either between themselves or between them and third parties, and which do not have any beneficial features[2]. Secondly, it will need to control attempts by monopolists or firms with market power to abuse their position and prevent new competition emerging[3]. Thirdly, it will need to ensure that workable competition is maintained in oligopolistic industries[4]. Fourthly, it will need to monitor mergers between independent undertakings which may concentrate the market and diminish the competitive pressures within it[5]. Common to each of these phenomena is a single idea: that competition law is concerned with the problem of one or more firms which individually or collectively possess power over the market. Where this happens, the firm or firms with market power will be able to restrict output and raise price above the level that would prevail in a competitive market, and profit from doing so. From the consumer's perspective, the benefits of competition are lost.

2. THE FUNCTION OF COMPETITION LAW

If the sole function of competition law were the maximisation of consumer welfare by achieving the most efficient allocation of resources and by reducing costs as far as possible, the formulation of legal rules and their application would be relatively simple. There would of course be the problem that such a policy would be essentially economic and that lawyers would have difficulties when asked to step outside the parameters of their own discipline, but at least it would be possible to proceed by reference to some single, unifying aim. In reality however many different policy objectives have been pursued in the name of competition law, some of which are not rooted in notions of consumer welfare in the technical sense at all, and some of which are plainly inimical to the pursuit of allocative and productive efficiency. The result can be inconsistency and contradiction, but

2　See in particular chs 13 and 15 on horizontal agreements and ch 16 on vertical agreements.
3　See in particular chs 17 and 18 on abusive non-pricing and pricing practices.
4　See in particular ch 14 on tacit collusion, oligopoly and parallel behaviour.
5　See chs 20–22 on mergers generally.

it is as well for the reader to be aware of this before coming to the law itself. There is no single, unifying policy which binds EC or UK law together: there is no simple premise from which decisions flow through the application of logic alone. In particular competition policy does not exist in a vacuum: it is an expression of the current values and aims of society and is as susceptible to change as political thinking generally. Because views and insights shift over a period of time, competition law is infused with tension. Different systems of competition law reflect different concerns, an important point when comparing the laws of the US, the EC and the UK[6]. As already noted, competition law has now been adopted in at least 80 countries, whose economies and economic development may be very different. It is impossible to suppose that each system will have identical concerns.

(A)   Consumer protection

Several different objectives other than the maximisation of consumer welfare in the technical sense can be ascribed to competition law. The first is that its essential purpose should be to protect the interests of consumers, not by protecting the competitive process itself, but by taking direct action against offending undertakings, for example by requiring dominant firms to reduce their prices. It is of course correct in principle that competition law should be regarded as having a 'consumer protection' function: ultimately the process of competition itself is intended to deliver benefits to consumers. However the possibility exists that competition law might be invoked in a more 'populist' manner; this appeared to happen in the UK in 1998 and 1999, at a time when the Government wished to be seen to be doing something about so-called 'rip-off Britain', where ministers suggested that excessive prices were being charged by both monopolists and non-monopolists[7]. A problem with using competition law to assume direct control over prices, however, is that regulators are ill-placed to determine what price a competitive market would set for particular goods or services, and indeed by fixing a price they may further distort the competitive fabric of the market. The UK Competition Commission declined to recommend price regulation following its report of *Supermarkets*[8], fearing that such intervention would be disproportionate and unduly regulatory. Populist measures taken to have electoral appeal may ultimately be more harmful than the high prices themselves. Similarly, the consumer may be harmed – or at least consider himself to be harmed – where a producer insists that all his goods should be sold by dealers at maintained prices, or that dealers should provide a combined package of goods plus after-sales service. Here the consumer's choice is restricted by the producer's decision. Competition law may proscribe resale price maintenance or tie-in sales for this reason, although there are those who argue that this intervention is undesirable: the producer is restricting intra-brand competition, but inter-brand competition may be enhanced as a result[9]. The obsession with protecting the consumer can

6   On the differences between the policies of competition law in the US and the EC, see eg Jebsen and Stevens 'Assumptions, Goals and Dominant Undertakings; the Regulation of Competition under Article 86 of the European Union' (1996) 64 Antitrust Law Journal 443.
7   See ch 18, pp 665-669 on the control of exploitative pricing practice under UK law.
8   Cm 4842 (2000).
9   See in particular ch 16 on vertical agreements.
10   This is one of Bork's most pressing arguments in *The Antitrust Paradox* (Basic Books, 1995).

also be considered short-sighted since, in the longer run, the producer might choose to abandon the market altogether rather than comply with an unreasonable competition law; short-term benefits will then be outweighed by long-term harm to consumer welfare[10].

(B) Redistribution

A second possible objective of competition law might be the dispersal of economic power and the redistribution of wealth: the promotion of economic equity rather than economic efficiency. Aggregations of resources in the hands of monopolists, multinational corporations or conglomerates could be considered a threat to the very notion of democracy, individual freedom of choice and economic opportunity. This argument was influential in the US for many years at a time when there was a fundamental mistrust of big business. President Roosevelt warned Congress in 1938 that 'The liberty of a democracy is not safe if the people tolerate the growth of a private power to a point where it becomes stronger than the democratic state itself... Among us today a concentration of private power without equal in history is growing'[11]. It was under the US antitrust laws that the world's largest corporation at the time, AT&T, was eventually dismembered. Some critics of the action brought by the Department of Justice against Microsoft were concerned that it amounted to an attack on a spectacularly successful business[12], while others welcomed the attempt to restrain its undoubted economic muscle[13].

(C) Protecting competitors

Linked to the argument that competition law should be concerned with redistribution is the view that competition law should be applied in such a way as to protect small firms against more powerful rivals: the competition authorities should hold the ring and ensure that the 'small guy' is given a fair chance to succeed. To put the point another way, there are those who consider that competition law should be concerned with competitors as well as the process of competition. This idea has at times had a strong appeal in the US, in particular during the period when Chief Justice Warren led the Supreme Court. However it has to be appreciated that the arrest of the Darwinian struggle, in which the most efficient succeed and the weak disappear, for the purpose of protecting small business can run directly counter to the idea of consumer welfare in the technical economic sense. It may be that competition law is used to preserve the inefficient and to stunt the performance of the efficient. In the US, the 'Chicago School' of economists has been particularly scathing of the 'uncritical sentimentality' in favour of the small competitor, and in the 1980s, in particular, US law developed in a noticeably less sentimental way[14]. To the Chicago School,

---

11 83 Cong Rec 5992 (1938).
12 For a highly critical view of the Microsoft case generally, see McKenzie *Antitrust on Trial: How the Microsoft Case Is Reframing the Rules of Competition* (Perseus Publishing, 2000).
13 See 'Now Bust Microsoft's Trust' *The Economist* 13 November 1999; 'Bill Rockefeller?' *The Economist* 29 April 2000.
14 See Fox 'The New American Competition Policy – from Anti-trust to Pro-Efficiency' (1981) 2 ECLR 439 where the author traces the change in the policy of the Supreme Court from judgments such as *Brown Shoe Co v US* 370 US 294 (1962) to the position in *Continental TV Inc v GTE Sylvania Inc* 433 US 36 (1977).

the essential question in an antitrust case should be whether the conduct under investigation could lead to consumers paying higher prices, and whether those prices could be sustained against the forces of competition; antitrust intervention to protect competitors from their more efficient rivals is harmful to consumer welfare. Even firms with high market shares are subject to competitive constraints provided that barriers to entry and exit are low, so that intervention on the part of the regulator is usually uncalled for.

There is no doubt that EC competition law has, in some cases, been applied with competitors in mind: this is particularly noticeable in some decisions under Article 82, and can be traced back to the influence of the so-called 'Freiburg School' of ordoliberalism[15]. Scholars of the Freiburg School, which originated in Germany in the 1930s, saw the free market as a necessary ingredient in a liberal economy, but not as sufficient in itself. The problems of Weimar and Nazi Germany were attributable in part to the inability of the legal system to control and, if necessary, to disperse private economic power. An economic constitution was necessary to constrain the economic power of firms, but without giving Government unrestrained control over their behaviour: public power could be just as pernicious as private. Legal rules could be put in place which would achieve both of these aims. It is not surprising that the beneficiaries of such thinking would be small and medium-sized undertakings, the very opposite of the monopolists and cartels feared by the members of the Freiburg School. There is no doubt that ordoliberal thinking had a direct influence on the leading figures involved in the establishment of the three European Communities in the 1950[16], and that this led to decisions and judgments in which the law was applied to protect competitors rather than the process of competition. However, without questioning the appropriateness of decisions taken in the early years of the Communities, it can be questioned whether it is appropriate in the new millennium to maintain this approach: there is much to be said for applying competition rules to achieve economic efficiency rather than economic equity. The two ideas sit awkwardly together: indeed they may flatly contradict one another, since an efficient undertaking will inevitably be able to defeat less efficient competitors, whose position in the market ought not to be underwritten by a competition authority on the basis of political preference or, as Bork might say, sentimentality. This is an issue that will be considered further in later chapters, and in particular in chapters 17 and 18 on abusive practices on the part of dominant firms.

(D)   Other issues

In some cases, particularly involving mergers, the relevant authorities might find that other issues require attention: whether they can be taken into account will depend on the applicable law[17]. For example, unemployment and regional policy are issues which arise in the analysis of mergers and cooperation agreements; the capacity of competition to dampen price-inflation may be considered to be important; merger controls may be used to prevent foreign

---

15 See Gerber *Law and Competition in Twentieth Century Europe: Protecting Promotheus* (Clarendon Press Oxford, 1998), ch VII; see also Gerber 'Constitutionalizing the Economy: German Neo-liberalism, Competition Law and the "New" Europe' (1994) 42 American Journal of Comparative Law 25.

16 Ibid, pp 263-265; ch IX.

17 On the relevant tests to be applied to mergers under EC and UK law see respectively ch 21, pp 770-783 and ch 22, pp 818-830.

takeovers of domestic companies; and there have been situations in which a competition authority may have been concerned with the problem of inequality of bargaining power between the parties to an agreement[18].

(E)   The single market imperative

Lastly, we must consider two more issues of particular significance. One is that competition policy in the context of the EC fulfils an additional but quite different function from those just described (although EC law may be applied with them in mind as well). This is that competition law plays a hugely important part in the overriding goal of achieving single market integration[19]. The very idea of the single market is that internal barriers to trade within the Community should be dismantled and that goods, services, workers and capital should have complete freedom of movement. Firms should be able to outgrow their national markets and operate on a more efficient, trans-national, scale throughout the Community. Competition law has both a negative and a positive rôle to play in the integration of the single market. The negative one is that it can prevent measures which attempt to maintain the isolation of one domestic market from another: for example national cartels, export bans and market-sharing will be seriously punished[20]. The largest fine ever to have been imposed on a single undertaking, of EUR 102 million, was in *Community v VW*[1] where Volkswagen sought to prevent exports of its cars from Italy to Germany and Austria. The positive rôle is that competition law can be moulded in such a way as to encourage trade between Member States, partly by 'levelling the playing fields of Europe' as one contemporary catchphrase puts it, and partly by facilitating cross-border transactions and integration. Horizontal collaboration between firms in different Member States may be permitted in some circumstances[2]; a producer in one Member State can be permitted to appoint an exclusive distributor in another and so penetrate a market which individually he could not have done[3]. Unification of the single market is an obsession of the Community authorities; this has meant that decisions have sometimes been taken prohibiting behaviour which a competition authority elsewhere, unconcerned with single market considerations, would not have reached. Faced with a conflict between the narrow interests of a particular firm and the broader problem of integrating the market, the tendency will be to subordinate the former to the latter. In the UK, the Competition Act 1998 will generally be interpreted consistently with the jurisprudence of the Community Courts under Article 81 and 82, but not in so far as it is motivated by single market as opposed to competition considerations[4].

18 The European Commission's block exemption for the distribution of motor cars seems, in part, to be influenced by the desire to 'protect' the car dealer from the supplier: see ch 16, pp 592-593; similarly, the block exemption on technology transfer agreements seems motivated in part by the need to protect licensees from licensors: see ch 19, pp 688-696.
19 See Ehlermann 'The Contribution of EC Competition Policy to the Single Market' (1992) 29 CML Rev 257; the Commission's XXIXth *Report on Competition Policy* (1999), point 3.
20 See ch 7 pp 237-239 on the powers of the European Commission to impose fines for infringements of Articles 81 and 82.
1   OJ [1998] L 124/60, [1998] 5 CMLR 33: on appeal the fine was reduced to EUR 90 million, Case T-62/98 [2000] 5 CMLR 853; the case is on appeal to the ECJ, Case C-338/00 (judgment pending).
2   See generally ch 15.
3   See generally ch 16.
4   See ch 9, pp 329-333.

(F) Who decides?

The other issue that should be mentioned is that competition law may not be so much about any particular policy – for example the promotion of consumer welfare or protection of the weak – but about who actually should make decisions about the way in which business should be conducted. The great ideological debate of the twentieth century was between capitalism and communism: whether to have a market or not. For the most part, that debate has been concluded in favour of the market mechanism. But competition law and policy by their very nature envisage that there may be situations in which some control of economic behaviour in the market-place may be necessary in order to achieve a desirable outcome (using this expression here in a deliberately non-specific sense). To some the market, and the vast rewards it brings to successful operators, remains an object of suspicion; to others, the spectre of the state as regulator is more alarming. These matters have been eloquently discussed by Amato[5]:

> 'It is a fact that within liberal society itself one of the key divisions of political identity (and hence identification) is between these two sides: the side that fears private power more, and in order to fight it is ready to give more room to the power of government; and the side that fears the expansion of government more, and is therefore more prepared to tolerate private power.'

In Europe there seems little doubt that, notwithstanding the demonopolisation and liberalisation of economic behaviour and the promotion of free enterprise in the late twentieth century, there remains a scepticism about the market, and that this results in 'active' enforcement of the competition rules by the European Commission and by the national competition authorities[6].

In the European Community there has been a fair degree of dirigism in the way that the Commission has developed its policy. For example, historically it has taken a wide view of the circumstances in which competition is restricted for the purposes of Article 81(1), but has then given block exemption under Article 81(3) to certain types of agreements which satisfy criteria, specified by it, in various regulations[7]. The legal adviser is highly likely to advise a client to comply with these criteria, whether suitable or not, because of the administrative and juridical advantages of doing so. In this case the invisible hand of competition is replaced by the much more visible hand of the Commission and, specifically, DG COMP, the Directorate of the Commission responsible for competition matters[8]. Competition law is then really a matter of who makes important commercial decisions: the market itself, or the competition authorities which control firms' behaviour. This in turn raises an additional, complex, issue: if there are to be competition authorities to decide on what is and what is not acceptable business behaviour, what type of institution should be asked to make these decisions (a court, a commission, an individual?); how should individuals be appointed to those institutions (by ministerial appointment, by election, by

5   Amato *Antitrust and the Bounds of Power: The Dilemma of Liberal Democracy in the History of the Market* (Hart Publishing, 1997) p 4.
6   See Gerber *Law and Competition in Twentieth Century Europe* (Clarendon Press Oxford, 1998) pp 421 ff.
7   The Commission's 'new style' regulations, of which Regulation 2790/99 is the first, are less formalistic, and therefore less dirigiste, than their predecessors: see ch 4, pp 144-145.
8   See further ch 2, pp 48-50 on the rôle of the Commission in EC competition law and policy.

open competition?); and how should those institutions themselves be controlled (by judicial review, or by an appellate court?). Here we leave law and economics and move into the world of political science which, though fascinating, is beyond the scope of this book[9].

(G) Competition advocacy

A final point about the function of competition law is that competition authorities can usefully be given a different task, which is to scrutinise legislation that will bring about a distortion of competition in the economy. The reality is that states and international regulatory authorities are capable of harming the competitive process at least as seriously as private economic operators on the market itself, for example by granting legal monopolies to undertakings, by limiting in other ways the number of competitors in the market or by establishing unduly restrictive rules and regulations. Some competition authorities are specifically mandated to scrutinise legislation that will distort competition[10]; in the US the Federal Trade Commission has adopted a Competition and Consumer Advocacy Programme[11]. Some developing countries might more usefully deploy their resources on this issue rather than adopting their own competition rules[12].

3. MARKET DEFINITION AND MARKET POWER

The discussion in this chapter has been intended to give the reader some idea of the theory of competition and of the function of competition law. However it might also be useful, before embarking upon a study of the substantive provisions of the law, to discuss the issues of market definition and market power, since these ideas will crop up regularly in the text that follows.

As suggested above, competition law is concerned, above all, with the problems that occur where one or more firms possess market power: market power presents undertakings with the possibility of limiting output and raising price, which are clearly inimical to consumer welfare. There are numerous ways in which this key concern – the exercise of market power – is manifested, by implication if not expressly, in EC and UK competition law: there are rules that firms should not enter into agreements to restrict competition (Article 81 EC; Chapter I prohibition, Competition Act 1998): however, there are various '*de minimis*' exceptions where the parties lack market power[13]; block exemption is not available to parties to

---

9   On these issues see generally Doern and Wilks (eds) *Comparative Competition Policy: National Institutions in a Global Market* (Clarendon Press Oxford, 1996) and, in particular, chs 1 and 2; Cini and McGowan *Competition Policy in the European Union* (Macmillan, 1998); Craig *Administrative Law* (Sweet & Maxwell, 4th ed, 1999) ch 11.

10 See eg s 21(k) of the South African Competition Act 1998, which requires the Competition Commission to 'review legislation and public regulations and report to the Minister concerning any provision that permits uncompetitive behaviour'.

11 See Celnicker *The Federal Trade Commission's Competition and Consumer Advocacy Programme* (1988-89) 33 St Louis University Law Journal 379.

12 Rodriguez and Coate *Competition Policy in Transition Economies: the Role of Competition Advocacy* (1997) 23 Brooklyn Journal of International Law 365.

13 See ch 3, pp 107-110; ch 9, pp 295-297.

agreements where the parties' market share exceeds a certain threshold[14]; firms should not abuse a dominant position (Article 82 EC; Chapter II prohibition, Competition Act 1998); concentrations can be prohibited under the ECMR that would create or strengthen a dominant position as a result of which competition would be significantly impeded; 'monopoly situations' and 'complex monopoly situations' can be investigated by the Competition Commission (Fair Trading Act 1973, UK). Other variants can also be found[15]. Without wishing to suggest that all these provisions operate in an identical manner and according to identical standards, which manifestly is not the case, each of them reflects a concern about the abuse or potential abuse of market power. Throughout this book and throughout competition law and practice generally, therefore, two key issues will recur: first, the definition of the relevant product and geographic (and sometimes the temporal) markets in relation to which market power may be found to exist; and secondly, the identification of market power itself. These concepts are so critical that they merit investigation at this early stage, before the legal provisions themselves are introduced.

(A)   Market definition

Pure monopoly is rare, but a firm or firms collectively may have sufficient power over the market to enjoy some of the benefits available to the true monopolist. If the notion of 'power over the market' is key to analysing competition issues, it becomes immediately obvious that it is necessary to understand what is meant by 'the market' or, as will be explained below, the 'relevant market' for this purpose. The concept is an economic one, and in many cases it may be necessary for lawyers to engage the services of economists to assist in the proper delineation of the market, as highly sophisticated economic and econometric analysis is sometimes called for. However, the fact that market definition is complex and is essentially economic does not mean that competition lawyers can afford to ignore it: in most competition law cases, progress cannot be made without some feel for the appropriate market definition, and all 'practitioners', using the term in a broad sense to include both advisers and competition policy officials, ought to be familiar with the relevant principles.

In recent years, the 'science' of market definition has evolved considerably. There are numerous sources of information on how to define markets. Of particular importance in Europe is the European Commission's *Notice on the Definition of the Relevant Market for the Purposes of Community Competition Law*[16]. This

14   See eg Article 3 of Regulation 2790/99, OJ [1999] L 336/21, [2000] 4 CMLR 398 on vertical agreements: 30% market share cap; Article 4 of Regulation 2658/2000, OJ [2000] L 304/3, [2001] 4 CMLR 800 on specialisation agreements: 20% market share cap; and Article 4 of Regulation 2659/2000, OJ [2000] L 304/7, [2001] 4 CMLR 808, on research and development agreements: 25% market share cap.

15   For example in the telecommunications sector specific provision is made for the control of 'significant market power': see eg Articles 1 and 2(3) of the Commission's Leased Lines Directive (92/44/EEC) OJ [1992] L 165/27 as amended, which provides for a presumption of significant market power at 25% or more; significant market power also appears in the licensing, interconnection and revised telephony Directives in the telecommunications sector: see ch 23, pp 868-869: for criticism of the use of the notion of significant market power, see Tarrant 'Significant Market Power and Dominance in the Regulation of Telecommunications Markets' (2000) 21 ECLR 320.

16   OJ [1997] C 372/5, [1998] 4 CMLR 177; the Notice can be accessed on the Commission's website at http://europa.eu.int/comm/competition/mergers/legislation/mergmrkt.html; see also OFT Research Paper 1 (OFT 049) *Market Definition in UK Competition Policy* (National

Notice attempts to capture the Commission's experience of market definition over many years, and explains some of the techniques that may be deployed when defining markets. While it is true to say that the Notice is without prejudice to the case law of the European Court of Justice and the Court of First Instance and that it does have limitations[17], it is nevertheless an extremely important and influential guide to this issue. The Notice itself adopts the approach taken by the antitrust authorities in the US in the analysis of horizontal mergers[18]; and the OFT in the UK has indicated that it will adhere to its principles[19]. Other competition authorities have also adopted the same approach[20].

Paragraph 2 of the Commission's Notice explains why market definition is important:

> 'Market definition is a tool to identify and define the boundaries of competition between firms. It serves to establish the framework within which competition policy is applied by the Commission. The main purpose of market definition is to identify in a systematic way the competitive constraints that the undertakings involved face. The objective of defining a market in both its product and geographic dimension is to identify those actual competitors of the undertakings involved that are capable of constraining those undertakings' behaviour and of preventing them from behaving independently of effective competitive pressure'.

This paragraph contains a number of important points. First, market definition is not an end in itself: it is an analytical tool that assists in determining the competitive constraints upon undertakings. Secondly, both the product and geographic dimensions of markets must be analysed. Thirdly, market definition enables the competitive constraints only from *actual* competitors to be identified: it tells us nothing about potential competitors. However, as paragraph 13 of the Notice points out, there are three main sources of competitive constraint upon undertakings: demand substitutability, supply substitutability and potential competition. As will be explained below, demand substitutability is the essence of market definition. In some, albeit fairly narrow, circumstances supply substitutability may also be part of the market definition; however normally supply substitutability lies outside market definition and is an issue of potential competition. This is a very important point to understand, since it means that a particular share of a market cannot, in itself, indicate that a firm has market power; an undertaking with 100% of the widget market would not have market power if there are numerous potential competitors and no barriers to entry into the market. Lawyers must not be seduced by numbers when determining whether a firm has market power; market shares, of course, are helpful; indeed there are

---

Economic Research Associates, 1992); *Market definition* OFT Guideline 403, http://www.oft.gov.uk/html/comp-act/technical_guidelines/oft403.html; Baker and Wu 'Applying the Market Definition Guidelines of the European Commission' (1998) 19 ECLR 273; Bishop and Walker *The Economics of EC Competition Law* (Sweet & Maxwell, 1999) ch 3; for a discussion of the position prior to the adoption of the Notice, see Kauper 'The Problem of Market Definition under EC Competition Law' [1996] Fordham Corporate Law Institute (ed Hawk), ch 13.

17 See pp 31-32 below.
18 See p 27 below.
19 *Market definition* OFT Guideline 403, para 1.3.
20 See eg the *Merger Guidelines* of the Australian Competition and Consumer Commission, available at http://www.accc.gov.au; the *Business Acquisition Guidelines* of the New Zealand Competition Authority, available at http://www.med.govt.nz/about/comp_ent/html/.

circumstances in which they are very important: a share of 50% or more of a market creates a legal presumption of dominance in a case under Article 82[1], and a market share of 30% or more will prevent the application of the block exemption in Regulation 2790/99 on vertical agreements[2]. However, calculating an undertaking's market share is only one step in determining whether it has market power.

(B)   Circumstances in which it is necessary to define the relevant market

The foregoing discussion may be rendered less abstract by considering the circumstances in EC and UK competition law in which it may be necessary to define the relevant market. Some, but not all, of the following situations are referred to specifically in the Commission's Notice[3] and in the OFT's Guideline on *Market Definition*[4].

(i)   EC competition law

- Under Article 81(1), when considering whether an agreement has the effect of restricting competition[5].
- Under Article 81(1) when considering whether an agreement *appreciably* restricts competition; in particular there are market share tests in the *Notice on Agreements of Minor Importance*: a horizontal agreement, that is one between competitors, will usually be *de minimis* where the parties' market share is 5% or less, and a vertical agreement, that is one between undertakings operating at different levels of the market, will usually be *de minimis* where their market share is 10% or less[6].
- Under the Commission's guidelines on the application of Article 81(1) to horizontal cooperation agreements, where further market share thresholds will be found[7].
- Under Article 81(3)(b) when considering whether an agreement would substantially eliminate competition[8].
- Under numerous block exemptions containing market share tests, for example Regulation 2790/99 on vertical agreements[9], Regulation 2658/2000 on specialisation agreements[10] and Regulation 2659/2000 on research and development agreements[11].
- Under Article 82, when considering whether an undertaking has abused a dominant position[12].

1   See ch 5, p 155.
2   See ch 16, pp 578-580.
3   OJ [1997] C 372/5, [1998] 4 CMLR 177, paras 10-12.
4   OFT 403, para 2.4.
5   See eg Case C-234/89 *Delimitis v Henninger Bräu* [1991] ECR I-935, [1992] 5 CMLR 210.
6   OJ [1997] C 372/13, [1998] 4 CMLR 192, para 9.
7   See ch 15, pp 501-508.
8   See ch 4, pp 132-133.
9   See ch 16, pp 578-580.
10 See ch 15, pp 517-520.
11 Ibid, pp 510-515.
12 See ch 5, p 152.

- Under the ECMR when determining whether a merger would create or strengthen a dominant position[13].

(ii) UK law

- When applying the Chapter I and Chapter II prohibitions of the Competition Act, which are based on the provisions in Articles 81 and 82[14].
- Specifically, in the case of the Chapter I prohibition, in determining whether non-hard-core horizontal agreements restrict competition: this will not be so where the parties' market share is less than 25%[15].
- When analysing scale and complex monopoly situations under the Fair Trading Act 1973[16].
- When determining the effects of a merger on competition under the Fair Trading Act 1973[17].

Market definition, therefore, plays a key part in much competition law analysis. Competition authorities have a considerable discretion in their delineation of the market; however various tests have been developed which endeavour to make market definition more scientific[18].

(C) The relevant product market

The ECJ, when it heard its first appeal on the application of Article 82 by the Commission in *Europemballage Corpn and Continental Can Co Inc v Commission*, held that when identifying a dominant position the delimitation of the relevant product market was of crucial importance[19]. This has been repeated by the ECJ on numerous occasions.[20] In *Continental Can Co Inc*[1] it was the Commission's failure to define the relevant product market that caused the ECJ to quash its decision. The Commission had held that Continental Can and its subsidiary SLW had a dominant position in three separate product markets – cans for meat, cans for fish and metal tops – without giving a satisfactory explanation of why these markets were separate from one another or from the market for cans and containers generally. The ECJ in effect insisted that the Commission should define the relevant product market and support its definition in a reasoned decision. However there have subsequently been many unsuccessful appeals on this matter to the Community Courts, the allegedly dominant firm usually claiming that its market power had been exaggerated by the Commission as a result of an unrealistically narrow definition of the market:[2] it is one thing

13 See ch 21, pp 771-772.
14 See ch 9, pp 291-321.
15 Ibid, pp 295-297.
16 See ch 11, pp 364-370.
17 See ch 22, pp 818-830.
18 See pp 30-31 below.
19 Case 6/72 [1973] ECR 215, [1973] CMLR 199, para 32.
20 See eg Case 27/76 *United Brands v Commission* [1978] ECR 207, [1978] 1 CMLR 429, para 10.
1   JO [1972] L 7/25, [1972] CMLR D11.
2   See eg Cases 6 and 7/73 *ICI and Commercial Solvents v Commission* [1974] ECR 223, [1974] 1 CMLR 309; Case 27/76 *United Brands v Commission* [1978] ECR 207, [1978] 1 CMLR 429; Case 322/81 *Nederlandsche Banden-Industrie Michelin NV v Commission* [1983] ECR 3461, [1985] 1 CMLR 282.

for the Court to require the Commission properly to reason its decision, quite another for it to substitute its own opinion for that of the Commission[3].

(i)   The legal test

The judgments of the ECJ show that the definition of the market is essentially a matter of interchangeability. Where goods or services can be regarded as interchangeable, they are within the same product market. Thus in *Continental Can* the ECJ enjoined the Commission, for the purpose of delimiting the market, to investigate:

> '[those] characteristics of the products in question by virtue of which they are particularly apt to satisfy an inelastic need and are only to a limited extent interchangeable with other products'.[4]

Similarly in *United Brands v Commission*, where the applicant was arguing that bananas were in the same market as other fruit, the ECJ said that this issue depended on whether the banana could be:

> 'singled out by such special features distinguishing it from other fruits that it is only to a limited extent interchangeable with them and is only exposed to their competition in a way that is hardly perceptible'.[5]

(ii)   Measuring interchangeability

Conceptually, the idea that a relevant market consists of goods or services that are interchangeable with one another is simple enough. In practice, however, the measurement of interchangeability can give rise to considerable problems for a variety of reasons: for example there may be no data available on the issue, or the data that exist may be unreliable, incomplete or deficient in some other way. A further problem is that, in many cases, the data will be open to (at least) two interpretations. It is often the case therefore that market definition is extremely difficult.

(iii)   Commission Notice on the Definition of the Relevant Market for the Purposes of Community Competition Law[6]

Useful guidance on market definition is provided by the Commission's Notice. The introduction of the ECMR had, as an inevitable consequence, that the Commission was called upon to define markets in a far larger number of situations than previously. Whereas it may have had to deal with complaints under Article 82, say, 20 times a year in the 1980s, by the 1990s it was having to deal with 100 or more notifications under the ECMR each year: the Merger Task Force (hereafter the 'MTF') received no fewer than 235 notifications under the ECMR

---

3   See eg Case T-65/96 *Kish Glass & Co Ltd v Commission* [2000] 5 CMLR 229, para 64.
4   Case 6/72 [1973] ECR 215, [1973] CMLR 199, para 32.
5   Case 27/76 [1978] ECR 207, [1978] 1 CMLR 429, para 22.
6   OJ [1997] C 372/5, [1998] 4 CMLR 177.

in 1998[7] and 301 in 1999[8]. Furthermore, whereas an Article 82 case would normally require the definition of just one market – the one in which the dominant firm was alleged to have abused its position – a case under the ECMR might be quite different, since the merging parties might conduct business in a number of different markets giving rise to competition considerations. This necessarily meant that the MTF was called upon to develop more systematic methods for defining the market, although it remains the case that a fair amount of subjective assessment is involved in this difficult process. There are still many cases in which, for example, the notifying parties under the ECMR may be in fundamental disagreement with the Commission over its delineation of the market; in an Article 82 case the disagreement may be between the complainant and the Commission on the one hand and the 'defendant' on the other. Furthermore, it may be that parties involved in an Article 82 case would favour a different definition of the market than they would in a merger case: a broad market under Article 82 may mean that a defendant is found not to have a dominant position; whereas very narrow markets under the ECMR may mean that two merging entities do not have any areas of horizontal overlap with the consequence that they are not creating or strengthening a dominant position. One can see, therefore, that much is at stake in the art, or science, of market definition.

(iv)   Demand-side substitutability

As mentioned above, the Commission explains at paragraph 13 of the Notice that firms are subject to three main competitive constraints: demand substitutability, supply substitutability and potential competition. It continues that, for the purpose of market definition, it is demand substitutability that is of the greatest significance; supply substitutability may be relevant to market definition in certain special circumstances, but normally this is a matter to be examined when determining whether there is dominance; potential competition in the market is always a matter of dominance.

Paragraph 14 of the Notice states that the assessment of demand substitution entails a determination of the range of products which are viewed as substitutes by the consumer. It then proposes a test whereby it becomes possible to determine whether particular products are within the same market. The so-called 'SSNIP' test, first deployed by the Department of Justice and the Federal Trade Commission under US competition law when analysing horizontal mergers[9], works as follows: suppose that a producer of a product – for example a widget – were to introduce a Small but Significant Non-transitory Increase in Price. In those circumstances, would consumers be inclined to switch their purchases to other makes of widgets, or indeed even to blodgets? If the answer is yes, this would suggest that the market is at least as wide as widgets generally and includes blodgets as well. The same test can be applied to the delineation of the geographic market. If a firm could raise its price by a significant amount and retain its customers, this would mean that the market would be worth monopolising: prices could be raised profitably, since there would be no competitive constraint. For this reason,

7   XXVIIIth *Report on Competition Policy* (1998), point 136.
8   XXIXth *Report on Competition Policy* (1999), point 147.
9   US Department of Justice *Horizontal Merger Guidelines*: see http://www.usdoj.gov/atr/
     public/guidelines/horiz_book/hmg1.html; the SSNIP test is not used in the US for the purpose
     of market definition in cartel and monopolisation cases under ss 1 and 2 Sherman Act 1890.

the SSNIP test is also – and more catchily – referred to sometimes as the 'hypothetical monopolist test'[10]. The hypothetical monopolist test is given formal expression in paragraph 17 of the Commission's Notice, where it states that:

> 'The question to be asked is whether the parties' customers would switch to readily available substitutes or to suppliers located elsewhere in response to a hypothetical small (in the range 5% to 10%) but permanent relative price increase in the products and areas being considered. If substitution were enough to make the price increase unprofitable because of the resulting loss of sales, additional substitutes and areas are included in the relevant market.'

This formulation of the test takes the 'range' of 5% to 10% to indicate 'significance' within the SSNIP formula.

(v)   The 'Cellophane Fallacy'

It is necessary to enter a word of caution on the hypothetical monopolist test. A monopolist may already be charging a monopoly price: if it were to raise its price further, its customers would cease to buy from it at all. In this situation, its 'own-price elasticity' – the extent to which consumers switch from its products in response to a price rise – is high. If a SSNIP test is applied in these circumstances between the monopolised product and another one, this might suggest a high degree of substitutability, since consumers are already at the point where they will cease to buy from the monopolist; the test therefore would exaggerate the breadth of the market. This error was committed by the US Supreme Court in *United States v EI du Pont de Nemour and Co*[11] in a case concerning packaging materials, including cellophane, since when it has been known as the 'Cellophane Fallacy'. This demonstrates clearly the care that must be taken in applying the SSNIP test: it may be appropriate in merger cases, where a competition authority is trying to predict what will happen in the future if the hypothetical monopolist were to raise its prices after the transaction[12]; but not in a dominance case, where a crucial issue is whether the defendant is a monopolist in the first place.

In the US, the SSNIP test is used only in merger cases. In the Commission's Notice, it states in the first paragraph that it is to be used for cases under Articles 81, 82 and the ECMR; the Cellophane Fallacy is briefly acknowledged at paragraph 19 of the Notice, where it says that in cases under Article 82 'the fact that the prevailing price might already have been substantially increased will be taken into account'. This is not the finest feature of the Notice, since it does not explain what methodology should be used in such cases. In the UK, the Guideline on *Market definition* states, at paragraph 5.14, that in these circumstances the Director General of Fair Trading would look not only at market definition but at other evidence of market power and the undertaking's conduct in determining a case under the Chapter II prohibition, acknowledging that market definition is not an end in itself but a tool for assessing whether an undertaking has market power. The OFT Guideline is more open than the Commission's Notice in

---

10   The term 'monopolist' is used here to mean the sole supplier of a product; it does not assume that the firm is question has market power which is, of course, the issue to be determined: see footnote 2 of the OFT's Guideline *Market definition* OFT 403.
11   351 US 377 (1956).
12   See *Bishop and Walker* para. 3.06.

acknowledging the problem of the Cellophane Fallacy, but does not go a great deal further in providing a convincing explanation of how the SSNIP test can be applied to cases of abuse under Article 82 and the Chapter II prohibition[12a].

(vi) Supply-side substitutability

In most cases, interchangeability will be determined by examining the market from the customer's perspective. However, it is also helpful in some situations to consider the degree of substitutability on the supply side of the market. Suppose that A is a producer of widgets and that B is a producer of blodgets: if it is a very simple matter for B to change its production process and to produce widgets, this might suggest that widgets and blodgets are part of the same market. Dicta of the ECJ in *Continental Can v Commission*[13] indicate that the supply side of the market should be considered for the purpose of defining the market. Among its criticisms of the Commission's decision,[14] the ECJ said that it should have made clear why it considered that producers of other types of containers would not be able to adapt their production to compete with Continental Can. The Commission has specifically addressed the issue of supply-side substitutability in some subsequent decisions[15]. A good example is *Tetra Pak 1 (BTG Licence)*[16], where it took into account the fact that producers of milk-packaging machines could not readily adapt their production to make aseptic packaging machines and cartons in arriving at its market definition.

In paragraphs 20-23 of the *Notice on Market Definition* the Commission explains the circumstances in which it considers that supply-side substitutability is relevant to market definition. At paragraph 20 the Commission says that where suppliers are able to switch production to other products and to market them 'in the short term' without incurring significant additional costs or risks in response to small and permanent changes in relative prices, then the market may be broadened to include the products that those suppliers are already producing. A footnote to paragraph 20 suggests that the short term means 'such a period that does not entail a significant adjustment of existing tangible and intangible assets'. A practical example is given in paragraph 22 of a company producing a particular grade of paper: if it could change easily to producing other grades of paper, they should all be included in the market definition. However, where supply substitution is more complex than this, it should be regarded as a matter of determining dominance rather than establishing the market. While it may seem unimportant whether this issue is dealt with at the stage of market definition or dominance, there is a sense that once a market has been narrowly defined, there is an unavoidable consequence that a defendant will be found to be dominant and to be guilty of abuse: it would normally prefer therefore a broader market definition, and try to demonstrate that it does not

---

12a These issues are considered further in the OFT's Economic Discussion Paper 2, *The Rôle of Market Definition in Monopoly and Dominance Inquiries* (prepared by National Economic Research Associates, July 2001).
13 Case 6/72 [1973] ECR 215, [1973] CMLR 199, paras 32 ff.
14 *Continental Can Co Inc* JO [1972] L7/25, [1972] CMLR D11.
15 See eg *Eurofix-Bauco v Hilti* OJ [1988] L 65/19, [1989] 4 CMLR 677, para 55, upheld on appeal to the CFI Case T-30/89 *Hilti AG v Commission* [1991] ECR II-1439, [1992] 4 CMLR 16 and on appeal to the ECJ Case C-53/92 P [1994] ECR I-667, [1994] 4 CMLR 614.
16 OJ [1988] L 272/27, [1988] 4 CMLR 47, upheld on appeal Case T-51/89 *Tetra Pak Rausing SA v Commission* [1990] ECR II-309, [1991] 4 CMLR 334 and on appeal to the ECJ Case C-333/94 P [1996] ECR I-5951, [1997] 4 CMLR 662.

have a dominant position. Furthermore, where competition law deploys a market share test, as for example in Article 3 of Regulation 2790/99[17], the possibility of broadening the market definition through the inclusion of supply-side substitutes may have a crucial effect on the outcome of a particular case: a market share test does not say anything about competitive constraints from potential competitors outside the relevant market. This point in itself illustrates the limits of market shares as an indicator of market power.

(vii) Evidence relied on to define relevant markets

In practice, the critical issue is to know what evidence is available and can be adduced to determine the scope of the relevant market. While it is relatively easy to understand the concepts of demand- and supply-side substitutability, the more problematic issue is to capture data that will provide meaningful results to a SSNIP test. If the world were composed of an infinite number of market research organisations devoted to asking SSNIP-like questions of consumers, market definition would be truly scientific. But of course the world is not so composed, and a variety of techniques, some of considerable sophistication, are deployed by economists and econometrists in order to seek solutions. The Commission's Notice, from paragraph 25 onwards[18], considers some of the evidence that may be available, but it quite correctly says that tests that may be suitable in one industry may be wholly inappropriate in another. A moment's reflection shows that this must be so: for example, the demand-substitutability of one alcoholic beverage for another in the ordinary citizen's mind is likely to be tested by different criteria than an airline choosing whether to purchase aeroplanes from Boeing or Airbus.

(viii) Examples of evidence that may be used in defining the relevant product market

As far as definition of the product market is concerned, the Commission suggests in the Notice that the following evidence may be available.

(A) EVIDENCE OF SUBSTITUTION IN THE RECENT PAST. There may recently have been an event – such as a price increase or a 'shock', perhaps a failure of the Brazilian coffee crop due to a late frost – and there may be direct evidence of the consequences that this had for consumers' consumption (perhaps a large increase in the drinking of tea).

(B) QUANTITATIVE TESTS. Various econometric and statistical tests have been devised which attempt to estimate own-price elasticities and cross-price elasticities for the demand of a product, based on the similarity of price movements over time, the causality between price series and the similarity of price levels and/or their convergence. Own-price elasticities measure the extent to which demand

---

17 OJ [1999] L 336/21, [2000] 4 CMLR 398; on market definition under this block exemption, see the Commission's *Guidelines on Vertical Restraints*, OJ [2000] C 291/1, [2000] 5 CMLR 1074, Section V, paras 78-90.

18 See also *Bishop and Walker*, chs 7-15, which consider techniques that may be relevant to market definition; also LECG Ltd *Quantitative techniques in competition analysis* OFT Research Paper 17, 1999; this can be obtained from the Office of Fair Trading's website at http://www.oft.gov.uk/html/rsearch/reports/oft266.htm.

for a product changes in response to a change in its price. Cross-price elasticities measure the extent to which demand for a product changes in response to a change in the price of some other product. Own-price elasticities provide more information about the market power that an undertaking possesses than cross-price elasticities; however cross-price elasticities help more with market definition, since they provide evidence on substitutability.

(c)   VIEWS OF CUSTOMERS AND COMPETITORS.   The Commission will contact customers and competitors in a case that involves market definition, and will, where appropriate, specifically ask them to answer the SSNIP test. This happens routinely, for example, when the MTF seek to delineate the market under the ECMR.

(d)   MARKETING STUDIES AND CONSUMER SURVEYS.   The Commission will look at marketing studies as a useful provider of information about the market, although it specifically states in paragraph 41 that it will scrutinise 'with utmost care' the methodology followed in consumer surveys carried out *ad hoc* by the undertakings involved in merger cases or cases under Articles 81 and 82. Its concern is that the selection of questions in the survey may be deliberately made in order to achieve a favourable outcome.

(e)   BARRIERS AND COSTS ASSOCIATED WITH SWITCHING DEMAND TO POTENTIAL SUBSTITUTES.   There may be a number of barriers and/or costs that result in two *prima facie* demand substitutes not belonging to one single product market. The Commission deals with these in paragraph 42 of the Notice, and gives as examples regulatory barriers, other forms of State intervention, constraints occurring in downstream markets, the need to incur capital investment and other factors.

(f)   DIFFERENT CATEGORIES OF CUSTOMERS AND PRICE DISCRIMINATION.   At paragraph 43, the Commission states that the extent of the product market might be narrowed where there exist distinct groups of customers for a particular product: the market for one group may be narrower than for the other, if it is possible to identify which group an individual belongs to at the moment of selling the relevant products and there is no possibility of trade between the two categories of customer.

(ix)   A word of caution on the Notice

The *Notice on Market Definition* is a useful document. It explains in a helpful way both the reasons for market definition and some of the possible techniques that are available; furthermore, it is based on the practical experience of the Commission – and in particular the MTF – in applying the competition rules. However, it is important to point out a few words of caution. The problem of the Cellophane Fallacy has already been mentioned[19]. There are three other points about the Notice. First, it is 'only' a Commission Notice: it does not have the force of law, and ought not to be treated as a legislative instrument. The ECJ has referred to demand substitutability in terms of price, physical characteristics[20] and intended use[1], whereas the Notice very much emphasises price. While the

19   See pp 28-29 above.
20   See pp 32-33 below.
1   See p 33 below.

emphasis in the Notice is no doubt in accord with how most economists approach the issue of market definition, it nevertheless remains the case, as a matter of law, that physical characteristics and intended use are also relevant to market definition.

A second point about the Notice is that, no matter how well it explains the SSNIP test and the evidence that may be used when applying it, the fact remains that in some sectors the data needed may simply not be available: the information that can be captured varies hugely from one sector to another, and in some cases one will be thrown back on fairly subjective assessments of the market for want of hard, scientific evidence. An example of this is the Commission's decision in *British Interactive Broadcasting*[2], where the Commission itself stated that it could not delineate the markets for interactive broadcasting services by applying a SSNIP test, since no data were available in relation to a product that had yet to be launched. Clearly this is always likely to be a problem in relation to products introduced into the 'new' economy[3].

A third point about the Notice is that there are by now very many cases – in particular under the ECMR – in which the Commission has been called upon to define the market. With more than 2,000 mergers having been notified to the Commission under the ECMR, there are few sectors in which it has not been called upon to analyse the market. As a consequence of this, there is a very considerable 'decisional practice' of the Commission in which it has opined – from cars, buses and trucks to pharmaceuticals and agrochemicals, from banking and insurance services to international aviation and deep-sea drilling[4]. Not unnaturally, an undertaking in need of guidance on the Commission's likely response to a matter of market definition will wish to find out what it has had to say in the past in actual decisions; however the caveat should be entered that the CFI has established that the market must always be defined in any particular case by reference to the facts prevailing at the time and not by reference to precedents.[5] Given these words of caution on the SSNIP test, it remains helpful to consider various issues that have been considered by the Commission and/or the Community Courts over the years when considering problems of market definition.

(x)   Physical characteristics

It may be legitimate to take into account the physical characteristics of products for the purpose of identifying the market, although this happens infrequently

2   OJ [1999] L 312/1, [2000] 4 CMLR 901.
3   On the issue of market definition in cases involving e-commerce, see *E-commerce and its implications for competition policy* (Frontier Economics Group, OFT Economic Discussion Paper 1, 2000) ch 4.
4   See ch 21, pp 742-743 on how to access the Commission's decisions under the ECMR.
5   In Joined Cases T-125/97 and T-127/97 *Coca-Cola v Commission* [2000] All ER (EC) 460, [2000] 5 CMLR 467, at para 82, the CFI stated that in the course of any decision applying Article 82, 'the Commission must define the relevant market again and make a fresh analysis of the conditions of competition which will not necessarily be based on the same considerations as those underlying the previous finding of a dominant position'; examples of how market definitions can change over a period of time are afforded by cross-channel ferry services between the UK and continental Europe, where the Channel Tunnel has altered the market: see *The Peninsular and Oriental Steam Navigation Corpn and Stena Line AB* Cm 4030 (1998); and the market for betting shops in the UK: see *Ladbroke Group plc and The Coral Betting Business* Cm 4030 (1998).

now. For example in *United Brands v Commission*[6] the ECJ considered that the softness, seedlessness, taste and handling quality of bananas were relevant in deciding that they could reasonably be considered to form a distinct market from that of fruit generally.

(xi) Intended use

In determining interchangeability, it is relevant to look at the use for which a particular purchaser requires a product. The rationale for this is that if a person needs a product for a specific purpose, that product will be within the same market only as other products which satisfy the same need. For example, in *ICI and Commercial Solvents Corpn v Commission*[7] Commercial Solvents (CSC) produced nitropropane and supplied it to Zoja, an Italian company; Zoja processed it into ethambutol, a drug used for the treatment of tuberculosis. CSC decided that it would no longer supply Zoja, which claimed that this amounted to an abuse within Article 82. CSC argued that it did not have a dominant position, as nitropropane was part of a wider market consisting of all raw materials from which ethambutol could be produced. The ECJ rejected this argument, as Zoja could not adapt its industrial process to produce ethambutol from other raw materials without great difficulty and expense. From Zoja's position, the relevant product market consisted of those products from which it could realistically continue to produce ethambutol: in other words it was the particular use that Zoja had for nitropropane which determined the issue of interchangeability.

(xii) Spare parts and the aftermarket[8]

There are numerous sectors in which a consumer of one product – for example a car – will need to purchase at a later date complementary products such as spare parts. The same can be true where a customer has to buy 'consumables', such as cartridges to be used in a laser printer, or maintenance services. In such cases, one issue is to determine how the relevant product market should be defined. If there is a separate market for the complementary product, it may be that an undertaking that has no power over the 'primary' market may nevertheless be dominant in the 'secondary' one. An illustration is *Hugin v Commission*,[9] where the ECJ upheld the Commission's finding that Hugin was dominant in the market for spare parts for its own cash machines. Liptons, a firm which serviced Hugin's machines, could not use spare parts produced by anyone else for this purpose because Hugin would have been able to prevent this by relying on its rights under the UK Design Copyright Act 1968. Therefore, although for other purposes it might be true to say that there is a market for spare parts generally, in this case, given the use to which Liptons intended to put them, the market had to be more narrowly defined. Liptons was 'locked in', as it was dependent on Hugin,

6 Case 27/76 [1978] ECR 207, [1978] 1 CMLR 429, para 31.
7 Cases 6, 7/73 [1974] ECR 223, [1974] 1 CMLR 309.
8 See *Bishop and Walker* paras 5.58-5.64; this issue often arises in cases concerning alleged 'tie-in transactions', as to which see ch 17, pp 605-611.
9 Cases 22/78 [1979] ECR 1869, [1979] 3 CMLR 345; the Commission's decision was quashed in this case as it had failed to establish the necessary effect on inter-state trade.

and this justified a narrow market definition. This case, and the judgments of the ECJ in *AB Volvo v Erik Veng*[10] and *CICRA v Régie Nationale des Usines Renault*,[11] establish that spare parts can form a market separate from the products for which they are needed. Likewise consumables, such as nails for use with nail-guns[12] and cartons for use with filling-machines,[13] have been held to be a separate market from the product with which they are used.

However, as a matter of economics it would be wrong to conclude that the primary and secondary markets are necessarily always discrete: it may be the case that a consumer, when deciding to purchase the primary product, will already have taken into account the price of the secondary products that will be needed in the future: in other words, high prices in the secondary market may act as a competitive constraint when the purchaser is making his initial decision as to which primary product to purchase. It is an empirical question whether there is a separate aftermarket, depending on the extent to which consumers are 'locked in' to a particular supplier. The Commission has stated that it regards the issue as one that needs to be examined on a case-by-case basis[14], and that it will look at all important factors such as the price and life time of the primary product, the transparency of the prices for the secondary product and the proportion of the price of the secondary product to the value of the primary one. In its investigation of *Kyocera/Pelikan*[15] it concluded that Kyocera was not dominant in the market for toner cartridges for printers, since consumers took the price of cartridges into account when deciding which printer to buy.

(xiii) *Structure of supply and demand*

It may be necessary to look at the structure of supply and demand on a market when testing interchangeability. This is best illustrated by *Nederlandsche Banden-Industrie Michelin v Commission*[16]. The ECJ upheld the Commission's identification of the market as *replacement* tyres for heavy vehicles. One issue was whether replacement tyres were in a separate market from the tyres with which a new vehicle is equipped: in both cases the product is identical. However, if one looked at the structure of supply and demand, one could see that replacement tyres are purchased and fitted in quite different circumstances from the tyres that are fitted to a new vehicle. It was therefore legitimate to distinguish the two markets.[17]

---

10 Case 238/87 [1988] ECR 6211, [1989] 4 CMLR 122.
11 Case 53/87 [1988] ECR 6039, [1990] 4 CMLR 265.
12 Case T–30/89 *Hilti AG v Commission* [1990] ECR II-163, [1992] 4 CMLR 16, upheld on appeal Case 53/92 P *Hilti AG v Commission* [1994] ECR I-667, [1994] 4 CMLR 614.
13 *Tetra Pak II* OJ [1992] L 72/1, [1992] 4 CMLR 551, upheld on appeal to the CFI Case T–83/91 *Tetra Pak International SA v Commission* [1994] ECR II-755, [1997] 4 CMLR 726, and on appeal to the ECJ: Case C-333/94 P *Tetra Pak International SA v Commission* [1996] ECR I-5951, [1997] 4 CMLR 662.
14 XXVth *Report on Competition Policy* (1995), point 86; see also the *Notice on Market Definition* (p 26, n 6 above), para 56; the *Guidelines on Vertical Restraints* (p 30, n 17 above), para 86.
15 XXVth *Report on Competition Policy* (1995), point 87.
16 Case 322/81 [1983] ECR 3461, [1985] 1 CMLR 282, paras 35-45.
17 See similarly *BBI/Boosey and Hawkes: Interim Measures* OJ [1987] L 286/36, [1988] 4 CMLR 67, para 17.

(xiv) Internal documents

In some cases, the Commission has relied on the internal documents of an undertaking when identifying the relevant market. In *BBI/Boosey and Hawkes: Interim Measures*,[18] it regarded documents in which Boosey and Hawkes had identified a discrete market for brass band instruments for British-style brass bands, distinguishable from the market for brass instruments generally, as a significant factor in adopting a narrow market definition. It obviously follows from this that an undertaking ought to exercise some caution about the claims it makes about particular products, both in internal documents and, for example, in advertising material: it is possible that the Commission will use statements that an undertaking makes as part of the proof in any particular proceedings that might be brought.

(xv) Statutory markets

In some situations, the relevant market may be defined by statute. For example in *British Leyland v Commission*[19] legislation provided that only BL could provide type-approval certificates, as required by the Department of the Environment, in respect of BL vehicles.

(xvi) Procurement markets

In some cases the business behaviour under scrutiny is that of buyers rather than sellers. For example where supermarkets merge[20], or where their procurement policies are under investigation[1], the market must be defined from the demand- rather than the supply-side of the market. In the case of an exclusive supply obligation, as that term is used in Regulation 2790/99 on vertical restraints, Article 3(b) requires that the market be defined from the demand side[2].

(xvii) Innovation markets[3]

In the US a 'market for innovation', separate from products already on the market, has been found in some cases involving high technology industries[4]. It is not yet clear whether the competition authorities in the EC and the UK will adopt this approach. The Commission's decision in *Shell/Montecatini*[5] suggested that it would be prepared to define a market for innovation, although in other cases it has made use of the more conventional idea of 'potential competition' to deal

---

18 OJ [1987] L 286/36, [1988] 4 CMLR 67.
19 Case 226/84 [1986] ECR 3263, [1987] 1 CMLR 185; this follows an earlier similar case, Case 26/75 *General Motors v Commission* [1975] ECR 1367, [1976] 1 CMLR 95.
20 See eg Case No IV/M.1221 *Rewe/Meinl* OJ [1999] L 274/1, [2000] 5 CMLR 256.
1   *Supermarkets* Cm 4842 (2000).
2   See ch 16, p 579.
3   See Rapp 'The Misapplication of the Innovative Market Approach to Merger Analysis' (1995) 64 Antitrust Law Journal 19.
4   *United States v Flow International Corpn* No 94-71320; US Department of Justice and Federal Trade Commission *Antitrust Guidelines for the Licensing of Intellectual Property* http://www.usdoj.gov/atr/public/guidelines/ipguide.htm.
5   OJ [1994] L 332/48.

with the situation[6]. The Commission's *Guidelines on Horizontal Cooperation Agreements*[7] provide some guidance on this issue.

(D)   The relevant geographic market

It is also necessary, when determining whether a firm or firms have market power, that the relevant geographic market should be defined. The definition of the geographic market may have a decisive impact on the outcome of a case, as in the *Volvo/Scania* decision under the ECMR: the Commission's conclusion that there were national, rather than pan-European, markets for trucks and buses led to an outright prohibition of that merger[8]. Some products can be supplied without difficulty throughout the Community or even the world. In other cases there may be technical, legal or practical reasons why a product can be supplied only within a narrower area. The delineation of the geographic market helps to indicate which other firms impose a competitive constraint on the one(s) under investigation. The cost of transporting products is an important factor: some goods are so expensive to transport in relation to their value that it would not be economic to attempt to sell them on distant markets. Another factor might be legal controls which make it impossible for an undertaking in one Member State to export goods or services to another. This problem may be dealt with by the Commission bringing proceedings against the Member State to prevent restrictions on the free movement of goods (under Articles 28 to 30 (ex Articles 30 to 36)) or of services (under Articles 49 to 55 (ex Articles 59 to 66)). With the completion of the internal market, there should be fewer claims that fiscal, technical and legal barriers to inter-state trade exist.

(i)   United Brands v Commission

That the geographic market should be identified is clear from the ECJ's judgment in *United Brands v Commission*[9]. It said that the opportunities for competition under Article 82 must be considered:

> 'with reference to a clearly defined geographic area in which [the product] is marketed and where the conditions are sufficiently homogeneous for the effect of the economic power of the undertaking concerned to be able to be evaluated'.

In that case the Commission had excluded the UK, France and Italy from the geographic market since in those countries special arrangements existed as to the importing and marketing of bananas. United Brands argued that, even so, the Commission had drawn the geographic market too widely, since competitive conditions varied between the remaining six Member States;[10] the ECJ however

6   See Temple Lang 'European Community Antitrust Law: Innovation Markets and High Technology industries' [1996] Fordham Corporate Law Institute (ed Hawk), ch 23; Landman 'Innovation Markets in Europe' (1998) 19 ECLR 21.
7   OJ [2001] C3/2, [2001] 4 CMLR 819, paras 51-53.
8   See ch 21, p 801.
9   Case 27/76 [1978] ECR 207, [1978] 1 CMLR 429, paras 10 and 11.
10   This decision was reached before the accession of Greece, Spain and Portugal etc.

concluded that the Commission had drawn it correctly. The significance of the geographic market in determining dominance was emphasised by the ECJ in *Alsatel v Novasam SA*[11]. There the ECJ held that the facts before it failed to establish that a particular region in France rather than France generally constituted the geographic market, so that the claim that Novasam had a dominant position failed in the absence of evidence of power over the wider, national, market.

(ii) Obvious cases

In many cases the geographic market is obvious. For example in *British Telecommunications*[12] the question was whether BT had abused its dominant position in its dealings with message-forwarding agencies in the UK. It was obvious that BT's geographic market was the UK, within which it had an absolute monopoly in the provision of telecommunication services. In the *TV Listings* case[13], where the CFI and the ECJ upheld the Commission's decision[14] that it was an abuse of a dominant position for television companies to refuse to make available listings of television programmes, the market was Ireland and Northern Ireland, where consumers would want information about the programmes of the three television companies in question, one in Eire and two in Ulster.

(iii) More difficult cases

In other cases there may be more difficulty in defining the geographic market. It is not clear from the ECJ's judgment in *United Brands* precisely what issues are relevant when defining it. The ECJ said that the geographic market must be an area in which the objective conditions of competition must be the same for all traders[15]. In *United Brands* this was not true of the UK, Italian and French markets, because of the special arrangements there for bananas. In the other six states of the EC at the time there were no particular factors which could be considered to disturb the unity of the geographic market.

(iv) The Commission's Notice on Market Definition

The Commission provides helpful guidance on the definition of the geographic market in its *Notice on Market Definition*[16]. At paragraph 28, it says that its approach can be summarised as follows:

'it will take a preliminary view of the scope of the geographic market on the basis of broad indications as to the distribution of market shares between

11 Case 247/86 [1988] ECR 5987, [1990] 4 CMLR 434.
12 OJ [1982] L 360/36, [1983] 1 CMLR 457, upheld on appeal Case 41/83 *Italy v Commission* [1985] ECR 873, [1985] 2 CMLR 368.
13 Cases T-69/89 etc *RTE v Commission* [1991] ECR II-485, [1991] 4 CMLR 586, upheld on appeal to the ECJ Case 241/91 P *RTE and ITP v Commission* [1995] ECR I-743, [1995] 4 CMLR 718.
14 *Magill TV Guide/ITP, BBC and RTE* OJ [1989] L 78/43, [1989] 4 CMLR 757.
15 See similarly *Decca Navigator System* OJ [1989] L 43/27, [1990] 4 CMLR 627, paras 88-90, where the Commission said that it was necessary to ask whether competitive conditions were similar.
16 See p 26, n 6 above.

the parties and their competitors, as well as a preliminary analysis of pricing and price differences at national and Community or EEA level. This initial view is used basically as a working hypothesis to focus the Commission's enquiries for the purposes of arriving at a precise geographic market definition.'

In the following paragraph, the Commission says that it will then explore any particular configuration of prices or market shares in order to test whether they really do say something about the possibility of demand substitution between one market and another: for example, it will consider the importance of national or local preferences, current patterns of purchases of customers and product differentiation. This survey is to be conducted within the context of the SSNIP test outlined above, the difference being that, in the case of geographic market definition, the question is whether, faced with an increase in price, consumers located in a particular area would switch their purchases to suppliers further away. Further relevant factors are set out in paragraphs 30 and 31 of the Notice, and at paragraph 32 the Commission points out that it will take into account the continuing process of market integration in defining the market, the assumption here being that, over time, the single market should become more of a reality, with the result that the geographic market should have a tendency to get wider. There is no reason in principle why the relevant geographic market should not extend to the entire world, and there have been decisions in which this has been so[17].

(v)   *Examples of evidence that may be used in defining the relevant geographic market*

As far as definition of the geographic market is concerned, the Commission suggests that the following evidence may be available.

(A)   PAST EVIDENCE OF DIVERSION OF ORDERS TO OTHER AREAS.   It may be that direct evidence is available of changes in prices between areas and consequent reactions by customers. The Commission points out that care may be needed in comparing prices where there have been exchange rate movements, where taxation levels are different and where there is significant product differentiation between one area and another.

(B)   BASIC DEMAND CHARACTERISTICS.   The scope of the geographic market may be determined by matters such as national preferences or preferences for national brands, language, culture and life style, and the need for a local presence.

(C)   VIEWS OF CUSTOMERS AND COMPETITORS.   As in the case of defining the product market, the Commission will take the views of customers and competitors into account when determining the scope of the geographic market.

(D)   CURRENT GEOGRAPHIC PATTERN OF PURCHASES.   The Commission will examine where customers currently purchase goods or supplies. If they already purchase across the Community, this would indicate a Community-wide market.

---

17 The Commission found global markets for top-level internet connectivity in Case No IV/ M.1069 *WorldCom/MCI* OJ [1999] L 116/1, [1999] 5 CMLR 876, para 82 and Case No COMP/M.1741 *MCI WorldCom/Sprint* decision of 28 June 2000, para 97.

(E)   TRADE FLOWS/PATTERNS OF SHIPMENTS.   Information on trade flows may be helpful in determining the geographic market, provided that the trade statistics are sufficiently detailed for the products in question.

(F)   BARRIERS AND SWITCHING COSTS ASSOCIATED WITH THE DIVERSION OF ORDERS TO COMPANIES LOCATED IN OTHER AREAS.   Barriers that isolate national markets, transport costs and transport restrictions may all contribute to the isolation of national markets.

(E)   The temporal market

It may also be necessary to consider the temporal quality of the market. Competitive conditions may vary from season to season, for example because of the variation of weather conditions or of consumer habits. A firm may find itself exposed to competition at one point in a year but effectively free from it at another. In this situation, it may be that its behaviour may be controlled under Article 82 during the part of the year in which it can be shown to be dominant.

The issue arose in *United Brands v Commission*[18]. There was evidence in that case which suggested that the cross-elasticity of demand for bananas fluctuated from season to season. When other fruit was plentiful in summer, demand for bananas dropped: this suggests that the Commission might have considered that there were two seasonal markets, and that United Brands had no market power over the summer months. The Commission however identified just the one temporal market and held that UBC was dominant within it. On appeal the ECJ declined to deal with this issue. In *ABG*[19] on the other hand the Commission did define the temporal market for oil more narrowly by limiting it to the period of crisis which followed the OPEC action in the early 1970s. The Commission held that during the crisis companies had a special responsibility to supply existing customers on a fair and equitable basis; the ECJ quashed the Commission's decision on the issue of abuse, but not on the definition of the market[20].

(F)   Barriers to entry and barriers to exit

In determining whether a firm or firms have market power, it is not simply market share that is relevant: a large market share may quickly be whittled away if a firm makes excessive profits in an industry, with the result that other firms quickly enter the market. The point has been made above that competitive constraints come in the form of demand substitutability, supply substitutability and potential competition. Market definition is predominantly concerned with the first, and partially with the second, of these. However market shares do not tell us all that needs to be known about market power, since they say nothing about potential competition; it is an intellectual short-circuit, and wrong in principle, to reach a finding of market power on the basis of market shares alone[1]. In particular it is necessary to consider how easily other undertakings

18   Case 27/76 [1978] ECR 207, [1978] 1 CMLR 429.
19   OJ [1977] L 117/1, [1977] 2 CMLR D1.
20   Case 77/77 *BP v Commission* [1978] ECR 1513, [1978] 3 CMLR 174; on the temporal market, see also *Market definition* OFT Guideline 403, paras 5.1-5.3.
1   The dangers of relying too much on market shares are pointed out in Baker and Coselli 'The Rôle of Market Shares in Differentiated Product Markets' (1999) 20 ECLR 412; in Harbord

could enter the market. This requires a consideration of the height of the barriers to entry to and exit from the market[2].

The definition of a barrier to entry in the Oxford Dictionary of Economics is 'Laws, institutions, or practices which make it difficult or impossible for new firms to enter some markets ...'[3]. However, the idea that it is difficult to enter a market is very different from it being impossible to do so. There has been much debate as to the appropriate definition of a barrier to entry for competition law purposes. It is obvious that legal provisions such as licensing laws and intellectual property rights conferring a legal monopoly can act as barriers to entry; so might the advantage of scale and anti-competitive practices designed to deter new entrants to the market. After this the consensus tends to break down. Some economists regard the superior efficiency of a dominant firm, its technological know-how, the cost of advertising, product differentiation and the difficulty of gaining access to risk capital as barriers. Much of this has been questioned, however. In particular it has been suggested that a barrier to entry means 'a cost ... which must be borne by a firm which seeks to enter an industry but is not borne by firms already in the industry'[4]. According to this view, there must be some asymmetry between the position of firms already on the market and newcomers. It would follow that the cost of advertising is not a barrier: the existing firm had to invest in the promotion of its product and the new one will not face a higher cost. Similarly access to capital might be a problem in the sense that the money markets are inefficient, but this is equally true for any borrower. As we shall see in chapter 5[5], the tendency of the European Commission and the Community Courts in applying Article 82 EC has been to adopt a wide approach to barriers to entry; this has had as its consequence that many firms have been found to be in a dominant position, even where their market shares fell considerably short of 100%. In the UK, the OFT's Guideline on the *Assessment of market power*[6] provides quite detailed guidance on how this issue will be handled under the Competition Act 1998, and is in many respects more principled and illuminating than the position under Article 82; in particular this Guideline identifies three types of barrier to entry: absolute advantages, strategic advantages that follow from being the 'first-mover' in the market, and exclusionary behaviour. This Guideline will be discussed in chapter 9[7].

Barriers to exit are also significant when considering market power. A customer of a powerful supplier will be more exploitable where it is difficult for him to leave the market on which he operates, for example because he owns assets that

---

and von Graevenitz 'Market Definition in Oligopolistic and Vertically Related Markets: Some Anomalies' (2000) 21 ECLR 151; and in Griffiths 'A Glorification of de minimis – the Regulation of Vertical Agreements' (2000) 21 ECLR 241.

2   A useful discussion of this topic will be found in OFT Research Paper No 2 *Barriers to Entry and Exit in UK Competition Policy* (1994, London Economics) and in the OFT Guideline *Assessment of market power* OFT 415, http://www.oft.gov.uk/html/comp-act/technical_guidelines/oft415.html, paras 5.1-5.29; see also the Commission's *Guidelines on Vertical Restraints* (p 30, n 17 above), paras 118-121; *Bishop and Walker* Appendix A (pp 301-303); Hardbord and Hoehn 'Barriers to Entry and Exit in European Competition Policy' (1994) 14 International Review of Law and Economics 411.

3   Black (Oxford University Press, 1997) p 27.

4   Stigler *The Organization of Industry* (Homewood, 1968) p 67; also Bork *The Antitrust Paradox* (Basic Books, 1995) pp 310-311.

5   See ch 5, pp 156-161.

6   OFT 415, paras 5.1-5.29.

7   See ch 9, pp 318-319.

are not easily adapted to other uses. In perfectly competitive markets, resources can move freely from one part of the economy to another.

(G) A final reflection on market shares

It has been said several times in this chapter that market share does not, in itself, determine whether an undertaking possesses market power; assessing market power is not and cannot be reduced simply to numbers. This having been said, however, it is interesting to consider the large range of situations in which EC and UK competition law require competition lawyers and their clients to consider market share figures for the purpose of deciding how to handle a particular case. This arises partly from numerous pieces of legislation, both hard and soft, which contain a market share threshold; and partly from case law which has attributed significance to particular market share figures. The following table sets out a series of market share thresholds that should be embedded in the mind of in-house counsel to *DoItAll*, a diversified conglomerate company conducting business in the EU. The list is not exhaustive, and was compiled in a more light-hearted mood than the rest of this chapter: it does nevertheless reveal how influential market share figures can be in analysing competition law cases in the EC and the UK.

Table of market share thresholds

0%   With a market share of 0%, even the most zealous of competition authorities is unlikely to take action against you.

5%   At 5% or more, your horizontal agreements are no longer *de minimis* under the European Commission's *Notice on Agreements of Minor Importance*[8]; however, if your market share is less than 5%, it is unlikely that your vertical agreements will contribute to any 'cumulative' effect on competition in the case of single branding[9] or selective distribution systems[10].

10%   At 10% or more, your vertical agreements are no longer *de minimis* under the *Notice on Agreements of Minor Importance*[11]; block exemption for certain co-insurance agreements ceases to be available[12]; and block exemption for certain specialisation[13] and research and development agreements[14] under the old Regulations ceases to be available if they extend to joint distribution.

15%   At 15%, block exemption for certain co-reinsurance, as opposed to co-insurance, agreements ceases to be available[15]; under the ECMR, in the case of horizontal mergers, markets in which your market share exceeds

---

8   OJ [1997] C 372/13, [1998] 4 CMLR 192, para 9: see ch 3, pp 108-110.
9   Commission's *Guidelines on Vertical Restraints* OJ [2000] C 291/1, [2000] 5 CMLR 1176, para 142.
10 Ibid, para 189.
11 OJ [1997] C 372/13, [1998] 4 CMLR 192, para 9.
12 Article 11(1)(a) of Regulation 3932/92, OJ [1992] L 398/7.
13 Article 3(2)(a) of Regulation 417/85, OJ [1985] L 53/1, as amended by Regulation 151/93.
14 Article 3(3a) of Regulation 418/85, OJ [1985] L 53/5, as amended by Regulation 151/93.
15 Article 11(1)(b) of Regulation 3932/92, OJ [1992] L 398/7.

15% are 'affected markets', necessitating the provision of substantial information on Form CO to the MTF[16]; you will no longer be eligible to take advantage of the 'simplified procedure' for certain horizontal mergers under the ECMR[17]; you have the benefit of a rule in Regulation 17/62 that certain specialisation agreements may benefit from individual exemption irrespective of notification[18]; it is unlikely that your group purchasing agreements[19] or your commercialisation[20] agreements infringe Article 81(1) where your market share is below 15%.

20%   At 20%, block exemption ceases to be available for specialisation and research and development agreements under the old Regulations, even if they do not extend to joint distribution[1]; furthermore, block exemption ceases to be provided for specialisation agreements under the new block exemption where the parties' market share exceeds 20%[2]; some marginal relief is available up to a market share cap of 25%[3].

25%   At 25%, block exemption ceases to be available for research and development agreements under the new block exemption[4]; some marginal relief is provided up to a market share cap of 30%[5] and even, exceptionally, beyond 30%[6]; under the ECMR, at 25% you cease to benefit from the presumption that your merger will not create or strengthen a dominant position[7], you will not benefit from the simplified procedure in the case of vertical mergers[8] and, in the case of vertical mergers, markets in which your market share exceeds 25% are affected markets[9]; your non hard-core horizontal agreements could infringe the Chapter I prohibition in the UK Competition Act[10]; you could be referred to the Competition Commission in the UK under the monopoly and under the merger provisions of the Fair Trading Act[11] where you supply or are supplied with 25% or more of the goods or services of a certain description; and you have significant market power for the purposes of the EC Directives on Leased Lines, Licensing, Interconnection and Voice Telephony[12].

30%   At 30%, your vertical agreements cease to benefit from the EC block exemption[13], although there is some marginal relief up to 35%[14]; also your liner consortia agreements run into problems under Commission

---

16   See ch 21, p 771.
17   Ibid, p 767.
18   Article 4(3)(c) of Regulation 17/62, OJ [1962] 13/204, OJ [1959-62] spec ed 87.
19   Commission's *Guidelines on Horizontal Cooperation Agreements* OJ [2001] C3/2, [2001] 4 CMLR 819, para 130.
20   Ibid, para 149.
1   See n 13 and n 14 above.
2   Article 4 of Regulation 2658/2000, OJ [2000] L 304/3, [2001] 4 CMLR 800.
3   Ibid, Article 6.
4   Article 4 of Regulation 2659/2000, OJ [2000] L 304/7, [2001] 4 CMLR 808.
5   Ibid, Article 6(2).
6   Ibid, Article 6(3).
7   Recital 15 of Regulation 4064/89; see ch 21, p 774.
8   Ibid, p 767.
9   Ibid, p 771.
10   See ch 9, pp 295-297.
11   See ch 11 (monopolies) and ch 22 (mergers).
12   See p 22 above.
13   Article 3 of Regulation 2790/99: see ch 16, pp 578-580.
14   Ibid, Article 9(2)(c).

Regulation 823/2000 if operated within a liner conference[15], with some marginal relief of up to 10% (ie up to a market share of 33%).

35% At 35%, your liner consortia agreements run into problems, even if operated outside a liner conference[16]; there is some marginal relief of up to 10%, so be careful as you approach 38.5%.

40% You may be dominant under Article 82 with a market share of 40% or more (there has been only one finding of dominance under Article 82 below 40%)[17]; if you are dominant, you have a special responsibility not to hinder competition[18]; the benefit of the block exemption for technology transfer agreements may be withdrawn where your market share exceeds 40%[19]; however, there is unlikely to be a cumulative foreclosure effect arising from your single branding agreements where all the companies at the retail level have market shares below 30% and the total tied market share is less than 40%[20].

45%

50% There is a legal presumption that, with 50% of the market, you have a dominant position[1]; this presumption does not apply in a case of collective dominance[2]; you can no longer take advantage of the opposition procedure for certain shipping consortia[3]; where the market share of the 5 largest suppliers in a market is below 50%, there is unlikely to be a single or cumulative anti-competitive effect arising from a single branding agreement[4]; also there is unlikely to be such an effect where the share of the market covered by selective distribution systems is less that 50%[5].

55%
60%
65%
70%
75%
80% At 80%, you may now be approaching a position of 'super-dominance', where you have a particularly special responsibility not to indulge in abusive behaviour[6].

85%
90% At 90%, you are approaching 'quasi-monopoly'[7].
95%
100% At 100%, you may need to go forth and multiply[8].

15 Article 6(1) of Regulation 823/2000 OJ [2000] L 100/24, [2000] 5 CMLR 92.
16 Ibid.
17 See *Virgin/British Airways* OJ [2000] L 30/1, [2000] 4 CMLR 999: dominance at 39.7% of the market.
18 On the special responsibility of dominant firms, see ch 5, p 162.
19 Article 7(1) of Regulation 240/96 OJ [1996] L 31/2.
20 Commission's *Guidelines on Vertical Restraints* (p 30, n 17 above), para 149.
1   See Case-62/86 *AKZO Chemie v Commission* [1991] ECR I-3359, [1993] 5 CMLR 215, para 60: see ch 5, p 155.
2   Cases C-68/94 and C-30/95 *France v Commission* [1998] ECR I-1375, [1998] 4 CMLR 829.
3   Article 7(1) of Regulation 823/2000.
4   Commission's *Guidelines on Vertical Restraints* (p 30, n 17 above) para 143.
5   Ibid, para 189.
6   See ch 5, pp 162-163.
7   Ibid.
8   This is a joke.

CHAPTER 2

Overview of EC and UK competition law

This chapter will provide a brief overview of EC and UK competition law and the relevant institutions. The rules of the European Economic Area are briefly referred to, and the trend on the part of Member States to adopt domestic competition rules modelled on those in the EC Treaty is noted. A diagram at the end of the chapter explains the institutional structure of EC and UK competition law[1]. The problems that might occur in the event of a conflict between domestic competition law and the rules in the EC Treaty are considered in chapter 9[2].

I. EC LAW

(A) The Rome Treaty

The Rome Treaty of 1957[3] established what is now known as the European Community[4]. The Treaty, as renumbered by the Amsterdam Treaty, consists of 314 Articles. It is a complex document which has generated a considerable body of jurisprudence[5]. Much of EC law is concerned with the elimination of obstacles to the free movement of goods, services, persons and capital. The removal of these obstacles in itself promotes competition within the Community; initiatives

---

1 See p 63 below.
2 See ch 9, pp 322-329.
3 The Treaty of Paris of 1951 had earlier established a special régime for coal and steel which contains provisions dealing specifically with competition; this Treaty will expire in 2002: it is discussed briefly in ch 23, pp 853-854.
4 The original name 'European Economic Community' was replaced by its current title by the Maastricht Treaty 1992, primarily to reflect the move away from a purely economic Community to one with a stronger political emphasis; following the Maastricht and Amsterdam Treaties, the EC constitutes one of three 'pillars' of the European Union, the other two, 'Police and Judicial Cooperation in Criminal Matters' and 'Common Foreign and Security Policy' being of an inter-Governmental nature, more akin to conventional international treaties.
5 For comprehensive analysis of EC law in general, see Craig and De Burca *EU Law: Texts, Cases and Materials* (Oxford University Press, 2nd ed, 1998); Kapteyn and van Themaat *Introduction to the Law of the European Communities*; (Kluwer Law International, 3rd ed, 1998, ed Gormley); Weatherill and Beaumont *EU Law* (Penguin, 3rd ed, 1999); Wyatt and Dashwood's *European Union Law* (Sweet & Maxwell, 4th ed, 2000, eds Arnull, Dashwood, Ross and Wyatt).

such as the establishment of a public procurement régime[6] and the creation of the Euro[7] contribute substantially to the competitiveness of the European economy. However, quite apart from this 'macro' effect of the Treaty on competition, it also contains specific competition rules that apply to undertakings and to the Member States themselves.

(i)   The competition chapter in the Treaty

EC competition law is contained in Chapter 1 of Part III of the EC Treaty, which consists of Articles 81 to 89. In understanding these provisions, it is necessary to read them in conjunction with the principles of the Treaty laid down in its early Articles. Of particular significance are Articles 2 and 3. The former provides that:

> 'The Community shall have as its task, by establishing a common market and an economic and monetary union and by implementing the common policies or activities referred to in Articles 3 and 4, to promote throughout the Community a harmonious, balanced and sustainable development of economic activities, a high level of employment and of social protection, equality between men and women, sustainable and non-inflationary growth, a high degree of competitiveness and convergence of economic performance, a high level of protection and improvement of the quality of the environment, the raising of the standard of living and quality of life, and economic and social cohesion and solidarity among Member States.'

Article 3 sets out certain activities of the Community intended to help the achievement of the task laid down in Article 2; paragraph (g) of Article 3 specifically refers to:

> 'a system ensuring that competition in the internal market is not distorted'.

Furthermore, Article 4 provides that the activities of the Member States and the Community shall be conducted in accordance with the principle of an open market economy with free competition. These references to competition in the constitution of the EC have a significant effect on the decisions and judgments of the European Commission (hereafter 'the Commission'), the Court of First Instance and the European Court of Justice ('the CFI' and 'the ECJ' respectively or, collectively, 'the Community Courts'), which have often interpreted the specific competition rules teleologically from the starting point of Articles 2 and 3(g)[8].

6   On public procurement, see Bovis *EC Public Procurement Law* (Longman, 1997); Medhurst *EC Public Procurement Law* (Blackwell Sciences, 1997); Cox *Public Procurement in the EC* (Earlsgate Press, 1997); Arrowsmith 'The Community's Legal Framework on Public Procurement: "The Way Forward" At Last?' (1999) 36 CML Rev 13.

7   On the Euro, see Herdegen 'Price Stability and Budgetary Restraints in Economic and Monetary Union: the Law as Guardian of Economic Wisdom' (1998) 35 CML Rev 9; Louis 'A Legal and Institutional Approach for Building a Monetary Union' (1998) 35 CML Rev 33; Swann *The Economics of the Common Market* (Penguin Books, 8th ed, 1999) ch 7; see further p 47 below.

8   For examples of teleological interpretation of the competition rules, see Cases C-68/94 and 30/95 *France v Commission* [1998] ECR I-1375, [1998] 4 CMLR 829, paras 169-178 and Case T-102/96 *Gencor v Commission* [1999] ECR II-753, [1999] 4 CMLR 971, paras 148-158.

Within Chapter 1 of Part III of the Treaty, Article 81(1) prohibits agreements, decisions by associations of undertakings and concerted practices that are restrictive of competition[9], although this prohibition may be declared inapplicable in the case of agreements which satisfy the conditions in Article 81(3)[10]. Article 82 prohibits the abuse by an undertaking or undertakings of a dominant position[11]. Article 86 imposes obligations on Member States in relation to the Treaty generally and the competition rules specifically and addresses the relationship between the competition rules and public sector undertakings and private undertakings to which a Member State entrusts particular responsibilities[12]. Articles 87-89 prohibit state aids to undertakings by Member States which might distort competition in the common market[13]. An important additional instrument of EC competition law is the EC Merger Regulation ('the ECMR') which applies to concentrations between undertakings[14].

(ii) The single market imperative

As mentioned in chapter one[15], it is important to stress that EC competition law is applied by the Commission and the Community Courts very much with the issue of single market integration in mind. Agreements and conduct which might have the effect of dividing the territory of one Member State from another will be closely scrutinised and may be severely punished. The existence of 'single market' competition rules as well as 'conventional' competition rules is a unique feature of Community competition law. The fact that there are a further 12 countries negotiating accession to the European Union[16] means that single market integration will remain a key feature of competition policy.

(iii) Economic and monetary union

The creation of the euro has an important influence on competition within the Community. As explained in chapter one, the competitive process depends, *inter alia*, on consumers having adequate information to enable them to make rational choices[17]. Price comparisons are difficult where the same goods and services are sold in different, variable currencies; the problem is compounded by the cost of exchanging money. The Euro brings a transparency to price information that fundamentally transforms the position, and that will have a considerable impact on the way in which business is conducted. The Commission has stressed the significance of the Euro for competition policy on a number of occasions[18].

---

9   On Article 81(1), see ch 3.
10 On Article 81(3), see ch 4.
11 On Article 82, see ch 5.
12 On Article 86, see ch 6, pp 189-210.
13 Articles 87-89 are briefly discussed in ch 6, pp 189-213.
14 OJ [1990] L 257/13, as amended by Regulation 1310/97, OJ [1997] L 180/1; on the ECMR, see ch 21.
15 See ch 1, p 19.
16 The 12 are Bulgaria, Cyprus, the Czech Republic, Estonia, Hungary, Latvia, Lithuania, Malta, Poland, Romania, Slovakia and Slovenia; negotiations are under way for the potential accession of Turkey, although this is likely to take somewhat longer to realise.
17 See ch 1, pp 5-6.
18 See eg the Commission's XXVIIth Report on Competition Policy (1997), pp 7-8 and XXVIIIth Report on Competition Policy (1998), pp 24-25.

(iv)   The modernisation of Community competition law

During the course of the 1990s it became apparent that many aspects of Community competition law were in need of modernisation; in particular the law on vertical agreements, on horizontal cooperation and on the obtaining of individual exemptions under Article 81(3) of the Treaty were perceived by many people, including Commission officials, to be in need of radical reform. Proposals for reform were set out by the Director General of Competition in an address to the 25th Annual Conference of the Fordham Corporate Law Institute in October 1998[19], and the modernisation programme gathered pace in 1999 and 2000[20]. The adoption of Regulation 2790/99 has radically changed the application of Article 81(3) to vertical agreements[1], and a transformation of the Commission's approach to horizontal cooperation agreements was completed at the end of 2000[2]. Even more radically, it is likely that the system of notifying agreements for individual exemption under Article 81(3), in place since 1962, will be abolished with effect from 1 January 2003 and replaced by a very different régime[3]. There is no question that these are major changes in the direction of competition law and policy in the Community.

(B)   Institutions[4]

(i)   Council of Ministers

The supreme legislative body of the European Community is the Council of Ministers. It is not involved in competition policy on a regular basis. However it has adopted several major pieces of legislation, including the ECMR[5]; it has delegated important powers to the Commission through regulations to enforce the competition rules in the Treaty, in particular Regulation 17/62[6]; and it has given the Commission power to grant block exemptions in respect of agreements caught by Article 81(1) but which satisfy the criteria of Article 81(3)[7]. The Commission's proposals for the modernisation of the procedural régime for the enforcement of Articles 81 and 82 will necessitate adoption by the Council of a regulation to replace Regulation 17/62[8].

(ii)   European Commission

The European Commission in Brussels is at the core of the development of Community competition policy and is responsible for fact-finding, taking action against infringements of the law, imposing penalties and granting individual

---

19   Schaub 'EC Competition System – Proposals for Reform' [1998] Fordham Corporate Law Institute (ed Hawk), ch 9; see also Ehlermann 'The Modernisation of EC Antitrust Policy: A Legal and Cultural Revolution' (2000) 37 CML Rev 537.
20   See the Commission's XXIXth Report on Competition Policy (1999), points 8-42.
1   See ch 16, pp 567-591.
2   See ch 15, pp 501-508.
3   See ch 4, pp 146-147 and ch 7, pp 246-258.
4   The institutional structure of EC and UK law is set out in diagrammatic form at the end of this chapter: see p 63 below.
5   See p 47 n 14 above.
6   OJ [1962] 13/204, OJ [1959-62] spec ed 87; on the Commission's powers of enforcement, see ch 7.
7   See ch 4, pp 142-144.
8   Ibid, pp 146-147 and ch 7, pp 246-258.

exemptions under Article 81(3)[9]. The Commission is also involved in the international aspect of competition law, including cooperation with competition authorities in jurisdictions such as the US, Canada and Japan[10]. One of the 20 Commissioners takes responsibility for competition matters; this is regarded as one of the most important portfolios within the Commission, and confers upon the incumbent a high public profile. DG COMP (formerly known as DG IV) is the Directorate of the Commission specifically responsible for competition policy. Its website is an invaluable source of material, including entries in the Official Journal, Press Releases, speeches, the Competition Policy Newsletter and competition legislation[11]. The Commission's Annual Report on Competition Policy provides essential information on matters of both policy and enforcement, as well as a statistical review of DG COMP's activities. In 2000 the Commission published a booklet *Competition Policy in Europe and the Citizen* with the intention of creating an awareness and interest in the general public in competition policy[12].

DG COMP has a Director General and two or more Deputy Directors General. There are also two Hearing Officers responsible for ensuring that the rights of the defence are respected in proceedings before the Commission and that draft decisions of the Commission take due account of the relevant facts; one of the Hearing Officers is responsible for cases under Articles 81 and 82 and the other for cases under the ECMR[13]. DG COMP is divided into eight administrative units. Directorate A is responsible for general competition policy and co-ordination. Directorate B is the Merger Task Force, which deals with concentrations notified under the ECMR. Directorates C, D, E and F are operational units which take responsibility for cases under Articles 81 and 82 from start to finish. These units are sub-divided, the constituent parts taking responsibility for specific sectors of the economy. Within Directorate E there is a specific unit with responsibility for tracking down cartels. Directorates G and H are responsible for the provisions in Articles 87–89 of the Treaty on state aids. Formal decisions of DG COMP must be vetted by the Legal Service of the Commission, with which it works closely. The Legal Service represents the Commission in proceedings before the Community Courts. The composition of DG COMP at the end of July 2001 is set out in the following diagram which can be accessed on DG Comp's website:[14]

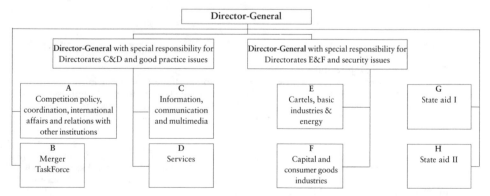

9 As noted above, the system of notification for individual exemption may be abolished by 2003.
10 On the international dimension of competition law, see ch 12.
11 The website is http://www.europe.en.int/comm/competition/index_en.html; the address of DG COMP is Commission of the European Communities, DG Competition, Antitrust Registry, Rue Joseph II, B-1049 Bruxelles.
12 This can be found at http://www.europa.eu.int/comm/competition/publications/ competition_policy_and_the_citizen.
13 On the rôle of the Hearing Officer, see ch 7, pp 234-235.
14 http://europa.eu.int/comm/dgs/competition/index_en.htm.

The staff and resources of DG COMP are insufficient to deal with its workload, and it is possible that the number of staff may be increased by up to 100[15]. There has been an ongoing debate as to whether an independent European Cartel Office should be established, perhaps modelled on the Bundeskartellamt in Germany, which would make decisions in competition cases rather than the Commission. The loudest calls for this have come from Germany[16]. The House of Lords Select Committee on the European Communities, however, expressly rejected the idea at the time of its *Report on the Enforcement of Community Competition Rules*[17]. The debate has abated since the middle of the 1990s, since when attention has been more on the modernisation of the existing system of competition law rather than on reform of the institutions themselves[18].

(iii)   Court of First Instance[19]

In general, actions against the Commission in competition cases (including cases on state aids) are brought in the first instance before the CFI[20]. Member States' actions are taken to the ECJ as happened, for example, in the case of *France v EC Commission*[1], an important judgment which established, *inter alia*, that the ECMR applies to collective dominance. It can happen that substantially similar matters are before both the CFI and the ECJ simultaneously, in which case it is likely that the CFI will suspend its proceedings pending the judgment of the ECJ: this happened, for example, in the case of the 'Irish ice-cream war', where the CFI stayed the appeal of Van den Bergh Foods Ltd against the Commission's decision[2] finding infringements of Articles 81 and 82 pending the outcome of the Article 234 reference in the case of *Masterfoods Ltd v HB Ice Cream Ltd*[3]. The website of the CFI (and of the ECJ) is an invaluable source of material, where, for example, recent judgments of the Courts, opinions of the Advocates General in the ECJ and information about pending cases can be found; there is also a bibliography listing literature on the case law of the Community Courts[4].

---

15   *Financial Times*, 27 July 2000.
16   For a summary of views and discussion, see Ehlermann 'Reflections on a European Cartel Office' (1995) 32 CML Rev 471; Wilks and McGowan 'Disarming the Commission: the Debate over a European Cartel Office' (1995) 33 Journal of Common Market Studies 259; Riley 'The European Cartel Office: A Guardian Without Weapons?' (1997) 18 ECLR 3.
17   1st Report 1993-94 HL Paper 7-I, point 104.
18   See p 48 above.
19   See the *Codified version of the Rules of Procedure of the CFI* OJ [2001] C34/39; on the CFI, see Kerse *EC Antitrust Procedure* (Sweet & Maxwell, 4th ed, 1998) para 1.34; Brown 'The First Five Years of the Court of First Instance and Appeals to the Court of Justice: Assessment and Statistics' (1995) 32 CML Rev 743.
20   On the actions that can be brought, see ch 7, pp 243-246.
1   Cases C-68/94 and 30/95 [1998] ECR I-1375, [1998] 4 CMLR 829; on collective dominance, see ch 14, pp 471-492.
2   *Masterfoods Ltd and Valley Ice Cream (Ireland) Ltd v Van den Bergh Foods Ltd (formerly HB Ice Cream Ltd)* OJ [1998] L 246/1, [1998] 5 CMLR 530, on appeal Case T-65/98 (judgment pending).
3   Case C-344/98 [2001] 4 CMLR 449.
4   The website is http://europa.eu.int/cj/en/index.htm.

(iv) European Court of Justice[5]

The ECJ hears appeals from the CFI on points of law only. The ECJ has been strict about what is meant by an appeal on a point of law, and it will not get drawn into factual disputes[6]. The ECJ also deals with points of law referred to it by national courts under Article 234[7]. As mentioned above, the ECJ's website contains much useful material[8]. The ECJ is assisted by an Advocate General, drawn from a panel of six, who delivers an opinion on each case that comes before it. Although not binding, this opinion is frequently followed by the ECJ, and is often more cogent than the judgment of the ECJ itself which may be delphic, particularly where it represents a compromise of the judges (no dissenting judgments are given by the ECJ). Students of competition law are strongly recommended to read the opinions of the Advocate General in competition cases, which are frequently of very high quality and contain a large amount of invaluable research material. The Community Courts are severely over-stretched, and there can be considerable delays in some cases. The ECJ published a document in May 1999 setting out proposals to deal with some of the problems it experiences[9]. The Treaty of Nice,[9a] if ratified, will make some changes to the structure of the Community Courts; in particular, judicial panels may be created to deal with specific types of case.

(v) Advisory Committee on Restrictive Practices and Monopolies

The Advisory Committee on Restrictive Practices and Monopolies consists of officials from each of the Member States[10]. They attend oral hearings, consider draft decisions of the Commission and comment on them; they also discuss draft legislation and the development of policy generally. It is in this forum that Member States can best hope to influence the content and application of EC competition law. The Committee is specially constituted when dealing with matters in the transport sector[11].

---

5   See the *Codified version of the Rules of Procedure of the CFI* OJ [2001] C34/1; on the ECJ, see Lasok *The European Court of Justice Practice and Procedure* (Butterworths, 2nd ed, 1994); Arnull *The European Union and its Court of Justice* (Oxford EC Law Library, 1999); Neville Brown and Kennedy *The Court of Justice of the European Communities* (Sweet & Maxwell, 5th ed, 2000).
6   See for example Case C-7/95P *John Deere v EC Commission* [1998] ECR I-3111, [1998] 5 CMLR 311, paras 17-22.
7   On the Article 234 procedure, see Collins *European Community Law in the United Kingdom* (Butterworths, 4th edn 1990) pp 142 et seq; Anderson *References to the European Court* (Sweet & Maxwell, 1995); Hartley *The Foundations of European Community Law* (Oxford University Press, 4th ed, 1998) ch 9; Kerse *EC Antitrust Procedure* (Sweet & Maxwell, 4th ed, 1998) para 1.33.
8   See n 4 above.
9   Press Release 36/99, 28 May 1999; see also the discussion paper of the President of the ECJ 'The Future of the Judicial System of the European Union', which can be found at http://curia.eu.int/en/txts/intergov/ave.pdf; also 'The EC Court of Justice and the Institutional Reform of the European Union' (April 2000), which can be found at http://curia.eu.int/en/txts/intergov/rod.pdf.
9a OJ [2001] C 80/1.
10 Provision is made for this Committee by Article 10(4) of Regulation 17/62, p 48, n 6 above; on the Advisory Committee, see ch 7, p 235.
11 See Council Regulation 4056/86, OJ [1986] L 378/4, Article 15(4); Council Regulation 3975/87, OJ [1987] L 374/1, Article 8(4).

(vi)   Advisory Committee on Concentrations[12]

The Advisory Committee on Concentrations consists of officials from each
Member State; they attend oral hearings and must be consulted on draft decisions
of the Commission under the ECMR[13].

(vii)   National courts

National courts are increasingly asked to apply the EC competition rules, which
are directly applicable and may be invoked by individuals (both as defendant
and as plaintiff)[14]. The rôle of national courts is likely to be enhanced if the
Commission's proposal to abolish the system of notification for individual
exemption is implemented[15].

(viii)   Parliament and ECOSOC

The European Parliament – in particular its Standing Committee on Economic
and Monetary Matters – and the Economic and Social Committee, ECOSOC,
are consulted on matters of competition policy and may be influential, for example,
in the legislative process or in persuading the Commission to take action in
relation to a particular issue.

(C)   European Economic Area

On 21 October 1991 the Member States of the EC and of the European Free
Trade Association ('EFTA') signed an Agreement to establish the European
Economic Area ('the EEA')[16]; it consists of the 15 Member States of the EC,
Norway, Iceland and Liechtenstein. The referendum in Switzerland on joining
the EEA led to a 'no' vote, so that that signatory country remains outside. The
EEA Agreement entered into force in 1994. It includes rules on competition which
follow closely the EC Treaty and the ECMR. Article 81 on agreements appears
as Article 53 of the EEA Agreement; Article 82 on the abuse of a dominant
position is mirrored in Article 54; the ECMR is reflected in Article 57; and
Article 86 on public undertakings and Article 87 on state aids appear as Articles
59 and 61 of the Agreement respectively.

The EEA Agreement and its associated texts establish a 'twin pillar' approach
to jurisdiction: there are two authorities responsible for competition policy, the
European Commission and the EFTA Surveillance Authority ('the ESA')[17], but

---

12 See Council Regulation 4064/89, p 47, n 14 above, Article 19(3)-(7).
13 On this Committee, see ch 21, p 789.
14 On the position of national courts, see ch 8.
15 See ch 4, pp 146-147 and ch 7, pp 246-258.
16 OJ [1994] L 1/1; see Blanchet, Piiponen and Wetman-Clément *The Agreement on the*
    European Economic Area (EEA) (Clarendon, 1999); Stragier 'The Competition Rules of the
    EEA Agreement and Their Implementation' (1993) 14 ECLR 30; Diem 'EEA Competition
    Law' (1994) 15 ECLR 263; Broberg 'The Delimitation of Jurisdiction with Regard to
    Concentration Control under the EEA Agreement' (1995) 16 ECLR 30; Forman 'The EEA
    Agreement Five Years On: Dynamic Homogeneity In Practice and Its Implementation by
    the Two EEA Courts' (1999) 36 CML Rev 751.
17 The website of the ESA is http://www.efta.int/structure/SURV/efta-srv.cfm.

any particular case will be investigated by only one of them. Article 108 of the EEA Agreement established the ESA; it mirrors the European Commission and is vested with similar powers. The ESA is subject to review by the EFTA Court of Justice[18], which sits in Luxembourg. Article 55 of the Agreement provides that the European Commission or the ESA shall ensure the application of Articles 53 and 54; Article 56 of the Agreement deals with the attribution of jurisdiction between these two bodies in cases caught by these Articles; Article 57 provides for the division of competence in respect of mergers.

An important principle of the EEA Agreement is that there should be cooperation between the European Commission and the ESA, in order to develop and maintain uniform surveillance throughout the European Economic Area and in order to promote a homogeneous implementation, application and interpretation of the provisions of the Agreement. Article 58 requires the authorities to cooperate, in accordance with specific provisions contained in Protocol 23 (dealing with restrictive practices and the abuse of market power) and Protocol 24 (dealing with mergers). Similarly, Article 106 of the Agreement establishes a system for the exchange of information between the two courts with a view to achieving a uniform interpretation of its terms[19].

(D) Modelling of domestic competition law on Articles 81 and 82[20]

Most Member States of the European Community and the EEA now have systems of competition law modelled upon Articles 81 and 82[21]. English translations are available of these laws on the website of DG COMP[1]. For example the Greek Act of 1977 was based on the EC competition rules, even before that country had acceded to the Community[2]. The French Ordonnance of 1986 is similar to EC law[3]. The Austrian Act of 1988, after a number of amendments, bears some similarity to EC law[4]. Spain altered its competition law in 1989, the new provisions

18 The EFTA States signed an *Agreement on the Establishment of a Surveillance Authority and a Court of Justice* on 2 May 1992; it is reproduced in (1992) 15 *Commercial Laws of Europe*, Part 10; the ECJ delivered two Advisory Opinions on these arrangements: Opinion 1/91 [1991] ECR I-6079, [1992] 1 CMLR 245; and Opinion 1/92 [1992] ECR I-2821, [1992] 2 CMLR 217.
19 The two courts reached different conclusions, however, on the international exhaustion of trade mark rights: see ch 19, pp 709-710.
20 See generally Gerber *Law and Competition in Twentieth Century Europe: Protecting Prometheus* (Clarendon Press Oxford, 1998), ch X; Maher 'Alignment of Competition Laws in the European Community' (1996) 16 Oxford Yearbook of European Law 223.
21 Many of them are reproduced in *Competition Laws of Europe* (Butterworths, 1995, ed Maitland-Walker); see also Drahos *The Convergence of Competition Law and Policies in the European Community* (Kluwer, 2001); for some sceptical comments on the alignment of the domestic competition laws of the Member States, see Ullrich 'Harmonisation within the European Union' (1996) 17 ECLR 178.
1   http://europa.eu.int/comm/competition/legislation/national/volume2/.
2   Act 703 of 26 September 1977.
3   Ordonnance n° 86-1243; the website of the French competition authority is http://www.finances.gouv.fr/DGCCRF/index-d.htm.
4   Cartel Act 1988; the website of the Austrian competition authority is http://www.bmwa.gv.at/service/weservice/start.htm.

being similar to the EC rules[5]. The Italian Protection of Competition and the Market Act 1990 introduced domestic competition rules in that country for the first time[6]. In Belgium, the Protection of Economic Competition Act 1991 closely follows Articles 81, 82 and the ECMR[7]. In Ireland the Competition Act 1991 which entered into force on 1 October 1991 is modelled on Articles 81 and 82[8]. Finland adopted a Competition Act in 1992[9]. Norway passed its Competition Act in 1993[10], the same year as the Portuguese decree[11] and the Icelandic Act of 1993 was amended in 2000 to conform with EC law[12]. The same year saw the adoption of the Swedish Competition Act[13]. Switzerland, a signatory to the EEA Agreement but which has yet to ratify it, adopted a new Competition Act in 1996[14]. The Dutch Competition Act was passed in 1997[15] and the same happened in Denmark[16]; new legislation, including the creation of a system of merger control, was adopted in Denmark in May 2000[17]. Even the UK eventually succumbed to temptation, adopting rules modelled upon Articles 81 and 82 in the Competition Act of 1998[18]. Changes in German law that entered into force

5   Act 16/89 of 17 July 1989; see Rubio de Casas 'The Spanish Law for the Defence of Competition' (1990) 11 ECLR 179 and Lage 'Significant Developments in Spanish Antitrust Law' (1996) 17 ECLR 194; on the 1999 amendments to the Act of 1989, see Varona 'Amendments to the Spanish Law for the Defence of Competition' (2000) 21 ECLR 234; the website of the Spanish competition authority is http://www.meh.es/commun/dgpedc.htm.
6   Law 287 of 10 October 1990; see Romani 'The New Italian Antitrust Law' [1991] Fordham Corporate Law Institute (ed Hawk) pp 479–485; Siragusa and Scassellati 'Italian and EC Competition Law: a New Relationship - Reciprocal Exclusivity and Common Principles' (1992) 29 CML Rev 93; Heimler 'National Priorities, National Law and European Law: The Italian Experience' (1998) 19 ECLR 315; the website of the Italian competition authority is http://www.agcm.it/.
7   Law 91–2790 of 5 August 1991; see Vanderelst and Wijckmans 'The Belgian Law on the Protection of Competition' (1992) 13 ECLR 120; the website of the Belgian competition authority is http://mineco.fgov.be/organization_market/index_fr.htm.
8   The Act was amended in 1996 by the Competition (Amendment) Act to introduce criminal sanctions and to provide new enforcement powers; see generally on Irish competition law Maher *Competition Law: Alignment and Reform* (Round Hall Sweet & Maxwell, 1999); the website of the Irish competition authority is http://www.irlgov.ie/compauth/home.htm.
9   Act 480/1992; see Laurila 'Finland: Act on Restrictions of Competition' (1994) 15 ECLR 225; Relander, Wik and Ratliff 'Finnish Competition Law and Practice: An Evolving Picture' (1998) ECLR 455; Finnish legislation on merger control was introduced in 1998 by Act 303/1998; the website of the Finnish competition authority is http://www.kilpailuvirasto.fi.
10   See Engzelius 'The Norwegian Competition Act 1993' (1995) 16 ECLR 384; the website of the Norwegian competition authority website is http://www.konkurransetilsynet.no/.
11   Law Decree 371/93, the website of the Portuguese competition authority is http://www.dgcc.pt/.
12   Law no 8/1993 as amended by Law no 107/2000.
13   See Carle and Simonsson 'Competition Law in Sweden' (1993) 14 ECLR 176; Mohamed 'Competition Rules of Sweden and the European Union Compared' (1998) 19 ECLR 237; Koponen 'The Swedish Competition Act: A Second View from Abroad' in *The Competition Act: A New Era for UK Competition Law* (Hart Publishing, 2000, eds Rodger and MacCulloch); the website of the Swedish competition authority is http://www.kkv.se/.
14   See Bonvin 'Competition Law in Switzerland' (1997) 18 ECLR 191; the website of the Swiss competition authority is http://wettbewerbskommission.ch/.
15   See VerLoren van Themaat 'The Dutch Competition Act of May 22, 1997' (1997) 18 ECLR 344; Wesseling 'Divergences in "Harmonised" Laws: A View from Abroad' in *The Competition Act: A New Era for UK Competition Law* (Hart Publishing, 2000, eds Rodger and MacCulloch); the website of the Dutch competition authority is http://www.NMa-org.nl/.
16   Statute 384 of 10 June 1997; see Kofmann 'The Danish Competition Act' (1998) 19 ECLR 269; for criticism of the reform, see Blomgren-Hansen and Møllgaard 'The Ineffective Harmonisation of Danish Competition Law' (1999) 20 ECLR 287; the website for the Danish competition authority is http://www.ks.dk/eng/index.html.
17   Statute 413 of 31 May 2000, which entered into force on 1 October 2000.
18   See pp 55-62 below and chs 9 and 10.

on 1 January 1999 brought it more closely into line in some respects with EC law[19]. Reform is under way in Luxembourg[20].

It should be added that the Community competition rules also have influenced legislative developments in many of the countries of central and eastern Europe[1]. There are also so-called 'Europe Agreements' between the European Communities, the Member States and many of the countries in this region, which themselves contain competition rules[2]. There are moves towards the establishment of a 'Euro-Mediterranean Economic Area', with the result that countries on the Mediterranean coast from Algeria to Turkey will be parties to Euro-Mediterranean (Association) Agreements containing, *inter alia*, provisions based on the Community competition rules[3].

2. UK LAW

(A) Competition Act 1998

In the UK the Competition Act 1998 received the Royal Assent on 9 November 1998; the main provisions entered into force on 1 March 2000. It radically reforms the domestic competition law of the UK. It contains two prohibitions. The so-called 'Chapter I prohibition' is modelled on Article 81 EC, and forbids agreements that restrict competition[4]. However, vertical agreements, with the exception of price-fixing agreements, are excluded from the Chapter I prohibition[5]. The Chapter II prohibition is modelled on Article 82 EC and forbids the abuse of a dominant position[6]. The Act gives to the Director General of Fair Trading (hereafter 'the DGFT') wide powers to obtain information, to carry out on-the-spot investigations, to adopt decisions and to impose fines[7]. In relation to certain sectors such as telecommunications and energy, the powers of the DGFT are shared concurrently with the relevant regulator, such as the Director General of Telecommunications and the Gas and Electricity Markets Authority[8]. As 'public

---

19 See Stadler 'The 1999 Changes to German Merger Control and Competition Law' (1998) 19 ECLR 542; the website of the German competition authority is http://www.bundeskartellamt.de/.
20 The Law of 17 June 1970 is in the process of being amended.
1 See Ojala *The Competition Law of Central and Eastern Europe* (Sweet & Maxwell, 1998); Pittman 'Competition Law in Central and Eastern Europe: Five Years Later' (1998) 43 Antitrust Bulletin 179.
2 See for example the Poland Agreement OJ [1993] L 348/2 and the implementing rules OJ [1996] L 208/24; Articles 63-67 of the Agreement contain the competition rules. It is possible in principle for agreements between the Community and third countries to have direct effect: see Case 104/81 *Hauptzollamt Mainz v Kupferburg* [1982] ECR 3641, [1983] 1 CMLR 1; Case C-192/89 *Sevince v Staatssecretaris van Justitie* [1990] ECR I-3461, [1992] 2 CMLR 57 and Wyatt and Dashwood's *European Union Law* (p 45, n 5 above) pp 104-109; however there has yet to be a judgment on whether the competition rules in the Europe Agreements themselves have direct effect; on one occasion the Commission required amendments to Chantel's distribution agreements to remove restrictions on exports to countries with which the Community had negotiated 'Free Trade Agreements', but this was done by agreement and without a reasoned decision on the part of the Commission: *Chanel* OJ [1994] C 334/11, [1995] 4 CMLR 108.
3 See Hakura 'The Extension of EC Competition Law to the Mediterranean Region' (1998) 19 ECLR 204.
4 On the Chapter I prohibition, see ch 9, pp 291-314.
5 See ch 16, pp 595-598.
6 See ch 9, pp 314-321.
7 On the enforcement powers under the 1998 Act, see ch 10, pp 348-356.
8 On concurrency, see ch 10, p 357.

authorities', each of these bodies is obliged under section 6 of the Human Rights Act 1998 (which received the Royal Assent on the same day as the Competition Act) to act in a manner that is compatible with the European Convention for the Protection of Human Rights and Fundamental Freedoms of 1950. In competition law, it can be anticipated that the right to a fair trial (Article 6 of the Convention), the right to respect for private life (Article 8) and the right to peaceful enjoyment of possessions (Article 1 of the First Protocol) will be of particular significance. Section 60 of the Competition Act contains provisions designed to maintain consistency between EC jurisprudence and the application of domestic law; however the duty to do so is subject to limitations, in particular with the result that judgments of the Community Courts motivated by single market considerations and the law of the EC on vertical agreements under Article 81 will not be followed in the UK[9].

(B)   Fair Trading Act 1973

The Fair Trading Act 1973 ('the FTA') enables so-called 'scale monopolies' and 'complex monopolies' to be referred to the Competition Commission for investigation[10]; such investigations are expected in the future to be less frequent than in the past, given that the Chapter II prohibition in the Competition Act 1998 forbids the abuse of a dominant position. However the retention of the monopoly provisions in the FTA is a useful 'safety net' in UK competition law, in particular since they could lead to a structural remedy where one is needed; the 1998 Act is concerned with the control of anti-competitive behaviour rather than the structure of the market. While scale monopoly investigations are likely to be rare, it can be anticipated that there will continue to be a reasonable number of complex monopoly references[11]. The FTA also contains the UK system of merger control[12]. There are proposals under consideration for reform of the provisions on mergers[13].

(C)   Institutions[14]

Competition law in the UK assigns rôles to the Secretary of State, the DGFT, the sectoral regulators, the Competition Commission and to the High Court.

(i)   The Secretary of State and the Department of Trade and Industry

The Secretary of State for Trade and Industry has extensive powers in relation to monopolies and mergers under the FTA. He is assisted by a Minister of State for Consumers and Corporate Affairs who has particular responsibility for competition matters and is able to make some decisions himself. The Secretary of State

---

9   See ch 9, pp 329-333
10 On the monopoly provisions in the FTA, see ch 11.
11 Ibid, pp 383-385.
12 On UK merger control, see ch 22.
13 See ch 22, pp 836; some further changes in UK competition law are in contemplation: see *Productivity in the UK: Enterprise and the Productivity Challenge* (HM Treasury, June 2001), pp 19-24; *A World Class Competition Régime* (DTI, July 2001), Cm 5233.
14 The institutional structure of EC and UK law is set out in diagrammatic form at the end of this chapter: see p 63 below.

makes the most senior appointments, for example of the DGFT, the Chairman and the President of the Appeal Tribunals of the Competition Commission. The Secretary of State refers mergers to the Competition Commission, and may refer 'monopoly situations' under the FTA, although the latter are usually made by the DGFT[15] and may be made, in some cases, by the sectoral regulator[16]. The Competition Commission sends its reports on mergers and monopolies to the Secretary of State, who decides what action is to be taken in the event of an adverse finding. The rôle of the Secretary of State in relation to mergers is currently under review[17]. The Secretary of State is given some rôles under the Competition Act 1998, for example to enact the procedural rules of the DGFT[18] and of the Appeal Tribunals of the Competition Commission[19]; also to make rules in relation to penalties and to approve the DGFT's Guidance on their level[20]. However it is important to appreciate that the Secretary of State has no function in relation to the practical enforcement of the Chapter I and Chapter II prohibitions: in this respect the 1998 Act makes an important shift from the FTA. Within the Department of Trade and Industry there is a Competition and Markets Group with a Director General responsible for competition policy; its website contains a wide variety of information and guidance on matters of competition law and on the personnel responsible for different matters[1]. Press releases on competition matters, such as the referral of and subsequent action in relation to mergers, are published on this site.

(ii)   The DGFT and the Office of Fair Trading

The position of DGFT was created by section 1 of the FTA. Many important functions are given to the DGFT, whose Annual Report is an important source of information on developments in domestic competition policy[2]. It is a notable feature of UK competition law that significant powers are entrusted to an individual rather than, as in the case of the EC, to a college of 20 Commissioners. The UK Government's view is that it is no longer appropriate that such extensive powers should be vested in an individual. It is intended that legislation will be introduced when time is available providing for the establishment of the OFT as a statutory fair trading authority, with its chairman heading a management board. The board would consist of the DGFT as chairman with at least four other members; in practice it would probably have between five and eight. Some of the members would be 'outsiders'. Minutes of the board and individual members' opinions would be routinely published. The board would involve itself in matters of strategy and would also be able to participate fully in decisions and in executive functions[3]. This model would, to some extent, reflect the Gas and Electricity Markets Authority, which, in 2000, replaced the individual posts of Director General of Gas Supply and Director General of Electricity Supply[4].

15   See ch 11, pp 371-373 on the making of monopoly references.
16   Ibid, p 373.
17   See ch 22, p 836 .
18   See ch 10, pp 348-349.
19   Ibid, p 358.
20   Ibid, p 352.
1   The website is http://www.dti.gov.uk/CACP/cp/default.htm.
2   See eg the 1999 *Annual Report of the DGFT*, pp 37-64; 2000 *Annual Report of the DGFT*, pp 13-32
3   See *A Consultation Document: Proposed Changes to the Structure of the Office of Fair Trading*, DTI, 21 September 2000.
4   See s 1 Utilities Act 2000.

The DGFT has responsibilities in various areas – for example in relation to consumer credit and misleading advertisements – but competition policy is a significant part of his brief. The DGFT has considerable powers under the Competition Act 1998. The DGFT will play the principal rôle in enforcing the Chapter I and Chapter II prohibitions, with significant powers to obtain information, enter premises to conduct investigations, make interim and final decisions and impose financial penalties[5]. Under the FTA, the DGFT has various functions, which include making recommendations to the Secretary of State on mergers and taking action, where necessary, following an adverse report by the Competition Commission[6]; the DGFT may make monopoly references under the FTA and, as in the case of mergers, will be involved in any action that needs to be taken pursuant to an adverse report[7]. The DGFT is also given specific responsibilities in relation to competition by the Financial Services Act 1986[8], the Companies Act 1989, the Broadcasting Act 1990[9], the Courts and Legal Services Act 1990, the Law Reform (Miscellaneous Provisions) (Scotland) Act 1990, the Water Industry Act 1991, the Environment Act 1995, the Financial Services and Markets Act 2000[10] and the Transport Act 2000. A new rôle is contemplated for the DGFT in relation to payment systems in the banking sector.[10a] The OFT liaises on competition matters with the European Commission in Brussels and attends meetings on competition policy on behalf of the UK at the Organisation for Economic Co-operation and Development and the United Nations Conference on Trade and Development.

The DGFT is assisted by the Office of Fair Trading ('the OFT'); the OFT is not mentioned anywhere in the legislation, but section 1(5) FTA provides that the DGFT 'may appoint such staff as he may think fit'. The OFT has a permanent staff of about 170 officials dealing with competition policy[11]. The Competition Policy Division has a Director and seven branches. Four branches, each with a mix of disciplines, are devoted to case-handling and are organised by industrial sectors. There is also a branch that handles cartel investigations and a policy co-ordination branch. The seventh branch handles mergers. The structure of the OFT bears a considerable resemblance to that of DG COMP of the European Commission[12]. The OFT also has a Director of Legal Affairs and, specifically, a Legal Director with responsibility for competition policy. The OFT's website is a vital source of information on UK competition law and includes, among other things, the numerous guidelines on the Competition Act 1998 and the Weekly Gazette[13]. The OFT has published a number of research papers on important issues in competition policy, for example on market definition, barriers to entry and exit and predatory behaviour, which are available on its website. The first of a new series of economic discussion papers, on *e-commerce and its Implications for Competition Policy*, was published in August 2000 and is also available on

---

5   See ch 10 , pp 335-342 and 348-356.
6   The rôle of the DGFT in merger cases, and the proposals for reform of this area, are discussed in ch 22, pp 809-813 and 836.
7   The rôle of the DGFT in monopoly investigations is discussed in ch 11, p 373.
8   See the 1999 *Annual Report of the DGFT*, pp 50-51.
9   Ibid, p 51.
10 See ch 9, p 303.
10a See *Competition in Payment Systems* (HM Treasury, August 2001).
11 The 2000 *Annual Report of the DGFT* explains the OFT's personnel and resources at pp 58-72; the address of the OFT is Fleetbank House, 2-6 Salisbury Square, London EC4Y 8JX.
12 See p 49 above.
13 The website that introduces the work of the OFT on competition law is http://www.oft.gov.uk/html/about/strct2.htm#encouraging.

the website; the second in the series, *The Rôle of Market Definition in Monopoly and Dominance Inquiries*, was published in July 2001.

The composition of the competition policy division of the OFT in July 2001 is set out in the following diagram.

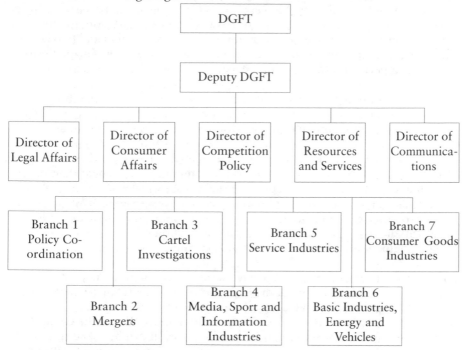

An OFT booklet, 'Helping You'[14], sets out the standards of service and response that can be expected when dealing with the OFT. It includes estimates of the time that it should take to discharge its various functions: for example it states that the OFT expects to advise the Secretary of State whether to refer a merger to the Competition Commission within 39 working days from the receipt of a satisfactory submission in 90% of cases. Work is also under way on improving the transparency of the OFT's operations[15].

(iii) *The sectoral regulators*

The sectoral regulators for telecommunications, gas and electricity, water and rail have concurrent power to enforce the Competition Act 1998 with the DGFT. Arrangements are in place for the coordination of the performance of the concurrent functions under the Act[16]. Appeals against the decisions of the sectoral regulators in the exercise of their Competition Act powers lie to the Appeal Tribunals of the Competition Commission. References in relation to their licensing functions and certain monopoly references may be made to the reporting panel of the Competition Commission. Regulators' decisions may therefore come up for review by the Competition Commission through two different routes.

---

14 OFT 107 May 2000, found at http://ww.oft.gov.uk/html/search/leaflets/oft107.pdf.
15 See *Opening the Door on Fair Trading: a Consultation Paper on Improving Transparency in the Operations of the OFT*, July 1999; 1999 *Annual Report of the DGFT*, pp 56-57; 2000 *Annual Report of the DGFT*, p 26.
16 On concurrency, see ch 10, p 357.

(iv)   The Competition Commission

The Competition Commission was established by section 45(1) of the Competition Act 1998 and came into existence on 1 April 1999. Section 45(3) of the Act dissolved the Monopolies and Mergers Commission, which had been in existence under various names since 1948, and transferred its functions to the new Commission[17]. The Competition Commission has a Chairman and two Deputy Chairmen. The Secretary of State announced changes to the terms of appointment to the Competition Commission in July 2000 in order to safeguard the independence of its members[18].

The Commission has a Council which acts as a management board, and which consists of the Chairman, the Deputy Chairman, the President of the Appeal Tribunals and the Secretary of the Commission[19]. The Commission has a permanent staff of about 80 officials[20], some of whom are civil servants and some of whom are direct employees. The Commission publishes an Annual Review and Accounts. It has a website that contains a wide variety of information, for example on current inquiries, press releases, past inquiries, reports, the Annual Review and the way in which it is organised[1]. The Commission has also been seeking to achieve greater transparency in its procedures, while maintaining the confidentiality of commercially sensitive information[2].

The Competition Commission has two functions.

(A)   THE REPORTING FUNCTION.   The functions that the old Monopolies and Mergers Commission had under the FTA, including the investigation of mergers and monopoly situations, were taken over by the so-called 'reporting panel'[3] of the Competition Commission. As well as its rôles under the FTA and the Competition Act 1998, the Competition Commission can be asked to conduct 'efficiency audits' of public sector bodies under the Competition Act 1980: such audits are now rare[4]. The Competition Commission has various functions in relation to privatised utilities such as undertakings in the telecommunications industry[5]: these will be found in the Telecommunications Act 1984, the Airports Act 1986 and the Airports (Northern Ireland) Order 1994, the Gas Acts 1986 and 1995 and the Gas (Northern Ireland) Order 1996, the Electricity Act 1989 and the Electricity (Northern Ireland) Order 1992, the Water Industry Act 1991, the Railways Act 1993, the Postal Services Act 2000, the Utilities Act 2000 and the Transport Act 2000. The Commission has an appellate capacity in respect of

---

17   For a fascinating account of the work of the Monopolies and Mergers Commission in the 50 years from 1948 to 1998, see Wilks *In the Public Interest: Competition Policy and the Monopolies and Mergers Commission* (Manchester University Press, 1999).
18   DTI Press Notice P/2000/543, 28 July 2000.
19   The Council was established by Competition Act 1998, Sch 7, Part I, para 5.
20   See the 1999/2000 Competition Commission's *Annual Review & Accounts*, p 15.
1   The website of the Competition Commission is http://www.competition-commission.gov.uk.
2   See the 2000/2001 Competition Commission's *Annual Review & Accounts*, p 3.
3   This terminology is introduced by Sch 7 of the 1998 Act.
4   On efficiency audits, see 47 *Halsbury's Laws of England* (4th edn reissue, 1994) paras 137-138.
5   The provisions on telecommunications, gas, electricity, water, rail and post are described briefly in ch 23, which deals with the application of the competition rules to particular sectors; the Airports Act 1986, ss 43–55 deal with references by the Civil Aviation Authority to the Commission: the most recent reports are *BAA plc: a report on the economic regulation of the London airports companies (Heathrow Airport Ltd, Gatwick Airport Ltd and Stansted Airport Ltd)* MMC 4 (1996) and *Manchester Airport plc: a report on the economic regulation of Manchester Airport plc* MMC 5 (1997).

decisions of the DGFT under the Broadcasting Act 1990. The Commission also has a rôle under the Financial Services and Markets Act 2000 in ensuring that the rules and practices of the Financial Services Authority do not impede competition. Each of these functions is carried out by the reporting side of the Commission.

The reporting side of the Competition Commission can have up to 50 members[6], although it normally has about 30.[7] Members are appointed by the Secretary of State following an open competition. They are appointed for their diversity of background, individual experience and ability, not as representatives of particular organisations, interests or political parties. In each case a group will be appointed to conduct the investigation. Until 1989 the groups usually consisted of six Commissioners, but it is now possible for a group to consist of just three[8]. In 1999, most of the investigations completed were conducted by groups of four or five[9]. There are also 'specialist group members' for investigations conducted in the newspaper, water, electricity and telecommunications industries. It is possible to be a member both of the reporting panel and a specialist panel[10]. The Chairman of the Competition Commission must be a reporting panel member, as must any Deputy Chairman. The Chairman of the Competition Commission has published Guidance for groups on the procedures to be adopted[11]. The decisions of the Competition Commission on the reporting side are subject to judicial review by the Divisional Court of the Queen's Bench Division of the High Court, but there is no system of appeal[12].

(B) THE APPEAL FUNCTION.   The other function of the Competition Commission is to hear full appeals from decisions of the DGFT and the sectoral regulators under the Competition Act 1998[13]. This function is discharged by the 'appeal panel', operating one or more Appeal Tribunals constituted by the President of the Competition Commission Appeal Tribunals, who must be legally qualified with 10 years' standing and must have appropriate experience and knowledge of competition law and practice. Once constituted, each Tribunal acts independently. There is a panel of Tribunal chairmen, comprising lawyers with seven years' standing and with appropriate specialised knowledge and experience, who chair Tribunals that are not being chaired by the President himself. An Appeal Tribunal must comprise a (legally qualified) Chairman and two other appeal panel members. The President constitutes the Tribunal and has issued a Practice Direction on arrangements for doing so[14]. A statutory instrument sets out the rules of the Appeal Tribunals[15]. The rules provide for the appointment of a

6   The number was increased to 50 by the Monopolies and Mergers (Increase in Membership) Order 1989, SI 1989/1240.
7   There were 36 members on 31 March 2001; see the Competition Commission's 2000/2001 *Annual Review and Accounts*, p 15.
8   Monopolies and Mergers Commission (Performance of Functions) Order 1989, SI 1989/122: see now Competition Act 1998, Sch 7, para 15(2).
9   Details of the groups will be found in the short discussions of each investigation in the Competition Commission's *Annual Report & Accounts*.
10 See 1999/2000 Competition Commission *Annual Review & Accounts*, p 14.
11 See ch 11, pp 376-378 in relation to monopoly investigations and ch 22, pp 817-818 in relation to merger investigations; the Guidance on procedures can be found at http://www.competiton-commission.org.uk/traind.htm.
12 See ch 11, pp 369 and 381 and ch 22, pp 835-836 for details of judicial review proceedings in the case of monopoly and merger investigations respectively.
13 On appeals, see ch 10, pp 358-359; it is possible that an action for judicial review may also be brought before the Divisional Court: ibid, p 358.
14 This can be found at http://www.competition-commission.gov.uk/appeals/practice.htm.
15 The Competition Commission Appeal Tribunal Rules 2000, SI 2000/261.

Registrar of Appeal Tribunals to support the President and the appeal panel members in the discharge of the tribunals' functions. The Commission itself has published a *Guide to Appeals under the Competition Act 1998*[16]. There is an appeal by virtue of section 49 of the Act from the Appeal Tribunals of the Competition Commission to the Court of Appeal on a point of law and on the amount of any penalty. From the Court of Appeal further appeal may be taken, with leave, to the House of Lords. It is also possible for the Competition Commission to refer a matter of Community law to the ECJ[17].

(v)   The High Court

Actions may be brought in the High Court where there are infringements of Articles 81 and 82 of the EC Treaty[18] or the Chapter I and II prohibitions[19].

3.   THE INSTITUTIONAL STRUCTURE OF EC AND UK COMPETITION LAW

The diagram opposite sets out the institutional structure of EC and UK competition law.

---

16 The first Guide was published on 1 June 2000 and is available on the Commission's website: http://www.competiton-commission.org.uk; it will be updated from time to time.
17 See The Competition Commission Appeal Tribunal Rules 2000, SI 2000/261, rule 31 and ch 9, pp 359-361.
18 On the enforcement of the EC competition rules in national courts, see ch 8.
19 On the enforcement of the Competition Act in the courts, see ch 10, pp 361-362.

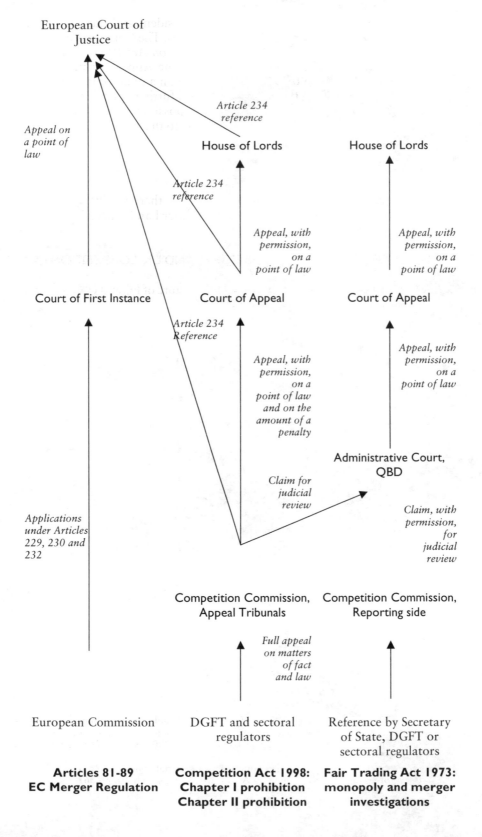

CHAPTER 3

Article 81(1)

This chapter is concerned with Article 81(1) EC which prohibits agreements, decisions by associations of undertakings and concerted practices that are restrictive of competition. Article 81(1) may be declared inapplicable where the criteria set out in Article 81(3) are satisfied: the provisions of Article 81(3) are considered in chapter 4. An agreement which is prohibited by Article 81(1) and which does not satisfy Article 81(3) is stated to be automatically void by virtue of Article 81(2)[1]. The full text of Article 81 is as follows:

'1. The following shall be prohibited as incompatible with the common market: all agreements between undertakings, decisions by associations of undertakings and concerted practices which may affect trade between Member States and which have as their object or effect the prevention, restriction or distortion of competition within the common market, and in particular those which:
(a) directly or indirectly fix purchase or selling prices or any other trading conditions;
(b) limit or control production, markets, technical development, or investment;
(c) share markets or sources of supply;
(d) apply dissimilar conditions to equivalent transactions with other trading parties, thereby placing them at a competitive disadvantage;
(e) make the conclusion of contracts subject to the acceptance by other parties of supplementary obligations which, by their nature or according to commercial usage, have no connection with the subject of such contracts.

2. Any agreements or decisions prohibited pursuant to this Article shall be automatically void.

3. The provisions of paragraph 1 may, however, be declared inapplicable in the case of:

---

1   See ch 8, p 260ff on the numerous issues that arise from the provision for automatic voidness in Article 81(2).

- any agreement or category of agreements between undertakings;
- any decision or category of decisions by associations of undertakings;
- any concerted practice or category of concerted practices;

which contributes to improving the production or distribution of goods or to promoting technical or economic progress, while allowing consumers a fair share of the resulting benefit, and which does not:

(a) impose on the undertakings concerned restrictions which are not indispensable to the attainment of these objectives;
(b) afford such undertakings the possibility of eliminating competition in respect of a substantial part of the products in question.'

Many aspects of the basic prohibition in Article 81(1) require elaboration. First, the meaning of 'undertakings' and then the terms 'agreements', 'decisions' and 'concerted practices' will be explained. The third section of this chapter will consider what is meant by agreements that 'have as their object or effect the prevention, restriction or distortion of competition'. The fourth section deals with the '*de minimis*' doctrine. Section 5 explains the requirement of an effect on trade between Member States. The chapter concludes with a checklist of agreements that, for a variety of reasons, normally will fall outside Article 81(1).

I.   UNDERTAKINGS

Three issues must be considered in respect of this term: first, its basic definition for the purpose of Article 81(1)[2]; secondly, whether two or more undertakings form a single economic entity and the significance of such a finding; thirdly, whether two or more firms may be treated as one undertaking where they are related by succession.

(A)   Basic definition

The Treaty does not define an 'undertaking'[3]. However it is a critically important term, since only agreements *between undertakings* are caught by Article 81(1). The term has been given extensive consideration by the Community Courts and the Commission. It can be particularly problematic where agreements are entered into by organs of the Member States (public authorities, municipalities, communes and so on) or by entities entrusted by the Member States with regulatory or other functions. The question that arises is whether such agreements can be challenged under Article 81. A separate question, considered in chapter 6, is whether Member States themselves may be liable for the anti-competitive behaviour of such entities[4].

The ECJ held in *Höfner and Elser v Macrotron*[5] *Gmb* that:

2   The term undertaking has the same meaning under Article 82: see ch 5, pp 150-151 .
3   Article 80 of the ECSC Treaty and Article 80 of the Euratom Treaty do contain definitions of an undertaking for their respective purposes.
4   See ch 6, pp 184-189 .
5   Case C-41/90 [1991] ECR I-1979, [1993] 4 CMLR 306, para 21.

'the concept of an undertaking encompasses every entity engaged in an economic activity regardless of the legal status of the entity and the way in which it is financed'.

This is a helpful starting point in understanding the meaning of the term.

(i) 'Engaged in an economic activity'

The idea in *Höfner* that any entity engaged in an economic activity, regardless of legal status, can qualify as an undertaking finds expression in numerous judgments of the Community Courts and decisions of the Commission. Companies and partnerships of course can qualify as undertakings, as can agricultural co-operatives[6], P and I clubs[7], and a firm, established by four independent companies, whose function was to supervise a quota-fixing agreement[8]. A trade association that carries on an economic activity can be an undertaking: it follows that agreements between trade associations may themselves be caught by Article 81(1)[9]. The fact that an organisation lacks a profit-motive[10] or does not have an economic purpose[11] does not disqualify it as an undertaking, provided always that it is carrying on some commercial or economic activity. On this basis, the Commission held in *Distribution of Package Tours During the 1990 World Cup*[12] that FIFA, the body responsible for the 1990 Football World Cup, as well as the Italian football association and the local organising committee, were undertakings subject to Article 81[13]. An individual has been held on numerous occasions to qualify as an undertaking[14], although an individual acting as an employee would not be[15].

6 See eg Case 61/80 *Coöperative Stremsel–en Kleurselfabriek v Commission* [1981] ECR 851, [1982] 1 CMLR 240; *MELDOC* OJ [1986] L 348/50, [1989] 4 CMLR 853.
7 *P & I Clubs* OJ [1985] L 376/2, [1989] 4 CMLR 178; *P & I Clubs* OJ [1999] L 125/12, [1999] 5 CMLR 646, paras 50–51.
8 *Re Italian Cast Glass* OJ [1980] L 383/19, [1982] 2 CMLR 61.
9 See eg Case 71/74 *FRUBO v Commission* [1975] ECR 563, [1975] 2 CMLR 123; Case 96/82 *IAZ International Belgium NV v Commission* [1983] ECR 3369, [1984] 3 CMLR 276; *Algemene Schippersvereniging v ANTIB* OJ [1985] L 219/35, [1988] 4 CMLR 698, on appeal Case 272/85 *ANTIB v Commission* [1987] ECR 2201, [1988] 4 CMLR 677.
10 Cases 209/78 etc *Van Landewyck v Commission* [1980] ECR 3125, [1981] 3 CMLR 134, para 88; *P & I Clubs* OJ [1985] L 376/2, [1989] 4 CMLR 178; *P & I Clubs* OJ [1999] L 125/12, [1999] 5 CMLR 646; Case C-244/94 *Fédération Française des Sociétés d'Assurance* [1995] ECR I-4013, [1996] 4 CMLR 536, para 21.
11 Case 155/73 *Italy v Sacchi* [1974] ECR 409, [1974] 2 CMLR 177, paras 13 and 14.
12 OJ [1992] L 326/31, [1994] 5 CMLR 253, para 43.
13 Ibid, paras 44–57; see similarly *UEFA's Broadcasting Regulations* OJ [2001] L 171/12, para 47.
14 See eg *AOIP v Beyrard* OJ [1976] L 6/8, [1976] 1 CMLR D14 where a patent licence between an individual and a company was held to fall within Article 81(1); *Reuter/BASF* OJ [1976] L 254/40, [1976] 2 CMLR D44; *RAI v UNITEL* OJ [1978] L 157/39, [1978] 3 CMLR 306 where two opera singers were undertakings; *Vaessen BV v Moris* OJ [1979] L 19/32, [1979] 1 CMLR 511; Case 35/83 *BAT v Commission* [1985] ECR 363, [1985] 2 CMLR 470; Case 42/84 *Remia BV and Verenigde Bedrijven Nutricia NV v Commission* [1985] ECR 2545, [1987] 1 CMLR 1; *Breeders' Rights: Roses* OJ [1985] L 369/9, [1988] 4 CMLR 193.
15 See p 71 below.

(ii)   'Regardless of legal status'

The ECJ in *Höfner* stated that the legal status of an entity does not determine whether it qualifies as an undertaking. Public authorities, such as the Federal Employment Office in *Höfner* itself or the Autonomous Administration of State Monopolies in the *Banchero*[16] case, have been held to be engaged in activities of an economic nature with regard to employment procurement and the offering of goods and services on the market for manufactured tobacco respectively. State-owned corporations may be undertakings[17], as may bodies entrusted by the state with particular tasks[18] and quasi-Governmental bodies which carry on economic activities[19]. Aéroports de Paris, responsible for the planning, administration and development of civil air transport installations in Paris, the Portuguese Airports Authority, ANA, and the Finnish Civil Aviation Administration were all found by the Commission to constitute undertakings[20]. In *Aluminium Products*[1] foreign trade organisations in eastern European countries were regarded as undertakings, even though they had no existence separate from the state under their domestic law: claims of sovereign immunity should be confined to acts which are those of Government and not of trade. The same point was made by the Commission in its decision in *Amministrazione Autonoma dei Monopoli di Stato*[2].

(iii)   Need to adopt a functional approach

To the formula in Höfner should be added a further point: that a particular entity might be acting as an undertaking when carrying out certain of its functions but not acting as an undertaking when carrying out others. For example a local authority in the UK might sometimes act under its public law powers in order to achieve a purpose set out in an Act of Parliament, in which case it would not be acting as an undertaking; but might at other times act as a commercial entity, in which manifestation it would be an undertaking for the purpose of Article 81 (and the Chapter I prohibition in the UK Competition Act 1998)[3]. A 'functional approach' must therefore be adopted when determining whether a particular entity qualifies as an undertaking for the purpose of the competition rules[4].

---

16   Case C-387/93 [1995] ECR I-4663, [1996] 1 CMLR 829, para 50.
17   See eg Case 155/73 *Sacchi* [1974] ECR 409, [1974] 2 CMLR 177; Case 41/83 *Italy v Commission* [1985] ECR 873, [1985] 2 CMLR 368.
18   Such bodies have a limited dispensation from the competition rules by virtue of Article 86(2) of the Treaty: see ch 6, pp 202-208.
19   Case 258/78 *Nungesser KG v Commission* [1982] ECR 2015, [1983] 1 CMLR 278.
20   See respectively *Alpha Flight Services/Aéroports de Paris* OJ [1998] L 230/10, [1998] 5 CMLR 611, paras 49-55; *Portugese Airports* OJ [1999] L 69/31, [1999] 5 CMLR 103, para 12 (in this case, a public undertaking in the sense of Article 86(1) EC); *Ilmailulaitos/ Luftfartsverket* OJ [1999] L 69/24, [1999] 5 CMLR 90, paras 21-23.
1   OJ [1985] L 92/1, [1987] 3 CMLR 813: see XIVth *Report on Competition Policy* (1984), point 57; see similarly *Re Colombian Coffee* OJ [1982] L 360/31, [1983] 1 CMLR 703.
2   OJ [1998] L 252/47, para 21.
3   See ch 9, pp 292-293.
4   On this point, see the opinion of Advocate General Jacobs in Cases C-67/96 etc *Albany International BV v SBT* [1999] ECR I-5751, [2000] 4 CMLR 446, para 207; this opinion contains an invaluable discussion of the meaning of 'undertakings' in Article 81(1); see also Case T-128/98 *Aéroports de Paris v Commission* [2001] 4 CMLR 1376, para 108.

(iv)   The professions[5]

Members of the liberal professions can be undertakings for the purpose of Article 81(1). In *Commission v Italy*[6] the ECJ held that customs agents in Italy, who offer for payment services consisting of the carrying out of customs formalities in relation to the import, export and transit of goods, were undertakings; it rejected the Italian Government's argument that the fact that the activity of customs agents is intellectual and requires authorisation and compliance with conditions meant that they were not undertakings. The ECJ further held that the National Council of Customs Agents was an association of undertakings, relying on *BNIC v Clair*[7] for the proposition that its public law nature did not remove it from the application of Article 81[8]. In *Coapi*[9] the Commission concluded that industrial property agents were undertakings, notwithstanding that they were members of a regulated profession, that their services were of an intellectual, technical or specialised nature, and that they provided services on a personal and direct basis. A similar conclusion was reached in *EPI code of conduct*[10] in relation to professional representatives before the European Patent Office. Self-employed medical specialists have been held to be undertakings[11], including when they are making contributions to their own supplementary scheme[12]. It is clear that it is possible that a Member State might be found to have breached the competition rules by delegating to a professional association the power to fix prices; and that the professional association itself might be liable for actually doing so[13]. The application of Article 81(1) to legal services is under consideration by the ECJ in two Article 234 references, one concerning fees[14] and the other the restriction on multi-disciplinary partnerships[15].

(v)   Certain bodies may not qualify as undertakings

Although it is clear that state-owned corporations or public authorities may qualify as undertakings for some purposes, they will not do so when conducting

5   On the application of the competition rules to the professions, see the Commission's XXIXth *Annual Report on Competition Policy* (1999), point 138.
6   Case C-35/96 [1998] ECR I-3851, [1998] 5 CMLR 889; see similarly Case T-513/93 *CNSD v Commission* [2000] 5 CMLR 614, upholding the Commission's decision in *CNSD* OJ [1993] L 203/27, [1995] 5 CMLR 889.
7   Case 123/83 [1985] ECR 391, [1985] 2 CMLR 430.
8   Case C-35/96 [1998] ECR I-3851, [1998] 5 CMLR 889, para 40; see similarly Case T-513/93 *CNSD v Commission* [2000] 5 CMLR 614; Cases C-180/98 etc *Pavel Pavlov v Stichting Pensioenfonds Medische Specialisten* [2001] 4 CMLR 30, paras 85-89.
9   OJ [1995] L 122/37, [1995] 5 CMLR 468.
10 OJ [1999] L 106/14, [1999] 5 CMLR 540, partially annulled on appeal to the CFI Case T-144/99 *Institut des Mandataires Agréés v Commission* (judgment of 28 March 2001).
11 Cases C-180/98 etc *Pavel Pavlov v Stichting Pensioenfonds Medische Specialisten* [2001] 4 CMLR 30, para 77.
12 Ibid, paras 78-82; the Commission, intervening, had argued that, when making such contributions, the specialists were acting as consumers rather than as undertakings.
13 *Coapi* OJ [1995] L 122/37, [1995] 5 CMLR 468, paras 44-48; Case T-513/93 *CNSD v Commission* [2000] 5 CMLR 614, para 73.
14 Case C-35/99 *Arduino* (grounds of reference OJ [1999] C 100/10: the opinion of Advocate General Léger was given on 10 July 2001).
15 Case C-309/99 *Wouters v Netherlands Bar Council* (grounds of reference OJ [1999] C 299/15: Advocate General Léger also gave his opinion in this case on 10 July 2001).

activities 'in the exercise of official authority'[16] or when acting 'as public authorities'. In *Corinne Bodson v Pompes Funèbres des Regions Libérées SA*[17] a French law entrusted the performance of funeral services to local communes; many of the communes in turn awarded concessions to provide those services to private undertakings. The ECJ held that Article 81 did not apply to 'contracts for concessions concluded between communes *acting in their capacity as public authorities* and undertakings entrusted with the provision of a public service' (emphasis added)[18]. An entity acts in the exercise of official authority where the activity in question is 'a task in the public interest which forms part of the essential functions of the State' and where that activity 'is connected by its nature, its aim and the rules to which it is subject with the exercise of powers ... which are typically those of a public authority'[19]. Many cases have concerned social protection, including social security, schemes, and specifically whether the operators of such schemes qualify as undertakings[20]. In *Poucet v Assurances Générales de France*[1] the ECJ concluded that French regional social security offices administering sickness and maternity insurance schemes to self-employed persons were not undertakings, but it reached the opposite conclusion in relation to a differently-constituted scheme in *Fédération Française des Sociétés d'Assurance*[2]. The difference between the cases was that in *Poucet* the benefits payable were identical for all recipients, contributions were proportionate to income, the pension rights were not proportionate to the contributions made and schemes that were in surplus helped to finance those which had financial difficulties; the schemes were based on the principle of solidarity. In the *Fédération Française* case on the other hand the benefits payable depended on the amount of the contributions paid by recipients and the financial results of the investments made by the managing organisation. Thus the manager of the scheme was carrying on an economic activity in competition with life assurance companies. In *Albany International BV v Stichting Bedrijfspensioenfonds Textielindustrie*[3] the ECJ held that the pension fund in that case was an undertaking, since it was carrying on an economic activity: its function was to make investments, the result of which determined the amount of benefits that the fund could pay to its members;[4] as such, this fund was different from the one in *Poucet*[5].

Two further examples of entities found not to be undertakings by the ECJ can be given. In *SAT Fluggesellschaft v Eurocontrol*[6] the ECJ concluded that Eurocontrol, an international organisation established for the safety of air navigation, was not an undertaking for the purpose of Articles 81 and 82[7]. In

---

16   Case C-343/95 *Cali e Figli* [1997] ECR I-1547, [1997] 5 CMLR 484, paras 16-17.
17   Case 30/87 [1988] ECR 2479, [1989] 4 CMLR 984.
18   Ibid, para 18.
19   Case C-343/95 *Cali e Figli* [1997] ECR I-1547, [1997] 5 CMLR 484, para 23.
20   See Winterstein 'Nailing the Jellyfish: Social Security and Competition Law' (1999) 20 ECLR 324.
1   Cases C–159/91 and 160/91 [1993] ECR I-637.
2   Case C-244/94 [1995] ECR I-4013, [1996] 4 CMLR 536.
3   Cases C-67/96 etc [1999] ECR I-5751, [2000] 4 CMLR 446; for commentary on this case, see Gyselen (2000) 37 CML Rev 425; see also Cases C-180/98 etc *Pavel Pavlov v Stichting Pensioenfonds Medische Specialisten* [2001] 4 CMLR 30, paras 102-119.
4   Ibid, paras 71-87.
5   See n 1 above.
6   Case C-364/92 [1994] ECR I-43, [1994] 5 CMLR 208.
7   A similar conclusion had earlier been reached by the Commercial Court in London in *Irish Aerospace (Belgium) NV v European Organisation for the Safety of Air Navigation* [1992] 1 Lloyd's Rep 383.

Calì e Figli[8] the ECJ held that a private company engaged in anti-pollution surveillance in Genoa harbour would not be acting as an undertaking when discharging that particular responsibility, since this was a task in the public interest, forming part of one of the essential functions of the state in protecting the maritime environment: this judgment is of particular interest as the public duty was being carried out by a private body. On the other side of the line, the Commission held in *Spanish Courier Services*[9] that the Spanish Post Office, in so far as it was providing services on the market, was an undertaking; in *Höfner and Elser v Macrotron*[10] the ECJ reached the same conclusion in respect of the German Federal Employment Office; and in *Merci Convenzionali Porto di Genova v Siderurgica Gabrielle SpA*[11] it held that the Port Authority at Genoa was an undertaking.

(vi) Employees and trades unions

In *Jean Claude Becu*[12] the ECJ held that workers are, for the duration of their employment relationship, incorporated into the undertakings that employ them and thus form part of an economic unit with them; as such they do not constitute undertakings within the meaning of Community competition law[13]. Nor should the dock workers in that case, taken collectively, be regarded as constituting an undertaking[14]. However an ex-employee who carries on an independent business would be[15]. In the *Albany* case[16] the ECJ was concerned with a case where organisations representing employers and employees collectively agreed to set up a single pension fund responsible for managing a supplementary pension scheme and requested the public authorities to make affiliation to the fund compulsory. One of the issues in the case was whether an agreement between such organisations was an agreement 'between undertakings'. The ECJ's answer was that they were not. The Treaty's activities include not only the adoption of a competition policy, but also a policy in the social sphere: this is stated in Article 3(1)(j) and revealed, for example, in Article 137 (ex Article 118), the purpose of which is to promote close cooperation between Member States in the social field, particularly in matters relating to the right of association and collective bargaining between employers and workers. The ECJ's view was that the social objectives pursued by collective agreements would be seriously undermined if they were subject to Article 81(1) of the Treaty and that therefore they fall outside it[17]. However the same exclusion does not apply in relation to a decision taken by members of the liberal professions, since it is not concluded in the context of collective bargaining between employers and employees[18].

8   Case C-343/95 [1997] ECR I-1547, [1997] 5 CMLR 484.
9   OJ [1990] L 233/19, [1991] 4 CMLR 560.
10 Case C-41/90 [1991] ECR I-1979, [1993] 4 CMLR 306.
11 Case C-179/90 [1991] ECR I-5889, [1994] 4 CMLR 422..
12 Case C-22/98 [1999] ECR I-5665, [2001] CMLR 968.
13 Ibid, para 26.
14 Ibid, para 27.
15 See eg *Reuter/BASF* OJ [1976] L 254/40, [1976] 2 CMLR D44.
16 See n 3 above.
17 Ibid, para 59; for critical comment, see Van den Bergh and Camesasca 'Irreconcilable Principles? The Court of Justice Exempts Collective Labour Agreements from the Wrath of Antitrust' (2000) 25 EL Rev 492; see also Case C-222/98 *Van der Woude v Stichting Beatrixoord* [2001] 4 CMLR 93.
18 Cases C-180/98 etc *Pavel Pavlov v Stichting Pensioenfonds Medische Specialisten* [2001] 4 CMLR 30, paras 67-70.

(B)   Undertakings that form a single economic entity

Article 81(1) does not apply to agreements between undertakings that form a single economic entity. The most obvious example of this is an agreement between a parent and a subsidiary company, though the relationship between a principal and agent and between a contractor and sub-contractor is analogous.

(i)   Parent and subsidiary

(A)   THE BASIC RULE.   Firms within the same corporate group can enter into legally enforceable contracts with one another. However such an agreement will not fall within the terms of Article 81(1) if the relationship between them is so close that economically it would be realistic to regard them as a single economic entity. Where this is the case, the agreement is regarded as the internal allocation of functions within a corporate group rather than a restrictive agreement between independent undertakings. In *Béguelin Import v GL Import Export*[19] the ECJ held that Article 81(1) would not apply to an agreement between a parent and its subsidiary 'which, although having separate legal personality, enjoys no economic independence'. In *Corinne Bodson v Pompes Funebres des Regions Libérées SA*[20] the ECJ stated that Article 81(1) would not apply if the undertakings 'form an economic unit within which the subsidiary has no real freedom to determine its course of action on the market, and if the agreements or practices are concerned merely with the internal allocation of tasks as between the undertakings'[1]. A logical consequence of the doctrine is that, when counting the number of undertakings that are party to an agreement for the purpose of applying one of the block exemptions, undertakings that form a single economic entity are counted as one[2].

(B)   THE *VIHO* JUDGMENT.   The issue was revisited in *Viho v Commission*[3]. Parker Pen had established an integrated distribution system for Germany, France, Belgium, Spain and the Netherlands, where it used subsidiary companies for the distribution of its products. The Commission concluded that Article 81(1) had no

---

19   Case 22/71 [1971] ECR 949, [1972] CMLR 81; see also Case 15/74 *Centrafarm BV v Sterling Drug Inc* [1974] ECR 1147, [1974] 2 CMLR 480 and Cases T–68/89 etc *Società Italiano Vetro v Commission* [1992] ECR II-1403, [1992] 5 CMLR 302, para 357; the Commission came to a similar conclusion in *Re Christiani and Nielsen NV* JO [1969] L 165/12, [1969] CMLR D 36 and in *Re Kodak* JO [1970] L 147/24, [1970] CMLR D19; see also *TFI/France 2 and France 3*, Commission's XXIXth *Report on Competition Policy* (1999) p 167.

20   Case 30/87 [1988] ECR 2479, [1989] 4 CMLR 984.

1   Ibid, para 19.

2   Case 170/83 *Hydrotherm Gerätebau v Andreoli* [1984] ECR 2999, [1985] 3 CMLR 224; this is relevant, for example, under Regulation 240/96 on technology transfer agreements, which confers block exemption only on bilateral agreements: see ch 19, p 689; and under Regulation 2790/99, which requires that, for the block exemption to apply, there must not be two undertakings to a vertical agreement operating at the same level of the market: see ch 16, p 571.

3   Case T-102/92 *Viho v Commission* [1995] ECR II-17, [1995] 4 CMLR 299, upheld by the ECJ in Case C-73/95 P [1996] ECR I-5457, [1997] 4 CMLR 419: Advocate General Lenz discusses the case law on the economic entity doctrine ('an inconsistent picture') at paras 48-73; see also Case T-198/98 *Micro Leader Business v Commission* [2000] All ER (EC) 361, [2000] 4 CMLR 886 at 895, para 38 (agreements within the Microsoft group not subject to Article 81(1)); on the similar position in US law, see *Copperweld Corpn v Independence Tube Corpn* 467 US 752.

application to this allocation of tasks within the Parker Pen group. This finding was challenged by a third party, Viho, which had been trying to obtain supplies of Parker Pen's products and which considered that the agreements between Parker Pen and its subsidiaries infringed Article 81(1). The CFI and the ECJ upheld the decision of the Commission, that Article 81(1) had no application. At paragraph 15 of its judgment, the ECJ noted that Parker Pen held 100% of the shares in the subsidiary companies, it directed their sales and marketing activities and it controlled sales, targets, gross margins, sales costs, cash flow and stocks:

> 'Parker and its subsidiaries thus form a single economic unit within which the subsidiaries do not enjoy real autonomy in determining their course of action in the market, but carry out the instructions issued to them by the parent company controlling them'[4].

The ECJ went on to say that in those circumstances the fact that Parker Pen could divide national markets between its subsidiaries was outside Article 81, although it pointed out that such unilateral conduct could fall foul of Article 82 where the requirements for its application were satisfied[5].

(C)   THE TEST OF CONTROL.   The crucial question, therefore, is whether parties to an agreement are independent in their decision-making or whether one has sufficient control over the affairs of the other that the latter does not enjoy 'real autonomy' in determining its course of action on the market. For these purposes it is necessary to examine various factors such as the shareholding that a parent company has in its subsidiary, the composition of the board of directors, the extent to which the parent influences the policy of or issues instructions to the subsidiary and similar matters[6]. Where a parent has a majority shareholding, the presumption will be that it controls the subsidiary's affairs[7]; the *Viho* case was a simple one, since Parker Pen held all the shares in the subsidiaries. What is less clear is whether a minority shareholder might be held to have sufficient control to negate autonomy on the part of the subsidiary. Under Article 3(3) of the ECMR, a minority shareholder which has the 'possibility of exercising decisive influence' over the affairs of another undertaking has sufficient control for there to be a concentration[8]. The case law has yet to explain whether the notion of control in the ECMR should be applied to the 'single economic entity' doctrine under Article 81(1), or whether the notions of control differ as between these two provisions. There would seem to be much to be said for the adoption of a consistent approach[9].

(D)   DECISIONS WHERE THE ECONOMIC ENTITY DOCTRINE DID NOT APPLY.   In *Ijsselcentrale*[10] the Commission rejected the argument that four Dutch electricity generating

4   Case C-73/95 P [1996] ECR I-5457, [1997] 4 CMLR 419, para 16.
5   Ibid, para 17; as to the possible application of Article 82, see *Interbrew* XXVIth *Report on Competition Policy* (1996), pp 139-140.
6   See also Case 107/82 *AEG-Telefunken v Commission* [1983] ECR 3151, [1984] 3 CMLR 325, paras 47–53.
7   See the Opinion of AG Warner in Cases 6, 7/73 *Commercial Solvents v Commission* [1974] ECR 223, [1974] 1 CMLR 309.
8   See ch 21 pp 745-748; note the different test of control for the purpose of calculating the turnover of 'undertakings concerned' in Article 5(4) of the ECMR: ibid, pp 754-755 .
9   See Wils 'The Undertaking as Subject of EC Competition Law and the Imputation of Infringements to Natural or Legal Persons' (2000) 25 EL Rev 99, pp 104-108.
10 OJ [1991] L 28/32, [1992] 5 CMLR 154, paras 22–24.

companies and the joint venture that they controlled formed a single economic entity, and that therefore Article 81(1) did not apply to agreements between them. The fact that the generators formed part of an indivisible system of public electricity supply did not mean that they were one unit, for they were separate legal persons, not controlled by a single natural or legal person, and were able to determine their own conduct independently. In *Gosmé/Martell-DMP*[11], DMP was a joint subsidiary of Martell and Piper-Hiedsieck. Each parent held 50% of the capital of DMP and the voting rights; half of the supervisory board members represented Martell shareholders and half Piper-Hiedsieck shareholders; DMP distributed brands not belonging to its parent companies; Martell and Piper-Hiedsieck products were invoiced to wholesalers on the same document; DMP had its own sales force and it alone concluded the contracts of sale with buying syndicates in France. In these circumstances the Commission concluded that Martell and DMP were independent undertakings, so that an agreement between them to identify and prevent parallel exports infringed Article 81(1) and attracted fines of EUR 300,000 in the case of Martell and EUR 50,000 in the case of DMP.

If a subsidiary becomes independent of its parent, for example by being sold off, an agreement between the two companies could be caught by Article 81(1) once the parent-subsidiary relationship ends. In *Austin Rover/Unipart*[12] the relationship between those undertakings following the privatisation of British Leyland and the selling off of Unipart was investigated by the Commission under Article 81(1), but exempted under Article 81(3).

(E)   CONCLUDING COMMENTS ON THE ECONOMIC ENTITY DOCTRINE.   Various points should be noted. First, although an agreement between connected firms may not itself infringe Article 81(1), the manipulation of a subsidiary company by a parent might mean that the competition rules are broken in other ways. A parent might order its subsidiaries to impose export bans on their distributors: the agreements containing such restrictions could themselves infringe Article 81[13]. Secondly, a parent company can be held liable for the activities of its subsidiaries: the Commission has frequently punished the former for the behaviour of the latter[14], and in the context of distribution agreements it is established that a parent has a particular responsibility to ensure that competition downstream in the market is not distorted[15]. Thirdly, it is also clear that a subsidiary may be fined for action which it takes in disobedience to the instructions of its parent[16]. Lastly, the immunity of agreements from Article 81(1) is in a sense a double-edged weapon: the Community Courts and the Commission have held that EC law can be applied to a parent company not present within the Community because of the conduct of its subsidiaries carried on there[17].

11   OJ [1991] L 185/23, [1992] 5 CMLR 586, para 30.
12   OJ [1988] L 45/34, [1988] 4 CMLR 513.
13   See eg *Re Kodak* JO [1970] L 147/24, [1970] CMLR D 19.
14   Case T–65/89 *BPB Industries plc v Commission* [1993] ECR II-389. [1993] 5 CMLR 32 paras 148–155; Case T-77/92 *Parker Pen Ltd v Commission* [1994] ECR II-549, [1995] 5 CMLR 435; Case T-354/94 *Stora v Commission* [1998] ECR II-2111, para 79; *Greek Ferry Services Cartel* OJ [1999] L 109/24, [1999] 5 CMLR 47, para 138, on appeal Cases T-56/99 etc *Marlines SA v Commission* (judgment pending); *Amino Acids* OJ [2001] L 152/24, [2001] 5 CMLR 322, paras 439-441.
15   *Johnson and Johnson* OJ [1980] L 377/16, [1981] 2 CMLR 287; Cases 100–103/80 *Musique Diffusion Française v Commission* [1983] ECR 1825, [1983] 3 CMLR 221.
16   Case 32/78 *BMW Belgium SA v Commission* [1979] ECR 2435, [1980] 1 CMLR 370.
17   See Case 48/69 *ICI v Commission* [1972] ECR 619, [1972] CMLR 557; Case 6/72 *Europemballage Corpn and Continental Can Co Inc v Commission* [1973] ECR 215, [1973] CMLR 199; see ch 12 on extra-territoriality generally.

(ii) Principal and agent

In some cases the relationship between a principal and agent will be dealt with in a similar way, with the result that Article 81(1) will not be applicable: this issue is dealt with in chapter 16[18].

(iii) Contractor and sub-contractor

Agreements between a contractor and a sub-contractor may also fall outside Article 81(1) because of the close relationship between them; this issue is also dealt with in chapter 16[19].

(C) Undertakings related by succession

Separate undertakings may be treated as one and the same where one undertaking succeeds another, so that the liabilities of the latter may be attributed to the former[20]. This issue has arisen on numerous occasions where the Commission, in the course of investigating a cartel, discovers that a member of it has become part of, or been taken over by, another firm. In such circumstances the question arises whether the second firm can be held responsible for the conduct of the first: obviously this is an important issue when the purchaser conducts its due diligence of the firm to be acquired. In *Compagnie Royale Asturienne des Mines SA and Rheinzink GmbH v Commission*[1] the ECJ held that 'a change in the legal form and name of an undertaking does not create a new undertaking free of liability for the anti-competitive behaviour of its predecessor when, from an economic point of view, the two are identical'. In *PVC*[2] the Commission held that it is a matter of Community law whether one undertaking can be liable for the past conduct of another: changes in organisation under national company law are not decisive. In order to decide whether there is 'undertaking identity', the expression used by the Commission in the *PVC* decision, the determining factor 'is whether there is a functional and economic continuity between the original infringer and the undertaking into which it was merged'[3]. It repeated this formulation in the second *PVC* decision[4]. In *All Weather Sports Benelux BV v Commission*[5] the CFI held that the Commission must adequately explain its reasoning when it imposes a fine on a successor to the entity that committed the

---

18 See ch 16, pp 538-540 and, in particular, the Commission's *Guidelines on Vertical Restraints* OJ [2000] C 291/1, [2000] 5 CMLR 1176, paras 12-20.

19 See ch 16, pp 593-594 and, in particular, the Commission's *Notice on Sub-contracting Agreements* OJ [1979] C 1/2, [1979] 1 CMLR 264.

20 See Garzaniti and Scassellati-Sforzolini 'Liability of Successor Undertakings for Infringements of EC Competition Law Committed Prior to Corporate Reorganisations' (1995) 16 ECLR 348.

1 Cases 29, 30/83 [1984] ECR 1679, [1985] 1 CMLR 688, para 9; see also Case T-134/94 *NMH Stahlwerke GmbH v Commission* [1999] ECR II-239, paras 122-141; Case C-297/98 P *SCA Holdings Ltd v Commission* [2001] 4 CMLR 13, paras 23-32.

2 OJ [1989] L 74/1, [1990] 4 CMLR 345, para 42.

3 Ibid, para 43; see similarly *LdPE* OJ [1989] L 74/21, paras 49–54; other decisions of the Commission dealing with this point are *Peroxygen Products* OJ [1985] L 35/1, [1985] 1 CMLR 481, *Polypropylene* OJ [1986] L 230/1, [1988] 4 CMLR 347 and *Welded Steel Mesh* OJ [1989] L 260/1, [1991] 4 CMLR 13, para 194.

4 OJ [1994] L 239/14, paras 14–43.

5 Case T-38/92 [1994] ECR II-211, [1995] 4 CMLR 43, paras 26-36.

infringement. Having determined that there is 'undertaking identity', the Commission must then decide which legal entity should be the addressee of the decision; this will depend on the facts of any particular case[6].

2.   AGREEMENTS, DECISIONS AND CONCERTED PRACTICES

The policy of Article 81 is to prohibit cooperation between independent undertakings which prevents, restricts or distorts competition: in particular it is concerned with the eradication of cartels and 'hard-core' restrictions of competition. Chapter 13 will examine this subject in detail. The application of Article 81(1) is not limited to legally enforceable agreements: this would make evasion of the law simple. Article 81 applies also to cooperation achieved through the decisions of trade associations and to more informal understandings, known as concerted practices. The Chapter I prohibition in the UK Competition Act 1998 has the same scope[7]. A broad interpretation has been given to each of the terms 'agreement', 'decision' and 'concerted practice'. A difficult issue is whether parallel behaviour by firms in an oligopolistic industry is attributable to an agreement or concerted practice between them, in which case Article 81(1) would be applicable; or whether it is a natural effect of the structure of the market, in which case a different competition law response might be needed. Chapter 14 will consider the issue of oligopoly, tacit collusion and so-called 'collective dominance' under Article 82, the EC Merger Regulation and the Chapter II prohibition in the Competition Act. In several decisions, particularly in the context of distribution systems, conduct which appeared to be unilateral has been held to be sufficiently consensual to fall within Article 81(1)[8].

(A)   Agreements

(i)   Examples of agreements

A legally enforceable contract of course qualifies as an agreement, including a compromise of litigation such as a trade mark delimitation agreement[9] or the settlement of a patent action[10]. 'Gentleman's agreements'[11] and simple understandings[12] have been held to be agreements, though neither is legally

---

6   Ibid, paras 44-46.
7   See ch 9, pp 292-294.
8   See pp 86-89, below.
9   See eg *Re Penney's Trade Mark* OJ [1978] L 60/19, [1978] 2 CMLR 100; *Re Toltecs and Dorcet* OJ [1982] L 379/19, [1983] 1 CMLR 412, upheld on appeal Case 35/83 *BAT v Commission* [1985] ECR 363, [1985] 2 CMLR 470; it is not entirely clear what effect embodiment of the compromise in an order of a national court has on the applicability of Article 81(1): see Case 258/78 *LC Nungesser KG v Commission* [1982] ECR 2015, [1983] 1 CMLR 278, paras 80–91, where the ECJ was delphic on this issue; the tenor of the ECJ's judgment in *BAT v Commission* would suggest that the agreement would be caught even where sanctioned by a national court. On trade mark delimitation agreements, see further ch 19, p 697.
10   See eg Case 65/86 *Bayer v Süllhöfer* [1988] ECR 5249, [1990] 4 CMLR 182.
11   Case 41/69 *ACF Chemiefarma NV v Commission* [1970] ECR 661.
12   *Re Stichting Sigarettenindustrie Agreements* OJ [1982] L 232/1, [1982] 3 CMLR 702 (an 'understanding' between trade associations held to be an agreement); *National Panasonic* OJ [1982] L 354/28, [1983] 1 CMLR 497, where there was no formal agreement between Panasonic and its dealers, but the Commission still held that there was an agreement as

binding; there is no requirement that an agreement should be supported by enforcement procedures[13]. A 'protocol' which reflects a genuine concurrence of will between the parties constitutes an agreement within the meaning of Article 81(1)[14]. Connected agreements may be treated as a single one[15]. An agreement may be oral[16]. The Commission will treat the contractual terms and conditions in a standard-form contract as an agreement within Article 81(1)[17]. An agreement which has expired by effluxion of time but the effects of which continue to be felt can be caught by Article 81(1)[18]. The constitution of a trade association qualifies as an agreement within Article 81[19]. An agreement entered into by a trade association might be construed as an agreement on the part of its members[20]. An agreement to create a European Economic Interest Grouping (EEIG), or the byelaws establishing it may be caught by Article 81(1)[1]. There may be 'inchoate understandings and conditional or partial agreement' during a bargaining process sufficient to amount to an agreement in the sense of Article 81(1)[2]. Guidelines issued by one person that are adhered to by another can amount to an agreement[3]. The fact that formal agreement has not been reached on all matters does not preclude a finding of an agreement[4]. Undertakings cannot justify infringement of the rules on competition by claiming that they were forced into an agreement by the conduct of other traders[5]. Where an agreement is entered into unwillingly, this may be significant in influencing the Commission to mitigate a fine[6], not to impose a fine[7] or not to institute proceedings at all. The Commission may abstain

opposed to a concerted practice between them; *Viho/Toshiba* OJ [1991] L 287/39, [1992] 5 CMLR 180, where the Commission found an understanding between Toshiba's German subsidiary and certain distributors that an export prohibition should apply, even though the standard distribution agreements had been amended to remove an export prohibition clause.

13 *Soda-ash/Solvay, CFK* OJ [1991] L 152/16, [1994] 4 CMLR 645, para 11; *PVC* OJ [1994] L 239/14, para 30.

14 *HOV SVZ/MCN* [1994] OJ L 104/34, para 46.

15 *ENI/Montedison* OJ [1987] L 5/13, [1988] 4 CMLR 444.

16 Case 28/77 *Tepea v Commission* [1978] ECR 1391, [1978] 3 CMLR 392; Cases T-25/95 etc *Cimenteries CBR SA v Commission* judgment of 15 March 2000, para 2341.

17 *Putz v Kawasaki Motors (UK) Ltd* OJ [1979] L 16/9, [1979] 1 CMLR 448; *Sandoz* OJ [1987] L 222/28, [1989] 4 CMLR 628, upheld on appeal Case 277/87 *Sandoz Prodotti Farmaceutici SpA v Commission* [1990] ECR I–45.

18 Case T–7/89 *SA Hercules NV v Commission* [1991] ECR II-1711, [1992] 4 CMLR 84, para 257; Case 51/75 *EMI Records Ltd v CBS UK Ltd* [1976] ECR 811, pp 848–849, [1976] 2 CMLR 235, p 267.

19 *Re Nuovo CEGAM* OJ [1984] L 99/29, [1984] 2 CMLR 484.

20 Cases 209/78 etc *Heintz Van Landewyck v Commission* [1980] ECR 3125, [1981] 3 CMLR 134.

1 *Orphe* (Commission's XXth *Report on Competition Policy* (1990), point 102); *Tepar* [1991] 4 CMLR 860; *Twinning Programme Engineering Group* OJ [1992] C 148/8, [1992] 5 CMLR 93.

2 *Pre-Insulated Pipe Cartel* OJ [1999] L 24/1, [1999] 4 CMLR 402, para 133, on appeal Cases T-9/99 etc *HFB Holding v Commission* (judgment pending).

3 *Anheuser-Busch Incorporated-Scottish & Newcastle* OJ [2000] L 49/37, [2000] 5 CMLR 75, para 26.

4 Ibid, para 134.

5 Case 16/61 *Modena v High Authority* [1962] ECR 289, [1962] CMLR 221; *Musique Diffusion Française v Commission* [1983] ECR 1825, [1983] 3 CMLR 221, paras 90 and 100.

6 *Hasselblad* OJ [1982] L 161/18, [1982] 2 CMLR 233; *Wood Pulp* OJ [1985] L 85/1, [1985] 3 CMLR 474, para 131.

7 *Burns Tractors Ltd v Sperry New Holland* OJ [1985] L 376/21, [1988] 4 CMLR 306; *Fisher-Price/Quaker Oats Ltd—Toyco* OJ [1988] L 49/19, [1989] 4 CMLR 553.

from fining parties which had no input in the drafting of the agreements into which they have entered[8].

(ii) Complex cartels

Many cartels are complex and of long duration. Over a period of time, some firms may be more active than others in the running of a cartel; some may 'drop out' for a while but subsequently re-enter; others may attend meetings or communicate in other ways in order to be kept informed, without necessarily intending to fall in line with the agreed plan; there may be few occasions on which all the members of a cartel actually meet or behave precisely in concert with one another. This presents a problem for a competition authority: where the shape and active membership of a cartel changes over a period of time, must the authority prove a series of discrete agreements or concerted practices, and identify each of the parties to each of those agreements and concerted practices? This would require a considerable amount of evidence and impose a very high burden on the competition authority; it might also mean that it would not be possible to impose fines in relation to 'old' agreements and concerted practices, in relation to which infringement proceedings had become time-barred[9]. The Commission, upheld by the Community courts, has addressed these problems in two ways: first, by developing the idea that it is not necessary to characterise infringements of Article 81(1) specifically as an agreement on the one hand or a concerted practice on the other; and secondly by establishing the concept of a 'single overall agreement' for which all members of a cartel bear responsibility, irrespective of their precise involvement from day to day[10].

(A)   AGREEMENT 'AND/OR' CONCERTED PRACTICE.   The Commission has stated that agreements and concerted practices are conceptually distinct[11]. However Advocate General Reischl has said that there is little point in defining the exact point at which agreement ends and concerted practice begins[12]. It may be that, in a particular case, linguistically it is more natural to use one term than the other, but legally nothing turns on the distinction: the important distinction is between collusive and non-collusive behaviour[13]. Where the Commission is satisfied that the parties are guilty of a concerted practice, it does not consider it necessary

---

8   *Viho/Toshiba* OJ [1991] OJ L 287/39, [1992] 5 CMLR 180, para 26; guidance on the Commission's fining policy can be found in two Commission notices, *Notice on the Non-imposition of Fines in Cartel Cases* OJ [1996] C 207/4, [1996] 5 CMLR 362 and *Notice on the Method of Setting Fines* OJ [1998] C 9/3, [1998] 4 CMLR 472: they are discussed in ch 7, pp 238-239 .

9   Under Regulation 2988/74 the Commission cannot impose fines in relation to an infringement that ended five years or more previously: see Kerse *EC Antitrust Procedure* (Sweet & Maxwell, 4th ed, 1998) paras 7.47-7.49; Smith *Competition Law: Enforcement & Procedure* (Butterworths, 2001) paras 9.96-9.104.

10 See generally Joshua 'Attitudes to Anti-Trust Enforcement in the EU and US: Dodging the Traffic Warden, or Respecting the Law' [1995] Fordham Corporate Law Institute (ed Hawk) 85.

11 See *Polypropylene* OJ [1986] L 230/1, [1988] 4 CMLR 347, para 86.

12 See Cases 209/78 etc *Van Landewyck v Commission* [1980] ECR 3125, p 3310, [1981] 3 CMLR 134, p 185.

13 *Polypropylene* OJ [1986] L 230/1, [1988] 4 CMLR 347, para 87, on appeal Case T-7/89 *SA Hercules NV v Commission* [1991] ECR II-1711, [1992] 4 CMLR 84, upheld on appeal to the ECJ Case C-51/92 P *Hercules Chemicals v Commission* [1999] 5 CMLR 976; *Soda-ash/Solvay, ICI* OJ [1991] L 152/1, [1994] 4 CMLR 645, para 55.

also to determine whether they are party to an express or tacit agreement[14]. In some decisions the Commission has said simply that cooperation between undertakings amounted to an agreement or at least a concerted practice, without actually deciding which[15]. In the *PVC*[16] decision, the Commission reached the conclusion that the parties to the cartel had participated in an agreement 'and/ or' a concerted practice. On appeal to the CFI, Enichem argued that the Commission was not entitled to have made this 'joint classification', which would be lawful only if it could prove the existence of both an agreement and a concerted practice. In its judgment the CFI rejected this argument and upheld the Commission[17]. It held that:

'In the context of a complex infringement which involves many producers seeking over a number of years to regulate the market between them the Commission cannot be expected to classify the infringement precisely, for each undertaking and for any given moment, as in any event both those forms of infringement are covered by Article [81] of the Treaty'[18].

The CFI went on to say that joint classification was permissible where the infringement includes elements both of an agreement and of a concerted practice, without the Commission having to prove that there was both an agreement and a concerted practice throughout the period of the infringement. This approach has been confirmed by the ECJ, in *Commission v ANIC*[19].

The Commission adopted a joint classification approach in *British Sugar*[20], stating at paragraph 70 of its decision that:

'The Court of First Instance in various judgments made it clear that it was not necessary, particularly in the case of a complex infringement of considerable duration, for the Commission to characterise it as exclusively an agreement or concerted practice, or to split it up into separate infringements. Indeed, it might not even be feasible or realistic to make any such distinctions, as the infringement as a whole might present characteristics of both types of prohibited conduct, while considered in isolation some of its manifestations could more accurately be described as one rather than the other. In particular, it would be artificial to subdivide continuous conduct, having one and the same overall objective, into several

14 Ibid.
15 See eg *Re Floral* OJ [1980] L 39/51, [1980] 2 CMLR 285.
16 OJ [1989] L 74/1, [1990] 4 CMLR 345; this decision was taken by the Commission after its earlier decision, OJ [1989] L 74/1, had been annulled by the ECJ for infringement of essential procedural requirements: Cases C-137/92 P etc *Commission v BASF* [1994] ECR I-2555.
17 Cases T-305/94 etc *NV Limburgse Vinyl Maatschappij v Commission* [1999] ECR II-931, [1999] 5 CMLR 303, paras 695-699; ICI has appealed this judgment to the ECJ, Case C-254/99P *ICI v Commission* (grounds of appeal OJ [1999] C 352/17, judgment pending); the CFI had noted the possibility of a joint classification in its earlier judgments in the *Polypropylene* case: see eg Case T-1/89 *Rhône-Poulenc v Commission* [1991] ECR II-867, paras 125-127 and Case T-8/89 Rev *DSM v Commission* [1991] ECR II-1833, paras 234-235.
18 Cases T-305/94 etc *NV Limburgse Vinyl Maatschappij v Commission* [1999] ECR II-931, [1999] 5 CMLR 303, para 696.
19 Case C-49/92 [1999] ECR I-4125, paras 132 and 133; see also Case T-62/98 *Volkswagen AG v Commission* [2000] 5 CMLR 853, para 237.
20 OJ [1999] L 76/1, [1999] 4 CMLR 1316, substantially upheld on appeal Cases T-202/98 etc *Tate & Lyle v Commission* (judgment of 12 July 2001).

discrete infringements. The Court of First Instance in its judgments therefore endorsed the Commission's dual characterisation of the single infringement as an agreement and a concerted practice, and stated that this had to be understood, not as requiring, simultaneously and cumulatively, proof that each of the factual elements contained in the continuous conduct presented the constituent elements both of an agreement and of a concerted practice, but rather as referring to a complex whole which comprised a number of factual elements some of which in isolation would be characterised as agreements whereas others would be considered concerted practices'.

The same approach can be found in *Cartonboard*[1] and in *Pre-Insulated Pipe Cartel*[2]. As one former Commission official has put it: the search should not be for an agreement on the one hand or a concerted practice on the other; rather for a 'partnership for unlawful purposes with all the possible disagreements about methods that may occur in such a venture without affecting the cohesion of the shared purpose and design'[3].

(B)   THE CONCEPT OF A 'SINGLE, OVERALL AGREEMENT'.   In a series of decisions from the mid-1980s the Commission has developed the concept of a 'single, overall agreement' for which undertakings bear responsibility, even though they may not be involved in its operation on a day-to-day or a continuing basis. For example, in *Polypropylene*[4] the Commission investigated a complex cartel agreement in the petrochemicals sector involving 15 firms over many years. It held that the detailed arrangements whereby the cartel operated were all part of a single, overall agreement: this agreement was oral, not legally binding, and there were no sanctions for its enforcement. Having established that there was a single agreement, the Commission concluded that all 15 firms were guilty of infringing Article 81, even though some had not attended every meeting of the cartel and had not been involved in every aspect of its decision-making: participation in the overall agreement was sufficient to establish guilt. Furthermore, the fact that some members of the cartel had reservations about whether to participate – or indeed intended to cheat by deviating from the agreed conduct – did not mean that they were not party to an agreement. The Commission reached similar conclusions in other cases, for example *PVC*[5], *LdPE*[6], in its second decision on *PVC*[7] and in *Amino Acids*[8]. The CFI has confirmed the concept of a 'single overall agreement'[9]. In the appeal against the second *PVC* decision, the CFI upheld the Commission's view that at an undertaking can be held responsible for an overall cartel, even though it participated in only one or some of its constituent elements, 'if it is shown that it knew, or must have known, that the collusion in which it participated ... was part of an overall plan intended to distort competition

---

1   OJ [1994] L 243/1, [1994] 5 CMLR 547, para 128.
2   OJ [1999] L 24/1, [1999] 5 CMLR 402, paras 131-132, on appeal Cases T-9/99 etc *HFB Holding v Commission* (judgment pending).
3   Johsua 'Attitudes to Anti-Trust Enforcement in the EU and US: Dodging the Traffic Warden, or Respecting the Law?' [1995] Fordham Corporate Law Institute (ed Hawk), 85.
4   OJ [1986] L 230/1, [1988] 4 CMLR 347.
5   OJ [1989] L 74/1, [1990] 4 CMLR 345.
6   OJ [1989] L 74/21, [1990] 4 CMLR 382, paras 49–54.
7   OJ [1994] L 239/14, paras 30-31.
8   OJ [2001] L 152/24, [2001] 5 CMLR 322, paras 237-238; the decision has been appealed to the CFI, Cases T-221/00 etc *Cheil Jedang Corpn v Commission* (judgment pending).
9   See Case T-1/89 *Rhône Poulenc v Commission* [1991] ECR II-867, para 126.

and that the overall plan included all the constituent elements of the cartel'[10]. In *Tréfileurope v Commission*[11], one of the appeals in the *Welded Steel Mesh* case, the CFI held that the fact that an undertaking does not abide by the outcome of meetings which have a manifestly anti-competitive purpose does not relieve it of full responsibility for its participation in the cartel, if it has not publicly distanced itself from what was agreed in the meetings; this has been repeated on various occasions, for example in *BPB de Eendracht NV v Commission*[12], an appeal in the *Cartonboard* case, and in the *Cement* cases[13]. The Commission repeated the point in *Amino Acids*[14]. In *Steel Beams*[15] the CFI held that attendance by an undertaking at meetings involving anti-competitive activities suffices to establish its participation in those activities in the absence of proof capable of establishing the contrary[16]. The Commission said the same thing in *Amino Acids*[17]. However, where there are numerous bilateral and multilateral agreements between a large number of undertakings, it cannot be presumed from this in itself that they form part of a single, overall agreement: it is necessary for the Commission to prove that this is the case[18].

The cumulative effect of these judgments must be beneficial to the Commission in its anti-cartel policy, since the Community Courts seem to have deliberately refrained from construing the expressions 'agreement' and 'concerted practice' in a legalistic or formalistic manner: what emerges, essentially, is that any contact between competitors that touches upon business behaviour such as pricing, markets, customers and volume of output is risky in the extreme.

(B) Decisions by associations of undertakings

Coordination between independent undertakings may be achieved through the medium of a trade association. The trade association may have a particularly important rôle where the cartel consists of a large number of firms, in which case compliance with the rules of the cartel needs to be monitored: where only a few firms collude, it is relatively easy for each firm to monitor what the others are doing[19]. The possibility that trade associations may play a part in cartel activity is explicitly recognised in Article 81(1) by the proscription of 'decisions by associations of undertakings' that could restrict competition. The application of Article 81(1) to decisions means that the trade association itself may be held liable and be fined[20].

---

10 Cases T-305/94 etc *NV Limburgse Vinyl Maatschappij v Commission* [1999] ECR II-931, [1999] 5 CMLR 303, para 773.
11 Case T-141/89 [1995] ECR II-791, para 85.
12 Case T-311/94 [1998] ECR II-1129, para 203.
13 Cases T-25/95 etc *Cimenteries CBR SA v Commission* judgment of 15 March 2000, paras 1353, 1389 and 3199.
14 OJ [2001] L 152/24, [2001] 5 CMLR 322, para 221.
15 Cases T-141/94 etc *Thyssen Stahl v Commission* [1999] ECR II-347, [1999] 4 CMLR 810.
16 Ibid, applying Case T-14/89 *Montedipe v Commission* [1992] ECR II-1155, [1993] 4 CMLR 110.
17 OJ [2001] L 152/24, [2001] 5 CMLR 322, para 185.
18 Cases T-25/95 etc *Cimenteries CBR SA v Commission* judgment of 15 March 2000, paras 4027, 4060, 4109 and 4112.
19 See ch 14, pp 460-467 on tacit collusion in oligopolistic markets.
20 See eg *AROW v BNIC* OJ [1982] L 379/1, [1983] 2 CMLR 240 where BNIC was fined EUR 160,000; *Fenex* OJ [1996] L 181/28, [1996] 5 CMLR 332 where Fenex was fined EUR 1,000.

It has been held that the constitution of a trade association is itself a decision[1], as well as regulations governing the operation of an association[2]. An agreement entered into by an association might also be a decision. A recommendation made by an association has been held to amount to a decision, and it has been clearly established that the fact that the recommendation is not binding upon its members does not prevent the application of Article 81(1)[3]. In such cases it is necessary to consider whether members in the past have tended to comply with recommendations that have been made, and whether compliance with the recommendation would have a significant influence on competition within the relevant market. In *IAZ International Belgium NV v Commission*[4] an association of water-supply undertakings recommended its members not to connect dish-washing machines to the mains system which did not have a conformity label supplied by a Belgian association of producers of such equipment. The ECJ confirmed the Commission's view that this recommendation, though not binding, could restrict competition, since its effect was to discriminate against appliances produced elsewhere in the EC. Regulations made by a trade association may amount to a decision within the meaning of Article 81(1)[5].

A decision does not acquire immunity because it is subsequently approved and extended in scope by a public authority[6], nor does a trade association fall outside Article 81(1) because it is given statutory functions or because its members are appointed by the Government[7]. The ECJ has specifically stated that the public law status of a national body (for example an association of customs agents) does not preclude the application of Article 81[8]. Article 81(1) also applies to decisions by associations of trade associations[9]. A trade association does not have to have a commercial or economic activity of its own to be subject to Article 81(1)[10]; it follows that that Article 81(1) may be applicable to the decisions of a trade association, even if it does not apply to its agreements since the

1   See eg *Re ASPA* JO [1970] L 148/9, [1970] CMLR D25; *National Sulphuric Acid Association* OJ [1980] L 260/24, [1980] 3 CMLR 429.
2   *Sippa* OJ [1991] L 60/19; *Coapi* OJ [1995] L 122/37, [1995] 5 CMLR 468, para 34; *Nederlandse Federative Vereniging voor de Grootlandel op Elektrotechnisch Gebied and Technische Unie (FEG and TU)* OJ [2000] L 39/1, [2000] 4 CMLR 1208, para 95.
3   Case 8/72 *Vereeniging van Cementhandelaren v Commission* [1972] ECR 977, [1973] CMLR 7; Case 71/74 *FRUBO v Commission* [1975] ECR 563, [1975] 2 CMLR 123, Cases 209/78 etc *Van Landewyck v Commission* [1980] ECR 3125, [1981] 3 CMLR 134; Case 45/85 *VDS v Commission* [1987] ECR 405, [1988] 4 CMLR 264, para 32; see also *Distribution of railway tickets by travel agents* OJ [1992] L 366/47, paras 62–69, partially annulled on appeal Case T–14/93 *UIC v Commission* [1995] ECR II-1503, [1996] 5 CMLR 40; *Fenex* OJ [1996] L 181/28, [1996] 5 CMLR 332, paras 32-42.
4   Cases 96/82 etc [1983] ECR 3369, [1984] 3 CMLR 276.
5   *Re Acier* JO [1970] L 153/14, [1970] CMLR D31; *Publishers' Association – Net Book Agreements* OJ [1989] L 22/12, [1989] 4 CMLR 825, upheld on appeal Case T–66/89 *Publishers' Association v Commission (No 2)* [1992] ECR II-1995, [1992] 5 CMLR 120, partially annulled on appeal to the ECJ in Case C–360/92 P *Publishers' Association v Commission* [1995] ECR I-23, [1995] 5 CMLR 33.
6   *AROW v BNIC* OJ [1982] L 379/1, [1983] 2 CMLR 240; *Coapi* OJ [1995] L 122/37, [1995] 5 CMLR 468, para 32.
7   Ibid and *Pabst and Richarz KG v BNIA* OJ [1976] L 231/24, [1976] 2 CMLR D63.
8   Case C-35/96 *Commission v Italy* [1998] ECR I-3851, [1998] 5 CMLR 889, para 40.
9   See eg *Cematex* JO [1971] L 227/26, [1973] CMLR D135 and *Milchförderungsfonds* OJ [1985] L 35/35, [1985] 3 CMLR 101.
10   Cases T-25/95 etc judgment of 15 March 2000, para 1320, citing many earlier judgments of the ECJ and CFI to similar effect.

association is not itself an undertaking[11] . Where the association is an undertaking, an agreement between it and other undertakings may be caught by Article 81(1)[12] .

(C)   Concerted practices

The inclusion of concerted practices within the proscription of Article 81 means that conduct which is not attributable to an agreement or a decision may nevertheless infringe Article 81(1). While it can readily be appreciated that loose, informal understandings to limit competition must be prevented as well as agreements, it is difficult both to define the type or degree of coordination within the mischief of the law and to apply that rule to the facts of any given case. In particular there is the problem that parties to a cartel may do all they can to destroy incriminating evidence of meetings, e-mails, faxes and correspondence, in which case the temptation of the competition authority will be to infer the existence of an agreement or concerted practice from circumstantial evidence such as parallel conduct on the market. This can be dangerous, for it may be that firms act in parallel not because of an agreement or concerted practice, but because their individual appreciation of market conditions tells them that a failure to match a rival's strategy could be damaging or even disastrous. The application of the law in this area is complex, and competition authorities must proceed with care in order to distinguish covert cartels from rational and innocent parallel commercial activities. The problem of parallel behaviour in oligopolistic markets will be examined in detail in chapter 14, which will consider not only the application of Article 81(1) to this phenomenon but also the utility of the concept of collective dominance in Article 82 and in the Chapter II prohibition in the UK Competition Act, and of the 'complex monopoly' provisions of the Fair Trading Act 1973, in dealing with it.

It is necessary at this stage to consider first the legal meaning of a concerted practice; secondly the question of whether a concerted practice must have been put into effect for Article 81(1) to have been infringed; and lastly the burden of proof in such cases.

(i)   Meaning of concerted practice[13]

ICI v Commission[14] (usually referred to as the *Dyestuffs* case) was the first important case on concerted practices to come before the ECJ. The Commission had fined several producers of dyestuffs which it considered had been guilty of price fixing through concerted practices[15] . Its decision relied upon various pieces of evidence, including the similarity of the rate and timing of price increases and of instructions sent out by parent companies to their subsidiaries and the fact that there had been informal contact between the firms concerned. The ECJ

---

11   AG Slynn in Case 123/85 *BNIC v Clair* [1985] ECR 391, p 396, [1985] 2 CMLR 430, p 442.
12   Cases T-25/95 etc *Cimenteries CBR SA v Commission* judgment of 15 March 2000, paras 1325 and 2622.
13   See Black 'Communication and Obligation in Arrangements and Concerted Practices' (1992) 13 ECLR 200.
14   Cases 48/69 etc [1972] ECR 619, [1972] CMLR 557.
15   *Re Aniline Dyes Cartel* JO [1969] L 195/11, [1969] CMLR D23.

upheld the Commission. It said that the object of bringing concerted practices within Article 81 was to prohibit:

> 'a form of coordination between undertakings which, without having reached the stage where an agreement properly so-called has been concluded, knowingly substitutes practical cooperation between them for the risks of competition'[16].

In *Suiker Unie v Commission*[17] (the *Sugar Cartel* case) the ECJ elaborated upon this test. The Commission had held[18] that various sugar producers had taken part in concerted practices to protect the position of two Dutch producers on their domestic market. The producers denied this as they had not worked out a plan to this effect. The ECJ held that it was not necessary to prove that there was an actual plan. Article 81 strictly precluded:

> 'any direct or indirect contact between such operators, the object or effect whereof is either to influence the conduct on the market of an actual or potential competitor or to disclose to such a competitor the course of conduct which they themselves have decided to adopt or contemplate adopting on the market'[19].

These two cases provide the legal test of what constitutes a concerted practice for the purpose of Article 81: there must be a mental consensus whereby practical cooperation is *knowingly* substituted for competition; however the consensus need not be achieved verbally, and can come about by direct or indirect contact between the parties. In *Züchner v Bayerische Vereinsbank AG*[20] the ECJ quoted both of these extracts when repeating the test of a concerted practice. In *Wood Pulp*[1] Advocate General Darmon noted at paragraphs 170 to 175 of his Opinion that the concept of a concerted practice implies the existence of reciprocal contact. However, this reciprocity can be quite easily established. In the *Cement* appeals[2] the CFI found that Lafarge was party to a concerted practice when it received information at a meeting about the future conduct of a competitor: it could not argue that it was merely the passive recipient of such information[3]. In the same case the CFI stated that a concerted practice does not require a formal undertaking to have been given as to future behaviour[4].

In *Polypropylene*[5], *PVC*[6] and *LdPE*[7] the Commission stressed that a concerted practice did not require proof of a plan, and it is notable that in *LdPE* BP, Monsanto and Shell were held to be parties to a concerted practice even though they were on the 'periphery' of the cartel[8]. In *Soda-ash/Solvay*[9] the Commission

---

16   [1972] ECR 619, [1972] CMLR 557, para 64.
17   Cases 40/73 etc [1975] ECR 1663, [1976] 1 CMLR 295.
18   *Re European Sugar Cartel* OJ [1973] L 140/17, [1973] CMLR D65.
19   [1975] ECR 1663, p 1942, [1976] 1 CMLR 295, p 425.
20   Case 172/80 [1981] ECR 2021, [1982] 1 CMLR 313.
1   Cases 89/85 etc *Ahlström v Commission* [1993] ECR I-1307, [1993] 4 CMLR 407.
2   Cases T-25/95 etc *Cimenteries CBR SA v Commission* judgment of 15 March 2000.
3   Ibid, para 1849.
4   Ibid, para 1852.
5   OJ [1986] L 230/1, [1988] 4 CMLR 347.
6   OJ [1989] L 74/1, [1990] 4 CMLR 345.
7   OJ [1989] L 74/21, [1990] 4 CMLR 382, paras 49–54.
8   Ibid, para 41.
9   OJ [1991] L 152/1.

pointed out that it would be unlikely, given the well-known legal risks under Article 81(1), that one would find a written record of an illegal resolution; it said that:

'There are many forms and degrees of collusion and it does not require the making of a formal agreement. An infringement of Article 81 may well exist where the parties have not even spelled out an agreement in terms but each infers commitment from the other on the basis of conduct.'[10]

(ii) Must a concerted practice have been put into effect?

The judgment of the ECJ in the *Polypropylene*[11] cases deals with the question of whether a concerted practice must have been put into effect in order for there to be an infringement of Article 81(1). If the answer to this is yes, it would follow, for example, that if competitors were 'merely' to meet or to exchange information, without actually producing any effects on the market by doing so, this would not amount to a concerted practice; the Commission would therefore have to prove there to be an agreement, the object or effect of which is to restrict competition. The Commission has been keen not to allow there to be legalistic distinctions between the treatment of agreements and concerted practices in Article 81(1), and has received the support of the Community Courts in this endeavour[12]. The ECJ held in *Hüls*, one of the *Polypropylene* cases, that 'a concerted practice ... is caught by Article 81(1) EC, even in the absence of anti-competitive effects on the market'[13]; however, in the *Cement* cases the CFI said that there would be no infringement if the parties can prove to the contrary[14]. In reaching its conclusion in *Hüls*, the ECJ stated that, as established by its own case law[15], Article 81(1) requires that each economic operator must determine its policy on the market independently. At paragraph 161, the ECJ acknowledged that the concept of a concerted practice implies that there will be common conduct on the market, but added that there must be a presumption that, by making contact with one another, such conduct will follow: the ECJ appears to be saying that, because of this presumption, the Commission does not have to go further and actually prove those effects. At paragraph 164 the ECJ specifically stated that a concerted practice may have an anti-competitive *object*, thus harnessing the words of Article 81(1) itself (agreements and concerted practices *the object or effect of which ...*) in support of the proposition that the concerted practice does not need to have produced effects on the market. Even if one has semantic, or indeed philosophical, problems with the proposition that a concerted practice need not have produced

10 Ibid, para 59.
11 Cases C-51/92 P etc *Hercules Chemicals NV v Commission* [1999] ECR I-4235, [1999] 5 CMLR 976.
12 See pp 78-80 above on complex cartels.
13 Case C-199/92 P etc *Hüls AG v Commission* [1999] ECR I-4287, [1999] 5 CMLR 1016, para 163; see similarly the CFI in Cases T-141/94 etc *Thyssen Stahl v Commission* [1999] ECR II-347, [1999] 4 CMLR 810, paras 269-272, dealing in this case with Article 65(1) ECSC.
14 Cases T-25/95 etc *Cimenteries CBR SA v Commission* judgment of 15 March 2000, para 1865.
15 Cases 40/73 etc *Suiker Unie v Commission* [1975] ECR 1663, [1976] 1 CMLR 295 at 296, para 73; Case 172/80 *Züchner v Bayerische Vereinsbank AG* [1981] ECR 2021, [1982] 1 CMLR 313, para 13; Cases 89/85 etc *Ahlström v Commission* [1993] ECR I-1307, [1993] 4 CMLR 407, para 63; Case C-7/95 P *John Deere v Commission* [1998] ECR I-3111, [1998] 5 CMLR 311, para 86.

effects on the market, the law is clearly stated in this judgment. In *British Sugar*[16] the Commission specifically concluded that there can be a concerted practice in the absence of an actual effect on the market.

(iii)   The burden of proof

An important issue, having established the legal definition of what constitutes a concerted practice, is to consider who bears the burden of proof. It is clear that the burden is on the Commission to establish that there has been a concerted practice; the Community Courts have annulled decisions where they were unhappy about the evidence on which the Commission relied[17]. In particular, the ECJ's judgment in *Compagnie Royale Asturienne des Mines SA and Rheinzink GmbH v Commission*[18] established that, whereas parallel behaviour can be circumstantial evidence of a concerted practice, it cannot be conclusive where there are other explanations of what has taken place[19]. In that case the Commission had concluded that the simultaneous cessation of deliveries to a Belgian customer, Schlitz, by CRAM and Rheinzink of Germany was attributable to a concerted practice to protect the German market. The ECJ held that there was a possible alternative explanation of the refusal to supply, which was that Schlitz had been failing to settle its accounts on the due date; as the Commission had not dealt with this possible explanation of the conduct in question its decision should be quashed.

The most difficult cases on concerted practices are those in which firms behave in a parallel manner, but claim to do so not because of collusion between them but because of the oligopolistic structure of the market. The difficulties that such cases give rise to, including the burden of proof on the Commission, are considered further in chapter 14[20].

(D)   'Unilateral' conduct and Article 81(1)

The scheme of the EC competition rules is that Article 81 applies to conduct by two or more undertakings which is consensual and that Article 82 applies to unilateral action by a dominant firm. It follows that unilateral conduct by a firm that is not dominant is not caught at all, which is why in some cases fairly outlandish claims of dominance have been made[1]. However it is important to appreciate that conduct which might at first sight appear to be unilateral has sometimes been held by the Commission to fall within Article 81(1) as an

---

16   *British Sugar plc, Tate & Lyle plc, Napier Brown & Co Ltd, James Budgett Sugars Ltd* OJ [1999] L 76/1, [1999] 4 CMLR 1316, paras 95ff, substantially upheld on appeal Cases T-202/98 etc *Tate & Lyle v Commission* (judgment of 12 July 2001).

17   See eg Case 40/73 *Suiker Unie v Commission* [1975] ECR 1663, [1976] 1 CMLR 295; Cases 29/83 and 30/83 *Compagnie Royale Asturienne des Mines SA and Rheinzink GmbH v Commission* [1984] ECR 1679, [1985] 1 CMLR 688; and Cases T–68/89 etc *Società Italiano Vetro v Commission* [1992] ECR II-1403, [1992] 5 CMLR 302, in each of which the Community Courts quashed some or all of the findings of concerted practices.

18   Cases 29/83 and 30/83 [1984] ECR 1679, [1985] 1 CMLR 688.

19   See Commission's XIVth *Report on Competition Policy* (1984), point 126.

20   See ch 14, pp 467-469.

1   See eg Case 75/84 *Metro v Commission (No 2)* [1986] ECR 3021, [1987] 1 CMLR 118, paras 79–92; Case 210/81 *Demo-Studio Schmidt v Commission* [1983] ECR 3045, [1984] 1 CMLR 63.

agreement or a concerted practice, and that the Commission's decisions in this respect have usually been upheld by the Community courts; however, in *Bayer AG/Adalat*[2] the Commission stretched the notion of an agreement too far, and the decision was annulled by the CFI[3].

The characterisation of apparently independent, unilateral action as an agreement is particularly likely to occur in the context of relations between a producer and the participants in its distribution system: the Commission is vigilant in these circumstances to monitor conduct which either has the effect of maintaining resale prices or which leads to the partitioning of national markets and the suppression of parallel trade.

(i) AEG Telefunken v Commission; Ford v Commission

In *AEG-Telefunken v Commission*[4] the ECJ rejected a claim that refusals to supply retail outlets which were objectively suitable to handle AEG's goods were unilateral acts falling outside Article 81(1). The ECJ held that the refusals arose out of the contractual relationship between the supplier and its established distributors and their mutual acceptance, tacit or express, of AEG's intention to exclude from the network distributors who, though qualified technically, were not prepared to adhere to its policy of maintaining a high level of prices and excluding modern channels of distribution. AEG's refusals to supply were not unilateral but provided proof of an unlawful application of its selective distribution system, as their frequency was sufficient to preclude the possibility that they were isolated cases not forming part of systematic conduct[5]. In *Ford v Commission*[6] the ECJ held that a refusal by Ford's German subsidiary to supply right–hand drive cars to German distributors was attributable to the contractual relationship between them. The *Ford* judgment is an extension of *AEG*. In *AEG* there was an obvious community of interest between the distributors who received supplies from AEG, that 'cut–price' outlets should not be able to obtain goods and undercut their prices; in this case it was easy to see that certain assumptions might creep into the relationship between AEG and its usual customers. In *Ford*, however, the German distributors with whom Ford had entered into contracts did not themselves benefit from the refusal to supply right–hand drive cars: the beneficiaries of this policy were distributors in the UK, who would be shielded from parallel imports. Here the 'unilateral' act held to be attributable to the agreements between supplier and distributors was not an act for the benefit of those very distributors.

(ii) Subsequent cases

In several decisions after *AEG* and *Ford* the Commission has applied Article 81(1) to apparently unilateral conduct. In *Sandoz*[7] it held that, where there was no written record of agreements between a producer and its distributors, unilateral measures, including placing the words 'export prohibited' on all invoices, were attributable to the continuing commercial relationship between the parties and

2   OJ [1996] L 201/1, [1996] 5 CMLR 416.
3   Case T-41/96 [2001] All ER (EC) 1, [2001] 4 CMLR 126; see pp 88-89 below.
4   Case 107/82 [1983] ECR 3151, [1984] 3 CMLR 325.
5   Ibid, paras 31–39.
6   Cases 25/84 and 26/84 [1985] ECR 2725, [1985] 3 CMLR 528.
7   OJ [1987] L 222/28, [1989] 4 CMLR 628.

were within Article 81(1). On appeal the ECJ upheld the Commission's decision[8]; in *Vichy*[9] the Commission specifically applied paragraph 12 of the *Sandoz* judgment. In *Tipp-Ex*[10] the Commission applied the ECJ's judgments in *AEG* and *Ford*, holding that there was an infringement of Article 81 consisting of agreements between Tipp-Ex and its authorised dealers regarding the mutual protection of territories. In *Konica*[11] the Commission held that the sending of a circular to its distributors requiring them not to export Konica film from the UK to Germany was an offer by Konica, and that by complying with the circular the distributors had accepted it, with the result that there was an agreement or at least a concerted practice within Article 81. In *Bayo-n-ox*[12] goods were supplied at a special price, on condition that customers use them for their own requirements: they could not resell them; this stipulation was contained in circulars sent by the supplier to the customers. The Commission said that by accepting the products at the special price the customers had tacitly agreed to abide by the 'own requirements' condition. The fact that a customer is acting contrary to its own best interests in agreeing to its supplier's terms does not mean that it is not party to a prohibited agreement under Article 81(1)[13]. In *Volkswagen AG v Commission*[14] the CFI rejected Volkswagen's argument that it had acted unilaterally, rather than entering into agreements with its distributors to restrict parallel trade[15].

(iii)   Bayer v Commission

The Commission again characterised apparently unilateral action as an agreement in *Bayer AG/Adalat*[16]; on this occasion, however, the CFI annulled the decision since, in its view, the Commission had failed to prove the existence of an agreement[17]. In order to prevent its French and Spanish wholesalers from supplying parallel exports to the UK, and thereby to protect its UK pricing strategy, Bayer had reduced supplies of the drug Adalat to France and Spain. Prices for pharmaceuticals in France and Spain were as much as 40% less than in the UK, so that the market was ripe for parallel trade. The Commission concluded that a tacit agreement existed between Bayer and its wholesalers not to export to the UK contrary to Article 81(1): in its view the agreement was evidenced by the wholesalers ceasing to supply the UK in response to Bayer's tactic of reducing supplies. It has to be said that this would appear to be counter-intuitive, given that the wholesalers had tried every means possible to defy Bayer and to obtain extra supplies for the purpose of exporting to the UK: there was no 'common interest' in this case between Bayer and its wholesalers, whose respective needs were diametrically opposed.

8   Case C–277/87 *Sandoz Prodotti Farmaceutici SpA v Commission* [1990] ECR I–45.
9   OJ [1991] L 75/57, upheld on appeal Case T–19/91 *Vichy v Commission* [1992] ECR II–415.
10   OJ [1987] L 222/1, [1989] 4 CMLR 425, upheld on appeal Case C–279/87 *Tipp-ex GmbH v Commission* [1990] ECR 1–261.
11   OJ [1988] L 78/34, [1988] 4 CMLR 848.
12   OJ [1990] L 21/71, [1990] 4 CMLR 930; see also *Bayer Dental* OJ [1990] L 351/46, [1992] 4 CMLR 61.
13   See eg *Gosmé/Martell-DMP* OJ [1991] L 185/23, [1992] 5 CMLR 586.
14   Case T-62/98 [2000] 5 CMLR 853.
15   Ibid, paras 236-239.
16   OJ [1996] L 201/1, [1996] 5 CMLR 416.
17   Case T-41/96 [2000] All ER (EC) 1, [2001] 4 CMLR 176.

Bayer did not deny that it had reduced the quantities delivered to France and Spain, but it argued that it had acted unilaterally rather than pursuant to an agreement. The Commission's decision was criticised[18] and Bayer obtained a suspension of the decision pending judgment[19]. In a very significant judgment in October 2000, the CFI held that there was no agreement and annulled the Commission's decision. After stressing that Article 81(1) applies only to conduct that is coordinated bilaterally or multilaterally[20], the Court reviewed the case law and stated that the concept of an agreement 'centres around the existence of a concurrence of wills between at least two parties, the form in which it is manifested being unimportant so long as it constitutes the faithful expression of the parties' intention'[1]. It acknowledged that there could be an agreement where one person tacitly acquiesces in practices and measures adopted by another[2]; however it concluded that the Commission had failed both to demonstrate that Bayer had intended to impose an export ban[3] and to prove that the wholesalers had intended to adhere to a policy on the part of Bayer to reduce parallel imports[4]. The CFI was satisfied that earlier judgments, including *Sandoz*, *Tipp Ex* and *AEG*, were distinguishable[5]. It also rejected the argument that the wholesalers, by maintaining their commercial relations with Bayer after the reduction of supplies, could thereby be held to have agreed with it to restrain exports[6]. The CFI specifically said that a measure taken by a manufacturer that would hinder parallel imports is lawful, provided that it is not adopted pursuant to a concurrence of wills between it and its wholesalers contrary to Article 81(1) and provided that it does not amount to an abuse of a dominant position contrary to Article 82[7]. The CFI was not prepared to extend the scope of Article 81(1), acknowledging the importance of 'free enterprise' when applying the competition rules[8].

The importance of this judgment cannot be overstated. Had the CFI upheld the decision of the Commission, the notion that an agreement for the purpose of Article 81(1) requires consensus between the parties would have been virtually eliminated; while this would have given the Commission greater control over restrictions of parallel trade within the Community, it would have done so at the expense of the integrity of the competition rules, which clearly apprehend unilateral behaviour only where a firm has a dominant position in the sense of Article 82. However the Commission is anxious to test the CFI's assessment of the meaning of 'agreement' in Article 81(1), and has therefore appealed against the CFI's judgment to the ECJ[9].

18 Kon and Schoeffer 'Parallel Imports of Pharmaceutical Products: a New Realism or Back to Basics?' (1997) 22 EL Rev 123; Lidgard 'Unilateral Refusal to Supply: an Agreement in Disguise?' (1997) 18 ECLR 352.
19 Order reported at Case T-41/96 R *Bayer AG v Commission* [1997] ECR II-381, [1996] 5 CMLR 290; see Lasok (1997) 34 CML Rev 1309.
20 Case T-41/96 [2001] CMLR 176, para 64.
1   Ibid, para 69.
2   Ibid, para 71.
3   Ibid, paras 78-110.
4   Ibid, paras 111-157.
5   Ibid, paras 158-171.
6   Ibid, paras 172-182.
7   Ibid, para 176.
8   Ibid, para 180.
9   Case C-3/01 *Commission v Bayer* (judgment pending).

3.   THE OBJECT OR EFFECT OF PREVENTING, RESTRICTING OR DISTORTING COMPETITION

Article 81(1) prohibits agreements which have as their object or effect the prevention, restriction or distortion of competition[10]. Article 81(1) contains an illustrative list of agreements that may be caught such as price fixing and market sharing, but this is insufficient in itself to explain the numerous intricacies involved in understanding how this Article works. Judgments of the CFI and, at the top of the hierarchy, the ECJ contain the most authoritative statements of the law, and some of the best analyses of it will be found in the Opinions of the Advocates General; the Commission's decisions and Notices also provide important guidance on the application of Article 81(1), as do its press releases, the Annual Report on Competition Policy and the quarterly Competition Policy Newsletter[11].

The application of Article 81(1) to agreements, in particular on the part of the Commission, has for many years been controversial. In essence, the complaint on the part of many commentators has been that Article 81(1) has been applied too broadly, catching many agreements that are not in reality detrimental to competition at all[12]. Agreements that are caught by Article 81(1) are void and unenforceable, and may attract a fine, unless they satisfy the criteria set out in Article 81(3). Under the existing law, only the Commission can grant an individual exemption to an agreement under Article 81(3); these are rarely given, and the procedure is time-consuming, costly and cumbersome[13]. A consequence is that many firms must satisfy the terms of one of the 'block exemptions' under Article 81(3) in order to be certain that their agreements are legally enforceable[14]. An obvious solution proposed by critics of the current position is that Article 81(1) should be applied to fewer agreements than is currently the case: only those agreements that pose a real threat to competition should be caught in the net of competition law: others should not be ensnared by the competition rules at all.

(A)   Some preliminary comments

These issues will be explored in the text that follows. However, a few preliminary comments may be helpful. First, there are many judgments of the Community Courts that demonstrate that a contractual restriction does not necessarily result

---

10 In the text that follows, the term 'restriction' of competition is taken to include the prevention and distortion of competition.

11 Available on DG COMP's website at http://europa.eu.int/comm/competition/publications/cpn/.

12 See eg Bright 'EU Competition Policy: Rules, Objectives and Deregulation' (1996) 16 Oxford Journal of Legal Studies 535; there is a considerable amount of academic literature criticising the 'over'-application of Article 81(1): see eg Joliet *The Rule of Reason in Antitrust Law; American, German and Common Market Laws in Comparative Perspective* (1967) pp 77–106, 117 to the end; Korah 'The Rise and Fall of Provisional Validity' (1981) 3 NJILB 320; Schechter 'The Rule of Reason in European Competition Law' [1982(2)] Legal Issues in European Integration 1; Forrester and Norall 'The Laicization of Community Law: Self–help and the Rule of Reason' (1984) 21 CML Rev 11; Korah 'EEC Competition Policy – Legal Form or Economic Efficiency' (1986) 39 CLP 85; Venit 'Pronuptia: Ancillary Restraints or Unholy Alliances?' (1986) 11 EL Rev 213; Holley 'EEC Competition Practice; a Thirty-Year Retrospective' in [1992] Fordham Corp L Inst (ed Hawk) 669, p 689.

13 See ch 4, p 136; the proposal of the Commission to abandon its 'monopoly' over individual exemptions is also described there, at pp 146-147; see also ch 7, pp 246-258.

14 On block exemptions see ch 4, pp 141-146.

in a restriction of competition[15]. It is essential to understand this key point: the concept of a restriction of competition is an economic one, and as a general proposition economic analysis is needed to determine whether an agreement could have an anti-competitive effect. A relatively small class of agreements are considered by law to have as their object the restriction of competition[16], and even then some market analysis is required to establish that any restriction of competition is appreciable and that trade between Member States will be affected[17]; in the case of all other agreements anti-competitive effects must be demonstrated for there to be an infringement of Article 81(1)[18]. Secondly, it is important to stress that it is the Community Courts, and not the Commission, which determine the scope of application of Article 81(1), and the Commission is bound by their judgments. In so far as there sometimes appears to be a dissonance in the application of Article 81(1) between the judgments of the Courts and the decisional practice of the Commission, it is of course the former that must be followed. Thirdly, in several judgments the Community Courts have made clear that the Commission must adequately demonstrate that an agreement is restrictive of competition, and that they will not simply 'rubber-stamp' its analysis: a particularly good example is *European Night Services v Commission*[19], where the CFI exposed the thorough inadequacy of the Commission's reasoning in its decision in that case[20]; the margin of discretion available to the Commission in competition cases is so great that effective judicial review by the CFI is essential. Fourthly, the Commission itself has become more amenable to the suggestion that it should adopt a 'reasonable' approach to the application of Article 81(1): in recent years it has appeared to be more willing to conclude that an agreement falls outside Article 81(1) altogether, rather than to find an infringement of Article 81(1) and then to grant an individual exemption or to close the file with an Article 81(3) comfort letter[1]. Finally, the CFI has said that in a case under Article 81(1) the definition of the market is relevant at the stage of determining whether there has been an impairment of competition or an effect on trade between Member States; it is not something that must be undertaken as a preliminary matter, as in the case of Article 82 where it is a necessary precondition to a finding of abuse[2].

(B)   Horizontal and vertical agreements

One point is absolutely clear: Article 81 is capable of application both to horizontal agreements (between undertakings at the same level of the market) and to vertical agreements (between undertakings at different levels of the market). It was at one time thought that Article 81 might have no application at all to vertical agreements, but that idea was firmly scotched by the ECJ's judgment in *Consten and Grundig v Commission*[3]. The application of Article 81 to vertical

---

15   See pp 99-100 below.
16   See pp 95-98 below.
17   See p 107 below.
18   See pp 98-103 below.
19   Cases T-374/94 etc [1998] ECR II-3141, [1998] 5 CMLR 718.
20   *European Night Services Ltd* OJ [1994] L 259/20, [1995] 5 CMLR 76.
1   See p 103 below; on Article 81(3) comfort letters, see ch 7, pp 217-218.
2   Case T-29/92 *SPO v Commission* [1995] ECR II-289, para 75; Cases T-25/95 etc *Cimenteries CBR SA v Commission* judgment of 15 March 2000, para 833; Case T-62/98 *Volkswagen AG v Commission* [2000] 5 CMLR 853, paras 230-232.
3   Cases 56 and 58/64 [1966] ECR 299, [1966] CMLR 418.

agreements has been one of the most controversial issues in EC competition law[4]. As part of the Commission's modernisation of the competition rules, major changes have taken place in recent years in relation to vertical agreements, in particular the adoption of a new block exemption in December 1999 which entered into force on 1 June 2000[5]. The Commission also published *Guidelines on Vertical Restraints*[6] in October 2000, which contain important guidance not only on the operation of the block exemption but also on the analysis of vertical restraints under Article 81(1). The application of Article 81 to vertical agreements will be considered in detail in chapter 16. A further step in the Commission's modernisation programme was the adoption in November 2000 of two new block exemptions for horizontal agreements, for specialisation[7] and for research and development[8] respectively, both of which entered into force on 1 January 2001. The Commission also published *Guidelines on Horizontal Cooperation Agreements*[9] which contain guidance on the operation of those block exemptions and also set out a framework for the analysis of horizontal cooperation agreements under Article 81(1). The application of Article 81 to such agreements will be considered in detail in chapter 15.

(C)   The 'object or effect' of preventing, restricting or distorting competition

Article 81(1) prohibits agreements 'which have as their their *object or effect* the prevention, restriction or distortion of competition' (emphasis added). It is important to understand the significance of the words 'object or effect' in Article 81(1).

(i)   *'Object or effect' to be read disjunctively*

It is clear that these are alternative, and not cumulative, requirements for a finding of an infringement of Article 81(1). In *Société Technique Minière v Maschinenbau Ulm*[10] the ECJ stated that the words were to be read disjunctively, so that it is first necessary to consider what the object of an agreement is; only if it is not clear that the object of an agreement is to harm competition is it necessary to consider whether it might have the effect of doing so.

(ii)   *'Object'*

There are some types of agreement the anti-competitiveness of which can be determined simply from their object; the word 'object' in this context means not the subjective intention of the parties when entering into the agreement, but the

---

4   See ch 16, p 564ff; note that, in the UK, the Chapter I prohibition in the Competition Act 1998 does not apply to vertical agreements other than the maintenance of minimum resale prices: ibid, pp 595-598.
5   Regulation 2790/99, OJ [1999] L 336/21, [2000] 4 CMLR 398.
6   OJ [2000] C 291/1, [2000] 5 CMLR 1176.
7   Regulation 2658/2000, OJ [2000] L 304/3, [2001] 4 CMLR 800.
8   Regulation 2659/2000, OJ [2000] L 304/7, [2001] 4 CMLR 808.
9   OJ [2001] C 3/2, [2001] 4 CMLR 819.
10   Case 56/65 [1966] ECR 235, p 249, [1966] CMLR 357, p 375.

objective meaning and purpose of the agreement considered in the economic context in which it is to be applied[11]. Where an agreement has as its object the restriction of competition, it is unnecessary to prove that the agreement would have an anti-competitive effect order to find an infringement of Article 81(1). This was repeated by the ECJ two weeks after the *Société Technique Miniere* judgment in *Consten and Grundig v Commission*[12]; in *VdS v Commission*[13] the ECJ again stated that if the object of an agreement is to restrict competition, there is no need for the Commission also to show that it might have an anti-competitive effect. The Community Courts have frequently reaffirmed the position[14], and have confirmed that a concerted practice can have the object of restricting competition as well as an agreement[15]. The Commission has also stated the same thing on a number of occasions; for example it said in its *TACA*[16] decision in 1998:

'There is no need to wait to observe the concrete effects of an agreement once it appears that it has as its object the prevention, restriction or distortion of competition'[17].

The apparent simplicity of this proposition is to some extent undermined by the two requirements that, for there to be an infringement of Article 81(1), an agreement must appreciably restrict competition and must have an appreciable effect on trade between Member States. Each of these propositions is examined later in this chapter[18]. At this stage it is necessary to acknowledge that some analysis of the impact of an agreement on the market is needed, even in the case of agreements that are held to have as their object the restriction of competition. The jurisprudence is somewhat confused and confusing on this issue, but it is possible to reconcile the statements of the Community Courts and the Commission set out above with the two requirements introduced in this paragraph. The classification of an agreement as having as its object the restriction of competition means that the parties, for example, to a price-fixing agreement cannot argue that the fixing of prices does not restrict competition: the law has decided, as a matter of policy, that it does; given that, generically, price fixing is considered to have as its object the restriction of competition, the parties can only defend the practice by proving, in a particular case, that it satisfies the criteria of Article 81(3)[19]. However it is open to them to argue that, in a quantitative sense, their

11 Cases 29/83 and 30/83 *Compagnie Royale Asturienne des Mines SA and Rheinzinc GmbH v Commission* [1984] ECR 1679, [1985] 1 CMLR 688, paras 25-26; Case C-277/87 *Sandoz Prodotti Farmaceutici v Commission* [1990] ECR I-45; Case T-148/89 *Tréfilunion v Commission* [1995] ECR II-1063, para 79; on the relevance of subjective intention, see Odudo 'Interpreting Article 81(1): Object as Subjective Intention' (2001) 26 ELRev 60.
12 Cases 56 and 58/64 [1966] ECR 299, p 342, [1966] CMLR 418, p 473
13 Case 45/85 [1987] ECR 405, [1988] 4 CMLR 264, para 39.
14 See eg Cases T-25/95 *Cimenteries CBR SA v Commission* judgment of 15 March 2000, paras 837, 1531 and 2589.
15 See eg Case C-199/92 P etc *Hüls AG v Commission* [1999] ECR I-4287, [1999] 5 CMLR 1016, para 164.
16 OJ [1999] L 95/1, [1999] 4 CMLR 1415.
17 Ibid, para 381; see similarly *FETTCSA* OJ [2000] L 268/1, [2000] 5 CMLR 1011, para 135, on appeal to the CFI, Case T-213/00 *CMA v Commission* (judgment pending); *Amino Acids* OJ [2001] L 152/24, [2001] 5 CMLR 322, para 230.
18 See pp 107-110 below on the *de minimis* doctrine and pp 110-120 below on the requirement of an effect on trade between Member States.
19 See the extract from the CFI's judgment in *European Night Services v Commission* set out below.

agreement does not appreciably affect competition or affect trade between Member States, because their position on the market is so weak; conceptually this is a different matter from arguing that the practice of price fixing is not restrictive of competition. The Community Courts themselves have not explicitly stated the law in these terms, but this would seem to offer a workable explanation of how two elements of the law of Article 81(1) that appear to pull in opposite directions can be reconciled. A separate point is that the effect that an agreement may have on the market is relevant to the gravity of the infringement and therefore to the amount of any fine[20].

(iii)   *'Effect'*

Where an agreement does not have as its object the restriction of competition, it is necessary to demonstrate that it would have a restrictive effect, a more onerous task for the Commission or the undertaking wishing to establish an infringement of Article 81(1). The position was stated clearly by the CFI in *European Night Services v Commission*[1]:

> '... it must be borne in mind that in assessing an agreement under Article [81(1)] of the Treaty, account should be taken of the actual conditions in which it functions, in particular the economic context in which the undertakings operate, the products or services covered by the agreement and the actual structure of the market concerned ... *unless it is an agreement containing obvious restrictions of competition such as price-fixing, market-sharing or the control of outlets* .... In the latter case, such restrictions may be weighed against their claimed pro-competitive effects only in the context of Article [81(3)] of the Treaty, with a view to granting an exemption from the prohibition in Article [81(1)]' (emphasis added).

(iv)   Comment on the 'object or effect' distinction

This passage of the CFI's judgment in *European Night Services v Commission* indicates that in most cases it is necessary to demonstrate that an agreement will have an anti-competitive effect; however, there is a limited class of agreements that have as their object the restriction of competition and which therefore automatically fall within Article 81(1), provided that the other requirements for an infringement are satisfied, for example that the restriction of competition is appreciable and that there is an appreciable effect on trade between Member States; the parties to agreements of this kind will be able to proceed lawfully only if their agreement qualifies for exemption under Article 81(3). As a matter of law, where an agreement has as its object the restriction of competition, the Commission (or any other person opposing the agreement) does not have to prove that that kind of agreement has an anti-competitive effect; the onus would be on the parties to the agreement to show that it satisfies Article 81(3)[2].

---

20   See eg *Amino Acids* OJ [2001] L 154/24, [2001] 5 CMLR 322, paras 261-298; see further ch 7, pp 237-239 .

1   Cases T-374/94 etc [1998] ECR II-3141, [1998] 5 CMLR 718, para 136.

2   On the burden of proof under Article 81(3) see ch 4, p 124.

Agreements that have as their object the restriction of competition involve an 'obvious' infringement of Article 81(1), the word used in *European Night Services*, and they are the agreements that are particularly likely to attract a fine[3]. Clearly, therefore, it is important to know which agreements can be classified as having as their object the restriction of competition.

It may be helpful to think of the position in terms of two boxes, as follows:

OBJECT	EFFECT
Agreements that have as their object the restriction of competition	Agreements that have as their effect the restriction of competition

Article 81(1), as interpreted by the Community courts, allocates particularly pernicious types of agreement to the object box, with the consequences just described. This is done as a matter of policy: certain agreements are so clearly inimical to the objectives of the Community that they can be permitted only where they can be shown to satisfy the requirements of Article 81(3). In all other cases, however, the lawfulness of an agreement under Article 81(1) must be tested according to its anti-competitive effects and this, as we shall see, requires a wide-ranging analysis of the market[4]. There is clearly an analogy here with the position under section 1 of the Sherman Act 1890 in the US, which characterises some agreements as *per se* infringements of the Act, whereas others are subject to a 'rule of reason'[5]. Where there is a *per se* infringement, this means that it is not open to the parties to the agreement to argue that it does not restrict competition: it belongs to a category of agreement that has, by law, been found to be restrictive of competition. However, there is an important difference in EC law in that, even if an agreement has as its object the restriction of competition, that is to say that it infringes Article 81(1) *per se*, the parties can still argue for exemption under Article 81(3)[6]. This possibility does not exist in US law, since there is no equivalent of Article 81(3) in that system.

(D)   Agreements that have as their object the prevention, restriction or distortion of competition

In *European Night Services v Commission*[7] the CFI referred to agreements 'containing obvious restrictions of competition such as price-fixing, market-sharing or the control of outlets'; without using the terminology used in this chapter, it seems clear that the CFI considered that agreements of this nature

---

3   On the Commission's power to impose fines see ch 7, pp 237-239.
4   See pp 98-99 below; the explanation of the law offered in the text is consistent with the approach taken by Advocate General Tesauro in his Opinion in Case C-250/92 *Gøttrup-Klim Grovvareforeninger v Dansk Landburgs Grovvareselskab AmbA* [1994] ECR I-5641, [1996] 4 CMLR 191 see also the Commission's *Guidelines on Horizontal Restraints* OJ [2001] C 3/2, [2001] 4 CMLR 819, paras 17-20.
5   For an interesting discussion of this topic, see Black 'Per Se Rules and Rules of Reason: What Are They?' (1997) 18 ECLR 145; this article contains extensive citation of the literature on the position under US law.
6   See ch 4, p 124 on the judgment in Case T-17/93 *Matra Hachette v Commission* [1994] ECR II-595; see also the Commission's decision in *Reims II* OJ [1999] L 275/17, [2000] 4 CMLR 704: individual exemption given to 'a price-fixing agreement with unusual characteristics' (ibid, para 65) in the postal sector.
7   See Cases T-374/94 etc [1998] ECR II-3141, [1998] 5 CMLR 718.

should be allocated to the 'object' box. Price fixing is specifically cited as an example of an anti-competitive agreement in Article 81(1)(a) of the Treaty, and it is unsurprising that it is dealt with harshly, whether horizontal[8] or vertical[9]; market sharing is specifically mentioned in Article 81(1)(c), and again its strict treatment is to be expected, in particular because it is likely to be harmful to the single market[10]. The CFI did not refer in *European Night Services* to agreements to limit output, but they must also be allocated to the object box on the basis that they obviously restrict competition, and they are specifically referred to in Article 81(1)(b) of the Treaty; analogous agreements, for example to limit sales, must also be included[11]. In the *Cement* cases[12] the CFI considered that the exchange of price information had as its object the restriction of competition; and the Commission has characterised collective exclusive dealing in the same way[13].

The CFI in *European Night Services* also referred to agreements to control outlets as containing obvious restrictions of competition; the control of outlets is not specifically referred to in Article 81(1), but the CFI presumably had in mind the imposition on distributors of export bans on sales from one Member State to another, which have consistently been found to have as their object the restriction of competition: nothing could be more obviously inimical to the goal of market integration than restrictions of this kind[14]. An example of the Community Courts' attitude to export bans is to be found in the judgment of the CFI in *BASF v Commission*[15], in which it dismissed two appeals against the Commission's finding that such bans in distribution agreements infringed Article 81(1), and in doing so confirmed its strict approach to such provisions:

> 'It is settled case law that, by its nature, a clause designed to prevent a buyer from reselling or exporting goods he has bought is liable to partition the markets and consequently to affect trade between Member States. The CFI finds that that agreement, *by virtue of its object*, constitutes a restriction on competition prohibited by Article 81(1) EC ...' (emphasis added).

Following the order of the text above, it seems that the contents of the 'object' box can be depicted as follows:

The object box[16]

Horizontal agreements:
- to fix prices
- to share markets
- to limit output
- to limit sales
- to exchange price information
- for collective exclusive dealing

---

8 See ch 13, pp 426-433.
9 See ch 16, pp 563-564.
10 See ch 13, pp 434-435.
11 Ibid, pp 436-438.
12 Cases T-25/95 etc *Cimenteries CBR SA v Commission* judgment of 15 March 2000, para 1531.
13 See eg *Nederlandse Federative Vereniging voor de Grootlandel op Elektrotechnisch Gebied and Technische Unie (FEG and TU)* OJ [2000] L 39/1, [2000] 4 CMLR 1208, para 105, and the further examples given in footnote 120 of that decision.
14 See ch 16, pp 550-553.
15 Cases T-175/95 and T-176/95 [1999] ECR II-1581, [2000] 4 CMLR 33; see similarly Case T-176/95 *Accinauto SA v Commission* [2000] 4 CMLR 67.
16 It will be seen that the contents of the box correspond to a large extent with the provisions

> **Vertical agreements:**
> - to fix minimum resale prices
> - to impose export bans

An important qualification must be made. This presentation of the position to some extent oversimplifies the law. For example, there have been a few occasions on which the ECJ has concluded that an export ban, in the context of a specific type of agreement, did not have as its object the restriction of competition. An example can be found in *Erauw-Jacquery Sprl v La Hesbignonne Société Coopérative*[17], where the ECJ held that a provision preventing a licensee from exporting seeds protected by plant breeders' rights could fall outside Article 81(1) where it was necessary to protect the right of the licensor to select his licensees. Another example is *Javico v Yves St Laurent*[18], where an export ban was imposed on distributors in Russia and the Ukraine:

'19. In the case of agreements of this kind stipulations of the type mentioned in the question must be construed not as being intended to exclude parallel imports and marketing of the contractual product within the Community but as being designed to enable the producer to penetrate a market outside the Community by supplying a sufficient quantity of contractual products to that market. That interpretation is supported by the fact that, in the agreements at issue, the prohibition of selling outside the contractual territory also covers other non-member countries'.

Having concluded that the agreement in *Javico* did not have as its object the restriction of competition, the ECJ went on to consider whether it might have this effect[19]. These, and other[20], cases indicate that the broad headings used in the box above may require refinement to exclude from the 'object' category some agreements that are not so obviously restrictive of competition. The size and content of the object box is capable of change over a period of time, as the Community Courts are called on to consider, or perhaps to reconsider, the restrictive nature of particular types of agreement. This process of categorisation and recategorisation is natural and to be expected, and has a parallel in the US where the courts are from time to time called upon to determine whether a particular type of agreement should be tested according to a *per se* or a rule of reason standard[1]. However the fact that such a process takes place does not call

---

that are black-listed in Article 4(a) and 4(b) of Regulation 2790/99 on vertical agreements (ch 16, pp 582-583), Article 5 of Regulation 2658/00 on specialisation agreements (ch 15, pp 517-520) and Article 5 of Regulation 2659/00 on research and development agreements (ch 15, pp 510-515).

17 Case 27/87 [1988] ECR 1919, [1988] 4 CMLR 576; see similarly the Commission's decision in *Sicasov* OJ [1999] L 4/27, [1999] 4 CMLR 192, paras 53-61.

18 Case C-306/96 [1998] ECR I-1983, [1998] 5 CMLR 172.

19 See p 119 below.

20 See eg Case 262/81 *Coditel v Ciné Vog Films SA (No 2)* [1982] ECR 3381, [1983] 1 CMLR 49: see pp 100-101 below.

1   In the US, see *Continental TV v GTE Sylvania* 433 US 36 (1977), where the Supreme Court overruled an earlier judgment, *US v Arnold Schwinn & Co* 388 US 365 (1967), subjecting non-price vertical restraints to a *per se* rule; *National Society of Professional Engineers v US* 435 US 679 (1978), where a trade association's rules prohibiting competitive bidding by members were tested under the rule of reason rather than a *per se* rule; *Broadcast Music Inc v CBS* 441 US 1 (1979), where the rule of reason was applied to the rules of a copyright collecting society: the Supreme Court accepted that the agreement was a price fixing agreement 'in the literal sense', but concluded that it was not a 'naked restraint', but instead enabled copyright owners to market their product more efficiently; and *State Oil Co v Khan* 118 S Ct 275 (1997), where the Supreme Court held that maximum resale price maintenance should be tested under the rule of reason and not a *per se* standard.

into question the underlying 'object or effect' distinction contained in Article 81(1).

(E)   Agreements that have as their effect the prevention, restriction or distortion of competition

(i)   Extensive analysis of an agreement in its market context is required to determine its effect

Where it is not possible to say that the object of an agreement is to restrict competition, it is necessary to conduct an extensive analysis of its effect on the market before it can be found to infringe Article 81(1). This has been stressed by the Community Courts on a number of occasions. For example, in *Brasserie de Haecht v Wilkin*[2] the ECJ said that:

'it would be pointless to consider an agreement, decision or practice by reason of its effect if those effects were to be taken distinct from the market in which they are seen to operate, and could only be examined apart from the body of effects, whether convergent or not, surrounding their implementation. Thus in order to examine whether it is caught by Article [81(1)] an agreement cannot be examined in isolation from the above context, that is, from the factual or legal circumstances causing it to prevent, restrict or distort competition. The existence of similar contracts may be taken into consideration for this objective to the extent to which the general body of contracts of this type is capable of restricting the freedom of trade'[3].

An important case which demonstrates the depth of analysis required in determining whether an agreement has the effect of restricting competition is *Delimitis v Henninger Bräu AG*[4]. There the ECJ considered a provision in an agreement between a brewery and a licensee of a public house owned by the brewery, whereby the licensee was required to purchase a minimum amount of beer each year. The litigation in the German courts concerned the refusal by the brewery, on termination, to return the full deposit to the licensee that he had paid when entering into the agreement: the brewery had deducted sums that it considered it was entitled to. The licensee claimed that the agreement was void and unenforceable under Article 81; an appeal court in Germany referred the case to the ECJ under Article 234 EC. The ECJ said that beer supply agreements of the type under consideration do not have as their object the restriction of competition[5]. Instead it stressed that the agreement had to be considered in the

2   Case 23/67 [1967] ECR 407, [1968] CMLR 26.
3   [1967] ECR 407, p 415, [1968] CMLR 26, p 40; see similarly Cases C-7/95 P and C-8/95 P *John Deere v Commission* [1998] ECR I-3111, [1998] 5 CMLR 311, paras 76 and 91 respectively and Cases C-215/96 and C-216/96 *Carlo Bagnsaco v BPN* [1999] ECR I-135, [1999] 4 CMLR 624, para 33.
4   Case C–234/89 [1991] ECR I-935, [1992] 5 CMLR 210, para 13; see Korah 'The Judgment in *Delimitis*: A Milestone Towards a Realistic Assessment of the Effects of an Agreement – or a Damp Squid' (1992) 14 EIPR 167; there is a longer version in (1998) 8 Tulane European and Civil Law Forum 17; Lasok 'Assessing the Economic Consequences of Restrictive Agreements: A Comment on the Delimitis Case' (1991) 12 ECLR 194; see similarly Case C-214/99 *Neste Markkinointi Oy v Yötuuli* [2001] All ER (EC) 76, [2001] 4 CMLR 993.
5   Ibid, para 13.

context in which it occurred[6]. To begin with it was necessary to define the relevant product and geographic markets[7]: these were defined as the sale of beer in licensed premises (as opposed to beer sold in retail outlets) in Germany. Having defined the markets, the Court then said that it was necessary to determine whether access to the market was impeded: could a new competitor enter the market, for example by buying an existing brewery together with its network of sales outlets or by opening new public houses?[8] If the answer was that access to the market was impeded, it was necessary to ask whether the agreements entered into by Henninger Bräu contributed to that foreclosure effect, for example because of their number and duration[9]. Only if the answer to both of these questions was yes could it be held that Article 81(1) was infringed. The analysis suggested in this case was specific to the issues raised by beer supply agreements, and is not necessarily the same to be deployed, for example, to restrictive covenants taken on the sale of a business[10] or to the rules of a group purchasing association[11]. However the important point about the judgment is its requirement that a full analysis of the agreement in its market context must be carried out before it is possible to determine whether its effect is to restrict competition.

(ii) A contractual restriction does not necessarily restrict competition

Judgments such as *Brasserie de Haecht v Wilkin* and *Delimitis v Henninger Bräu AG* explain a technique: how to determine whether an agreement has as its effect the restriction of competition; they do not state a conclusion as to whether a particular type of agreement infringes Article 81(1), since the very point that they make is that this is an empirical question. It is necessary therefore to look more closely at the jurisprudence of the Community Courts and the decisional practice of the Commission in order to understand better how Article 81(1) may apply to agreements that do not have as their object the restriction of competition. As has already been mentioned, there has been much criticism that Article 81(1) has been applied to too many agreements, with all the problems that this can entail[12]. A particular problem has been the tendency, particularly on the part of the Commission, to reach the conclusion that a contractual restriction amounts to a restriction of competition. This is clearly wrong in principle: a restriction of competition is an economic concept, and is something that happens in relation to a market; a determination cannot be made simply from a provision in a contract that competition is restricted, except in so far as the law allocates particular types of agreements to the 'object' box discussed above[13]. Where anti-competitive effects are in issue, something more than a reading of the agreement is needed to determine whether Article 81(1) applies. This is not to say that a contractual restriction cannot restrict competition, but that it is not possible to reach such a finding without analysis of the effect of the agreement in its market context. It

---

6   Ibid, para 14.
7   Ibid, paras 16-18; on market definition see ch 1, pp 22-39.
8   Ibid, paras 19-23.
9   Ibid, paras 24-27.
10 On agreements of this kind, see *Remia BV and Verenidge Bedrijven and Nutricia v Commission*, pp 100-101 below.
11 On agreements of this kind, see *Gøttrup-Klim Grovvareforeninger v Dansk Landburgs Grovvareselskab AmbA*, p 101 below.
12 See p 90 above.
13 See pp 95-98 above.

should be added that an agreement may be found to have as its effect the restriction of competition even though it does not contain any contractual restrictions[14].

(iii)   Cases in which agreements containing restrictions were found not to have anti-competitive effects

There have been many judgments in which the Community Courts have concluded that agreements containing contractual restrictions did not result in a restriction of competition. Several of these cases were Article 234 references, where one party was trying to avoid a contractual restriction freely entered into by invoking Article 81(2) of the Treaty: it would not be entirely surprising if some of the judges in these cases felt unsympathetic to litigants trying to use competition law in order to escape from their contractual responsibilities. The first case of note was as long ago as 1966: in *Société Technique Minière v Maschinenbau Ulm*[15] the ECJ said that a term conferring exclusivity on a distributor might not infringe Article 81(1) where this seemed to be 'really necessary for the penetration of a new area by an undertaking'. Two weeks later, the ECJ in *Consten and Grundig v Commission*[16] reached the conclusion that an agreement conferring absolute territorial protection on a distributor had as its object the restriction of competition and was not eligible for exemption under Article 81(3). These two judgments are highly instructive. *Société Technique Minière* shows that simply granting exclusive rights to a territory, without export bans, may not infringe Article 81(1) at all: it is an empirical question whether such an agreement, assessed in its market context, has a restrictive effect; *Consten and Grundig*, however, shows that where an agreement goes further, imposing export bans and preventing the possibility of parallel trade, it is considered by law to have as its object the restriction of competition and, furthermore, to be ineligible for exemption. There is no better illustration of the impact of the 'single market imperative'[17] than this.

In *Metro SB–Grossmärkte v Commission*[18] the ECJ held that restrictive provisions contained in a selective distribution system may fall outside Article 81(1) where they satisfy objective, qualitative criteria and are applied in a non-discriminatory manner[19]. In *L C Nungesser KG v Commission*[20] the ECJ held that an open exclusive licence of plant breeders' rights would not infringe Article 81(1) where, on the facts of the case, the licensee would not have risked investing in the production of maize seeds at all without some immunity from intra–brand competition[1]. In *Coditel v Ciné Vog Films SA (No 2)*[2] the ECJ held that an exclusive copyright licence to exhibit a film in a Member State would not necessarily infringe Article 81(1), even where this might prevent transmission of that film by cable broadcasting from a neighbouring Member State, where this was necessary to protect the investment of the licensee. Restrictive covenants may fall outside Article 81(1), provided that they are duly limited in time, space

---

14 See for example the discussion of information agreements in ch 13, pp 444-450 where Article 81(1) may be infringed irrespective of whether the parties restrict themselves.
15 Case 56/65 [1966] ECR 235, p 250, [1966] CMLR 357, p 375.
16 Cases 56 and 58/64 [1966] ECR 299, [1966] CMLR 418.
17 See ch 1, p 19 and ch 2, p 47.
18 Case 26/76 [1977] ECR 1875, [1978] 2 CMLR 1.
19 See ch 16, pp 556-561.
20 Case 258/78 [1982] ECR 2015, [1983] 1 CMLR 278.
1   See ch 19, pp 681-683.
2   Case 262/81 [1982] ECR 3381, [1983] 1 CMLR 49.

and subject-matter; in other words that they satisfy the principle of proportionality. This was established by the Commission in *Reuter/BASF*[3], and confirmed by the ECJ in *Remia BV and Verenidge Bedrijven and Nutricia v Commission*[4]: there the Court recognised that, in order to effect the sale of a business together with its associated goodwill, it may be necessary that the vendor should be restricted from competing with the purchaser; in the absence of such a covenant it may not be possible to sell the business at all. The *Remia* doctrine allows the purchaser of a business to be protected from its vendor: it does not apply in the reverse situation[5].

In *Pronuptia de Paris v Schillgalis*[6] the ECJ held that many restrictive provisions in franchising agreements designed to protect the intellectual property rights of the franchisor and to maintain the common identity of the franchise system fall outside Article 81(1). In *Erauw-Jacquery Sprl v La Hesbignonne Société Coopérative*[7] the ECJ held that a provision preventing a licensee from exporting seeds protected by plant breeders' rights could fall outside Article 81(1) where it was necessary to protect the right of the licensor to select his licensees. In *Gøttrup-Klim Grovvareforeninger v Dansk Landburgs Grovvareselskab AmbA*[8] the ECJ held that a provision in the statutes of a cooperative purchasing association, forbidding its members from participating in other forms of organised cooperation which were in direct competition with it, did not necessarily restrict competition, and may even have beneficial effects on competition[9]; it was necessary to consider the effect of the provision on the market, and it would not be caught by Article 81(1) if it was restricted to what was necessary to ensure that the cooperative could function properly and maintain its contractual power in relation to the suppliers with which it had to deal[10]. The ECJ subsequently applied *Gøttrup-Klim* in *Dijkstra v Friesland Coöperatie BA*[11] and in *Luttikhuis v Verenigde Coöperatieve Melkindustrie Coberco BA*[12]; so did the Commission in *P and I Clubs*[13].

These judgments of the ECJ show that, when considering whether an agreement has the effect of restricting competition, it is possible to argue that restrictions which are necessary to enable the parties to an agreement to achieve a legitimate purpose fall outside Article 81(1), provided that they are no more restrictive than is necessary; in other words that they are proportionate. They clearly support the proposition in the previous section, that a contractual restriction does not necessarily restrict competition.

3 OJ [1976] L 254/40, [1976] 2 CMLR D44.
4 Case 42/84 [1985] ECR 2545, [1987] 1 CMLR 1.
5 *Quantel International-Continuum/Quantel SA* OJ [1992] L 235/9, [1993] 5 CMLR 497, para 42.
6 Case 161/84 [1986] ECR 353, [1986] 1 CMLR 414.
7 Case 27/87 [1988] ECR 1919, [1988] 4 CMLR 576, see similarly the Commission's decision in *Sicasov* OJ [1999] L 4/27, [1999] 4 CMLR 192, para 53-61.
8 Case C-250/92 [1994] ECR I-5641, [1996] 4 CMLR 191.
9 Ibid, para 34.
10 Ibid, paras 35-45.
11 Cases 319/93 etc [1995] ECR I-4471, [1996] 5 CMLR 178.
12 Case C-399/93 [1995] ECR I-4515, [1996] 5 CMLR 178, paras 14 and 18.
13 OJ [1999] L 125/12, [1999] 5 CMLR 646, para 66 ff.

(iv)   Has the ECJ embraced the 'rule of reason'?

As mentioned above, critics of Article 81(1) complain that it is applied to too many agreements[14]; they argue for the application of a 'rule of reason', which would result in fewer agreements being caught. The judgments that have just been discussed raise the question of whether the ECJ has adopted a rule of reason under Article 81(1). Discussion of the rule of reason under Article 81(1) is often very imprecise. It is sometimes used as little more than a slogan by opponents of the judgments of the Court and, in particular, decisions of the Commission. In so far as the call for a rule of reason is a request for good rather than bad, or reasonable rather than unreasonable, judgments and decisions, no-one could disagree with it. However, if proponents of the rule of reason mean that US jurisprudence on the rule of reason under the Sherman Act 1890 should be incorporated into EC competition law, this seems to be quite misplaced. EC law is different in many ways from US law, not least in that it has the 'bifurcation' of Article 81(1) and Article 81(3), which does not exist in the Sherman Act, and that it is concerned with the promotion of a single market as well as with 'conventional' competition law concerns[15]. US and EC competition law are materially different in numerous respects, and terminology should not be imported from US law that could blur this significant fact[16]. The fact that the ECJ has handed down reasonable judgments does not mean that it has adopted the rule of reason in the sense in which that expression is used in the US. Various commentators have argued against incorporation into EC law of a rule of reason modelled upon US experience[17]. In its *White Paper on Modernisation*[18] the Commission said that it did not see the adoption of the rule of reason as a solution to the problems of enforcement and procedure that it had identified. It can be anticipated that the Community Courts and the Commission will continue to refine their approaches to Article 81(1), and to be more receptive to the argument that restrictions in contracts are justifiable where they enable parties successfully to achieve legitimate objectives; also it is to be expected that the CFI will require the Commission to explain its reasoning more carefully where it considers that competition is restricted, as in *European Night Services v Commission*[19]. However it does not seem necessary to adopt the US rule of reason as part of Community law.

(v)   Actual and potential competition

In deciding whether Article 81 is infringed, the Commission and the Community Courts will not limit their consideration to whether existing competition will be restricted by the agreement; they will also take into account the possibility that an agreement might affect potential competition in a particular market. Following considerable criticism, the Commission has shifted its perception of 'potential

---

14   See p 90 above.
15   See ch 1, p 19 and ch 2, p 47.
16   See Whish and Sufrin 'Article 85 and the Rule of Reason' (1987) 7 Ox YEL 1.
17   Ibid; Waelbroeck 'Vertical Agreements: is the Commission Right not to Follow the US Policy?' (1985) 25 Swiss Rev ICL; Schroter 'Antitrust Analysis and Article 85(1) and (3)' [1987] Fordham Corp L Inst (ed Hawk), ch 27; Caspari (formerly Director General of DG IV at the Commission) [1987] Fordham Corp L Inst (ed Hawk), p 361.
18   OJ [1999] C 132/1, [1999] 5 CMLR 208.
19   See below.

competition' under Article 81(1), and now adopts a more realistic view of the expression so that fewer agreements are caught than previously[20]. The CFI in *European Night Services v Commission*[1] rejected in its entirety a finding of the Commission that the establishment of the joint venture European Night Services Ltd could restrict actual or potential competition between its parents: the Court considered this to be 'a hypothesis unsupported by any evidence or any analysis of the structure of the relevant market from which it might be concluded that it represented a real, concrete possibility[2]. However, the Commission would be erring in law if it were to disregard altogether the impact of an agreement on potential competition[3].

(vi)   Joint ventures

Article 81(1) does not apply to full-function joint ventures, which are dealt with under the provisions on merger control: this is explained in chapter 21[4].

(vii)   The Commission's current practice in the application of Article 81(1)

The Commission has responded to the criticism that it applies Article 81(1) too extensively. In recent years there appear to have been more occasions on which it has been prepared to conclude that an agreement did not infringe Article 81(1), rather than to apply Article 81(1) and to exempt (or issue a comfort letter) under Article 81(3). Specific illustrations of this will be provided in later chapters of this book, dealing with horizontal cooperation agreements (chapter 15), vertical agreements (chapter 16) and intellectual property licences (chapter 19). The two new *Guidelines*, on horizontal and vertical agreements, also reveal a less formalistic (more economic) approach[5]. For example, paragraph 115 of the Commission's *Guidelines on Vertical Restraints*[6] sets out eight situations in which vertical restraints may have 'positive effects', in particular by promoting non-price competition and improved quality of service. It would be reasonable for critics of the Commission to acknowledge that its current decisional practice is somewhat different from what it was in the past.

(F)   Article 86(2)

Article 86(2) precludes the application of the competition rules to certain undertakings in so far as compliance with them would obstruct them in the

---

20   See eg *Konsortium ECR 900* OJ [1990] L 228/31, [1992] 4 CMLR 54; *Elopak/Metal Box—Odin* OJ [1990] L 209/15, [1991] 4 CMLR 832; Commission's *Guidance on Horizontal Cooperation Agreements* OJ [2001] C 3/2, [2001] 4 CMLR 819, para 9 and footnotes 8 and 9; see further ch 15, pp 501-502.
1   Cases T-374/94 etc [1998] ECR II-3141, [1998] 5 CMLR 718.
2   Ibid, paras 139-147.
3   See Case C-504/93 *Tiercé-Ladbroke v Commission* [1997] ECR II-923, [1997] 5 CMLR 309, where the CFI annulled a Commission decision which failed to take into account a possible restriction of potential competition.
4   Ch 21, pp 748-751.
5   See ch 15, pp 501-508 and ch 16, pp 542-545 respectively.
6   OJ [2000] C 291/1, [2000] 5 CMLR 1176.

performance of a task entrusted to them by a Member State. This subject is dealt with in chapter 6[7].

(G) State compulsion

The competition rules do not apply to undertakings in so far as they are compelled by law to behave in a particular way. The 'state compulsion' defence has been raised on numerous occasions, but has always failed. In *Wood Pulp*[8] the Commission concluded that the defence was not available to parties to an agreement within the US Webb–Pomerene Act 1918, which allows US exporters to form cartels, as that Act merely authorises cartels, but does not compel firms to enter into them. In *ENI/Montedison*[9] the parties to a restructuring agreement in the thermoplastics sector sought negative clearance and/or individual exemption. One ground for applying for negative clearance was that they were acting under directives from the Italian Government as set out in its 'Chemical Plan'. The Commission rejected this: the rôle of Government planning in this case was not so large as to absolve the parties of responsibility for their agreements. In *Aluminium Products*[10] parties to a cartel agreement in the aluminium industry argued that their conduct was known of and encouraged by the UK Government. The Commission held that there was no compulsion by the Government, nor indeed did there appear to be any legislative mechanism whereby there could be such compulsion. The fact of approval and encouragement did not in itself override the free will of the undertakings in question to make their own commercial decisions. In *SSI*[11] Dutch cigarette producers argued that they had entered into various agreements because, at meetings with Government representatives, the Government had explained its objectives which included the raising of substantial tax revenue; the undertakings had merely fallen in line with what they considered the Government expected of them. The Commission rejected this argument, holding that the Government had not compelled any particular form of behaviour or required them to enter into agreements prohibited by Article 81. On appeal, the ECJ upheld the Commission's decision[12]. In *French-West African Shipowners' Committee*[13] the Commission rejected the Committees' argument that the cargo–sharing system they operated fell outside Article 81 as it was imposed upon them by the public authorities in various African states. In *CNSD v Commission*[14] the CFI explained that if anti-competitive conduct is required of undertakings by national legislation, or if the latter creates a legal framework which itself eliminates any possibility of competitive activity on their part, Articles 81 and 82 do not apply; however, where the legislation does not preclude them from engaging in autonomous conduct, the competition rules can apply to their behaviour.

---

7   See ch 6, pp 202-208.
8   OJ [1985] L 85/1, [1985] 3 CMLR 474.
9   OJ [1987] L 5/13, [1988] 4 CMLR 444, para 25.
10   OJ [1985] L 92/1, [1987] 3 CMLR 813.
11   OJ [1982] L 232/1, [1982] 3 CMLR 702.
12   Cases 240/82 etc *SSI v Commission* [1985] ECR 3831, [1987] 3 CMLR 661.
13   OJ [1992] L 134/1, [1993] 5 CMLR 446, paras 32–38.
14   Case T-513/93 [2000] 5 CMLR 614, paras 58-59; see also Cases C-359/95 and 379/95 P *Commission v Ladbroke Racing* [1997] ECR I-6265, [1998] 4 CMLR 27, para 33; Case T-228/97 *Irish Sugar v Commission* [1999] 5 CMLR 1300, para 130.

It is clear from the foregoing that the defence of state compulsion will succeed only rarely. For a successful defence, it would seem that three requirements must be satisfied. First, the state must have made certain conduct *compulsory*: mere persuasion is insufficient; secondly, the defence is available only where there is a legal basis for this compulsion: this was considered by the Commission to be relevant in *Aluminium Producers*[15]; and thirdly, there must be no latitude at all for individual choice as to the implementation of the governmental policy.

(H) Highly regulated markets

In some cases undertakings accused of infringing Article 81 have argued that the market on which they were operating was so highly regulated by the state that there was no latitude left for competition; therefore they could not be found guilty of agreeing to restrict competition. In *Suiker Unie v Commission*[16] such a plea succeeded. In Italy the sugar industry was highly regulated in order that supply and demand be kept in balance; for example suppliers and customers were not allowed to negotiate with one another at all. The ECJ accepted that there was no competition capable of being distorted[17]. On subsequent occasions, however, this defence has failed. It was rejected by the ECJ in two judgments involving appeals against Commission decisions applying Article 81 to the Belgian[18] and Dutch[19] tobacco industries. In the latter decision, *Re Stichting Sigarettenindustrie Agreements*[20], the Commission refused to accept that the restriction of price competition in the Dutch cigarette market did not infringe Article 81(1) because Government regulations fixed the maximum price for retailing cigarettes: the regulations still left open the possibility of competing on price, albeit within a narrower band. Indeed if anything the Governmental restriction of competition meant that it was all the more important to preserve what latitude for competition remained. The Commission also rejected such an argument in *Greek Ferries*[1].

(I) Commission Notices

There are a number of Commission Notices, some of which have been mentioned in the course of the preceding text, in which the Commission has provided guidance on the application of Article 81(1) to various types of agreement. It might be helpful to provide a checklist of Commission Notices, arranged chronologically, that are of particular significance to the application of Article 81(1), with some brief comments where appropriate.

15 OJ [1985] L 92/1, [1987] 3 CMLR 813.
16 Cases 40/73 etc [1975] ECR 1663, [1976] 1 CMLR 295.
17 In different proceedings the national regulations were themselves held to be unlawful under the Treaty provisions on the free movement of goods: Cases 65/75 and 88/75 *Tasca and SADAM v Comitato Interministeriale dei Prezzi* [1976] ECR 291 and 323, [1976] 2 CMLR 183.
18 Cases 209/78 etc *Van Landewyck v Commission* [1980] ECR 3125, [1981] 3 CMLR 134.
19 Cases 240/82 etc *SSI v Commission* [1985] ECR 3831, [1987] 3 CMLR 661 and Case 260/82 *NSO v Commission* [1985] ECR 3801, [1988] 4 CMLR 755.
20 OJ [1982] L 232/1, [1982] 3 CMLR 702.
1 *Greek Ferry Services Cartel* OJ [1999] L 109/24, [1999] 5 CMLR 47, paras 98-108, on appeal Cases T-56/99 etc *Marlines SA v Commission* (judgment pending); see also *French–West Africa Shipowners' Committees* OJ [1992] L 134/1, [1993] 5 CMLR 446; Cases C-359/95 P *Commission and France v Ladbroke Racing Ltd* [1997] ECR I-6265, [1998] 4 CMLR 27; Cases T-202/98 etc *Tate & Lyle plc v Commission*, judgment of 12 July 2001, paras 44-45.

(i)   Notice on sub-contracting agreements[2]

Article 81(1) does not apply to sub-contracting agreements.

(ii)   Notice regarding restrictions directly related and necessary to the concentration[3]

Article 81(1) does not apply to ancillary restrictions; this Notice is relevant to the analysis of concentrations under the EC Merger Regulation, but it provides useful insights into the Commission's thinking more generally.[4]

(iii)   Notice on the application of the competition rules to cross-border credit transfers[5]

This Notice has specific application in the banking sector.

(iv)   Notice on agreements of minor importance[6]

This Notice is explained below.

(v)   Notice on the application of the competition rules to the postal sector[7]

This Notice has specific application in the postal sector.

(vi)   Notice on the concept of full-function joint ventures[8]

Article 81 does not apply to full function joint ventures.

(vii)   Notice on the application of the competition rules to access agreements in the telecommunications sector[9]

This Notice has specific application in the telecommunications sector.

(viii)   Guidelines on vertical restraints[10]

This Notice deals, at length, with the application of Article 81(1) and Article 81(3) to vertical agreements. The *Guidelines* include guidance on the application of Article 81(1) to agreements between a principal and agent.

2   OJ [1979] C1/2, [1979] 1 CMLR 264.
3   OJ [2001] C 188/5.
4   The Notice is discussed in ch 21, pp 783-784.
5   OJ [1995] C 251/3.
6   OJ [1997] C 372/13, [1998] 4 CMLR 192.
7   OJ [1998] C 39/2, [1998] 5 CMLR 108; see ch 23, pp 871-875.
8   OJ [1998] C 66/1, [1998] CMLR 542; see ch 21, pp 748-751.
9   OJ [1998] C 265/2, [1998] 5 CMLR 821; see ch 23, pp 868-871.
10   OJ [2000] C 291/1, [2000] 5 CMLR 1074; see ch 16, pp 542-546.

(ix)   Guidelines on horizontal cooperation agreements[11]

This Notice deals, at length, with the application of Article 81(1) and Article 81(3) to horizontal agreements.

4.   THE *DE MINIMIS* DOCTRINE

(A)   Introduction

Some agreements which affect competition within the terms of Article 81(1) may nevertheless not be caught because they do not have an appreciable impact either on competition or on inter-state trade. This *de minimis* doctrine was first formulated by the ECJ in *Völk v Vervaecke*[12]. There a German producer of washing-machines granted an exclusive distributorship to Vervaecke in Belgium and Luxembourg and guaranteed it absolute territorial protection against parallel imports. Volk's market share was negligible[13]. On an Article 234 reference the ECJ held that:

'an agreement falls outside the prohibition in Article 81(1) where it has only an insignificant effect on the market, taking into account the weak position which the persons concerned have on the market of the product in question'.

In *Pavel Pavlov v Stichting Pensioenfonds Medische Specialisten*[14] the ECJ concluded that a decision by medical specialists to set up a pension fund entrusted with the management of a supplementary pension scheme did not appreciably affect competition within the common market: the cost of the scheme had only a marginal and indirect influence on the final cost of the services that they offered.

The *de minimis* doctrine applies both to agreements whose object or effect is to prevent competition, which means that even horizontal restraints of a clearly anti-competitive nature or export bans in a vertical agreement could fall outside Article 81 because of their diminutive impact; having said this, it is to be expected that a stricter approach will be taken to agreements in the 'object' category within Article 81(1) than those that have as their effect the restriction of competition. Formal decisions applying the doctrine are rare: the Commission would normally settle such cases informally. The *de minimis* doctrine is in practice of considerable significance. Many agreements escape EC competition law, and hence problems such as the need to notify and the possibility of unenforceability, because they are of minor importance. The Commission has given guidance on the *de minimis* doctrine in a series of Notices, the most recent of which appeared in 1997[15]. This Notice will in many cases give a reasonably clear idea of whether an agreement is within the *de minimis* doctrine, although it must be treated with

11   OJ [2001] C 3/2, [2001] 4 CMLR 819; see ch 15, pp 504-508.
12   Case 5/69 [1969] ECR 295, [1969] CMLR 273.
13   0.2% and 0.5% of production in Germany in 1963 and 1966 respectively.
14   Cases C-180/98 etc [2001] 4 CMLR 30, paras 90-97.
15   *Notice on Agreements of Minor Importance* OJ [1997] C 372/13, [1998] 4 CMLR 192, replacing the previous Notice, OJ [1986] C 231/2 amended by OJ [1994] C 368/20.

some caution as it is not legally binding. In some circumstances an agreement might be held to fall within Article 81(1) even though it is below the quantitative criteria established by it[16]. An agreement may be found not to have an appreciable effect on competition even where the criteria in the Notice are exceeded[17]. It is anticipated that a revised Notice will be adopted in the near future which will take into account developments in the Commission's policy, in particular following the adoption of the *Guidelines* on vertical and horizontal agreements[18].

(B)   The Commission's *Notice on Agreements of Minor Importance*

The first six paragraphs of the Notice contain important statements on the *de minimis* doctrine. Paragraph 1 points out that the doctrine is consistent with the Commission's desire to facilitate cooperation between undertakings where such cooperation is economically desirable and does not present difficulties from the point of view of competition policy. Paragraph 2 reiterates the principle that agreements which are not capable of affecting trade between Member States should be examined on the basis of national legislation alone. In paragraph 3 the Commission states that the Notice provides quantitative criteria which should indicate to undertakings whether their agreements are within Article 81(1); it also says that these quantitative criteria are not an absolute yardstick and that agreements exceeding them may, in some situations, not have an appreciable effect and so be outside the competition rules. Paragraph 4 points out that, where the Notice applies, it should not be necessary to notify agreements to the Commission: it intends by this Notice to obviate the need for firms to send their agreements to Brussels. The administrative problems for DG COMP are great enough without firms notifying insignificant agreements to it.

Paragraph 5 is important: it states that the Commission will not as a general rule open proceedings in respect of agreements covered by the Notice; that where, owing to exceptional circumstances, an agreement covered by the Notice falls within Article 81(1), the Commission will not impose fines; and that it will not impose fines where firms fail to notify agreements because they assumed in good faith that the agreement was covered by the Notice. Paragraph 7 states that the Notice is without prejudice to the competence of national courts to apply Article 81(1) on the basis of their own jurisdiction, although it constitutes a factor which they may take into account. It also makes the obvious point that it is without prejudice to any interpretation of the *de minimis* doctrine by the ECJ. Paragraph 8 similarly states that the Notice is without prejudice to the application of national competition laws.

The main provision in the Notice is contained in Part II, at paragraph 9. It provides as follows:

> 'the Commission holds the view that agreements between undertakings engaged in the production or distribution of goods or in the provision of services do not fall under the prohibition in Article 81(1) if the aggregate

---

16   See p 110 below.
17   Case T-7/93 *Langnese-Iglo GmbH v Commission* [1995] ECR II-1533, [1995] 5 CMLR 602, para 98; *Notice on Agreements of Minor Importance*, OJ [1997] C 372/13, [1998] 4 CMLR 192, para 3; Case T-374/94 etc *European Night Services v Commission* [1998] ECR II-3141, [1998] 5 CMLR 718, paras 102–103.
18   See p 110 below.

market shares held by all of the participating undertakings do not exceed, on any of the relevant markets:

(*a*) the 5% threshold, where the agreement is made between undertakings operating at the same level of production or of marketing ("horizontal" agreements); or

(*b*) the 10% threshold, where the agreement is made between undertakings operating at different economic levels ("vertical" agreements).'

In the case of a mixed horizontal/vertical agreement, or where it is difficult to classify the agreement as either horizontal or vertical, the 5% threshold is applicable.

A particular problem with the Notice is that firms may outgrow these limits, although some marginal relief is provided by paragraph 10 where the thresholds are exceeded by no more than 10% during two successive years. Guidance on market definition is provided by the Commission *Notice on the Definition of Relevant Market for the Purpose of Community Competition Law*[19].

The Notice states that agreements that have as their object to fix prices or production or sales quotas or to share markets or sources of supply, that is to say agreements that have as their object the restriction of competition[20], may infringe Article 81(1) even below the Notice thresholds[1]. However, paragraph 11 indicates that even in such *per se* cases 'in the first instance it is for the authorities and courts of the Member States to act'.

It is not clear what happens to an agreement when it has outgrown the Notice, including the provisions for marginal relief: one possibility is that it becomes retrospectively void; a second is that it becomes unenforceable from the moment that the Notice ceases to apply; a third is that it should be enforceable until the Commission takes action to terminate it; no guidance on this difficult and commercially important issue is available. The third solution is perhaps the fairest, although the second is the most consistent with the scheme of Article 81 of the EC Treaty. In the UK, the Court of Appeal held in *Passmore v Morland plc*[2] that an agreement can infringe Article 81(1) at some times and at other times not do so, depending on the surrounding facts: in other words it can drift into and out of voidness.

The Notice indicates a continuation of the Commission's policy towards small- and medium-sized enterprises (hereafter 'SMEs') by affirming that agreements between them are 'rarely capable of significantly affecting trade between Member States and competition within the Common Market'. Even if they do so exceptionally, paragraph 19 of the Notice states that they will not be of sufficient Community interest to justify intervention, and on this basis the Commission will not institute proceedings either upon request or on its own initiative, even if the thresholds set out in paragraphs 9 and 10 are exceeded. However, in paragraph 20 it reserves the right to intervene in relation to significant restrictions, even on the part of SMEs, such as price fixing: it did so in its decision on *Greek Ferries*[3]. In paragraph 20 it also reserves the right to intervene where the cumulative effect of similar agreements in a particular market restricts competition. This refers to the doctrine elaborated by the ECJ in relation to brewers' supply

---

19 See OJ [1997] C 372/5, [1998] 4 CMLR 177; see ch 1, p 26ff.
20 See pp 95-98 above.
1 See similarly para 10 of the *Guidelines on Vertical Restraints* OJ [2000] C 291/1, [2000] 5 CMLR 1176.
2 [1999] 1 CMLR 1129, CA.
3 See below.

agreements[4] and by the Commission in relation to licences of plant breeders' rights[5].

The first application of the new Notice was in *Relais et Chateaux*[6] which concerned the notification of the rules of an association of small independent hotels in France. Applying the policy set out in paragraph 19 of the Notice, the Commission considered that the notified arrangements did not have an appreciable effect on trade between Member States because they were between SMEs, and because there were no similar agreements operating within the market in question. However, in *Greek Ferries*[7] the Commission imposed fines on Marlines and Ventouris, which were SMEs, since they were party to price-fixing agreements, a particularly serious infringement[8].

(C)   Limitations of the Notice

It is important to note the limitations of this Notice. The Commission itself may consider it inappropriate where it is dealing with an agreement in a tightly oligopolistic market where competition is already severely limited[9]; also the Commission expressly restricts the right to intervene in the circumstances specified in paragraph 20 of the Notice. The ECJ has indicated that it is wrong to adopt a purely quantitative approach to the issue of *de minimis* agreements and in *Distillers Co Ltd v Commission*[10] it concluded that an agreement affecting the distribution of Pimms was of importance, notwithstanding the minute proportion of the market held by that drink, because Distillers was a major producer occupying an important position on the market for drinks generally. In *Musique Diffusion Française v Commission*[11] the ECJ held that a concerted practice was not within the *de minimis* doctrine where the parties' market shares were small but the market was a fragmented one, their market shares exceeded those of most competitors and their turnover figures were high.

(D)   The Commission's Draft Notice of 2001

The Commission has published a draft Notice to replace the existing one.[11a] The new Notice will be relevant only to the question of whether competition is appreciably restricted: it is not concerned with the effect on trade between Member States. The market share cap for horizontal agreements will be raised to 10% and for vertical agreements to 15%. In markets where there may be a cumulative effect arising from parallel networks of agreements the market share cap will be

---

4   See Case 23/67 *Brasserie de Haecht SA v Wilkin* [1967] ECR 407, (1968) CMLR 26; Case 43/69 *Bräuerei Bilger v Lehle* [1970] ECR 127, [1974] 1 CMLR 382; Case 47/76 *De Norre v Brouwerij Concordia* [1977] ECR 65, [1977] 1 CMLR 378; and Case C-234/89 *Stergios Delimitis v Henninger Bräu* [1991] ECR I-935, [1992] 5 CMLR 210.

5   See *Royon v Meilland* OJ [1985] L 369/9, [1988] 4 CMLR 193.

6   Case IV/36180, unreported; see the Commission's Competition Policy Newsletter (1998) No 1 February.

7   *Greek Ferry Services Cartel* OJ [1999] L 109/24, [1999] 5 CMLR 47, on appeal Cases T-56/99 etc *Marlines SA v Commission* (judgment pending).

8   Ibid, para 151.

9   *Floral* OJ [1980] L 39/51, [1980] 2 CMLR 285.

10   Case 30/78 [1980] ECR 2229, [1980] 3 CMLR 121; see similarly Case 19/77 *Miller International v Commission* [1978] ECR 131, [1978] 2 CMLR 334; Case 107/82 *AEG-Telefunken v Commission* [1983] ECR 3151, [1984] 3 CMLR 325, para 58.

11   Cases 100/80 etc [1983] ECR 1825, [1983] 3 CMLR 221; see also *Yves Saint Laurent Parfums* OJ [1992] L 12/24, [1993] 4 CMLR 120.

11a See Peeperkorn 'Revision of the 1997 Notice on Agreements of Minor Importance', Commission's Competition Policy Newsletter, June 2001, p 4.

5%. Hard-core restrictions of the kind black-listed in Regulation 2790/99 on vertical agreements and Regulation 2658/00 on specialisation agreements will not be covered by the new Notice.

5.   THE EFFECT ON TRADE BETWEEN MEMBER STATES[12]

The application of Article 81(1) is limited to agreements, decisions or concerted practices which may affect trade between Member States. The scope of Article 82 is similarly limited. The inter-Member State trade clause is therefore of central importance in EC competition law, since it defines 'the boundary between the areas respectively covered by Community law and the law of the Member States'[13]. Historically both the Commission and the Community courts have adopted a liberal interpretation of the inter-state trade clause, thereby enlarging the scope of Articles 81 and 82[14]; the fact that most of the Member States now have domestic competition laws modelled upon Articles 81 and 82[15], in conjunction with the principle of subsidiarity, which is found in Article 5 (ex 3(b)) of the Treaty, means that there is less need now for the European Commission to assert jurisdiction on such a broad basis, and the judgment of the ECJ in *Carlo Bagnasco v BPN*[16] and the decision of the Commission in *Dutch Banks*[17], in which national agreements were found not to affect inter-state trade, may reflect this.

Some agreements obviously produce an effect on inter-state trade. A contract which prohibits a distributor from selling goods other than on his own national market would do so[18]; so would an agreement whereby producers agree to protect each other's national markets[19]. However it is not only in such obvious cases that this jurisdictional requirement is satisfied.

(A)   The STM test

In *Société Technique Minière v Maschinenbau Ulm*[20] the ECJ stated that for Article 81 to apply:

> 'it must be possible to foresee with a sufficient degree of probability on the basis of a set of objective factors of law or of fact that the agreement in question may have an influence, direct or indirect, actual or potential, on the pattern of trade between Member States'[1].

It has repeated this test in a number of subsequent cases[2]. Various comments should be made about this approach.

---

12 See Faull 'Effect on Trade Between Member States' [1989] Fordham Corporate Law Institute (ed Hawk) p 485.
13 Case 22/78 *Hugin Kassaregister AB v Commission* [1979] ECR 1869, p 1899, [1979] 3 CMLR 345, p 373.
14 Cp the position in the US where the inter-state commerce clause has also been construed flexibly: see eg *Manderville Island Farms v American Crystal Sugar Co* 342 US 143 (1951).
15 See ch 2, pp 53-55.
16 Case 215/96 etc [1999] ECR I-135, [1999] 4 CMLR 624, paras 50-53.
17 OJ [1999] L 271/28, [2000] 4 CMLR 137.
18 There have been many such cases: see ch 16, pp 550-553.
19 On horizontal market sharing see ch 13, pp 433-435.
20 Case 56/65 [1966] ECR 235, [1966] CMLR 357.
1   Ibid, pp 249 and 375 respectively.
2   Eg Cases 209/78 etc *Van Landewyck v Commission* [1980] ECR 3125, [1981] 3 CMLR 134; Case 126/80 *Salonia v Poidomani* [1981] ECR 1563, [1982] 1 CMLR 64; it has also been applied by the CFI: see eg Case T–66/89 *Publishers' Association v Commission (No 2)* [1992] ECR II-1995, [1992] 5 CMLR 120, para 55.

(i)   Windsurfing International Inc v Commission[3]

It is clear from this case that, where an agreement has an effect on inter-state trade, it follows that the restrictions of competition in the agreement may infringe Article 81(1) even though they themselves do not have that effect[4]. In *Welded Steel Mesh*[5] the Commission held that if undertakings participated in an agreement which affects inter-state trade they will be bound by Article 81(1) even if their conduct does not, viewed independently, have such an effect.

(ii)   Increases in trade

In *Consten and Grundig v Commission* the ECJ specifically held that the test would be satisfied where there was an *increase* in trade[6]. It might seem strange that this should be so; however the inter-Member State trade requirement relates only to the jurisdictional issue of the scope of application of EC law, whereas the qualitative effects of an agreement should be considered under the heading of restriction of competition. The Commission has applied this rule in several decisions[7].

(iii)   Actual or potential effects

It is not necessary that an agreement can be shown to have already affected inter-state trade; it is sufficient that it is reasonably foreseeable that it might do so. In *AEG-Telefunken v Commission*[8] the ECJ held that the fact that there was little trade between Member States in the relevant goods did not mean there was no infringement of Article 81(1), since it could reasonably be expected that patterns of trade in the future might change. In *Scottish Nuclear, Nuclear Energy Agreement*[9] an agreement whereby Scottish Power plc and Scottish Hydro–Electric plc agreed to purchase all the electricity produced by Scottish Nuclear Ltd was held by the Commission to be likely to affect trade between Member States. There was in the Commission's view an increasing interdependence of networks and an interconnection already linked the French electricity grid to that in England and Wales: such development meant that an agreement in the Scottish market would have a likely impact on inter-state trade. In *Trans-Atlantic Agreement*[10] the Commission, relying on the ECJ in *Höfner and Elser v Macrotron*[11] and the CFI in *BPB Industries plc v Commission*[12], again stated it was unnecessary to establish an *actual* effect on trade between Member States provided that a potential one could be demonstrated.

3   Case 193/83 [1986] ECR 611, [1986] 3 CMLR 489.
4   Ibid, paras 95–97; the Commission specifically applied this principle in *Cewal* OJ [1993] L 34/20, [1995] 5 CMLR 198, para 93.
5   OJ [1989] L 260/1, [1991] 4 CMLR 13 para 162, on appeal Cases T–141/89 etc *Tréfileurope Sales Sarl v Commission* [1995] ECR II-791.
6   Cases 56 and 58/64 [1966] ECR 299 at 341–342, [1966] CMLR 418 at 472.
7   See eg *Re Central Stikstof Verkoopkantoor* OJ [1978] L 242/15, [1979] 1 CMLR 11; *Re Italian Cast Glass* OJ [1980] L 383/19, [1982] 2 CMLR 61; *Milchförderungsfonds* OJ [1985] L 35/35, [1985] 3 CMLR 101; *Napier Brown – British Sugar* OJ [1988] L 284/41, [1990] 4 CMLR 196, para 80.
8   Case 107/82 [1983] ECR 3151, [1984] 3 CMLR 325, para 60.
9   OJ [1991] L 178/31.
10   OJ [1994] L 376/1.
11   Case C-41/90 [1991] ECR I-1979, [1993] 4 CMLR 306, paras 32-33.
12   Case T-65/89 [1993] ECR II-389, [1993] 5 CMLR 32, para 134.

(iv) Direct or indirect effects

It is necessary that indirect as well as direct effects of an agreement should be considered. In *Re Zanussi SpA Guarantee*[13] the Commission held that Zanussi's former practice of limiting the application of its guarantees to goods bought and used in the same Member State infringed Article 81(1), as this would discourage the import of Zanussi goods from other Member States which would not have the benefit of guarantees. In *Gosmé/Martell-DMP*[14] the Commission held that any practice or agreement directly or indirectly discouraging exports or making them less profitable, such as the refusal to grant discounts on goods for export, is liable to affect trade between Member States. In *Eirpage*[15] the Commission considered that a joint venture between Irish Telecom and Motorola Ireland Limited to provide a radio-paging service in Ireland affected inter-state trade as, in the Commission's view, the activities of Motorola Ireland Limited must be seen as part of the Motorola Group's European operations and therefore they necessarily would have repercussions outside Ireland.

In *Compagnie Maritime Belge Transports SA v Commission*[16] the CFI upheld a Commission decision, following a series of complaints, that various agreements between three liner conferences operating between northern Europe and west Africa breached Articles 81 and 82. The agreements in question sought to exclude companies belonging to one conference from operating as independent shipping companies in the areas of activity of the other two conferences. The appellants argued *inter alia* that, as the condemned practices only related to Africa and not to homeward transit to the Community, they did not affect inter-state trade. The Commission had disagreed with this, reasoning that outbound and inbound transport markets, being inter-dependent, could not be separated, and that agreements concerned with outbound transport could therefore have an impact on trade between Member States. The CFI upheld this approach. It also reasoned that even if such agreements did not directly affect competition between Community ports, the sort of market partitioning which the decision condemned might affect activities in the ports' catchment areas. In addition it held (in relation to Article 82) that behaviour seeking to eliminate a competitor from the market in the EC was inherently capable of affecting the structure of competition in that market[17]. The Commission has found trade to be affected between Member States in several other decisions concerning liner shipping to and from the Community, where at first sight it is not obvious that there is such an effect: for example it has found that the restriction of competition between shipowners could influence and alter trade flows in transport services within the common market[18] and that it could have an effect on competition between ports by altering their respective catchment areas and between activities in those catchment areas[19].

13 OJ [1978] L 322/26, [1979] 1 CMLR 81.
14 OJ [1991] L 185/23, [1992] 5 CMLR 586, para 37.
15 OJ [1991] L 306/22, [1993] 4 CMLR 64, para 13.
16 Cases T-24/93 R etc [1996] ECR II-1201, [1997] 4 CMLR 273; see also *TACA* OJ [1999] L 95/1, [1999] 4 CMLR 1415, paras 386-396, on appeal Cases T-191/98, *Atlantic Container Line v Commission* (judgment pending); and *EATA* OJ [1999] L 193/23, [2000] 5 CMLR 1380, paras 157-175.
17 Ibid.
18 *FETTCSA* OJ [2000] L 258/1, [2000] 5 CMLR 1011, para 140.
19 Ibid, para 141.

(v)   National agreements

The fact that the parties to an agreement are from the same Member State does not mean that there can be no effect on trade between Member States. This is in practice an extremely important point, and the Commission has on several occasions held that Article 81 applies to agreements between undertakings in the same Member State[20]. Various judgments of the Community Courts point to the same conclusion[1]. As the CFI has said:

'anti-competitive conduct confined to the territory of a single Member State is capable of having repercussions on patterns of trade and competition in the Common Market'[2].

If an agreement is intended to operate across an entire national market there is a strong presumption that it will affect inter-state trade, although the ECJ in *Carlo Bagnasco* and the Commission in *Dutch Banks* have recently retreated from this position to some extent[3]. In *Vereeniging van Cementhandelaren (VCH) v Commission*[4] the ECJ refused to overturn the Commission's decision[5] that a price-fixing scheme limited to the sale of cement on the Dutch market and which did not affect imports or exports infringed Article 81(1). The ECJ held that an agreement:

'extending over the whole of the territory of a Member State by its very nature has the effect of reinforcing the compartmentalization of markets on a national basis, thereby holding up the economic interpenetration which the Treaty is designed to bring about and protecting domestic production'[6].

In *Salonia v Poidomani*[7] it adopted the same view in its judgment on an Article 234 reference from Italy. There the Italian court asked whether a national selective distribution system in respect of newspapers could affect inter-state trade. The ECJ repeated its statement in *VCH*, and suggested that in the case of newspapers the test should be applied more strictly than for other products, presumably because of the particular need to ensure the free circulation of news and opinion. The ECJ's dictum in *VCH* has been applied by the Commission on

---

20 See eg *Vacuum Interrupters Ltd* [1977] L 48/32, [1977] 1 CMLR   D67; *Italian Cast Glass* OJ [1980] L 383/19, [1982] 2 CMLR 61; *Italian Flat Glass* OJ [1981] 326/32, [1982] 3 CMLR 366; *Eirpage* OJ [1991] L306/22, [1993] 4 CMLR 64, and *Dutch Mobile Cranes* OJ [1995] L 312/79, [1996] 4 CMLR 565, upheld on appeal Cases T-213/95 and T-18/96 *SCK and FNK v Commission* [1997] ECR II-1739, [1998] 4 CMLR 259.
1   Case 246/86 *S C Belasco v Commission* [1989] ECR 2117, [1991] 4 CMLR 96; Cases T-68/89 etc *Società Italiano Vetro v Commission* [1992] ECR II-1403, [1992] 5 CMLR 302.
2   Case T–66/89 *Publishers' Association v Commission (No 2)* [1992] ECR II-1995, [1992] 5 CMLR 120, para 57, citing Case 322/81 *NV Nederlandsche Banden-Industrie Michelin v Commission* [1983] ECR 3461, [1985] 1 CMLR 282, para 103; see also Case 246/86 *S C Belasco v Commission* [1989] ECR 2117, [1991] 4 CMLR 96, para 38.
3   See p 115 below.
4   Case 8/72 [1972] ECR 977, [1973] CMLR 7.
5   *VCH* JO [1972] L 13/34, [1973] CMLR D16.
6   Case 8/72 [1972] ECR 977, p 991, [1973] CMLR 7, p 23.
7   Case 126/80 [1981] ECR 1563, [1982] 1 CMLR 64; see also Case 61/80 *Cöoperative Stremsel–en Kleurselfabriek v Commission* [1981] ECR 851, [1982] 1 CMLR 240 and Case 42/84 *Remia BV and Verenigde Bedrijven Nutricia NV v Commission* [1985] ECR 2545, [1987] 1 CMLR 1.

several occasions[8]. Where a national cartel has the object, *inter alia*, of acting defensively against foreign imports, the Commission and the Community courts have no hesitation in finding an effect on inter-state trade[9]. In *MELDOC* the Commission rejected the argument that the *VCH* test applied only to agreements between traders and not to manufacturing cartels[10]. In *Pronuptia de Paris v Schillgalis*[11] the ECJ held that clauses in distribution franchise agreements which partition markets between franchisor and franchisee or between franchisees are *per se* capable of affecting inter-state trade, even if they are concluded between enterprises in the same Member State, to the extent that they prevent the franchisees from setting themselves up in other Member States[12].

The ECJ has rejected an argument in *VBVB v Commission*[13] that the Flemish–speaking parts of Belgium and the Netherlands should be regarded as a homogeneous territory for the purpose of the market in books so that there can be no inter-state trade between them.

In *Carlo Bagnasco v BPN*[14] the ECJ held that standard banking conditions relating to the provision of general guarantees to secure current account credit facilities in Italy were not liable to affect trade between Member States[15]. There seems little doubt that, had the Court wished to come to the opposite conclusion, the precedents would have enabled it to do so. In *Dutch Banks*[16] the Commission concluded that the acceptance giro system in operation, although anti-competitive in the sense of Article 81(1)(a), was not capable of appreciably affecting inter-state trade. Having reiterated the ECJ's case law, the Commission took into account that the cross-border nature of acceptance giros is very limited; that non-Dutch banks played only a very modest rôle in the system; and that participating in the GSA agreement was not an important factor for non-Dutch banks when deciding to enter the Netherlands market. This decision, which unusually sees the Commission renouncing jurisdiction, is indicative of its increased willingness to see the national competition authorities apply their own competition laws to matters that have only a national (or more local) impact. At a time when many Member States lacked a system of competition law, the Commission may have felt that it needed to assert jurisdiction on a wide scale; this is not necessary any longer, as Member States have effective laws of their own.

(vi) Raw materials

The ECJ has held that, where an agreement relates to a semi–finished product which is not itself the subject of inter-state trade but which is incorporated into a product which is, Article 81(1) does apply[17].

---

8   See eg *MELDOC* OJ [1986] L 348/50, [1989] 4 CMLR 853; *Belgische Vereniging der Banken/Association Belge des Banques* OJ [1987] L 7/27, [1989] 4 CMLR 141; *Eirpage* OJ [1991] L 306/22, [1993] 4 CMLR 64.
9   *Belgian Roofing Felt* OJ [1986] L 232/15, [1991] 4 CMLR 130, upheld on appeal Case 246/86 *Belasco v Commission* [1989] ECR 2117, [1991] 4 CMLR 96.
10   OJ [1986] L 348/50, paras 71–72.
11   Case 161/84 [1986] ECR 353, [1986] 1 CMLR 414.
12   Ibid, para 26.
13   Cases 43 and 63/82 [1984] ECR 19, [1985] 1 CMLR 27.
14   Case 215/96 [1999] ECR I-135, [1999] 4 CMLR 624.
15   Ibid, paras 47-53
16   OJ [1999] L 271/28, [2000] 4 CMLR 137.
17   Case 123/83 *BNIC v Clair* [1985] ECR 391, [1985] 2 CMLR 430 and Case 136/86 *BNIC v Aubert* [1987] ECR 4789, [1988] 4 CMLR 331, para 18; Cases C–89/85 etc *A Ahlström Oy*

(vii)   Proximity to the frontier

Undertakings situated near to national frontiers are particularly likely to find they have made agreements which affect inter-state trade. This was true for example in *Re Industrial Timber*[18], a case settled informally where the agreements in question operated in Belgium and the border areas of other timber–producing Member States. In *AEG–Telefunken v Commission*[19] one relevant point in establishing the necessary effect on inter-state trade was that, despite problems in selling television sets in other Member States caused by different technical standards, there was a demand for AEG sets in the frontier regions of Germany and France[20].

(viii)   Governmental barriers to trade

In *Van Landewyck v Commission*[1] the Court rejected the submission of the members of a Belgian trade association that its recommendations had not affected inter-state trade since the Belgian tax system rendered parallel importing impossible. The policy of the Commission and the Community Courts is to ensure that where competition is already restricted by Governmental action, the remaining latitude of firms to compete should be carefully preserved, and they do not want this to be subverted by narrowing the application of the inter-state trade clause[2].

(ix)   Meaning of trade

Articles 81 and 82 refer to an effect on *trade* between Member States. This word has been given a wide meaning, so that effects on any commercial activities may be taken into account. Trade includes the services sector and areas such as banking[3], insurance[4] and maritime transport[5] have been subjected to the competition rules. Electricity is capable of being imported and exported, so that an agreement restricting Dutch distributors of electricity supplying into Belgium affected inter-state trade and infringed Article 81(1)[6]. Even opera singers are involved in trade[7].

---

    v Commission [1993] ECR I-1307, [1993] 4 CMLR 407, para 142; *Trans-Atlantic Agreement* OJ [1994] L 376/1, para 296.

18 IP (75) 198, [1976] 1 CMLR D11.

19 Case 107/82 [1983] ECR 3151, [1984] 3 CMLR 325.

20 Ibid, para 65; see also Case T-213/95 etc *SCK and FNK v Commission* [1997] ECR II-1739, [1998] 4 CMLR 259.

1   Cases 209/78 etc [1980] ECR 3125, [1981] 3 CMLR 134.

2   See similarly Case 45/85 *VdS v Commission* [1987] ECR 405, [1988] 4 CMLR 264, paras 44–51; Cases C-359/95 P etc *Commission and France v Ladbroke Racing Ltd* [1997] ECR I-6265, [1998] 4 CMLR 27, paras 33-34.

3   See eg Case 172/80 *Züchner v Bayerische Vereinsbank AG* [1981] ECR 2021, [1982] 1 CMLR 313.

4   See eg *Re Nuovo CEGAM* OJ [1984] L 99/29, [1984] 2 CMLR 484; Case 45/85 *VdS v Commission* [1987] ECR 405, [1988] 4 CMLR 264.

5   See eg *French-West African Shipowners' Committees* OJ [1992] L 134/1, [1993] 5 CMLR 446.

6   *Ijsselcentrale* OJ [1991] L 28/32, [1992] 5 CMLR 154.

7   *RAI v UNITEL* OJ [1978] L 157/39, [1978] 3 CMLR 306.

(x) De minimis

In order to come within Article 81 or 82 there must be an *appreciable* effect both on inter-state trade and on competition. The *de minimis* doctrine was dealt with above[8]. The influence which an agreement may have on trade between Member States is to be determined by taking into account in particular the position and importance of the parties on the market for the products concerned[9]. The ECJ has held that a US export cartel in wood pulp with a market share of between 14%–17% cannot claim to have an insignificant effect on inter-state trade[10]. In *Compagnie Royale Asturienne des Mines SA and Rheinzink GmbH v Commission*[11] the ECJ rejected an argument that an agreement fell within the doctrine where it was entered into by competitors on an oligopolistic market (where there were only six zinc sheet rolling mills in the Community) and where the object of the agreement was to isolate the German market. In *Erauw-Jacquery Sprl v La Hesbignonne Société Cooperative*[12] the ECJ held, in an Article 234 reference, that it would be for the national court to decide, on the basis of all the economic evidence before it, whether an agreement had a sufficiently appreciable impact on inter-state trade to fall within Article 81(1). In reaching its decision, the national court would have to take into account the cumulative effect of a network of similar agreements in a particular market, which might render penetration by imports impossible. The same point arose in *Breeders' rights: Roses*[13], where the Commission held that a licence between two French nationals of plant breeders' rights had an appreciable effect on inter-state trade because of the cumulative effect of the existence of thousands of similar agreements[14]. In *Vichy*[15] the Commission again pointed, at paragraph 19, to the cumulative effect of parallel systems of exclusive distribution through pharmacies for all brands of cosmetics sold through the pharmaceutical channel in deciding that there was an effect on inter-state trade when reaching a decision under Article 15(6) of Regulation 17/62.

(xi) The 'inter-state trade' clause as interpreted by the UK courts

Whereas the Commission has found it relatively easy to determine that there is an effect on trade between Member States in a case in which it asserts jurisdiction, in domestic litigation it may be more difficult to persuade a judge in a national court on this point. A number of cases in the UK have failed because the party raising a point under Article 81 or 82 has been unable to satisfy the court on this point[16].

---

8 See pp 107-110.
9 Case 99/79 *Lancôme v ETOS* [1980] ECR 2511, para 24, [1981] 2 CMLR 164; Case T-77/92 *Parker Pen Ltd v Commission* [1994] ECR II-549, [1995] 5 CMLR 435, para 40.
10 Cases 89/85 etc *A Ahlström Oy v Commission* [1993] ECR I-1307, [1993] 4 CMLR 407, para 144.
11 Cases 29 and 30/83 [1984] ECR 1679, [1985] 1 CMLR 688, paras 29–31.
12 Case 27/87 [1988] ECR 1919, [1988] 4 CMLR 576.
13 OJ [1985] L 369/9, [1988] 4 CMLR 193, para 24.
14 See similarly *Bloemenveilingen Aalsmeer* OJ [1988] L 262/27, [1989] 4 CMLR 500, paras 124–134; Case C–234/89 *Delimitis v Henninger Bräu* [1991] ECR I-935, [1992] 5 CMLR 210: see paras 10-27.
15 OJ [1991] L 75/57, upheld on appeal Case T-19/91 *Vichy v Commission* [1992] ECR II-415.
16 See for example *Panayiotou v Sony Music Entertainment (UK) Ltd* [1994] ECC 395 and *Heathrow Airport Ltd v Forte (UK) Ltd* [1998] Eu LR 98.

(B)   The structural test

On some occasions the ECJ has applied a different test to decide whether there has been an effect on inter-state trade; instead of attempting to identify actual or potential effects, it has suggested that the phrase will be satisfied by any alteration in the structure of competition within the common market[17]. This test is of more significance in Article 82 cases where *ex hypothesi* one firm is in a dominant position so that the structural fabric of the market is already a matter for concern: the elimination of a competitor in these circumstances may have serious effects[18]. However the structural test has also been applied by the Commission in decisions under Article 81[19].

(C)   Agreements concerning trade outside the common market

The fact that an agreement relates to trade outside the common market does not necessarily mean that it is not caught by Article 81. It is necessary to consider whether the agreement might produce effects on trade between the Member States of the EC. An agreement between undertakings in the EC and overseas firms intended to limit imports into the common market may affect inter-state trade and so be caught[20]. It is not permissible to take private initiatives to prevent the 'dumping' of cheap goods in the EC: this problem is one which the Commission insists should be dealt with at Community level under Article 133 (ex Article 113) of the Treaty. Article 81(1) will not be infringed however if it can be shown that, because of the nature of the product, importation into the EC and a consequent effect on inter-state trade is inherently unlikely[1].

An agreement between firms within the common market as to their exports outside it may be caught if it is clear that a necessary side effect of it will be to prevent, distort or restrict competition within the Community and that this will affect inter-state trade. For example in *Suiker Unie v Commission*[2] a collusive tendering agreement was caught for this reason. In *Compagnie Royale Asturienne des Mines SA and Rheinzink GmbH v Commission*[3] an agreement between Rheinzink and Schlitz that Schlitz would export goods to countries in the Middle East and in particular to Egypt was held to have an effect on inter-state trade as it was really a way of protecting the German market from parallel imports.

---

17   See in particular Cases 6/73, 7/73 *Commercial Solvents v Commission* [1974] ECR 223, [1974] 1 CMLR 309; Case 22/79 *Greenwich Film Production v SACEM* [1979] ECR 3275, [1980] 1 CMLR 629; Case 7/82 *GVL v Commission* [1983] ECR 483, [1983] 3 CMLR 645.
18   See ch 5, pp 151-152.
19   See eg *Re Vacuum Interrupters Ltd* OJ [1977] L 48/32, [1977] 1 CMLR D67; *Polypropylene* OJ [1986] L 230/1, [1988] 4 CMLR 347, para 95.
20   See eg *Re Franco-Japanese Ballbearings Agreement* OJ [1974] L 343/19, [1975] 1 CMLR D8; *Re French and Taiwanese Mushroom Packers* OJ [1975] L 29/26, [1975] 1 CMLR D83; *Aluminium Products* OJ [1985] L 92/1, [1987] 3 CMLR 813; *Siemens/Fanuc* OJ [1985] L 376/29, [1988] 4 CMLR 945.
1   See eg *Re A Raymond & Co and Nagoya Rubber Ltd Agreement* JO [1972] L 143/39, [1972] CMLR D45.
2   Cases 40/73 etc [1975] ECR 1663, [1976] 1 CMLR 295; where no such effect is likely, the agreement will fall outside Article 81(1): see eg *Re VVVF* JO [1969] L 168/22, [1970] CMLR D1.
3   Cases 29, 30/83 [1984] ECR 1679, [1985] 1 CMLR 688, paras 24 et seq; see also Cases T-25/95 etc *Cimenteries CBR SA v Commission* judgment of 15 March 2000.

In its first application of the competition rules to maritime transport, *French-West African Shipowners' Committees*[4], the Commission applied both Article 81 and Article 82 to the provision of transport services between the Community and third countries, *in casu*, France and parts of West and Central Africa. The Commission held that agreements between shipowners concerning cargo–sharing on these routes did affect trade between Member States because, firstly, French shipping lines thereby acquired privileged access to the routes and so gained a competitive edge in world trade over the lines of other Member States; secondly, competition between French importers and exporters and those in other Member States was distorted; and thirdly, trade could be deflected away from ports in France to those elsewhere in the Community[5]. In *Tretorn*[6] the Commission found that a ban on exports from the Community and into Switzerland affected trade between Member States, since it prevented Swiss traders from buying goods from one Member State and reselling them into another.

In *Javico v Yves Saint Laurent*[7] the ECJ was asked to consider whether export bans imposed upon distributors in the Ukraine and Russia infringed Article 81(1). The ECJ held export bans in these circumstances did not have as their object the restriction of competition[8]. However it went on to say that there might be some cases in which the enforcement of restrictions on resale outside a non-EU contractual territory might be found to infringe Article 81(1) where (a) they have an appreciable effect on competition within the EU and (b) they produce an appreciable effect on trade between Member States. This would require the court making this appraisal, or the Commission if it were to investigate, to take account of the 'economic and legal context' of the agreement[9]. It would be necessary to show a risk of 'an appreciable effect on the pattern of trade *between the Member States* such as to undermine attainment of the objectives of the common market' (emphasis added)[10]. To produce an appreciable effect on competition within the EU, the ECJ suggested that the EU market in the relevant products must be oligopolistic, so that there is limited competition there; and that there should be a substantial difference in the prices charged for the products inside the EU and in the country(ies) from which the transhipments originate, after allowing for relevant duties and transport costs. Further, to produce an appreciable effect on trade between Member States, the volume of products put onto the market in non-Member States must be more than a 'very small percentage' of the total market for those products within the EU. No figure was offered by the Court as to what would constitute a 'very small percentage'. More recently, in *Micro Leader Business*[11] the CFI annulled the Commission's decision to reject a complaint against the resale prices of Microsoft products and implicitly accepted that a prohibition on imports into France of French-language Microsoft products from Canada was capable of affecting trade in the Community. These cases illustrate that care must be taken in relation to non-EU agreements, since the possibility that they might infringe Article 81(1) cannot be ruled out.

4   OJ [1992] L 134/1, [1993] 5 CMLR 446; see also the CFI's judgment in Cases T-24/93 etc *Compagnie Maritime Belge SA v Commission* [1996] ECR II-1201, [1997] 4 CMLR 273.
5   See similarly on the deflection of trade point *Cewal* OJ [1993] L 34/20, [1995] 5 CMLR 198, paras 39–40.
6   OJ [1994] L 378/45, [1997] 4 CMLR 860.
7   Case C-306/96 [1998] ECR I-1983, [1998] 5 CMLR 172.
8   See p 97 above.
9   Ibid, para 22.
10 Ibid, para 25.
11 Case T-198/98 [2000] All ER (EC) 361, [2000] 4 CMLR 886.

(D)   Review by the CFI

A finding by the Commission that an agreement may have an effect on inter-state trade may be challenged before the CFI. Generally speaking the Community Courts have adopted an equally wide approach to this phrase as the Commission. In *Groupement des Fabricants de Papiers Peints de Belgique v Commission*[12] the ECJ overturned the Commission's finding that a national system of collective resale price maintenance affected inter-state trade, since the case was a relatively novel one and the Commission had not explained in sufficient detail the precise way in which inter-state trade would be affected. In *Hugin v Commission*[13] the Commission's decision that Hugin had abused a dominant position within the meaning of Article 82 was quashed, because on the facts the Court could not see how inter-state trade could be affected by the refusal of a Swedish producer to supply spare parts to a London-based firm which operated only on a local market (at the relevant time Sweden was not a Member State). Apart from these isolated examples the Community Courts have always upheld the Commission's findings on the inter-state trade clause.

6.   CHECKLIST OF AGREEMENTS THAT FALL OUTSIDE ARTICLE 81(1)

At the end of this chapter, it may be helpful to set out a checklist of the circumstances in which an agreement might be found not to infringe Article 81(1): the list follows the order of the text of this chapter:
*   Article 81(1) applies only to an agreement between undertakings[14]
*   Article 81(1) does not apply to collective agreements between employers and workers[15]
*   Article 81(1) does not apply to an agreement between undertakings that form a single economic entity[16]
*   Article 81(1) does not normally apply to agreements between a principal and agent[17]
*   Article 81(1) does not normally apply to an agreement between a contractor and a sub-contractor[18]
*   Article 81(1) does not apply to unilateral conduct which is not attributable to a concurrence of wills between two or more undertakings[19]
*   Article 81(1) does not apply to an agreement that has neither the object nor the effect of preventing, restriction or distorting competition[1]
*   Article 81(1) does not apply to contractual restrictions that are entered into to enable undertakings to achieve a legitimate purpose and which are not disproportionate[2]

12   Case 73/74 [1975] ECR 1491, [1976] 1 CMLR 589.
13   Case 22/78 [1979] ECR 1869, [1979] 3 CMLR 345.
14   See pp 66-71 above.
15   See p 71 above.
16   See pp 72-74 above.
17   See p 75 above and ch 16, pp 538-540.
18   See p 75 above and ch 16, pp 593-594.
19   See p 89 above.
1   See pp 90-107 above.
2   See pp 100-101 above.

- Article 81 does not apply to full-function joint ventures[3]
- A realistic view must be taken of potential competition[4]
- Article 81(1) does not apply to an agreement if this would obstruct an undertaking or undertakings in the performance of a task of general economic interest entrusted to them by a Member State[5]
- Article 81(1) does not apply to an agreement which undertakings were compelled to enter into by law[6]
- Article 81(1) does not apply to an agreement in a market that is so highly regulated that there is no latitude left for competition[7]
- Article 81(1) does not apply to an agreement that has no appreciable effect on competition[8]
- Article 81(1) does not apply to an agreement that does not have an appreciable effect on trade between Member States.[9]

3   See ch 21, pp 748-751.
4   See pp 100-102 above.
5   See pp 103-104 above and ch 6, pp 202-208.
6   See pp 104-105 above.
7   See p 105 above.
8   See pp 107-110 above.
9   See pp 110-120 above.

CHAPTER 4

Article 81(3)

An agreement which falls within Article 81(1) of the Treaty is not necessarily 'automatically void' as Article 81(2) states. Article 81(3) provides that the provisions of Article 81(1) may be declared inapplicable in respect of agreements, decisions or concerted practices[1], or of categories[2] of agreements, decisions or concerted practices, which satisfy four conditions, the first two positive and the last two negative. To satisfy Article 81(3), an agreement must improve the production or distribution of goods or promote technical or economic progress and consumers must receive a fair share of the resulting benefit; furthermore the agreement must not contain dispensable restrictions nor substantially eliminate competition in the relevant market[3]. A favourable decision under Article 81(3) may be obtained in two ways: either by applying to the Commission for a so-called 'individual exemption' in respect of a particular agreement or by drafting an agreement to satisfy one of the 'block exemptions' issued by the Commission under powers conferred on it by the Council of Ministers (hereafter 'the Council')[4].

This chapter will begin with a discussion of the provisions of Article 81(3) itself. It will then discuss the mechanism whereby parties to an agreement may seek an individual exemption. The system of block exemptions will then be explained. On 28 April 1999 the Commission adopted a White Paper on *Modernisation of the Rules Implementing Articles 81 and 82*[5]. The proposals, if adopted, will revolutionise the way in which EC competition law is enforced: in particular the existing system of notification of agreements to the Commission for individual exemption will be eliminated. This aspect of the modernisation proposals will be briefly discussed in the final section of this chapter; the White Paper and the proposed regulation to replace Regulation 17/62 will be considered in detail in chapter 7[6].

1 The reference to decisions is useful since it means eg that the rules of a trade association can be approved; it will only be rarely that exemption is sought for a concerted practice, but this can happen: see eg *Re International Energy Agency* OJ [1983] L 376/30, [1984] 2 CMLR 186; renewed in 1994, OJ [1994] L 68/35.
2 The inclusion of 'categories' of agreements is important, since it paves the way for 'block' exemptions: see further pp 141-146 below.
3 Note that the UK Competition Act 1998 contains similar provisions in ss 4-11: see ch 9, pp 309-313.
4 In a few cases, the Council itself has adopted a block exemption: see p 141 below.
5 OJ [1999] C 132/1, [1999] 5 CMLR 208.
6 See ch 7, pp 246-258.

1.   THE CRITERIA FOR EXEMPTION UNDER ARTICLE 81(3)

(A)   The four requirements in Article 81(3)

To qualify for exemption, an agreement must overcome the four hurdles set out in Article 81(3). In the case of notifications for individual exemption, the burden is on the notifying parties to prove that their agreement satisfies each of the four conditions[7]. The Commission will require the parties to show that it would not be possible for the beneficial effects claimed to be experienced in competitive conditions[8]. All four of the requirements must be satisfied if an agreement is to benefit from exemption: the Court of Justice ('the ECJ') and the Court of First Instance ('the CFI') have stressed this on a number of occasions; an example of this is the CFI's judgment in *Métropole Télévision SA v Commission*[9]. In *Auditel*[10] the Commission was satisfied that an agreement contained provisions that were not indispensable and that it would substantially eliminate competition; it refused to grant an exemption without considering the other criteria in Article 81(3).

A separate point is that the CFI, in *Matra Hachette v Commission*[11], has stated that there are no anti-competitive agreements which, *as a matter of law*, could never be eligible for exemption: in each case the Commission would have to consider whether all the conditions laid down in Article 81(3) are satisfied. Of course, it is highly unlikely that price-fixing and market-sharing agreements would be granted exemption, but in exceptional circumstances this may be possible: indeed Articles 3 to 5 of Council Regulation 4056/86 on maritime transport[12] provide block exemption for horizontal price-fixing in the case of international liner conferences[13]. In *Reims II*[14] the Commission granted individual exemption to an agreement between the public postal operators in Europe as to the amount that one operator would pay to another for the onward delivery of letters in the latter's territory. The agreement did entail the 'fixing' of prices, in that participants in the scheme were committed to its principles; but this was price fixing of an 'unusual' nature[15], and the Commission could identify a number of economic efficiencies that would follow from it[16].

Each of the four requirements of Article 81(3) will be examined in turn.

---

7   Cases 43/82 and 63/82 *VBVB and VBBB v Commission* [1984] ECR 19, [1985] 1 CMLR 27; Case 42/84 *Remia BV and Verenigde Bedrijven Nutricia NV v Commission* [1985] ECR 2545, [1987] 1 CMLR 1; Case T–66/89 *Publishers' Association v Commission (No 2)* [1992] ECR II-1995, [1992] 5 CMLR 120, para 69; *Trans-Atlantic Agreement* OJ [1994] L 376/1, para 383; the Commission is expected to cooperate in establishing the relevant facts and circumstances: Cases 56 and 58/64 *Consten and Grundig v Commission* [1966] ECR 299, p 347, [1966] CMLR 418, p 477.
8   See eg *Re Vereeniging van Cementhandelaren* JO [1972] L 13/34, [1973] CMLR D 16 and the XIVth *Annual Report on Competition Policy* (1984), point 150.
9   Joined Cases T-528/93 etc [1996] ECR II-649, [1996] 5 CMLR 386, para 93.
10   OJ [1993] L 306/50, [1995] 5 CMLR 719, paras 28-34.
11   Case T-17/93, [1994] ECR II-595, para 85.
12   OJ [1986] L 378/1.
13   See ch 23, p 861.
14   OJ [1999] L 275/17, [2000] 4 CMLR 704.
15   Ibid, para 65.
16   Ibid, paras 69-76.

(i)   An improvement in the production or distribution of goods or in technical or economic progress

The 'benefit' produced by the agreement must be something of objective value to the Community as a whole, not a private benefit to the parties themselves[17]. Any advantages claimed of the agreement must outweigh the detriments it might produce[18]; the Commission will not accept that an agreement produces an improvement if, in practice, its effect is a disproportionate distortion of competition in the market in question[19]. The benefits that may be claimed are specified in Article 81(3): the agreement must either contribute to an improvement in the production or distribution of goods[20] or promote technical or economic progress. These concepts overlap, and in many cases the Commission has considered that more than one – or even that all – the heads were satisfied[1]. In other cases a particular type of benefit may be obviously appropriate for the agreement in question. When permitting specialisation agreements, which can lead to economies of scale and other efficiencies, the Commission has considered that there would be an improvement in the production of goods[2], while it has often held that research and development projects would lead to technical and economic progress[3]. Vertical agreements between suppliers and distributors naturally come under the head of improvements in distribution[4].

An important question is to determine how broad the criteria in Article 81(3) are: to use an analogy from many card games, in what circumstances can a 'benefit' under Article 81(3) 'trump' a restriction of competition under Article 81(1), with the result that an agreement which would have been prohibited under Article 81(1) is in fact permitted under Article 81(3)? The issue is significant not only in assessing the relationship of competition policy with other policies of the Community, but also in deciding which institutions should be called upon to make decisions. Specifically, if, as the Commission envisages in its *White Paper on Modernisation*, decisions under Article 81(3) will in the future be made by national competition authorities ('NCAs') and national courts, this would suggest that it would be preferable to interpret Article 81(3) in a narrow and legalistic manner.

(A)   A NARROW VIEW OF ARTICLE 81(3).   A narrow view of Article 81(3) is that it permits improvements in economic efficiency to be invoked by parties to an agreement so that they may obtain exemption notwithstanding the fact that their agreement restricts competition: according to this view, the very wording of

---

17   Cases 56/64 and 58/64 *Consten and Grundig v Commission* [1966] ECR 299, p 348, [1966] CMLR 418, p 478; *Astra* OJ [1993] L 20/23, [1994] 5 CMLR 226, para 22.
18   Cases 56/64 and 58/64 *Consten and Grundig v Commission* [1966] ECR 299, p 348, [1966] CMLR 418, p 478.
19   *Screensport/EBU* OJ [1991] L 63/32, [1992] 5 CMLR 273, para 71.
20   Note that services are not included here: this means that agreements on services are usually granted exemption under the heads of improvements to technical or economic progress, although in *Nuovo CEGAM* OJ [1984] L 99/29, [1984] 2 CMLR 484 the provisions on production and distribution were applied in the insurance services sector by analogy; see similarly *ABI* [1987] L 43/51, [1989] 4 CMLR 238 (banking); in the UK, section 9 of the Competition Act 1998 specifically includes improvements in the production or distribution of goods *or services*.
1   See eg *Re United Reprocessors GmbH* OJ [1976] L 51/7, [1976] 2 CMLR D1.
2   On specialisation agreements see ch 15, pp 517-520.
3   Ibid, pp 510-515.
4   On vertical agreements see ch 16, p 540ff.

Article 81(3), which speaks of improvements to production and distribution and to technical and economic progress, is suggestive of an efficiency standard. Article 81(3), therefore, allows a balancing of the restrictive effects of an agreement under Article 81(1) against the enhancement of efficiency under Article 81(3); in striving to achieve the right balance, the other criteria of Article 81(3) – a fair share to consumers, no dispensable restrictions and no substantial elimination of competition – should ensure that a reasonable outcome in the public interest is achieved. The Commission's *White Paper on Modernisation* explains Article 81(1) and 81(3) in this way[5].

(B)   A BROADER APPROACH TO ARTICLE 81(3).   However an alternative, and broader, view of Article 81(3) is possible: that it allows policies other than economic efficiency to be taken into account when deciding whether to allow agreements that are restrictive of competition. There are many important policies in the Community, for example on industry[6], the environment[7], employment[8], the regions[9] and culture[10], which go beyond the simple enhancement of efficiency. According to a broad view of Article 81(3), a benefit in terms of any of these policies could 'trump' a restriction of competition under Article 81(1).

Some of these broader considerations do seem to have had an influence on the application of Article 81(3) over the years. For example, in the early days competition policy was influenced by industrial policy, and this can still be detected in matters presented in the guise of competition law[11]: Amato points to the block exemption for specialisation agreements, with its acceptance that rationalisation in production fulfils the Article 81(3) criteria, as reflecting industrial policy rather than competition thinking[12]. Another example is cultural policy: in the case of the Commission's action on fixed prices for the retailing of German-language books, Commissioner Monti announced that the solution reached was fully supported by the Commissioner for Culture and Education 'with whom I have maintained regular contacts on this matter'[13]. To some extent the issue was side-stepped on this occasion by the Commission's conclusion that the agreement in question did not have an effect on trade between Member States, so that Article 81(1) was not applicable anyway[14].

There are other instances where non-competition matters have intruded into Article 81(3). In *Metro v Commission*[15] the ECJ considered that employment was

5   *White Paper*, para 57.
6   On industry under the EC Treaty, note Article 157 (ex Title XIII).
7   On environmental protection under the EC Treaty, note Article 6 (ex Article 3c) and Articles 174-176 (ex Title XVI).
8   On employment under the EC Treaty, note Articles 125-130 (ex Title VIa)
9   On economic and social cohesion under the EC Treaty, note Articles 158-162 (ex Title XIV).
10   On culture under the EC Treaty, note Article 151 (ex Article 128).
11   Note that by Article 157 EC the Community's industrial policy is to be conducted 'in accordance with a system of open and competitive markets'.
12   Amato *Antitrust and the Bounds of Power* (Hart Publishing, 1997) pp 63-64; the relevant block exemption is now Regulation 2658/2000, OJ [2000] L 304/3, [2001] 4 CMLR 800.
13   IP/00/183 of 23 February 2000; the German Government had called upon the Commission to remember cultural policy when deciding whether to unpick the resale price maintenance scheme for German language books, and the Council had made the same point; see the Council *Resolution on fixed book prices in homogeneous cross-border linguistic areas* OJ [1999] C 42/3.
14   OJ [2000] C 162/5, [2000] 5 CMLR 364.
15   Case 26/76 [1977] ECR 1875, [1978] 2 CMLR 1, para 43; see similarly Case 42/84 *Remia BV and Verenigde Bedrijven Nutricia NV v Commission* [1985] ECR 2545, [1987] 1 CMLR 1.

a relevant factor under the first condition in Article 81(3), saying the agreement was 'a stabilising factor with regard to the provision of employment which, since it improves the general conditions of production, especially when market conditions are unfavourable, comes within the framework of the objectives to which reference may be had pursuant to Article [81(3)]'. When considering whether an exemption might be given to a joint venture to produce a 'multi-purpose vehicle' in Portugal in *Ford/Volkswagen*[16], the Commission 'took note' of 'exceptional circumstances' in that it would bring a large number of jobs and substantial foreign investment to one of the poorest regions of the Community, promoting harmonious development, reducing regional disparities and furthering European market integration[17]. The Commission emphasised, however, that this would not be enough in itself to make an exemption possible unless the other conditions of Article 81(3) were fulfilled[18]. In its submissions to the CFI when the decision was challenged, the Commission argued that it was possible to take into account factors other than those expressly mentioned in Article 81(3), including, for example, the maintenance of employment[19]. The Commission has been considering the question of exempting the collective selling of broadcasting rights for football and appears unwilling to limit the analysis to 'simple economic considerations', and recognises the need to redistribute revenue in order 'to promote sporting activities within the population, as well as providing for interesting sporting competitions'[20]. The issue of the application by the Commission of the competition rules to the system of transfer fees in football was taken up in the UK at prime ministerial level in September 2000[1]. In *Stichting Baksteen*[2] the Commission considered that the restructuring of the Dutch brick industry, involving coordinated closures 'carried out in acceptable social conditions, including the redeployment of employees', promoted technical and economic progress[3]. In *CECED*[4] the Commission granted an individual exemption to an agreement between manufacturers of domestic appliances (washing-machines etc) which would lead to energy efficiencies, and in doing so noted not only individual economic benefits to consumers from lower energy bills but also the 'collective environmental benefits' that would flow from the agreement[5], referring specifically to the Community's environmental policy in its decision.

It is clear, therefore, that a number of factors have been influential in decisions under Article 81(3), not all of which can be considered to be 'narrow' improvements in efficiency. There are significant proponents of the view that Article 81(3) does admit broad, non-competition considerations[6].

16 OJ [1993] L 20/14, [1993] 5 CMLR 617.
17 Ibid, paras 23, 28 and 36; see also the Commission Press Release, IP/92/1083 of 23 December 1992.
18 Ibid, para 36.
19 Case T-17/93 *Matra Hachette v Commission* [1994] ECR II-595, para 96; on this case generally, see Swaak (1995) 32 CML Rev 1271.
20 See Jean-François Pons, *Sport and European Competition Policy* [1999] Fordham Corporate Law Institute (ed Hawk), ch 6; this speech can be accessed at http://europa.eu.int/search/s97.vts.
1   See eg Financial Times, 7 September 2000.
2   OJ [1994] L 131/15, [1995] 4 CMLR 646.
3   Ibid, paras 27-28.
4   OJ [2000] L 187/47, [2000] 5 CMLR 635.
5   Ibid, paras 55-57.
6   See eg Siragusa in *European Competition Law Annual 1997: Objectives of Competition Policy* (eds Ehlermann and Laudati, Hart Publishing, 1998) p 39; Faull, giving the Burrell lecture in London, 21 February 2000, said that social policy can 'reasonably credibly' be brought within Article 81(3).

(C)   IS A RESOLUTION OF THE NARROW AND THE BROADER APPROACHES POSSIBLE?   This discussion suggests that there is uncertainty – even confusion – as to the proper application of Article 81(3). However, it is necessary to achieve a resolution of the various approaches, in particular because, under the Commission's *White Paper* proposals, decisions under Article 81(3) will, in the future, be made by NCAs and national courts as well as by the Commission itself. These institutions must know the limits of their discretion under Article 81(3); furthermore, they seem ill-placed to balance the restriction of competition that an agreement might entail against a broad range of Community policies; they would have less difficulty, however, in applying a 'narrow' interpretation of Article 81(3), limited to a consideration of economic efficiencies.

These considerations suggest that Article 81(3) ought to be interpreted in a narrow rather than a broad manner, according to standards and by reference to principles that can properly be regarded as justiciable in courts of law. This may require some *ex post* rationalisation of earlier judgments of the Community courts such as *Metro* and *Remia and Nutricia*, coupled with a more restrained and legalistic approach on the part of the Commission in its future decision-making and other pronouncements on Article 81(3). This may explain why in recent decisions, such as *Reims II*[7] and *CECED*[8], the Commission has provided quite detailed explanations for the application of Article 81(3): in doing so, it has given guidance on the scope of that provision. Further insights into its thinking can be obtained from the *Guidelines on Vertical Restraints*[9] and from the *Guidelines on Horizontal Cooperation Agreements*[10]. Paragraph 32 of the *Horizontal Guidelines* specifically refers to the benefits in Article 81(3) as 'economic benefits', and makes no reference to the broader considerations of policy considered above. For the post-modernisation provisions to work, it is necessary that Article 81(3) should be operated according to proper legal standards, and the Commission has an important rôle to play in making this possible.

As a postscript to this discussion, it is interesting to note that the European Community Merger Regulation ('the ECMR') also refers in Article 2(1)(b) to 'technical and economic progress'[11], but only as one of the 'appraisal criteria' to be taken into account by the Commission when making a decision on the compatibility of a concentration with the common market, and only provided that it is to consumers' advantage and is not an obstacle to competition; it appears from this formulation that technical and economic progress cannot trump the anti-competitive effect of the creation or strengthening of a dominant position, in the way that Article 81(3) can trump the restriction of competition under Article 81(1)[12]. There seems to be an asymmetry between Article 81(3) and the treatment of technical and economic progress in the ECMR, and Ehlermann has remarked that it may not be sustainable in the long run to have a strictly economic competition goal in the ECMR but non-economic considerations included in Article 81(3)[13].

---

7   OJ [1999] L 275/17, [2000] 4 CMLR 704.
8   OJ [2000] L 187/47, [2000] 5 CMLR 635.
9   OJ [2000] C 291/1, [2000] 5 CMLR 1176.
10   OJ [2001] C 3/2, [2001] 4 CMLR 819.
11   Council Regulation 4064/89 OJ [1989] L 395/1, [1990] 4 CMLR 286, as amended by Regulation 1310/97 OJ [1997] L 180/1.
12   See ch 21, pp 778-779.
13   See Ehlermann in *Ehlermann and Laudati* (n 6 above) p 480.

(ii) Fair share to consumers

The parties must show that a fair share of the benefit that results from an agreement will accrue to consumers. Generally the transmission of benefits to the consumer depends on the intensity of competition within the relevant market[14]. For the purpose of this limb of Article 81(3) a 'consumer' does not necessarily mean a member of the public who purchases goods or services for personal use: in many cases such a person may be too far removed from the level of the market at which the agreement takes effect to be shown to receive any benefit. Undertakings which acquire products in the course of their trade qualify as consumers[15]. This does not mean that Article 81(3) is unconcerned about the interest of the public 'at large'. On the contrary, the fourth head of Article 81(3) should protect this wider interest by ensuring that competition in the relevant market is not substantially eliminated.

The Commission has not tried to give a definition of a 'fair share' for this purpose, and it is doubtful that fairness for these purposes could be given precise meaning. The expression clearly gives the Commission a broad discretion. On several occasions it has held that an agreement failed to yield a fair share to consumers. In *Re VBBB and VBVB Agreement*[16] it concluded that resale price maintenance in the books market failed under this head, since the system deprived consumers of choice and prevented them from seeking and obtaining lower prices. In *Vichy*[17] the Commission did not accept that consumers benefited from a restriction that a certain brand of skin care products could be distributed only through pharmacies. In *Screensport/EBU*[18] the Commission did accept that the establishment of Eurosport, a transnational satellite television channel dedicated to sport, might be beneficial to consumers in the short term, but in the longer term it considered that the consumer might be better served by having a choice of channels, differing in style, content and quality. In *Re VNP and COBELPA*[19] the Commission held that an information agreement which made information available on the selling but not on the buying side of the market failed to yield a fair share to consumers. In other cases the Commission has been more sanguine about this issue, particularly where the intensity of competition in the market was likely to ensure the transmission of any benefits to customers, or where consumers themselves had indicated their approval of and enthusiasm for the agreement in question[20].

In *SPO v Commission*[1] SPO, a Dutch building association, appealed to the CFI to overturn a Commission decision[2] refusing to grant an Article 81(3) exemption to various of its rules which were designed to combat the effects of

---

14 See the *Guidelines on Horizontal Cooperation Agreements* (n 10 above), para 34.
15 See eg *Re ACEC/Berliet Agreements* JO [1968] L 201/7, [1968] CMLR D35; *Kabel–und Metallwerke Neumeyer AG and Etablissements Luchaire SA Agreement* OJ [1975] L 222/34, [1975] 2 CMLR D40.
16 OJ [1982] L 54/36, [1982] 2 CMLR 344, upheld on appeal Cases 43/82 and 63/82 *VBVB v Commission* [1984] ECR 19, [1985] 1 CMLR 27.
17 OJ [1991] L 75/57 upheld on appeal Case T–19/91 *Société d'Hygiene Dermatologique de Vichy v Commission* [1992] ECR II-415.
18 OJ [1991] L 63/32, [1992] 5 CMLR 273.
19 OJ [1977] L 242/10, [1977] 2 CMLR D28.
20 See eg *GEC Ltd and Weir Group Ltd Agreement* OJ [1977] L 327/26, [1978] 1 CMLR D42.
1   Case T-29/92 [1995] ECR II-289, upheld on appeal to the ECJ, Case C-137/95P [1996] ECR I-1611.
2   OJ [1992] L 92/1, [1993] 5 CMLR 135.

'ruinous competition'. Neither the Commission nor the CFI considered whether this aim could constitute a benefit for the purposes of the first limb of Article 81(3) (although the CFI doubted whether it would be possible to distinguish 'ruinous competition' from healthy competition, stating that all competition is ruinous to inefficient companies). However, when assessing whether a fair share of the possible benefits resulting from the agreement accrued to consumers, the CFI upheld the Commission's reasoning that this would not be the case since, by restricting competition, the rules necessarily deprived consumers of any potential benefits arising from the arrangements.

In *Reims II*[3] the Commission acknowledged that prices might rise for some consumers, but it was satisfied that other benefits – for example, the elimination of cross-subsidisation in the postal sector and improved service standards – were sufficient to offset this.

(iii) No dispensable restrictions

The Commission will not grant an exemption if the restriction of competition which it would entail is greater than is necessary to procure the benefit in question: there must be no restrictions that are 'not indispensable'. This is, in effect, a manifestation of the Community principle of proportionality. A helpful way of discovering what type of clauses the Commission will object to is to look at the so-called 'black lists' in its block exemption Regulations, such as Article 4 of Regulation 2790/99[4]; the inclusion of black–listed provisions will prevent the block exemption from applying. Price-fixing or geographic market-sharing would normally not be regarded as indispensable, although the possibility of an exemption even for these practices cannot be entirely ruled out[5]. Export and import bans will almost inevitably be considered not indispensable, since they are so clearly contrary to the 'single market imperative'[6]. However it has consistently been held that some measure of exclusivity for distributors and licensees may be an indispensable feature of distribution agreements and licences of intellectual property rights which is why, for example, it is permissible under Regulation 2790/99 on vertical agreements[7] to grant territorial and customer exclusivity, and even to have a ban on active sales outside the territory or customer group, provided that passive sales remain possible: this is the compromise that is struck between the goal of market integration and the legitimate needs of producers and their distributors and licensees[8]. In horizontal agreements the Commission has accepted that various restrictions may be indispensable: for example in specialisation agreements it is acceptable that each party agrees to forego production of the goods that the other is to produce[9]; in research and development agreements it may be necessary for parent companies to agree to refrain from research in an area entrusted to a jointly-owned subsidiary[10].

3   OJ [1999] L 275/17, [2000] 4 CMLR 704; see p 128 above.
4   OJ [1999] L 336/21, [2000] 4 CMLR 398.
5   See p 124 above.
6   See ch 1, p 19 and ch 2, p 47.
7   OJ [1999] L 336/21, [2000] 4 CMLR 398.
8   See further on Regulation 2790/99 ch 16, pp 567-591; on Regulation 240/96 for technology transfer agreements, see ch 19, pp 688-696.
9   See further ch 15, pp 517-520.
10   Ibid, pp 510-515.

Much of the Commission's attention when dealing with notifications for exemption goes into the issue of indispensability, and under this head it will encourage the parties to remove those elements of their agreement which it considers to be objectionable. The Commission will often impose conditions or obligations upon firms when granting an exemption to ensure that they do not operate the agreement in a way which is more restrictive than it is willing to countenance[11].

In *Publishers' Association v Commission*[12] the ECJ annulled a decision of the Commission[13], and set aside a judgment of the CFI[14], for errors in relation to the indispensability of restrictions under Article 81(3). The Publishers' Association had sought exemption for the Net Book Agreement, under which publishers agreed that 'net books' would not be sold to the public at less than the net published price. The Commission found that the Agreement infringed Article 81(1), and that a collective system of fixed prices was not indispensable to the attainment of the objectives of the Publishers' Association. The CFI upheld the Commission's decision refusing exemption. The ECJ, however, held that the CFI had erred in law in doing so. It had wrongly failed to consider whether there existed a 'single language area' forming a single market for books in Ireland and the UK; without doing so, it could not have carried out a detailed review of the indispensability of the restrictions arising from the Agreements. Furthermore, the Commission's decision was found to have been insufficiently reasoned, since it failed to show why the Publishers' Association's argument, that the 1962 judgment of the Restrictive Practices Court in the UK upholding the Net Book Agreements was evidence of the benefits flowing therefrom for the purpose of Article 81(3), was unsound[15].

In *Métropole Télévision SA v Commission*[16] the CFI, on the application of third party complainants, annulled a decision of the Commission granting individual exemption to the regulations of the European Broadcasting Union on the ground that it had erred in law on the issue of indispensability. The judgment is considered in some detail below[17]; *inter alia* it is of interest in showing that the Commission's determination of indispensability must conform to the proper legal standard. In *European Night Services*[18] the CFI held that a condition attached to an individual exemption by the Commission, that the operators of certain railways services should supply equivalent services to third parties on non-discriminatory terms, should be overturned since the Commission had failed to show that it was necessary to prevent the restrictions in the agreement from going beyond what was indispensable[19].

---

11 See pp 140-141 below.
12 Case C-360/92 P *Publishers' Association v Commission* [1995] ECR I-23, [1995] 5 CMLR 33.
13 OJ [1989] L 22/12, [1989] 4 CMLR 825.
14 [1992] ECR II-1995, [1992] 5 CMLR 120.
15 Resale price maintenance for books was authorised in the UK by the Restrictive Practices Court from 1962 (LR 3 RP 246, [1962] 3 All ER 751, RPC) until 13 March 1997, when the Restrictive Practices Court concluded that the practice should discontinue: see the 1997 *Annual Report of the DGFT*, p 49.
16 Cases T-528/93 etc [1996] ECR II-649, [1996] 5 CMLR 386.
17 See pp 135-136 below.
18 Cases T-374/94 etc [1998] ECR II-3141, [1998] 5 CMLR 718.
19 Ibid, paras 205-221.

(iv)   No substantial elimination of competition

If the result of an agreement would be substantially to eliminate competition it will not be given an exemption. For example in *Van Landewyck v Commission*[20] the ECJ upheld the Commission's decision that an agreement affecting over 80% of the market for cigarettes in Belgium failed under this head, while in *Re WANO Schwarzpulver GmbH*[1] the Commission refused exemption to an agreement which would effectively seal off the UK market. In some cases the Commission has not paid a great deal of attention to this head of Article 81(3), either because an agreement has already failed under the other provisions, or because it has already clocked up sufficient merit marks under the other heads to qualify for lenient treatment under this one. On some occasions the Commission has noted that an agreement, far from eliminating competition, would have a pro-competitive effect: for example, in *TPS*[2] it said that the agreement in question would stimulate competition in the French pay-TV market. This part of Article 81(3) is important because it underpins the philosophy of Article 81 generally, and the Commission will be sceptical of agreements which are entered into by firms with large market shares. Even so, there have been a few notable occasions on which major companies have satisfied this part of Article 81(3) where they wished to implement an important technological project, particularly where they faced substantial competitive pressure from non-EC undertakings[3].

In some cases, particularly on crisis or 'restructuring' cartels, a problem for the Commission has been to show convincingly that an agreement would not substantially eliminate competition. In *Bayer/BP Chemicals*[4] the Commission was clearly sensitive to this problem and explained at length that the geographic market for polyethylene, the subject-matter of the agreement, was the entire EC as it could be transported cheaply and safely; there were 14 producers in the EC; imports from third countries were increasing; there was considerable inter-state trade; and barriers to entry were minimal. This being so there was a reasonable degree of workable competition in the market, so that a restructuring arrangement between two major undertakings did not substantially eliminate competition[5].

In deciding whether an agreement might substantially eliminate competition, it is necessary to define the relevant product and geographic markets. The Commission's *Notice on Market Definition*[6] gives guidance on these concepts. In each case the definition of the product and geographic markets must turn on the particular facts. An incorrect assessment by the Commission can be challenged before the CFI. In *Kali und Salz AG v Commission*[7] the Commission's decision was annulled for its failure to identify the product market.

It will be seen below that some of the block exemption Regulations apply only to agreements between undertakings with less than a specified market share: this is an expression of the requirement in Article 81(3) that an exempted agreement must not result in a substantial elimination of competition. Similarly, the

20 Cases 209/78 etc [1980] ECR 3125, [1981] 3 CMLR 134.
1   OJ [1978] L 322/26, [1979] 1 CMLR 403.
2   OJ [1999] L 90/6, [1999] 5 CMLR 168, paras 135-138.
3   See eg *Re Bayer AG and Gist-Brocades NV Agreement* OJ [1976] L30 13, [1976] 1 CMLR D 98; *Olivetti/Canon* OJ [1988] L 52/51, [1989] 4 CMLR 940.
4   OJ [1988] L 150/35, [1989] 4 CMLR 24.
5   See similarly *Enichem/ICI* OJ [1988] L 50/18, [1989] 4 CMLR 54.
6   OJ [1997] C 372/5, [1998] 4 CMLR 177; see ch 1, p 26ff.
7   Cases 19, 20/74 [1975] ECR 499, [1975] 2 CMLR 154.

Regulations provide the Commission with the power to withdraw the benefit of a block exemption in relation to a particular agreement where it could result in a substantial elimination of competition.

(B) Unilateral action and Article 81(3)

The decision of the Commission in *Re Ford Werke AG Agreement (No 2)*[8] revealed an additional and significant feature of its attitude to Article 81(3). In that case Ford notified its standard distribution agreement to the Commission. The Commission refused to grant an exemption, not because it objected to any particular clauses in the agreement, but because Ford's distribution policy as actually implemented produced effects which overall were inimical to the underlying objectives of competition policy. Ford had ceased to supply right–hand drive cars to the German market in the numbers it had formerly done. This was intended to protect the position of Ford of Britain and its dealers there, and deprived consumers of the possibility of acquiring cars from the Continent at considerably lower prices. Viewed in its overall context, Ford Werke was acting in a way which compartmentalised the common market and so its distribution agreement was ineligible for exemption. The decision, which was upheld by the ECJ on appeal[9], means that, when applying for an exemption, the practical operation of an agreement must be considered as well as its actual provisions. The Commission therefore has some power over the unilateral conduct of a single undertaking through the way in which it reaches decisions under Article 81(3).

(C) Relationship between Article 81(3) and Article 82

The relationship between conduct exempted from the prohibition of Article 81(1) under Article 81(3) and the application of Article 82, which forbids the abuse of a dominant position, can be problematic. A claim that the Commission ought not to have granted an exemption to a dominant undertaking failed in *ANCIDES v Commission*[10], where the complainant failed to adduce evidence to show that the recipient of the exemption was dominant. However, the Commission would be unlikely to grant an individual exemption where there was a danger of serious harm to competition: the last limb of Article 81(3) requires it to consider whether an agreement might substantially eliminate competition. In *Decca Navigator System*[11] the Commission refused to grant individual exemption to conduct that amounted to an abuse under Article 82.

The relationship between the block exemptions and Article 82 was considered by the CFI in *Tetra Pak Rausing SA v Commission* (Tetra Pak I)[12], reviewing the Commission's decision in *Tetra Pak I (BTG Licence)*[13]. The Commission had

8   OJ [1983] L 327/31, [1984] 1 CMLR 596.
9   Cases 25, 26/84 *Ford v Commission* [1985] ECR 2725, [1985] 3 CMLR 528; the ECJ decided the case differently from the Commission (see ch 3, p 87), but it specifically upheld the Commission on this point at para 33 of its judgment.
10 Case 43/85 [1987] ECR 3131, [1988] 4 CMLR 821.
11 OJ [1989] L 43/27, [1990] 4 CMLR 627, para 122.
12 Case T–51/89 [1990] ECR II-309, [1991] 4 CMLR 334; see also Case T-65/89 *BPB Industries plc v Commission* [1993] ECR II-389, [1993] 5 CMLR 32, para 75.
13 OJ [1988] L 272/27, [1988] 4 CMLR 47.

held that Tetra Pak had abused a dominant position by acquiring, through its purchase of another company, an exclusive patent licence. This licence benefited from block exemption under Regulation 2349/84[14] (since replaced by Regulation 240/96[15]). During the Commission's administrative procedure Tetra Pak offered to abandon all claims to exclusivity in the licence. Nonetheless the Commission adopted a decision that, until such time as the exclusivity was abandoned, Tetra Pak had been abusing its dominant position on the market, rejecting Tetra Pak's argument that it could not be guilty of abuse until such time as the Commission had withdrawn the block exemption in accordance with Regulation 2349/84. The CFI upheld the decision of the Commission. The mere fact that an agreement benefits from block exemption does not mean that a dominant undertaking cannot be found to be abusing its dominant position by entering into or operating the agreement or becoming a party to it by acquisition. It would be wrong to require the Commission always to withdraw the benefit of the block exemption by individual action in order to prevent dominant firms from abusing their dominant position in such circumstances. The CFI said that the fact of a dominant undertaking acquiring an exclusive licence did not in itself constitute an abuse: the circumstances surrounding the acquisition, and in particular its effect on the competitive structure of the relevant market, had to be taken into account[16]. In this particular case the acquisition of the licence constituted an abuse because the right to use the technology protected by the licensed patent afforded the only opportunity that a competitor might have of effectively competing with Tetra Pak.

The CFI's judgment in *Tetra Pak* is of considerable importance. It eschews the two simplest answers to the question of the relationship of Article 81(3) with Article 82, that on the one hand conduct exempt under Article 81(3) cannot infringe Article 82 until the Commission withdraws the exemption and on the other that being party to an exclusive agreement inevitably involves an abuse of a dominant position. In each case one must analyse the market to determine the effect of the dominant firm's conduct. In *Cewal*[17] the Commission held, in the context of maritime transport, that the fact that some of Cewal's activities were covered by the block exemption for liner conferences contained in Article 3 of Regulation 4056/86[18] did not prevent the application of Article 82. This was upheld on appeal by the CFI[19] and the ECJ.[20]

(D)   Review by the CFI

The Commission's decisions on the application of Article 81(3) are subject to review by the CFI (formerly the ECJ). In *Consten and Grundig v Commission*[1] the ECJ indicated that it would not adopt an interventionist stance on applications for review; Article 81(3) involves complex evaluations of economic issues, and

14 Commission Regulation 2349/84, OJ [1984] L 219/5.
15 On Regulation 240/96 see ch 19, pp 688-696.
16 Case T-51/89 [1990] ECR II-309, [1991] 4 CMLR 334, para 23.
17 OJ [1993] L 34/20, [1995] 5 CMLR 198, para 50.
18 OJ [1986] L 378/4.
19 Cases T-24/93 etc *Compagnie Maritime Belge v Commission* [1996] ECR II-1201, [1997] 4 CMLR 273.
20 Cases C-395/96 P etc *Compagnie Maritime Belge Transports SA v Commission* [2000] All ER (EC) 385, [2000] 4 CMLR 1076, para 130.
1   Cases 56/64 and 58/64 [1966] ECR 299, [1966] CMLR 418.

the ECJ considered that this task is essentially one for the Commission. The Court will confine itself to examining the relevant facts and the legal consequences deduced therefrom; it will not substitute its decision for the Commission's. The Community Courts have maintained this approach, emphasising the extent of the discretion available to the Commission when dealing with notifications for exemption and (by implication) its unwillingness to interfere with the exercise of this discretion[2]. However, it is essential that the Commission's decision should be adequately reasoned, and where there is a defect in this respect the courts will be prepared to annul the decision in question[3]. Similarly, the CFI will annul a Commission decision where it has seriously misapprehended the facts of a particular case[4].

In *Métropole v Commission*[5] a third party successfully persuaded the CFI that an individual exemption granted by the Commission to the European Broadcasting Union should be annulled due to an error of law on the Commission's part. The Commission had granted an individual exemption to the regulations of the European Broadcasting Union governing the joint negotiation, acquisition and sharing of television rights to sports events, subject to conditions designed to permit third parties to have access to the television rights in question and to ensure that the Commission would be kept informed of the practical application of the regulations[6]. A number of television companies, not members of the EBU, sought the annulment of the Commission's decision granting individual exemption. The CFI, having decided that the applications were admissible (in so far as the Commission had contested this in the first place), considered, first, whether the restrictions on competition arising from the rules on membership of the EBU were 'indispensable' in the sense of Article 81(3)(a); and, second, whether the 'particular public mission' of members of the EBU was relevant to an assessment of the EBU regulations under Article 81(3), and in particular paragraph (a) thereof, as opposed to Article 86(2).

As to the first issue, the CFI considered, as in its view the Commission was obliged to do, whether the EBU membership rules were objective and sufficiently determinate so as to enable them to be applied uniformly and in a non-discriminatory manner vis-à-vis all potential active members: unless this pre-condition was satisfied, it would be impossible to be sure that the restriction of competition inherent in the rules was indispensable. The CFI found that the Commission had not carried out such an investigation, and had consequently not considered whether the rules were indispensable: it had therefore committed an error of law warranting the annulment of the exemption. On the second point, the CFI found that, in as much as the Commission had concluded in its decision that Article 86(2) was not applicable, it could not then take into account factors coming within its ambit in the context of Article 81(3). This also constituted an error of law.

This judgment demonstrates that a third party may be able successfully to challenge the grant of an exemption, though it should be said that this is the only

---

2   See eg Case 26/76 *Metro SB-Grossmärkte v Commission* [1977] ECR 1875, [1978] 2 CMLR 1; Case T-7/93 *Langnese-Iglo GmbH v Commission* [1995] ECR II-1533, [1995] 5 CMLR 602, para 178.
3   Case C-360/92 P *Publishers' Association v Commission* [1995] ECR I-23, [1995] 5 CMLR 33.
4   Cases T-79/95 R etc *SNCF and BRB v Commission* [1996] ECR II-1491, [1997] 4 CMLR 334.
5   Cases T-528/93 etc [1996] ECR II-649, [1996] 5 CMLR 386.
6   OJ [1993] L 179/23, [1995] 4 CMLR 56.

occasion in which this has been achieved. In the *Métropole* case the Commission at a later stage adopted a further decision granting exemption to the rules in question in *Eurovision*[7].

2. NOTIFICATION FOR INDIVIDUAL EXEMPTION

(A) The Commission's monopoly over the grant of individual exemptions

The Commission has sole power (subject to review by the Community Courts) to grant individual exemptions[8]. This monopoly over the grant of individual exemptions means that the Commission has had the opportunity to develop its policy towards various types of agreement over a period of time, and in some cases to give expression to this policy in its block exemption Regulations. However the monopoly has its drawbacks, since the Commission has insufficient staff to deal with the enormous volume of agreements that are notified to it: the result is that severe delays can be experienced, considerable business time is spent collecting the data and preparing Form A/B, and substantial expense is incurred, not least on legal fees. The Commission itself is overburdened with notifications, many of which concern agreements that have no seriously anti-competitive effect, with the consequence that it is distracted from other tasks, such as the pursuit of cartels and abusive behaviour. For example, in 1997, it received 221 notifications[9]; in 1998, it received a further 216[10]; the number dropped a little in 1999 to 162[11], and to 101 in 2000[11a], over this period, the total number of formal exemptions given was negligible. The problems noted have been ameliorated to some extent by issuing Notices providing guidance on the application of the competition rules[12]; by the adoption of block exemption Regulations[13], in some cases containing an opposition procedure[14]; by the informal settlement of some cases[15]; and by other procedural changes[16]. However, the 'problem' of the monopoly over the grant of individual exemptions has not been eliminated[17]; this is what led the Commission, in the White Paper of 1999, to propose abolition of notification altogether[18].

---

7   OJ [2000] L 151/18, [2000] 5 CMLR 650; the case has been appealed by third parties to the CFI, Cases T-185/00 etc *Métropole Television (M6) v Commission* (judgment pending).
8   Regulation 17/62, Article 9(1).
9   See the Commission's XXVIIth *Report on Competition* Policy (1997), point 20.
10 See the Commission's XXVIIIth *Report on Competition Policy* (1998), pp 45 and 46.
11 See the Commission's XXIXth *Report on Competition Policy* (1999), point 7.
11a See the Commission's XXXth *Report on Competition Policy* (2000) Table D.
12 See ch 3, pp 105-107.
13 See pp 141-146 below.
14 See p 146 below.
15 See ch 7, pp 217-218.
16 Eg by requiring more information on Form A/B in the case of certain joint ventures in order to accelerate the procedure for dealing with them: see pp 139-140 below.
17 The stock of 'antitrust' cases pending before the Commission at the end of 2000, that is to say of cases under Articles 81 and 82 as well as Articles 31 and 86 on state monopolies and monopoly rights, amounted to 931: XXXth *Report on Competition Policy* (2000), p 61; this figure was down from 1,204 at the end of 1998.
18 See pp 146-147 below.

(B) Procedure for obtaining an individual exemption

(i) Article 4(1) of Regulation 17/62: notification a pre-requisite for individual exemption

As a general proposition, an agreement can benefit from an individual exemption only where it has been notified to the Commission[19] and exemption can be given only prospectively from the date of notification, not retrospectively to an earlier date[20].

(ii) Article 4(2) of Regulation 17/62: agreements in respect of which notification is not necessary

There are some exceptions to the two basic rules just discussed; these exceptions were fairly minor until 1999, but they have been significantly amended by Regulation 1216/99[1] with the highly important consequence that all vertical agreements can now benefit from a retrospective exemption, whether notified or not. Article 4(2) of Regulation 17/62, as amended by Regulation 1216/99, provides that the following agreements do not require to have been notified in order to be eligible for individual exemption:
- agreements where the parties are from the same Member State and the agreement does not relate to imports or exports (Article 4(2)(1));
- vertical agreements between two or more undertakings each operating, for the purpose of the agreement, at a different level of the production or distribution chain, relating to the conditions under which the parties may purchase, sell or resell certain goods or services (Article 4(2)(2)(a));
- certain bilateral assignments or licences of intellectual property rights (Article 4(2)(2)(b));
- agreements that have as their sole object the development or uniform application of standards or types, joint R&D or specialisation, where the parties' market share is below 15% and their turnover is below EUR 200 million (Article 4(2)(3)).

Article 6(2) of Regulation 17/62 provides for the possibility of retrospective exemption in the case of the agreements described in Article 4(2): for example in June 1999 the Commission granted retroactive exemption to the terms in Scottish and Newcastle's leases of public houses, which contained a 'beer tie', on the basis of Article 4(2)(1)[2]. Historically the provisions of Article 4(2) have been interpreted narrowly by the Commission and the Community Courts, and their use has been quite limited; however, the extension of Article 4(2) to vertical agreements, coupled with the desire of the Commission to be relieved from the burden of notifications so that it can concentrate on the task of pursuing cartels and abusive behaviour, mean that this provision will be of more significance in the future, until such time as the system of notification is abolished altogether. Legal advisers, faced with the possibility that an individual exemption may be needed for an agreement, ought always to pause to consider whether non-notification is an option. In relation to vertical agreements, it would appear to be the case that Regulation 1216/99 has retrospective effect: that is to say *any*

19 Regulation 17/62, Article 4(1).
20 Ibid, Article 6(1).
1   OJ [1999] L 148/5.
2   *Scottish and Newcastle* OJ [1999] L 186/28, [1999] 5 CMLR 831; see similarly *Bass* OJ [1999] L 186/1, [1999] 5 CMLR 782.

vertical agreement may benefit from retrospective exemption, irrespective of notification, whether it was entered into before or after Regulation 1216/99 entered into force.

There are some other exceptions to the requirement of notification in order to obtain an exemption in the procedural Regulations in the maritime and air transport sectors[3].

(iii)   No provisional validity

As a general proposition agreements do not benefit from 'provisional validity'. That is to say an agreement which infringes Article 81(1) and which is denied an exemption is not valid and enforceable until the date of the Commission decision rejecting exemption: it will have been unenforceable *ab initio*. If exemption is given, it can be effective from the date of notification, where notification is required, or from an earlier date, where no notification is required. There are exceptions to the rule that there is no provisional validity, for example in relation to 'old' agreements entered into before Regulation 17/62 came into force, but for commercial agreements entered into today the possibility of provisional validity does not exist[4].

(iv)   Immunity from fines

A benefit that follows from notification is that the parties cannot be fined for operating the agreement after it has been notified[5]. This immunity from fines can be withdrawn by a Commission decision, and this has happened on a few occasions[6]. The position on immunity from fines in the procedural Regulations in the transport sector needs to be examined by reference to the provisions of each Regulation[7].

(v)   Procedural regulations

When notifying an agreement for individual exemption, recourse must be had to the relevant procedural Regulation. The position is complicated, since the Commission's powers to implement Articles 81 and 82 derive from different Council Regulations according to the sector in question. Regulation 17/62 is the 'general' Regulation under which most of the Commission's enforcement activity takes place. However there are separate Council Regulations for rail, road and inland waterway transport (Regulation 1017/68[8]), maritime transport (Regulation 4056/86[9]) and air transport (Regulation 3975/87[10]). It was formerly the case that each of these Regulations gave rise to a procedural Regulation of the Commission explaining *inter alia* how notifications should be made; it was

3   See ch 23, p 859ff on these Regulations.
4   On provisional validity, see further ch 8, pp 262-263.
5   Regulation 17/62, Article 15(5); notification to the Commission also provides immunity from being fined under UK domestic competition law: Competition Act 1998, s 41(2).
6   Regulation 17/62, Article 15(6); see ch 7, p 230.
7   See ch 23, p 859ff on these Regulations.
8   OJ [1968] L 175/1.
9   OJ [1986] L 378/1.
10   OJ [1987] L 374/1.

essential to use the correct procedural Regulation for the agreement in question[11]. The position was simplified to some extent with effect from 1 February 1999, when Regulation 2843/98[12] entered into force and provided for a single form for the notification of agreements in the transport sector (the so-called 'Form TR'). Form A/B is used for all other notifications. The position can be presented in the following tabular form:

Sector	The economy generally	Rail, road and inland waterways	Maritime transport	Air transport
Council Implementing Regulation	17/62	1017/68	4056/86	3975/87
Commission Procedural Regulation	3385/94	2843/98	2843/98	2843/98
Form	A/B	TR	TR	TR

Where Regulation 17/62 is the relevant procedural Regulation, the format for Form A/B is set out in Regulation 3385/94[13]. The format for Form TR is set out in Regulation 2843/98. The 'form' is not a proforma document that has to be obtained from the Commission, completed and sent to it; rather it is a document that the parties themselves must create and submit to the Commission in the form, and subject to the other requirements, set out in the relevant Regulation.

(vi) Fast-track procedure for structural joint ventures

This chapter has noted the procedural problems that can be encountered in obtaining an individual exemption under Article 81(3); a particular difficulty can be the delay involved in obtaining a decision from the Commission. One way of dealing with this, in the case of structural joint ventures subject to Article 81(1), has been for the Commission to require more information to be provided in the notification than would be given in other cases: the *quid pro quo* for this is that the Commission will then be able to give a quicker decision (by comfort letter, if not by formal decision) than would otherwise have been the case. Regulation 3385/94 makes specific provision for this: in particular sections 6-10 (pages 42-45 of the Regulation as printed in the Official Journal) of chapter 11 of the Form A/B set out the additional information required. Many joint ventures are classified for the purpose of EC competition law as concentrations, which means that they are dealt with under the procedures of the ECMR (where they have a Community dimension) or under domestic law (where they do not). As a result they will not be subject to Article 81(1) and so will not be notified on Form

11 See Case C-264/95 P *Commission v UIC* [1997] ECR I-1287, [1997] 5 CMLR 49 for an
    example of the Commission proceeding under the wrong procedural Regulation.
12 OJ [1998] L 354/22, [1999] 4 CMLR 236.
13 OJ [1994] L 377/28.

A/B, but will instead be dealt with under the relevant procedural rules of EC or domestic merger control. However, in so far as a structural joint venture does not amount to a concentration, it might benefit from the fast-track procedure mentioned in this paragraph. The complex subject of determining whether a joint venture is subject to the ECMR is dealt with in chapter 21[14].

(vii)   Regulation 17/62, Article 8(1): specified period; conditions and obligations

When the Commission grants an individual exemption under Regulation 17/62, Article 8(1) provides that it shall do so for a specified period, and that it may attach conditions and obligations. Similar provisions will be found in the transport Regulations.

(A)   SPECIFIED PERIOD.   Exemption cannot be granted in perpetuity. The period permitted will depend on the circumstances and may range from a relatively short period, for example 5 to 10 years, to as much as 20 years in an exceptional case[15]. In *European Night Services v Commission*[16] the Commission had limited an individual exemption for an agreement to operate overnight passenger rail services between the UK and the Continent through the Channel Tunnel to a period of eight years; on appeal to the CFI, the parties successfully argued that the limited duration for the exemption, which in their view would prevent them from earning an adequate return on what was a major long-term investment, was vitiated by a lack of reasoning on the part of the Commission explaining why it thought that such a short period should be allowed. A particularly short duration for an individual exemption arose in *P & O Stena*[17], where the Commission allowed a joint venture for cross-channel ferry services from 10 March 1998 to 9 March 2001: the Commission wanted to be able to reconsider the situation once the effects of the abolition of duty-free concessions on the tourist travel market were known.

(B)   CONDITIONS AND OBLIGATIONS.   The Commission may impose conditions and obligations: an example will be found in *British Interactive Broadcasting*[18], where detailed conditions and obligations were attached to an individual exemption. Breach of a condition automatically terminates the exemption; breach of an obligation could lead to termination of the exemption, but not automatically so, and could lead to a fine under Article 15(2)(b) of Regulation 17/62. In some cases there are protracted discussions between the Commission and the parties in relation to conditions and obligations, in order that an adequate remedy is in place to prevent what might otherwise amount to an unacceptable restriction of competition. On a number of occasions the Commission has imposed reporting obligations on the parties to agreements, for example on the operation of a research and development agreement or the establishment of links between the parties to a joint venture. It may be possible to persuade the Commission that conditions and obligations attached to an individual exemption are no longer needed, as happened in the case of *Unisource*[19].

14 See ch 21, pp 748-751.
15 See eg *Delta Chemie/DDD* OJ [1988] L 309/34, [1989] 4 CMLR 535.
16 Joined Cases T-374/94 etc [1998] ECR II-3141, [1998] 5 CMLR 718.
17 OJ [1999] L 163/61, [2000] 5 CMLR 682; the exemption was renewed in June 2001: Commission Press Release IP/01/806, 7 June 2001.
18 OJ [1999] L 312/1, [1999] 4 CMLR 901.
19 OJ [2000] C 217/35, [2000] 5 CMLR 741.

In *Transocean Marine Paint Association v Commission*[20] the ECJ established an important procedural point that, should the Commission wish to impose conditions and obligations, it must give the parties an opportunity to be heard on this issue.

(viii) Renewal of individual exemptions

In several cases the Commission has renewed an exemption for a further period or periods[1], or sent a comfort letter effectively prolonging an earlier exemption. However the Commission will analyse carefully the legal, factual and economic context of the agreement in question before renewing an exemption. Renewal should not be anticipated as a mere administrative act: for example, the Commission conducted an in-depth investigation of whether individual exemption should be renewed for UIP[2], a joint distribution company for films established by Paramount, Universal Studios and MGM; the outcome was that the Commission sent a comfort letter renewing the exemption on 9 September 1999, after the parties had amended their agreements in material respects and after certain commitments had been offered[3].

(ix) Revocation of individual exemption

An individual exemption may be revoked or amended in certain circumstances, although there is no known case of this happening[4].

3. BLOCK EXEMPTIONS[5]

(A) Rôle of block exemptions

Article 81(3) foreshadowed the advent of block exemptions by providing both that agreements and *categories* of agreements could be granted exemption; in other words it envisaged the exemption of agreements on a generic basis as well as pursuant to individual notification. Block exemptions are normally produced by the Commission, acting under powers conferred upon it by regulations of the Council[6]. There are two exceptions to this, where the Council itself has granted the block exemption: the block exemption for certain agreements in the road and inland waterway sectors is provided by Article 4 of Council Regulation 1017/68[7] and block exemption for various agreements in the maritime transport sector is granted by Articles 3 to 6 of Council Regulation 4056/86[8]. Agreements within the terms of a block exemption do not need to be notified to the Commission:

---

20 Case 17/74 [1974] ECR 1063, [1974] 2 CMLR 459.
1 See Regulation 17/62, Article 8(2).
2 The initial exemption was given in July 1989, OJ [1989] L 226/25, [1990] 4 CMLR 749.
3 Commission Press Release IP/99/681; see OJ [1999] C 205/6, [1999] 5 CMLR 732.
4 Regulation 17/62, Article 8(3).
5 The terms 'bloc' and 'group' exemptions are also used: the expression 'block exemption' is used here as it is the most common one, and the one normally used by the Commission.
6 See pp 142-144 below for details.
7 OJ [1968] L 175/1.
8 OJ [1986] L 378/1.

they are valid without specific authorisation. The block exemptions therefore provide desirable legal certainty for firms; they are also important from the Commission's point of view, since they relieve it from a substantial number of notifications for individual exemption.

(B)   Vires and block exemptions currently in force

The Commission requires authority from the Council to issue block exemptions[9]. The Council has published a number of Regulations; these are listed below, along with the Commission Regulations currently in force under each Council Regulation.

(i)   *Council Regulation 19/65*

Regulation 19/65[10], as amended by Regulation 1215/99[11], authorises the Commission to grant block exemption to vertical agreements and to bilateral licences of intellectual property rights. The following Commission Regulations are in force under Council Regulation 19/65:
(a)   Regulation 1475/95 on distribution agreements for motor cars[12];
(b)   Regulation 240/96 on technology transfer agreements[13];
(c)   Regulation 2790/99 on vertical agreements[14]; this Regulation replaces, and is wider in effect than, Regulation 1983/83 on exclusive distribution agreements[15], Regulation 1984/83 on exclusive purchasing agreements[16] and Regulation 4087/88 on franchising agreements[17].

(ii)   *Council Regulation 2821/71*

Regulation 2821/71[18] authorises the Commission to grant block exemption in respect of standardisation agreements, research and development agreements and specialisation agreements. The following Commission Regulations are in force under Council Regulation 2821/71:
(a)   Regulation 2658/2000[19] on specialisation agreements; this Regulation replaces Regulation 417/85[20], as amended by Regulation 151/93[1];
(b)   Regulation 2659/2000[2] on research and development agreements; this Regulation replaces Regulation 418/85[3], as amended by Regulation 151/93[4].

9   The Council has power to confer such vires by virtue of Article 83(2)(b) of the Treaty.
10   JO [1965] p 533, OJ [1965–66] p 35.
11   OJ [1999] L 148/1.
12   OJ [1995] L 145/25; see ch 16, pp 592-593.
13   OJ [1996] L 31/2, [1996] 4 CMLR 405; see ch 19, pp 688-696.
14   OJ [1999] L 336/21, [2000] 4 CMLR 398; see ch 16, pp 567-591.
15   OJ [1983] L 173/1.
16   OJ [1983] L 173/5.
17   OJ [1988] L 359/46.
18   JO [1971] L 285/46, OJ [1971] p 1032.
19   OJ [2000] L 304/3, [2001] 4 CMLR 800; see ch 15, pp 517-520.
20   OJ [1985] L 53/1.
1   OJ [1993] L 121/8.
2   OJ [2000] L 304/7, [2001] 4 CMLR 808; see ch 15, pp 510-515.
3   OJ [1985] L 53/5.
4   See n 1 above.

(iii) Council Regulation 1017/68

Regulation 1017/68[5] itself provides block exemption for certain agreements between small-and medium-sized undertakings[6]. There are no Commission Regulations granting block exemption under Regulation 1017/68.

(iv) Council Regulation 4056/86

Regulation 4056/86[7] itself provides block exemption for certain liner conferences[8] and for certain agreements between transport users and conferences concerning the use of scheduled maritime transport services[9]. There are no Commission Regulations granting block exemption under Regulation 4056/86.

(v) Council Regulation 3976/87

Regulation 3976/87[10] authorises the Commission to grant block exemptions for certain agreements in the air transport sector. There is one Commission Regulation in force under Regulation 3976/87:
(a) Regulation 1617/93[11] as amended by Regulation 1523/96[12] on joint planning and coordination of schedules, joint operations, consultations on passenger and cargo tariffs on scheduled air services and slot allocation at airports; this Regulation was extended in force until 30 June 2002 in relation to passenger transit consultations and slot allocations, but not for joint planning and scheduling and joint operations[13].
(b) Regulation 3652/93[14] on agreements relating to computerised reservation systems for air transport services expired in 1998.

(vi) Council Regulation 1534/91

Regulation 1534/91[15] authorised the Commission to grant block exemptions in the insurance sector. The Commission adopted Regulation 3932/92[16] under the vires of this Council Regulation. The operation of Regulation 3932/92 was reviewed in 1999, the Commission having delivered a report to the Parliament on its operation to date[17].

---

5   OJ [1968] L 175/1.
6   See Article 4.
7   OJ [1986] L 378/1.
8   See Articles 3-5.
9   See Article 6.
10 OJ [1987] L 374/9.
11 OJ [1993] L 155/18.
12 OJ [1996] L 190/11.
13 Commission Regulation 1083/99, OJ [1999] L 131/27, [1999] 5 CMLR 205 and Commission Regulation 1324/2001, OJ [2001] L 177/56.
14 OJ [1993] L 333/37.
15 OJ [1991] L 143/1.
16 OJ [1992] L 398/7.
17 This can be accessed at http://europa.eu.int/comm/competition/antitrust/others/.

(vii)   Council Regulation 479/92

Regulation 479/92[18] authorised the Commission to grant block exemptions to consortia between liner shipping companies. The Commission adopted Regulation 823/2000[19] under the vires of this Regulation.

(C)   The format of block exemptions

The typical format of most block exemptions[20] is that they begin with a series of recitals which explain the policy of the Commission in adopting the regulation in question; these recitals may themselves be of legal significance, as they may be referred to for the purpose of construing the substantive provisions of the regulation itself where there are problems of interpretation. Each regulation will then confer block exemption upon a particular category of agreements: for example, Regulation 2790/99 block exempts vertical agreements, as defined in Article 2(1) thereof. The older block exemptions were very specific as to the clauses that could benefit from block exemption: only those set out in the so-called 'white list' would do so. This was considered by many critics to be too prescriptive and formalistic, and the three most recent block exemptions of the Commission are significantly different. Regulations 2790/99, 2658/2000 and 2659/2000, on vertical agreements, specialisation agreements and research and development agreements, eschew white lists. They do, however, contain black lists (as did all earlier regulations), setting out provisions that must not be included if an agreement is to enjoy block exemption. The exclusion of white lists from these new Regulations is a deliberate attempt on the part of the Commission to respond to the criticism that the block exemptions operate in too mechanical and legalistic a manner; they can usefully be referred to as 'new-style' block exemptions.

Most block exemptions have market share thresholds. For example each of the three new Regulations just referred to has one: under Regulation 2790/99, Article 3 provides that undertakings with a market share of more than 30% will not qualify for block exemption, although they may still be able to ask for individual exemption; as already noted, this may be available for a vertical agreement irrespective of whether it was notified[1]. Article 4 of the Regulation for specialisation agreements has a market share cap of 20%, and Article 4 of the Regulation for research and development agreements has one at 25%.

Each block exemption confers on the Commission a power of withdrawal in the event that a particular agreement has a detrimental effect on competition. Block exemption has been withdrawn from an agreement on only one occasion, in *Langnese-Iglo GmbH*[2]; the Commission's decision to do so was upheld on appeal by the CFI[3].

Regulation 2790/99 on vertical agreements contains a novel provision in Article 7, which gives a Member State the power to withdraw the benefit of the block exemption from vertical agreements which have effects incompatible with the

---

18   OJ [1992] L 55/3.
19   OJ [2000] L 100/24, [2000] 5 CMLR 92; this block exemption replaced the earlier Regulation 870/95, OJ [1995] L 89/7.
20   The block exemptions in the transport sector are, in some cases, drafted rather differently.
1   See pp 137-138 above.
2   OJ [1993] L 183/19, [1994] 4 CMLR 51.
3   Case T-7/93 [1995] ECR II-1533, [1995] 5 CMLR 602.

conditions of Article 81(3) within its territory or a part thereof, where that territory has all the characteristics of a distinct geographic market. Another novel provision of Regulation 2790/99 is Article 8, which gives power to the Commission, by regulation, to withdraw the benefit of the block exemption from an entire sector, where parallel networks of similar vertical restraints cover more than 50% of a relevant market.

(D) Characterisation of agreements to determine if block exemption is available

In order to benefit from a block exemption, an agreement must be generically of the type envisaged by the Commission when producing the regulation in question. This means that there is a need to ensure that the agreement is within the spirit as well as the letter of any particular regulation. On several occasions an agreement has failed at the point of 'characterisation'. For example in *Italian Cast Glass*[4] the Commission rejected an argument that what it regarded as a horizontal market-sharing agreement was within the block exemption on specialisation agreements; in *Boussois/Interpane*[5] the parties failed to persuade the Commission that a licence of know-how with associated patents fell within the block exemption on patent licensing; in *Siemens/Fanuc*[6] the Commission rejected an argument that a horizontal market-sharing agreement was covered by the block exemption on exclusive distribution agreements. In *Moosehead/ Whitbread*[7] the Commission concluded that a licence agreement between those two undertakings related primarily to the Moosehead trade mark, to which any know-how was ancillary; the consequence of this was that the now-repealed Regulation 556/89 on know-how licences was inapplicable and the parties had to notify the agreement in order to obtain an individual exemption[8]. In the case of Regulation 2790/99, the definition of a vertical agreement is a broad one, with the result that a much wider range of agreements will be block exempted than under the Regulations it replaces[9].

(E) *Delimitis v Henninger Bräu*

In order to benefit from a block exemption, an agreement must satisfy all the requirements of the relevant regulation. The ECJ held in *Delimitis v Henninger Bräu*[10] that where an agreement fails to do so, albeit only in a marginal way, block exemption will be unavailable and individual exemption required. Provisions in a block exemption derogating from the prohibition in Article 81(1) cannot be interpreted widely, nor in such a way as to extend the effects of the regulation further than is necessary for the protection of the interests that it is intended to safeguard[11].

---

4 OJ [1980] L 383/19, [1982] 2 CMLR 61.
5 OJ [1987] L 50/30, [1988] 4 CMLR 124.
6 OJ [1985] L 376/29, [1988] 4 CMLR 945.
7 OJ [1990] L 100/32, [1991] 4 CMLR 391.
8 See also *Quantel International-Continuum/Quantel SA* OJ [1992] L 235/9, [1993] 5 CMLR 497, paras 45–49 (non-application of Regulation 418/85).
9 See ch 16, pp 570-571.
10 Case C–234/89 [1991] ECR I-935, [1992] 5 CMLR 210.
11 Case T-9/92 *Automobiles Peugeot SA v Commission (No 2)* [1993] ECR II-493, [1995] 5 CMLR 696, para 37.

(F)   Compliance with a block exemption is not mandatory

It is not mandatory to comply with a block exemption. This point may seem obvious, but this did not prevent a French court referring this very question to the ECJ in *VAG France SA v Etablissements Magne SA*[12]. The Court held that the block exemption on the distribution of motor vehicles presented undertakings with the possibility of invoking its terms, but that it was not obligatory for them to do so. They might instead wish, for example, to apply for an individual exemption if they find it impossible to comply with the terms of a block exemption.

(G)   Opposition procedure

The Regulation on technology transfer contains what is known as an 'opposition procedure' whereby certain agreements which do not satisfy the terms of a block exemption can nonetheless benefit from an accelerated exemption procedure. The opposition procedure is an attempt to overcome the twin objections that block exemptions have a 'strait-jacketing' effect since they require parties to comply with provisions which may be inappropriate, and that (where parties do not submit to the strait–jacket) individual exemption involves an unacceptable delay. Opposition procedures will also be found in various regulations in the transport sector. Where the parties wish to invoke the opposition procedure, they must notify the agreement to the Commission on Form A/B (or the equivalent Form TR used in the transport sector). Then, unless the Commission takes objection to the agreement within a specified period, the agreement will qualify for exemption. It is possible that the Commission will agree that, where the parties notify an agreement under the opposition procedure, they may be permitted to omit some of the information that would normally have to be provided on Form A/B or Form TR. Regulation 3385/94 on Form A/B states, in its sixth recital, that the Commission is prepared to have discussions with the parties prior to notification, and this is something that should be considered where there is a possibility of invoking the opposition procedure.

The opposition procedure has not been a success in practice; very few notifications have been made, and of those several were unsuccessful. Regulation 2790/99 on vertical agreements does not contain an opposition procedure; nor do the new Regulations for specialisation and research and development agreements. It follows that the only opposition procedures extant are the one for technology transfer agreements and those in the transport sector. The procedure, therefore, will be of marginal significance in the future, and may lapse altogether; the abolition of the notification system proposed in the White Paper makes this all the more likely.

4.   THE COMMISSION'S WHITE PAPER ON MODERNISATION

As mentioned at the start of this chapter, in April 1999 the Commission adopted a White Paper on *Modernisation of the Rules Implementing Articles 81 and 82*[13]. In it, the Commission made two radical proposals. First, that its monopoly

---

12   Case 10/86 [1986] ECR 4071, [1988] 4 CMLR 98; see similarly Case C-41/96 *VAG-Händlerbeirat eV v SYD-Consult* [1997] ECR I-3123, [1997] 5 CMLR 537, para 16.
13   OJ [1999] C 132/1, [1999] 5 CMLR 208.

over the grant of individual exemptions should be abandoned: national courts and NCAs should be able to share with it the right to apply the provisions of Article 81(3). Secondly, the system of notifying agreements to the Commission for individual exemption should be abandoned: instead, Article 81 in its entirety, and not just Article 81(1), as at present, will be made directly applicable. In the autumn of 2000, the Commission published a draft Council Regulation which would carry these proposals into effect together with an explanatory memorandum[14]. The Commission's intention is that the new régime will enter into force on 1 January 2003, although it is obviously possible that there could be some slippage in this timetable. The changes proposed in the draft regulation go considerably beyond the way in which decisions under Article 81(3) will be made in the future: many other issues affecting enforcement and procedure are at stake, which is why detailed consideration of the White Paper will be delayed until chapter 7. However, a few comments on the White Paper as it affects Article 81(3) should be made here.

First, it is important to understand that, under the new régime, there will be no such thing as an 'individual exemption'. The procedure of notifying an agreement to the Commission, and the Commission 'granting' an exemption, as an administrative or 'constitutive' act, will be discontinued. Article 81 in its entirety will be applied by national courts, NCAs and the Commission, and they will conclude either that Article 81 does, or that it does not, apply to a particular agreement. This will be explained further in chapter 7, as will some of the arguments that this aspect of the proposal has generated[15]. However, although there will no longer be such a creature as an individual exemption in Community competition law, the system of block exemptions will remain in place; future block exemptions will be in the 'new style' of Regulations 2790/99, 2658/00 and 2659/00[16].

Secondly, the fact that national courts and NCAs will be making decisions on Article 81 in its entirety makes it important that a clear, and justiciable, application of Article 81(3) should be possible: as suggested earlier in this chapter, a narrow interpretation of this provision is needed if the new system is to be workable[17].

A third point is that, if the White Paper proposals are implemented, businesses and their legal advisers will have to be more self-reliant than they are at the moment. It will no longer be possible to notify agreements to the Commission and to ask it for a view, enjoying in the meantime immunity from being fined[18]. Instead, a view will have to be taken by the companies themselves with their lawyers as to whether an agreement satisfies the terms of both Article 81(1) and Article 81(3). This is a very different position from the current one, and will obviously have a considerable effect on the application of competition law in practice. From the Commission's point of view, the elimination of the notification system will mean that it will be able to use its resources to pursue cartels and abusive behaviour, rather than to process notifications on behalf of the notifying parties. Indeed this is one of driving motivations between the entire modernisation proposal. The post-modernisation régime will be discussed in chapter 7.

14 OJ [2000] C 365 E/28, [2001] 5 CMLR 1148.
15 See ch 7, pp 246-258.
16 See pp 144-145 above.
17 See pp 125-128 above.
18 On immunity from fines see p 138 above and ch 7, pp 230.

CHAPTER 5

Article 82

1. INTRODUCTION

Article 82 is an important companion of Article 81. Whereas Article 81 is concerned with agreements, decisions and concerted practices which are harmful to competition, Article 82 is directed towards the unilateral conduct of dominant firms which act in an abusive manner. Many of the most controversial decisions of the Commission have been taken under Article 82, and the largest fine so far imposed in a single decision – EUR 273 million against the members of the Trans-Atlantic Conference Agreement[1] – was in an Article 82 case, where the members of the Conference were considered to have abused their collective dominant position.

A frequent complaint against the Commission is that it tends, when applying Article 82, not to concern itself solely with the maintenance of the competitive process but also with the protection of competitors, a quite different matter[1a]. To put the point another way, in any competition, whether economic, sporting or of some other kind, the most efficient or the fittest person will win: this is an inevitable part of the competitive process so that, if a firm ends up as a monopolist by virtue of its superior efficiency, this should be applauded, or at the very least it should not be condemned. A criticism of the Commission has been that it prohibits business practices of dominant firms that would be perfectly acceptable if the firm were not dominant and yet which are considered to be abusive if they are dominant; this amounts to the imposition of a handicap upon those firms, effectively penalising them because of their success. Whatever the merits may be of this criticism, it is undoubtedly the case that a dominant firm (or one that might be characterised as dominant) must behave on the market with caution: a transgression of Article 82, as can be seen from the *TACA* case, can have serious consequences. It is also important to point out that, where there is an infringement

---

1   *TACA* OJ [1999] L 95/1, [1999] 4 CMLR 1415: this decision is on appeal to the CFI, Cases T-191/98 etc *Atlantic Container Line v Commission* (judgment pending); see also *Tetra Pak II* OJ [1992] L 72/1, [1992] 4 CMLR 551 where the Commission imposed a fine of EUR 75 million for abuse of dominance under Article 82, upheld on appeal to the CFI, Case T–83/91 *Tetra Pak International SA v Commission* [1994] ECR II-755, [1997] 4 CMLR 726, paras 136-140, and on appeal to the ECJ, Case C-333/94 P *Tetra Pak International SA v Commission* [1996] ECR I-5951, [1997] 4 CMLR 662.

1a See the discussion of this issue, and of the influence of 'ordoliberalism' in the early days of the European Communities, in ch 1, p 18.

of Article 82, not only can the Commission impose a fine: an injured third party might also bring an action in a national court, seeking an injunction and/or damages[2].

The purpose of this chapter is to provide a general sense of how Article 82 works. More detailed, and critical, discussion of its application to abusive practices will be found later in the book, and in particular in chapters 6, 17 and 18.

Article 82 of the EC Treaty provides as follows:

'Any abuse by one or more undertakings of a dominant position within the common market or in a substantial part of it shall be prohibited as incompatible with the common market in so far as it may affect trade between Member States. Such abuse may, in particular, consist in:
(a) directly or indirectly imposing unfair purchase or selling prices or unfair trading conditions;
(b) limiting production, markets or technical development to the prejudice of consumers;
(c) applying dissimilar conditions to equivalent transactions with other trading parties, thereby placing them at a competitive disadvantage;
(d) making the conclusion of contracts subject to acceptance by the other parties of supplementary obligations which, by their nature or according to commercial usage, have no connection with the subject of such contracts.'

Article 82 does not forbid dominance itself. Nor does it contain an exhaustive list of the matters within its mischief: it has been applied to many practices not specifically mentioned in it[3]. The first formal decision under Article 82 was adopted by the Commission in 1971[4]; since then it has been applied with increasing frequency. Quite a number of cases have been closed by settlement between the dominant firm and the Commission, without a formal decision.

2.   UNDERTAKINGS

The term 'undertaking' has the same meaning in Article 82 as in Article 81, and reference should be made to the relevant section of the previous chapter[5]. The issue of the application of the competition rules to public undertakings and undertakings entrusted with exclusive or special rights will be discussed in chapter 6[6]; a few particular points about Article 82 and the public sector should, however, be noted here. First, the fact that an undertaking has a monopoly conferred upon it by statute does not remove it from the ambit of Article 82[7]. Secondly, Member States have a duty under Article 10 of the Treaty not to do anything 'which could jeopardise the attainment of the objectives of this Treaty', one of which is expressed in Article 3(g) to be the institution of a system ensuring that competition is not

2   See ch 8, pp 167-182.
3   See pp 276-284 below.
4   *GEMA* JO [1971] L 134/15, [1971] CMLR D35.
5   See ch 3, pp 66-71.
6   See ch 6, pp 189-212.
7   Case 311/84 *Centre Belge d'Etudes de Marché Télé-marketing v CLT* [1985] ECR 3261, [1986] 2 CMLR 558, para 16; also see Case 26/75 *General Motors v Commission* [1975] ECR 1367, [1976] 1 CMLR 95; Case 41/83 *Italy v Commission* [1985] ECR 873, [1985] 2 CMLR 368; Case 226/84 *British Leyland v Commission* [1986] ECR 3263, [1987] 1 CMLR 185; Case C–41/90 *Höfner v Macrotron* [1991] ECR I–1979, [1993] 4 CMLR 306, para 28;

distorted[8]. This means that a Member State cannot confer immunity on undertakings from Article 82, except to the limited extent provided for in Article 86(2)[9]. Thirdly, the provisions in Article 86(2) permitting derogation from the competition rules to the extent that their application would 'obstruct the performance, in law or in fact, of the particular tasks assigned to them' have consistently been interpreted narrowly by both the Commission and the Community Courts[10]. Lastly, it is important in this context to bear in mind Article 31 of the Treaty (ex Article 37), the function of which is to prevent Member States discriminating in favour of their own state monopolies of a commercial character. This provides the Commission with a useful alternative weapon for dealing with some monopolies in the public sector[11].

3. THE EFFECT ON INTER-STATE TRADE

The meaning of this phrase was analysed in chapter 3, to which reference should be made[12]. For the purpose of Article 82 particular attention should be paid to the ECJ's judgment in *Commercial Solvents v Commission*[13] in which it held that this requirement would be satisfied where conduct brought about an alteration in the structure of competition in the common market[14]. This test, which has been applied by both the Community Courts and the Commission on subsequent occasions[15], is of particular importance in Article 82 cases, where the existence of market power means that the structure of the market will be carefully monitored and safeguarded. In the *Soda-ash* decisions under Article 82[16] the Commission held that rebates offered by ICI and Solvay in their respective markets had the effect of reinforcing the structural rigidity of the EC market as a whole and its division along national lines. What is of interest about these decisions is that it was US exporters who were excluded from the EC market, but the Commission still held that there was an effect on inter-state trade: imports would have helped to undermine the dominant positions of ICI and Solvay in their respective markets.

Prior to the Competition Act 1998 entering into force in the UK, there was no provision making the abuse of dominance illegal there; as a result, in a number of cases it was essential, for the success of a complaint against a dominant firm,

---

Case C-18/93 *Corsica Ferries* [1994] ECR I-1783, para 43; Case C-242/95 *GT-Link v De Danske Statsbaner (DSB)* [1997] ECR I-4349, [1997] 5 CMLR 601, para 35; see also the Commission's decision in *French-West African Shipowners' Committees* OJ [1992] L 134/1, [1993] 5 CMLR 446, para 64.

8   See eg Case C–260/89 *Elliniki Radiophonia Tiléorassi-Anonimi Etairia (ERT) v Dimotiki Etairia Pliroforissis (DEP)* [1991] ECR I–2925, [1994] 4 CMLR 540, para 27.
9   Case 13/77 *INNO v ATAB* [1977] ECR 2115, [1978] 1 CMLR 283; see ch 6, pp 202-208.
10   See ch 6, pp 202-208.
11   Ibid, pp 211-212.
12   See ch 3, pp 110-120.
13   Cases 6/73 and 7/73 [1974] ECR 223, [1974] 1 CMLR 309.
14   See ch 3, p 118.
15   See eg Case 27/76 *United Brands v Commission* [1978] ECR 207, [1978] 1 CMLR 429; *Tetra Pak 1 (BTG Licence)* OJ [1988] L 272/27, [1988] 4 CMLR 881, para 48; *Napier Brown – British Sugar* OJ [1988] L 284/41, [1990] 4 CMLR 196, paras 77–80; *London European – Sabena* OJ [1988] L 317/47, [1989] 4 CMLR 662, para 33.
16   *Soda-ash/Solvay* OJ [1991] L 152/21 and *Soda-ash/ICI* OJ [1991] L 152/1; these decisions were annulled on procedural grounds by the CFI: Cases T-30/91 etc *Solvay SA v Commission* [1995] ECR II-1775, [1996] 5 CMLR 57; the Commission's appeal to the ECJ failed, Cases C-286/95 P etc [2001] All ER (EC) 439, [2000] 5 CMLR 413 and 454; the Commission readopted the decisions in December 2000: Commission Press Release IP/00/1449, 13 December 2000.

for there to be an effect on trade between Member States in order for Article 82 to be applicable. The Chapter II prohibition under domestic law is closely modelled upon Article 82, but requires only an effect on trade within the UK [17]; this will mean that it is no longer necessary for a complainant to show that Community law is applicable, since a remedy may be available under domestic law.

4.   DOMINANT POSITION

Article 82 applies only where an undertaking has a 'dominant position'[18]. A finding of dominance involves a two-stage procedure. The first is to determine the relevant market: market definition has been discussed in detail in chapter 1[19]. Having defined the market, it is necessary in an Article 82 case to determine what is meant by a dominant position: this expression needs to be considered in some detail. Unfortunately the Commission has not published a Notice on market power to accompany its *Notice on the Definition of the Relevant Market for the Purposes of Community Competition Law*[20]; some helpful insights into the identification of market power can however be gained from the UK Office of Fair Trading's Guideline *Assessment of Market Power*[1].

(A)   The legal test

The ECJ in *United Brands v Commission*[2] laid down the following test:

> '38 ... The dominant position thus referred to by Article [82] relates to a position of economic strength enjoyed by an undertaking which enables it to prevent effective competition being maintained on the relevant market by affording it the power to behave to an appreciable extent independently of its competitors, customers and ultimately of its consumers[3].'

This definition contains two elements – the ability to prevent competition and the ability to behave independently – without explaining how these two ideas

---

17   See ch 9, p 316.
18   For a critical commentary on the Commission's and the Community Courts' approach to the meaning of dominance see Jebsen and Stevens 'Assumptions, Goals and Dominant Undertakings; the Regulation of Competition under Article [82] of the European Union' (1996) 64 Antitrust Law Journal 443.
19   See ch 1, p 262ff.
20   OJ [1997] C 372/5, [1998] 4 CMLR 177.
1   OFT Guideline 415; it can be accessed at http://www.oft.gov.uk/html/comp-act/technical_guidelines/oft415.html.
2   Case 27/76 [1978] ECR 207, [1978] 1 CMLR 429; it has used the same formulation on several other occasions, eg in Case 85/76 *Hoffmann-La Roche v Commission* [1979] ECR 461, [1979] 3 CMLR 211, para 38.
3   This definition does not adequately reflect (what is undoubtedly true), that Article 82 also applies to market power on the buying as well as the selling side of the market, since that was not in issue in *United Brands*; a powerful purchaser may also be able to behave independently of its sellers who are not exactly 'customers' in the normal sense of that word; for action taken against buying power, see *Re Eurofirma* [1973] CMLR D217; *Re GEMA* OJ [1971] L 134/15, [1971] CMLR D35; Case 298/83 *CICCE v Commission* [1985] ECR 1105, [1986] 1 CMLR 486; *UK Small Mines* XXIst *Report on Competition Policy* (1991), point 107; see also ch 1, p 35 on procurement markets and ch 21, p 774 on the *Enso/Stora* merger.

relate to each other. Does the ECJ mean that they are cumulative, that is to say that both elements must be proved? Or is one idea parasitic upon the other, in which case which is the parasite? It is suggested that the essential issue is the ability to act independently on the market; this would accord with economists' notion of market power, which is the ability of a firm or firms to restrict output and thereby to increase price above the competitive level[4]. The ability to restrict output and increase price derives from independence or, to put the matter another way, freedom from competitive constraint[5]. The inclusion of the phrase about the power 'to prevent effective competition' in the *United Brands* judgment is therefore to be regarded as descriptive rather than prescriptive: it may have been inserted because of the application of Article 82 to anti-competitive as well as exploitative behaviour.

(B) Measuring market power[6]

True monopoly is rare, except where conferred by the State. The majority of cases have therefore had to deal with the problem of deciding at what point an undertaking, though not a true monopolist, has sufficient power over the market to fall within the ambit of Article 82.

(i) Statutory monopolies

Various cases have concerned undertakings with a statutory monopoly in the provision of goods or services. The ECJ has rejected the argument that, because a monopoly is conferred by statute, this immunises the undertaking from Article 82;[7] where an undertaking has a statutory monopoly it must comply with Article 82, its only special privilege being that conferred by Article 86(2)[8]. A different point is that the fact that an undertaking has a dominant position as a result of rights derived from national legislation does not in itself mean that it has exclusive rights in the sense of Article 86[9].

(ii) Market shares

In cases where there is no statutory monopoly, market shares are an important issue in assessing market power, but not to the exclusion of other 'factors indicating dominance' which must also be taken into account[10]. Market shares are not conclusive: mere numbers cannot in themselves determine whether an undertaking has power over the market. This point was stressed several times in chapter 1, and it should be borne firmly in mind in the discussion that follows. Having said this, however, it is natural that market shares are looked at, and they may be

---

4 See eg Bishop and Walker *The Economics of EC Competition Law* (Sweet & Maxwell, 1999), paras 2.27-2.38.
5 This is the terminology used by the Commission in its *Notice on Market Definition*: see ch 1, p 26ff.
6 See *Bishop and Walker* paras 2.39-2.60.
7 See the cases cited at p 150, n 8 above.
8 See ch 6, pp 202-208.
9 Ibid, p 192.
10 See pp 156-162 below.

regarded as a proxy, albeit an imperfect one, for determining dominance: the range of situations in which market shares are used in competition law analysis was set out at the end of chapter 1[11]. As far as Article 82 is concerned, it is obvious that the larger the market share, the more likely the finding of dominance. A market share of 100% is rare in the absence of statutory privileges, although not unheard of[12]. However some firms have been found to very large market shares. For example in *Tetra Pak 1 (BTG Licence)*[13] Tetra Pak's market share in the market for machines capable of filling cartons by an aseptic process was 91.8%; and in *BPB Industries plc*[14] BPB was found to have a market share in plasterboard of 96–98% in Great Britain and of 92–100% in Ireland, although the Commission had excluded wet plastering from the market definition.

In *Hoffmann-La Roche v Commission*[15] the ECJ said:

'41 ... Furthermore although the importance of the market shares may vary from one market to another the view may legitimately be taken that very large shares are in themselves, and save in exceptional circumstances, evidence of the existence of a dominant position. An undertaking which has a very large market share and holds it for some time ... is by virtue of that share in a position of strength ....'

The Court says here that large market shares may in themselves be evidence of a dominant position, but this assertion is qualified in two ways: first, by recognising that in 'exceptional circumstances' large market shares may not mean that a firm is dominant; and secondly, by referring to the notion that the market share must exist 'for some time'. In assessing market power, economists would argue that it is the exercise of market power *over time* which is of particular significance. A large market share held only briefly before the emergence of new competition would suggest that there was never any market power. This extract from *Hoffmann-la Roche* makes clear that a firm could argue, for example, that barriers to entry in an industry are low so that new competition might soon emerge or that it was charging only at marginal cost so that its market share did not reflect true power over the market. In practice the Community Courts and the Commission habitually look to see what other factors indicate market power: they do not content themselves merely with quantifying market shares[16]. This is correct in principle, in particular as market shares cannot say anything about *potential* entrants to the market.

(iii)   The AKZO presumption of dominance where an undertaking has a market share of 50% or more

In *AKZO v Commission*[17] the ECJ referred to the passage from *Hoffmann-La Roche* quoted above and continued that a market share of 50% could be

---

11 See ch 1, pp 41–43.
12 In *GVL* OJ [1981] L 370/49, [1982] 1 CMLR 221 that body had a 100% market share in the market in Germany for the management of performing artists' rights of secondary exploitation.
13 OJ [1988] L 272/27, [1988] 4 CMLR 881, para 44.
14 OJ [1989] L 10/50, [1990] 4 CMLR 464.
15 Case 85/76 [1979] ECR 461, [1979] 3 CMLR 211; the Commission specifically referred to this paragraph in *Van den Bergh Foods Ltd* OJ [1998] L 246/1, [1998] 5 CMLR 530, para 258.
16 In an interim case where it was necessary to act expeditiously the Commission considered that high market shares sufficed: see *ECS/AKZO* OJ [1983] L 252/13, [1983] 3 CMLR 694.
17 Case C-62/86 [1991] ECR I-3359, [1993] 5 CMLR 215.

considered to be very large so that, in the absence of exceptional circumstances pointing the other way, an undertaking with such a market share will be presumed dominant; that undertaking will bear the burden of establishing that it is not dominant. The CFI applied this test in *Hilti AG v Commission*[18]. Clearly this is a very significant rule, which indicates that firms are at risk of being found to be dominant where they fall considerably short of being monopolists in the strict sense of that term.

(iv) Findings of dominance below the 50% threshold

It is necessary to consider at what point a firm's market share is so small that it could not be considered to have a dominant position. Both the ECJ and the Commission held in *United Brands* that a firm with a market share in the 40–45% range was dominant. In that case other factors were considered to be significant: the market share alone would not have been sufficient to sustain a finding of dominance. The case shows that a firm supplying less than 50% of the relevant products may be held to have a dominant position. Even an undertaking subject to lively competition on the market, as UBC was at certain periods of the year, may be held to be dominant for the purposes of Article 82. In *United Brands* there was argument over the definition of the product, geographical and temporal markets: if they were drawn too narrowly or widely, United Brand's market share of between 40 and 45% may have considerably overstated its position, especially as it had faced fierce competition from other undertakings from time to time[19]. Given that it was subject to this competition, that its market share had been falling, and that it had not been in profit in its banana operations, one might say that UBC was as close to the threshold of dominance as one could get. Not everyone has been so charitable about the findings of the Commission and the ECJ in this case[20].

In *Hoffmann-La Roche v Commission*[1] the ECJ quashed the Commission's decision[2] that Roche was dominant in the vitamin B3 market where its market share was 43%, as it was not satisfied that there were sufficient additional factors indicating dominance for so deciding. The Commission has said that it takes the view that a dominant position can generally be taken to exist when a firm has a market share of 40–45% and even that one cannot be ruled out in the region of 20–40%[3]. Its decision in *Virgin/British Airways*[4] marked the first occasion on which an undertaking with a market share of less than 40% was found to be in a dominant position under Article 82. BA was held to be dominant in the UK air travel agency services market with a market share of 39.7%. When looking at market shares, it is relevant to look at the largest firm's share relative to its competitors': the smaller the shares of the competitors, the likelier the Commission will be to hold that the largest firm is dominant[5]. However, where one firm has

18 Case T–30/89 [1991] ECR II-1439, [1992] 4 CMLR 16.
19 The ECJ itself accepted that UBC had at times faced lively competition: Case 27/76 [1978] ECR 207, [1978] 1 CMLR 429, paras 113–117.
20 See eg Valgiurata 'Price Discrimination under Article [82] of the EEC Treaty: the *United Brands* case' (1982) 31 ICLQ 36.
1   Case 85/76 [1979] ECR 461, [1979] 3 CMLR 211.
2   *Hoffmann-La Roche AG* OJ [1976] L 223/27, [1976] 2 CMLR D25.
3   See the Commission's Xth *Report on Competition Policy* (1980), point 50.
4   OJ [2000] L 30/1, [2000] 4 CMLR 999, on appeal to the CFI Case T-219/99 *British Airways v Commission* (grounds of appeal OJ [2000] C 20/21, judgment pending).
5   See Case 322/81 *Nederlandsche Banden-Industrie Michelin v Commission* [1983] ECR 3461, [1985] 1 CMLR 282 where the nearest rivals of NBIM had shares between 4% and 8%.

a market share of, say, 45%, and the nearest rival has 35%, this would open up the possibility of the Commission reaching a finding of collective dominance[6].

(v)   How to calculate market shares

In its *Notice on Market Definition*[7] the Commission deals with the method of calculating market shares at paragraphs 53 to 55. Data on these may be available from market sources, for example trade association statistics or from studies commissioned within the industry. However, it will often be necessary to calculate market shares within the context of a particular investigation – whether under Article 81, Article 82 or the EC Merger Regulation (hereafter 'the ECMR') – and the Commission will normally expect to do so by reference to the sales of figures of the firms operating on the market. However, sales figures are not the only data capable of revealing market shares. For example, paragraph 54 indicates that in aviation it may be as informative to look at the relative size of airlines' fleets, and in a sector such as mining the reserves held by different operators may be of importance. As for sales data themselves, the Commission states in paragraph 55 of the Notice that both sales by volume and sales by value are significant, and in the case of differentiated products it considers that sales by value and their associated market share are more revealing.

(vi)   'Factors indicating dominance': barriers to entry

Market shares are not the sole issue in determining whether a firm has market power. As was stressed in chapter 1, market shares cannot indicate the competitive pressure exerted by firms not yet operating on the market but with the capacity to enter it. It is necessary therefore to consider various other 'factors indicating dominance' which help to establish an undertaking's position on the market: the most obvious factor will be barriers to entry[8].

A firm with a large market share will be in a much better position to earn monopoly profits if it knows that in doing so it will not attract new competition. In economic terms the relevant question is whether there are any barriers to entry which would prevent anyone else entering the market. What constitutes a barrier to entry is controversial among economists. Some argue that in the absence of statutory regulation, and provided that supplies of raw materials are available, a barrier to entry exists only where a new entrant will face higher costs than those already in the industry[9]. A less stringent view would be that anything which might make it particularly difficult for a firm to enter the market is a barrier. Clearly if the former, narrow, view of barriers to entry is adopted, fewer firms will be found to be dominant than if the latter, wide, approach is taken. In practice the position is more complicated than this, and it is helpful to distinguish between 'absolute' barriers to entry, such as the ownership of intellectual property

6   On collective dominance, see pp 163-164 below and, in more detail, ch 14 generally.
7   OJ [1997] C 372/5, [1998] 4 CMLR 177.
8   On barriers to entry, see ch 1, pp 39-41; note the reference there to the UK OFT's Guideline *Assessment of Market Power* OFT 415: whilst this provides guidance on the application of the UK Competition Act 1998, it contains a useful discussion of the issue of barriers to entry generally; see also *Bishop and Walker* paras 2.52-2.58 and Appendix A .
9   See eg Stigler *The Organisation of Industry* (1968) at p 67: he says that a barrier to entry is 'a cost of producing (at some or every rate of output) which must be borne by a firm which seeks to enter an industry but is not borne by firms already in the industry'.

rights, which may impede access to a market, from 'strategic' advantages that may accrue to a firm or firms from having been the first to enter a market[10]. Where the first mover in a market incurs substantial sunk costs[11], it may enjoy a substantial advantage over firms that subsequently wish to enter. The Community Courts and the Commission have not attempted to lay down a general definition of a barrier to entry for these purposes; however their judgments and decisions have adopted a wide approach, which has led to criticism that the market power of some undertakings has been exaggerated.

Some of the barriers to entry and other matters considered by the Courts and the Commission to amount to 'factors indicating dominance' are as follows.

(A) LEGAL PROVISIONS. It is clear that the provisions of national legal systems can operate as barriers to entry: in *Hugin v Commission*[12] the ECJ seems to have accepted that Hugin was dominant in the market for spare parts for its cash registers because other firms could not produce spares for fear of being sued by Hugin in the UK under the Design Copyright Act 1968. In the same way the ownership of patents, trade marks and other intellectual property may constitute barriers to entry[13]. It does not follow that the owner of intellectual property rights is automatically dominant: there might be other products which compete with the product protected by the intellectual property rights and which can be manufactured without infringing them. In *Tetra Pak 1 (BTG Licence)*[14] the acquisition by Tetra Pak of a company that had the benefit of an exclusive patent and know-how licence was regarded as a factor indicating dominance, as it made entry to the market more difficult for other firms that would be unable to gain access to the licensed technology. Other obvious legal barriers to entry are Government licensing requirements and planning regulations, Governmental control of frequencies for the transmission of radio signals[15], statutory monopoly power[16] and provisions of domestic law which shield producers on the home market from foreign competition. Legal provisions such as these give the incumbent firm an absolute advantage[17], so that a would-be entrant to the market cannot gain access to an asset or resource at all, or only at considerable cost (for example by paying for a licence of the intellectual property right). The control of an essential facility, which may or may not be attributable to legal provisions, could confer the same absolute advantage on an incumbent undertaking[18].

---

10 See *Barriers to Entry and Exit in UK Competition Policy* (London Economics, 1994, OFT Research Paper No 2); *Bishop and Walker* Appendix A.
11 On this expression see ch 1, p 6.
12 Case 22/78 [1979] ECR 1869, [1979] 3 CMLR 345.
13 See eg *Eurofix-Bauco v Hilti* OJ [1988] L 65/19, [1989] 4 CMLR 677, para 66; *Magill TV Guide/ITP, BBC and RTE* OJ [1989] L 78/43, [1989] 4 CMLR 757, para 22 (copyright protection of TV listings relevant to finding of dominance), upheld on appeal to the CFI, Cases T–69/89 etc *RTE v Commission* [1991] ECR II-485, [1991] 4 CMLR 586, and further on appeal to the ECJ, Cases C-241 and C-242/91 P [1995] ECR I-743, [1995] 4 CMLR 718.
14 OJ [1988] L 272/27, [1988] 4 CMLR 881, para 44, upheld on appeal Case T-51/89 *Tetra Pak Rausing SA v Commission* [1990] ECR II-309, [1991] 4 CMLR 334.
15 *Decca Navigator System* OJ [1989] L 43/27, [1990] 4 CMLR 627.
16 Case 311/84 *Centre Belge d'Etudes de Marché Télé-marketing v CLT* [1985] ECR 3261, [1986] 2 CMLR 558; see Marenco 'Legal Monopolies in the Case law of the Court of Justice of the European Communities' (1991) Fordham Corp L Inst (ed Hawk), pp 197–222.
17 The UK Guideline on *Assessment of Market Power* (n 8 above) deals with absolute advantages at paras 5.4-5.8.
18 On essential facilities, see p 177 below and ch 17, pp 611-614.

(B)   SUPERIOR TECHNOLOGY.   The Community Courts and the Commission consider that the technology of a firm is relevant when deciding whether it has market power, although this has attracted criticism. If one takes the 'Stigler approach' to the concept of a barrier to entry[19], one would say that a new firm wishing to enter a market will not face any greater cost than the alleged dominant firm which has itself had to expend money and take risks in building up its technical know-how. Indeed the newcomer may be in a superior position if patents or know-how possessed by the allegedly dominant firm are now in the public domain. Some critics would assert that to rely on technological superiority as an indicator of dominance is to punish a firm for its innovative efforts. The riposte to this, that a finding of dominance is not an accusation in itself[20] but merely anterior to an investigation of abuse, is little comfort to a firm faced with the cost of defending itself under Article 82, perhaps before both the Commission and a national court. However it is clearly the case that superior technology may bestow on an incumbent firm a strategic advantage over would-be entrants. The ECJ has relied on technology as an indicator of dominance in several cases, including *United Brands v Commission*[1], *Hoffmann-La Roche v Commission*[2] and *Michelin v Commission*[3] so that, as a matter of law, this is clearly a factor that may be taken into account.

(C)   DEEP POCKET.   Access to capital is an important issue. In *Continental Can*[4] the Commission regarded that firm's access to the international capital market as significant, and this factor was stressed in *United Brands v Commission*[5]. Some economists would argue that access to capital ought not to be regarded as a barrier to entry, either because they consider that capital markets are not inefficient or because they think that any problem of inefficiency should be dealt with by restructuring the market for financial services[6].

(D)   ECONOMIES OF SCALE.   Economies of scale may be a barrier to entry[7]. The ECJ in *United Brands v Commission*[8] considered scale to be a factor indicating dominance, and the Commission in *BPB Industries plc* referred to this matter specifically[9].

(E)   VERTICAL INTEGRATION AND WELL-DEVELOPED DISTRIBUTION SYSTEMS.   Vertical integration, which may give incumbent undertakings a strategic advantage over new entrants, is regarded as a significant indicator of dominance. In *United Brands v Commission*[10] the ECJ described the extent to which UBC's activities were integrated – it owned banana plantations and transport boats and it marketed

19   See p 157 above.
20   See Case 322/81 *Nederlandsche Banden-Industrie Michelin v Commission* [1983] ECR 3461, [1985] 1 CMLR 282, para 57.
1   Case 27/76 [1978] ECR 207, [1978] 1 CMLR 429, paras 82–84.
2   Case 85/76 [1979] ECR 461, [1979] 3 CMLR 211, para 48.
3   Case 322/81 [1983] ECR 3461, [1985] 1 CMLR 282; see also *Eurofix-Bauco v Hilti* (n 13 above), para 69 and *Tetra Pak 1 (BTG Licence)* (p 154, n 13 above), para 44.
4   JO [1972] L 7/25, [1972] CMLR D11.
5   Case 27/76 [1978] ECR 207, [1978] 1 CMLR 429, para 122.
6   For further discussion see Bain *Barriers to New Competition* (1956) ch 5; on the treatment of access to finance in the UK, see OFT Guideline *Assessment of Market Power* OFT 415, paras 5.18-5.19.
7   Economies of scale are discussed in ch 1, pp 8-9; see also *Bain*, ch 3.
8   Case 27/76 [1978] ECR 207, [1978] 1 CMLR 429.
9   See p 154, n 14 above, para 116.
10   Case 27/76 [1978] ECR 207, [1978] 1 CMLR 429, paras 69-81, 85-90.

its bananas itself – and said that this provided that firm with commercial stability which was a significant advantage over its competitors. In *Hoffmann-La Roche v Commission*[11] the ECJ pointed to Roche's highly developed sales network as a relevant factor conferring upon it commercial advantages over its rivals. The Commission has often treated vertical integration and the benefit of well-established distribution systems as a factor indicating dominance,[12] since this could impede access for a would-be entrant to the market.

(F)　PRODUCT DIFFERENTIATION.　In *United Brands v Commission*[13] the ECJ considered that United Brand's advertising campaigns and brand image were significant factors indicating dominance: it had spent considerable resources establishing the Chiquita brand name which was well-protected by trade marks. The Commission has often noted (in cases under the ECMR) that advertising expenditure could make entry difficult into the market for fast-moving consumer goods such as soft drinks[14], sanitary protection[15] and toilet tissue[16].

(G)　OVERALL SIZE AND STRENGTH.　In *Hoffmann-La Roche v Commission*[17] the ECJ rejected the Commission's argument that the fact that Roche produced a wider range of products than its rivals and that it was the largest producer of vitamins in the world were relevant for the purposes of establishing dominance[18]. The mere fact that a firm is large does not in itself mean that it is dominant in respect of any particular product market; size and strength *within* a market will however be relevant[19].

(H)　OPPORTUNITY COSTS.　Opportunity costs are the value of something that has to be sacrificed in order to achieve something else. In *British Midland v Aer Lingus*[20] the Commission considered that opportunity costs could act as a deterrent to potential entrants to the market in question. There the Commission was looking at the air-route from Heathrow to Dublin. An airline operating from Heathrow is allowed a certain number of 'slots' for taking off and landing. If it were to compete on the London–Dublin route it would have to sacrifice slots currently used for other destinations. As the Dublin route was not particularly profitable, the Commission considered that the opportunity costs involved in switching to it from other more lucrative ones were high and acted as a deterrent. The Commission did not ask whether the opportunity costs for a new entrant would be higher than those for the incumbent airline, which would be the relevant question according to the Stigler definition suggested above[1].

(I)　OBLIGATORY TRADING PARTNER.　A customer may be so dependent upon a firm for the supply of goods or services that the supplier can be regarded as an

---

11　Case 85/76 [1979] ECR 461, [1979] 3 CMLR 211, para 48.
12　See eg *Eurofix-Bauco v Hilti* OJ [1988] L 65/19, [1989] 4 CMLR 677, para 69; *Napier Brown – British Sugar* OJ [1988] L 284/41, [1990] 4 CMLR 196, para 56.
13　Case 27/76 [1978] ECR 207, [1978] 1 CMLR 429, paras 91-94.
14　See eg Case No IV/M.190 *Nestlé/Perrier* OJ [1992] L 356/1, [1993] 4 CMLR M17.
15　See eg Case No IV/M.430 *Procter & Gamble/VP Schickendanz* OJ [1994] L 352/32.
16　See eg Case No IV/M.623 *Kimberly-Clark/Scott Paper* OJ [1996] L 183/1.
17　Case 85/76 [1979] ECR 461, [1979] 3 CMLR 211.
18　Ibid, paras 44–47.
19　See Case 322/81 *Nederlandsche Banden-Industrie Michelin v Commission* [1983] ECR 3461, [1985] 1 CMLR 282.
20　OJ [1992] L 96/34, [1993] 4 CMLR 596.
1　See p 157.

'obligatory trading partner'[2]. In some findings under Article 82 the Commission and the Community Courts have been influenced by this relationship in reaching a finding a dominance; for example in *Deutsche Bahn v Commission*[3] the CFI, in upholding the Commission's finding of dominance, noted the economic dependence of railway operators on the statutory monopolist in the provision of railway services within Germany. In *Virgin/British Airways*[4] the Commission noted that BA's position on the markets for air transport made it an obligatory business partner for travel agents.

(J) CONDUCT.   The ECJ in *United Brands v Commission*[5] agreed with the idea that the conduct of an alleged dominant firm could be taken into account in deciding whether it is dominant. This means, for example, that it might be legitimate to take into account the fact that a firm has offered discriminatory rebates to certain customers in deciding whether it is dominant: the rebates may themselves prevent competitors entering the market and so constitute a barrier to entry. In *Michelin v Commission*[6] the Commission had relied on Michelin's price discrimination as an indicator of dominance. Michelin argued before the ECJ that this approach was circular: the Commission was saying that because it had offered discriminatory prices, it was dominant, and because it was dominant its discriminatory prices were an abuse. The ECJ did not explicitly deal with this issue in its judgment, but in affirming the Commission's decision there is at least tacit approval of considering conduct as a factor indicating dominance. Despite criticism of the circularity of this approach, the Commission has continued to regard conduct as a relevant factor indicating dominance: for example in *Eurofix-Bauco v Hilti*[7] it regarded that firm's behaviour as 'witness to its ability to act independently of, and without due regard to, either competitors or customers...'[8]; and in *AKZO* it found that that undertaking's ability to weaken or eliminate troublesome competitors was an indicator of dominance[9]. There is increasing recognition that there are types of behaviour that may deter entry[10], and it would be wrong to discount such conduct from the consideration of whether an undertaking is dominant.

(K) PERFORMANCE.   The economic performance of an undertaking, as well as its conduct, may be a factor indicating dominance. The fact that a firm had idle capacity was regarded as significant in *Hoffmann-La Roche v Commission*[11], as

2   The concept of a 'partenaire obligatoire' was found originally in French law on pricing policy: see Ordonnance No 86-1243 on Freedom in Pricing and Competition.
3   Case T-229/94 [1997] ECR II-1689, [1998] 4 CMLR 220, para 57.
4   OJ [2000] L 30/1, [2000] 4 CMLR 999, para 92.
5   Case 27/76 [1978] ECR 207, [1978] 1 CMLR 429, para 122.
6   Case 322/81 [1983] ECR 3461, [1985] 1 CMLR 282.
7   OJ [1988] L 65/19, [1989] 4 CMLR 677.
8   Ibid, para 71; the objection to the 'circularity' argument may be met if the Commission uses conduct as an indicator only in clear cases, and provided that it is not relied on exclusively to support a finding of dominance.
9   *ECS/AKZO* OJ [1985] L 374/1, [1986] 3 CMLR 273, para 56, upheld on appeal Case 62/86 *AKZO Chemie BV v Commission* [1991] ECR I-3359, [1993] 5 CMLR 215, para 61; see also *Soda-ash/ICI* OJ [1991] L 152/40, paras 6 and 48.
10 See eg Ordovar and Salonen 'Predation, Monopolisation and Antitrust' in *The Handbook of Industrial Organisation* (Amsterdam, North-Holland, 1989, eds Schmalensee and Willig); *Barriers to Entry and Exit in UK Competition Policy* (London Economics, 1994, OFT Research Paper No 2) and in the OFT Guideline *Assessment of Market Power* OFT 415, paras 5.20-5.23.
11 Case 85/76 [1979] ECR 461, [1979] 3 CMLR 211.

was the ability of a firm unilaterally to increase its prices, which the market followed, in *Napier Brown – British Sugar*[12].

(L) EVIDENCE OF MANAGERS. In *BBI/Boosey and Hawkes: Interim Measures*[13] the Commission regarded internal documents of Boosey and Hawkes, in which it had described its instruments as 'automatically first choice' of all the top brass bands, as significant in its finding that Boosey and Hawkes was dominant. This presents a warning to firms to take care over the preparation and record of internal memoranda. In-house counsel may need to exercise restraint over hawkish commercial personnel, given to describing their position in the global widget market in written memoranda and advertising copy as 'world-beating', 'the biggest' or 'clearly the dominant player'. Whilst shareholders might like to hear this, and whilst no doubt individuals' bonuses may be linked to their performance, it is not always easy to convince Commission officials that one's market share is *de minimis* in the face of such assertions.

(C) Previous findings of dominance

In *Coca-Cola Co v Commission*[14] the CFI held that, whenever the Commission adopts a decision applying Article 82 (or the ECMR), it must define the relevant market and make a fresh analysis of the conditions of competition within it on the basis of the available evidence at the appropriate time; this may lead to a determination of the market which is different from a previous finding[15]. Furthermore a national court (or a national competition authority) would not be bound in a later case by a previous finding of dominance by the Commission in a different case[16]. However the actual decision in an Article 82 case may serve as a basis for an action for damages brought by a third party before a national court in relation to the same facts, even where the Commission's decision did not impose a fine[17].

(D) The 'special responsibility' of dominant firms

It is not an offence for a firm to have a dominant position; what is offensive is to abuse the position of dominance, but the ECJ in *Michelin v Commission*[18] stated that a firm in a dominant position 'has a special responsibility not to allow its conduct to impair undistorted competition on the common market'[19]. This statement is routinely repeated in the judgments of the Community Courts and the decisions of the Commission. In one sense it is a statement of the obvious: it is clear that Article 82 imposes obligations on dominant firms that non-dominant

---

12 OJ [1988] L 284/41, [1990] 4 CMLR 196, para 55; on the treatment of this issue in the UK, see OFT Guideline *Assessment of Market Power* OFT 415, paras 6.3-6.5.
13 OJ [1988] L 286/36, [1988] 4 CMLR 67, para 18.
14 Joined Case T-125/97 and T-127/97 [2000] 5 CMLR 467.
15 Ibid, para 82.
16 Ibid, para 85.
17 Ibid, para 86; see also Case C-344/98 *Masterfoods Ltd v HB Ice Cream Ltd* [2001] All ER (EC) 130, [2001] 4 CMLR 449.
18 Case 322/81 [1983] ECR 3461, [1985] 1 CMLR 282, para 57.
19 See also Case T-65/89 *BPB Industries plc v Commission* [1993] ECR II-389, [1993] 5 CMLR 32, para 67.

firms do not bear. Unilateral behaviour is not controlled under Article 81, which applies only to conduct which is attributable to a concurrence of wills; unilateral acts can however amount to an infringement of Article 82[20]. The important question is whether the 'special responsibility' amounts to something more than this, and in particular whether it means that dominant firms must refrain from harming competitors, even where the behaviour of the dominant firm is attributable to its superior efficiency: should Article 82 be deployed to protect competitors as well as the process of competition? This matter has been discussed in chapter 1[1], and will be considered further in the treatment of abusive practices below and in chapters 17 and 18.

(E)   The emergence of super-dominance

It would appear to be the case that the responsibility of a dominant firm becomes greater, so that a finding of abuse becomes more likely, where the firm under investigation is not merely dominant, but rather 'enjoys a position of dominance approaching a monopoly'[2]. The ECJ has said that the scope of the special responsibility of a dominant firm must be considered in the light of the special circumstances of each case[3]. It follows that behaviour may be considered not to be abusive when carried out by some dominant firms but to be abusive when carried out by others. An example of the distinction is afforded by the practice of a dominant firm which selectively cuts its prices to some customers, but not to below cost in the sense of the law on predatory pricing[4], whilst charging higher prices to others. There are strong arguments for not condemning this practice: if the dominant firm is not losing money, it would appear to be competing on the basis of efficiency, which competition law should encourage[5]. In *Compagnie Maritime Belge Transports SA v Commission*[6] the ECJ refrained from deciding generally on the practice of selective price cutting[7]; however, at paragraph 119 it said that:

> 'It is sufficient to recall that the conduct at issue here is that of a conference having a share of over 90 per cent of the market in question and only one competitor. The appellants have, moreover, never seriously disputed, and indeed admitted at the hearing, that the purpose of the conduct complained of was to eliminate G&C from the market'.

---

20 The respective rôles of Articles 81 and 82 are spelt out particularly clearly in the judgment of the CFI in Case T-41/96 *Bayer v Commission* [2001] All ER (EC) 1, [2001] 4 CMLR 126.
1   See ch 1, pp 15-21.
2   See para 136 of the Opinion of AG Fennelly in Cases C-395/96 P etc *Compagnie Maritime Belge SA v Commission* [2000] 4 CMLR 1076.
3   Case C-334/94 P *Tetra Pak v Commission* [1996] ECR I-5951, [1997] 4 CMLR 662, para 24; Cases 395/96 P etc *Compagnie Maritime Belge SA v Commission* [2000] 4 CMLR 1076, para 114.
4   See p 178 below and, in more detail, ch 18, pp 653-657.
5   It is possible that this pricing policy may amount to a different type of abuse, namely price discrimination (see p 178 below), but the issue here is whether the selective price cutting *in itself* amounts to an abuse.
6   Cases C-395/96 P and C-396/96 P [2000] 4 CMLR 1076.
7   Ibid, para 118.

On this basis the ECJ upheld the finding that there had been an abuse of a dominant position, whilst leaving open the possibility that the same conduct on the part of an undertaking with less than 90% of the market and facing more competition would not have been found guilty.

The idea that the obligations on dominant firms become more onerous depending on the special circumstances of the case (to use the language of the ECJ in *Tetra Pak*), finds expression in decisions and judgments that seem to have turned on the degree of market power that the dominant undertaking enjoys. For example Tetra Pak's market share in the market for aseptic cartons and carton-filling machines was in the region of 90 to 95%, and it was found to have abused a dominant position where its conduct did not take place in the market in which it was dominant, and was not intended to benefit its position in that market[8]. In *Compagnie Maritime Belge* the conference's market share was 90% or more[9]. This would also help to explain why firms that control 'essential facilities' have an obligation in certain circumstances to provide access to them, since their market power is particularly strong[10]. It may be helpful, therefore, to identify a concept over and above dominance, that we might call 'super-dominance', where the risks of being found to be acting abusively are correspondingly higher: if a dominant undertaking has a 'special' responsibility, a super-dominant has one that is even greater. The expression 'super-dominance' has not been used by the Community Courts or the Commission themselves, and it remains to be seen whether it will be. However a dominance/super-dominance calibration may be a helpful one in understanding why certain types of behaviour, such as selective price cutting and refusal to supply, are treated more seriously in some cases than in others.

(F) Collective dominance

An important issue in Community competition law has been whether Article 82 is capable of application not only to 'single firm dominance', where one firm or group of firms comprising a single economic unit enjoys a dominant position, but also to so-called 'collective' or 'joint' dominance, where two or more independent firms enjoy power over the market. After much uncertainty and no little confusion it is now clear that Article 82 is capable of application to collective dominance, the judgment of the ECJ in *Compagnie Maritime Belge SA v Commission*[11] being particularly important in this respect. The concept of collective dominance is also to be found in Article 82, the EC Merger Regulation ('the ECMR') and the Chapter II prohibition in the UK Competition Act 1998. UK law possesses, in the complex provisions of the Fair Trading Act 1973, a different mechanism for dealing with some of the problems raised by markets that could be considered to be collectively dominated. Collective dominance,

8   See pp 173-175 below.
9   See similarly, on the responsibility of a monopolist, Case 7/82 *GVL v Commission* [1983] ECR 483, [1983] 3 CMLR 645, para 56; this was cited by the Commission in *1998 Football World Cup* OJ [2000] L 5/55, [2000] 4 CMLR 963, para 85.
10 On essential facilities see p 177 below and ch 17, pp 611-624.
11 Cases 395/96 P and 396/96 P etc [2000] 4 CMLR 1076.

and the concepts of tacit collusion and oligopoly, will be treated separately in chapter 14.

5.   A SUBSTANTIAL PART OF THE COMMON MARKET

Once it has been established that a firm has a dominant position on the market, one further jurisdictional question must be answered before going on to the issue of abuse. Is that dominant position held in the whole or a substantial part of the common market? If not, Article 82, by its own terms, does not apply. This issue is not the same as the delimitation of the relevant geographical market: that concept is used as part of the investigation into a firm's market power. The requirement that market power should exist over a substantial part of the common market is in a sense the equivalent of the *de minimis* doctrine under Article 81, according to which agreements of minor importance are not caught[12].

Obviously there is no problem with the issue of substantiality where it is decided that an undertaking is dominant throughout the EC. The position may be more difficult where dominance is more localised than this. Suppose that a firm is dominant in just one Member State, or even in a part of one Member State: when will that area be considered to constitute a substantial part of the EC? Three points must be noted. The first is that the issue is not solely a geographical one. In *Suiker Unie v Commission*[13] the ECJ said that for this purpose:

> 'the pattern and volume of the production and consumption of the said product as well as the habits and economic opportunities of vendors and purchasers must be considered'[14].

This indicates that substantiality is not simply a question of relating the *physical* size of the geographical market to the EC as a whole. In *Suiker Unie* the ECJ considered the ratio of the volume of Belgian and South German production of sugar to Community production overall and concluded on this basis that each of those markets could be considered to be substantial.

The second point is that it is likely that each Member State would be considered to be a substantial part of the common market, in particular where an undertaking enjoys a statutory monopoly[15], and *Suiker Unie* further established that parts of a Member State can be[16]. The third point about this issue is that neither the Community Courts nor the Commission has laid down that any particular percentage of the common market as a whole is critical in determining what is substantial. In *BP v Commission*[17] Advocate General Warner took the view that

---

12   See ch 3, pp 107-110.
13   Cases 40/73 etc [1975] ECR 1663, [1976] 1 CMLR 295, para 371.
14   Ibid, para 371.
15   Case 127/73 *BRT v SABAM* [1974] ECR 313, [1974] 2 CMLR 238, para 5; Case T-229/94 *Deutsche Bahn AG v Commission* [1997] ECR II-1689, [1998] 4 CMLR 220; Case T-228/97 *Irish Sugar v Commission* [1999] ECR II-2969, [1999] 5 CMLR 1300, para 99.
16   It is important to remember however that the abuse must also have an effect on inter-Member State trade to fall within Article 82: see pp 151-152 above.
17   Case 77/77 [1978] ECR 1513, [1978] 3 CMLR 174.

sole reliance should not be placed on percentages in such cases and was of the opinion that the Dutch market for petrol, which represented only about 4.6% of the Community market as a whole, could be considered substantial. The ECJ did not comment on this issue, as it quashed the Commission's finding of abuse on other grounds[18].

There are numerous examples of the test of substantiality having been satisfied in relation to a single facility: in each of *Merci Convenzionali Porto di Genova v Siderugica Gabriella*[19], *Sealink/B and I – Holyhead: Interim Measures*[20], *Sea Containers v Stena Sealink – Interim Measures*[1], *Flughaven Frankfurt/Main*[2], *Corsica Ferries*[3], *Portuguese Airports*[4], *Ilmailulaitos/Luftfartsverket*[5] and *Spanish Airports*[6] ports or airports have been found to be sufficiently substantial. Furthermore, the ECJ has held that, where national law confers a contiguous series of monopolies within a Member State which, taken together, cover the entire territory of that State, that law creates a dominant position in a substantial part of the common market[7].

6. SMALL FIRMS AND NARROW MARKETS

(A) Small firms

It might be assumed that Article 82 is applicable only to large undertakings. It is certainly true that the Commission has used it to investigate some of the industrial giants of the world such as Roche, Commercial Solvents, United Brands, IBM and Microsoft. However it would be quite wrong to suppose that only firms such as this fall within the risk of Article 82. The significant issue under Article 82 is market power, not the size of an undertaking. Given that the relevant market may be drawn very narrowly, small firms may be found guilty of an abuse of Article 82. In *Hugin*[8], that firm was fined by the Commission for refusing to supply its spare parts to Liptons, the market for these purposes being spare parts for Hugin machines; Hugin's share of the cash register market was 12–14%, but its share of the spare parts market for its machines was 100%. On appeal[9] the

---

18 See ch 17, p 625.
19 Case C-179/90 [1991] ECR I-5889, [1994] 4 CMLR 422, para 15.
20 [1992] 5 CMLR 255, para 40.
1   OJ [1994] L 15/8, [1995] 4 CMLR 84.
2   OJ [1998] L 72/30, [1998] 4 CMLR 779.
3   Case C-18/93 [1994] ECR I-1783.
4   OJ [1999] L 69/31, [1999] 5 CMLR 103, upheld on appeal Case C-163/99 *Portugal v Commission* judgment of 29 March 2001.
5   OJ [1999] L 69/24, [1999] 5 CMLR 90.
6   OJ [2000] L 208/36, [2000] 5 CMLR 967.
7   Case C-323/93 *La Crespelle* [1994] ECR I-5077, para 17; this reasoning was applied by the Commission in, for example, *Portuguese Airports* OJ [1999] L 69/31, [1999] 5 CMLR 103, paras 21-22.
8   OJ [1978] L 22/23, [1978] 1 CMLR D19.
9   Case 22/78 *Hugin v Commission* [1979] ECR 1869, [1979] 3 CMLR 345.

ECJ quashed the Commission's decision because it considered there to be no effect on inter-state trade, but it upheld the finding on dominance. A vivid illustration of the vulnerability of small firms under Article 82 is afforded by *BBI/Boosey and Hawkes: Interim Measures*[10]. It was found by the Commission, in an interim decision, to have abused its dominant position when it refused to supply musical instruments to customers who were threatening to enter into competition with it. Boosey and Hawkes' world-wide sales in all products were worth £38 million in 1985, and the market it was accused of dominating was defined as instruments for British-style brass bands, in which its market share was 80–90%.

(B)   Narrow markets

In the *Hugin* case a small part of its activities, the supply of spare parts, constituted the relevant market within which it was dominant. Similarly in *General Motors v Commission*[11], where the Belgian Government had given General Motors the exclusive power to grant test certificates to second-hand imports of Opel cars, this function was held to constitute a separate market, and General Motors' exclusive right meant that it was in a dominant position. The decision in *British Leyland v Commission*[12] was similar, that firm being held to have a dominant position in the provision of national type approval certificates for its vehicles. Two further cases illustrate how narrowly a market can be defined. In *Porto di Genova v Siderurgica Gabrielli*[13] the ECJ held that the organisation of port activities at a single port could constitue a relevant market; and in *Corsica Ferries*[14] it reached the same conclusion in relation to the provision of piloting services at the same port. Similarly narrow markets have been found by the Commission in a series of decisions on services linked to access to airports[15].

The *Football World Cup 1998*[16] decision epitomises the possibility of very narrow market definitions. The Commission proceeded on the basis of abuse in the market for 574,300 'blind pass' tickets to matches at the 1998 World Cup, a blind pass consisting of a ticket where the consumer does not know, at the time of purchase, what game he or she will be seeing[17]. The CFO, responsible for the ticketing arrangements, was found to have abused its dominant position by selling tickets only to customers having a postal address in France: this had caused complaints, not surprisingly, that it was guilty of discrimination in favour of French nationals. A token fine of EUR 1000 was imposed.

10   OJ [1987] L 286/36, [1988] 4 CMLR 67.
11   OJ [1975] L 29/14, [1975] 1 CMLR D20; the decision was quashed by the ECJ on the excessive pricing issue: Case 26/75 *General Motors Continental NV v Commission* [1975] ECR 1367, [1976] 1 CMLR 95: see ch 18, p 635.
12   Case 226/84 [1986] ECR 3263, [1987] 1 CMLR 185.
13   Case C-179/90 [1991] ECR I-5889, [1994] 4 CMLR 422.
14   Case C-18/93 [1994] ECR I-1783.
15   See p 165 above.
16   OJ [2000] L 5/55, [2000] 4 CMLR 963.
17   For example, the third place play-off between, as yet, unidentified teams.

7. ABUSE

Once it has been decided that a firm has a dominant position in a substantial part of the common market, it is necessary to consider what constitutes an abuse of that position. Article 82 gives examples – charging unfair prices, limiting production and discrimination – but this list is not exhaustive[18] and Commission decisions and the case law of the Community Courts have revealed Article 82 to be a formidable weapon. Of particular importance is the ECJ's teleological interpretation of the Treaty whereby it applies the competition rules against the backdrop of the overall objectives expressed in Articles 2 and 3(g). This has been highly significant in the case of anti-competitive abuses[19]. It is not an offence for a firm to have a dominant position, but, as already noted, a firm in a dominant position has a special responsibility not to allow its conduct to impair undistorted competition on the common market[20]; and it would appear that this responsibility becomes greater, so that a finding of abuse becomes more likely, where the firm under investigation is not merely dominant, but super-dominant[1]. The ECJ has often said that the concept of abuse is an objective one[2], meaning that behaviour can be abusive even where the dominant undertaking had no intention of infringing Article 82. Conduct may be harmful to the structure of the market whether it was intended to be harmful or not. The fact that there are certain abuses – for example predatory pricing above average variable cost[3] and selective price cutting[4] – where evidence of intention is an integral part of establishing an infringement does not contradict this idea: intention is not a key component of the concept of abuse.

The most obvious objection to a monopolist is that he is in a position to reduce output and thereby increase the price of his products above the competitive level[5]. However in the absence of barriers to entry a monopolist earning monopoly profits would be expected to attract new entrants to the market: in other words exploitation of a monopoly position may in itself increase competition. Of greater long-term significance is behaviour by a monopolist designed to, or which might have the effect of, preventing the development of competition, and much of the case law of the Community Courts and the decisional practice of the Commission has been concerned with anti-competitive behaviour of this kind. In order to illustrate the kind of behaviour which falls within the mischief of Article 82 it is helpful to consider exploitative and anti-competitive abuses separately, although this is not to suggest that there is a rigid demarcation between these two categories: the same behaviour may feature both. A dominant firm which charges discriminatory prices may be both exploiting its position by earning the maximum profit it can at the expense of customers and harming competition by making it harder for other firms to enter the market. In the same way a refusal to supply may have an exploitative purpose (for example where it is threatened or effected

---

18 Case 6/72 *Continental Can v Commission* [1973] ECR 215, [1973] CMLR 199, para 26; Cases C–395/96 P and C-396/96 P *Compagnie Maritime Belge Transports v Commission* [2000] 4 CMLR 1076, para 112.
19 See p 169ff below.
20 See p 162 above.
1   See pp 162-163 above
2   See eg Case 85/76 *Hoffmann-La Roche v Commission* [1979] ECR 461, [1979] 3 CMLR 211, para 91.
3   See p 178 below and ch 18 pp 646-653.
4   See p 178 below and ch 18 pp 653-657.
5   See the analysis of price theory in ch 1.

in order to make a customer pay a higher price) and an anti-competitive one (where it is intended to remove a competitor from the market). A third category of cases under Article 82 is concerned with practices that are considered to be detrimental to the single market. For example, excessive pricing, as well as being exploitative, may be a ploy to impede parallel imports and to limit intra-brand competition, as in the case of *British Leyland v Commission*[6]. It is also necessary to consider the significance of the doctrines of objective justification and proportionality when determining whether an undertaking is acting abusively.

Abusive practices will be considered in greater detail in later chapters of this book, and in particular in chapters 6, 17 and 18. At this stage it is intended to provide an overview of the type of practices that might be found to be abusive.

(A)   Exploitation

(i)   Exploitative prices, terms and conditions

It is clear from its very wording that Article 82 is capable of application to exploitative behaviour: Article 82(2)(a) gives as an example of an abuse the imposition of unfair purchase or selling prices or other unfair trading conditions. However as a general proposition competition authorities are not keen to establish themselves as price regulators: where prices are high there may be a need for a bespoke regulator, for example where utilities such as telecommunications or water companies are privatised and yet retain a position of monopoly or near monopoly[7]. Competition authorities tend to be keener to apply Article 82-like provisions to prohibit anti-competitive abuses which are harmful to existing competitors or which deter new entrants to the market. Furthermore, even if a competition authority wishes to intervene to control prices, it is not easy to decide when a price is excessive for these purposes. For these reasons there has been relatively little examination of high prices or other exploitative behaviour by the Commission, and the case law of the Community Courts has not authoritatively defined what is meant by an excessive price. Having said this, there may be exceptional cases in which the Commission will investigate high prices: for example in 1997 it began an investigation of the prices in several Member States for international telephone calls[8] and in 1998 it looked at the prices of mobile telephone calls[9]. These files were closed, either because prices came down or because the relevant national competition or regulatory bodies took the investigations over[10]. Exploitative pricing practices are considered further in chapter 18[11]. There have been numerous cases on the activities of collecting societies in which their rules have been scrutinised in order to ensure that they do not act in a way that unfairly exploits the owner of the copyright or the would-be licensee of it; collecting societies are considered in chapter 19[12]. Unfair trading conditions were condemned by the Commission in *1998 Football World Cup*[13],

---

6   Case 226/84 [1986] ECR 3263, [1987] 1 CMLR 185; see p 179-180 below and ch 18, p 637.
7   See ch 23, p 870.
8   Commission Press Release IP(97)1180, 19 December 1997.
9   Commission Press Release IP(98)707, 27 July 1998.
10   See the Commission's XXVIIIth *Report on Competition Policy* (1998), points 79-82.
11   See ch 18, pp 633-639.
12   See ch 19, pp 701 and 719.
13   OJ [2000] L 5/55, [2000] 4 CMLR 963, para 91; see also paras 99-100.

where it considered that the arrangements for the sale of tickets were unfair to consumers resident outside France.

(ii) Other examples of exploitation

In its colloquial sense, exploitation suggests the earning of monopoly profits at the expense of the customer. One of the other 'benefits' of the monopolist is the 'quiet life' and the freedom from the need to innovate and improve efficiency in order to keep up with or ahead of competitors[14]. This raises the question whether inefficiency or inertia could be considered to be an abuse under Article 82. Article 82(2)(b) gives as an example of abuse the limitation of production, markets or technical development to the prejudice of the consumer, and in *British Telecommunications*[15] the Commission objected to behaviour on BT's part which, *inter alia*, meant that the possible use of new technology was impeded. In *Höfner & Elser v Macrotron*[16] the German Federal Employment Office ('the FEO') had a statutory monopoly in respect of the recruitment of executive personnel; in practice private agencies also provided this service, albeit unlawfully, the FEO itself being incapable of satisfying market demand. The ECJ held that it could be an abuse for the FEO to prevent private agencies from offering recruitment services where it was unable to offer them sufficiently itself. In *Merci Convenzionali Porto di Genova v Siderurgica Gabrielli*[17] a port undertaking had exclusive rights under national law to organise or carry out various port operations. The ECJ held that one of the abuses to which these statutory arrangements led was a refusal to use modern technology, which meant that unloading operations were more expensive and protracted than they would otherwise be. These judgments indicate that inefficient monopolies may be challenged under Article 82, and in each of these cases this meant that exclusive rights conferred upon the undertakings in question were themselves substantially undermined. This case law is of particular significance when the special or exclusive rights conferred on undertakings by the State are called into question under the competition rules. These cases are dealt with in more detail in chapter 6[18].

(B) Anti-competitive practices

Article 82 has most frequently been applied to behaviour which the Commission and Community Courts consider to be anti-competitive. In particular many of the cases have involved anti-competitive behaviour aimed specifically at new entrants to a market: the Commission will readily investigate such practices and is likely to impose large fines[19]. The Commission is particularly vigilant to ensure that undertakings in recently liberalised markets do not act in an abusive manner which could eliminate the benefits of liberalisation[20]. The cases on anti-competitive abuses have caused more controversy than those on exploitation do:

14 See ch 1, pp 4-5.
15 OJ [1982] L 360/36, [1983] 1 CMLR 457, upheld on appeal Case 41/83 *Italy v Commission* [1985] ECR 873, [1985] 2 CMLR 368.
16 Case 41/90 [1991] ECR I–1979, [1993] 4 CMLR 306.
17 Case 179/90 [1991] ECR I–5889, [1994] 4 CMLR 422.
18 Ch 6, pp 190-202.
19 See eg the Commission's decisions referred to in p 149, n 1 above.
20 See the Commission's XXVIIIth *Report on Competition Policy* (1998), point 71.

the dominant firm will argue that it is simply competing – as it should do – whereas the complainant will argue that it has departed from competition 'on the merits' and is guilty of abusive behaviour. There is a very fine – sometimes invisible – line between these two positions.

(i)   *Continental Can v Commission*[1]

The ECJ's judgment in this case is a classic example of EC jurisprudence. Whether one agrees with it or not the reasoning and conclusion are remarkable, particularly to the English lawyer attuned to the inductive shifts of the common law. The question before the ECJ was whether mergers could be prohibited under Article 82. One argument against this was that Article 82 was designed to prevent the direct exploitation of consumers and not to deal with the more indirect adverse effects that might be produced by harming the competitive process[2]; therefore structural changes in the market could not be caught. The ECJ rejected this. It was not possible to draw a distinction between direct and indirect effects on the market; instead it was necessary to interpret Article 82 in the light of the spirit of the Treaty generally. Article 3(g) (ex Article 3(f)) required the institution of a system ensuring that competition in the common market is not distorted and Article 2 called for the promotion of a continuous and balanced expansion in economic activities. Articles 81 and 82 had to be interpreted with these aims in mind: it would be futile to prevent agreements which distort competition under Article 81 but then to allow mergers which resulted in the elimination of competition. The adoption in 1989 of the EC Merger Regulation means that Article 82 is now largely redundant in respect of mergers[3]; however *Continental Can* remains immensely important to the law on Article 82, since it confirmed that it could be applied to anti-competitive abuses as well as to exploitative ones.

(ii)   *Causation*

One of the arguments raised by Continental Can was that, even if mergers were caught by Article 82, it had not *used* its market power to effect the merger in question; thus there was a break in the chain of causation between its position on the market and the behaviour alleged to amount to an abuse. It had not, for example, threatened to drive the target firm out of the market by predatory price cutting if it refused to merge[4]. The ECJ rejected this argument as well. It was possible to abuse a dominant position without actually exercising or relying on market power. It was an abuse simply for a dominant firm to strengthen its

---

1   Case 6/72 *Europemballage Corpn and Continental Can Co Inc v Commission* [1973] ECR 215, [1973] CMLR 199; the impact of the judgment is discussed in Vogelenzang 'Abuse of a Dominant Position in Article 86' (1976) 13 CML Rev 61.

2   See eg Joliet *Monopolisation and Abuse of Dominance* (Martinus Nijhoff, 1970); it was also argued in *Continental Can* that mergers were not caught by Article 82 as the ECSC Treaty dealt with them explicitly so that, by inference, the EC Treaty, which was silent on the issue, could not apply to them; and that anyway behaviour could not be abusive unless it was attributable to and caused by the use of the position of dominance (see below).

3   For a further examination of its application to mergers, see ch 21, p 737-738.

4   Cp *ECS/AKZO* OJ [1985] L 374/1, [1986] 3 CMLR 273 at para 85, upheld on appeal Case 62/86 *AKZO Chemie BV v Commission* [1991] ECR I-3359, [1993] 5 CMLR 215.

position and substantially to eliminate competition by taking over a rival. Abuse is an objective concept, and the conduct of an undertaking may be regarded as abusive in the absence of any fault and irrespective of the intention of the dominant undertaking[5]. The scope of Article 82 would obviously be reduced if the Commission could apply it only to practices which were attributable to the exercise of market power that a dominant undertaking enjoys[6]. In *Hoffmann-La Roche* the ECJ said that:

'The interpretation suggested by the applicant that an abuse implies that the use of the economic power bestowed by a dominant position is the means whereby the abuse has been brought about cannot be accepted'[7].

In *Tetra Pak II*[8] the ECJ stated at paragraph 27 of its judgment that 'application of Article [82] presupposes a link between the dominant position and the alleged abusive conduct'. This may appear to contradict the causation point in *Continental Can*. However, the issue in *Tetra Pak* was whether it is possible for the abuse to take place in a market different from the one in which an undertaking is dominant[9]; the Court was not concerned with the issue of whether the market power had to have been used in order to bring about the abuse.

(iii) Abusive conduct and 'traders' performance'[10]

Some conduct may be exclusionary because it reflects greater efficiency. In *Michelin v Commission*[11] the ECJ said that:

'Article [82] covers practices which are likely to affect the structure of a market where, as a direct result of the presence of the undertaking in question, competition has already been weakened and which, through recourse to methods different from those governing normal competition in products or services based on traders' performance, have the effect of hindering the maintenance or development of the level of competition still existing on the market.'[12]

---

5   Case 85/76 *Hoffmann-La Roche v Commission* [1979] ECR 461, [1979] 3 CMLR 211, para 91; Case T–65/89 *BPB Industries v Commission* [1993] ECR II-389, [1993] 5 CMLR 32, para 70.
6   See Vogelenzang 'Abuse of a Dominant Position in Article 86: the Problem of Causality and Some Applications' (1976) 13 CML Rev 61; the Commission relied specifically on this aspect of the *Continental Can* judgment in para 46 of its decision in *Tetra Pak 1 (BTG Licence)* OJ [1988] L 272/27, [1988] 4 CMLR 881.
7   At para 91; note the suggestion by AG Reischl at para 7c of his Opinion in *Hoffmann-la Roche* that causation might be treated differently according to the nature of the abuse in question.
8   Case C-333/94 P *Tetra Pak International v Commission* [1996] ECR I-5951, [1997] 4 CMLR 662.
9   See pp 173-175 below.
10 See Faull and Nikpay *The EC Law of Competition* (Oxford University Press, 1999), paras 3.124-3.130; Al-Dabbah 'Conduct, Performance and Abuse in 'Market Relationship': Analysis of Some Conceptual Issues under Article 82' (2000) 21 ECLR 45.
11 Case 322/81 [1983] ECR 3461, [1985] 1 CMLR 282, para 70.
12 This paragraph in the *Michelin* judgment mirrors quite closely the second part of paragraph 91 of the ECJ's judgment in *Hoffmann-la Roche* (n 12 above), 'normal competition in products or services on the basis of the transactions of commercial operators'; the *Michelin* version 'traders' performance' is more suggestive of taking efficiency into account than the one in *Hoffmann-la Roche*.

This is an important statement: abusive conduct is conduct which is not based on traders' performance; it should follow that a dominant undertaking which 'defeats' a competitor because of its superior economic efficiency should not be condemned under Article 82, since its conduct is based on its performance. An undertaking that wins business 'on the merits', whether dominant or not, must be allowed to do so. In *Irish Sugar plc v Commission*[13] the CFI said that, where a dominant firm takes action to protect its commercial position, its conduct 'must, at the very least, in order to be lawful, be based on criteria of economic efficiency and consistent with the interests of consumers'[14].

There is a second point arising from the extract from the judgment in *Michelin*: it says that practices are abusive where they 'have the effect' of hindering the maintenance or development of the level of competition in the market[15]. This presumably means that, where a particular practice could not produce such an effect, it should not be found to be abusive. This is not to say that the anti-competitive effect must already have been felt: Article 82 can apply to practices that entail a serious risk of anti-competitive effects in the future[16], although the Commission must demonstrate on the basis of convincing evidence that the risk is a real one[17]. However, in the absence of an actual or potential effect on the market, conduct should not be characterised as abusive under Article 82. This raises the question of whether some types of conduct are considered, by law, as having an abusive effect without this having to be demonstrated empirically on the facts of the case; an analogy would be with the position under Article 81(1), according to which some agreements are considered as having as their object the restriction of competition so that it is unnecessary to demonstrate a restrictive effect[18]. Another way of putting this point is that there may be some types of conduct that amount to *per se* infringements of Article 82.[18a] Case law does not provide very much guidance on this point, although some judgments suggest a *per se* standard for some kinds of conduct: for example in *Irish Sugar plc v Commission*[19] the CFI stated that 'where an undertaking in a dominant position actually implements a practice aimed at ousting a competitor, the fact that the result hoped for is not achieved is not sufficient to prevent that being an abuse of a dominant position within the meaning of Article 82'[20]. The economics of abuse are complex and controversial, considerably more so, for example, than those of horizontal price fixing. This being so, it may be questioned whether it is really

---

13 Case T-228/97 [1999] ECR II-2969, [1999] 5 CMLR 1300.
14 Ibid, para 189.
15 On exclusionary effect, see *Faull and Nikpay*, paras 3.131-3.135.
16 Case 6 and 7/73 *Commercial Solvents v Commission* [1974] ECR 223, [1974] 1 CMLR 309, para 25.
17 This would be consistent with the requirement of the CFI in Cases T-374/94 etc *European Night Services v Commission* [1998] ECR II-3141, [1998] 5 CMLR 718 that, where the Commission considers that an agreement might restrict potential as opposed to actual competition under Article 81(1), it must adduce convincing evidence to that effect: see ch 3, pp 102-103.
18 See ch 3, pp 92-95.
18a For a discussion of the issue of whether there sould be *per se* infringements of s 2 of the US Sherman Act 1890 on monopolisation, see Muris 'The FTC and the Law of Monopolisation'(2000) 67 Antitrust Law Journal 693, concluding that there should not be: see further (2000) 168 Antitrust Law Journal 309 (a response by Balto and Nagato) and (2000) 68 Antitrust Law Journal 325 (a response by Muris); Muris is the chairman of the Federal Trade Commission.
19 Case T-228/97 [1999] ECR II-2969, [1999] 5 CMLR 1300
20 Ibid, para 191; see also Case 62/86 *AKZO Chemie BV v Commission* [1991] ECR I-3359, [1993] 5 CMLR 215, suggesting a *per se* rule on predatory pricing below average variable cost: see ch 18, pp 648-649.

appropriate to adopt *per se* rules under Article 82, even thought they may be appropriate for obvious restrictions of competition under Article 81(1); all the more so given that it is always possible to argue that an agreement that infringes Article 81(1) may satisfy the criteria of Article 81(3)[1]. There is much to be said to condemning conduct as abusive only where it can convincingly be demonstrated that there will be adverse effects on the market.

The great difficulty with Article 82 is that it can be very difficult to distinguish those practices that amount to competition 'on the merits' from those that are characterised as abusive. Dominant firms must be allowed to compete, as the Community Courts have regularly acknowledged[2]; however some competitive responses, for example selective price cutting and rebating, might be considered to depart from competition on the merits and so be held to be abusive. There is a fine line, but it is one that has to be drawn. In the absence of an intellectually convincing synthesis of all the cases in which conduct has been found to be abusive, the second-best solution is to try to define those categories of abuse which reflect the case law of the Community Courts. This process is somewhat jejune, but nevertheless it provides insights into the application of Article 82. Some categories will be suggested below[3]; they will be considered in further detail in chapters 6[4], 17[5] and 18[6].

(iv) The dominant position, the abuse and the effects of the abuse may be in different markets

It has become clear from the jurisprudence of the Community Courts and from the decisional practice of the Commission that it is not necessary for the dominance, the abuse and the effects of the abuse all to be in the same market. In a simple case, X may be dominant in the market for widgets and charge high prices to exploit its customers or drop its prices in order to eliminate competitors from the widget market: clearly Article 82 can apply to this behaviour. However, more complex situations can be imagined. X might be present on both the widget market and the neighbouring blodget market, and may act on one of those markets in order to derive a benefit in the other. At risk of over-simplification, the widget and blodget markets may be related 'horizontally' to one another: for example they may be different types of vitamins or building materials; or they may be related 'vertically': widgets may be 'upstream' from blodgets, where they are a raw material or some other kind of input, or they may be 'downstream' from blodgets, for example where they are a derivative product.

Some examples should assist in understanding these somewhat abstract statements.

(A) *MICHELIN V COMMISSION*[7]: Michelin was dominant in the market for replacement tyres and committed various abuses in order to protect its position in that market.

1   See ch 4, p 124ff.
2   See eg Case T-228/97 *Irish Sugar plc v Commission* [1999] ECR II-2969, [1999] 5 CMLR 1300, paras 112 and 189.
3   See pp 175-179 below.
4   Ch 6, pp 197-202.
5   Ch 17, pp 601-627.
6   Ch 18, pp 639-662.
7   Case 322/81 [1983] ECR 3461, [1985] 1 CMLR 282.

(B)   *COMMERCIAL SOLVENTS*[8] : Commercial Solvents supplied a raw material in which it was dominant to a customer which used it to make an anti-tuberculosis drug. The raw material was 'upstream' of the drug, the 'downstream' or 'derivative' product: the relationship between the markets was vertical. Commercial Solvents decided to produce the drug itself and ceased to supply the customer. Commercial Solvents was found to have abused its dominant position: it refused to supply the raw material in relation to which it was dominant, but this was done to benefit its position in the drug market, where it was not yet present at all.

(C)   *TÉLÉMARKETING*[9] : the dominant undertaking, a broadcasting authority with a statutory monopoly, decided to enter the downstream telemarketing sector. It ceased to supply broadcasting services to the only other telemarketer, thereby eliminating it from the market and effectively reserving the telemarketing business to itself.

(D)   *SEALINK/B AND I – HOLYHEAD: INTERIM MEASURES*[10] : Sealink, which owned and operated the port at Holyhead, was considered to have committed an abuse on the market for the provision of port facilities for passenger and ferry services, in which it was dominant, by structuring the sailing schedules there to the advantage of its own downstream ferry operations and to the disadvantage of its competitor at that level of the market, B&I. The same point can be noted in *Sea Containers v Stena Sealink – Interim Measures*.[11]

(E)   *BRITISH GYPSUM V COMMISSION*[12] : British Gypsum was dominant in the plasterboard market, but not dominant in the neighbouring plaster market (these markets were 'horizontally' related in the sense used above). Among its abuses, British Gypsum gave priority treatment to customers for plaster who remained loyal to it in relation to plasterboard. This differs from the above examples, since in *British Gypsum* the abuse was committed in the non-dominated market in order to protect British Gypsum's position in its dominated market.

(F)   *TETRA PAK II*[13] : the ECJ concluded that Tetra Pak had infringed Article 82 by tying practices and predatory pricing[14] in the market for non-aseptic liquid repackaging machinery and non-aseptic cartons. It was not dominant in this market, but the abusive conduct was intended to benefit its position in that market. Tetra Pak was dominant in the (horizontally) associated market for aseptic machinery and cartons. The ECJ, after citing *Commercial Solvents*, *Télémarketing* and *British Gypsum*, held that 'in special circumstances'[15], there could be an abuse of a dominant position 'where conduct on a market distinct from the dominated market produces effects on that distinct market'[16] . The ECJ then went on to describe the 'close associative links' between the aseptic and non-aseptic markets which amounted to sufficiently special circumstances to engage Article 82: for example Tetra Pak had or could have customers in both markets, it could

---

8   Case 6/73 etc [1974] ECR 223, [1974] 1 CMLR 309.
9   Case 311/84 *Centre Belge d'Etudes de Marché Télémarketing v CTL* [1985] ECR 3261, [1986] 2 CMLR 558.
10   [1992] 5 CMLR 255.
11   OJ [1994] L 15/8, [1995] 4 CMLR 84.
12   Case C-310/93 P [1995] ECR I-865, [1997] 4 CMLR 238.
13   Case C-333/94 P [1996] ECR I-5951, [1997] 4 CMLR 662; the ECJ's approach to the issue of abuse was different from that of the Commission's in its decision.
14   On these practices in detail, see ch 17, pp 605-611 and ch 18, pp 646-653 below.
15   Case 333/94 P [1996] ECR I-5951, [1997] 4 CMLR 662, paras 25-31.
16   Ibid.

rely on having a favoured status in the non-dominated market because of its position in the dominated one, and it could concentrate its efforts on the non-aseptic market independently of other economic operators because of its position in relation to the aseptic market. This case undoubtedly extends the scope of application of Article 82 beyond, even, *British Gypsum*.

A table may help to explain the propositions set out in this paragraph.

Dominance, abuse and neighbouring markets

Case	Market A	Market B
Michelin v Commission	Dominance Abuse Benefit	
Commercial Solvents; Télémarketing; Sealink decisions	Dominance	Abuse Benefit
British Gypsum v Commission	Dominance Benefit	Abuse
Tetra Pak v Commission II	Dominance	Abuse Benefit

Many of the Commission's decisions under Article 82 in recent years have involved two rather than one market. A good example is *Virgin/British Airways*[17]: BA's dominant position was in the market for the procurement of travel agents' services; its abuse in that market was found by the Commission to have effects on the neighbouring market for air transport[18]. It may be that the Commission can apply the reasoning just described in the context of neighbouring product markets to dominance, abuse and benefits in neighbouring geographical markets[19].

(v) *Examples of anti-competitive abuses*

The Commission and the Community Courts have condemned many practices which could have anti-competitive effects.

(A) HARMING THE COMPETITIVE STRUCTURE OF THE MARKET.   As we have seen, the application of Article 82 to mergers was established in *Continental Can*[20]. There has been one other decision since actually condemning a merger[1], and the Commission was sometimes able to prevent the consummation of other mergers by threatening Article 82 proceedings. However, the inadequacy of Article 82 as

17 OJ [2000] L 30/1, [2000] 4 CMLR 999, on appeal to Case T-219/99 *British Airways v Commission* (grounds of appeal OJ [2000] C 20/21) (judgment pending).
18 Ibid, paras 96-111.
19 See eg *Interbrew* in the Commission's XXVIth *Report on Competition Policy* (1996), point 53, where Interbrew was considered to have acted in non-dominated geographical markets to protect its dominant position in Belgium.
20 Case 6/72 [1973] ECR 215, [1973] CMLR 199.
1   *Warner-Lambert/Gillette* OJ [1993] L 116/21, [1993] 5 CMLR 559.

a tool for controlling EC mergers lay behind the Commission's eagerness for a specific regulation, which finally emerged in 1989 after a gestation period of 16 years[2]. The application of Article 82 to mergers after the ECMR is dealt with in chapter 21[3]. Even though mergers would now be dealt with under the ECMR, the Commission considers that the *Continental Can* case is authority for the proposition that it can be an abuse to alter the competitive structure of a market where competition on that market is already weakened as a result of the very presence of the dominant undertaking on it. This is demonstrated by *Tetra Pak 1 (BTG Licence)*[4], where the Commission objected to the acquisition, by merger, of an exclusive licence of patents and know-how which would prevent competitors entering Tetra Pak's market; a further example of such an abuse would be the elimination of potential competition on the market by inducing would-be competitors to join a liner conference that has a collective dominant position rather than leaving them to enter the market on a normal competitive basis[5].

(B)   REQUIREMENTS CONTRACTS AND TIE-INS.   The ECJ condemned requirements contracts in *Hoffmann-La Roche v Commission*[6], whereby customers were required to purchase all or most of their requirements of vitamins from Roche, because the effect could be to foreclose opportunities for other competitors. The Commission has on numerous occasions taken action against requirements contracts and other exclusive dealing agreements under Article 82[7]. It has also condemned tie-in sales whereby a customer, as a condition of acquiring one product, is required to purchase another one[8]: the abusive nature of tie-in transactions is explicitly recognised in Article 82(2)(d). In these cases the concern is that customers are tied to the dominant undertaking, with the consequence that access to the market is foreclosed to competitors. Pricing practices that have a tying effect are also condemned[9].

(C)   CABINET EXCLUSIVITY.   In one of its most far-reaching decisions to date, the Commission decided in *Van den Bergh Foods*[10] that it could be abusive for a firm in a dominant position (in that case in relation to the market for 'impulse' ice-cream) to induce retailers to take free-on-loan freezer cabinets, in which only the dominant undertaking's ice-creams, but not those of its competitors, could be stored. The Commission's view was that, in the context of the market for such ice-cream in Ireland, such a practice foreclosed access in relation to a particular retail outlet for other competitors on that market. The Commission also found that the agreements with the retailers infringed Article 81. In paragraphs 211 to 220 of its decision it rejected an argument that such a finding would unreasonably interfere with the property rights of Van den Bergh stating that, whilst the Treaty

2   Council Regulation 4064/89/EEC, OJ [1990] L 257/13, as amended by Council Regulation 1310/97/EC, OJ [1997] L 180/1.
3   See ch 21, pp 737-738.
4   OJ [1988] L 272/27, [1988] 4 CMLR 881, upheld on appeal Case T–51/89 *Tetra Pak Rausing SA v Commission* [1990] ECR II-309, [1991] 4 CMLR 334.
5   See *TACA* OJ [1999] L 95/1, [1999] 4 CMLR 1415, paras 559-567, on appeal to the CFI, Case T-191/98 etc *Atlantic Container Line v Commission* (judgment pending).
6   Case 85/76 [1979] ECR 461, [1979] 3 CMLR 211.
7   See ch 17, pp 601-605.
8   See ch 17, pp 605-611.
9   See ch 18, pp 639-645.
10   OJ [1998] L 246/1, [1998] 5 CMLR 530; the Commission's decision was suspended by the CFI pending the result of the appeal: Case T-65/98 R *Van den Bergh Foods v Commission* [1998] ECR II-2641, [1998] 5 CMLR 475; the appeal itself was stayed pending the ECJ's judgment in a related case referred to it under Article 234, Case C-344/98 *Masterfoods Ltd v HB Ice Cream Ltd* [2001] All ER (EC) 130, [2001] 4 CMLR 449.

respected the existence of property rights, it could in certain circumstances be improper to exercise those rights in a way that would lead to a detriment to competition[11].

(D)   REFUSALS TO SUPPLY AND THE ESSENTIAL FACILITIES DOCTRINE.   The ECJ upheld the Commission's decision[12] in *Commercial Solvents v Commission*[13] that Commercial Solvents had abused its dominant position by refusing to supply nitropropane to Zoja. The Court agreed that it was an abuse to refuse to supply an existing customer which would, as a result, be eliminated from the downstream market. In *Hugin v Commission*[14] the ECJ did not comment on the Commission's decision that Hugin had abused its position by refusing to supply spare parts to Liptons because it held there was no effect on inter-state trade. Refusals to supply motivated by an intention to eliminate an actual or potential competitor have been condemned in several Commission decisions[15]. The Commission will need to be satisfied that there is an objective justification for the refusal to supply (for example that the customer was in debt) if it is to be persuaded that there is no abuse.

Refusal to supply as a technique for dividing markets may be an abuse[16]. Even a refusal to supply a new customer (as opposed to an existing one) may be an abuse, for example where it is based on the nationality of the customer[17] or where an undertaking has a very large market share[18]. A refusal to grant copyright licences to third parties may be regarded as an anti-competitive exercise of intellectual property rights in some circumstances[19].

The Commission has over a number of years been developing a doctrine of 'essential facilities' whereby a dominant undertaking which both owns and controls a facility or infrastructure to which competitors need access in order to provide services to customers, cannot refuse access to such competitors or grant them access only on terms less favourable than those it gives to its own operations. This doctrine has emerged from the cases on refusal to supply, and is discussed in detail in chapter 17[20].

(E)   PRICING PRACTICES HAVING A TYING EFFECT[1].   Just as requirements contracts and tie-ins are condemned, so too are pricing practices which could have the same effect. Loyalty rebates,[2] across the board rebates,[3] target discounts,[4] uniform

---

11   See pp 181-182 below on the abuse of dominance and property rights.
12   *Zoja/CSC-ICI* JO [1972] L 299/51, [1973] CMLR D50.
13   Cases 6/73 and 7/73 [1974] ECR 223, [1974] 1 CMLR 309.
14   Case 22/78 [1979] ECR 1869, [1979] 3 CMLR 345.
15   See eg *BBI/Boosey and Hawkes: Interim Measures* OJ [1987] L 286/36, [1988] 4 CMLR 67; *Napier Brown – British Sugar* OJ [1988] L 284/41, [1990] 4 CMLR 196.
16   Case 226/84 *British Leyland v Commission* [1986] ECR 3263, [1987] 1 CMLR 185: see pp 179-180 below on abuses that are harmful to the single market.
17   Case 7/82 *GVL v Commission* [1983] ECR 483, [1983] 3 CMLR 645.
18   Case 311/84 *Centre Belge d'Etudes de Marché Télé-marketing v CLT and IPB* [1985] ECR 3261, [1986] 2 CMLR 558 (where the dominance was conferred by statute).
19   Cases T–69/89 etc *RTE v Commission* [1991] ECR II-485, [1991] 4 CMLR 586; Case 53/87 *CICRA etc v Regie Nationale des Usines Renault* [1988] ECR 6039, [1990] 4 CMLR 265; Case 238/87 *AB Volvo v Erik Veng* [1988] ECR 6211, [1989] 4 CMLR 122: see ch 19, pp 698-701 on these decisions.
20   See ch 17, pp 611-624.
1   See ch 18 pp 639-645.
2   See eg Case 85/76 *Hoffmann-La Roche v Commission* [1979] ECR 461, [1979] 3 CMLR 211.
3   Ibid.
4   Case 322/81 *Michelin v Commission* [1983] ECR 3461, [1985] 1 CMLR 282.

delivered pricing[5] and 'top-slice' rebates[6] have all been condemned under Article 82.

(F) PRICING PRACTICES THAT ARE INTENDED TO ELIMINATE COMPETITORS. Predatory pricing, that is to say selling at less than cost, may be an abuse of a dominant position[7]; in certain circumstances a dominant undertaking that adopts a policy of selective price-cutting, though at prices above cost, may be guilty of an abuse where the pricing strategy is part of a determined policy to eliminate a competitor and where the dominant firm has a very large market share[8].

(G) PRICE DISCRIMINATION[9]. Price discrimination might be unlawful (and anti-competitive) in the sense of Article 82(2)(c) where dissimilar conditions are applied to equivalent transactions, thereby placing one trading party at a competitive disadvantage with others. This type of offence looks at injury to competitors not at the level of the discriminating firm, but at the level of its customers, so-called 'secondary-line injury'. Since one customer has to pay a higher price than another for a particular input, it will be at a comparative disadvantage when it conducts business in the downstream market. Article 82(2)(c) infringements have been relatively few, but there have been more in recent years than used to be the case: an example is *Aéroports de Paris – Alpha Flight Services*[10], where different ground-handlers at two Parisian airports were treated in a discriminatory manner by the airport operator. In *Deutsche Bahn v Commission* the CFI stated that maintaining 'artificial price differences so as to place customers at a disadvantage and to distort competition' is an abuse.[11]

In some cases, pricing practices may be found to be abusive both because of their exclusionary effect and because they are discriminatory. An example of this is the decision in *Virgin/British Airways*[12] where the rebates offered to travel agents by BA were found not only to have an unlawful tying effect[13] but also to be discriminatory contrary to Article 82(2)(c), since travel agents handling the same number of BA tickets could receive different commission rates.

5   *Napier Brown – British Sugar* OJ [1988] L 284/41, [1990] 4 CMLR 196.
6   *Soda – Solvay* OJ [1991] L 152/51 and *Soda-ash – ICI* OJ [1991] L 152/40: these decisions were annulled on procedural grounds by the CFI, Cases T-30/91 etc *Solvay SA v Commission* [1995] ECR II-1775, [1996] 5 CMLR 57; the Commission readopted them in December 2000: see p 151, n 16 above.
7   See ch 18, pp 646-653.
8   Cases C-395/96 P and C-396/96 P *Compagnie Maritime Belge Transports* v *Commission* [2000] 4 CMLR 1076; *Irish Sugar* OJ [1997] L 258/1, [1997] 5 CMLR 666, upheld on appeal, Case T-228/97 *Irish Sugar plc v Commission* [1999] ECR II-2969, [1999] 5 CMLR 1300.
9   See ch 18, pp 657-662.
10   OJ [1998] L 230/10, [1998] 5 CMLR 611 (upheld on appeal Case T-128/98 *Aéroports de Paris v Commission* [2001] 4 CMLR 1376); see similarly *Portuguese Airports* OJ [1999] L69/31, [1999] 5 CMLR 103; upheld on appeal, Case 163/99 *Portugal v Commission* judgment of 29 March 2001; similar matters were dealt with in *Ilmailulaitos/Luftfartsverket* on Finnish Airports, although this decision did not involve a state measure, the airport authority in this case being a self-financing public undertaking: OJ [1999] L 69/24, [1999] 5 CMLR 90.
11   Case T-229/94 *Deutsche Bahn v Commission* [1997] ECR II-1689, [1998] 4 CMLR 220, para 78, upheld on appeal to the ECJ, Case 436/97 P [1999] ECR I-2387, [1999] 5 CMLR 776.
12   OJ [2000] L 30/1, [2000] 4 CMLR 999, on appeal Case T-219/99 *British Airways v Commission* (grounds of appeal OJ [2000] C 20/21) (judgment pending).
13   Ibid, para 101, where the Commission reviewed the ECJ's judgments in Case 85/76 *Hoffmann-La Roche* [1979] ECR 461, [1979] 3 CMLR 211 and Case 322/81 *Michelin v Commission* [1983] ECR 3461, [1985] 1 CMLR 282.

(H)   OTHER ANTI-COMPETITIVE ABUSIVE PRACTICES.   The Commission held in *Decca Navigator System*[14] that it is an abuse for an undertaking in a dominant position to enter into an agreement with an actual or potential competitor with the intention of sharing markets or stunting the efforts of competitors. In the course of the *Promedia* case[15], the Commission stated that entering into litigation, which is the expression of the fundamental right of access to a judge, is not an abuse; however, where a dominant firm brings an action '(i) which cannot reasonably be considered as an attempt to establish its rights and can therefore only serve to harass the opposite party, and (ii) which is conceived in the framework of a plan whose goal is to eliminate competition', this could be abusive. The CFI's judgment, in which it upheld the decision of the Commission not to proceed against Belgacom following a complaint from Promedia, appears, at paragraphs 72 and 73, to have confirmed the Commission's view that vexatious litigation could amount to an abuse in the circumstances envisaged by it. The CFI also stated in this judgment that a claim for the performance of a contractual obligation could amount to an abuse where the claim 'exceeds what the parties could reasonably expect under the contract or if the circumstances applicable at the time of the conclusion of the contract have changed in the meantime'[16].

It should be said that several of these findings are controversial, and that it is by no means obvious that all of these practices should have been condemned as abusive: however, a firm that is dominant or that fears that it might be considered to be dominant will wish to peruse these precedents carefully in order to understand where the potential pitfalls are to be found.

(C)   Abuses that are harmful to the single market

As one would expect, abuses that are harmful to the single market are condemned[17]. The pressure not to export sugar to other Member States applied to Belgian customers by Raffinerie Tirlemontoise was held to be an abuse within Article 82 in *Suiker Unie v Commission*[18] and, had the evidence supported the allegation, the Court would have condemned import bans in that case too[19]. In *British Leyland v Commission*[20] BL's pricing policy in respect of type approval certificates had the effect of reducing imports of BL cars from the continent into the UK, and the Commission's condemnation of this conduct was upheld on appeal by the ECJ. In *Eurofix-Bauco v Hilti*[1] one of Hilti's abuses was to have imposed pressure on its distributors in the Netherlands not to supply Hilti compatible cartridge strips to the UK. In *AAMS*[2] the Commission concluded that both contractual and unilateral practices on the part of an Italian cigarette producer and distributor intended to limit access for foreign cigarettes to the

14   OJ [1989] L 43/27, [1990] 4 CMLR 627.
15   Case T-111/96 *ITT Promedia v Commission* [1998] ECR II-2937, [1998] 5 CMLR 491; see Preece 'ITT *Promedia v EC Commission*: Establishing an Abuse of Predatory Litigation?' (1999) 20 ECLR 118.
16   Ibid, para 140.
17   See ch 1, p 19 and ch 2, p 47 on the single market imperative.
18   Cases 40/73 etc [1975] ECR 1663, [1976] 1 CMLR 295.
19   See also the fate of the 'green banana' clause in Case 27/76 *United Brands v Commission* [1978] ECR 207, [1978] 1 CMLR 429.
20   Case 226/84 [1986] ECR 3263, [1987] 1 CMLR 185.
1   OJ [1988] L 65/19, [1989] 4 CMLR 677.
2   OJ [1998] L 252/47, on appeal Case T-139/98 *Amministratzione Autonoma dei Monopoli di Stato v Commission* (judgment pending).

Italian market amounted to an abuse of a dominant position; a fine of EUR 6 million was imposed. Rebates and discounts intended to keep imports out of a dominant firm's territory will be condemned[3].

(D) Objective justification and the principle of proportionality

The term abuse bears great intellectual strain, particularly as there is no equivalent to Article 81(3) whereby conduct may be exonerated because of some compensating benefit and as transgressions of Article 82 have serious consequences for the guilty party. In order to distinguish abusive behaviour caught by Article 82 from legitimate behaviour outside it, the Community Courts and Commission will use two tools – objective justification and proportionality – as a way of distinguishing legitimate commercial behaviour from conduct which is within the mischief of Article 82.

The language of objective justification and proportionality can be found in many judgments and decisions. For example in *Centre Belge d'Etudes de Marché Télé-marketing v CLT*[4] the ECJ, in an Article 234 reference from the Tribunal de Commerce in Brussels, held that an undertaking in a dominant position in television broadcasting which entrusted 'telemarketing' to its own subsidiary, thereby excluding other firms from entering this market, would be guilty of an abuse where there was no objective necessity for such behaviour[5]. The Commission in *Eurofix-Bauco v Hilti*[6] considered at length whether there was any objective justification, such as safety considerations and the prevention of false and misleading advertising, for Hilti's practice of requiring purchasers of Hilti nail cartridges to also purchase Hilti nails, but concluded that there was no such justification. When dismissing Hilti's appeal, the CFI concluded that there are laws in the UK attaching penalties to the sale of dangerous products and to the use of misleading claims as to the characteristics of products, as well as authorities vested with powers to enforce those laws; it was not for Hilti to take steps on its own initiative to eliminate products which, rightly or wrongly, it regarded as dangerous or inferior to its own[7]. In *Tetra Pak 1 (BTG Licence)*[8] the Commission considered whether there was any objective justification for Tetra Pak's acquisition of an exclusive patent and know-how licence, and concluded that there was not; in his Opinion in the appeal by Tetra Pak to the CFI, Advocate General Kirschner considered at length the proportionality of its behaviour. The Commission rejected claims in *Tetra Pak II* that the tie-in provisions were necessary to protect health and to avoid product liability[9]. The principles of objective justification and

3   *BPB Industries* OJ [1989] L 10/50, [1990] 4 CMLR 464, upheld on appeal to the CFI Case
      T-65/89 *BPB Industries plc and British Gypsum v Commission* [1993] ECR II-389, [1993] 5
      CMLR 32 and further on appeal to the ECJ Case 310/93P *BPB Industries plc and British
      Gypsum v Commission* [1995] ECR I-865, [1995] 4 CMLR 238.
4   Case 311/84 [1985] ECR 3261, [1986] 2 CMLR 558.
5   Ibid, para 26.
6   OJ [1988] L 65/19, [1989] 4 CMLR 677.
7   Case T–30/89 *Hilti AG v Commission* [1991] ECR II-1439, [1992] 14 CMLR 16, paras
      102–119.
8   OJ [1988] L 272/27, [1988] 4 CMLR 881, paras 49–52, upheld on appeal Case T-51/89
      Tetra Pak Rausing SA v Commission [1990] ECR II-309, [1991] 4 CMLR 334.
9   OJ [1992] L 72/1, [1992] 4 CMLR 551, paras 118-120; upheld on appeal to the CFI Case T–
      83/91 *Tetra Pak International SA v Commission* [1994] ECR II-755, [1997] 4 CMLR 726,
      paras 136-140; on appeal to the ECJ Case 333/94 *Tetra Pak International SA v Commission*
      [1996] ECR I-5951, [1997] 4 CMLR 662, para 37.

proportionality have been invoked on other occasions[10] and are now firmly part of Article 82 analysis. In *Portuguese Airports*[11] the Commission rejected as an objective justification for the discount system operated for the use of airports in Portugal that Barcelona and Madrid operated a similar system the Commission was proceeding against them anyway, and a Member State cannot justify an infringement of the Treaty by arguing that another Member State was guilty of the same infringement.

8. ABUSE OF DOMINANCE AND PROPERTY RIGHTS

In a number of cases under Article 82 a particular issue has been the extent to which a dominant undertaking could be held to have acted abusively in relation to the way in which it chose to use, or not to use, its own property. Article 295 EC (ex Article 222) provides that 'This Treaty shall in no way prejudice the rules in Member States governing the system of property ownership'. If it is possible for the Commission, under Article 82, to order the owner, for example, of an essential facility to provide access to it to a third party[12], this clearly affects that undertaking's property rights; but has it affected them to the point where the rules on property ownership in Member States have been prejudiced? The issue arose in relation to *Frankfurt Airport*[13] where the Commission required FAG, the owner and operator of that airport, to allow competition in the market for ground-handling services there. The Commission rejected the argument that this would interfere with the property rights of FAG. The Commission noted that the ECJ in *Hauer v Land Rheinland Pfalz*[14] had acknowledged the existence of a fundamental right to property in the Community legal order; however it had also noted that the constitutions of the Member States recognised that the exercise of property rights may be restricted in the public interest. In the *Frankfurt Airport* decision, the Commission said that it followed from the *Hauer* judgment that the competition rules in the Treaty may be considered to constitute restrictions on the right of property which correspond to objectives of general interest pursued by the Community[15]. In its view, allowing the provision of ground-handling services within the airport would not constitute an excessive or intolerable interference with its rights as owner of the airport; it would not interfere with its own ability to provide these services, and it could charge a reasonable fee to third parties for their right to do so. In his Opinion in *Masterfoods Ltd v HB Ice Cream Ltd*[16] Advocate General Cosmas had no doubt that 'it is perfectly comprehensible for restrictions to be placed on the right to property ownership pursuant to Articles [81] and [82] of the EC Treaty, to the degree to which they might be necessary to protect competition'[17].

10 See eg *BBI/Boosey and Hawkes* OJ [1987] L 286/36, [1988] 4 CMLR 67; *BPB Industries plc* OJ [1989] L 10/50, [1990] 4 CMLR 464, para 132, upheld on appeal Case T–65/89 *BPB Industries plc and British Gypsum v Commission* [1993] ECR II-389, [1993] 5 CMLR 32 and further on appeal to the ECJ Case C-310/93 P *BPB Industries plc and British Gypsum v Commission* [1995] ECR I-865, [1997] 4 CMLR 238; *Napier Brown – British Sugar* OJ [1988] L 284/41, [1990] 4 CMLR 196, paras 64 and 70.
11 OJ [1999] L 69/31, [1999] 5 CMLR 103, para 29.
12 See p 177 above and ch 17, pp 611-624.
13 *Flughafen Frankfurt* OJ [1998] L 72/30, [1998] 4 CMLR 779.
14 Case 44/79 [1979] ECR 3727, [1980] 3 CMLR 42, para 17.
15 *Flughafen Frankfurt* OJ [1998] L 72/30, [1998] 4 CMLR 779, para 90.
16 [2001] All ER (EC) 130, [2001] 4 CMLR 449.
17 Ibid, para 105.

9. POWERS OF THE COMMISSION UNDER ARTICLE 82 AND REGULATION 17/62

Where the Commission finds an abuse of a dominant position, it has power, pursuant to Article 15 of Regulation 17/62, to impose a fine[18], and to order the dominant undertaking to cease and desist from the conduct in question[19]; where necessary, it may also order a dominant undertaking to adopt positive measures in order to bring an infringement to an end[20]. It would appear to be the case that it is not possible for the Commission to order the divestiture of an undertaking's assets, or to break an undertaking up, under the powers conferred by Regulation 17/62, except to reverse a transaction which itself amounted to an abuse[1].

In many cases the Commission has negotiated a settlement with the undertaking under investigation, without reaching a formal decision and imposing a fine, in return for an agreed remedy. Through the use of informal settlements of this kind the Commission can sometimes achieve as much if not more than it would have done if it had gone through the formal procedure and reached a final decision: an undertaking may agree to change its conduct in the future, and perhaps agree even to a structural remedy, that could not have been forced upon it by formal decision. It is noticeable that a number of important cases have been settled in this way. An important example in the early 1980's was the settlement in the *IBM* case[2]. Subsequent examples include *IRI/Nielsen*[3], *SWIFT*[4], *Belgacom*[5], *Digital*[6], *Athens Airport*[7] and *IRE/Nordion*[8].

10. CIVIL CONSEQUENCES OF ARTICLE 82

The civil law consequences of infringing Article 82 are discussed in chapter 8[9].

---

18 See ch 7, pp 237-239.
19 See ibid, pp 235-237.
20 Ibid, p 236.
1   Ibid, pp 236-237.
2   See ch 17, p 613.
3   See the Commission's XXVIth *Report on Competition Policy* (1996), pp 144-148 (termination of exclusivity contracts, unbundling of products)
4   XXVIIth *Report on Competition Policy* 1997, pp 143-145 (non-discriminatory access to cross-border payment services).
5   Ibid, pp 152-153 (access to date regarding subscribers to Belgacom's voice telephony services).
6   Ibid, pp 153-154 (unbundling of products and amendment to pricing policies); see Dolmans and Pickering 'The 1997 Digital Undertaking' (1998) 19 ECLR 108; Andrews 'Aftermarket Power in the Computer Services Market: The Digital Undertaking' (1998) 19 ECLR 176.
7   Commission's XXVIIth *Report on Competition Policy* (1997), points 131-134 (improvements to airport terminal, abolition of monopoly over ground-handling services).
8   Commission's XXVIIIth *Report on Competition Policy* (1998), point 74 and pp 169-170 (renunciation of exclusivity clauses in sales contracts).
9   See pp 275-284.

CHAPTER 6

The obligations of Member States under the EC competition rules

1. INTRODUCTION

This chapter will examine the obligations of Member States in relation to the competition rules in the EC Treaty. Specifically it is necessary to consider the obligations that Article 10 (former Article 5), Article 31 (former Article 37) and Article 86 (former Article 90) place upon Member States; Articles 87 to 89 (former Articles 92 to 94) will be briefly mentioned at the end of the chapter. Article 10 imposes a general duty of 'sincere cooperation' or 'loyalty' on Member States; Article 31 deals specifically with state monopolies of a commercial character; and Article 86 is concerned with measures that are contrary to the Treaty. In *France v Commission*[1] Advocate General Tesauro spoke of the 'obscure clarity' of Article 31 as opposed to the 'clear obscurity' of Article 86. These provisions are complex and the law has taken a long time to develop: the encroachment of the Treaty on national monopolies and state activity is inevitably political and contentious.

The Treaty itself provides, in Article 3(g) (former Article 3(f)), that one of the activities of the Community shall be to institute 'a system ensuring that competition in the internal market is not distorted'. Article 4 (former Article 3a) provides that the activities of the Member States and the Community shall be conducted in accordance with the principle of an open market economy with free competition. State involvement in economic activities may work against this goal; however Member States may take offence at too much interference at an EC level in domestic economic policy. Articles 81 and 82 are essentially private law provisions, conferring rights and imposing obligations on undertakings; many other Articles in the Treaty are primarily of a public law nature, imposing obligations on Member States. The extent to which Member States and undertakings which enjoy special or exclusive rights are subject to Articles 81 and 82 is an issue that is still being explored by the Commission and the Community Courts.

The Treaty is neutral on the issue of public ownership of industry in itself. Article 295 (former Article 222) provides that the Treaty 'shall in no way prejudice the rules in Member States governing the system of property ownership'. This means that Member States may confer legal monopolies on organs of the State

---

1   Case C-202/88 [1991] ECR I-1223, [1992] 5 CMLR 552, at para 11 of his Opinion.

or on undertakings that are not publicly owned, and in cases under Article 86(1) such as *Sacchi*[2], *ERT v Dimotiki*[3] and *Höfner & Elser v Macrotron*[4] the ECJ has held that the conferment of special or exclusive rights on an undertaking is not, in itself, an infringement of the Treaty. However, there is a tension between this principle and the obligation imposed on Member States by Article 86(1) not to enact or maintain in force measures contrary to the competition rules in the Treaty, with the result that property rights are not as inviolable as the wording of Article 295 suggests[5].

2.   ARTICLE 10

Article 10(1) requires Member States to take all appropriate measures to ensure fulfilment of the obligations arising out of the Treaty; Article 10(2) imposes an obligation on Member States to abstain from any measure which could jeopardise the attainment of the objectives of the Treaty. There have been many cases in which individuals and undertakings have invoked Article 10(2) in proceedings in the criminal and civil courts of Member States, both as plaintiff and defendant, to claim that a particular law of a Member State is unenforceable because of its incompatibility with the competition rules in the Treaty; many of these cases have led to references to the ECJ under Article 234 (former Article 177), and will be discussed in this section of the chapter. Where a Member State is in breach of its Treaty obligations under Article 10, it would also be possible for the Commission to take action against it, either under Article 226 (former Article 169), as in the case of *Commission v Italy*[5a], or, where there is an infringement of Article 86(1), under Article 86(3)[6].

(A)   The relationship between Article 10 and Articles 81 and 82

The case law on Article 10 is complex, for reasons that are not difficult to understand[7]. It is obvious that measures adopted by Member States may distort competition: they might do so for example by imposing minimum or maximum prices for goods or services; by adopting discriminatory measures of taxation; by imposing regulatory rules that make it difficult for undertakings to enter

---

2   Case 155/73 [1974] ECR 409.
3   Case C–260/89 [1991] ECR I–2925, [1994] 4 CMLR 540, para 16.
4   Case C–41/90 [1991] ECR I–1979, [1993] 4 CMLR 306, para 29.
5   See further pp 190-202 below.
5a   Case C-35/96 [1998] ECR I-3851, [1998] 5 CMLR 889; see pp 187-188 below.
6   See further pp 208-210 below.
7   For interesting discussions of the issues involved, see Bacon 'State Regulation of the Market and EC Competition Rules: Articles [81] and [82] Compared' (1997) 18 ECLR 283; Ehle 'State Regulation under the US Antitrust State Action Doctrine and under EC Competition Law: a Comparative Analysis' (1998) 19 ECLR 380; Gagliardi 'United States and European Union Antitrust Versus State Regulation of the Economy: Is There a Better Test?' (2000) 25 ELRev 353; on the position in the US in relation to state regulatory measures, see *Parker v Brown* 317 US 341 (1943).

markets; or by operating restrictive licensing régimes for particular economic activities. Each of these measures might have quite serious implications for the competitiveness of markets. However, the issue that arises in relation to Article 10, when read in conjunction with Articles 81 and 82, is the extent to which those measures can be challenged, and be found to be unlawful, under EC law.

Article 10 is addressed to Member States; Articles 81 and 82 are directed to undertakings. The conundrum is to decide when a Member State can be held liable for anti-competitive behaviour on the part of undertakings that infringes the competition rules. On the one hand, Member States are naturally jealous of their sovereignty, and would not countenance the use of Article 10 to undermine national laws, delegated legislation, regulatory régimes and other measures because they happen to have an effect on the competitiveness of markets; a broad use of Article 10 would be particularly objectionable given that there are clear legal bases for proceeding against Member States under other parts of the Treaty dealing, for example, with the free movement of goods and services. On the other hand, the *effet utile* of Articles 81 and 82 could be seriously undermined if Member States could act as the agent of cartels and undertakings that act abusively, by adopting measures that have the same effect on the market as the undertakings would have achieved themselves. The case law of the ECJ has sought to achieve a balance, and to identify those infringements of Articles 81 and 82 for which Member States must bear responsibility.

(B) The case law predominantly concerns Article 10 in conjunction with Article 81

It is noticeable that state measures that raise issues in relation to abusive behaviour under Article 82 usually arise in the context of Article 86(1), which imposes a specific duty on Member States not to enact nor maintain in force measures in the case of 'public undertakings and undertakings to which Member States grant special or exclusive rights' which infringe the Treaty and, specifically, the competition rules[8]. The case law on Article 10 therefore has been predominantly concerned with the liability of Member States for infringements of Article 81. Before considering the cases themselves, it may be helpful to illustrate the type of problem that arises. Suppose the following: in Member State A, all lawyers belong to a privately-established bar association, and agree to comply with the fees that it recommends for legal services; in Member State B, the State itself fixes legal fees; in Member State C, the bar association is established by law, but the association is free to decide whether to recommend fees and, if so, to determine the level of those fees; in Member State D, the state requires the bar association to fix fees, but leaves it to determine what they should be; in Member State E the state has the power, by order, to decree that all lawyers will comply with any fee recommendations on the part of the bar association. In each of these cases, the likely outcome will be that there is little competition in relation to legal fees: the effect is that of a horizontal cartel. However, in EC competition law the important question is which, if any, of these situations is unlawful; and, specifically in the case of Article 10, whether any state measure itself violates the Treaty, with the consequence that it is void and unenforceable. These questions will be considered after the case law has been analysed.

(C)   The case law of the ECJ on Article 10 and the competition rules

(i)   The INNO doctrine

In *INNO v ATAB*[9] the ECJ, dealing in that case with the taxation of tobacco in the Netherlands, held that the combined effect of Articles 3(g), 10, 81 and 82 meant that a Member State could infringe the Treaty by maintaining in force legislation which could deprive the competition rules of their effectiveness. Subsequent cases have had to search out the implications of this judgment. A challenge to French legislation requiring retailers of books to comply with minimum resale prices imposed by publishers failed, since the ECJ was not certain that this practice was unlawful under Article 81 anyway[10]; a challenge to fixed minimum prices for petrol also failed, since this was a pure state measure unrelated to any agreement between undertakings[11]. Opposition to a French law forbidding the undercutting of tariffs for air fares approved by the Minister for Civil Aviation and made binding upon all traders also failed since, at the time, there was no implementing regulation for the application of the competition rules to the air transport sector; this meant *inter alia* that there was no mechanism in place for determining whether any agreements satisfied the terms of Article 81(3)[12]. In *BNIC v Clair*[13] a French trade association, BNIC, was suing Clair for undercutting minimum prices established by it, but then extended by Ministerial decree to the entire industry. Under French law these 'extension orders' became binding on everyone in the industry, and BNIC was given the right to bring an action against anyone selling at less than the fixed price. The ECJ, in an Article 234 reference from a French court, held that the involvement of the Minister did not deprive the activities of BNIC of illegality under Article 81(1). This confirmed the Commission's decisions in *BNIA*[14] and *BNIC*[15]; however the ECJ was not asked in this reference to consider the legality of the French legislation or of the Ministerial order themselves, so that Article 10 was not discussed.

(ii)   Successful application of the INNO doctrine

(A)   BNIC V YVES AUBERT.   The *INNO* doctrine was successfully applied in a similar case, *BNIC v Yves Aubert*[16]. There the ECJ held that the Minister's extension order, which in this case fixed quotas for wine-growers and permitted fines to be imposed on anyone who exceeded them, was itself unlawful. The order had the effect of strengthening the impact of the prior agreement made within the

8   See pp 190-202 below.
9   Case 13/77 [1977] ECR 2115, [1978] 1 CMLR 283.
10   See Case 229/83 *Association des Centres Distributeurs Edouard Leclerc v Au Blé Vert* [1985] ECR 1, [1985] 2 CMLR 286; Case 254/87 *Syndicat des Libraires de Normandie v L'Aigle Distribution SA* [1988] ECR 4457, [1990] 4 CMLR 37.
11   Case 231/83 *Cullet v Centre Leclerc, Toulouse* [1985] ECR 305, [1985] 2 CMLR 524.
12   Cases 209/84 etc *Ministère Public v Asjes* [1986] ECR 1425, [1986] 3 CMLR 173, paras 46-69; however the ECJ continued that, if an adverse finding had been made under Articles 84 or 85(2) (former Articles 88 and 89(2)), it would have been contrary to Article 10 for France to have reinforced the effects of an unlawful agreement: ibid, paras 70-77; Regulation 3975/87 was subsequently adopted in relation to air transport: see ch 7, pp 216-217 and ch 23, pp 864-866.
13   Case 123/83 [1985] ECR 391, [1985] 2 CMLR 430.
14   OJ [1976] L 231/24, [1976] 2 CMLR D63.
15   OJ [1982] L 379/1, [1983] 2 CMLR 240.
16   Case 136/86 [1987] ECR 4789, [1988] 4 CMLR 331.

membership of BNIC and was a breach of France's obligations under the Treaty; it followed that an action brought against Yves Aubert by BNIC for infringement of the extension order would fail.

(B) VLAAMSE REISBUREAUS V SOCIALE DIENST. In *Vlaamse Reisbureaus v Sociale Dienst*[17] a tour operator in Belgium brought an action against an association of travel agents which was passing on to its customers the commission it received from tour operators. By Belgian law, the tour operator was permitted in these circumstances to bring an action for unfair competition against the price–cutter. The defendant raised the incompatibility of this law with Article 81(1). The ECJ held that there was a constellation of agreements in the industry between tour operators and agents intended to dampen price competition and which infringed Article 81(1); the Belgian legislation buttressed this anti–competitive system by giving it permanent effect, extending it to non–participating undertakings, and by providing penalties for firms which passed on their commission. Therefore the legislation violated the Treaty and the plaintiff's action for unfair competition should fail.

(C) AHMED SAEED. In *Ahmed Saeed Flugreisen v Zentrale zur Bekämpfung Unlauteren Wettbewerbs eV*[18] the ECJ held that the approval by aeronautical authorities of air tariffs fixed by agreement by airlines involved a breach by Member States of their obligations under Articles 3(g) and 10 of the Treaty. The material distinction between this case and *Ministère Public v Asjes*[19] was that by the time of the litigation in *Ahmed Saeed* the implementing regulation in the air transport sector had come into effect[20], so that there was no longer the problem that existed at the time of the earlier case.

In each of these cases an infringement of Article 10 was found where the legislation of the Member State strengthened or encouraged anti-competitive agreements that were already in existence, and in *Yves Aubert* and *Ahmed Saeed* the Member States had delegated the power to fix prices to private operators, subsequently reinforcing the effect of their decisions. In *P Van Eycke v ASPA SA*[1] a plaintiff, disappointed at the interest rate payable on a deposit of his savings, claimed that the rate had been reduced below his expectations because of tax legislation which contravened Article 81. The ECJ held that the INNO doctrine was inapplicable as there was no suggestion that the legislation in question encouraged or extended a prior anti–competitive private agreement. In its judgment, the ECJ said that the case law showed that a Member State would be in breach of Article 10 in conjunction with Article 81 if it were:

'to require or favour the adoption of agreements, decisions or concerted practices contrary to Article [81] or to reinforce their effects, or to deprive its own legislation of its official character by delegating to private traders responsibility for taking decisions affecting the economic sphere'.

---

17 Case 311/85 [1987] ECR 3801, [1989] 4 CMLR 213.
18 Case 66/86 [1989] ECR 803, [1990] 4 CMLR 102.
19 Cases 229/84 etc [1986] ECR 1425, [1986] 3 CMLR 173.
20 See n 12 above.
1   Case 267/86 [1988] ECR 4769, [1990] 4 CMLR 330.

This is a formulation that the ECJ has repeated on subsequent occasions[2]. A particularly clear application of the doctrine is to be found in *Commission v Italy*[3], an action brought by the Commission under Article 226, challenging – successfully – Italian legislation which required the National Council of Customs Agents to set compulsory tariffs for customs agents. The ECJ concluded that the National Council had itself infringed Article 81(1) by adopting the tariff[4]. However it held further that Italy had also infringed the Treaty by requiring the Council to compile a compulsory, uniform tariff[5]; by wholly relinquishing to private economic operators the powers of the public authorities to set tariffs[6]; by prohibiting, in the primary legislation, any derogation from the tariff[7]; and by adopting a Decree having the appearance of approving the tariff by public regulation[8].

(iii)   No liability where there is no agreement between undertakings

On a number of occasions, challenges to national legislation have failed where the final determination of prices remained with a Member State: Article 10 in conjunction with Article 81 is infringed only where a Member State requires, favours or reinforces an anti-competitive agreement or abandons its own price-setting powers and delegates them to private operators. Thus in *Meng*[9] the ECJ declined to strike down a German regulation which prohibited insurance companies from passing on commissions to their customers: unlike the position in *Vlaamse*, where Belgium had acted to reinforce prior agreements between travel agents, there was no agreement in the *Meng* case[10]; similar conclusions were reached in *Ohra*[11] and *Reiff*[12] and in a number of later judgments[13]. The insistence that

2   See eg Case C-185/91 *Reiff* [1993] ECR I-5801, [1995] 5 CMLR 145, para 14; Case C-153/93 *Delta Schiffahrts- und Speditionsegesellschaft* [1994] ECR I-2517, [1996] 4 CMLR 21, para 14; Case C-38/97 *Autotrasporti Librandi v Cuttica Spedizioni e Servizi Internazionali* [1998] ECR I-5955, [1998] 5 CMLR 966, para 26.
3   Case C-35/96 [1998] ECR I-3851, [1998] 5 CMLR 889; the Commission's decision finding that the National Council itself had infringed Article 81(1) (OJ [1993] L 203/27, [1995] 5 CMLR 495) was upheld on appeal by the CFI in Case T-513/93 *CNSD v Commission* [2000] 5 CMLR 614.
4   Ibid, para 51.
5   Ibid, para 56.
6   Ibid, para 57.
7   Ibid, para 58.
8   Ibid, para 59.
9   Case C-2/91 [1993] ECR I-5751; note that *Meng* was decided at about the same time as *Keck and Mithouard*, Case C-267/91 [1993] ECR I-6097, [1995] 1 CMLR 101, in which the ECJ declined to apply Article 28 (former Article 30) to national marketing rules forbidding the use of loss-leaders (selling below cost) in retail outlets: see Reich 'The 'November Revolution' of the European Court of Justice: *Keck, Meng* and *Audi* Revisited' (1994) 31 CMLR 459.
10   Ibid, para 14.
11   Case C-245/91 [1993] ECR I-5851.
12   Case C-185/91 [1993] ECR 5801, [1995] 5 CMLR 145.
13   See eg Case C-153/93 *Delta Schiffahrts- und Speditionsegesellschaft* [1994] ECR I-2517, [1996] 4 CMLR 21; Case C-412/93 *Société d'Importaton Edouard Leclerc-Siplec v TFI and M6* [1995] ECR I-179, [1995] 3 CMLR 422; Case C-96/94 *Centro Servizi Spediporto v Spedizioni Marittima del Golfo* [1995] ECR I-2883, [1996] 4 CMLR 613; Cases C-140/94 etc *DIP SpA v Commune di Bassano del Grappa* [1995] ECR I-3257, [1996] 4 CMLR 157; Case C-38/97 *Autotrasporti Librandi v Cuttica Spedizioni e Servizi Internazionali* [1998] ECR I-5955, [1998] 5 CMLR 966; Case C-266/96 *Corsica Ferries* [1998] ECR I-3949, [1998] 5 CMLR 402.

there must be an agreement contrary to Article 81 before a Member State can be found to have infringed Article 10 places an obvious limit on the extent to which it is possible to use the *INNO* doctrine to challenge state measures; in particular it is clear that Article 10 cannot be used simply because a state measure produces effects similar to those of a cartel.

(D) Application of the case law to lawyers' fees

Having analysed the case law under the *INNO* doctrine, we should return briefly to the alternative situations set out above in relation to legal fees[14]. In the case of Member State A, lawyers agreed to comply with the recommendations of a privately-established bar association: this could clearly amount to an infringement of Article 81(1), assuming an appreciable effect on competition and inter-state trade; however there is no involvement on the part of the State, so the application of Article 10 does not arise[15]. In the second situation, Member State B itself fixed the fees: however in this case there is no suggestion of an agreement, and so there can be no infringement of Article 10. In the third case, Member State C established a regulatory mechanism, but left it to the bar association to fix the fees: the association in doing so would be infringing Article 81, but it is not clear whether the Member State has acted unlawfully; it has given freedom to the bar association to decide how to act, rather than requiring it to act. In the case of Member State D, however, it has delegated its regulatory rôle to the bar association and required it to fix fees, so that it would be held responsible for the price fixing that ensues. Member State E would be strengthening the effect of an agreement contrary to Article 81 by issuing a decree compelling compliance with the bar association's recommendations, and would therefore be in breach of Article 10; a lawyer wishing to charge fees lower than the recommended ones could not be prosecuted for doing so[16].

3. ARTICLE 86[17]

Article 86 provides that:

> '1. In the case of public undertakings and undertakings to which Member States grant special or exclusive rights, Member States shall neither enact nor maintain in force any measure contrary to the rules contained in this Treaty, in particular to those rules provided for in Article 12 [former Article 6] and Articles 81 to 89.

---

14 See p 185 above.
15 On the application of the competition rules to the professions see ch 3, pp 69.
16 Some of these issues may be decided by the ECJ in a case concerning legal fees in Italy in Case C-35/99 *Arduino* (judgment pending): Advocate General Léger gave his Opinion in this case on 10 July 2001; he also gave an opinion in Case C-309/99 *Wouters* on the same day, and in Case C-221/99 *Conte* on 12 July 2001.
17 See generally Buendia Sierra *Exclusive Rights and State Monopolies under EC Law* (Oxford University Press, 1999): this book contains an extensive bibliography of literature on Article 86 at pp 431-451; see also Blum and Logue *State Monopolies under EC Law* (Wiley, 1998); Edwards and Hoskins 'Article [86]: Deregulation and EC Law: Reflections Arising from the XVI FIDE Conference' (1995) 32 CML Rev 157.

2. Undertakings entrusted with the operation of services of general economic interest or having the character of a revenue–producing monopoly shall be subject to the rules contained in this Treaty, in particular to the rules on competition, in so far as the application of such rules does not obstruct the performance, in law or in fact, of the particular tasks assigned to them. The development of trade must not be affected to such an extent as would be contrary to the interests of the Community.

3. The Commission shall ensure the application of the provisions of this Article and shall, where necessary, address appropriate directives or decisions to Member States'.

Article 86(1) is a prohibition addressed to Member States themselves; Article 86(2) provides a limited exception for certain undertakings from the application of the competition rules; Article 86(3) provides the Commission with important powers to ensure compliance with the provisions of Article 86. The law of Article 86 is complex and still developing. After a long period when it was little used, it has proved to be a formidable provision in the process of liberalising numerous markets in Europe, in particular in 'utility' sectors such as telecommunications, energy and post and related services.

(A)   Article 86(1)

Article 86(1) is closely related to Article 10: each seeks to ensure effective adherence to the Treaty on the part of Member States. However Article 86 goes beyond Article 10, in that it has its own sphere of application and is not limited to compliance with general principles of law. Article 86(1) imposes an obligation on Member States not to enact nor to maintain in force measures *'contrary to those rules contained in this Treaty, in particular to those rules provided for in Article 12 and Articles 81 to 89'*. Two important features of Article 86(1) should be noted at the outset. The first is that Article 86(1) is a 'renvoi' provision or a 'reference rule', that is to say it does not have an independent application but applies only in conjunction with another Article or other Articles of the Treaty. The second point is that Article 86(1) is not limited in its scope only to infringements of the competition rules; although the competition rules (and the rule of non-discrimination in Article 12) are specifically mentioned, measures that infringe, for example, Article 28 on the free movement of goods[18], Article 39 on the free movement of workers[19], Article 43 on the freedom of establishment[20] and Article 49 on the free movement of services[1], could all result in an infringement of Article 86(1). It follows that Article 86(1) did not need to have been placed in the chapter of the Treaty on competition law; however, the fact that it is there indicates that the authors of the Treaty were aware of the potential for Member States to distort competition through the legislative and other measures that they adopt. The importance of Article 86(1) in relation to the competition rules is that, in certain circumstances, a Member State can be liable for the abuses that have been, or would be, carried out by undertakings.

---

18 See eg Case C-18/88 *RTT* [1991] ECR I-5941.
19 See eg Case C-179/90 *Merci* [1991] ECR I-5889, [1994] 4 CMLR 422.
20 See eg *Greek Insurance* OJ [1985] L 152/25.
1   See eg Case C-260/89 *ERT v DEP* [1991] ECR I-2925, [1994] 4 CMLR 540.

(i) Undertakings

Article 86(1) applies to measures concerning 'public undertakings and undertakings to which Member States grant special or exclusive rights'. The term 'undertaking' has been considered in the context of Articles 81 and 82 in earlier chapters[2]. In particular it should be noted that state–owned bodies can be undertakings, but that organs of the state that are not involved in any economic activity may fall outside the definition[3].

(ii) Public undertakings[4]

The term 'public undertaking' appears only in Article 86(1) of the Treaty, and is not defined. There is not a uniform notion of this expression among the Member States, and state intervention in and control of economic behaviour takes many different forms. For this reason, Advocate General Reischl has stated that the term must be a concept of Community law which should be given a uniform interpretation for all Member States[5]. In Article 2(1)(b) of the Transparency Directive[6] the Commission said that a public undertaking means 'any undertaking over which the public authorities may exercise, directly or indirectly, a dominant influence by virtue of their ownership of it, their financial participation therein, or the rules which govern it'. On appeal the ECJ approved this, without providing a more exhaustive definition[7]. The crucial question in each case should be whether the State does have such influence, not the legal form of the undertaking in question.

(iii) Undertakings with 'special or exclusive rights'

Article 86(1) applies to measures in the case both of public undertakings and of undertakings having 'special or exclusive rights': sometimes the latter are referred to as 'privileged undertakings' to distinguish them from public undertakings. It is important to understand what each of the expressions 'special' and 'exclusive' means. The Treaty itself does not define them, but definitions can be found in Article 2(1)(f) and (g) of the Commission Transparency Directive[8]. Often special or exclusive rights will have been given to a public undertaking, in which case it is unnecessary to give separate consideration to this head of Article 86(1). However, many undertakings may have exclusive or special rights without being 'public'. More is known about 'exclusive' rights than 'special' ones.

(A) EXCLUSIVE RIGHTS[9]. A company established by insurance undertakings to perform a specific statutory task[10], an agricultural marketing board[11], an entity

2   See ch 3, pp 66-71 and ch 5, pp 150-151.
3   See in particular ch 3, pp 69-70.
4   For detailed discussion of this concept, see Buendia Sierra (p 189, n 17 above), paras 1.113-1.139.
5   Cases 188/80 etc *France v Commission* [1982] ECR 2545, p 2596.
6   OJ [1980] L 195/35, as amended most recently by OJ [2000] L 193/75; see p 213 below.
7   Cases 188/80 etc *France v Commission* [1982] ECR 2545, [1982] 3 CMLR 144.
8   See n 6 above.
9   On the concept of exclusive rights, see *Buendia Sierra* (p 189, n 17 above), paras 1.01-1.214.
10 Case 90/76 *Van Ameyde v UCI* [1977] ECR 1091.
11 Case 83/78 *Pigs Marketing Board v Redmond* [1978] ECR 2347, [1979] 1 CMLR 177.

granted a monopoly over the provision of recruitment services[12], a dock-work undertaking entrusted with the exclusive right to organise dock work for third parties[13] and a limited partnership between a Member State, a district authority and eight industrial undertakings responsible for waste management[14] are examples of bodies that were considered to have been granted exclusive rights. It would appear that an 'exclusive' right can be granted to more than one undertaking: in *Entreprenørforeningens Affalds v Københavns Kommune*[15] the ECJ held that three undertakings authorised to receive building waste in Copenhagen had been granted an exclusive right, but it did not explain why these rights were exclusive rather than special, which would have been a more natural finding.

In principle, it seems appropriate that a functional rather than a formalistic approach should be taken to the meaning of 'exclusive rights'. Rights may be exclusive in substance, even though they are not described as such (or as monopolies) in the measure in question. For example, in *La Crespelle*[16] the ECJ concluded that a scheme for the artificial insemination of cattle in France involved exclusive rights, because of the way the national legislation was operated in practice[17]. Furthermore, the exclusive rights may derive from a series of different legislative and administrative measures rather than just one[18]. On the other hand, the ECJ has held that the mere fact that a body exercises powers conferred upon it by the state and that it has a dominant position in the market is not sufficient in itself to establish that it has exclusive rights[19]. This is consistent with an early Commission decision, holding that a copyright collecting society that could derive benefits from national copyright legislation did not have exclusive rights where there was no impediment to other such societies claiming the same benefit[20]; nevertheless the Commission did conclude that the society in question had a dominant position for the purpose of Article 82. The concepts of 'exclusive rights' and 'dominant position' are independent of one another.

Intellectual property rights are not exclusive rights in the sense of Article 86(1). Although it is true to say, for example, that a patent gives an exclusive right (to exclude others from the patented product or process), the patent itself was available to anyone who applied for it and who satisfied the relevant legal requirements. For a measure to fall within Article 86(1), it must entail some element of discretion on the part of the State: where an intellectual property right is given pursuant to the terms of a given Act, there is no *discretion* on the part of the State. The same is true in the case of public procurement, when practised in accordance with the law[1]; the fact that an undertaking is awarded a contract does not give it an exclusive right in the sense of Article 86(1), since the award is not discretionary. This is a helpful, and perhaps overlooked, way of

---

12   Case C–41/90 *Höfner & Elser v Macrotron* [1991] ECR I–1979, [1993] 4 CMLR 306, para 34.
13   Case C–179/90 *Merci* [1991] ECR I-5889, [1994] 4 CMLR 422.
14   Case C-203/96 *Dusseldorp* [1998] ECR I-4075, [1998] 3 CMLR 873, para 58.
15   Case C-209/98 judgment of 23 May 2000.
16   Case C-323/93 [1994] ECR I-5077.
17   Although the ECJ did not address the point directly, the Opinion of AG Gulmann indicates that it was common ground between the parties that exclusive rights existed.
18   See *Exclusive Rights to Broadcast Television Advertising in Flanders* OJ [1997] L 244/18, [1997] 5 CMLR 718, paras 1 and 2, upheld on appeal Case T-266/97 *Vlaamse Televisie Maatschappij NV v Commission* [2000] 4 CMLR 1171.
19   Case C-387/93 *Banchero* [1995] ECR I-4663.
20   *GEMA* OJ [1971] L 134/15, [1971] CMLR D35.
1   See ch 2, p 46, n 6 for relevant literature on public procurement law.

explaining why some state-conferred exclusivities are not covered by Article 86(1).

(B) SPECIAL RIGHTS[2] . The ECJ's judgment in *France v Commission*[3] indicates that there is a distinction between exclusive and special rights. The Court held that the provisions in the Commission's Directive on *Telecommunications Equipment*[4] were void in so far as they required Member States to remove special rights from national telecommunications services providers, since it had failed to specify which rights were special or why they were incompatible with the Treaty. In the subsequent amended Directive on *Telecommunications Liberalisation*[5] the Commission stated at recital 11 that, in the telecommunications sector, special rights are 'rights that are granted by a Member State to a limited number of undertakings, through any legislative, regulatory or administrative instrument which, within a given geographical area, limits to two or more, otherwise than according to objective, proportional and non-discriminatory criteria, the number of undertakings which are authorised to provide any such service ...'[6] . This definition can presumably be carried over to other sectors of the economy. In *Second Operator of GSM Radiotelephony Services in Italy*[7] the Commission decided that the grant to Telecom Italia of the right to operate a GSM radiotelephony network qualified as a special right, since the operator had been designated otherwise than according to objective and non-discriminatory criteria.

(iv) *'Measures'*

For a Member State to be in breach of Article 86(1), it must have adopted a 'measure'. The expression 'measure' has been given a wide meaning by the Commission, and its approach has been endorsed by the ECJ. In an early Directive under Article 28[8], the Commission said that measures in that Article included 'laws, regulations, administrative provisions, administrative practices, and all instruments issued from a public authority, including recommendations'; there is no reason to suppose that the expression should have a different meaning under Article 86(1). In another case under Article 28, *Commission v Ireland*[9] , the ECJ said that a measure did not have to be legally binding, provided that it might be capable of exerting an influence and of frustrating the aims of the Community as set out in Articles 2 and 3 of the Treaty[10] . The measure does not have to have been adopted by central Government or by a national Parliament: a measure of

2   On the concept of special rights, see *Buendia Sierra* (p 189, n 17 above), paras 2.01-2.22.
3   Case C–202/88 [1991] ECR I-1223, [1992] 5 CMLR 552, paras 31–47; see similarly Cases 271/90 etc *Spain v Commission* [1992] ECR I-5833, paras 32 and 34.
4   Commission Directive (EEC) 88/301 on competition in the markets for telecommunications terminal equipment OJ [1988] L 131/73, [1991] 4 CMLR 922.
5   Commission Directive (EC) 94/46 amending Directive (EEC) 88/301 and Directive (EEC) 90/388 in particular with regard to satellite communications OJ [1994] L 268/15.
6   See similarly Article 2(1)(g) of the Commission's Transparency Directive, p 191, n 6 above.
7   OJ [1995] L 280/49, para 6; see similarly *Second Operator of GSM Radio Telephony Services in Spain* OJ [1997] L 76/19, para 10.
8   Commission Directive (EEC) 70/50 based on the provisions of Article 33(7) on the abolition of measures which have an effect equivalent to quantitative restrictions on imports and are not covered by other provisions adopted in pursuance of the EEC Treaty 70/50/EEC JO [1970] L 13/29.
9   Case 249/81 [1982] ECR 4005 (the *'Buy Irish'* case).
10   Ibid, para 28.

any body that is a manifestation of the state could fall within Article 86(1), such as the local communes in *Corinne Bodson v Pompes Funèbres*[11].

Numerous examples can be given to support the view that the expression 'measures' has a wide meaning under Article 86(1): for example in *Second Operator of GSM Radio Telephony in Italy*[12] and *Second Operator of GSM Radio Telephony in Spain*[13] the grant of a second mobile licence subject *inter alia* to a substantial licence fee which had not been levied on the incumbent operator amounted to measures; in *Port of Rødby*[14] the refusal to grant a ferry company access to a state-run Danish port was a measure; and in *Brussels National Airport (Zaventem)*[15], *Portuguese Airports*[16] and *Spanish Airports*[17] systems of stepped landing fee discounts at various national airports did so.

In each of the above cases, the Member State had adopted specific measures which affected the conduct of the public undertaking or the undertaking given special or exclusive rights. In some cases a public authority enters into an agreement with another undertaking granting the latter an exclusive right to perform a particular task: for example to provide funeral services[18]. The question here is whether this amounts to a measure granting exclusive rights, in which case Article 86(1) may apply, or an agreement between undertakings that restricts competition, in which case Article 81(1) may apply. In *Bodson* the ECJ considered that Article 81(1) would not be applicable where a local authority was acting pursuant to its public law powers, since it would not be acting as an undertaking[19]. In *British Telecommunications*[20], however, BT was acting as an undertaking, and so subject to Article 82 when, notwithstanding that it had a regulatory function, it was carrying on a business activity in retransmitting messages.

(v)   The obligations on Member States under Article 86(1)

Article 86(1) requires Member States to refrain from enacting or maintaining in force any measure contrary to the Treaty, and in particular one which would contravene Article 12, Article 81 or Article 82. The relationship of Article 86(1) with Articles 81 and 82 is one of the most difficult areas of competition law. Articles 81 and 82 are addressed to undertakings, but Article 86 to Member States: as in the case of Article 10[1], the conceptual issue is to determine how, and in what circumstances, these provisions can operate in such a way as to lead to an infringement of the Treaty by a Member State. As has been seen, under Article 10 the liability of Member States in relation to Article 81 is quite limited; however the jurisprudence of the ECJ has been more dramatic in cases dealing with Article 86(1) in conjunction with Article 82. For many years, this issue was barely addressed at all; however, the position began to change as a result of a

---

11   Case 30/87 [1988] ECR 2479, [1989] 4 CMLR 984.
12   OJ [1995] L 280/49.
13   OJ [1997] L 76/19.
14   OJ [1994] L 55/62.
15   OJ [1995] L 216/8, [1996] 4 CMLR 232.
16   OJ [1999] L 69/31, [1999] 5 CMLR 103 upheld on appeal Case C-163/99 *Portugal v Commission* judgment of 29 March 2001.
17   OJ [2000] L 208/36, [2000] 5 CMLR 967.
18   Case 30/87 *Corinne Bodson v Pompes Funèbres* [1988] ECR 2479, [1989] 4 CMLR 984.
19   See ch 3, p 70.
20   *British Telecommunications* [1982] OJ L 360/36, upheld on appeal Case 41/83 *Italy v Commission (British Telecommunications)* [1985] ECR 873, [1985] 2 CMLR 368.
1   See pp 184-189 above.

remarkable series of cases in 1991 in which the ECJ delivered four judgments on the relationship between Article 86(1) and other Treaty Articles, including in particular Article 82. A further landmark judgment, in the *Corbeau* case, followed in 1993[2].

(vi)   The judgments of 1991

(A)   *HÖFNER & ELSER V MACROTRON.*   In April 1991, the ECJ held in *Höfner & Elser v Macrotron*[3] that a Member State which had conferred exclusive rights on a public employment agency could be in breach of Article 86(1) where the exercise by that agency of its rights would inevitably involve an infringement of Article 82. In Germany the Federal Employment Office ('the FEO') had a legal monopoly as an intermediary in the employment market, though in practice it was unable to satisfy demand and tolerated 'head–hunting' agencies which, strictly, were acting illegally. An agency seeking payment of its fee for having recruited on behalf of a client was met with the defence that, as the agency was acting unlawfully, it could not enforce the contract; thus the alleged infringement by Germany of the Treaty was raised as a defence to a contract action between two private undertakings. The matter was referred to the ECJ under Article 234. The conclusion of the ECJ was that the fact that Germany had granted a legal monopoly to the FEO did not in itself entail a breach of Articles 82 and 86(1)[4]; however there would be a breach if the mere exercise of its right would inevitably lead to an abuse under Article 82. This could be the case if the undertaking was manifestly unable to satisfy demand, as was the case here by the admission of the FEO, and if the legal monopoly prevented a competitor from trying to satisfy that demand[5].

(B)   *ERT V DIMOTIKI.*   In June 1991, the ECJ was asked in *ERT v Dimotiki*[6] to consider the compatability with the Treaty of the Greek television and radio station's monopoly over broadcasting. The Court held that the existence of the monopoly in itself was not contrary to the Treaty, but that the manner in which it was exercised could be so[7]. Specifically on Article 82 the ECJ held that, if a Member State which had granted the exclusive right to transmit television broadcasts then granted the same undertaking the right to retransmit broadcasts, it would infringe Article 86(1) if this created a situation in which the broadcaster would be led to infringe Article 82 by virtue of a discriminatory policy which favours its own broadcasts.

(C)   *MERCI CONVENZIONALE PORTO DI GENOVA V SIDERURGICA GABRIELLI.*   In December 1991 the ECJ gave its judgment in *Merci Convenzionale Porto di Genova v Siderurgica Gabrielli*[8]. Merci was a private undertaking given an exclusive concession for the handling of loading operations in the harbour of Genoa. As a result of a strike at Merci, Siderurgica was unable to unload goods imported in a ship from Germany. Siderurgica sued for damages. The ECJ stated that the

2   Case C-320/91 [1993] ECR I-2533, [1995] 4 CMLR 621.
3   Case C–41/90 [1991] ECR I–1979, [1993] 4 CMLR 306.
4   Ibid, para 29.
5   Ibid, paras 30-31.
6   Case C–260/89 [1991] ECR I–2925, [1994] 4 CMLR 540.
7   Ibid, paras 12 and 32.
8   Case C–179/90 [1991] ECR I–5889, [1994] 4 CMLR 422; see Gyselen (1992) 29 CML Rev 1229.

simple fact of creating a dominant position by granting exclusive rights is not as such incompatible with Article 86(1)[9]; however the Court repeated the ideas in *Höfner* and *ERT* that there could be an infringement by a Member State if the undertaking in question, merely by exercising the exclusive rights granted to it cannot avoid abusing its dominant position (*Höfner*), or when such rights are liable to create a situation in which that undertaking is induced to commit such abuses (*ERT*)[10]. In this case the Court observed that Merci appeared to have been induced to demand payment for services which had not been requested, to charge disproportionate prices, to refuse to have recourse to modern technology and to treat customers in a discriminatory manner: matters which are specifically mentioned as possible abuses in Article 82(2)(a), (b) and (c) of the Treaty[11].

(D)   *RTT V GB-INNO-BM.*   The ECJ delivered a further judgment in December 1991, three days after the judgment in *Merci*, in *RTT v GB–Inno–BM*[12]. RTT had exclusive rights in Belgium for the operation of telephone services and for the approval of telecommunications terminal equipment such as telephones; it also was a supplier of telephones itself. GB–Inno sold telephones in Belgium which had been imported from the Far East. RTT asked for an injunction to prevent such sales, since this encouraged people to connect equipment which had not been approved according to Belgian law. The ECJ referred to earlier case law, that an abuse is committed where an undertaking holding a dominant position on a particular market reserves to itself an ancillary activity which might be carried out by another undertaking as part of its activities on a neighbouring but separate market, with the possibility of eliminating all competition from such an undertaking[13]. The ECJ went on to say that where a state measure brings about such a reservation of an ancillary activity, the measure in question infringes Article 86(1)[14]. RTT argued that there would be an infringement of Article 86(1) only where the Member State favoured an abuse, for example by acting in a discriminatory manner[15], but the ECJ rejected this, stating that the extension of RTT's monopoly was itself a state measure contrary to Article 86(1)[16]. The establishment of a regulatory system which gave RTT the power to determine at will which telephone equipment could be connected to the public telephone network, thereby placing itself at an obvious advantage over its competitors, was unlawful[17].

(vii)   The Corbeau judgment

A further judgment of great significance was *Corbeau* in 1993[18]. Criminal proceedings had been brought against Corbeau, a businessman from Liège, for infringing the Belgian legal monopoly for postal services. Corbeau was operating

9   Ibid, para 16.
10   Ibid, para 17.
11   Ibid, paras 18 and 19.
12   Case C–18/88 [1991] ECR I-5941; see Gyselen, n 8 above.
13   Ibid, para 18, referring to Case 311/84 *CBEM* (the *Télémarketing* judgment) [1985] ECR 3261, [1986] 2 CMLR 558.
14   Ibid, para 21.
15   Ibid, para 22.
16   Ibid, para 23.
17   In reaching this finding, the ECJ relied on another of its judgments in 1991, the *Telecommunications Directive* case, p 193, n 3 above, at para 51.
18   Case C-320/91 [1993] ECR I-2533, [1995] 4 CMLR 621; see Hancher (1994) 31 CML Rev 105.

a door-to-door express delivery service in the Liège area: he was not conducting the service of delivering letters on a daily-delivery basis. The ECJ, after referring to the requirement in Article 86(1) not to enact nor to maintain in force measures contrary to the competition rules[19], spent the rest of its judgment considering, under Article 86(2), whether the breadth of the monopoly given to the Belgian Post Office was greater than was necessary to enable it to carry out the task of general economic interest entrusted to it[20]. The significance of the judgment for Article 86(1) was that the ECJ, in effect, was ruling that the breadth of the monopoly granted to the Belgian Post Office was, to the extent that it could not be justified under Article 86(2), unlawful under the Treaty. In other words, the Court was challenging the exclusive rights themselves, despite its numerous statements that the creation of dominance is not in itself incompatible with the Treaty.

(viii) Making sense of the case law on Article 82 in conjunction with Article 86(1)

The difficulty with these cases, and with the ECJ's subsequent judgments[1], has been to determine the circumstances in which a Member State can be liable under Article 86(1) for an infringement of Article 82. Two points can be made at the outset. First, as Advocate General Jacobs explained at paragraph 388 of his Opinion in *Albany*[2], Member States cannot be held responsible for independent anti-competitive behaviour on the part of undertakings simply because it takes place within their jurisdiction. Article 86(1) can be infringed 'only where there is a causal link between a Member State's legislative or administrative intervention on the one hand and anti-competitive behaviour of undertakings on the other hand'. Secondly, the mere creation of a dominant position by the grant of exclusive rights does not normally infringe Article 86(1) in itself; this has been said by the ECJ on many occasions[3]: the point is exemplified by the judgment in *Crespelle*[4], where the Court concluded that French legislation conferring legal monopolies on insemination centres for the provision of certain services to cattle breeders did not lead to an abuse for which France was responsible.

---

19 Ibid, para 12.
20 For discussion of Article 86(2), and of the *Corbeau* judgment on this issue, see pp 202-208 below.
1   There have been several subsequent judgments on the relationship between Article 82 and Article 86(1): see in particular Case C-393/92 *Almelo* [1994] ECR I-1477; Case C-18/93 *Corsica Ferries Italia srl v Corpo del Piloti del Porto de Genoa* [1994] ECR I-1783; Case C-323/93 *Centre d'Insémination de la Crespelle v Coopérative de la Mayenne* [1994] ECR I-5077; Case C-111/94 *Job Centre (I)* [1995] ECR I-3361; Case C-242/95 *GT-Link A/S v De Danske Statsbaner* [1997] ECR I-4349, [1997] 5 CMLR 601; Case C-387/93 *Banchero* [1995] ECR I-4663; Case C-55/96 *Job Centre (II)* [1997] ECR I-7119, [1998] 4 CMLR 708; Case C-70/95 *Sodemare v Regione Lombardia* [1997] ECR I-3395, [1998] 4 CMLR 667; Case C-163/96 *Silvano Raso* [1998] ECR I-533, [1998] 4 CMLR 737; Case C-266/96 *Corsica Ferries France SA v Gruppo Antichi Ormeggiatori del Porto di Genova* [1998] ECR I-3949, [1998] 5 CMLR 402; Case C-203/96 *Dusseldorp* [1998] ECR I-4075, [1998] 3 CMLR 873; Cases C-67/96 etc *Albany International BV v SBT* [2000] 4 CMLR 446; Cases C-147/97 and C-148/97 *Deutsche Post Ag v GZS* [2000] 4 CMLR 838; Case C-238/98 *Giovanni Carra* judgment of 14 September 2000; Case C-209/98 *Entreprenørforeningens Affalds/Miljøsektion v Københavns Kommune* judgment of 23 May 2000; Case C-340/99 *TNT Traco SpA v Poste Italiane SpA*, judgment of 17 May 2001.
2   Cases C-67/96 etc *Albany International BV v SBT* [2000] 4 CMLR 446.
3   Specific paras in which the ECJ has said this were cited above in relation to the 1991 judgments in *Höfner*, *ERT* and *Merci*: see pp 195-196 above.
4   Case C-323/93 *Centre d'Insémination de la Crespelle v Coopérative de la Mayenne* [1994] ECR I-5077.

Helpful though these two points are, they do not in themselves shed any light on the circumstances in which a Member State will be found to have infringed Article 86(1) as a result of an abuse that infringes Article 82. Furthermore, the frequently-repeated statement that the mere creation of dominance does not in itself infringe Article 86(1) does not sit easily with judgments such as *ERT*, *RTT* and *Corbeau* which do seem, in effect, to have concluded that the monopoly rights in question were incompatible with the Treaty. The judgments of the ECJ on the necessary causal link between the measure under Article 86(1) and the abuse under Article 82 are neither clear nor consistent: in *Höfner* the Court considered that a measure would be unlawful where it led to an 'inevitable' abuse; in *ERT* if it would induce an infringement; in *Banchero*[5] the ECJ considered that there would be an infringement only if the Member State created a situation in which the undertaking in question 'cannot avoid abusing its dominant position'[6]. In *Dusseldorp*[7] however the Court was much less guarded: a Member State infringes Article 86(1) in conjunction with Article 82 'if it adopts any law, regulation or administrative provision which enables an undertaking on which it has conferred rights to abuse its dominant position'[8]. Some formulations of the necessary causal link impose quite a high standard before a Member State will be found liable; others, such as the one in *Dusseldorp*, are much stricter. What seems clear is that the causal link must be stronger in some kinds of cases than others, depending on how likely it is that abusive behaviour will follow from the measure in question.

Many attempts have been made to make sense of the cases, in particular by identifying specific categories[9]; this is a natural response to the case law, but it is noticeable that different commentators have devised different categories, or have assigned the cases differently. This is not surprising: the cases can be explained in different, and sometimes in overlapping, ways, and the jurisprudence is still evolving. As Advocate General Fennelly stated in his Opinion in *Silvano Raso*[10]:

> 'I do not think that any general test can be enunciated for determining in advance the existence of such a [causal] link. Instead, in each individual case, it will be necessary to assess the impact of impugned national rules in the economic and factual circumstances in which they operate'[11].

The text that follows attempts a categorisation, but must be read subject to the caveat that it is simply one way, among several others, of trying to make sense of the jurisprudence of the ECJ and the decisional practice of the Commission.

---

5   Case C-387/93 [1995] ECR I-4663.
6   Ibid, para 51.
7   Case C-203/96 [1998] 3 CMLR 873.
8   Ibid, para 61, citing the *RTT* judgment (see p 196, n 12 above).
9   See eg *Buendia Sierra* (p 189, n 17 above), paras 5.68-5-109; see also Buendia Sierra in Faull and Nikpay *The EC Law of Competition* (Oxford University Press, 1999) paras 5.52-5.79; Edward and Hoskins 'Article [86]: Deregulation and EC Law: Reflections arising from the XVI FIDE Conference' (1995) 32 CML Rev 157; Advocate General Jacobs in his Opinion in *Albany* (n 2 above), paras 396-440; Ritter, Braun and Rawlinson *European Competition Law: a Practitioner's Guide* (Kluwer Law International, 2nd ed, 2000), pp 764-767; see also, on the issue of causation, the Opinion of Advocate General Fennelly in Case C-163/96 *Silvano Raso* [1998] ECR I-533, [1998] 4 CMLR 737, paras 57-66.
10   Ibid.
11   Ibid, para 65.

(A)   MANIFEST INABILITY TO MEET DEMAND.   In *Höfner & Elser v Macrotron*[12] the ECJ held that there would be an infringement of Article 86(1) where Germany had created a situation in which the FEO was 'manifestly not in a position to satisfy demand' for recruitment services, and its legal monopoly prevented a competitor from satisfying that demand. The idea that inability to meet demand can be abusive can be traced back to Article 82(2)(b) EC, which gives as an example of abuse 'limiting production, markets or technical development to the prejudice of consumers'. On similar facts to *Höfner*, in *Job Centre (II)*[13] the ECJ concluded that the enforcement of an employment procurement monopoly enforced in Italy through criminal proceedings was a measure contrary to Article 86(1). In the *Albany* judgment[14] the ECJ seems to have considered that the exclusive right given to the operator of a sectoral pension fund amounted to a limitation of demand[15], although it went on to decide that this could be justified under Article 86(2)[16]. The judgment in *Merci*[17] can be explained, in part, on the basis that the entrusted undertaking had refused to have recourse to modern technology, which resulted in a failure to satisfy the demand of customers. In *Dusseldorp*[18] a requirement that waste for recovery could be supplied only to the entrusted undertaking, and could not be exported to a third undertaking, was held to restrict outlets and to contravene Article 86(1) in conjunction with Article 82[19]. The Commission's decisions on courier services, *Dutch Express Delivery Services*[20] and *Spanish International Courier Services*[1], and on licences for mobile telephony operators, *Second Operator of GSM Telephony Services in Italy*[2] and *Second Operator of GSM Telephony Services in Spain*[3], can be included, in part, in this category of cases[4].

(B)   CONFLICT OF INTEREST.   In *ERT v Dimotiki*[5] the ECJ held that there would be an infringement of Article 86(1) where Greece had created a situation in which the broadcaster ERT would be led to infringe Article 82 by virtue of a discriminatory policy in favour of its own broadcasts. A notable feature of this case was that it was not necessary for ERT to have actually abused its dominant position in the manner suggested: the granting of the exclusive right made this sufficiently likely that the measure in question infringed Article 86(1). The ECJ seems to have considered it to be inevitable that an undertaking in the position of ERT, because of its conflict of interest, would act abusively. The same idea was presumably present in *RTT v GB-Inno-BM*[6], since the regulatory function

12 Case C–41/90 [1991] ECR I–1979, [1993] 4 CMLR 306.
13 Case C-55/96 [1997] ECR I-7119, [1998] 4 CMLR 708; see also Case C-258/98 *Giovanni Carra* judgment of 14 September 2000.
14 Cases C-67/96 etc [2000] 4 CMLR 446.
15 Ibid, para 97.
16 On Article 86(2), see pp 202-208 below.
17 Case C–179/90 [1991] ECR I–5889, [1994] 4 CMLR 422.
18 Case C-203/96 [1998] ECR I-4075, [1998] 3 CMLR 873.
19 Ibid, para 63.
20 OJ [1990] L 10/47, [1990] 4 CMLR 947 quashed on appeal Cases C-48/90 and C-66/90 *Netherlands and Koninklijke PTT Nederland v Commission* [1992] ECR I-565, [1993] 5 CMLR 316.
1   OJ [1990] L 233/19, [1991] 4 CMLR 560, para 11.
2   OJ [1995] L 280/49, [1996] 4 CMLR 700, para 17(ii).
3   OJ [1997] L 76/19, para 21(ii).
4   The same decisions can also be included in the 'reservation of an ancillary activity' category: see p 200 below.
5   See p 195, n 6 above.
6   See p 196, n 12 above.

of RTT inevitably gave rise to a conflict of interest, although the ECJ specifically relied there on the extension of monopoly rights to neighbouring markets[7]. A further example of a conflict of interest case is *Silvano Raso*[8], where a dock-work scheme granted an undertaking the exclusive right to supply temporary labour to terminal concessionaires, but also enabled it to compete with them on the market for the provision of dock services: merely by exercising its monopoly rights the entrusted undertaking would be able to distort competition in its favour, for example by imposing on its competitors unduly high costs or by supplying them with labour less suited to the work to be done[9]. The ECJ specifically mentioned the conflict of interest of the entrusted undertaking in this judgment[10].

(C)   RESERVATION OF AN ANCILLARY ACTIVITY.   In *RTT v GB–Inno–BM*[11] the ECJ held that a measure that resulted in the extension of RTT's monopoly to an ancillary activity on a neighbouring but separate market infringed Article 86(1). As noted in the preceding paragraph, the ECJ could have reached the same conclusion on the basis of a conflict of interest, but it decided the case specifically on the basis of its earlier judgment in the *Télémarketing* case[12]. The Commission considered that there were abuses under this head in *Dutch Express Delivery Services*[13] and *Spanish International Courier Services*[14]. In each of *Second Operator of GSM Telephony Services in Italy*[15] and *Second Operator of GSM Telephony Services in Spain*[16] the Commission decided that, in requiring a second mobile operator to make a substantial payment for a mobile telephony licence that had not been paid by the incumbent telecommunications companies, there had been state measures capable of extending the monopoly rights of the latter. The Commission also considered that there was an abuse under this head in *Port of Rødby*[17] where the refusal by a port operator, DSD, to allow Euro-Port A/S access to the port of Rødby eliminated competition in the downstream market for ferry services from Rødby to Puttgarden, in which it was collectively dominant with Deutsche Bahn. A further decision under this head is *New Postal Services in Italy*.[18]

(D)   CORBEAU.   In *Corbeau*[19] the ECJ did not discuss Article 86(1) in any detail, but instead considered the extent to which the postal monopoly of the Belgian Post Office could be justified under Article 86(2)[20]. However, the interest of the case under Article 86(1) is that, to the extent that the monopoly was not justifiable under Article 86(2), the ECJ seems to have considered that it would amount to a

7   See below.
8   Case C-163/96 [1998] ECR I-533, [1998] 4 CMLR 737; the Commission condemned various aspects of the same dock-work legislation in *Provisions of Italian Ports Legislation Relating to Employment* OJ [1997] L 301/17; it noted the conflict of interest created by the legislation at paras 30(b) and (c) of its decision, referring to this as 'inherently an abuse'.
9   Case C-163/96 [1998] ECR I-533, [1998] 4 CMLR 737, paras 28-31.
10   Ibid, para 28.
11   Case C–18/88 [1991] ECR I-5941.
12   See p 196, n 13 above; see also Cases C-271/90 etc *Spain v Commission* [1992] ECR I-5833, para 36.
13   OJ [1990] L 10/47 quashed on appeal Cases C-48/90 and C-66/90 *Netherlands and Koninklijke PTT Nederland v Commission* [1992] ECR I-565, [1993] 5 CMLR 316.
14   OJ [1990] L 233/19, [1991] 4 CMLR 560, para 10.
15   OJ [1995] L 280/49, [1996] 4 CMLR 700, para 17(i).
16   OJ [1997] L 76/19, para 21(i).
17   OJ [1994] L 55/52.
18   OJ [2001] L 63/59; on appeal to the ECJ, Case C-102/01 *Italy v Commission* (judgment pending).
19   Case C-320/91 [1993] ECR I-2533, [1995] 4 CMLR 621.
20   See p 206 below.

measure contrary to Article 86(1). This could be seen as an example of the unlawful extension of a monopoly right to an ancillary activity, as in the cases just discussed. More radically, however, the case seems to suggest that it is possible to strike down monopolies that are too broad: in *RTT*, for example, that company would be able to use its monopoly right to extend its activities into the neighbouring market; in *Corbeau* the Court seems simply to have regarded the monopoly of the Belgian Post Office as too broad in itself. To the extent that this is a correct interpretation of *Corbeau* the judgment is very radical, and seems to go beyond the often-repeated assertion that the grant of an exclusive right is not, in itself, unlawful. Since *Corbeau* a specific Directive has been adopted in the postal sector determining the permitted extent of the 'reserved area' (that is to say the monopoly) in the postal sector[1]. As for the judgment itself, it is possible that this was the 'high-tide' of intervention under Article 86(1), and that the ECJ has since taken a more cautious approach, as the judgments in *Crespelle*[2] and *Banchero*[3] seem to suggest[4].

(E)   DISCRIMINATION.   In *Merci*[5] the ECJ referred to the discriminatory treatment of customers as an abuse for which a Member State could be responsible under Article 86(1). In *GT-Link A/S v De Danske Statsbaner*[6] the Court stated that, where a public undertaking which owns and operates a commercial port waives the port duties on its own ferry services and some of its trading partners whilst charging the full duties to other customers, there could be an infringement of Article 82(2)(c), that is to say the application of dissimilar conditions to equivalent transactions placing other trading parties at a competitive disadvantage[7]. Appropriately transparent accounting would be needed to show that this was not the case[8]. In a series of decisions in relation to charges levied for the use both of airports[9] and ports[10] the Commission has expressly condemned price discrimination contrary to Article 82(2)(c), and found the Member State in question to have adopted a measure contrary to Article 86(1). In these cases the airport or port was a natural monopoly, which would result in a particularly strict responsibility not to act in an abusive manner[11]; and it may be necessary, under the essential facilities doctrine[12], for the owner of such infrastructure to grant access to third parties on non-discriminatory terms[13].

(F)   THE CATEGORIES ARE NOT CLOSED.   The caveat has already been entered that this categorisation of the cases is simply an attempt to make sense of the judgments and decisions on Article 86(1) in conjunction with Article 82. It should be added

1   See ch 23, p 872.
2   Case C-323/93 *Centre d'Insémination de la Crespelle v Coopérative de la Mayenne* [1994] ECR I-5077.
3   Case C-387/93 [1995] ECR I-4663.
4   On these two judgments, see *Buendia Sierra* (p 189, n 17 above), paras 5.110-5.128.
5   Case C–179/90 [1991] ECR I–5889, [1994] 4 CMLR 422.
6   Case C-242/95 [1997] ECR I-4349, [1997] 5 CMLR 601.
7   Ibid, para 41; on Article 82(2)(c) generally, see ch 18, pp 657-662.
8   Ibid, para 42.
9   See *Brussels National Airport (Zaventem)* OJ [1995] L 216/8, [1996] 4 CMLR 232, paras 12-18; *Portuguese Airports* OJ [1999] L 69/31, [1999] 5 CMLR 103, paras 24-40; *Spanish Airports* OJ [2000] L 208/36, [2000] 5 CMLR 967, paras 45-56.
10   See *Tariffs for Piloting in the Port of Genoa* OJ [1997] L 301/27, paras 11-21.
11   See ch 5, pp 162-163 on the responsibilities of dominant, and super-dominant, undertakings.
12   See ch 5, p 177 and ch 17, pp 611-624.
13   See eg *Port of Rødby* OJ [1994] L 55/52, where the Commission decided that a refusal to allow access to the port was an unlawful extension of the monopoly right enjoyed by the port operator: see p 200 above.

that there is no reason why there should not be further cases in the future that do not fall into any of these categories at all. In each case, the question is whether a Member State has adopted a measure that infringes or might infringe Article 82 for which it bears responsibility under Article 86(1): the categories set out above do not include all the examples of abusive behaviour found to have infringed Article 82[14].

(ix)   Remedies and direct effect

Article 86(1) has direct effect, with the consequence that individuals can bring an action in a national court against a Member State which has infringed it[15]. An interesting question is whether an individual or a third party is able to bring an action for damages against a Member State which has acted in breach of Article 86(1). After *Francovich v Italy*[16], in which the ECJ held that in certain circumstances a Member State may have to compensate individuals who suffer as a result of the non-implementation of a Directive, this must at least be arguable.

(B)   Article 86(2)

Article 86(2) is a somewhat awkwardly drafted provision[17]. It is in three parts. To begin with, it states that undertakings entrusted with the operation of services of general economic interest or having the character of a revenue–producing monopoly shall be subject to the rules in the Treaty, and in particular to the competition rules. It then states, however, that this subjection to the rules applies only 'in so far as the application of such rules does not obstruct the performance, in law or in fact, of the particular tasks assigned to them'. Article 86(2) represents an exception to the application of Articles 81 and 82, and therefore must be interpreted strictly[18]. Article 86(2) requires that any restriction of competition should satisfy the principle of proportionality[19]. The burden of proof is on the undertaking seeking to rely on this provision[20]; however, to succeed under Article 86(2) it is not necessary to show that an undertaking's survival would be threatened if it were to be subjected to the competition rules[1]; nor to prove that there is no other conceivable measure that could secure that the task in question could be

---

14 On abusive behaviour under Article 82, see further ch 5, pp 167-181 and chs 17 and 18 generally.
15 See for example Case 155/73 *Sacchi* [1974] ECR 409, [1974] 2 CMLR 177, para 18; Case C-179/90 *Merci Convenzionale Porto di Genova SpA v Siderurgica Gabrielli SpA* [1991] ECR I-5889, [1994] 4 CMLR 422, para 23; for a recent statement to the same effect, and citing other judgments of the ECJ on the point, see Case C-238/98 *Giovanni Carra* judgment of 14 September 2000, para 11.
16 Cases 6/90 etc [1991] ECR I-5357, [1993] 2 CMLR 66.
17 Its counterpart in UK law will be found in the Competition Act 1998, Sch 3, para 4, although that provision is drafted rather more elegantly; for detailed discussion of Article 86(2), see *Buendia Sierra* (p 189, n 17 above) paras 8.01-8.324; also Buendia Sierra in *Faull and Nikpay* (p 198, n 9 above) paras 5.122-5.155.
18 See Cases C-157/94 etc *Commission v Netherlands* [1997] ECR I-5699, [1998] 2 CMLR 373, para 37; see also *Reims II* OJ [1999] L 275/17, [2000] 4 CMLR 704, para 92.
19 See *Buendia Sierra* (p 189, n 17 above) paras 8.115-8.261; also Buendia Sierra in *Faull and Nikpay* (p 198, n 9 above) paras 5.134-5.147.
20 See Cases 157/94 etc *Commission v Netherlands* [1997] ECR I-5699, [1998] 2 CMLR 373, para 51.
1 Ibid, para 43.

performed[2]. A third limb to Article 86(2) adds that the development of trade must not be affected to such an extent as would be contrary to the interests of the Community. The burden is on the Commission or third party complainants to prove this[3].

The effect of Article 86(2) is that some undertakings can claim to be excepted[4] from the application of Articles 81 and 82 where their application would prevent them from carrying on the tasks assigned to them; however, a Member State's interest in doing this must be balanced against the Community's interest in ensuring free competition and a single market. A good example of circumstances in which Article 86(2) may be applicable is afforded by postal services: all Member States require their national postal operator to observe a 'minimum service obligation': this is defined in Article 1 of the Postal Services Directive[5] as 'a universal service involving the permanent provision of a postal service of specified quality at all points in their territory at affordable prices for all users'. The postal operator will usually[6] be given a monopoly over the basic letter service, which will charge the same price for the delivery of letters to all parts of the country. Effectively, this means that the inhabitants of urban areas subsidise the postal services of those living in rural ones: delivering a letter from one part of London to another is cheaper than from the south-west of England to the north-east of Scotland. In a sense, therefore, the uniform tariff is discriminatory and could be attacked as such under Article 82. However, in so far as the uniform tariff provides an income to the postal operator that enables it to maintain the universal service, Article 86(2) is applicable and the undertaking is not subject to the competition rules.

A number of points require consideration.

(i) Services of general economic interest

An undertaking can claim to be excluded from the rules in the Treaty only if it has been entrusted with services of general economic interest or if it has the character of a revenue producing monopoly. It is not enough in itself that the undertaking performs that service; it must have been entrusted with that performance, which will mean that it is under certain obligations[7]. It is not necessary that the undertaking has been entrusted with the performance of the service by a legislative measure; this could have come about, for example, as a result of the terms and conditions of a concession agreement[8]. The expression 'services of general economic interest' is not defined in the Treaty. Obvious

---

2 Ibid, para 58.
3 See p 207 below.
4 Article 86(2) provides for the non-application of the rules in the Treaty in the circumstances specified, and so entails an exception or exclusion from them; it is not quite the same as Article 81(3), which provides that Article 81(1) 'may be declared inapplicable' to agreements that infringe Article 81(1).
5 Directive 97/67/EC of the European Parliament and of the Council on *Common Rules for the Development of the Internal Market of Community Postal Services and the Improvement of Quality of Service* OJ [1998] L 15/14.
6 There is no legal monopoly for postal services in Sweden or Finland.
7 See the opinion of AG Jacobs in Case 203/96 *Dussesldorp* [1998] ECR I-4075, [1998] 3 CMLR 873, para 103.
8 Case 30/87 *Corinne Bodson v Pompes Funèbres* [1988] ECR 2479, [1989] 4 CMLR 984.

examples of such services are the operation of the basic postal service[9] and the provision of services, for example in the transport sector, which are not economically viable in their own right[10]. The Commission has said that basic utilities would amount to services of general economic interest[11]. The protection afforded to services of general economic interest is a sensitive political issue and was addressed at the 1997 Inter-Governmental Conference. Proposals to amend Article 86(2) itself were rejected in favour of the insertion of Article 16 EC by the Treaty of Amsterdam. This expressly preserves the application of Article 86 because of:

> '...the place occupied by services of general economic interest in the shared values of the Union as well as their rôle in promoting social and territorial cohesion...'[12].

Article 16 reinforces the commitment of the Community and Member States to supporting undertakings required to provide services of general economic interest. In 1996 the Commission adopted a communication on services of general interest in Europe[13] in which it confirms that both public and private undertakings can be entrusted with the operation of services of general economic interest;[14] a further communication (replacing the 1996 one) was adopted in September 2000[15].

(ii)   *Undertakings having the character of a revenue-producing monopoly*

This expression is not defined in the Treaty. It would apply to a monopoly created in order to raise revenue for the State; usually this monopoly would be conferred upon a public undertaking which would contribute its profits to the State, but it could also be conferred upon a private undertaking in exchange for revenue. Undertakings that have the character of a revenue-earning monopoly may also be subject to Article 31, and the ECJ has established that Article 86(2) may be invoked as a defence in an action under that provision[16].

(iii)   *Scope of the exception: obstruction of the performance of the tasks assigned*

In a number of cases undertakings have argued that they were shielded from the competition rules by virtue of Article 86(2); in *BRT v SABAM*[17] the ECJ ruled that, as Article 86(2) involves a derogation from the application of the competition

---

9   Case 320/91 *Corbeau* [1993] ECR I-2533, [1995] 4 CMLR 621, para 15: 'it cannot be disputed that Régie des Postes is entrusted with a service of general economic interest consisting in its obligation to collect, carry and distribute mail on behalf of all users throughout the territory of the Member State concerned, at uniform tariffs ...'
10   See eg Case 66/88 *Ahmed Saeed* [1989] ECR 803, [1990] 4 CMLR 102, para 55.
11   XXth *Report on Competition Policy* (1990), p 12.
12   Article 16 EC; see further the Commission's XXVIIth *Report on Competition Policy* (1997), points 96-98; Ross 'Article 16 EC and Services of General Economic Interest: from Derogation to Obligation' (2000) 25 EL Rev 22.
13   Commission Communication OJ [1996] C 281/3; see further the Commission's XXVIIth *Report on Competition Policy* (1997), point 99.
14   Ibid, para 10.
15   OJ [2001] C 17/4, [2001] 4 CMLR 882.
16   See p 212 below.
17   Case 127/73 [1974] ECR 313, [1974] 2 CMLR 238.

rules, it should be construed narrowly, and the Commission and Community Courts have consistently done so, thereby maximising the application of Articles 81 and 82. In particular, they have been sceptical of the assertion that anti–competitive behaviour is *necessary* to enable undertakings to carry out the tasks assigned to them.

(A)   UNSUCCESSFUL CLAIMS BASED ON ARTICLE 86(2).   Claims based on Article 86(2) have often been rejected[18]. For example, in *EEC v ANSEAU–NAVEWA*[19] the Commission held that an agreement requiring purchasers in Belgium to acquire 'conformity labels' before washing-machines and dishwashers could be plumbed in infringed Article 81(1), because it had the effect of discriminating against imports from other Member States. The association of Belgian water authorities involved in running the scheme claimed the benefit of Article 86(2). The Commission accepted that they qualified as a body to whom services of a general economic interest had been entrusted, but went on to hold that the scheme in question was much more restrictive than necessary, saying that:

'a possible limitation of the application of the rules on competition can only be envisaged in the event that the undertaking concerned has no other technically and economically feasible means of performing its particular task'[20].

Similarly in *British Telecommunications*[1] the Commission rejected British Telecommunications's defence based on Article 86(2); when the Italian Government challenged this decision before the ECJ the Commission's decision was upheld[2]. The ECJ held that Italy had failed to show that the Commission's censure of BT, for prohibiting private message–forwarding agencies from using its network to forward messages from other EC Member States, put the performance of its tasks in jeopardy. Article 86(2) also failed in *Air Inter v Commission*[3], where the CFI rejected TAT's appeal against a Commission decision requiring the termination of exclusive rights on French air routes. The CFI accepted that the airline was entrusted with a public task of maintaining unprofitable domestic air routes. However it held that subjection to the competition rules would merely hinder or make more difficult the performance of this task; for Article 86(2) to apply, it was necessary to show that this would obstruct it, in fact or in law[4].

18   As well as the cases mentioned in the text, see also Case 172/80 *Züchner v Bayerische Vereinsbank* [1981] ECR 2021, [1982] 1 CMLR 313 and *Uniform Eurocheques* OJ [1985] L 35/43, [1985] 3 CMLR 434, paras 29 and 30 (both cases on banking); *Decca Navigator System* OJ [1989] L 43/27, [1990] 4 CMLR 627, para 128; *Magill TV Guide/ITP, BBC and RTE* OJ [1989] L 78/43, [1989] 4 CMLR 757, para 25; *Dutch Express Delivery Services* OJ [1990] L 10/47, paras 16-18; *Spanish International Courier Services* OJ [1990] L 233/19, [1991] 4 CMLR 560, paras 13–14; Case C-179/90 *Merci Convenzionale Porto di Genova v Siderurgica Gabrielli* [1991] ECR I-5889, [1994] 4 CMLR 540, paras 25-28; Case C-18/88 *RTT v GB-Inno-BM* [1991] ECR I-5941, paras 14-28; *IJsselcentrale* OJ [1991] L 28/32, [1992] 5 CMLR 154, paras 39–42; Case C-242/95 *GT-Link A/S v De Danske Statsbaner* [1997] ECR I-4349, [1997] 5 CMLR 601, paras 47-55; Case C-393/92 *Almelo* [1994] ECR I-1477, paras 46-51; when this case returned to the Dutch court, the claim based on Article 86(2) was unsuccessful: see Hancher (1997) 34 CML Rev 1509.
19   OJ [1982] L 167/39 as amended at L 325/20, [1982] 2 CMLR 193; upheld on appeal, Cases 96/82 etc *IAZ International Belgium SA v Commission* [1983] ECR 3369, [1984] 3 CMLR 276.
20   OJ [1982] L 167/39, [1982] 2 CMLR 193, para 66.
1   OJ [1982] L 360/36, [1983] 1 CMLR 457.
2   Case 41/83 *Italy v Commission* [1985] ECR 873, [1985] 2 CMLR 368.
3   Case T-260/94 [1997] ECR II-997, [1997] 5 CMLR 851.
4   Ibid, paras 134-141.

A particularly important judgment on Article 86(2) is *Corbeau*[5]. As we have seen, the case concerned the operation of an express delivery service, in contravention of the Belgian Post Office's postal monopoly[6]. The core of the ECJ's judgment dealt with the extent to which the postal monopoly could be justified under Article 86(2)[7]. The Court acknowledged that the Post Office was entrusted with a service of general economic interest[8], and that it might be necessary for it to benefit from a restriction of competition in order to be able to offset less profitable activities against profitable ones[9]: put more colloquially, it may be legitimate to prevent an entrant into the market from 'cream-skimming' or 'cherry-picking', leaving the incumbent postal operator to carry out unprofitable services pursuant to its universal service obligation. However, the Court continued that:

> 'the exclusion of competition is not justified as regards specific services dissociable from the service of general interest which meet special needs of economic operators and which call for certain additional services not offered by the traditional postal service, such as collection from the senders' address, greater speed or reliability of distribution or the possibility of changing the destination in the course of transit, in so far as such services, by their nature and the conditions in which they are offered, such as the geographical area in which they are provided, do not compromise the economic equilibrium of the service of general economic interest performed by the holder of the exclusive right'[10].

Since this was an action under Article 234, the ECJ then stated that it would be for the national court to make a decision under Article 86(2) on the particular facts of the case[11], but it is clear that it was giving a strong indication that it should not be possible to maintain a monopoly over express courier services in order to sustain the basic service of the daily delivery of letters.

(B)   SUCCESSFUL CLAIMS BASED ON ARTICLE 86(2).   It would be wrong to suppose from the foregoing that claims based on Article 86(2) are always unsuccessful. In particular, as the competition rules have come to be applied with greater regularity to the utilities (gas, electricity, water and similar sectors) and to areas of activity for which the state has historically taken responsibility, so too Article 86(2) has been invoked more often with successful effect. This point can be demonstrated by reference to four judgments of the ECJ from 1998 to 2000. In *Corsica Ferries France SA v Gruppo Antichi Ormeggiatori del Porto di Genova*[12] the Court was concerned with Italian legislation requiring ships from other Member States using the ports of Genoa and La Spezia in Italy to use the services of local mooring companies. It considered that mooring operations were of general economic interest: mooring groups are obliged to provide at any time and to any user a universal mooring service, for reasons of safety in port waters[13]. As a

---

5   Case C-320/91 [1993] ECR I-2533, [1995] 4 CMLR 621.
6   See pp 196-197 above.
7   Case C-320/91 [1993] ECR I-2533, [1995] 4 CMLR 621, paras 13-21.
8   Ibid, para 15.
9   Ibid, paras 17-18.
10   Ibid, para 19.
11   Ibid, para 20.
12   Case C-266/96 [1998] ECR I-3949, [1998] 5 CMLR 402.
13   Ibid, para 45.

result it was not incompatible with Article 86(1) in conjunction with Article 82 to include in the price of the service a component designed to cover the cost of maintaining the universal mooring service, and Article 86(2) was applicable[14]. In the *Albany* judgment[15] the ECJ held that the exclusive right of a pension fund to manage supplementary pensions in a particular sector could be justified under Article 86(2), since otherwise 'young employees in good health engaged in non-dangerous activities' would leave the scheme, leaving behind members who would be bad insurance risks, thereby undermining the success of the system[16]. In *Deutsche Post AG v Gesellschaft für Zahlungssysteme mbH and Citicorp Kartenservice GmbH*[17] the ECJ considered that Article 86(2) justified the grant by a Member State to its postal operators of a statutory right to charge internal postage on items of so-called 'remail'[18]. Environmental considerations led to the successful application of Article 86(2) in *Entreprenørforeningens Affalds/ Miljøsektion v Københavns Kommune*[19].

Although Article 86(2) is drafted in terms of the position of undertakings, it has become clear that Member States themselves can rely on it. For example in *Dusseldorp*[20] the ECJ, following the Opinion of Advocate General Jacobs, confirmed that the Netherlands could rely on Article 86(2) in relation to its 'Long Term Plan' relating to waste disposal. The same point arose in *Commission v Netherlands*[1].

(iv)   Adverse development of trade

It is not possible to rely on Article 86(2) if the development of trade would be affected to such an extent as would be contrary to the interest of the Community. This must mean something more than an effect on trade in the sense of Articles 81 and 82, since without such an effect the EC competition rules would not be applicable anyway. The ECJ has held in *Commission v Netherlands* that the Commission must prove whether the exclusive right has affected and continued to affect the development of intra-Community trade 'to an extent which is contrary to the interests of the Community'[2]. An application will be dismissed where it fails to do so[3].

(v)   Direct effect

In *Belgische Radio en Televisie (BRT) v SABAM*[4] the ECJ established that Articles 81 and 82 are directly applicable to the undertakings described in Article 86(2) so that an action may be brought against them in domestic proceedings, whether the Commission has acted under Article 86(3) or not. A national court should

---

14   Ibid, paras 46-47.
15   Cases C-67/96 etc *Albany International BV v SBT* [2000] 4 CMLR 446.
16   Ibid, paras 98-111.
17   Joined Cases C-147/97 and 8/97 [2000] 4 CMLR 838.
18   Ibid, paras 41-54.
19   Case C-209/98 judgment of 23 May 2000, paras 74-83.
20   Case C-203/96 [1998] ECR I-4075, [1998] 3 CMLR 873, para 67.
1   Cases C-157/94 etc. [1997] ECR I-5699, [1998] 2 CMLR 373, paras 51-64.
2   Ibid, paras 65-68.
3   See Case C-159/94 *Commission v France* [1997] ECR I-5815, [1998] 2 CMLR 373, paras 109-116.
4   Case 127/73 [1974] ECR 313, [1974] 2 CMLR 238.

investigate whether the undertaking falls within Article 86(2); if it does not, the court may go ahead and apply the competition rules[5]. In this sense, Article 86(2) could be said to be 'negatively' directly effective. What was not clear was whether a national court should proceed if satisfied that an undertaking is within Article 86(2): could the court in those circumstances ask whether application of the competition rules would obstruct the undertaking in the performance of the tasks assigned to it? It was arguable that this matter was exclusively within the competence of the Commission, so that the court could not deal with it[6]; a preferable solution was that the national court could address this issue and, in clear cases, reach a conclusion on it: in other words, that Article 86(2) should be 'positively' as well as 'negatively' directly effective. In cases of doubt the national court could stay the action whilst the opinion of the Commission is sought. The latter view was apparently favoured by the ECJ in *Ahmed Saeed*[7] and was actually decided in *ERT v Dimotiki*[8]; it was affirmed by the Court in *Almelo*[9].

It remains uncertain whether the final sentence of Article 86(2), which requires that trade must not be affected contrary to the interests of the Community, has direct effect. It is arguable that only the Commission should be entitled to carry out the task of assessing the interests of the Community.

(C)   Article 86(3)[10]

Article 86(3) provides that the Commission shall ensure the application of Article 86(1) and (2) and that, where necessary, it shall address appropriate decisions or directives to Member States. This is a power which for many years lay dormant; however the Commission began to employ it in the 1980s, most notably in the context of the telecommunications sector[11], and it is now an important part of its armoury. The advantage of Article 86(3) from the Commission's perspective is that it can adopt a decision or directive itself; in doing so, it is not subject to any particular procedural framework, although it must of course comply with the general principles of EC law, and must provide adequate reasons for its action, in accordance with Article 253 EC[12]. The Commission liaises with other interested parties, including the Parliament, when exercising its powers under Article 86(3), and particularly when adopting a Directive[13]. If the Commission did not have its Article 86(3) powers, it would be able to proceed against measures that offend Article 86(1) only by taking proceedings before the ECJ under Article 226 or by persuading the Council of Ministers to adopt the measures it favours.

Article 86(3) enables the Commission to adopt both decisions and directives: a decision can be adopted, establishing that a Member State is in breach of a Community obligation; but a directive can go further and legislate for the elimination of existing violations of the Treaty and the prevention of future ones.

---

5   Case 155/73 *Italy v Sacchi* [1974] ECR 409, [1974] 2 CMLR 177.
6   See Case 10/71 *Public Prosecutor v Müller* [1971] ECR 723.
7   Case 66/86 [1989] ECR 803.
8   Case C–260/89 [1991] ECR I–2925, [1994] 4 CMLR 540, para 34.
9   Case C–393/92 [1994] ECR I-1477, para 50.
10 On Article 86(3) generally, see *Buendia Sierra* (p 189, n 17 above) paras 10.01-10.184 and *Buendia Sierra* in *Faull and Nikpay* (p 198, n 9 above) paras 5.156-5.186.
11 See p 210 below.
12 The Commission's decision in *Dutch Express Delivery Services* was quashed for various procedural improprieties: see n 17 below.
13 See XXVth *Report on Competition Policy* (1995), point 100.

(i) Decisions

In *Greek Public Property Insurance*[14] the Commission required Greece, by decision under Article 86(3), to alter its domestic legislation requiring that all public property in Greece be insured by Greek public sector insurance companies and that staff of Greek state–owned banks recommend to their customers insurance with companies affiliated to the public banking sector and controlled by it. When Greece failed to take the necessary measures to do this within the prescribed period, the Commission brought an action under Article 226 for failure to fulfil its Treaty obligations. The ECJ made the declaration[15], holding in the course of its judgment that a decision by the Commission under Article 86(3) is 'binding in its entirety' on the person to whom it is addressed so that the addressee must comply with it until it obtains from the ECJ a suspension of its operation or a declaration that it is void. In *Spanish Transport Fares*[16] the Commission addressed a decision to Spain condemning its discriminatory fares for passengers from mainland Spain to the Balearic and Canary Islands. The Commission also adopted decisions under Article 86(3) in *Dutch Express Delivery Services*[17], *Spanish International Courier Services*[18], *Port of Rødby*[19], *Second Operator of GSM Radiotelephony Services in Italy*[20], *Second Operator of GSM Radiotelephony Services in Spain*[1], *Brussels National Airport (Zaventem)*[2], *Exclusive Right to Broadcast Television Advertising in Flanders*[3], *Italian Ports Legislation Relating to Employment*[4], *Tariffs for Piloting in the Port of Genoa*[5], *Portugese Airports*[6], *Spanish Airports*[7], and in *New Postal Services in Italy*[8].

(ii) Directives

The competence of the Commission to adopt directives under Article 86(3) has been considered by the ECJ on three occasions. The Transparency Directive[9] was challenged in *France v Commission*[10], *inter alia* on the basis that, since it concerned the superveillance of state aids, it should have been adopted under Article 89 (former Article 94) rather than Article 86(3). The ECJ ruled that the

14 OJ [1985] L 152/25.
15 Case 226/87 *Commission v Greece* [1988] ECR 3611, [1989] 3 CMLR 569.
16 OJ [1987] L 194/28.
17 OJ [1990] L 10/47 quashed on appeal Cases C-48/90 and C-66/90 *Netherlands and Koninklijke PTT Nederland v Commission* [1992] ECR I-565, [1993] 5 CMLR 316 as the Commission had failed to give the Dutch Government a fair hearing.
18 OJ [1990] L 233/19, [1991] 4 CMLR 560.
19 OJ [1994] L 55/52.
20 OJ [1995] L 280/49, [1996] 4 CMLR 700.
1   OJ [1997] L 76/19.
2   OJ [1995] L 216/8, [1996] 4 CMLR 232.
3   OJ [1997] L 244/18, [1997] 5 CMLR 718, upheld on appeal Case T-266/97 *Vlaamse Televisie Maatschappij NV v Commission* [2000] 4 CMLR 1171.
4   OJ [1997] L 301/17.
5   OJ [1997] L 301/27.
6   OJ [1999] L 69/31, [1999] 5 CMLR 103; upheld on appeal Case C-163/99 *Portugal v Commission*, judgment of 29 March 2001.
7   OJ [2000] L 208/36, [2000] 5 CMLR 967.
8   OJ [2001] L 63/59, on appeal to the ECJ Case C-102/01 *Italy v Commission* (judgment pending).
9   Commission Directive (EEC) 80/723 OJ [1980] L 195/35, amended most recently by OJ [2000] L 193/75.
10 Cases 188/80 etc [1982] ECR 2545, [1982] 3 CMLR 144; for a later challenge related to this Directive, see Case C-325/91 *France v Commission* [1993] ECR I-3283.

fact that the Commission could have proceeded under Article 89 did not mean that it could not also do so under Article 86(3). Towards the end of the 1980s, the Commission's concern about the fragmented nature of the telecommunications market in the EC and the consequent lack of competition led to the adoption of two directives, the first on the telecommunications terminal equipment market[11] and the second on telecommunications themselves[12]. Opposition from Member States to these Directives was considerable and both were challenged before the ECJ. In each case the ECJ upheld the competence of the Commission to have proceeded under Article 86(3)[13]. In *France v Commission*[14] three Member States complained that the Commission should have proceeded under Article 226 rather than Article 86(3). The ECJ held that there had been no misuse of powers: the Commission may use the powers conferred upon it by Article 86(3) to specify in general terms the obligations that arise under Article 86(1); however the Commission may not use a directive under Article 86(3) to rule upon specific infringements of the Treaty, for which the Article 226 procedure must be used[15]. The ECJ also held that the fact that the Council had competence to adopt legislation relating to telecommunications did not mean that the Commission had no competence[16]. The ECJ annulled Articles 2, 7 and 9 of the Directive on terminal equipment since the Commission had failed to explain which rights were 'special' nor why they were contrary to Community law[17]. It is not possible to use Article 86(3) for the purpose of achieving harmonisation, the legislative base for which is provided by Articles 94 and 95 EC (former Articles 100 and 100(a)): this explains why in the telecommunications sector there are Article 86(3) Directives, dealing with the conditions of competition, and a raft of separate measures under Article 94 and 95 on harmonisation[18].

(iii)   Judicial review of the Commission's powers under Article 86(3)

In *Bundesverband der Bilanzbuchhalter v Commission*[19] the ECJ held that individuals may, in some circumstances, be entitled to bring an action for annulment against a decision of the Commission taken on the basis of Article 86(3); and that, in exceptional situations, an individual may have standing to challenge a refusal by the Commission to make a decision[20]. However the Commission enjoys a wide discretion in the field covered by Article 86(1) and (3)[1] and an individual may not indirectly compel a Member State to legislate by way of judicial review[2].

---

11   Commission Directive (EEC) 88/301 OJ [1988] L 131/73, [1991] 4 CMLR 922.
12   Commission Directive (EEC) 90/308 OJ [1990] L 192/10, [1991] 4 CMLR 932.
13   See Case C–202/88 *France v Commission* [1991] ECR I-1223, [1992] 5 CMLR 552 (terminal equipment); Cases C–271/90 etc *Spain, Belgium and Italy v Commission* (telecommunications) [1992] ECR I-5833, [1993] 4 CMLR 100.
14   See n 13 above.
15   Ibid, paras 16–18.
16   Ibid, paras 19–27; see similarly Cases 188/80 etc *France v Commission* [1982] ECR 2545, [1982] 3 CMLR 144, para 14.
17   Case C-208/88 (n 13 above), paras 45-47 and 53-58.
18   See ch 23, pp 868-869.
19   Case C-107/95 P [1997] ECR I-947, [1997] 5 CMLR 432.
20   Ibid, para 25.
1   Ibid, para 27; see also Case T-266/97 *Vlaamse Televisie Maatschappij NV v Commission* [2000] 4 CMLR 1171, para 75.
2   Ibid, para 28.

4. ARTICLE 31 – STATE MONOPOLIES OF A COMMERCIAL CHARACTER[3]

Article 31(1) of the Treaty provides that:

'Member States shall adjust any State monopolies of a commercial character so as to ensure that no discrimination regarding the conditions under which goods are procured and marketed exists between nationals of Member States'[4].

Article 31(1) goes on to state that it applies to any body through which a Member State supervises, determines or appreciably influences imports or exports between Member States, and also that it applies to monopolies delegated by the State to others. Article 31(2) obliges Member States not to introduce any new measure contrary to the principles in Article 31(1) or which restricts the scope of the Treaty Articles dealing with the prohibition of customs duties and quantitative restrictions between Member States. However Article 31 does not require the abolition of existing monopolies; only that they should be adjusted to prevent discrimination.

Article 31 is designed to prevent state monopolies of a commercial character discriminating against nationals of other Member States. This provision appears in the chapter of the Treaty on the free movement of goods rather than on the competition rules: it might have been more natural for it to appear alongside Article 86, which was contemplated at one stage during the writing of the Treaty. At some stage, however, these siblings became separated, and subsequent amendments to the Treaty have not reunited them. One way of ensuring that Member States do not discriminate in this way is to alter their public procurement policies, in which area the Council has been active[5]. The Commission continues to monitor the conduct of Member States under Article 31; details of its application of Article 31 will be found in its annual reports on competition policy[6]. In *Commission v Greece*[7] the ECJ held that Greece was obliged to terminate exclusive rights to import and sell petroleum derivatives since those rights discriminated against exporters of such products in other Member States and since they upset the normal conditions of competition between Member States. Where the Commission suspects infringement of Article 31, it may take proceedings against the Member State under Article 226 of the Treaty or it could make use of the powers available to it under Article 86(3)[8]. Where the Commission takes Article 226 proceedings, it must prove that a Member State has failed to fulfil its obligations and it must place before the ECJ the information needed to enable it

---

3 See generally Buendia Sierra *Exclusive Rights and State Monopolies under EC Law* (OUP, 1999) paras 3.01-3.201; also Buendia Sierra in *Faull and Nikpay* (p 198, n 9 above) paras 5.97-5.112.
4 Note that Article 31 of the Treaty is not identical to the original Article 37, which contained transitional rules that had become redundant.
5 See ch 2, p 46 n 6.
6 See eg the Commission's XXVIth *Report on Competition Policy* (1996), points 132-135; XXVIIth *Report on Competition Policy* (1997), points 137-144; there is nothing in the 1998 and 1999 Reports on Article 31.
7 Case C–347/88 [1990] ECR I-4747.
8 See pp 208-210 above.

to decide whether this is the case[9]. An injured undertaking could bring an action in a national court, as Article 31 is directly effective[10].

In *Commission v Netherlands*, the ECJ found that import and export monopolies for gas and electricity in the Netherlands, Italy, and France amounted to an infringement of Article 31(1)[11]. However, the Court considered that Article 86(2) could be invoked by Member States in proceedings brought under Article 31 to justify such monopolies. They could be, provided that the maintenance of monopoly rights was necessary to enable the undertaking in question to perform the tasks of general economic interest entrusted to it under economically acceptable conditions; it was not necessary that the survival of the undertaking itself would be threatened in the absence of such a monopoly. On the facts the Commission failed to satisfy the ECJ that the monopolies could not be justified under Article 86(2).

5.   ARTICLES 87 TO 89 – STATE AIDS

The Treaty provides the Commission with power under Articles 87 to 89 (ex Articles 92-94) of the Treaty to deal with state aids that could distort competition in the common market. A considerable amount of DG COMP's energies go into this issue, but lack of space prevents a detailed discussion of the topic here[12].

Article 87(1) provides that:

'Save as otherwise provided in this Treaty, any aid granted by a Member State or through State resources in any form whatsoever which distorts or threatens to distort competition by favouring certain undertakings or the production of certain goods shall, in so far as it affects trade between Member States, be incompatible with the common market.'

Article 87(2) provides that aids having a social character granted to individual consumers, aids to make good the damage caused by national disasters or exceptional occurrences and aids granted to the economy of certain areas of West Germany affected by the division of Germany after the Second World War shall be compatible with the common market. Article 87(3) gives the Commission discretion to permit other aids, for example to promote the economic development of areas where the standard of living is abnormally low or where there is serious unemployment, or to promote the execution of an important project of common European interest or to remedy a serious disturbance in the economy of a Member State.

9   See eg Cases C-157/94 etc *Commission v Netherlands* [1997] ECR I-5699, [1998] 2 CMLR 373, para 59.
10   Case 91/78 *Hansen v Hauptzollamt Flensberg* [1979] ECR 935.
11   See Cases C-157/94 etc *Commission v Netherlands* [1997] ECR I-5699, [1998] 2 CMLR 373: the nature of the monopolies varied from state to state.
12   See for further discussion Farr in Div VIII of *Butterworths Competition Law* (eds Freeman and Whish); Harden *State Aid: Community Law and Policy* (Bundesanzeiger: Köln, 1993); Evans *European Community Law of State Aid* (Clarendon Press, 1997); Hancher, Ottervanger and Slot *EC State Aids* (Chancery Law Publishing, 2nd ed, 1999); Wyatt and Dashwood *European Union Law* (Sweet & Maxwell, 4th ed, 2000) ch 24; D'Sa *European Community Law on State Aid* (Sweet & Maxwell, 1998); Bellamy and Child *European Community Law of Competition* (Sweet & Maxwell, 5th ed, 2001, ed Roth) ch 19; the Commission's annual *Report on Competition Policy* contains a detailed account of its activities under the state aids provisions; see eg the XXIXth *Report on Competition Policy* pp 81-110 and 221-317.

Article 88 deals with procedure. The Commission may, by Article 88(2)(i), adopt a decision that a state aid which is incompatible with the common market shall be abolished or altered. If the Member State does not comply with this decision within the stated time, the Commission or another Member State may take the matter to the ECJ under Article 87(3)(ii) without having to resort to the procedure under Articles 226 and 227 (former Articles 169 and 170) of the Treaty[13]. Repayment of state aids may be demanded. Article 88(3) requires plans to grant or alter aids to be notified to the Commission in sufficient time to enable it to submit its comments. The aid may not be implemented until the Commission has reached a decision. Article 88(3) is directly effective[14] and an individual may seek relief in a domestic court where aid is granted without notification under Article 88(3) or put into effect before the Commission's decision[15].

It can be difficult to tell, in the absence of relevant information, whether competition is being distorted where a Member State controls part of the economy directly or grants financial aids to certain firms. To overcome this problem, the Commission issued a Directive in 1980 to increase the transparency of the relationship between Member States and public undertakings[16], which was unsuccessfully challenged in *France v Commission*[17]; the Directive has been amended a number of times, most recently in July 2000[18]. The Commission uses the data that it receives through this Directive to monitor the compatibility of state aids with Article 87[19].

Council Regulation 994/98[20] confers powers on the Commission to adopt 'group exemptions' for certain categories of state aid, and to adopt a regulation on 'de minimis' aids. Three block exemptions and a de minimis regulation were adopted on 6 December 2000.[1] Council Regulation 659/1999[2] lays down detailed rules for the application of Article 88 of the Treaty. The Commission has also adopted a number of guidelines on the application of the state aid rules[3].

---

13 It cannot proceed under Article 88(2)(ii) in respect of a later state aid which was not within the scope of an earlier decision: Case C–294/90 *British Aerospace plc v Commission* [1992] ECR I-493, [1992] 1 CMLR 853.
14 Case 120/73 *Lorenz v Germany* [1973] ECR 1471.
15 See eg *R v A-G, ex p ICI* [1987] 1 CMLR 72, CA.
16 OJ [1980] L 195/35.
17 See p 191, n 7 above.
18 Commission Directive 2000/52/EC OJ [2000] L 193/75
19 See the Commission's XIVth *Report on Competition Policy*, points 281–283.
20 OJ [1998] L 142/1.
1   Commission Press Release IP/00/1415, 6 December 2000.
2   OJ [1999] L 83/1; see Sinnaeve and Slot 'The New Regulation on State Aid Procedures' (1999) 36 CML Rev 1153.
3   See eg the *Community Guidelines on State Aid for Rescuing and Restructuring Firms in Difficulty* OJ [1994] C 368/12; *Notice on Cooperation between National Courts and the Commission in the State Aid Field* OJ [1995] C 312/8; *Community Guidelines on State Aid for Small and Medium-sized Enterprises* OJ [1996] C 213/4.

CHAPTER 7

Articles 81 and 82: enforcement by the European Commission

I. INTRODUCTION

Infringement of Articles 81 and 82 may have serious consequences for guilty undertakings. Such is the importance of competition law that companies must put in place effective compliance programmes to ensure that the competition rules are not infringed and that employees understand what types of behaviour must be avoided[1]. The European Commission has wide powers to enforce compliance with the competition rules, as do some national competition authorities ('NCAs')[2]. This chapter will consider the enforcement of Articles 81 and 82 by the Commission and judicial review of its decisions; it will conclude with a discussion of the Commission's modernisation programme. Articles 81 and 82 are directly applicable and may be invoked in proceedings in the domestic courts of the Member States; this subject will be considered in chapter 8.

The enforcement of EC competition law is a substantial subject in its own right and there are several works for practitioners which deal with the topic in detail[3]. In understanding the extent of – or rather the limits to – the Commission's powers, it is important to have reference to the general principles of Community law some of which, such as respect for fundamental rights and for the rights of the defence and the principle of proportionality, have obvious significance for the enforcement of the competition rules[4]. A developing issue is the relationship

---

1   On compliance programmes generally see Smith, *Competition Law: Enforcement & Procedure* (Butterworths, 2001), ch 2; Rodger 'Compliance with Competition Law: A View from Industry' [2000] Commercial Law Liability Review 249.
2   NCAs will become more involved in enforcement of the competition rules under the Commission's modernisation programme: see pp 246-258 below.
3   See in particular Ortiz Blanco *European Community Competition Procedure* (Clarendon Press Oxford, 1996); Kerse *EC Antitrust Procedure* (Sweet & Maxwell, 4th ed, 1998); Smith *Competition Law: Enforcement & Procedure* (Butterworths, 2001); Bellamy and Child *European Community Law of Competition* (Sweet & Maxwell, 5th ed, 2001) chs 11 and 12; the Commission has produced a helpful booklet *Dealing with the Commission: notifications, complaints, inspections and fact-finding powers under Articles 81 and 82 of the EEC Treaty* (Brussels and Luxembourg, 1997).
4   On general principles of EC law see Kerse (n 3 above) ch 8; Smith (n 3 above) ch 11; Hartley *The Foundations of European Community Law* (Oxford University Press, 4th ed, 1998), ch 5; Wyatt and Dashwood *European Union Law* (Sweet & Maxwell, 4th ed, 2000) ch 6; Usher, *General Principles of EC Law* (Addison Wesley Longman, 1998); Tridimas *The General Principles of EC Law* (Oxford University Press, 1999).

between the Commission's procedures and the standards required by the European Convention on Human Rights. The Convention contains important provisions such as Article 6, which recognises the right to a fair and public hearing in matters of criminal law. In *Société Stenuit v France*[5] the European Commission on Human Rights concluded that proceedings under French competition law, which were characterised in French law as administrative, were in fact criminal and so within the scope of Article 6 of the Convention. Under EC law, however, competition proceedings are said to be administrative rather than criminal[6]. The ECJ has said in *Al Jubail v Council*[7] (an anti-dumping case) that it has a duty to avoid conspicuous discrepancies between its construction of the right to a fair trial and the requirements established by the European Court of Human Rights[8].

(A)   The legal basis for the Commission's powers

Article 83(1) EC (ex Article 87(1)) gives the Council of Ministers a general power to adopt any 'appropriate regulations or directives to give effect to the principles set out in Articles 81 and 82'. Acting on the basis of Article 83(1) the Council adopted Regulation 17/62[9], which confers wide powers upon the Commission, for example to request information, to carry out on-the-spot investigations, to grant negative clearances (that Articles 81(1) or Article 82 do not apply to an agreement or practice), to grant individual exemptions (that the terms of Article 81(3) are satisfied) and to impose penalties for transgression of the competition rules. Regulation 17/62 applies to all sectors of the economy with the exception of transport[10]; there are specific implementing regulations for rail, road and inland waterways[11]; for maritime transport[12] and for air transport[13]. Tramp vessel services in the maritime transport sector are not covered by any of these regulations[14]; nor is air transport other than between Community airports[15]. It follows that in relation to these sectors the Member States may exercise the powers conferred on them by Article 84 EC (ex Article 88) and that the Commission may proceed on the basis of Article 85 EC (ex Article 89): the proposed alliance between BA and American Airlines was reviewed both in the UK and by the

---

5   (1992) 14 EHRR 509; see in particular paras 62 and 63 of the Commission's opinion.
6   See Regulation 17/62, Article 15(4).
7   Case C–49/88 [1991] ECR I-3187, [1991] 3 CMLR 377, paras 111 and 112.
8   See also the Opinion of Darmon AG in Cases 89/85 etc *A Ahlström Oy v Commission*, [1993] ECR I-1307, [1993] 4 CMLR 407, paras 143–145; Case T-112/98 *Mannesmannröhren-Werke AG v Commission* judgment of 20 February 2001, paras 59-60.
9   JO 204/62, OJ (Special Edition 1959–62) p 57; note that this Regulation has been amended in important respects, in particular by Regulation 1216/99, OJ [1999] L 148/5, and that it is essential to use an updated, consolidated, version: a consolidated version will be found at http://europa.eu.int/comm/competition/antitrust/legislation/.
10 This exception was effected by Regulation 141/62, OJ (Special Edition 1959-62) p 291; see ch 23, pp 859-866 on the application of the competition rules to transport.
11 Regulation 1017/68, JO [1968] L 175/1, OJ [1968] 302.
12 Regulation 4056/86, OJ [1986] L 378/4.
13 Regulation 3975/87, OJ [1987] L 374/1, corrected at OJ [1988] L 30/40 and OJ [1989] L 43/56 and amended by Regulation 1284/91, OJ [1991] L 122/2 and Regulation 2410/92, OJ [1992] L 240/18.
14 See Regulation 4056/86, Article 1(3).
15 See Regulation 3975/87, Article 1(2).

Commission on the basis of these Treaty provisions, since it was concerned with air transport between the Community and the US[16].

Article 24 of Regulation 17/62 gives the Commission the power to adopt regulations on notifications and on hearings. The Commission has adopted Regulation 3385/94 on notifications under Regulation 17/62[17] and Regulation 2843/98 on notifications in the transport sector[18]. It has also adopted Regulation 2842/98 on hearings[19]. These regulations replace earlier regulations, now repealed[20].

(B) Formal decisions and informal settlements

(i) The small number of formal decisions

The Commission has for a long time been hopelessly short of the resources necessary to enable it to enforce Articles 81 and 82 throughout the Community and to respond to notifications for individual exemption while at the same time discharging its numerous other functions such as the development of competition policy, the drafting of new legislation, the application of the ECMR and the rules on state aid and international cooperation with other competition agencies and international institutions such as the OECD, UNCTAD and the WTO. In any one year the Commission adopts a very small number of formal decisions compared with the number of new cases opened; in 1999 it adopted a total of 68 decisions compared with 388 new cases[1]; the corresponding figures in 2000 were 36 formal decisions and 297 new cases[2]. The formal decisions that the Commission adopts tend to deal either with important points of principle indicating the way in which it wishes to develop competition policy or to involve serious transgressions of the competition rules where deterrent punishment is thought necessary.

(ii) Informal settlements[3]

The Commission deals with many other cases informally; there is no specific legal basis for this practice, but it has developed over many years as a sensible and pragmatic way of disposing of cases. In some cases the Commission may consider that an agreement or practice notified gives rise to no competition concern; in others it may negotiate with undertakings and try to persuade them to alter features of agreements or practices considered to be objectionable. The outcome is often that the Commission informs the party by 'comfort letter' that it considers that there is no infringement of Article 81(1) or Article 82, or, in the

---

16 See the Commission's XXVIII *Report on Competition Policy* (1998), points 101-104; the *BA/American Airways (Articles [84] and [85]) Enforcement Regulations 1996*, SI 1996/ 2199 were adopted to enable an effective investigation to take place in the UK, as to which see Kerse 'Enforcing Community Competition Policy under Articles [84] and [85] of the EC Treaty: New Powers for UK Competition Authorities' (1997) 18 ECLR 17.

17 OJ [1994] L 377/28, [1995] 5 CMLR 507.

18 OJ [1998] L 334/22, [1999] 4 CMLR 236.

19 OJ [1998] L 354/18, [1999] 4 CMLR 228.

20 See eg Regulation 99/63 on hearings, which was replaced by Regulation 2842/98.

1 See the XXIXth *Report on Competition Policy* (1999), p 57.

2 See the XXXth *Report on Competition Policy* (2000), p 60.

3 See *Kerse* paras 6.53-6.66; *Smith* paras 8.72-8.89.

case of an agreement that infringes Article 81(1), that the terms of Article 81(3) appear to be satisfied, and that therefore it intends to close its file. When notifying agreements to the Commission for negative clearance and/or individual exemption the parties are specifically asked whether they would be satisfied with a 'comfort letter' rather than a formal decision. Sometimes infringement proceedings are settled between the parties and the Commission, also leading to the closure of the file. In 1999 514 cases were settled informally[4] and in 2000 the corresponding number was 343[5].

Disposal of cases by comfort letter is therefore an important fact of life as far as the Commission and notifying parties are concerned. However there is one problem with the use of comfort letters from the parties' point of view, which is that the ECJ held in the so-called *Perfumes* cases that they are not binding, as a matter of law, on national courts[6]. The possibility exists therefore that A and B may have received a comfort letter from the Commission saying that an agreement does not infringe Article 81(1), or that it infringes Article 81(1) but that it satisfies the requirements of Article 81(3); years later A may wish to be released from its contractual commitment and therefore acts in breach of it, with the result that it is sued by B. In its defence A claims that the agreement infringes Article 81(1), has not been granted individual exemption by a formal decision under Article 81(3), and is therefore void under Article 81(2); in addition A argues that the comfort letter of the Commission is not binding on the judge of the national court in which the litigation takes place, and succeeds in persuading the judge that there has indeed been an infringement of the competition rules. Clearly this would be a very unsatisfactory outcome for B. However in practice this does not appear to have caused major problems for the recipients of comfort letters, and it seems unlikely that a national court would depart from the stance taken by the Commission; the fact of the matter is that, notwithstanding the technical problem that comfort letters are not formal decisions, undertakings are prepared to accept them as a pragmatic way of settling cases[7]. The 'problem' of comfort letters, in so far as it exists, will be eliminated if the Commission's modernisation proposals are implemented; the procedure of notification to the Commission for negative clearance and individual exemption, out of which the comfort letter system has grown, will be abolished in its entirety[8].

The Commission maintains a helpful list on its website of both the formal and the informal decisions it adopts each year[9].

---

4   See the XXIXth *Report on Competition Policy* (1999), p 57.
5   See the XXXth *Report on Competition Policy* (2000), p 60.
6   See Cases 253/78 *Procureur de la République v Giry and Guerlain* [1980] ECR 2327, [1981] 2 CMLR 99; as to whether a comfort letter is binding on the Commission see Case T-7/93 *Langnese-Iglo GmbH v Commission* [1995] ECR II-1533, [1995] 5 CMLR 602, upheld on appeal Case C-279/95 P [1998] ECR I-5609, [1998] 5 CMLR 933, and Case T-241/97 *Stork Amsterdam BV v Commission* [2000] 5 CMLR 31, para 80.
7   See further ch 8, p 265.
8   See pp 246-258 below.
9   See, for 2001, http://europa.eu.int/comm/competition/antitrust/cases/2001/; the Commission's *Annual Report on Competition Policy* provides a statistical survey each year of the number of notifications, decisions, rejections of complaints etc: see eg the XXXth *Report on Competition Policy* (2000), points 10 to 15, which states that in 2000 there were 297 new cases under Articles 81, 82 and 86, a decrease from the previous year; in all 379 cases were closed, thereby reducing the backlog of cases to 931, a decrease from 1,013 the previous year.

(C) The Commission's modernisation programme

In April 1999 the Commission published its White Paper on Modernisation[10] in which it proposed very significant changes in relation to the enforcement of Articles 81 and 82. In essence, the system of notifying agreements to the Commission for individual exemption under Article 81(3) would be abandoned; Article 81(3) would become directly applicable on the part of NCAs and national courts; and the burden of enforcing Articles 81 and 82 would be shared with the latter, the Commission concentrating on cases of major significance. These immensely important proposals, and the likely timetable for their implementation, will be considered in the final section of this chapter[11].

2. FACT-FINDING POWERS OF THE COMMISSION

The Commission's fact-finding powers are an important part of the enforcement procedure. The availability of written evidence is particularly important to the Commission since it lacks the ability to take oral evidence on oath[12]. The Commission obtains information from various sources. It receives many complaints; its responsibilities towards complainants are described below[13]. It receives information from firms which apply to it for negative clearance or notify if for individual exemption[14]. The Commission also gathers information by acting on its own initiative. It will follow the financial press and trade journals, while Article 12 of Regulation 17/62 authorises it to conduct an inquiry into any sector of the economy in which there is reason to believe that competition is being distorted in some way; it has rarely used this procedure.

Of particular importance to the Commission are the powers conferred by Articles 11 and 14 of Regulation 17/62 (and by equivalent provisions in the transport Regulations[15]) to request information from undertakings and to carry out investigations. The position of information containing business secrets, privileged material and self-incriminating evidence will be considered after Articles 11 and 14 have been looked at.

(A) Article 11: requests for information[16]

Article 11 deals with requests for information; information for this purpose includes documents[17]. The Commission may request from the Governments and competent

---

10 Commission Programme No 99/027, OJ [1999] C 132/1, [1999] 5 CMLR 208.
11 See pp 246-258 below.
12 As part of the modernisation proposals the Commission is seeking a power to interview natural or legal persons and to record their statements: see p 256 below.
13 See pp 240-243.
14 Article 10 of Regulation 17/62 requires the Commission to transmit a copy of any applications and notifications that it receives together with supporting documentation to the competent authorities of Member States; the ECJ has held in Case C-67/91 *Dirección Géneral de Defensa de la Competencia v Asociación Espanola de Banca Privada* [1992] ECR I-4785 – the so-called *Spanish Banks* case – that a domestic competition authority may not use this information for the purpose of its own investigations into anti-competitive behaviour.
15 See p 216 above.
16 See *Kerse* paras 3.02-3.15; *Smith* paras 6.02-6.26.
17 Case 374/87 *Orkem v Commission* [1989] ECR 3283, [1991] 4 CMLR 502; Case 27/88 *Solvay & Cie v Commission* [1989] ECR 3355, [1991] 4 CMLR 502.

authorities of Member States and from undertakings and associations of undertakings 'all necessary information,[18] to enable it to carry out its duty to enforce the application of Articles 81 and 82 of the Treaty; information may be requested from undertakings which are not themselves the subject of the investigation. It would be *ultra vires* the Commission to request information for a purpose other than the enforcement of the competition rules, and in exercising its discretion under Article 11 it must have regard to the principle of proportionality[19]. Quite often the Commission requests information under Article 11 *after* it has carried out an on-the-spot investigation under Article 14[20], for example because it needs to check particular points that have arisen out of the investigation or to pursue certain matters further.

Article 11 contains a two-stage procedure. In the first place the Commission must send a request for information. When doing so Article 11(3) provides that the Commission must state the legal basis and the purpose of its request and inform the person addressed of the penalties for supplying incorrect information. There is no duty to comply with the Commission's request, but Article 15(1)(b) provides penalties for making false or misleading replies; the Commission has imposed fines for supplying misleading information[1]. It is important to note that the Commission adopts a strict approach in these cases: undertakings must reply not only to the specific questions asked by the Commission, but should also take into account the general objective behind the Commission's request.

Where a firm fails to supply information, or supplies information that is incomplete, Article 11(5) provides that the Commission may by formal decision require it to be furnished. The Commission must tell the undertaking concerned what information is required and that its decision may be reviewed by the CFI. At this stage not only are there penalties for providing inaccurate information, but also for failing to supply any at all[2]. A decision under Article 11(5) can be challenged before the CFI (formerly the ECJ)[3], for example if it was thought that the Commission was exercising its powers for an improper purpose, or if it was seeking privileged information to which it was not entitled. The fact that an undertaking considers that the Commission has no grounds for action under Article 81 does not entitle it to resist a request for information[4].

(B)   Article 14: investigations[5]

Article 14 gives the Commission power to carry out 'on-the-spot' investigations necessary to enable it to ensure compliance with the competition rules. When

18   On the meaning of 'necessary information' see Case C-36/92 P *SEP v Commission* [1994] ECR I-1911; see also Case T-46/92 *Scottish Football Association v Commission* [1994] ECR II-1039.
19   Case C-36/92 P *SEP v Commission* [1994] ECR I-1911.
20   See below.
1   See eg *Telos* OJ [1982] L 58/19, [1982] 1 CMLR 267; *National Panasonic (Belgium) NV* OJ [1982] L 113/18, [1982] 2 CMLR 410; *National Panasonic (France) SA* OJ [1982] L 211/32, [1982] 3 CMLR 623; *Comptoir Commercial d'Importation* OJ [1982] L 27/31, [1982] 1 CMLR 440; *Peugeot* OJ [1986] L 295/19, [1989] 4 CMLR 371; *Anheuser-Busch Incorporated – Scottish & Newcastle* OJ [2000] L 49/37, [2000] 5 CMLR 75.
2   Regulation 17/62, Articles 15(1)(b) and 16(1)(c); see eg *Baccarat* OJ [1991] L 97/16, [1992] 5 CMLR 189 (fine of EUR 10,000 imposed).
3   See eg Case 374/87 *Orkem v Commission* [1989] ECR 3283, [1991] 4 CMLR 502 and Case 27/88 *Solvay & Cie v Commission* [1989] ECR 3355, [1991] 4 CMLR 502.
4   See eg *Fire Insurance* OJ [1982] L 80/36, [1982] 2 CMLR 159 and *Deutsche Castrol* OJ [1983] L 114/26, [1983] 3 CMLR 165.
5   See *Kerse* paras 3.16-3.42; *Smith* paras 6.27-6.73.

carrying out an investigation Article 14(1) provides that the Commission may examine books and business records, take copies thereof, ask for oral explanations of them on the spot and enter any premises, land and means of transport of the undertaking concerned; there is no power under Regulation 17/62 to enter domestic premises, although such a power is contemplated under the Commission's modernisation proposals[6]. It is normal for officials of the competent authority in the Member State in which an investigation takes place to accompany the Commission's inspectors on such occasions.

Article 14 envisages two types of investigation: a voluntary one carried out by agreement with the firm in question, and a mandatory one to which it is obliged to submit. There is no duty on the Commission first to have attempted to conduct a voluntary investigation: it is entitled to proceed straight to a compulsory one if this is appropriate[7].

(i)   Voluntary investigations

In the case of a voluntary investigation, Article 14(2) requires that the Commission's officials produce an authorisation in writing specifying the subject-matter and purpose of the investigation and the penalties which may be imposed for incomplete production of the required books and business records. If during a voluntary inspection the undertaking provides incomplete information, Article 15(1)(c) enables fines to be imposed[8]. The Commission has held that a firm being investigated is under a positive duty to assist the Commission's officials in finding the information they want: it is not sufficient simply to grant them unlimited access to all the filing cabinets or the IT system[9].

(ii)   Mandatory investigations

Where it considers it appropriate the Commission may, instead of carrying out an investigation by agreement, adopt a formal decision under Article 14(3) requiring an undertaking to submit to an inspection. The Commission must consult with the national authorities before carrying out such an investigation, but this can be done in an informal manner, by telephone if necessary[10]. The Commission has used its powers under Article 14(3) with increasing frequency, sometimes launching simultaneous 'dawn raids'[11] in different parts of the Community on undertakings suspected of being members of a cartel. The Commission is entitled to arrive unannounced at the premises in question and to

---

6   See p 256 below.
7   Case 136/79 *National Panasonic (UK) Ltd v Commission* [1980] ECR 2033, [1980] 3 CMLR 169, paras 8–16.
8   This happened in *FNICF* OJ [1982] L 319/12, [1983] 1 CMLR 575; see Korah 'Inspections under the EEC Competition Rules: Dangers of Voluntary Submission' (1983) 4 Business Law Review 23.
9   See *Fabbrica Pisana* OJ [1980] L 75/30, [1980] 2 CMLR 354 and *Pietro Sciarra* OJ [1980] L 75/35, [1980] 2 CMLR 362; the same would be true of an investigation under Article 14(3).
10   Case 5/85 *AKZO Chemie BV v Commission* [1986] ECR 2585, [1987] 3 CMLR 716, para 24.
11   The expression is, of course, a misnomer in the absence of a Community Directive on the harmonisation of dawn.

insist that the investigation shall commence straightaway, though this power is tempered by the principle of proportionality[12].

There is no entitlement to the presence of a lawyer, although the Commission will usually be prepared to wait for a reasonable period for one to arrive if there are no in-house counsel[13]. The Commission's officials must provide various information to the undertaking concerned[14]. A firm subjected to a compulsory investigation has the same duty to supply complete information as a firm that submits voluntarily, and the comments made above on voluntary investigations would be equally applicable here. A firm to which an Article 14(3) decision is addressed is under the further duty to submit to the investigation, and Articles 15(1)(c) and 16(1)(d) provide that failure to do so may be penalised. In *Sugar*[15] a fine of EUR 3,000 was imposed on CSM NV for preventing Commission officials from taking copies of particular documents during the course of an investigation. The Commission stressed in its decision that, if the undertaking concerned considered that the Commission was not entitled to certain documents, the matter should be determined by the CFI: the undertaking cannot decide this itself. In the maritime transport sector a fine of EUR 5,000 was imposed on *Ukwal*[16] under Article 18(3) of Regulation 4056/86, the equivalent of Article 14(3) of Regulation 17/62, for refusing to submit to an investigation. In *AKZO*[17] the Commission imposed a fine of EUR 5000 for failing to submit fully to the investigation and rejected arguments that it could investigate the offices of AKZO Chemicals only at two named sites and not premises that belonged to AKZO NV, a different undertaking.

Financial sanctions may not be sufficient to persuade an undertaking to allow the Commission's officials to carry out an inspection, but the Commission does not have a power of forcible entry under Article 14[18]. Where a firm steadfastly refuses to allow entry, Article 14(6) provides that the Member State concerned has a duty to provide such assistance as may be necessary to enable the investigation to take place. A difficulty may arise if the Member State is unwilling to provide that assistance or if the procedure under domestic law for gaining entry is so cumbersome that the necessary element of surprise is lost. Obstructive action by a Member State would put it in breach of its Community obligations, entitling the Commission to proceed against it under Article 230 EC (ex Article 169); this would not in itself be sufficient to enable the Commission to carry out any particular investigation, however. In *Hoechst v Commission*[19] the ECJ held that the Member State called upon to render assistance has no right to substitute its own assessment of the need for an investigation for that of the Commission.

12 Case 136/79 *National Panasonic v Commission* [1980] ECR 2033, [1980] 3 CMLR 169 and Joshua 'The Element of Surprise: EEC Competition Regulations under Article 14(3) of Regulation 17' (1983) 8 ELRev 3.
13 See the XIIth *Report on Competition Policy* (1982), point 32.
14 See the XIIIth *Report on Competition Policy* (1983), point 74(a) and pp 271–272; the information annexed to an authorisation under Article 14(3) is slightly different from that in an Article 14(2) case.
15 OJ [1992] L 305/16.
16 OJ [1992] L 121/45, [1993] 5 CMLR 632; see also *Mewac* OJ [1993] L 20/6, [1994] 5 CMLR 275.
17 OJ [1994] L 294/31.
18 Case 46/87 *Hoechst v Commission* [1989] ECR 2859, [1991] 4 CMLR 410.
19 See n 18 above.

(iii)   Article 14 investigations in the UK

Although the Commission's powers of investigation have been applicable in the UK since 1973, it was not until the Competition Act 1998 that specific powers were given to the Director General of Fair Trading ('the DGFT') for this purpose. The DGFT is given power to enter premises with a warrant, using reasonable force as necessary, in the event of obstruction of either (a) a Commission investigation in which the DGFT is assisting (a 'Director's investigation); or (b) an investigation carried out by the DGFT under EC law at the request of the Commission (a 'Director's investigation'); or (c) a Director's investigation carried out by the DGFT in connection with a Commission investigation (a 'Director's special investigation')[20]. The powers, offences and penalties are similar to those in the case of investigations by warrant under domestic law provided for by section 28 of the Act[1].

(C)   Confidentiality: professional secrecy and business secrets[2]

Undertakings that are investigated by the Commission or that make complaints to it, will be anxious to ensure that any information acquired by the Commission will be treated as confidential. For example they will not want details of joint venture agreements, data about market shares, plans for the expansion of capacity and similar matters to become public knowledge or to be handed over to competitors or customers. Nor would they want a dominant firm about which they had complained to discover the source of the complaint: there would be an obvious anxiety that in due course the dominant undertaking might take reprisals[3]. On the other hand the Commission has a duty to ensure that undertakings are given a fair hearing, and this inevitably means that in some cases information must be divulged which was gathered from one source in order to prosecute a case against another firm.

Regulation 17/62 provides in Article 20(2), which is based on Article 287 EC (ex Article 214), that 'the Commission ... shall not disclose information acquired as a result of this Regulation and of the kind covered by the obligation of professional secrecy'. Article 19(3) provides that publication of Commission decisions 'shall have regard to the legitimate interest of undertakings in the protection of business secrets'.

(i)   Professional secrecy

The meaning of the phrase 'professional secrecy' has not been defined with precision. It seems that in some cases the Commission may be permitted to divulge information containing professional secrets where this is necessary, for

---

20 Competition Act 1998, ss 61-65: see also DGFT's Guideline *Powers of investigation* (OFT 404), paras 10.1 and 10.9; note the position of Crown premises under s 73(6)-(8).
1   See ch 10, pp 338-342.
2   See *Kerse* paras 8.22-8.26; *Smith* paras 11.02-11.11; see also Joshua 'Balancing the Public Interests: Confidentiality, Trade Secrets and Disclosure of Evidence in EC Competition Procedures' (1994) 15 ECLR 68.
3   See Case C-310/93 P *BPB Industries plc v Commission* [1995] ECR I-865, [1997] 4 CMLR 238, paras 26-27, where the ECJ held that the Commission is not obliged to disclose documents to a dominant firm which would reveal the identity of a complainant.

example, to enable a third party to receive a fair hearing; however, before doing so the Commission should give the owner of such information an opportunity to give its views on whether it should be divulged[4].

(ii)   Business secrets

Business secrets benefit from greater protection than professional secrets. Guidance on what the Commission regards as business secrets can be found in its *Notice on the Internal Rules of Procedure for Processing Requests for Access to the File*[5]. In *AKZO Chemie BV v Commission*[6] the ECJ held that business secrets must never be divulged. Where there is a dispute between an undertaking and the Commission as to whether something qualifies as a business secret, the Commission must reach a formal decision on the issue which can then be reviewed by the CFI[7]. In *Adams v Commission*[8] the ECJ held that, where a complainant supplies information to the Commission, the Commission owes a duty of care to safeguard his anonymity; in this case it ought to have warned the complainant of the risk he was running in providing information which rendered him liable to prosecution under Swiss law.

(D)   Privilege[9]

Regulation 17/62 is silent on the issue of privilege. That some documents are privileged under Community law was established by the ECJ in *AM and S Europe Ltd v Commission*[10], where certain papers had been withheld from Commission officials acting under Article 14(3); the same principle must surely apply under Article 11. The *AM & S* case dealt with two issues: first, whether there is a doctrine of privilege in Community law; secondly, if there is one, what mechanism should be adopted to ascertain whether any particular document is privileged. On the first question the ECJ held that some, but not all, correspondence between a client and an independent lawyer based in the EC was privileged, but that dealings with an in-house lawyer or with a lawyer in a third country were not. Privilege mainly extends to correspondence relating to the defence of a client after the initiation of proceedings by the Commission, although it also applies to correspondence before the initiation of proceedings though intimately linked with their subject-matter. The privilege belongs to the client, not the lawyer.

The ECJ limited privilege to dealings with independent lawyers because in many Member States employed lawyers are not subject to professional codes of discipline. In some Member States, for example the UK, in-house counsel may

---

4   Case T-353/94 *Postbank NV v Commission* [1996] ECR II-921, [1997] 4 CMLR 33.
5   OJ [1997] C 23/3, [1997] 4 CMLR 490, Part A.1.
6   Case 53/85 [1986] ECR 1965, [1987] 1 CMLR 231; see also Cases 142/84 and 156/84 *BAT v Commission* [1987] ECR 4487, [1988] 4 CMLR 24, paras 21–24.
7   This is the same procedure adopted in respect of claims to privilege: see below; it may be that the Hearing Officer could play a useful rôle in such cases: on the position of the Hearing Officer see pp 234–235 below.
8   Case 145/83 [1985] ECR 3539, [1986] 1 CMLR 506; see March Hunnings 'The Stanley Adams Affair or the Biter Bit' (1987) 24 CML Rev 65.
9   See *Kerse* paras 8.16-8.21; *Smith* paras 11.14-11.30; see also Christoforou 'Protection of Legal Privilege in EEC Competition Law: The Imperfections of a Case' [1985–86] Fordham International Law Journal 1.
10 Case 155/79 [1982] ECR 1575, [1982] 2 CMLR 264.

remain subject to the rules of the Bar Council or the Law Society, so that this reason for excluding privilege ought not to apply; however the ECJ's judgment is quite clear that there is no privilege in these circumstances[11]. The position was slightly relaxed in *Hilti v Commission*[12] where the CFI held that privilege does extend to an internal memorandum prepared by an in-house lawyer which simply reports what an independent lawyer has said. In *John Deere*[13] the Commission relied on written advice by an in-house lawyer to show that an undertaking knew that it was infringing Article 81.

The limitation of privilege to correspondence with EC lawyers is overtly discriminatory, and the Commission at one point intended to try to persuade the Council to rectify this[14]; it is understood that this has since been dropped, although the case for refinement of the position continues to be heard[15].

On the question of how claims to privilege should be adjudicated the ECJ, in effect, held that it (or, now, the CFI) should fulfil this task. This seems cumbersome, but is better than allowing the Commission itself to see the documents: even if a Commission official were to accept that they were privileged, a firm would be bound to suspect that he or she had been influenced by what had been seen. It follows that what has to happen in the case of a dispute as to privilege is that the Commission must make a formal decision, requiring the documents in question; this decision may then be appealed to the CFI, which will resolve the issue[16].

(E)   Self-incrimination[17]

In the *Orkem* and *Solvay* cases[18] the ECJ had to consider whether, in the context of an Article 11 request for information, undertakings could refuse to answer certain questions on the basis that to do so would be self-incriminating. The ECJ's conclusion was that there is a limited privilege against self-incrimination in Community law, which entitles undertakings to refuse to answer questions that would require them to admit to the very infringement the Commission is seeking to establish; however this privilege does not entitle them to refuse to

11   See however the cogent argument of Advocate General Slynn to the contrary in the *AM & S* case; note that under s 30 UK Competition Act 1998 communications with in-house lawyers do enjoy privilege: see ch 10, pp 339-340.
12   Case T–30/89 A [1990] ECR II-163, [1990] 4 CMLR 16.
13   OJ [1985] L 35/58, [1985] 2 CMLR 554; see similarly *London European-Sabena* OJ [1988] L 317/47, [1989] 4 CMLR 662; privilege was unsuccessfully claimed in *VW* OJ [1998] L 124/60, [1998] 5 CMLR 33, para 199.
14   See the XIIIth *Report on Competition Policy* (1983), point 78 and Faull 'Legal Professional Privilege *(AM and S)*: the Commission Proposes International Negotiations' (1985) 10 ELRev 119.
15   See Faull 'The Enforcement of Competition Policy in the European Community: a Mature System' in [1991] Fordham Corporate Law Institute (ed Hawk), p 139 at p 151.
16   A possible alternative method would be to allow the Hearing Officer to adjudicate; on the position of the Hearing Officer see pp 234-235 below.
17   See *Kerse* para 3.44; *Smith* paras 6.74-6.77; see also Riley '*Saunders* and the Power to Obtain Information in Community and UK Competition Law' (2000) 25 ELRev 264.
18   Case 374/87 *Orkem v Commission* [1989] ECR 3283, [1991] 4 CMLR 502: see Lasok 'The Privilege against Self-incrimination in Competition Cases' (1990) 11 ECLR 90; Case 27/88 *Solvay & Cie v Commission* [1989] ECR 3355, [1991] 4 CMLR 502; see also Case T-34/93 *Société Générale v Commission* [1995] ECR II-545, [1996] 4 CMLR 665, paras 72-74; as to privilege against self-incrimination in domestic courts, see Case C-60/92 *Otto v Postbank* [1993] ECR I-5683: for comment on this case see Kerse (1994) 31 CML Rev 1375; Cumming '*Otto v Postbank* and the Privilege Against Self-Incrimination in Enforcement Proceedings of Articles [81] and [82] before the English Courts' (1995) 16 ECLR 401.

hand over documents to the Commission which might serve to establish an infringement by the undertaking concerned or by another one. It is presumably the case that the same doctrine must apply in the case of investigations under Article 14. In *Mannesmann-Röhrenwerke AG v Commission*[19] the CFI held that there is no absolute right to silence in competition proceedings[20], except in so far as a compulsion to provide answers would involve an admission of the existence of an infringement[1]; in the Court's view certain questions asked by the Commission did go beyond what it was entitled to ask[2]. Judgments of the European Court of Human Rights in *Funke v France*[3] and *Saunders v United Kingdom*[4] have recognised a right to remain silent in criminal cases, but it seems after the *Mannesmann* judgment that Community law will not extend privilege this far in relation to cases under Articles 81 and 82, unless the ECJ overrules the judgment of the CFI in this case.

3.   INTERIM DECISIONS[5]

The ECJ established in *Camera Care v Commission*[6] that the Commission has power under Article 3 of Regulation 17/62 to grant interim relief, albeit subject to limitations. In practice the Commission has adopted interim measures on very few occasions; it would prefer to see third parties seek interim relief in their domestic courts or from NCAs. On some occasions the Commission has been able to negotiate an interim settlement with undertakings without having formally to adopt an interim decision. Several points about the ability of the Commission to adopt interim measures should be noted.

(i)   Urgency

First the case must be one of urgency, where interim measures are necessary:

'to avoid a situation likely to cause serious and irreparable damage to the party seeking their adoption, or which is intolerable for the public interest'[7].

This means that the Commission may act either because of damage to an undertaking or because of harm to the public interest. The Commission intervened on the former basis, for example, in *ECS/AKZO*[8], *BBI/Boosey and Hawkes*:

19   Case T-112/98 judgment of 20 February 2001.
20   Ibid, para 66.
1   Ibid, para 67.
2   Ibid, paras 69-74.
3   [1993] 1 CMLR 897; for comment on *Funke* see van Overbeek 'The Right to Remain Silent in Competition Investigations' (1994) 15 ECLR 127.
4   (1996) 23 EHRR 313.
5   See *Kerse* paras 6.02-6.12; *Smith* paras 8.05-8.28.
6   Case 792/79 R [1980] ECR 119, [1980] 1 CMLR 334; the power to order interim measures had previously been in doubt as Regulation 17/62 is not explicit on this issue. Article 66(5) of the ECSC Treaty specifically provides that interim action can be taken against prohibited agreements and the ECJ held in Case 109/75R *National Carbonising Co v Commission* [1975] ECR 1193, [1975] 2 CMLR 457 that interim relief was available in cases of abuse of a dominant position.
7   Case 792/79 R *Camera Care v Commission* [1980] ECR 119, [1980] 1 CMLR 334, para 19.
8   OJ [1983] L 252/13, [1983] 3 CMLR 694.

Interim Measures[9], *Ecosystem SA v Peugeot SA*[10] and in *Irish Continental Group v CCI Morlaix*[11]; it acted on the basis of harm to the public interest in *Ford Werke AG-Interim Measure*[12].

In English law an applicant for an interlocutory injunction will not succeed where an award of damages at the trial of the action would be an adequate remedy[13]. If the test is the same under *Camera Care*, the Commission would be unable to act (or could choose not to act) where an applicant for interim measures could claim damages for the competition law infringement in a national court. This seems to have been the Commission's approach in rejecting an application for interim measures by La Cinq, which had complained that it had been excluded from membership of the European Broadcasting Union. On appeal in *La Cinq v Commission*[14] the CFI considered that the Commission had adopted too narrow a view of serious and irreparable damage: it should have asked itself whether the damage to La Cinq could be remedied by the decision which it, the Commission, could take on a final disposal of the case[15]; the fact that La Cinq might obtain an award of damages in domestic litigation was an irrelevant consideration.

Following *La Cinq*, the Commission adopted two interim measures decisions in 1992. In *Sealink/B & I – Holyhead: Interim Measures*[16] it dealt with a complaint by B & I that Sealink's schedules at Holyhead harbour had the effect of damaging B & I's position on the market for ferry services between Holyhead and Ireland. The Commission concluded that compensation for B & I would not be an adequate remedy as it would be impossible to quantify the compensation to which B & I would be entitled; that no final decision that it could take would provide an adequate remedy; and that B & I's exclusion from the market for the summer season would seriously tarnish its reputation for efficiency. The Commission's decision in *Mars*[17] was adopted on the basis that Mars would suffer grave and irreversible injury by being excluded from the ice-cream market in Germany as a result of exclusivity clauses in purchasing agreements between German producers of ice-cream and their distributors. The decision was suspended in part in *Langnese-Iglo GmbH v Commission*[18] because of the greater harm that would be caused to the German producers by the Commission's decision than to Mars by its suspension. The President of the CFI adopted a compromise solution, allowing Mars access to a specific part of the market, ice-cream sold at petrol stations.

9   OJ [1987] L 286/36, [1988] 4 CMLR 67.
10 [1990] 4 CMLR 449, upheld on appeal Case T–23/90 *Peugeot v EC Commission* [1991] ECR II-653, [1993] 5 CMLR 540.
11 [1995] 5 CMLR 177.
12 OJ [1982] L 256/20, [1982] 3 CMLR 267; see Burnside 'Enforcement of EEC Competition Law by Interim Measures: the Ford Case' (1985) 19 JWTL 34.
13 This was why the plaintiff failed in *Garden Cottage Foods v Milk Marketing Board* [1984] AC 130, [1983] 2 All ER 770, HL; see ch 8, pp 279-280.
14 Case T–44/90 [1992] ECR II-1, [1992] 4 CMLR 449.
15 Ibid, paras 78–83.
16 [1992] 5 CMLR 255.
17 Unreported decision of 25 March 1992; see XXIInd *Report on Competition Policy* (1992), point 195.
18 Cases T–24/92 and 28/92 R [1992] ECR II-1839.

(ii)   Prima facie case

There must be a reasonably strong *prima facie* case that the competition rules are being infringed if interim measures are to be adopted, although it is not necessary for the Commission at the interim stage to be certain that there has been an infringement[19]. In *La Cinq v Commission*[20] the CFI held that the Commission had gone wrong in law in having asked itself whether there was a clear, flagrant infringement of Articles 81 and 82: this was too rigorous a standard to apply at an interim stage in proceedings[1].

(iii)   Temporary and conservatory measures

The measures imposed by the Commission must be temporary and conservatory in nature[2]. Furthermore the Commission cannot make an order at an interim stage that it would not have authority to make in a final decision. In *Ford Werke AG v Commission*[3] the ECJ quashed the Commission's interim decision requiring Ford Germany to supply right-hand drive cars to German distributors, since the refusal to supply did not in itself infringe either Article 81 or Article 82. The Commission adopted the wrong procedure in this case. Ford had notified its distribution agreements to the Commission which, given its objection to the operation of Ford's distribution policy in practice, should have withdrawn the immunity from fines conferred by notification by issuing a provisional decision under Article 15(6) of Regulation 17/62[4].

(iv)   Essential procedural safeguards

When adopting interim measures the Commission must maintain the essential safeguards guaranteed to the parties concerned by Regulation 17/62[5]. In particular this means that interested undertakings, including perhaps third parties, must be given an opportunity to be heard. It seems unlikely that an *ex parte* order would be given. In cases of dire emergency it would probably be better to go before a domestic court where *ex parte* injunctions can be given.

(v)   Proportionality and the balancing of interests

When making decisions the Commission has an obligation to observe the Community principle of proportionality. In the context of interim measures this means that it must balance the interests of the applicant with those of the defendant, which may suffer serious harm if it is forbidden to behave in a way which, upon further investigation, turns out to be perfectly lawful. One way of balancing

---

19 The ECJ did not actually say this in *Camera Care* but see the Commission's *Practice Note* [1980] 2 CMLR 369 and *BBI/Boosey and Hawkes: Interim Measures* OJ [1987] L 286/36, [1988] 4 CMLR 67, para 14.
20 Case T–44/90 [1992] ECR II-1, [1992] 4 CMLR 449.
1   Ibid, paras 60–66.
2   Case 792/79 R *Camera Care v Commission* [1980] ECR 119, [1980] 1 CMLR 334, para 19.
3   Cases 228/82 and 229/82 [1984] ECR 1129, [1984] 1 CMLR 649.
4   See p 230 below.
5   Case 792/79 R *Camera Care v Commission* [1980] ECR 119, [1980] 1 CMLR 334, para 19.

these competing interests would be to require the applicant to give a binding undertaking to compensate the defendant for any loss suffered as a result of the interim measures should the defendant's behaviour ultimately be vindicated. The Commission has indicated that it will do this in appropriate cases[6].

(vi) Review

The Commission's decision must be in a form which is capable of review by the CFI[7]. In particular this means that it should be properly reasoned as required by Article 253 EC (ex Article 190) of the Treaty. The addressee of the decision may apply for interim relief, pending the CFI's final judgment[8].

(vii) Enforcement

It is not entirely clear what would happen where an undertaking refuses to comply with an interim decision. Article 15(2) of Regulation 17/62 enables a fine to be imposed where there has been an infringement of Articles 81 or 82: *ex hypothesi* this has not been established in interim cases. Article 16(1)(a) enables periodic penalties to be imposed for continuing infringements of Articles 81 and 82 but the same problem applies; however the Commission has not been deterred by this, and its imposition of periodic penalties on various occasions[9] has not been challenged. A refusal to comply with an interim order would be likely to aggravate the size of any fine subsequently imposed in a final decision under Articles 81 or 82.

(viii) 'Fast-track' procedure in air transport

The Council has adopted a Regulation in the air transport sector which provides a procedure for 'fast-track' interim measures where the Commission has clear *prima facie* evidence of an infringement of Articles 81 or 82 which has 'the object or effect of directly jeopardising the existence of an air service, and where recourse to normal procedures may not be sufficient to protect the air service or the airline company'[10]. This is achieved by adding a new para 4a to Regulation 3975/87, the implementing Regulation in the air transport sector[11]. This 'fast-track' procedure is without prejudice to the normal interim measures procedure under the *Camera Care* case.

---

6   See *Sealink/B & I – Holyhead: Interim Measures* [1992] 5 CMLR 255, para 13.
7   Case 792/79 R [1980] ECR 119, [1980] 1 CMLR 334, paras 19 and 20.
8   See eg Case T–23/90 *Peugeot v Commission* [1991] ECR II–653, [1993] 5 CMLR 540; Cases T–24/92 and 28/92 R *Langnese-Iglo GmbH v Commission* [1992] ECR II-1713 and 1839; see also p 246 below.
9   *Ford Werke AG* OJ [1982] L 256/20, [1982] 3 CMLR 267; *BBI/Boosey and Hawkes* OJ [1987] L 286/36, [1988] 4 CMLR 67; *Ecosystem SA v Peugeot SA* [1990] 4 CMLR 449.
10 Council Regulation 1284/91, OJ [1991] L 122/2.
11 See p 216, n 13 above.

4.   PROVISIONAL DECISIONS[12]

Where an agreement has been notified to the Commission for individual exemption, Article 15(5) of Regulation 17/62 provides that no fine can be imposed on the parties for infringement of Article 81 for the period between the notification and the Commission's final decision. This means that a seriously anti-competitive agreement could be safely operated for a considerable period. Article 15(6) enables the Commission to withdraw the benefit of this provision where, following a preliminary investigation, it considers that an agreement falls within Article 81(1) and that the application of Article 81(3) is not justified. Such a decision can be challenged before the CFI[13]. A complainant to the Commission cannot insist that the Commission should remove the immunity from fines enjoyed by parties to an agreement notified under Regulation 17/62[14]. The Commission has adopted provisional decisions under Article 15(6) on very few occasions; an example is *SCK/FNK*[15]. A statement of objections based on Article 15(6) was sent in the case of *Agence et Messageries de la Presse*[16] as a result of which various aspects of a selective distribution system for newspapers and periodicals in Belgium were altered. The ECJ considered that the Commission ought to have used the Article 15(6) procedure in the *Ford* case[17].

5.   NEGATIVE CLEARANCE[18]

Article 2 of Regulation 17/62 enables the Commission to certify that, on the basis of the facts known to it, there are no grounds for proceeding under Article 81(1) or Article 82 against an agreement or practice. A 'negative clearance' is of use to the undertakings concerned, although it does not afford complete security for two reasons. First circumstances may alter, so that behaviour apparently outside the competition rules subsequently comes within them. This could happen, for example, where an agreement which originally fell within the terms of the *Notice on Agreements of Minor Importance*[19] subsequently ceases to do so because the market share of the parties rises above the relevant thresholds; a different possibility is that, as actually implemented, an agreement which apparently falls outside Article 81(1) in fact restricts competition[20]. Secondly negative clearance does not prevent the application of stricter provisions of domestic law, so that the parties will also have to overcome this additional hurdle[1].

Where negative clearance (or individual exemption) is sought for an agreement under Article 81, Form A/B must be used; its use is not obligatory in the case of applications for negative clearance from Article 82[2]. Applications for negative

---

12   See *Kerse* paras 6.13-6.15; *Smith* paras 8.29-8.31.
13   Cases 8–11/66 *SA Cimenteries v Commission* [1967] ECR 75, [1967] CMLR 77.
14   Case T–3/90 *Vereniging Prodifarma v Commission* [1991] ECR II-1.
15   OJ [1994] L 117/30; the other instances are referred to in both *Kerse* and *Smith* (n 12 above).
16   OJ [1987] C 164/2, paras 2–3.
17   See p 228 above.
18   See *Kerse* para 6.26; *Smith* paras 8.32-8.33.
19   See ch 3, pp 108-111.
20   See *AEG/Telefunken* OJ [1982] L 117/15, [1982] 2 CMLR 386, upheld on appeal Case 107/82 [1983] ECR 3151, [1984] 3 CMLR 325.
1   See ch 9, pp 327-328.
2   The information required in Form A/B is set out in Regulation 3385/94, OJ [1994] L 377/38; in the transport sector Form TR must be used in the form set out in Regulation 2843/98, OJ [1998] L 354/22, [1999] 4 CMLR 236.

clearance alone are rare: most firms would seek negative clearance and, in the alternative, individual exemption under Article 81(3). If, having received an application for negative clearance, the Commission considers that the undertakings involved are infringing Articles 81 or 82 and it wishes to adopt a formal decision to that effect, it will have to issue a statement of objections outlining its reasons for thinking so and giving them an opportunity to be heard[3]. A statement of objections is not necessary, however, where the Commission intends to grant negative clearance. The Commission is obliged by Article 19(3) of Regulation 17/62 to give third parties an opportunity to be heard before adopting a final decision on negative clearance, and to consult with the Advisory Committee on Restrictive Practices and Monopolies[4]. The Commission is required by Article 21 of Regulation 17/62 to publish a decision granting negative clearance. Third parties with sufficient standing may appeal against the decision[5]; however the parties themselves cannot appeal against a negative clearance that they have been granted: even if they object to the reasoning or findings in the Commission's decision, their legal position cannot be harmed by a decision that confirms that they are not infringing the competition rules[6].

6. INDIVIDUAL EXEMPTION[7]

Article 9 of Regulation 17/62 enables the Commission – and only the Commission – to grant individual exemption to agreements which satisfy the criteria in Article 81(3). The mechanics and the benefits of notification have been discussed in chapter 4, as have issues such as the duration of individual exemptions, the conditions and obligations that can be attached to them and the renewal and revocation of exemptions[8]. The exclusive jurisdiction of the Commission to grant individual exemptions causes problems where agreements are litigated in domestic courts: they can decide whether agreements fall within or outside Article 81(1), or within a block exemption[9], but they cannot, under the existing law, decide whether individual exemption is available under Article 81(3). Under the Commission's modernisation proposals national courts will, in future, be able to apply Article 81(3) as well as Article 81(1)[10].

Where individual exemption is granted the sanction of nullity in Article 81(2) does not apply, and the exemption can be relied on against a third party[11]. The Commission may or may not issue a statement of objections prior to a decision granting individual exemption, but in any event it must allow interested third parties to be heard and consult the Advisory Committee. The Commission's decision must be published[12] and can be challenged by the parties themselves

---

3 This procedure is discussed below in the context of infringement proceedings.
4 On the Advisory Committee, see ch 2, p 51.
5 Case 26/76 *Metro SB-Grossmärkte GmbH & Co KG v Commission* [1977] ECR 1875, [1978] 2 CMLR 1.
6 Case T-138/89 *Nederlandse Bankiersvereniging v Commission* [1992] ECR II-2181, [1993] 5 CMLR 436; see similarly (under the ECMR) Joined Cases T-125/97 and T-127/97 *Coca-Cola Co v Commission* [2000] 5 CMLR 467.
7 See *Kerse* paras 6.27-6.40; *Smith* paras 8.34-8.48.
8 See ch 4, pp 136-141.
9 Case 59/77 *De Bloos v Bouyer* [1977] ECR 2359, [1978] 1 CMLR 511.
10 See pp 246-258 below.
11 Case 31/80 *L'Oreal NV v De Nieuwe AMCK PVBA* [1980] ECR 3775, [1981] 2 CMLR 235.
12 Regulation 17/62, Article 21(1).

where, for example, conditions and obligations are attached to the exemption to which they object[13] and by third parties[14]. In practice few individual exemptions are granted. In 1999 the Commission granted seven individual exemptions; in 2000 five exemptions were given. As has already been noted, many cases are settled informally[15]. It has never been decided whether undertakings which notify an agreement to the Commission for an exemption are entitled to insist upon it proceeding to a final decision; a paragraph in the CFI's judgment in *Automec(2) v Commission*[16] hints that there may be an obligation to proceed where individual exemption is sought.

7.   INFRINGEMENT PROCEEDINGS[17]

Article 3(1) of Regulation 17/62 enables the Commission to require undertakings to terminate infringements of Articles 81 and 82. It may do so either upon its own initiative or upon application by Member States or undertakings claiming a legitimate interest[18]. There is a limitation Regulation which determines the time within which the Commission must commence proceedings[19]. In *Polypropylene* the ECJ observed that the presumption of innocence, resulting in particular from Article 6(2) of the European Convention on Human Rights, is one of the fundamental rights which, according to the Court's settled case law, the preamble to the Single European Act and Article F(2) of the Treaty on European Union, are protected in the Community legal order, and that this right applies to competition rules that may result in the imposition of fines or periodic payments[20]. A frequent criticism is that the Commission acts as policeman, prosecutor, judge and jury in infringement proceedings and that the lack of separation of powers is inherently unfair. However the ECJ has rejected the suggestion that the system established by Regulation 17/62 is contrary to the rules of natural justice[1].

(i)   Statement of objections and reply

If the Commission decides to initiate a procedure under Article 3 of Regulation 17/62 it must serve on the firms concerned a statement of objections indicating its objections to their behaviour, unless it has no intention of imposing a fine; in the latter case proceedings can be commenced simply by a notice in the Official Journal[2]. The Commission is not entitled to take action against firms in respect of matters which have not been dealt with in the statement of objections. Allegations of infringements must be precisely formulated, and the essential facts upon which the Commission relies must be stated succinctly; however the

---

13   See eg Cases T-374/94 etc *European Night Services v Commission* [1998] ECR II-3141, [1998] 5 CMLR 718.
14   See ch 4, pp 135-136.
15   See pp 217-218 above.
16   Case T-24/90 [1992] ECR II-2223, [1992] 5 CMLR 431, para 75.
17   See *Kerse* ch 4 generally and paras 6.17-6.25; *Smith* ch 7 generally and paras 8.49-8.71.
18   Regulation 17/62, Article 3(2).
19   Regulation 2988/74, OJ [1974] L 319/1.
20   Case C-199/92 P *Hüls v Commission* [1999] ECR I-4287, [1999] 5 CMLR 1016, paras 149-150.
1   See eg Cases 100/80 etc *Musique Diffusion Française SA v Commission* [1983] ECR 1825, [1983] 3 CMLR 221, paras 6–8.
2   See Regulation 2842/98, Article 3.

Commission's ultimate decision need not be a replica of the statement of objections[3]. In some cases the Commission may send a supplementary statement of objections, for example where further possible infringements are alleged or where the Commission's case changes as a result of new facts that become available to it. The Commission may not rely on information which it is unable to divulge to a defendant because it amounts to a business secret[4]. The statement of objections may be drawn up, signed and sent by the Director General of DG COMP: it is not necessary that the Commissioner responsible for competition matters do this[5]. If the Commission intends to impose a fine, the statement of objections must state the period of the infringement in question. In *Compagnie Maritime Belge Transports SA v Commission*[6] the fines on the members of a liner conference were annulled since the possibility of a fine was mentioned only in the statement of objections sent to the conference itself, and not in the statements sent to the members. It is not normally possible to seek judicial review of a statement of objections[7].

The recipient of a statement of objections must be given the right to reply in writing within a period fixed by the Commission; the period is often two months, though in complex cases it may be longer.

(ii)   Access to the file

It is now clearly established that the recipient of a statement of objections has a right of access to the Commission's files. This right was not always recognised[8]; however a practice arose whereby the Commission permitted access to its files, except for internal working documents and information protected by the rules on professional secrecy[9]. When the issue came before the CFI in 1992 in *SA Hercules v Commission*[10] it concluded that the Commission was under an obligation to make its files available, subject to the exceptions referred to above. Subsequent cases have developed the law further, in particular the *Soda Ash* cases[11]; there the CFI acknowledged a general principle of 'equality of arms', meaning that in a competition case the knowledge of the defendant of the contents of the Commission's file should be the same as that of the Commission. In response to the developing case law the Commission has issued a *Notice on the Internal Rules for Processing Requests for Access to the File*[12], in which it sets out its

---

3   Case T–66/89 *Publishers' Association v Commission (No 2)* [1992] ECR II-1995, [1992] 5 CMLR 120, para 65.
4   Case 85/76 *Hoffmann-La Roche v Commission* [1979] ECR 461, [1979] 3 CMLR 211, para 14; on business secrets, see p 225 above.
5   Cases 43, 63/82 *VBVB and VBBB v Commission* [1984] ECR 19, [1985] 1 CMLR 27.
6   Joined Cases C-395/96 P and 396/96 P [2000] 4 CMLR 1076; see similarly Cases T-95/95 etc *Cimenteries CBA SA v Commission* judgment of 15 March 2000, para 480.
7   See pp 244-245 below.
8   See eg Cases 43, 63/82 *VBVB and VBBB v Commission* [1985] ECR 19, [1985] 1 CMLR 27.
9   See XIIth *Report on Competition Policy* (1982), points 34–35; XIIIth *Report on Competition Policy* (1983), point 74b.
10   Case T–7/89 [1991] ECR II-1711, [1992] 4 CMLR 84, paras 46–57.
11   Cases T-30/91 etc *Solvay v Commission* [1995] ECR II-1775, [1996] 5 CMLR 57; see Moore (1996) 33 CML Rev 355; see also Case C-51/92P *Hercules v Commission* [1999] ECR I-4235, paras 61-83; Case T-175/95 *BASF Coatings AG v Commission* [1999] ECR II-1581, [2000] 4 CMLR 33, paras 35-60.
12   OJ [1997] C 23/3, [1997] 4 CMLR 490; see Levitt 'Commission Notice on Internal Rules of Procedure for Access to the File' (1997) 18 ECLR 187; Levitt 'Access to the File: The

current practice. The *Notice* explains which documents are non-communicable[13] and which are communicable[14]. It then proceeds to explain the practical arrangements that will be made for access to the file.

(iii)   Oral hearing and the rôle of the Hearing Officer

The parties have the right to an oral hearing. This takes place in Brussels in the presence of the interested parties (including third parties with a legitimate interest), the Commission and the Advisory Committee on Restrictive Practices and Monopolies, which consists of representatives of the Member States[15]. In some cases the oral hearing may last for just one or perhaps two days, though in complicated cartel cases, where there are sometimes many defendants, it can be much more protracted.

In 1982 the Commission appointed a Hearing Officer whose function is to preside over hearings and to ensure that the rights of the defence are properly respected throughout the administrative procedure[16]. The Hearing Officer must be present throughout the hearing, and has direct access to the Commissioner responsible for competition. The parties are not entitled to see his report[17], although the Commission decided in May 2001 that it will be made available to them at the same time as the decision itself[18]. Disquiet about the Commission's procedures in competition cases, and in particular about the combination of rôles played by it, led to calls for the position of the Hearing Officer to be enhanced; indeed Dr Temple Lang resigned his position as Hearing Officer in September 2000 as he was dissatisfied with the Commission's unwillingness to countenance substantial changes to the rôle. The UK House of Lords Select Committee on the European Union published a report in November 2000, *Strengthening the Rôle of the Hearing Officer in EC Competition Cases*[19], in which it made a number of recommendations for reform. In May 2001 the Commission announced some changes in the mandate of the Hearing Officer[20]. The main aspects of the reform are that the Hearing Officer will no longer be attached to the Directorate General for Competition, but instead will be part of the office of the Commissioner in charge of competition policy; his report on the draft decision of the Commission will be communicated to the Member States; it will also be attached to the draft Commission decision submitted to the College of Commissioners and will be

---

Commission's Administrative Procedures in Cases under Articles [81] and [82]' (1997) 34 CML Rev 1413; Levitt 'Commission Hearings and the Rôle of the Hearing Officer: Suggestions for Reform' (1998) 19 ECLR 404; Carreras and Valiente 'Access to File as a Right of the Defence in Competition Procedures Before the EC Commission' (1998) 21(4) World Competition 5.

13 Ibid, Part A.1: this section deals with business secrets, confidential documents and internal documents of the Commission.

14 Ibid, Part B.

15 See p 235 below.

16 See XIIth *Report on Competition Policy* (1982), points 36–37; XIIIth *Report on Competition Policy* (1983), points 75 and 76 and pp 273–274; Johannes 'The Rôle of the Hearing Officer' [1989] Fordham Corporate Law Institte (ed Hawk), pp 347–382; van der Woude 'Hearing Officers and EC Antitrust Procedures: The Art of Making Subjective Procedures More Objective' (1996) 33 CML Rev 531.

17 Case T–13/89 *ICI v Commission* [1992] ECR II-1021; the ECJ had reached the same conclusion in an earlier judgment, Case 212/86 *ICI v Commission* [1987] 2 CMLR 500.

18 See below.

19 This report is available at http://www.publications.parliament.uk/pa/ld/ldselect.htm.

20 See Commission decision of 23 May 2001 on *The Terms of Reference of Hearing Officers in Certain Competition Proceedings* OJ [2001] L 162/21.

disclosed to the parties and published together with the final decision; the Hearing Officer will also have more involvement in discussion of whether remedies proposed to deal with competition concerns are acceptable to other undertakings with a legitimate interest: this point is of particular importance in merger cases, where commitments are often required from the parties as a condition of clearance[1].

(iv)   The Advisory Committee on Restrictive Practices and Monopolies

Before adopting its decision the Commission must consult the Advisory Committee on Restrictive Practices and Monopolies, but the undertakings concerned do not have a right to be informed of its deliberations. This has been the subject of criticism[2], but the ECJ rejected an argument that the Committee's report should be available in order to protect the rights of the defence in *Musique Diffusion Française v Commission*[3]. Consultation of the Advisory Committee is an essential procedural safeguard; a breach of this safeguard will affect the legality of the Commission's final decision if it is proved that failure to forward certain material information to the Committee prevented it from delivering an opinion in full knowledge of the facts[4].

(v)   Termination of infringement and remedies

Having gone through the procedure just described, the College of Commissioners may adopt a formal decision pursuant to Article 3(1) of Regulation 17/62 finding that Article 81 and/or Article 82 have been infringed; the decision may require that the infringement should be terminated and may impose a fine[5].

(A)   DECLARATORY DECISIONS.   In some cases the parties may have ended their anti-competitive behaviour by the time the Commission adopts its decision; however it is still permitted to adopt a final decision recording the infringement[6]. For example in *Bloemenveilingen Aalsmeer*[7] the Commission published a decision condemning the rules of a Dutch trade association, although they had been changed to the satisfaction of the Commission, in order to provide a clear statement on the illegality of the original rules; this would be of benefit to a national court in which the legality of the rules was being litigated and to other undertakings that might wish to challenge similar rules of other trade associations. In *Distribution of Package Tours During the 1990 World Cup*[8] the Commission adopted a decision in order to clarify the legal position in respect of exclusive rights to sell tickets for sporting events.

---

1   See ch 21, pp 784-787.
2   See *Kerse* para 5.26.
3   Cases 100–103/83 [1983] ECR 1825, [1983] 3 CMLR 221, paras 34-36.
4   Cases T-25-104/95 etc *Cimenteries CBR SA v Commission* judgment of 15 March 2000, para 742.
5   See pp 237-239 below on fines.
6   This was confirmed in Case 7/82 *GVL v Commission* [1983] ECR 483, [1983] 3 CMLR 645.
7   OJ [1988] L 262/27, [1989] 4 CMLR 500, paras 164-168; see similarly *Zera/Montedison* OJ [1993] L 272/28, [1995] 5 CMLR 320, para 132; *Europe Asia Trades Agreement* OJ [1999] L 193/23, [1999] 5 CMLR 1380, paras 182-185.
8   OJ [1992] L 326/31.

(B)   POSITIVE ORDERS.   In requiring the discontinuation of an infringement the Commission may make positive as well as negative orders. This was established in *Commercial Solvents Co v Commission*[9], where a dominant firm was ordered to resume supplies to a former customer. In *Magill TV Guide*[10] three broadcasting organisations were ordered to supply each other and third parties with advance weekly programme listings. However, whereas an undertaking can be ordered to supply a distributor or customer where it has infringed Article 82, this cannot be done following an infringement of Article 81. In *Automec v Commission (No 2)*[11] Automec complained to the Commission that it had been wrongly excluded from BMW's distribution system and asked it to order BMW to make supplies of BMW cars available. The Commission told Automec that it had no power to make such an order, and this was upheld on appeal by the CFI. Articles 81 and 82 have a different logic: Article 81 prohibits agreements, and the Commission may make an order to terminate them; Article 82 prohibits abuse, and again the Commission can make an order to terminate an abuse. However a refusal to supply under Article 81 cannot in itself be unlawful. The Commission could order an undertaking to terminate an agreement not to supply, but it does not follow that it can also make an order to supply. Any further civil law consequences of an infringement of Article 81 should be determined in the domestic courts of Member States[12].

(C)   STRUCTURAL REMEDIES.   The Commission may, in limited circumstances, make a structural order where Articles 81 or 82 have been infringed. For example if two undertakings were to enter into a partial-function joint venture[13] which, by its nature, was restrictive of competition, the only remedy that could deal with the problem would appear to be a requirement that the joint venture be abandoned; similarly if a completed merger was found to infringe Article 82, the obvious remedy would be to require its reversal[14]. However the reason why a structural remedy could be adopted in these cases is that it was a structural occurrence – the creation of the joint venture or the consummation of the merger – that constituted the infringement; requiring the infringement to end by its nature requires a return to the *status quo ante*. What has never been decided under Regulation 17/62 is whether the Commission could adopt a structural remedy to break up a dominant firm because of its record of acting in an abusive manner. For example it is not clear whether the Commission could require a vertically-integrated dominant undertaking to divest itself of a subsidiary operating in a downstream market because of its repeated tendency to treat the subsidiary more favourably than other customers in that market[15]. The wording of Article 3(1) of Regulation 17/62 does not seem to envisage a remedy as drastic as this, and the Commission has never adopted a decision to this effect. There have been occasions when the Commission has required a dominant firm to deal with a subsidiary on an arm's-length basis and to maintain separate and transparent accounts[16]; this, however, does not amount to a structural remedy in the sense of requiring a divestment of the subsidiary. An important feature of the Commission's

9   Cases 6/73 and 7/73 [1974] ECR 223, [1974] 1 CMLR 309.
10   OJ [1989] L 78/43, [1989] 4 CMLR 757.
11   Case T–24/90 [1992] ECR II-2223, [1992] 5 CMLR 431.
12   Ibid para 50; this issue generally is dealt with in paras 34–54 of the CFI's judgment.
13   The creation of a full-function joint venture would be treated as a merger: see ch 21, pp 748-751.
14   Mergers would now be dealt with under the ECMR: on Article 82 and mergers see ch 21, pp 737-738.
15   Problems of this kind will be discussed, in particular, in chapters 17 and 18 on abusive practices under Article 82.
16   See eg *Deustsche Post* OJ [2001] L 125/27.

modernisation proposals is that it does intend that structural remedies will be available for infringements of Articles 81 and 82 in the future[17].

(D) SUSPENDED DECISIONS. Most decisions of the Commission requiring the termination of infringements have immediate effect, but in appropriate circumstances the Commission may allow the parties a period of time in which to comply[18].

(vi) Fines[19]

The Commission has power under Articles 15 and 16 of Regulation 17/62 to impose fines on undertakings that infringe Articles 81 or 82. A natural person could be fined only in so far as he or she is an undertaking for the purpose of these Articles[20]. There is no criminal liability under EC competition law, and no provision whereby individuals may be imprisoned: imprisonment is possible in some jurisdictions, most notably the US[1]. A firm may be fined a maximum of EUR 1,000,000 or 10% of its turnover in all products, worldwide, in the preceding year, whichever is greater. Where the infringement is a serious one the fines may be substantial. In *Tetra Pak (II)*[2] the Commission imposed a fine of EUR 75 million on that company for abusing its dominant position. The largest fine so far to have been imposed on one undertaking occurred in *Volkswagen*[3], which was fined EUR 102 million for preventing parallel imports of its cars from Italy into Austria and Germany; the fine was reduced to EUR 90 million on appeal to the CFI[4]. The largest fine in a single decision was on the members of the *Trans-Atlantic Conference Agreement*[5], amounting to EUR 273 million. There is no doubt that the Commission will take an increasingly serious view of blatant infringements of the competition rules, and the level of fines can be expected to be increased in such cases. One of the reasons behind the Commission's modernisation proposals is to free up its resources to be able to deal with serious infringements[6], and there is a concerted attempt on the part of competition authorities around the world to pursue and punish international cartels[7].

The appropriate amount of a fine has become a substantial subject in its own right. The chapter in Kerse's *Antitrust Procedure* devotes no less than 51 pages to the subject. It is not proposed to enter into the detail of the level of fines in this chapter, especially when both Kerse and Smith's *Competition Law: Enforcement & Procedure* deal with it so thoroughly. However it is appropriate to draw

17 See p 255 below.
18 See eg *IJsselcentrale* OJ [1991] L 28/32, [1992] 5 CMLR 154.
19 See *Kerse* ch 7; *Smith* ch 9.
20 On the meaning of undertaking see ch 3, pp 66-71.
1   See ch 13, pp 416-417; see also Wils 'Does the Effective Enforcement of Articles 81 and 82 EC Require Not Only Fines on Undertakings But Also Individual Penalties, in particular Imprisonment?' in European Competition Law Annual (Hart Publishing, ed Ehlermann, 2002).
2   OJ [1992] L 72/1, [1992] 4 CMLR 551, upheld on appeal to the CFI, Case T-83/91 *Tetra Pak International SA v Commission* [1994] ECR II-755, [1997] 4 CMLR 726, and on appeal to the ECJ, Case C-333/94 P *Tetra Pak International SA v Commission* [1996] ECR I-5951, [1997] 4 CMLR 662.
3   OJ [1998] L 124/60, [1998] 5 CMLR 33.
4   Case T-62/98 *Volkswagen AG v Commission* [2000] 5 CMLR 853; the case is on appeal to the ECJ, Case C-338/00 (judgment pending).
5   OJ [1999] L 95/1, [1999] 4 CMLR 1415; the case is on appeal to the CFI, Cases T-191/98 etc *Atlantic Container Line AB v Commission* (judgment pending).
6   See pp 248-249 below.
7   See ch 13, pp 415-419.

attention to one Notice and one Guideline of the Commission which set out the framework for its current approach.

(A)   THE WHISTLEBLOWERS' NOTICE.   In 1996 the Commission adopted its *Notice on the Non-imposition or Reduction of Fines in Cartel Cases* ('the *Leniency Notice*')[8]. It formalises the idea of granting 'leniency' – that is to say imposing a reduced fine – to a member of a cartel that voluntarily approaches the Commission to admit its participation in the cartel and to provide evidence that will enable the Commission successfully to bring proceedings. This is the notion of 'whistleblowing', which has proved to be immensely successful in the US in recent years in tracking down and prosecuting cartels: as just mentioned, the pursuit of cartels is very high on the agenda of competition authorities around the world, and the whistleblowing programme is an important part of this policy[9]. The policy in the US, which was adopted in its current form in 1993, can be accessed on the home page of the Department of Justice[10].

Under the Commission's *Leniency Notice* an undertaking may obtain the benefit of a reduced fine in specified circumstances. The Notice explains the circumstances in which a 'very substantial', a 'substantial' and a 'significant' reduction may be earned, as well as the procedure to be followed. To benefit from a 'very substantial' reduction, the undertaking must inform the Commission about a secret cartel before the Commission has begun an investigation; it must be the first to adduce decisive evidence of the cartel's existence; it must terminate its own participation in the cartel; it must provide the Commission with all the relevant evidence in its possession and cooperate with the Commission throughout the procedure; and it must not have been the ring-leader of the cartel. In these circumstances the undertaking may enjoy a reduction in its fine of 75%, or even from a total exemption from being fined[11]. Undertakings that fail to satisfy all these criteria may benefit from lesser reductions[12].

The system of leniency in the EC differs from the one in operation in the US: for example the US rules allow an automatic 100% amnesty for a successful whistleblower, whereas the EC one envisages a reduction of 'at least 75% or even from total exemption'; the tests set out in the Commission's *Notice* are also, cumulatively, stricter than the US model. A leniency programme has been adopted under the UK Competition Act 1998[13] which is modelled on the US rather than the EC system. The reason for the preference for the US model is clear: offering an automatic, 100% amnesty is more likely to encourage whistleblowing, and is therefore more effective. It is unsatisfactory that there should be different systems of whistleblowing in the EC and the US[14], in particular in an era of increasing cooperation between competition authorities, and it may be that the EC model will be altered to bring it more into line with the one in the US.[14a] It is important

---

8   OJ [1996] C 207/4, [1996] 5 CMLR 362; see Wils 'The Commission's Notice on the Non-Imposition of Fines in Cartel Cases: A Legal and Economic Analysis' (1997) 22 ELRev 125.

9   See ch 13, pp 415-419; major cases such as *Vitamins*, *Citric Acid* and *Sotheby's/Christies* all came to light as a result of whistleblowing.

10   See US Department of Justice, Antitrust Division, Corporate Leniency Policy of 10 August 1993, available as an Annex to speeches of Gary Spratling, Deputy Assistant Attorney General, on http://www.usdoj.gov/atr/speeches.

11   *Leniency Notice*, Part B.

12   Ibid, Parts C and D.

13   See ch 10, pp 353-355.

14   See Brokx 'A Patchwork of Leniency Programmes' (2001) 22 ECLR 35.

14a See the Commission's *Draft Commission Notice on Immunity from Fines and Reductions in Cartel Cases* OJ [2001] C 205/18.

to add that, whereas whistleblowing may result in immunity from being fined, or, if not immunity, at any rate lower fines, it does not affect the liability of the whistleblower to pay damages to victims of a cartel as a matter of civil law.

(B)   THE COMMISSION'S GUIDELINES.   As well as the *Leniency Notice* the Commission has adopted *Guidelines on the Method of Setting Fines Imposed Pursuant to Article 15(2) of Regulation No 17 and Article 65(3) of the ECSC Treaty*[15] . The *Guidelines* respond to the criticism that the Commission ought not to have an unfettered discretion in relation to the level of fines; in the US, for example, there are sentencing guidelines that enable the level of a fine (and a prison sentence) to be predicted with a fairly high degree of accuracy[16] . Guidance on the amount of a penalty is also available under UK law[17] .

Under the Commission's *Guidelines* a number of factors are relevant. To begin with a 'basic amount' for the fine will be calculated by reference to the gravity and duration of the infringement[18] . As to gravity, the *Guidelines* place infringements into one of three categories: minor, serious and very serious; the last of these categories includes horizontal restrictions such as price-fixing cartels and market-sharing quotas, other practices that jeopardise the functioning of the single market and clear-cut abuses. For very serious cases the basic fine is likely to be above EUR 20 million. Duration is then taken into account: infringements may be short, medium or long. For infringements of long duration, the basic fine is likely to be increased by 10% of the basic amount for each year of the infringement.

Having determined the basic amount of the fine, the Commission then explains circumstances that will be regarded as aggravating, so as to increase the level of the fine[19]; and those that are regarded as attenuating, so as to reduce it[20] . Examples of the former are the fact that an undertaking repeatedly has committed the same infringement (recidivism), is uncooperative with the Commission, or that it was the ringleader of a cartel. Examples of the latter would be that an undertaking terminated the infringement at the commencement of the Commission's investigation or that it committed the infringement negligently or unintentionally.

It is a noticeable feature of recent Commission decisions that they explain in a great deal more detail than they formerly did how the level of the fine was arrived at: the *Guidelines* require that the Commission should do so, and it is to be anticipated that the CFI will carefully review the exercise of the Commission's discretion in setting fines in order to ensure that the requisite standards are being applied.

---

15 OJ [1998] C 9/3, [1998] 4 CMLR 472; see Wils 'The Commission's New Method for Calculating Fines in Antitrust Cases' (1998) 23 ELRev 252; Spink 'Recent Guidance on Fining Policy' (1999) 20 ECLR 101; Richardson 'Guidance Without Guidance – A European Revolution in Fining Policy?' (1999) 20 ECLR 360; Castellot 'The Application of the Guidelines on Fines: An Overview' Competition Policy Newsletter October 2000, p 5.
16 See the Sentencing Reform Act 1984 and the US Sentencing Commission *Guidelines Manual*.
17 See ch 10, pp 352-353.
18 *Guidelines*, Part 1.
19 Ibid, Part 2.
20 Ibid, Part 3.

8. THE POSITION OF COMPLAINANTS[1]

The Commission receives numerous complaints each year about infringements of Articles 81 and 82; in 1999 it received 149 complaints and in 2000 112[2]. Article 3(2) of Regulation 17/62 states that Member States and 'natural or legal persons who claim a legitimate interest' may make an application to the Commission asking it to carry out an investigation under the competition rules. The Community Courts have not laid down a test of what is meant by a 'legitimate interest' under Article 3(2) of Regulation 17/62. Regulation 2842/98 contains provisions of relevance to the position of complainants[3]. There is no legal requirement for complaints to be made in a specific format, in the way that notifications for negative clearance or individual exemptions must be made in the manner specified by Regulation 3385/94 (or, in the case of transport, by Regulation 2843/98)[4]. The rights of a complainant to be heard are not as extensive as those of an undertaking that is the subject of an investigation[5]; nor do complainants have the same rights of access to the file[6]. There have been many cases on the rights of complainants brought before the Community Courts, very often where the Commission has decided not to initiate an investigation of an alleged infringement to a complainant's disappointment. A short account of the essential principles follows; however specialist works should be referred to on this complex subject, the law on which is still evolving.

(A) The Commission's duty of vigilance

The Commission is under an obligation to give attention to the complaints that it receives: this is sometimes referred to as a 'duty of vigilance'[7]. If the Commission were simply to refuse to give any consideration to a complaint at all, or if it were to select cases on an arbitrary or discriminatory basis, a complainant could bring an action under Article 232 (ex Article 175) for failure to act[8].

---

1 See *Kerse* paras 2.29-2.37; *Smith* ch 5; see also Vesterdorf 'Complaints Concerning Infringements of Competition Law within the Context of European Community Law' (1994) 31 CML Rev 77; Kerse 'The Complainant in Competition Cases: A Progress Report' (1997) 34 CML Rev 213; Pirie 'The Complainant in EC Competition Law' (2000) 23(1) World Competition 107.
2 See the XXIXth *Report on Competition Policy* (1999), point 7 and the XXXth *Report on Competition Policy* (2000), point 11.
3 OJ [1998] L 354/18, [1999] 4 CMLR 228.
4 See ch 4, pp 136-141 above.
5 Cases 142 and 156/84 *BAT and Reynolds v Commission* [1987] ECR 4487, [1987] 2 CMLR 551, para 19; Case T-65/96 *Kish Glass & Co v Commission* [2000] 5 CMLR 229, para 33.
6 Case T-17/93 *Matra Hachette v Commission* [1994] ECR II-595, para 33; Case T-83/96 *Van der Wal v Commission* [1998] ECR II-545, upheld on appeal Cases C-174/98 P and C-198/98P *Netherlands and van der Wal v Commission* [2000] ECR I-1; Case T-65/96 *Kish Glass & Co v Commission* [2000] 5 CMLR 229, para 34.
7 See eg Case 210/81 *Demo-Studio Schmidt v EC Commission* [1983] ECR 3045, [1984] 1 CMLR 63.
8 See p 243 below.

(B) The Commission's discretion in determining whether to investigate

The duty of vigilance requires the Commission to consider the contents of the complaint. However it does not follow from this duty that the Commission can be required to proceed with the complaint and to investigate it fully. The Commission has scarce resources and numerous responsibilities: it would be placed in an impossible position if it was required, as a matter of law, to pursue every complaint to a final determination. The problem for the Commission and the Community Courts has been to strike a reasonable balance between the Commission's right to reject complaints that do not merit consideration on its part on the one hand and the rights of complainants to invoke the assistance of the Commission in eliminating anti-competitive behaviour on the other. Relevant to this discussion is the Commission's desire, expressed in its *Notice on Cooperation between National Courts and the Commission in Applying Articles [81] and [82] of the EC Treaty*[9], in the companion *Notice on Cooperation between National Competition Authorities and the Commission in handling cases falling within the scope of Articles [81] or [82] of the EC Treaty*[10], and, most recently, in the *White Paper on Modernisation*[11] to decentralise the enforcement of the competition rules by giving national courts and NCAs a greater rôle.

In *GEMA v Commission*[12] the ECJ established that the rights conferred upon complainants by Regulation 17/62 and Regulation 99/63 (the predecessor of Regulation 2843/98) do not include a right to obtain a decision. In *Automec (No 2) v Commission*[13] the CFI held[14] that it followed from this that the Commission could not be compelled to conduct an investigation: if it could not be required to issue a decision, it would be futile to order it to carry out an investigation. However the Commission, when deciding whether to investigate or not, must evaluate with the requisite care the factual and legal aspects adduced by the complainant and have proper reasons for deciding to close its file[15]. The crucial point about *Automec (No 2)* is that the CFI held that, in making its decision whether to proceed or not, the Commission is entitled to accord different degrees of priority to the complaints it receives[16], and that in doing so it may choose to deal with cases that have a 'Community interest'[17]. In *Automec (No 2)* itself the CFI concluded that the Commission was entitled to conclude that there was not a sufficient Community interest to require it to investigate: there were already civil proceedings between Automec and BMW in Italy, the national court could apply Article 81(1) and the block exemption for motor cars[18], and points of Community law could be referred by the national court to the ECJ under Article

9   OJ [1993] C 39/6, [1993] 4 CMLR 12.
10 OJ [1997] C 313/3, [1997] 5 CMLR 884.
11 OJ [1999] C 132/1, [1999] 5 CMLR 208.
12 Case 125/78 [1979] ECR 3173, [1980] 2 CMLR 177.
13 Case T–24/90 [1992] ECR II-2223, [1992] 5 CMLR 431; see similarly Case T-7/92 *Asia Motor France v Commission* [1993] ECR II-669, [1994] 4 CMLR 30; Case T-154/98 *Asia Motor France v Commission* [1999] ECR II-1703, [2001] 4 CMLR 189, paras 55 and 56.
14 Case T–24/90 *Automec v Commission (No 2)* [1992] ECR II-2223, [1992] 5 CMLR 431, para 76.
15 Ibid, para 81.
16 Ibid, para 83.
17 Ibid, paras 84–86.
18 The relevant block exemption at the time was Regulation 123/85; national courts are able to apply block exemptions: see p 231, n 9 above.

234 (ex Article 177)[19]. In the Commission's *Notice on Cooperation between National Courts and the Commission in Applying Articles [81] and [82] of the EC Treaty*[20] the Commission said that, following *Automec (No 2)*, it would henceforth concentrate on notifications, complaints and own-initiative proceedings 'having particular political, economic or legal significance for the Community'[1].

From the Commission's point of view *Automec (No 2)* was an important judgment, since it confirmed that it did not have to proceed to investigate every complaint. However the CFI will review the reasoning of the Commission when it decides not to proceed in order to determine whether it exercised its discretion lawfully in accordance with the test laid down. For example in *Tremblay v Commission*[2] the CFI upheld the Commission's finding that a complaint raised no point of Community interest. However on several occasions the CFI or the ECJ have disagreed with the basis on which the Commission reached its decision. For example the CFI annulled the Commission's rejection of complaints in *BEUC v Commission*[3]. In *Commission and France v Ladbroke Racing Ltd*[4] and in *Union Française de l'Express (Ufex) v Commission*[5] the ECJ concluded that the CFI had been incorrect in law in deciding that the Commission had correctly decided to reject complaints.

(C)   The procedure to be followed when rejecting a complaint

If the Commission decides to reject a complaint, Article 6 of Regulation 2842/98 requires it to inform the complainant and to fix a time-limit within which it may submit any further comments in writing[6]. If the Commission fails to do this it could be challenged under Article 232 for failure to act[7]. If the Commission informs the complainant under the Article 6 procedure that it does not intend to pursue the complaint, this could not be challenged under Article 230, since the complainant still has the right to make further comments[8]. However if the complainant does make such comments the Commission must then decide whether to proceed or not; in accordance with the principle of good administration this

19 Case T–24/90 *Automec (No 2)*, paras 87–98.
20 OJ [1993] C 39/6, [1993] 4 CMLR 12.
1   Ibid, para 14.
2   Case T-5/93 [1995] ECR II-185, [1996] 4 CMLR 305, upheld on appeal Case C-91/95 P [1996] ECR I-5547, [1997] 4 CMLR 211; see similarly Cases T-185/94 and 190/94 *Riviera Auto Service Établissements Dalmasso SA v Commission* [1999] ECR II-93, [1999] 5 CMLR 31.
3   Case T-37/92 [1994] ECR II-285, [1995] 4 CMLR 167; see similarly the annulment of the Commission's rejection of a complaint under Article 82 in Case T-198/98 *Micro Business Leader v Commission* [2000] 4 CMLR 886.
4   Cases C-359/95 P and C-379/95 P [1997] ECR I-6265, [1998] 4 CMLR 27.
5   Case C-119/97 P [1999] ECR I-1341, [2000] 4 CMLR 268, para 89; when this case was returned to the CFI, it decided that the Commission's rejection of the complaint should be annulled: see Case T-77/95 *UFEX v Commission* [2001] 4 CMLR 35; see also Cases T-189/95 etc *Service pour le Groupement d'Acquisitions v Commission* [2001] 4 CMLR 215, paras 39-41.
6   See Case C-282/95 P *Guérin Automobiles v Commission* [1997] ECR I-1503, [1997] 5 CMLR 447; Case T-127/98 *UPS Europe SA v Commission* [1999] ECR II-2633, [2000] 4 CMLR 94.
7   See Case T–28/90 *Asia Motor France v Commission* [1992] ECR II-2285, [1992] 5 CMLR 431, paras 29–30.
8   Case T–64/89 *Automec v Commission* [1990] ECR II-367, [1991] 4 CMLR 177, para 46; Case T–28/90 *Asia Motor France v Commission* [1992] ECR II-2285, [1992] 5 CMLR 431, para 42.

must be done within a reasonable time after receipt by the Commission of the complainant's observations. If the Commission then decides to reject the complaint, this amounts to an act in relation to which the complainant may seek judicial review under Article 230[9]. There have been and continue to be many such cases. The Commission's decision to reject a complaint must state its reasons and be sufficiently precise to enable the CFI to review the exercise of its discretion.

9. JUDICIAL REVIEW[10]

It is possible to bring an action before the CFI in respect of Commission decisions on competition matters; Article 232 (ex Article 175) of the Treaty deals with failures to act, Article 230 (ex Article 173) with actions for annulment and Article 229 (ex Article 172) with penalties. Proceedings before the CFI must be completed within a reasonable time; reasonableness is tested by reference to the importance of the case for the person concerned, its complexity and the conduct of the applicant and the competent authorities[11].

(A) Article 232: failure to act

Under Article 232 it is possible to bring an action against the Commission where, in infringement of the Treaty, it has failed to act. The Commission must have been under a specific duty to carry out the act in question. An action may be brought only where the Commission has been required to act and has failed to do so within two months; the action itself must be brought within the following two months[12]. If an action for failure to act is commenced under Article 232 and the Commission subsequently performs the act required of it, the action becomes devoid of purpose and the CFI will not give a ruling on it[13]. Article 232 is often invoked by complainants wishing to force the Commission to investigate complaints against undertakings suspected of infringing the competition rules[14].

Where the Commission is guilty of a failure to act, an undertaking that suffers damage in consequence may bring an action against the Commission for compensation under Article 288 EC (ex Article 215); to date such actions in the context of the competition rules have failed, for example because the undertaking omitted to specify the damage it had suffered[15] or because it calculated damage in respect of an incorrect period[16].

9   See pp 244-246 below.
10 See *Kerse* ch 9; *Smith* ch 10.
11 Case C-185/95 P *Baustahlgewebe GmbH v Commission* [1998] ECR I-8417, [1999] 4 CMLR 1203; the fine was reduced by EUR 50,000 in this case because of the delay in the proceedings.
12 Article 232(2); time-limits are applied strictly by the CFI: see Case T-12/90 *Bayer v Commission* [1991] ECR II-219, [1993] 4 CMLR 30.
13 Case T–28/90 *Asia Motor France v Commission* [1992] ECR II-2285, [1992] 5 CMLR 431, paras 34–38.
14 On the position of complainants see pp 240-243 above.
15 Case T–64/89 *Automec Srl v Commission* [1990] ECR II-367, [1991] 4 CMLR 177.
16 Case T-28/90 *Asia Motor France v Commission* [1992] ECR I-2285, [1992] 5 CMLR 431, paras 48–51.

(B)   Article 230: Action for annulment

Under Article 230 it is possible to bring an action to have various 'acts' of the Commission annulled. Proceedings must be commenced within two months of the applicant hearing of the act in question[17]. Where an action succeeds in part only, Article 231 enables the bad parts of a decision to be severed, leaving the remainder intact. Three issues in particular need consideration: who may sue; what 'acts' may be challenged; and on what grounds an action may be brought.

(i)   Locus standi

Apart from Member States and the Council, Article 230(4) provides that any undertaking may challenge a decision addressed to it or to another person if it is of 'direct and individual concern' to it. This clearly entitles third parties in some situations to sue. In *Metro v Commission*[18] the ECJ confirmed that a complainant under Article 3(2) of Regulation 17/62 could proceed under Article 230[19]; it is presumably the case that in appropriate circumstances a third party who has not actually complained under Regulation 17/62 could do so. In some cases however the applicant's interest may be altogether too vague to give standing[20]. Of course, the recipients of adverse decisions may themselves bring an action under Article 230, and their right to do so is not limited to cases in which fines have been imposed. The recipients of a negative clearance (and of an unconditional clearance under the ECMR) have been held to have no right to challenge the reasoning of the Commission's decision, since their legal position has not been adversely affected[1].

(ii)   Acts

It is not only decisions, but other 'acts' which may be challenged under Article 230. Formal decisions under Regulation 17/62 such as negative clearances, individual exemptions and decisions imposing penalties may be the subject of review. Some difficulty however has been encountered in establishing what other acts of the Commission can be. In the *Perfumes* cases[2] the ECJ held that comfort letters were not capable of review, but were merely administrative. In *Coca-Cola Co v Commission*[3] the CFI held that it is settled law that any measure which

---

17   Article 230(5); see n 12 above on the CFI's approach to time-limits.
18   Case 26/76 [1977] ECR 1875, [1978] 2 CMLR 1.
19   See also Case 43/85 *ANCIDES v Commission* [1987] ECR 3131, [1988] 4 CMLR 821; a third party successfully challenged the grant of an individual exemption in Cases T-528/93 etc *Métropole v Commission* [1996] ECR II-649, [1996] 5 CMLR 386.
20   See eg Case 246/81 *Bethell v Commission* [1982] ECR 2277, [1982] 3 CMLR 300; Case C-70/97 P *Kruidvat BVBA v Commission* [1998] ECR I-7183, [1999] 4 CMLR 68.
1   Case T-138/89 *Nederlandse Bankiersvereniging v Commission* [1992] ECR II-2181, [1993] 5 CMLR 436 (negative clearance under Article 81); Joined Cases T-125/97 and T-127/97 *Coca-Cola Co v Commission* [2000] 5 CMLR 467 (clearance under the ECMR).
2   See eg Case 99/79 *Lancôme v Etos* [1980] ECR 2511, [1981] 2 CMLR 164; see generally on this and the other Perfumes cases Korah 'Comfort Letters – Reflections on the Perfumes Cases' (1981) 6 ELRev 14; Case T-241/97 *Stork Amsterdam BV v Commission* [2000] ECR II-309, [2000] 5 CMLR 31, para 84.
3   Joined Cases T-125/97 and T-127/97 [2000] 5 CMLR 467.

produces binding legal effects such as to affect the interest of an applicant by bringing about a distinct change in its legal position is an act or decision which may be the subject of an action under Article 230[4]. In *IBM v Commission*[5] the ECJ held that a statement of objections could not normally be challenged, because it was simply a preliminary step in the formal procedure[6]. Similarly in *Automec Srl v Commission*[7] the CFI held that a letter from the Commission under Article 6 of Regulation 99/63 (the predecessor of Regulation 2842/93) which contained merely a provisional statement of its opinion could not be challenged. In *BAT v Commission*[8] the ECJ held that letters from the Commission to two complainants, finally rejecting their complaints, were acts capable of challenge under Article 230. The CFI held in the *Omni-Partijeu Akkord* judgments[9] that a letter from the Commissioner responsible for competition policy to a Member State that was purely factual in nature produced no legal effects and could not be challenged under Article 230. Mere silence on the part of a Community institution cannot produce binding legal effects unless express provision to this effect is made for it in Community law[10].

(iii)   Grounds of review

The grounds of review are specified in Article 230(1). The Commission may be challenged on grounds of:

'lack of competence, infringement of an essential procedural requirement, infringement of this Treaty or of any rule of law relating to its application, or misuse of powers'.

To some extent these grounds overlap with one another, and their cumulative effect is to provide a basis of review which is similar to the position in the administrative law of the UK. Of particular significance will be a failure by the Commission to give a fair hearing[11]; a failure to articulate properly the reasoning behind its decision[12]; and a failure to base a decision on adequate evidence[13]. The Commission is not required to set out in its decision exhaustively all the

---

4   The CFI cited for this proposition the judgments in Case 60/81 *IBM v Commission* [1981] ECR 2639, [1981] 3 CMLR 635, para 9; Joined Cases C-68/94 and C-30/95 *France v Commission* [1998] ECR I-1375, [1998] 4 CMLR 829, para 62; and Case T-87/95 *Assuriazioni Generali v Commission* [1999] ECR II-203, [2000] 4 CMLR 312, para 37.
5   Case 60/81 [1981] ECR 2639, [1981] 3 CMLR 635.
6   See similarly Cases T–10/92 etc *SA Cimenteries CBR v Commission* [1992] ECR II-2667, [1993] 4 CMLR 259.
7   Case T–64/89 [1990] ECR II-367, [1991] 4 CMLR 177, para 42.
8   Cases 142, 156/84 [1987] ECR 4487, [1988] 4 CMLR 24; see also Case 210/81 *Demo-Studio Schmidt v Commission* [1983] ECR 3045, [1984] 1 CMLR 63.
9   Cases T–113/89 etc *Nefarma v Commission* [1990] ECR II–797.
10 Cases T–189/95 etc *Service pour le Groupement d'Acquisitions v Commission* [2001] 4 CMLR 215, paras 26-29.
11 See eg Case 17/74 *Transocean Marine Paint Association v Commission* [1974] ECR 1063, [1974] 2 CMLR 459 where the members of the association were not given an opportunity to be heard on the conditions which the Commission intended to attach to an individual exemption.
12 See eg Case 73/74 *Groupement des Fabricants des Papiers Peints de Belgique v Commission* [1975] ECR 1491, [1976] 1 CMLR 589 where the Commission failed to explain the mechanism whereby the agreement in question could affect inter-state trade.
13 See eg Case 41/69 *ACF Chemiefarma v Commission* [1970] ECR 661 where the Commission's decision was partially annulled for lack of evidence.

evidence available; it is sufficient if it refers to the conclusive evidence[14]. The CFI will not annul an act or decision unless it is reasonably likely that an error on the part of the Commission may have affected it in a material respect.

(C)   Article 229: penalties

Under Article 229 the CFI has unlimited jurisdiction in respect of penalties imposed by the Commission. Article 17 of Regulation 17/62 provides that the CFI may cancel, reduce or increase fines or periodic penalties imposed. In the exercise of its unlimited jurisdiction the CFI may review a decision in its entirety – on factual as well as legal grounds – and many of its judgments have dealt exhaustively with the facts of the case. In the first cartel case to come before the CFI, *Italian Flat Glass*[15], it conducted an exhaustive review of the Commission's findings and was extremely critical of them, leading to annulment of the decision and the fines. There have many occasions since that case on which the CFI has adopted a similarly robust approach[16].

(D)   Interim measures

It is possible to apply to the CFI for interim measures suspending the operation of a Commission decision pending an appeal. Examples of this having occurred are *Bayer v Commission*[17] and *Van den Bergh Foods Ltd v Commission*[18].

10.   MODERNISATION[19]

It became increasingly obvious over many years that the system established by Regulation 17/62 for the enforcement of the competition rules was in need of fundamental reform. The problems have been mentioned several times already in this book; in particular the Commission's monopoly over the grant of individual exemptions under Article 81(3) meant that delay, expense and uncertainty were experienced on the part of undertakings that entered into agreements that might be considered to infringe Article 81(1) – in particular as a result of the expansive interpretation given to that provision by the Commission – and which did not benefit from any of the block exemptions. At the same time, notifications for individual exemptions imposed burdens on the staff of the Commission who were diverted from other more gainful tasks, such as the investigation of cartels and serious abuses of dominance.

Serious consideration of the possibilities for reform began in the 1990s. Several papers were given at the 1996 Fordham Corportate Law Institute dealing with

14 Case T–2/89 *Petrofina SA v Commission* [1991] ECR II-1087.
15 Cases T-68/89 etc *Società Italiano Vetro SpA v Commission* [1992] ECR II-1403, [1992] 5 CMLR 302.
16 See in particular the *Table of major cartel cases since 1986* in ch 13, pp 419-424 which shows the outcome of appeals to the CFI and ECJ.
17 Case T-41/98 R [1997] ECR II-381; Bayer's appeal in this case was successful: see Case T-41/98, [2001] 4 CMLR 126.
18 Case T-65/98 R [1998] ECR II-2641, [1998] 5 CMLR 475; the appeal in this case is pending.
19 Part of what follows is based on an essay by the author co-written with Brenda Sufrin of the University of Bristol 'Community Competition Law: Notification and Individual Exemption – Goodbye to All That' in Hayton (ed) *Law's Future(s)* (Hart Publishing, 2000), ch 8.

the issue[20]. In 1999 the Commission published its *White Paper on Modernisation*[1] which offers a solution to these problems which is both breathtakingly simple and yet complex in its implications: the abandonment of the Commission's monopoly of granting individual exemptions under Article 81(3) and the abolition of notification for individual exemptions altogether.

In understanding these proposals it is important to point out that the Treaty itself does not use the expression 'exemption' at all: Article 81(3) provides that Article 81(1) 'may be declared inapplicable' to agreements which satisfy its criteria, without designating such a declaration as an 'exemption' and without saying by what mechanism the declaration should be made. At the time that the Treaty was drafted there was disagreement, in particular between the Germans and the French, on this issue. Two choices were available. One, that an agreement that infringed Article 81(1) could escape the prohibition of that Article (and the voidness provided for by Article 81(2)) only where a prior authorisation was given to it by a public agency such as the Commission: a 'constitutive' act was needed in order to invest the agreement with a validity that it would otherwise lack. The alternative choice was the idea of a directly applicable exception (*'de l'exception légale'*), according to which all the provisions of Article 81 – both Article 81(1) and Article 81(3) – should be applied to an agreement to determine whether or not it was lawful, without the need for a positive, constitutive act by a public agency. The inability to agree which of these two approaches was appropriate led to a compromise: by phrasing Article 81(3) in a negative manner (Article 81(1) *'may be declared inapplicable ...'*), rather than a positive one (agreements *'may be declared valid'*), the choice between an authorisation system

---

20 See Schaub 'EC Competition Law – The Millennium Approaches' [1996] Fordham Corporate Law Institute (ed Hawk), ch 12; see also Fennelly, ibid, ch 13; Hope and Thorsen, ch 14; Siragusa 'Rethinking Article [81]: Problems and Challenges in the Design and Enforcement of the EC Competition Rules', ibid, ch 15; Temple Lang 'Community Antitrust Law and National Regulatory Procedures', ibid, ch 16; other interesting pieces on the need for reform, but dealing with the position prior to the White Paper on modernisation, include Rodger and MacCulloch 'Community Competition Law Enforcement Deregulation and Re-regulation: The Commission, National Authorities and Private Enforcement' (1998) 4 Columbia Journal of European Law 579; Wils 'Notification, Clearance and Exemption in EC Competition Law: An Economic Analysis' (1999) 24 ELRev 139; Klimish and Krueger 'Decentralised Application of EC Competition Law: Current Practice and Future Prospects' (1999) 24 ELRev 463; see generally Wesseling *The Modernisation of EC Antitrust* (Hart Publishing, 2000).

1 OJ [1999] C 132/1, [1999] 5 CMLR 208; for a thorough analysis of the Commission's proposals see Wils 'The Modernisation of the Enforcement of Articles 81 and 82 EC: A Legal and Economic Analysis of the Commission's Proposal for a new Council Regulation Replacing Regulation 17/62' [2000] Fordham Corporate Law Institute (ed Hawk) (not yet published); see also Schaub 'Modernisation of the Rules Implementing Articles 81 and 82' [1999] Fordham Corporate Law Institute (ed Hawk), ch 10; Forrester 'Modernisation of EC Competition Law', ibid, ch 12; Kon 'The Commission's White Paper on Modernisation: The Need for Procedural Harmonisation', ibid, ch 13; Mersing 'The Modernisation of EC Competition Law: The Need for a Common Competition Culture', ibid, ch 14; Siragusa 'A Critical Review of the White Paper on the Reform of the EC Competition Law Enforcement Rules', ibid, ch 15; Wolf 'Comment on the Reform of EC Competition Law', ibid, ch 16; see also for further critical comment Wesseling 'The Commission White Paper on Modernisation of EC Antitrust: Unspoken Consequences and Incomplete Treatment of Alternative Options' (1999) 20 ECLR 420; Rodger 'The Commission White Paper on Modernisation of the Rules Implementing Articles 81 and 82 of the EC Treaty' (1999) 24 ELRev 653; Paulweber 'The End of a Success Story? The European Commission's White Paper on the Modernisation of European Competition Law' (2000) 23(3) World Competition 3; Gerber 'Modernising European Competition Law: A Developmental Perspective' (2001) 22 ECLR 122; see also the Commission's XXXth *Report on Competition Policy* (2000), points 37-67.

on the one hand and a directly applicable exception system on the other was deliberately left to the Community legislator, rather than being settled in the Treaty itself. The Council subsequently made that choice in Article 9(1) of Council Regulation 17/62, which adopted a system of prior authorisation. The White Paper proposes that the system established by Article 9(1) should now be abolished, and that a directly applicable system should take its place.

(A)   The reasons for the proposals

The White Paper begins by explaining that when Regulation 17/62 was adopted, it was decided that there should be a centralised authorisation system for exemption under Article 81(3) so that the Commission could create a 'culture of competition' in Europe and ensure the integration of national markets. However, the centralised system devised in 1962 when there were six Member States 'is no longer appropriate for the Community of today with 15 Member States, 11 languages and over 350 million inhabitants'[2]. The system of exclusive notification to the Commission of agreements requiring exemption has thwarted its attempts to achieve decentralisation of the enforcement of the competition rules. The Notices in 1993 and 1997 which were intended to give impetus to increased enforcement of the rules by national courts and NCAs respectively[3] 'have now reached their limits within the existing legal framework'[4].

The need for the Commission to devote resources to dealing with notifications hinders it in the performance of tasks that it considers more important: dealing with cross-border cartels, maintaining competitive market structures, merger control, the liberalisation of hitherto monopolised markets and international co-operation[5]. The Commission notes the numerous steps that have been taken to alleviate the burden of notification such as the provision of guidance as to those agreements that fall outside Article 81(1) in a series of Notices[6]; the adoption of block exemptions[7]; and speedier settlement of cases, in particular by so-called 'comfort letters'[8]. However, further accessions to the Community in the near future would be likely to lead to more notifications, exacerbating the Commission's problems.

In the Commission's view, the time has come for 'radical reforms' to be considered; it is no longer possible to retain a centralised prior authorisation system in Brussels[9]. The notification system tends to force the Commission to adopt an essentially reactive stance, dealing with the agreements notified to it[10]. Instead, the burden of enforcement, *including a determination of whether the criteria of Article 81(3) are satisfied*, should be the prime responsibility of national

2   *White Paper*, Executive Summary, para 5.
3   Commission *Notice on Cooperation between National Courts and the Commission Applying Articles [81] and [82] of the EEC Treaty* OJ [1993] C 39/6, [1993] 5 CMLR 95; Commission *Notice on Cooperation Between the National Competition Authorities and the Commission in Handling Cases Falling Within the Scope of Articles [81] and [82]* OJ [1997] C 313/3, [1997] 5 CMLR 884.
4   *White Paper*, para 39.
5   Ibid, Executive Summary, para 8.
6   See ch 3, pp 105-107.
7   See ch 4, pp 141-146.
8   See pp 217-218 above.
9   Ibid, para 40.
10   Ibid, paras 44-45, where the Commission points out that of new cases commenced between 1988 and 1998, only 13% were commenced as a result of its own initiatives, whereas 58% arose from notifications and 29% from complaints.

courts and NCAs. The Commission therefore proposes that the notification and exemption system in Regulation 17/62 should be abolished and replaced by a Council Regulation which would render the criteria in Article 81(3) directly applicable without prior decision of the Commission. Prior authorisation would be replaced by directly applicable exceptions[11]: 'Article 81 would then become *a unitary norm comprising a rule establishing the principle of prohibition unless certain conditions are met*' (Commission's own emphasis)[12]. However, one particular category of agreement, partial-function joint ventures, should continue to be subject to an authorisation system[13].

Crucially, there are two strands to this proposal. The first is that the system of notification should be abandoned; there will no longer be 'individual exemptions' at all, only decisions as to whether Article 81, in its entirety, applies to an agreement or not. The system of block exemption will continue, however. The second strand to the proposal is that the Commission should abandon its monopoly of decision-making under Article 81(3).

The Commission notes[14] the workload and expense involved in having to notify under the existing system, but says that notification proved useful 'as long as the interpretation of Article 81 and in particular of paragraph 3 was uncertain.'[15] In a system of *ex post* control, undertakings would have to make their own assessment of the compatibility of their restrictive practices with Community law, which would lighten their administrative burden, but would require them to take on added responsibility[16].

The Commission says that in the new system 'undertakings' legal certainty will remain at a globally satisfactory level, and will in some respects even be strengthened'[17]. Among the reasons given for this statement are that, after forty years of the competition rules, the conditions for the application of Article 81(3) have been largely clarified[18]; that a new generation of block exemptions with a wider scope of application is about to come into being[19]; that the Commission will adopt a more economic approach to Article 81(1) when dealing with individual cases (so that Article 81(3) would not be relevant to the analysis of many cases where there is no market power); and that there will be 'preventive and corrective mechanisms' to ensure consistent and uniform application of Community law by national authorities and courts.

11 *White Paper*, paras 55-73, where the Commission considers the respective merits of the authorisation system and a directly applicable exception system.
12 Ibid, para 69.
13 Ibid, paras 79-81: such cases would be brought within the regime for dealing with concentrations, including 'full-function joint ventures'; see ch 21, p 748-751.
14 Ibid, para 76.
15 Ibid, para 77.
16 Ibid.
17 Ibid, para 78.
18 See however ch 4, pp 125-128 on the debate surrounding the criteria in Article 81(3), and the suggestion that a narrow approach to those criteria will be needed if the White Paper proposals are to be implemented.
19 Regulation 2790/99 on vertical agreements (see ch 16, pp 567-591), Regulation 2658/2000 on specialisation agreements (see ch 15, pp 517-520) and Regulation 2659/2000 on research and development agreements (see ch 15, pp 510-515) are the first examples of these 'new style' block exemptions.

(B)   Decentralised application of the competition rules

There will be a new division of responsibilities. The Commission will continue to determine competition policy in various ways[20]. It will retain the sole right to propose legislative texts, regulations (including block exemptions), notices and guidelines; and will continue to adopt prohibition decisions, which will be of great importance as precedents. As the Commission will be concentrating on the most serious restrictions of competition rather than scrutinising notified agreements which tend to be innocuous, the number of individual prohibition decisions can be expected to increase substantially[1]. However, the Commission will no longer grant individual exemptions: the whole point is that the new system will not require a constitutive act by the Commission in order to declare the prohibition of Article 81(1) inapplicable. Nevertheless the Commission says that it will sometimes adopt decisions that are not prohibition decisions, for example where new questions arise and a declaration of the Commission's position in relation to them is needed[2].

The Commission proposes[3] a new kind of decision, terminating proceedings that would otherwise have led to a prohibition, where suitable commitments have been offered by the parties. The possibility of fines and periodic penalty payments would have to be introduced in order to ensure that such commitments are complied with. The Commission does not say so specifically, but there is an obvious precedent for such decisions in Article 8(2) of the ECMR[4].

The Commission wishes to see NCAs play an enhanced rôle in the application of the competition rules[5]. It notes that, although there has been pragmatic cooperation between itself and the NCAs to date, this has been limited as a result of its exclusive right to grant exemptions. For the new system to work, each NCA will have to be given the power, as a matter of domestic law, to apply Community law.

The national courts are also to play an enhanced rôle in the application of the competition rules[6]. The Commission has for a long time been keen to see more enforcement of Articles 81 and 82 in national courts and this is seen in the 1993 *Cooperation Notice*[7]. The inability of national courts to exempt agreements under Article 81(3) has been a major obstacle and there has been relatively little recourse to national courts. With a directly applicable exception the Commission says that parties to agreements will be able to obtain a judgment from national courts both on Article 81(1) and Article 81(3), and this will provide them with greater legal certainty; furthermore third parties will be able to obtain damages more quickly, without the national action being stayed pending a decision of the Commission on the application of Article 81(3). The judgments of national courts

20   *White Paper*, paras 83-90.
1   Ibid, para 87.
2   Ibid, paras 88-89.
3   Ibid, para 90.
4   Council Regulation 4064/89 OJ [1989] L 395/1, corrected version OJ [1990] L 257/13, as amended by Council Regulation 1310/97 OJ [1997] L 180/1; on commitments under the ECMR see ch 21, pp 784-787.
5   *White Paper*, paras 91-98; also Temple Lang 'The Duties of National Authorities under Community Constitutional Law' (1998) 23 ELRev 109; Temple Lang 'Decentralised Application of Community Competition Law' (1999) 22(4) World Competition 3; Temple Lang 'The Duties of Cooperation of National Authorities and Courts under Article 10': Two More Reflections' (2001) 26 ELRev 84.
6   On the enforcement of Articles 81 and 82 in national courts generally see ch 8, p 260ff.
7   See p 248, n 3 above.

would be *res judicata* (subject to any appeal), and would be entitled to recognition in all other Member States of the EU and Contracting States of the EEA under the Brussels and Lugano Conventions respectively[8].

Paragraphs 101 to 107 of the White Paper address the need to maintain consistency and uniform application of the competition rules. In one of the less convincing passages of the document, the Commission sets out various principles for the resolution of conflicts that, it claims, should allow any problems that may arise to be resolved. The Commission suggests that mechanisms should be set up to buttress the need for consistency. First, NCAs would have to inform the Commission of the initiation of proceedings or of the withdrawal of the benefit of block exemption[9]. The Commission would be able to take a case out of the jurisdiction of an NCA where appropriate. NCAs would also be obliged to inform the Commission of any proceedings under national law that might have implications for Community proceedings. The Advisory Committee on Restrictive Practices and Monopolies would have a reinforced rôle and become a full-scale forum in which important cases would be discussed irrespective of the competition authority dealing with them[10]. The Commission proposes that national courts would be obliged by regulation to make the Commission aware of any proceedings involving the Community competition rules, a precedent for which exists in paragraph 96 of the German Act against Restrictions of Competition, which obliges the German courts to inform the Bundeskartellamt of any proceedings[11]. The Commission would be given the right to intervene as *amicus curiae* in domestic proceedings, and the rules in the 1993 *Cooperation Notice* would also be incorporated in the regulation amending Regulation 17/62.

(C) Implications of the proposals

(i) Responses to the White Paper

The White Paper triggered a wide-ranging debate. Responses were submitted to the Commission by individuals, companies, trade associations, Community and national institutions and by the Member States themselves. The German Government issued a statement[12] setting out its doubts about the proposals, questioning the very legality of the suggestion that Article 81(3) could be directly applicable and that notification should be eliminated. The European Parliament investigated and presented a report on 30 November 1999 which was broadly supportive of the proposals[13]. The Economic and Social Committee (ECOSOC) wholeheartedly supported the reform proposals[14]. In the United Kingdom the CBI's Position Paper of 29 September 1999 was critical of many features of the

---

8 *Brussels Convention on Jurisdiction and the Enforcement of Judgments in Civil and Commercial Matters* (1968); *Lugano Convention* OJ [1988] L 391/1.

9 Provision has been made for withdrawal of block exemption by NCAs by Article 1(4) of Regulation 1215/1999 OJ [1999] L 148/1, amending Article 7 of Regulation 19/65, where an agreement has a detrimental effect on competition in a 'distinct market' in that Member State; Article 6 of the new block exemption on vertical agreements, Regulation 2790/1999 OJ [1999] L 336/21, [2000] 4 CMLR 398, expressly provides for this.

10 *White Paper*, para 106; on the Advisory Committee, see ch 2, p 51.

11 Ibid, para 107.

12 *Statement by the Government of the Federal Republic of Germany*, November 1999.

13 *Report on the Commission White Paper on modernisation of the rules implementing Articles [81] and [82] of the EC Treaty* Final A5-0069/1999.

14 ECOSOC Opinion of 29 March 2001, COM(2000)582 final.

proposals, in particular on decentralisation and the abolition of notification. The House of Lords Select Committee on the European Communities published a wide-ranging Report and accompanying evidence on 29 February 2000[15] ; this Report acknowledged the 'bold and imaginative initiative' of the Commission[16] , but concluded that much more work needs to be done before the proposals could be implemented: otherwise, adoption of the White Paper would 'involve a great step into the unknown'[17] . The Report also raised the question of whether the time might not be approaching when Article 81 itself might be reformulated, so as to make it more amenable to application by national judges[18] .

(ii) Specific issues

A number of issues arise from the White Paper and the responses to it[19] . The first is whether the proposal to make Article 81(3) directly applicable is lawful under the Treaty at all: some have argued that Article 81(3) can only ever be applied by virtue of a constitutive act, and that the system established by Regulation 17/62 cannot be reversed. A second issue is whether the criteria of Article 81(3) are themselves capable of being directly applicable: this raises the question, discussed in chapter 4, of what Article 81(3) is really about: a balancing of beneficial effects on efficiency against the restrictive effects on competition; or a more wide-ranging trade-off between competition policy on the one hand and other Community policies on the other[20] . Thirdly, some commentators have expressed doubts as to whether national courts are appropriate fora for determinations on the competition rules generally and more specifically on the criteria in Article 81(3), and how they will cope under the new system. In considering whether national courts are appropriate fora for making decisions under Article 81(3), the problem is not that economic decision-making is too difficult for judges; the issue of whether there is a restriction of competition, which is already within the ambit of national judges given that Article 81(1) is directly applicable, in itself demands economic analysis, which may be more complex than the application of Article 81(3) in its narrow 'efficiency' sense. The point is rather that, if the question asked by Article 81(3) requires the consideration of *non-competition matters*, it is arguable that this needs a public body to do it because the nature of the decision, which involves a balancing of public and private interests and of the requirements of different Community policies, is unsuited to judicial determination. In the UK exemptions under the Competition Act 1998 in the UK are given by the DGFT, not the courts[1] . There seems little judicial enthusiasm in the UK for applying Article 81(3)[2] . A fourth issue is the maintenance of consistency of decisions across the Community in the event of further decentralisation, including the application of Article 81(3), to Member States.

---

15 HL 33 (2000); this document can be found on the internet at http://www.publications.parliament.uk/pa/ld199900/ldselect/ldeucom/33/3301.htm.
16 Ibid, para 145.
17 Ibid, para 147.
18 Ibid, para 149.
19 Each of these issues is explored in some detail in See Whish and Sufrin 'Community Competition Law: Notifications and Individual Exemption – Goodbye to all that', p 246, n 19 above.
20 See ch 4, pp 125-128.
1 Competition Acy 1998, s 4.
2 See eg Eady J in *Williams v Welsh Rugby Union* [1999] Eu LR 195 and the evidence of Ferris J and Laddie J to the House of Lords Select Committee, HL 33 (2000), para 59.

Perhaps most controversial of all has been the proposal to scrap notifications altogether. The elimination of *mandatory* notification if exemption is to be granted has generally been welcomed; however the removal of the right to notify at all is another matter. This is more than a procedural alteration: it involves a fundamental change in the way that undertakings operate in relation to the competition rules. Hitherto the problem has been that, for most agreements, an individual exemption required pre-notification to the Commission, and yet the Commission does not have the resources to deal with the volume of notifications it receives. The majority of agreements receive nothing more than a comfort letter. The system is flawed, but at least it offers a relatively safe haven. Under the proposals in the White Paper, notification will be abolished altogether: sending in a Form A/B to the Commission and relying on immunity from being fined[3] will no longer be available. In the words of the Commission at paragraph 77 of the White Paper:

'undertakings would have to make their own assessment of the compatibility of their restrictive practices with Community law, in the light of the legislation in force and the case law'.

The abolition of notification will present significant challenges to companies and their advisers. The position will be closer to that in the US, where companies have to be more self-reliant, or else reliant on being able to sue their lawyers who may have reached a wrong judgment on the compliance of an agreement with the Sherman Act or other relevant statutes.

The degree to which the directly applicable exception will create a diminution of legal certainty for undertakings should not be entirely dismissed. The Commission itself recognises that, in some cases, a decision *ex ante* may be required, for example where substantial investment is to be made in a particular case and legal certainty on the compliance of the agreement is needed: for this reason it proposes that partial-function joint ventures would be dealt with in accordance with the procedures of the ECMR, where the system is one of prior notification followed by a binding decision. The Commission suggests this because 'operations of this kind generally require substantial investment and far-reaching integration of operations which makes it difficult for them to unravel afterwards at the behest of a competition authority'. This is an admission that legal certainty is reduced without a prior authorisation system. Given this favoured treatment of partial-function joint ventures it can be predicted that a new tactic will emerge: the structuring, where possible, of horizontal transactions not covered by block exemptions so that they can be notified under the ECMR, which will not only deliver clearance to many transactions, but clearance, in most cases, within four weeks[4].

The Commission says at paragraph 88 of the White Paper that it would still take positive decisions 'in the general interest' in certain cases, where a transaction raises a 'new' question and where 'it may be necessary to provide the market with guidance'. This recognises the important function which individual exemptions have played in the past in developing competition policy. 'Positive decisions' of this kind would be able to contain commitments entered into by the parties in the same way that commitments can be attached to decisions under Article 6(1)(b) of the ECMR. These decisions would be of a declaratory nature, and would have the same legal effect as a negative clearance at present.

3   This immunity is provided by Article 15(5) of Regulation 17/62; it can be removed by decision under Article 15(6); see further ch 4, p 138.
4   On the procedural timetables under the ECMR see ch 21, pp 768-770.

(D)   The Commission's draft regulation

The Commission published its *Proposal for a Council Regulation* to replace Regulation 17/62 and to implement the modernisation proposals in September 2000[5]. It is inevitable that alterations will be made to the proposed regulation prior to its eventual adoption; because of this it is not intended to discuss it extensively at this stage: the reader will need to follow the progress of the regulation on DG COMP's website and in the periodical literature. However it may be helpful to point out some of the more significant aspects of the draft regulation as published in September 2000. It contains 11 chapters.

(i)   Chapter I: principles

Article 1 of the proposed regulation is headed 'direct applicability' and provides that agreements caught by Article 81(1) which do not satisfy the conditions of Article 81(3), and the abuse of a dominant position contrary to Article 82, shall be prohibited, no prior decision to that effect being required. Article 2 states the existing law on the burden of proof: that a party alleging an infringement must prove that Article 81(1) or Article 82 are being infringed, but that undertakings claiming that the conditions of Article 81(3) are satisfied bear the burden of proving that this is the case.

Article 3 contains one of the most controversial and complicated proposals of all, not mentioned in the *White Paper*. The suggestion is that, where an agreement or practice is caught by Article 81 or Article 82, 'Community competition law shall apply to the exclusion of national competition law'. The neatness and attraction of this proposal are obvious: there would no longer be any need to determine the relationship of Community and national law, since there would be no dual application[6]; consistent application of the law would be promoted; and a 'simplicity' would be injected into the law. However there are domestic rules of competition law that are, in some circumstances, more effective or more responsive to the conditions of the market in individual Member States which, arguably, should not be excluded by Community law; an obvious example is the UK Fair Trading Act 1973, which contains provisions for the investigation of scale and complex monopolies[7]. It may be that this radical proposal will be dropped from the eventual regulation, or at least that a more nuanced version of it will be adopted.

(ii)   Chapter II: powers

Articles 4 to 6 deal with the powers of the Commission, the NCAs and national courts respectively. Article 4(2) contains a somewhat surprising idea, that the Commission will have the power, by regulation, to require that certain types of agreement may be made registrable; penalties may be imposed where registration is not effected. This would mean that, if the Commission were to be concerned about a particular type of agreement, it could require them to be registered; it would then have the opportunity to adopt a policy on the type of agreement in

5   COM(2000)583 final, OJ [2000] C 365 E/28, [2000] 5 CMLR 1148.
6   The discussion in ch 9, pp 321-333 on the relationship between EC and national law would become otiose.
7   See ch 11.

question. UK lawyers, nostalgic for the Restrictive Trade Practices Act 1976, will be reminded of the practice of 'calling up' services agreements and information agreements under that legislation. It is unlikely that the Commission would actually make use of this power except in highly unusual circumstances. Article 5 provides that NCAs shall have the power to apply Article 81(1), Article 81(3) and Article 82 in individual cases. In some Member States – including the UK – the domestic competition authorities do not at present have the power to apply the EC competition rules; under the proposed new system enforcement of EC law by NCAs will be an important part of the enforcement mechanism, consistent with the policy of decentralisation. Article 36 of the draft regulation requires Member States to designate a competition authority for this purpose. Article 6 provides specifically that national courts will have the power to apply Article 81(3).

(iii)   Chapter III: Commission decisions

Articles 7 to 10 deal with Commission decisions. Article 7 provides for decisions finding and terminating infringements. The most interesting point is that Article 7(1) specifically provides that the Commission may adopt 'remedies of a structural nature'; there is no specific power of this kind in Regulation 17/62[8]. Article 8 enables the Commission to adopt interim measures, and Article 9 provides for the adoption of decisions subject to commitments: this replicates the system in the ECMR, which permits the clearance of a merger subject to modification of the transaction[9]. Article 10 provides for the Commission to adopt a 'finding of inapplicability': such a decision could be made under both Article 81 and Article 82. Decisions of this kind could be adopted, for example, where the Commission considers that there is uncertainty about the lawfulness of a particular type of agreement or practice; by adopting a decision it could provide legal certainty to the business and legal communities. It is important to appreciate however that this type of decision would be adopted at the volition of the Commission; the current system of notification to the Commission requesting a decision will no longer exist.

(iv)   Chapter IV: cooperation with national authorities and courts

Articles 11 to 16 deal with cooperation with NCAs and national courts. Article 11(3) requires NCAs to inform the Commission of cases in which they are proposing to apply Articles 81 and 82, and Article 11(4) provides that they must consult with the Commission before adopting a decision. An important provision is Article 11(6) which states that, if the Commission initiates proceedings, the NCAs will be relieved of their competence to apply Articles 81 and 82. This is one of the ways in which the Commission will seek to avoid the uneven application of the competition rules across the Community, and it means that it could assert exclusive competence in relation, for example, to a cross-border cartel. Article 12 provides for the exchange of information between the Commission and NCAs: this is to be possible 'notwithstanding any national provision to the contrary'. Article 12(2) enshrines the rule in *Spanish Banks* in the regulation[10]. Article 13

8   See pp 236-237 above.
9   See ch 21, pp 784-787.
10 See p 219, n 14 above.

contains provisions to avoid the duplication of investigations, while Article 14 explains the rôle of the Advisory Committee on Restrictive Practices and Monopolies: an innovation, in Article 14(4), is the possibility of the Committee to consult by written procedure rather than by physically meeting. Article 15 deals with cooperation with national courts. As a result of Article 15(2) they will be obliged to send to the Commission copies of judgments applying Articles 81 and 82 within one month of delivery; Article 15(3) will enable the Commission to submit written or oral observations to national courts. Article 16 provides that NCAs and national courts must use every effort to avoid decisions that conflict with those of the Commission.

There has been much concern about the possibility that the modernisation proposals will lead to inconsistent enforcement of the competition rules; Chapter IV of the draft regulation makes a start towards addressing these complex issues, but it can be anticipated that more detailed proposals will be developed before the new system enters into force.

(v)   Chapter V: powers of investigation

Articles 17 to 21 deal with powers of investigation. Article 17 contains the power, currently found in Article 12 of Regulation 17/62, to conduct inquiries into particular sectors of the economy. Article 18 is the equivalent of Article 11 of Regulation 17/62, which provides for requests for information. Article 19 contains a novel idea, which is that the Commission will have the power to interview 'any natural or legal person' in order to ask questions relating to the subject-matter of an investigation and to record the answers. The draft regulation does not provide any penalties for non-attendance or for giving incorrect or misleading answers, and there is no discussion of issues such as privilege against self-incrimination and the right to silence. It is perhaps surprising that 'any' person may be asked to be interviewed: one might have expected this power to be limited to senior officers of an undertaking. It seems desirable that the regulation, when adopted, should explain in greater detail how this power is to be exercised.

Article 20 contains the power, currently found in Article 14 of Regulation 17/62, to conduct 'on-the-spot' investigations. The most notable change from the current law is that the Commission will be able to inspect the homes of directors, managers and other members of staff of undertakings, in so far as there is a suspicion that business records are being kept there. Clearly the exercise of this power will raise important questions in relation to human rights, but it is hard to object in principle to this power, given that examples have been found in the past of undertakings adopting a deliberate policy of filing certain documents at home as an insurance policy against a dawn raid on business premises. Article 21 deals with investigations by NCAs. Article 21(1) provides for one NCA to conduct an investigation on behalf of another one.

(vi)   Chapter VI: penalties

Articles 22 and 23 deal with penalties. Of particular importance is the proposal that fines for offences such as the provision of incorrect or misleading information and other procedural offences of this kind will be much higher than at present: 1% of the preceding year's turnover in the case of fines and 5% of average daily turnover in the case of periodic penalty payments. Article 22(4) specifically provides that, where a trade association is insolvent, fines can be imposed on undertakings that were members of it at the time of the infringement.

(vii)   *ChapterVII: limitation periods*

Articles 24 and 25 contain the rules on limitation periods; these are currently to be found in Regulation 2988/74[11].

(viii)   *ChapterVIII: hearings and professional secrecy*

Articles 26 and 27 deal with hearings and professional secrecy. Article 26(2) specifically acknowledges the right of access to the file[12].

(ix)   *Chapter IX: block exemptions*

The vires for block exemptions will be contained in Articles 28 to 30 of the new regulation. This is a useful 'tidying up' of the current position, in which there are a number of different enabling regulations, some of which have been materially amended over the years[13].

(x)   *Chapter X: general provisions*

Articles 31 to 34 contain general provisions. Article 33 excludes from the scope of the new regulation those maritime and air transport services that are not subject to any of the existing implementing regulations[14]. Article 34 gives the Commission the power to take measures in order to apply the regulation, for example as to the registration of agreements pursuant to Article 4(2) or the form of complaints.

(xi)   *Chapter XI: transitional and final provisions*

Articles 35 to 42 contain transitional and final provisions. Article 35(1) provides that all existing notifications to the Commission shall lapse, as will any existing individual exemptions. The latter proposition is controversial, since it removes the benefit of a privilege that has already been conferred on the recipients of the exemption; on the other hand it is consistent with the concept of Article 81(3) being directly applicable, rather than requiring the constitutive act of the Commission. In practice there are relatively few individual exemptions extant; a pragmatic solution might be to allow existing individual exemptions to remain in place, notwithstanding the intellectual inconsistency between this idea and the direct applicability of Article 81(3). Article 36 requires Member States to designate the domestic competition authority responsible for the application of

---

11   OJ [1974] L 319/1.
12   On access to the file see pp 233-234 above.
13   See ch 4, pp 141-146.
14   See above.

Articles 81 and 82. An interesting issue in the UK is whether the designated authority should be the Director General of Fair Trading alone, or whether the sectoral regulators should also be designated coterminously with their powers to enforce the Competition Act 1998: the latter solution would seem to be a sensible solution. Article 41 provides for the repeal of Regulation 17/62 and the various Council Regulations conferring on the Commission the vires to adopt block exemptions.

(E)   Timing and conclusion

The Commission's intention at the time of its *White Paper* was that the regulation to replace Regulation 17/62 would be adopted by the end of 2001; this would mean that the new system would enter into force a year later, at the beginning of 2003. At the time of writing (July 2001), however, it seems that this timetable may be optimistic. It would appear that the replacement for Regulation 17/62 is unlikely to be adopted before the middle of June 2002 at the earliest, and that the new system may not come into effect until the start of 2004.

CHAPTER 8

Articles 81 and 82: enforcement in the courts of Member States

I. INTRODUCTION[1]

Article 81(1) and Article 82 are directly applicable and produce direct effects: they give rise to rights and obligations on the part of individuals which national courts have a duty to safeguard[2]. Agreements that infringe Article 81(1) and that do not satisfy the terms of Article 81(3) are void as a result of Article 81(2). It follows that it is open to one of the parties to an agreement to argue that a contractual obligation is unenforceable because it infringes Article 81, and that a judge of a national court must rule accordingly where an infringement is demonstrated; Article 82 does not contain a specific provision on voidness, but it seems clear that a dominant undertaking could not enforce a contractual term that amounts to an abuse of its dominant position[3]. A third party harmed by an infringement of the competition rules may bring an action in a domestic court for an injunction, to bring the harm to an end, and (probably) for damages for any loss that it has suffered. This chapter will consider the effect that infringements of Articles 81 and 82 have on the enforceability of agreements in sections 2 and 3; section 4 will consider the position of third parties.

The Commission has for a long time been eager that Articles 81 and 82 should be applied more frequently in national courts, thereby relieving it of some of the burden of enforcement: 'enforcement' for this purpose would include not only the award of injunctions and/or damages to third parties harmed by anti-competitive behaviour, but also declarations that anti-competitive agreements are void. The Commission lacks the resources to police the competition rules across a Community of 15 Member States with well over 350 million inhabitants;

1 See generally on this issue *EEC Competition Rules in National Courts* (Nomos Verlagsgesellschaft, Baden-Baden, ed Behrens), which surveys the enforcement of the competition rules in several of the Member States: see Part I, UK and Italy (1992); Part II, Benelux and Ireland (1994); Part III, Germany (1996); and Part IV, France (1997); Braakman *The Application of Articles 81 and 82 of the EC Treaty by National Courts in the Member States* (European Commission, 1997); Kerse *EC Antitrust Procedure* (Sweet & Maxwell, 4th ed, 1998) ch 10; Jones *Private Enforcement of Antitrust Law in the EU, UK and USA* (Oxford University Press, 1999); Smith *Competition Law: Enforcement & Procedure* (Butterworths, 2001) chs 17-20; Bellamy and Child *European Community Law of Competition* (Sweet & Maxwell, 5th ed, 2001) ch 10.
2 Case 127/73 *BRT v SABAM* [1974] ECR 51, [1974] 2 CMLR 238.
3 See pp 275-276 below.

the problem will intensify if, as intended, at least 10 new Member States accede to the European Union in the first decade of the new millennium. The Commission is strongly of the view that it should concentrate its efforts on prosecuting serious infringements of the law, while also developing competition policy and legislation and engaging in dialogue at the international level in order to deal with the complex issues arising from an increasingly global economy. Private enforcement of the competition rules has a part to play in enabling it to achieve these objectives.

The Commission has produced important guidance in its *Notice on Cooperation between National Courts and the Commission in Applying Articles [81] and [82] of the EC Treaty*[4] ('the *Cooperation Notice*'); in this Notice the Commission has indicated the circumstances in which, in its view, it would be appropriate for a national court to deal with a case, and the extent to which it (the Commission) might be able to assist with questions arising during the proceedings. In a companion *Notice on Cooperation between National Competition Authorities and the Commission in Handling Cases Falling Within the Scope of Articles [81] or [82] of the EC Treaty*[5] the Commission has also encouraged national competition authorities to become more involved in the enforcement of the competition rules. Both Notices are part of a movement towards the decentralisation of the enforcement of the competition rules. While it is probably true to say that there has been less litigation of the competition rules in domestic courts than might have been anticipated (and than had been hoped for on the part of the Commission), there can be no doubt that the combination of the Commission's determination to achieve decentralisation, the proposals contained in its *White Paper on Modernisation of the Rules Implementing Articles [81] and [82] of the EC Treaty*[6] and the fact that society is more litigious anyway, means that there will be a lot more cases in the future. Competition law litigation is here to stay[7]. Commissioner Monti reaffirmed the Commission's desire for more private enforcement of the competition rules in a speech to the Sixth EU Competition Law and Policy Workshop in Florence in June 2001[8].

2.   THE ENFORCEABILITY OF AGREEMENTS: ARTICLE 81[9]

(A)   Article 81(2)

(i)   *The sanction of voidness*

Many systems of competition law deploy an important sanction, in addition to the imposition of fines, in order to persuade undertakings to obey the law: the sanction of voidness. Article 81(2) of the EC Treaty provides that an agreement

---

4   OJ [1993] C 39/6, [1993] 5 CMLR 95.
5   OJ [1997] C 313/3, [1997] 5 CMLR 884.
6   Commission Programme No 99/027, OJ [1999] C 132/1, [1999] 5 CMLR 208; see ch 7, pp 246-258.
7   This raises the interesting question of the extent to which a court asked to adjudicate upon competition law cases should be assisted by economists, as to which see Brunt 'Antitrust in the Courts: The Role of Economics and Economists' [1998] Fordham Corporate Law Institute (ed Hawk), ch 20.
8   The speech is available at http://europa.eu.int/comm/competition/speeches/index_speeches_by_the_commissioner.html.
9   This and the following section are based in part on the author's essay 'The Enforceability of Agreements under EC and UK Competition Law' in Rose (ed) *Lex Mercatoria: Essays on International Commercial Law in Honour of Francis Reynolds* (LLP, 2000) ch 15.

that restricts competition in the sense of Article 81(1) and that does not satisfy the terms of Article 81(3) is void. The sanction of voidness may not always be a very real one: the members of a price-fixing or a market-sharing cartel would not normally think of trying to enforce their agreement in a court. Their main concern will be to conceal the cartel from the Commission, although it has considerable powers to unearth this type of practice[10] and to penalise the recalcitrant firms[11]. In other cases, however, the sanction of voidness may be much more significant. If a patentee grants a licence of a patent, it will calculate carefully what rate of royalties the licensee should pay and protracted negotiations may take place to settle the other terms of the bargain, for example on the quantities to be produced, the areas in which the products are to be sold and the treatment and ownership of any improvements made by the licensee. For its part, the licensee will often have been granted an exclusive territory in which to manufacture and sell. If it transpires that certain aspects of the licence are void and unenforceable, this will undermine the deal struck between the parties. The same would be true of an exclusive purchasing term imposed by a supplier on a distributor, as typically occurs in agreements for the sale and purchase of beer and petrol; and of non-competition covenants imposed, for example, when a vendor sells a business as a going concern to a purchaser. In these cases the threat that competition law poses is not normally that the Commission or some other competition authority will impose a fine, but that a key term of a contract will be unenforceable in commercial litigation. It will be noted from this that the sanction of voidness, as a general proposition, impacts not on serious infringements of the competition rules, such as the operation of cartels, but on more innocuous agreements where the harm to competition is much less obvious; this is a powerful reason for urging competition authorities to adopt a 'realistic' approach to the application of Article 81(1) and its progeny in the Member States to agreements[12].

(ii) Eco Swiss China Time Ltd v Benetton

Judges tend to be hostile by instinct to what may be seen as technical – even scurrilous – attempts to avoid contractual obligations by invoking points of competition law. However the ECJ's judgment in *Eco Swiss China Time Ltd v Benetton*[13] has confirmed how significant the sanction of voidness is considered to be in the legal system of the Community: where an agreement infringes Article 81(1), voidness is an important consequence. At the risk of over-simplification, the ECJ was asked by the Dutch Supreme Court to determine whether the competition rules in the Treaty could be considered to be rules of public policy: on this question turned the possibility of an appeal being brought against an arbitral award[14]. The ECJ was quite clear:

'36 However, according to Article 3(g) of the EC Treaty (now, after amendment, Article 3(1)(g) EC), Article 81 EC (ex Article 85) constitutes a fundamental provision which is essential for the accomplishment of the tasks entrusted to the Community and, in particular, for the functioning of

10 See ch 7, pp 219-226 .
11 Ibid, pp 237-239 .
12 See ch 3, pp 98-103, in particular on what is meant by an agreement having as its 'effect' the restriction of competition.
13 Case C-126/97 [1999] ECR I-3055, [2000] 5 CMLR 816.
14 The case is discussed further at pp 273-274 below.

the internal market. The importance of such a provision led the framers of the Treaty to provide expressly, in Article 81(2) EC (ex Article 85(2)), that any agreements or decisions prohibited pursuant to that Article are to be automatically void.

37. It follows that where its domestic rules of procedure require a national court to grant an application for annulment of an arbitration award where such an application is founded on failure to observe national rules of public policy, it must also grant such an application where it is founded on failure to comply with the prohibition laid down in Article 81(1) EC (ex Article 85(1))'.

(B)   The 'problem' of Article 81(3) and the Commission's rôle in relation to individual exemptions[15]

As has been explained in chapter 4 the Commission has sole power to grant individual exemptions under Article 81(3); this is a result of the 'monopoly' conferred upon it by Article 9(1) of Regulation 17/62[16]. This monopoly has frequently caused problems for national courts; they are permitted to apply Article 81(1), but cannot grant an individual exemption under Article 81(3). The same problem does not arise in relation to block exemptions, since national courts are able to apply them[17]; literally thousands of agreements, the enforceability of which might otherwise be in doubt, are drafted in such a way that they benefit from the 'safe haven' of a block exemption. The difficulty in relation to agreements needing individual exemption would be avoided if they were 'provisionally valid' until the time when the Commission decides not to grant an exemption, since in that case a national court would be able to enforce the agreement unless and until the Commission reaches a contrary conclusion; however it is clear that 'new' agreements do not benefit from provisional validity[18]. What this means is that new agreements that are caught by Article 81(1) and that need individual exemption under Article 81(3) are valid only if a favourable decision is taken by the Commission in respect of them, although that validity may be conferred retrospectively[19]; if, however, the Commission does not adopt a favourable decision, the agreement will have been void *ab initio* (from the beginning). An additional complicating factor is that some agreements can benefit from individual exemption only where they have been notified to the Commission; others can be

15   The problems about to be discussed will be eliminated if the Commission's *Modernisation* proposals are implemented, since its monopoly over individual exemptions and the process of notification to the Commission will both be abolished: see ch 7, pp 246-258.
16   See ch 4, p 136.
17   Case 59/77 *De Bloos v Bouyer* [1977] ECR 2359, [1978] 1 CMLR 511; Case 170/83 *Hydrotherm v Compact* [1984] ECR 2999, [1985] 3 CMLR 224.
18   That is to say agreements entered into after Regulation 17/62 came into effect or, in the case of Member States that have joined the European Community since it was originally formed, agreements entered into after their accession; 'old' agreements entered into prior to Regulation 17/62 do benefit from provisional validity: see Case C–234/89 *Delimitis v Henninger Bräu* [1991] ECR I-935, [1992] 5 CMLR 210, para 49; Case C-39/96 *Koninklijke Vereeniging ter Bevordering van de Belangen des Boekhandels v Free Record Shop BV* [1997] ECR I-2303, [1997] 5 CMLR 521: for comment on the latter case see Travers 'The Protracted Longevity of Provisional Validity' (1998) 23 ELRev 83; provisional validity is probably also enjoyed by 'accession' agreements, although the point has not been dealt with by the ECJ; on the provisional validity of old and accession agreements see *Kerse* paras 10.05-10.11; *Smith* paras 18.06-18.10.
19   Regulation 17/62, Article 6(1).

granted whether notified or not: vertical agreements are included in the latter category as a result of an amendment to Article 4(2) of Regulation 17/62 effected by Regulation 1216/99[20].

The difficulty that arises in relation to the Commission's monopoly over the grant of individual exemptions is that the ECJ has held, in *Delimitis v Henninger Bräu*[1], that a national court has a duty, deriving from Article 10 EC (ex Article 5), not to reach a conclusion that would be inconsistent with that of the Commission. The point has been restated and explained further in the ECJ's judgment in *Masterfoods Ltd v HB Ice Cream Ltd*[2]. The predicament for a national court is that, if it were to strike down an agreement on the basis that it infringes Article 81(1), this might prove to be inconsistent with an eventual decision of the Commission to grant an exemption; on the other hand a national court has an obligation to enforce Article 81(1), and may feel that it ought to condemn an agreement even though, technically, it may be possible for the Commission to exempt it.

The position of a national court varies according to whether an agreement is one that must be notified in order to benefit from individual exemption, or whether it is one that can be exempted whether it has been notified or not.

(i) Agreements that must be notified in order to benefit from individual exemption

(A)   THE POSITION IF THE PARTIES HAVE NOTIFIED THEIR AGREEMENT   Where the parties have notified their agreement, the Commission has exclusive competence to decide the case; the national court cannot apply Article 81(3), and so must await the Commission's decision. However the court may decide to allow preliminary steps to be taken in preparation of the case for trial[3].

(B)   THE POSITION IF THE PARTIES HAVE NOT NOTIFIED THEIR AGREEMENT.   Where a national court is asked to enforce an agreement that needs to be, but has not been, notified for individual exemption[4], it has the following possibilities open to it:

- if it is obvious that the agreement is not caught by Article 81(1), the court may continue with its proceedings and rule on the agreement in issue[5]: this is stated specifically at paragraph 23 of the Commission's *Cooperation Notice*:
- if the agreement comes entirely within a block exemption, the court should apply the block exemption[6]: this is stated at paragraph 26 of the *Cooperation Notice*;
- if it is obvious that the agreement infringes Article 81(1) and that it will not benefit from a block exemption, the court may continue with its proceedings[7]: this is stated at paragraph 28 of the *Cooperation Notice*;
- if the agreement falls outside a block exemption, albeit only to a marginal extent, there is no discretion in the national court to authorise the agreement[8];

---

20   See ch 4, pp 137-138.
1   Case C-234/89 [1991] ECR I-935, [1992] 5 CMLR 210.
2   Case C-344/98 [2001] 4 CMLR 449, [2001] All ER (EC) 130, para 51.
3   See pp 265-266 below on *MTV Europe v BMG Records*.
4   See para 28 of the *Cooperation Notice*.
5   Case C–234/89 *Delimitis v Henninger Bräu* [1992] ECR I-935, [1992] 5 CMLR 210, para 50.
6   Ibid, para 46.
7   Ibid, para 50.
8   Ibid, paras 39 and 46.

- if the national court has doubts about the application of Article 81(1) or about the interpretation of a block exemption, it could seek information from the Commission about any proceedings it may have in motion and it could also ask it for any economic and legal information which it can supply: the Commission has a duty under Article 10 of the Treaty to cooperate with the judicial authorities in Member States in this way[9]. In the *Cooperation Notice* the Commission specifically mentions the possibility of a stay in paragraph 22, and explains ways in which the court may seek the assistance of the Commission in paragraphs 33 to 44;
- the national court could make a reference to the ECJ under Article 234 (ex Article 177) of the Treaty[10]. The House of Lords would be obliged to do so under the provisions of Article 234(3), unless the case is one of acte clair as explained by the ECJ in *CILFIT v Minister of Health*[11]; the *Cooperation Notice* specifically mentions this possibility in paragraphs 22 and 32;
- 'old' and 'accession'[12] agreements benefit from provisional validity and so can be enforced until the Commission has taken a decision against them: the *Cooperation Notice* deals with this at paragraph 31.

(ii)   Agreements that can be exempted whether notified or not

(A)   THE POSITION IF THE PARTIES HAVE NOTIFIED THEIR AGREEMENT.   The national court would have to await the decision of the Commission, as in *(i)*(A) above.

(B)   THE POSITION IF THE PARTIES HAVE NOT NOTIFIED THEIR AGREEMENT.   Where a national court is asked to enforce an agreement that can be exempted whether notified or not, and which has not been notified, it has the following possibilities open to it:
- if it appears that the agreement does not infringe Article 81(1), the national court could proceed[13]: paragraph 23 of the *Cooperation Notice* states this specifically;
- if it is obvious that the agreement infringes Article 81(1) and that there is no chance of the Commission granting an individual exemption, regard being had to the Commission's previous decisions, the national court may continue with its proceedings and rule on the agreement in issue[14]: this is stated specifically in paragraph 30 of the *Cooperation Notice*;
- if the national court considers that there is a possibility that an exemption might be given, it could stay the domestic proceedings or adopt interim measures pursuant to national procedures[15]: the *Cooperation Notice* states this at paragraph 32 and sets out cooperation procedures between national courts and the Commission at paragraphs 33 to 44;
- the national court may refer the matter to the ECJ under Article 234[16]: the *Cooperation Notice* mentions this possibility at paragraphs 22 and 32;

9   Ibid, para 53; on the Commission's duty of sincere cooperation, see Case C–2/88 R *Zwartveld* [1990] ECR 3365.
10   Ibid para 54; Case T–24/90 *Automec v Commission (No 2)* [1992] ECR II-2223, [1992] 5 CMLR 431, para 92.
11   Case 283/81 [1982] ECR 3415, [1983] 1 CMLR 472.
12   See p 262, n 18 above.
13   Case C–234/89 *Delimitis v Henninger Bräu* [1992] ECR I-935, [1992] 5 CMLR 210, para 50.
14   Ibid.
15   Ibid, para 52.
16   Ibid, para 54.

- the national court cannot apply Article 81(3) itself[17];
- if individual exemption has been given, the national court must respect this and give effect to the agreement: this is stated in paragraph 25 of the *Cooperation Notice*;
- if the agreement benefits from block exemption, the national court can enforce it: this is envisaged by paragraph 26 of the *Cooperation Notice*;
- 'old' and 'accession'[18] agreements benefit from provisional validity and so can be enforced until the Commission has taken a decision against them: the *Cooperation Notice* deals with this at paragraph 31.

(iii)   Comfort letters

An additional complicating factor is that most notifications do not result in the Commission adopting a formal decision, but in the sending of a comfort letter stating that the Commission intends, on the basis of the information in its possession, to take no further action on the case and to close its file[19]; comfort letters sometimes say that the Commission considers that Article 81(1) or Article 82 do not apply to an agreement or practice, while others may say that an agreement appears to infringe Article 81(1) but that the requirements of Article 81(3) are satisfied. Comfort letters do not bind national courts[20], with the result that the 'rule' in *Delimitis* – that a national court must avoid conflicts with decisions of the Commission – does not apply. It would be very unfortunate for legal certainty if national judges were to deviate from the Commission's position as stated in comfort letters, and this does not appear to have been a significant problem in practice. In its *Cooperation Notice* the Commission points out at paragraph 20 that the ECJ has said that national courts may take comfort letters into account which state that Articles 81(1) or 82 do not apply; and at paragraph 25 the Commission expresses its hope that national courts will also take account of Article 81(3) comfort letters[1], a point yet to be specifically dealt with by the ECJ.

(iv)   Parallel proceedings and the UK courts

The issue of parallel Commission investigations and domestic proceedings came before the Court of Appeal in *MTV Europe v BMG Records*[2]. In this case MTV was a third party claiming damages against seven defendants for infringements of Article 81. A notification of the agreement in question had been made to the Commission. Lord Bingham MR (as he then was) said that, as a general proposition, the national court should stay proceedings pending a decision by the Commission in the interests of legal certainty, unless the answer to the complaint is clear. However he went on to add that it did not follow from this that there should be a general stay of all steps in the action: it may, for example,

---

17 Regulation 17/62, Article 9.
18 See p 262, n 18 above.
19 See ch 7, pp 217-218.
20 Ibid, p 218.
1   In one case, *Inntrepreneur Estates Ltd v Mason* [1993] 2 CMLR 293, Deputy Judge Barnes QC expressed some uncertainty as to how a national court should deal with a letter from the Commission, but the letter in that case was not a comfort letter closing a file.
2   [1997] 1 CMLR 867, [1997] Eu LR 100, CA.

be reasonable to allow the preparation of an action for trial, provided that this did not lead to a decision in advance of that made by the Commission. Litigants should be treated fairly, and this was a matter for the national court to assess. The Court of Appeal upheld the order of Evans-Lombe J at first instance: he had ordered a stay of the action over the summer months of 1994 while the matter was being argued in Brussels, but ordered that preparation of the case should be permitted thereafter, subject to an agreement not to set it down for trial.

In *Williams v Welsh Rugby Union*[3] Eady J ordered a stay of proceedings where a dispute had arisen between Cardiff Rugby Football Club and the Welsh Rugby Union ('the WRU'). Cardiff RFC had brought an action against the WRU; the International Rugby Union sought to be joined in the action. The IRU's rules had been notified to the Commission, and the WRU intended to notify. Eady J allowed the IRU's application to be joined as a party to the proceedings, and agreed to its and the WRU's applications for the action to be stayed. His view was that the issues at hand – professionalism in sport and the social and economic implications thereof – were typical and ripe for consideration by the Commission; this was demonstrated by the Commission's own document *Broadcasting of Sports Events and Competition Law*[4]. In *Philips Electronics v Ingman Ltd*[5] Laddie J applied Lord Bingham's ruling in *MTV Europe* and ordered a stay of proceedings pending the outcome of a complaint by the defendants to the Commission, that the plaintiff's commencement of a patent action entailed infringements of the competition rules.

(C)   The classic 'Euro-defence'

As suggested above, there seems little doubt that the judicial mind is unsympathetic to an Article 81(2) defence where one party to an agreement freely entered into attempts to walk away from it on the ground that it is void under competition law. The maxim *'pacta sunt servanda'* – contracts should be honoured – has a powerful influence where an undertaking purports, on the basis of a 'technicality' of competition law, to avoid a contractual obligation.

In the *George Michael* case[6] the singer sought to argue that his recording contract with Sony was in restraint of trade at common law and amounted to an infringement of Article 81(1), and that it was therefore void and unenforceable: on this occasion the matter came before the court not as a Euro-defence, but in an action by George Michael for a declaration. The court rejected both claims; as to Article 81(1), Parker J was not satisfied that the recording contract was capable of producing an appreciable effect on trade between Member States. More generally, the judge was clearly unimpressed at an attempt to avoid an agreement which had been entered into as a settlement of earlier litigation between the parties, the singer at the time of such settlement having received legal advice form leading lawyers in the UK and US with specialisation in the law of publishing agreements. The maxim *'interest rei publicae ut finis litium sit'* – it is in the public interest that litigation should be settled – in conjunction with *pacta sunt servanda* formed a powerful combination on this occasion.

3   [1999] Eu LR 195, QBD.
4   2 June 1998; see also *Application of EC competition law to sport*, Commission Press Release IP(99)133.
5   [1998] 2 CMLR 839, [1998] Eu LR 666, ChD; see also *Harrison v Matthew Brown* [1998] Eu LR 493, ChD and CA.
6   *Panayiotou v Sony Music Entertainment (UK) Ltd* [1994] ECC 395, ChD.

Euro-defences were invoked in two cases arising from the plight of individuals – known as 'names' – called upon by Lloyd's of London to contribute substantial sums of money as a result of insurance losses, *Society of Lloyd's v Clementson*[7] and *Higgins v Marchant & Eliot Underwriting Ltd*[8]. In *Clementson*, Lloyds itself was suing Clementson; his defence was that the Central Fund Byelaw of the Society of Lloyds itself infringed Article 81(1). The Court of Appeal had concluded that it was at least arguable that Clementson would be able to run such a Euro-defence, and therefore allowed an appeal against its having been struck out. Subsequently, however, the defence did indeed fail. In the *Marchant* case, two cash calls had been made on a Lloyds name, Higgins, by Marchant & Elliott Underwriting Ltd. Higgins' case was that the agreement between him and Marchant & Elliott infringed Article 81(1) and was therefore unenforceable. Rix J considered that the *Clementson* case was distinguishable, as what was in issue in that case was whether the Central Fund Byelaw of Lloyds itself infringed Article 81(1). In the *Higgins* case the agreement that Marchant & Elliott sought to enforce was a separate agreement between it and Higgins. For Higgins, it was argued that this agreement was entered into pursuant to the Lloyds régime, and that it amounted, effectively, to an attempt to enforce the rules of the overall system; as a result it was also tainted and unenforceable. This was rejected by Rix J[9]:

'No case has been cited to me in which A has been unable to enforce his lawful rights under contract with B because A has been instigated to litigate against B by C in furtherance of C's unlawful agreement or decision. Such a doctrine would be immensely far-reaching and damaging to lawful rights'.

In the Court of Appeal the judgment of Rix J was upheld[10]. Judicial disfavour of Euro-defences shone through: 'through the ingenuity of his lawyers [Higgins] relies upon the Article to evade payment of his debts. It is our task to see whether that ingenuity has been well directed and will avail him' (per Leggatt LJ).

Another failed Euro-defence can be seen in *Oakdale (Richmond) Ltd v National Westminster Bank plc*[11]. Chadwick J dismissed an argument that the restrictive terms of an all-moneys debenture arrangement, which provided for a lender to have control over the borrower company's book debts and which was necessary to protect the bank against the risks it had assumed, were anti-competitive. On the contrary the judge was satisfied that these terms were necessary to such agreements and, as such, promoted competition. This judgment is of interest in that the judge did not 'merely' reject the defence, but positively recognised that contractual restrictions can be pro-competitive: as such it sits happily with judgments of the ECJ such as *Delimitis v Henninger Bräu*[12] and *Gøttrup Klim v DLG*[13] in which that court has provided an important lead in showing that contractual restrictions are not necessarily restrictions of competition; indeed contractual restrictions often provide a positive contribution to the competitive process[14].

---

7   [1995] 1 CMLR 693, [1995] CLC 117, CA.
8   [1996] 1 Lloyd's Rep 313, QBD.
9   [1996] 1 Lloyd's Rep 313, pp 331-332.
10 [1996] 3 CMLR 349, CA.
11 [1997] Eu LR 27, ChD, affirmed on appeal [1997] 3 CMLR 815, CA.
12 Case C–234/89 [1991] ECR I-935, [1992] 5 CMLR 210.
13 Case C-250/92 [1994] ECR I-5641, [1996] 4 CMLR 191.
14 See ch 3, pp 98-101.

(D)   Severance

The preceding section reveals that judges may view with distaste technical invocations of the competition rules in order to avoid contractual obligations. However, there will be occasions when voidness does follow from an infringement of Article 81(1); the facts of *Eco Swiss China Time v Benetton*[15] reveal how this might happen. Where Article 81(1) is successfully invoked in litigation, a problem can arise over the effect of the voidness upon the remainder of the agreement. The ECJ has held that, provided that it is possible to sever the offending provisions of the contract from the rest of its terms, the latter remain valid and enforceable[16]. However the Court did not lay down a Community-wide principle of severance, so that the mechanism whereby this is to be effected is a matter to be decided according to the domestic law of each Member State[17]. This in turn gives rise to issues under the Brussels[18] and Rome Conventions[19]; the former determines where litigation may take place in civil and commercial cases, while the latter determines the law that should be applied in contractual disputes. Assuming that severability is regarded as a matter of substance rather than procedure, the Brussels Convention ought not to affect the outcome of litigation, since in principle the Rome Convention should lead to the same finding of the applicable law, wherever the litigation takes place; however, the determination of the applicable law may be crucial to the outcome of the litigation, since different Member States have different methods of severing unlawful restrictions from contracts.

As a matter of English contract law severance is possible in certain circumstances, although the rules on this subject are complex[20]. The Court of Appeal was called upon to examine severability in a competition law context in *Chemidus Wavin Ltd v Société pour la Transformation*[1]. A patentee was suing for royalties payable under an agreement that arguably infringed Article 81(1). The Court held that the minimum royalties provision was enforceable, irrespective of whether other parts of the agreement might infringe Article 81(1). Buckley LJ said:

'It seems to me that, in applying Article [81] to an English contract, one may well have to consider whether, after the excisions required by the Article of the Treaty have been made from the contract, the contract could be said to fail for lack of consideration or on any other ground, or whether the contract would be so changed in its character as not to be the sort of contract that the parties intended to enter into at all'.

In *Inntrepreneur Estates Ltd v Mason*[2] M Barnes QC, sitting as a Deputy Judge of the High Court, held that, where a beer tie infringed the competition

---

15 See Case C-126/97 [1999] ECR I-3055, [2000] 5 CMLR 816; the facts of the case are discussed at pp 273-275 below.
16 Case 56/65 *Société Technique Minière v Maschinenbau Ulm* [1966] ECR 235, [1966] CMLR 357; Case 319/82 *Société de Vente de Ciments et Bétons de l'Est v Kerpen and Kerpen GmbH* [1983] ECR 4173, [1985] 1 CMLR 511.
17 Case 319/82 *Ciments et Bétons* (n 16 above); Case 10/86 *VAG France SA v Establissements Magne SA* [1986] ECR 4071, [1988] 4 CMLR 98.
18 *Brussels Convention on Jurisdiction and the Enforcement of Judgments in Civil and Commercial Matters* 1968; note that this Convention will be replaced by Council Regulation 44/2001, OJ [2001] L 12/1, which will enter into force on 1 March 2002.
19 *Rome Convention on the Law Applicable to Contractual Obligations 1980.*
20 See *Chitty on Contracts* (Sweet & Maxwell, 28th ed, 1999), chapter 17, ¶¶185 ff.
1   [1978] 3 CMLR 514, CA.
2   [1993] 2 CMLR 293, QBD.

rules, it did not follow that a covenant to pay rent would also be unenforceable. Applying the test in *Chemidus Wavin* the judge had no difficulty in severing the tie, leaving the rest of the agreement intact. A similar result was reached by the Court of Appeal in *Inntrepeneur Estates (GL) Ltd v Boyes*[3]. It is unsurprising that the judges in these cases found the argument unappealing that the tenant of a public house could be relieved of the obligation to pay rent to the landlord as a collateral consequence of an (arguably) unlawful beer tie. A contrary finding would have devastating consequences for landlords holding large portfolios of public houses.

If the effect of severing certain clauses from an agreement would be that its scope and intention would be entirely altered, the entire agreement would become unenforceable[4].

(E) Void or illegal?

Agreements which infringe Article 81(1) are stated by Article 81(2) to be void; however an important question is whether they are 'merely' void or whether they are also illegal. On this classification turn the important issues of whether any money paid under the contract by one party to the other would be irrecoverable, applying the principle *in pari delicto potior est conditio defendentis*[5], and whether one party to the agreement could bring an action against the other for damages for harm suffered as a result of the operation of the agreement. The question of whether agreements contrary to Article 81(1) are illegal has been brought before UK courts in numerous cases in recent years. Typically, the cases have involved exclusive purchasing agreements between tenants of public houses and landlords of public houses, who may or not themselves be brewers. The tenants have raised numerous complaints against the landlords – about the exclusive purchasing tie itself, about the high rents that may be payable for the premises, about the price that they have to pay for the beer, and about the competitive disadvantage that they suffer compared to publicans in the 'free' trade, who may be able to obtain beer more cheaply. Disgruntled tenants in these circumstances have deployed a range of arguments in order to remedy their situation by recourse to principles of the laws of contract, tort, set-off and restitution. It should be said straightaway that these claims have for the most part been unsuccessful, and a raft of recent Commission decisions in the brewery sector, either clearing[6] or exempting[7] standard tenancy agreements in this sector may, in large part, bring an end to this particular round of litigation. Similar arguments have arisen in relation to exclusive purchasing agreements for the purchase of petrol, where the tenants' complaints resemble those of publicans.

---

3 [1993] 2 EGLR 112, CA; see similarly *Trent Taverns Ltd v Sykes* [1998] Eu LR 571, QBD, upheld on appeal [1999] Eu LR 492, CA.
4 See *Richard Cound Ltd v BMW (GB) Ltd* [1997] Eu LR 277, QBD and CA; *Benford Ltd v Cameron Equipment Ltd* [1997] Eu LR 334 (Mercantile Court); *Clover Leaf Cars Ltd v BMW (GB) Ltd* [1997] Eu LR 535, CA; *First County Garages Ltd v Fiat Auto (UK) Ltd* [1997] Eu LR 712, ChD; *Fulton Motors Ltd v Toyota (GB) Ltd* [1998] Eu LR 327, ChD.
5 See Goff and Jones *The Law of Restitution* (Sweet & Maxwell, 5th ed, 1998) ch 24.
6 That is to say declaring the non-application of Article 81(1), for example on the ground that an agreement does not restrict competition to an appreciable extent, as in the case of Greene King's tenancy agreements: see *Roberts/Greene King* Commission Press Release IP(98)967.
7 See eg *Whitbread* OJ [1999] L 88/26, [1999] 5 CMLR 118; *Bass* OJ [1999] L 186/1, [1999] 5 CMLR 782; *Scottish and Newcastle* OJ [1999] L 186/28, [1999] 5 CMLR 831.

It has been settled by the Court of Appeal that, as a matter of UK law, an agreement that infringes Article 81(1) is illegal rather than merely void. In *Gibbs Mew plc v Gemmel*[8] it held (admittedly *obiter*, as the Court was satisfied that the agreement in question did not offend Article 81(1) anyway) that the parties to an agreement that infringes Article 81 cannot bring an action in tort or in restitution for compensation for any harm suffered, since they are themselves party to an illegal agreement:

'the parties to a beer tie offending Article [81] are the cause, not the victims, of the distortion, restriction or prevention of competition'[9].

The Court of Appeal therefore considered that, where two parties enter into an agreement that infringes Article 81(1), they are acting *in pari delicto* (they are equally responsible for the wrongdoing), with the consequence that neither can bring an action against the other that would have the effect of enforcing an illegal contract. It is interesting to speculate whether an argument could be made to the contrary: that the tenant in a case such as *Gibbs Mew* is not truly *in pari delicto*, but is rather the weaker of two parties and the victim of oppressive, and anti-competitive, conduct on the part of the more powerful landlord/brewer. A similar characterisation could be made of the relationship of an oil company and the tenant of a petrol station or a powerful patentee and a weak and oppressed licensee. There are arguments to the effect that there should be at least a possibility of restitutionary recovery[10], and that Community law should ensure that, in these relationships, the more powerful of the two parties should not be able to benefit from its oppressive behaviour by retaining money had and received. Backing for the idea that a weaker person should have a remedy could be found in the opinion of Advocate General van Gerven who argued, at paragraph 23 of his Opinion in the *Delimitis* case[11], that certain provisions of Regulation 1984/83 on exclusive purchasing agreements in the brewery sector seemed precisely to reflect such a policy:

'[Article 8(2)(b) of Regulation 1984/83] reveals the intention of affording better protection to the competitive freedom of contracting parties in a weak economic position and of granting less readily exemption from the prohibition under Article [81(1)]'.

It could be argued that provisions of the block exemptions on car dealerships[12] and on technology transfer agreements[13] are similarly motivated. This issue was referred by the Court of Appeal to the ECJ in 1999 in what, for ease of reference, may be referred to as the *Crehan* case[14]. Advocate General Mischo delivered his Opinion on 22 March 2001, in which he supported the view that, in some circumstances, a co-contractor should be able to bring an action for damages against another party to the agreement. In his view the rule expounded by the

8   [1998] Eu LR 588, CA.
9   [1998] Eu LR 588, p 604.
10   See Jones *Recovery of Benefits Conferred Under Contractual Obligations Prohibited by Article 81 or 82 of the Treaty of Rome* (1996) 112 LQR 606; Jones *Restitution and European Community Law* (Mansfield Press, 2000) ch 6.
11   Case C-234/89 [1991] ECR I-935, [1992] 5 CMLR 210.
12   Regulation 1475/95.
13   Regulation 240/96.
14   *Crehan v Courage Ltd* [1999] Eu LR 409, ChD; on appeal [1999] Eu LR 834, [1999] ECC 455, CA, referring the case, Case C-453/99, to the ECJ under Article 234.

Court of Appeal in *Gibbs Mew plc v Gemmell*[15] was too formalistic, and threatened the effective application of the competition rules. While acknowledging that normally one party to an agreement that infringes Article 81(1) ought not to have a right to damages against the other, there could be 'exceptional circumstances' where one party bears 'no significant responsibility for the distortion of competition'[16]. If one party is in a significantly weaker position than the other, so that it had no freedom to choose the terms of the contract, it would not be in *in pari delicto* and could bring an action for damages.

(F) Transient voidness

A different issue to have come before the Court of Appeal is whether the statutory prohibition in Article 81(2) may be 'turned on and off' depending on the surrounding facts. In *Passmore v Morland plc*[17] the Court of Appeal upheld the Chancery Division's judgment that an agreement could move from voidness to validity (and back again) according to the effect that it might be having on the market. Passmore was the publican of a pub in Aldershot, under a tenancy granted by the Inntrepreneur Pub Co ('IPC'). The tenancy contained an exclusive purchasing term that Passmore should purchase beer exclusively from IPC. Subsequently the reversion of the lease was acquired by Morland plc, a relatively small brewer. In a dispute between Morland and Passmore the latter claimed that the beer tie was unenforceable as a result of the application of Article 81. Essentially, the question for the Court of Appeal was as follows[18]. Suppose that the exclusive purchasing term was unenforceable when entered into, since IPC owned 4,500 pubs containing similar ties which, cumulatively, could foreclose access to the market by other brewers (this being the essential issue according to the judgment of the ECJ in *Delimitis*[19]). If some of those pubs were subsequently to come into the hands of a small brewer such as Morland, might it follow that, because those agreements did not contribute to any foreclosure because of its much weaker position in the market, they would cease to be unenforceable? In other words, is the logic of the prohibition in Article 81(1), in conjunction with the declaration of voidness in Article 81(2), that agreements can, over a period of time, float into and out of voidness, depending on market conditions? The Court of Appeal, upholding the order of Laddie J below[20], was clear that this was indeed the position. Three passages of the judgment of Chadwick LJ state the position clearly:

> '[A]n agreement which is not within Article [81(1)] at the time when it is entered into – because, in the circumstances prevailing in the relevant market at that time, it does not have the effect of preventing, restricting or distorting competition – may, subsequently and as the result of change in those circumstances, come within Article [81(1)], because, in the changed circumstances, it does have that effect'[1].

15 See n 8 above.
16 Ibid, para 44.
17 [1998] 4 All ER 468, [1998] Eu LR 580, ChD; affd [1999] Eu LR 501, [1999] 1 CMLR 1129, CA.
18 Note that the claims for damages and restitution could not be pursued because of the Court of Appeal judgment in *Gibbs Mew plc v Gemmell*, n 8 above.
19 See ch 3, pp 98-99.
20 [1998] 4 All ER 468.
1   [1999] Eu LR 501, p 511, [1999] 1 CMLR 1129, para 26.

Later:

'It must follow, also, by a parity of reasoning, that an agreement which is within the prohibition of Article [81(1)] at the time when it is entered into – because, in the circumstances prevailing in the relevant market at that time, it does have the effect of preventing, restricting or distorting competition – may, subsequently and as a result of a change in those circumstances, fall outside the prohibition contained in that Article, because, in the changed circumstances, it no longer has that effect'[2].

Later again:

'The prohibition is temporaneous (or transient) rather than absolute, in the sense that it endures for a finite period of time – the period of time for which it is needed – rather than for all time'[3].

Towards the end of his judgment Chadwick LJ dealt with an argument on behalf of Passmore that the principle of legal certainty should have as its consequence that the tie was and remained unenforceable, consistently with the Court of Appeal's judgment in *Shell UK Ltd v Lostock Garage*[4]: the Court of Appeal (Lord Denning MR dissenting) held there that a restrictive covenant that was valid when entered into should remain valid, even if subsequent circumstances made it unreasonable or unfair to enforce it. Ormrod LJ felt that the opposite conclusion 'would introduce into the law an unprecedented discretion in the court to suspend for a time a term in a contract; the repercussions of this are quite unforeseeable and unmanageable'[5]. On this, Chadwick LJ concluded in *Passmore* that 'it has to be recognised that what was seen, in *Shell UK Ltd v Lostock Garage Ltd*, as a wholly novel doctrine is now enshrined in Community competition law'[6].

It will readily be appreciated that the combination of transient voidness as in *Passmore v Moreland plc* and illegality that is consequent upon that voidness as in *Gibbs Mew plc v Gemmell* may give rise to some exquisitely complex litigation in the future. For example a restitutionary claim could be successful where money has been paid during the enforceable period of an agreement's lifetime, but not where made during its void period; evidence will be required that successfully pinpoints the moment when validity turned to voidness and vice versa. It remains to be seen how the position might be affected as a result of the ECJ's judgment in the pending *Crehan* case.[6a]

(G)   The duties of a national court

An issue that has occupied the courts of some Members States and the ECJ has been the extent to which a national court is obliged, of its own motion, to raise and consider points of Community law: should a domestic court simply adjudicate upon those matters that the parties have chosen to litigate, or should it adopt an active rôle in raising, for example, the possibility that a contract violates the competition rules? This issue came before the ECJ in *Van Schijndel v Stichting*

2   [1999] Eu LR 501, pp 511-512, [1999] 1 CMLR 1129, para 26.
3   [1999] Eu LR 501, p 512, [1999] 1 CMLR 1129, para 28.
4   [1977] 1 All ER 481, [1976] 1 WLR 1187, CA.
5   Ibid, pp 492, 1202 respectively.
6   [1999] Eu LR 501, [1999] 1 CMLR 1129, para 54.
6a   See n 14 above.

Pensioensfonds voor Fysiotherapeuten[7] and *Peterbroeck Van Campenhout &
Cie v Belgium*[8]. In *Van Schijndel* the appellants were sued for unpaid contributions
to a compulsory professional pension scheme in the Netherlands. They had
contested, unsuccessfully, in the Dutch court of first instance and in the first
appellate court that they could not be obliged to join the scheme under Dutch
law. Their appeal reached the Dutch Supreme Court, where the question was
raised whether the first appellate court should have considered, of its own motion
if necessary, whether the national law in issue was compatible with the competition
rules in the Treaty. The Dutch Supreme Court referred the matter to the ECJ. The
ECJ dealt with two issues. First (and uncontroversially) it held that, if national
law provided that domestic courts must raise of their own motion points of law
based on binding domestic rules, they must also do so where binding Community
rules are concerned: anything else would amount to a discriminatory treatment
of Community law. The second issue was more complex. What should the position
be where under domestic law a court may raise points of its own motion, but
only within the subject-matter of the dispute and based on the facts before it:
does Community law impose in such circumstances an obligation on the domestic
courts to go beyond this 'passive rôle'? The ECJ's answer was that there was no
such obligation. This ruling is consistent with the policy of 'procedural autonomy',
according to which the ECJ will abstain from dictating to the courts of the Member
States how litigation should be conducted and what remedies should be available.
The decision in *Van Schijndel* not to require judges pro-actively to investigate
whether an agreement infringes the competition rules is a reasonable restraint
on the part of the ECJ.

In the *Peterbroeck* case the facts were rather different. There the question was
not whether judges had a positive duty to raise points of competition law, including
going beyond the facts of the case as disputed between the parties. Rather the
ECJ was asked in *Peterbroeck* whether a domestic rule was void which prevented
a national court from considering of its own motion, after a fixed period, whether
a measure of domestic law is compatible with a provision of Community law.
On this point the Court held that such a rule could be void if it would prevent the
effective application of Community law, for example because the period was
excessively short. This judgment shows that there are occasions on which the
principle of procedural autonomy may have to yield to the importance of *effet
utile*.

(H)   The duties of an arbitrator[9]

In *Eco Swiss China Time Ltd v Benetton International NV*[10] the ECJ was asked
to consider the impact of the competition rules on arbitration proceedings.

---

7   Cases C-430/93 and 431/93 [1995] ECR I-4705, [1996] 1 CMLR 801; on these two cases
    see Heukels (1996) 33 CML Rev 337-353; Prechal 'Community Law in National Courts:
    The Lessons from *Van Schijndel*' (1998) 35 CML Rev 681.
8   Case C-312/93 [1995] ECR I-4599, [1996] 1 CMLR 793.
9   See *Competition and Arbitration Law* (International Chamber of Commerce, 1993); Atwood
    'The Arbitration of International Antitrust Disputes: A Status Report and Suggestions'
    [1994] Fordham Corporate Law Institute (ed Hawk), ch 15; von Mehren 'Some Reflections
    on the International Arbitration of Antitrust Issues' ibid, ch 16; Atwood, von Mehren and
    Temple Lang 'International Arbitration' ibid, ch 17; Schmitthoff 'The Enforcement of EC
    Competition Law in Arbitral Proceedings' [1996] Legal Issues in European Integration 101;
    Lugard 'EC Competition Law and Arbitration: Opposing Principles?' (1998) 19 ECLR 295
    (written prior to the judgment in *Eco Swiss*); on arbitration and the antitrust rules in the US
    see *Mitsubishi Motors v Soler Chrysler-Plymouth Inc* 473 US 614 (1985)
10 Case C-126/87 [1999] ECR I-3055, [2000] 5 CMLR 816; see Komninos (2000) 37 CML
    Rev 459.

Benetton had granted a trade mark licence to Eco Swiss to market watches under the Benetton name. Benetton subsequently terminated the licence and Eco Swiss referred the matter to an arbitrator, under Dutch law, in accordance with the agreement. The arbitrator awarded Eco Swiss substantial damages. No competition law point was taken by the parties, and the arbitrator did not raise one. In fact the trade mark licence infringed Article 81(1) and was ineligible for block exemption under Regulation 240/96 on technology transfer agreements[11]. Benetton decided to try to prevent the enforcement of the award of damages on the basis that to do so would amount to enforcing an agreement that was contrary to EC competition law. Under Dutch law an arbitration award can be challenged before the courts, in the absence of agreement between the parties, only on grounds of public policy. The Dutch Supreme Court held that the enforcement of competition rules did not amount to public policy in Dutch law, so that if the matter were purely domestic Benetton would be unsuccessful. However, since Benetton's case rested on the Community competition rules, the matter was referred to the ECJ under Article 234.

As noted above, the ECJ stressed the fundamental importance of the competition rules in the Treaty, and the importance of the sanction of voidness in ensuring compliance with them[12]. A consequence of this was that, if domestic law allowed an appeal against an arbitration award on grounds of public policy, the possibility that there might be a breach of the Community competition rules should be investigated. On a separate point, the ECJ recognised that domestic procedural rules which prescribe time limits for the challenging of arbitral awards could have the effect of preventing an appeal based on the competition rules; provided that the time limits were not so fierce as to infringe the requirement of effective application of the competition rules, they would themselves be valid.

The ECJ did not say anything specifically about the obligations of arbitrators themselves, but the case is of obvious importance to their rôle. Arbitration is intended to enable parties to disputes to reach a reasonably rapid and cheap settlement of disputes. If an arbitrator ignores points of competition law, but these can subsequently be raised on appeal as, subject to the time limit point, in *Eco Swiss*, the speedy and cheap conclusion of cases would be undermined. The arbitrator ought, therefore, to apply his or her mind to the issue, albeit that, according to *Van Schijndel*, there is no obligation pro-actively to root out infringements of the competition rules. It seems likely that the ECJ will be asked in due course to look further into the precise obligations of both judges and arbitrators in circumstances such as these[13].

It would appear to be the case that an arbitrator could not refer an issue of competition law to the ECJ under Article 234; the establishment of an arbitration panel is a consensual process, with the result that it is not a 'court or tribunal of a Member State'[14].

---

11   This Regulation is discussed in ch 19, pp 688-696.
12   See pp   261-262 above.
13   An interesting question is whether an arbitrator in a non-EU country would apply the competition rules, as a matter of public policy, where an agreement infringes Article 81 (or Article 82).
14   Case 102/81 *Nordsee Deutsche Hochseefisherei GmbH v Reederei Mond* [1982] ECR 1095; see further the Opinion of Advocate General Colomer in Case C-17/00 *de Coster v Collège des Bourgmestres*, 28 June 2001.

3. THE ENFORCEABILITY OF AGREEMENTS: ARTICLE 82

It may be that a contractual term infringes Article 82, because it amounts to an abuse of a dominant position, as well as infringing Article 81. For example an agreement to purchase one's entire requirements of a particular product from a dominant firm is quite likely to infringe both Article 81 and Article 82[15], because it might foreclose access to the market on the part of competitors; it is irrelevant for this purpose whether the undertaking that accepts the obligation is willing or unwilling to accept it[16]. Similarly a system of loyalty rebates, which falls short of a contractual requirement not to buy from competitors but which may have the same effect, may amount to an abuse[17]. In this situation it has been assumed that the prohibition of Article 82 means that the offending provisions are void, although there is nothing on the face of Article 82, as there is in the case of Article 81(2), to say so. It would follow that a customer tied by an exclusive purchasing commitment which infringes Article 82 could safely ignore it and purchase supplies elsewhere. The impact of any such invalidity on the remainder of the agreement would raise the same question of severability discussed above[18]. Of course a judge will wish to be satisfied on the facts that there is indeed an infringement of Article 82, which requires *inter alia* a demonstration of an appreciable effect on trade between Member States; a Euro-defence based on Article 82, by a tenant of buildings used for the provision of flight catering services at Heathrow Airport, failed for lack of such an effect in *Heathrow Airport Ltd v Forte (UK) Ltd*[19]. Where Article 82 is raised before a national court the task for the judge is not complicated by the problem of notification which was discussed above[20], because it is not possible to apply for an exemption under Article 82 as it is under Article 81(3). A judge does have discretion to adjourn a case if the Commission is investigating the same matter, and he or she could refer an issue of legal uncertainty to the ECJ under Article 234.

It will be recalled that in *Gibbs Mew* the Court of Appeal held that an agreement than infringes Article 81(1) is illegal, so that no action in restitution, tort or contract can be brought by one party against the other[1]; judgment is awaited in *Crehan v Courage*, in which this rule of English law is in question[2]. In the case of Article 82 there is a good argument that, whatever the position under Article 81, a party to an agreement imposed by a dominant undertaking should be able to enforce it, and where appropriate to sue the dominant firm for damages: the argument that the parties are *in pari delicto* is unconvincing where one of them is in a dominant position. Article 82(2)(a) provides that an abuse is committed where a dominant firm imposes 'unfair purchase or selling prices or other unfair trading conditions' on its customers: a party to an agreement who has been abused in this way ought, presumably, to be able to claim that it has been improperly treated. This would suggest that the same agreement, which would be regarded as illegal if the dominant firm sought to enforce it, and which is illegal for the purposes of Article 81, ought not to be so regarded where a claim is brought by the customer.

15 See eg Case 85/76 *Hoffmann-La Roche v Commission* [1979] ECR 461, [1979] 3 CMLR 211.
16 On agreements of this kind see ch 17, pp 601-605.
17 On practices of this kind see ch 18, pp 639-644.
18 See pp 268-269 above.
19 [1998] ECC 357, [1998] Eu LR 98, ChD.
20 See pp 262-266 above.
1 See pp 269-271 above.
2 See pp 270-271 above.

Authority that the customer ought to have a remedy under Article 82 can perhaps be found in the ECJ's judgment in *GT-Link A/S v De Danske Statsbaner*[3]. Charges were imposed by De Danske Statsbaner ('DDS'), the Danish state-owned railway undertaking, on GT-Link, a ferry operator making use of DDS-owned ports. These charges were arguably in breach of Article 82. A Danish court asked the ECJ a series of questions concerning the compatibility of the charges with Community law, including whether GT-Link could recover then, assuming them to be unlawful. The ECJ held that charges levied by a Member State in breach of Community law must be repaid (citing *Comateb v General des Douanes et Droits Indirects*[4]); it added that the same would be true of a public undertaking such as DDS which was responsible to the Danish Ministry of Transport and governed by the Budget Act. What is of interest about this judgment is whether the ECJ would have decided the same way had the defendant not been a public undertaking of the type specified in the judgment, but a 'normal' private-sector dominant firm. It is clearly arguable that, since Article 82 is directly effective and since national courts must give practical effect to the rights that this entails, any victim of abusive behaviour should be able to recover. In other words, the *GT-Link* case should not be regarded, or regarded only, as a state liability case, but as a case on the obligations of dominant firms to compensate those whom they abuse.

4.   THIRD PARTIES

Sections 2 and 3 of this chapter considered the extent to which Articles 81 and 82 may affect litigation in domestic courts between the parties to an agreement that is in violation of them. This section is concerned with the extent to which a third party can bring an action for an injunction and/or damages against undertakings that infringe the competition rules.

(A)   A right to damages?

An important question is whether third parties can invoke the unlawfulness of agreements under Article 81 and the abuse of a dominant position under Article 82 in order to bring an action for damages against the offending undertakings. The Commission is keen to see more enforcement of Articles 81 and 82 in national courts[5], and the possibility of obtaining damages in particular would encourage litigants to sue.

(i)   Actions for damages in US antitrust

The availability of damages is an important feature of the enforcement process in US antitrust[6]. Approximately 90% of all antitrust cases in the US involve private rather than public action, and as many as 2,000 cases have been brought

---

3   Case C-242/95 [1997] ECR I-4349, [1997] 5 CMLR 601.
4   Cases C-192/95 etc [1997] ECR I-165, [1997] 2 CMLR 649.
5   See pp 259-260 above and the Commission's *Cooperation Notice* OJ [1993] C 39/6, [1993] 4 CMLR 12, in particular at paras 13–16.
6   See generally Jones *Private Enforcement of Antitrust Law in the EU, UK and USA* (Oxford University Press, 1999).

in a single year[7]. To the extent that victims of anti-competitive behaviour can bring an action for damages, the enforcement mechanism is privatised and the burden on public institutions is correspondingly diminished. In US law the award of damages is in many cases trebled, and this acts as an inducement to private parties to take the enforcement initiative themselves[8]; the right to negotiate contingency fees, to the effect that the plaintiff's lawyers will recover fees only if a case is successful, adds to this inducement[9]. However it should be acknowledged that, if the incentive to litigate is excessively generous, this, in itself, may have a distorting effect on economic behaviour: it may have as its consequence that defendants agree to out-of-court settlements not because they are guilty of anti-competitive behaviour or because a court is likely to make such a finding, but because it is the cheapest way of avoiding expensive court proceedings[10]. Partly because of this danger, there are various limitations in US law upon the rights of plaintiffs to bring private actions, for example that direct injury must have been sustained and that firms that are harmed only incidentally cannot sue, and that damages can be awarded only for injury to business or property[11]; the courts have also developed a series of principles relevant to the quantification of damages[12], including whether a plaintiff can recover damages for losses that have been 'passed on' to customers and/or consumers[13]. An interesting recent example of a suit leading to an award of damages is the *Sotheby's/Christies'* case: a judge approved a legal settlement in February 2001 in which customers of Sotheby's and Christies' were awarded damages of $537 million for losses incurred as a result of their illegal price-fixing cartel[14].

(ii) *The availability of damages for infringements of Articles 81 and 82 as a matter of Community law*

Perhaps surprisingly, there has not yet been a judgment of the ECJ dealing with the question of whether Member States have an obligation, as a matter of EC law, to provide a remedy in damages where there has been an infringement of the competition rules. There are several judgments and principles of Community law which illuminate the path towards a finding that damages should be available in such cases, but there is still no judgment that actually says so.

(A) FRANCOVICH AND FACTORTAME. In *Francovich v Italy*[15] the ECJ held that a Member State may, in certain circumstances, be liable in damages to an individual

---

7 Ibid, p 79.
8 See the Clayton Act 1914, s 4 and *Jones*, pp 79-84; an interesting point noted at p 35 of *Jones* is that, under Article IV of the now-repealed UK Statute of Monopolies 1623, a victim of an unlawful monopoly 'shall recover three times the damages that he sustained': several other early English statutes contained similar provisions.
9 See ch 10, p 362 on the possibility of agreeing 'conditional fees' in the UK.
10 On the possible problems associated with 'excessive' private enforcement, see Elzinga and Breit *The Antitrust Penalties: A Study in Law and Economics* (New Haven, 1976); Schwartz *Private Enforcement of the Antitrust Laws: An Economic Critique* (Washington, 1981).
11 See *Jones*, chs 14 and 15.
12 Ibid, chs 17 and 18.
13 See Coutroulis and Allen 'The Pass-on Problem in Indirect Purchaser Class Litigation' (1999) 44 Antitrust Bulletin 179.
14 Financial Times, 23 February 2001.
15 Cases C–6/90 and 9/90 [1991] ECR I-5357, [1993] 2 CMLR 66; see Ross 'Beyond *Francovich*' (1993) 56 MLR 55; see also Case C-5/94 *R v Ministry of Agriculture, Fisheries and Food, ex p Hedley Lomas* [1996] ECR I-2553, [1992] 2 CMLR 391; Cases C-178/94 etc *Dillenkofer v Germany* [1996] ECR I-4845, [1996] 3 CMLR 469.

who suffers loss as a result of the non-implementation of a Directive. That case concerned a Directive on the non-payment of salaries in the event of an employer's insolvency; an important feature of the case was that the Directive in question was not directly effective, but nevertheless the ECJ held that Italy could be liable in damages. The UK Court of Appeal, applying the rule in *Francovich*, held in *R v Secretary of State for Transport, ex p Factortame*[16] that the UK was liable for damages for having infringed Community law by adopting the Merchant Shipping Act 1988; this judgment was upheld on appeal to the House of Lords[17]. Of course these cases concerned the liability of Member States themselves to pay damages, whereas the question under Articles 81 and 82 is whether undertakings can be liable. Nevertheless the *Francovich* and *Factortame* cases are important in that they assign an important rôle to damages actions in the enforcement of Community law.

(B)   THE PRINCIPLES OF NON-DISCRIMINATION AND EFFET UTILE.   Where a Community provision is directly effective, individuals must be afforded remedies in their national courts which are as effective as the remedies they would enjoy under domestic law: this principle of 'equality of treatment' or non-discrimination has been expressed in several judgments of the ECJ[18] and in paragraphs 10 and 11 of the Commission's *Cooperation Notice*[19]. In so far as a Member State allows a damages action for infringements of its domestic competition law, it could be argued on this basis that damages must also be available where the Community competition rules are infringed. Furthermore the ECJ has held that Member States must not render the enforcement of Community rights impossible or excessively difficult, irrespective of discrimination[20], and it may be that a right to damages could be claimed on this basis: for example where a firm has already suffered economic harm as a result of anti-competitive behaviour, and perhaps has been put out of business, injunctive relief will be of no benefit; in this case the only effective remedy would be the award of damages.

(C)   *HJ BANKS V BRITISH COAL CORPN.*   In *HJ Banks v British Coal Corpn*[1] Advocate General van Gerven addressed the issue of whether damages were available for breaches of Articles 4(d), 60 , 65 and/or 66(7) of the ECSC Treaty: these Articles are similar, but not identical to, Articles 81 and 82 of the EC Treaty[2]. The Advocate General's view was that 'as a result of its obligation to ensure that Community law is fully effective and to protect the rights thereby conferred on individuals, the national court is under an obligation to award damages for loss sustained by an undertaking as a result of the breach by another undertaking of a directly effective provision of Community competition law'[3].

16 [1998] 3 CMLR 192, CA.
17 [1999] 4 All ER 906, [1999] 3 CMLR 597, HL.
18 See eg Case 158/80 *REWE v Hauptzollamt Kiel* [1981] ECR 1805, [1982] 1 CMLR 449, para 44; Case 199/82 *Ammistrazione delle Finanze dello Stato v San Giorgio* [1983] ECR 3595, [1985] 2 CMLR 658.
19 OJ [1993] C 39/6, [1993] 5 CMLR 95.
20 See eg *San Giorgio* (n 18 above).
1   Case C-128/92 [1994] ECR I-1209, [1994] 5 CMLR 30; for comment on this case see Friend 'Enforcing the ECSC Treaty in National Courts' (1995) 20 ELRev 59.
2   For other cases litigated in the UK courts under the provisions of the ECSC Treaty see Case C-18/94 *Hopkins v National Power* [1996] ECR I-2281, [1996] 4 CMLR 745; the claims in these cases were subsequently struck out: see *Doublerange Ltd v National Power plc* [1997] Eu LR 589; *HJ Banks & Co Ltd v British Coal Corpn* [1997] Eu LR 597; see also *Coal Authority v HJ Banks & Co Ltd* [1997] Eu LR 610.
3   Ibid, para 45.

In his Opinion the Advocate General went on to give detailed consideration to a number of more specific issues in relation to the award of damages, including the necessary causal connection between the breach of the competition rules and ensuing damage, the illegality of the conduct alleged, damages and interest[4]. Unfortunately, however, the ECJ concluded that the relevant provisions of the ECSC Treaty were not directly effective; in the Court's view the Commission had sole jurisdiction to determine whether there was an infringement of Articles 65 and 66 of that Treaty, with the result that national courts could not entertain actions for damages.

(D)   FURTHER SUGGESTIONS OF A RIGHT TO DAMAGES.   Further suggestions that there is a right to damages where the competition rules are infringed can be found. For example the Opinion of Advocate General Mischo in the *Crehan* case seems to assume that there is a right to damages; and paragraph 16 of the Commission's *Cooperation Notice* also assumes that such a right exists. The various authorities reviewed in this and the preceding paragraphs seem to suggest strongly that the ECJ will, in due course, conclude that damages should be available where the competition rules are infringed; however it may well be that it will develop various refinements to this general proposition.

(iii)   The availability of damages for infringements of Articles 81 and 82 as a matter of UK law[5]

Notwithstanding the fact that the ECJ has not given a ruling on the availability of damages when the competition rules are infringed, the UK courts have addressed the issue on a number of occasions. The leading case in the UK is the House of Lords' judgment in *Garden Cottage Foods v Milk Marketing Board*[6]. The case arose out of the appellant's complaint that the Milk Marketing Board's refusal to supply it with bulk butter was an abuse of a dominant position. The appeal in the House of Lords was specifically concerned with the appellant's application for an interlocutory injunction; however Lord Diplock, with whom three other Law Lords agreed, concluded that an interlocutory injunction should not be given, since damages would be an adequate remedy when the matter came on for final trial. The frustrating aspect of the judgment is that it did not formally decide that damages are available, but proceeded on the basis that, if damages are available, they would provide an adequate remedy[7]. Lord Wilberforce powerfully dissented in *Garden Cottage Foods* on this issue which, in his view, required further consideration; he considered that it was possible that Community rights could adequately be protected by injunctions without

4   Ibid, paras 46-54.
5   See Picanol 'Remedies in National Law for Breach of Articles [81] and [82] of the EEC Treaty' [1983] LIEI 1; Jacobs 'Damages for Breach of Article [82] EEC' (1983) 8 ELRev 353; Hoskins '*Garden Cottage* Revisited: The Availability of Damages in the National Courts for Breaches of EEC Competition Rules' (1992) 13 ECLR 257; Whish 'The Enforcement of EC Competition Law in the Domestic Courts of Member States' (1994) 15 ECLR 60; Winterstein 'A Community Right in Damages for Breach of EC Competition Rules' (1995) 16 ECLR 49; Brealey and Hoskins *Remedies in EC Law* (Sweet & Maxwell, 2nd ed, 1998) chs 6, 7 and 8; on the position of third party actions under the UK Competition Act 1998 see ch 10, pp 361-362 and in particular the articles cited at n 17.
6   [1984] AC 130, [1983] 3 CMLR 43.
7   For a similar finding in Ireland see *Curust Financial Services Ltd v Loewe-Lack-Werk Otto Loewe GmbH* [1993] 2 CMLR 808.

also conferring on complainants a right to damages, which involved an extension of those rights. Several subsequent cases in the UK courts have assumed that damages are available[8]. In *Arkin v Borchard Lines Ltd*[9] the court proceeded on the basis that it was common ground between the parties that somebody who suffers loss by reason of breach of Article 81 or 82 has a private action for damages analogous to a claim for breach of statutory duty.

It seems, therefore, to be uncontroversial in the UK that there is a right to damages, although there has yet to be a case in which a court has actually made an award; it is understood that there have been several cases that have been settled out of court but which have not been publicised: indeed a party that agrees to pay damages out of court will probably include, as a condition of the settlement, that the matter must be kept confidential.

If damages are available in the UK for breaches of Articles 81 and 82, a separate question is how the action should be framed. In *Garden Cottage Foods* Lord Diplock was of the view that the action should be for breach of statutory duty, the relevant statutory provision being section 2 of the European Communities Act 1972, which gives effect to directly applicable provisions of Community law. However it is not obvious that this action is appropriate where the competition rules are broken. For example, the 'abuse' of a dominant position is an objective concept[10] and a dominant undertaking may abuse its position without intention or even recklessness. It is not obvious that an action for breach of statutory duty should lie in these circumstances, since it could render dominant undertakings liable to actions for damages on a very strict basis. Furthermore it is the normal rule that, where a financial penalty is available under a statute, there is no right to bring an action for breach of statutory duty[11]; as infringements of Article 82 can be penalised under Regulation 17/62, it could be argued that there should not be a right to bring an action for breach of statutory duty as well. A more discriminating cause of action might be the tort of wrongful interference, since liability there requires an intention on the part of the defendant to harm the plaintiff, although this does not have to have been the defendant's predominant motive[12]. This approach may enable the domestic court to distinguish particularly reprehensible cases, where a plaintiff ought to be compensated by the defendant, from those where the harm suffered by the plaintiff is an incidental effect of the defendant's infringement of the competition rules.

A further interesting question is whether there would be a possibility of a claimant recovering exemplary damages in a case of particularly blatant and deliberate anti-competitive behaviour. UK law adopts a narrow approach towards

---

8   See eg *An Bord Bainne Co-operative Ltd v Milk Marketing Board* [1984] 1 CMLR 519, affd [1984] 2 CMLR 584, CA; *Bourgoin S A v Minister of Agriculture Fisheries and Food* [1985] 1 CMLR 528; on appeal [1986] 1 CMLR 267, CA (this case was concerned with whether damages could be recovered from a Member State that had acted in breach of Article 28 of the Treaty, but the judgments in the Court of Appeal deal also with actions under the competition rules: the case was settled after the Court of Appeal's judgment, the plaintiff recovering substantial damages, and before an appeal to the House of Lords had been heard: see [1987] 1 CMLR 169); *Plessey v GEC* [1990] ECC 384, para 37 (injunction refused *inter alia* on grounds that damages at the trial would be an adequate remedy); *Norbain SD Ltd v Dedicated Micros Ltd* [1998] Eu LR 266 (QBD: interlocutory injunction refused *inter alia* since this would complicate rather than simplify the calculation of damages).
9   [2001] Eu LR 232, QBD.
10   See para 47 of the opinion of Jacobs AG in Case C–41/90 *Höfner and Elser v Macrotron* [1991] ECR I–1979, [1993] 4 CMLR 306.
11   *Cutler v Wandsworth Stadium* [1949] AC 398.
12   See *Lonrho v Fayed* [1990] 2 QB 479, CA.

awards of exemplary damages[13]; however the Law Commission has recommended that a less restrictive rule should be formulated[14].

(iv) The position in other Member States

It is not easy to follow developments in relation to this subject in other Member States. There is no official reporting system which brings together all the judgments in national courts dealing with competition cases, and in some jurisdictions there may be no written judgment at all setting out a court's findings. Some attempts have been made to review national enforcement: the work edited by Behrens referred to in the first footnote of this chapter is very helpful, as is the analysis produced for the Commission under the editorial supervision of Braakman, also referred to there. What is needed, however, is a database that is regularly updated so that the pattern of enforcement in national courts can be continuously monitored. It may be that, once the Commission's *Modernisation* proposals are implemented, the position will improve, since national courts will be required to provide details of all judgments to the Commission within one month of their delivery[15]. In the meantime it is far from easy to follow the pattern of enforcement in other jurisdictions.

A few examples of damages being awarded, or of judgments for damages to be assessed, are known of. In Germany this happened in the cases of *BMW*[16] and of *British Telecommunications plc and Viag Interkom GmbH v Deutsche Telecom*[17]. In Ireland the Irish Supreme Court held that damages were available for a breach of section 5 of the Competition Act 1991, the domestic equivalent there of Article 82, in *Dermot Donovan v Electricity Supply Board*[18]; the Court held in this case that the motives or the intention of the defendant were irrelevant to the issue of whether damages were available, and that damages would be awarded on the same basis as any other tort or civil wrong. In the Netherlands the Amsterdam District Court awarded damages in the case of *Theal BV and Watts v Wilkes*[19].

(B) Relying on Commission decisions

A would-be litigant in an action based on the EC competition rules would be in a much better position if it had the benefit of a Commission decision establishing that the conduct complained of was an infringement of Article 81 or 82. Article 249 EC (ex Article 189) provides that a decision of the Commission is binding upon the person to whom it is addressed; it could be argued, therefore, that in domestic proceedings a defendant is prevented by Community law from contesting findings of law or fact in a decision that has been addressed to it. The argument would be even stronger where the Commission's decision has been upheld on appeal by the CFI or the ECJ.

---

13 On exemplary damages see *Rookes v Barnard* [1964] AC 1129; *R v Secretary of State for Transport, ex p Factortame* [1997] Eu LR 475, QBD, pp 524-532; *Kuddus v Chief Constable of Leicestershire Constabulary* [2001] 3 All ER 193, HL; see *Jones*, pp 232-240, for an interesting discussion of this subject.
14 *Aggravated, Exemplary and Restitutionary Damages* (Law Commission 247, 1997).
15 See ch 7, pp 246-258 on the Commission's *Modernisation* proposals.
16 [1980] ECC 213.
17 [1998] 2 CMLR 114 (Landgericht, Düsseldorf).
18 [1998] Eu LR 212.
19 Judgment of 11 January 1979.

The issue arose in *Masterfoods Ltd v HB Ice Cream Ltd*[20]. The High Court in Ireland had dismissed a claim by Masterfoods that HB Ice Cream, a subsidiary of the Unilever group and subsequently known as Van den Bergh Foods, had infringed the competition rules by supplying freezer cabinets to retailers on condition that they were used exclusively for HB products (the 'exclusivity clause'). Masterfoods appealed against this judgment to the Irish Supreme Court. In the meantime the Commission adopted a decision that the exclusivity clause infringed Articles 81 and 82[1]. Van den Bergh appealed to the CFI[2]. The Irish Supreme Court at this stage stayed its own proceedings in the appeal and made a reference to the ECJ, under Article 234, essentially asking what it should do in these somewhat complex circumstances. The CFI then decided that it should stay its own hearing of the appeal against the Commission's decision pending the outcome of the Article 234 reference to the ECJ. The ECJ gave its judgment in December 2000. After noting the rule in *Delimitis v Henninger Bräu*[3] that the courts of Member States must avoid giving decisions which would conflict with a decision contemplated by the Commission[4], the ECJ added that it is even more important that national courts should not reach decisions which conflict with a decision that the Commission has already adopted[5]; this would apply even where, as in this case, the lower Irish court had reached a conclusion in favour of Van den Bergh prior to the Commission's finding to the opposite effect: the Irish Supreme Court would be bound not to reach a conclusion at variance with the Commission's decision. The ECJ added that, where the outcome of a dispute in a national court depends on the outcome of an appeal against a Commission decision, the national court should stay its proceedings pending final judgment in the action for annulment in the Community Courts, unless it thinks that it would be appropriate to make an Article 234 reference to the ECJ for a preliminary ruling on the validity of the Commission decision[6].

(C) Standard of proof

A separate question is the standard of proof that should be required by a national court where a plaintiff claims there has been an infringement of Articles 81 and/ or 82. In *Shearson Lehman Hutton Inc v Watson Co Ltd*[7] Webster J in the UK High Court was of the view that, as an infringement of Article 81 carries with it a liability to penalties, he should apply the standard of 'a high degree of probability': this is a higher standard than in civil proceedings generally but

20 Case C-344/98 [2001] 4 CMLR 449, [2001] All ER (EC) 130; see Preece '*Masterfoods Ltd v HB Ice Cream*' [2001] ECLR 281.
1 *Van den Bergh Foods Ltd* OJ [1998] L 246/1, [1998] 5 CMLR 530; the Commission's decision is discussed in ch 17, p 605.
2 Case T-65/98 (judgment pending); the President suspended the operation of the Commission's decision in Case T-65/98 R [1998] ECR II-2641, [1998] 5 CMLR 475, pending the appeal.
3 Case C-234/89 [1991] ECR I-935, [1992] 5 CMLR 210.
4 Ibid, para 51.
5 Ibid, para 52.
6 Ibid, para 57; see also *Iberian UK Ltd v BPB Industries* [1996] 2 CMLR 601, [1997] Eu LR 1, ChD, where a UK court followed the Commission's decision in *Plasterboard*: for comment see Laddie (the judge in that case) 'Community Competition Law in English Courts' in Andenas and Jacobs (eds) *European Community Law in the English Courts* (Clarendon Press Oxford, 1998) ch 11; see also Advocate General van Gerven in *HJ Banks v British Coal Corpn* Case C-128/92 [1994] ECR I-1209, paras 55-61.
7 [1989] 3 CMLR 429 at 570; see also *Application by Anley Maritime Agencies Ltd for Judicial Review* [1999] Eu LR 97.

lower than the requirement in a criminal case. In *Masterfoods Ltd v HB Ice Cream Ltd*[8], however, Kean J in the Irish High Court decided to apply the standard of proof normally applicable in civil proceedings, namely proof on the balance of probabilities.

(D) Interlocutory relief

Experience to date suggests that the domestic courts in the UK are reluctant to grant interlocutory relief in cases based on Articles 81 and 82[9]. In commercial cases the tendency of the court will be to conclude that, as damages would be an adequate remedy, interim orders will not be made. In *Garden Cottage Foods v Milk Marketing Board*[10], *Argyll Group plc v Distillers Co plc*[11], *Plessey Co plc v General Electric Co*[12], *Megaphone v British Telecom*[13] and *Macarthy v UniChem*[14] applications for interim relief were rejected. Some applications have been successful, particularly where individuals' livelihoods were at stake[15], and occasionally between more substantial litigants[16]. The Commission's view is that interim measures may be more easily and quickly obtained in national courts[17].

(E) Third party as defendant

Where a third party raises Article 82 as a defence to an action by a dominant firm, but there is no contractual relationship between the parties, the defence may fail. In several cases the owner of an intellectual property right such as a patent, registered design or copyright has brought an action against a defendant for infringement; the defendant has then claimed that it has a defence under Article 82, since the plaintiff is guilty of abusing its dominant position. In particular, the defendant may claim that, by refusing to grant a licence of the intellectual property right in question, it (the plaintiff) is guilty of an abuse under Article 82. Whether or not a refusal to license can be abusive is itself a vexed question; it is considered in chapter 18[18]. However, even if the plaintiff is abusing its dominant position, this will not in itself confer on the defendant a valid defence. The courts have established that there must be a sufficient nexus between the plaintiff's abusive behaviour and the defendant to entitle it to rely on Article 82. In *Chiron Corpn v Organon Teknika Ltd*[19] Aldous J said (at paragraph 44) that:

8   [1992] 3 CMLR 830 at 873.
9   See Rodger and MacCulloch 'Wielding the Blunt Sword: Interim Relief for Breaches of EC Competition Law before the UK Courts' (1996) 17 ECLR 393.
10 [1984] AC 130, [1983] 3 CMLR 43.
11 [1986] 1 CMLR 764.
12 [1990] ECC 384.
13 28 February 1989, unreported, QBD.
14 24 November 1989, unreported.
15 *Cutsforth v Mansfield Inns* [1986] 1 CMLR 1; *Holleran and Evans v Thwaites plc* [1989] 2 CMLR 917.
16 For example ECS succeeded in obtaining an interim injunction against AKZO in the High Court as well as persuading the Commission to proceed under Article 82 in *ECS/AKZO* OJ [1983] L 252/13, [1983] 3 CMLR 694; see also *Sockel GmbH v Body Shop International plc* [1999] Eu LR 276, ChD.
17 *Cooperation Notice* OJ [1993] C 39/6, [1993] 4 CMLR 12, para 16.
18 See ch 17, pp 612-613 and ch 19, pp 688-701.
19 [1992] 3 CMLR 813, upheld on appeal, judgment of 7 April 1993.

'The fact that a person is abusing a dominant position does not mean that all wrongdoers have a defence in respect of all actions brought by that person. It is only in those cases where the exercise or existence of that right creates or buttresses the abuse will the court refuse to give effect to the exercise of the right.'

In several cases the necessary nexus has been lacking[20] and the defence therefore struck out. Where there is a sufficient nexus between the parties, for example where the dominant undertaking is abusing its market power specifically in order to harm the defendant, a defence based on Article 82 may be pleaded[1].

---

20 See eg *ICI v Berk Pharmaceuticals* [1981] 2 CMLR 91, [1981] FSR 1; *British Leyland Motor Corpn v Armstrong Patents Co Ltd* [1984] 3 CMLR 102 (this decision was overturned in the House of Lords on the issue of copyright protection for functional objects: [1986] AC 577); *Ransburg-GEMA AG v Electrostatic Plant Systems* [1989] 2 CMLR 712, QBD; *Philips Electronics v Ingman Ltd* [1998] Eu LR 666, ChD; *Sandvik Aktiebolag v KR Pfiffner (UK) Ltd* [1999] Eu LR 755, ChD; *HMSO v Automobile Association Ltd* [2001] Eu LR 80, ChD.
1 See eg *British Leyland v TI Silencers* [1981] 2 CMLR 75, CA; *Lansing Bagnall v Buccaneer Lift Parts* [1984] 1 CMLR 224, [1984] FSR 241, CA; *Pitney Bowes Inc v Francoyp-Postalia GmbH* [1990] 3 CMLR 466, [1991] FSR 72; see also *Intergraph Corpn v Solid Systems* [1998] Eu LR 221, ChD.

CHAPTER 9

Competition Act 1998 – substantive provisions

1. INTRODUCTION

The Competition Act 1998, the main provisions of which entered into force on 1 March 2000[1], radically reforms the domestic law of the UK on restrictive agreements and anti-competitive practices. The 1998 Act sweeps away much of the system that had formed over the preceding 50 years; the Restrictive Trade Practices Acts 1976 and 1977, the Resale Prices Act 1976 and the provisions on anti-competitive practices in the Competition Act 1980 are repealed. The investigative system in the Fair Trading Act 1973 ('the FTA') for monopolies[2] and mergers[3] is retained; the system of merger control is itself the subject of a consultation procedure, pursuant to a Department of Trade and Industry document published in August 1999[4]; this was followed in October 2000 by a document setting out the framework for the new merger régime[5]. Further changes in domestic competition law are in contemplation, including the possibility of the introduction of criminal penalties for individuals involved in cartel cases, and the disqualification of company directors.[5a] The basic shape of UK competition now is that anti-competitive conduct is dealt with by the Competition Act 1998, while issues of market structure can be investigated under the FTA. After a brief consideration of the background to this reform, this chapter will consider in turn the so-called Chapter I and Chapter II prohibitions in the Act; the relationship between EC and domestic competition law, including the very important 'governing principles' clause in section 60 of the 1998 Act which is intended to achieve consistency with EC law; and, briefly, the transitional provisions. Matters of enforcement and procedure are considered in chapter 10.

---

1 The Competition Act (Commencement No 5) Order 2000, SI 2000/344.
2 See ch 11.
3 See ch 22.
4 *Mergers: A Consultation Document on Proposals for Reform* (August 1999): see ch 22, p 836.
5 *Mergers: The Response to the Consultation on Proposals for Reform*: URN 00/805.
5a See HM Treasury Press Release 67/01, 18 June 2001; *Productivity in the UK: Enterprise and the Productivity Challenge* (HM Treasury, June 2001), pp 19-24; *A World Class Competition Régime* (DTI, July 2001), Cm 5233.

(A) The movement towards reform[6]

Dissatisfaction with the old domestic law of the UK was widespread, among regulators, lawyers and their business clients. The law was defective in various ways: it was ineffective in punishing cartels, in particular since there were very weak sanctions; the powers of the Director General of Fair Trading ('the DGFT') to obtain information about cartel activity were weak; the law on restrictive trade practices was enormously complicated, and often caught innocuous agreements while failing to apply to seriously anti-competitive ones; there was little effective control over the unilateral behaviour of firms with significant market power; and it was very different from EC law, with which firms also had to comply. These, and other, problems led to numerous Consultation Documents, Green Papers and White Papers suggesting proposals for reform. As long ago as 1978/79 two Green Papers were published, *A Review of Monopolies and Mergers Policy*[7] and *A Review of Restrictive Trade Practices Policy*[8] suggesting the need for modifications of the law. The latter led to the provisions for the control of anti-competitive practices in the Competition Act 1980, but the legislation on restrictive trade practices, resale price maintenance and on monopoly situations remained in place.

(i) A period of inertia

Dissatisfaction, specifically with the law on restrictive trade practices, led to the publication in 1988 of a Green Paper *Review of Restrictive Trade Practices Policy: a Consultative Document*[9]. In this Green Paper the Conservative Government of the time suggested that the restrictive trade practices legislation should be fundamentally altered, and should be modelled upon Article 81 EC. After a period of consultation, the Government published a White Paper *Opening Markets: New Policy on Restrictive Trade Practices*[10] in which it confirmed its intention to proceed along these lines. However no Bill was forthcoming, so that the highly unsatisfactory Restrictive Trade Practices Act remained in place, notwithstanding the numerous weaknesses that had been set out so clearly in the Green and White Papers.

The next Green Paper on the reform of domestic competition law dealt not with restrictive trade practices but with the control of firms with significant market power. In *Abuse of Market Power: a Consultative Document on Possible Legislative Options*[11] the Government examined the case for introducing stronger provisions to deal with this issue. Views were sought from the business community and other interested parties on a range of options, including, most radically, the introduction of a prohibition system based on Article 82 EC. The responses to the Green Paper were varied and inconsistent, and the Government announced that it would not go for the radical option, but would instead seek to strengthen the existing legislation (the FTA and the Competition Act 1980) to deal with

---

6 See generally Wilks 'The Prolonged Reform of UK Competition Policy' in *Comparative Competition Policy* (Clarendon Press, 1996, eds Doern and Wilks); Whish 'The Competition Act 1998 and the Prior Debate on Reform' in *The Competition Act: A New Era for UK Competition Law* (Hart Publishing, 2000, eds Rodger and MacCulloch).
7 Cm 7198 (1978).
8 Cmnd 7512 (March 1979).
9 Cm 331 (March 1988).
10 Cm 727 (July 1989).
11 Cm 2100 (November 1992).

some of the criticisms of them. As in the case of the restrictive trade practices proposals, however, no Bill was forthcoming, and the law remained unreformed.

(ii) Mounting criticism of the failure to reform the law

The House of Commons Select Committee on Trade and Industry took evidence on the current state of competition law in the UK in March 1995. *The Economist* reported in an article entitled '*Screaming at the Umpire*'[12] that members of the Committee 'found themselves listening to one long stream of rage. Those testifying before the committee have unleashed a barrage of criticism at the country's competition laws and regulatory bodies'. The Select Committee said that the Government's excuses for not proceeding with reform of the legislation – for example that there was no Parliamentary time – were wearing thin[13]. In the debate on the Queen's Speech in the autumn of 1995, the President of the Board of Trade, Ian Lang, announced to the House of Commons on 20 November that the Government would proceed with a consultation exercise for fundamental reform of domestic competition law, and in March 1996 it published a consultation document *Tackling Cartels and the Abuse of Market Power: Implementing the Government's Policy for Competition Law Reform*[14]. This repeated the proposals that had been suggested earlier, namely that legislation modelled upon Article 81 should be introduced to deal with the problems of restrictive trade practices but that the issue of market power should be addressed by a strengthening of the current law rather than by adopting a prohibition system based upon Article 82. There then followed a period of consultation, during which a large number of responses were received from business, consumers' representatives, associations, law firms and others[15]. The Government published, in August 1996, an explanatory document *Tackling Cartels and the Abuse of Market Power: a Draft Bill*[16] which set out not only its proposals and a summary of the results of the consultation procedure, but also a draft Bill running to 54 clauses and five schedules. It seemed that, at last, reform of the law would become reality. However, the Queen's Speech of November 1996 did not contain any mention of a Competition Bill, and the Conservative Government lost the general election on 1 May 1997[17].

(iii) The new Labour administration of 1997

The Labour Party manifesto of 1997 said that, if elected, the new Government would adopt a tough prohibition approach for competition law. After its landslide victory on 1 May of that year the Government announced, in the Queen's Speech on 14 May 1997, its intention to 'bring forward legislation to reform and strengthen competition law'. In relation to restrictive trade practices, the Government broadly agreed with its predecessor that a system modelled upon Article 81 should be introduced. In relation to the abuse of market power,

---

12 1 April 1995, p 27.
13 See generally the report of the Committee *UK Policy on Monopolies* HC 249-I (HMSO).
14 URN 96/905, DTI March 1996.
15 A list of the respondents will be found in Annex A to the August document; the CBI produced two substantial documents, *Reform of UK Competition Law* and *Tackling Cartels and the Abuse of Market Power: CBI Response* (May 1996).
16 DTI, August 1996.
17 For a chronology of the lethargic progress in reforming UK competition law, see Wilks *In the Public Interest* (Manchester University Press, 1999) pp 296-305 and Whish in *The Competition Act: A New Era for UK Competition Law* (n 6 above) pp 1-11.

however, the new Government announced that it would opt for the 'radical' solution of introducing a prohibition based upon Article 82 EC, although it would also retain the scale and complex monopoly provisions in the FTA.

The bill was introduced in the House of Lords on 15 October 1997 and received the Royal Assent on 9 November 1998[18]. It was decided that the main provisions would not enter into force until 1 March 2000, so that the business community would have an adequate opportunity to adapt to the radically different new system. The debates in the House of Lords were often of a high quality, and a reading of Hansard can be instructive and, indeed, essential at times to understand fully the meaning of the Act. There will be occasions, particularly in the light of the House of Lords' judgment in *Pepper v Hart*[19], on which it will be necessary to refer to the debates in Parliament, and in particular to many of the statements of Lord Simon of Highbury in the House of Lords, in order to understand how some of the Act's provisions are intended to operate[20]. The debates in the House of Commons, by contrast, are not very illuminating, although some important statements were made by Ministers, in particular Nigel Griffiths.

(B) The Competition Act 1998 – overview

(i) Part I: the Chapter I and Chapter II prohibitions

The Competition Act 1998 is a complex and technical piece of legislation. The Act is divided into four parts, consisting of 76 sections. It also contains 14 schedules which contain much important detail, for example on exclusions, notifications, the rôle of the sectoral regulators and transitional provisions. The most important provisions are found in Part I of the Act, which is divided into five chapters. In particular it introduces prohibitions that are modelled upon Article 81 EC (the 'Chapter I prohibition') and Article 82 EC (the 'Chapter II prohibition'). The Act confers substantial powers of investigation and enforcement on the DGFT and the sectoral regulators such as the Director General of Telecommunications[1], and establishes a new Competition Commission with a variety of rôles, including the hearing of appeals against decisions of the DGFT and the regulators. A key aim of the Competition Act is the eradication of cartels, which will be treated much more harshly than under the old Restrictive Trade Practices Act 1976.

(ii) Part II: European investigations

Part II of the Act is concerned with investigations in relation to Articles 81 and 82, giving specific powers for the first time to a High Court judge to issue a warrant authorising the DGFT to enter premises in connection with an investigation requested by the European Commission[2].

---

18 On the passage of the Bill through Parliament, see Borrie 'Lawyers, Legislators and Lobbyists – the Making of the Competition Act 1998' [1999] JBL 205.
19 [1993] AC 593, [1993] 1 All ER 42, HL on the application of the rule in *Pepper v Hart,* see *R v Secretary of State, ex p Spath Holme* [2001] 1 All ER 195, HL.
20 See Whish in *The Competition Act: A New Era for UK Competition Law* (n 6 above) pp 11-15.
1 See ch 10, p 357 on the concurrent powers of the DGFT and the sectoral regulators.
2 See ch 10, p 336.

(iii)   Part III: amendments to the FTA

Part III of the Act makes some changes to the monopoly provisions of the FTA, in particular by amending the powers of the DGFT in order to make it easier for him to obtain information for the purposes of his functions under that Act. The monopoly provisions contained in the FTA have been retained, notwithstanding the introduction of the Chapter II prohibition for the abuse of dominance; it is likely that the FTA system will be used less in the future, but the Competition Act makes a few improvements to the system for those cases in which it will continue to be used[3].

(iv)   Part IV: miscellaneous amendments

Part IV of the 1998 Act contains various supplemental and transitional provisions, including the repeal of sections 44 and 45 of the Patents Act 1977[4], and provisions on Crown application.

(v)   DGFT guidance

The Competition Act 1998 requires the DGFT to publish general advice and information as to how he will apply the law in practice[5]. The sectoral regulators may issue similar advice and information in relation to their respective sectors and have done so in conjunction with the DGFT[6]. A number of guidelines have been published, and they are an essential accompaniment to the Act itself[7]; it is intended that there will be further guidelines in due course on intellectual property and on the exclusion for services of general economic interest provided for by paragraph 4 of Schedule 3 of the Act[8]. On 31 July 2001 the following guidelines had been published:

- *The Major Provisions* (OFT 400)
- *The Chapter I prohibition* (OFT 401)
- *The Chapter II prohibition* (OFT 402)
- *Market definition* (OFT 403)
- *Powers of investigation* (OFT 404)
- *Concurrent application to regulated industries* (OFT 405); this guideline was revised in January 2001 to take account of the Competition Act 1998 (Concurrency) Regulations 2000[9] (OFT 433).
- *Transitional arrangements* (OFT 406)
- *Enforcement* (OFT 407)
- *Trade associations, professional bodies and self-regulatory organisations* (OFT 408)
- *Assessment of individual agreements and conduct* (OFT 414)

3   On the relationship between the 1998 Act and the FTA, see ch 11, pp 383-385.
4   See ch 19, p 715.
5   Competition Act, s 52.
6   Competition Act, Sch 10, para 2(6) for telecommunications, para 3(5) for gas, para 4(5) for electricity, para 5(8) for water, para 6(5) for railways.
7   The Guidelines can be found on the OFT website at http://www.oft.gov.uk/html/comp-act/ technical_guidelines/index.html#guidelines and as the case may be on the sectoral regulators' websites.
8   See p 304 below.
9   SI 2000/260.

- *Assessment of market power* (OFT 415)
- *Exclusion for mergers and ancillary restrictions* (OFT 416)
- *The application of the Competition Act in the telecommunications sector* (OFT 417)
- *Vertical agreements and restraints* (OFT 419)
- *Land agreements* (OFT 420)
- *The application of the Competition Act in the water and sewerage sectors* (OFT 422)
- *Guidance as to the appropriate amount of a penalty* (OFT 423)[10]
- *The application of the Competition Act in the energy sector* (OFT 428)
- *The application of the Competition Act to railway services* (OFT 430)
- *Guidance notes on completing Form N* (OFT 431)[11]; Form N itself is set out in the Director's Rules[12]
- *Application to the Northern Ireland energy sectors* (OFT 437).

(vi)   Publicising the Act

The OFT took a very active rôle in publicising the new Act. Staff of the OFT gave many conference speeches and spoke at numerous seminars. The OFT issued a video *The Competition Act 1998: Compliance Matters*, together with a series of introductory guides on particular aspects of the Act, including *What your business needs to know, How your business can achieve compliance, Under investigation?, Making a complaint, Is notification necessary?, Cartels and the Competition Act 1998: a guide for purchasers, Leniency in cartel cases* and *Public sector bodies and the Competition Act 1998* these guides are available on its website[13]. It is intended to produce a guide on the DGFT's leniency programme[14]. The OFT publishes a Weekly Gazette which contains details of cases being investigated under the Competition Act 1998 and under the Fair Trading Act 1973. It is available from the OFT both in electronic form and by post.

(vii)   Delegated legislation under the Act

The Secretary of State has made a number of Orders, Rules and Regulations pursuant to his powers under the Competition Act 1998, including in particular:
- The Competition Act 1998 (Concurrency) Regulations[15]
- The Competition Commission Appeal Tribunal Rules[16]
- The Competition Act 1998 (Small Agreements and Conduct of Minor Significance) Regulations[17]
- The Competition Act 1998 (Notification of Excluded Agreements and Appealable Decisions) Regulations[18]

---

10   This is not a formal Guideline under s 52 of the Act, but guidance under s 38.
11   This is not a formal Guideline under s 52 of the Act.
12   See n 19 below,
13   http://www.oft.gov.uk/html/comp-act/technical_guidelines/index.html#leaflets.
14   On leniency, see ch 10, pp 353-355.
15   SI 2000/260.
16   SI 2000/261.
17   SI 2000/262.
18   SI 2000/263.

- The Competition Act 1998 (Director's Rules) Order[19]
- The Competition Act 1998 (Determination of Turnover for Penalties) Order[20]
- The Competition Act 1998 (Land and Vertical Agreements Exclusion) Order[1].

(viii)   Literature

A large number of books and articles have been written on the new Act[2].

(ix)   DTI consultation documents

The DTI has also published consultation documents[3] dealing respectively with vertical agreements[4], land agreements[5], concurrent powers of regulators[6], the Competition Commission appeal tribunal rules[7] and draft regulations on concurrency[8].

2.   THE CHAPTER I PROHIBITION

The Chapter I prohibition is contained in sections 1 to 16 of the Act. In addition, section 50 provides for the exclusion, by order, of vertical agreements and agreements relating to land: this was effected by SI 2000/310[9]. Section 1 provides that the following four Acts will cease to have effect: the Restrictive Practices Court Act 1976; the Restrictive Trade Practices Act 1976; the Resale Prices Act 1976; and the Restrictive Trade Practices Act 1977. These repeals took effect on 1 March 2000.

Section 2 contains the Chapter I prohibition itself[10]. Section 3 provides for excluded agreements. Sections 4 to 11 deal with exemptions. The provisions in

19 SI 2000/293; there has been a consultation on minor amendments to the Director's Rules.
20 SI 2000/309.
1   SI 2000/310.
2   On the background to the Act, see Wilks (see p 286 n 6 above), and *The Europeanisation of UK Competition Law* (Hart Publishing, 1998, eds Green and Robertson); on the Act itself, see Coleman and Grenfell *The Competition Act 1998* (Oxford University Press, 1999); Flynn and Stratford *Competition: Understanding the 1998 Act* (Palladian Law Publishing, 1999); Frazer and Hornsby *The Competition Act 1998: a Practical Guide* (Jordans, 1999); Freeman and Whish *A Guide to the Competition Act 1998* (Butterworths, 1999); Latham *A Practitioner's Guide to the Competition Act 1998* (Sweet & Maxwell, 2000); Livingstone *The Competition Act 1998: A Practical Guide* (Sweet & Maxwell, 2001); Singleton *Blackstone's Guide to the Competition Act 1998* (Blackstone Press, 1999); SJ Berwin and Co *Competition Law of the UK* (Juris Publishing, Inc, 2000); Kellaway and Rose *Tolley's Competition Act 1998: A Practical Guide* (Tolley's, 1999); Willis *The Competition Act 1998: A Guide for Businesses* (Monitor Press Ltd, 2nd ed, 2000); Maher 'Juridification, Codification and Sanction in UK Competition Law' (2000) 63 MLR 544; Parker 'The Competition Act 1998: Change and Continuity in UK Competition Policy' [2000] JBL 283.
3   These are available on the DTI's website: http://www.dti.gov.uk.
4   URN 98/1030.
5   URN 98/1029.
6   URN 99/586.
7   URN 98/1154.
8   URN 98/1169.
9   See pp 307-309 below and ch 16, pp 595-598 .
10 See generally *The Major Provisions* OFT Guideline 400, *The Chapter I prohibition* OFT Guideline 401 and *Trade associations, professions and self-regulating bodies* OFT Guideline 408.

sections 12 to 16 on notification are considered in chapter 10. The Chapter I prohibition is closely modelled upon Article 81(1), although it is by no means identical in every respect[11].

(A)   Section 2(1): the prohibition

Section 2(1) provides that:

> 'Subject to section 3, agreements between undertakings, decisions by associations of undertakings or concerted practices which–
> (a) may affect trade within the UK, and
> (b) have as their object or effect the prevention, restriction or distortion of competition within the UK,
> are prohibited unless they are exempt in accordance with the provisions of this Part.'

(i)   'subject to section 3'

Section 3 provides for a wide range of agreements to be excluded from the Chapter I prohibition. These exclusions are considered below[12]. It is also necessary to bear in mind the exclusion for vertical and land agreements under section 50[13].

(ii)   Agreements between undertakings, decisions by associations of undertakings or concerted practices

These words are identical to those in Article 81(1), with the minor exception that the word 'or' in section 2(1) replaces 'and' in Article 81(1). These expressions are ones that have been considered in numerous judgments of the Community Courts which, as a general proposition, the DGFT and sectoral regulators, the Competition Commission and the domestic courts in the UK are obliged to follow as a result of section 60 of the Act[14].

(iii)   'Undertakings'

As in the case of Community law[15], this term will be interpreted broadly by the DGFT to include any natural or legal persons capable of carrying on commercial or economic activities relating to goods or services[16]. Informal guidance has been published on the position of local authorities under the Act, which may sometimes amount to undertakings for the purpose of the Chapter I and II prohibitions.[16a] Also, depending on the facts of each case, a parent company and

11 For a detailed discussion of Article 81(1), see ch 3.
12 See pp 299-307 below.
13 See pp 307-309 below and ch 16, pp 595-598.
14 For discussion of s 60, see pp 329-333 below.
15 On the meaning of undertakings in Community law, see ch 3, pp 66-76 and ch 5, pp 150-151.
16 See *The Major Provisions* OFT Guideline 400, para 1.9 and *The Chapter I prohibition*, OFT Guideline 401, para 2.5.
16a *Public sector bodies and the Competition Act 1998.*

its subsidiaries will be treated as one undertaking where the subsidiaries lack economic independence[17].

The Chapter I prohibition applies to agreements 'between undertakings', but certain provisions of the Act refer to 'persons' rather than undertakings. The reason for this appears to be that in certain contexts the word 'person' is a more appropriate expression. However, in order to prevent undertakings arguing to the contrary, section 59 provides that the expression 'persons' includes 'undertakings'[18].

(iv) 'Agreements'

This term is construed widely in Community law[19]. The Guidelines state that agreements may be spoken or written and need not be legally binding[20]. A reluctant participant to an agreement can still be liable[1].

(v) 'Decisions by associations of undertakings'

This expression has been broadly interpreted in Community law[2], and the DGFT will rely on EC law in its interpretation. The term 'decision' will have a broad meaning, including recommendations, the management decisions of trade associations and their rules. The crucial issue for the DGFT is not the form of the decision nor the method by which it was adopted, but the possibility of it having the effect of limiting the freedom of action of an association's members in commercial matters[3]. The Guideline on *Trade associations, professional bodies and self-regulatory bodies*[4] provides examples of 'decisions': recommendations to members which can be said to have an appreciable effect on competition in the market in question; oral statements which are intended to be followed by members; and constitutional rules of an association which are an agreement that all members must follow.

The effect that a decision of an association might have on the UK market will depend to a certain extent on the size of the membership of the association concerned: the broader the membership of an association, the greater the influence of the association is likely to be[5].

(vi) 'Concerted practices'

This expression will be interpreted in line with the jurisprudence of the Community Courts[6] which identifies the main elements of a concerted practice as a form of

---

17 *The Chapter I prohibition*, OFT Guideline 401, para 2.6.
18 See HL Report Stage, 23 February 1998, cols 511–512.
19 See ch 3, pp 76-81.
20 See *The Major Provisions* OFT Guideline 400, para 1.9, and *The Chapter I prohibition*, OFT Guideline 401, para 2.7.
1   *The Chapter I prohibition*, OFT Guideline 401, para 2.8.
2   See ch 3, pp 81-83.
3   *Trade associations, professional bodies and self-regulatory bodies* OFT Guideline 408, para 2.2.
4   Ibid, paras 2.3-2.5.
5   Ibid, para 5.3.
6   See ch 3, pp 83-86.

practical co-operation, knowingly entered into by the parties, which is intended to amount to a substitution for competition in the market[7]. Contacts or communications which influence market behaviour, depending on the nature of the contact or the effect, or even potential effect, on competition, may be caught if the conduct leads to, or would have led to, a different result had the undertakings not embarked on this conduct[8].

In any consideration of a concerted practice, the DGFT will conduct an economic assessment[9]. He will take into account the structure of the relevant market, the nature of the products involved and the number of undertakings in the market; where there are only a few undertakings he will consider whether they have similar cost structures and outputs[10]. In oligopolistic markets, the DGFT recognises that there may be similar behaviour by undertakings without collusion[11]. The DGFT will examine the form of any apparent co-ordination in order to determine whether there is a concerted practice or not; for example price leadership on its own may be innocent, but where there is price leadership coupled with frequent communication this could fall foul of the Chapter I prohibition.

(vii) 'May affect trade within the UK'

The obvious point about this expression is that there is no requirement under section 2(1) that trade *between Member States* may be affected as in the case of Article 81(1), only that trade *within the UK* should be affected. The result is that, in so far as an agreement affects both trade between Member States and trade within the UK, it may be subject both to Article 81(1) and to the Chapter I prohibition[12]. The consequences of this situation are threefold. First, there is a possibility of an undertaking or undertakings being fined more than once in relation to the same agreement. However section 38(9) of the Act provides that the DGFT must take into account any fine that has been imposed by the European Commission or any court or body in another Member State. Secondly, there may be circumstances in which both the DGFT and the European Commission will have jurisdiction in relation to the same agreement[13]. In that case, the question will arise as to which of the two authorities is the appropriate one to investigate[14]. Thirdly, there may be circumstances in which the parties to an agreement will consider notifying for an individual exemption both under Article 81(3) and under section 4 of the 1998 Act[15].

---

7 Case 48/69 *ICI v EC Commission ('Dyestuffs')* [1972] ECR 619, [1972] CMLR 557.
8 Cases 40/73 etc *Suiker Unie v EC Commission* [1975] ECR 1663, [1976] 1 CMLR 295.
9 *The Chapter I prohibition*, OFT Guideline 401, para 2.12.
10 Ibid, para 2.13.
11 See generally ch 14 on tacit collusion, oligopoly and collective dominance.
12 *The Chapter I prohibition*, OFT Guideline 401, para 7.2; note, however, the European Commission's proposal for the mutual exclusivity of domestic and EC competition law: see pp 321-322 below and ch 7, p 254.
13 See Case 14/68 *Walt Wilhelm v Bundeskartellamt* [1969] ECR 1, [1969] CMLR 100 and para 21 of AG Jacobs opinion in Case C-7/97 *Oscar Brönner v Mediaprint* [1998] ECR I-7791, [1999] 4 CMLR 112.
14 On this issue see *The Chapter I prohibition*, OFT Guideline 401, paras 7.4-7.9.
15 Ibid.

(B) Section 2(2): illustrative list

Section 2(2) provides that:

> 'Subsection (1) applies, in particular, to agreements, decisions or practices which—
> (a) directly or indirectly fix purchase or selling prices or any other trading conditions;
> (b) limit or control production, markets, technical development or investment;
> (c) share markets or sources of supply;
> (d) apply dissimilar conditions to equivalent transactions with other trading parties, thereby placing them at a competitive disadvantage;
> (e) make the conclusion of contracts subject to acceptance by the other parties of supplementary obligations which, by their nature or according to commercial usage, have no connection with the subject of such contracts.'

This list, which exemplifies the sorts of agreement which would infringe section 2(1), is identical to the list in Article 81(1). However, it is important to stress that Article 81(1) has been applied to many other agreements that are *not* explicitly mentioned in the list, and that the same will be true in the case of the Chapter I prohibition. For example, an agreement to exchange information about sales, which enables manufacturers to know the market position and strategy of their competitors in an oligopolistic market, has been found by the ECJ to be caught by Article 81(1)[16], although there is no specific reference to information exchanges in the Article itself. This is because the list is merely illustrative and in each case the critical issue is whether the agreement has as its object or effect the prevention, restriction or distortion of competition. The DGFT's Guideline *The Chapter I prohibition* sets out numerous examples of agreements that could infringe section 2(2) at paragraphs 3.5 to 3.28; these will be examined further in chapter 13 on cartels and hard-core restrictions of competition[17].

Section 2(2)(d) and (e) suggest that agreements to discriminate and tie-ins may amount to infringements of Article 81 or the Chapter I prohibition. It is fair to point out, however, that in the history of the application of Article 81 by the Commission there have been few such cases under Article 81(1)(d) and (e). Discrimination and tie-ins are matters which usually give rise to concern in competition policy only where there is market power on the part of the party which is practising discrimination or which is imposing the tie. For this reason, these phenomena are usually investigated, if at all, under Article 82 rather than under Article 81[18].

(C) Appreciability

The Chapter I prohibition will be applicable only where an agreement brings about an *appreciable* restriction of competition. This is a key feature of the prohibition: the Government and the DGFT have no desire that the new legislation

---

16 Case C-7/95 P *John Deere Ltd v EC Commission* [1998] ECR I-3111, [1998] 5 CMLR 311.
17 See ch 13, pp 455-457.
18 On price discrimination see ch 18, pp 657-662 and on tie-ins see ch 17, pp 605-611.

should catch agreements that could not, in practice, have a significant impact upon the market. However, the requirement that the impact on competition should be appreciable is not to be found in the legislation itself, but rather is to be found in the case law of the Community Courts[19] and the DGFT's Guideline on the *Chapter I prohibition*. This issue was the subject of debate in the House of Lords, where it was argued by some of their Lordships that a specific linguistic amendment ought to be made in order to show that a finding of appreciability was needed. Lord Simon however rejected the argument that the wording of the Chapter I prohibition needed to be changed to include 'significant' or 'appreciable'[20], since the relevant EC jurisprudence would apply anyway by virtue of section 60. This view is sensible: section 60 will indeed bring in the jurisprudence of the Community Courts on this matter, which is likely itself to develop over time. Had the UK attempted to legislate specifically for appreciability, there is every possibility that the words used domestically might turn out to be at variance with the evolving case law in Europe.

The view that the DGFT intends to take in relation to appreciability[1] is that, as a general proposition, an agreement will have no appreciable effect on competition if the undertakings' combined market share of the relevant market[2] does not exceed 25%[3]. However the DGFT will generally consider that any agreement which directly or indirectly fixes prices or shares markets, which imposes minimum resale prices or which is one of a network of similar agreements which have a cumulative effect on the market in question will be capable of having an appreciable effect, even where the undertakings' combined market share falls below the 25% threshold[4]. In calculating the market share, the DGFT will take into account the parties to the agreement and also parents, subsidiaries and affiliates[5]. The DGFT has indicated that an agreement may not have an appreciable effect even where the parties have a market share in excess of 25%[6]. The DGFT will not look at turnover when considering appreciability, since turnover in itself is unlikely to provide much indication of the parties' market power. However turnover will be one of the relevant criteria under section 36 of the Act in determining whether immunity from fines will be available for small agreements[7].

The DGFT's approach to appreciability is significant when considering the policy behind the Chapter I prohibition, which is above all to eradicate cartels. 'Non hard-core' agreements of a horizontal nature where the parties' market share is below 25% will not be subject to the Chapter I prohibition, and vertical agreements, with the exception of minimum and fixed prices, will be outside it

---

19   Case 5/69 *Völk v Vervaecke* [1969] ECR 295, [1969] CMLR 273; Case 22/71 *Béguelin Import v GL Import Export SA* [1971] ECR 949, [1972] CMLR 81; Cases T-374, 375, 384, 388/94 *European Night Services v EC Commission* [1998] ECR II-3141, [1998] 5 CMLR 718: see ch 3, pp 107-110.

20   See eg HL Report Stage, 9 February 1998, cols 884–888.

1   *The Chapter I prohibition* OFT Guideline 401, paras 2.18–2.22.

2   On market definition, see the European Commission's 'Notice on the definition of the relevant market for the purposes of Community competition law' OJ [1997] C 372/5, [1998] 4 CMLR 177; *Market definition* OFT Guideline 403, and in particular para 1.3 which states that the DGFT, in defining markets for the purposes of this Act, will do so consistently with the Commission Notice.

3   Compare the position under EC law: see ch 3, pp 107-110.

4   *The Chapter I prohibition*, OFT Guideline 401, para 2.20.

5   Ibid, para 2.22.

6   Ibid, para 2.21.

7   See ch 10, pp 355-356.

altogether[8]. It follows that fairly few agreements will be caught by the Chapter I prohibition except for cartels; and also, therefore, that there will be relatively few notifications for exemption[9]. Therefore the OFT's resources will be able to be devoted to cartel investigations and to the investigation of the abuse of market power under the Chapter II prohibition, rather than the processing of notifications.

(D)   Section 2(3): extra-territorial application

The extra-territorial scope of the Act is considered in chapter 12[10].

(E)   Section 2(4): voidness

Section 2(4) provides that:

'Any agreement or decision which is prohibited by subsection (1) is void.'

This mirrors Article 81(2) EC. The possibility that agreements may be void is of considerable significance: for many firms it is the possibility that their agreements may turn out to be unenforceable that has as much, and in many cases more, significance than the possibility of being fined. A considerable compliance effort has to be maintained in order to ensure that important commercial transactions will not be undermined by one or more parties to an agreement subsequently reneging on it and claiming it to be unenforceable. These issues are considered, in relation to EC law, in chapter 8[11]. A couple of points are worthy of mention here.

(i)   Severance

Section 2(4) provides that 'any agreement' which violates section 2(1) is void. It does not say that the voidness might relate only to the provisions in the agreement that violate the Chapter I prohibition, nor does it say anything about the consequence of such voidness on the remaining provisions of the agreement. However, despite the clear wording of both section 2(4) and Article 81(2) EC that the agreement is void, it has been established by the ECJ that it may be possible to sever the offending clauses, leaving the remainder of the agreement enforceable[12]. The intention is that the courts in the UK should interpret section 2(4) in the same way as the ECJ has interpreted Article 81(2)[13], and this will be possible by virtue of section 60 of the Act.

English contract law provides that severance is possible in certain circumstances, although the rules on this subject are complex[14]. It is presumably a matter for the applicable law of the contract, rather than the *lex fori* of the

---

8   See p 307 below and ch 16, pp 595-598.
9   This is borne out by the experience of the first 17 months of the Act: by 31 July 2000 only seven notifications for a decision had been made: see p 311, n 3 below.
10   See ch 12, pp 404-405.
11   See also Whish 'The Enforceability of Agreements under EC and UK Competition Law' in *Lex Mercatoria: Essays on International Commercial Law in Honour of Francis Reynolds* (ed Rose, LLP, 2000).
12   See ch 8, pp 268-269.
13   HL Report Stage, 9 February 1998, col 890.
14   See *Chitty on Contracts* (Sweet & Maxwell, 28th edn, 1999, ed Beale), paras 17–185 to 17–194.

court in which the action is brought, to determine whether, and, if so, by what criteria, severance is to be effected[15].

(ii)   Void or illegal?

In *Gibbs Mew plc v Gemmell*[16] the Court of Appeal concluded that an agreement that infringes Article 81(1) is not only void and unenforceable, but is also illegal. This has serious consequences: for example a party who has paid money to another under an illegal agreement cannot recover that money unless it can be shown that the parties were not *in pari delicto*[17]. It will presumably follow from this that agreements that infringe the Chapter I prohibition will likewise be held to be illegal. The Guidelines do not say anything on this issue, nor was it discussed in Parliament. Further light should be shed on this issue when the ECJ gives judgment in *Crehan v Courage Ltd*[18], a case referred from the UK under Article 234 EC.

(iii)   Transient voidness

In *Passmore v Morland plc*[19] the Court of Appeal held that an agreement may, in its lifetime, drift into and out of unlawfulness under Article 81(1), and therefore be void and unenforceable at some times but not at others. The same presumably will be true of section 2(4).

(F)   Sections 2(5) and 2(6): interpretation

These provisions explain that, except where the context otherwise requires, any reference in the Act to an agreement includes a reference to a concerted practice and a decision by an association of undertakings. This overcomes the clumsiness of having to use all three expressions throughout the text of the Act.

(G)   Section 2(7): the UK

Section 2(7) provides that '"the UK" means, in relation to an agreement which operates or is intended to operate only in a part of the UK, that part.' The UK for this purpose includes England, Wales, Scotland plus the subsidiary islands (excluding the Isle of Man and the Channel Islands) and Northern Ireland[20].

---

15 See Rome Convention on the law applicable to contractual obligations 1980 (consolidated version OJ [1998] C 27/34, p 34); *Dicey and Morris on the Conflict of Laws* (Sweet & Maxwell, 13th edn, 2000, ed Collins) chs 32 and 33.
16 [1998] Eu LR 588; see also *Trent Taverns Ltd v Sykes* [1999] Eu LR 492, CA.
17 See Goff and Jones *Law of Restitution* (Sweet & Maxwell, 5th ed, 1998) ch 24, p 607.
18 [1999] Eu LR 834, [1999] 2 EGLR 145; Case C-453/99 (judgment pending); Advocate General Mischo gave his opinion in this case on 22 March 2001.
19 [1999] 3 All ER 1005, [1999] 1 CMLR 1129, CA; see ch 8, pp 271-272.
20 *The Chapter I prohibition* OFT Guideline 401, para 2.15.

(H) Section 2(8): the 'Chapter I prohibition'

Section 2(8) provides that:

'The prohibition imposed by subsection (1) is referred to in this Act as "the Chapter I prohibition".'

The expression 'the Chapter I prohibition' is therefore a legislative one, and is mirrored by section 18(4) which recognises the companion 'Chapter II prohibition'[1].

(I) The Chapter I prohibition: excluded agreements

Section 3 provides for a number of exclusions from the Chapter I prohibition. These exclusions will be of considerable importance in practice, and in some cases are complex. Some, but not all, of these exclusions apply also in the case of the Chapter II prohibition[2]. Section 50 also provides for most vertical and land agreements to be excluded[3]. Section 59(2) provides that if the effect of one or more exclusions is that the Chapter I prohibition is inapplicable to one or more provisions of an agreement, those provisions do not have to be disregarded when considering whether the agreement itself infringes the prohibition for other reasons. In other words, the effect of the agreement as a whole can be considered.

Section 3(1) provides that the Chapter I prohibition does not apply in any of the cases in which it is excluded by or as a result of Schedule 1 on mergers and concentrations; Schedule 2 on competition scrutiny under other enactments; Schedule 3 on planning obligations and other general exclusions; and Schedule 4 on professional rules. Sections 3(2) to (5) make provision for the Secretary of State to amend Schedules 1 and 3 in certain circumstances, whether by adding additional exclusions or by amending or removing existing ones[4]. Section 3(6) notes that Schedule 3 itself enables the Secretary of State himself in certain circumstances to exclude agreements from the Chapter I prohibition[5].

(i) Schedule 1: mergers and concentrations

Schedule 1 deals with the application of the Chapter I and II prohibitions to mergers and concentrations. The basic policy of the Schedule is that the prohibitions will not apply to mergers under the FTA nor to concentrations in respect of which the European Commission has exclusive jurisdiction under the EC Merger Regulation ('the ECMR')[6]. The exclusion in Schedule 1 is automatic and does not require an application to the DGFT or to the Secretary of State. Guidelines have been published by the DGFT on these provisions[7].

1　See pp 314-321 below.
2　See pp 320-321 below.
3　See pp 307-309 below and ch 16, pp 595-598.
4　This order-making power is subject to 71 of the Act, which requires an affirmative resolution of each House of Parliament.
5　See pp 305-306 below on Sch 3, para 7.
6　Council Regulation 4064/89/EEC, OJ [1990] L 257/13, as amended by Council Regulation 1310/97/EC, OJ [1997] L 180/1.
7　*Exclusion for mergers and ancillary restrictions* OFT Guideline 416.

(A)   RELATIONSHIP OF THE CHAPTER I AND II PROHIBITIONS WITH UK MERGER CONTROL.   Schedule 1, paragraph 1(1) provides that the Chapter I prohibition does not apply to an agreement or combination of agreements which results or would result in any two enterprises 'ceasing to be distinct enterprises' for the purposes of Part V of the FTA[8]. The exclusion applies to any transaction whereby enterprises cease to be distinct, irrespective of whether the merger in question would be one that 'qualifies for investigation' for the purposes of the FTA[9]. If this were otherwise, the 1998 Act would have revolutionised the control of mergers in the UK by bringing all those transactions that are not subject to the FTA because they fall below the relevant thresholds within the scope of the new Act, which would be an absurdity.

Schedule 1, paragraph 1(2) provides in addition that the exclusion extends to 'any provision directly related and necessary to the implementation of the merger provisions'. Thus, 'ancillary restraints' will also fall outside the Chapter I prohibition[10]. To be ancillary, the restraint must be both 'directly related [to]' and 'necessary to the implementation of' the merger provisions. Examples of ancillary restraints are given in the DGFT's guidelines[11] and include, for example, appropriately limited non-compete clauses, licences of intellectual property rights and purchase and supply agreements. Whether a restraint is to be treated as ancillary is something that will be determined by the DGFT[12]. The relevant regulator for gas and electricity, water, telecommunications and railways will be consulted where appropriate[13]. The expression 'merger provisions' is defined in paragraph 1(3) as meaning the provisions of the agreement which cause, or if carried out would cause, the agreement to lead to enterprises ceasing to be distinct. The purpose of this definition is to demarcate those provisions which are ancillary to the merger, and therefore fall outside the Chapter I prohibition, from other provisions which would remain subject to its provisions.

(B)   NEWSPAPER MERGERS.   Schedule 1, paragraph 3 provides the same exclusion from the Chapter I prohibition for newspaper mergers as defined in section 57 of the FTA 1973, and any ancillary restraints[14].

(C)   CLAWBACK.   Schedule 1, paragraph 4 provides for the possibility of 'withdrawal of the paragraph 1 exclusion' by the DGFT; such a provision is known as a 'clawback', a device that can be found elsewhere in the 1998 Act[15]. The clawback applies only to the Chapter I prohibition; it does not apply to the Chapter II prohibition. There is no clawback provision in relation to newspaper mergers, which are within the exclusive competence of the Secretary of State. In the House of Lords Lord Simon explained the reason for the inclusion of the

8   For the meaning of 'ceasing to be distinct', see ch 22, pp 805-807; the UK exclusion is wider than the disapplication of Article 81 to concentrations in the EC, effected by Article 21(2) of the ECMR, since 'ceasing to be distinct' is a broader term than concentration: see ch 22, pp 806; see also HL Third Reading, 5 March 1998, col 1365 (Lord Simon of Highbury).
9   See ch 22, pp 807-809 on the meaning of mergers that qualify for investigation.
10   On ancillary restraints under the ECMR, see ch 21, p 783.
11   *Exclusion for mergers and ancillary restrictions* OFT Guideline 416, paras 4.9–4.16.
12   Ibid, paras 4.17–4.21.
13   Ibid, para 4.22.
14   On newspaper mergers, see ch 22, pp 844-850.
15   See eg Competition Act 1998, Sch 3, para 2(3) (clawback possible in relation to agreements that benefit from directions under s 21(2) Restrictive Trade Practices Act 1976); Competition Act 1998, Sch 3, para 9(7) (clawback possible for agreements relating to agricultural products); and Article 7 of The Competition Act 1998 (Land and Vertical Agreements Exclusion) Order 2000, SI 2000/310 (clawback available for both types of agreement).

clawback provision: that the breadth of the exclusion – even to include the acquisition of control or material influence by one business over another – 'creates some risk of providing a loophole for anti-competitive agreements'[16]. The guidelines cite as an example a price-fixing agreement deliberately structured in such a way that it falls within the definition of a merger, but which falls below the thresholds at which it would qualify for investigation[17]. Paragraph 4(5) therefore provides that the DGFT may, by a direction in writing[18], remove the benefit of the exclusion where he considers that (*a*) an agreement would, if not excluded, infringe the Chapter I prohibition; and (*b*) he would not be likely to grant it an unconditional exemption (that is to say an exemption to which no conditions or obligations are attached under section 4(3)(*a*))[19]; and (*c*) the agreement is not a protected agreement[20].

The cumulative effect of these provisions is that the clawback power will be exercised only rarely, which is acknowledged in the Guideline[1]. Furthermore, exercise of the clawback would not in itself mean that the agreement infringes the Chapter I prohibition: this would have to be the subject of a separate assessment[2].

(D)   PROTECTED AGREEMENTS.   The DGFT cannot exercise the right of clawback in relation to a 'protected agreement'. The Act defines four categories of protected agreement. First, an agreement in relation to which the Secretary of State has announced that he will not be making a reference to the Competition Commission; the DGFT cannot override a decision by the Secretary of State not to refer a merger under the FTA by instituting his own investigation under the 1998 Act. Second, an agreement in relation to which the Competition Commission has found there to be a merger qualifying for investigation. Third, an agreement that would result in enterprises ceasing to be distinct in the sense of section 65 of the FTA, other than by virtue of the provisions of paragraph 1(4) of Schedule 1[3]. Fourth, an agreement which the Competition Commission has found gives rise to a merger in the sense of section 32 of the Water Industry Act 1991.

(E)   RELATIONSHIP OF THE CHAPTER I AND II PROHIBITIONS WITH EC MERGER CONTROL[4].   Schedule 1, paragraph 6 provides that the Chapter I prohibition does not apply to concentrations which have a Community dimension in relation to which the European Commission has exclusive jurisdiction. This provision is necessary in order to comply with Article 21(2) of the ECMR[5], which provides that no Member State may apply its national legislation on competition to any concentration that has a Community dimension. Paragraph 6 does not mention ancillary restraints specifically, but since the European Commission can deal with these under the ECMR, it presumably follows that Article 21(2) prevents Member States from taking action in relation to them as well.

16   HL Committee, 13 November 1997, col 328.
17   *Exclusion for mergers and ancillary restrictions* OFT Guideline 416, para 3.1.
18   CA, Sch 3, para 4(7)(a); the direction cannot be retrospective: see para 4(7)(b).
19   CA, Sch 3, para 4(6).
20   CA, Sch 3, para 5; on protected agreements, see below.
1   *Exclusion for mergers and ancillary restrictions* OFT Guideline 416, para 3.6.
2   Ibid, para 3.8.
3   See above
4   On the ECMR generally, see ch 21.
5   See ch 21, pp 756-757.

(F)   NO CLAWBACK.   Since Schedule 1, paragraph 6 deals with matters that are within the exclusive jurisdiction of the European Commission, it follows that the DGFT does not in this situation enjoy a right of clawback as he does under paragraph 4 in relation to mergers that are subject to the FTA.

(ii)   Schedule 2: competition scrutiny under other enactments

Schedule 2 excludes agreements which are subject to competition scrutiny under the Financial Services Act 1986, the Companies Act 1989 and its Northern Irish equivalent[6], the Broadcasting Act 1990 or the Environment Act 1995. The view was taken by the Government that, in so far as particular agreements are subject to competition scrutiny under régimes constructed to deal with the circumstances of specific sectors, it is inappropriate to subject them to the Chapter I prohibition as well, as 'that would just create an unwelcome and unjustified double jeopardy'[7]. In each case, the exclusion from the Chapter I prohibition is effected by amending the provisions of the legislation that provides for 'other' competition scrutiny. There is no exclusion from the Chapter II prohibition for these cases. Further exclusions, from both the Chapter I and Chapter II prohibitions, have been added by sections 164, 311 and 312 of the Financial Services and Markets Act 2000.

(A)   FINANCIAL SERVICES ACT 1986.   The Financial Services Act 1986 deals with the regulation of investment business, and provides for firms to comply with the rules of the regulatory authorities[8]. Schedule 2, paragraph 1 of the 1998 Act amends sections 125 to 127 of the 1986 Act in order to provide for exclusion from the Chapter I prohibition of agreements and recognised professional bodies that are dealt with according to those provisions. These provisions will cease to have effect, by virtue of an order under section 426 of the Financial Services and Markets Act 2000, when the arrangements under that Act, described below, enter into force.

(B)   COMPANIES ACT 1989 AND COMPANIES (NORTHERN IRELAND) ORDER 1990[9]. Paragraphs 2 and 3 of Schedule 2 of the 1998 Act amend Schedule 14 of the Companies Act 1989 and Schedule 14 of the Companies (Northern Ireland) Order 1990 respectively. These Schedules deal with the supervision and qualification of company auditors. The amendments provide for such matters to be dealt with under the rules of recognised professional bodies[10].

(C)   BROADCASTING ACT 1990.   Section 194A of the Broadcasting Act 1990 deals with the Channel 3 news provision and networking arrangements, and provides for the Secretary of State to exempt agreements from Chapter I which are not considered to pose a threat to competition[11]. Paragraph 4 of Schedule 2 of the 1998 Act amends section 194A of the 1990 Act, in relation to news provision for Channel 3, and paragraph 5 makes provision for the exclusion from the Chapter I prohibition of networking arrangements to the extent that they are subject to Schedule 4 of the Broadcasting Act 1990, or contain provisions which have been

6   Companies (Northern Ireland) Order 1990, SI 1990/593.
7   HL Committee, 13 November 1997, col 342.
8   See 3(2) *Halsbury's Laws of England* (Butterworths, 4th ed reissue) para 158.
9   SI 1990/593.
10   See 7(2) *Halsbury's Laws of England* (Butterworths, 4th ed reissue) para 955.
11   See 45 *Halsbury's Laws of England* (Butterworths, 4th ed reissue) para 425.

considered thereunder. Paragraph 5(2) of Schedule 2 provides that a list of such arrangements must be published by the Independent Television Commission, which must consult the DGFT before doing so and must ensure that the list will be brought to the attention of persons who would be affected by it or have an interest in it. As required by the Act, the ITC published a list of excluded networking arrangements in August 2000[12].

(D) ENVIRONMENT ACT 1995. Section 94 of the Environment Act 1995 provides for the responsibility of producers in relation to the materials they use[13]. Paragraph 6 of Schedule 2 of the Act allows the Secretary of State to exclude agreements from the Chapter I prohibition which relate to exemption schemes.

(E) NO POWER TO AMEND SCHEDULE 2. There is no power to amend Schedule 2. Section 3 of the 1998 Act provides the power to amend only in relation to Schedule 1 and Schedule 3.

(F) FINANCIAL SERVICES AND MARKETS ACT 2000. This Act establishes the Financial Services Authority ('the FSA') with the regulatory objectives of achieving market confidence, public awareness, the protection of consumers and the reduction of financial crime[14]. Section 95 makes provision for the Treasury, by order, to establish competition scrutiny of the FSA in relation to the official listing of securities. Sections 159 to 163 provide for competition scrutiny in relation to regulating provisions and practices adopted by the FSA. The DGFT must keep them under review and may report on provisions and practices having a significant adverse effect on competition[15]. Where he makes a report to this effect, the Competition Commission will investigate the matter further[16]. Where the Commission's report is adverse, the Treasury is given power to give directions, although it is not always bound to do so[17]. Section 164 provides for exclusion from both the Chapter I and Chapter II prohibitions for agreements, practices or conduct that are encouraged by any of the FSA's regulating provisions. Similar provisions are to be found in sections 302 to 312 in relation to recognised investment exchanges and clearing houses.

(iii) Schedule 3: planning obligations and other general exclusions

Schedule 3 is entitled 'General Exclusions' and sets out various matters that are excluded, some of which are of considerable importance.

(A) PLANNING OBLIGATIONS. Paragraph 1 of Schedule 3 provides that the Chapter I prohibition does not apply to agreements involving planning obligations, for example where planning permission is given subject to the developer agreeing to provide certain services or access to facilities[18].

---

12 ITC Press Release 66/00, 2 August 2000.
13 See 8(2) *Halsbury's Laws of England* (Butterworths, 4th ed reissue) para 458.
14 Financial Services and Markets Act 2000, ss 1 and 2.
15 Ibid, ss 159 and 160.
16 Ibid, s 162 and Sch 14.
17 Ibid, s 163.
18 See Town and Country Planning Act 1990, s 106.

(B)   SECTION 21(2) RESTRICTIVE TRADE PRACTICES ACT 1976.   Paragraph 2 of Schedule 3 provides that agreements that are the subject of directions under section 21(2) of the Restrictive Trade Practices Act 1976 are excluded from the Chapter I prohibition. Under the 1976 Act, agreements containing restrictions having an insignificant effect on competition could, effectively, be excluded from the Act as a result of directions given by the Secretary of State. Many thousands of agreements were dealt with in this way[19]. Such agreements are also excluded from the 1998 Act. Paragraph 2(2) of Schedule 3 provides that, if a material variation is made to an agreement that has been the subject of directions under section 21(2) of the Restrictive Trade Practices Act, the exclusion shall cease to apply from the coming into force of the variation. This provision removes the benefit of exclusion without any reference to the competitive impact of the material variation. However, in so far as the varied agreement has no appreciable impact upon competition, it would not come within the Chapter I prohibition anyway, so that the removal of the exclusion would not make any difference[20]. The DGFT has indicated that a material variation would be one that has as its object or effect an appreciable restriction of competition, and that a minor adjustment in the trading relationship of the parties to an agreement would not be caught[1]. Paragraph 2(3) of Schedule 3 provides the DGFT with a power of clawback in relation to excluded s 21(2) agreements, similar to those found in Schedule 1 for mergers under the FTA[2].

(C)   EEA REGULATED MARKETS.   Paragraph 3 of Schedule 3 provides that the Chapter I prohibition does not apply to various matters concerning 'EEA regulated [financial services] markets'. This expression is defined in paragraph 3(5) as meaning a market which is listed by another EEA state[3] and which does not require a dealer on the market to have a presence where trading facilities are provided or on any other trading floor of that market.

(D)   SERVICES OF GENERAL ECONOMIC INTEREST.   Paragraph 4 of Schedule 3 provides that neither the Chapter I nor the Chapter II prohibition shall apply to an undertaking:

> 'entrusted with the operation of services of general economic interest or having the character of a revenue-earning monopoly in so far as the prohibition would obstruct the performance, in law or in fact, of the particular tasks assigned to it'.

This important provision is modelled upon Article 86(2) EC[4], although the language of the Schedule is somewhat less tortuous than that to be found in the Treaty. It is intended that the DGFT in conjunction with the sectoral regulators will produce guidelines on this provision in due course.[4a]

---

19   On the section 21(2) procedure see Div I *Butterworths Competition Law* (Butterworths, eds Freeman and Whish) paras [1104]-[1199]; Green and Robertson *Commercial Agreements and Competition Law* (Kluwer Law International, 2nd ed, 1997) paras 4.96-4.114.
20   See Case C-39/96 *KVB v Free Record Shop BV* [1997] ECR I-2303, [1997] 5 CMLR 521 on the treatment of 'old' agreements under Article 81 of the Treaty, and the impact on the provisional validity of subsequent variations.
1   *Transitional arrangements* OFT Guideline, para 4.16.
2   See pp 299-302 above; see also *Transitional Arrangements* OFT Guideline 406, paras 5.6-5.12.
3   Pursuant to Article 16 of Council Directive 93/22/EEC, OJ [1993] L 141/27.
4   See ch 6, pp 202-208; see also the European Commission's *Communication on services of general economic interest* OJ [2001] C 17/4, [2001] 4 CMLR 882.
4a   A draft was published in July 2001, OFT 421.

(E) COMPLIANCE WITH LEGAL REQUIREMENTS. Paragraph 5 of Schedule 3 provides that neither the Chapter I nor the Chapter II prohibition applies to an agreement or to conduct that is required to comply with a legal requirement. For this purpose, a legal requirement is one imposed by or under any enactment in force in the UK, by or under the EC Treaty or the EEA Agreement and having legal effect in the UK without further enactment, or under the law in force in another Member State having legal effect in the UK. An example of the operation of this exclusion could occur where an undertaking in one of the utility sectors was subject to a licence condition requiring it to behave in a certain way[5]: in such circumstances it could not be guilty of infringing the Chapter I or II prohibitions where it had simply complied with the licence condition. Similarly it could not be found liable under the Act where it had done something required, for example, by a Commission Directive adopted under Article 86(3) of the Treaty[6]. However, this exclusion applies only where the regulated undertaking is required to act in a certain way; it does not apply to the discretionary behaviour of that undertaking.

(F) AVOIDANCE OF CONFLICT WITH INTERNATIONAL OBLIGATIONS. Paragraph 6(1) of Schedule 3 gives power to the Secretary of State to make an order to exclude the application of the Chapter I prohibition from an agreement or a category of agreements where this would be appropriate in order to avoid a conflict between the provisions of the Competition Act and an international obligation of the UK. The order can provide that the exclusion shall apply only in specified circumstances[7] and may be retrospective[8]. Similar provisions are contained in Schedule 3 paragraph 6(4) and (5) for exclusion from the Chapter II prohibition. Schedule 3 paragraph 6(6) was introduced in the House of Lords as a Government amendment to extend the meaning of the term 'international obligation' to include inter-Governmental arrangements relating to civil aviation: the reason for this is that such arrangements, permitting flights between the UK and other countries, are often not made as treaties[9] and so do not give rise to international 'obligations' as such.

(G) PUBLIC POLICY. Paragraph 7 of Schedule 3 gives power to the Secretary of State to make an order to exclude the application of the Chapter I prohibition from an agreement or a category of agreements where there are 'exceptional and compelling reasons of public policy' for doing so. The order can provide that the exclusion shall apply only in specified circumstances[10], and may be retrospective[11]. Similar provisions are contained in paragraph 7(4) and (5) of Schedule 3 for exclusion from the Chapter II prohibition. It is questionable how much this provision will be used in practice: the other exclusions in the Act are reasonably specific, and the Secretary of State has power to vary some of them in the manner laid down in the Act. This provision allows him to make an exclusion on public policy grounds, a concept that is necessarily vague. However, the requirement that the reasons must be 'exceptional and compelling' clearly imposes a heavy burden on the Secretary of State to demonstrate that he should be able to exercise the power. It might be that the power would be invoked, for

---

5   HL Deb 13 November 1997, col 334.
6   On Article 86(3), see ch 6, pp 208-210.
7   Competition Act 1998, Sch 3, para 6(2).
8   Ibid, Sch 3, para 6(3).
9   HL Deb 9 February 1998, cols 972-3.
10   Competition Act 1998, Sch 3(7)(2).
11   Ibid, Sch 3(7)(3).

example, in relation to the defence industry. The EC Treaty provides a specific exclusion from the competition rules for certain matters related to defence in Article 296 (ex Article 223), but there are no specific exclusions for this area from the Competition Act.

(H)   COAL AND STEEL.   Paragraph 8 of Schedule 3 provides that the Chapter I and Chapter II prohibitions do not apply to agreements and conduct within the exclusive jurisdiction of the European Commission under the ECSC Treaty. These exclusions will cease to have effect when the ECSC Treaty expires in 2002[12].

(I)   AGRICULTURAL PRODUCTS.   Paragraph 9 of Schedule 3 provides exclusion from the Chapter I prohibition for agreements that fall outside Article 81 EC by virtue of Regulation 26/62[13]. If the European Commission decides that an agreement is not excluded from Article 81 by Regulation 26/62, the exclusion from paragraph 9 of Schedule 3 ceases on the same date[14]. Provision is made for clawback[15].

(iv)   Schedule 4: professional rules

The Government considered that professional rules which serve to protect the public, which contain disciplinary arrangements and which are liable to judicial review should fall outside the Chapter I prohibition[16]. Pursuant to paragraph 1(1) of Schedule 4, the Chapter I prohibition does not apply to an agreement which constitutes a designated professional rule; which imposes obligations arising from designated rules; or which constitutes an agreement to act in accordance with such rules. It is important to appreciate that the exclusion is for the professional rules and the consequences of the rules: it is not an exclusion for the professions as such, in the way that professional services were excluded from the Restrictive Trade Practices Act 1976. Schedule 1(2) defines professional rules widely as those regulating a professional service or the people providing that service. Professional services themselves are set out in Part II of the Schedule and include, for example, legal, medical, dental and ophthalmic services. Paragraph 2 of Schedule 4 gives the power to designate professional rules for the purposes of the exclusion to the Secretary of State. Application must be made to him for designation[17]: the Competition Act (Application for Designation of Professional Rules) Regulations 1999[18] set out the means by which professional bodies can do so. Alterations in professional rules must be notified to the Secretary of State as soon as is reasonably practicable, but a rule does not cease to be designated simply because it has been altered[19]. Provision is made for the DGFT to keep the list of professional rules under review and to advise the Secretary of State whether the exclusion should be restricted in relation to the rules of a particular body[20]. The Secretary of State has power, if he receives such advice from the DGFT, to remove particular rules from the designated list[1]. There is no power to amend Schedule 4, for example by adding additional services to the list in Part II. The

12   Ibid, Sch 3(8)(2) and (4); see ch 23, pp 853-854.
13   See ch 23, pp 855-858.
14   Competition Act 1998, Sch 3, para 9(2).
15   Ibid, Sch 3, para 9(6) and (7).
16   HL Committee, 13 November 1997, col 292; see also HL Deb 9 February 1998, cols 896-898.
17   Competition Act 1998, Sch 4, para 3.
18   SI 1999/2546.
19   Competition Act 1998, Sch 4, para 4.
20   Ibid, Sch 4, para 5.
1   Ibid, Sch 4, para 6.

DGFT published, in the spring of 2000, a consultation document, *A review of competition restrictions in the professions*[2]. In March 2001 the DGFT published a report, *Competition in professions*, in which he recommended that a number of restrictions on competition in three professions – lawyers (in particular barristers), accountants and architects – should be removed[3]; the DGFT considered that there was a strong case for repealing Schedule 4 of the Competition Act 1998, a view with which the Secretary of State expressed agreement.[3a] Further action on this matter is awaited.

(v) Section 50: vertical agreements[4]

Section 50 of the Act makes provision for the exclusion or exemption of vertical agreements from the Chapter I, but not the Chapter II, prohibition. This has been effected, except in relation to vertical price fixing, by the Competition Act 1998 (Land and Vertical Agreements Exclusion) Order[5]; Article 7 of the Order makes provision for clawback. A Guideline has been published on the application of the Act to vertical agreements[6]. The policy background to and the extent of this exclusion is dealt with in detail in chapter 16 on vertical agreements. It should be mentioned in passing that the exclusion of vertical agreements does not extend to licences of intellectual property rights; however, many licences will benefit from parallel exemption by virtue of the combination of section 10 of the 1998 Act with Regulation 240/96 on technology transfer agreements[7].

(vi) Section 50: land agreements

As the Competition Bill passed through Parliament, the Government recognised that there was a compelling case for excluding certain agreements relating to land from the Chapter I, though not the Chapter II, prohibition: an obvious case would be commercial leases containing covenants and conditions imposed for the sake of good estate management[8]. In particular, it would be undesirable if there was widespread uncertainty as to whether such covenants and conditions might be rendered void and unenforceable as a result of section 2(4) of the Act. However, the difficulties of framing a specific exclusion were noted by Lord Simon in the House of Lords[9]; rather than defining land agreements in the Act itself, power was given to exclude or exempt them in section 50, which gave the same power in relation to vertical agreements. The DTI published a Consultation Document in February 1999 together with a draft order[10]. After initially proposing

---

2   http://www.oft.gov.uk/html/new/professions5-00.htm.
3   The report is available at http://www.oft.gov.uk/html/rsearch/reports/oft328.htm and was concluded under s 2 of the Fair Trading Act 1972.
3a DTI Press Release P/2001/141, 9 March 2001.
4   On vertical agreements generally, see ch 16.
5   SI 2000/310.
6   *Vertical agreements and restraints* OFT Guideline 419.
7   On parallel exemptions, see pp 312-313 below; on Regulation 240/96, see ch 19, pp 688-696.
8   The registrability of restrictive covenants in commercial leases under the Restrictive Trade Practices Act 1976 was the subject of a test case in *Re Ravenseft Property Ltd's Application* [1978] QB 52, [1977] 1 All ER 47, RPC; on the position of shopping centre leases in Ireland, see Maher *Competition Law: Alignment and Reform* (Round Hall Sweet & Maxwell, 1999) pp 430-431.
9   HL Committee, 13 November 1997, col 340.
10 URN 98/1029.

separate orders for vertical and land agreements, the Secretary of State enacted a single Order covering both, the Competition Act 1998 (Land and Vertical Agreements Exclusion) Order[11]. The Order itself came into force on 1 March 2000[12] and was accompanied by a Guideline on land agreements[13].

(A)   THE EXCLUSION.   Article 5 of the Order provides that the Chapter I prohibition shall not apply to an agreement to the extent to which it is a land agreement. To the extent that an agreement is a vertical agreement, it is not a land agreement[14]; however, the same agreement may benefit partly from the exclusion for vertical agreements and partly from the exclusion for land agreements[15]: typically a lease of a public house or of a petrol station might be partially excluded as a vertical agreement, where the tenant accepts an obligation to purchase beer or petrol only from the landlord, and partly as a land agreement, where the tenant is subject to obligations and restrictions in his capacity as a holder of an interest in land[16]. To the extent that an agreement is not a land agreement, it could be subject to the Chapter I prohibition[17]; this would require an analysis of the various criteria for application of that provision[18]. It will be recalled that there is a specific exclusion in paragraph 1 of Schedule 3 for planning obligations[19].

Article 2 provides that a land agreement means:

> 'an agreement between undertakings which creates, alters, transfers or terminates an interest in land, or an agreement to enter into such an agreement, together with any obligation and restriction to which Article 6 applies; and to the extent that an agreement is a vertical agreement it is not a land agreement'.

The same Article defines further what is meant by an 'interest in land', which includes licences and references to Scottish property concepts; and 'land', which includes buildings and other structures on land covered with water. Examples of land agreements include transfers of freeholds, leases or assignments of leasehold interests and easements[20]. The exclusion applies only to an agreement as defined in Article 2; an agreement between landlords to fix rents, or between tenants as to the goods they will sell from their properties, would not be land agreements since they do not *create, alter, transfer or terminate* an interest in land[1].

(B)   ARTICLE 6 OBLIGATIONS AND RESTRICTIONS.   The exclusion of land agreements extends, by virtue of Article 6, to obligations[2] and restrictions[3] which relate to 'relevant land'[4]. For obligations to be excluded, they must be accepted by a party to a land agreement 'in his capacity as holder of an interest' in relevant land: if the obligation is not accepted in this capacity, it may amount to a

11   SI 2000/310.
12   Ibid, Article 1.
13   *Land Agreements* OFT Guideline 420.
14   SI 2000/310, Article 2.
15   *Land Agreements* OFT Guideline 420, paras 3.3 and 3.4.
16   On the expression 'in his capacity as a holder of an interest in land', see p 309 below.
17   On the expression 'to the extent that' see paras 3.1 and 3.2 of the Guideline.
18   Ibid, paras 1.9-1.14.
19   See p 303 above.
20   Ibid, para 2.3.
1   Ibid, para 2.4.
2   SI 2000/310, Article 6(1).
3   SI 2000/310, Article 6(2).
4   Relevant land is defined in Article 2 of the Order.

restriction of competition and must be tested according to the criteria of the Chapter I prohibition[5]. The critical term here is 'capacity', which is considered in paragraphs 2.6 to 2.9 of the Guideline[6]. For restrictions to be excluded, they must restrict the activity that may be carried out on or in connection with the relevant land, and again must be accepted by a party to the agreement in his capacity as holder of an interest in that land; here again, the term 'capacity' is critical, as is the expression 'activity': it is considered in paragraphs 2.10 and 2.11 of the Guideline. Paragraph 2.12 states that reciprocal restrictions may benefit from the exclusion: for example a restriction imposed on one tenant of premises in a shopping centre only to sell widgets on condition that other tenants in the same centre will not sell widgets[7].

(C) CLAWBACK. Provision is made for clawback of the exclusion for land agreements by Article 7 of the Order. Where a direction for clawback is made, Article 8 provides that the exclusion for land agreements will not apply to any agreement that is made 'to the like object or effect' as the one that was the subject of the direction. The DGFT has indicated that this power will rarely be used[8]. Where it is used, it does not follow that the agreement automatically will infringe the Chapter I prohibition: it simply enables the DGFT to consider whether there is in fact an infringement[9]. Any infringement would be found only from the date of withdrawal; any voidness of the agreement would start from that date, and penalties could be imposed only from then[10].

(J) The Chapter I prohibition: exemptions

(i) Introduction

As in the case of Article 81(3), the Competition Act makes provision for exemption from the Chapter I prohibition. The relevant provisions are contained in sections 4 to 11, and provide for four kinds of exemption: individual exemptions, under sections 4 and 5, which the DGFT may grant in relation to an agreement that has been notified to him; block exemptions pursuant to sections 6 to 8; parallel exemptions in accordance with section 10, where an agreement satisfies one of the EC block exemptions, or would do if it were to affect trade between Member States[11]; and 'exemptions for other agreements' contained in section 11.

Each of these will be explained below, after a consideration of the criteria according to which exemption may be available.

(ii) Exemption criteria

The exemption criteria are set out in section 9 of the 1998 Act. Exemption is available for any agreement which:

5   *Land Agreements* OFT Guideline 420, paras 1.9-1.14.
6   See p 308, n 16 above.
7   If the tenants were to agree this between themselves, the exclusion would not apply (see n 1 above); however it seems that the same effect can be achieved where the restrictions are agreed with the landlord.
8   Ibid, para 4.2.
9   Ibid, para 4.4.
10   Ibid, para 4.5.
11   On the EC block exemptions, see ch 4 pp 141-146.

'(*a*) contributes to-
    (i)   improving production or distribution, or
    (ii) promoting technical or economic progress,
    while allowing consumers a fair share of the resulting benefit; but
(*b*) does not—
    (i)   impose on the undertakings concerned restrictions which are not
        indispensable to the attainment of those objectives; or
    (i)   afford the undertakings concerned the possibility of eliminating
        competition in respect of a substantial part of the products in
        question.'

The wording of section 9 is very similar to, but not quite identical with, Article 81(3) EC. The latter refers to 'improving the production or distribution of goods', but the domestic provision is not so limited, and can therefore be applied to services as well. The DGFT has said that parties involved in an agreement are responsible for demonstrating that all the conditions of section 9 are satisfied so that an agreement merits an exemption[12].

(A)   THE AGREEMENT MUST CONTRIBUTE TO AN IMPROVEMENT IN PRODUCTION OR DISTRIBUTION OR TO TECHNICAL OR ECONOMIC PROGRESS.   The DGFT has given examples of improvements in production or distribution in his Guideline *The Chapter I prohibition*, such as lower costs from longer production or delivery runs, improvements in product quality and increases in the range of products produced or services provided[13]; and examples of the promotion of technical or economic progress such as efficiency gains from economies of scale and specialisation in research and development[14].

(B)   A FAIR SHARE OF ANY BENEFITS MUST ACCRUE TO CONSUMERS.   The DGFT has said that the views of customers and consumers will be an important consideration when deciding whether to give an exemption, and that their views will, in appropriate cases, be sought[15]. 'Consumers' here can mean trade purchasers as well as final consumers.

(C)   INDISPENSABLE RESTRICTIONS.   The DGFT has said that the agreement should contain the least restrictive means of achieving its aims. The DGFT will look carefully for any restrictions beyond those necessary for securing those benefits[16].

(D)   COMPETITION MUST NOT BE SUBSTANTIALLY ELIMINATED.   The DGFT has said that an exemption will be unlikely if the parties cannot show that there will continue to be effective competition in the market for the goods or services concerned[17].

Lord Simon stated twice in the House of Lords that he expected the criteria in section 9 of the Competition Act to be interpreted in the same broad way as Article 81(3) EC[18].

(iii)   Individual exemptions

Section 4 of the Act makes specific provision for the grant by the DGFT of individual exemption. The irony will not be lost that the Act is modelled on the

12 *The Chapter I prohibition* OFT Guideline 401, para 4.10.
13 Ibid, para 4.11.
14 Ibid, para 4.12.
15 Ibid, para 4.13.
16 Ibid, para 4.15.
17 Ibid, para 4.16.
18 On the exemption criteria under Article 81(3), see ch 4, pp 124-133.

system that has been in force in the EC since the adoption of Regulation 17/62, but that the European Commission's White Paper on Modernisation proposes that the idea of granting individual exemptions to agreements should be abolished altogether[19]. It is conceivable that the UK Government will decide in due course that, if notification is to be abolished at EC level, it should also be abolished under the 1998 Act. Section 4(1) of the Act provides that individual exemption may be granted by the DGFT if a request has been made under section 14 and if the exemption criteria in section 9 are satisfied. The procedure for notifying agreements to the DGFT is described in chapter 10[20]. The DGFT may impose conditions and obligations pursuant to section 4(3)(*a*) and according to sections 4(3)(*b*) and (4) he must specify a period for which the exemption will have effect. Section 4(5) allows for retrospective individual exemption, which can be to a date before the date of the notification; a key policy of the Act is that the DGFT should not be overburdened with notifications, and this provision is consistent with this. In the EC, as a general proposition, agreements can be exempted only in relation to a period beginning on the date when they were notified; there have always been some minor exceptions to this, and the position was radically altered in 1999 with the result that vertical agreements can now be exempted to a date earlier than notification[1]. As a separate matter, section 4(6) allows the DGFT to extend the period of an individual exemption.

Section 5(1) of the Act enables the DGFT to cancel an individual exemption, to vary or remove any condition or obligation or to impose additional ones. Section 5(2) specifies that this may be done by notice in writing where he has a reasonable suspicion that he based his decision to grant an exemption on information that was incomplete, false or misleading. Breach of a condition has the effect of automatically cancelling an exemption in accordance with section 5(3); section 5(4) provides that breach of an obligation entitles the DGFT by notice in writing to take the steps set out in section 5(1). Section 5(5) requires the DGFT to specify the time from which his decision is to have effect where he takes any of the steps in section 5(1). Where an exemption is cancelled because the DGFT based his decision on wrong information under section 5(2), or because of breach of an obligation, section 5(6) provides that the time from which his decision is to have effect may be earlier than the date on which he gave his notice in writing. Section 5(7) empowers the DGFT to proceed under section 5 on his own initiative or on a complaint made by any person.

The first notification for an individual exemption was made on 2 March 2000 in the case of *MasterCard/Europay UK Ltd*[2]; by 31 July, a total of seven notifications for a decision had been received[3]. Details of notifications, including a short summary of the agreement, are posted on the OFT's website[4].

---

19 See ch 4, pp 146-147.
20 See ch 10, pp 343-348.
1 See ch 7.
2 Case 00090/00.
3 See Case CP/0642/00 *Link Interchange Network Ltd* (11 May 2000); Case CP/1071/00/S *The General Insurance Standards Council* (20 July 2000), cleared by decision of the DGFT, 24 January 2001; third parties have appealed against this clearance in *IIIB v DGFT* (Cases 1002 and 1003/2/1/01 and *Association of British Travel Agents v DGFT* (Case 1004/2/1/01), judgment pending; Case CP/1058/00/S *The British Horseracing Board and The Jockey Club* (3 August 2000); Case CP/1321/00/S *The Society of Film Distributors* (22 September 2000) Case CP/1687-00/P; *BSkyB/NTL Channel Supply Agreement* (22nd November 2000); Case CP/1730-00/S *Memorandum of Understanding on the Supply of Oil Fuels in an Emergency* (6 December 2000).
4 http://www.oft.gov.uk/html/comp-act/case_register/notifications.html; the OFT has published an information leaflet *Is notification necessary?*, available from the OFT's website.

(iv)   Block exemptions

Section 6 allows the Secretary of State to adopt block exemptions, acting upon a recommendation from the DGFT. A block exemption may contain conditions and obligations and may be of limited duration, by virtue of section 6(5) and section 6(7) respectively. Section 7 provides that a block exemption may include an 'opposition procedure', a device that has been used in some EC block exemptions, albeit not particularly successfully[5]. The procedure for adopting block exemptions is set out in section 8. There are a number of EC block exemptions, and these will be applicable to agreements caught by the Chapter I prohibition by virtue of the parallel exemption provisions in section 10[6]; furthermore vertical agreements are excluded from the Chapter I prohibition so that they do not require exemption anyway[7]. It follows that it is likely that the block exemption procedure will be used infrequently; however one block exemption has been adopted, for public transport ticketing schemes, with effect from 1 March 2001[8].

(v)   Parallel exemptions

A novel, and effective, device in the 1998 Act is the concept of 'parallel exemptions' contained in section 10. Many agreements are block exempted by a Community block exemption; there are others that would be exempt but for the fact that they do not produce an effect on trade between Member States: since such agreements would not infringe Article 81(1) they would not require or benefit from block exemption under Article 81(3). Section 10(1) and (2) of the Act provide that any agreement that benefits from a block exemption, an individual exemption or an opposition or objection procedure under Community law, or that would do if it were to affect trade between Member States, will also be exempted from the Chapter I prohibition under domestic law. A consequence of this is that the parties to such agreements will not need to obtain an individual exemption or to satisfy the provisions of a block exemption under domestic law. Quite apart from the simplicity that this introduces for the parties, it reduces the burden on the DGFT, who will not need to grant such agreements individual exemption or to make recommendations to the Secretary of State that a block exemption should be adopted. Section 10(3) provides that such an exemption is to be known as a 'parallel exemption', while section 10(4) ensures that the duration of the parallel exemption is in line with the position in EC law. The most important effect of section 10 is in relation to licences of intellectual property rights which, if caught by the Chapter I prohibition, may benefit from the provisions of Regulation 240/96[9]. Since vertical agreements are excluded from the Chapter I prohibition, they do not require, as a matter of domestic law, to benefit from parallel exemption; to the extent that they infringe Article 81(1), however, they will have to satisfy Regulation 2790/99 in order to be block exempted under Community law[10]. It is unlikely that parallel exemption will be necessary for specialisation agreements

---

5   On the opposition procedure in EC law, see ch 4 p 416.
6   See below.
7   See p 307 above and ch 16, pp 595-598.
8   Competition Act 1998 (Public Transport Ticketing Schemes Block Exemption) Order 2001, SI 2001/319; a draft guideline has been published on this block exemption, available at http://www.oft.gov.uk/html.comp-act/technical guidelines/oft 439.html.
9   See ch 19, pp 688-696 above.
10   See ch 16, pp 567-591.

or research and development agreements by virtue of the relevant Community block exemptions[11] since such agreements would be caught by the Chapter I prohibition only where the parties have a market share of 25% or more; and if they did have that high a market share, they would not benefit from the EC block exemptions which are themselves subject to a market share cap[12].

Section 10(5) makes provision for the DGFT, in accordance with rules made under section 51 of the Act, to impose, vary or remove conditions and obligations subject to which a parallel exemption is to have effect, or even to cancel a parallel exemption. Section 10(6) enables this cancellation to be retrospective from before the date of the DGFT's notice. It is not entirely clear, as a matter of Community law, whether it is open to the DGFT to impose stricter standards than those agreed by the Commission under Article 81(3) of the Treaty[13], and this is a matter which might, in due course, be the subject of an Article 234 reference to the ECJ. What is clear is that Article 7 of the new EC block exemption for vertical agreements and concerted practices[14] specifically authorises a Member State to withdraw the benefit of it in certain, specified, circumstances; it is not known what power in the domestic law of the UK could be used to achieve such a withdrawal.

(vi) EC comfort letters[15]

The provisions in section 10 of the 1998 Act will prove important in practice where an agreement is exempt from EC law by virtue of an individual or block exemption. However, it is important to note that parallel exemption is *not* available for an agreement that has been the subject of a so-called 'comfort letter'. However the DGFT would have regard to such a comfort letter where it was issued pursuant to an Article 19(3) Notice in the Official Journal, as a result of section 60(3) of the 1998 Act[16].

(vii) 'Exemption for other agreements'

Section 11 makes provision for 'other' agreements to be exempt: this section, which will rarely be applied in practice, may be applicable in a very narrow range of cases where exemption may be given under Article 84 of the EC Treaty[17].

(K) Comment

The Chapter I prohibition is, above all, concerned with the elimination of cartels. This is a key policy of the Competition Act, and is manifested in a number of

11 See ch 15, pp 510-515 and 517-520.
12 Ibid, pp 513-514 and 519.
13 See pp 323-327 below; the DGFT would presumably be under no constraint in a s 10(2) case, where there is, *ex hypothesi*, no Community jurisdiction, but a real problem of conflict could arise in a s 10(1) case.
14 Commission Regulation 2790/99 OJ [1999] L 336/21, [2000] 4 CMLR 398; for a detailed account of this Regulation, see ch 16, pp 567-591.
15 *The Chapter I prohibition* OFT Guideline 401, paras 7.11-7.12.
16 See *The Chapter I prohibition* OFT Guideline 401, paras 7.11-7.12 and, on s 60(3) of the Act, pp below; on comfort letters in EC law, see ch 7, pp 217-218.
17 For example, as there is still no implementing regulation for air transport between a Community airport and an airport in a third country, exemption can be given only under Article 84: see ch 23, pp 864-866.

ways: vertical agreements are excluded from the Chapter I prohibition, except for price fixing; non hard-core horizontal agreements will not be considered as having an appreciable effect on competition where the parties' market share is below 25%; cartels will be caught even below that threshold; individual exemption can be backdated to a date prior to notification: this should reduce the number of precautionary notifications and, as a result, free up the resources of the DGFT to pursue cartels[18]; furthermore, as the next chapter will demonstrate, the DGFT, for the first time in UK competition law, has the powers of investigation and to fine that mean that it should be possible to detect and to punish hard-core infringements.

The Chapter I prohibition is modelled upon Article 81(1), but there are some differences. The appreciability threshold for non hard-core horizontal infringements in the UK is much higher at 25% than in the case of the European Commission's *De Minimis* Notice, where it is set at 5% for horizontal agreements[19]; however, the Commission's Guidelines on Horizontal Cooperation Agreements[20] suggest that, in some cases, it would not proceed against agreements where the parties' market share is above 15%, so that the difference between UK and EC practice may not be as great as the *De Minimis* Notice suggests[1]. Vertical agreements are often caught by Article 81(1), albeit subject to the possibility of exemption under Regulation 2790/99[2], whereas they are excluded from the Chapter I prohibition, except in the case of vertical price-fixing. Again, however, the differences between the two régimes will not be as great in practice as this suggests, given that in the EC vertical agreements that do not contain hard-core restrictions will be exempt provided that the parties' market shares are below 30%. There are other exclusions from the Chapter I prohibition which do not exist under EC law, for example for professional rules and for land agreements, but some of these would not normally fall within Article 81 anyway for lack of an effect on trade between Member States. Section 60 of the Act requires consistency with EC law 'so far as is possible (having regard to any relevant differences between the provisions concerned)': in particular this means that the 'single market' jurisprudence of the Community Courts will not be applied in the interpretation of the UK Act. It is unlikely that this will cause a significant divergence between the outcome of cases in the UK and in the EC. A reasonable conclusion is that, although Article 81(1) and the Chapter I prohibition are not identical twins, they are related by blood and can be expected to develop in close harmony.

3.   THE CHAPTER II PROHIBITION[3]

The Competition Act 1998 controls the abuse of a dominant position by means of a new prohibition introduced to operate alongside the existing controls on

---

18   The fact that there are fees for notifications also acts as a disincentive to notify: see ch 10, p 348.
19   See ch 3, pp 107-110.
20   OJ [2001] C 3/2, [2001] 4 CMLR 819.
1   Note that it is intended that the Commission's *De Minimis* Notice will be revised in the course of 2001, with the effect of raising the market share thresholds: see ch 3, p 107, n 15.
2   See ch 16, pp 567-591.
3   See Sufrin 'The Chapter II Prohibition' in *The Competition Act: A New Era for UK Competition Law* (p 286, n 6 above).

monopoly situations contained in the FTA[4]. The control of anti-competitive conduct under the Competition Act 1980 is abolished by section 17 of the 1998 Act. For the first time in UK competition law, firms with market power that abuse their position are subject to the possibility of substantial fines and actions for injunctions and, probably, damages[5]. This reflects the position that has prevailed under EC competition law since 1962, when Article 82 was brought into effect by Council Regulation 17/62[6]. The first two fines to be imposed by the DGFT involved infringements of the Chapter II prohibition.[6a]

(A) The prohibition

(i) Section 18

The prohibition of the abuse of a dominant position is contained in section 18 of the 1998 Act. Section 18 draws heavily on the text of Article 82[7], and provides:

'(1) Subject to section 19, any conduct on the part of one or more undertakings which amounts to the abuse of a dominant position in a market is prohibited if it may affect trade within the UK.

(2) Conduct may, in particular, constitute such an abuse if it consists in-
(a) directly or indirectly imposing unfair purchase or selling prices or other unfair trading conditions;
(b) limiting production, markets or technical development to the prejudice of consumers;
(c) applying dissimilar conditions to equivalent transactions with other trading parties, thereby placing them at a competitive disadvantage;
(d) making the conclusion of contracts subject to acceptance by the other parties of supplementary obligations which, by their nature or according to commercial usage, have no connection with the subject of the contracts.

(3) In this section-
"dominant position" means a dominant position within the UK; and
"the UK" means the UK or any part of it.

(4) The prohibition imposed by subsection (1) is referred to in this Act as "the Chapter II prohibition".'

(ii) 'The Chapter II prohibition'

As in the case of the Chapter I prohibition, section 18(4) of the Act establishes the term 'the Chapter II prohibition' to refer to the prohibition set out in section 18.

4   On the relationship between the Competition Act and the FTA, see ch 11, pp 383-385.
5   On third party actions under the Act, see ch 10, pp 361-362; a claimant in a court would no longer fail simply because an abuse has no effect on trade between Member States: see eg *Heathrow Airport Ltd v Forte (UK) Ltd* [1998] Eu LR 98.
6   OJ [1962] 13/204, OJ [1959-1962] spec ed 87.
6a   *Napp Pharmaceutical Holdings Ltd* (30 March 2001), fine of £3.21m, on appeal Case 1000/ 1/1/01, judgment pending; *Aberdeen Journals Ltd* (16 July 2001), fine of £1.32m.
7   For a detailed discussion of EC law on the abuse of a dominant position see chs 5, 17 and 18.

(iii)   Affecting trade within the UK

As with the Chapter I prohibition, there is a requirement that trade within the UK be affected; however, this is unlikely to have great significance in the context of Chapter II, as most conduct that is an abuse of a dominant position within the UK will also affect trade there. This requirement could have the effect of excluding from the scope of the prohibition an abuse of a dominant position within the UK that has its effects entirely outside the UK[8].

(iv)   Voidness

The 1998 Act does not refer explicitly to voidness in the case of Chapter II. Prohibited conduct can nevertheless include agreements. Under EC law, an agreement that is prohibited by Article 82 is probably void, although there is no direct ECJ authority on this point[9]. The same consequence would presumably follow, by virtue of section 60, in the case of an agreement that was prohibited by Chapter II.

(v)   Market size

Section 18(3) provides that a dominant position means a dominant position in the UK, and that the UK means the UK 'or any part of it.' Unlike Article 82[10], which refers to a dominant position '... within the common market or in a substantial part of it', there is no need for the dominant position to be in the whole or a 'substantial' part of the UK, and a relatively small part of the UK could constitute a 'market' within the meaning of section 18. The Chapter II prohibition is therefore a potentially far-reaching instrument for competition authorities and litigants alike. Firms that have market power which is on only a local scale and which therefore run little risk of infringing Article 82 for lack of any effect on inter-state trade, or are dominant only in an insubstantial part of the common market, might well find that they are infringing the Chapter II prohibition. Local dominance can be expected to be found in several sectors, such as the operation of bus services: there were numerous investigations of bus services under the old Competition Act 1980[11] and the monopoly provisions of the FTA 1973[12].

(vi)   The relevant market

As in the case of Community law, a finding of dominance requires a determination of the relevant market. Market definition has been discussed in some detail in chapter 1[13]. In the UK, the DGFT has issued a Guideline on *Market Definition*[14]

---

8   See ch 12, p 405.
9   On this point, see ch 8, pp 275-276.
10   See ch 5, p 150.
11   See eg *Thamesway Ltd* (OFT, August 1993); *Fife Scottish Omnibuses Ltd* (OFT, March 1994); *United Automobile Services Ltd* (OFT, March 1995).
12   See eg *The supply of bus services in the north-east of England* Cm 2933 (1995).
13   See ch 1, pp 22-39.
14   OFT Guideline 403.

for the purposes of the Chapter I and II prohibitions. In general, the Guideline follows the approach of the European Commission's *Notice on the definition of the relevant market for the purposes of Community competition law*[15]; this is a matter of choice rather than legal obligation, since section 60 of the Act requires only that the DGFT and other regulators should 'have regard' to statements of the Commission, not that they maintain consistency with them[16].

The DGFT describes market definition as important because market shares can be determined only after the boundaries of the market have been defined, and because it 'sets the stage on which competition takes place'[17]. Market definition is important in determining whether an agreement has an appreciable effect on competition for the purpose of the Chapter I prohibition and in determining whether a firm is dominant for the purpose of the Chapter II prohibition[18]. In relation to the product market, the DGFT will start by trying to identify products which can be substituted for each other so that competing undertakings can be identified[19]. In ascertaining the relevant product market, he will usually use the 'hypothetical monopolist' or 'SSNIP' test[20] to ascertain which group of products could be supplied at prices maintained above competitive levels, and will usually apply the narrowest potential definition[1]. On the demand side, he will consider the proportion of captive customers, whether the hypothetical monopolist is able to discriminate between customers and, sometimes, issues arising from chains of substitution[2]. On the supply side, he will consider whether other suppliers could switch relatively quickly (in a typical case the time period would be one year) to supplying products to compete with the hypothetical monopolist[3]. The DGFT will add the estimated market shares of the products that could be switched when trying to ascertain total market size, accepting that this may not be easy[4].

The DGFT will consider demand-side and supply-side issues as well as the possibility of imports in assessing the size of the geographic market. Demand-side factors include the value of the product, the mobility of customers and chains of substitution[5]; while supply-side factors include transport from one area to another[6]. The DGFT stresses that the prevalence of imports does not necessarily mean a market is international and that the lack of imports need not mean it is not international[7]. The DGFT will also analyse the temporal market where appropriate, although this has not been a prominent issue under Article 82[8].

---

15 OJ [1997] C 372/5, [1998] 4 CMLR 177.
16 See p 333 below.
17 *Market definition* OFT Guideline 403, para 2.3.
18 Ibid, para 2.4.
19 Ibid, para 2.6.
20 On the SSNIP test, see ch 1, p 26ff.
1   Ibid, paras 2.9 and 3.3.
2   Ibid, paras 3.1-3.12.
3   Ibid, paras 3.13-3.22.
4   Ibid, para 3.21.
5   Ibid, paras 4.3-4.6.
6   Ibid, paras 4.7-4.8.
7   Ibid, paras 4.9-4.10.
8   Ibid, paras 5.1-5.3, giving as examples of temporal markets peak and off-peak services, for example in the case of transport or the supply of electricity; seasonal variations, for example between winter and summer; and 'inter-generational products', meaning products in relation to which consumers may delay expenditure while they await a new product to come onto the market: obvious examples of this would be computer software and hardware and various broadcasting services where the pace of innovation is great.

(vii)   Assessing dominance

The DGFT has issued a Guideline on *Assessment of market power*[9] . As paragraph 1.2 of the Guideline points out, the concept of market power itself is not part of the statutory framework of the 1998 Act, which forbids restrictive agreements and the abuse of dominance; however, it is a useful tool in assessing potentially anti-competitive behaviour. The same paragraph states that market power refers to a situation in which 'the constraints which would usually ensure that' an undertaking behaves in a competitive matter are not working effectively. In determining whether a firm is dominant, the DGFT will consider, consistently with the ECJ's judgment in *United Brands Co v EC Commission*[10] , the extent to which an undertaking faces constraints on its ability to behave independently; those constraints may be existing competitors, potential competitors and other factors such as strong buying power from the undertaking's customers[11] . There is no particular market share test in the Act itself for determining dominance, but the DGFT notes that the ECJ has held that there is a presumption of dominance at 50% or more of the market, and that it is unlikely, although it cannot be ruled out, that dominance would be found below 40%[12] .

The Guideline proceeds to discuss market shares (paragraph 4), entry barriers (paragraph 5) and other factors relevant to an assessment of market power (paragraph 6). In the absence of a Notice of the European Commission on market power, these paragraphs are particularly helpful.

(A)   MARKET SHARES.   Paragraph 4 of the Guideline explains that market shares are important when considering the intensity of existing competition, and points out that it is the development of market shares over a period of time that is important, not the calculation of them at a single point in time[13] . In some markets, for example aerospace or defence products, one firm may have a large market share in one year and another firm in another year: it may be sensible in these circumstances to look at the figures over a five-year period in order to get a realistic view of their market shares. Paragraph 4.3 points out that market shares cannot in themselves be determinative of market power: one firm may have a large market share but barriers to entry may be low, so that potential entrants are able to constrain its behaviour on the market; while another firm may regularly produce new products ahead of its competitors, so that its high market share is a reflection of its successful innovation rather than its market power. Paragraphs 4.4 to 4.6 provide insights into the method of calculating market shares.

(B)   ENTRY BARRIERS.   Paragraph 5 of the Guideline deals with entry barriers; as it explains, they are important in the assessment of potential competition[14] . The Guideline distinguishes three types of barriers to entry, absolute advantages, strategic advantages and exclusionary behaviour. Absolute advantages exist where an incumbent undertaking owns or has access to important assets or resources which are not accessible to a potential entrant: this could be the case, for example,

9   OFT Guideline 415.
10   Case 27/76 [1978] ECR 207, [1978] 1 CMLR 429; see ch 5, pp 152-153.
11   *Assessment of market power* OFT Guideline 415, para 2.10; see also paras 3.1-3.6, which also refer to the extent of economic regulation in the market and the conduct and economic performance of undertakings as relevant to a determination of market power.
12   Ibid, para 2.11; the DGFT concluded that Dixon's, whose market share was 'considerably below the 40% threshold', was not dominant in the supply of home computers: OFT Press Release PN 15/01, 6 April 2001.
13   Ibid, paras 4.1 and 4.2.
14   Ibid, para 5.1.

where a system of regulation exists which limits the number of operators that can act on the market[15]; where one undertaking controls an essential facility[16]; or as a result of intellectual property rights[17]. Strategic advantages are those which arise from being the first into the market; examples are sunk costs, that is to say the costs that an undertaking will incur when entering a market that it will not be able to recover when it exits[18]; economies of scale, information constraints and time lags[19]; and access to finance[20]. The Guidelines also note that exclusionary behaviour such as predatory pricing and refusals to supply can act as a barrier to entry[1]. Paragraphs 5.25 to 5.29 provide insights into the way in which the DGFT will assess these matters.

(c)   OTHER FACTORS RELEVANT TO AN ASSESSMENT OF MARKET POWER.   Paragraph 6 considers other matters that are relevant to an assessment of market power, including the amount of buyer power in the market[2], the conduct and performance of the undertaking under investigation: for example it could be evidence of market power that an undertaking is able to raise prices consistently in excess of cost or to earn persistently excessive profits[3]; and it may be necessary to consider how a system of economic regulation (for example the prices that water companies can charge to customers) affects market power[4].

(viii)   Abuse

Section 18(2) sets out a non-exhaustive list of abuses, in identical terms to those in Article 82 EC. Unlike Article 82, sections 18(1) and 18(2) refer to 'conduct' which amounts to an abuse, rather than merely an abuse. It is hard to see how the use of the term 'conduct' improves on the EC version, and indeed it is not entirely apt: there is no doubt, for example, that a refusal to supply could, in certain circumstances, amount to an abuse of a dominant position; semantically it is somewhat strange to characterise inaction as conduct.

The DGFT has issued a Guideline on *Assessment of individual agreements and conduct*[5], much of which is relevant to the application of section 18 and which supplements the explanation in the general Guideline *The Chapter II prohibition*[6]. The Guideline on *Agreements and conduct* describes the DGFT's approach to each of the following in turn:

(*a*)   excessive prices[7];
(*b*)   price discrimination[8];
(*c*)   predation[9];

---

15   Ibid, para 5.5.
16   Ibid, para 5.6; see ch 17, pp 614-624 on the essential facilities doctrine.
17   Ibid, paras 5.7-5.8.
18   Ibid, paras 5.12-5.15.
19   Ibid, paras 5.16-5.17.
20   Ibid, paras 5.18-5.19.
1   Ibid, paras 5.20-5.23.
2   Ibid, paras 6.1-6.2.
3   Ibid, paras 6.3-6.5.
4   Ibid, paras 6.6-6.7.
5   OFT Guideline 414.
6   OFT Guideline 402.
7   *Assessment of individual agreements and conduct* OFT Guideline 414, paras 2.1-2.23.
8   Ibid, paras 3.1-3.17.
9   Ibid, paras 4.1-4.28.

(*d*) discounts[10];
(*e*) vertical restraints[11];
(*f*) refusal to supply and access to essential facilities[12];
(*g*) actions in related markets[13].

The Guideline concludes with a useful glossary of terms, such as average costs, bundling and economies of scale. Community jurisprudence on abuse will be highly influential in the application of the Chapter II prohibition, not least because of the 'general principles' clause in section 60 of the Act[14]: as a result, the reader is referred to chapter 5 for a general discussion of the meaning of abuse under Article 82[15]. Abusive practices themselves are considered in detail in chapter 17, which deals with non-pricing abuses, and chapter 18, which deals with pricing abuses. In each chapter, specific attention is given to the application of the Chapter II prohibition[16].

(ix)   Undertakings

This term has the same meaning as in the case of the Chapter I prohibition[17].

(B)   Exclusions[18]

(i)   Exclusions for mergers subject to UK or EC merger control

The Chapter II prohibition does not apply to conduct resulting in a merger situation[19] or in a concentration having a Community dimension[20]. This exclusion is closely related to the exclusion of mergers from the Chapter I prohibition, which was described above[1].

(ii)   Financial Services and Markets Act 2000

When this Act comes into force, the Chapter II prohibition will not apply to certain conduct pursuant to the regulating provisions of the FSA[2].

---

10 Ibid, paras 5.1-5.2.
11 Ibid, paras 6.1-6.33.
12 Ibid, paras 7.1-7.5.
13 Ibid, paras 8.1-8.6.
14 See pp 329-333 below.
15 See ch 5, pp 167-182.
16 See ch 17, pp 627-632 and ch 18, pp 664-673.
17 See pp 292-293 above.
18 See the detailed discussion of exclusions in the context of the Chapter I prohibition at pp 299-309 above.
19 Competition Act 1998, s 19 and Sch 1, paras 2 ('normal' mergers) and 3(2) ('newspaper mergers').
20 Ibid, s 19 and Sch 1, para 6.
1   See pp 299-302 above.
2   See pp 303 above.

(iii) Other exclusions

Section 19(1) provides that the Chapter II prohibition does not apply to cases excluded by Schedule 3. Some of the exclusions in Schedule 3 apply only to the Chapter I prohibition; however paragraph 4 of Schedule 3 (services of general economic interest), paragraph 5 (compliance with legal requirements), paragraph 6 (avoidance of conflict with international obligations), paragraph 7 (exceptional and compelling reasons of public policy) and paragraph 8 (conduct falling under the exclusive jurisdiction of the Commission under the ECSC Treaty) also exclude the application of the Chapter II prohibition.

(C) Comment

The Chapter II prohibition is a very important feature of the Competition Act 1998. Prior to the entry into force of the Act, UK law was weak in its treatment of undertakings that abused their market power. Whereas Article 82 prohibited the abuse of a dominant position which affected trade between Member States, purely domestic conduct was subject only to the investigative system in the FTA, or the similar system embodied in sections 2 to 10 of the now-repealed Competition Act 1980. Undertakings with market power at a local level within the UK are, for the first time, vulnerable to investigation by the DGFT (or the sectoral regulators, given that market power is still quite common in utility sectors) and to actions in the courts for an injunction and/or damages as a result of the 1998 Act. It is important to recall that the Chapter II prohibition is an addition to, and not a replacement of, the monopoly provisions contained in the FTA; under the FTA, structural remedies are available where there are persistent problems in a particular sector: this issue is discussed further in chapter 11[3].

4. THE RELATIONSHIP BETWEEN EC AND DOMESTIC COMPETITION LAW[4]

Following the enactment of the Competition Act 1998, much of UK competition law bears direct resemblance to the rules in the EC. Nevertheless, the possibility for conflict between EC and UK competition law will remain for four reasons. First, UK competition law on merger control and the administrative control of scale and complex monopolies remain different from EC law. Secondly, there are limited but specific differences between the substance of EC and UK competition law even in the harmonised area, for example in the treatment of vertical agreements[5]. Thirdly, UK competition law does not have the market unifying objective of EC competition law. Lastly, even in cases where the law itself is in harmony, the authorities may reach opposite conclusions on a given case. The relationship between EC and domestic competition law therefore is complex. It is important to appreciate, however, that this relationship will be dramatically changed if the Commission's proposed regulation to replace Regulation 17/62 is adopted[6]. Article 3 of the draft regulation provides that, where Community law

3   See ch 11, pp 383-385.
4   See Rodger 'Interrelationship with Community Competition Law Enforcement' in *The Competition Act: A New Era for UK Competition Law* (p 286, n 6 above).
5   See p 307 above and ch 16, pp 595-598.
6   See ch 7, pp 254-258.

applies to an agreement or to an abuse, it shall apply to the exclusion of national competition laws; in this case there will be no possibility of the conflicting application of differing laws[7].

In this section, two issues will be considered. First, as a matter of Community law, what should happen if there is a true conflict between Community law and domestic law; and secondly the very important 'governing principles clause' found in section 60 of the Competition Act, the purpose of which is to attain consistency, where possible, between the 1998 Act and Community law.

(A)   Conflicts between EC and domestic competition law

The basic position is that Community law takes precedence over national law so that where a clash occurs it is the former which must be applied[8]. Furthermore Article 10 of the Treaty specifically imposes a duty on Member States to ensure fulfilment of the obligations arising out of the Treaty, to facilitate the achievement of the Community's tasks and to abstain from any measure which could jeopardise the attainment of the Treaty's objectives; restraint on the part of the domestic authorities may mean that the possibility of conflict is avoided. The ECJ has held that the European Commission has a similar duty to co-operate with Member States[9], and the Commission has given advice to the former Monopolies and Mergers Commission in a number of its investigations[10]. The duty of co-operation is further manifested in Article 10 of Regulation 17/62 and Article 19 of the ECMR which require liaison between the European Commission and Member States in the enforcement of Articles 81 and 82 and in the control of mergers respectively.

In *Walt Wilhelm v Bundeskartellamt*[11] the ECJ ruled that conflicts between the rules of the Community and national rules in the matter of the law on cartels must be resolved by applying the principle that Community law takes precedence. However behind the simplicity of this statement there are some difficult issues, yet to be fully resolved in Community law and where, until such time as the proposal outlined above for the exclusion of domestic law where Community law applies is adopted, clear guidance will continue to be needed from the ECJ. The particular problem is that *Walt Wilhelm* was concerned only with the situation where conduct is condemned both under EC and domestic law. It did not deal

---

7   On this idea, see Walz 'Rethinking Walt Wilhelm, on the Supremacy of Community Competition Law over National Law' (1996) 21 ELRev 449; note also that conflict can already be avoided where there is a domestic rule that, if EC law applies, domestic law will not: see eg Art 1 of the Italian Competition Act, Law 287/90, which provides that domestic law should apply only to agreements falling outside Community law; however, this has been interpreted to mean that the domestic jurisdiction ceases only where the European Commission commences proceedings: see Heimler 'National Priorities, National Law and European Law: the Italian Experience' (1998) 19 ECLR 315, at 316.

8   See Case 6/64 *Costa v ENEL* [1964] ECR 585, [1964] CMLR 425; Case 106/77 *Amministrazione delle Finanze dello Stato v Simmenthal* [1978] ECR 629, [1978] 3 CMLR 263; Case C–213/89 *R v Secretary of State for Transport, ex p Factortame (No 2)* [1991] 1 AC 603, [1990] 3 CMLR 1; Case C–221/89 *R v Secretary of State for Transport, ex p Factortame Ltd (No 3)* [1991] ECR I-3905, [1991] 3 CMLR 589.

9   Case C–2/88 *Zwartveld* [1990] ECR I-4405, [1990] 3 CMLR 457.

10   See eg *British Steel plc/C Walker and Sons (Holdings) Ltd* Cm 1028 (1990); *British Airways plc/Sabena SA* Cm 1155 (1990); *Carbonated Soft Drinks* Cm 1625 (1991); *New Motor Cars* Cm 1808 (1991); *Motor Car Parts* Cm 1818 (1991); *Domestic Electrical Goods I* Cm 3675 (1997) paras 2.436 and 2.439.

11   Case 14/68 [1969] ECR 1, [1969] CMLR 100.

fully with other questions that can arise, such as the relationship of Commission exemptions with stricter provisions of domestic law, and the judgment does not provide conclusive answers to them. The academic literature has considered this issue at length[12].

It is necessary to distinguish various types of conflict.

(i)   Community prohibition; domestic authorisation

The first arises where conduct is prohibited by Article 81(1) or Article 82 but permitted at the domestic level. This is the simplest case: there is no doubt that Community law must prevail and that it is not possible for the conduct to be permitted by a national authority. The fact that an agreement has been approved by the competition authority of a Member State cannot prevent the Commission from subsequently condemning it under Community law[13], although, where the parties to an agreement draw the attention of the Commission to the reasoning deployed by a domestic authority, the Commission should explain why it declines to follow that reasoning if that is the case[14]. It may be that particular behaviour is prohibited under both systems, in which case both the Commission and the domestic authority are permitted to proceed against it. Where penalties have already been imposed by a domestic authority, these ought to be taken into account by the Commission when fixing the level of fines[15], though this does not mean that an undertaking cannot be fined twice in respect of the same matter. In the UK, the DGFT must take into account fines that have been imposed for the same offence by the Commission or in another Member State[16].

(ii)   Community individual exemption; domestic prohibition

In the second situation, it may happen that an agreement which would not be permitted under domestic law is granted an individual exemption by the Commission under Article 81(3). The question then arises whether the more stringent provisions of domestic law should be or can be applied, or whether the Community authorisation overrides the domestic prohibition[17]; a more refined

12   See eg Markert 'Some Legal and Administrative Problems of the Co-existence of Community and National Competition Law in the EC' (1974) 11 CML Rev 92; Stockmann 'EC Competition Law and Member State Competition Laws' [1987] Fordham Corporate Law Institute (ed Hawk) pp 265-300; Kerse *EC Antitrust Procedure* (Sweet & Maxwell, 4th ed 1998) pp 445–458; Goyder *EC Competition Law* (Oxford EC Law Library, 3rd ed 1998) pp 502–510; Bellamy and Child *European Community Law of Competition* (Sweet & Maxwell, 5th ed, 2001) paras 10-074 to 10-080.
13   Cases 43 and 63/82 [1984] ECR 19, [1985] 1 CMLR 27, para 40; Case T–66/89 *Publishers Association v EC Commission (No 2)* [1992] ECR II-1995, [1992] 5 CMLR 120, para 74.
14   Case C–360/92P *Publishers Association v EC Commission* [1995] ECR I-23, [1995] 5 CMLR 33, paras 36-44; this was the appeal to the ECJ from the judgment of the CFI cited in the previous footnote.
15   Case 14/68 *Walt Wilhelm v Bundeskartellamt* [1969] ECR 1, [1969] CMLR 100, para 11; in *Cast Iron and Steel Rolls* OJ [1983] L 317/1, [1984] 1 CMLR 694 the Commission took into account the fact that a majority of the undertakings concerned had been fined in earlier proceedings before the German Cartel Office; there were also proceedings in the UK in respect of this cartel: 1988 *Annual Report of the DGFT* p 38.
16   See ch 10, p 352.
17   According to the 'double barrier' theory, an agreement will be permitted only where it satisfies both EC and domestic law; this was the approach of Markert in the article referred to in n 12 above; Markert was then head of the German Cartel Office, and was reluctant to

version of the question is whether a national authority could impose more stringent conditions and obligations before permitting an agreement than those required by the European Commission.

There are dicta in *Walt Wilhelm* stating that:

'if the ultimate general aim of the Treaty is to be respected, this parallel application of the national system can only be allowed in so far as it does not prejudice the uniform application throughout the Common Market of the Community rules on cartels and of the full effect of the measures adopted in implementation of those rules'.

Later the ECJ says that, in order to achieve the objectives of the Treaty, the Community authorities are permitted:

'to carry out certain positive, though indirect, action with a view to promoting a harmonious development of economic activity within the whole Community'.

Precisely how this applies to individual (or block) exemptions is not clear. Conferment of an exemption by the Commission could be regarded not so much as an *application* of Community law, but as a concession from its application[18] : in this case there would be nothing to prevent the application of stricter domestic law. Furthermore the parties cannot be compelled to carry out the exempted agreement, they can only be permitted to operate it. Since the Community cannot insist upon performance, it is for the parties to decide whether to proceed or not. This may be considered to support the view that the national authorities should be allowed to prohibit the agreement.

An argument the other way is that the grant of an individual exemption is 'positive action' in the sense envisaged by the ECJ in *Walt Wilhelm*, and that national authorities should not be able to thwart such action. The Commission has used Article 81(3) to encourage certain types of behaviour: for example research and development agreements, the licensing of intellectual property rights and the efficient supply of goods and services. The argument would therefore run that exemptions are not just a grudging concession on the part of the Commission but rather have a positive rôle in the economic policy of the EC; the language of Article 81(3) itself seems to support this view. Furthermore, in the case of an individual exemption, the Commission has to have considered the very agreement in question, and to have given it its imprimatur; this would not be the case in respect of an agreement that falls within a block exemption. Seen in this light, there is a strong argument that the position adopted under EC law should prevail over a domestic prohibition. In *Walt Wilhelm* the Kammergericht in Germany had asked the ECJ to consider the effect of Community exemptions on national law, so that it is possible to read the dicta in that case on the basis that the ECJ was considering both prohibitions and exemptions under Community law. Furthermore, the Advocate General had suggested the adoption of the double-barrier test: the ECJ did not specifically accept it, so that perhaps by implication it rejected it. The Commission's own view is that a national authority is bound

---

see its power to prevent agreements taken away by the grant of Community exemptions; the Advocate General in *Walt Wilhelm* also adopted the 'double barrier' approach: Case 14/68 [1969] ECR 1, p 23, [1969] CMLR 100, p 119.

18 See *Markert* and *Kerse* para 10.34, see n 12 above.

to respect the exemption and to refrain from applying its own stricter standards[19], though it has not elaborated upon this in detail.

A more complex analysis has been suggested: that some exemptions are purely permissive, in which case national law could override them, while others represent positive Community policy, in which case they must be respected[20]. However Commission decisions do not make this distinction and it would be acutely difficult to apply such a test unless the Commission were to do so expressly.

Against this, the European Commission indicated in the investigation by the UK Monopolies and Mergers Commission (now the Competition Commission) into *British Airways/Sabena*[1] that it might allow the imposition by a national authority of stricter exemption conditions than it had intended to apply in the same case. In *Director General of Fair Trading v Publishers' Association (Net Book Agreement 1957)*[2] the Restrictive Practices Court accepted that 'there is clearly a serious argument that it is not open to the national court to condemn under the national law an agreement which has received an exemption under Community law'. On a slightly different point, in *Bundeskartellamt v Volkswagen AG and VAG Leasing GmbH (VAG Händlerbeirat ev intervening)*[3] the ECJ held, at paragraphs 18 and 19, that an individual (or block) exemption affected only the enforceability of an agreement between the parties and was not capable of affecting third parties; it followed that the fact that an agreement was exempted under Article 81(3) would not affect the application of the German law on unfair competition to third parties.

The Competition Act 1998 includes provision for 'parallel exemptions' where an agreement enjoys individual or block exemption from the prohibition of Article 81(1) or where it benefits from the opposition procedure in any of the block exemptions[4]. However the Act also empowers the DGFT to impose conditions, to modify or to cancel the parallel, that is to say the domestic, exemption[5]: thus, as a matter of domestic law, the Act suggests that there are circumstances in which a stricter approach could be taken than the result achieved in the Community. It is clearly arguable that a purported exercise of this power by the DGFT would be unlawful as a matter of Community law[6]. The Restriction on Agreements and Conduct (Specified Domestic Electrical Goods) Order 1998[7], made under the FTA following the investigation of *Domestic Electrical Goods*[8], specifically excludes from the prohibition of various practices agreements that are exempt under EC law, or that would be if they were to affect trade between Member States[9].

19 See the 4th *Report on Competition Policy*, points 43–47 and its reply to a Parliamentary question in OJ [1981] C 85/6; see also the Commission's submissions to the ECJ in Case C-266/93 *Bundeskastellamt v Volkswagen and VAG Leasing GmbH* [1995] ECR I-3477, [1996] 4 CMLR 478 and the *Notice on co-operation between national competition authorities and the Commission* OJ [1997] C 313/3, [1997] 5 CMLR 884, para 19.
20 See the *Stockmann* paper cited in n 12 at p 323 above.
1   Cm 1155 (1991).
2   Judgment dated 9 August 1995, per Ferris J; the same Court also refused a stay in *British Sugar v DGFT*, judgment dated 9 August 1995, on similar grounds to those in the *Publishers' Association* case.
3   Case C-266/93 [1995] ECR I-3477, [1996] 4 CMLR 478.
4   Competition Act 1998, s 10(1); see pp 312-313 above.
5   Ibid, s 10(5).
6   Section 60 of the Act requires only that the DGFT should 'have regard to' a Commission exemption, not that it should maintain consistency with it: see p 333 below.
7   SI 1998/1271.
8   Cm 3675 and Cm 3676 (1997).
9   SI 1998/1271, Article 12.

(iii)   Community block exemption; domestic prohibition

The third situation is similar to the last, except that the conflict arises not because an agreement is granted individual exemption by the Commission, but because it benefits from one of the block exemptions[10]. Again it is unclear whether it would be improper for a national authority to apply its own stricter law and to condemn the agreement. On the one hand one can argue that the block exemption, like an individual exemption, is merely a concession from the application of Article 81(1), in which case national authorities should be free to apply their own stricter standards. This is consistent with several judgments of the ECJ which have held that it is not mandatory for parties to comply with the provisions of a block exemption[11] : these judgments were concerned with Regulation 123/85 on the distribution of motor cars, but their reasoning is capable of application to any block exemption. On the other hand one can argue that the block exemptions positively encourage certain types of agreement (for example to collaborate in research and development or to grant licences of patents and know-how). The recitals of each block exemption elaborate the reasons why particular types of agreement should be permitted. In this case, the block exemptions could be said to express a positive act on the part of the Council of Ministers, through its empowering legislation, or the Commission itself, in the block exemptions, from which national authorities ought not to derogate through the application of their own stricter laws. Furthermore, the block exemption regulations always confer power on the Commission to withdraw the benefit of block exemption in particular circumstances: to allow a national authority to apply its stricter provisions would seem to run counter to this. Interestingly, Article 7 of Regulation 2790/99[12] specifically allows a Member State to withdraw the benefit of that block exemption where there are detriments to competition within its national market[13]. This could be taken to suggest that, in the absence of such a provision, the Member State would not be entitled to apply its own stricter law.

Apart from Regulation 2790/99, the Commission's own view is not entirely clear. In some respects it seems to consider that a block exemption does override the position under domestic law. This would make sense of recital 19 of the now-repealed Regulation 1984/83[14], in which the Commission specifically stated that national authorities may apply stricter national laws on exclusive purchasing agreements in the petrol industry: this can be read as a concession on the part of the Commission, that is to say that the normal position would be that the block exemption authorises agreements, notwithstanding the position under national law. However the Commission's approach has not always been consistent with the view that the block exemption overrides national law unless it contains an explicit concession. After the former Monopolies and Mergers Commission's report on *The Supply of Beer*[15] conditions were imposed upon brewers that were stricter than those permitted by Regulation 1984/83; the Commission was content to allow this to happen[16].

---

10 On the block exemptions, see ch 4, pp 141-146.
11 See eg Case C-266/93 *Bundeskartellamt v Volkswagen AG and VAG Leasing GmbH (VAG Händlerbeirat ev intervening)* (n 19 above); on this point, see ch 4, p 146.
12 OJ [1999] L 336/21, [2000] 4 CMLR 398.
13 See ch 16, pp 588-589.
14 OJ [1983] L 173/5.
15 Cm 651 (1989).
16 Commission Press Release IP(90) 472 of 14 June 1990.

An alternative approach to this problem might be to distinguish between conflicts between national law and the 'core' purpose of a block exemption (for example to encourage research and development agreements or the transfer of technology), in which case the block exemption must prevail; and situations in which the conflict is between national law and an aspect of a block exemption which is 'periforal', in which the national rule could be applied. A further possibility is that national law might be applicable, notwithstanding the provisions of a block exemption, where a particular national sensitivity is at stake or where an agreement could be particularly detrimental to competition in a national market[17]. This approach may have some conceptual attraction, but one can foresee that there would be serious difficulties in its practical application.

Advocates General VerLoren Van Themaat in *Metro-SB-Grossmärket GmbH v Commission*[18] and Tesauro in *Bayerisch MotorenWerke AG v ALD Auto-Leasing* and *Bundeskartellamt v Volkswagen ACT and VAG Leasing GmbH*[19] both considered that where an agreement benefits from block exemption, this precludes the contrary application of national law. However the ECJ did not opine on the issue, since it found that the agreements in question were not covered by the block exemption for the distribution of motor cars which was in issue in those cases.

The parallel exemption provisions in the Competition Act 1998 apply to EC block exemptions, and the Act further provides that they extend to agreements which fall within the categories covered by those block exemptions but which do not affect trade between Member States (that is to say they do not infringe Article 81(1) and are therefore not subject to Article 81(3) at all)[20]. Again, however, the DGFT's power to modify, to add conditions or to cancel the parallel exemption applies[1]. It is not known what power the DGFT could use, as a matter of domestic law, to withdraw a Community block exemption.

(iv) Non-application of Article 81 or 82; domestic prohibition

The next situation which one must consider is where conduct infringes national law but the European Commission or the Community Courts indicate that it is not caught by Article 81 or Article 82. For example it might be that the operation of a selective distribution network is compatible with Article 81(1) under the doctrine established in *Metro v EC Commission*[2]. It can be argued in this situation that the non-application of the EC rules invests the conduct in question with a validity at Community level which overrides the harsher provisions of domestic law. For some while this was a controversial issue, but after the *Perfumes* cases it would seem clear that it is permissible for stricter provisions of national law to be applied, at least where the reason for the non-application of Article 81(1) is that the agreement does not have an effect on inter-state trade or that it is an

---

17 There is a parallel provision to this in Article 9 of the ECMR: see ch 21, pp 758-761.
18 Case 75/84 [1986] ECR 3021, [1987] 1 CMLR 118.
19 Case C-70/93 [1995] ECR I-3439, [1996] 4 CMLR 478 and C-266/93 [1995] ECR I-3477; the Commission supported this view in its submission to the ECJ in these cases.
20 Competition Act, s 10(2).
1 Ibid, s 10(5).
2 Case 26/76 [1977] ECR 1875, [1978] 2 CMLR 1, ECJ; see ch 16, pp 556-561.

agreement of minor importance[3]. Agreements given negative clearance in this way do not benefit from parallel exemption under the Competition Act 1998. While there is nothing in the Act requiring the DGFT to follow the Commission, under section 60(3) he must have regard to any relevant decision or statement of the Commission.

(v)   Comfort letters

A further conflict could occur where the European Commission sends a comfort letter stating that, in its view, an agreement would benefit from an exemption under Article 81(3), but that it intends to close its file without proceeding to a final decision[4]. In this case there is no binding legal decision on the part of the Commission which could override domestic law. However, if the position is that individual and block exemptions prevail over national prohibitions, it would seem to be correct in principle that comfort letters of this type should also do so: it would be unfortunate if the legal position varied according to the point at which the Commission's assessment of an agreement is terminated. In practice far more cases are settled by comfort letter than by decision, and the distinctions between these two methods of disposal ought to be kept to a minimum. In the *Notice on co-operation between national competition authorities and the Commission*[5] the Commission calls on national authorities to consult it before deciding whether to overrule such a comfort letter[6]. Section 60(3) requires the DGFT to 'have regard to any statement by the Commission' and the Guideline on *The Chapter I prohibition* indicates that he will liaise with the Commission and will generally follow its assessment[7].

(vi)   Mergers

Article 21(1) of the ECMR[8] provides that the European Commission shall have exclusive jurisdiction over mergers that have a 'Community dimension'; this term is defined in Article 1 of the Regulation by reference to the turnover of the undertakings involved. The Commission's exclusive jurisdiction is a manifestation of the 'one-stop' principle, according to which mergers should be subject either to investigation at the domestic level under a Member State's domestic law or at the EC level under the Regulation[9]. It would be unduly burdensome to subject the same merger to investigation at both levels. However there are exceptions to the one-stop principle in Article 9, which allows the Commission to refer mergers that have a Community dimension but which may cause harm to competition within a national market back to the domestic authorities, and Article 21(3),

---

3   See eg Case 253/78 *Procureur de la République v Giry and Guerlain SA* [1980] ECR 2327, [1981] 2 CMLR 99; see also report of the UK Monopolies and Mergers Commission (as it then was) on *Domestic Electrical Goods I* Cm 3675 at paras 2.425 and 2.426 where the European Commission stated that a selective distribution system that does not fall within Article 81(1) can be prohibited under national law.
4   See ch 7, pp 217-218 on comfort letters generally.
5   OJ [1997] C 313/3 [1997] 5 CMLR 884.
6   Ibid, para 21.
7   OFT Guideline 401, paras 7.11–7.12; see further p 333 below.
8   See ch 21, pp 756-757.
9   Ibid.

which allows a Member State to take action to protect its 'legitimate interests' other than competition interests[10]. Such cases are relatively rare. It may also be possible, at least theoretically, for a national court to apply Article 82 to a merger that has a Community dimension[11].

The Treaty of Paris, which established the European Coal and Steel Community, gave the European Commission exclusive jurisdiction over products listed in the Annex to that Treaty (known as 'Paris' products). In *British Steel plc/C Walker and Sons (Holdings) Ltd*[12] the former Monopolies and Mergers Commission declined to investigate whether a merger was against the public interest under the FTA in so far as it related to Paris products, limiting its inquiry to non-Paris products; it concluded that there was no detriment to the public interest in respect of them.

(vii) Diagonal conflicts

A quite different conflict can arise where the competition policy of the Community is in conflict with a domestic policy such as the protection of cultural values: this has been a notable feature of the Commission's investigation of resale price maintenance for books in the German language[13]. Since this conflict is not a 'vertical' one, that is to say between a higher and a lower system of competition law, the expression 'diagonal' conflict has been deployed to describe it[14]. Such conflicts, in the absence of a legal system of resolution, may require to be resolved at a political level, by the Commission or even the Council of Ministers.

(B) Section 60: the 'governing principles' clause[15]

In recognition of the potential for conflict and the need for consistency in interpretation, section 60 of the Competition Act 1998 sets out the governing principles to be applied in determining questions which arise in relation to competition within the UK; essentially, the principle is that there will be close conformity between the Act and the EC régime. Section 60 is an important provision, which enables the UK competition authorities to apply Community competition law when making decisions under the Act. However there are numerous subtleties to section 60, and it can be anticipated that it will be the subject of a fair amount of litigation: for this reason it has been variously described as the 'Klondike' or the 'El Dorado' clause, due to the riches, if not actually gold, that practising lawyers can hope to earn from it.

10 See ch 21, pp 761-763.
11 See ch 21, pp 757-758.
12 Cm 1028 (1990); in Ireland the Minister prohibited this merger but had to revoke the prohibition order when the merger was authorised by the European Commission: see Rowley and *International Mergers: the Antitrust Process* (Sweet & Maxwell, 3rd ed, 2000) para 28.009.
13 See Bellamy and Child *European Community Law of Competition* (Sweet & Maxwell, 5th ed, 2001) para 4-036, n 5.
14 See Rodger 'Interrelationship with Community Competition Law Enforcement' in *The Competition Act: A New Era for UK Competition Law* (p 285, n 6 above).
15 See Middleton 'Harmonization with Community Law – the Euro Clause' in *The Competition Act: A New Era for UK Competition Law* (p 286, n 6 above).

(i)   Section 60(1)

Section 60(1) sets out the purpose of the governing principles clause: the duties to which it gives rise are imposed by sections 60(2) and 60(3). Section 60(1) provides that:

> 'The purpose of this section is to ensure that so far as is possible (having regard to any relevant differences between the provisions concerned), questions arising under this Part in relation to competition within the UK are dealt with in a manner which is consistent with the treatment of corresponding questions arising in Community law in relation to competition within the Community'[16].

The objective of consistency is not absolute: consistency is envisaged only 'so far as is possible', having regard to 'relevant differences' and only 'in relation to competition'. The Government stated that 'we are satisfied that the drafting of [section] 60 accurately expresses the concept that Community jurisprudence is to be followed unless the court is driven to some different interpretation by some provision in that part of the [Act]'[17].

(A) 'SO FAR AS IS POSSIBLE'. The purpose of the Act is to achieve consistency 'so far as is possible'. Clearly this will not be possible where the Act explicitly differs from EC law: examples of this are given in the next section. Where there is some doubt in a particular case, these words indicate that there is a policy preference towards maintaining consistency with EC law.

(B) 'HAVING REGARD TO ANY RELEVANT DIFFERENCES'. A critical issue will be the identification of any 'relevant differences' between Community law and the Act. Some examples appear on the face of the Act itself: for example, it contains some exclusions which are not available under EC law[18]; the Act provides a wider privilege for correspondence with lawyers than in the Community[19]; the exclusion under the 1998 Act for mergers is wider than that provided for under EC law; and the Act makes specific provision for vertical and land agreements to be excluded, which has been done by statutory instrument[1]. Secondly, the procedural and enforcement rules under the Act are not identical to those in EC law: for example there is a full appeal to the Appeal Tribunals of the Competition Commission against decisions of the DGFT and the sectoral regulators; in the Community, judicial review may provide a less effective remedy to an applicant; in the UK, the provisions on leniency are different from those in the EC[2], as is the method of calculating the level of a fine[3].

---

16 For the meaning of 'the Community' see the Interpretation Act 1978 and European Communities Act 1972.
17 HL Consideration of Commons' Amendments, 20 October 1998, col 1383 (Lord Simon of Highbury).
18 On the exclusions from the Chapter I and Chapter II prohibitions, see pp 299-309 and pp 320-321 above.
19 See ch 10, pp 339-340 .
1   The Competition Act (Land and Vertical Agreements Exclusion) Order 2000, SI 2000/310; see pp 307-309 above on land agreements and ch 16, pp 595-598 on vertical agreements.
2   See ch 10, pp 353-355.
3   Ibid, pp 352-353.

A further example of a relevant difference, but one that is not apparent on the face of the Act, is that the EC competition rules are applied, *inter alia*, with the objective of single market integration in mind, a point repeatedly stressed in earlier chapters of this book[4]. The 1998 Act, presumably, does not have to be applied for this purpose, since the goal of market integration is 'relevantly different' from one arising in relation to competition within the UK: this could lead to some divergence in the way in which the Chapter I and II prohibitions and Articles 81 and 82 are applied. The OFT Guideline on *The Major Provisions* specifically states that the Community single market objectives would not be relevant to the domestic prohibition system[5]. For example, an agreement restricting exports from the UK to other Member States might not restrict competition within the UK but would be a cardinal offence under EC competition law; a Report prepared by Bill Bishop and this author for the Department of Trade and Industry on the *Treatment of Vertical Agreements under the Competition Bill*[6] revealed that every fine but one imposed by the Commission in relation to a vertical agreement had been attributable to the inclusion of export bans: the one exception was for discriminatory application of a selective distribution system in *AEG Telefunken AG v EC Commission*[7]. The task for the competition authorities in the UK will be to determine which judgments, or indeed which parts of which judgments, of the Community Courts were motivated by single market considerations and which by 'normal' competition law considerations: a not inconsiderable task, given that the judgments themselves will not have been written with this distinction in mind, and indeed that some judgments may savour of both[8]. It would be wrong to suggest that the non-application of 'single market' jurisprudence will lead to a wide divergence between the outcome of cases under EC and domestic law, but it can be anticipated that it will arise from time to time. When it does, it will be possible to obtain access to the ECJ from the Appeal Tribunals of the Competition Commission[9] and from the higher courts in the UK in order to obtain a preliminary ruling on the appropriate interpretation of earlier judgments, and it will be of interest to see how the ECJ deals with this issue.

A further area in which relevant differences might exist will arise in the substantive analysis of particular cases; for example it is provided by the OFWAT Guidelines that a different measure of costs will be used to assess alleged predatory pricing[10] due to the 'specific nature of the water industry as a network industry' from the one suggested by the ECJ in the *AKZO* judgment[11].

---

4   See ch 1, p 19; ch 2, p 47.
5   OFT Guideline 400, para 6.3.
6   3 February 1998.
7   Case 107/82 [1983] ECR 3151, [1984] 3 CMLR 325.
8   This may arise, in particular, in relation to licences of intellectual property rights which, unlike vertical agreements, are not specifically excluded from the Chapter I prohibition. Where an exclusive licence does not enjoy parallel exemption under s 10 of the Competition Act in conjunction with Regulation 240/96 on transfer of technology agreements, the question will arise whether it infringes the Chapter I prohibition; EC law on this issue has developed very much with the issue of single market integration in mind: see ch 19, pp 680-683.
9   See ch 10, pp 359-361.
10 *Application in the water and sewerage sector* OFT Guideline 422, paras 4.11-4.13, where instead of the Community assessment of predation using average variable costs and average total costs, the DGFT and regulator will consider long run marginal costs.
11 Ibid, para 4.12; on *AKZO*, see ch 18, pp 648-649.

(C)   'QUESTIONS ARISING ... IN RELATION TO COMPETITION'.   The policy of maintaining consistency arises only where there are 'questions arising in relation to competition'. The view of the UK Government was that it was not necessary for the DGFT (or sectoral regulators) to follow the same detailed procedures as the European Commission: indeed that might be undesirable, given that it is a very different institution from the OFT; it can reasonably be argued that the procedural rules do not themselves raise questions 'in relation to competition'[12]. However it was accepted in the House of Lords by Lord Simon of Highbury that section 60 does import the general principles of Community law as well as the specific jurisprudence on Articles 81 and 82 themselves, save where there is a relevant difference[13]. Examples of what have come to be termed in discussion of the Act as 'high level principles' are equality, legal certainty, legitimate expectation, proportionality and privilege against self-incrimination: each of these is well-established in Community law[14]. Other general principles noted by the Community courts include the duty to state reasons for a decision with sufficient precision[15], the principle of good administration[16], the right of access to the file[17] and equality of arms[18].

(ii)   Section 60(2) and (3)

Section 60(2) and (3) provide that:

'(2) At any time when the court[19] determines a question arising under this Part, it must act (so far as is compatible with the provisions of this Part[1] and whether or not it would otherwise be required to do so with a view to securing that there is no inconsistency[2] between-

(*a*)   the principles applied, and decision reached, by the court in determining that question; and

(*b*)   the principles laid down by the Treaty[3] and the European Court[4], and any relevant decision of that Court, as applicable at that time in determining any corresponding question arising in Community law'.

---

12   On this issue generally, see Willis 'Procedural Nuggets from the "Klondike Clause": The Application of s 60 of the Competition Act 1998 to the Procedure of the OFT' (1999) 20 ECLR 314.

13   HL Committee, 25 November 1997, cols 960–963.

14   See Wyatt and Dashwood's *European Union Law* (Sweet & Maxwell, 4th ed, 2000) ch 6.

15   Case T-241/97 *Stork Amsterdam BV v EC Commission* [2000] 5 CMLR 31, para 74.

16   Case T-127/98 *UPS Europe SA v EC Commission* [1999] ECR II-2633, [2000] 4 CMLR 94, para 37.

17   Cases T-25-104/95 etc *Cimenteries CBR SA v Commission* judgment of 15 March 2000, para 142.

18   Ibid, para 143.

19   'Court' in this context includes the Competition Commission, the DGFT and the sectoral regulators: Competition Act 1998, s 60(5).

1   'This Part' of the Act deals with all matters to do with the prohibitions and their enforcement of them, but not investigations under the FTA.

2   Section 60(1) puts the objective positively and is preferable to this double negative.

3   'Treaty' in this context refers to the EC Treaty: Competition Act 1998, s 59(1); it would not apply to jurisprudence or decisions under the ECSC Treaty, nor under the EEA Agreement.

4   'European Court' refers to both the ECJ and the CFI: ibid; it does not refer to the opinions of the Advocates General, nor to the EFTA Court.

(3) The court must, in addition, have regard to any relevant decision or statement of the Commission.'

(A) THE DUTY OF CONSISTENCY. Consistency must be maintained between the principles applied and the decision reached by the domestic authority and the principles laid down by the Treaty and the Community Courts and any decisions of those Courts in determining corresponding questions that may be applicable at that time. As already noted, 'high level' principles such as equality and proportionality will be imported by virtue of section 60(2). What is less clear is whether the twin principles of Community law that Articles 81 and 82 have direct effect and are capable, in certain circumstances, of overriding national laws, could also imported by section 60. If so, it might be possible to challenge a domestic statute in so far as it is in conflict with the Act[5]. There is nothing in Hansard nor in the various Guidelines under the Act to suggest that section 60 could have such a radical effect as this.

(B) HAVING 'REGARD TO' DECISIONS OR STATEMENTS OF THE COMMISSION. The competition authorities under section 60(3) must 'have regard to' any relevant decision[6] or statement of the Commission; this is a lesser obligation than the obligation to ensure that there is no inconsistency under section 60(2). Decisions and statements of other bodies such as the Council of Ministers[7] or the European Parliament are not included. The Act itself does not explain what is meant by Commission statements. However the DGFT's view is that the statements must carry the authority of the Commission itself: this would include decisions on individual cases adopted by the Commission and clear statements about its policy such as the Annual Report on Competition Policy[8]. It is understood that the DGFT also regards comfort letters which have been preceded by a notice in the Official Journal under Article 19(3) of Regulation 17/62[9] and the various Notices of the Commission as having the authority of the Commission.

(C) REFERENCES TO THE ECJ. The Appeal Tribunals of the Competition Commission, the Court of Appeal and the House of Lords will be able to make references to the ECJ for a preliminary ruling under Article 234 of the EC Treaty. This is considered further in chapter 10[10].

5. TRANSITIONAL PROVISIONS

The Chapter I prohibition and the Chapter II prohibition entered into force on 1 March 2000. There were no transitional provisions in relation to the Chapter II prohibition. However, transitional arrangements were made in relation to agreements that were already in force at the time that the Chapter I prohibition

---

5   See Green 'Some Observations on the Civil Consequences of the Chapter I and Chapter II Prohibitions' in *The Europeanisation of UK Competition Law* (Hart Publishing 1999, eds Green and Robertson, pp 29-30); as to the circumstances in which this could happen in EC law, see ch 6, pp 190-202.
6   See Competition Act 1998, s 60(6).
7   Documents such as the Minutes of the Council's deliberations about the ECMR would therefore not need to be considered, although they could be relevant in a particular case.
8   *The Major Provisions* OFT Guideline 400, para 6.2.
9   See ch 7, pp 217-218 on the informal settlement of cases.
10 See ch 10, pp 359-361.

entered into force. They are set out in Schedule 13 of the Act and are accompanied by a detailed Guideline[11] . The transitional provisions are complex, and reference should be made to Schedule 13 and the Guideline where issues arise.

---

11 *Transitional arrangements* OFT Guideline 406.

CHAPTER 10

Competition Act 1998: enforcement and procedure

The Competition Act 1998 gives wide powers of enforcement to the Director General of Fair Trading ('the DGFT') and to the sectoral regulators. The exercise of these rights will have to satisfy the Human Rights Act 1998, which received the Royal Assent on the same day as the Competition Act (9 November 1998) and which entered into force on 2 October 2000[1]. The possible application of the Human Rights Act will be discussed at appropriate points in the text that follows. This chapter will begin with a consideration of the way in which inquiries and investigations are carried out under the Act. After a section on complaints it will consider the provisions on notification for guidance and decisions. Section 4 deals with the powers of enforcement and section 5 with concurrency. The chapter then contains a discussion of appeals and concludes with a consideration of third party actions in the courts.

1. INQUIRIES AND INVESTIGATIONS[2]

One of the fundamental weaknesses of the former competition law of the UK was that it did not confer on the DGFT effective powers to obtain information and to conduct investigations. The purpose of the 1998 Act is to eradicate cartels and abusive behaviour and it provides the DGFT and the sectoral regulators with wide powers to conduct inquiries and investigations. These powers are set out in sections 25 to 29 of the Act; they are explained in some detail in the OFT's Guideline *Powers of investigation*[3]. The OFT has also published an information leaflet *Under investigation?*[4].

Section 25 provides that the DGFT may conduct an investigation if there are 'reasonable grounds for suspecting' that either of the prohibitions has been

---

1   On the Human Rights Act, see Gordon and Ward *Judicial Review and the Human Rights Act* (Cavendish Publishing, 2000); on procedural issues under the Competition Act generally, see Smith *Competition Law: Enforcement and Procedure* (Butterworths, 2001), ch 15.

2   See McNeil 'Investigations under the Competition Act 1998' in *The Competition Act: A New Era for UK Competition Law* (Hart Publishing, 2000, eds Rodger and MacCulloch).

3   OFT Guideline 404; this can be accessed on the DGFT's website, http://www.oft.gov.uk/html/comp-act/technical_guidelines/index.html.

4   This is available on the website referred to in n 3 above.

infringed[5]. The terms of the section anticipate the DGFT's delegation to authorised officers and do not require his personal suspicion in each case[6]. Section 25 requires there to be grounds for suspecting: this deals with one of the DGFT's complaints about the previous régime, under which he had to have 'reasonable cause to believe'[7] that an infringement had occurred before he could investigate: in other words, he had to be able to show that an infringement existed before he could find out whether or not it did.

As in the case of Regulation 17/62, which gives the European Commission power to obtain information (Article 11) and to conduct on-the-spot investigations (Article 14), the Act gives the DGFT the power to make written inquiries (section 26) and to enter premises (sections 27 to 29)[8].

(A)   Written inquiries[9]

A written request for information is made by a notice under section 26 requiring a person to produce to the DGFT a specified document or specified information which the DGFT considers relevant to the investigation[10]. The notice must indicate the subject-matter and purpose of the investigation[11] and the offences involved in non-compliance[12]. Specification can be by reference to a particular item or by category and the notice may state when and where the document or information is to be provided as well as how and in what form[13]. The DGFT has the further power to take copies or extracts from a document produced in response to the notice and to ask for an explanation of it, or, if the document is not produced, to ask where it is believed to be[14]. Notices can be addressed to any person, which is defined to include an undertaking[15] and the DGFT regards this as extending to an association of undertakings[16]. It should be noted that while section 26 applies equally to documents and to information, the *Guideline* makes it clear that the power to obtain information can effectively require a person to create a document comprising that information 'using the knowledge or experience of the sales manager'[17].

---

5   On the circumstances in which the DGFT's powers can be used, see *Powers of investigation* OFT Guideline 404, para 2; the DGFT's powers are equally available to the sectoral regulators listed in s 54 and it should be assumed throughout this chapter that anything which applies to the DGFT applies equally to them, unless otherwise stated.
6   See HL Report Stage, 9 February 1998, cols 986–7 (Lord Haskel); *Powers of investigation* OFT Guideline 404, para 1.5.
7   Restrictive Trade Practices Act 1976, s 36.
8   Note that sections 61-64, in conjunction with the Competition Act (Commission Investigation and Director's Investigation) Order 1999, SI 1999/3027 deal with investigations under Articles 81 and 82 EC.
9   *Powers of investigation* OFT Guideline 404, para 3.
10   Competition Act, s 26(1), (2).
11   Ibid, s 26(3)(a).
12   Ibid, s 26(3)(b).
13   Ibid, s 26(4) and (5); s 59(3) provides that, if information is not in legible form, the DGFT may require a copy in legible form.
14   Competition Act, s 26(6); see pp 340-341 below for discussion of the scope of the power to request explanations and the law on self-incrimination.
15   Ibid, s 59(1), which refers to the Interpretation Act 1978 ('person' includes a body of persons corporate or unincorporate); see p 342 below.
16   *Powers of investigation* OFT Guideline 404, para 3.11; in the case of an undertaking or an association, an authorised person should respond on its behalf.
17   Ibid, para 3.7.

(B) Power to enter premises without a warrant[18]

Section 27 provides that any officer of the DGFT who is authorised in writing by the DGFT to do so ('an investigating officer') may enter any premises in connection with an investigation under section 25[19].

The operation of the power of entry varies depending on whether the premises are occupied by a party under investigation for possible infringement of the Chapter I or Chapter II prohibitions or by a 'third party', that is to say someone who is not suspected of an offence. In the case of the former, the investigating officer must have written authority from the DGFT, together with a document including details of the subject-matter and the purpose of the investigation and the offences involved in non-compliance. On entry, he must produce this document and show evidence of his authorisation[20]. There is no requirement to give prior warning or notice; nor is it necessary for the DGFT first to have attempted to obtain information under the powers in section 26[1].

In the case of entry to third party premises, the investigating officer must give two working days' prior written notice and the notice itself must indicate the subject-matter and the purpose of the investigation[2]. If, however, the officer has taken all reasonable steps to give notice but has been unable to do so, he may dispense with the notice requirement and enter as if the premises were occupied by a party under investigation. This, presumably, will happen only rarely.

When entering the premises, the officer may take with him any necessary equipment: this could be a laptop computer or tape recording equipment[3]; may require 'any person'[4] to produce any documents which the officer considers relevant, to say where a document may be found, and, in relation to any document produced, may require an explanation of it; may take copies of or extracts from any document produced (but not take the originals); and may require the production in visible, legible and portable form of any relevant information that is held on computer[5].

Premises are defined in section 59(1) of the Act as not including domestic premises unless they are also used in connection with an undertaking's affairs or an undertaking's documents are kept there, but are taken to include any vehicle; relevant documents cannot therefore safely be hidden at home or in a car. Where the DGFT wishes to enter domestic premises, it can be anticipated that the Human Rights Act 1998 might be invoked, since one of the 'Convention Rights' protected by that Act is the right to respect for private and family life[6]. Documents kept at

---

18 Ibid, para 5.
19 As to investigations under s 27 on Crown land, see Competition Act s 73(4)(a) and the Competition Act 1998 (Definition of Appropriate Person) Regulations 1999, SI 1999/2282; the Secretary of State may certify in the interests of national security that specified Crown premises may not be entered under this section (see s 73(8)).
20 Competition Act, s 27(3), (4); *Powers of investigation* OFT Guideline 404, paras 4.7-4.9.
1 *Powers of investigation* OFT Guideline 404, para 3.2.
2 Competition Act, s 27(2)
3 *Powers of investigation* OFT Guideline 404, para 4.5.
4 In this instance, this term presumably (although not necessarily) refers to an individual rather than to an undertaking, but there is no restriction as to who the person needs to be; it could include secretaries, IT personnel and messengers as well as directors; see HL Committee, 17 November 1997, col 391 (Lord Simon of Highbury).
5 Competition Act, s 27(5); see also s 59(3).
6 Article 8 of the European Convention for the Protection of Human Rights and Fundamental Freedoms 1950: see in particular *Niemietz v Germany* (1992) 16 EHRR 97; that case suggests that Article 8 may apply in the case of business as well as domestic premises; under

the offices of an undertaking's lawyers would be disclosable also, subject to legal professional privilege[7].

It is not permissible under section 27 to use force to enter or once on the premises and permitted equipment would not therefore include crowbars or other tools[8]. Section 27 entry may therefore be described as a 'right of peaceable entry'[9]. Where force might be required, the powers in section 28 must be used.

(C) Power to enter premises with a warrant[10]

The DGFT may apply for a warrant giving him a power of entry: the warrant may be issued in specified circumstances by a judge of the High Court (Court of Session in Scotland) and in this case he may use reasonable force to obtain entry[11]. The circumstances are that there are reasonable grounds for suspecting that a document sought by written notice, or by an investigation without a warrant, but not produced, is on the premises; that there are reasonable grounds for suspecting that a document that the DGFT could obtain by written notice is on the premises but would be interfered with if it were required to be produced; or that entry without a warrant for the purpose of investigation has been impossible and there are reasonable grounds for suspecting that documents are on the premises that could have been required if entry had been obtained[12]. The section 28 powers therefore confer a 'right of forcible entry'[13].

Investigation by warrant is a serious matter and the investigator's powers are more extensive than under sections 26 or 27. Section 28(2) states that the warrant must authorise the investigating officer and any others delegated by the DGFT by name. The subject-matter and purpose of the investigation, and the offences for non-compliance, must be indicated in the warrant itself[14]. It follows that the party being investigated should inspect this document carefully.

The investigators may use reasonable force to gain entry, but must lock the premises up in as secure a manner as they found them before leaving[15]. They may take 'equipment' to exercise such force but may not use force against any person[16]. As with investigations without a warrant, the authorised officer may require documents to be produced but the scope of this power depends on the situation in which the warrant was issued. The warrant will accordingly specify

---

EC law, see Cases 46/87 & 227/88 *Hoechst AG v EC Commission* [1989] ECR 2859, [1991] 4 CMLR 410.
7   See *Powers of investigation* OFT Guideline 404, para 4.6.
8   Ibid, para 4.5 which refers to portable computers and recording equipment.
9   See pp 339-341 below for discussion of legal professional privilege, the right of access to lawyers and the right against self-incrimination.
10 *Powers of investigation* OFT Guideline 404, para 5; it is intended that a Practice Direction will be issued in due course which will include, *inter alia*, examples of warrants under these provisions. The first 'dawn raids' under these provisions were carried out in October 2000, at the premises of two bus operators, Arriva and FirstGroup: *Financial Times*, 23 October 2000; it is understood that by the end of July 2001 there had been eight 'on-site' investigations with a warrant.
11 Competition Act, s 28.
12 Ibid, s 28(1).
13 A section 28 investigation cannot be conducted on Crown land: Competition Act, s 73(4)(b).
14 Ibid, s 29(1).
15 Competition Act, s 28(2), (5); a curiosity is that s 62(5) allows the use of force when searching as well as entering when conducting an EC investigation: s 28 allows the use of force for entry only.
16 *Powers of investigation* OFT Guideline 404, paras 5.4-5.5.

documents of 'the relevant kind'[17], that is to say those subject to a specific request under sections 26 or 27, or those of the kind that could have been required on investigation under section 27 but were not provided. The DGFT envisages the second category as requiring a generic definition only[18]. In addition to all the powers investigators would have on entry without a warrant, including the power to require information to be accessed from computers[19], they can also take away *originals* of documents and retain them for three months if copying them on the premises is not practicable or if taking them away appears necessary to prevent their disappearance[20]. The investigators can also take any other necessary steps to preserve the existence of documents[1].

(D) Access to lawyers

In the case of an investigation with or without a warrant, there is no statutory right to obtain outside legal help, and certainly none to delay the start of an investigation until an undertaking's external lawyer arrives on the scene. Such situations are familiar in the context of EC investigations; during the passage of the Bill through Parliament, the Government stated that, even though there was nothing in the statute itself, the DGFT would follow European Commission practice in this regard, by giving a firm without internal legal assistance a reasonable period (in practice usually an hour or so) to obtain external help[2]. The Director's Rules provide expressly for this right 'if the officer considers it reasonable in the circumstances to do so and if he is satisfied that such conditions as he considers ... appropriate ... will be complied with'[3]. The Guideline on *Enforcement* provides further guidance on this issue[4]. The investigating officer will not wait for an external lawyer to arrive if the firm being investigated has an internal legal adviser[5], apparently irrespective of whether he or she is specialised in competition law.

(E) Limitation on the use of the powers of investigation[6]

(i) Legal professional privilege

The requirement to produce documents, whether by written notice or on investigation, does not extend to privileged communications[7]. These are defined as communications either between a professional legal adviser and his client or those made in connection with, or in contemplation of, legal proceedings and which, for the purposes of those proceedings, would be protected from disclosure in High Court proceedings (Court of Session in Scotland) on grounds of legal

17 Competition Act, s 28(2)(*b*).
18 *Powers of investigation* OFT Guideline 404, para 5.6.
19 Competition Act, s 28(3).
20 Ibid, s 28(2)(c), (7).
1 Ibid, s 28(2)(*d*).
2 HL Committee, 17 November 1997, col 404 (Lord Simon of Highbury); for a description of European Commission practice see ch 7, pp 232-239.
3 SI 2000/293, r 13(1).
4 See *Powers of investigation* OFT Guideline 404, paras 4.10-4.11.
5 Ibid, para 4.11.
6 *Powers of investigation* OFT Guideline 404, para 6.
7 Competition Act, s 30.

professional privilege (confidentiality of communications in Scotland)[8]. 'Professional legal adviser' includes professionally qualified lawyers employed by firms (in-house counsel) as well as those practising in their own right, and in this respect privilege under the 1998 Act is more extensive than under EC competition law[9]. Not only does EC law not extend to correspondence with 'in-house' (that is to say employed) lawyers; nor does it apply to dealings with independent professional lawyers not qualified in a Member State[10]. It follows that some documents could legitimately be withheld where the investigation takes place under the Competition Act 1998 but not where it is conducted under EC law; if the investigators were combining a UK with an EC investigation into a single visit under dual authority, the situation could become quite Gilbertian; for this reason, combined investigations are unlikely. The problem of a combined investigation would be exacerbated by the fact that disputed claims of privilege in an EC context are referred to the Court of First Instance, but a dispute under UK law would either be 'stored up' for an appeal against the DGFT's final decision, or be subject to an application for judicial review[11]. Neither the Act nor the *Guidelines* indicate how disputes under the 1998 Act should be handled where there is disagreement as to whether a document is privileged; one suggestion is that the documents should be sealed in an envelope and that the matter should be determined by a judge[12]. A correct handling of this issue is required by the Human Rights Act 1998.

(ii)   Self-incrimination

The DGFT acknowledges the EC jurisprudence on the subject of self-incrimination[13] and accepts that this is one of those 'high level' principles which will apply to his actions by virtue of section 60[14]. It remains to be seen how this difficult area will be addressed in practice, not least since the position is additionally complicated as a result of the Human Rights Act 1998, which brings in the case law of the European Court of Human Rights: that Court's judgment in *Funke v France*[15] would appear to confer a more ample privilege than the ECJ did in *Orkem v Commission*[16]. The DGFT accepts that he may not ask for explanations that might involve admissions of an infringement and will instead seek explanations of matters of fact[17], but the distinction between these two will not always be clear-cut.

8   For the law of privilege in court proceedings see 13 *Halsbury's Laws* (4th edn), paras 71–85.
9   See *Powers of investigation* OFT Guideline 404, paras 6.1-6.2 and 10.7 and 10.8; HL Committee, 17 November 1997, col 416 (Lord Haskel).
10   For a discussion of privilege in EC competition law, see ch 7 pp 224-225.
11   On appeals and applications for judicial review, see pp 358-359 below.
12   Murphy 'A Proposed Strategy to Settle Legal Professional Privilege Claims' (2000) 21 ECLR 180.
13   See ch 7, pp 225-226.
14   *Powers of investigation* OFT Guideline 404, para 6.3.
15   [1993] 1 CMLR 897; see also *Saunders v United Kingdom* (1996) 2 BHRC 358, distinguished in *Brown v Stott* [2001] All ER 97, PC.
16   Case 347/87 [1989] ECR 3283; see also Case T-112/98 *Mannesmannröhren-Werke AG v Commission* judgment of 20 February 2001, discussed at ch 7, p 226; on self-incrimination. On this issue, see Cumming '*Otto v Post Bank* and the Privilege Against Self-Incrimination in Enforcement Proceedings of Articles [81] and [82] before the English Courts' (1995) 16 ECLR 401.
17   Ibid, para 6.4: the example given is whether a particular employee attended a particular meeting.

The power to demand an 'explanation' of a document is expressly linked to and limited to documents that are produced[18]. However, in the case of an investigation, an explanation can be sought in relation to 'any document appearing to be of the relevant kind'[19] without any specific reference to the document having been produced: this is because, in the case of a search, documents may be found as well as produced. The investigator could in theory require explanation of a document that appears to exist but which he has been unable to find, but the DGFT's guidelines do not indicate any intention to act in this way[20].

(iii) Confidentiality

There are detailed provisions in the 1998 Act about restrictions on the disclosure of information obtained during the course of an investigation (and as a result of the operation of Part I of the Act generally)[1] and these provide a degree of reassurance to disclosing parties. However, parties subject to an investigation or to a request for information would be well advised to identify any confidential information that is supplied to the DGFT or to his investigators in order to support any subsequent claim that it should not be published or disclosed to anyone else. There is, moreover, no right to withhold information from the investigators on grounds of confidentiality[2]. The DGFT's guidelines explain his rights and obligations as regards publication[3].

(F) Offences[4]

There are criminal sanctions for non-compliance with the powers of investigation. Individuals as well as legal persons may commit offences; the penalties in some cases include imprisonment[5]. The relevant offences are set out in sections 42 to 44 of the Act and fall into five main categories: failing to comply with a requirement imposed under sections 26, 27 or 28[6]; intentionally obstructing an officer investigating without a warrant[7]; intentionally obstructing an officer investigating with a warrant[8]; intentionally or recklessly destroying, disposing of, falsifying or concealing documents, or causing or permitting those things to happen[9]; and knowingly or recklessly supplying information which is false or misleading in a material particular either directly to the DGFT, or to anyone else, knowing it is for the purpose of providing information to the DGFT[10].

The Act allows various defences to these penal provisions. If a person is charged with not producing a document, it is a defence to show that he did not have it in

---

18 Competition Act, ss 26(6)(*a*)(ii), 27(5)(*b*)(ii).
19 Ibid, s 28(2)(*e*).
20 SI 2000/293: the Director's Rules, r 13(3) provides that any person required under s 26(6)(*a*)(ii) (ie by written notice) to provide an explanation of a document may be accompanied by a legal adviser; note that they do not offer such a right during an on-the-spot investigation.
1   See Competition Act, s 55, together with Sch 11, and s 56.
2   See rule 27 of the Director's Rules in relation to information provided by third parties.
3   *Powers of investigation* OFT Guideline 404, paras 6.5–6.9.
4   Ibid, OFT Guideline 404, para 7.
5   See p 342 below.
6   Competition Act, s 42(1).
7   Ibid, s 42(5).
8   Ibid, s 42(7).
9   Ibid, s 43(1).
10 Ibid, s 44(1), (2).

his possession or control and it was not reasonably practical for him to get it[11]. A similar defence applies to failure to provide information. In relation to all requirements under sections 26 and 27 (written notice and investigation without a warrant) there is a general defence if the investigator failed to act in accordance with the section[12]. This shows the importance of ensuring that all the procedural steps are properly taken; there is no such defence in relation to investigations with a warrant, although it is possible to appeal against the issue of the warrant itself. There are no statutory defences to the charges of knowingly or recklessly destroying documents or providing false or misleading information.

The penalties can be substantial and depend on whether the offence is tried summarily or is serious enough to be taken on indictment to the High Court (or Court of Session in Scotland). Usually the penalties are financial but in the case of any obstruction of investigators with a warrant, destruction of documents or provision of false or misleading information, imprisonment for up to two years is possible (as well as a fine in some cases)[13].

As already described, the powers of investigation, and the offences, are applicable to 'persons', which can include an undertaking[14]. In addition, under section 72, officers of bodies corporate are liable to punishment if they have consented to or connived at an offence or it is due to neglect on their part[15]. Officer means a director, manager, secretary or other similar officer, or anyone purporting to act as such[16]. There are similar provisions applicable to companies managed by their members (who can be liable) and, in Scotland, to partners and partnerships[17]. The fact that individuals themselves can be liable in certain circumstances under the 1998 Act, and that there is even a possibility of imprisonment, will no doubt concentrate the minds of those responsible for ensuring compliance with the legislation.

2.   COMPLAINTS

Although the Competition Act 1998 contains no reference to any procedure for complaining to the authorities, the DGFT has made it clear that complaints both to himself and to the sectoral regulators are to be encouraged. Officials of the OFT have been heard to say many times 'Don't notify, do complain' since the Act was adopted. There is no specific form for making a complaint, and no fee is payable. The OFT has published Information Leaflets *Making a complaint*[18] and on *Cartels and the Competition Act 1998: a Guide for Purchasers*[19]. Part 8 of the DGFT's Guideline on *The Major Provisions*[20] describes what a potential complainant should do and what information a complaint should preferably

---

11 Ibid, s 42(2), (3).
12 Ibid, s 42(4).
13 Ibid, ss 42(6), (7), 43(2), 44(3); *Powers of investigation* OFT Guideline 404, para 7.7 describe the penalties in detail.
14 Competition Act, s 59(1); see *Powers of investigation* OFT Guideline 404, para 4.3.
15 Competition Act, s 72(2); see *Powers of investigation* OFT Guideline 404, para 7.4; similar provisions were contained in the RTPA 1976, but never attracted particular attention (see s 38(6), (7) of that Act).
16 Competition Act, s 72(3).
17 Ibid, s 72(4)–(6).
18 This can be obtained directly from the OFT or found on the OFT's website at http://www.oft.gov.uk/html/comp-act/download/oft427.pdf.
19 Ibid, oft435.pdf.
20 OFT Guideline 400.

include. It is helpful for the DGFT to know the identity of the complainant and whether it is a customer or competitor of the undertaking complained about or a final consumer, and to have an explanation of the complaint together with any relevant correspondence and notes. Information on the relevant market and market shares should also be provided if possible and appropriate. OFT officials are willing to discuss the situation before any complaint is made.

Complaints raise questions of confidentiality which can be difficult. Some complainants wish to remain anonymous and this can make it difficult for the DGFT or sectoral regulator to pursue the complaint. The complainant's identity may also have to be disclosed to the undertaking complained about in order to enable it to respond adequately, in the interests both of fairness and the proper pursuit of the investigation. The DGFT emphasises that claims for anonymity and confidentiality of materials or correspondence should be made at the earliest opportunity, and that confidential matters should be put in a separate annex. The DGFT would normally consult the complainant before disclosing its identity or any confidential material: under sections 55 and 56 the DGFT and regulators are subject to a qualified obligation to respect confidentiality.

What happens to a complaint depends on whether the DGFT (or sectoral regulator) considers that it reveals a possible breach of the prohibition. If it does, the complaint may trigger an investigation, although the DGFT may also need further information from the complainant. If no possible breach is indicated, the DGFT (or regulator) will inform the complainant as soon as possible that he intends to take no further action[1].

3. NOTIFICATION

(A) Introduction

An agreement may be notified to the DGFT[2] for the purpose of assessing whether it infringes the Chapter I prohibition[3]. Conduct may also be notified to the DGFT for the purpose of assessing whether it infringes the Chapter II prohibition[4]. The procedure to be followed is outlined in the 1998 Act[5] and further guidance is contained in the Director's Rules[6], the notification Form N[7] and the DGFT's Guidance Notes[8]; there is also an Information Leaflet, *Is notification necessary?*[9]. There are two sorts of notification provided for by the 1998 Act, namely for guidance and for a decision. Where guidance only is sought, the DGFT will not consult third parties: the procedure is confidential, and the possibility exists that the DGFT could change his opinion at a later date, if and when third party representations are made[10]. The rules on guidance and decisions are explained

---

1   *The Major Provisions* OFT Guideline 400, para 8.3.
2   The regulators have all the powers of the DGFT to receive and process notifications to give guidance and make decisions granting exemption.
3   Competition Act, s 12.
4   Ibid, s 20.
5   Ibid, ss 12-16, as amended by the Competition Act 1998 (Notification of Excluded Agreements and Appealable Decisions) Regulations 2000, SI 2000/263, ss 20-24 and Schs 5 and 6.
6   SI 2000/293.
7   *Form N* OFT Guideline 409.
8   *Guidance Notes on Completing Form N* OFT Guideline 431.
9   http://www.oft.gov.uk/html/comp-act/download/oft434.pdf.
10 A parallel system exists in the procedure for confidential guidance on mergers under the Fair Trading Act 1973: see ch 22, p 811.

below. Fees are payable when notifying for guidance or a decision. The relevant sectoral branch of the OFT will deal with notifications[11]. Where a notification is made, but it seems to the DGFT that the agreement or conduct does not infringe either of the prohibitions in the Act, he may exercise his discretion not to give guidance or a decision at all[12]. If notification under EC law is abolished, it may be that the provisions in the Competition Act on notification will also be repealed[13]; if they are not, undertakings wishing to obtain certainty as to the validity of their agreements will be likely to notify to the OFT on a precautionary basis, a practice which it has been at pains to discourage.

(B)   Guidance

(i)   Notification of agreements for guidance

Notification for guidance must be made by a party to the agreement. When the DGFT has received such a notification he may give the applicant guidance as to whether or not the agreement is likely to infringe the Chapter I prohibition[14]. A fee of £5,000 is payable[15]. If he considers that an infringement is likely (in the absence of any exemption) the guidance may indicate either whether a block, parallel or section 11 exemption applies or whether he would grant individual exemption if asked to do so[16].

(ii)   Effect of notification of agreements for guidance

If the DGFT determines an application under section 13 by giving guidance to the effect either that the agreement is unlikely to infringe, that it benefits from block, parallel or section 11 exemption, or that he would be likely to exempt it individually, the consequences listed in section 15 follow. The first is that the DGFT cannot proceed further against the agreement unless he has reasonable grounds to believe there has been a material change of circumstance; or he has a reasonable suspicion that he was given information that was incomplete, false or misleading in a material particular; or one of the parties asks him for a decision under section 14; or he receives a complaint from a third party[17]. The second consequence is that he cannot impose a penalty[18].

(iii)   Notification of conduct for guidance and its effect

Notification of conduct for guidance must be made by the person whose conduct is at issue, and when the DGFT has received the notification he may give the person guidance as to whether the Chapter II prohibition is likely to be infringed[19].

11   See ch 2, pp 57-59 on the organisation of the OFT.
12   *Guidance Notes on Completing Form N* OFT Guideline 431, para 2.4.
13   See ch 4, pp 146-147 and ch 7, pp 246-248 on the proposed amendments to the system of notification in the EC.
14   Competition Act, s 13(1), (2).
15   Competition Act 1998 (Director's Rules) Order 2000, SI 2000/293, Annex 2 Part 1.
16   Competition Act, s 13(3).
17   Competition Act, s 15(2).
18   Ibid; for discussion of immunity from penalties, see pp 355-356 below.
19   Competition Act, s 21.

A fee of £5000 is payable[20]. The effect of guidance is similar to that given under the Chapter I prohibition[1].

(C) Decisions

(i) Notification of an agreement for a decision

For an agreement to be examined under section 14 a party to the agreement must notify the DGFT, who may then take a decision as to whether the Chapter I prohibition has been infringed and, if not, whether that is because of the effect of an exclusion or because the agreement is exempt[2]. A fee of £13,000 is payable[3]. Section 14(3) of the 1998 Act provides that the application 'may include' a request for individual exemption. In practice it is likely that this will be the rule rather than the exception: if the agreement benefits from a block, parallel or a section 11 exemption, notification is unlikely to be justified, first as the exemptions are automatic and secondly because the benefits of a further decision on the subject are small. A decision confirming that an agreement falls within one of the exclusions could have benefits in some situations of doubt, but the main purpose of section 14 notifications is likely to be for individual exemption. Seven notifications for a decision had been made by 31 July 2001[4].

(ii) Effect of notification of an agreement for a decision

If the DGFT takes a decision as a result of a notification under section 14 to the effect that the agreement has not infringed the Chapter I prohibition, the consequences set out in section 16 follow. First, the DGFT cannot proceed further against the agreement unless he has reasonable grounds to believe there has been a material change of circumstance since his decision; or he has a reasonable suspicion that he was given information that was incomplete, false or misleading in a material particular[5]. Secondly, he may impose no penalty[6]. If he takes a decision that the agreement has infringed the prohibition (because no exemption or exclusion applies and the agreement restricts competition to an appreciable extent) the enforcement procedure will apply.

A statutory requirement for the DGFT to give reasons in the case of decisions following notifications is contained in Schedules 5 and 6[7].

(iii) Notification of conduct for a decision and its effect

Notification of conduct for a decision must be made by the person whose conduct is at issue, and when the DGFT has received the notification he may make a decision as to whether the Chapter II prohibition has been infringed and, if not,

---

20 See n 15 above.
1   Competition Act, s 23.
2   Ibid, s 14(2).
3   Director's Rules, SI 2000/293, Annex 2 Part 2.
4   See ch 9, p 311, n 3.
5   Competition Act, s 16(2).
6   Ibid, s 16(3); for discussion of immunity from penalties, see pp 355-356 below.
7   Ibid, Sch 5, para 6 and Sch 6, para 6.

whether that is on account of an exclusion[8]. There are no exemptions from the Chapter II prohibition of the 1998 Act. A fee of £13,000 is payable[9]. The effect of a decision on conduct is the same as that given under the Chapter I prohibition[10].

(D) Procedure

(i) Form N

Notification in all cases must be made using Form N[11], and an original must be supplied together with two copies (and an extra copy for any relevant regulator). Copies must be duly certified by the applicant. Joint applications may be made by a jointly-nominated representative; notifications made by a representative of an applicant must include written proof of the authority to act. Time starts to run on the date the notification is received by the DGFT provided that this is before 6.00pm. If Form N is incomplete, the DGFT must inform the applicant(s) in writing and the effective date of the notification is delayed until full information is received. The DGFT has one month within which to inform the applicant of incomplete information, otherwise the notification is deemed to be complete. Confidential information should be put in a separate annex together with an explanation. Material changes to the relevant facts must be communicated without delay to the DGFT or the relevant regulator, as the case may be.

(ii) Concurrency[12]

In the case of the DGFT and one or more of the sectoral regulators having concurrent jurisdiction, Form N must still be sent to the DGFT with an extra copy for any relevant sectoral regulator[13]. It is advisable to send an additional copy direct to the regulator in question. The DGFT must inform the applicant that he has passed the Form N to the relevant regulator (there may be more than one) and the applicant is to be kept informed of which regulator is handling the case[14].

(iii) Notification of other parties

The applicant must take all reasonable steps to notify all other parties of whom he is aware that an application has been made, and what sort of application it is[15]. This must be in writing and be given within seven working days of receipt of the DGFT's acknowledgement of receipt. In addition a copy of the notice must be given to the DGFT.

---

8   Ibid, s 22.
9   See p 345, n 3 above.
10 Competition Act, s 24.
11 The information required by From N is set out in the Director's Rules, SI 2000/293, Annex 1.
12 See p 357 below.
13 Ibid, r 3(2).
14 Competition Act 1998 (Concurrency) Regulations 2000, SI 2000/260, art 5 (1).
15 That is to say whether it is for guidance or a decision: see Director's Rules, SI 2000/293 and the 1998 Act, Sch 5, para 2 and Sch 6, para 2.

(iv)   Public register

In the case of notifications for a decision (but not for guidance) the DGFT keeps a register containing a summary of the agreement or conduct in question, and an indication of the result of the application[16]. However there is nothing under the new régime which resembles the practice under the Restrictive Trade Practices Act 1976, where the actual agreements submitted for registration under that Act could be scrutinised and copied. Form N contains a section in which the applicants are asked to provide a summary of the agreement or conduct. The OFT publishes a Weekly Gazette in which the summary is reproduced. The Gazette is available in hard copy and electronically[17].

(v)   Provisional decisions

Paragraph 3 of Schedule 5 and paragraph 3 of Schedule 6 of the Act provide for the DGFT to make provisional decisions after a preliminary investigation[18]. In the case of agreements, he must consider it likely that the Chapter I prohibition will be infringed and that individual exemption would not be appropriate[19]; in the case of conduct, he must consider it likely that the Chapter II prohibition will be infringed[20]. In each case he must notify the applicant in writing of the decision[1]. The DGFT must consult the applicant and other parties to the agreement or engaged in the conduct and state in the written notification his reasons for the decision and the facts on which it is based. Provisional decisions in relation to notified agreements remove the provisional immunity from penalties[2]. There is no such immunity for notified conduct. Provisional decisions are not subject to appeal to the Competition Commission[3], and do not affect the final determination of the application[4]. Provisional decisions following notifications should be distinguished from interim measures[5].

(vi)   Procedure on giving guidance

Where the DGFT gives guidance, this must be in writing together with the supporting facts and reasons[6]. Guidance is not published. It may be negative, or favourable[7]. If the DGFT proposes to take further action after favourable guidance, for example because he has received a complaint, he must consult the recipient of the guidance[8]. Having given negative guidance, he is, of course, free to enforce

16   Director's Rules, SI 2000/293, r 8.
17   http://www.oft.gov.uk/html/comp.
18   Director's Rules, r 9.
19   Competition Act, Sch 5, para 3(1).
20   Ibid, Sch 6, para 3(1).
1   Ibid, Sch 5, para 3(2)(a) and Sch 6, para 3(2).
2   Ibid, Sch 5, para 3(2)(b); on immunities, see pp 355-356 below.
3   On appealable decisions, see pp 358-359 below.
4   Ibid, Sch 5, para 3(4), (5); Sch 6, paras 3(4), (5).
5   Ibid, s 35; see pp 350-351 below.
6   Director's Rules, SI 2000/293, r 10.
7   Negative guidance would be to the effect that the agreement or conduct is likely to infringe a prohibition and is not subject to an exclusion or (for an agreement only) an exemption; the limitations on DGFT action under Competition Act, ss 15, 16, 23 and 24 only apply in the event of favourable guidance.
8   Director's Rules, SI 2000/293, r 11.

the prohibitions against the applicants by taking either a provisional decision or a final decision, or both, and in either case with directions which would be considered appropriate to bring any infringement to an end[9].

(vii)   *Consultation of the public*

When an agreement or conduct is notified for a decision, the Director's Rules provide for varying degrees of consultation[10]: if the DGFT proposes to grant an exemption for an agreement, whether or not subject to conditions or obligations, he *must* consult the public; if he proposes to decide that the Chapter I or Chapter II prohibitions have not been infringed he *may* consult the public.

(viii)   *Fees*

The charging of fees for guidance and for decisions will, in some cases, have a deterrent effect on notifications: from the DGFT's point of view this is to be welcomed, since he is keen that he should not be swamped with notifications; the intention is that instead his resources should be used in the fight against cartels and serious abuses. Calculation of the fee level is based on the principle of full economic cost recovery on the part of the OFT in evaluating a case; this has been done by estimating the cost of the work for an average case. Fees are chargeable only in respect of guidance and decisions; informal advice may be obtained from the OFT without payment of a fee. The fees apply to all undertakings irrespective of their turnover.

4.   ENFORCEMENT

(A)   Introduction

Sections 32 to 41 of the Act deal with enforcement. The DGFT and sectoral regulators[11] are given powers to order the cessation of infringements and to impose penalties. In the case of an infringement, the DGFT may give directions to bring the infringement to an end[12], may request market conduct to be modified[13] and may require an infringing undertaking to pay him a penalty[14]. Sections 34 and 37 of the Act deal with enforcement of directions and with the recovery of penalties respectively. There are immunities from penalties; these immunities can be withdrawn[15]. There are also provisions for interim measures[16]. These provisions are supplemented by various statutory instruments, in particular the Director's Rules[17] and by two DGFT Guidelines on *Enforcement*[18] and *Guidance*

---

9   See p 350 below.
10   See the Director's Rules, SI 2000/293, r 12; these broadly reflect similar requirements under EC law, but Council Regulation 17/62/EEC, Art 19(3) (OJ [1962] 13/204, OJ [1959-62] spec ed 87) requires publication of the intention to grant both negative clearance and exemption.
11   As defined in Competition Act, s 54.
12   Competition Act, ss 32, 33.
13   *Enforcement* OFT Guideline 407, para 2.2.
14   Competition Act, s 36 and *Enforcement* OFT Guideline 407, para 4.
15   Competition Act, ss 39-40 and see pp 355-356 below.
16   Ibid, s 35.
17   Competition Act 1998 (Director's Rules) Order 2000, SI 2000/293.
18   *Enforcement* OFT Guideline 407; this Guideline is made under s 52 of the Act.

as to the appropriate amount of penalty[19]. The following paragraphs discuss each of these matters in turn. Private actions for damages or injunctive relief are discussed at the end of the chapter[20].

(B) Procedure

Where the DGFT suspects an infringement of the Act, he will first carry out an investigation pursuant to section 25. If, as a result of that investigation, he proposes to adopt a decision that there has been an infringement of the Chapter I or Chapter II prohibition, section 31 of the Act requires him to give written notice to the person or persons 'likely to be affected'[1] and give that person (or persons) an opportunity to make representations[2]. There is no such statutory requirement in relation to infringement or conditional exemption decisions following an application under sections 14 or 22, although the Director's Rules provide for this[3]. The form of the written notice is set out in rule 14 of the Director's Rules and is the equivalent of a statement of objections in Community law[4]. Subsequently, the parties may request the opportunity to make oral representations to the DGFT, but this is limited to commenting on the DGFT's rule 14 notice, and does not involve an *inter partes* hearing: it is not the same as the oral hearing that takes place in proceedings before the European Commission[5]. The DGFT, on request, must give the parties an opportunity to inspect the DGFT's file on the proposed decision, excluding confidential information or internal DGFT documents[6]. At the end of this procedure the DGFT may adopt a decision that there has been an infringement of the Chapter I or Chapter II prohibition; there is no express requirement in the Act for the DGFT to give reasons, but the Director's Rules provide that reasons will be given[7].

An important question is whether the proceedings before the DGFT should be characterised as criminal for the purpose of the Human Rights Act 1998. If so, it could be argued that the procedure to be followed by him fails to satisfy Article 6 of the European Convention, which establishes the right to a fair trial. In particular it is arguable that the DGFT is insufficiently independent from the team of investigators within the OFT; that there should be a right to cross-examine witnesses; and that there should be a presumption of innocence. If the proceedings are not criminal, the Convention is probably satisfied by the fact that there is a full right of appeal to the Appeal Tribunals of the Competition Commission, at which any defect can be cured[8]; this argument may not prevail if the proceedings before the DGFT were to be regarded as criminal[9].

---

19   *Guidance on the appropriate amount of a penalty* OFT Guideline 423; this Guideline is made under s 38 of the Act.
20   See pp 361-362.
1   Competition Act, s 31(2)(a).
2   Ibid, s 31(2)(*b*).
3   Director's Rules, SI 2000/293, r 14(1).
4   See ch 7, pp 232-233.
5   On the oral hearing in EC law, see ch 7, pp 234-235.
6   See *Enforcement* OFT Guideline 407, para 2.5.
7   See *Enforcement* OFT Guideline 407, para 2.6 and Director's Rules, SI 2000/293, r 15.
8   See *Albert and Le Compte v Belgium* (1982) 5 EHRR 533, Series A 58 (1983) para 29; see also *Kingsley v United Kingdom* (Application No 35605/97), judgment of 7 November 2000, para 59; on appeals to the Competition Commission, see pp 358-359 below.
9   See *Findlay v United Kingdom* (1997) 24 EHRR 221; note that in *Han & Yau v Customs and Excise Comrs* (judgment of 3 July 2001) the Court of Appeal held that the imposition of civil penalty charges for dishonest evasion of tax gives rise to criminal charges within the meaning of Article 6 of the European Convention on Human Rights.

(C)   Directions

Section 32(1) of the Competition Act provides that, when the DGFT has made a decision that an agreement infringes the Chapter I prohibition, he may give to such person or persons as he considers appropriate such directions as he considers appropriate to bring the infringement to an end. Section 32(3) expands on the content of these directions, which may require the parties to the agreement to modify the agreement or require them to terminate the agreement.

There are corresponding provisions in section 33 for directions in the case of infringements of the Chapter II prohibition; in this case the direction may require the person concerned to modify the conduct in question, or require him to cease that conduct. In either case, directions may also include other provisions such as positive action and reporting obligations[10]. The DGFT gave directions to Napp Pharmaceuticals in May 2001 requiring it to terminate abusive practices; these were amended later in the month.[10a] It is probably the case that directions under section 33(3) would not be able to require divestment or transfer of part of the undertaking or assets of the dominant firm found to have abused its position contrary to the Chapter II prohibition; certainly the section does not explicitly give such a power, and it would require a bold interpretation to include divestiture within the meaning of the modification or cessation of conduct; structural remedies could, however, follow from a monopoly investigation under the relevant provisions of the Fair Trading Act 1973[11].

(D)   Persons who may be the subject of directions

It should be noted that directions may be given to 'appropriate' persons, who will not necessarily be the parties to the agreement or perpetrators of the conduct. The purpose of this is to enable the DGFT to give directions to parents, affiliates or private individuals with the ability to influence or procure actions by the infringing persons[12]. Section 34 of the Act allows the court to order an undertaking or its officers to obey a direction relating to the management of that undertaking if the person subject to the direction has failed to comply.

(E)   Interim measures

If the DGFT has a 'reasonable suspicion' that either the Chapter I or the Chapter II prohibition has been infringed, but has not completed his investigation, he may give directions for the purpose either of preventing serious, irreparable damage to a particular person, or of protecting the public interest, if he considers that it is necessary to act as a matter of urgency[13]. Interim measures therefore require a reasonable suspicion of infringement, a valid purpose and a need for urgent action[14]. It is not entirely clear why section 35 requires 'reasonable

---

10 See *Enforcement* OFT Guideline 407, para 2.3.
10a See OFT Press Release PN 23/01, 23 May 2001.
11 See ch 11, pp 380 and 383-385; note that Article 7(1) of the regulation proposed by the European Commission to replace Regulation 17/62 would specifically provide the possibility of structural remedies under Articles 81 and 82: see ch 7, p 255.
12 See *Enforcement* OFT Guideline 407, para 2.2.
13 Competition Act, s 35(1), (2).
14 For EC law on interim measures see ch 7, pp 226-229; para 3.3 of *Enforcement* OFT Guideline 407 suggests that the burden of proof in EC law is too high to make the use of interim measures effective and that they will therefore feature to a greater extent under the 1998 Act; see also HL Report Stage, 19 February 1998, col 354 (Lord Simon of Highbury).

suspicion' if the DGFT is to adopt interim measures, whereas section 25 provides that he may conduct an investigation if there are 'reasonable grounds for suspecting' an infringement: was the draftsman intending to impose different tests when choosing these formulations? If so, the test for interim measures must require a higher standard, since section 35 itself envisages that the DGFT will already have commenced his investigation, so that he must at some prior point in time have had reasonable grounds for suspecting an infringement. An alternative view would be that these are simply alternative ways of formulating the same test. This may have to be tested before the Competition Commission or the courts.

The DGFT must give notice to the affected persons before giving directions, thus giving them an opportunity to make representations[15]. Such notice must indicate the nature of the proposed direction and the DGFT's reasons[16]. Any direction given may be similar in terms to a final direction and can be enforced in a similar way[17]. The DGFT attaches considerable importance to the power to take interim measures[18]; under the Fair Trading Act 1973 a serious problem was the lack of any power to adopt interim measures pending the outcome of a Competition Commission investigation, with the result that in some cases a complainant had gone out of business long before any remedial steps could be taken to assist it[19]. The DGFT gave notice in June 2001 to Robert Wiseman Dairies of his intention to adopt interim measures in relation to its pricing practices in Scotland for fresh, processed milk.[19a]

The DGFT's powers to make final decisions under the prohibitions are based on damage to competition; however he may give interim directions to protect the public interest. This term is not defined in the Act[20]. During the Parliamentary debates on the Bill the Government said that, in accordance with EC principles of proportionality, the DGFT's interim measures should not exceed what was necessary to achieve the proposed objective[1].

(F)   Enforcement of compliance with directions

If a person subject to directions (whether interim or final) fails to comply without reasonable excuse, the DGFT may apply to the court[2] for an order requiring compliance within a specified time or, if the direction concerns the management of an undertaking, ordering another officer to carry it out[3]. Breach of such an order would be contempt of court, punishable by fines or imprisonment, at the court's discretion[4]. There is nothing in section 34 that limits the court's order-making powers to persons within the UK[5].

---

15 Competition Act, s 35(3).
16 Ibid, s 35(4).
17 Ibid, s 35(5)–(7).
18 *Enforcement* OFT Guideline 407, Part 3.
19 See eg *Highland Scottish Omnibuses Ltd* Cm 1129 (1990).
19a OFT Press Release 25 June 2001.
20 A definition exists in s 84 of the Fair Trading Act 1973 for the purposes of that Act: see ch 11, pp 374-375; see also *Enforcement* OFT Guideline 407, para 3.6, which refers to the need to protect an 'industry'.
1   HL Report Stage, 19 February 1998, col 356 (Lord Simon of Highbury).
2   'Court' is defined in Competition Act, s 59(1).
3   Ibid, s 34.
4   *Enforcement* OFT Guideline 407, para 2.9.
5   On the territorial scope of the Act, see ch 12, pp 404-405.

(G)   Penalties

A key feature of the Act is that penalties can be imposed for infringements of the Chapter I and Chapter II prohibitions. The most obvious failing of the old legislation was that there was no credible sanction. Section 36(1) of the Act provides that a penalty may be imposed for an infringement of the Chapter I prohibition; while section 36(2) provides correspondingly for an infringement of the Chapter II prohibition. As a prerequisite for the imposition of a penalty, section 36(3) requires that the DGFT must be satisfied that the infringement has been committed intentionally or negligently. Intention may be deduced from internal documents, or from deliberate concealment of the agreement or conduct in question[6]. The Act does not establish criminal liability for infringements of the Chapter I and II prohibitions, as has been done in some jurisdictions[7]; as has been noted, however, individuals may commit offences where, for example, they obstruct investigations or provide false information,[8] and the Government announced in June 2001 that it is contemplating the introduction of criminal penalties for participation in cartels.[8a]

(i)   Maximum amount of a penalty

Section 36(8) provides that penalties may not exceed 10% of the turnover of the penalised undertaking. In Parliament, this was confirmed as turnover arising in the UK[9], a position which is different from that under Council Regulation 17/62[10] where worldwide turnover can be taken into account. Turnover is to be determined in accordance with provisions specified by order of the Secretary of State. This was effected by the Competition Act 1998 (Determination of Turnover for Penalties) Order 2000[11] and this allows turnover for up to three years to be taken into account if the infringement has continued for as long as that. The Schedule to the statutory instrument sets out how to determine what qualifies as applicable turnover. In setting penalties, the DGFT must take account of fines imposed by the European Commission or by a court or other body in another Member State (though apparently not a Contracting State of the EEA), as must the Appeal Tribunals of the Competition Commission or any court hearing appeals on levels of penalties[12]. This raises interesting questions concerning whether the same agreement or conduct is at issue, as there may be different effects in different Member States. EC principles applied through section 60 may assist in resolving them[13].

---

6   Ibid, paras 4.6–4.8; for negligence see paras 4.9–4.10 and for duress see para 4.11.
7   See ch 13, pp 415-416.
8   See pp 341-342 above.
8a   See HM Treasury Press Release 67/01, 18 June 2001; *A World Class Competition Régime* (July 2001), Cm 5233, ch 7; an Enterprise Bill is likely to be introduced in March 2002.
9   HC SC G, 16 June 1998, col 454 (Nigel Griffiths): 'The power to penalise an undertaking by up to 10% of its UK turnover will give the new prohibition régime real teeth'; see also HL Committee, 17 November 1997, col 425 (Lord Haskel) and HL Consideration of Commons' Amendments, 20 October 1998, cols 1373–6 (Lord McIntosh of Haringey).
10   Council Regulation 17/62/EEC, OJ [1962] L13/204 (S edn 1959–62, p 87).
11   SI 2000/309.
12   Competition Act, s 38(9); fines under US anti-trust law are not covered.
13   See eg the judgment of the ECJ Case 45/69 in *Boehringer Mannheim Gmb* [1970] ECR 769.

(ii) The Commission's Guidance as to the appropriate amount of a penalty

The DGFT's Guideline of March 1999 on *Enforcement*[14] provided some indications of his likely approach to the level of penalties. However this Guideline has, to some extent, since been superceded by his *Guidance as to the appropriate amount of a penalty*[15] of March 2000. This Guidance is given pursuant to section 38 of the Act, and has been approved by the Secretary of State, as required by that provision. The DGFT and the sectoral regulators must take this guidance into account when setting the level of the penalty; the guidance is not binding, however, on the Appeal Tribunals of the Competition Commission.

Paragraph 1.8 of the *Guidance* sets out the DGFT's policy objectives in setting the level of penalties: to reflect the seriousness of the infringement and to deter undertakings from engaging in anti-competitive practices. Severe penalties can therefore be expected for price-fixing and market-sharing agreements and for serious abuses of market power. However, 'whistleblowing' is encouraged, and lenient treatment will be given to those that do blow the whistle[16]. Paragraph 2 sets out the various steps to be taken when calculating the level of the fine: these are explained in detail in paragraphs 2.3 to 2.7. The provisions on whistleblowing and leniency are set out in paragraph 3.

The starting point in any case will be to determine the relevant turnover of the undertaking to be fined and to consider how serious the infringement is[17]. This will determine how near to the maximum 10% figure the penalty should be. Having made this initial calculation, the DGFT will then consider the duration of the infringement[18]; he will take into account 'other factors', such as the gains made by the infringing undertaking from its behaviour[19]; and he will consider whether there are any aggravating and mitigating factors[20]. Among the mitigating factors will be that adequate steps have been taken with a view to compliance[1] and co-operation in the DGFT's investigation[2]. The DGFT will make any necessary adjustments to ensure that the maximum penalty is not exceeded and that the undertaking is not subjected to double jeopardy[3].

(iii) Whistleblowing: the leniency programme

'Whistleblowing' is strongly encouraged by the DGFT as a way of assisting it in the fight against cartels[4]. By the end of July 2001, it is understood that the DGFT had applied the leniency procedure in five cases. A firm seeking to take advantage of the leniency programme should contact the Director of Cartel Investigations at the OFT, or the equivalent thereof at the sectoral regulators[5]. A lawyer can approach the OFT with a potential claim to leniency and the OFT will allow a short period, of perhaps a week, during which no other claims will be admitted while the lawyer has time to advise and seek instructions from his or her client.

---

14 OFT Guideline 407.
15 OFT Guideline 423.
16 Ibid, para 1.9: see below.
17 Ibid, paras 2.3-2.7.
18 Ibid, para 2.7.
19 Ibid, para 2.8.
20 Ibid, paras 2.10-2.12.
1   Ibid, paras 2.12.
2   Ibid.
3   Ibid, paras 2.13-2.15.
4   *Enforcement* OFT Guideline 407, paras 4.37–4.39; *Guidance as to the appropriate amount of a penalty* OFT Guideline 423, Part 3.
5   Ibid, para 3.9.

Where leniency is agreed, the Director of Cartel Investigations, on behalf of the DGFT, and the firm concerned will sign letters setting out the terms of the total or partial immunity, as the case may be[6]. The DGFT will endeavour, where possible, to keep the identity of any whistleblower confidential throughout the investigation. The UK leniency policy is set out in paragraphs 4.37 to 4.39 of the DGFT Guideline on *Enforcement*[7] and, in greater detail, in paragraph 3 of the DGFT's *Guidance as to the appropriate amount of a penalty*[8]. The DGFT has published an Information Leaflet *Leniency in Cartel Cases: a guide to the Leniency Provisions for Cartel Cases under the Competition Act 1998*[9].

The leniency programme in the UK differs from that in the EC[10], and is modelled on the approach taken in the US[11]. In particular, the EC leniency régime requires that any evidence furnished to the Commission must be 'decisive', a higher standard than in the UK[12]; the EC system does not guarantee total immunity, which the UK one does[13]; and the EC system restricts the reduction in a fine that is available to the ringleader *or ringleaders* of a cartel[14], whereas the UK does not recognise the idea of 'multiple' ringleaders and restricts immunity only to a single ringleader[15]. Furthermore, the UK system provides greater certainty than the EC one, which in itself should encourage undertakings to avail themselves of its terms.

Paragraph 3.3 to 3.7 of the *Guidance as to the appropriate amount of a penalty* on penalties provides for total immunity and paragraph 3.8 for partial immunity.

(A) TOTAL IMMUNITY. Paragraph 3.3 provides for total immunity, which is automatic in the circumstances set out in paragraph 3.4 and is discretionary in the circumstances in paragraphs 3.5 to 3.7. Paragraph 3.3 provides automatic full immunity to the first member of a cartel to provide the DGFT with evidence of it *before* he has commenced an investigation. To qualify, the DGFT must not already have sufficient information to establish the existence of the alleged cartel; the firm in question must provide the DGFT with all the information, documents and evidence available to it; it must maintain continuous and complete cooperation throughout the investigation; it must not have compelled another undertaking to participate in the cartel and must not have acted as the instigator or played the leading rôle in the cartel (there is no total immunity for the ringleader); and it must refrain from partaking any further in the cartel once it has blown the whistle.

6   Drafts of these letters are available on the OFT's website at http://www.oft.gov.uk/html/comp-act/leniency/index.html.
7   OFT Guideline 407.
8   OFT Guideline 423.
9   Available on the OFT website, OFT436.pdf.
10   See ch 7, pp 238-239.
11   See US Department of Justice, Antitrust Division, Corporate Leniency Policy of 10 August 1993; it can be accessed as an Annex to speeches of Gary Spratling, Deputy Assistant Attorney General, on http://www.usdoj.gov/atr/speeches.
12   Compare OFT Guideline 423, para 3.4 with the Commission's *Notice on the non-imposition or reduction of fines in cartel* cases OJ [1996] C 207/4, [1996] 5 CMLR 362, para B(b).
13   Compare OFT Guideline 423, para 3.3 with the Commission's Notice, which refers to a reduction of 'at least 75% or even from total exemption ...'
14   Commission Notice, para B(e) restricts the reduction available to an enterprise that has compelled another to take part in the cartel or that has been an instigator or played a determining rôle in the illegal activity.
15   OFT Guideline 423, para 3.4 refers to 'the instigator' and 'the leading rôle', both expressed in the singular.

Paragraphs 3.5 to 3.7 confer discretionary full immunity for the first firm to come forward *after* the DGFT has embarked on an investigation but *before* the DGFT has issued a rule 14 written notice of a proposed infringement decision. The conditions set out above on eligibility for automatic total immunity apply, but the DGFT has a discretion whether to grant immunity in this case. In deciding whether to grant immunity the DGFT will have regard to the time when the undertaking comes forward, and to whether, at that point, he has sufficient evidence to make a decision that the Chapter I prohibition has been infringed.

Paragraphs 3.10 and 3.11 of the *Guideline* provide for an 'amnesty-plus' or 'two for one' policy: if a firm is already cooperating with an investigation in respect of one cartel, and comes forward with information that entitles it to total immunity in relation to a second cartel, it may receive an additional reduction in the penalty to be applied in relation to the first cartel.

The provisions of paragraph 3 of the *Guideline* are clearly powerful incentives to blow the whistle, and may encourage a race to be the first to arrive at the door of the OFT or to contact the Director of Cartel Investigations.

(B) PARTIAL IMMUNITY. Paragraph 3.8 provides for reduced penalties of up to 50% for firms that provide evidence of the existence and activities of a cartel but are not the first to do so. The evidence must be provided before the rule 14 notice is sent; furthermore the firm must satisfy the other conditions set out in paragraph 3.4, except that the 'ringleader' is also eligible for partial immunity.

Other information which is provided to the OFT during the course of its investigation does not expressly qualify for a reduction in penalties in respect of that infringement. Nevertheless it may constitute a mitigating factor on the amount of the fine if such cooperation specifically enables the enforcement process to be concluded more effectively and speedily[16].

(iv) Immunity for small agreements, conduct of minor significance and other cases

In addition to providing for the level of penalties and the conditions for their application, the Act confers immunity from penalties in the case of 'small agreements', other than price-fixing agreements, where the DGFT is satisfied that an undertaking acted on the reasonable assumption that being party to such an agreement gave it immunity[17]; 'conduct of minor significance', where the DGFT is similarly so satisfied[18]; an application for guidance or a decision on the Chapter I (but not the Chapter II) prohibition, for the period from the date of notification to the date specified by a notice (which cannot be retrospective) from the DGFT[19]; guidance being given under either prohibition[20]; or a decision that neither prohibition has been infringed[1]. An agreement which has been notified to the European Commission for exemption under Article 81(3), for the period

---

16 Ibid, para 2.12.
17 Competition Act, ss 36(4), 39 and the Competition Act 1998 (Small Agreements and Conduct of Minor Significance) Regulations 2000, SI 2000/262, Article 3 of which establishes that a small agreement is one where the combined turnover of the parties in the preceding calendar year was £20 million or less.
18 Competition Act, ss 36(5), 40 and SI 2000/262 (n 17 above), Article 4 of which establishes that conduct is of minor significance where the perpetrator's world turnover in the preceding calendar years was £50 million or less.
19 Competition Act, ss 13(4), (5), 14(4), (5).
20 Ibid, ss 15(3), 23(3).
1   Ibid, ss 16(3), 24(3).

from notification until the Commission determines the matter, is also immune[2]. There is no immunity, however, from the voidness of agreements provided for in section 2(4), nor from third party actions.

(v)   Withdrawing immunities

The immunities in respect of small agreements and conduct of minor significance are liable to be withdrawn by the DGFT if, after investigation, he considers an infringement is likely, after all, subject to his observation of some basic procedures[3].

In the case of guidance or decisions following notification, the grounds for the DGFT withdrawing the immunity are that he has reasonable grounds for believing there is a material change of circumstances, or has a reasonable suspicion that the information on which he based his guidance or decision was incomplete, false or misleading in a material particular[4]. In the case of guidance, additional grounds for withdrawal are given: in the case of an agreement where one of the notifying parties has applied for a decision, or, in the case of an agreement or conduct, when a complaint has been made by a non-party[5]. In each case, the DGFT must take action in one of these circumstances[6] and he must consider it likely that the Chapter I prohibition or the Chapter II prohibition will be infringed. He must give notice of removal and specify a date. If he reasonably suspects that information was provided which was false, incomplete or misleading in a material particular, the DGFT may backdate the notice of withdrawal[7].

In the case of notification of agreements, the notification itself gives immunity from penalties while the application is being considered[8]. This 'provisional' immunity may be withdrawn by a provisional decision of the DGFT, which has the effect of deeming the immunity never to have existed[9]. This is similar to a decision of the European Commission under Council Regulation 17/62, Article 15(6) but, unlike the position under EC law, such a decision is not subject to an appeal[10].

Immunity from penalties under the Act following a notification to the European Commission cannot be withdrawn by the DGFT, but if the European Commission takes an interim decision under Article 15(6) of Council Regulation 17/62[11] to remove the provisional immunity from penalties under that Regulation[12], this has the effect of withdrawing the corresponding immunity under UK law[13].

2   Ibid, s 41 and see the Competition Act 1998 (Provisional Immunity from Penalties) Order 1999, SI 1999/2281.
3   Ibid, ss 39(4), 40(4); the DGFT must give the parties or persons in respect of which the immunity is withdrawn written notice of his decision and must specify a date which gives them time to adjust (ss 39(5), (8), 40(5), (8)).
4   Ibid, ss 15(2), 16(2), 23(2) and 24(2).
5   Ibid, ss 15(2), 23(2).
6   Ibid, ss 15(4), 16(4), 23(4) and 24(4).
7   Ibid, ss 15(5), 16(5), 23(5) and 24(5).
8   Ibid, s 15(3).
9   Ibid, Sch 5, para 3(2)(b).
10   See Council Regulation 17/62/EEC, OJ [1962] L13/204 (S edn 1959–62, p 87); see ch 7, p 230; provisional decisions under Sch 5 (or Sch 6) do not appear in the list of appealable decisions in s 46.
11   Council Regulation 17/62/EEC, OJ [1962] 13/204, OJ [1959-62] spec ed 87).
12   Such a decision can be appealed to the CFI under EC law (Cases 8-11/66 SA *Cimenteries CBR Cementbedrijven NV* [1967] ECR 75, [1967] CMLR 77).
13   Competition Act, s 41; the DGFT is not precluded from investigating the agreement and the phrase 'provisional immunity from penalties' is defined in the Competition Act 1998 (Provisional Immunity from Penalties) Order 1999, SI 1999/2281.

5. CONCURRENCY[14]

An interesting feature of the 1998 Act is that concurrent powers are given to the DGFT and the sectoral regulators to enforce the Chapter I and Chapter II prohibitions. In their respective spheres of influence, the Director General of Telecommunications, the Gas and Electricity Markets Authority, the Director General of Water Services and the Rail Regulator enjoy concurrent powers. For the regulators, the availability of the Competition Act powers raises the interesting dilemma of whether to use the Act against anti-competitive behaviour, or whether to enforce the specific provisions of the regulated company's licence[15]. As far as the Act itself is concerned, provisions have been put in place in order to ensure that concurrency operates in a satisfactory manner. The Act deals with this issue in section 54 and Schedule 10. The DGFT, in conjunction with the regulators published a Guideline on *Concurrent application to regulated industries*[16]. Following a DTI consultation document[17], the Secretary of State has adopted the Competition Act (Concurrency) Regulation 2000[18], and an amended *Guideline* has been published in consequence[19]. The revised *Guideline* provides the best picture of the operation of the concurrency provisions. It explains that the regulators have the same powers as the DGFT, save that only the latter can issue guidance on penalties and make amendments to the Director's Rules[20]. It describes the purpose of the Concurrency Regulation[1] and explains the rôle of the Concurrency Working Party (the 'CWP'), which is chaired by a representative of the OFT and brings together officials from all the regulators[2]. The CWP discusses, among other things, general principles and information sharing, the guidelines and disagreements over who should exercise jurisdiction in a particular case[3]. The proceedings of the CWP are confidential, and no minute of its meetings is made publicly available. The *Guideline* considers how cases will be allocated: in the event of a dispute on jurisdiction, the matter will be referred to the Secretary of State[4]: it can reasonably be assumed that this will happen only exceptionally. Parties to a notification and complaint are not given any rights to specify which regulator should take action. Notifications must be sent to the DGFT[5], but complaints may go to the DGFT or the relevant regulator[6]; the same is true for applications for interim measures[7]. The *Guideline* also discusses the relation between the regulators' powers under the Competition Act 1998 and their sector-specific powers[8] and explains the law on confidentiality and disclosure of information[9].

---

14 See Prosser 'Competition, Regulators and Public Service' in *The Competition Act: A New Era for UK Competition Law* (Hart Publishing, 2000, eds Rodger and MacCulloch).
15 See ch 23, pp 866-867.
16 OFT Guideline 405.
17 URN 99/586.
18 SI 2000/260.
19 OFT Guideline 433.
20 Ibid, paras 2.3-2.4.
1   Ibid, para 3.1.
2   Ibid, para 3.3.
3   Ibid, para 3.4.
4   Ibid, para 3.9.
5   Ibid, paras 3.11-3.12.
6   Ibid, para 3.13.
7   Ibid, para 3.4.
8   Ibid, paras 4.1-4.3.
9   Ibid, paras 5.1-5.3.

6.   APPEALS AND REFERENCES UNDER ARTICLE 234 EC

(A)   Appeals

The powers available to the DGFT and the sectoral regulators under the Act are considerable. To balance this it was felt that a full right of appeal – not merely the possibility of judicial review – should be available; furthermore that the appellate body should be one with appropriate expertise in matters of competition law and policy. For this reason the Competition Commission Appeal Tribunals were created[10].

The Act deals with appeals in sections 46 to 49 and in Schedule 8. Following a DTI consultation document[11], the Secretary of State has adopted the Competition Commission Appeal Tribunal Rules 2000[12]. The Commission itself has published *A Guide to Appeals under the Competition Act 1998*[13]. The rules of the Appeal Tribunals are based on five main principles: first, early disclosure of each party's case, and of the evidence relied on; secondly, active case management by the Tribunals to identify the main issues early on and avoid delays; thirdly, strict timetables; fourthly, effective procedures to establish contested facts; and fifthly the conduct of oral hearings within defined time limits[14]. The procedure before the Tribunals will be predominantly written; submissions should be kept as short as possible. The oral hearing should be regarded as an opportunity to debate contentious issues rather than to state a case which has already been made in writing. The decisions that can be appealed are specifically set out in section 46[15], and include decisions finding infringements of the Chapter I and II prohibitions and decisions whether to grant an individual exemption. Limited rights of appeal are available to third parties[16]. In so far as the Act does not provide for an appeal, it can be anticipated that claims for judicial review will be brought before the Administrative Court of the Queen's Bench Division of the High Court under Part 54 of the Civil Procedure Rules[17]. Claims for judicial review can be anticipated in relation to perceived procedural irregularities, but it may be that permission will be refused where the Administrative Court considers that the issue can be addressed within the statutory appeal procedure[18].

The powers of the Appeal Tribunals of the Competition Commission are extensive: they are set out in paragraph 3 of Schedule 8 of the Competition Act, and include the power to adopt interim measures[18a], to confirm or set aside the decision that is the subject of the appeal, to remit the matter to the DGFT or sectoral regulator, to impose or revoke or vary the amount of a penalty[19] and to

---

10 See ch 2, pp 61-62.
11 URN 99/1154, October 1999.
12 SI 2000/261.
13 1 June 2000.
14 *Annual Review & Accounts of the Competition Commission* 1999/2000, p 10.
15 As amended by Article 10 of the Competition Act 1998 (Notification of Excluded Agreements and Appealable Decisions) Order 2000, SI 2000/263.
16 Competition Act 1998, s 47.
17 http://www.open.gov.uk/lcd/civil/procrules_fin/crulesfr.htm.
18 See *Harley Development Inc v IRC* [1996] 1 WLR 727, at 736C (Privy Council); on judicial review where an appeal system is in place, see Craig *Administrative Law* (Sweet & Maxwell 4th ed, 1999) pp 807-809.
18a See *Napp Pharmaceuticals Holdings Ltd v DGFT*, judgment of 22 May 2001 (Case 1000/1/1/01 (IR), where the President of the Tribunal followed judgments of the Community Courts, pursuant to s 60 Competition Act, in determining the appropriate test for the adoption of interim measures.
19 The penalty is suspended pending the appeal (Competition Act, s 46(4)), but the Appeal Tribunals may order that interest is payable (ibid, Sch 8, para 10 and the Competition Commission Appeal Tribunal Rules 2000, SI 2000/261, rule 27).

grant or cancel an individual exemption. These powers are much more extensive than those of the Court of First Instance[20]. Appeals on points of law lie, with leave, from the appeal tribunals to the Court of Appeal[1]. Proceedings before the Appeal Tribunals must comply with the Human Rights Act 1998[2].

(B)   Article 234 references

An important aid to the consistency of application of EC law in Member States is the preliminary ruling procedure of Article 234 EC which enables the ECJ to rule on questions referred by national courts or tribunals. Given the objective of consistency between the Act and EC competition law, an important question is whether it is possible for a UK court or tribunal when applying the provisions of the Act rather than EC competition law to make a reference to the ECJ, in circumstances where domestic law is to be interpreted consistently with the Treaty as a result of the governing principles clause in section 60. It is also important to consider which courts or tribunals in the UK can make an Article 234 reference.

(i)   Can an Article 234 reference be made where a court or tribunal is applying the Competition Act 1998?

The jurisprudence of the ECJ strongly suggests that references under Article 234 will be possible in cases involving the UK prohibitions. The ECJ has faced the problem in the past that its rulings are intended to be binding and that it does not give 'merely' advisory opinions: its rulings must not merely be indicative; and yet it would not want a position to develop in which national laws based upon Articles 81 and 82 are interpreted in a substantially different way from the meaning given to them by Community institutions. In *Kleinwort Benson Ltd v Glasgow City Council*[3] the ECJ declined to give a ruling on the interpretation of the Civil Jurisdiction and Judgments Act 1982 in so far as it related to the allocation of jurisdiction as between the courts of England and Wales on the one hand and the courts of Scotland on the other. There, the ECJ noted that the domestic court in the UK, when applying the so-called 'modified Convention' (dealing with intra-UK matters), had only an obligation 'to have regard to the Court's case law'; there was no obligation to apply 'absolutely and unconditionally' the Court's case law. This sets up the possibility of distinguishing *Kleinwort Benson* since, in the case of section 60(1) of the Competition Act, there is a duty, albeit a qualified one, to maintain consistency with EC jurisprudence[4]. Subsequent judgments have suggested that the ECJ may indeed be willing to deal with a reference where a ruling on a point of Community law is necessary to enable a proper interpretation to be made of purely internal rules of a Member State: this can be seen, for example, in *Bernd Giloy v Hauptzollamt Frankfurt am Main-Ost*[5] and *Leur Bloem v Inspecteur der Belastingdienst*[6], citing earlier judgments

20   See ch 7, pp 243-246.
1   Competition Act, s 49.
2   See p 349 above on the issue of whether proceedings under the Competition Act are to be characterised as criminal.
3   Case C-346/93 [1995] ECR I-615.
4   See ch 9, pp 329-333.
5   Case C-130/95 [1997] ECR I-4291.

in *Masam Dzodzi v Belgium*[7] and *Gmurzynska-Bscher Oberfinanzdirektion Köln*[8].

In *Leur-Bloem*, the ECJ was asked to interpret provisions of domestic Dutch law on income tax, but the national court asked the Court whether that domestic law should be interpreted in conformity with Article 2 and 11 of Council Directive 90/434/EEC on the common system of taxation applicable to mergers, etc. The ECJ held that:

> 'The Court of Justice has jurisdiction under Article [234] of the EC Treaty to interpret Community law when the situation is not governed directly by Community law but the national legislature, in transposing the provisions of a directive into domestic law, has chosen to apply the same treatment to purely internal situations and to those governed by the directive so that it has aligned its domestic legislation to Community law'[9].

In *Giloy* the ECJ was asked to interpret provisions of domestic German law on the levying of turnover taxes, and specifically whether they should be interpreted in conformity with Article 244 of Council Regulation 2913/92 establishing the Community Customs Code[10]. The ECJ repeated the *Leur-Bloem* formulation[11].

In *Bronner*[12], the Austrian court of first instance in competition matters referred questions to the ECJ to interpret Article 82 in the context of a refusal to provide access to a daily newspaper distribution system. Although the Austrian court was applying its own domestic law to the case, and although this was not written in the same terms as EC law, it nonetheless felt that an interpretation of Article 82 would enable it to reach a decision, as it would not wish to apply its own law inconsistently with EC competition law. The European Commission argued that the reference was inadmissible as the Austrian court was not applying EC law. The ECJ held as follows:

> 'A request from a national court may be rejected only if it is quite obvious that the interpretation of Community law bears no relation to the actual facts of the case or to the subject matter of the main action' (paragraph 17).

Later it said that:

> '... the fact that a national court is dealing with a restrictive practices dispute by applying national competition law should not prevent it from making a reference to the Court on the interpretation of Community law on the matter, and in particular on the interpretation of Article [82] of the Treaty in relation to that same situation, when it considers that a conflict between Community law and national law is capable of arising' (paragraph 20).

This ruling would appear to establish that references may be made to the ECJ on the interpretation of Articles 81 and 82 when the domestic court or tribunal is considering corresponding issues under Chapters I and II.

6   Case C-28/95 [1997] ECR I-4161.
7   Cases C-297/88 and C-197/89 [1990] ECR I-3763.
8   Case C-231/89 [1990] ECR I-4003.
9   Case C-28/95 [1997] ECR I-4161, para 34.
10   OJ [1992] L 302/1.
11   Case C-130/95 [1997] ECR I-4291, para 23.
12   Case C-7/97 *Oscar Brönner GmbH v Mediaprint* [1998] ECR I-7791, [1999] 4 CMLR 112.

(ii) Which courts or tribunals in the UK can make an Article 234 reference in a case under the Competition Act 1998?

It is obvious that the House of Lords and the Court of Appeal can make Article 234 references. It is also assumed that the Appeal Tribunals of the Competition Commission can do so: provision is made for this in the Rules[13]. What is less clear is whether the DGFT or the sectoral regulators could make a reference. Lord Simon, in the debate on the third reading of the Bill, thought that this would be possible[14], although he subsequently was more equivocal on the point[15]. It is a matter of Community law whether the DGFT and the regulators qualify as courts or tribunals[16]. It may be that the point will not arise, should the DGFT and the regulators determine of their own volition not to attempt to make such a reference.

7. THIRD PARTY ACTIONS[17]

In its consultation paper prior to the Competition Bill[18], the Government envisaged third party civil actions as an important buttress to the deterrent effect of the prohibitions and as a safeguard for the victims of anti-competitive behaviour. During the passage of the Bill through Parliament the Government was at pains to confirm that the right of third parties to seek redress in the courts was available. Thus, Lord Simon stated '[I]t is an important part of the new régime that businesses and consumers who have been seriously harmed by anti-competitive behaviour should be able to seek redress. To that end, we are including provisions to facilitate rights of private action in the courts for damages'[19]. The then Secretary of State, Margaret Beckett, similarly confirmed that 'Companies and individuals who have been harmed by infringements of the prohibitions will be entitled to seek damages in the Courts'[20]. The DTI also issued a press release confirming the Government's intention that private actions for damages should be available[1]. However the Act itself does not explicitly provide such an action, although it is not entirely silent on the issue of private actions. Section 58(1) provides that, unless the court directs otherwise or the DGFT intends to take further action, his

---

13 Rule 31 of the Competition Commission Appeal Tribunal Rules 2000, SI 2000/261.
14 25 November 1997, col 963.
15 Ibid, col 975.
16 See eg Case C-54/96 *Dorsch Consult Ingenieurgesellschaft mbH v Bundesbaugessellschaft Berlin mbH* [1997] ECR I-4961, [1998] 2 CMLR 237; on this point, see Brown and Jacobs *The Court of Justice of the European Communities* (Sweet & Maxwell, 5th ed, 2000) pp 223-227; Wyatt and Dashwood's *European Union Law* (Sweet & Maxwell, 4th ed, 2000) pp 267-268.
17 See Yeung 'Privatizing Competition Regulation' (1998) 18 Oxford Journal of Legal Studies 581; Kon and Maxwell 'Enforcement in National Courts of the EC and New UK Competition Rules: Obstacles to Effective Enforcement' (1998) 19 ECLR 443; Turner 'The UK Competition Act 1998 and Private Rights' (1999) 20 ECLR 62; MacCulloch 'Private Enforcement of the Competition Act Prohibitions' in *The Competition Act: A New Era for UK Competition Law* (Hart Publishing, 2000, eds Rodger and MacCulloch); Roth 'The New UK Competition Act – The Private Perspective' in [2000] Fordham Corporate Law Institute (ed Hawk) (not yet published); see also the Government's White Paper of 31 July 2001, *A World Class Competition Régime* (Cm 5233), ch 8, proposing that the Competition Commission Appeal Tribunals should be able to hear claims for damages by third parties.
18 'A prohibition approach to anti-competitive agreements and abuse of dominant position' (URN 97/803) (August 1997), para 7.26.
19 HL 2R, 30 October 1997, col 1148.
20 HC 2R, 11 May 1998, col 35; the Government 'considered carefully' whether the Appeals Tribunals of the Competition Commission should be the forum for private actions but decided against it for reasons of economy and speed of process (Consultation Paper, August 1997, para 7.25).
1 DTI Press Release P/98/552 (9 July 1998).

findings of fact are binding on the parties in court proceedings brought by the infringing parties or third parties, provided that the time for appeal has expired, or the DGFT's findings are confirmed on appeal[2]. This means that parties bringing such proceedings will not have to go through the process of producing all the evidence once again, but can proceed on the 'coat-tail' of the DGFT's actions. Section 58(3) of the Act enables rules to be made for the DGFT to provide assistance to the court in private actions. Furthermore, the restriction on the disclosure of information by the DGFT and the sectoral regulators does not apply where it is made for the purpose of civil proceedings[3]. Actions for damages may be facilitated by resort to the concept of a 'group litigation order', a procedure available in England and Wales since 2 May 2000[4] which provides for the case management of claims which give rise to common or related issues of fact or law; the fact that lawyers are entitled to work on a conditional fee basis may also be of assistance to would-be claimants[5].

The apparent explanation for the absence from the 1998 Act itself of any express right to bring civil actions is that UK law should develop consistently with the jurisprudence of the ECJ on this subject, such consistency to be achieved through the 'general principles' clause in section 60. Although it is probably the case that the ECJ will eventually rule that, in principle, there should be damages where Articles 81 and/or 82 are infringed, it does not follow that damages should be available in every case[6]. The ECJ may wish to consider issues such as causation, remoteness of damage and the degree of intention or recklessness that must be demonstrated before firms that infringe the competition rules should incur financial liability in civil actions. Such an approach might resemble a number of cases beginning with *Francovich v Italy*[7] on state liability. From the UK's perspective, therefore, it may be preferable to leave the law on private actions to develop consistently with the case law in the EU.

It is understood that a number of claims were brought in domestic courts quite early in the life of the new Act; the first judgment, rejecting an application by Claritas (UK) Ltd for an interim injunction against the Post Office under the Chapter II prohibition, was given on 2 November 2000.[8] It is likely that the High Court will stay proceedings if an appeal is pending before the Competition Commission Appeal Tribunal which related to the same subject-matter, in order to avoid the risk of inconsistent decisions.[9] It seems reasonable to expect that there will be numerous cases in which the liability of undertakings that infringe the Chapter I and II prohibitions will be determined. If proceedings before the DGFT are to be classified as criminal for the purposes of the Human Rights Act 1998, it would follow that he would bear a higher burden of proof than a claimant in civil proceedings; this might encourage more litigation than would otherwise be the case.

2   Decisions of the European Commission have been held to be admissible in English court proceedings as evidence of the correctness of the conclusions they contain; see *Iberian UK Ltd v BPB Industries and British Gypsum* [1996] 2 CMLR 601, [1997] Eu LR 1 (per Laddie J).
3   Competition Act, s 55(3)(b).
4   Civil Procedure Rules, rules 19.10-15.
5   Courts and Legal Services Act 1990, s 58; Conditional Fee Agreements Regulations 2000, SI 2000/692; Conditional Fee Agreements Order 2000, SI 2000/823.
6   For discussion of private actions for breach of EC competition law and the remedies that may be available see ch 8, pp 276-281; for a case in which it was ordered that damages should be paid under Irish law, see *Dermot Donovan v Electricity Supply Board* [1998] Eu LR 212 (Irish Supreme Court).
7   Cases C-6 and 9/90 [1991] ECR I-5357, [1993] 2 CMLR 66.
8   See also the DGFT's decision rejecting the complaint of Claritas: Case CA 98/4/2001, 15 June 2001.
9   See *Synstar Computer Services (UK) Ltd v ICL (Sorbus) Ltd*, judgment of 30 March 2001, Ch D; the DGFT concluded that ICL had not infringed the Chapter II prohibition on 20 July 2001, Case No CA 98/6/2001.

CHAPTER 11

The monopoly provisions of the Fair Trading Act 1973

1. INTRODUCTION

The modern law of competition in the UK began with the Monopolies and Restrictive Practices (Inquiry and Control) Act 1948. The investigative system established by the 1948 Act was essentially benign. Under the Act the Board of Trade could require the Monopolies and Restrictive Practices Commission[1] to investigate situations in which at least one third of the goods of any description were being supplied by or to the same person, or two or more persons who in some way were acting to prevent or restrict competition in relation to those goods. The decision to refer a situation to the Commission was discretionary; the Act contained no presumption against all or any particular anti-competitive practices; the concept of the public interest for the purposes of the Act was extremely broad and did not accord any pre-eminence to the value of competition: indeed it did not even mention the term. The Act did not confer or impose any enforceable rights or obligations upon individuals who were harmed by or who indulged in anti-competitive behaviour; there was not even a requirement that adverse findings by the Commission had to be translated into remedial action: there was simply a power on the part of the Minister to do so. The Act was suffused with discretion. These basic characteristics of the investigative system introduced in 1948 remain essentially the same today, although the range of practices and problems within its scope has since changed considerably, as have the *dramatis personae*.

The monopoly provisions are now found in the Fair Trading Act 1973 ('the FTA'). Under this Act 'monopoly situations' can be referred to the Competition Commission ('the Commission[2]') for investigation, and where it considers that there are detriments to the public interest arising from such a situation, a range of remedies is available to the Secretary of State, including, if appropriate, a structural remedy.

---

1   This body was subsequently renamed the Monopolies and Mergers Commission by the Fair Trading Act, s 4(1); its functions have now been transferred to the Competition Commission by s 45(3) Competition Act 1998.
2   For the sake of simplicity, the term 'Commission' will be used to comprehend both the current Competition Commission and its predecessors.

The coverage of these provisions will be briefer than in earlier editions of this book[3]. The reason is simple. With the entry into force of the Competition Act 1998, the UK has adopted, for the first time, a prohibition of the abuse of a dominant position. Many, though not necessarily all[4], firms in a monopoly situation in the sense of the FTA will also be dominant in the sense of Chapter II: if they behave in an abusive manner they will be infringing the Chapter II prohibition and vulnerable to fines and (perhaps) to private actions in the courts[5]. It should follow that resort to the monopoly provisions of the FTA will be less frequent than in the past; however it would be wrong to regard the monopoly provisions as otiose: the fact that a 'scale' monopolist might be subjected to a structural remedy following an FTA investigation[6], and that 'complex' monopolists might be subjected to an industry-wide investigation under that Act[7], mean that there is life yet in the system originally introduced in 1948: indeed the Government announced in June 2001 its intention to legislate further to reform the complex monopoly provisions of the Act.[7a] The relationship between the FTA and the Competition Act 1998 is considered further below[8]. The Department of Trade and Industry has published guidance on its own procedures for handling monopoly references and reports[9].

2. MONOPOLY SITUATIONS

The FTA enables the Secretary of State and, in most cases, the DGFT to refer monopoly situations to the Competition Commission for investigation; the sectoral regulators also have power to make references. Monopoly situations for this purpose are separately defined in relation to goods, services and exports.

(A) Monopoly situations in relation to goods

Section 6 of the FTA describes four types of monopoly situation in relation to goods. Two of these are sometimes termed 'structural' or 'scale' monopolies and two 'behavioural' or (in the vocabulary of the Act) 'complex' monopolies.

(i)   Structural or scale monopolies

Section 6(1)(*a*) provides that a monopoly situation shall be taken to exist where at least one quarter of the goods of any description supplied in the UK are supplied by or to one and the same person[10]. Section 6(1)(*b*) provides that a monopoly

---

3   A detailed account of the monopoly provisions in the FTA will be found in *Butterworths Competition Law* (eds Freeman and Whish) Div VI [91]-[223]; in 47 *Halsbury's Laws* (4th ed reissue, 1994), paras 111-125; and in Smith *Competition Law: Enforcement & Procedure* (Butterworths, 2001), ch 14.
4   A firm that supplies 25% or more of goods or services of a certain description may be in a monopoly situation under the FTA; as a general proposition, firms are unlikely to have a dominant position with a market share of less than 40%: see ch 5, pp 155-156 and ch 9, p 318.
5   On private actions, see ch 10, pp 361-362.
6   See pp 380 and 383-384 below.
7   See pp 365 and 385 below.
7a See HM Treasury Press Release 67/01, 18 June 2001; *A World Class Competition Régime* (July 2001), Cm 5233, ch 6. An Enterprise Bill is expected in March 2002.
8   See pp 383-385 below.
9   http://www2.dti.gov.uk/CACP/cp/monopoly.htm.
10 Note that the definition means that buying as well as selling power may be investigated: see eg *Supermarkets* Cm 4842 (2000) where the Competition Commission found a complex

situation shall also be taken to exist where the goods in question are supplied by or to two or more companies possessing separate legal personalities but which are, in economic terms, part of a single economic unit: the Act refers to such companies as 'interconnected bodies corporate'[11]. The essential point about these situations is that one firm or group of firms alone is responsible for a certain percentage of the supply or acquisition of goods of a certain description. It should be noted that the definition focuses upon who supplies or is supplied with the goods and not upon who produces them. Thus a firm which produces goods solely for its own consumption would not come within either subsection; while an overseas firm with no production facilities in the UK would do if it was responsible for the supply there of one quarter of the relevant goods[12].

(ii) Behavioural or complex monopolies

Section 6(1)(c) provides that a 'complex monopoly situation'[13] shall be taken to exist where at least one quarter of the goods of any description supplied in the UK are supplied by or to two or more of the persons described in section 6(2). These persons are:

> 'any two or more persons (not being a group of interconnected bodies corporate) who whether voluntarily or not, and whether by agreement or not, so conduct[14] their respective affairs as in any way to prevent, restrict or distort competition in connection with the production or supply of goods of that description, whether or not they themselves are affected by that competition and whether the competition is between persons interested as producers or suppliers or between persons interested as customers or producers or suppliers.'

The practical implications of this concept will be discussed once the provisions on services and exports have been outlined. At this stage it should be noted that this type of monopoly situation differs from the structural monopolies in that it is defined by reference to the way in which firms *behave*.

Section 6(1)(d) describes a second type of complex or behavioural monopoly which is more readily comprehensible, namely where, as a result of one or more agreements, goods of a particular description are not supplied in the UK at all. Again this situation is defined by reference to the behaviour of firms (in implementing an agreement), but in practice it has never been the source of a monopoly reference. Furthermore, such an agreement would be likely to infringe the Chapter I prohibition of the Competition Act 1998 anyway.

---

monopoly situation on the part of five supermarkets which adversely affected the competitiveness of some of their suppliers and distorted competition in the supplier market.

11 FTA, s 137(5) defines this term by reference to the Companies Act 1985, s 736; in some reports the Commission has had to deal with arguments as to which companies fall within this expression: see eg *Plasterboard* Cm 1224 (1990) paras 9.2–9.6.

12 Note however that it is possible to make an order under the Act only against UK companies or citizens or persons carrying on business in the UK: FTA, s 90(3); see ch 12, pp 405-407 on the extra-territorial application of the FTA.

13 FTA, s 11(1) provides that the situations described in s 6(1)(c) and (d), s 7(1)(c) and (d) and s 8(2) and (3) shall be termed 'complex monopoly situations'.

14 The Commission has said that the use of the word 'conduct' does imply that the firms must have some discretion in the way in which they behave: *Credit Card Services* Cm 718 (1989) para 7.32.

(B)   Monopoly situations in relation to services

Section 7 contains provisions defining monopoly situations in relation to services which are almost identical to those in relation to goods in section 6. In particular the same distinction is made between structural and behavioural monopolies. Two features of section 7 call for specific mention. First is the problem of deciding where services are 'supplied'. In goods cases this issue is quite simple, but it is not always easy to identify where a service is provided. Section 7(3) provides that, in cases of uncertainty, services may be regarded as supplied in the UK if the person supplying them has a place of business in the UK, controls the relevant activities from there or, in the case of a company, is incorporated under the law of Great Britain or Northern Ireland. It does not matter that the services would not otherwise be regarded as supplied in the UK. The second point to note is that the supply of services does not include services relating to land. However section 68 of the Competition Act 1998 gives the Secretary of State power, by order, to provide that section 7 of the FTA includes, or ceases to include, any activity which consists in, or in making arrangements in connection with, permitting the use of land.

(C)   Monopoly situations in relation to exports

It is possible for the Competition Commission to be asked to investigate the performance of UK firms in export markets. In practice there have been few export references; the last one was *Insulated Electric Wires and Cables*[15] in 1979. Anti-competitive behaviour in export markets would very possibly infringe either EC or another State's competition law, so that it is unlikely that these provisions would be used.

(D)   Local monopoly situations

As a jurisdictional matter, a monopoly reference may be limited to a part only of the UK. This has occurred on various occasions[16]. Even where a reference does not specifically ask the Competition Commission to consider local monopolies, it will do where it is appropriate to do so[17].

(E)   Supplementary provisions

Section 10 of the FTA contains supplementary provisions relating to monopoly situations. Sections 10(3) and 10(4) establish that it is possible to frame a monopoly reference either in relation to the supply of goods or services generally, or by reference to a particular form of supply. This means that there is considerable flexibility in determining the scope of a monopoly inquiry. Examples of references limited to a particular form of supply include *Fresh Processed Milk to Middle-*

15 HCP (1978-79) 243.
16 See eg *The Supply of Bus Services in the North-East of England* Cm 2933 (1995); *Solicitors' Estate Agency Services in Scotland* Cm 3699 (1997); *Fresh Processed Milk to Middle-Ground Retailers in Scotland* Cm 5002 (2000).
17 See eg *Concrete Roofing Tiles* (1981–82) 12 HCP where competition in the tile market was particularly muted in some regions of the UK.

Ground Retailers in Scotland, where the Commission was asked to investigate the supply of fresh processed milk to 'middle ground' customers, meaning retailers other than supermarket chains[18]; and *Supermarkets*[19] where the Commission was asked to investigate the supply of groceries from stores exceeding a specified size.

(F) Comments

These provisions invite various comments.

(i)   Non-economic meaning of 'monopoly situation'

The first concerns the very idea of a 'monopoly situation' as defined by the Act. This term is a misnomer in that it is not related to the word monopoly as used by an economist. A monopoly situation may be defined by reference to goods or services 'of any description': for example, in *Ice Cream* the reference was limited to the supply of ice cream intended for immediate consumption[20]. There is no obligation to limit the class so defined to goods or services within a relevant market, as is required under Article 82 EC and the Chapter II prohibition[1]. Section 10(7) of the Act emphasises this point by providing that the person making a monopoly reference may select whatever criteria seem suitable in the circumstances when deciding whether goods or services are of the same description. This is not to say that the DGFT and the Secretary of State do not attempt to be rational in selecting the goods or services to be referred: only that there is no *legal* obligation to identify the relevant market at the stage of making a reference. A full market analysis is conducted by the Commission as part of its inquiry. It is theoretically possible, but unlikely, that a wholly unreasonable classification of goods or services for the purposes of a reference might be the subject of a successful administrative law challenge in accordance with the principles laid down by Lord Greene MR in *Associated Provincial Picture Houses Ltd v Wednesbury Corpn*[2].

As far as the meaning of 'monopoly' is concerned, again the Act obviates the need to adopt an economic approach. It simply states that a monopoly situation exists where a firm or firms supply one quarter or more of the class of goods or services described[3]. Not only is there no obligation to define the market in an economic sense; the Act also selects an arbitrary figure of 25% for the purpose of defining a 'monopoly situation'. This may sound like criticism: in fact the FTA system has much to commend it. The real issue in monopoly inquiries is whether any firm or firms are acting in a way that is harmful to the public interest. This question is inextricably bound up with the structure of the market and the power of individual firms operating on it. These are matters for the Commission to consider in the course of its investigation, and it would be inappropriate for

18 Cm 5002 (2000).
19 Cm 4842 (2000).
20 Cm 4510 (2000).
1   On the relevant market in EC and UK law, see ch 1, pp 22-39.
2   [1948] 1 KB 223, [1947] 2 All ER 680, CA.
3   FTA, s 10(6) provides that the 25% threshold may be calculated by reference to such criteria – eg value, cost, price, quantity, capacity – as may appear suitable in the circumstances; see eg *Postal Franking Machines* Cmnd 9747 (1986) where the Commission concluded that monopoly situations existed by reference both to value and volume.

them to have to be dealt with in detail at the prior, jurisdictional, stage of deciding whether to refer a particular situation to the Commission in the first place. There is much to be said for providing the referring agencies with a relatively simple jurisdictional test of referability which leaves the substantive issues to be considered by the Commission.

(ii)   Complex monopolies[4]

A second comment about the Act's definition of monopoly situations concerns the notion of complex or behavioural ones. The subjection of complex monopolies to the investigative system is useful since it means that certain matters, for example parallel conduct on the part of firms in an oligopoly or networks of similar agreements in a particular market, which may not be covered by the Competition Act 1998, can be scrutinised by the Competition Commission under the FTA. There are many reasons why certain industries do not function competitively; it is not only cartel agreements or the abuse of market power that have this effect. Failure of the market mechanism may occur without there being any 'misconduct' at all. UK law provides a system whereby the Commission can conduct an industry-wide inquiry and make recommendations on a case-by-case basis as to how competition could be enhanced. On some occasions it concludes that this can best be achieved by alterations in the behaviour of people other than the firms that are in the complex monopoly[5]. The power to investigate in this *ad hoc* way provides a system of control which is not concerned exclusively with a search for misconduct on someone's part. It is clear that firms may be complex monopolists under the FTA that would not be collectively dominant for the purpose of Article 82 EC or the Chapter II prohibition[6].

An example of the Competition Commission's approach is afforded by its report in 1989 on *The Supply of Beer*[7]. The Brewers' Society argued strongly that the tied-house system operated by many brewers could not amount to a complex monopoly situation: the system was a manifestation of horizontal competition between brewers, rather than restrictive of competition. The Society's view was that the effects of the vertical relationships between brewers and retail outlets should be assessed in the overall market context and that, analysed in this way, there was no restriction of competition giving rise to a complex monopoly. The Commission declined to follow this reasoning: as the identification of a complex monopoly situation is merely a jurisdictional trigger, enabling an investigation to be carried out, it preferred not to give the term a narrow, economic meaning. It remarked that:

> 'The test to be applied is whether competition is prevented, restricted or distorted and not, as The Brewers' Society suggests, whether competition is altered for the worse.'[8]

Later it said that:

4   See Brent 'The Meaning of "Complex Monopoly"' (1993) 56 MLR 812.
5   See pp 379, n 9 below.
6   On collective dominance generally, see ch 14, pp 471–492.
7   Cm 651 (1989) paras 11.2–11.26; see similarly *The Supply of Petrol* Cm 972 (1990) paras 8.16–8.23.
8   Ibid, para 11.16.

'The finding of a complex monopoly does not mean that any practices of those in whose favour the monopoly has been found to exist necessarily constitute facts which operate or may be expected to operate against the public interest. We examine whether the practices which have been taken into account in arriving at the monopoly finding do give rise to detriments later . . .[9]'.

As more than 90% of brewers carried out practices that restricted competition, for example by owning retail premises and by making preferential loans in return for exclusive purchasing commitments, the Commission was satisfied that there was a complex monopoly situation. Numerous examples can be given of findings of complex monopoly. Sometimes substantial numbers of undertakings have been found to be complex monopolists: for example in *Contact Lens Solutions*[10] the Commission found that retailers generally were in a complex monopoly situation through their practice of selling branded solutions at or only just below the recommended resale price; in *Private Medical Services*[11] 12,000 consultant doctors were; and in *Residential Mortgage Valuations*[12] more than 100 lenders were party to the complex monopoly situation. In 2000, complex monopolies were found in *The Supply of Impulse Ice Cream*[13], in the way that Unilever, Mars and Nestlé practised both freezer and outlet exclusivity; in *New Cars*[14], resulting from suppliers' practices in distributing new cars in the UK; and in *Supermarkets*[15] the Commission concluded that various pricing practices of supermarkets and aspects of their commercial dealings with suppliers amounted to complex monopolies[16].

On two occasions the Commission's finding of a complex monopoly situation has been challenged in an application for judicial review, each time unsuccessfully. The report on *Credit Card Services*[17] was challenged in *R v Monopolies and Mergers Commission, ex p Visa International*[18]. Visa International argued that it could only be party to a 'group' within the meaning of section 7(1)(*c*) of the FTA (and so a 'complex monopolist') if it was itself a supplier of the services referred to the Commission. The Court of Appeal saw no reason to accept this limitation on the definition in the legislation: the important question was whether the group, once identified, supplied at least 25% of the reference services. The report on *Electrical Contracting at Exhibition Halls*[19] was challenged in *R v Monopolies and Mergers Commission, ex p Ecando Systems*[20] where the Court of Appeal rejected arguments that the alleged 'complex monopolists' were not within the scope of section 7(1)(c) since their conduct in restricting competition was forced upon them by hall owners for whom they provided services and since their conduct was dissimilar from one another.

---

9   Ibid, para 11.25.
10 Cmnd 2242 (1993).
11 Cm 2452 (1994).
12 Cm 2542 (1994).
13 Cm 4510 (2000).
14 Cm 4660 (2000).
15 Cm 4842 (2000).
16 Ibid, paras 2.321 ff.
17 Cm 718 (1989); the Commission deals with the complex monopoly situations at paras 7.19–7.41.
18 [1991] CCLR 13, 10 Tr LR 97, CA.
19 Cm 995 (1990); the Commission deals with the complex monopoly situation at paras 6.1–6.11 of its report.
20 (30 September 1991, unreported); affd (12 November 1992, unreported), CA.

The non-technical approach adopted by the Commission to complex monopoly means that many industries, and in particular oligopolies, can be investigated where competition is muted. However, even if the term is interpreted widely, there must be some restriction of competition if a reference is to be made. It is arguable that this requirement should be taken out of the reference criteria entirely: it should be for the Commission to investigate the restriction of competition and any detriments flowing therefrom and not for the person that makes the reference in the first place. A solution would be to amend the FTA's definition of a 'complex monopoly situation' by adding a third type of structural monopoly situation which would be specifically drafted with oligopolistic markets in mind[1]. Power could be given to refer 'oligopoly situations' where, for example, four or fewer firms supply more than 50% of the goods or services of a certain description. The opportunity to make this change was not taken in the Competition Act 1998. However, the Government announced in June 2001 that amendments would be made to complex monopoly provisions in the Act.[1a]

3.   GATHERING INFORMATION ABOUT MONOPOLY SITUATIONS

The monopoly situations described above may be referred for investigation to the Commission. Most references are made by the DGFT although some are made, and some can only be made, by the Secretary of State[2]. It is important that relevant information about the existence of monopoly situations should be readily available and the DGFT plays an important rôle in acquiring and updating such information. The Act imposes a general duty upon him to review the carrying on of commercial activities in the UK and to gather information about such activities which may adversely affect consumers' interests[3]; and a specific one to collect information about monopoly situations and uncompetitive practices[4] and to give relevant advice and assistance to the Secretary of State[5]. The latter may give directions as to the performance of these duties, though no such directions have been made[6].

The DGFT, in pursuance of the duties just described, has established a monitoring system, the operation of which is briefly explained from time to time in his Annual Reports. The OFT watches for information in the press and is also dependent upon receiving information and complaints from individuals. It gathers statistical information on the structure of particular markets and the conduct of firms (for example their pricing behaviour, the ratio of advertising expenditure to sales and merger activity) and their performance (for example changes in their profit margins and their return on capital). Particular attention is paid to the economic performance of large firms, taking into account import penetration[7]. The DGFT is given power under the FTA to require information from firms; these powers have been extended by sections 66 and 67 of the Competition Act 1998. The powers now enjoyed by the DGFT under the FTA are described in the OFT's Guideline *Powers of investigation*.[8] Where the DGFT is considering whether

---

1   The problems raised by oligopoly for competition policy are considered further in ch 14.
1a   See p 364, n 7a above.
2   See p 373 below.
3   FTA, s 2(1).
4   Ibid, s 2(2); uncompetitive practices are defined in s 137(2) as practices having the effect of preventing, restricting or distorting competition in connection with any commercial activities in the UK.
5   Ibid, s 2(3).
6   Ibid, s 12.
7   *Annual Report of the DGFT* for 1987, p 27.
8   OFT Guideline 404, paras 9.1-9.5.

to make a monopoly reference or whether to propose that undertakings should be accepted in lieu of a reference, he may require any person (not just the monopolist) who supplies or is supplied with the goods or services in the UK to provide him with information about his business[9]. The information that may be required is specified in section 44(2) as amended, and the DGFT is given power to enter premises in order to obtain it[10], to require any person on the premises to give an explanation of relevant documents[11] and to take copies[12]. Any person found to have tampered with documents which he has been asked to provide[13] or not complying with a requirement imposed under section 44(2) by the DGFT[14] will be liable to a fine and/or a term of imprisonment no more than two years[15]. The obstruction of the DGFT in the exercise of his duties may also lead to a fine[16]. Penalties are provided for failing to comply with a request for information under these sections[17]; and more serious ones for giving false replies[18]. In practice firms are normally prepared to provide the DGFT with information without his having to have recourse to the exercise of these powers.

4. MONOPOLY REFERENCES[19]

A reference may be made to the Commission whenever it appears that a monopoly situation exists or may exist. As has been explained, the monopoly situation itself may be defined by reference to goods or services of any description and by reference to different forms of supply and to different parts of the UK[20]. The reference itself may further particularise the issues which the Commission should consider: the Act allows considerable flexibility in the framing of monopoly references. The Commission may be asked to limit itself to a consideration of any particular agreements or practices[1]. An example of this is afforded by the report on *Domestic Electrical Goods*[2] where the reference was limited to considering the practices of recommending resale prices and refusal to supply.

(A) Monopoly references limited to the facts

A monopoly reference may be framed in such a way that the Commission is asked to make only a factual investigation[3] in which case it has to decide whether and in whose favour a monopoly situation exists, whether it is being exploited or

---

9 FTA, s 44, as amended by s 66 Competition Act 1998.
10 FTA s 44(2)(c); note that this does not give the power to conduct an unannounced dawn raid.
11 Ibid, s 44(2)(c)(ii).
12 Ibid, s 44(5)(a)(i).
13 Ibid, s 46(8) as amended by s 67 Competition Act 1998.
14 FTA, s 46(4).
15 Ibid.
16 Ibid, s 46(7); see also *Powers of investigation* OFT Guideline 404, para 9.5.
17 Ibid, s 46(2).
18 Ibid, s 46(3).
19 The powers of the Secretary of State to make 'general references' and 'restrictive labour references' are described briefly at the end of this chapter: see pp 388-389 below.
20 See pp 366-367 above.
1 FTA, s 47(2).
2 Cm 3675 and Cm 3676 (1997).
3 FTA, s 48.

maintained in any way and whether any action[4] or omission is attributable to it. The Commission in making its report has a duty to come to definite conclusions on these questions[5]. In the jargon of the Act, this is known as a 'monopoly reference limited to the facts'. In practice, there have been hardly any such references[6].

(B)   Monopoly references not limited to the facts

The remaining references require the Commission to go further and to consider whether any of the facts it has found to exist operate or may be expected to operate against the public interest[7]. As one might expect, the Act describes this as a 'monopoly reference not limited to the facts'. In such a case the Commission must also consider what action should be taken to prevent damage to the public interest and may make appropriate recommendations[8]. A reference not limited to the facts may require the Commission to investigate an industry generally[9]; this type of reference is known as a 'full public-interest reference'. Alternatively it may be asked to comment upon practices of particular concern[10]; this is known as a 'restricted public interest reference'. Many references are on a 'full public-interest' basis, but by no means all. For example in *Residential Mortgage Valuations* the Commission was limited to examining agreements and practices relating to the making or procuring of mortgage valuations and the making of charges[11]; and in *Foreign Package Holidays*[12] the Commission was specifically asked to investigate the practice among travel agents of linking travel insurance with holiday discounts and to address the DGFT's concern over vertical integration within the industry.

(C)   Variation and duration of monopoly inquiries

Monopoly references may in certain circumstances be varied[13]. They must specify time limits within which the investigation is to be completed, though extensions are possible and sometimes asked for[14]. Failure to report within the relevant period means that the reference lapses[15]. It is apparently not possible for a reference to be withdrawn.

---

4   In *Tampons* Cmnd 9705 (1986) the Commission rejected an argument that an 'action' for these purposes must mean some positive act to exploit a monopoly situation or something wholly attributable to it, so that the mere setting of prices at a particular level could not be commented upon by the Commission: ibid, paras 8.5–8.8.
5   FTA, s 54(2); see p 374 below.
6   *Wallpaper* HCP (1963–64) 59 was the only report to have dealt only with the facts; *Copper and Copper Alloys* HCP (1955–56) 56 was originally a reference limited to the facts, though it was later varied to become a full public-interest reference.
7   FTA, s 49(1).
8   Ibid, s 54(3); see p 374 below.
9   Ibid, s 49(1).
10   Ibid, s 49(2) and (3).
11   Cm 2542 (1994).
12   Cm 3813 (1997).
13   FTA, s 52.
14   Ibid, s 55; this most recently occurred in the *Supermarkets* inquiry, where the completion date for the Commission to report was extended from 1 April 2000 to 31 July 2000, and in *Banking Services*, where the date was extended from 19 June 2001 to 19 October 2001.
15   Ibid, s 55(1)(*b*).

(D) Who may make monopoly references

Most monopoly references may be made by the DGFT[16]. The Secretary of State may make any reference[17], and there are some situations which can be referred to the Commission only by the Secretary of State[18]. These situations are described in Part I of Schedule 5 and in Schedule 7 of the FTA and include matters such as mail, certain transport services and various agricultural matters[19]. If these areas are referred by the Secretary of State, he must normally act with the consent of the relevant minister in that sector[20]. References can also be made to the Commission by the Director General of Telecommunications, the Gas and Electricity Markets Authority, the Director General of Water Services, by the Civil Aviation Authority and by the Rail Regulator[1]. The Secretary of State may veto a reference by the DGFT, though this has never been done (but it has sometimes been requested)[2]. Two references in respect of gas were made by the Secretary of State in 1992, which were not within the competence of the DGFT or the sectoral regulators; at the same time two further references were made by the Director General of Gas Supply, whose functions are now carried out by the Gas and Electricity Markets Authority[3].

(E) Undertakings in lieu of a reference

Provision is made in section 56A to G of the FTA for undertakings to be given in lieu of a monopoly reference. These provisions were inserted into the Act by section 7 of the Deregulation and Contracting Out Act 1994. They have never been used. Voluntary, non-statutory, assurances were given by Milk Marque for the OFT in August 1996 in relation to its prices, but abandoned in 1998; a reference to the Commission followed[4].

5. INVESTIGATION BY THE COMPETITION COMMISSION

Once a monopoly reference has been made to the Commission, it must carry out an investigation in accordance with its terms[5].

---

16 FTA, s 50(1).
17 FTA, s 51(1); references by the Secretary of State are rare, but on 20 March 2000 the Secretary of State and the Chancellor of the Exchequer referred the supply of banking services by clearing banks to small- and medium-sized enterprises to the Commission.
18 Ibid, s 50(2)-(5).
19 There have been several alterations to the original provisions of these two Schedules: eg the DGFT can now refer charter flights (Monopoly References (Alteration of Exclusions) Order 1984, SI 1984/1887) and some aspects of airport management (s 83(5) Airports Act 1986: the Secretary of State has power under the Airports Act, s 56 to make regulations to ensure that there is no duplication of functions between the Civil Aviation Authority and the DGFT); the DGFT cannot refer licensed cable programmes (Cable and Broadcasting Act 1984); the Monopoly References (Deletion of Exclusions) Order 1998, SI 1998/2253 deleted the exclusions of liquid cow's milk and potatoes, which formerly had been the subject of statutory marketing schemes, from Part II of Schedule 7, and revoked the Monopoly References (Alteration of Exclusions) Order 1994, SI 1994/1922.
20 FTA, s 51(2)-(4).
1 See 47 *Halsbury's Laws* (Butterworths, 4th ed reissue), para 120.
2 FTA, s 50(6).
3 See Cms 2314, 2315 and 2316 (1993).
4 *The Supply of Raw Milk* Cm 4286 (1999).
5 The basic duty of the Commission is imposed by FTA, s 5(1).

(A)   The Commission's report

The Commission must make its report either to the Secretary of State if the reference was made by the DGFT[6] or to whichever Minister or Ministers made the reference otherwise[7]. In the case of a monopoly reference limited to the facts[8], the Commission must come to definite conclusions on the questions contained in the reference, namely whether a monopoly situation exists, in whose favour, whether any steps are being taken by the persons involved to exploit or maintain that situation and whether any action or omission by them is attributable to the monopoly situation[9]; in doing so, it is sufficient that the Commission establishes a causal link between the action and the monopoly situation: this does not preclude that there might be other concurrent causes for the action[10]. The Court of Appeal has said that the Commission ought to deal in its reports with each of these matters specifically[11]. In doing so it must give an account of its reasons for these conclusions and of the general position regarding the subject-matter of the reference and of the developments which have led to that position, so as to facilitate a proper understanding of that situation generally[12]. The latter provision in particular means that the Commission's investigation tends to be time-consuming as it is required to conduct a detailed survey of the industry in question. If the reference was not limited to the facts[13], the Commission must also consider the public interest. If it considers that the public interest is being or may be expected to be harmed by the monopoly situation itself or by any acts done to exploit or maintain that position or by any action or omission attributable to it, it shall specify the adverse effects and consider what action may be taken to overcome them and make appropriate recommendations[14]. The Commission must make its report within the specified time-limit[15].

(B)   Meaning of 'the public interest'

In considering whether the public interest is being harmed section 84 of the FTA provides that:

> 'the Commission shall take into account all matters which appear to them in the particular circumstances to be relevant and, among other things, shall have regard to the desirability—
> (a) of maintaining and promoting effective competition between persons supplying goods and services in the UK;

---

6   FTA, s 54(1)(a).
7   Ibid, s 54(1)(b).
8   See pp 371-372 above.
9   See FTA, s 54(2) read in conjunction with s 48.
10   *R v Monopolies and Mergers Commission, ex p National House Building Council* [1993] ECC 388 (QBD), [1995] ECC 89, CA.
11   *R v Monopolies and Mergers Commission, ex p Visa International* [1991] CCLR 13, [1991] ECC 291 per Dillon LJ.
12   FTA, s 54(2)(a) and (b).
13   See pp 371-372 above.
14   FTA, s 54(3); the Commission may recommend that such action be taken by the person or persons with the monopoly situation or the relevant Minister or public authority: ibid, s 54(4); a judicial review of the Commission practice under s 54(4) failed in *R v Monopolies and Mergers Commission, ex p Ecando Systems Ltd* (30 September 1991, unreported); affd (12 November 1992, unreported), CA.
15   See p 372, n 14 above.

(b) of promoting the interests of consumers, purchasers and other users of goods and services in the UK in respect of the prices charged for them and in respect of their quality and the variety of goods and services supplied;

(c) of promoting, through competition, the reduction of costs and the development and use of new techniques and new products, and of facilitating the entry of new competitors into existing markets;

(d) of maintaining and promoting the balanced distribution of industry and employment in the UK;

(e) of maintaining and promoting competitive activity in markets outside the UK on the part of producers of goods, and of suppliers of goods and services, in the UK.'

Clearly this concept of the public interest is of great breadth[16]. While it is true to say that, in practice, the Commission will devote most of its time to the issue of competition, section 84 itself does not give pre-eminence to any particular matter. The maintenance of competition is not, as a matter of law, the predominant issue, for this could not be squared with the desirability of the balanced distribution of industry and employment nor with the requirement to take into account *all* relevant matters. In *Tampons*[17] the Commission specifically rejected an argument that the maintenance of competition expressed in section 84(1)(*a*) was of paramount importance in construing the section, so that nothing could be recommended by it that might have the effect of stifling price competition[18]. The section amply illustrates the pragmatism of the investigative system. A DTI Consultation Document of 1999 questioned whether the public interest test should be retained in merger cases[19]; a later document of October 2000 confirmed the intention of the Government to introduce a competition test for mergers, with a possibility of the Secretary of State deciding a very small minority of cases on the basis of exceptional public interest issues[20]. It may be, however, that the Government will replace the public interest test for monopolies if it introduces new legislation in 2002[1].

The structure of the Act is such that the question of market power is relevant at the public interest stage of an inquiry. The Commission is more likely to consider, for example, that requirements contracts or tie-in sales harm the public interest when they are employed by a firm which controls a preponderant part of the market. The Commission will therefore carry out an economic analysis in order to see whether a particular firm does possess market power and it will look at market shares, countervailing power on the buying side of the market and barriers to entry; it will also consider the extent to which a firm might be subject to competitive pressure from outside the particular market in which it operates. However on its face the FTA does not *require* the Commission to define what the relevant market consists of: the Commission is simply required (by section 48(d) of the FTA in conjunction with section 54(2)) to confirm that a monopoly situation within the meaning of the Act exists, not to identify the market in economic terms.

16 Note that s 84 is also applicable when the Commission is considering the public interest in merger investigations (other than newspaper mergers) under the FTA (ch 22, pp 816-817).
17 Cmnd 9705 (1986).
18 Ibid, paras 8.9–8.10.
19 See ch 22, p 836.
20 URN 00/805.
1   See p 364, n 7a.

(C)   The Commission's procedure

The FTA says little about the manner in which the Commission should conduct its investigations. It has a duty to take into consideration any representations made to it by persons appearing to have a substantial interest in the subject-matter of the reference and, if not impractical, to hear such persons orally[2]. Other than this it is provided that the Commission may determine its own procedure[3] subject to any directions given by the Secretary of State[4]; none have been given. In carrying out its investigations, the Commission is under a duty to act fairly[5]. A number of claims for judicial review of the Commission's procedures have been made, but the Courts, while stating that the Commission must act reasonably, have shown no inclination to place the Commission in a procedural strait-jacket. The provisions in the FTA dealing with the constitution of the Commission and the performance of its functions have been replaced by Schedule 7 of the Competition Act 1998. Schedule 7 provides that the Commission's functions in respect of particular references may be assigned to a group consisting of not less than three of its members[6]. One member will be appointed chairman of the group and, in the event of a tied vote, he or she has a casting vote[7]. In practice individual inquiries are always assigned to a group. If a group concludes that the public interest is being harmed as a result of a monopoly situation, a majority of two thirds of its members is required before the Secretary of State can make an order[8]; since there was not a two-thirds majority that the public interest was being harmed, no order could be made in *Fresh Processed Milk to the Middle-Ground Retailers in Scotland*[8a]. Dissentients may attach a dissenting opinion[9]. The Report must not contain confidential or sensitive information unless this is unavoidable[10]. The Act gives the Commission power to compel the attendance of witnesses for the purpose of its investigation and to take evidence on oath[11]. It has rarely been necessary for the Commission to use these powers. It is a criminal offence to provide the Commission with information in the knowledge that it is materially false or misleading or to provide such information to another person knowing that it is to be given to the Competition Commission[12].

The Commission has adopted a clear procedure over the years. The progress of inquiries can easily be tracked on the Commission's website[13]. Each group may determine its own procedure[14], but the Chairman has published guidance for them pursuant to paragraph 19(3) of Schedule 7 of the Competition Act 1998[15]. When the reference is first made the group begins by collecting as much

2   FTA, s 81(1).
3   Ibid, s 81(2).
4   Ibid, s 81(3).
5   See *Hoffmann-La Roche and Co AG v Secretary of State for Trade* and Industry [1975] AC 295, [1974] 2 All ER 1128, HL.
6   CA, Sch 7, Part II, para 15(2).
7   107 Ibid, para 21; this happened in *Fresh Processed Milk to the Middle-Ground Retailers in Scotland* Cm 5002 (2000).
8   CA, Sch 7, Part II, para 20(2).
8a   Cm 5002 (2000).
9   FTA, s 82(4) and CA, Sch 7, Part II, para 18(2)(*b*); see eg the note of dissent in *The Supply of Beer* Cm 651 (1989) pp 296–303.
10   FTA, s 133.
11   FTA, s 85(1)(a) and s 85(7) inserted by the Companies Act 1989: failure to comply with the Commission's request entitles any member of the Commission group to certify that fact in writing to a court and it may then inquire into the case.
12   FTA, s 93B.
13   http://www.competition-commission.gov.uk/index.html.
14   CA Sch 7, Part II, para 19(1).
15   February 2000; it can be found on the Commission's website: see n 13 above.

evidence about the industry in question as it can. The Commission makes great use of written questionnaires at this stage, although it may hold an oral hearing in order to ascertain the facts. The Commission has its own economists, lawyers and accountants to assist it, and it may appoint consultants to help. Site visits are often arranged. Having assembled the relevant materials it proceeds to consider the impact upon the public interest. It prepares an 'issues letter' which is sent out to the firms involved for them to make relevant representations. The contents of this letter have become fairly formalised, and it will typically contain a provisional finding as to any monopoly or complex monopoly situations, a draft description of the industry under investigation, a list of public interest issues and details of any third party complaints. The Commission will make public an 'issues statement' based on the issues letters sent to the parties under investigation. The issues statement is made available on the Commission's website.

Where appropriate a group may decide to hold a public meeting[16]; it may also hold a joint meeting, at which more than one of the main parties to the proceedings will be present. There are then public interest hearings, which the Chairman's guidance says should usually be held in private and usually should not be held in the presence of other parties; these hearings are relatively informal, and give the parties an opportunity to present their arguments. Counsel often appear at public interest hearings[17], although the Commission will use this occasion to direct questions to company executives rather than to listen to rhetorical flourishes from lawyers. There may be discussion of hypothetical remedies for public interest detriments that the Commission may identify, although no conclusions on the public interest will have been reached at this stage. The Commission will make public on its website a 'remedies statement', on which third parties may comment. Where remedies are under discussion, the Chairman of the Commission in his guidance advises groups to hold a meeting with representatives of the OFT to discuss their relative advantages and disadvantages. It is the Commission's practice to send the parties who have given oral evidence a copy of the full transcript of the hearing which they attended, asking them to confirm its accuracy and to make any additional substantive points in a separate note.

After the public interest hearings the Commission prepares its draft report. Sections of the background chapters are sent to the parties who provided the information contained in those sections to enable any factual inaccuracies to be corrected; at the same time it will prepare its final chapter containing the group's conclusions on the public interest, though this will not be sent to the parties. An important section of the report will contain the Commission's recommendations as to how any public interest detriments might be remedied; it is rare for the Commission to recommend no remedies at all, although this did happen in the case of *Supermarkets*[18] in relation to the pricing of grocery products: it was unable to suggest any remedy that would not be disproportionate and unduly regulatory. The final report is sent to the Secretary of State or other Minister. It has been suggested that the parties themselves ought to be allowed to see the final report before it is released by the Commission so that they are in a better position to deal with press criticism and to counteract any findings by the

---

16 The first public hearing was held in *Cars* Cm 4660, 2000; another took place in the investigation of *Banking Services by Clearing Banks to SMEs* in 2001.
17 This practice is confirmed by the Commission's own explanation of its procedures on its website at http://www.competition-commission.gov.uk/role3.htm.
18 Cm 4842 (2000).

Commission which they consider to be unfair or improper. In 1980 the Competition Act made a small concession in this direction by providing that, before a report is laid before Parliament[19], any firm found to be in a monopoly situation must receive a copy of it at least 24 hours in advance, but this was repealed by section 69 of the Competition Act 1998.

6.   CONSEQUENCES OF THE COMPETITION COMMISSION'S REPORT

A copy of the report must be sent to the Secretary of State or other Minister[20]. It must also be presented to Parliament[1]. It is not always published immediately: there may for example be a delay because of problems of confidential information[2]; in some cases a report may raise sensitive matters or be politically embarrassing to the Government; and careful consideration may need to be given to the advice given by the Competition Commission on remedies. It may be the case that the Minister is out of the country, resulting in delay; and the DTI may wish to avoid publishing more than one report at the same time. The DTI aims to publish reports within 10 weeks of receipt. Rumours sometimes circulate as to the contents of the report prior to its publication. On 1 October 2000 *The Observer* published an extensive account of the Commission's report on *Supermarkets*[3], claiming to have read a copy of it even though it had yet to be published. It is extremely undesirable that the contents of Commission reports should be divulged prior to publication, since they invariably contain sensitive information which can affect share prices.

What happens after receipt of the report by the Secretary of State will depend on whether the Competition Commission has concluded that it may be expected that the public interest may be harmed or not.

(A)   No harm to the public interest

If the Commission does not conclude that the public interest is being or may be expected to be harmed in some way, no further action can be taken; the Secretary of State can act only where the Commission has found there to be a detriment to the public interest. However the Commission may recommend that the DGFT should keep the situation 'under review' if it is anxious about a particular activity or industry. In its report on *Supermarkets*[4] the Commission expressed concern about the level of concentration in the market in certain parts of the country, and noted that existing planning laws could not be used to address the issue. Since this problem was not attributable to a scale or complex monopoly there was no power under the FTA to deal with the problem; nevertheless the Commission recommended that in certain clearly defined circumstances the DGFT's approval should be required before some operators would be allowed to acquire or develop large new stores, and that a dedicated unit should be established within the OFT

19   See below.
20   FTA, s 54(1).
1   Ibid, s 83.
2   See FTA, s 83(3) which requires the Minister to excise from reports information which would be against the public interest; also s 83(3A) which requires the excision of information related to individuals, publication of which would cause serious prejudice.
3   Cm 4842 (2000).
4   Ibid.

to deal with such cases. It may be that such a system will be negotiated on a voluntary basis with the supermarkets in question; if not, primary legislation would be needed to make it enforceable. The Secretary of State asked the DGFT to monitor the situation and said that, should there be signs of the situation deteriorating, 'appropriate legislation would be considered'[5].

It is worth pointing out that by no means all monopoly investigations end with the Commission making an adverse report. On numerous occasions it has made no criticisms at all. For example, in *Scottish Solicitors*[6] the Commission concluded that the supply of estate agency services in Scotland via 'Solicitor Property Centres' did not impede competition from non-solicitor estate agents. It found that the Property Centres were not 'essential facilities' and that non-solicitor estate agents could collaborate on providing their own services; its opinion was buttressed by the high level of consumer satisfaction regarding estate agency and conveyancing in Scotland. In *Historical On-Line Database Services*[7] the availability of other service providers meant that the Commission upheld the *Financial Times'* copyright licensing practice to prevent competitors from using its articles in providing on-line access to archival business and financial information. In *Recorded Music*[8] the Commission concluded that concern over the price differential of compact discs between the US and UK was misplaced, in particular because of different taxes; the Commission was satisfied that excessive profits were not being earned and that the record companies' complex monopoly and a recorded music retailer's scale monopoly did not operate against the public interest. It is not unusual for the Commission to suggest that regulatory rules or Governmental procedures ought to be amended in order to overcome restrictive effects on competition[9].

(B) Harm to the public interest

(i) Remedies

If the Commission concludes that there are public interest detriments the Secretary of State has power to take a large range of action to remedy the position[10]. The Commission is required to consider recommendations to remedy any public interest detriments that it identifies and its reports usually contain such recommendations. As noted above, in *Supermarkets*[11], unusually, it was unable to recommend remedies to deal with the problem of below-cost selling by supermarkets that would not be disproportionate and harmful to competition in themselves[12]. The OFT actually negotiates remedies with the parties concerned, and it will be closely involved with the Secretary of State and the Competition and Markets Group of the DTI at the stage of discussing them.

---

5   DTI Press Notice P/2000/674, 10 October 2000.
6   Cm 3699 (1997).
7   Cm 2554 (1994).
8   Cm 2599 (1994).
9   See eg *Postal Franking Machines* Cmnd 9749 (1986); *Contact Lens Solutions* Cm 2242 (1993), where the Commission considered that regulatory changes would be preferable to price control; *Exhaust Gas Analysers* Cm 2386 (1993).
10 FTA, ss 56 and 90; the territorial scope of such orders is considered in ch 12, pp 405-407.
11 Cm 4842 (2000).
12 Ibid, paras 1.7 and 1.8.

(ii)   The powers of the Secretary of State

The powers of the Secretary of State are specified in Parts I and II of Schedule 8 of the Act. The difference between the two parts is that the powers in Part II, which are more drastic and enable even the divestiture of companies or the division of businesses, are exercisable only with the positive approval of Parliament[13]. Orders may be made under Part I to terminate agreements[14]; to prohibit refusals to supply[15], tie-in transactions[16] and discrimination[17]; to fix and control prices[18]; and to prevent the acquisition of businesses[19]. Under Part II orders may be made to divide up a business. Part II powers cannot be exercised against public sector bodies[20]. The Minister may also apply to the Comptroller General of Patents to regulate the licensing behaviour of patentees[1]. A major gap in the powers contained in the FTA was the inability to control copyright licences or to grant copyright licences of right: this was remedied by s 144 of the Copyright, Designs and Patents Act 1988. If an order is made under the foregoing provisions, there are no criminal sanctions to ensure compliance with it[2], but an action may be brought in respect of any contravention or apprehended contravention of it both by the Crown and by an individual[3]. Section 93 does not state specifically whether an individual may bring an action *for damages* if he is harmed by disobedience to an order. In *Mid Kent Holdings v General Utilities plc*[4], in the context of a merger investigation, Knox J held that section 93A, which applies where an undertaking as opposed to an order is broken[5], did not confer on a private person a right of action to enforce undertakings given to the Secretary of State following a Commission merger inquiry since they had been given to avoid possible detriment to the public interest and not to prevent damage to Mid Kent; it seems that each case must be assessed on its own merits according to the intention behind the order or the undertaking.

(iii)   Orders

Orders are made quite frequently following Commission inquiries which identify public interest detriments. The report on *Beer*[6] led to the Supply of Beer (Loan Ties, Licensed Premises and Wholesale Prices) Order 1989[7] and the Supply of Beer (Tied Estate) Order 1989[8]. These orders were under review by the OFT in 2000, due to the consolidation of the beer industry and the consolidation of

---

13   Ibid, s 91(1); s 91(2) describes the procedure to be adopted when making an order under Part I of the Schedule.
14   Ibid, Sch 8, Part I, para 2.
15   Ibid, para 4.
16   Ibid, para 5.
17   Ibid, paras 6 and 7.
18   Ibid, paras 8–11.
19   Ibid, para 12.
20   Ibid, s 56(5) and (6).
1   Patents Act 1977, s 51, as substituted by Copyright, Designs and Patents Act 1988, s 295, Sch 5, para 14 and amended by Competition Act 1998 (Competition Commission) Transitional, Consequential and Supplemental Provisions Order 1999, SI 1999/506.
2   Ibid, s 93(1).
3   Ibid, s 93(2).
4   [1996] 3 All ER 132, [1997] 1 WLR 14; for critical comment, see Rodger (1997) 18 ECLR 273.
5   See p 381 below.
6   Cm 651 (1989).
7   SI 1989/2258.
8   SI 1989/2390.

powerful pub chains[9]. The Electrical Contracting (London Exhibition Halls) Order 1995[10] followed the Commission's Report on *Electrical Contracting at Exhibition Halls*[11]. The Foreign Package Holidays (Tour Operators and Travel Agents) Order[12] was partially annulled as a result of a successful judicial review[13]; a fresh order was made in August 2000[14]. The Restriction of Agreements and Conduct (Specified Domestic Electrical Goods) Order 1998[15] prohibited the practice of recommended resale prices in the case of domestic electrical goods, following the Commission's two reports on that industry. The Supply of New Cars Order 2000[16] was made following the Commission's report on *New Cars*[17].

(iv) Undertakings

Despite the availability of the order-making procedure, in many cases it is preferred to try to reach agreement informally by negotiation between the firms in question and the DGFT. The Act itself provides machinery that envisages this approach. Apart from requiring that the DGFT be sent a copy of the Report[18], it is also provided that, if requested to do so by the Secretary of State, he should consult the parties concerned with a view to securing undertakings designed to overcome any adverse effects upon the public interest[19]. Any undertakings so negotiated will actually be given to the Secretary of State, though the DGFT negotiates them[20] and will then monitor them and give advice to the Minister should they need to be varied or superseded or if they are not being carried out[1]. If no undertaking is likely to be forthcoming, the DGFT must tell the Secretary of State who can then consider exercising his order-making powers[2]. In some cases, an interim undertaking might be taken pending a final solution to a case: this happened, for example, after the Commission's report on *The Supply of Impulse Ice-Cream* in 2000, when Birds Eye Wall's guaranteed minimum terms of supply to independent wholesalers pending a final remedy[3].

(v) Continuing surveillance of undertakings

An important aspect of the work of the OFT is that it may continue to monitor undertakings given, and the industry to which they relate, for many years after

---

9   See DTI Press Release P/2000/805, 1 December 2000, proposing that a new order will be made amending the earlier ones.
10 SI 1995/3299.
11 Cm 995 (1990).
12 SI 1998/1945; this Order was made following the Commission's report on *Foreign Package Holidays* Cm 3813 (1997).
13 *R v Secretary of State for Trade and Industry, ex p Thomson Holidays* [2000] ECC 321, CA.
14 SI 2000/2110.
15 SI 1998/1271; this Order was made following the Commission's reports on the *Supply of Domestic Electrical Goods* Cm 3675 and Cm 3676 (1997).
16 SI 2000/2088; see ch 16, p 599.
17 Cm 4660 (2000).
18 FTA, s 86.
19 Ibid, s 88.
20 Ibid, s 88(2).
1   Ibid, s 88(4).
2   Ibid, s 88(3).
3   Cm 4510 (2000); see DTI Press Release P/2000/108, 16 February 2000; see also P/2000/260, 7 April 2000 and P/2000/509, 20 July 2000 for the additional undertakings given in this case.

the Commission's original report: for example, in his 1999 Annual Report, the DGFT said he was reviewing the undertakings given after *Petrol* in 1965 and *Metal Containers* in 1972[4]. The OFT publishes a register of all continuing undertakings[5].

(vi)   The advice of the DGFT and the recommendations of the Competition Commission are not binding on the Secretary of State

It may be that the Secretary of State declines to accept the advice of the DGFT or the Commission and decides not to require or to accept undertakings from the firm or firms concerned. The procedure under the FTA is essentially discretionary and the last word lies with the Secretary of State. The reports on *Credit Card Franchise Services*[6] and *Trading Check Franchise and Financial Services*[7] recommended that retailers should be permitted to levy a surcharge on customers paying by credit card rather than by cash and the DGFT agreed. The Secretary of State decided not to change the system for fear that this might rebound to the consumer's disadvantage[8]. In 1987 the DGFT made a second reference of credit cards, leading to a further adverse report and, on this occasion, to statutory orders to terminate practices detrimental to the public interest[9]. In 1999, the Secretary of State declined to accept the advice of the Commission in its entirety in relation to *The Supply in Great Britain of Raw Cow's Milk*[10]. The Commission had recommended that Milk Marque, a farmers' cooperative that was the successor to the Milk Marketing Board, should be broken up into three or more parts, since it was engaged in practices that enabled it to raise the price of milk beyond those that would obtain in competitive conditions. The Secretary of State declined to accept the recommendation for divestiture, but asked the DGFT to seek other solutions to the problem. In the event, Milk Marque voluntarily split into three separate companies, while contesting whether the Commission's report was lawful since it was inconsistent with the EC Treaty[11]; the Secretary of State asked the DGFT to continue to monitor the situation[12]. The Secretary of State did not follow the advice of the Commission in 2000 in relation to *The Supply of Impulse Ice-Cream*[13]; the remedies in this case were secured in three tranches[14]. When the Secretary of State declines to follow the advice of the Commission there is sometimes vociferous criticism in the media; however, as a matter of law, it is quite clear that the ultimate decision as to how any public interest issues should be dealt with does indeed lie with the Minister.

---

4   1999 *Annual Report of the DGFT*, pp 42-43.
5   This can be found on the OFT's website – http://www.oft.gov.uk/html/rsearch/reports/ oft138.htm.
6   Cmnd 8034 (1980).
7   HCP (1981–82) 62.
8   The Parliamentary Statement by the Minister is reproduced in the 1980 *Annual Report of the DGFT* pp 83–84.
9   Cm 718 (1989).
10   DTI Press Release P/99/587, 6 July 1999.
11   See the 1999 *Annual Report of the DGFT*, p 41; the issue of whether the Commission had jurisdiction to conduct this investigation, given the rules of the Common Agricultural Policy, was referred to the ECJ under Article 234 EC: Case C-137/00 *R v Monopolies and Mergers Commission and the Secretary of State for Trade and Industry, ex p Milk Marque Ltd* (judgment pending).
12   DTI Press Release P/99/895, 5 November 1999; see also P/2000/304 of 2 May 2000.
13   Cm 4510 (2000).
14   See n 3 above.

(vii) Breach of an undertaking

If an undertaking is broken the Secretary of State can consider making an order under Schedule 8. It would also be possible for the DGFT to make a second reference to the Commission under the FTA[15], and a second reference may be made where a company asks to be released from undertakings given after an earlier report[16]. Section 93A of the FTA gives anyone harmed by the breach of an undertaking a right to bring civil proceedings against the person responsible[17].

7. THE RELATIONSHIP OF THE MONOPOLY PROVISIONS WITH CHAPTER II OF THE COMPETITION ACT 1998

The advent of the Chapter II prohibition in the Competition Act 1998 means that undertakings which abuse a dominant position are acting unlawfully if trade within the UK is affected. Article 82 EC applies only where trade *between* Member States is affected. Prior to the 1998 Act, a 'purely' domestic abuse was not unlawful, but could be investigated only under the FTA or the old Competition Act 1980, which was a largely ineffective piece of legislation. Not unnaturally, during the passage of the Competition Bill through Parliament in 1997-1998, it was questioned whether it was necessary or appropriate to retain the scale and complex monopoly provisions of the FTA, given that the Chapter II prohibition would now be available to deal with abusive behaviour[18]. In particular it was argued that this would expose dominant firms to double jeopardy, that is to say the possibility of investigation under both Acts. The Government resisted calls for the abolition of the monopoly provisions, in the view of this author for compelling reasons[19]. Since the monopoly provisions have been retained, consideration will be given, in later chapters of this book, to some of the more significant reports of the Commission over the years on practices such as requirements contracts and tie-ins, excessive and anti-competitive pricing and other practices which it might be required to investigate again in the future[20]. At this stage it is necessary to consider when, if at all, scale and complex monopoly inquiries might be launched in the future.

(A) The future of scale monopoly investigations

In the case of scale monopolies, Lord Simon stated in the House of Lords that these powers would be used in the future only where a firm had already been

---

15 For example, the Commission has reported no less than four times on aspects of the ice-cream market in the UK under the FTA and the now-repealed anti-competitive practices provisions of the Competition Act 1980, in 1979, 1994, 1998 and, most recently, in 2000, Cm 4510 (2000).

16 This was the procedure adopted in the case of *Plasterboard* Cm 1224 (1990).

17 See however the outcome of the *Mid Kent* case discussed at p 380 above.

18 On this issue, see Furse 'Monopolies, the Public Interest, the Fair Trading Act and the Chapter II Prohibition' in *The Competition Act: A New Era for UK Competition Law* (Hart Publishing, 2000, eds Rodger and MacCulloch).

19 In support of the retention of the monopoly provisions, see Hay 'Is More Like Europe Better?: An Economic Evaluation of Recent Changes in UK Competition Policy' in *The Europeanisation of UK Competition Law* (Hart Publishing, 1999, eds Green and Robertson), pp 54-58.

20 See in particular ch 14, pp 493-494 on tacit collusion; ch 16, p 594 on vertical integration; ch 17, pp 627-632 on non-pricing anti-competitive practices and ch 18, pp 664-673 on pricing practices.

found to have abused its dominant position under the Chapter II prohibition, and where the DGFT believed that further abuses were likely[1]. The point is repeated in the OFT's Guideline *The Major Provisions*[2]; however it says that a scale monopoly reference may be made in relation to the utility sectors irrespective of whether there have been past abuses[3]. It should be recalled that the remedies available under the Competition Act 1998 are behavioural: for example to give such directions to the dominant firm as may be appropriate to bring an infringement to an end[4]. Fines may also be imposed under the 1998 Act. Where a scale monopolist has abused its market power several times, and may be likely to do so again, there is much to be said for retaining the possibility of a monopoly investigation, at the end of which the powers are more extensive, and include the possibility of a structural remedy.

The Commission has only rarely recommended divestiture. It did conclude in *Roadside Advertising Services*[5] that the scale and complex monopoly situations it discovered operated against the public interest as they led to higher prices, and it recommended that a company, British Posters Ltd, be wound up. However this company was not a true monopolist, but rather a company jointly owned by competitors in the provision of advertising sites: its existence had the effect of blunting competition between them. In *Domestic Gas Appliances*[6] the Commission recommended the selling-off of British Gas' retailing activities as a possible remedy to the problem it identified. In its first report on *Beer*[7] the Commission considered the possibility of requiring brewers to sell off their retail outlets, but concluded that there were numerous problems associated with such a solution. In 1989, however, it recommended in *The Supply of Beer*[8] that no brewer should be allowed to own more than 2,000 retail outlets: this would involve six brewers[9] selling off a total of 21,900 public houses[10]. An order was made, although in different terms from those recommended by the Commission. Divestiture was recommended in *Artificial Lower Limbs*[11] though this proved unnecessary[12]; it was also recommended in *Gas*[13], but not ordered as British Gas chose to restructure itself. In *The Supply of Raw Cow's Milk*[14] the Commission recommended that Milk Marque, a scale monopolist in the supply of raw milk, should be divided into a number of quota holding and independent bodies; this was achieved voluntarily without resort to the order-making powers. The record shows, therefore, that divestiture is rare in monopoly cases, but nevertheless that it is among the remedial possibilities following an adverse report.

1　See HL Committee, 13 November 1997, col 300 and HL 3R, 5 March 1998, col 1333; the same policy would presumably be applied by the sectoral regulators where they are able to make references.
2　OFT Guideline 400, para 13.4.
3　Ibid, para 13.5; see also *Concurrent Application to Regulated Industries* OFT Guideline 433, para 4.8.
4　See ch 10, p 350.
5　HCP (1980–81) 365.
6　HCP (1979–80) 703.
7　HCP (1969–70) 216.
8　Cm 651 (1989).
9　Allied, Bass, Courage, Grand Metropolitan, Scottish and Newcastle and Whitbread: ibid, Table 12.1.
10　The Beer Orders (The Supply of Beer (Tied Estate) Order 1989 SI 1989/2390 and The Supply of Beer (Loan Ties, Licensed Premises and Wholesale Prices Order SI 1989 2258) are the subject of a review: see pp 380-381 above.
11　Cm 594 (1989).
12　1989 *Annual Report of the DGFT* p 36.
13　Cm 2314, Cm 2315 and Cm 2316 (1993).
14　Cm 4286 (1999).

(B) The future of complex monopoly investigations

The case for retention of the complex monopoly provisions is even stronger than in the case of scale monopolies. In recent years there have been several major complex monopoly investigations: for example *Domestic Electrical Goods I and II*[15]; *Foreign Package Holidays*[16]; *New Cars*[17]; and *Supermarkets*[18]. Typically in these cases there is parallel behaviour between a number of independent undertakings, but the parallel behaviour is not attributable to an agreement or concerted practice in the sense of Article 81 EC or the Chapter I prohibition. Furthermore, it may not be appropriate to characterise the behaviour as amounting to an abuse of a collective dominant position under Article 82 EC or the Chapter II prohibition[19]. In so far as the complex monopolists are parties to vertical agreements, for example with distributors and retailers, that cumulatively have an anti-competitive effect, these agreements are excluded from the Chapter I prohibition of the Competition Act 1998[20]. The retention of the complex monopoly provisions means that it remains possible to conduct an industry-wide investigation in order to examine how the conditions of competition might be improved. It is perhaps unfortunate that EC law does not possess a similar legal instrument. In the House of Lords, Lord Simon specifically stated that the complex monopoly provisions might be used where the competition authorities discover problems that fall outside the Chapter I and II prohibitions[1].

It is interesting to reflect that, if the European Commission's proposal that domestic competition law should be disapplied in the case of agreements and abuses that have an effect on trade between Member States is implemented, the scale and complex monopoly provisions would no longer be available, to that extent, to the domestic competition authorities[2]. It is likely, however, that the new EC regulation will be drafted in such a way that the provisions in the FTA will not be disapplied. In the meantime the Government has announced its intention to reform the complex monopoly provisions in the FTA.[2a]

---

15   Cms 3675 and 3676 (1997).
16   Cm 3813 (1997).
17   Cm 4660 (1999).
18   Cm 4842 (2000).
19   See ch 14, p 480.
20   See ch 16, pp 595-598.
1   HL Report State, 19 February 1998, col 351; see similarly *The Major Provisions* OFT Guideline 400, para 13.4.
2   See ch 7, p 254.
2a   See p 364, n 7a above.

8.   TABLE OF MONOPOLY INVESTIGATIONS 1994-2001

The following Table provides details of monopoly investigations completed since the last edition of this book, from 1994 to the end of July 2001.

1994			
Title	Command Number	Date Published	Finding of detriments to the public interest?
Private medical services	Cm 2452	11.2.94	Yes
Ice cream	Cm 2524	29.3.94	Yes
Contraceptive sheaths	Cm 2529	30.3.94	Yes
The supply of residential mortgage valuations	Cm 2542	28.4.94	Yes
Historical on-line database services	Cm 2554	12.5.94	No
The supply of recorded music	Cm 2599	23.6.94	No
Films	Cm 2673	6.10.94	Yes

1995			
Title	Command Number	Date Published	Finding of detriments to the public interest?
Video games	Cm 2781	9.3.95	Yes
The supply of bus services in the north-east of England	Cm 2933	3.8.95	Yes

1996			
Title	Command Number	Date Published	Finding of detriments to the public interest?
Performing rights	Cm 3147	1.2.96	Yes

1997			
Title	Command Number	Date Published	Finding of detriments to the public interest?
Domestic electrical goods I	Cm 3675	30.7.97	Yes
Domestic electrical goods II	Cm 3676	30.7.97	Yes
Solicitors' estate agency services in Scotland	Cm 3699	29.8.97	No
Foreign package holidays	Cm 3813	19.12.97	Yes

No reports in 1998

1999			
Title	Command Number	Date Published	Finding of detriments to the public interest?
Underwriting services for share offers	Cm 4168	24.02.99	No (but recommendations concerning transparency)
Supply of raw milk	Cm 4286	06.07.99	Yes

2000			
Title	Command Number	Date Published	Finding of detriments to the public interest?
The supply of impulse ice-cream	Cm 4510	28.01.00	Yes
New cars	Cm 4660	10.04.00	Yes
Supermarkets	Cm 4842	10.10.00	Yes
Supply of fresh processed milk to middle-ground retailers in Scotland	Cm 5002	22.12.00	Yes, but not by a two thirds majority, so no remedies

9.   OTHER REFERENCES

The Secretary of State may make references of two other kinds to the Commission relating to monopolistic or anti-competitive problems.

(A)   General references

Section 78 of the FTA enables him to make general references of practices of a specified class which are commonly adopted as a result of or for the purpose of preserving monopoly situations[3] or which appear to be uncompetitive practices[4]. Uncompetitive practices for this purpose are defined in section 137 as practices 'having the effect of preventing, restricting or distorting competition in connection with any commercial activities in the UK'. In the case of uncompetitive practices, section 78(1)(b) does not refer to monopoly situations at all. Eight references have been made under section 78 or its predecessor[5]: *Collective Discrimination*[6]; *Recommended Resale Prices*[7]; *Refusal to Supply*[8]; *Professional Services*[9]; *Parallel Pricing*[10]; *Full-line Forcing and Tie-in Sales*[11]; *Discounts to Retailers*[12]; and,

---

3   Ibid, s 78(1)(a).
4   Ibid, s 78(1)(b).
5   Monopolies and Restrictive Practices (Inquiry and Control) Act 1948, s 15. That provision was more limited than FTA, s 78 since a general reference could be made only of practices of a class that had already been dealt with in context by the Commission's earlier reports.
6   Cmd 9504 (1955).
7   HCP (1968–69) 100.
8   Cmnd 4372 (1970).
9   Cmnd 4463 (1970).
10   Cmnd 5330 (1973).
11   HCP (1980–81) 212.
12   HCP (1980–81) 311.

most recently, *Collective Licensing*[13]. This reference was made by the Secretary of State in conjunction with the Home Office in March 1988 following complaints from local commercial radio stations about the royalties they had to pay to copyright collecting societies and the restrictions on needle-time imposed by them. The Commission came to the conclusion that on the whole such societies produce favourable effects, although it did make several recommendations for possible improvements[14]. In its report, it rejected the argument that it should not question existing or prospective legislation, remarking that it is in the nature of a general report that it should be able to make suggestions for changes in the law[15]. The DGFT recommended to the Secretary of State in the former Conservative Government that a general reference should be made of the supermarket sector, but the advice was not accepted; in May 1999 the DGFT himself made a monopoly reference to the Commission[16].

A general reference may ask the Commission to report on what action if any could be taken to remedy or prevent adverse effects resulting from monopoly situations or practices described in section 78(1)[17]. There is no order-making power after an investigation under this section, but reports may be influential.

(B)   Restrictive labour references

The Secretary of State may refer restrictive labour practices to the Commission for it to consider their impact upon the public interest[18]. In March 1988 the Secretary of State for Employment acting with the Home Secretary made the first, and only, reference under section 79, of labour practices in television and film-making. The reference required the Commission to investigate the operation of the closed shop, demarcation disputes and manning levels. The Commission concluded that the practices in question did not operate against the public interest[19]. After that reference, there were hints from the Conservative Government that more may be made: a possible reference would have been of the National Dock Labour Scheme, but instead specific legislation was passed in 1989[20].

13   Cm 530 (1988).
14   On the activities of collecting societies see further ch 19, p 719.
15   Ibid, para 7.5.
16   See the 1999 *Annual Report of the DGFT*, p 12 and *Supermarkets* Cm 4842 (2000).
17   FTA, s 78(2).
18   FTA, s 79.
19   *Labour Practices in TV and Film-making* Cm 666 (1989).
20   Dock Work Act 1989.

CHAPTER 12

The international dimension of competition law

1. INTRODUCTION

This book so far has described the main provisions, other than those dealing with mergers[1], of EC and UK law, and the way in which those provisions are enforced. This chapter is concerned with an issue of growing importance: the international dimension of competition law.

Dramatic changes have taken place in the world's economy in a remarkably short period of time. State-controlled economies have been exposed to the principles of the market; legal monopolies have been reduced or entirely eliminated; and domestic markets have been increasingly opened up to foreign trade and investment. The World Trade Organisation ('the WTO') performs a central rôle in promoting international trade. These developments present significant challenges for systems of competition law. The economic effects of cartels and anti-competitive behaviour on the part of firms with market power and of mergers are not constrained by national boundaries. It is perfectly possible for a few producers to operate a cartel that has significant effects throughout the world: the OPEC oil cartel is an obvious example of this, although there are both legal and political constraints that prevent competition authorities from tackling this particular organisation[2]. Many of the cartels investigated in recent years by the Department of Justice in the US and the European Commission in Brussels have had a wide geographical reach, the *Lysine* and *Vitamins* cartels being good examples of this[3]. Undertakings such as Microsoft produce products, such as its computer operating system, that are truly global, and it has been the subject of competition law investigations in several jurisdictions, including the US and the EC. International mergers, for example between car manufacturers, aluminium

---

1   On mergers see chs 20-22.
2   To the extent that the actors in this cartel are sovereign states as opposed to undertakings, the doctrine of sovereign immunity prevents the application of the EC competition rules: see ch 3, pp 66-71 on the meaning of 'undertakings' in Articles 81 and 82; on sovereign immunity in US law, see the Foreign Sovereign Immunity Act 1976, 28 USC §§ 1602-1611 (1988) and the joint Department of Justice and Federal Trade Commission *Antitrust Enforcement Guidelines for International Operations* (April 1995), para 3.31: these *Guidelines* can be accessed on the Department of Justice's website at http://www.usdoj.gov/atr/public/guidelines/guidelin.htm; note also the position in the US on foreign sovereign compulsion, ibid, para 3.32, and the Act of State doctrine, ibid, para 3.33.
3   See ch 13, pp 416-419.

producers or telecommunications companies, may produce effects in a multitude of countries, and may be subject to notification to a large number of different competition authorities[4]. It is now common practice for competition authorities to cooperate closely with one another when they are conducting investigations that have an international dimension[5].

Until relatively recently the international component of competition law was predominantly concerned with the question of whether one country could apply its competition rules extraterritorially against an undertaking or undertakings in another country, where the latter behave in an anti-competitive manner having adverse effects in the territory of the former; and whether there should be laws (so-called 'blocking statues') to prevent the 'excessive' assertion of extraterritorial jurisdiction. These issues are considered in sections 2 to 5 of this chapter. However the international dimension of competition law has undoubtedly evolved beyond these somewhat parochial concerns: for the future the interesting question will be how to develop an international system that can address the competition policy issues that arise from the globalisation of markets. A new competition law architecture is needed to deal with this phenomenon: this will be discussed briefly in section 6 of this chapter.

2. EXTRATERRITORIALITY: THEORY AND US LAW

The limits upon a State's jurisdictional competence – and therefore upon its ability to apply its competition laws to overseas undertakings – are matters of public international law[6]. There are two elements to a State's jurisdictional competence. First, a State has jurisdiction to make laws, that is to say to 'lay down general or individual rules through its legislative, executive or judicial bodies'[7]: this is known variously as a State's legislative, prescriptive or subject-matter jurisdiction. Secondly, a State has jurisdiction to enforce its laws, that is 'the power of a State to give effect to a general rule or an individual decision by means of substantive implementing measures which may include even coercion by the authorities'[8]: this is known as a State's enforcement jurisdiction. It is not necessarily the case that the limits of subject-matter and enforcement jurisdiction should be the same: they do not have to be coextensive. An assertion of subject-matter jurisdiction by one State over natural or legal persons in another may not lead to a conflict at all, provided that the former does not seek to enforce its law in the territory of another State. However when a State goes further and seeks enforcement – for example by serving a writ on a person located in another State or demanding the production of evidence there – the possibility of conflict is obvious. Most of the controversial conflicts between States in these matters have

4   See ch 20, pp 723-724.
5   On international cooperation, see pp 409-414 below.
6   For a general account of the relevant principles of public international law see Brownlie *Principles of Public International Law* (Clarendon Press, 5th ed, 1998) ch XV; see also Mann 'The Doctrine of Jurisdiction in International Law' 111 RDC (1964) 9; Akehurst 'Jurisdiction in International Law' (1972–73) 46 British Yearbook of International Law 145; Mann 'The Doctrine of International Jurisdiction Revisited' 186 RDC (1984) 18; Rosenthal and Knighton *National Laws and International Commerce: the Problem of Extraterritoriality* (1982); Lowe *Extraterritorial Jurisdiction* (1983); Olmstead *Extraterritorial Application of Laws and Responses Thereto* (1984).
7   Per Advocate General Darmon in Cases 114/85 etc *A Ahlström Oy v Commission* (the *Wood Pulp* case) [1988] ECR 5193, p 5217, [1988] 4 CMLR 901, p 923.
8   Ibid.

concerned enforcement rather than subject-matter jurisdiction, and it is essentially against enforcement measures that States have adopted blocking statutes[9]. An issue that has arisen relatively recently in the US is whether it is possible to apply its competition law (or 'antitrust law') extraterritorially as a way of gaining access to foreign markets[10].

(A)   Subject-matter jurisdiction

As far as subject-matter jurisdiction is concerned, it is generally accepted in public international law that a State has power to make laws affecting conduct within its territory (the territoriality principle) and to regulate the behaviour of its citizens abroad, citizens for this purpose including companies incorporated under its law (the nationality principle). The territoriality principle has been extended in a logical way so that a State is recognised as having jurisdiction not only where acts originate in its territory (known as subjective territoriality), but also where the objectionable conduct originates abroad but is completed within its territory (objective territoriality). The classic textbook illustration is of a shot being fired across a national boundary: although part of the conduct happened outside the State, it will have jurisdiction as the harmful event occurred within it. A consequence of this is that more than one State may assert jurisdiction in the same matter where the conduct in question straddles national borders. What is controversial is whether, in the area of economic law, it is legitimate to apply the idea of objective territoriality to the *effects* of an agreement entered into, or an anti-competitive act committed, in another State.

For the purpose of subject-matter jurisdiction the territoriality and nationality principles are sufficient to comprehend a great number of infringements of competition law, either because the overseas undertaking will have committed some act – for example taking over a competitor or charging predatory prices – within the territory of the State concerned to apply its law, or because an agreement will have been made between a foreign undertaking and a firm established within the State in question. Alternatively it may be that an act has been committed within that State by a subsidiary company of an overseas parent. In this case the question arises whether it is legitimate to treat the two companies as being in reality one economic entity, so that the conduct of the subsidiary can be considered to be that of the parent. If so the territoriality principle will suffice to establish jurisdiction over the parent company. The economic entity approach is a significant feature of EC law[11].

However even the objective territoriality principle and the economic entity theory may not be sufficient to account for all cases in which a State may wish to assume jurisdiction over foreign undertakings. For example if all the producers of widgets in Japan were to agree not to export widgets to the UK, their agreement could obviously produce commercial effects in the UK; however it is hard to see how it can be meaningfully said that there is any conduct there. The controversial public international law question is whether a State may assert subject-matter jurisdiction simply on the basis that foreign undertakings produce commercial effects within its territory, even though they are not present there and have not committed any act there. The traditional principles of public international law are inadequate to deal with these issues, since they were developed with physical

---

9   See pp 407-409 below.
10 See p 397 below.
11 See pp 398-399 below.

rather than economic conduct in mind. As a matter of logic, it does not seem absurd to suggest that harmful economic effects as well as physical ones emanating from another State ought in some cases to establish jurisdiction: it is not difficult to see the analogy between a shot being fired across the border of one State into a neighbouring one and a conspiracy by firms in one State to charge fixed and excessive prices or to boycott customers in another one. However some commentators reject the notion of jurisdiction based on effects alone, and the Government of the UK has consistently objected to the idea[12].

(B)   Enforcement jurisdiction

Enforcement jurisdiction tends to give rise to the most acute conflicts between States[13]. It is generally recognised that even if subject-matter jurisdiction exists in relation to the conduct of someone in another State, it is improper to attempt to enforce the law in question within that State's territory without its permission. For these purposes enforcement does not mean only the exaction of penalties and the making of final orders such as perpetual injunctions, but refers to all authoritative acts such as the service of a summons, a demand for information or carrying out an investigation. Gathering information can be a particular problem for competition authorities: as business becomes increasingly global, the likelihood of a national authority requiring information which is located outside its jurisdiction increases correspondingly. A problem is that jurisdictional rules developed in the nineteenth century are not particularly well-suited to the business context or the information technology of the twenty-first century.

Many legal systems contain provisions whereby States assist one another in relation to these matters. For example the Hague Convention on the Taking of Evidence Abroad[14] provides for one State to assist another in the gathering of evidence: this Convention is given effect in UK law by the Evidence (Proceedings in Other Jurisdictions) Act 1975. The recognition and enforcement of foreign judgments is an important part of private international law: most foreign judgments can be enforced in the UK[15], though not where they are penal[16]. However cooperation on evidence and the enforcement of judgments is often not provided by one State to another where the former takes exception to an attempt by the latter to assert its law extraterritorially, and most legal systems contain restrictions on the divulging by competition authorities of confidential information. However negotiations have been taking place between the UK and the US for the relaxation of these rules insofar as this might assist the pursuit of cartels, leading to an exchange of diplomatic notes in April and May 2001 extending the scope of the UK/US Mutual Assistance Treaty to criminal infringements of competition law.

12   See Jennings 'Extraterritorial Jurisdiction and the United States Antitrust Laws' (1957) 33 British Yearbook of International Law 146; Higgins 'The Legal Bases of Jurisdiction' in Olmstead *Extraterritorial Application of Laws and Responses Thereto* (1984); *Lowe* pp 138–186; on the UK's position, see further pp 404-407 below.

13   See *Brownlie* (n 6 above), pp 310-312.

14   Cmnd 3991 (1968); Dodge 'Antitrust and the Draft Hague Judgments Convention' (2001) 32 Law and Policy in International Business 363.

15   See Dicey and Morris *The Conflict of Laws* (Sweet & Maxwell, 13th ed, 2000); Cheshire and North's *Private International Law* (Butterworths, 13th ed, 1999).

16   Treble damage awards in the US are probably penal: *British Airways Board v Laker Airways Ltd* [1984] QB 142 at 163, and in the CA, ibid 201; see also the Protection of Trading Interests Act 1980, s 5, which introduced a statutory prohibition on the enforcement of awards of multiple damages: p 409 below.

(C) The 'effects doctrine' in US antitrust law

(i) The Alcoa and Hartford Fire Insurance cases

As has been mentioned, it is not clear that public international law permits jurisdiction to be taken on the basis of effects alone. However US law has undoubtedly embraced the 'effects doctrine'. In *United States v Aluminium Co of America*[17] (*Alcoa*) Judge Learned Hand said that:

> 'it is settled law ... that any State may impose liabilities, even upon persons not within its allegiance, for conduct outside its borders which has consequences within its borders which the State reprehends; and these liabilities other States will ordinarily recognise'[18].

The US courts had not always accepted this view[19]; the statement may not have been necessary to the case[20]; and as formulated the doctrine was extremely wide. However *Alcoa* was of seminal importance and triggered off much controversy between the US and other countries. The most recent Supreme Court judgment on extraterritoriality is *Hartford Fire Insurance Co v California*[1], where the Court repeated that jurisdiction could be taken over 'foreign conduct that was meant to produce and did in fact product some substantial effect in the United States'. The joint Department of Justice/Federal Trade Commission *Antitrust Enforcement Guidelines for International Operations* ('the *International Guidelines*') of 1995[2] explain, by reference to a series of illustrative examples, how those enforcement agencies interpret the jurisdictional scope of US antitrust law in the light of these, and other, judgments.

(ii) Comity

Some US courts, drawing on the principle of judicial comity, have attempted to apply the effects doctrine in a relatively restrictive way, requiring not only that there should be a direct and substantial effect within the US, but also that the respective interests of the United States in asserting jurisdiction and of other

17 148 F 2d 416 (2d Circ, 1945).
18 Ibid, p 444.
19 See eg *American Banana Co v United Fruit Co* 213 US 347 (1909) in which the Supreme Court held that the Sherman Act did not apply to activities outside the US.
20 It is arguable that there was conduct within the US since one of the firms involved in the alleged conspiracy, Aluminium Ltd of Canada, had its effective business headquarters in New York and was in the same group as the Aluminium Company of America.
1 509 US 764 (1993); for comment on this case, see Roth 'Jurisdiction, British Public Policy and the US Supreme Court' (1994) 110 LQR 194; Robertson and Demetriou 'The Extraterritorial Application of US Antitrust Laws in the US Supreme Court' (1994) 43 ICLQ 417; also, by the same authors, 'US Extraterritorial Jurisdiction in Antitrust Matters: Recent Developments' (1995) 16 ECLR 461; Trenor 'Jurisdiction and the Extraterritorial Application of Antitrust Laws after *Hartford Fire*' (1995) 62 University of Chicago Law Review 1582; Waller 'From the Ashes of *Hartford Fire*: The Unanswered Questions of Comity' [1998] Fordham Corporate Law Institute (ed Hawk), ch 3; see also *United States v Nippon Paper* 109 F 3d (1st Circ, 1997), for comment on which see Reynolds, Sicilian and Wellman 'The Extraterritorial Application of the US Antitrust Laws to Criminal Conspiracies' (1998) 19 ECLR 151.
2 See p 391, n 2 above; for commentary on the Guidelines, see Griffin *US International Antitrust Enforcement: A Practical Guide to the Agencies' Guidelines* (Bureau of National Affairs, 1996).

States which might be offended by such assertion should be weighed against one another[3]. The origins of this approach can be traced back to Brewster's *Antitrust and American Business Abroad* in 1958 in which he called for a 'jurisdictional rule of reason'. The DoJ/FTC *International Guidelines* set out various factors relevant to comity analysis, including the relative significance to the alleged violation of conduct within the US, as compared to conduct abroad; the nationality of the persons involved or affected by the conduct; the presence or absence of an intention to affect US consumers, markets or exporters; the relative significance and foreseeability of the effects on the US compared to the effects abroad; the existence of reasonable expectations that would be furthered or defeated by the action; the degree of conflict with foreign law or articulated foreign economic policies; the extent to which the enforcement activities of another country may be affected; and the effectiveness of foreign as opposed to US enforcement[4]. Dealing with the problem of conflicts of jurisdiction by resort to the criterion of reasonableness has its critics, not least because a court hardly seems an appropriate forum in which to carry out such a delicate balancing process[5]. The principle of comity, however, is an important one which has been recognised by the CFI in *Gencor v Commission*[6] and in the two EC/US Cooperation Agreements[7].

(iii)   *Extraterritorial application of US antitrust law*

The competition authorities in the US have had little compunction about enforcing their antitrust laws against overseas companies and have sometimes demanded, for example, that commercial documents located abroad should be handed over; the courts have even issued final orders requiring that foreign companies should change their commercial practices or restructure their industry[8]. An example of extraterritorial action in the US in relation to a foreign merger arose in the case of *Institut Mérieux*[9], where the Federal Trade Commission took action in respect of the acquisition by Institut Mérieux, a French company, of Connaught BioSciences, a Canadian company, because of perceived detriments to competition in the US in the market for anti-rabies vaccines[10].

The International Antitrust Enforcement Assistance Act 1994[11] is intended to improve the ability of the US enforcement agencies to obtain evidence located abroad by providing for reciprocal agreements to be entered between the US and other countries to facilitate the exchange of information, including confidential

---

3   See *Timberlane Lumber Co v Bank of America* 549 F 2d 597 (9th Circ, 1976) and *Mannington Mills v Congoleum Corpn* 595 F 2d 1287 (3 Circ. 1979); for an account of this development see Fox 'Reasonableness and Extraterritoriality' [1986] Fordham Corporate Law Institute (ed Hawk), p 49.

4   See the *International Guidelines*, para 3.2.

5   See Judge Wilkey in *Laker Airways Ltd v Sabena* 731 F 2d 909 at 945–952 (DC Circ, 1984), [1984] ECC 485; Rosenthal and Knighton *National Laws and International Commerce: the Problem of Extraterritoriality* (1982); Mann 'The Doctrine of International Jurisdiction Revisited After Twenty Years' 186 RDC (1984) 19.

6   Case T-102/96 [1999] ECR II-753, [1999] 4 CMLR 971: see pp 402-403 below.

7   See pp 411-412 below.

8   See eg *United States v ICI* (1952) 105 F Supp 215 (1952) where the US court ordered ICI to refrain from relying upon its patent rights under UK law: for the response, and other examples of the extraterritorial assertion of US law, see pp 407-409 below.

9   55 Fed Reg 1614 (1990).

10   See Owen and Parisi 'International Mergers and Joint Ventures: a Federal Trade Commission Perspective' in [1990] Fordham Corporate Law Institute (ed Hawk), ch 1 at pp 5–14.

11   15 USC §§ 6201-6212 (Supp 1995).

information. It is relevant also to note that US law makes certain antitrust offences criminal, and that it is possible for individuals to be sentenced to terms of imprisonment. This explains why the executives of some companies have a policy of not visiting the US at all, and why the same executives earnestly hope that aeroplanes will not be diverted for operational reasons to US airports. There have been recent examples of European executives being required to serve terms of imprisonment in the US for violations of the antitrust rules[12].

(D)   The extraterritorial application of US competition law to gain access to foreign markets

The antitrust laws in the US are applied not only to extraterritorial behaviour that affects imports into the US. Jurisdiction may also be asserted where US companies are obstructed by anti-competitive behaviour in their attempts to gain access to foreign markets. The so-called 'Structural Impediments Initiative'[13] in the US identified the lax enforcement of the Japanese Anti-Monopoly Act against Japanese undertakings as a contributing factor to the difficulties of US firms in expanding into Japanese markets; the Japanese Large Scale Retail Stores Act was considered to be an additional obstacle to would-be importers. The Department of Justice threatened to apply the US antitrust rules against Japanese restrictive practices having the effect of excluding US exporters from Japanese markets[14]. Subsequently the Japanese Government substantially increased the penalties that can be imposed for infringement of the Japanese legislation[15]. The first case in which the US challenged conduct abroad that denied foreign access was in the case of *United States v Pilkington*[16]: the case was settled through a consent decree whereby Pilkington agreed not to enforce certain provisions in technology licences against US undertakings. The enforcement agencies in the US may also take action against foreign cartels that have no effect within the US, but that raise prices in relation to transactions where the US Government contributes more than half the funding[17].

---

12 See ch 13, pp 416-417.
13 See Anwar 'The Impact of the Structural Impediments Initiative on US-Japan Trade' (1992-93) 16(2) World Competition 53; see also the dispute between Eastman-Kodak and Fuji, which ended up as a complaint by the US to the disputes settlement body of the World Trade Organisation, noted by Furse 'Competition Law and the WTO Report: "Japan – Measures Affecting Consumer Photographic Film and Paper"' (1999) 20 ECLR 9.
14 See the DOJ's *Antitrust Enforcement Policy Regarding Anticompetitive Conduct that Restricts US Exports* 3 April 1992; see also Rill 'International Antitrust Policy – A Justice Department Perspective' in [1991] Fordham Corporate Law Institute (ed Hawk), pp 29–43; Coppel 'A Question of Keretsu: Extending the Long Arm of US Antitrust' (1992) 13 ECLR 192; Ohara 'The New US Policy on the Extraterritorial Application of Antitrust Laws, and Japan's Response' (1993-94) 17(3) World Competition 49; Davidow 'Application of US Antitrust Laws to *Keiretsu* Practices' (1994-95) 18(1) World Competition 5; Yamane and Seryo 'Restrictive Practices and Market Access in Japan – Has the JFTC been Effective in Eliminating Barriers in Distribution?' (1999) 22(2) World Competition 1.
15 See Yamada 'Recent Developments of Competition Law and Policy in Japan' [1997] Fordham Corporate Law Institute (ed Hawk), ch 5.
16 (1994-2) Trade Cases (CCH) ¶ 70,482 (1994); for comment see Byowitz 'The Unilateral Use of US Antitrust Laws to Achieve Foreign Market Access: A Pragmatic Assessment' [1996] Fordham Corporate Law Institute (ed Hawk), ch 3.
17 See ch 13, p 417, n 11.

3. THE EXTRATERRITORIAL APPLICATION OF EC COMPETITION LAW[18]

Many non-EC undertakings have been held to have infringed the EC competition rules. The ECJ has not yet ruled whether there is an effects doctrine under EC law, since it has always been possible in cases under Articles 81 and 82 to base jurisdiction on some other ground, such as the economic entity doctrine or the fact that an agreement entered into outside the Community was implemented within it. In both the *Dyestuffs*[19] and *Wood Pulp*[20] cases the question of whether EC law should recognise the effects doctrine was argued at length, but the ECJ was able to avoid a pronouncement upon the issue since jurisdiction could be taken on one or other of these bases. The EC Merger Regulation ('the ECMR') has often been applied to mergers outside the Community; the CFI has given an important judgment on the territorial application of the ECMR in *Gencor v Commission*[1], but again without explicitly adopting the effects doctrine[2]. This section will deal with subject-matter and enforcement jurisdiction under Articles 81 and 82, and will then discuss the position under the ECMR.

(A) Subject-matter jurisdiction

Articles 81 and 82 apply only to the extent that an agreement or abuse have an effect upon inter-state trade. However there is no reason in principle why, for example, conduct by a US firm might not satisfy this test, particularly given the liberal way in which it has been applied[3]. In *Javico v Yves St Laurent*[4] the ECJ held that it was possible that an export ban imposed upon distributors in the Ukraine and Russia could infringe Article 81(1)[5].

(i) The economic entity doctrine

In the *Dyestuffs* case[6] the ECJ developed the economic entity doctrine. The Court came to the conclusion that Geigy, Sandoz and ICI, three non-EC undertakings, had participated in illegal price fixing within the EC through the medium of subsidiary companies located in the EC but under the control of non-EC parents. The ECJ was willing to go beyond the legal façade of the separate legal personalities of the parent and subsidiary companies, and to say that in reality each parent and subsidiary formed one economic entity. This approach was criticised, not only because of the refusal to respect the independent legal personalities of the companies concerned, but also because the ECJ seemed

---

18 See Allen 'The Development of EC Antitrust Jurisdiction over Alien Undertakings' [1974] 2 L1E1 35; Kuyper 'European Community Law and Extraterritoriality: Some Trends and Recent Developments' (1984) 33 ICLQ 1013; Slot and Grabandt 'Extraterritoriality and Jurisdiction' (1986) 23 CML Rev 544; Brittan 'Jurisdictional Issues in EC Competition Policy' in *Merger Control in the Single European Market* (Grotius Publications, 1991).
19 Cases 48/69 etc *ICI v Commission* [1972] ECR 619, [1972] CMLR 557.
20 Cases 114/85 etc *A Ahlström Oy v Commission* [1988] ECR 5193, [1988] 4 CMLR 901.
1 Case T-102/96 [1999] ECR II-753, [1999] 4 CMLR 971.
2 See pp 402-403 below.
3 See ch 3, pp 110-120.
4 Case C-306/96 [1998] ECR I-1983, [1998] 5 CMLR 172.
5 See ch 3, p 119.
6 See n 19 above.

prepared to hold that a parent controlled its subsidiary on limited evidence[7]; however the economic entity doctrine is now undoubtedly a part of EC competition law. The Community Courts and the Commission have relied on the economic entity approach on a number of subsequent occasions, both in the subject-matter and enforcement jurisdiction contexts[8]. The crucial issue is whether the parent controls the subsidiary, for which purpose the size of the shareholding, the representation on the board of directors of the subsidiary, the ability to influence the latter's affairs and actual evidence of attempts to do so will all be relevant[9].

(ii) Does EC law recognise the effects doctrine?

Many of the Commission's decisions have involved and been addressed to non-EC undertakings[10], but in every case the non-EC firm, either itself or through a subsidiary company[11], entered into an agreement with an EC undertaking[12] or committed some act within the EC. In other words jurisdiction in these cases did not depend upon the existence in Community law of an effects doctrine, since it could be explained in more orthodox ways. The Commission has quite often asserted that Community law does indeed recognise the effects doctrine[13], and this belief was supported by Advocate General Mayras in the *Dyestuffs* case[14] and by Advocate General Darmon in *Wood Pulp*[15]; other Advocates General have also appeared to support this view[16]. However there has been no definitive statement from the ECJ on this issue.

(iii) The ECJ's judgment in Wood Pulp

Against this background the appeal to the ECJ against the Commission's decision in *Wood Pulp*[17] was eagerly awaited. The Commission, in finding that there was a concerted practice between undertakings in several non-EC countries, had held that jurisdiction could be based on the effects of the concerted practice in the EC.

---

7   On *Dyestuffs* see Mann 'The Dyestuffs Case in the Court of Justice of the European Communities' (1973) 22 ICLQ 35; Acevedo 'The EC Dyestuffs Case: Territorial Jurisdiction' (1973) 36 MLR 317.

8   The doctrine may be used to overcome any perceived difficulty in sending a decision to a company in a non-EC State by serving instead on the EC subsidiary.

9   See ch 3, pp 72–74.

10 See eg *Genuine Vegetable Parchments Association* OJ [1978] L 70/54, [1978] 1 CMLR 534; *Zinc Producer Group* OJ [1984] L 220/27, [1985] 2 CMLR 108; *Associated Lead Manufacturers* OJ [1979] L 21/16, [1979] 1 CMLR 464; *Cast Iron and Steel Rolls* OJ [1983] L 317/1, [1984] 1 CMLR 694; in each of these cases a non-EC firm was fined.

11 See eg *Johnson and Johnson* OJ [1980] L 377/16, [1981] 2 CMLR 287.

12 See eg *French-Japanese Ballbearings* OJ [1974] L 343/19, [1975] 1 CMLR D8; *Franco-Taiwanese Mushroom Packers* OJ [1975] L 29/26, [1975] 1 CMLR D83.

13 See eg the XIth *Report on Competition Policy* (1981), points 34–42; the Commission's decisions in *Wood Pulp* OJ [1985] L 85/1, [1985] 3 CMLR 474 and *Aluminium Products* OJ [1985] L 92/1, [1987] 3 CMLR 813 were explicitly adopted on the basis of the effects doctrine.

14 Cases 48/69 etc [1972] ECR 619, pp 687–694, [1972] CMLR 557, pp 593–609.

15 Cases 114/85 etc *A Ahlström Oy v Commission* [1988] ECR 5193, p 5227, [1988] 4 CMLR 901, p 932.

16 See eg Advocate General Roemer in Case 6/72 *Continental Can v Commission* [1973] ECR 215, [1972] CMLR 690; Advocate General Warner in Cases 6/73, 7/73 *Commercial Solvents v Commission* [1974] ECR 223, [1974] 1 CMLR 309.

17 OJ [1985] L 85/1, [1985] 3 CMLR 474.

However the ECJ, no doubt keen to avoid the adoption of this controversial doctrine if possible, concluded that the case could be settled by reference to conventional public international law criteria. It held[18] that, on the facts of the case, the agreement had been *implemented* within the EC; it was immaterial for this purpose whether this implementation was effected by subsidiaries, agents, sub-agents or branches within the Community. Since the agreement was implemented within the Community, it was unnecessary to have recourse to the effects doctrine: the universally recognised territoriality principle was sufficient to deal with the matter. The ECJ did not comment on what the position would have been if the agreement had been formed *and implemented* outside the EC, but had produced economic effects within it; an example would be a collective boycott by members of a non-EC cartel, whereby they refuse to supply customers within the EC: could one argue in such circumstances that this agreement is 'implemented' within the EC by the refusal to supply there? Linguistically this seems hard to sustain; however there is no doubt in this situation that the *effects* of the agreement would be felt within the EC. This issue is unresolved. However there will be relatively few cases in which the pure effects doctrine is crucial in jurisdictional terms: in most cases the economic entity doctrine or the reasoning of the ECJ in *Wood Pulp* will be sufficient to establish jurisdiction.

(B)   Enforcement jurisdiction

(i)   Initiating proceedings

Where proceedings are started by the Commission under Articles 81 or 82, Article 3 of Regulation 2842/98[19] requires that the undertakings concerned must be informed. If the undertaking cannot be served within the EC, the question arises whether a statement of objections may be sent to it abroad. As suggested above this could be considered to contravene public international law, since it amounts to an enforcement of one State's law in the territory of another[20]. However the ECJ has rejected the notion that service without the consent of the foreign State is invalid and vitiates the proceedings. Provided that the non-EC undertaking has received the statement in circumstances which enabled it to take cognizance of the objections held against it, the service is valid. In *Geigy v Commission*[1] the Commission sent its statement of objections to Geigy's Swiss offices. Geigy returned it, acting on instructions from the Swiss authorities, claiming that the service was unlawful both under internal and public international law. The ECJ rejected this. It is sufficient for Community law purposes, therefore, for the Commission to send a registered letter to the non-EC undertaking concerned.

18   Cases 114/85 etc *A Ahlström Oy v Commission* [1988] ECR 5193, [1988] 4 CMLR 901 paras 11–23; for comment see Ferry 'Towards Completing the Charm: the *Wood Pulp* Judgment' (1989) 11 EIPR 19; Mann 'The Public International Law of Restrictive Trade Practices in the European Court of Justice' (1989) 38 ICLQ 375; Lowe 'International Law and the Effects Doctrine in the European Court of Justice' (1989) 48 CLJ 9; Christoforou and Rockwell 'EC Law: the Territorial Scope of Application of EC Antitrust Law – the *Wood Pulp* Judgment' (1989) 30 Harvard International Law Journal 195; Lange and Sandage 'The *Wood Pulp* Decision and its Implications for the Scope of EC Competition Law' (1989) 26 CML Rev 137; Van Gerven 'EC Jurisdiction in Antitrust Matters: the *Wood Pulp* Judgment' [1989] Fordham Corporate Law Institute (ed Hawk), ch 21.
19   OJ [1998] L 354/18, [1999] 4 CMLR 228.
20   It is arguable that the *initiation* of proceedings is not an issue of enforcement, as it is not in itself a coercive act.
1   See Case 52/69 [1972] ECR 787, [1972] CMLR 557 (one of the *Dyestuffs* cases).

(ii)   Information and investigations

The ECJ has not been called upon to consider the extent to which the Commission may require information from or conduct investigations of undertakings abroad under Articles 11 and 14 respectively of Regulation 17/62[2] (or the equivalent regulations in the transport sector)[3]. There would seem to be little objection to the Commission simply asking for information under Article 11(3), there being no compulsion to comply with such a request; in practice the Commission does send Article 11(3) requests to non-EC undertakings. It is less certain whether the Commission can make a demand for information under Article 11(5) of the Regulation, and the better view is that this is not possible. It is inconceivable that Article 14 entitles the Commission to carry out an investigation abroad, unless it has the authority of the State concerned. However the fact that the Commission intends to investigate a trade association within the EC which represents non-EC undertakings does not entitle that association to refuse to submit to the investigation[4]; and if the Commission carries out an investigation in a new Member State of the EC and discovers information relating to infringements carried out by undertakings prior to that State's accession to the Community, the Commission is entitled to take that information into account[5]. The Commission will not be sympathetic to the argument that a non-EC undertaking is unable to provide it with information because of some constraint imposed upon it by its domestic law[6].

(iii)   Final decisions

Two issues arise. First, there is the problem of whether a final decision, for example finding an infringement of the competition rules and imposing penalties, may be served on non-EC undertakings. This is more an act of enforcement than merely serving a statement of objections, and so is more open to objection in terms of public international law. For this reason the Commission will often look to serve the decision on a subsidiary within the EC, as it did in the *Dyestuffs* cases, or seek the assistance of the foreign State concerned[7]. However the ECJ has held that service direct upon the non-EC undertaking is valid provided that, as in the case of a statement of objections, it reaches the undertaking and enables it to take cognizance of it. It is no defence that the undertaking received the decision and sent it back without reading it.

The second problem is whether it is possible for the final decision to include orders against and impose penalties upon an overseas undertaking. It is clear

---

2   In Case 27/76 *United Brands Continental BV v Commission* [1978] ECR 207, [1978] 1 CMLR 429 the ECJ suggested at one point that the Commission might have obtained some information which it needed from United Brands; however United Brands had subsidiaries within the EC, so that it cannot be deduced from this remark that the ECJ was advocating extraterritorial requests for information under Article 11(3).

3   See ch 7, pp 219-226.

4   *Ukwal* OJ [1992] L 121/45 [1993] 5 CMLR 632.

5   Cases 97–99/87 *Dow Chemical Ibérica SA v Commission* [1989] ECR 3165, [1991] 4 CMLR 410, paras 61–65.

6   See *Centraal Stikstof Verkoopkantoor (CSV)* OJ [1976] L 192/27.

7   In the *Dyestuffs* cases the Commission tried in the first place to serve the final decision on the non-EC undertakings by using diplomatic channels; only when this failed did it serve the EC subsidiaries.

that the ECJ does not object to orders being made against foreign undertakings[8], although it is recognised by both the Commission and the Community Courts that it would not be possible actually to enforce the order in the territory of a foreign State. It would however be possible to seize any assets that were present within the EC.

(C)   EC Merger Regulation

(i)   *The jurisdictional criteria in the ECMR*

Under Article 1(2) of the ECMR[9], concentrations that have a Community dimension must be pre-notified to the Commission in Brussels. Concentrations have a Community dimension where the combined turnover of the undertakings involved exceeds EUR 5,000 million worldwide, provided that at least two of the undertakings have a turnover within the Community of at least EUR 250 million and that their business is not primarily within one and the same Member State[10]; an alternative set of criteria were inserted into the ECMR by Regulation 1310/97 in an attempt to deal with the problem of multiple notification to Member States[11]. The jurisdictional criteria in the ECMR clearly mean that concentrations involving undertakings which conduct a very substantial proportion of their business outside the EC, or which involve transactions far removed physically from the EC, may, nevertheless, have a Community dimension. Countless numbers of concentrations that have little or no effect within the Community have to be notified because of the operation of the thresholds in the ECMR. For example a joint venture between two substantial undertakings that brings about a merger of their widget businesses in Thailand could be notifiable under the ECMR, even though the joint venture will have no presence or effect on the EC market, if the parents exceed the turnover thresholds in Article 1. Cases such as this may, however, benefit from the simplified procedure introduced for the speedy disposal of some notifications under the ECMR in 2000[12].

(ii)   *Gencor v Commission*

In *Gencor/Lonrho*[13] the Commission prohibited a merger between two South African undertakings on the basis that it would have created a dominant duopoly (collective dominance) in the platinum and rhodium markets, as a result of which

---

8   See eg Cases 6/73 & 7/73 *Commercial Solvents v Commission* [1974] ECR 223, [1974] 1 CMLR 309 where the ECJ upheld the Commission's order that supplies to Zoja be resumed; this would clearly affect CSC in the US; see also *Warner-Lambert/Gillette* OJ [1993] L 116/21, [1993] 5 CMLR 559, where the Commission ordered the Gillette Company of the US to reassign trade marks in third countries to Eemland Holdings NV in order to remove distortions of competition within the EC; the decision was not appealed to the CFI.
9   Council Regulation 4064/89; see ch 21, p 738ff for a general discussion of this Regulation.
10   The thresholds are considered in detail in ch 21, pp 751-756.
11   See ch 21, p 752 on Article 1(3) of the ECMR.
12   See the Commission's *Notice on a Simplified Procedure for Treatment of Certain Concentrations under Council Regulation (EEC) No 4064/89* OJ [2000] C 217/32, [2000] 5 CMLR 774; this procedure is explained briefly in ch 21, p 767; for discussion generally of the application of the ECMR to non-EC concentrations, see Ezrachi 'Limitations on the Extraterritorial Reach of the European Merger Regulation' (2001) 22 ECLR 137.
13   OJ [1997] L 11/30, [1999] 4 CMLR 1076.

competition would be significantly impeded in the common market[14]. Gencor appealed to the CFI, *inter alia* on the ground that the Commission did not have jurisdiction under the ECMR to prohibit activities in South Africa which, furthermore, the Government there had approved. In *Gencor v Commission*[15] the CFI upheld the Commission's decision, and reviewed at some length the jurisdictional position[16]. The Court's findings on jurisdiction were divided into two parts, first an assessment of the territorial scope of the ECMR[17] and secondly a consideration of the compatibility of the Commission's decision with public international law[18]. As to the former, the CFI noted that the parties to the merger exceeded the turnover thresholds in Article 1(2) of the ECMR. It acknowledged that Recital 11 of the Regulation required that the parties should have substantial operations in the Community, but stated that these operations could as well consist of sales as production. The Court added that the *Wood Pulp* judgment, requiring 'implementation' within the Community, did not contradict the Commission's assertion of jurisdiction in this case: indeed the requirement in Article 1(2) of the ECMR, that the parties should have turnover in excess of EUR 250 million within the Community, was consistent with the *Wood Pulp* judgment, since it meant that they must have acted in some way on the EC market.

On the issue of public international law, the CFI said that application of the ECMR is justified under public international law where it is foreseeable that a proposed concentration will have an immediate and substantial effect in the Community[19]. The Court's view was that these criteria were satisfied, but went on to consider whether the exercise of jurisdiction in this case 'violated a principle of non-interference or the principle of proportionality'[20]: in other words it acknowledged that comity analysis should be undertaken when applying the ECMR. The Court's view was that neither principle was violated, so that there was no jurisdictional objection to the Commission's decision.

Clearly this judgment is of considerable significance. It will be noted that the CFI did not adopt an effects doctrine *as a matter of Community law*, since it determined the Commission's subject-matter jurisdiction on the basis of the turnover thresholds in the ECMR and equated them to the 'implementation doctrine' in *Wood Pulp*; rather the CFI considered the effects of the merger, and the possible comity objections to jurisdiction, as a matter of public international law. As in the case of the ECJ's judgments in *Dyestuffs* and *Wood Pulp*, the CFI avoided the adoption of the effects doctrine. In practice, of course, the Commission could have great problems in enforcing a prohibition decision against non-EC undertakings which are unwilling to cooperate and which are protected by their national Governments. However the Commission works very closely with the competition authorities in other jurisdictions, and in particular with the Department of Justice and the Federal Trade Commission in the US, in order to try to prevent serious conflicts breaking out. However it is not always possible to avoid disputes, as the high-profile cases of *Boeing/McDonnell Douglas*[1] in 1997 and *GE/Honeywell*[2] in 2001 demonstrate.

14   See ch 14, pp 486-488 for a discussion of the finding of collective dominance in this case.
15   Case T-102/96 [1999] ECR II-753, [1999] 4 CMLR 971; for comment, see Fox 'The Merger Regulation and Its Territorial Reach: *Gencor Ltd v Commission*' (1999) 20 ECLR 334.
16   Case T-102/96 [1999] ECR II-753, [1999] 4 CMLR 971, paras 48-111.
17   Ibid, paras 78-88.
18   Ibid, paras 89-111.
19   Ibid, para 90.
20   Ibid, para 102.
1   Case No IV/M.877 OJ [1997] L 336/16; see pp 411-413 below for discussion of EC/US cooperation, including this case.
2   Case No COMP/M.2220.

4.   THE EXTRATERRITORIAL APPLICATION OF UK COMPETITION LAW

The view has always been taken in the UK that jurisdiction cannot be based simply upon commercial effects, but that the territoriality and nationality principles alone are applicable in this area. This is clearly stated in the Aide-Memoire which the UK Government submitted to the ECJ following the Commission's decision in the *Dyestuffs* litigation[3], and is further illustrated by the Protection of Trading Interests Act 1980 which is considered later in this chapter. The submissions of the UK Government in the *Wood Pulp* case maintained its traditional hostility to the effects doctrine. The competition law statutes themselves do not always deal explicitly with jurisdictional issues, but, even where they do not do so, in practice they are not applied extraterritorially on the basis of effects.

(A)   Competition Act 1998

(i)   Chapter I prohibition

The Chapter I prohibition in the Competition Act 1998 has been discussed in chapter 9[4]. On the issue of jurisdiction section 2(1), which sets out the Chapter I prohibition, provides that an agreement will be caught only where it may affect trade and competition within the UK. This in itself does not answer the jurisdictional issue of whether the Act is applicable to undertakings that are located outside the UK. The answer to this question is given by section 2(3), which provides that:

> 'Subsection (1) applies only if the agreement, decision or practice is, or is intended to be, implemented in the UK.'

Section 2(3) is specifically intended to give legislative effect in the UK to the 'implementation doctrine' espoused by the ECJ in the *Wood Pulp* case[5]. This is a sensible resolution on the part of the Government: as already mentioned, the *Wood Pulp* doctrine falls short of being an 'effects doctrine', with the result that section 2(3) does not amount to a reversal of the traditional attitude of the UK described above. At the same time, the 1998 Act is able to adopt a position in relation to jurisdiction which is consistent with EC law as set out in *Wood Pulp*. It follows that agreements implemented in the UK by non-UK undertakings would be caught by the Chapter I prohibition, provided that they meet all the other requirements. What would be interesting in the future would be a situation in which the ECJ extends the jurisdictional reach of the competition rules to include an effects doctrine. In such a situation, the basic rule in section 60 of the Competition Act, that there should be no inconsistency between interpretation of the UK legislation and the principles laid down in the Treaty and by the Community Courts, would suggest that the UK should adopt the effects doctrine.

3   Cases 48/69 *ICI Ltd v Commission* [1972] ECR 619, [1972] CMLR 557. The Aide-Memoire is produced in full in *Lowe* pp 144–147; details are given there of various diplomatic exchanges between the US and UK Governments on jurisdictional conflicts and other expressions of the UK's views at pp 147–186; see also the UK Government's Amicus Curiae brief in *Washington Public Power Supply System v Western Nuclear Inc* [1983] ECC 261.
4   See ch 9, pp 291-314.
5   HL Committee, 13 November 1997, col 261 (Lord Simon of Highbury).

However, section 60(1) of the Act specifically provides that consistency must be achieved, 'having regard to any relevant differences between the provisions concerned'[6]. Presumably this would be a situation in which the clear wording of section 2(3) would indicate a relevant difference between the 1998 Act and the new case law of the ECJ, with the consequence that the UK authorities would not be required under the Act to adopt the effects doctrine. The DGFT's guidelines are silent on the issue of extraterritoriality, which perhaps is itself indicative of the delicate and complex nature of this issue.

(ii) Chapter II prohibition

The Chapter II prohibition has also been discussed in chapter 9[7]. There is no mention of extraterritorial application in section 18, which sets out the Chapter II prohibition, and in particular there is no equivalent of section 2(3) which limits the ambit of the Chapter I prohibition to agreements that are implemented in the UK. Section 18(3) does require that the dominant position must be within the UK. In the debate during the passage of the Bill Lord Simon explained that this would not be the case if the market in which the dominant position is held was entirely outside the UK; however there could be a case in which the dominant position extends beyond the UK, provided that it includes some part of the UK territory[8].

An interesting question is whether the Chapter II prohibition would apply in a case where the dominant position is (wholly or partly) within the UK but the abuse occurs in a related market outside the UK, or its effects are felt entirely outside the UK (for example a refusal by a UK company to supply an overseas customer). Here the requirement that trade must be affected within the UK would come into play and determine whether the prohibition applies.

(B) Fair Trading Act 1973

(i) Monopoly situations[9]

Subject-matter jurisdiction could be taken over foreign undertakings under this Act. For example under section 6(1)(a), which defines monopoly situations in relation to goods, a monopoly situation shall be taken to exist where at least one quarter of the goods of a certain description supplied in the UK are supplied by one and the same person. That person might be established abroad, but section 6(1)(a) would still be satisfied. Similarly, under section 6(1)(d) a monopoly situation shall be taken to exist in relation to goods if, as a result of an agreement, no goods of a particular description are supplied in the UK at all[10]. Such an agreement might infringe the Chapter I prohibition of the Competition Act 1998, in which case that Act would apply. However the monopoly provisions could, perhaps, catch the case of a foreign cartel which agrees to boycott UK purchasers, a situation which would appear to escape the Chapter I prohibition for want of

6   See ch 9, pp 329-333.
7   See ch 9, pp 314-321.
8   HL Third Reading, 5 March 1998, col 1336 (Lord Simon of Highbury).
9   The monopoly provisions of the Fair Trading Act 1973 are described in ch 11.
10 See similarly s 7(1)(a) and (d) respectively in relation to services.

'implementation' in the UK[11]. However it is a discretionary matter whether a particular monopoly situation is referred to the Competition Commission and it can be assumed, given the traditional UK view of jurisdiction, that an investigation would not be launched unless some serious issue of conduct within the UK was involved. Foreign firms have been considered in various monopoly investigations, but only to the extent that they have acted on the UK market[12]; an example of such an investigation is *Razors and Razor Blades*[13], discussed in the context of merger investigations below[14].

As far as enforcement powers are concerned, under sections 44 to 46 of the Fair Trading Act 1973 the DGFT can require information from persons within the UK by or to whom goods or services are supplied. There is no explicit provision that these powers cannot be exercised against persons not resident in the UK, but it is highly unlikely that they would be. Section 85 of the Act, which allows the Commission when conducting an investigation to require any person to attend, to give evidence, to produce documents and to provide information, does not limit these powers to persons within the jurisdiction; however the Commission has taken the view that it has no power to require evidence from overseas affiliates of companies whose activities in the UK are being investigated[15].

The Secretary of State's powers to make an interim[16] or final[17] order following a monopoly investigation are limited by section 90(3) of the Act. It provides that nothing in an order under the Act shall apply to a person's conduct outside the UK unless that person is a UK citizen, a company incorporated in the UK or a person carrying on business in the UK[18]. In the case of any such person, an order may extend to acts or omissions outside the UK. This is a statutory embodiment of the orthodox territoriality and nationality principles to which the UK adheres and which were described above.

(ii)   Mergers[19]

Section 64(1) of the Act provides that merger references may be made to the Commission where two or more enterprises cease to be distinct and where at least one of them was carried on in the UK, provided that certain other criteria are satisfied. The enforcement powers in merger cases are the same as those already described in the context of monopoly situations[20]. There have been various occasions on which overseas undertakings have been required to divest themselves of their interest in UK undertakings[1].

It may be that the events leading to a qualifying merger are themselves extraterritorial. For example in *Stora Koppabergs Bergslags AB/Swedish Match*

---

11   See p 404 above.
12   See eg *Chlordiazepoxide and Diazepam* HCP (1972–73) 197.
13   Cm 1472 (1991).
14   See pp 404-407 below.
15   *Chlordiazepoxide and Diazepam* HCP (1972–73) 197, para 208.
16   FTA 1973, s 89.
17   Ibid, s 56.
18   Section 90(3) does not say specifically that no order can be made against *other* persons than those mentioned in the section, but this must be implicit.
19   The merger provisions of the Fair Trading Act 1973 are described in ch 22.
20   See pp 405-406 above.
1   Apart from the *Gillette* case (below), see eg *MiTek Industries Inc/Gang-Nail Systems Inc* Cm 429 (1988); *Government of Kuwait/British Petroleum plc* Cm 477 (1988).

NV and Stora Koppabergs Bergslags AB/The Gillette Co[2] a merger had taken place between the Gillette group and Swedish Match NV, a Dutch company which itself controlled Wilkinson Sword, Gillette's main competitor in the UK. The Commission concluded that the merger (and the corresponding monopoly situation of Gillette[3]) could be expected to operate against the public interest, and recommended that Gillette UK Ltd should dispose of its equity interest in Swedish Match NV and all preemption and conversion rights. A draft order was prepared in 1992 to carry out the Commission's recommendation, but the matter was settled without its adoption. In accordance with the traditional UK view of territoriality, the order would have been addressed to two UK companies, Gillette UK Ltd and Lustrasilk International UK Ltd (an associated company); paragraph 1(3) of the draft order specified that it would extend to acts and omissions of these two UK companies outside the UK.

5. RESISTANCE TO EXTRATERRITORIAL APPLICATION OF COMPETITION LAW

(A) Introduction

The judgment of the Supreme Court in *United States v Aluminium Co of America*[4] triggered off a number of battles between the US and other States which objected to the extraterritorial application of US antitrust laws[5]. Apart from diplomatic protests, several countries have passed 'blocking statutes', whereby they attempt to thwart excessive assumptions of jurisdiction[6]. There are no provisions in EC law which have this effect: the Commission considers that this is essentially a matter for the Governments of individual Member States. The UK has taken a consistently hostile view of US practice, which culminated in the Protection of Trading Interests Act 1980.

The earliest attempt made by the UK Government to prevent the extraterritorial application of US law came in 1952[7]; thereafter it secured the passage of the Shipping Contracts and Commercial Documents Act 1964, the provisions of which were used on several occasions to prevent disclosure of information to US authorities[8]. The courts in the UK have also objected to US practice. In *British Nylon Spinners v ICI*[9] the Court of Appeal ordered ICI not to comply with a court order in America, requiring it to reassign certain patents to Du Pont; the US court considered that the parties were dividing the market horizontally. In *Rio Tinto Zinc v Westinghouse Electric Corpn*[10] the House of Lords declined to assist in the process of discovery in a US court, investigating an alleged uranium cartel, where it considered that the information so acquired would subsequently be used for an improper assertion of extraterritorial jurisdiction. The UK courts are obliged by the Evidence (Proceedings in Other Jurisdictions) Act 1975 to

2   Cm 1473 (1991).
3   See the separate report on *Razors and Razor Blades* Cm 1472 (1991).
4   See p 395 above.
5   See Griffin 'Foreign Governmental Reactions to US Assertions of Extraterritorial Jurisdiction' (1998) 19 ECLR 64, and the references in n 1 thereof.
6   See *Lowe* pp 79 et seq where he lists the many blocking statutes that have been passed; further blocking statutes have been passed since then.
7   See *Lowe* pp 138–139.
8   See *Lowe* pp 139–143.
9   [1955] Ch 37, [1954] 3 All ER 88, CA and [1953] Ch 19, [1952] 2 All ER 780, CA.
10   [1978] AC 547, [1978] 1 All ER 434, HL.

assist in requests for discovery by foreign courts. However the Act provides exceptions to this obligation, and the House of Lords considered that this case fell within these exceptions for two reasons: first, because the request for information was in reality a 'fishing expedition'; and secondly, because Rio Tinto might incriminate itself under EC competition law by divulging the documents sought.

The 1975 Act did not allow a court to resist a request for information simply because the foreign court was making a claim to extraterritorial jurisdiction; this is now dealt with by section 4 of the Protection of Trading Interests Act 1980 (below). At common law, a UK court has discretion to order a litigant to restrain foreign proceedings which are oppressive: in *Midland Bank plc v Laker Airways plc*[11] the Court of Appeal ordered Laker to discontinue proceedings against Midland Bank in the US which would have involved the extraterritorial application of US antitrust law. In *British Airways v Laker Airlines*[12], however, the House of Lords refused British Airway's application for a stay; in this case there was no doubt that BA was carrying on business in the US, so that it was subject to US law on conventional jurisdictional principles. If Laker were deprived of the opportunity to litigate in the US, it would have been unable to sue in the UK since it had no cause of action under UK law. In those circumstances the House of Lords was prepared to allow the US litigation to go ahead.

(B)   Protection of Trading Interests Act 1980

The Protection of Trading Interests Act 1980 contains wide-ranging provisions[13]. It is not limited to blocking US enforcement of antitrust laws, but may be invoked in any case in which US law is being applied in a way which could harm the commercial interests of the UK[14]. Section 1 enables the Secretary of State to make orders requiring UK firms to notify him of, and forbidding them to comply with, measures taken under the law of a foreign country affecting international trade and which threaten to damage the trading interests of the UK. This power has been exercised on three occasions[15]. The first order was not concerned with antitrust laws, but with the saga of the Siberian pipe-line[16]. The second was concerned with competition law, but not with the specific issue of extraterritoriality; the objection to the US action in question was that it involved a breach of Treaty obligations concerning air travel between the US and the UK[17].

11 [1986] QB 689, [1986] 1 All ER 526, CA.
12 [1985] AC 58, [1984] 3 All ER 39, HL.
13 See generally on this Act Huntley 'The Protection of Trading Interests Act – Some Jurisdictional Aspects of Enforcement of Antitrust Laws' (1981) 30 ICLQ 213; Lowe 'Blocking Extraterritorial Jurisdiction – The British Protection of Trading Interests Act 1980' (1981) 75 American Journal of International Law 257; Collins 'Blocking and Clawback Statutes: the UK Approach' [1986] JBL 372 and 452.
14 The Shipping Contracts and Commercial Documents Act 1964 could be invoked only where there was an infringement of UK *jurisdiction*; the 1980 Act is wider, as it applies where there is harm to UK commercial interests, whether there is an infringement of jurisdiction or not.
15 See the Protection of Trading Interests (US Re-export Control) Order 1982, SI 1982/885; the Protection of Trading Interests (US Antitrust Measures) Order 1983, SI 1983/900; and the Protection of Trading Interests (US Cuban Assets Control Regulations) Order 1992, SI 1992/2449.
16 See *Lowe* pp 197–219.
17 The vires of the Order in this case were challenged, unsuccessfully, by the plaintiff in the US antitrust action: see *British Airways Board v Laker Airways Ltd* [1984] QB 142, [1983] 3

Section 2 of the Act gives the Secretary of State power to prohibit compliance with a requirement by an overseas authority to submit commercial information to it which is not within its territorial jurisdiction. This provision replaces the Shipping and Commercial Documents Act 1964. Section 3 provides for the imposition of penalties upon anyone who fails to comply with orders under the foregoing provisions, but, consistently with the UK approach to these issues, these may be imposed only in accordance with the UK's conventional interpretation of the international law principles of territoriality and nationality. Section 4 provides that a UK court should not comply with a foreign tribunal's request for assistance in the discovery process where this would infringe UK sovereignty. This is statutory reinforcement of the House of Lords' judgment in *Rio Tinto Zinc v Westinghouse Electric Corpn*[18].

Section 5 provides that foreign multiple damages awards shall not be enforceable in the UK. This means that a plaintiff in the UK could not enforce a treble damages award obtained in the US[19]. Section 6 goes even further and provides that, where a UK defendant has actually paid US multiple damages, he may bring an action in the UK to 'claw back' the excess of such damages over the amount actually required to compensate the plaintiff. This provision symbolises the degree of antipathy in the UK towards various aspects of US antitrust practice.

6. THE INTERNATIONALISATION OF COMPETITION LAW

It is clearly unsatisfactory that there should be acrimonious disputes between States over the extraterritorial application of competition law. Principles of public international law do not provide an adequate answer to the problems that arise when true conflicts occur between competition authorities, and yet the scope for such conflicts is likely to increase as more States adopt their own codes of competition law and as business becomes increasingly international. Transnational mergers pose a particular problem where several competition authorities investigate the same transaction and have different perceptions of whether it should be permitted or not. A different, and more positive, point is that competition authorities have become increasingly aware that, since national systems of competition law are not always adequate to deal with cartels, anti-competitive practices and mergers that transcend national boundaries, international cooperation between them may increase the chances of achieving a successful solution. Many steps have been taken towards greater international cooperation between competition authorities, some of which are considered below. However there are complex issues to be confronted before a truly internationalised approach can be taken to the enforcement of competition law.

All ER 375, CA; on appeal [1985] AC 58, [1984] 3 All ER 39, HL; the House of Lords also reversed the Court of Appeal's decision that Laker should discontinue its US action against British Airways as this would mean there was no forum in which it could sue: see n 12 above.
18 [1978] AC 547, [1978] 1 All ER 434; see p 407 above.
19 At common law foreign judgments can normally be enforced in the UK but 'penal' judgments cannot be; note that under s 5 of the Act the whole sum is unenforceable, not just the penal element; one order has been made under s 5, the *Protection of Trading Interests Act (Australian Trade Practices) Order 1988*, SI 1988/569.

(A) UNCTAD

The United Nations Conference on Trade and Development ('UNCTAD') has taken an interest in the development of competition policy for many years. In 1980 it adopted a voluntary, non-binding code, *The Set of Multilaterally Agreed Equitable Principles and Rules for the Control of Restrictive Business Practices*', setting out suggested core principles to be adopted in systems of competition law. UNCTAD fulfils an important rôle in providing technical assistance to developing countries that have adopted, or intend to adopt, a domestic system of competition law.

(B) OECD

The Organisation for Economic Cooperation and Development ('the OECD') is active in matters of competition policy. In 1995 it published a *Revised Recommendation Concerning Cooperation between Member Countries on Restrictive Business Practices Affecting International Trade*[20] which provides for voluntary notification, consultation and cooperation in competition law cases involving the legitimate interests of foreign Governments; this Recommendation replaced an earlier one of 1986. The OECD has published numerous studies on aspects of competition policy, details of which can be found on its website[1]. In 1992 it commissioned research on the problems of international merger control, leading to the publication of a report containing some recommendations in 1994[2]. In 1998 the OECD published a *Recommendation on Hard-Core Cartels*[3].

(C) International cooperation agreements[4]

International cooperation between competition authorities has been advanced by the adoption of several bilateral and multilateral agreements. For example the United States has negotiated agreements in relation to competition law enforcement with Germany[5], Australia[6] and Canada[7]. US-Canadian cooperation is also facilitated by the Mutual Legal Assistance Treaty which applies to criminal law enforcement generally, but which can be used in relation to criminal law prosecutions in competition law cases[8]. The Closer Economic Relations Agreement, which entered into force between Australia and New Zealand on 1 January 1983[9], provides for close cooperation between those two countries, even allowing for one country to apply the other's law where it is appropriate to do

---

20 OECD Doc C(95) 130 (final), 27 July 1995.
1   http://www.oecd.org//daf/clp/.
2   *Merger Cases in the Real World* (OECD, 1994).
3   http://www.oecd.org//daf/clp/Recommendations/Rec9com.htm.
4   A useful summary of such agreements will be found in Parisi 'Enforcement Cooperation Among Antitrust Authorities' (1999) 20 ECLR 133.
5   4 Trade Reg Rep (CCH) para 13,501.
6   Ibid, para 13,502.
7   Ibid, para 13,503.
8   See Goldman and Kissack 'Current Issues in Cross-Border Criminal Investigations: A Canadian Perspective' [1995] Fordham Corporate Law Institute (ed Hawk) ch 4.
9   See Brunt 'Australian and New Zealand Competition Law and Policy' [1992] Fordham Corp L Inst (ed Hawk), ch 7.

so. Regional agreements have an important rôle to play in developing a cooperative approach to competition issues; the EC itself is an example of regional cooperation, and Chapter 15 of the North American Free Trade Agreement contains provisions for consultation, cooperation and coordination between the US, Canada and Mexico in matters of competition policy.

(D)   The EC/US Cooperation Agreements

Two Cooperation Agreements have been entered into between the EC and the US[10].

(i)   The Cooperation Agreement of 23 September 1991[11]

The first Cooperation Agreement was entered into on 23 September 1991[12]. The French Government successfully challenged the legal basis on which the Commission had proceeded, since the Council of Ministers should have been involved in the adoption of the Agreement[13]. The position was rectified by the adoption of a joint decision of the Council and the Commission of 10 April 1995[14].

The Agreement sets out detailed rules for cooperation on various aspects of the enforcement of EC and US competition law. Article II requires the competent authorities in each jurisdiction to notify each other whenever they become aware that their enforcement activities may affect important interests of the other party. Article II(3) contains special provisions on the timing of notifications in the case of mergers. Article III deals with the exchange of information between the authorities in each jurisdiction, and provides for regular meetings between officials of the EC and the US to discuss matters of mutual interest. Article IV deals with cooperation and coordination in enforcement activities, in relation to which each agency will assist the other. Article V is a novel provision going beyond Article IV, as it embodies the idea of 'positive comity': one agency may ask the other to take action in order to remedy anti-competitive behaviour in the *former's* territory[15]. The idea of positive comity is taken further in the second Cooperation Agreement, discussed below. Article VI requires the parties to avoid conflicts in enforcement activities, and lays down certain criteria that should be taken into account when an agency is deciding whether to proceed. These criteria reflect the principle of (negative) comity discussed in the context of the US 'jurisdictional rule of reason'[16]. Article VII of the Agreement requires the parties to consult with

---

10   The EC has also entered into a Cooperation Agreement with Canada, OJ [1999] L 175/49, [1999] 5 CMLR 713, and is in negotiations for one with Japan.

11   See Ham 'International Cooperation in the Antitrust Field and in particular the Agreement between the United States and the Commission of the European Communities' (1993) 30 CML Rev 571; Torremans 'Extraterritorial Application of EC and US Competition Law' (1996) 21 ELRev 280.

12   [1991] 4 CMLR 823.

13   Case C–327/91 *France v Commission* [1994] ECR I-3641, [1994] 5 CMLR 517: see Riley *Nailing the Jellyfish: the Illegality of the EC/US Government Competition Agreement* (1992) 13 ECLR 101 and again in (1995) 16 ECLR 185.

14   OJ [1995] L 95/45.

15   See Atwood 'Positive Comity – is it a Positive Step?' [1992] Fordham Corporate Law Institute (ed Hawk), ch 4.

16   See pp 395-396 above.

one another in relation to the matters dealt with by it. Article VIII provides that neither party to the Agreement can be required to provide information to the other where this is prohibited by the law of the party possessing it or where to do so would be incompatible with important interests of the party possessing it; furthermore each party agrees to keep the information it receives from the other confidential to the fullest extent possible. Article IX provides that neither party can be required to do anything under the Agreement that would be inconsistent with existing laws. The Agreement is terminable on 60 days' notice by either party.

(ii)   The Positive Comity Agreement of 4 June 1998

A second EC/US Cooperation Agreement was entered into on 4 June 1998, and develops the principle of positive comity in Article V of the first Agreement. The Council and the Commission gave their approval to the Positive Comity Agreement in a joint Decision of 29 May 1998[17]. Article I provides that the Agreement is to apply where one party can demonstrate to the other that anti-competitive activities are occurring within the latter's territory which are adversely affecting the interests of the former. Article II contains definitions; it is important to note that mergers do not fall within the scope of this Agreement as a result of the definition of 'competition law(s)' in Article II(4). Article III contains the principle of positive comity: the competition authorities of a 'Requesting Party' may request the authorities in the 'Requested Party' to investigate and, if warranted, to remedy anti-competitive activities in accordance with the latter's competition laws. Article IV provides that the Requesting Party may defer or suspend the application of its law while the Requested Party is applying its. Article V deals with confidentiality and the use of information. Article VI provides that the Positive Comity Agreement shall be interpreted consistently with the 1991 Agreement. The Positive Comity Agreement is terminable on 60 days' notice by either party.

(iii)   EC/US cooperation in practice

The Commission reports each year to the Council of Ministers and the Parliament on the application of the Cooperation Agreements[18], and these are also reproduced in its *Annual Report on Competition Policy*[19]. The Cooperation Agreements have been highly successful in practice. Cooperation between the competition authorities in the EC and the US is now a fact of daily life: if anything the degree of cooperation has probably been greater than could have been imagined in the early 1990s. A great deal of attention, including press coverage, is given to the few cases where there is real friction between the EC and the US, as in the cases

---

17   OJ [1998] L 173/26, [1999] 4 CMLR 502; the first case to be initiated on the basis of positive comity was *Sabre*: see the Commission's XXXth *Report on Competition Policy* (2000), point 453.

18   These can be accessed on DG COMP's website at http://europa.eu.int/comm/competition/international/bilateral/.

19   See eg the XXIXth *Annual Report on Competition Policy* (1999), pp 319-332; see also pp 333-335 on the EC/Canada Cooperation Agreement (see n 10 above).

of *Boeing/McDonnell Douglas*[20] and *GE/Honeywell*[1]. In the *Boeing* case the FTC in the US reached a majority decision not to oppose the merger, while the European Commission seemed likely, at one point, to prohibit it in its entirety; in the event commitments to modify the transaction were offered to the Commission with the result that it was given conditional clearance. Exceptional cases such as *Boeing/McDonnell Douglas* and *GE/Honeywell* ought not to obscure the fact that a large number of cases, particularly mergers, are successfully completed without any friction between the two jurisdictions. No matter how sophisticated the machinery for cooperation between the EC and the US, there will always be some cases in which there is disagreement as to the appropriate outcome. The success of the Cooperation Agreements should be assessed on the basis of how rare these cases are, and on this basis they have been very successful. It remains to be seen whether friction will increase in the future as a result of any ideological differences that may emerge between the Bush administration in the US and the position of the Commission in Europe.

(E)   The future

A huge amount of intellectual capital has been invested in recent years in the complex issues that arise from the profound changes, noted at the beginning of this chapter, in the global economy and from the proliferation of systems of competition law around the world. The relationship between competition and trade policy is a major subject in its own right, as is the debate as to the institutional mechanisms needed to deal with the new economic order[2]. Three particular issues will be discussed briefly below.

(i)   The WTO

The first is the rôle of the WTO in relation to competition policy. The post-war Havana Charter contained an antitrust code; however this was not incorporated into the General Agreement on Tariffs and Trade of 1947, the organisation from which the WTO developed. The WTO is predominantly concerned with trade,

---

20   Case IV/M.877 OJ [1997] L 336/16; for comment, see Bavasso '*Boeing/McDonnell Douglas*: Did the Commission Fly Too High?' (1998) 19 ECLR 243; Banks 'The Development of the Concept of Extraterritoriality under European Merger Law Following the *Boeing/McDonnell Douglas* Decision' (1998) 19 ECLR 306; Fiebig 'International Law Limits on the Extraterritorial Application of the European Merger Control Regulation and Suggestions for Reform' (1998) 19 ECLR 323.

1   Case COMP/M.2220.

2   The literature on these matters is vast, and the subject merits a separate book. Many of the issues are captured in an interesting series of essays in the Journal of International Economic Law for 1999, for example by Pitofsky 'Competition Policy in a Global Economy' (1999) 3 JIEL 403 and Roessler 'Should Principles of Competition Policy be Incorporated into WTO Law Through Non-Violation Complaints?' ibid, 413; see also Matsushita 'Reflections on Competition Policy/Law in the Framework of the WTO' [1997] Fordham Corporate Law Institute (ed Hawk), ch 4; *New Dimensions of Market Access in a Globalising World Economy* (OECD 1995), in particular the chapters in Part III on Trade and Competition Policies in the Global Market Place; a series of essays on the relationship between competition and trade policy will be found in [1998] Fordham Corporate Law Institute (ed Hawk), chs 13-19; see also Iacobucci 'The Interdependence of Trade and Competition Policies' (1997-98) 21(2) World Competition 5; see Rodgers 'Competition Policy, Liberalism and Globalisation: A European Perspective' (2000) 6 Columbia Journal of European Law 289.

rather than competition policy. The rules in the WTO do not impose obligations on companies in relation to competition. A working group has been established to examine the interaction between trade and competition policy. However it seems unlikely at the current stage of its development that the WTO will metamorphose into a global competition authority, not least because the US is staunchly opposed to such an idea.

(ii)   The ICPAC report

A very important contribution to the debate on the future of international competition policy is the *Final Report of the International Competition Policy Advisory Committee to the US Attorney General and Assistant Attorney General for Antitrust* (the so-called 'ICPAC Report'), published in February 2000[3]. The Report recommended that the US should explore the scope for collaboration among interested Governments and international agencies to create a new venue in which ideas could be exchanged and work undertaken towards common solutions of competition law and policy problems: the Report referred to this as the 'Global Competition Initiative'. The Initiative would foster dialogue in relation to a range of matters, including the multilateralisation and deepening of positive comity; the development of consensus principles on best practice in relation to phenomena such as hard-core cartels; consideration and review of the scope of governmental exemptions and immunities from competition law; rationalisation of systems of merger notification and review; new subjects such as e-commerce; collaborative analysis of issues such as global cartels; and, perhaps, the provision of dispute mediation and technical assistance services. This Report examined three particular issues: multi-jurisdictional mergers, the interface of trade and competition policies and anti-cartel enforcement and international cooperation.

(iii)   The Global Competition Forum

Following the ICPAC Report, a meeting took place at Ditchley Park in the UK at which the issues raised in it were debated by senior competition officials and practitioners from all over the world. From this there followed the establishment of a Global Competition Forum; the Forum is not a new institution, but rather is intended to act catalytically to bring together all interested parties, both public authorities and private parties including business, professional, consumer and academic bodies, to discuss the competition issues arising from the rapid transformation of the world economy. A particular concern of the Forum should be the position of developing countries and countries with fledgling systems of competition law. Its first meeting was scheduled to be held in Paris in October 2001.

3   Copies are available from the US Government Printing Office.

CHAPTER 13

Horizontal agreements (1) – cartels

The previous chapters have described the main principles of EC and UK competition law. The focus of attention in this and the following chapters is different. Instead of looking at the individual provisions of competition law, such as Articles 81 and 82 of the EC Treaty and the Chapter I and II prohibitions in the UK Competition Act 1998, a contextual approach will be adopted and the application of the law to various types of agreements and business practices will be analysed.

There are 11 'contextual' chapters. The first three consider horizontal issues: first, cartels; then the 'problem' of tacit collusion and oligopoly; and lastly horizontal cooperation agreements that the competition authorities might be willing to countenance. Chapter 16 deals with vertical agreements. Chapters 17 and 18 analyse practices that might be found to be abusive under Article 82 EC and/or the Chapter II prohibition in the Competition Act 1998; the possible application of the UK Fair Trading Act 1973 to such practices will also be briefly considered. Chapter 19 considers the relationship between intellectual property rights and competition law. In each of these chapters the primary focus will be on EC law, although the final section of each one will consider the position in the UK. Chapters 20 to 22 deal with merger control in the EC and UK, and the book concludes with a discussion of how competition law impacts on specific sectors of the economy, in particular so-called utilities such as telecommunications, postal services and energy markets.

1. THE HARDENING ATTITUDE OF COMPETITION AUTHORITIES TOWARDS CARTELS

Horizontal agreements between independent undertakings to fix prices, divide markets and to restrict output are perhaps the most obvious target for any system of competition law and they are prohibited by both EC and UK law[1]. So too are horizontal agreements which are designed to foreclose competition from other

---

1 For a general discussion of cartels and competition law, see Guerrin and Kyriazis 'Cartels: Proof and Procedural Issues' [1992] Fordham Corporate Law Institute (ed Hawk), ch 29; Joshua 'Attitudes to Anti-Trust Enforcement in the EU and US: Dodging the Traffic Warden, or Respecting the Law?' [1995] Fordham Corporate Law Institute (ed Hawk), ch 8.

firms in order to protect the privileged position of the cartel members. This chapter deals with these 'hard-core' cartels, although where appropriate it will be pointed out that even these most blatant restrictions of competition may, in exceptional circumstances, have compensating advantages of which account should be taken[2].

A particularly noticeable feature of competition policy in recent years – not only in Europe but also in the United States, Canada and elsewhere – has been that competition authorities generally are taking a much keener interest in the eradication of hard-core cartels. There have been and continue to be fierce debates about many issues in competition policy: for example the appropriate treatment of vertical agreements, 'abusive' pricing by dominant firms, refusals to supply, the inter-relationship of competition law and intellectual property rights and the standards for intervention against mergers. However if competition policy is about one thing, it is surely about the condemnation of horizontal price fixing, market sharing and analogous practices: on both a moral and practical level, there is not a great deal of difference between price fixing and theft; US law has for many decades treated hard-core cartels as *per se* infringements of the Sherman Act and as criminal offences, punishable, *inter alia*, by imprisonment. Investigation of and argumentation about the other issues mentioned above may afford greater intellectual stimulation to inhabitants of the world of competition policy, but pursuit of the hum-drum cartel ought to lie at the heart of any competition authority's agenda.

In several of the countries of the OECD – for example the US, Canada, Ireland, Japan, Korea, Norway, France and Greece – criminal sanctions, including in some cases terms of imprisonment, can be imposed on individuals where they bear responsibility for the operation of hard-core cartels. As a deterrent, there is no question that in the US, for example, being in prison rather than with the family on Thanksgiving Day is going to have a greater deterrent effect than the imposition of a corporate fine, no matter how large that fine might be. There are no criminal sanctions in the EC, but substantial fines can be imposed on undertakings[3]; in the UK there are no criminal sanctions for anti-competitive behaviour, although offences may be committed by individuals who, for example, provide inaccurate information to the competition authorities or obstruct competition investigations[4].

(A)   Recent cartel cases in the US[5]

Enforcement activity against cartels has been particularly severe in recent years in the US. It is easy to trace the progress of these cases on the website of the Department of Justice, in particular through its Press Releases[6]. In the case of *Vitamins*, several executives of Hoffmann-La Roche of Switzerland and BASF of Germany agreed to plead guilty, to serve sentences of imprisonment in the US

2   See eg the block exemption for horizontal price fixing in the transport of containerised cargo in the maritime transport sector: p 432 below and ch 23, p 861.
3   See ch 7, pp 237-239.
4   See ch 10, pp 348-357; criminal penalties may be introduced in the UK in due course: see *Productivity and Enterprise: A World Class Competition Régime* (Cm 5233, 2001), ch 7.
5   See Griffin 'An Inside View of an International Cartel at Work' in *Fighting Cartels – Why and How?* (Swedish Competition Authority, 2001) for a discussion of recent action in the US and, specifically, for an account of the investigation of the lysine cartel; for discussion of US law on price fixing, see Scherer and Ross *Industrial Market Structure and Economic Performance* (Houghton Mifflin, 3rd ed, 1990) ch 9.
6   http://www.usdoj.gov/atr/public/press_releases/2001/index01.htm.

and to pay personal fines for their rôles in the cartel[7]; the total fines in this case amounted to $1 billion. The European Commission began an investigation of the same cartel under Article 81 EC, sending out statements of objections in the summer of 2000. In *Graphite Electrodes* a former executive of UCAR International agreed to serve a 17-month jail term and to pay a personal fine for conspiring to fix the price and allocate the volume of graphite electrodes sold in the US and elsewhere; the total fines imposed in this case amounted to $434 million[8]. In the case of *Lysine* three jail sentences and fines of $120 million were imposed[9], and in *Citric Acid* fines of $85 million[10]. In August 2000 a German company, Holzmann, was sentenced to pay a fine of $30 million for its part in a conspiracy to rig bids on construction contracts funded by the US in Egypt[11]. In October 2000 the Department of Justice announced that Sothebys had agreed to pay a fine of $45 million for its participation in a price fixing cartel with Christies[12]; there remains a possibility that individuals involved in this case may have to serve terms of imprisonment. A browse through the Department of Justice's Press Releases will reveal many other actions against cartels, including a number of bid-rigging cases. The picture of vigorous enforcement is a very clear one.

(B) Cartels and globalisation

The OECD has pointed out that cartels are an increasingly international phenomenon and that they thwart the gains that should follow from global market liberalisation[13]. In its view, increased cooperation is needed between antitrust authorities to combat such cartels: cooperation, for example, between the EC, the US and Canada is now a notable and important feature of competition law enforcement[14]. In recent years several cartels have come to light which had a genuinely global reach: the vitamins and lysine cartels are obvious examples of this[15]. An anti-cartel enforcement workshop was held in the autumn of 1999 in the US, attended by representatives of competition authorities from 25 countries, to share learning and experience on how to address the problem of international cartels. A similar event was held in the UK in the autumn of 2000[16]. Canada is the host in 2001.

---

7   See the Press Releases of 6 April and 5 May 2000.
8   See Press Releases of 29 September 1999, 17 November 1999 and 10 May 2001; fines totalling EUR 218.8m were imposed by the European Commission on the members of this cartel in July 2001: Commission Press Release IP/01/1010, 18 July 2001.
9   The jail sentences on two of the individuals were subsequently increased from 24 months to 36 and 33 months respectively: Press Releases of 17 September 1998 and 22 September 2000; a book has been published about this cartel: see Eichenwald *The Informant: A True Story* (Broadway Books, 2000). The Department of Justice in this case obtained from the FBI filmed evidence of members of the cartel meeting to fix prices and to determine their quotas, and has shown the video at a number of conferences on antitrust enforcement against cartels; the same cartel was fined under EC law in 2000: see *Amino Acids* OJ [2001] L 154/24, [2001] 5 CMLR 322, on appeal Cases T-221/00 etc *Cheil Jedang* (judgment pending).
10 See Press Release of 23 June 1998.
11 See Press Release of 18 August 2000.
12 See Press Release of 5 October 2000.
13 See generally *Hard Core Cartels* (OECD, 2000) available at http://www.oecd.org.
14 See ch 12, pp 411-413.
15 See n 7 and n 9 above.
16 See *Fair Trading* (OFT, Issue 29, February 2001) pp 12-15.

(C)   The European Commission's approach to cartels

The European Commission is attaching a higher priority to cartels than at any time in its history. In a speech delivered by Commissioner Monti to the 3rd Nordic Competition Policy Conference on 11 September 2000 in Stockholm, he referred to cartels as 'cancers on the open market economy which forms the very basis of our Community'[17]. One obvious expression of the Commission's determination to eradicate cartels was the creation within DG COMP of the 'Cartel Unit', Unit E1, under the supervision of Maurice Guerrin (now Georg de Bronett), which was announced by Commissioner Karel Van Miert on December 3 1998[18]. This unit has a staff of some twenty of DG COMP's most experienced officials in this type of investigation and focusses on the pursuit, unveiling and elimination of cartels. The Commission's commitment to a tougher policy towards cartels is also demonstrated in other ways. First, the *Leniency Notice*[19] encourages participants in cartels to provide evidence to the Commission of their unlawful behaviour in return for a reduction in fines. In the US, the amnesty for whistleblowers introduced by the Department of Justice has been very successful in bringing cartels to light: this was true of the *Vitamins* and *Citric Acid* cases referred to above[20] and more recently of *Sothebys/Christies*[1]. The Commission's Notice allows a reduction of 75% of the fine, or even a total amnesty in some cases, although this degree of leniency will not be available to the 'ring leader' of the cartel. In other cases, the reduction of the fine may be 'substantial' and in others 'significant'. In the UK, whistleblowing has been encouraged under the Competition Act, which entered into force on 1 March 1998[2]. The encouragement of whistleblowing, therefore, has become an important feature of competition authorities' fight against cartels, and it would be reasonable to suppose that numerous undertakings will be considering whether to 'blow the whistle' in order to reduce the level of possible fines; however one can imagine that the possibly less savoury reprisals of the other members of, for example, a sulphuric acid or ready-mixed concrete cartel may cause some hesitation on the part of would-be whistleblowers when deciding whether to set out on the path to confession.

A second manifestation of the Commission's determination to combat cartels is that this is a key driving force behind its *White Paper on Modernisation*[3]: the Commission's intention is to abandon its monopoly over decision-making under Article 81(3) of the Treaty and to abolish the system of notifying agreements to it: this would enable it to redeploy its resources, enabling it, *inter alia*, to concentrate on tracking down serious infringements of Articles 81 and 82[4]. Third, actual evidence of the Commission's eagerness to punish and eradicate cartels

17   The speech is available at http://europa.eu.int/comm/competition/speeches/index_speeches_by_the_commissioner.html; see also the Commission's XXXth *Report on Competition Policy* (2000), points 68-69.
18   Commission Press Release IP/98/1060.
19   Commission *Notice on the Non-imposition or Reduction of Fines in Cartel Cases* OJ [1996] C 207/4, [1996] 5 CMLR 362; see also the *Guidelines on the Method of Setting Fines* published by the Commission in 1998, OJ [1998] C 9/3, [1998] 4 CMLR 472: it is noticeable that recent Commission decisions in cartel cases contain quite detailed discussion of the appropriate level of the fines, pursuant to the adoption of these Notices; for discussion of them see ch 7, pp 237-239.
20   See nn 7 and 10 above.
1   See n 12 above.
2   *Guidance as to the Appropriate Amount of a Penalty*, OFT Guideline 423, para 9; see ch 10, pp 353-355.
3   OJ [1999] C 132/1, [1999] 5 CMLR 208.
4   For discussion of the White Paper and its aftermath, see ch 7, pp 246-258.

has been the recent adoption of a number of decisions imposing substantial fines on hard-core cartels. In its 1999 *Report on Competition Policy* the Commission specifically stated that it is 'committed to an extremely tough stance against cartels, particularly following the adoption of the euro as a common currency'[5]. A table of the major cartel cases since 1986 is set out below[6]. The Commission's *Guidelines on Horizontal Cooperation Agreements*[7] for the most part do not apply to the types of horizontal agreement considered in this chapter.

2. MAJOR CARTEL CASES SINCE 1986

At the outset it may be helpful to examine a table of the major cartel cases since 1986, beginning with the Commission's decision in *Polypropylene*; this decision was taken on appeal to the CFI and the ECJ and many important points of law were argued in it. Most of the decisions in the table involved price fixing; in several, however, the price fixing was practiced in conjunction with other infringements of Article 81(1), such as the sharing of markets, the allocation of quotas or the exchange of information[8]. In some cases there was no price fixing; for example, the *Seamless Steel Tubes* decision was concerned exclusively with the geographical sharing of markets. Most of the decisions were appealed to the CFI and, in some cases, to the ECJ. The table provides references to these appeals; all of them are reported in the European Court Reports, the official reports of the Community Courts, but the Common Market Law Reports has reported only some of them. After the table of cases, this chapter will examine the application of Article 81 to various types of cartels, for example price fixing, market sharing and agreements to fix quotas and limit production.

Table of major cartel cases since 1986

Date	Commission decision	CFI judgment	ECJ judgment
1986	*Polypropylene*[9] Fines of EUR 57.85 million	Decision substantially upheld on appeal; some marginal reduction of fines[10]	CFI's judgment affirmed on appeal to the ECJ[11]
1986	*MELDOC*[12] Fines of EUR 6.565 million		

5   Ibid, point 44; on its activities against cartels in 1999, see points 46-52 of the same Report.
6   See pp 419-424.
7   OJ [2001] C 3/2, [2001] 4 CMLR 819; on these *Guidelines* see ch 15, p 501ff.
8   See pp 428-429 below.
9   OJ [1986] L 230/1, [1988] 4 CMLR 347.
10 Cases T-1/89 etc *Rhône-Poulenc SA v Commission* [1991] ECR II-867; the judgment in the case of *Hercules NV v Commission* is reported at [1991] ECR II-1711, [1992] 4 CMLR 84.
11 Cases C-51/92 P etc *Hercules Chemicals NV v Commission* [1999] 5 CMLR 976; see also [1999] 5 CMLR 1016 (*Hüls v Commission*), [1999] 5 CMLR 1110 (*ICI v Commission*); [1999] 5 CMLR 1142 (*Shell v Commission*); [2001] 4 CMLR 602 (*Anic v Commission*); and [2001] 4 CMLR 691 (*Montecatini v Commission*).
12 OJ [1986] L 348/50, [1989] 4 CMLR 853.

Date	Commission decision	CFI judgment	ECJ judgment
1986	*Belgian Roofing Felt*[13] Fines of EUR 1 million	Decision upheld in its entirety on appeal[14]	
1988	*Italian Flat Glass*[15] Fines of EUR 13.4 million	Decision mostly annulled on appeal[16]	
1988	*PVC*[17] Fines of EUR 23.5 million **Note: a second decision was adopted in 1994**[18]	Decision found to be so flawed on appeal as to be 'non-existent'[19]	CFI's judgment that the decision was non-existent reversed on appeal to the ECJ, but the decision of the Commission annulled[20]
1989	*LdPE*[1] Fines of EUR 37 million	Decision annulled on appeal[2]	
1989	*Welded Steel Mesh*[3] Fines of EUR 9.5 million	Decision substantially upheld on appeal; partial annulment of decision and some reduction of fines[4]	Small reduction of the fine on one undertaking due to the delay in the appeal before the CFI[5]; appeal by Ferriere Nord dismissed[6]

13 OJ [1986] L 232/15, [1991] 4 CMLR 130.
14 Case 246/86 *Belasco v Commission* [1989] ECR 2117, [1991] 4 CMLR 96.
15 OJ [1989] L 33/44, [1990] 4 CMLR 535.
16 Cases T–68/89 etc *Società Italiano Vetro SpA v Commission* [1992] ECR II-1403, [1992] 5 CMLR 302.
17 OJ [1989] L 74/1, [1990] 4 CMLR 345.
18 See p 421, n 16 below.
19 Cases T–79/89 etc *BASF AG v Commission* [1992] ECR II-315, [1992] 4 CMLR 357.
20 Cases C-137/92 P *Commission v BASF AG* [1994] ECR I-2555; see Toth (1995) 32 CML Rev 271.
1 OJ [1989] L 74/21, [1990] 4 CMLR 382.
2 Cases T–80/89 etc *BASF AG v Commission* [1995] ECR II-729.
3 OJ [1989] L 260/1, [1991] 4 CMLR 13.
4 Cases T-141/89 etc *Tréfileurope Sales SARL v Commission* [1995] ECR II-791.
5 Case C-185/95 P *Baustahlgewebe GmbH v Commission* [1998] ECR I-8417, [1999] 4 CMLR 1203; see Toner (1999) 36 CML Rev 1345.
6 Case C-219/95 P [1997] ECR I-4411, [1997] 5 CMLR 575.

Date	Commission decision	CFI judgment	ECJ judgment
1991	*Soda-Ash*[7] Fines of EUR 48 million for infringements of both Article 81 and 82 **Note: a second decision was adopted in 2000**[8]	Decision annulled on appeal[9]	The CFI judgment annulling the decision upheld on appeal[10]
1992	*Eurocheque: Helsinki Agreement*[11] Fines of EUR 6 million	Decision annulled in part and fines reduced on appeal[12]	
1992	*Building and Construction Industry in the Netherlands*[13] Fines of EUR 22.5 million	Decision upheld on appeal[14]	Appeal against the judgment of the CFI dismissed[15]
1994	*PVC*[16] Fines of EUR 19.25 million	Decision substantially upheld on appeal; some reduction of fines[17]	Appeal against the judgment of the CFI pending[18]
1994	*Steel Beams*[19] Fines of EUR 104.35 million	Decision substantially upheld on appeal[20]	Appeal against the judgment of the CFI pending[1]

7   This case consists of four separate Commission decisions, OJ [1991] L 152/1, [1994] 4 CMLR 454; OJ [1991] L 152/16, [1994] 4 CMLR 482; OJ [1991] L 152/21 and OJ [1991] L 152/40, [1994] 4 CMLR 645.
8   See p 424, n 12 below.
9   Cases T-30/91 etc *Solvay v Commission* [1995] ECR II-1775, [1996] 5 CMLR 57.
10 Cases C-286/95 P etc *Commission v ICI* [2000] 5 CMLR 413 and 454.
11 OJ [1992] L 95/20, [1993] 5 CMLR 323.
12 Cases T-39/92 and T-40/92 *Groupement des Cartes Bancaires v Commission* [1994] ECR II-49, [1995] 5 CMLR 410.
13 OJ [1992] L 92/1, [1993] 5 CMLR 135.
14 Case T-29/92 *SPO v Commission* [1995] ECR II-289.
15 Case C-137/95 P *SPO v Commission* [1996] ECR I-1611.
16 OJ [1994] L 239/14.
17 Cases T-305/94 etc *Limburgse Vinyl Maatschappij v Commission* [1999] ECR II-931, [1999] 5 CMLR 303.
18 Cases C-238/99 P *Limburgse Vinyl Maatschappij v Commission*.
19 OJ [1994] L 116/1, [1994] 5 CMLR 353.
20 Cases T-141/94 etc *Thyssen Stahl v Commission* [1999] ECR II-347, [1999] 4 CMLR 810.
1   Cases C-176/99 P *ARBED v Commission*.

Date	Commission decision	CFI judgment	ECJ judgment
1994	*Cartonboard*[2] Fines of EUR 132 million	Decision substantially upheld on appeal; some small reduction of fines[3]	Three fines reduced on appeal to the ECJ, two cases referred back to the CFI for reassessment; the remaining appeals dismissed[4]
1994	*Cement*[5] Fines of EUR 248 million	Substantial reduction of fines on appeal[6]	Appeal against the judgment of the CFI pending[7]
1994	*Transatlantic Agreement*[8] No fine	Appeal pending[9]	
1994	*Far East Freight Conference*[10] Fines of EUR 13 million	Appeal pending[11]	
1995	*Dutch Mobile Cranes*[12] Fines of EUR 11.8 million	Decision upheld on appeal[13]	
1997	*Ferry operators*[14] Fines of EUR 0.645 million		

2   OJ [1994] L 243/1, [1994] 5 CMLR 547.
3   See Cases T-295/94 etc *Buchmann GmbH v Commission* [1998] ECR II-813.
4   See Cases C-248/98 P etc *Koninklijke v Commission* [2001] 4 CMLR 322, 370 and 413.
5   OJ [1994] L 343/1, [1995] 4 CMLR 327.
6   Cases T-25/95 etc *Cimenteries SA v Commission* judgment of 15 March 2000.
7   Cases C-204/00 P *Aalborg Portland A/S v Commission*.
8   OJ [1994] L 376/1.
9   Cases T-395/94 etc *Atlantic Container Line AB v Commission*.
10   OJ [1994] L 378/17.
11   Cases T-86/95 etc *Compagnie Générale Maritime v Commission*.
12   OJ [1995] L 312/79, [1996] 4 CMLR 565.
13   Cases T-213/95 and T-18/96 *SCK and FNK v Commission* [1997] ECR II-1739, [1997] 4 CMLR 259.
14   OJ [1997] L 26/23, [1997] 4 CMLR 798.

Date	Commission decision	CFI judgment	ECJ judgment
1998	*TACA*[15] Fines of EUR 273 million imposed for abuse of a collective dominant position under Article 82	Appeal pending[16]	
1998	*Alloy Surcharge*[17] Fines of EUR 27.3 million		
1998	*Pre-insulated Pipes*[18] Fines of EUR 92 million	Appeal pending[19]	
1998	*Greek Ferries*[20] Fines of EUR 9.12 million	Appeal pending[1]	
1998	*British Sugar*[2] Fines of EUR 43.9 million	Substantially upheld on appeal[3]	
1999	*Dutch Electrotechnical Equipment*[4] Fines of EUR 6.55 million	Appeal pending[5]	
1999	*Seamless Steel Tubes*[6] Fines of EUR 99 million	Appeal pending[7]	

15 OJ [1999] L 95/1, [1999] 4 CMLR 1415.
16 Cases T-191/98 etc *Atlantic Container Line AB v Commission*.
17 OJ [1998] L 100/55, [1998] 4 CMLR 973: note that this decision was actually adopted under Article 65 ECSC Treaty, the equivalent provision in that Treaty to Article 81(1) EC.
18 OJ [1999] L 24/1, [1999] 4 CMLR 402.
19 Cases T-9/99 etc *HFB Holding v Commission*.
20 OJ [1999] L 109/24, [1999] 5 CMLR 47.
1 Cases T-56/99 etc *Marlines SA v Commission*.
2 OJ [1999] L 76/1, [1999] 4 CMLR 1316.
3 Cases T-202/98 etc *Tate & Lyle v Commission*, judgment of 12 July 2001.
4 OJ [2000] L 39/1, [2000] 4 CMLR 1208.
5 Cases T-5/00 *NAVEG v Commission*.
6 See the Commission's XXIXth *Report on Competition Policy* (1999), p 137.
7 Cases T-78/00 *Sumitomo v Commission*.

Date	Commission decision	CFI judgment	ECJ judgment
2000	*FETTCSA*[8] Fines of EUR 6.932m	Appeal pending[9]	
2000	*Amino Acids*[10] Fines of EUR 109m	Appeal pending[11]	
2000	*Soda Ash*[12] Fines of EUR 33m	Appeal pending[12a]	
2001	*Graphite Electrodes* Fines of EUR 218.8m[12b]		
2001	*SAS/Maersk* Fines of EUR 52.5m[12c]		

3.   HORIZONTAL PRICE FIXING[13]

Horizontal price fixing would be regarded by most people as the most blatant and undesirable of restrictive trade practices. As Adam Smith observed in *The Wealth of Nations* in 1776[14]:

> 'People of the same trade seldom meet together, even for merriment and diversion, but the conversation ends in a conspiracy against the public, or in some contrivance to raise prices'[15].

It is interesting in passing to note that price fixing has not always attracted the opprobrium that it does today. In the UK, for example, it was characteristic of most industries during the first half of the twentieth century that prices were set at an agreed level; this was thought to provide stability, to protect firms against cyclical recession and overseas competition, and to facilitate orderly and rational marketing from which purchasers too would benefit[16]. The introduction of power to inhibit price fixing in the Monopolies and Restrictive Practices (Inquiry and Control) Act 1948 was resented and even now resistance to price competition remains deep-rooted in some parts of the economy.

---

8   OJ [2000] L 268/1, [2000] 5 CMLR 1011.
9   Case T-213/00 *CMA v Commission*.
10   OJ [2001] L 154/24, [2001] 5 CMLR 322.
11   Cases T-220/00 etc *Cheil Jedang v Commission*.
12   Commission Press Release IP/00/1449, 13 December 2000.
12a Cases T-50/01 and T-58/01 *Solway v Commission* (judgment pending).
12b Commission Press Release 10/01/1010, 18 July 2001.
12c Commission Press Release 10/01/1009, 18 July 2001.
13   For further detail, see Pheasant and Bright in Division II of *Butterworths Competition Law* (eds Freeman and Whish), ch 10; Bellamy and Child *European Community Law of Competition* (Sweet & Maxwell, 5th ed, 2001, ed Roth), paras 4-006 to 4-040.
14   Modern Library Edition, 1937.
15   Ibid, p 128.
16   See eg Allen *Monopoly and Restrictive Practices* (George Allen & Unwin, 1968) ch 14.

It might be assumed that in the absence of antitrust laws – or at any rate in the absence of any significant prospect of being detected and punished for breaking them – all competitors would find the urge to cartelise and to maximise profits an irresistible one. However participation in a cartel itself has its price and membership will be more profitable to some firms than others[17]. Costs will be incurred in negotiating to fix the price at which the product is to be sold and these costs will inevitably increase as more firms are brought into the agreement and the range of products to be comprehended by it is extended. Firms may find it difficult both to agree a price and to remain faithful to the level set. It will be to the advantage of more efficient firms to fix a lower price, since output (and so their revenue) will then be greater; the producer of strongly differentiated goods will want a higher price, which will cover the cost of promoting their brand image. Having fixed prices, further expense will be incurred in operating and monitoring the agreement. Meetings will be necessary to reappraise matters from time to time, resources will need to be expended in policing it to ensure that individual firms are not cheating by cutting prices secretly, offering discounts and bonuses or altering the quality of the product[18]. To prevent cheating, the agreement may fix quotas and provide for the imposition of fines upon firms that exceed them. Further resources may have to be devoted to arrangements such as collective boycotts, patent pooling and the offer of aggregated rebates in order to prevent new entrants coming on to the market with a view to sharing in any supra-competitive profits that are being earned. A system of collective resale price maintenance may have to be established to buttress the stability of the cartel. Operating an effective cartel may involve sophisticated arrangements for monitoring and punishing members so that the price chosen can be sustained. A trade association may have to be established to reinforce the cartel.

The problems inherent in the cartelisation process itself explain why in some industries price fixing has a tendency to break down in the long term and why the parties may attempt to limit competition in other ways than by direct limitations on pricing strategy. For example, it may be easier to prevent 'cheating' where each firm is given an exclusive geographical market or a particular class of customers with which to deal. Furthermore the fact that price fixing becomes more difficult as the number of participants involved in the agreement increases may be considered to signify that competition authorities ought to expend their enforcement resources on those markets where collusion is most likely to be privately profitable because of the high level of concentration that exists or the homogeneity of the products sold[19].

It should not be assumed from the foregoing comments that price fixing is rare. Even the existence of antitrust laws backed up by severe penalties has not dissuaded some firms from attempts to control the market. Experience shows that some industries are particularly prone to cartelisation. It is also important to appreciate that prices can be fixed in numerous different ways, and that a fully effective competition law must be able to comprehend not only the most blatant forms of the practice but also a whole range of more subtle agreements whose object is to limit price competition. For example, where firms agree to restrict credit to customers, to abstain from offering discounts and rebates, to

---

17 See Scherer and Ross *Industrial Market Structure and Economic Performance* (Houghton Mifflin, 3rd ed, 1990) chs 7 and 8; Neven, Papandropoulos and Seabright *Trawling for Minnows* (CEPR, 1998) ch 3; Bishop and Walker *The Economics of EC Competition Law* (Sweet & Maxwell, 1999), paras 4.06-4.23.

18 It is not uncommon for a cartel agreement to break down, or to run the risk of doing so, because of the extent of cheating indulged in by members: see eg *Zinc Producer Group* OJ [1984] L 220/27, [1985] 2 CMLR 108, paras 23-63.

19 See Posner *Antitrust Law* (The University of Chicago Press, 1976) ch 4.

refrain from advertising prices, to notify one another of the prices they charge to customers or intend to recommend their distributors to charge, or to adopt identical cost accounting methods, the object or effect of the agreement may be to diminish or totally prevent price competition. Indeed, agreements to divide markets or produce fixed quotas can in a sense be seen as covert price-fixing agreements, in that they limit the extent to which firms can compete with one another on price. These and other similar agreements will be dealt with separately later in this chapter.

(A)   Article 81(1)

Article 81(1) specifically provides that agreements, decisions and concerted practices which 'directly or indirectly fix purchase or selling prices or any other trading conditions' may be caught. Many aspects of Article 81(1) have been discussed earlier in this book. The expressions 'agreement' and 'concerted practice' are given a wide meaning[20]: specifically, the Commission may find a 'single, overall agreement'[1], may adopt a dual classification of an agreement 'and/or' a concerted practice[2]; and attendance at meetings at which prices are discussed between competitors is highly incriminating[3]. The Community Courts and the Commission regard price-fixing agreements as having as their *object* the restriction of competition for the purposes of Article 81(1), so that there is no need also to show that they have the effect of doing so[4]. However, it is necessary to show that an agreement will have an appreciable effect on competition in a quantitative sense[5] and an appreciable effect on trade between Member States[6] for there to be an infringement of Article 81(1). Furthermore Article 81(1) is capable of being applied extraterritorially to agreements entered into outside but implemented within the Community[7]. This section examines more closely the application of Article 81(1) to price-fixing agreements.

(i)   Price fixing in any form is caught

It is clear from the decisions of the Commission and the judgments of the Community Courts that it is not just blatant price fixing that is caught, but that Article 81(1) will catch any agreement that might directly or indirectly suppress price competition. In *IFTRA Rules on Glass Containers*[8] the Commission condemned rules of a glass manufacturers' association which might reduce price competition by including an obligation not to offer discounts, an open information scheme, the adoption of a common accounting procedure and a term providing for the charging of uniform delivered prices. In this decision the Commission pointed out that in the particular product market the potential for non-price competition was weak, the corollary being that maintenance of price competition

20   See ch 3, pp 76-89.
1   Ibid, pp 80-81.
2   Ibid, pp 78-80.
3   Ibid, p 81.
4   Ibid, pp 95-98.
5   Ibid, pp 107-110.
6   Ibid, pp 110-120.
7   See ch 12, pp 398-402.
8   OJ [1974] L 160/1, [1974] 2 CMLR D50; see similarly *IFTRA Rules for Producers of Aluminium Containers* OJ [1975] L 228/10, [1975] 2 CMLR D20.

was particularly important. An agreement not to discount off published prices was held to infringe Article 81(1) in *FETTCSA*[9], even though the parties had not expressly agreed on the level of their published prices. In *Vimpoltu*[10] an agreement to observe maximum discounts and to offer the same credit terms was caught. In *Italian Flat Glass*[11] the participants in the cartel had agreed not only to fix prices, but also to offer identical discounts and to ensure that these were applied downstream in the market.

Many other decisions have condemned agreements which might directly or indirectly facilitate level pricing. Prior consultation on price lists, with a commitment not to submit quotations before such consultation, is prohibited[12]. A substantial body of material on information agreements now exists[13], restrictions upon advertising may be caught[14], as are agreements on terms and conditions which limit price competition[15], agreements on recommended prices[16], maximum pricing[17], and collective resale price maintenance[18]. Objection has been taken to a scheme whereby members of a cartel at times refused to sell and at others themselves purchased zinc on the London Metal Exchange in order to maintain its price[19]. Where an industry considers that cooperation is necessary because of the depressed state of the market, this should be negotiated with the Commission: undertakings should not take unilateral action which restricts competition[20].

In the case of *British Sugar*[1] the Commission did not find that the prices for sugar had *actually* been fixed, but that the parties to the agreement/concerted practice could rely on the other participants to pursue a collaborative strategy of higher pricing in 'an atmosphere of mutual certainty'[2]. In *Fenex*[3] the Commission considered that the regular and consistent practice of drawing up and circulating recommended tariffs to members of a trade association infringed Article 81(1)[4]. In *Ferry Operators Currency Surcharges*[5] the Commission considered that an agreement on the amount of surcharges, and the timing of their introduction, to be imposed on freight shipments following the devaluation of the pound infringed Article 81(1). Price fixing as part of a strategy to isolate national markets is caught[6], and agreements between distributors are caught as well as between

9　OJ [2000] L 268/1, [2000] 5 CMLR 1011, paras 132-139, citing *IFTRA Rules on Glass Containers* and *IFTRA Rules for Producers of Aluminium Containers*.
10　OJ [1983] L 200/44, [1983] 3 CMLR 619.
11　OJ [1989] L 33/44, [1990] 4 CMLR 535, annulled on appeal Cases T-68/89 etc *Società Italiano Vetro SpA v Commission* [1992] ECR II-1403, [1992] 5 CMLR 302.
12　*Re Cast Iron Steel Rolls* OJ [1983] L 317/1, [1984] 1 CMLR 694: the parties here had established an 'alarm system' in the event that antitrust authorities should become aware of their cartel; upheld on appeal Cases 29/83 and 30/83 *Compagnie Royale Asturienne des Mines SA and Rheinzink GmbH v Commission* [1984] ECR 1679, [1985] 1 CMLR 688.
13　See pp 441-450 below.
14　See pp 450-453 below.
15　See pp 439-441 below.
16　Case 8/72 *Cementhandelaren v Commission* [1972] ECR 977, [1973] CMLR 7.
17　*European Glass Manufacturers* OJ [1974] L 160/1, [1974] 2 CMLR D50.
18　Cases 43, 63/82 *VBVB & VBBB v Commission* [1984] ECR 19, [1985] 1 CMLR 27.
19　*Zinc Producer Group* OJ [1984] L 220/27, [1985] 2 CMLR 108.
20　Ibid.
1　OJ [1999] L 76/1, [1999] 4 CMLR 1316, substantially upheld on appeal Cases T-202/98 etc *Tate & Lyle v Commission*, judgment of 12 July 2001.
2　See the Commission's XXVIIIth *Report on Competition Policy* (1998), pp 138-140.
3　OJ [1996] L 181/28, [1996] 5 CMLR 332.
4　Ibid, paras 45-74
5　OJ [1996] L 26/23, [1997] 4 CMLR 798.
6　Case 41/69 *ACF Chemiefarma NV v Commission* [1970] ECR 661.

producers[7]. An agreement the effect of which is to maintain a traditional price differential between two geographical markets will infringe Article 81(1)[8]. Fixing the price of imports into the EC has been caught[9]. In *Milchförderungsfonds*[10] the Commission prohibited the German Milk Promotion Board from financially supporting promotion of exports of German milk products to other EC countries, as this meant that exporters could charge lower prices than without this benefit, so that competition on the market was distorted.

(ii)   Joint selling agencies[11]

The Commission is wary of joint selling agencies, which it regards as horizontal cartels and generally ineligible for exemption[12], unless they are established pursuant to some other permissible form of cooperation, such as a research and development agreement or a specialisation agreements[13]. In the case of *Britannia Gas Condensate Field*[14] the Commission said that an agreement between several oil and gas companies participating in the development of the Britannia gas field in the UK North Sea was restrictive of competition; however the Commission considered that Article 81(1) was not applicable since the agreement had no effect on trade between Member States.

(iii)   Horizontal price fixing in conjunction with other infringements of Article 81(1)

In many cases, undertakings have been found guilty of price fixing in conjunction with other types of horizontal collusion. In *Polypropylene*[15] the Commission found price fixing and market sharing; in *Belgian Roofing Felt*[16] the parties were found guilty of price fixing, establishing production quotas and taking collective action to prevent imports into Belgium; in *Italian Flat Glass*[17] the Commission condemned firms for the apportionment of quotas and agreements

---

7   Cases 100–103/80 *Musique Diffusion Française SA v Commission* [1983] ECR 1825, [1983] 3 CMLR 221.
8   *Scottish Salmon Board* OJ [1992] L 246/37, [1993] 5 CMLR 602.
9   *Re Franco-Japanese Ballbearings Agreement* OJ [1974] L 343/19, [1975] 1 CMLR D8; *Re French and Taiwanese Mushroom Packers* OJ [1975] L 29/26, [1975] 1 CMLR D83; *Wood Pulp* OJ [1985] L 85/1, [1985] 3 CMLR 474; *Aluminium Imports* OJ [1985] L 92/1, [1987] 3 CMLR 813.
10   OJ [1985] L 35/35, [1985] 3 CMLR 101.
11   On joint selling, see Pheasant and Bright in Div II of *Butterworths Competition Law* (eds Freeman and Whish), ch 7; Bellamy and Child *European Community Competition Law* (Sweet and Maxwell, 5th ed, 2001, ed Roth), paras 4-089 to 4-100.
12   *Re Cimbel* OJ [1972] L 303/24, [1973] CMLR D167; *Re Centraal Stikstof Verkoopkantoor* OJ [1978] L 242/15, [1979] 1 CMLR 11; *Re Floral* OJ [1980] L 39/51, [1980] 2 CMLR 285; *Re Italian Flat Glass* OJ [1981] L 326/32, [1982] 3 CMLR 366; *Ansac* OJ [1991] L 152/54; *Astra* OJ [1993] L 20/23, [1994] 5 CMLR 226; *HOV SVZ/MCN* OJ [1994] L 104/34, upheld on appeal Case T-229/94 *Deutsche Bahn AG v Commission* [1997] ECR II-1689, [1998] 4 CMLR 220 and on appeal to the ECJ Case C-436/97 P [1999] ECR I-2387, [1999] 5 CMLR 776; see also the Commission's *Guidelines on Horizontal Cooperation Agreements* OJ [2001] C 3/2, [2001] 4 CMLR 819, paras 144 and 145.
13   On horizontal cooperation agreements generally see ch 15.
14   OJ [1997] C 291/10, [1996] 5 CMLR 627; see also the Commission's XXVIIth *Report on Competition Policy* (1997), p 139.
15   OJ [1986] L 230/1, [1988] 4 CMLR 347.
16   OJ [1986] L 232/15, [1991] 4 CMLR 130.
17   OJ [1989] L 33/44, [1990] 4 CMLR 535.

to exchange products as well as for fixing prices. In *Pre-Insulated Pipes*[18] the Commission identified infringements of virtually every kind, including market sharing, systematic price fixing, collective tendering, exchanging sensitive sales information and attempts to eliminate the only substantial non-member of the cartel. As the Commissioner responsible for competition policy at the time, Karel Van Miert, said: 'it is difficult to imagine a worse cartel'[19]. In *Amino Acids*[20] the Commission found agreements to fix prices, to determine quotas, and to exchange information.

(iv) Price fixing in the services sector

Price fixing in the services sector is also subject to Article 81(1)[1]. For example, in *Eurocheque: Helsinki Agreement*[2] the Commission imposed a fine of EUR 6 million where French banks had agreed between themselves on the commissions they would charge to customers and on their amount[3]; the decision was partially annulled and the fines reduced on appeal[4]. The Commission has been investigating the Visa International payment card scheme in so far as the interchange fee may amount to collective price fixing[5]; and it sent statements of objections to a number of banks in relation to a possible cartel agreement to fix the charges for exchanging currencies in the euro zone[6]. A fine of EUR 1,000,000 was imposed in *Distribution of Railway Tickets by Travel Agents*[7] where the Commission found that the International Union of Railways was responsible for price fixing in the sale of railway tickets; the decision was annulled on appeal, as the Commission had proceeded under the wrong procedural regulation[8]. In 1999, in the *Greek Ferries* decision, fines were imposed in the case of price fixing in ferry services between Italy and Greece[9]. Price fixing in the professions has come under Commission scrutiny in recent years[10]. The Commission has also been investigating the joint selling of sports rights[11].

---

18 *Pre-Insulated Pipe Cartel* OJ [1999] L 24/1, [1999] 4 CMLR 402, on appeal Cases T-9/99 etc *HFB Holding v Commission* (judgment pending).
19 Commission Press Release IP/98/917, 21 October 1998.
20 OJ [2001] L 154/24, [2001] 5 CMLR 322, on appeal Cases T-220/00 etc *Cheil Jedang v Commission* (judgment pending).
1 See eg *Re Nuovo CEGAM* OJ [1984] L 99/29, [1984] 2 CMLR 484 (common tariff system infringed Article 81(1)); *Re Fire Insurance* OJ [1985] L 35/20, [1985] 3 CMLR 246, upheld on appeal Case 45/85 *VdS v Commission* [1987] ECR 405, [1988] 4 CMLR 264 (recommendations on tariffs infringed Article 81(1)).
2 OJ [1992] L 95/50, [1993] 5 CMLR 323.
3 Ibid, paras 46-55.
4 Cases T-39/92 and T-40/92 *Groupement des Cartes Bancaires v Commission* [1994] ECR II-49, [1995] 5 CMLR 410.
5 Commission Press Release IP/00/1164, 16 October 2000; the Commission announced its intention to clear the rule that merchants must not add charges to customers who use their visa card: OJ [2000] C 293/18, [2000] 5 CMLR 1067.
6 Commission Press Release IP/00/784, 14 July 2000, [2000] 5 CMLR 369.
7 OJ [1992] L 366/47.
8 Case T–14/93 *Union Internationale des Chemin de Fer* [1995] ECR II-1503, [1996] 5 CMLR 40.
9 OJ [1999] L 109/24, [1999] 5 CMLR 47, on appeal Cases T-56/99 etc *Marlines v Commission* (judgment pending).
10 See ch 3, p 69.
11 XXIXth *Report on Competition Policy* (1999), pp 54-55; see Brinckman and Vollebreght 'The Marketing of Sport and its Relation to EC Competition Law (1998) 19 ECLR 281; Nitsche 'Collective Marketing of Broadcasting by Sports Associations in Europe' (2000) 21 ECLR 208.

(v)   Price fixing in regulated markets

The Commission will examine particularly carefully markets in which price competition is already limited by extraneous factors, in order to ensure that the parties themselves do nothing further to limit competition[12], and its decision will not be affected by the fact that a Government agency has itself sanctioned or extended the effect of a price-fixing agreement[13].

(vi)   Appeals against decisions of the Commission in cartel cases

There have been many high-profile cases where the Commission has condemned price-fixing cartels and has imposed considerable fines. Many of these cases have been taken on appeal to the CFI and the ECJ, in some cases with fairly disastrous outcomes from the Commission's point of view. Where the Commission imposes a fine, the CFI has an unlimited jurisdiction to review the Commission's decision, by virtue of Article 229 (former Article 172) of the Treaty. Some of these cases have run for a very long time, as can be seen from the table of major cartel cases above[14].

In 1986 the Commission condemned price-fixing cartels in *Polypropylene*[15] and *Belgian Roofing Felt*[16]; whilst in 1988 it found price fixing in the *Italian Flat Glass*[17], *PVC*[18] and *LdPE* cases[19]. In these five decisions, the total of the fines imposed was no less than EUR 132.25 million. Each decision was appealed. In *Polypropylene*[20] the CFI substantially upheld the Commission's decision, reducing the fines marginally in five cases; the CFI's judgment was affirmed by the ECJ[1]. The *Belgian Roofing Felt* decision was upheld in its entirety[2].

In the *Italian Flat Glass* and the *PVC* appeals the Commission fared much less well. In the case of *Italian Flat Glass* the CFI was extremely critical of the Commission and annulled most of the decision[3]. In *PVC*[4] the CFI went so far as to hold that the Commission's procedural errors were so serious as to render the decision non-existent. The ECJ disagreed and confirmed the existence of the

12   Cases 209/78 etc *Van Landewyck v Commission* [1980] ECR 3125, [1981] 3 CMLR 134; similarly see Case 85/76 *Hoffmann-la Roche v Commission* [1979] ECR 461, [1979] 3 CMLR 211, para 123; and *British Sugar plc* OJ [1999] L 76/1, [1999] 4 CMLR 1316, para 87, upheld on appeal, Cases T-202/98 *Tate & Lyle v Commission*, judgment of 12 July 2001.
13   *AROW v BNIC* OJ [1982] L 379/1, [1983] 2 CMLR 240; *Zinc Producer Group* OJ [1984] L 220/27, [1985] 2 CMLR 108; *Benelux Flat Glass* OJ [1984] L 212/13, [1985] 2 CMLR 350 (where competition was also limited by the similar costs faced by glass producers and the structure of the market); see ch 3, pp 104-105 and ch 6 generally on the relationship of the competition rules with state regulation of economic activity.
14   See pp 419-424 above.
15   OJ [1986] L 230/1, [1988] 4 CMLR 347.
16   OJ [1986] L 232/15, [1991] 4 CMLR 130.
17   OJ [1989] L 33/44, [1990] 4 CMLR 535.
18   OJ [1989] L74/1, [1990] 4 CMLR 345.
19   *LdPE* OJ [1989] L 74/21, [1990] 4 CMLR 382.
20   Cases T-1/89 etc *Rhône-Poulenc SA v Commission* [1991] ECR II-867; the judgment in the case of *Hercules NV v Commission* is reported at [1991] ECR II-1711, [1992] 4 CMLR 84.
1   Cases C-51/92 P etc *Hercules Chemicals NV v Commission* [1999] 5 CMLR 976; see also [1999] 5 CMLR 1016 (*Hüls v Commission*), [1999] 5 CMLR 1110 (*ICI v Commission*) and [1999] 5 CMLR 1142 (*Shell v Commission*).
2   Case 246/86 *Belasco v Commission* [1989] ECR 2117, [1991] 4 CMLR 96.
3   Cases T-68/89 etc *Società Italiano Vetro SpA v Commission* [1992] ECR II-1403, [1992] 5 CMLR 302.
4   Cases T-79/89 etc *BASF AG v Commission* [1992] ECR II-315, [1992] 4 CMLR 357.

decision, but annulled it for infringement of essential requirements[5]. Thereafter the Commission adopted another decision in 1994, almost identical to the 1988 one[6]. In *PVC II*[7] the CFI substantially upheld the Commission's second decision; nine of the appeals were rejected, although in three cases the fines were reduced since the Commission had erred in its assessment. This long-running case has now been taken on appeal to the ECJ[8]. The Commission's decision in *LdPE*[9] was also annulled by the CFI on procedural grounds.

In 1989 the Commission condemned arrangements fixing prices and quotas in *Welded Steel Mesh*[10] and imposed fines totalling EUR 9,501,000 and ranging from EUR 13,000 to 4,500,000. The CFI upheld the decision, reducing the fines and partially annulling the decision in four cases[11]. In *Baustahlgewebe v Commission*[12] this judgment was annulled by the ECJ in so far as it upheld a fine of EUR 3,000,000 on the appellant since the proceedings before the CFI, which had taken six years, did not satisfy the requirement of completion within a reasonable time. A sum of EUR 50,000 would constitute reasonable satisfaction for the excessive duration of the proceedings, so that a fine of EUR 2,950,000 was substituted by the ECJ; the appellant was required to pay its own costs and three quarters of those of the Commission.

In the 1990s, the Commission continued to uncover and punish price-fixing agreements, for example in *Steel Beams*[13], *Cartonboard*[14] and in *Cement*[15]; in the *Cement* case it imposed one of the highest fines ever, a total of EUR 248 million. The CFI largely upheld the Commission's decision in *Cartonboard*[16]. In *Cement*[17], however, the CFI annulled a considerable part of the Commission's decision due to procedural impropriety on its part and because it had either failed to establish, or had exaggerated the duration of, some parties' participation in the agreement. The total amount of fines was reduced on appeal from EUR 248 million to approximately EUR 110 million. In *Steel Beams*[18] the CFI mostly affirmed the Commission's decision, but reduced the fine on Thyssen since the Commission had exaggerated the effect of the infringement on the market. The CFI in this judgment affirmed that an agreement not to *increase* prices may constitute a price-fixing agreement[19] and that the Commission's inaction in relation to the price fixing for a long period of time did not alter the fact that there had been a breach of the competition rules[20]. This was the first judgment of a Community Court on price fixing under Article 65 of the ECSC Treaty rather

---

5   Cases C-137/92 P *Commission v BASF AG* [1994] ECR I-2555.
6   OJ [1994] L 239/14.
7   Cases T-305/94 etc *Limburgse Vinyl Maatschappij v Commission* [1999] ECR II-931, [1999] 5 CMLR 303.
8   Case C-254/99 P *ICI v Commission*.
9   Cases T–80/89 etc *BASF AG v Commission* [1995] ECR II-729.
10 OJ [1989] L 260/1, [1991] 4 CMLR 13.
11 Cases T-141/89 etc *Tréfileurope Sales SARL v Commission* [1995] ECR II-791.
12 Case C-185/95 P *Baustahlgewebe GmbH v Commission* [1998] ECR I-8417, [1999] 4 CMLR 1203.
13 OJ [1994] L 116/1, [1994] 5 CMLR 353.
14 OJ [1994] L 243/1, [1994] 5 CMLR 547.
15 OJ [1994] L 343/1, [1995] 4 CMLR 327.
16 See Cases T-295/94 etc *Buchmann GmbH v Commission* [1998] ECR II-813.
17 Cases T-25-104/95 etc *Cimenteries SA v Commission* judgment of 15 March 2000.
18 Cases T-141/94 etc *Thyssen Stahl v Commission* [1999] ECR II-347, [1999] 4 CMLR 810.
19 Ibid, paras 227 and 233.
20 Ibid, para 554.

than Article 81(1) of the EC Treaty[1]. The CFI held that the expressions 'agreement' and 'concerted practice' have the same meaning under the EC and the ECSC Treaty[2]. It also held that the fact that, under the ECSC Treaty, undertakings must publish price lists, thereby creating a transparency in the market to competitors as well as to customers, does not absolve them of their obligation to determine their prices independently; the fact that Article 60 tends to restrict competition by making prices more transparent does not prevent the application of Article 65(1)[3]. The case has been appealed to the ECJ[4].

(B)   Article 81(3)

As would be expected the Commission has regularly refused to grant exemption to price-fixing agreements. In its 10th *Report on Competition Policy* it stated at point 115 that a price cartel falls into 'the category of manifest infringements under Article 81(1) which it is almost always impossible to exempt under Article 81(3) because of the total lack of benefit to the consumer'. The same attitude is manifested in Regulation 2658/2000 on specialisation agreements[5] and Regulation 2659/2000 on research and development agreements[6]: Article 5 of each provides that block exemption will not be available to agreements containing obvious restrictions of competition, such as the fixing of prices, the limitation of output or the allocation of markets or customers.

However it should be recalled that, as a matter of law, it is always open to the parties to an agreement to argue for an individual exemption, even if they are highly unlikely to be successful[7]. On a few occasions the Commission has permitted arrangements which could limit price competition. For example in *Uniform Eurocheques*[8] the Commission granted individual exemption to an agreement whereby commissions for the cashing of Eurocheques were fixed: this meant that consumers using such cheques knew that they would be charged a common amount throughout the Community. In *Insurance Intermediaries*[9] the Commission indicated its intention to grant exemption to agreements between non-life insurers to fix maximum discounts. These and other[10] decisions suggest that the Commission might take a slightly more indulgent approach towards agreements that limit price competition in the services sector than in the goods sector. Indeed in the case of containerised maritime transport, block exemption is granted by Articles 3 to 5 of Council Regulation 4056/86 for price fixing for liner conferences[11]. In *Reims II*[12] the Commission granted individual exemption

1   A second decision imposing a fine in the steel sector was adopted in *Alloy Surcharges* OJ [1998] L 100/55, [1998] 4 CMLR 973.
2   Ibid, paras 262 and 266.
3   Ibid, para 312.
4   Case C-199/99 P *British Steel v Commission* (judgment pending).
5   OJ [2001] L 304/3, [2001] 4 CMLR 800; for commentary on this Regulation, see ch 15, pp 517-520.
6   OJ [2001] L 304/7, [2001] 4 CMLR 808; for commentary on this Regulation, see ch 15, pp 510-515.
7   Case T-17/93 *Matra Hachette SA v Commission* [1994] ECR II-595; see ch 4, p 124.
8   OJ [1985] L 35/43, [1985] 3 CMLR 434.
9   OJ [1987] C 120/5.
10 See also *Nuovo CEGAM* OJ [1984] L 99/29, [1984] 2 CMLR 484; *P and I Clubs* OJ [1985] L 376/2, [1989] 4 CMLR 178; *Associazione Bancaria Italiana* OJ [1987] L 43/51, [1989] 4 CMLR 238; *Tariff Structures in the Combined Transport of Goods* OJ [1993] L 73/38.
11 See Regulation 4056/86, OJ [1986] L 378/1.
12 OJ [1999] L 275/17, [2000] 4 CMLR 704.

to an agreement between the major postal operators in the Community relating to 'terminal dues' payable by one post office to another when a letter posted in Member State A has to be delivered to an address in Member State B: the Commission's view was that this case involved price fixing with 'unusual characteristics'[13] and that improvements in efficiency and the elimination of cross-subsidy that would flow from the agreement satisfied the terms of Article 81(3).

(C)   Collective dominance

The extent to which parallel pricing might amount to an abuse of a collective dominant position is considered in chapter 14[14].

4.   HORIZONTAL MARKET SHARING[15]

Competition may be eliminated between independent undertakings in other ways than through direct or indirect price fixing. One way of doing so is for firms to agree to apportion particular markets between themselves. For example, three firms in the UK might agree that each will have exclusivity in a particular geographical area and that none will poach on the others' territories; a similar device is division of the market according to classes of customers, for example that one firm will supply trade customers only, another retailers and another public institutions. Geographical market-sharing agreements may be more effective than price fixing from the cartel's point of view, because the expense and difficulties of fixing common prices are avoided: the agreement means that there will be no price competition anyway. Policing the agreement is also relatively simple, because the mere presence of a competitor's goods on one's own 'patch' reveals cheating. Geographical market sharing is particularly restrictive from the consumer's point of view since it diminishes choice: at least where the parties fix prices a choice of product remains and it is possible that the restriction of price competition will force the parties to compete in other ways. Market-sharing agreements in the EC context may be viewed particularly seriously because, apart from the obviously anti-competitive effects already described, they serve to perpetuate the isolation of geographical markets and to retard the process of single market integration which is a prime aim of the EC Treaty.

It is sometimes argued in favour of geographical market-sharing agreements that they should be permitted since they reduce the distribution costs of producers, who are relieved of the need to supply outside their exclusive geographical territories or to categories of customers other than those allotted to them. This is unconvincing, as it does not explain why the benefit claimed is dependent upon the horizontal agreement. If a producer found it profitable to do so, it would want to sell outside its allotted territory or class of customer and in determining the profitability of doing so it would take distribution costs into account. All the agreement does is to foreclose this possibility. Potential competition is removed with the same adverse effect upon consumer welfare that other horizontal restrictions may produce: a reduction in output and an increase in price.

13 Ibid, para 65.
14 See ch 14 pp 467-469.
15 For further detail, see Pheasant and Bright in Div II of *Butterworths Competition Law*, ch 13; *Bellamy and Child*, paras 4-055 to 4-075.

It is not inconceivable that in some cases market sharing might be beneficial: in other words that restrictions accepted might be regarded as ancillary to some legitimate objective. Market sharing might enhance efficiency by enabling firms to compete more effectively with large undertakings. For example, a number of small retailers may decide to combine to promote their own 'house-label' in order to try to match other multiple chains. Individually they may be weak and unable to undertake the enormous costs involved in advertising and promotion, but in combination they may be able to do so. It could be argued that each retailer should be able to claim an exclusive sales territory so that it will be encouraged to take its full part in the campaign in the knowledge that it will reap the benefit in its area. The corollary is that without this incentive it will not promote the brand label so actively and enthusiastically. The argument is similar to that applicable to many vertical restraints[16]. The conclusion ought therefore to be that in some cases horizontal market sharing should be permitted.

(A)   Article 81(1)

There have been many decisions under Article 81 on market sharing, which is specifically mentioned in Article 81(1)(c)[17]. There are two obvious reasons for this. First, geographical market sharing can be achieved relatively easily in the EC context, since there are many ways of segregating national markets from one another. Until a truly single market is established, the factual, legal and economic disparities between national markets will continue to act as an obstacle to inter-state trade. Secondly, the policy of the Commission is to take action to prevent anything which might inhibit market penetration and it therefore has tended to expend much of its resources on dealing with this problem. It can be anticipated that horizontal market sharing will be punished increasingly severely in the future. In *Peroxygen Products*[18] fines totalling EUR 9,000,000 were imposed on five producers which, from 1961 until at least 1980, operated a 'home market' agreement which covered most of the EC. A consequence of this was that prices for consumers varied widely between different geographical markets. In *Soda-ash – Solvay/ICI*[19] the Commission imposed fines on Solvay and ICI for geographical market sharing.

In *Quinine*[20] the ECJ upheld the Commission's decision[1] to fine the members of the Quinine Cartel who had indulged in price fixing, the allocation of quotas

---

16   See ch 16, pp 543-545.
17   See ch 3, p 65; market division can be facilitated by the reliance upon intellectual property rights conferred by national laws in order to keep products out of domestic markets: this issue is considered in ch 19.
18   OJ [1985] L 35/1, [1985] 1 CMLR 481.
19   OJ [1991] L 152/1, [1994] 4 CMLR 454: this investigation resulted in three other decisions imposing fines on ICI and Solvay for breaches of Article 82: *Soda-ash – Solvay* OJ [1991] L 152/21, *Soda-ash – ICI* OJ [1991] L 152/40, both reported at [1994] 4 CMLR 645 and on Solvay and CFK for market sharing: *Soda ash – Solvay, CFK* OJ [1991] L 152/16, [1994] 4 CMLR 482; the decisions were annulled for procedural reasons in Cases T–30/91 etc *Solvay v Commission* [1995] ECR II-1775, [1996] 5 CMLR 57, and the CFI's judgment was upheld in Cases C-286/95 P etc *Commission v ICI* [2000] 5 CMLR 413 and 454; the Commission readopted the decisions against Solvay and ICI in December 2000: Commission Press Release IP/00/1449, 13 December 2000.
20   Cases 41/69 etc *ACF Chemiefarma NV v Commission* [1970] ECR 661.
1   *Re Quinine Cartel* JO [1969] L 192/5, [1969] CMLR D41.

and market division, and there have been many other similar cases since[2]. The infringements in the *Pre-Insulated Pipes*[3] decision were wide-ranging. The Commission accused the parties of dividing national markets and, ultimately, the whole European market amongst themselves; of price fixing; and of taking measures to hinder the one substantial competitor outside the cartel and to drive it out of the market. The fines amounted to EUR 92,000,000. In some cases there have been elements both of vertical and horizontal market divisions; distributors must refrain from market division as well as producers[4]. In *Cement*[5] the Commission found that cement producers had agreed on the 'non-transshipment of cement to home markets', which prohibited any export of cement within Europe which could threaten neighbouring markets. In *Seamless Steel Tubes*[6] the Commission found that eight producers of stainless steel tubes had colluded to protect their respective domestic markets; Commissioner Monti stated that this amounted to 'a very serious breach of the principles of competition and calls for a really dissuasive penalty'[7].

Article 81(1) has also been applied to horizontal agreements involving customer restrictions[8], and there is little to suggest that they would be granted exemption.

(B)   Article 81(3)

There is no formal provision to prevent the advancement of efficiency arguments under Article 81(3), but it is unlikely that the Commission would grant exemption to a horizontal geographical market-sharing case, in view of the overriding goal of achieving single market integration. However in exceptional circumstances individual exemption may be granted where it is ancillary to some legitimate objective[9].

5.   QUOTAS AND OTHER RESTRICTIONS ON PRODUCTION[10]

A further way in which a cartel might be able to earn supra-competitive profits is by agreeing to restrict its members' output. If output is reduced, price will rise;

2   Cases 40/73 etc *Coöperatieve Vereniging Suiker Unie UA v Commission* [1975] ECR 1663, [1976] 1 CMLR 295; *Re Van Katwijk NV's Agreement* JO [1970] L 242/18, [1970] CMLR D43; Cases 29/83 and 30/83 *Compagnie Royale Asturienne des Mines SA etc v Commission* [1984] ECR 1679, [1985] 1 CMLR 688; *Zinc Producer Group* OJ [1984] L 220/27, [1985] 2 CMLR 108.
3   *Pre-Insulated Pipe Cartel* OJ [1999] L 24/1, [1999] 4 CMLR 402, on appeal Cases T-9/99 etc *HFB Holding v Commission* (judgment pending).
4   See eg Cases 100–103/80 *Musique Diffusion Française SA v Commission* [1983] ECR 1825, [1983] 3 CMLR 221 in which the ECJ upheld the Commission's decision (OJ [1980] L 60/21, [1980] 1 CMLR 457) that distributors had engaged in concerted practices *amongst themselves* to isolate the French market.
5   OJ [1994] L 343/1, [1994] 4 CMLR 327, para 45.
6   See the Commission's XXIXth *Report on Competition Policy* (1999), p 137, on appeal Cases T-78/00 *Sumitomo v Commission* (judgment pending).
7   Commission Press Release IP/99/957, 8 December 1999; see also *SAS/Maersk* (Commission Press Release IP/01/1009, 18 July 2001): fines of EUR 52.5m for market sharing in the aviation sector
8   See eg *Re William Prym-Werke and Beka Agreement* OJ [1973] L 296/24, [1973] CMLR D250 where the Commission required the deletion of a customer restriction clause; *Atka A/S v BP Kemi A/S* OJ [1979] L 286/32, [1979] 3 CMLR 684 where BP was to supply customers with consumption of at least 100,000 gallons; *Belgian Roofing Felt* OJ [1986] L 232/15, [1991] 4 CMLR 130.
9   See *Transocean Marine Paint Association* JO [1967] L 163/10, [1967] CMLR D9.
10 For further detail, see Pheasant and Bright in Div II of *Butterworths Competition Law*, ch 12; *Bellamy and Child*, paras 4-046 to 4-054.

the oil cartel operated by OPEC does not fix prices as such, but instead determines how much oil each member country will export. Horizontal agreements to limit production need to be carefully monitored, because over-production by some members of the cartel would result in the market price falling, unless the scheme is run in conjunction with a price-fixing system, as often happens. In the absence of direct price fixing, the cartel members will often agree on a quota system whereby they will each supply a specified proportion of the entire industry output within any given period. As in the case of price fixing there will be costs involved in negotiating these quotas, because some firms will be larger or more efficient or expanding more rapidly than others so that there may have to be hard and protracted bargaining. The quotas having been fixed, some mechanism will have to be established to prevent cheating. This may be done, for example, by requiring detailed information about production and sales to be supplied to a central information-gathering agency. The agreement will also commonly provide a system whereby those that exceed their allocated quotas have to make compensating payments to those who, as a necessary corollary, fail to dispose of theirs. Complicated rules may have to be settled on how such payments are to be made. A firm which 'over-produces' will have to sell its products on the market at a higher price than it would wish if it is to make a profit and make a payment to the other cartel members; the loss to the consumer of such schemes is clear.

Some agreements which involve restrictions of production may be beneficial: specialisation agreements, joint production, research and development agreements, restructuring cartels and standardisation agreements may in some circumstances be considered desirable. This chapter is concerned with 'naked' restrictions on production which limit output without producing any compensating benefits; agreements involving restrictions of production which may be ancillary to some legitimate objective will be discussed in chapter 15.

(A)   Article 81(1)

Article 81(1)(b) specifically applies to agreements to 'limit or control production, markets, technical development, or investment' and has been applied to agreements to limit production on many occasions. Straightforward quota systems have often been condemned[11].

In *Peroxygen Products*[12] the Commission found that, as well as sharing markets geographically, members of the cartel had entered into a series of detailed national agreements dividing markets in agreed percentages. In *MELDOC*[13] a quota and compensation scheme in the dairy sector in the Netherlands was held to infringe Article 81, and the Commission imposed fines totalling EUR 6,565,000. An exacerbating fact in this decision was the fact that the Dutch milk producers also agreed to a coordinated response to the threat posed to their market position by imports from other Member States. An agreement not to expand production

---

11   See eg *Zinc Producer Group* OJ [1984] L 220/27, [1985] 2 CMLR 108; *Benelux Flat Glass* OJ [1984] L 212/13, [1985] 2 CMLR 350; also the various cement cases decided by the Commission involving quota arrangements: see *Re Cementregeling voor Nederland* JO [1972] L 303/7, [1973] CMLR D149; *Re Cimbel* JO [1972] L 303/24, [1973] CMLR D167; *Re Nederlandse Cement-Handelmaatshappij NV* JO [1972] L 22/16, [1973] CMLR D257; see also *Belgian Roofing Felt* OJ [1986] L 232/15, [1991] 4 CMLR 130; *Welded Steel Mesh* OJ [1989] L 260/1, [1991] 4 CMLR 13.
12   OJ [1985] L 35/1, [1985] 1 CMLR 481.
13   OJ [1986] L 348/50, [1989] 4 CMLR 853.

without the approval of rival firms infringes Article 81(1)[14] and the Commission will not easily be persuaded that a quota scheme will bring about beneficial specialisation[15]. It is not permissible to establish a joint venture to apportion orders between competitors[16], nor will the Commission allow joint production which simply limits competition without producing any compensating benefits[17]. Not infrequently quota agreements confer on particular undertakings exclusive or priority rights in supplying their own domestic markets: they will certainly not be tolerated[18].

An interesting example of a quota scheme condemned by the Commission is *Associated Lead Manufacturers Ltd (White Lead)*[19]. Firms producing white lead in the UK, Germany and the Netherlands agreed that each would supply one third of the white lead to be exported to non-EC countries. A central office was established which gathered information from them on their deliveries of white lead. The producers supplied this office with details of *all* deliveries, including exports to other EC countries. The Commission held that in practice the quota scheme related to all exports, that is to say to intra-Community as well as extra-Community trade, and that it clearly amounted to an attempt to limit and control markets within the terms of Article 81(1)(b). Furthermore the Commission held that it was irrelevant that the quotas were not always meticulously observed: an agreement did not cease to be anti-competitive because it was temporarily or even repeatedly circumvented by one of the parties to it[20].

In *Compagnie Royale Asturienne des Mines SA and Rheinzink GmbH v Commission*[1] the ECJ held that it was an infringement of Article 81(1) for competitors to supply products to each other on a continuing basis. Whereas this might be acceptable to deal with certain emergencies, it was not permissible for competitors to enter into agreements of indeterminate length and for considerable quantities. The effect of doing so was to institutionalise mutual aid in lieu of competition, producing conditions on the market analogous to those brought about by quota arrangements. In *Soda-ash – Solvay/CFK*[2] the Commission condemned an agreement whereby Solvay agreed to allow CFK a guaranteed minimum sales tonnage and to purchase from it any shortfall in order to compensate it. In *Italian Flat Glass*[3] the Commission condemned an agreement between manufacturers to exchange products and agree quantities sold to particular customers. The CFI overturned this aspect of the decision for lack of evidence[4], but it did not question the principle that such an agreement restricts competition. The first fine for a substantive infringement of Article 81 in the maritime transport sector was imposed in *French-West African Shipowners' Committees*[5] upon shipowners which had agreed to a cargo-sharing system in respect of traffic between France and various west African countries.

14   *Re Cimbel* JO [1972] L 303/24, [1973] CMLR D167.
15   *Re Italian Cast Glass* OJ [1980] L 383/19, [1982] 2 CMLR 61.
16   *Air Forge* XIIth *Report on Competition Policy* (1982), point 85.
17   *Re WANO Schwarzpulver GmbH* OJ [1978] L 322/26, [1979] 1 CMLR 403.
18   Case 41/69 *ACF Chemiefarma NV v Commission* [1970] ECR 661.
19   OJ [1979] L 21/16, [1979] 1 CMLR 464.
20   Similarly see *Re Cast Iron and Steel Rolls* OJ [1983] L 317/1, [1984] 1 CMLR 694 where the Commission fined various French undertakings which operated a quota scheme in respect of deliveries to the Saarland in Germany.
1   Cases 29/83 and 30/83 [1984] ECR 1679, [1985] 1 CMLR 688.
2   OJ [1991] L 152/16, [1994] 4 CMLR 482.
3   OJ [1989] L 33/44, [1990] 4 CMLR 535.
4   Cases T–68/89 etc *Società Italiana Vetro SpA v Commission* [1992] ECR II-1403, [1992] 5 CMLR 302.
5   OJ [1992] L 134/1, [1993] 5 CMLR 446.

An elaborate 'price before tonnage scheme' was found to be anti-competitive by the Commission in *Cartonboard*[6] which involved the 'freezing' of market shares, the constant monitoring and analysis of them, and the coordination of 'machine downtime' in an effort to sustain prices and control supply. In *Europe Asia Trades Agreement*[7] the Commission concluded that an agreement for 'capacity non-utilisation' coupled with the exchange of information in relation to maritime transport infringed Article 81(1); in its view, the agreement artificially limited liner shipping capacity, thereby reducing price competition[8]. In *Danish Association of Pharmaceutical Producers and the Danish Ministry for Health*[9] the Commission investigated a quota arrangement aimed at controlling public spending on price subsidies for pharmaceuticals. The Commission was concerned that the scheme infringed Article 81(1) and sought a settlement with the parties that would be less restrictive: the parties agreed not to renew the quota scheme when it terminated on 1 March 2001.

(B)   Article 81(3)

It is unlikely that the type of agreements discussed in this section would be given an exemption by the Commission, although agreements on capacity and production volume may be permitted when ancillary to a legitimate specialisation agreement[10].

6.   COLLUSIVE TENDERING[11]

Collusive tendering is a practice whereby firms agree amongst themselves to collaborate over their response to invitations to tender. It is particularly likely to be encountered in the engineering and construction industries where firms compete for very large contracts; often the tenderee will have a powerful bargaining position and the contractors feel the need to concert their bargaining power. From a contractor's point of view collusion over tendering has other benefits apart from the fact that it can lead to higher prices: it may mean that fewer contractors actually bother to price any particular deal (tendering itself can be a costly business) so that overheads are kept lower; it may mean that a contractor can make a tender which it knows will not be accepted (because it has been agreed that another firm will tender at a lower price) and yet which indicates that it is still interested in doing business, so that it will not be crossed off the tenderee's list; and it may mean that a contractor can retain the business of its established, favoured customers without worrying that they will be poached by its competitors.

Collusive tendering takes many forms. At its simplest, the firms in question simply agree to quote identical prices, the hope being that in the end each will receive its fair share of orders. Level tendering however is extremely suspicious

6   OJ [1994] L 243/1, [1994] 5 CMLR 547, paras 129-132.
7   OJ [1999] L 193/23, [1999] 5 CMLR 1380.
8   Ibid, paras 148-156.
9   Press Release IP/99/633, 17 August 1999; XXIXth *Report on Competition Policy* (1999), p 170.
10   See Article 5(2)(a) of Regulation 2658/2000, OJ [2000] L 304/3, [2001] 4 CMLR 800; for commentary on this Regulation, see ch 15, pp 517-520.
11   For further detail, see Pheasant and Bright in Div II of *Butterworths Competition Law*, ch 4.

and is likely to attract the attention of the competition authorities, so that more subtle arrangements are normally made. The more complicated these are, the greater will be the cost to the tenderers themselves. One system is to notify intended quotes to each other, or more likely to a central secretariat, which will then cost the order and eliminate those quotes which it considers would result in a loss to some or all of the association's members. Another system is to rotate orders, in which case the firm whose turn it is to receive an order will ensure that its quote is lower than everyone else's. Again it may be that orders are allocated by the relevant trade association which will advise each member how it should proceed.

There is no doubt that collusive tendering is caught by Article 81(1). The practice was condemned by the Commission in *Re European Sugar Cartel*[12]. In *Building and Construction Industry in the Netherlands*[13] the Commission imposed a fine of EUR 22,500,000 for regulating prices and tendering in the Dutch building and construction industry. Twenty-eight associations of firms had established an organisation, the SPO, which established a system of uniform price-regulating rules which were binding on all members. The rules had the effect of restricting or distorting competition, as members exchanged information with one another prior to tendering, concerted their behaviour in relation to the prices for tenders and operated a system whereby the 'entitled' undertaking could be certain of winning a particular contract. The fact that the Dutch Government approved of the system did not provide a defence under Article 81(1): rather it led to the Commission threatening proceedings against the Netherlands under Article 226 (former Article 169) for having encouraged this anti-competitive behaviour. The Commission rejected arguments in favour of exemption under Article 81(3) in this decision[14]. In *Pre-Insulated Pipes*[15] the Commission concluded that the allocation of contracts on the basis of 'respect for existing "traditional" customer relationships' as well as various measures to support the bid-rigging, amounted to an infringement of Article 81(1)[16].

In *FIEC/CEETB*[17] the Commission published a notice in which it indicated its intention to take no action in respect of an agreement between building contractors and sub-contractors which would standardise tendering procedures; the Commission required various amendments before announcing this indulgence. The agreement as amended would not limit price competition, nor would it prevent people from tendering who wished to do so; the advantage of the scheme was that it would reduce the cost of the tendering procedure.

7. AGREEMENTS RELATING TO TERMS AND CONDITIONS[18]

We have seen above that apart from agreements directly fixing prices, supra-competitive profits can also be earned in other ways, for example by limiting

---

12 OJ [1973] L 140/17, [1973] CMLR D65.
13 OJ [1992] L 92/1, [1993] 5 CMLR 135, upheld on appeal Case T–29/92 *SPO v Commission* [1995] ECR II-289.
14 Ibid, paras 115–131.
15 OJ [1999] L 24/1, [1999] 4 CMLR 402, on appeal Cases T-9/99 etc *HFB Holding v Commission* (judgment pending).
16 Ibid, para 147.
17 OJ [1988] C 52/2.
18 For further detail, see Pheasant and Bright in Div II of *Butterworths Competition Law*; *Bellamy and Child*, paras 4-041 to 4-042.

production, fixing quotas and dividing markets geographically. Similarly restrictive agreements which limit competition in the terms and conditions offered to customers can have this effect. An agreement not to offer discounts is in effect a price restriction, as would be an agreement not to offer credit; it may well exist to buttress a price-fixing agreement. In some market conditions it might be that non-price competition is particularly significant because of the limited opportunities that exist for price-cutting; for example, in an oligopolistic market one oligopolist might be able to attract custom because it can offer a better after-sales service or guarantees or a free delivery service[19].

Although competition in terms and conditions is an important part of the competitive process, it is also true to say that in some circumstances standardisation of terms and conditions can be beneficial. This might have the effect of enhancing price transparency: that is to say a customer might be able more easily to compare the 'real' cost of goods or services on offer if he or she does not have to make some (possibly intuitive) allowances for the disparity in two sets of terms and conditions on offer. Again a trade association may have the knowledge and expertise (and legal resources) to draft appropriate standard form contracts which suit the needs of individual members whereas, acting individually, they would be unable to negotiate and conclude a set of terms and conditions suitable for their purpose. Competition law monitors the activities of trade associations carefully in order to ensure that they do not act as a medium for the restriction of competition, but will usually tolerate this function. Industry-based codes of practice may fall within the ambit of competition legislation, although they may be desirable and may be encouraged or even required by consumer legislation[20].

Article 81 is capable of catching agreements which limit competition on terms and conditions, and to the extent that this is effected through the medium of trade associations the application of that Article to 'decisions by associations of undertakings' will be particularly apposite. The Commission has condemned agreements only to supply on prescribed general conditions of sale[1] and it has also objected to them where they formed part of wider reciprocal exclusive dealing arrangements[2]. In *Vimpoltu*[3] the Commission condemned an agreement on terms and conditions which limited important 'secondary aspects of competition'. In *Publishers' Association: Net Book Agreements*[4] agreements to impose on resellers standard conditions of sale and measures taken to implement this were condemned, as they deprived retailers of the ability to deviate from fixed retail prices. In *TACA*[5] the Commission concluded that an agreement that prohibited members of a liner conference from entering into individual service contracts at rates negotiated between a shipper and an individual line infringed Article 81(1); under the agreement members were permitted to offer standard service contracts only on the terms negotiated by the TACA secretariat, which constituted a serious fetter on their ability to compete with one another.

The Commission has recognised the advantages for undertakings in having access to suitably drafted standard terms and conditions and has indicated that

19 On oligopoly generally see ch 14, pp 460-467.
20 See eg s 124 of the Fair Trading Act 1973.
1   See *Re Groupment des Fabricants de Papiers Peints de Belgique* OJ [1974] L 160/1, [1974] 2 CMLR D50; see similarly *FEDETAB* OJ [1978] L 224/29, [1978] 3 CMLR 524.
2   See eg *Donck v Central Bureau voor de Rijwielhandel* OJ [1978] L 20/18, [1978] 2 CMLR 194.
3   OJ [1983] L 200/44, [1983] 3 CMLR 619.
4   OJ [1989] L 22/12, [1989] 4 CMLR 825.
5   OJ [1999] L 95/1, [1999] 4 CMLR 1415, paras 379-380, on appeal to the CFI Cases T-191/98 etc *Atlantic Container Line AB v Commission* (judgment pending).

their use will not attract the application of Article 81(1) in the absence of tacit agreements to standardise prices, rebates or conditions of sale[6]. Also the Commission granted individual exemption in the fire insurance sector to an agreement whereby insurance companies would be likely (though not obliged) to adopt the standard terms and conditions of Concordato, a non-profit making trade association[7].

8. INFORMATION AGREEMENTS[8]

(A) The arguments in favour of and against information agreements

Not infrequently competitors agree to exchange information with one another[9]. Such agreements can pose problems for competition authorities. They may be highly beneficial. Competitors cannot compete in a statistical vacuum: the more information they have about market conditions, the volume of demand, the level of capacity that exists in an industry and the investment plans of rivals, the easier it is for them to make rational and effective decisions on their production and marketing strategies. They may benefit by exchanging information on methods of accounting, stock control, bookkeeping or on the draftsmanship of standard-form contracts. Benchmarking, whereby companies measure their performance against the 'best practice' in their industry, may enable them to improve their efficiency[10]. Information may also be exchanged about new forms of technology and the results of research and development projects. By spreading technological know-how, information agreements can help to increase the number of firms capable of operating on the market[11]. Buyers too will benefit from an increase in information: the more they know about the products available and their prices, the easier it will be to make satisfactory choices. Indeed perfect competition is dependent on consumers having perfect information about the market[12]: market transparency is, in general, to be encouraged.

Against this the dangers of information agreements have to be borne in mind. The essence of competition is that each producer should act independently on the market and not co-ordinate its behaviour with that of its rivals. If competitors agree to divulge to one another detailed information about their pricing policies, investment plans or research and development projects, it becomes easier for them to act in concert. Indeed in some circumstances it may be that the mere exchange of information will in itself be sufficient to eliminate normal competitive

6   *Notice on Cooperation Agreements* 29 July 1968, para 11(2); the Commission's *Guidelines on Horizontal Cooperation Agreements* OJ [2001] C 3/2, [2001] 4 CMLR 819 replaced the 1968 Notice and do not deal with the point in the text; however there is no reason to suppose that the Commission has changed the view expressed in the 1968 Notice.
7   *Concordato Incendio* OJ [1990] L 15/25, [1991] 4 CMLR 199.
8   For further detail, see Pheasant and Bright in Div II of *Butterworths Competition Law*, ch 3; *Bellamy and Child*, paras 4-115 to 4-126.
9   See generally O'Brien and Swann *Information Agreements, Competition and Efficiency* (1968); Evans 'Trade Associations and the Exchange of Price and Non-price Information' [1989] Fordham Corp Law Institute (ed Hawk), pp 709–746.
10 See Henry 'Benchmarking and Antitrust' (1993) 62 Antitrust Law Journal 483; on benchmarking and EC law, see Carle and Johnsson 'Benchmarking and EC Competition Law' (1998) 19 ECLR 74; Boulter 'Competition Risks in Benchmarking' (1999) 20 ECLR 434.
11 See Teece 'Information Sharing, Innovation and Antitrust' (1993) 62 Antitrust Law Journal 465.
12 See ch 1, pp 5-6.

rivalry. The problem for competition law is to distinguish those exchanges of information which have a neutral or a beneficial effect upon efficiency from those which seriously threaten the competitive process by facilitating collusive behaviour[13]. The line between these situations is a fine one and proper characterisation can be difficult. From a theoretical perspective however it is possible to say a little more about the type of information agreements which could harm competition.

(B)   The relevance of the structure of the market

In the first place it is important to consider the structure of the market. As the comments earlier in this chapter on the economics of price fixing showed[14], it will be easier to restrict or distort competition in an oligopolistic market where the products are homogeneous. The greater the degree of product differentiation and the more atomistic the structure of competition, the more difficult and expensive it will be to fix prices and prevent cheating. This suggests that information agreements should be considered in their economic context and that they should be particularly carefully monitored in oligopolistic markets, and that scarce enforcement resources would be most beneficially concentrated on such areas[15].

(C)   The nature of the information exchanged

Another important consideration is the type or quality of information which is imparted. Whilst it may be beneficial to firms in an industry to exchange statistical information of a general nature which enables them to build up an overall picture of the level of demand or output in it, or the average overhead costs of each competitor, it does not follow that they should be permitted to inform each other of matters such as pricing policies or research and development projects which in the normal course of things might be regarded as secret matters. Also the effect of an information agreement might be considered less serious where purchasers as well as sellers have access to the information in question. Furthermore a distinction may be drawn between pre-notification and post-notification agreements: in the former case, firms inform one another of their intended future conduct; this can obviously be more anti-competitive than in the latter case, where firms simply pass on information of action which has already been implemented. Where historic information is exchanged, it will be relevant to consider how recent it is: the older it is, the less impact it is likely to have on competition.

(D)   The means by which the information is exchanged

In practice information may be exchanged in a variety of different ways. The method chosen will depend on the needs of the industry. Parties may simply

---

13   See Kühn and Vives 'Information Exchanges Among Firms and their Impact on Competition' (European Commission, June 1994, revised ed, February 1995).
14   See pp 424-425 above.
15   The problem of detecting horizontal restraints upon competition in oligopolies is explored in greater detail in ch 14.

agree to exchange information with one another at periodic intervals. Alternatively this may be – and in practice often is – achieved through the medium of a trade association, whose duty is to accumulate relevant information and disseminate it amongst its members[16]. Information may be transmitted to competitors through articles or notices in the press or trade journals. In principle however the method chosen to exchange information ought not to colour its analysis for the purpose of competition law. In each case the important question is whether the agreement might impair competition or enhance efficiency and the form the practice takes does not determine this issue.

(E) 'B2B' market places

A specific issue that has been of interest to competition authorities in recent years has been whether the establishment of 'B2B' electronic markets may give rise to competition law problems, and specifically whether they could facilitate collusion and/or foreclose access to the market. Clearly the competition authorities would not be happy if Internet chat rooms were to become the twenty-first century equivalent of the 'smoke-filled rooms' of the nineteenth and twentieth centuries. In a B2B market undertakings establish an electronic market place where it is possible, for example, to sell and purchase goods and services. Typically electronic market places such as this may result in a considerable exchange of information, both between sellers and purchasers but also between competitors themselves, on both the selling and purchasing side of the market. Universal access to the Internet means that this information is instantly accessible to everyone involved in the electronic market. In the US, the Federal Trade Commission ('the FTC') held a public workshop on 29 and 30 June 2000 to consider whether B2B exchanges of information could give rise to antitrust problems[17]. On 26 October it published a staff report[18] representing the views of the staff, though not necessarily of the Commissioners, of the FTC. In this report, the potential of B2B marketplaces to generate efficiencies is noted, including the promotion of transparency in the market; however the possibility that they might facilitate collusion is also mentioned; other problems could be the exercise of buyer power and the possibility that B2Bs might operate in an exclusionary manner. The FTC closed its investigation of the Covisint B2B, established between a number of car manufactures in relation to the purchase of components[19], without taking any action against it.

In the UK, the OFT commissioned a study on E-commerce which considered some of these issues and which was published in August 2000[20]; the study noted that internet technology could potentially offer an 'ideal micro-climate for collusion, due to increased communication and transparency in the market'[1]. It also contained a table of the existing B2B e-markets, demonstrating how rapidly this particular form of business behaviour has grown.

16 See Bissocoli 'Trade Associations and Information Exchange under US and EC Competition Law' (2000) 23(1) World Competition 29.
17 See 'Entering the 21st Century: Competition Policy in the World of B2B Electronic Market Places'; this can be accessed on the FTC's website at http://www.ftc.gov/bc/b2b/index.htm; see further Baker 'Identifying Horizontal Price Fixing in the Electronic Marketplace' (1996) 65 Antitrust Law Journal 41.
18 Available at http://www.ftc.gov/os/2000/10/index.htm#26.
19 See www.ftc.gov/os/2000/09/covisintchrysler.htm; Covisint was approved by the European Commission in July 2001: see Commission Press Release IP/01/1155, 31 July 2001.
20 *E-Commerce and Its Implications for Competition Policy* OFT 308.
1   Ibid, para 6.54.

(F)   Information agreements under US law

In the US the application of section 1 of the Sherman Act 1890 to information agreements has produced some anomalous decisions. In *American Column and Lumber Co v United States*[2] the Supreme Court ruled that an agreement to exchange price information in an atomistic market where conditions for collusion were unpropitious infringed the Act whilst in *Maple Flooring Manufacturers' Association v United States*[3] it reached the opposite conclusion where the market was oligopolistic and the opportunity for price fixing much greater. It would seem that these cases are classic examples of the problems which can be caused where courts fail to analyse competition cases in their economic context. More recently the Supreme Court's decisions seem to have involved a greater sensitivity to the economic issues raised by information agreements, even if its actual decisions on the facts can be criticised[4]. The present position would appear to be that there is no *per se* rule against the exchange of information; rather, a rule-of-reason standard is applied, albeit that information agreements are presumptively illegal where the market is oligopolistic[5].

(G)   Article 81(1)

The Commission has accepted that information agreements may have beneficial consequences and has attempted to indicate the point at which an agreement will begin to come within Article 81(1). In its 1968 *Notice on Cooperation Agreements*[6] it described various types of agreement which could be regarded as beneficial and unlikely to infringe Article 81(1). Amongst the list were agreements whose sole object was an exchange of opinion or experience, joint market research, the joint carrying out of comparative studies of enterprises or industries and the joint preparation of statistics and calculation models. Clearly these agreements involve the exchange of information, but the Commission considered they were not objectionable if they simply enabled firms to determine their future marketing behaviour freely. However it did warn that it would watch to ensure that an agreement does not lead to a restraint of competition and it specifically remarked that competition could be restrained by exchanges of information on an oligopolistic market for homogeneous products. The Commission stressed this in its decision in *UK Agricultural Tractor Registration Exchange*[7]. The 1968

2   257 US 377 (1921).
3   268 US 563 (1925); see Posner *Antitrust Law* (The University of Chicago Press, 1976) pp 135–143 for a critique of these two cases.
4   See *United States v Container Corpn of America* 393 US 333 (1969); *United States v Citizens Southern National Bank* 422 US 86 (1975); and *United States v United States Gypsum Co* 438 US 422 (1978).
5   On current US law see the Department of Justice and Federal Trade Commission *Antitrust Guidelines for Collaborations Among Competitors* (April, 2000, reprinted in 4 Fed Reg Rep (CCH) ¶ 13,160, also available at http://www.usdoj.gov/atr/public/guidelines/jointindex.htm); Scherer and Ross *Industrial Market Structure and Economic Performance* (Houghton Mifflin, 3rd ed 1990) pp 347–352; *Bissocoli* (n 16 above) pp 84-91; DeSanti and Nagata 'Competitor Communications: Facilitating Practices or Invitations to Collude?' (1994) 63 Antitrust Law Journal 93.
6   JO [1968] C 75/3, [1968] CMLR D5.
7   See *UK Agricultural Tractor Registration Exchange* OJ [1992] L 68/19, [1993] 4 CMLR 358, paras 37 and 38, upheld on appeal to the CFI in Cases T-34 and T-35/92 *Fiatagri UK Ltd v Commission* [1994] ECR II-905 and 957 and on appeal to the ECJ in Cases C-7/95 and C-8/95 P *John Deere v Commission* [1998] ECR I-3111 and 3175, [1998] 5 CMLR 311; on the Commission's decision in this case, see Lenares 'Economic Foundations of EU Legislation on Information Sharing Among Firms' (1997) 18 ECLR 66.

Notice is no longer in force, having been replaced by the Commission's *Guidelines on Horizontal Cooperation Agreements*[8]; these Guidelines do not deal with information agreements[9], but they do not say anything to cast doubt on the views expressed in the earlier Notice.

In a series of decisions the Commission has objected to information agreements which it considered might restrict competition. Many of the decisions in which the Commission has considered the exchange of information have been prompted by other infringements or suspected infringements of Article 81; for example, in *Wood Pulp*[10] the Commission was concerned about concerted practices to fix prices in that industry (on appeal its decision was substantially annulled[11]), whilst in *UK Agricultural Tractor Registration Exchange*[12] the Commission's action followed allegations of interference with parallel imports of tractors into the UK: subsequently in *Ford Agricultural*[13] Ford was found to have infringed Article 81(1) by doing so. In *Building and Construction Industry in the Netherlands*[14] the Commission condemned the exchange of information which supported the anti-competitive tendering arrangements in that industry.

From the Commission's decisions, and the appeals in the *Tractors* case, the following picture of the application of Article 81(1) to information agreements emerges.

(i) Agreement to exchange information

To infringe Article 81(1), undertakings must have agreed to exchange information. It is not sufficient simply that they are able to obtain information about each other's behaviour, for example through the press or by discussions with customers; this in itself does not involve the necessary ingredient of an agreement. Where a third party collects, compiles and supplies information to customers, Article 81(1) would not be infringed. In *Wood Pulp*[15] the ECJ ruled that the fact that pulp producers announced price rises to users before those rises came into effect was not, in itself, sufficient to constitute an infringement of Article 81(1)[16]. On the other hand, exchanges of information which were not obligatory in a contractual sense could amount to a 'gentleman's agreement' or a concerted practice and so be caught by Article 81(1) where they have the effect of restricting or distorting competition[17].

(ii) Market structure

The Commission will investigate the structure of the market in which the information agreement is operable: the more concentrated the market is, the

---

8   OJ [2001] C 3/2, [2001] 4 CMLR 819, para 8.
9   Ibid, para 10.
10 OJ [1985] L 85/1, [1985] 3 CMLR 474.
11 Cases C–89/95 etc *A Ahlstrom Oy v Commission* [1993] ECR I-1307, [1993] 4 CMLR 407.
12 See p 444, n 7 above.
13 OJ [1993] L 20/1, [1993] 5 CMLR 135.
14 OJ [1992] L 92/1 [1993] 5 CMLR 135, paras 98–99, on appeal Case T–29/92 *SPO v Commission* [1995] ECR II-289.
15 Cases C–89/85 etc *A Ahlstrom Oy v Commission* [1993] ECR I-1307, [1993] 4 CMLR 407.
16 Ibid, paras 59–65.
17 See eg *IFTRA Free Trade Rules on Glass* OJ [1974] L 160/1, [1974] 2 CMLR D50: the Commission concluded that the exchanges of information that took place were an integral part of the participants' intention to protect national markets.

more likely the Commission is to hold that competition is being restricted. For example, in both *International Energy Program*[18] and *Non-ferrous Semi-manufacturers*[19] it specifically referred to the oligopolistic structure of the markets in question. In *UK Agricultural Tractor Registration Exchange*[20] the Commission condemned an information exchange system, placing considerable emphasis on the fact that the UK tractor market was oligopolistic: in particular it took into account that four firms on the UK market had a combined market share of approximately 80% and that in some geographical areas the concentration was higher; that barriers to entry were high, especially as extensive distribution and servicing networks were necessary; that the market was stagnant or in decline and there was considerable brand loyalty; and that there was an absence of significant imports[1]. The Commission seems to have considered that the exchange of detailed information about retail sales and market shares broken down by product, territory and time periods was a *per se* infringement in an oligopolistic market[2]. The Commission published a Press Release after this decision in which it said that the same result would not necessarily arise in the car market, which is much more competitive[3]. In its decision in *Wirtschaftsvereinigung Stahl*[4], condemning an information agreement under Article 65 ECSC, the Commission stressed at paragraphs 39 and 44 to 46 of its decision that the market in question was concentrated and had high barriers to entry. In *Eudim*[5] the Commission was more relaxed about the exchange of information between wholesalers of plumbing, heating and sanitary materials. The information related both to the purchasing and the selling activities of members of the association; even though some of the information was of a kind that would normally be regarded as confidential, the Commission had no concern at all about the purchasing side of the market, which was highly competitive, and considered that, since there was no oligopoly on the selling side, there could be no appreciable effect on competition.

(iii)   Type of information exchanged

In *Re VNP and COBELPA*[6] the Commission said that, whilst it was permissible to exchange general statistical information which could give a picture of aggregate sales and output in an industry without identifying individual companies, it would be contrary to Article 81(1) for firms to provide competitors with detailed information about matters which would normally be regarded as confidential[7]. It also suggested in this decision that Article 81(1) would more likely be infringed where the information exchanged was concealed from customers[8]. In *UK Agricultural Tractor Registration Exchange*[9] the Commission was influenced in

18 OJ [1983] L 376/30, [1984] 2 CMLR 186.
19 Vth *Report on Competition Policy* (1975), point 39.
20 See p 444, n 7 above.
1   Ibid, para 35.
2   Ibid, paras 37–43.
3   Commission Press Release IP/92/148, 4 March 1992.
4   OJ [1998] L 1/10, [1998] 4 CMLR 450; this decision was annulled on appeal, Case T-16/98 *Wirtschaftsvereinigung Stahl v Commission* [2001] 5 CMLR 310.
5   OJ [1996] C 111/8, [1996] 4 CMLR 871.
6   OJ [1977] L 242/10, [1977] 2 CMLR D28.
7   This formula has been repeated on subsequent occasions: see eg *Re Italian Cast Glass* OJ [1980] L 383/19, [1982] 2 CMLR 61.
8   See similarly *Genuine Vegetable Parchment Association* OJ [1978] L 70/54, [1978] 1 CMLR 534.
9   See p 444, n 7 above.

its adverse view of the information exchange by the fact that participants in the system had kept the information confidential amongst themselves; when this decision was upheld by the ECJ, it noted that the information exchanged was not available to purchasers, but only to the parties to the agreement[10]. This shows that where the availability of the information is asymmetric, there is more likely to be an infringement of Article 81(1): the private enhancement of market transparency between competitors gives cause for concern whereas improved public transparency may not.

The critical question therefore is to decide what type of information the Commission considers would normally be regarded as confidential: at what point do firms cross the threshold from innocent exchanges to infringements of Article 81(1)? One would expect the Commission to object most strongly to agreements to exchange information about prices and it has done on various occasions[11]. It has also objected to information agreements relating to other matters. In *Re Cimbel*[12] it condemned the obligation upon members of a trade association that they should inform each other of projected increases in industrial capacity: such an obligation could prevent one firm from gaining an advantage over competitors by expanding in time to meet an increase in demand. Similarly it condemned the obligation to inform rivals of investment plans in *Zinc Producer Group*[13]. It has condemned exchanges of information which specifically identify the output and sales figures of individual firms[14] and which might have the effect of rigidifying the operation of a distribution system, particularly if it might facilitate the partitioning of the market[15]. In 1999 the Commission closed its files in relation to a number of cases involving the exchange of information between manufacturers of tractors and agricultural machinery and their trade associations, in the aftermath of its *Tractors* decision[16], after it had ensured that individual data would not be exchanged earlier than one year after the event to which it pertained and that aggregated data would not be exchanged if it could be used to identify individual information about the position of undertakings[17]. In *EATA*[18] the Commission objected to the exchange of information as to capacity, percentage utilisation and forecast capacity in the maritime transport sector, noting, specifically, that the information was not aggregated but clearly stated to which party it related[19].

10 Cases C-7/95 P and C-8/95 P *John Deere v Commission* [1998] ECR I-3111, [1998] 5 CMLR 311, para 91.
11 See eg *Ship's Cables* Bull EC 9–1975, point 2107; *IFTRA Fair Trade Rules on Glass* OJ [1974] L 160/1, [1974] 2 CMLR D50; *Dutch Sporting Cartridges* Bull EC 7–8/73, point 211; *Re Vimpoltu* OJ [1983] L 200/44, [1983] 3 CMLR 619; exchange of information by buyers could also be caught: *Belgian Industrial Timber* Bull 10–75, point 2104, [1976] 1 CMLR D11.
12 OJ [1972] L 303/24, [1973] CMLR D167.
13 OJ [1984] L 220/27, [1985] 2 CMLR 108.
14 See *Associated Lead Manufacturers* OJ [1979] L 21/16, [1979] 1 CMLR 464; *Atka A/S v BP Kemi A/S* OJ [1979] L 286/32, [1979] 3 CMLR 684; *Benelux Flat Glass* OJ [1984] L 212/13, [1985] 2 CMLR 350; *UK Agricultural Tractor Registration Exchange* (p 444, n 7 above).
15 *Camera Care Ltd v Victor Hasselblad* OJ [1982] L 161/18, [1982] 2 CMLR 233; *UK Agricultural Tractor Registration Exchange* (p 444, n 7 above), paras 53–56.
16 See p 444, n 7 above.
17 See the Commission's XXIXth *Report on Competition Policy* (1999), pp 156-157.
18 OJ [1999] L 193/23, [1999] 5 CMLR 1380.
19 Ibid, paras 153-155.

In *Steel Beams*[20] the Commission found an information exchange on orders and deliveries of beams by individual companies in each Member State to go 'beyond what is admissible'[1], since the figures exchanged showed the deliveries and orders received by each individual company for delivery to their respective markets; this information was updated every week and circulated rapidly among the participants. The Commission added that the exchange was not limited to figures 'of a merely historical value with no possible impact on competition'[2]. The CFI confirmed the Commission's assessment, since the exchange of confidential information undermined the principle that every trader must determine its market strategy independently. In *Wirtschaftsvereingung Stahl*[3] the Commission decided that an exchange of information on deliveries and market shares in relation to various products infringed Article 65(1) ECSC; the data were individualised, not aggregated and were exchanged monthly. In *CEPI/ Cartonboard*[4] the Commission indicated its intention to approve an information exchange agreement once it had been amended so that only historical, aggregated data would be involved.

(iv)   Alternative sources of information

The fact that information might be obtainable from other sources does not diminish the unlawfulness of an agreement between competitors to exchange information[5].

(v)   Mode of exchanging information

The Commission has been equally prepared to condemn information agreements operated through the medium of trade associations as straight contractual arrangements. For example, in *Re Italian Cast Glass*[6] manufacturers provided information to FIDES, a trust company whose function was to monitor the operation of a quota scheme. The Commission in this case fined both the producers and FIDES. In *UK Agricultural Tractor Registration Exchange*[7] the information was exchanged through the Agricultural Engineers Association.

(vi)   B2B markets

The Commission has yet to adopt a decision on a B2B case under Article 81, although a comfort letter was sent in the case of *Covisint*.[7a] However, it would be reasonable to expect that the principles set out in this section on information agreements would be applied to e-markets; and specifically that the Commission

---

20   OJ [1994] L 116/1, [1994] 5 CMLR 353, paras 263-272, upheld on appeal to CFI in Cases T-141/94 etc *Thyssen Stahl v Commission* [1999] ECR II-347, [1999] 4 CMLR 810, paras 385-412; this case is on appeal to ECJ in Case C-199/99 P *British Steel v Commission* (judgment pending).
1   Ibid, para 267.
2   Ibid, para 268.
3   OJ [1998] L 1/10, [1998] 4 CMLR 450.
4   OJ [1996] C 310/3, [1996] 5 CMLR 725.
5   *VNP/COBELPA* OJ [1977] L 242/10, [1977] 2 CMLR D28; *Genuine Vegetable Parchment Association* OJ [1978] L 70/54, [1978] 1 CMLR 534.
6   OJ [1982] L 383/19, [1982] 2 CMLR 61.
7   See p 444, n 7 above.
7a   Commission Press Release IP/01/1155, 31 July 2001.

would not be concerned about agreements that increase the transparency of the marketplace in such a way as to increase customer information, but would be concerned if the exchange of information could facilitate collusion. The Commission's decision on the B2B market in *UTC/Honeywell/i2/Myaircraft.com*[8] was adopted under the EC Merger Regulation rather than Article 81[9].

(vii)   Exchange of information as evidence of a concerted practice

In *Wood Pulp*[10] the Commission had regarded the exchange of information, both direct and indirect through the press, as supporting evidence of a concerted practice to fix prices; according to this view, not only is it an offence to exchange information, but this fact may be taken to show a further, and more serious, infringement of Article 81. On appeal, however, the ECJ overturned the Commission's decision in this respect, concluding that the system of price announcements could be regarded as a rational response to the fact that both buyers and sellers needed information in advance in order to limit their commercial risks. The fact that price announcements were made at similar times could be regarded as a consequence of the natural degree of transparency of the market rather than an artificial transparency established by the pulp producers[11]. However, despite the fact that the Commission lost on this occasion, an unlawful exchange of price information could be taken as evidence of a concerted practice to fix price in a clear case[12].

(viii)   Fines

In the Commission's early decisions on information agreements it refrained from imposing fines on the parties, even though they were held to have infringed Article 81(1), in view of the novelty of its application in this area. However in subsequent cases it made it clear that in appropriate cases it would not hesitate to punish undertakings which participate in anti-competitive information agreements. This turned to reality in *Fatty Acids*[13]. The Commission imposed a fine of EUR 50,000 on firms which entered into an agreement to exchange information which enabled each to identify the individual business of its two main rivals on a quarterly basis, thereby removing an important element of uncertainty on the part of each as to the activities of the others. This means that firms must be careful not to divulge information to competitors which could be considered confidential or sensitive, particularly in oligopolistic markets; it also means that if and when competitors do meet, for example at conferences or trade association meetings, they should studiously avoid exchanging such information. The Commission clearly intends to signal to firms that they will be at risk if they

8   Case No COMP/M.1969.
9   See Vollebregt 'E-Hubs, Syndication and Competition Concerns' (2000) 21 ECLR 437; Lancefield 'The Regulatory Hurdles Ahead in B2B' (2001) 22 ECLR 9.
10 OJ [1985] L 85/1, [1985] 3 CMLR 474.
11 Cases C–89/85 etc *A Ahlstrom Oy v Commission* [1993] ECR I-1307, [1993] 4 CMLR 407.
12 In *Wood Pulp* the ECJ considered that the fact that members of the US trade association, KEA, exchanged information on prices could be taken to mean they had also concerted on those prices: ibid, paras 130–132.
13 OJ [1985] L 3/17, [1989] 4 CMLR 445.

contact one another in any way in respect of sensitive business matters; it is important not artificially to increase the transparency of the market[14].

(H)   Article 81(3)

Under EC law the main question has revolved around the application of Article 81(1) to information agreements, and in *Re VNP and COBELPA*[15] the Commission indicated that an information agreement within Article 81(1) would be unlikely to be given an individual exemption. In *UK Agricultural Tractor Registration Exchange*[16] the Commission rejected the parties' request for an exemption in terse terms. However in exceptional circumstances an agreement may be exempted under Article 81(3) because of its beneficial effects. In *International Energy Program*[17] a programme was drawn up between 21 States belonging to the OECD. The purpose of the programme was to establish co-operation between States in the event of disruptions in the supply of oil. The participation of companies was an important element in this programme and they were required *inter alia* to supply important and normally secret information in the event of a disruption. The Commission granted an individual exemption: not surprisingly it felt that the strategic importance of maintaining supplies of oil outweighed the loss of competition occasioned by the exchange of information. In *EWIS* the Commission indicated that it intended to take a 'favourable decision' in respect of an agreement for the exchange of statistical data, stock levels, consumption, quarterly forecasts, usage capacity and other matters in the waste paper industry. The information was to be divulged confidentially to a central agency, which would then circulate it in an aggregated form. It is not clear whether, by taking a favourable decision, the Commission was indicating that the agreement fell outside Article 81(1) altogether or whether it considered it was worthy of individual exemption; the former seems more likely than the latter[18].

9.   ADVERTISING RESTRICTIONS[19]

The function of advertising in competition policy raises important and controversial issues which can be dealt with only briefly here[20]. Advertising is an essential part of the competitive process. Unless the consumer knows what goods and services are on offer and what their price is he or she will be unable to choose what to buy and competition between suppliers will be diminished.

---

14 See also ch 3, p 78ff.
15 OJ [1977] L 242/10, [1977] 2 CMLR D28.
16 See p 444, n 7 above.
17 OJ [1983] L 376/30, [1984] 2 CMLR 186; see Brands 'The International Energy Agency and the EC Competition Rules' [1984(1)] LIEI 49.
18 OJ [1987] C 339/7.
19 For further detail, see Pheasant and Bright in Div II of *Butterworths Competition Law*, chs 9 and 11.
20 See eg Cowling *Advertising and Economic Behaviour* (1975); Telser 'Advertising and Competition' 72 J Pol Ec 536 (1964); Brozen 'Entry Barriers: Advertising and Product Differentiation' in *Industrial Concentration: The New Learning* (1974); Scherer and Ross *Industrial Market Structure and Economic Performance* (Houghton Mifflin, 3rd ed, 1990) pp 436 et seq.

Competition is about attracting business and a vital part of the process is to advertise one's products. Therefore competition law should ensure that advertising is not restricted[1]. Indeed it may be thought appropriate to impose upon businesses a duty to advertise prices, terms and conditions or details of quality in order to provide the consumer with the information needed to enable him or her to make a rational choice. Also the significance of advertising means that steps should be taken to ensure the truth of advertisements and, perhaps, to prevent the appropriation of innovative advertising ideas by competitive rivals; comparative advertising, whereby a competitor's products are unfavourably compared with one's own, might also be objected to.

In some circumstances collaboration between independent undertakings in their advertising activities may not be harmful. For example, a group of small producers may decide to sell a product under a common label and agree on the specifications and publicity of the product in question; they will all contribute to the advertising costs of this product. By doing this they may be able to present a strong brand image which will enhance their ability to compete with other firms on the market. Such schemes may be pro-competitive, although it will be necessary to ensure that nothing in the agreement limits competition unnecessarily, such as direct price fixing or market sharing. Again there may be a case for some collaboration on advertising – for example by agreeing to limit the number of industrial exhibitions visited in a year – if this will have the effect of rationalising advertising efforts and reducing advertising costs.

The importance of advertising in competition policy has an important side effect: namely that the advertising media themselves should function efficiently and be free from restrictive trade practices which might reduce the availability of advertising space. Various cases in the US have endeavoured to maintain an open advertising market[2].

Against the above line of reasoning there runs a quite different argument. This is that advertising costs are a serious barrier to entry to new firms wishing to enter a market as well as being a wasteful use of resources[3]. In some markets, such as lager, detergents and breakfast cereals, enormous amounts of money are spent in building up a brand image and it is argued that new entrants would be unable to expend the money on advertising necessary to match this. The problem, it is said, is accentuated by the fact that established firms have the accumulated advantage of past advertising and also that they have the capacity to indulge in 'predatory' advertising, that is short-term expensive campaigns designed to prevent the new entrant establishing a toe-hold in the market. Opinion on the barrier-raising effect of advertising is divided. Bork and other commentators have argued forcefully that it should not be treated as a barrier and there is empirical evidence which sheds doubt on the argument[4].

A separate objection to advertising comes from a quite different quarter, namely the liberal professions. They have argued that advertising is inimical to their ethical standards and that consumer protection in their spheres of activity is best served by maintaining professional standards through self-regulation, codes of practice and professional ethics.

1 Restrictions on advertising in the US are regarded as an indirect form of price fixing and are accordingly per se illegal.
2 See eg *United States v Lorain Journal* 342 US 143 (1951).
3 See eg Turner 'Conglomerate Mergers and s 7 of the Clayton Act' 78 Harv L Rev 1313 (1965).
4 See eg Bork *The Antitrust Paradox* (1978) pp 314–320.

(A)   Article 81(1)

Article 81(1) does apply to agreements to restrict advertising which have anti-competitive effects. In several decisions the Commission has stated that it considers that such restrictions limit an important aspect of competitive behaviour[5]. In the case of trade fairs, it has often held that the rules for participation infringe Article 81(1), although it has gone on to permit exemption subject to conditions (see below). Trade fair rules may affect competition in various ways: participants may be required not to take part in other fairs, thus limiting their competitive opportunities; other organisers of such fairs will lose business as a result of such exclusivity rules; and potential participants might be excluded from a trade fair by its rules, thus limiting their impact on the market. In 1988 the Commission, for the first time in a trade fair case, imposed a fine (of EUR 100,000) on the *British Dental Trade Association*[6] for anti-competitive exclusion of would-be exhibitors.

In a number of decisions[7] the Commission has revealed a benevolence towards advertising restrictions which might promote a particular brand image without seriously impairing competition in other ways. However in *Belgian Roofing Felt*[8] the Commission condemned joint advertising of roofing felt under the Belasco trade mark where this led to the uniform image of products in a sector in which individual advertising may facilitate differentiation and therefore competition. The Commission's *Guidelines on Horizontal Cooperation Agreements*[9] provide guidance on the application of Article 81 to so-called 'commercialisation agreements', which may involve joint advertising[10].

Restrictions on comparative advertising by patent agents practicing at the European Patent Office in Munich were held to infringe Article 81(1) in *EPI code of conduct*[11], but to be exemptable for a short period whilst new rules were adopted[12].

(B)   Article 81(3)

The Commission has accepted that in appropriate circumstances it can be advantageous to rationalise and coordinate advertising efforts. In a series of cases on trade fairs it has granted exemptions to agreements which contain rules requiring participants to limit the number of occasions on which they exhibit elsewhere and restricting the extent to which they are allowed to advertise in

---

5   See eg *Re Vimpoltu* OJ [1983] L 200/44, [1983] 3 CMLR 619.
6   OJ [1988] L 233/15, [1989] 4 CMLR 1021; an exemption was given for the Association's rules as modified to satisfy the Commission.
7   *Re VVVF* OJ [1969] L 168/22, [1970] CMLR D1; *Re Association pour la Promotion du Tube d'Acier Soude Electriquement* JO [1970] L 153/14, [1970] CMLR D31; *Re Industrieverband Solnhofener Natursteinplatten* OJ [1980] L 318/32.
8   OJ [1986] L 232/15, [1991] 4 CMLR 130, upheld on appeal Case 246/86 *Belasco v Commission* [1989] ECR 2117, [1991] 4 CMLR 96.
9   OJ [2001] C 3/2, [2001] 4 CMLR 819.
10 See ch 15, pp 523-524.
11 OJ [1999] L 106/14, [1999] 5 CMLR 540, paras 39-45, partially annulled on appeal to the CFI, Case T-144/99 *Institut des Mandataires Agréés v Commission* (judgment of 28 March 2001); see the Commission's XXIXth *Report on Competition Policy* (1999), pp 53 and 159-160.
12 Ibid, paras 46-48.

other ways[13]. The Commission often applies conditions to such exemptions. When renewing the exemption in *UNIDI*[14] the Commission required the introduction of an arbitration procedure to deal with complaints by exhibitors excluded from an exhibition. In *VIFKA*[15] it required the removal of a provision requiring exhibitors of office equipment not to exhibit elsewhere for a period of two years, as this was too long.

10. ANTI-COMPETITIVE HORIZONTAL RESTRAINTS[16]

The agreements so far considered have been concerned with cartels limiting competition and raising prices to earn supra-competitive profits. It is likely however that, in the absence of barriers to entry, this in itself will attract new entrants into the market. It is because of this that the members of a cartel will frequently take further action designed to fend off the possibility of new competition in just the same way that a monopolist might. For example, a collective reciprocal exclusive dealing arrangement might be negotiated whereby a group of suppliers agree with a group of dealers to deal only with one another. The effect may be to exclude other producers from the market if they cannot find retail outlets for their products. This is not an inevitable result however: to have a serious foreclosing effect there would have to be a lack of alternative retail outlets, for example due to barriers to entry at the retail level. A common pricing system may be supported by an aggregated rebates cartel, whereby purchasers are offered rebates calculated according to their purchases from all the members of the cartel; the disincentive to buy elsewhere is obvious[17]. Again it may be decided to boycott any dealer who handles the products of producers outside the cartel. As one would expect, exclusionary devices such as these which can cause serious harm to the competitive process are *per se* illegal in the US[18], although it has been argued that the breadth of the rule against collective boycotts is inappropriate[19]. The pejorative label given to group boycotts conceals the fact that in some cases independent firms will inevitably decide to refuse to deal with certain people, for example by refusing inadequately trained people entrance to a profession or inefficient dealers access to a branded product. A distinction should be made between naked restraints which are clearly intended to be exclusionary on the one hand and agreements which promote efficiency and which therefore may be permitted.

13 *Re CECIMO* OJ [1969] L 69/13, [1969] CMLR D1, renewed OJ [1979] L 11/16, [1979] 1 CMLR 419 and again OJ [1989] L 37/11; *Re BPICA* OJ [1977] L 299/18, [1977] 2 CMLR D43, renewed OJ [1982] L 156/16, [1983] 2 CMLR 40; *Re Cematex* JO [1971] L 227/26, [1973] CMLR D135, renewed OJ [1983] L 140/27, [1984] 3 CMLR 69; *Re UNIDI* OJ [1975] L 228/14, [1975] 2 CMLR D51, renewed OJ [1984] L 322/10, [1985] 2 CMLR 38; *Re Society of Motor Manufacturers and Traders Ltd* OJ [1983] L 376/1, [1984] 1 CMLR 611; *VIFKA* OJ [1986] L 291/46; *Internationale Dentalschau* OJ [1987] L 293/58; *Sippa* OJ [1991] L 60/19, [1992] 5 CMLR 529.
14 OJ [1984] L 322/10, [1985] 2 CMLR 38, challenged unsuccessfully in Case 43/85 *ANCIDES v Commission* [1987] ECR 3131, [1988] 4 CMLR 821.
15 OJ [1986] L 291/46.
16 For further detail, see Pheasant and Bright in Div II of *Butterworths Competition Law*, chs 5 and 6; *Bellamy and Child* paras 4-078 to 4-088.
17 Aggregated rebates cartels are unlikely where prices are *not* fixed, because they would discriminate against those offering lower prices.
18 See eg *Klors Inc v Broadway – Hale Stores Inc* 359 US 207 (1959).
19 See eg Bork *The Antitrust Paradox* (Basic Books, 1978) ch 17.

The Commission and the Community Courts have had to deal with a great number of collective exclusive dealing arrangements and other potentially exclusionary practices. Often such agreements are entered into by a national association which is keen to keep imports out of the domestic market. A more obvious target for the Commission it is hard to imagine and the Community Courts have usually upheld its findings. A scheme designed to keep washing machines out of the Belgian market was found by the ECJ to infringe Article 81(1)[20], as was a marketing system which could prevent imports of fruit into Holland[1]. The ECJ agreed with the Commission that an exclusive purchasing agreement which obliged members of an association to acquire rennet solely from a Dutch cooperative was unlawful[2]. The ECJ also held that practices designed to buttress the collective resale price maintenance of Dutch and Belgian books infringed Article 81[3].

The rigid collective exclusive dealing systems in two cigarettes cases, affecting the Belgian and Dutch markets respectively, were both condemned by the ECJ[4]. The Commission has dealt with many other similar situations, always striking such agreements down[5]. In *Hudson's Bay – Dansk Pelsdyravlerforening*[6] the Commission imposed a fine of EUR 500,000 on a Danish trade association for imposing an obligation on its members that they should sell their entire production to a subsidiary of the association, thereby preventing them from selling their products to other Member States. The decision on this point was upheld on appeal to the CFI[7]. In *Dutch Mobile Cranes*[8] the Commission imposed fines on a trade association found to have operated a price-fixing system whereby its members were obliged to charge 'recommended' rates for the hiring of mobile cranes; it also condemned the rules of a second association that effectively prohibited members from hiring cranes from firms not affiliated to it.

In *Dutch Electrotechnical Equipment*[9] the Commission imposed fines of EUR 4.4 million on FEG and EUR 2.15 million on TU for entering into collective exclusive dealing arrangements intended to prevent supplies to non-members of the associations by directly and indirectly restricting the freedom of members to

20   Cases 96/82 etc *IAZ International Belgium NV v Commission* [1983] ECR 3369, [1984] 3 CMLR 276; note the additional fine subsequently imposed by the Commission in this case: *Re IPTC Belgium SA* OJ [1983] L 376/7, [1984] 2 CMLR 131.
1   Case 71/74 *FRUBO v Commission* [1975] ECR 563, [1975] 2 CMLR 123; see similarly *Irish Timber Importers Association* XXth *Report on Competition Policy* (1990), point 98.
2   Case 61/80 *Coöperatieve Stremsel-en Kleurselfabriek v Commission* [1981] ECR 851, [1982] 1 CMLR 240.
3   Cases 43/82 and 63/82 *VBVB & VBBB v Commission* [1984] ECR 19, [1985] 1 CMLR 27.
4   Cases 209/78 etc *Van Landewyck v Commission* [1980] ECR 3125, [1981] 3 CMLR 134; Cases 240/82 etc *SSI v Commission* [1985] ECR 3831, [1987] 3 CMLR 661 and Case 260/82 *NSO v Commission* [1988] 4 CMLR 755.
5   *Re Gas Water-Heaters* OJ [1973] L 217/34, [1973] CMLR D231; *Re Stoves and Heaters* OJ [1975] L 159/22, [1975] 2 CMLR D1; *Re Bomée Stichting* OJ [1975] L 329/30, [1976] 1 CMLR D1; *Groupement d'Exportation du Leon v Société d'Investissements et de Cooperation Agricoles (Cauliflowers)* OJ [1978] L 21/23, [1978] 1 CMLR D66; *Donck v Centraal Bureau voor de Rijweilhandel* OJ [1978] L 20/18, [1978] 2 CMLR 194; *Re IMA Rules* OJ [1980] L 318/1, [1981] 2 CMLR 498; *Re Italian Flat Glass* OJ [1981] L 326/32, [1982] 3 CMLR 366.
6   OJ [1988] L 316/43, [1989] 4 CMLR 340.
7   Case T–61/89 *Dansk Pelsdyravlerforening v Commission* [1992] ECR II-1931.
8   OJ [1995] L 312/79, [1996] 4 CMLR 565, upheld on appeal Cases T-213/95 and T-18/96 *SCK and FNK v Commission* [1997] ECR II-1739, [1997] 4 CMLR 259.
9   OJ [2000] L 39/1, [2000] 4 CMLR 1208, on appeal Cases T-5/00 *NAVEG v Commission* (judgment pending); see also the Commission's XXIXth *Report on Competition Policy* (1999), p 135.

determine their selling prices independently. The facts of this case resemble many of the decisions of the Commission on collective exclusive dealing from the 1970s and 1980s[10]: the fact that there are still arrangements like this in existence is perhaps a vindication of the Commission's desire to focus its resources on the elimination of practices that one might have assumed had long since been discontinued. In this decision, the Commission reduced the fine it would otherwise have imposed due to the prolonged period of the proceedings, which had begun in 1991, for which it was partly to blame[11].

11. UK LAW[12]

The UK competition authorities share the European Commission's determination to eliminate cartels. The Competition Act 1998 gives to the DGFT substantial powers of investigation and enforcement[13], resembling those of the Commission, to enforce the Chapter I and II prohibitions and to achieve this goal. Some general points can be made in respect of the approach that is likely to be adopted. First, pursuant to section 60 of the Act, the UK authorities have a qualified obligation to achieve consistency between domestic and Community law[14]. Secondly, the DGFT has published a number of Guidelines on the Competition Act[15]; in them, the DGFT has adopted the OECD definition of 'hardcore cartels'[16]. Thirdly, the DGFT has published a booklet designed to enable purchasers to identify cartel activity and to encourage them to bring their suspicions to the attention of the OFT[17]. Fourthly, the OFT has a branch specifically established to investigate cartels[18]. Finally UK policy is to encourage whistle-blowers, and the OFT received several applications for immunity in the year after the Act entered into force[19].

(A) Horizontal price fixing

The DGFT's takes the view that agreements that explicitly and directly fix prices are likely to infringe the Chapter I prohibition and that they have appreciable effects on competition[20]. The DGFT will generally regard price-fixing agreements as appreciably restricting competition even where the combined market share of the parties falls below the 25% market share threshold[1]. The Guidelines recognise,

---

10 See n 5 above.
11 See paras 151-153 of the decision: the Commission was applying the judgment of the ECJ in Case C-185/95 P *Baustahlgewebe v Commission* [1998] ECR I-8417, [1999] 4 CMLR 1203, reducing (very slightly) a fine due to the protracted hearing of the appeal to the CFI: see p 431 above.
12 See generally chs 9 and 10 on the substantive and procedural rules of the Competition Act 1998.
13 See ch 10, pp 335-342 and 348-356.
14 See ch 9, pp 329-333.
15 Ibid, pp 289-290.
16 *DGFT's Guidance as to the Appropriate Amount of a Penalty* OFT Guideline 423, para 2.1
17 *Cartels and the Competition Act 1998: a Guide for Purchasers*, available at http://www.oft.gov.uk/html/comp-act/technical_guidelines/index.html#leaflets.
18 See ch 2, p 59.
19 See ch 10, pp 353-355.
20 *Chapter I Prohibition* OFT Guideline 401, para 3.5.
1 *The Major Provisions* OFT Guideline 400, para 3.6 and *Chapter I Prohibition* OFT Guideline 401, para 2.20.

and set out, a variety of ways in which prices can be fixed[2]. The DGFT states that:

> 'Price-fixing...and other cartel activities are among the most serious infringements caught under the Chapter I prohibition'[3].

Severe penalties will therefore be imposed[4]. The DGFT will operate a leniency policy for members of cartels that blow the whistle and that act in a cooperative manner with investigations[5].

In a Press Release in January 2001 the DGFT warned that allegations of price fixing, even between small businesses such as private cab firms, would be investigated under the Competition Act 1998[6].

(B)   Horizontal market sharing

The DGFT's Guidelines indicate that agreements to share markets, 'whether by territory, type or size of customer or in some other way' are likely to have an appreciable effect on competition[7]; the prohibition may also apply to market sharing that is incidental to the main object of an agreement, if it could appreciably affect competition[8]. The DGFT will generally regard market-sharing agreements as restricting competition to an appreciable extent, even when the aggregate market share of the undertakings is less than 25%[9].

(C)   Quotas and other restriction on production

Agreements to limit or control production will be caught[10].

(D)   Collusive tendering

The Guidelines note that tendering procedures are designed to promote competition, so that any form of collusion or 'bid-rigging' between supposedly rival bidders is likely to be prohibited[11].

---

2   *Chapter I Prohibition* OFT Guideline 401, para 3.5-3.8.
3   *DGFT's Guidance as to the Appropriate Amount of a Penalty* OFT Guideline 423, para 2.1.
4   Ibid.
5   Ibid, para 2.2; the rules on leniency and whistle-blowing are set out in the rest of this Guideline: for commentary, see ch 10, pp 353-355.
6   OFT Press Release, PN 01/01.
7   *Chapter I Prohibition* OFT Guideline 401, para 3.10.
8   Ibid, para 3.11.
9   *Main Provisions* OFT Guideline 400, para 3.6 and *Chapter I Prohibition* OFT Guideline 401, para 2.20.
10   Ibid, paras 3.12-3.13.
11   *Chapter I Prohibition* OFT Guideline 401, para 3.14.

(E)   Agreements relating to terms and conditions

Agreements on terms and conditions and codes of practice may be caught by the Chapter I prohibition[12].

(F)   Information agreements

Information agreements may infringe the Chapter I prohibition[13]. The Guidelines note that the more information that is available to market participants, the more effective competition is likely to be. However, they also note that the exchange of information may facilitate collusion. Price information in particular might have this effect[14], though not, for example, where it is historical[15]. The exchange of non-price information would normally be of less concern, in particular where it is historical and unlikely to influence market behaviour[16].

(G)   Advertising restrictions

The DGFT accepts that the restriction of advertising may diminish competition; however, attempts to curb misleading advertising, or to ensure that advertising is legal, truthful and decent, are unlikely to have an appreciable effect on competition[17].

(H)   Anti-competitive horizontal restraints

Other anti-competitive agreements could also be subject to the Chapter I prohibition[18].

---

12 Ibid, para 3.9; see also *Trade Associations, Professions and Self-Regulating Bodies* OFT Guideline 408, paras 3.18 and 4.4.
13 *Chapter I Prohibition* OFT Guideline 401, paras 3.17-3.24; see also *Trade Associations, Professions and Self-Regulating Bodies* OFT Guideline 408, paras 3.8-3.13.
14 *Chapter I Prohibition* OFT Guideline 401, para 3.21.
15 Ibid, para 3.22.
16 Ibid, paras 3.23-3.24.
17 Ibid, para 3.25 and *Trade Associations, Professions and Self-Regulating Bodies* OFT Guideline 408, para 3.14.
18 See eg *Chapter I Prohibition* OFT Guideline 401, para 3.15-16 (joint buying and selling) and paras 3.27-28 (aggregated rebate schemes and specialisation agreements).

CHAPTER 14

Horizontal agreements (2) – oligopoly, tacit collusion and collective dominance

1. INTRODUCTION

This chapter is concerned with the related topics of oligopoly, tacit collusion and collective dominance. Put at its simplest, a problem for competition policy arises in markets in which there are only a few operators who are able, by virtue of the characteristics of the market, to behave in a parallel manner and to derive benefits from their collective market power, without, or without necessarily, entering into an agreement or concerted practice to do so in the sense of Article 81 EC or the Chapter I prohibition of the Competition Act 1998. This phenomenon is known in economics as 'tacit collusion', an expression which jars with lawyers, who associate the notion of collusion with actively conspiratorial behaviour of the kind captured by the expressions 'agreement' and 'concerted practice' in Article 81 and the Chapter I prohibition. The terms 'conscious parallelism' or 'tacit coordination' may be preferable to tacit collusion, in that they connote the idea of parallel behaviour without attaching the opprobrious term 'collusion'[1]. Nevertheless 'tacit collusion' is included in the title of this chapter in deference to the weight of the economics literature which uses it.

The issue for competition policy is to determine, assuming that the problem just described does indeed exist, how to deal with it: is the 'oligopoly problem' one of behaviour, in which case is it possible to deal with it through the application of Articles 81 and 82 and their domestic equivalents; or is it one that arises from the structure of the industry in question, in which case structural solutions, most obviously through the system of merger control but also, in the UK, through the monopoly provisions of the Fair Trading Act 1973 ('the FTA'), may be needed to address it?

This chapter will begin with discussion of oligopolistic interdependence. It will then consider in turn the extent to which Article 81, Article 82 and the EC Merger Regulation ('the ECMR') can be used to address it; in the case of Article 82 and the ECMR it is of particular importance to understand whether the concept of 'collective dominance' can be used to deal with oligopoly. The final section of the chapter discusses UK law and, in particular, the possible use of the monopoly provisions of the FTA.

---

1 See p 462 below.

2. THE THEORY OF OLIGOPOLISTIC INTERDEPENDENCE

(A) Outline of the theory

The objection to monopoly is that a monopolist is able to restrict output and thereby increase the price of its goods or services. As a result it earns supra-competitive profits and society is deprived of the output it has suppressed. In perfect competition no firm has sufficient power over the market to affect prices by alterations in its rate of output; each firm 'takes' the price from the market and that price will coincide with the cost of producing the product in question[2]. Competition law typically intervenes to prevent independent undertakings coordinating their marketing behaviour and earning quasi-monopoly profits by reducing their output: Article 81 EC and Chapter I of the Competition Act 1998 prohibit horizontal price-fixing agreements and analogous 'hard-core' cartels and punish them severely[3].

(i)   The meaning of oligopoly and a warning about the term

In reality few markets are perfectly competitive and many are oligopolistic; the general trend in recent years has undoubtedly been towards an increase in industrial concentration. There is a vast literature on the 'problem' of oligopoly[4]. Oligopoly is a phenomenon that exists somewhere on the continuum that begins at monopoly and ends at perfect competition, or 'polypoly', where 'mono' means one, 'oligo' a few and the first 'poly' in polypoly means many. The expression oligopoly is not entirely helpful in describing the situation of concern for competition authorities, since there are many markets in which there are only a few sellers and yet which are highly competitive; and there are others in which there may be many economic operators and yet a failure of the competitive market mechanism. Some oligopolies are 'benign' in terms of competition; others may be malign where they are particularly conducive to uncompetitive outcomes. For this reason, it is increasingly recognised that to address the problem of 'oligopoly', as if the problem were purely numerical, is to miss the correct target. The expression oligopoly means 'sale by a few sellers', but it is not the fact of 'fewness', in itself, that is the problem. To depict the problem as a matter of numbers does not do full justice to economists' concept of 'power over a market'; it is market power, whether individual or collective, that confers the ability to suppress output and to raise

---

2   See ch 1, pp 2-5.
3   See ch 13 generally.
4   See eg Turner 'The Definition of Agreement under the Sherman Act: Conscious Parallelism and Refusals to Deal' (1962) 75 Harvard Law Review 655; Tirole *The Theory of Industrial Organisation* (The MIT Press, 1988) ch 6; Scherer and Ross *Industrial Market Structure and Economic Performance* (Houghton Mifflin, 3rd ed, 1990) chs 6–8; Stevens 'Covert Collusion and Conscious Parallelism in Oligopolistic Markets: A Comparison of EC and US Competition Law' (1995) Oxford Yearbook of European Law 47; Monti 'Oligopoly: Conspiracy? Joint Monopoly? Or Enforceable Competition?' (1996) 19(3) World Competition 59; Lopatka 'Solving the Oligopoly Problem: Turner's Try' (1996) 41 Antitrust Bulletin 843; Bishop and Walker *The Economics of EC Competition Law* (Sweet & Maxwell, 1999) paras 2.19–2.26; Lipsey and Chrystal *Principles of Economics* (Oxford University Press, 9th ed, 1999) pp 176-181; National Economic Research Associates *Merger Appraisal in Oligopolistic Markets* (OFT Research Paper 19, 1999); see also some of the earlier economics literature, eg Hall and Hitch 'Price Theory and Business Behaviour' (1939) 2 Oxford Economic Papers 12–45; Sweezy 'Demand under Conditions of Oligopoly' (1937) 47 J Pol Ec 568–575; Stigler 'The Kinky Oligopoly Demand Curve' (1947) 55 J Pol Ec 431.

price to the detriment of consumers. It may be true that the fewer the number of players in a market, the more likely it is that collective market power will exist; however, the identification of market power is not simply a matter of counting heads. There is, nevertheless, a certain catchiness in talking of 'the oligopoly problem', and there is no harm in using the expression provided that the caveat just entered is kept in mind.

(ii) The oligopoly problem

The main argument against oligopoly is that the structural conditions of the market in which oligopolists operate are such that they will not compete with one another on price and will have little incentive to compete in other ways; furthermore they will be able to earn supra-competitive profits without entering into the type of collusive agreement or concerted practice generally proscribed by competition law. In a perfectly competitive market a firm which cuts its price will have an imperceptible effect on its competitors, so that they will not need to respond. In an oligopoly a reduction in price would swiftly attract the customers of the other two or three rivals, the effect upon which would be so devastating that they would have to react by matching the cut. Similarly an oligopolist could not increase its price unilaterally, because it would be deserted by its customers if it did so. Thus the theory runs that in an oligopolistic market rivals are interdependent: they have a heightened awareness of each other's presence and are bound to match one another's marketing strategy. The result is that price competition between them will be minimal or non-existent; oligopoly produces non-competitive stability. The literature on so-called 'game theory' and 'the Prisoner's Dilemma', which recognises that firms take into account the likely actions (and reactions) of competitors when deciding how to behave, is supportive of this view of oligopoly[5].

The argument can be taken further. All firms have a will to maximise profits: profits are greater in monopolistic markets in which output is suppressed. Oligopolists recognise their interdependence as well as their own self-interest. By matching each other's conduct they will be able to achieve and charge a profit-maximising price which will be set at a supra-competitive level, without actually communicating with one another in any way at all. There does not need to be a collusive agreement: the structure of the market is such that, through interdependence and mutual self-awareness, prices will rise towards the monopolistic level. Also the non-competitive environment in which oligopolists function will enable them to act in an inefficient and wasteful manner. These theoretical arguments have been buttressed by empirical research which purports to show that there is a direct correlation between industrial structure and profit levels, which are said to increase in line with the concentration ratio of the industry in question[6], although the soundness of much of this evidence has been called into question[7]. The logical conclusion of the case against oligopoly is

---

5   See *Tirole* pp 205-208; *Scherer and Ross* pp 208-215; *Bishop & Walker* paras 2-20-2.21; *Lipsey and Chrystal* p 181; Franzosi 'Oligopoly and the Prisoner's Dilemma: Concerted Practices and 'As If' Behaviour' (1988) 9 ECLR 385; see generally Phlips *Competition Policy: A Game Theoretic Perspective* (Cambridge University Press, 1995).
6   See eg Bain 'Relation of Profit Rate to Industry Concentration' (1951) 65 Qu J Ec 293–324.
7   See eg Weiss 'The Concentration and Profits Issue' in *Industrial Concentration: The New Learning* (1974); Brozen 'The Concentration-Collusion Doctrine' (1977) 46 Antitrust Law Journal 826.

that, since it is the industrial structure itself which produces the problem, structural measures should be taken to remedy it by deconcentrating the market. Unless this is done, there will be an area of consciously parallel action in pricing strategies which is beyond the reach of conspiracy laws and yet which has serious implications for consumer welfare.

(iii)   Terminology:'tacit collusion';'conscious parallelism';'tacit coordination'

There is little doubt that there are markets in which it is possible for economic operators to coordinate their behaviour without entering into an agreement or being party to a concerted practice in the sense of Article 81(1) or the Chapter I prohibition; such behaviour will be to their own self-advantage and to the disadvantage of customers and ultimately consumers. This situation is often described by economists as 'tacit collusion': enjoying the benefits of a particular market structure without actually entering into an agreement to do so. If the firms in question had achieved the same end through explicit collusion, economists would have the same objection – that prices would be higher than they would be without coordination. Economists have no particular interest in whether collusion is 'tacit' or 'explicit': it is the effects of the collusion that matter. Lawyers however are considerably less comfortable with the expression tacit collusion. 'Collusion' is the evil at which Article 81 and the Chapter I prohibition are directed ('any *agreement* ... or *concerted practice* ... which has as its object or effect the prevention, restriction or distortion of competition'); in the same way section 1 of the US Sherman Act forbids 'every *contract* in restraint of trade', where the notion of collusiveness is inherent in the idea of contract. For many lawyers, to ask whether tacit collusion could be caught, for example, by the concept of collective dominance under Article 82 or the Chapter II prohibition in the UK is bizarre, since any behaviour that could be called collusive in a legal sense would be caught by Article 81 or the Chapter I prohibition anyway. If behaviour is not collusive under Article 81, lawyers not unnaturally feel uncomfortable at characterising the same behaviour as tacitly collusive under Article 82. An alternative expression for the conduct in question, 'conscious parallelism', may cause lawyers slightly less discomfort, the opprobrious word 'collusive' being avoided; but even 'consciousness' seems to move the enquiry back to a search for something sufficiently conspiratorial that it should really be investigated, if at all, under Article 81. In the interests of finding terminology which is meaningful and tolerable both to economists and to lawyers when considering the application of Article 82 it might be better to use the expression 'tacit coordination', since this at least eliminates the pejorative word 'collusion' whilst retaining the notion of parallel behaviour which is beneficial to the collectively dominant operators on the market and disadvantageous to customers and consumers.

(iv)   The conditions needed for the successful exercise of collective market power

For tacit coordination to occur, it is necessary for firms to indulge in a common form of behaviour. Typically this would involve the charging of similar prices; however it might also involve parallel decisions to reduce production or not to expand capacity: such decisions would, through the suppression of output, in themselves have an impact on prices in the industry in question. Tacit coordination also requires that each firm will be able to monitor quickly and easily how the others are behaving on the market: successful parallel behaviour requires that no one should deviate from the common conduct; transparency is therefore vital to each economic operator to enable it to know what the others are doing, both in terms of their prices and their output. Finally it is important that discipline among the firms with collective market power can be maintained. The benefits to the few of tacit coordination will be lost if one or more firms depart from the appropriate behavioural standard; in order to prevent this from happening, it is necessary that some retaliatory mechanism should be in place to impose sanctions on deviant firms. The most obvious sanction would be a sharp price war which would be harmful to everyone, and would send a severe warning that abandonment of tacit coordination will be to everyone's disadvantage[8].

(B) Criticisms of the theory

The theory of oligopolistic interdependence has attracted criticism[9]. Four particular problems have been pointed out. The first is that the theory overstates the interdependence of oligopolists. Even in a symmetrical three-firm oligopoly one firm might be able to steal a march on its rivals by cutting its price if, for example, there would be a delay before the others discovered what it had done: in the meantime the price-cutter may make sufficient profit to offset the cost of any subsequent price-war. It may also be that the rivals will be unable to expand their capacity in order to meet the increased demand that could be expected to follow a price cut. Anyway, an expansion in output may simply mean that new customers are attracted to the price-cutter, not that existing ones are drawn from its rivals.

A second problem is that the theory of oligopoly presents too simplistic a picture of industrial market structures. In a symmetrical oligopoly where producers produce identical goods at the same costs interdependence may be strong, but in reality market conditions are usually more complex. The oligopolists themselves will almost inevitably have different cost levels; they may be producing differentiated goods and will usually command at least some consumer loyalty; and their market shares will often not be equal. Furthermore there may be a fringe of smaller sellers which exert some competitive pressure upon the oligopolists and other firms not operating on the market may be capable of entering it if and when it becomes clear that supra-competitive profits are available. Many other factors affect the competitive environment in which oligopolists operate. The concentration of the market on the buying side is also important: the more concentrated it is, the less the oligopolists might compete with one another since it will be relatively easy to detect attempts to attract the custom of particular customers. The transparency of price information is significant: the easier it is to conceal the price of goods from competitors, the less will be the interdependence or mutual awareness of the oligopolists. Similarly oligopolists may be able, through rebates and discounts, secretly to charge prices lower than those in their published price lists. These and many other factors mean that oligopolistic markets differ considerably from one another and this in turn makes

8   The question of whether an effective retaliatory mechanism is a legal requirement to a finding of collective dominance under the ECMR arose, and was the subject of disagreement between the Commission and Airtours, in the *Airtours/First Choice* decision; the issue will be considered in the appeal pending before the CFI: see pp 490-492 below.
9   See eg Bork *The Antitrust Paradox* (Basic Books, 1978) ch 8.

it difficult to provide a convincing theoretical explanation of how such markets function and how they should be dealt with.

A third problem with the theory of interdependence is that it fails to explain why in some oligopolistic markets competition is intense. Firms quite clearly do compete with one another in some oligopolies. Such competition may take various forms. Open price competition may be limited, although price wars do break out periodically in some oligopolistic markets, for example between supermarkets or petrol companies. Where open price competition is restricted, this does not mean that secret price cutting does not occur. Non-price competition may be particularly strong in oligopolistic markets. This may manifest itself in various ways: offering better quality products and after-sales service; striving for a lead in technical innovation and research and development (sometimes described as the 'grass-roots' of competition in oligopoly); by introducing loyalty schemes of the kinds offered by airlines and supermarkets; and by making large investments in advertising to improve brand image[10]. Whilst expenditure on advertising has been objected to because it is wasteful of resources and amounts to a barrier to entry to new firms wanting to enter the market, it is inconsistent with the theory that oligopolists do not compete with one another[11].

A fourth objection to the theory of oligopolistic interdependence is that it does not explain satisfactorily its central proposition, which is that oligopolists can earn supra-competitive profits without actually colluding. The interdependence theory says they cannot increase price unilaterally because they will lose custom to their rivals and yet, to earn supra-competitive profits, prices must have been increased from time to time: how could this have been achieved without collusion? A possible answer to this is that a pattern of price leadership develops whereby one firm raises its price and this acts as a signal to the others to follow suit. Prices therefore remain parallel without conspiracy amongst the oligopolists, although this is not particularly convincing. Economists have suggested that price leadership may take three forms[12]. Dominant price leadership exists where a dominant firm raises its price and other firms in the industry follow suit because it is in their best interests to do so. *Ex hypothesi* this is not what happens in an oligopoly, where no firm is dominant. Secondly, barometric price leadership occurs where one firm raises its price because increased costs (for example, in wages or raw materials) force it to do so: other firms faced with the same increase in costs then follow suit. It would be unreasonable to condemn parallel increases in price if they are explicable on an objective basis in this way. The third type of price leadership is termed collusive: here there is an understanding that firms in an industry will follow the signal emitted from time to time by the price leader. However in this case it would seem to be perfectly reasonable to brand their action as an agreement or a concerted practice under Article 81 or the Chapter I prohibition.

Besides these criticisms, there are other objections to the theory of interdependence. One is that it concentrates solely on the tendency to non-collusive price fixing without asking other questions such as why a market is oligopolistic in the first place: this might be because of the superior efficiency associated with economies of scale. In this case, it is necessary to consider at what point the

10   This is a particular feature of certain markets such as breakfast cereals, household detergents and alcoholic drinks such as lagers.
11   See *Scherer and Ross* pp 592–610.
12   See Markham 'The Nature and Significance of Price Leadership' (1951) 41 Am Ec Rev 891–905; the classification suggested there was adopted in the former Monopolies and Mergers Commission's report *Parallel Pricing* Cmnd 5330 (1973).

advantages arising from these economies are offset by the adverse effects of a loss of price competition. Others would argue that, even if supra-competitive profits are earned in an oligopolistic market over a short period, that would attract new entrants to the market and increase competition in the long run unless there are significant barriers to entry to the market. In this case the 'problem' of oligopoly is ephemeral: the market could be left to heal the problem itself.

(C) Possible ways of dealing with oligopoly

Having considered this theoretical debate, the pertinent question is what, if anything, should be done about oligopoly in competition law, assuming that a problem exists.

(i) A structural approach

If economic theory were to demonstrate convincingly that oligopoly inevitably leads to non-collusive parallelism of price and an absence of non-price competition, and also that there are no redeeming features of oligopolistic markets, this would suggest that the problem should be seen as a structural one and dealt with as such. In this case it would be necessary to establish a system capable of preventing the structure of the market from becoming conducive to tacit coordination in the first place: as will be seen, there have been important developments in this regard under the ECMR, where the Commission examines carefully the possibility that mergers might lead to collective dominance[13]; in the UK, the test for the Competition Commission is whether a merger may be expected to operate against the public interest, which is broad enough to address the problem of oligopoly without any need to ask whether firms will be collectively dominant[14]. Logic might suggest that further structural powers are needed to deconcentrate industries that become oligopolistic other than through the process of mergers. However it would seem from the discussion above that the theory of oligopoly is lacking in too many respects to justify the dismantlement of oligopolistic market structures other than in the most exceptional situations. Structural remedies do not exist under Article 82, although it is possible that this position will change when the Council of Ministers adopts the 'new' Regulation 17/62[15]. A structural solution to the problem of oligopolistic markets is possible under the monopoly provisions of the FTA, although this approach is taken only in a very exceptional case[16].

(ii) A behavioral approach

An alternative approach is to see the problem as essentially behavioral, in which case control is necessary to prevent oligopolists behaving in a way that is uncompetitive. Some would favour making any parallelism in price between oligopolists illegal. This however would be quite inappropriate: it would be absurd to forbid firms from behaving in a parallel manner if this is an inevitable

13 See pp 482-492 below.
14 See pp 493-495 below.
15 See ch 7, p 255.
16 See p 493 below and ch 11, p 384 .

consequence of the structure of the market. To put the point another way, it would be strange indeed if competition law were to mandate that firms should behave irrationally, by not acting in parallel, in order to avoid being found to have infringed competition law.

Where oligopolists really do collude, for example to fix prices or to share markets, there is no reason why they – like firms in less concentrated markets – should not be subject to the provisions of Article 81 and the Chapter I prohibition of the Competition Act 1998. The term 'concerted practice' catches any situation in which firms abandon the risks of competition and substitute for them practical co-operation. However when this concept is applied to oligopolists a different problem arises: it can be difficult to distinguish conduct which is collusive in the sense of Article 81 and the Chapter I prohibition from parallel conduct which is attributable to the oligopolistic structure of a market. This problem is compounded by the fact that in many cases there is little or no evidence of actual contact between alleged conspirators: firms that really do intend to rig the market are wise enough usually to destroy incriminating evidence. The danger is that a competition authority will too readily reach the conclusion that parallel conduct means that there is collusion; this can be avoided only by thorough economic analysis of the market in question. An understanding of pricing theory and of the nature of oligopoly is vital when trying to decide whether parallel conduct is collusive (in the legal sense) or not[17].

As a separate matter, it may be appropriate in oligopolistic markets to prohibit 'facilitating practices' that lead to parallel behaviour: an obvious example is the exchange of information between oligopolists that makes it easier for them to behave in the same way. As we have seen, the structure of the market is one of the factors taken into account when analysing information agreements under Article 81 and the Chapter I prohibition[18]. The possibility that an agreement might lead to parallel behaviour may also be taken into account when considering whether it should be exempted under Article 81(3)[19]. Finally, it may be sensible to prevent anti-competitive abuses of a collective dominant position which have the effect of eliminating actual or potential competitors from oligopolistic markets; as will be seen, there have been some cases in recent years in which Article 82 has been used to deal with behaviour of this sort.

(iii)   A regulatory approach

A different possibility would be to introduce direct regulation of oligopolistic industries so that prices would be fixed at what might be considered to be a 'competitive', or at any rate a 'reasonable', level by a Government agency. An alternative suggestion is that oligopolists might be required periodically to notify their prices to a central agency and then to stick to the notified price for a specified time; this would considerably reduce the extent to which they could react to one another's market behaviour[20]: this has been a remedial solution that has been deployed on a few occasions following mergers of bus companies in the

---

17 See further the discussion of 'concerted practices' in ch 3, pp 83-86.
18 See ch 13, pp 445-446 and pp 469-470 below.
19 See pp 470-471 below.
20 Bishop 'Oligopoly Pricing: a Proposal' (1983) 28 Antitrust Bulletin 311; such a system would be known as 'bid-pricing': a particular merit of it would be that the firm itself bids for its price rather than a Government agency setting it.

UK[1]. However there are problems with the regulatory approach to oligopoly. Direct regulation is enormously cumbersome and requires extensive bureaucratic resources. It is also difficult to establish what a competitive or reasonable price should be: in so far as it is possible, it is preferable to let the market itself determine this issue rather than a Governmental body or a competition authority[2].

3. ARTICLE 81

(A) Does parallel behaviour amount to a concerted practice under Article 81?

Both the Commission and the Community Courts appreciate that price competition in an oligopoly may be muted and that oligopolists react to one another's conduct, so that parallel behaviour does not, in itself, amount to a concerted practice under Article 81(1)[3]. In *Dyestuffs*[4] the ECJ said at paragraphs 65 and 66 that:

'By its very nature, then, the concerted practice does not have all the elements of a contract but may *inter alia* arise out of coordination which becomes apparent from the behaviour of the participants. *Although parallel behaviour may not itself be identified with a concerted practice*, it may however amount to strong evidence of such a practice if it leads to conditions of competition which do not respond to the normal conditions of the market, having regard to the nature of the products, the size and number of the undertakings, and the volume of the said market. Such is the case especially where the parallel behaviour is such as to permit the parties to seek price equilibrium at a different level from that which would have resulted from competition, and to crystallise the status quo to the detriment of effective freedom of movement of the products in the Common Market and free choice by consumers of their suppliers' (emphasis added).

The ECJ added at paragraph 68 that the existence of a concerted practice could be appraised correctly only:

'if the evidence upon which the contested decision is based is considered, not in isolation, but as a whole, account being taken of the specific features of the products in question'.

In *Dyestuffs* the parties argued that they had acted in a similar manner only because of the oligopolistic market structure. The ECJ rejected this assertion since the market was not a pure oligopoly: rather it was one in which firms could realistically be expected to adopt their own pricing strategies, particularly in view of the compartmentalisation of the markets along national boundaries. The ECJ recognised that there might be situations in which a firm must take into account a rival's likely responses, but said that this did not entitle them actually to coordinate their behaviour:

---

1   See ch 22, p 823.
2   See ch 18, pp 633-639.
3   On concerted practices generally, see ch 3, pp 83-86.
4   Cases 48/69 [1972] ECR 619, [1972] CMLR 557.

'Although every producer is free to change his prices, taking into account in so doing the present or foreseeable conduct of his competitors, nevertheless it is contrary to the rules on competition contained in the Treaty for a producer to cooperate with his competitors, in any way whatsoever, in order to determine a coordinated course of action relating to a price increase and to ensure its success by prior elimination of all uncertainty as to each other's conduct regarding the essential elements of that action, such as the amount, subject–matter, date and place of the increases.'[5]

In *Züchner v Bayerische Vereinsbank AG*[6] the ECJ repeated that intelligent responses to a competitor's behaviour would not bring firms within the scope of Article 81(1). In *Zinc Producer Group*[7] the Commission said that it did not intend to condemn parallel action between 1977 and 1979 which might be explicable in terms of 'barometric price leadership'[8], saying that in such circumstances 'parallel pricing behaviour in an oligopoly producing homogeneous goods will not in itself be sufficient evidence of a concerted practice'[9]. In *Peroxygen Products*[10] however the Commission rejected an argument that an agreement between oligopolists fell outside Article 81(1) since, even without the agreement, the structure of the market would have meant that they would have behaved in the same way. In the Commission's view, the very fact that the firms had entered into an agreement at all indicated that the free play of competition might have led to different market behaviour.

In *Wood Pulp*[11] the Commission held that producers of wood pulp were guilty of a concerted practice to fix prices in the EC. There had been parallel conduct on the market from 1975 until 1981, but there was no evidence of explicit agreements to fix prices. However the Commission concluded that there was a concerted practice, basing its finding on two factors. The first was that there had been direct and indirect exchanges of information which had created an artificial transparency of price information on the market. The second was that, in the Commission's view, an economic analysis of the market demonstrated that it was not a narrow oligopoly in which parallel pricing might be expected. On appeal, the ECJ substantially annulled the Commission's findings[12]. The fact that pulp producers announced price rises to users in advance on a quarterly basis did not in itself involve an infringement of Article 81(1): making information available to third parties did not eliminate the producers' uncertainty as to what each other would do[13]. Furthermore, there were alternative explanations for the system of and simultaneity of price announcements, and the parallelism of prices could be explained other than by the existence of a concerted practice. Information was freely available on the market as buyers informed each other of the prices available, some agents acted for a number of different producers and so were

5   Ibid, para 118.
6   Case 172/80 [1981] ECR 2021, [1982] 1 CMLR 313, para 14.
7   OJ [1984] L 220/27, [1985] 2 CMLR 108.
8   See p 464 above.
9   OJ [1984] L 220/27, [1985] 2 CMLR 108, paras 75–76.
10   OJ [1985] L 35/1, [1985] 1 CMLR 481, para 50.
11   OJ [1985] L 85/1, [1985] 3 CMLR 474.
12   Cases C–89/85 etc *A Ahlstrom Oy v Commission* [1993] ECR I-1307, [1993] 4 CMLR 407; see Jones '*Wood Pulp*: Concerted Practice and/or Conscious Paralellism?' (1993) 14 ECLR 273; Van Gerven and Varano 'The *Wood Pulp* Case and the Future of Concerted Practices' (1994) 31 CML Rev 575; see also Alese 'The Economic Theory of Non-collusive Oligopoly' (1999) 20 ECLR 379.
13   Ibid, paras 59–65.

well-informed about prices and the trade press was dynamic; as to parallelism, the ECJ's experts considered that the market was more oligopolistic than the Commission had supposed, and that economic problems had discouraged producers from engaging in price cutting which their competitors would inevitably follow; the experts also considered that there was evidence to suggest that there could not have been concertation: for example, market shares had varied from time to time, which would be unlikely if there was a concerted practice; and the alleged cartel members had not tried to establish production quotas, which they could be expected to have done if they wished to control the market[14]. This important judgment demonstrates that the burden is on the Commission to prove the existence of a concerted practice, and in particular to deal with any alternative explanations of parallelism on the market. The judgment does acknowledge, however, that, in an appropriate case, parallelism could be evidence of a concerted practice where there is no plausible alternative explanation[15].

In *British Sugar*[16] British Sugar deployed the argument that the oligopolistic nature of the market meant that price competition was limited, and that its price leadership should not be regarded as evidence of a concerted practice. The Commission's reply to this was that, where competition in a market is already restricted, it should be particularly vigilant to ensure that the competition which does exist is not restricted[17]. This is consistent with the judgment of the CFI in the appeal against the Commission's decision in *Steel Beams*[18].

(B) Article 81(1), the exchange of information and other facilitating practices

The previous section has discussed the difficulties in determining whether parallel behaviour may be attributable to a concerted practice. A competition authority must avoid reaching a conclusion that parallel behaviour is unlawful if it can be explained by reference to the conditions of the market. However this is not to say that Article 81(1) cannot be deployed in other ways to deal with the problem of parallel behaviour: in particular it can be applied to what are often referred to as 'facilitating practices', that is to say practices that make it easier for firms to achieve the benefits of tacit coordination. The most obvious of these is the exchange of information which increases the transparency of the market and so makes parallel behaviour easier. It is for this reason that the application of Article 81(1) to information agreements focuses, *inter alia*, on the structure of the market[19]: it was the oligopolistic structure of the market in *UK Agricultural Tractor Registration Exchange*[20] that led the Commission to conclude that Article 81(1) had been infringed; and the more competitive nature of the cars' market

14 Ibid, paras 66–127.
15 Ibid, para 71.
16 OJ [1999] L 76/1, [1999] 4 CMLR 1316, substantially upheld on appeal Cases T-202/98 etc *Tate & Lyle v Commission*, judgment of 12 July 2001.
17 Ibid, para 87.
18 Case T-141/94 *Thyssen Stahl AG v Commission* [1999] ECR II-347, [1999] 4 CMLR 810, para 302.
19 See ch 13, pp 445-446.
20 OJ [1992] L 68/19, [1993] 4 CMLR 358, para 16, upheld on appeal to the CFI in Cases T-34/92 and T-35/92 *Fiatagri UK Ltd v Commission* [1994] ECR III-905 and 957 and on appeal to the ECJ in Cases C-7/95 and C-8/95 P *John Deere v Commission* [1998] ECR I-3111, and 3175, [1998] 5 CMLR 311.

that led it to the opposite conclusion in relation to it[1]. In *Thyssen Stahl AG v Commission*[2] the CFI held that, where the structure of a market is oligopolistic, it is all the more important to ensure the decision-making independence of undertakings and residual competition, and that therefore the exchange of recent data on market shares could infringe Article 81(1)[3].

The Commission will look for other facilitating practices. For example, at paragraph 20 of its *Guidelines on Vertical Restraints*[4] it says that it will examine agency agreements, even where the principal bears all the financial and commercial risks, if they could facilitate collusion[5]. This could happen, in the Commission's view, if a number of principals use the same agents whilst collectively preventing others from doing so, or where they use agents to collude on marketing strategy or to exchange sensitive information between themselves. Similar concerns are expressed throughout the *Guidelines* as to the possibility of vertical agreements facilitating collusion[6]. To give just one example, the Commission expresses the concern that in a narrow oligopoly the practice of using or publishing maximum or recommended resale prices may facilitate collusion by reducing the likelihood of lower prices[7].

The Commission's *Guidelines on Horizontal Cooperation Agreements*[8] state that, in assessing horizontal cooperation agreements other than 'hard-core' cartels of the kind that almost always fall within Article 81(1)[9], the concentration of the market will be taken into account[10]: some agreements may be found not to be anti-competitive where the market is reasonably competitive, but to be problematic where it is oligopolistic. The application of these *Guidelines* is considered in some detail in chapter 15[11].

The Commission has applied the *de minimis* rule narrowly in the case of an oligopoly[12] and has taken a strict approach to the appreciability of the effect on inter-state trade of an agreement where the market was oligopolistic[13].

(C)   Article 81(3)

The structure of the market will be relevant to the Commission's analysis of agreements which are notified to it for individual exemption under Article 81(3), in particular since that provision requires that there should be no substantial elimination of competition[14]. The fact that the Commission's block exemptions

1   See ch 13, p 446.
2   See n 18 above.
3   Ibid, paras 393-412.
4   OJ [2000] C 291/1, [2000] 5 CMLR 1176.
5   As a general principle agency agreements fall outside Article 81(1): see ch 16, pp 538-540.
6   See for example the following paragraphs in the *Guidelines*, all of which refer to the possibility of the facilitation of collusion: paras 103(ii), 107, 110, 112, 114, 133, 138, 142, 152, 161, 176 (specifically on exclusive dealerships in an oligopolistic market), 178, 185, 188, 191, 192, 226 and 227.
7   Ibid, para 228.
8   OJ [2001] C 3/2, [2001] 4 CMLR 819.
9   That is to say those agreements that have as their object the restriction of competition: see ch 3, pp 95-98 and ch 13 generally.
10   OJ [2001] C 3/2, [2001] 4 CMLR 819, para 29.
11   See ch 15, p 501ff.
12   *Floral* OJ [1980] L 39/51, [1980] 2 CMLR 285.
13   *Cast Iron and Steel Rolls* OJ [1983] L 317/1, [1984] 1 CMLR 694, upheld on appeal Cases 29/83 and 30/83 *Compagnie Royale Asturienne des Mines SA and Rheinzinc GmbH v Commission* [1984] ECR 1679, [1985] 1 CMLR 688.
14   See ch 4, pp 132-133.

contain market share caps in itself means that firms in an oligopoly will often not be able to avail themselves of these legal instruments[15]. In *P&O Stena Line*[16] the Commission granted exemption to a joint venture for cross-channel ferry services for a limited period of three years. The decision considered at length whether there was a risk that the joint venture would create a duopoly on the 'short sea tourist market', but concluded that the joint venture and Eurotunnel, the operator of the Channel Tunnel, could be expected to compete with each other rather than to act in parallel to raise prices[17]. An interesting feature of the decision is that the analysis under Article 81(3) is conducted in much the same way as the Commission approaches collective dominance under the ECMR[18]; indeed, the joint venture would now be regarded as a full-function joint venture subject to the ECMR, since its amendment by Regulation 1310/97[19].

The Commission may grant an exemption which it considers will have the effect of introducing more competition into an oligopolistic market[20].

4. ARTICLE 82 AND COLLECTIVE DOMINANCE[1]

One of the most complex and controversial issues in Community competition law has been the application – or non-application – of Article 82 EC and the ECMR to so-called 'collective dominance'[2]. Discussion of this question in relation to Article 82 can be traced back at least to the early 1970s[3]; an enormous body of literature has developed[4]. The law and decisional practice on collective

---

15 On the market share caps in the block exemptions, see ch 4, p 144.
16 OJ [1999] L 163/61, [2000] 5 CMLR 682.
17 Ibid, para 127.
18 See pp 482-492 below.
19 See ch 21, pp 748-751.
20 See eg *Carlsberg* OJ [1984] L 207/26, [1985] 1 CMLR 735.
1   The text that follows is based, in part, on *Collective Dominance*, the author's contribution to the Liber Amicorum in Honour of Lord Slynn of Hadley *Judicial Review in European Union Law* (Kluwer Law International, 2000, eds O'Keefe and Bavasso), ch 37.
2   The expressions 'collective dominance', 'joint dominance' and 'oligopolistic dominance' tend to be used interchangeably. In Cases C-395/96 P etc *Compagnie Maritime Belge NV v Commission* [2000] 4 CMLR 1076 Advocate General Fennelly indicated that he saw no meaningful distinction between these terms, but used the expression 'collective dominance' as this was the one that the Court itself usually employed; in its judgment in the same case, the ECJ used the expression 'collective dominance' throughout: see in particular para 36; in Case No IV/M.1524 *Airtours/First Choice* OJ [2000] L 93/1, [2000] 5 CMLR 494 the Commission said that it would use the terms 'collective dominance' and 'oligopolistic dominance' interchangeably.
3   See n 16 below.
4   See eg Whish and Sufrin 'Oligopolistic Markets and EC Competition Law' (1992) 12 Oxford Yearbook of European Law 59; Winkler and Hansen 'Collective Dominance under the EC Merger Control Regulation' (1993) 30 CML Rev 787; Ridyard 'Economic Analysis of Single Firm and Oligopoly Dominance under the European Merger Regulation' (1994) 15 ECLR 255; Rodger 'Market Integration and the Development of European Competition Policy to Meet New Demands: A Study of Oligopolistic Markets and the Concept of a Collective Dominant Position under Article [82] of the Treaty' [1994(2)] Legal Issues of European Integration 1; Rodger 'Oligopolistic Market Failure: Collective Dominance versus Complex Monopoly' (1995) 16 ECLR 21; Briones 'Oligopolistic Dominance: is there a Common Approach in Different Jurisdictions?' (1995) 16 ECLR 334; Soames 'An Analysis of the Principles of Concerted Practice and Collective Dominance: a Distinction without a Difference' (1996) 17 ECLR 24; Morgan 'The Treatment of Oligopoly under the European Merger Control Regulation' (1996) 41 Antitrust Bulletin 203; Tillotson and MacCulloch 'EC Competition Rules, Collective Dominance and Maritime Transport' (1997) 21(1) World Competition 51; Venit 'Two Steps Forward and No Steps Back: Economic Analysis and

dominance, under both legal instruments, developed considerably in 1998, 1999 and 2000; of particular importance are the ECJ's judgments in *France v Commission* (the so-called *Kali und Salz* case)[5] and *Compagnie Maritime Belge Transports SA v Commission*[6], the CFI's judgment in *Gencor v Commission*[7] and the Commission's decision under the ECMR in *Airtours/First Choice*[8]. This section will consider the development of the law under Article 82 and the following one the position under the ECMR, although it would appear now to be the case that the expression 'collective dominance' has the same meaning under each legal instrument.

(A)   The linguistic background

There is a linguistic background to the issue of collective dominance under Article 82 and the ECMR. Article 82 applies to '[a]ny abuse *by one or more undertakings* of a dominant position within the common market' (emphasis added). The same wording has been adopted in numerous domestic systems of competition law, both in the Member States themselves[9] and in third countries, particularly those in the 'queue' for accession to the Union[10]. The fact that Article 82 is capable of application to dominance held on the part of more than one undertaking clearly envisages the possibility, though not the inevitability, of 'collective' dominance being enjoyed by legally and economically separate undertakings; a narrow reading would be that the reference to more than one undertaking refers to different legal entities within the same corporate group.[11] In contradistinction to Article 82, Article 2(3) of the ECMR provides that a concentration that creates or strengthens a dominant position as a result of which competition would be significantly impeded in the common market or a substantial part of it may be declared incompatible with the common market; however this provision does not refer specifically to a dominant position *enjoyed by one or more undertakings*. Linguistically, therefore, it could be argued – as indeed it was by France, Société Commerciale des Potasses et de l'Azote (SCPA) and Entreprise Minière et Chemique (EMC) in the *Kali und Salz* case[12] – that the ECMR applies only to single firm dominance, even if Article 82 is capable of application to collective dominance. It has taken many years for the Community Courts to determine the proper scope of Article 82 and the ECMR: in each case in favour of the application of the measure in question to collective dominance.

Oligopolistic Dominance after *Kali und Salz*' (1998) 35 CML Rev 1101; Elliott 'The Gencor Judgment: Collective Dominance, Remedies and Extraterritoriality under the Merger Regulation' (1999) 24 EL Rev 638; Korah '*Gencor v Commission*: Collective Dominance' (1999) 20 ECLR 337; Stroux 'Is EC Oligopoly Control Outgrowing Its Infancy?' (2000) 23(1) World Competition 3; Fernández 'Increasing Powers and Increasing Uncertainty: Collective Dominance and Pricing Abuses' (2000) 25 ELRev 645; Stroux, commenting on *CMBT v Commission*, (2000) 37 CML Rev 1249; Etter 'The Assessment of Mergers in the EC under the Concept of Collective Dominance' (2000) 23(3) World Competition 103; Monti 'The Scope of Collective Dominance under Article 82' (2001) 38 CML Rev 131; Kloosterhuis 'Joint Dominance and the Interaction Between Firms' (2000) ECLR 79; Niels 'Collective Dominance – More than Just Oligopolistic Interdependence' (2001) 22 ECLR 168.

5   Cases C-68/94 and 30/95 *France v Commission* [1998] ECR I-1375, [1998] 4 CMLR 829.
6   Cases C-395/96 and 396/96 P [2000] 4 CMLR 1076.
7   Case T-102/96 [1999] ECR II-753, [1999] 4 CMLR 971.
8   Case IV/M.1524 *Airtours/First Choice* OJ [2000] L 93/1, [2000] 5 CMLR 494; the case is on appeal to the CFI in Case T-342/99 *Airtours v Commission* (judgment pending).
9   See eg s 18 of the UK Competition Act 1998.
10   See eg s 9 of the Maltese Competition Act 1994.
11   See p 473 below.
12   See n 5 above.

(B) The definition of collective dominance under Article 82

(i) 'One or more undertakings': the narrow view of Article 82

Article 82 prohibits the abuse of a dominant position 'by one or more undertakings'. The 'narrow' view of the reference to more than one undertaking is that it means that the market power and behaviour of undertakings within the same corporate group can be aggregated and dealt with under Article 82. In several of the cases on Article 82 a dominant position was found to exist among the members of a group. For example in *Continental Can*[13] three different companies in the same group were involved in the Commission's analysis: Continental Can (a US company), SLW (its German subsidiary) which held a dominant position in Germany and Europemballage (also its subsidiary) which acquired a competitor, TDV. It was the overall effect of these companies' position and behaviour which led to a finding of abuse of dominance. Similarly in *Commercial Solvents v Commission*,[14] there were two legal undertakings within the same corporate group, the US parent, Commercial Solvents, and its Italian subsidiary, ICI. The difficult question in cases such as these is whether the companies are so closely related to one another that it is reasonable to consider them as essentially one economic unit[15]. However, assuming that this issue is not in doubt, it is easy enough to see that the reference in Article 82 to an abuse by one or more undertakings might simply amount to separate legal entities within the same corporate group.

(ii) 'One or more undertakings': the wide view of Article 82

An alternative approach to the reference in Article 82 to one or more undertakings is that it has a wider meaning, so that legally and economically independent firms might be considered to hold a 'collective dominant position'. It would follow that abusive market behaviour on the part of the collectively dominant firms could be controlled under Article 82 (and, since the adoption of the ECMR, that the Commission would have control over a larger number of concentrations if the same approach could be taken in relation to that legal instrument). The Commission dabbled with the idea of collective dominance under Article 82 in the early 1970's[16], but the ECJ appeared to have rejected it in *Hoffmann-la Roche v Commission*[17]. There the Court seemed to suggest that problems of tacit coordination could not be controlled under Article 82:

'A dominant position must also be distinguished from parallel courses of conduct which are peculiar to oligopolies in that in an oligopoly the courses

---

13   JO [1972] L 7/25, [1972] CMLR D11, on appeal Case 6/72 *Europemballage Corpn and Continental Can Co Inc v Commission* [1973] ECR 215, [1973] CMLR 199.
14   JO [1972] L 299/51, [1973] CMLR D50, on appeal Cases 6/73 etc [1974] ECR 223, [1974] 1 CMLR 309.
15   See ch 3, pp 72-74.
16   See eg the *Report on the Behaviour of the Oil Companies during the period from October 1973 to March 1974*: COM (75) 675 10 December 1975; *Sugar Cartel* OJ [1973] L 140/17, [1973] CMLR D65 where the Commission held that two Dutch producers held a collective dominant position: the ECJ on appeal said nothing about this because it considered there was no abuse by the companies anyway: Cases 40/73 etc *Suiker Unie v Commission* [1975] ECR 1663, [1976] 1 CMLR 295.
17   Case 85/76 [1979] ECR 461, [1979] 3 CMLR 211.

of conduct interact, whilst in the case of an undertaking occupying a dominant position the conduct of the undertaking which derives profits from that position is to a great extent determined unilaterally.'[18]

This apparent rejection of Article 82 as a tool for controlling oligopolistic behaviour was understandable. Oligopolists who actively participate in agreements or concerted practices would be caught by Article 81 anyway. The ECJ appears to have taken the view that where oligopolists behave in an identical fashion because of the structure of the market on which they operate, rather than because of active participation in an agreement or concerted practice, they should not be condemned for abusing their position if their conduct is rational – even inevitable – behaviour. An approach to the 'oligopoly problem' which is based on the concept of abuse in Article 82 seemed inappropriate: or to put it another way, where there was no explicit collusion contrary to Article 81, the Court was not prepared to characterise the economist's notion of tacit collusion as abusive under Article 82. After *Hoffmann-la Roche* a period or relative inactivity followed. For example in *Alcatel v NOVASAM*[19] the Commission invited the ECJ to adopt a theory of collective dominance in an Article 234 case, but the Court declined to comment on the point in its judgment. In the *Magill* case[20] the Commission took objection to the refusal of three television companies to grant licences of copyright in their TV schedules to a third party wishing to produce a TV listings magazine. The Commission could have tried a collective dominance approach to the case, holding that the companies had collectively abused a collective dominant position in the TV schedules market; instead it found three individual dominant positions on the part of each company, and three individual abuses.

(iii)   Confirmation of the wide view

Any suggestion that the concept of collective dominance had been laid to rest was subsequently shown to be wrong. In *Italian Flat Glass*[1] the Commission held that three Italian producers of flat glass had a collective dominant position and that they had abused it. As participants in a tight oligopolistic market they enjoyed a degree of independence from competitive pressures that enabled them to impede the maintenance of effective competition, notably by not having to take into account the behaviour of other market participants. The conduct held to fall within Article 82 had already been condemned earlier in the decision as a concerted practice under Article 81. However the decision opened up the possibility that in other situations the conduct of oligopolists, *though not within Article 81*, might be attacked under Article 82. On appeal the CFI overturned the Commission's decision on collective dominance on the ground that the Commission had simply 'recycled' the facts relied on as constituting an infringement of Article 81, instead of properly defining the relevant product and geographic markets in order to weigh up the undertakings' economic power, as is necessary in Article 82 cases.

---

18   Ibid, para 39; similarly see Case 172/80 *Gerhard Züchner v Bayerische Vereinsbank* [1981] ECR 2021, [1982] 1 CMLR 313, para 10.
19   Case 247/86 [1988] ECR 5987.
20   *Magill TV Guide* OJ [1989] L 78/43, [1989] 4 CMLR 757, upheld on appeal Cases T-69/89 etc *RTE v Commission* [1991] ECR II-485, [1991] 4 CMLR 586 and further, on appeal to the ECJ, Case C-241/91 P [1995] ECR I-743, [1995] 4 CMLR 718.
1   OJ [1989] L 33/44, [1990] 4 CMLR 535.

Nevertheless, the CFI confirmed the principle of collective dominance at paragraph 358 of its judgment:

'There is nothing, in principle, to prevent two or more independent economic entities from being, on a specific market, united by such economic links that, by virtue of that fact, together they hold a dominant position vis-à-vis the other operators on the same market. This could be the case, for example, where two or more independent undertakings jointly have, through agreements or licences, a technological lead affording them the power to behave to an appreciable extent independently of their competitors, their customers and ultimately of their consumers (judgment of the Court in *Hoffmann-la Roche*, cited above, paragraphs 38 and 48)'[2].

The judgment in *Italian Flat Glass* was exciting and frustrating in equal measure. Collective dominance on the part of 'two or more independent entities' could exist under Article 82, although the Commission had failed to demonstrate that it existed in this particular case. Clearly, the CFI considered that infringements of Articles 81 and 82 were conceptually independent of one another: this is why the Commission was not permitted simply to 'recycle the facts' used to find an infringement of Article 81 in order to determine an abuse of collective dominance[3]. Each Article must be applied according to its own terms. Behaviour that amounts to a concerted practice is not automatically also abusive; and *vice versa*[4]. However, what is frustrating about the judgment is that it does not really advance our understanding of what collective dominance consists of. Did the judgment *require* that collectively dominant entities must be economically linked, or did it simply say that links were an example of collective dominance[5]? If 'links' were required, what exactly did this expression mean? Must the link consist of an agreement between the entities in question: the Court had given as examples 'agreements or licences'? If so, would not such agreements be likely to infringe Article 81, in which case what was the purpose of the principle of collective dominance under Article 82? Could cross-shareholdings amount to an economic link? Or interlocking directorships[6]? Or the sharing of a common infrastructure such as an electricity grid or a gas pipeline? More radically, could firms be economically linked simply by being in a market in which the opportunity for tacit coordination existed? Quite apart from these questions, which concern the identification of the legal concept of collective dominance, the judgment did not ask the more fundamental one: what was the function of the doctrine of collective dominance, and what could amount to an abuse of collective dominance? The judgment failed to provide adequate answers to any of these questions. Given

2   Cases T-68/89 etc *Società Italiano Vetro SpA v Commission* [1992] ECR II-1403, [1992] 5 CMLR 302; note that the reference to *Hoffmann-la Roche* in this paragraph is a reference to the meaning of market power as defined in that judgment, *not* to the meaning of collective dominance which, as mentioned earlier, the Court appeared to reject.

3   The differences between Articles 81 and 82 are very clearly stated in the judgment of the CFI in Case T-41/96 *Bayer v Commission* [2001] All ER (EC)1, [2001] 4 CMLR 126, paras 174-180.

4   This point is specifically confirmed at paras 43 and 44 of the ECJ's judgment in Cases C-395/96 and C-396/96 P *Compagnie Maritime Belge NV v Commission* [2000] 4 CMLR 1076: see pp 478-479 below.

5   Note the sentence in para 358 that begins 'This could be the case, *for example*, where two or more independent undertakings jointly...' (emphasis added).

6   AG Fennelly thought that each of these matters could give rise to collective dominance: para 28 of his opinion in the *CMBT* case.

that we now have the benefit of the judgments in *Compagnie Maritime Belge Transports v Commission* under Article 82 and *France v Commission* and *Gencor v Commission* under the ECMR it is perhaps no longer necessary to spend time in trying to understand what was meant by paragraph 358 of *Italian Flat Glass*. It is sufficient to say that an important landmark had been reached in this judgment, but that later case law has shed much more light on the concept of collective dominance.

(iv)   Further judgments and decisions on collective dominance under Article 82

In the years after *Italian Flat Glass* there were several more judgments and decisions in which collective dominance was referred to, but not until *France v Commission* and *Gencor v Commission* under the ECMR and *Compagnie Maritime Belge Transports v Commission* under Article 82 did a true picture begin to emerge of what was meant by the concept. In *Almelo*[7] the ECJ said that:

'42 However, in order for such a collective dominant position to exist, the undertakings in the group must be linked in such a way that they adopt the same conduct on the market ...

43 It is for the national court to consider whether there exist between the regional electricity distributors in the Netherlands links which are sufficiently strong for there to be a collective dominant position in a substantial part of the common market'.

This formulation refers back to the concept of a link in *Italian Flat Glass*, without further elaborating on what this means. However it introduces the idea that the significance of the link is that it enables the collectively dominant firms to adopt the same conduct on the market; the second part of the sentence in paragraph 42 suggests that the ECJ is looking at what economists would look at: the adoption of the same conduct on the market or, in other words, tacit coordination. This was an improvement on *Italian Flat Glass*, in that it provides an economic rationale for collective dominance, but it still left the mystery of 'links' to be explained. In particular, paragraph 43 of *Almelo* appeared to require a link as an essential component of collective dominance, without shedding much more light on what the link should consist of.

In *Spediporto*[8], *DIP*[9] and *Sodemare*[10] the ECJ repeated the *Almelo* formulation, but did not advance its notion of collective dominance. In the *Bosman* case[11] Advocate General Lenz assumed that football clubs in a professional football league could be 'united by such economic links' as to be regarded as collectively dominant; the ECJ did not address the issue. In the meantime the Commission began to reach findings of collective dominance in a number of decisions, both

7   Case C-393/92 *Almelo v NV Energiebedrijf Ijsselmij* [1994] ECR I-1477.
8   Case C-96/94 *Centro Servizi Spediporto Srl v Spedizioni Marittime del Golfo Srl* [1995] ECR I-2883, [1996] 4 CMLR 613, para 33.
9   Cases C-140/94 etc *DIP Spa v Commune di Bassano del Grappa* [1995] ECR I-3257, [1996] 4 CMLR 157, para 26.
10 Case C-70/95 *Sodemare SA, Anni Azzurri Holding SpA and Anni Azzurri Rezzato Srl v Regione Lombardia* [1997] ECR I-3395, [1998] 4 CMLR 667, para 46.
11 Case C-415/93 *Union Royale Belge des Sociétés de Football Association v Bosman* [1995] ECR I-4921, [1996] 1 CMLR 645.

under Article 82 and under the ECMR. The decisions under Article 82 did not greatly add to the notion of collective dominance, since they involved undertakings which unmistakably were economically linked in some way. For example in three decisions in the maritime transport sector the undertakings were members of liner conferences. In *French-West African Shipowners' Committees*[12] the Commission concluded that members of the shipowners' committees had abused a collective dominant position by taking action designed to prevent other shipping lines establishing themselves as competitors on routes between France and 11 west African states[13]. This decision was adopted after the CFI's judgment in the *Italian Flat Glass* case, and the Commission specifically imposed a fine for the infringement of Article 82 as well as the agreements that were caught by Article 81. In its decision on *Cewal*[14] the Commission found collective dominance between shipping lines that were members of a liner conference. The Commission's finding of collective dominance was upheld on appeal to the CFI[15] and to the ECJ: the latter judgment is of major importance on collective dominance under Article 82 and is considered in some detail below[16]. In *TACA*[17] the Commission imposed fines totalling EUR 273 million on the members of a liner conference for abuses of collective dominance, the largest fine to have been imposed in a single decision.

The Commission also reached a finding of collective dominance in *Port of Rødby*[18], where it considered that two ferry undertakings that fixed common rates, coordinated timetables and marketed their services jointly were collectively dominant. In *Irish Sugar*[19] the Commission found 'vertical' collective dominance between Irish Sugar and a distributor of sugar, Sugar Distributors Ltd (SDL). Without finding legal or *de facto* control of SDL, the Commission concluded that the combination of Irish Sugar's equity holding, the structure of policy-making of the two companies and the communication process established to facilitate it led to direct economic ties between them which created a clear parallelism of interest which amounted to collective dominance of the markets for industrial and retail sugar in Ireland[20]. On appeal the CFI upheld this finding of vertical collective dominance, without shedding any particular light on what this concept consists of[1].

These judgments and decisions under Article 82 after the CFI's judgment in *Italian Flat Glass* see the concept of collective dominance being quite regularly applied, and thereby becoming more familiar to officials, courts and practitioners. However, they did relatively little to answer any of the questions raised by that judgment, other than to introduce the idea of the adoption of common conduct on the market as a significant feature of collective dominance. An interesting glimpse of the way in which the Commission's view of collective dominance was developing was provided by its *Notice on Access Agreements in the Telecommunications Sector*[2]. At paragraph 79 it said that:

12 OJ [1992] L 134/1, [1993] 5 CMLR 446.
13 Ibid, paras 52-69.
14 OJ [1993] L 34/20, [1995] 5 CMLR 198.
15 Cases T-24/93 etc *Compagnie Maritime Belge Transports SA v Commission* [1996] ECR II-1201, [1997] 4 CMLR 273.
16 See pp 478-479 below.
17 OJ [1999] L 95/1, [1999] 4 CMLR 1415, on appeal Cases T-191/98 etc *Atlantic Container Line v Commission* (judgment pending).
18 OJ [1994] L 55/52, [1994] 5 CMLR 457.
19 OJ [1997] L 258/1, [1997] 5 CMLR 666.
20 Ibid, paras 111-113.
1   Case T-228/97 [1999] ECR II-2969, [1999] 5 CMLR 1300, paras 61-64.
2   OJ [1998] C 265/2, [1998] 5 CMLR 521.

'79. In addition, for two or more companies to be jointly dominant it is necessary, though not sufficient, for there to be no effective competition between the companies on the relevant market. This lack of competition may in practice be due to the fact that the companies have links such as agreements for cooperation, or interconnection agreements. *The Commission does not, however, consider that either economic theory or Community law implies that such links are legally necessary for a joint dominant position to exist.* It is a sufficient economic link if there is the kind of interdependence which often comes about in oligopolistic situations. *There does not seem to be any reason in law or in economic theory to require any other economic link between jointly dominant companies.* This having been said, in practice such links will often exist in the telecommunications sector where national [Telecomunications Operators] nearly inevitably have links of various kinds with one another' (emphasis added).

(v)   The judgment of the ECJ in Compagnie Maritime Belge Transports v Commission

Important light is shed on the meaning of collective dominance by the judgment of the ECJ in *Compagnie Maritime Belge Transports v Commission*[3], an appeal from the CFI's judgment[4] upholding the Commission's decision in *Cewal*[5] that there had been an infringement of Article 82. The ECJ deals with collective dominance at paragraphs 28 to 59 of its judgment. At paragraph 36 it states that collective dominance implies that a dominant position may be held by two or more economic entities legally independent of each other provided that from an economic point of view 'they present themselves or act together on a particular market as a collective entity'. The Court says that this is how the expression 'collective dominant position' should be understood in the judgment. It will be noted that this definition of collective dominance focuses on the notion of a collective entity, and not on the links between the undertakings in question. The ECJ then states that, in order to establish collective dominance, it is necessary to examine 'the economic links or factors which give rise to a connection between the undertakings concerned'[6], citing as precedents its earlier judgments in *Almelo*[7] under Article 82 and *France v Commission*[8] under the ECMR: the Court does not appear to consider that collective dominance has a different meaning under these two provisions. It continues that 'in particular' it must be asked whether economic links exist which enable them to act independently of their competitors[9]. However it then says that the fact that undertakings have entered into agreements does not in itself mean that they are collectively dominant[10]; but they might be if it caused them to appear as a collective entity[11]. Importantly, the ECJ then says that:

'the existence of an agreement or of other links in law is not indispensable to a finding of a collective dominant position; such a finding may be based

---

3   See p 475, n 4 above; for commentary on this judgment, see Stroux (2000) 37 CML Rev 1249.
4   See p 477, n 15 above.
5   See p 477, n 14 above.
6   Ibid, para 41.
7   See p 476, n 7 above.
8   See p 472, n 5 above.
9   Ibid, para 42.
10   Ibid, para 43.
11   Ibid, para 44.

on other connecting factors and would depend on an economic assessment and, in particular, on an assessment of the structure of the market in question[12] '.

This passage is consistent with the ECJ's judgment in *France v Commission* on collective dominance under the ECMR, where it had placed emphasis on 'connecting factors' rather than on economic links in determining whether there was collective dominance[13], and it is explicit that the existence of an agreement or concerted practice is not a pre-requisite to a finding of collective dominance. On the actual facts of the case the ECJ was satisfied that the members of the liner conference in question were collectively dominant[14].

This is clearly a very important judgment on collective dominance under Article 82: specifically, it would appear that the ECJ considers that the test of collective dominance is the same under Article 82 and the ECMR; and the Court specifically states that there is no legal requirement of an agreement or other links in law for there to be a finding of collective dominance. It would seem to be possible therefore that firms could be held to be collectively dominant where the oligopolistic nature of the market is such that they behave in a parallel manner, thereby appearing to the market as a collective entity, although there has yet to be a decision reaching such a conclusion in a particular case.

(C)   Abuse of collective dominance under Article 82

Having established that Article 82 is applicable to collective as well as single firm dominance, it is necessary to consider what kind of conduct would constitute an abuse of a collective dominant position under that provision: it is important to recall that it is not unlawful, in itself, under Article 82 to have a dominant position (whether individual or collective); for there to be an infringement of Article 82, there must be conduct which amounts to an abuse[15]. What qualifies as an abuse of collective dominance is under-developed in the case law. The economic theory around which the doctrine of collective dominance has developed under the ECMR is that in certain market conditions firms may be able to derive benefits from tacit coordination; and the very reason why the Commission might prohibit under the ECMR a concentration that would create or strengthen a collective dominant position is that it would make it easier for firms to benefit from this phenomenon[16]. Does it follow from this that tacit coordination, when actually practised, should be condemned as an abuse of a collective dominant position under Article 82? Is price parallelism in itself an abuse? To put the point another way, does symmetry require that, since predicted tacit coordination can be prevented through the prohibition of a concentration under the ECMR, actual coordination should be condemned under Article 82? If the answer to this question is no, what types of behaviour ought to be condemned under Article 82?

---

12 Ibid, para 45.
13 See pp 484-486 below.
14 Ibid, paras 46-56.
15 See ch 5, p 167; the point is made specifically in relation to collective dominance by the ECJ in its judgment in *CMBT v Commission* at paras 37-38.
16 See pp 482-492 below.

(i)   Exploitative abuse of a collective dominant position

Textbooks on Article 82 habitually make a distinction between those abuses that are 'exploitative' and those that are 'anti-competitive', whilst recognising that this is not a watertight distinction[17]. It could be argued that tacit coordination by collectively dominant undertakings is exploitative, since prices are charged which are higher than they would be in a competitive market, albeit without the need to enter into an explicit agreement. However the Commission has not attempted to condemn tacit coordination itself under Article 82, and it is submitted that, as a matter of law, it should not be able to do so. As explained earlier in this chapter[18], parallel behaviour *per se* is not caught by Article 81(1) if it does not arise from an agreement or a concerted practice in the sense of that provision. Tacit coordination comes about in certain market conditions, not because of an agreement or concerted practice between the collectively dominant firms in the legal sense of those terms, but because they react rationally according to the conditions of the market on which they operate. To condemn their parallel behaviour as abusive in itself would be a nonsense: if Article 82 were to mandate that firms must behave *irrationally* in order to comply with the law, it would indeed be an odd provision. This explains the position taken by the ECJ as long ago as *Hoffmann-la Roche*: parallel behaviour should be condemned where it is attributable to an agreement or concerted practice contrary to Article 81(1); it is not, in itself, abusive under Article 82[19]. It might seem that this shows an inconsistency between the law under Article 82 and the ECMR: how can it be that the prospect of tacit coordination can be condemned under the Merger Regulation and yet the actuality of the same behaviour cannot be condemned under Article 82? The truth is that the difference makes perfect sense: it is precisely because of the difficulty that competition law has in addressing the problem of tacit coordination when it does occur that competition authorities, through their systems of merger control, endeavour to prevent a market structure that will be conducive to this phenomenon from arising in the first place. This explains the emphasis that has been placed upon tacit coordination in merger control in the US[20].

A distinct issue is whether collectively dominant firms could be held to have abused their position by charging excessively high prices: here the abuse would lie not in the *parallelism* of the prices, but in their level. Article 82(2)(a) does condemn unfairly high prices, and it is not obvious that collectively dominant firms should enjoy an immunity from this offence which an individually dominant firm would not enjoy. In principle, therefore, it would seem that action could be taken against excessive pricing in an oligopoly. Such actions are likely to be rare, however, since the Commission does not want to establish itself as a price regulator: there have been very few investigations of high prices under Article 82, and those that have been conducted were often motivated by different considerations, for example that the excessive prices amounted to an obstacle to parallel imports[1]. The Commission contemplated a finding of an exploitative abuse of a collective dominant position of a different nature in its *P&I* decision[2].

---

17   See ch 5, pp 167-168; the Commission itself made this distinction in its decision on *P&I Clubs* OJ [1999] L 125/12, [1999] 5 CMLR 646, paras 127-136.
18   See pp 467-469 above.
19   See pp 473-474 above.
20   See pp 482-483 below.
1   See ch 18, pp 637 and 662-663.
2   OJ [1999] L 125/12, [1999] 5 CMLR 646.

The P&I clubs were members of the International Group, and were found to be collectively dominant. They had limited the level of insurance cover available to customers: this was considered by the Commission to be contrary to Article 82(2)(b), since it 'left a very substantial share of the demand unsatisfied'; however an alteration in the rules of the Group meant that the Commission did not reach a formal finding to this effect[3].

(ii) Anti-competitive abuse of a collective dominant position

Article 82 has been applied by the Commission to anti-competitive abuses of collective dominance on several occasions. Anti-competitive abuses are considered in some detail in chapters 17 and 18. It seems reasonable in principle that Article 82 should be applicable to the anti-competitive behaviour not only of individually but also of collectively dominant undertakings. Given that tacit coordination arises where a few firms, without explicit collusion, are able to set prices above the competitive level, the 'subversive' effect of new entrants into markets conducive to this phenomenon is likely to be welcomed by competition authorities: their entry may make tacit coordination less easy to achieve. In *Cewal*[4] the Commission held that Article 82 had been infringed where collectively-dominant members of a liner conference were found to have engaged in various practices with the intention of eliminating competitors from the market, such as selective price cutting and the grant of loyalty rebates. The findings of abuse were upheld on appeal to the CFI[5] and the ECJ[6], although the fines were annulled by the ECJ since the Commission had not referred to the possibility that they might be imposed in the statements of objections sent to the individual members of the conference[7]. In *TACA*[8] the abuses consisted of a refusal by members of a liner conference to offer individual service contracts to customers: various transport services were offered only pursuant to terms collectively agreed by the members of the conference; and of the abusive alteration of the competitive structure of the market by acting to eliminate potential competition: members of TACA had taken steps to induce any would-be entrants to the trans-Atlantic liner shipping market to do so within the TACA system. This smothered the emergence of new competition in the market. It can be anticipated that the Commission will investigate closely allegations of abusive behaviour by collectively dominant firms where the complainants are actual or potential competitors which might be able to subvert tacit coordination on the market.

(iii) Individual abuse of a collective dominant position

The final question under Article 82 is whether a collective dominant position can be abused only by all of the undertakings which hold that position, or whether

3   Ibid, paras 128-132.
4   OJ [1993] L 34/2, [1995] 5 CMLR 198; anti-competitive abuse was also found in the earlier *French-West African Shipowners' Committees* decision: OJ [1992] L 134/1, [1993] 5 CMLR 446; see also *P&I Clubs* (n 17 above) paras 134-136.
5   Cases T-24/93 etc *Compagnie Maritime Belge Transports SA v Commission* [1996] ECR II-1201, [1997] 4 CMLR 273.
6   See p 475, n 4 above.
7   See ch 7, p 233.
8   OJ [1999] L 95/1, [1999] 4 CMLR 1415, on appeal Cases T-191/98 etc *Atlantic Container Line v Commission* (judgment pending).

it is possible for one or some of them to commit an abuse. To put the matter another way, must there be 'collective' abuse of collective dominance, or can there also be 'individual' abuse? This has been clearly answered by the CFI in the *Irish Sugar* appeal[9]: 'undertakings occupying a joint dominant position may engage in joint or individual abusive conduct'. In principle this seems to be correct: if it is appropriate that action should be taken against anti-competitive abuses that foreclose access to a market in which there is collective dominance, it should not matter whether the abusive conduct is individual or collective, since it could have equally detrimental effects in either case.

5.   THE ECMR AND COLLECTIVE DOMINANCE[10]

(A)   Adoption of the ECMR

The ECMR does not expressly refer to collective dominance; nor does it refer to a dominant position on the part of one *or more* undertakings[11]. The Merger Task Force ('the MTF') looked for problems of tacit coordination when investigating concentrations from the earliest days of the ECMR[12]. This was not surprising. A study carried out for the Commission by Kantzebach and Kruse[13] as early as 1986, before the Regulation had been adopted, had been quite clear: 'it should be the aim of competition policy to prevent situations arising which form a hotbed for tacit collusive behaviour'. No doubt the fact that national officials were seconded to the MTF from Member States, such as the UK and Germany, where existing merger controls were already concerned with tacit coordination as well as single firm dominance, added to the pressures to apply the ECMR to collective dominance. Furthermore, experience in the US demonstrated that tacit coordination was a legitimate concern in merger analysis. Section 2 of the 1992 Horizontal Merger Guidelines of the Department of Justice and Federal Trade Commission[14], which discusses the potentially adverse competitive effects of mergers, begins with section 2.1 on the lessening of competition through coordinated interaction and then goes on in section 2.2 to discuss the lessening of competition through unilateral effects; to put this point another way, the US Guidelines suggest that collective dominance (coordinated interaction) is at least as important as, if not more important than, single firm dominance (unilateral effects). The first paragraph of section 2.1 of the 1992 US Guidelines states that:

'A merger may diminish competition by enabling firms selling in the relevant market more likely, more successfully, or more completely to engage in coordinated interaction that harms consumers. Coordinated interaction

---

9   Case T-228/97 [1999] ECR II-2969, [1999] 5 CMLR 1300, para 66.

10   For detailed texts on collective dominance under the ECMR, readers are referred in particular to Brandenburger, Spearing and Swift in *Butterworths Competition Law* (eds Freeman and Whish) Div VII paras [856]-[874]; Hawk and Huser *European Community Merger Control: A Practitioner's Guide* (Kluwer Law International, 1996) ch VII; Cook and Kerse *EC Merger Control* (Sweet & Maxwell, 3rd ed, 2000) para 5.7; Levy 'The Control of Concentrations between Undertakings' in *Competition Law of the European Community* (Matthew Bender, 2000) ¶ 8.08.

11   On the ECMR generally, see ch 21.

12   Several articles on collective dominance under the ECMR are cited in p 471, n 4 above.

13   See the Commission's XVIth *Annual Report on Competition Policy* (1986), p 285.

14   The Guidelines can be accessed at http://www.usdoj.gov/atr/public/guidelines/guidelin.htm.

is comprised of actions by a group of firms that are profitable for each of them only as a result of the accommodating reactions of the others. This behaviour includes tacit or express collusion, and may or may not be lawful in and of itself'.

The substantive test in US merger control is whether the effect of the merger 'may be substantially to lessen competition'[15]: there is no need to establish 'collective dominance', which is a concept that is specific to EC law and those systems that have subsequently been modelled upon it. It is interesting to speculate whether the European Commission might prefer the US standard to the test of dominance in the ECMR; the current proposal in the UK is to replace the 'public interest' test in the merger control system with a substantial lessening of competition test rather than one based on dominance[16].

(B)   The Commission's early practice under the ECMR

The possibility that concentrations could lead to market structures conducive to tacit coordination was considered in a very early case, *Varta/Bosch*[17], and again in *Alcatel/AEG Kabel*[18], but on neither occasion did the Commission reach an adverse finding. The first occasion on which the Commission required commitments from the parties to a concentration as a condition for clearing, rather than prohibiting, a concentration that it considered would create or strengthen a collective dominant position occurred in *Nestlé/Perrier*[19]. The decision attracted enormous attention, since it demonstrated that the Commission was prepared to intervene on the basis of collective as well as single firm dominance under the ECMR: it would not have had power to demand the commitments in the absence of a finding of collective dominance. The parties to the concentration did not appeal against the finding of collective dominance, presumably since they were content with the outcome even though they had been required to divest themselves of certain brands[20]. Other decisions on collective dominance followed, including *Kali und Salz*[1]. In this case the Commission required commitments as a condition of clearing a concentration which, in its view, raised problems of collective dominance. France, SCPA and EMC appealed, contesting, *inter alia*, whether the ECMR was applicable to collective dominance at all. Since a Member State was among the appellants, the case came before the ECJ rather than the CFI. The first outright prohibition on the basis of collective dominance occurred in *Gencor/Lonrho*[2], where the Commission found that the platinum and rhodium markets would have been collectively dominated by two firms, each with about 35% of the world market. Gencor appealed to the CFI. The ECJ's judgment in *France v Commission*[3] was handed down on 31 March

15   Clayton Act 1914, s 7.
16   On the UK proposals see ch 22, p 836; on the position in the EC, see the discussion of the *Airtours/First Choice* decision at pp 490-492 below.
17   Case No IV/M.012, OJ [1991] L 302/26.
18   Case No IV/M.165.
19   See Case No IV/M.190, OJ [1992] L 356/1, [1993] 4 CMLR M17.
20   Appeals by two trades unions against the decision were found to be inadmissible: see Case T–96/92 R *CCE v Commission* [1992] ECR II-2579 and Case T–12/93 *CCC de la Société Anonyme Vittel v Commission* [1995] ECR II-1247.
1   Case No IV/M.308, OJ [1994] L 186/38.
2   Case No IV/M.619, OJ [1997] L 11/30, [1999] 4 CMLR 1076.
3   Cases C-68/94 and 30/95 [1998] ECR I-1375, [1998] 4 CMLR 829.

1998; the CFI's in *Gencor v Commission*[4] on 25 March 1999. Between them, these judgments on the substance of the Commission's decisions under the ECMR have advanced the law of collective dominance considerably, and they appear to be consistent with the ECJ's judgment under Article 82 in *CMBT v Commission*[5]. The second outright prohibition under the ECMR on the basis of collective dominance, in *Airtours/First Choice*[6], has also been appealed, and the judgment of the CFI in that case should shed important further light on the concept[7].

(C)   France v Commission[8]

This case concerned a concentration between two German undertakings, Kali und Salz AG and Mitteldeutsche Kali AG ('MdK'), in the potash sector. The Commission considered that the concentration would create a collective dominant position on the part of Kali und Salz and another undertaking, SCPA, in particular because of structural links that already existed between them in the form of a joint venture in Canada, an export cartel and because of distribution arrangements that existed between them on the French market; in consequence the Commission required commitments on the part of Kali und Salz to terminate its links with SCPA as a condition of clearing the concentration. Kali und Salz gave the commitments required of it and the Commission cleared the transaction. It is important to stress that SCPA was not itself a party to the concentration, but that the Commission concluded that, if consummated, it would have made it collectively dominant with Kali und Salz[9]. France, SCPA and ECM, of which SCPA was a subsidiary, appealed. The ECJ concluded that the ECMR was capable of application to collective dominance; however it concluded that the Commission had failed adequately to demonstrate that there would be collective dominance on the facts of the case, and the decision was therefore annulled[10].

The ECJ emphatically rejected, at paragraphs 169 to 172, the arguments of the applicants that the ECMR did not apply to collective as well as single firm dominance: in the Court's view the goal of achieving undistorted competition within the Community meant that the Regulation must apply to collective dominance. As to the meaning of this concept, the ECJ said that:

> '221 In the case of an alleged collective dominant position, the Commission is therefore obliged to assess, using a prospective analysis of the reference

4   Case T-102/96 *Gencor v Commission* [1999] ECR II-753, [1999] 4 CMLR 971.
5   See p 475, n 4 above.
6   Case No IV/M. 1524 *Airtours/First Choice* OJ [2000] L 93/1, [2000] 5 CMLR 494, on appeal Case T-342/99 *Airtours v Commission* (judgment pending).
7   On the *Airtours* decision, see pp 490-492 below.
8   See p 483, n 3 above; for comment on the ECJ's judgment in this case see Ysewyn and Caffarra 'Two's Company, Three's a Crowd' (1998) 19 ECLR 468; Venit 'Two Steps Forward and No Steps Back: Economic Analysis and Oligopolistic Dominance after Kali und Salz' (1998) 35 CML Rev 1101; Bishop 'Power and Responsibility: The ECJ's Kali-Salz Judgment' (1999) 20 ECLR 37.
9   Advocate General Tesauro had advised the Court that collective dominance was not covered by the ECMR, in particular since there were no procedural safeguards in the Regulation for a firm in the position of SCPA that would be found to be collectively dominant without itself having brought this situation about.
10   Subsequently the Commission adopted a second decision clearing the concentration unconditionally: Commission's XXVIIIth *Annual Report on Competition Policy* (1998), paras 175-179.

market, whether the concentration which has been referred to leads to a situation in which effective competition in the relevant market is significantly impeded by the undertakings involved in the concentration and one or more other undertakings which together, in particular because of factors giving rise to a connection between them[11], are able to adopt a common policy on the market and act to a considerable extent independently of their competitors, their customers, and also of consumers'.

The ECJ stated at paragraphs 223 and 224 that the Commission enjoyed a certain discretion in making its assessment in relation to matters of such an economic nature; however, it concluded that the Commission's decision on the facts of the case should be annulled. At paragraph 226 the ECJ noted that, after the concentration, Kali und Salz and SCPA would have market shares of 23% and 37% respectively. 'A market share of approximately 60%, subdivided in that way, cannot in itself point conclusively to the existence of a dominant position on the part of those undertakings'. Thus the rule in *AKZO v Commission*[12] that dominance can be presumed where there is a market share of 50% or more must be seen as applicable only to cases of single, and not collective, dominance. The Court therefore analysed other motivations for the Commission's decision. In particular, since the Commission had placed so much emphasis on the 'structural links'[13] that existed between Kali und Salz and SCPA, the ECJ looked carefully to consider whether those links could contribute to any creation or strengthening of collective dominance on their part, but considered that the Commission had failed to demonstrate this to the necessary legal standard.

The important issue arising from the ECJ's judgment and its actual annulment of the Commission's decision is the light that it sheds on the notion of collective dominance under the ECMR. In paragraph 221, the ECJ emphasised the issue of whether the firms would be able to adopt a common policy on the market: it will be recalled that this was the feature of collective dominance under Article 82 that the ECJ introduced in paragraph 42 of the *Almelo* judgment[14]. In *France v Commission* the possibility of the adoption of a common policy is taken to be the key feature of collective dominance in the context of the ECMR. Such a common policy may arise 'in particular because of factors giving rise to a connection between them': it is important to note that this clause is subordinate to the main thrust of the sentence. As to the factors themselves, the ECJ does not provide an exhaustive list of those that are to be taken into account, nor does it prioritise them; more specifically, it does not state that economic or structural links between the collectively dominant firms are either the most important factor or even a requisite factor at all. Paragraph 222 of the judgment says that there must be a close examination of the particular circumstances of each case in order to consider the effects of a concentration in any particular market. The ECJ then went on to consider the impact of the structural links on the facts of the case, given that the Commission had placed so much emphasis on them, and disagreed with its assessment. In the Court's view the Commission had failed to demonstrate that the structural links on which it had relied were capable of sustaining a finding of

---

11 Note that this is the English translation in the official European Court Reports, and that it differs from the unofficial, and more opaque, translation in the Common Market Law Reports, 'in particular because of correlative factors which exist between them'.
12 Case C-62/86 [1991] ECR I-3359, [1993] 5 CMLR 215.
13 See p 488 below on the (possible) meaning of 'economic' as opposed to 'structural' links.
14 See p 476 above.

collective dominance. However it does not follow from this that the ECJ was saying that structural links were a pre-requirement for a finding of collective dominance; it was merely saying that, if the Commission adopted a decision on collective dominance on the basis of structural links, its reasoning on those links must be convincing.

(D)   Gencor v Commission[15]

In *Gencor/Lonrho*[16] the Commission prohibited a concentration that would have brought together the interests of those two undertakings in South Africa in platinum group metals. Gencor and Lonrho would jointly control these metals through a jointly-owned entity, Implats Ltd. As a result of the concentration, each of Implats and Amplats (a separate South African undertaking) would have had about 35% of the world production of platinum and rhodium. In the view of the Commission, this would result in the creation or strengthening of a 'dominant duopoly position'[17] as a result of which effective competition would be significantly impeded within the common market. The concentration was prohibited, the first occasion on which there had been an outright prohibition in the case of collective dominance.

At paragraph 140 of its decision, the Commission spelt out the 'problem' of what it terms 'oligopolistic dominance':

'a mere adaptation by members of the oligopoly to market conditions causes anti-competitive parallel behaviour whereby the oligopoly becomes dominant. Active collusion would therefore not be required for the members of the oligopoly to become dominant and to behave to an appreciable extent independently of their remaining competitors and, ultimately, the consumers'.

At paragraph 141, the Commission sets out those features of the platinum market that appeared to render it an uncompetitive oligopoly:

'(a) on the demand side, there is moderate growth, inelastic demand and insignificant countervailing buyer power. Buyers are therefore highly vulnerable to a potential abuse;

(b) the supply side is highly concentrated with high market transparency for a homogeneous product, mature production technology, high entry barriers (including high sunk costs) and suppliers with financial links and multi-market contacts. These supply side characteristics make it easy for suppliers to engage in parallel behaviour and provide them with incentives to do so, without any countervailing checks from the demand side'.

---

15   Case T-102/96 [1999] ECR II-753, [1999] 4 CMLR 971; see González-Díaz 'Recent Developments in EC Merger Control Law' (1999) 22 World Competition 3; Caffara and Kühn 'Joint Dominance: the CFI Judgment on *Gencor/Lonrho*' (1999) 20 ECLR 355; Elliott 'The *Gencor* Judgment: Collective Dominance, Remedies and Extraterritoriality under the Merger Regulation' (1999) 24 EL Rev 638; Korah '*Gencor v Commission*: Collective Dominance' (1999) 20 ECLR 337.
16   Case No IV/M.619 OJ [1997] L 11/30, [1999] 4 CMLR 1076.
17   Ibid, para 219; this term should be regarded as interchangeable with 'collective dominant position'.

In the succeeding paragraphs of the decision, the Commission considered each of these factors, concluding at paragraph 159 that '[t]he transparency of the market and the product homogeneity in combination with the other demand and supply characteristics have created a situation conducive to oligopolistic dominance'. It then went on to look at the position of the platinum market historically (over the previous two decades), and found that the evidence was consistent with the suggestion that the industry was conducive to oligopolistic behaviour. The Commission concluded that the concentration would create oligopolistic dominance and, effectively, a duopoly for Implats and Amplats.

Gencor appealed on a number of grounds to the CFI. The Court upheld the Commission's decision[18]. On the issue of collective dominance, the CFI confirmed (as it was bound to do, given the judgment of the ECJ in *France v Commission*[19]) that the ECMR was capable of being applied to collective dominance. Paragraphs 159 to 298 deal with the Commission's actual analysis of collective dominance. The CFI considered the Commission's analysis of each of the matters set out in paragraph 141, concluding that there were no errors on its part. Of particular interest are the Court's comments on structural links. Gencor had argued that the Commission had failed to apply the test in *Italian Flat Glass* correctly which, it asserted, 'requires for findings of collective dominance that there be structural links between the two undertakings ...'[20]. The CFI answered this point clearly at paragraphs 273 to 275:

'273 In its judgment in the *Flat Glass* case, the Court referred to links of a structural nature only by way of example *and did not lay down that such links must exist in order for a finding of collective dominance to be made.* (emphasis added)

274 It merely stated (at paragraph [358] of the judgment) that there is nothing, in principle, to prevent two or more independent economic entities from being united by economic links in a specific market and, by virtue of that fact, from together holding a dominant position *vis-à-vis* the other operators on the same market. It added (in the same paragraph) that that could be the case, for example, where two or more independent undertakings jointly had, through agreements or licences, a technological lead affording them the power to behave to an appreciable extent independently of their competitors, their customers and, ultimately, of consumers.

275. Nor can it be deduced from the same judgment that the Court has restricted the notion of economic links to the notion of structural links referred to by the appellant' (emphasis added).

A number of points can be made about these paragraphs. First, the CFI stresses that the *Italian Flat Glass* judgment did not require that there should be structural links in order for there to be a finding of collective dominance; rather such links were given as an example of when there might be such a finding. Secondly, the *Italian Flat Glass* case concerned Article 82; the Court in *Gencor* does not distinguish Article 82 cases and ECMR cases in paragraph 273 of its judgment: in other words, it must be taken to be saying that structural links are not a pre-

18 See p 484, n 4 above.
19 See p 483, n 3 above.
20 See para 264 of the judgment.

requisite under either legal instrument; this would be consistent with the subsequent judgment of the ECJ on Article 82 in *CMBT v Commission*[1]. Thirdly, the Court says that agreements or licences are simply examples of structural links, but that they are not the only economic links that might be found. Fourthly, the language of these paragraphs is confusing, since the CFI does not explain whether it considers that there is a difference between a 'structural' and an 'economic' link, and if so what that difference consists of. As was noted above, the CFI in *Italian Flat Glass* had used the expression 'economic links', whereas the Commission in *Gencor* referred to 'structural links'. In *Gencor* it is not obvious from paragraphs 273 to 275 how the CFI considers that these two terms relate to one another.

Paragraphs 276 and 277 may provide an answer to this conundrum:

'276 Furthermore, there is no reason whatsoever in legal or economic terms to exclude from the notion of economic links the relationship of interdependence existing between the parties to a tight oligopoly within which, in a market with the appropriate characteristics, in particular in terms of market concentration, transparency and produce homogeneity, those parties are in a position to anticipate one another's behaviour and are therefore strongly encouraged to align their conduct on the market, in particular in such a way as to maximise their joint profits by restricting production with a view to increasing prices. In such a context, each trader is aware that highly competitive action on its part designed to increase its market share (for example a price cut) would provoke identical action by the others, so that it would derive no benefit from its initiative. All the traders would thus be affected by the reduction in price levels.

277. That conclusion is all the more pertinent with regard to the control of concentrations, whose objective is to prevent anti-competitive market structures from arising or being strengthened. Those structures may result from the existence of economic links in the strict sense argued by the applicant or from market structures of an oligopolistic kind where each undertaking may become aware of common interests and, in particular, cause prices to increase without having to enter into an agreement or resort to a concerted practice'.

These paragraphs would appear to suggest that, where links are taken into account in establishing collective dominance, the controlling issue is whether links exist between firms which would facilitate tacit coordination. Such links could be 'merely' economic, that is to say a consequence of the economic conditions of the market itself: this is what is envisaged in paragraph 276. However, they might also be structural, where for example the firms in question are bound to one another in some other way, through agreements, licences, cross-shareholdings or shared infrastructure[2]. According to this view, structural links would be a 'sub-species' of economic links; the real issue being whether the links are conducive to tacit coordination. This is this author's attempt to explain a rather awkward passage in the judgment: further light may be shed on this in the *Airtours* appeal[3].

---

1   See p 475, n 4 above.
2   See the examples given at p 475 above.
3   See pp 490-492 below.

(E)   The Commission's decisional practice under the ECMR since *Gencor*

The Commission has paid close attention to collective dominance in several subsequent decisions under the ECMR; it is noticeable that the factors set out in paragraph 141 of its *Gencor/Lonrho* decision tend to form the starting point of its analysis[4]. Whilst it is reasonable and helpful to have such a checklist, it goes without saying that this should not be applied in too mechanistic a manner: as the ECJ said at paragraph 22 of its judgment in *France v Commission*, each case must turn on its particular facts. Different items on the checklist will have greater or lesser significance according to the industry in question. Two decisions on collective dominance under the ECMR are of particular interest.

(i)   *Price Waterhouse/Coopers & Lybrand*[5]

In *Price Waterhouse/Coopers & Lybrand* the Commission investigated the proposed concentration between these two firms of accountants, in particular in relation to the market for auditing and accounting services for large clients. In considering whether collective dominance would be created, the Commission did so on the basis of a 'dual-merger scenario'[6], since two other major firms of accountants, KPMG and Ernst & Young, had also notified their proposed concentration. The Commission's preliminary view had been that, if both of these transactions were to have been completed, the position 'would be consistent with a hypothesis of collective dominance'[7]; however, KPMG and Ernst & Young announced the termination of their own plans, so that the Commission did not have to reach a conclusion on this 'scenario'. What is intriguing is the possibility that the Commission might have been prepared to prohibit each of these concentrations because of a reduction in the 'Big Six' firms of accountants to only four. As noted below, the *Airtours/First Choice* concentration was blocked where the transaction would have taken the industry from four to three players; but this decision might have been preceded by a prohibition on the basis of a reduction from six players to four. With the KPMG/Ernst & Young deal having collapsed, the Commission then had to consider whether there were grounds for prohibiting the Price Waterhouse transaction, and concluded that there were not. In the course of its decision the Commission pointed out that a consequence of the ECJ's judgment in *France v Commission* is that it has a high burden of proof where it is considering whether it should adopt a finding of collective dominance[8]; presumably the burden on the Commission is higher where the merger will not create a duopoly of two, as in *Gencor/Lonrho*, but an oligopoly of three or more, as in *Price Waterhouse/Coopers & Lybrand*.

4   Apart from the decisions mentioned in the text, the Commission found collective dominance in the following Phase II investigations since *Gencor*: Case No IV/M.1225 *Enso/Stora* OJ [1999] L 254/9, [1999] 4 CMLR 21, paras 66-68; Case No IV/M.1313 *Danish Crown/ Vestjydske Slagterier* OJ [2000] L 20/1, [2000] 5 CMLR 296, paras 174-181; Case No IV/ M.1383 *Exxon/Mobil*; Case No COMP/M.1663 *Alcan/Alusuisse*; Case No COMP/M.1673 *VEBA/VIAG*; Case No COMP/M.2097 *SCA/Metsä Tissue*.
5   Case No IV/M. 938 OJ [1997] L 50/27, [1999] 4 CMLR 665.
6   Ibid, paras 108 ff.
7   Ibid, para 110.
8   Ibid, paras 104-106.

(ii)   *Airtours/First Choice*[9]

In *Airtours/First Choice* the Commission investigated a proposed hostile acquisition by Airtours of First Choice. The Commission concluded that the acquisition would create a collective dominant position in the market for short-haul package holidays in the UK on the part of the merged entity, Airtours/First Choice, and the two other leading tour operators, Thomson Travel Group and Thomas Cook. The Commission was not satisfied that commitments offered by Airtours could remedy the problems that it foresaw, and prohibited the concentration outright. This was the second outright prohibition under the ECMR on the basis of collective dominance; the decision has been appealed to the CFI[10].

An obvious point of distinction from *Gencor/Lonrho* was that in that decision the collective dominance would be held by two entities, Implats and Amplats, whereas in *Airtours/First Choice* three firms would be collectively dominant. Without wishing to suggest that there is any magic in numbers, the first prohibition in a 'four to three' case, *Airtours*, as opposed to a 'three to two' case, *Gencor*, is of interest. However, this in itself should not be regarded as the key factor in the case. To suggest that the identification of collective dominance is a matter of numbers is jejune: the critical issue in each case is whether a concentration will make it easier for firms to achieve tacit coordination; as seen in *Price Waterhouse/ Coopers & Lybrand*, the Commission might have been prepared, in the context of the market under consideration there, to conclude that a reduction from six to four players should be prohibited under the 'dual merger scenario'.

The Commission analysed a number of market characteristics in *Airtours/ First Choice* in order to determine whether the market was conducive to oligopolistic dominance: product homogeneity, low demand growth, low price sensitivity of demand, similar cost structures of the main suppliers, high market transparency, extensive commercial links between the major suppliers, substantial entry barriers and insignificant buyer power. On the basis of this assessment, and of a review of the history of competition in the industry, the Commission concluded that the concentration would result in an oligopolistic market in which it would be rational for the three collectively dominant undertakings to restrict supply to the market, thereby increasing price.

There was fundamental disagreement between Airtours and the Commission on various aspects of this decision. In particular, in relation to collective dominance, Airtours disagreed with three features of the decision. First, the issue of tacit coordination itself. Prior to *Airtours*, the Commission's decisional practice and the Courts' judgments in *France v Commission* and *Gencor v Commission* seemed to have established that the key issue in a case of collective dominance under the ECMR was whether the concentration enabled the undertakings 'to adopt a common policy on the market' and to act to a considerable extent independently of competitors, customers and consumers[11]. However, in *Airtours* the Commission stated at paragraph 54:

'Furthermore – contrary to the apparent view of Airtours – it is not a necessary condition of collective dominance for the oligopolists always to behave as if there were one or more explicit agreements (eg to fix prices or

---

9   Case IV/M.1524 *Airtours/First Choice* OJ [2000] L 93/1, [2000] 5 CMLR 494; see Motta 'EC Merger Policy and the *Airtours* Case' (2000) 21 ECLR 199; Christiansen and Rabassa 'The *Airtours* Decision: Is there a New Commission Approach to Collective Dominance?' (2001) 22 ECLR 227.

10   Case T-342/99 *Airtours v Commission* (judgment pending).

11   See *France v Commission*, see p 483, n 3 above, para 221.

capacity, or share the market) between them. *It is sufficient that the merger makes it rational for the oligopolists, in adapting themselves to market conditions, to act – individually – in ways which will substantially reduce* competition between them, and as a result of which they may act, to an appreciable extent, independently of competitors, customers and consumers' (emphasis added).

This language may be taken to suggest a departure by the Commission from its previous decisions, in that it refers to the individual actions of the oligopolists, rather than to their likely tacit coordination. This raises the question of whether the paragraph introduces a new approach to collective dominance, by creating a third ground of intervention which combines elements of the 'unilateral' and the 'coordinated effects' standards applied in US law[12]. To put the point another way, it can be argued that the Commission has attempted to lower the threshold for a finding of collective dominance, by looking at the rational unilateral behaviour of individual entities rather than their tacit coordination. The US standard in merger cases – whether the merger will substantially lessen competition – avoids the need that arises under the ECMR to establish individual or collective dominance, which are legal constructs rather than economic concepts. It may be that the Commission prefers the US standard, and that it would like to stretch the concept of collective dominance so that the two systems could apply effectively the same substantive test, that is to say the substantial lessening of competition. However it is not clear whether the Commission deliberately intended in this paragraph to extend the notion of collective dominance in this way. It is possible that the Commission was simply stating the basic point about oligopoly, which is that each firm makes an individual choice based on what it expects its competitors to do: tacit coordination occurs even though there is no agreement or concerted practice. The question of whether paragraph 54 goes beyond the established test of collective dominance under the ECMR will be dealt with in the appeal pending before the CFI.

A second disagreement between Airtours and the Commission concerned the application of the tacit coordination 'checklist' in paragraph 141 of *Gencor/Lonrho*: in the view of Airtours the Commission failed to apply the factors in that list in a way that was convincing in the circumstances of the industry in question, which was, of course, very different from a 'commodity' industry, such as platinum and rhodium in *Gencor/Lonrho*. This will also be examined on appeal.

A third disagreement arose from the fact that, in the opinion of Airtours, tacit coordination could be feasible only where there is a plausible retaliatory mechanism in place that would deter the other firms from cheating; the retaliation could take the form, for example, of a price war or a substantial increase in capacity[13]. The Commission's response to this was first, that neither the Commission nor the CFI in *Gencor* had required that a specific punishment mechanism was necessary for a finding of collective dominance; and secondly that there were anyway significant possibilities for punishment[14]. As to the former point, the US Horizontal Merger Guidelines state that:

> 'Successful coordinated interaction entails reaching terms of coordination that are profitable to the firms involved and an ability to detect and punish

12 See pp 482-483 above.
13 See paras 52, 55 and 148-149.
14 See paras 151-152.

deviations that would undermine the coordinated interaction. Detection and punishment of deviations ensure that coordinating firms will find it more profitable to adhere to the terms of coordination than to pursue short-term profits from deviating, given the costs of reprisal'[15].

The Commission however concluded at paragraph 150 of its Decision that:

'it is not necessary to show that there would be a strict punishment mechanism: what matters for collective dominance in the present case is whether the degree of interdependence between the oligopolists is such that it is rational for the oligopolists to restrict output, and in this sense reduce competition in such a way that a collective dominant position is created'.

In the Commission's view, strict punishment systems are necessary to support full-blown cartels, but not for tacit coordination: these two phenomena should not be confused with one another. The CFI has also been asked to examine this important issue in the *Airtours* appeal.

6.   UK LAW

(A)   Competition Act 1998

The Chapter I and Chapter II Prohibitions in the Competition Act 1998 are based on Articles 81 and 82 EC, and section 60 of the Act requires that consistency should be maintained with the jurisprudence of the Community Courts and that account should be taken of the decisional practice of the Commission[16]. It follows that the discussion in the earlier part of this chapter of the application of Articles 81 and 82 to tacit coordination and oligopolistic markets is directly relevant under the UK Act. However two additional points should be made about the domestic law of the UK in relation to this issue. First, the scale and complex monopoly provisions of the Fair Trading Act 1973 ('the FTA') have been retained, so that an alternative mechanism exists whereby oligopolistic markets may be investigated[17]. Secondly, the system of merger control in the UK requires the Competition Commission to determine whether a merger may be expected to operate against the public interest[18]. There is no reference in the legislation to 'collective dominance', nor to a substantial lessening of competition[19]. The following two sections will briefly examine the Competition Commission's investigations of oligopolistic markets under the monopoly and merger provisions respectively of the FTA.

---

15 US Guidelines, para 2.1; para 2.12 goes into greater detail on 'conditions conducive to detecting and punishing deviations'.
16 On s 60 of the Act see ch 9, pp 329-333.
17 For a general description of the monopoly provisions of the FTA, see ch 11.
18 See ch 22, pp 816-817.
19 Note however that the Government has proposed that the law should be amended in favour of a substantial lessening of competition test: ibid, p 836.

(B)   Monopoly investigations under the Fair Trading Act 1973[20]

Oligopolies can be referred to the Competition Commission by virtue of the complex monopoly provisions of the FTA. A reference may be made both where one firm supplies or is supplied with 25% or more of the goods or services of a particular description, but also where this threshold is satisfied by:

'two or more persons who ... whether voluntarily or not, and whether by agreement or not, so conduct their affairs, as to prevent, restrict or distort competition'[1].

Thus the Competition Commission can be asked to investigate a market even though no one firm has dominance over it. A complex monopoly situation can consist of a substantial number undertakings[2]: as a result it is a wider than the concept of collective dominance, which has been applied only to situations in which a few firms presented themselves the market as a common entity. The Competition Commission can consider whether the market structure itself or any things done by the oligopolists operate or may be expected to operate against the public interest and if so make suitable recommendations. This means that, in those situations where competition in an oligopoly seems to be weak and yet where it is unlikely that there is an agreement or concerted practice, it is possible for the Competition Commission to conduct an industry-wide investigation. The FTA therefore provides a useful safety-net to deal with the type of case which falls or may fall short of unlawful collusion.

Among the powers that the Secretary of State can exercise after a report is the power to order divestiture of assets. In practice however structural remedies have rarely been recommended[3]; various behavioural remedies are also available following a monopoly investigation, including the possibility of regulating prices[4].

The Competition Commission's reports have often been concerned with oligopolistic markets and sometimes specifically with pricing behaviour. Two aspects of oligopolistic pricing in particular have been considered: the problem of price parallelism and the possibility that oligopolists are charging supra-competitive prices without actually conspiring to do so.

(i)   Price parallelism

The Commission published a general report on *Parallel Pricing*[5] in 1973 in which it concluded that parallel pricing in the absence of parallel costs was generally detrimental to consumer welfare. On subsequent occasions it has noted the tendency of oligopolists to align their prices and has recommended ways in which competition between oligopolists could be intensified, thereby reducing

---

20   See Rodger 'Oligopolistic Market Failure: Collective Dominance versus Complex Monopoly' (1995) 16 ECLR 21; Brent 'The Certain Pursuit of Oligopoly: A Reply' (1996) 17 ECLR 163; Rodger 'A Response to Brent: 'Complex Monopoly: Oligopoly, the Public Interest and the Pursuit of Certainty' (1996) 17 ECLR 344.

1   FTA, s 6(2) in respect of goods; ss 7 and 8 contain similar provisions in respect of services and exports: see ch 11, p 365.

2   See ch 11, p 369.

3   See ch 11, p 384.

4   See ch 11, p 380; see also ch 18, pp 666-669.

5   Cmnd 5330 (1973).

the extent of parallelism. For example, in *Electricity Supply Meters*[6] and in *Concrete Roofing Tiles*[7] the Commission was of the view that if powerful customers (electricity boards in the first case and local authorities in the second) were to use their purchasing power more aggressively, the supply side of the market might become more competitive. In *Postal Franking Machines*[8] the Commission considered that a relaxation of the Post Office's regulations on the supply and maintenance of franking machines could improve the competitive environment[9]. In *White Salt*[10] it was concerned that the prices of ICI and British Salt had tended to be very similar and recommended that the prices of British Salt, the more efficient of the two, should be controlled directly: ICI could in future charge a 'parallel' price only if it significantly improved its efficiency.

In its report on *Supply of Petrol*[11] the Competition Commission concluded that the parallel pricing which was normal in the retailing of petrol was caused by the fact that oil was an internationally traded commodity the price of which was primarily determined by movements on the international markets: wholesaling and retailing margins were not large and it was inevitable that the prices of the five major companies would move closely together, as they were all affected by the same cost factors. The Commission therefore confined itself to recommending that the situation should be monitored. In *Credit Card Services*[12], a market where, like petrol, there had been public disquiet about high charges and parallel behaviour, the Commission found that matters such as high profits would now be cured by the increased competition which had entered the market even since the onset of the Commission investigation. The point to note about these reports is that they reflect perfectly the investigative system in the FTA: non-doctrinaire, pragmatic, case-by-case analysis. Given the theoretical problems posed by oligopoly, it would seem that there is much to be said for having a power to investigate industries in this way.

(ii)   Excessive pricing

In the Competition Commission's reports on excessive pricing, which will be considered in greater detail in chapter 18[13], one again sees the pragmatism of the Commission's approach. Where it finds that excessive prices are being charged it will make whatever recommendations, in the circumstances of the particular industry, appear appropriate. This can lead to the same phenomenon being treated very differently. For example, the Commission has sometimes recommended that prices should be directly controlled[14] or, in the first *Tampons* report[15], that the DGFT should monitor an industry for a period of time in the hope that it might become more competitive. When the Commission looked at this matter a second time it found that excessive pricing was still a problem, but it was satisfied

6   Cmnd 7639 (1979).
7   HCP (1981–82) 12.
8   Cmnd 9747 (1986).
9   The regulations were altered in 1987: 1987 *Annual Report of the DGFT* p 28.
10   Cmnd 9778 (1986); this report is discussed further in ch 18, p 668.
11   Cm 972 (1990).
12   Cm 718 (1989): this was the second Commission investigation into this market, the first being *Credit Card Franchise Services* Cm 8034 (1980).
13   See in particular pp 666-669.
14   See eg *Breakfast Cereals* HCP (1972–73) 2; *Household Detergents* HCP (1965–66) 105; *White Salt* Cmnd 9778 (1986).
15   Cmnd 8049 (1980).

that the market would correct itself over time so that price regulation was unnecessary[16].

(C)   Merger investigations under the Fair Trading Act 1973

When conducting a merger investigation under the FTA, the Competition Commission is asked to determine whether the merger may be expected to operate against the public interest[17]; it is not required to look for dominance, whether individual or collective, as under the ECMR. This means that the Commission has not had to undergo the tortuous experience of the European Commission and the Community Courts of working out what is meant by collective dominance. However, the Competition Commission does consider whether a merger could lead to a market structure in which tacit coordination could arise as part of its approach to the public interest. Examples are *Elders IXL Ltd/Scottish & Newcastle Breweries plc*[18], where it was concerned at the reduction of national brewers from six to five; and *Bond Helicopters Ltd/British International Helicopters Ltd*[19], where there would have been a duopoly in the provision of North Sea services to oil and gas installations.

A particularly striking report is *Interbrew SA/Bass plc*[20]. Interbrew, the owner, *inter alia*, of Stella lager, acquired Bass, owner of Carling lager. The concentration had a Community dimension under the ECMR, and was therefore notified to the European Commission. The UK Government asked for a reference back under Article 9 of the ECMR, which was granted[1]. The merger, which was conditional upon approval by the European Commission but not upon clearance under UK law, was referred to the Competition Commission. The Commission concluded that it could be expected to operate against the public interest, since it would create a duopoly between Interbrew and Scottish & Newcastle, the second largest brewer after the merged Interbrew/Bass. This would reduce competition in the market place, lead to higher prices and reduce consumer choice. The Commission's recommendation was that Interbrew should divest itself of Bass, and the Secretary of State accepted this advice[2]. It was reported that the loss to Interbrew of having to divest itself of Bass could be as much as £750 million, and a judicial review was sought of the required divestiture on the ground that it was a disproportionate response to the problem identified by the Commission. Though largely unsuccessful, the judicial review necessitated further consideration of the appropriate remedy in this case[3].

---

16   Cmnd 9470 (1985).
17   See ch 22, pp 816-817.
18   Cm 654 (1989).
19   Cm 2060 (1992); note that in a later report the Commission took a more relaxed view of a merger in this sector: see ch 22, p 822 on *CHC Helicopter/Helicopter Services Group* Cm 4556 (2000).
20   Cm 5014 (2001).
1   On Article 9 of the ECMR see ch 21, p 758-761.
2   DTI Press Release P/2001/11, 3 January 2001.
3   See Competition Commission Press Release 20/01, 23 May 2001.

CHAPTER 15

Horizontal agreements (3) – cooperation agreements

1. INTRODUCTION

The previous two chapters have considered the law on hard-core cartels and the phenomenon of tacit collusion in oligopolistic markets. However it is important to appreciate that there may be circumstances in which firms that operate at the same level of the market enter into cooperation agreements with one another that have economic benefits. It follows that competition law cannot simply prohibit all horizontal agreements outright: efficiency gains may follow from cooperation that are sufficient to outweigh any restriction of competition that it might entail. This chapter is concerned with horizontal cooperation agreements which the competition authorities in the EC and the UK may be prepared to countenance. The chapter is predominantly concerned with the treatment of such agreements under Article 81 EC, although the final section considers the position under the UK Competition Act 1998[1].

2. FULL-FUNCTION JOINT VENTURES

Where firms decide to cooperate with one another, the medium for their collaboration can vary widely from one case to another. For example firms that wish to cooperate in research and development ('R&D') may simply meet on a periodic basis to discuss matters of common interest; they may share out research work and pool the results; they may establish a committee to oversee the R&D programme; or they may go further and establish a joint venture company to conduct their R&D, while maintaining their independence as producers and suppliers to the market. The same range of possibilities exists in relation to other types of cooperation, for example on production and commercialisation. As a matter of competition law the medium chosen for the horizontal cooperation will not normally affect the legal analysis of an agreement, with one very important exception: where the parties to an agreement establish a joint venture company to carry out their objectives, this may amount to a concentration (to use the language of the EC Merger Regulation ('the ECMR')) or a merger (the term used in the UK Fair Trading Act 1973); if so, the joint venture will be considered not

---

1   See pp 531-533 below.

under Article 81 or the Chapter I prohibition of the Competition Act 1998, but under the ECMR or the relevant domestic merger control provisions of the Member States. It follows that it is necessary in any particular case to begin by considering whether parties intend to create a full-function joint venture amounting to a concentration or a merger: the meaning of a concentration under the ECMR is dealt with in chapter 21[2]; and chapter 22 considers what is meant by a merger in UK law[3]. It may even be the case that contractual integration, without the establishment of a joint venture company, will amount to a full-function joint venture under the ECMR[4]. Only where it is clear that there is no concentration or merger will it be relevant to consider the possible application of Article 81 and the Chapter I prohibition to horizontal cooperation agreements.

3. THE APPLICATION OF ARTICLE 81 TO HORIZONTAL COOPERATION AGREEMENTS AND THE COMMISSION'S *HORIZONTAL GUIDELINES*[5]

(A) Introduction

The general principles involved in the application of Article 81(1) and Article 81(3) have been described in chapters 3 and 4. In chapter 3, the distinction between agreements that have as their object the restriction of competition and those that have the effect of doing so was explained: as a general proposition the agreements considered in this chapter fall into the 'effect' rather than the 'object' box[6]. The important point was made in chapter 3 that not every contractual restriction necessarily restricts competition, and examples were given to explain this[7]. The application of Article 81(1) to potential as well as actual restrictions of competition was dealt with, and the point made that a realistic approach must be taken to restrictions of potential competition[8]. Reference was made to a greater willingness on the part of the Commission in recent years to conclude that agreements notified to it were not restrictive of competition, so that they could be cleared under Article 81(1), rather than being found to infringe Article 81(1) and then being exempted under Article 81(3)[9]. The *de minimis* doctrine[10] and the meaning of an effect on inter-state trade[11] were considered, and the chapter concluded with a checklist of agreements that would normally fall outside Article 81(1)[12]. In chapter 4 the criteria for the application of Article 81(3) were explained[13], as were the Commission's monopoly over, and the procedure for

---

2   See ch 21, pp 748-751; note that it may be that partial-function production joint ventures will be brought within the scope of the ECMR: see ibid, p 751.
3   See ch 22, pp 748-751.
4   See ch 21, p 751 on Case COMP/JV.19 *KLM/Martinair*.
5   For a very helpful analysis of the Commission's approach to the application of Article 81 to horizontal cooperation agreements, see Faull and Nikpay *The EC Law of Competition* (Oxford University Press, 1999) paras 6.39-6.342, noting, however, that this was written prior to the adoption of the Commission's *Horizontal Guidelines* and the two new block exemptions.
6   See ch 3, pp 92-95.
7   Ibid, pp 99-100.
8   Ibid, pp 102-103.
9   Ibid, p 103.
10   Ibid, pp 107-110.
11   Ibid, pp 110-120.
12   Ibid, pp 120-121.
13   Ch 4, pp 124-133.

obtaining, an individual exemption[14]. The point was made that there is no kind of agreement which is, by its nature, incapable of being exempted[15]. The system of block exemptions was described, including the recent adoption of 'new-style' block exemptions of a less formalistic and more economics-oriented nature[16]. Finally the Commission's *White Paper on Modernisation* was considered which, if implemented, will result in abandonment of the system of notification of agreements to the Commission and the abolition of individual (though not block) exemptions[17]. This chapter assumes a knowledge of the contents of chapters 3 and 4, and explains the current position in relation to horizontal cooperation agreements under Article 81[18].

A common criticism of the Commission has been that it has too readily applied Article 81(1) to horizontal cooperation agreements, with the result that the parties had to notify in order to obtain individual exemption under Article 81(3); and further that the block exemptions for specialisation agreements and R&D agreements were too narrow and formalistic to be of much utility. At the end of 2000 the Commission adopted new *Guidelines on Horizontal Cooperation Agreements*[19] as well as two 'new-style' block exemptions, Regulation 2658/2000 for specialisation agreements[20] and Regulation 2659/2000 for R&D agreements[1]. This package of measures on the part of the Commission represents a major overhaul of its practice in relation to horizontal cooperation agreements[2], and the intention is that this chapter should concentrate on the new régime; for this reason there will be relatively little discussion of the prior decisional practice of the Commission, although reference will be made to some particularly significant decisions.

(B) The Community Courts and horizontal cooperation agreements

There is very little case law of the Community Courts specifically on the application of Article 81 to horizontal cooperation agreements. A few cases have reached the ECJ under Article 234, such as *Gøttrup-Klim Grovvareforeninger v Dansk Landburgs Grovvareselskab AmbA*[3]. As for Commission decisions, where the parties to an agreement receive an exemption under Article 81(3) there is usually little incentive for them to appeal against the finding that the agreement infringed

---

14 Ibid, pp 136-141.
15 Ibid, p 124.
16 Ibid, pp 141-146.
17 Ibid, pp 146-147; see also ch 7, pp 246-258.
18 For discussion of the position in the US, see the Department of Justice *Antitrust Guidelines for Collaboriations Among Competitors*, available at http://www.usdoj.gov/atr/public/guidelines/jointindex.htm; see also Brodley 'Joint Ventures and Antitrust Policy' (1982) 95 Harvard Law Review 1523; McFalls 'The Rôle and Assessment of Classical Market Power in Joint Venture Analysis' (1997-98) 66 Antitrust Bulletin 651; Werden 'Antitrust Analysis of Joint Ventures: An Overview' ibid, 701; Correia 'Joint Ventures: Issues in Enforcement Policy' ibid, 737; Gutterman *Innovation and Competition Policy: A Comparative Study of the Regulation of Patent Licensing and Collaborative Research & Development in the United States and the European Community* (Kluwer Law International, 1997).
19 OJ [2001] C 3/2, [2001] 4 CMLR 819.
20 OJ [2001] L 304/3, [2001] 4 CMLR 800.
1 OJ [2001] L 304/7, [2001] 4 CMLR 808.
2 On the background to these reforms, see the Commission's XXVIIth *Report on Competition Policy* (1997), points 46 and 47; XXVIIIth *Report on Competition Policy* (1998), points 54 and 55; and XXIXth *Report on Competition Policy* (1999), points 37-39.
3 Case 250/92 [1994] ECR I-5641, [1996] 4 CMLR 191; see also Cases C-399/93 etc *HG Oude Luttikhuis v Coberco* [1995] ECR I-4515, [1996] 5 CMLR 178.

Article 81(1). A notable exception to this is the judgment of the CFI in *European Night Services v Commission*[4] where an appeal was successfully launched against the Commission's decision, in which it had attached conditions and obligations to an individual exemption which the parties considered to be unduly onerous. The CFI concluded that the Commission had failed to demonstrate that the agreement would appreciably restrict competition, as a result of which the decision was annulled. There have been some other cases in which a third party has challenged the Commission's decision to grant an exemption, but these have usually been unsuccessful[5]. A notable exception was *Métropole Télévision SA v Commission*[6], where the CFI upheld an appeal by a third party that the Commission had erred in law in granting an exemption to the European Broadcasting Union[7].

(C)   The Commission's *Guidelines on Horizontal Cooperation Agreements*

The Commission adopted its *Guidelines on Horizontal Cooperation Agreements* at the end of 2000; they were published in the Official Journal on 6 January 2001[8]. The *Guidelines* consist of seven chapters. In the first, the Commission sets out its position generally in relation to horizontal cooperation agreements and establishes an analytical framework for the most common types of agreement. Chapters then follow on each of the following six types of agreement: R&D[9]; production agreements, including specialisation agreements[10]; purchasing agreements[11]; commercialisation agreements[12]; agreements on standards[13]; and environmental agreements[14]. The *Guidelines* do not deal with other types of agreement, such as the exchange of information and the acquisition of minority shareholdings[15]. This chapter will follow the pattern of the *Guidelines*, considering first the general framework for the analysis of horizontal cooperation agreements and then each of the six types of agreement specified. It will conclude with a discussion of various other cases, such as restructuring agreements, under EC law and with a brief review of the position under UK law.

---

4   Cases T-374/94 etc [1998] ECR II-3141, [1998] 5 CMLR 718: see ch 3, p 91ff; see similarly Cases T-79/85 and 80/95 *SNCF v Commission* [1996] ECR II-1491, [1997] 4 CMLR 334; the recipients of an individual exemption in *TPS* OJ [1999] L 90/6, [1999] 5 CMLR 168 have appealed the decision to the CFI in Case T-112/99 *Métropole v Commission* (judgment pending); on *TPS* see Nikolinakos 'Strategic Alliances in the Pay TV Market: The *TPS* case' [2000] 21 ECLR 334.

5   See eg Case 43/85 *ANCIDES v Commission* [1987] ECR 3131, [1988] 4 CMLR 821; Case T-17/93 *Matra Hachette SA v Commission* [1994] ECR II-595.

6   Cases T-528/93 etc [1996] ECR II-649, [1996] 5 CMLR 386.

7   See ch 4, pp 135-136; note that the Commission subsequently adopted a second decision granting individual exemption, which was again challenged by Métropole: ibid, p 136, n 7.

8   OJ [2001] C 3/2, [2001] 4 CMLR 819.

9   *Guidelines*, ch 2: paras 39-77.

10   Ibid, ch 3: paras 78-114.

11   Ibid, ch 4: paras 115-138.

12   Ibid, ch 5: paras 139-158.

13   Ibid, ch 6: paras 159-178.

14   Ibid, ch 7: paras 179-198.

15   Ibid, para 10; on information agreements, see ch 13, pp 441-450; on minority shareholdings, see ch 21, pp 736-737.

4. THE ANALYTICAL FRAMEWORK IN THE COMMISSION'S *GUIDELINES* FOR THE MOST COMMON TYPES OF HORIZONTAL COOPERATION AGREEMENTS UNDER ARTICLE 81

(A) Purpose of the *Guidelines*

The *Guidelines* state that horizontal cooperation agreements may lead to competition problems where the parties agree to the fixing of prices, output or the sharing of markets or where cooperation enables the parties to maintain, gain or increase their market power, thereby causing negative effects with respect to prices, output, innovation or the variety and quality of products[16]. However the *Guidelines* go on to say that substantial economic benefits can flow from horizontal cooperation, in particular given the dynamic nature of markets, globalisation and the speed of technological progress. Cooperation can be a means for firms to share risk, save costs, pool know-how and launch innovation faster; the benefits to small and medium-sized enterprises are specifically noted[17]. The Commission states that, when analysing horizontal cooperation agreements, greater emphasis should be placed on economic criteria[18], for example on market power and on market structure[19]. The *Guidelines* replace the Commission's 1968 *Notice on agreements, decisions and concerted practices in the field of cooperation between enterprises*[20] and the 1993 *Notice concerning the assessment of cooperative joint ventures under Article [81]*[1], and complement the two new block exemptions on specialisation agreements and R&D agreements[2].

(B) Scope of the *Guidelines*

(i)   The Guidelines apply to agreements between actual and potential competitors

The *Guidelines* apply to agreements entered into between two or more competitors operating at the same level in the market: the expression 'competitor' is taken to include both actual and potential competitors[3]. Somewhat strangely, the meaning of 'actual' and of 'potential' competitors is relegated to footnotes 8 and 9 of the *Guidelines*.

(A)   ACTUAL COMPETITORS.   Footnote 8 states that an undertaking is an actual competitor either if it is active on the same relevant market or if, in the absence of the agreement, it is able to switch production to the relevant products and market them in the short term without incurring significant additional costs or risks in response to a small and permanent increase in relative prices: the Commission refers to this as 'immediate supply-side substitutability', and cross-refers to paragraphs 20 to 23 of its 1997 *Notice on Market Definition*[4], which explain this phenomenon in greater detail.

16 *Guidelines*, para 2.
17 Ibid, para 3.
18 Ibid, para 6.
19 Ibid, para 7.
20 OJ [1968] C 75/3.
1   OJ [1993] C 43/2.
2   *Guidelines*, para 8.
3   Ibid, para 9; on actual and potential competition under Article 81(1), see also ch 3, pp 102-103.
4   OJ [1997] C 372/5, [1998] 4 CMLR 177: see ch 1, p 26ff.

(B)   POTENTIAL COMPETITORS.   Footnote 9 provides that an undertaking is a potential competitor where, in the absence of the agreement, it would be likely to undertake the necessary investments or other switching costs so that it could enter the relevant market in response to a small and permanent increase in prices; the assessment must be based on realistic grounds, and a theoretical possibility is not sufficient[5]. In this formulation of the meaning of potential competition, the Commission refers to a policy statement that it made at point 55 of its XIIIth *Report on Competition Policy* in 1983[6], and to its decision in *Elopak/Metal Box-Odin*[7], where it concluded that a joint venture between those two undertakings to design a new kind of carton did not infringe Article 81(1) since they were not actual or potential competitors. The Commission could have, but did not, cite other decisions in which it reached similar conclusions, such as *Optical Fibres*[8], *Mitchell Cotts/Sofiltra*[9], *Konsortium ECR 900*[10], *Iridium*[11], *Cégétel+4*[12] and *P&I Clubs*[13]. It is interesting to compare these decisions with others in which the Commission concluded that undertakings were potential competitors, such as *British Interactive Broadcasting/Open*[14] and *GEAE/P&W*[15]; a consequence of this conclusion in each case was that the agreements in question were granted individual exemption subject to conditions and obligations[16], as opposed to being granted negative clearance.

(ii)   Relationship with the Guidelines on Vertical Restraints

Where an agreement is entered into between undertakings that operate at different levels of the market, it should be considered under the *Guidelines on Vertical Restraints* and Regulation 2790/99, the block exemption for vertical agreements[17]. However, to the extent that a vertical agreement is entered into between competitors, its effects should also be considered under the *Horizontal Guidelines*[18].

---

5   One of the criticisms of the Commission by the CFI in *European Night Services v Commission* (p 500, n 4 above) was that it had failed convincingly to demonstrate that the agreement was entered into between potential competitors: see ch 3, pp 102-103.
6   See also Faull 'Joint Ventures under the EEC Competition Rules' (1984) 9 ELRev 358.
7   OJ [1990] L 209/15, [1991] 4 CMLR 832.
8   OJ [1986] L 236/30.
9   OJ [1987] L 41/31, [1988] 4 CMLR 111.
10   OJ [1990] L 228/31, [1992] 4 CMLR 54.
11   OJ [1997] L 16/87, [1997] 4 CMLR 1065.
12   OJ [1999] L 218/14, [2000] 4 CMLR 106; see also a related decision, *Télécom Développement* OJ [1999] L 218/24, [2000] 4 CMLR 124.
13   OJ [1999] L 125/12, [1999] 5 CMLR 646.
14   OJ [1999] L 312/1, [2000] 4 CMLR 901, paras 141-144.
15   OJ [2000] L 58/16, [2000] 5 CMLR 49, paras 71-75.
16   See ch 4, pp 140-141 on the Commission's right to attach conditions and obligations to individual exemptions.
17   *Guidelines*, para 11: on the application of Article 81 to vertical agreements generally see ch 16, p 546ff.
18   Ibid; an agreement whereby one party supplies goods or services to another is vertical where, *for the purposes of that agreement*, the parties operate at different levels of the market, irrespective of the fact that, for other purposes, they are actual or potential competitors: see the definition of a vertical agreement in Article 2 of Regulation 2790/99, explained in ch 16, pp 569-573.

(iii)   The 'centre of gravity' of an agreement

As mentioned above, the *Guidelines* apply to six types of agreements, R&D, production, purchasing, commercialisation, standardisation and environmental. In any particular case, it is therefore necessary to characterise the agreement in order to be able to determine whether it falls into any of these six categories, and if so which one. Not surprisingly, agreements in commercial practice do not divide themselves neatly in this way: for example undertakings that agree to conduct R&D together will often decide to produce and commercialise the product if the R&D is successful, while the parties to a joint production agreement might agree to some joint R&D as a by-product of their cooperation. Paragraph 12 of the *Guidelines* attempts to provide a basis for allocating agreements to the appropriate category by introducing the notion of an agreement's 'centre of gravity'.

The Commission states that account should be taken of two factors: the first is the starting point of the cooperation and the second is the degree of integration of the different functions that are being combined. Two examples are given. In the first, the parties enter into an R&D agreement and envisage the possibility of proceeding, if successful, to joint production: here, the cooperation originates as an R&D agreement and is characterised as such. In the second, the parties agree to integrate their production facilities, but only partially to integrate their R&D: here, the agreement is essentially concerned with production and should be analysed as such. The Commission adds that so-called 'strategic alliances', which are not narrowly focussed on one or a few functions but instead involve undertakings agreeing to cooperate with one another in a fairly vague and aspirational sense, do not fall within the *Guidelines* at all. There have been several occasions on which the Commission has taken a favourable view of strategic alliances in the telecommunications and IT industries[19].

(iv)   The Guidelines apply to both the goods and services sectors

The *Guidelines* apply to both the goods and the services sectors. Many of the Commission's early decisions concerned horizontal cooperation in the goods sector; however there are plenty of decisions, in particular in recent years, that have concerned a range of services sectors, including banking, telecommunications, broadcasting, IT, the media and postal services. Many cases are settled each year as a result of the sending of comfort letters: the Commission's Annual Reports indicate the extent of this activity[20]. The *Guidelines* do not apply to the extent that sector-specific rules, for example on agreements in the transport and insurance sectors, are in place[1].

---

19 See eg *BT/MCI* OJ [1994] L 223/36, [1995] 5 CMLR 285 and *Olivetti/Digital* OJ [1994] L 309/24, both discussed in the Commission's XXIVth *Report on Competition Policy* (1994), points 156-162; *Atlas* OJ [1996] L 239/29, [1997] 4 CMLR 89 and *Phoenix/GlobalOne* OJ [1996] L 239/57, [1997] 4 CMLR 147, discussed in the Commission's XXVth *Report on Competition Policy* (1995), point 57 and the XXVIth *Report on Competition Policy* (1996), point 67; *Global European Network*, discussed in the XXVIIth *Report on Competition Policy* (1997), point 73 and p 128; and *Unisource* OJ [1997] L 381/1, [1998] 4 CMLR 105 and *Unisource* OJ [1997] L 381/24, [1998] 4 CMLR 145, discussed in the XXVIIth *Report*, points 71-72 and p 133; note the revised *Unisource* decision at OJ [2001] L 52/30.

20 See eg the Commission's XXIXth *Report on Competition Policy* (1999), pp 141-160, 174-180

1   *Guidelines*, para 13; on the block exemptions in the transport sector, see ch 23 pp 859-866; on the insurance sector, see below, pp 529-530 .

(C)   Basic principles for the assessment of horizontal cooperation agreements under Article 81

(i)   Article 81(1)

The Commission begins by noting that Article 81(1) applies both to agreements that have as their object the restriction of competition and to agreements that have this effect[2]. Some agreements have as their object the restriction of competition – price fixing, output limitation or the sharing of markets or customers – so that it is unnecessary to consider whether they have this effect[3]. However where agreements do not have as their object the restriction of competition, it is necessary to consider their effects. The Commission states that it is not sufficient simply to consider whether competition between the parties is limited; it is further necessary to consider whether an agreement is 'likely to affect competition in the market to such an extent that negative effects as to prices, output, innovation or the variety or quality of goods and services can be expected'[4]. This is an illustration of the Commission's acceptance that economic criteria should be taken into account when applying Article 81(1) or, to put the point another way, that Article 81(1) should not be applied in a formalistic manner. In considering whether an agreement is likely to cause negative effects on the market, the economic context must be considered, taking into account the nature of the agreement and the parties' market power which, together with other structural factors, determines the likelihood that horizontal cooperation would affect overall competition to a significant extent[5]. The Commission then proceeds to provide guidance on how the nature of the agreement affects its analysis, and on the relevance of the parties' market power and other structural factors.

(A)   THE NATURE OF THE AGREEMENT.   The relevance of the nature of the agreement to its assessment under Article 81(1) is that some forms of cooperation are entered into between undertakings that are unlikely to affect the marketing of goods or services. Cooperation on R&D, standards and environmental matters would not normally have a direct effect on the parties' prices and output when they take their products to the market: the Commission says that in these cases agreements are only likely to have negative effects, if at all, on the degree of innovation and the variety of products that the parties produce; they may also give rise to a foreclosure of third party access to the market[6]. Other agreements, for example on joint production and purchasing, are more likely to lead to coordination of pricing and output decisions, in particular where this leads to a high degree of common costs, for example through joint manufacture.

In paragraphs 24 to 26 of the *Guidelines* the Commission considers respectively those agreements that, by their very nature, would fall outside Article 81(1); those that almost always fall within it; and those that may fall within it because they have restrictive effects. In each of the subsequent chapters of the *Guidelines*, the Commission follows the same pattern of analysis.

In the first of these categories, the Commission says that cooperation between non-competitors and agreements between competing companies that cannot

2   Ibid, para 17.
3   Ibid, para 18: note the correspondence between the Commission's approach in the *Guidelines* and the commentary on the application of Article 81(1) in ch 3, p 92ff.
4   Ibid, para 19.
5   Ibid, para 20.
6   Ibid, para 22.

independently carry out the project or activity covered by the cooperation would normally fall outside Article 81(1); the same is said to be true of 'cooperation concerning an activity which does not influence the relevant parameters of competition', a phrase that does not have any obvious meaning[7]. In the case of the agreements described in paragraph 24, the Commission concludes that Article 81(1) could be infringed only if the parties enjoyed significant market power and if there could be a foreclosure effect[8]. In *Eirpage*[9] the Commission considered that a joint venture in Ireland to establish a nationwide paging service between Bord Telecom Eireann, the national postal and telecommunications company, and Motorola, one of the world's leading manufacturers of mobile telecommunications equipment, could have a deterrent effect on potential market entrants and thereby restrict competition[10]; an individual exemption was granted for a period of 11 years[11]. In *Screensport/EBU Members*[12] the Commission considered that a joint venture to establish a transnational satellite sports channel covering most of western Europe infringed Article 81(1) partly because of its foreclosure effects on third parties[13]; individual exemption was refused[14].

In the second category fall those agreements that have as their object the restriction of competition, such as price fixing and output limitation; the Commission states that these will almost always be prohibited[15]. However it acknowledges that an exception to this may arise in the case of a production joint venture, where the parents may agree on the output of the joint venture; they may even collaborate on sales, which therefore involves coordination on prices[16].

In other cases – that is to say in cases that might have as their effect the restriction of competition – the Commission states that further analysis is needed to determine whether Article 81(1) is applicable, and in particular it is necessary to consider the market shares of the parties and other structural factors[17].

(B) MARKET POWER AND MARKET STRUCTURE. Where it is necessary to consider whether an agreement could have the effect of restricting competition, the starting point for the analysis is the position of the parties on the market[18]. The starting point is the definition of the relevant market, using the methodology of the Commission's *Notice on Market Definition*[19]. The *Guidelines* provide some additional guidance on market definition, for example in relation to innovation and purchasing markets; where appropriate this further guidance will be referred to later in this chapter, where particular types of agreement are discussed. Paragraph 28 states that if the parties have a low combined market share, a restrictive effect is

---

7   Ibid, para 24.
8   Ibid; the Commission states at footnote 17 that firms may have significant market power even though they are not dominant in the sense of Article 82.
9   OJ [1991] L 306/22, [1993] 4 CMLR 64, para 12.
10 Ibid, para 12.
11 Ibid, paras 14-24.
12 OJ [1991] L 63/32, [1992] 5 CMLR 273, paras 57-66; see also *Astra* OJ [1993] L 20/23, [1994] 5 CMLR 226, where the Commission refused individual exemption for a joint venture to provide a television distribution service by satellite.
13 Ibid, paras 57-66.
14 Ibid, paras 70-76.
15 *Guidelines*, para 25.
16 Ibid, footnote 18; see further pp 515-520 below on joint production.
17 Ibid, para 26.
18 Ibid, para 27.
19 See p 501, n 4 above; the Notice is described in some detail in ch 1, p 26ff.

unlikely and no further analysis is required; furthermore if one party has a high market share and the other party to a bilateral agreement has only an insignificant market share there would normally be no problem, since there would be little increment to market power. However, the paragraph does not lay down a general market share figure for all the types of agreement covered by the *Guidelines*. It is of course the case that the *Notice on Agreements of Minor Importance*[20] lays down a threshold of 5%, below which horizontal agreements normally do not infringe Article 81(1); and that this threshold is likely to be raised to 10% in the course of 2001[1]. In so far as the *Guidelines* give further indications as to the significance of market share figures, these will be dealt with in the context of specific types of agreement later in this chapter.

(C)   ASSESSING MARKET CONCENTRATION.   Paragraphs 29 and 30 consider the relevance of structural factors when deciding whether an agreement could have the effect of restricting competition. This cannot be determined on the basis of market shares alone: the concentration of the market is relevant, as are other factors. The Commission suggests two ways of determining how concentrated a market is[2]. The first is to use the so-called 'Herfindahl-Hirschman Index' ('the HHI'). This sums up the squares of the individual market shares of all the competitors in a market: the higher the total, the more concentrated the market. The concentration level will be low where the total is below 1000; moderate if between 1000 and 1800; and high where it is above 1800. This is a relatively simple way of calculating market concentration, and its effectiveness is demonstrated by the following three examples (these are not taken from the *Guidelines*):

Example 1

In the widget industry there are 15 competitors: 5 of them each has a market share in the region of 10%, and 10 of them each has a market share in the region of 5%

$$HHI = 5 \times 10^2 + 10 \times 5^2 = 500 + 250 = 750$$

The market concentration is low

Example 2

In the blodget industry, there are 8 competitors: 2 of them each has a market share in the region of 20%, and 6 of them each has a market share in the region of 10%

$$HHI = 2 \times 20^2 + 6 \times 10^2 = 800 + 600 = 1400$$

The market concentration is moderate

20   OJ [1997] C 372/13, [1998] 4 CMLR 192; see ch 3, pp 107-110.
1   Ibid, p 110.
2   *Guidelines*, para 29.

Example 3

In the sprocket industry, there are 4 competitors: 2 of them each has a market share in the region of 30% and the other 2 each has a market share in the region of 20%

$$HHI = 2 \times 30^2 + 2 \times 20^2 = 1800 + 800 = 2600$$

The market concentration is high

The same approach can be used to work out the consequences for the concentration of the market of any of the competitors entering into an agreement with one another[3]. For example if, in Example 2, the two firms with 20% were to enter into an agreement (or merger) with one another, the HHI after the agreement would be:

$$40^2 + 6 \times 10^2 = 1600 + 600 = 2200$$

The market concentration will have moved from moderate to high

If however, in Example 2, two of the firms with 10% had entered into an agreement with one another, the HHI after the agreement would be:

$$2 \times 20^2 + 1 \times 20^2 + 4 \times 10^2 = 800 + 400 + 400 = 1600$$

The market concentration will remain moderate

Thus, the HHI demonstrates arithmetically the difference between the two situations, indicating that greater caution should be exercised by a competition authority in relation to the former than the latter case.

The Commission also suggests, in paragraph 29 of the *Guidelines*, that, in determining the concentration level of the market, another possible indicator is the leading firm concentration ratio. For example the three-firm concentration ratio is the sum of the market shares of the leading three competitors in a market, and is depicted as 'CR3'. 'CR4' would indicate the outcome of the same exercise in relation to the leading four firms[4].

(D)   OTHER STRUCTURAL FACTORS.   Paragraph 30 of the *Guidelines* suggest that other factors, such as the stability of market shares over time, entry barriers and the countervailing power of suppliers and buyers should also be taken into account in determining the position of the parties to a horizontal cooperation agreement and their ability to produce negative effects on the market.

(ii)   Article 81(3)

Where an agreement is caught by Article 81(1), it remains possible for the parties to argue that it satisfies the terms of Article 81(3). This provision has been discussed

---

3   The Herfindahl-Hirschman Index is used, in particular in the US, in the context of merger analysis: see ch 20, p 730.
4   *Guidelines*, para 29, footnote 23.

at length in chapter 4[5], and the Commission discusses the position briefly in paragraphs 31 to 36 of the *Guidelines*. Under the law as it currently stands, an agreement may be given an individual exemption by the Commission, acting under Article 9 of Regulation 17/62[6]; or it may be possible to bring it within the terms of one of the block exemptions[7]. It is likely that the system of individual exemption will be abolished in the fairly near future[8]; however the system of block exemptions will be maintained[9]. For as long as the possibility of individual exemption remains, an accelerated procedure is available for partial-function, structural joint ventures[10].

5. RESEARCH AND DEVELOPMENT AGREEMENTS[11]

Chapter 2 of the *Guidelines*[12] deals with agreements that have as their centre of gravity R&D, other than concentrations falling within the ECMR[13]. The *Guidelines* point out the benefits of R&D[14] and specifically refer to the benefits for small and medium-sized undertakings of cooperation at this level[15]. Paragraphs 43 to 54 deal with market definition in R&D cases, first in relation to existing markets and then in relation to markets for innovation.

Where an agreement concerns improvements to existing products, they and their close substitutes form the relevant market[16]. This is not the case where there will be a significant change to an existing product, or the development of an entirely new one, although in this situation the possibility exists that cooperation in the new market could lead to coordination in the old one[17]. Where the parties cooperate in relation to components, it is possible that the market for the final products in which the components will be incorporated will be relevant, where the component is a key element in the final product and the parties are important competitors in that market[18]. In some cases, the market may be one for technology rather than products, and paragraphs 47 to 49 explain how the market should be defined and market share calculated in those circumstances.

Where the parties conduct R&D in relation to entirely new products, the position is more complex. In paragraph 51 the Commission says that it may be possible to identify competing 'poles' of R&D, in which case it is necessary to consider whether, if two competing undertakings were to enter into a horizontal cooperation agreement, there will be a 'sufficient number of R&D poles left'. No guidance is given as to what would qualify as 'sufficient' for this purpose.

---

5   See ch 4, pp 124-133.
6   OJ [1962] 13/204, [1959-62] spec ed 87.
7   See ch 4, pp 141-146.
8   See ch 4, pp 146-147 and ch 7, pp 246-258.
9   See ch 7, p 249.
10   See ch 4, pp 139-140; for an example of the use of this procedure, see *General Motors Corporation/Fiat SpA*, described by Laschena and Dussart in the Commission's October 2000 *Competition Policy Newsletter*, p 54.
11   For a useful discussion of the position prior to the adoption of the *Guidelines* and the new block exemption, see *Faull and Nikpay* (p 498, n 5 above), paras 6.124-6.216.
12   *Guidelines*, paras 39-77.
13   Ibid, para 39.
14   Ibid, para 40.
15   Ibid, para 41.
16   Ibid, para 44.
17   Ibid, para 45.
18   Ibid, para 46.

The credibility of an R&D pole is assessed according to the nature, scope and size of other R&D efforts, their access to financial and human resources, know-how, patents and other specialised assets and their capability to exploit the results[19]. Where it is not possible to identify R&D poles, the Commission would limit its assessment to related product and/or technology markets[20].

(A)   The application of Article 81(1) to R&D agreements

(i)   Agreements that normally fall outside Article 81(1)

The Commission considers that R&D agreements 'at a rather theoretical level, far removed from the exploitation of the results', fall outside Article 81(1)[1]. So too would agreements between non-competitors[2], unless there is a possibility of a foreclosure effect and one of the parties has significant market power with respect to key technology[3]. The outsourcing of R&D to research institutes and academic bodies which are not active in the exploitation of the results is not caught by Article 81(1)[4]; and 'pure' R&D agreements, that do not extend to joint exploitation of the results, would rarely do so: they would do so only where they significantly reduce effective competition in innovation[5].

(ii)   Agreements that almost always fall within Article 81(1)

The Commission says that if the true object of an agreement is not R&D but the creation of a disguised cartel, Article 81(1) would apply; however it adds that an R&D agreement which includes the joint exploitation of future results is not necessarily restrictive of competition[6].

(iii)   Agreements that may fall within Article 81(1)

Paragraphs 60 to 67 deal with R&D agreements that may have the effect of restricting competition. They must be analysed in their economic context where the cooperation is 'close to the market launch' and is between competitors on existing product or technology markets or on innovation markets[7]. Three possible effects are noted: a restriction in innovation, coordination in existing markets and foreclosure; however the Commission acknowledges that these are unlikely in the absence of significant market power[8]. No market share figure is given for the application of Article 81(1) to R&D agreements, although the Commission points out that a safe haven is provided by Article 4 of Regulation 2659/00, the block exemption for R&D agreements where the parties' market share is below

19   Ibid, para 51.
20   Ibid, para 52.
1   Ibid, para 55.
2   Ibid, para 56.
3   Ibid, footnote 30.
4   Ibid, para 57.
5   Ibid, para 58.
6   Ibid, para 59.
7   Ibid, para 60.
8   Ibid, para 61.

25%[9]. The *Guidelines* say that where the parties have a market share of more than 25%, it does not automatically follow that Article 81(1) is infringed, but they continue by saying that an infringement becomes more possible as the parties' position on the market becomes stronger[10]. The *Guidelines* then provide guidance on R&D agreements in relation to existing products[11], entirely new products (acknowledging that cooperation in relation to new products is, in general, pro-competitive)[12] and agreements in between these two situations[13].

(B)   The application of Article 81(3) to R&D agreements[14]

Paragraphs 68 to 74 discuss the assessment of R&D agreements under Article 81(3). Paragraph 70 states that the hard-core restrictions that are listed in Article 5 of Regulation 2659/00, and which prevent the application of the block exemption, would be unlikely to be regarded as indispensable in the case of the individual assessment of an agreement under Article 81(3). Paragraphs 73 and 74 deal with the likely permitted duration of cooperation, both under the block exemption and in the case of a notification for individual exemption. Where R&D leads to the launch and marketing of a new product, a period of cooperation of 7 years beyond the R&D phase will be permitted, even though the market shares of the parties at this stage may be high: the Commission acknowledges that a strong market position is likely due to the 'first mover advantage' that is a consequence of successful R&D. The Commission further acknowledges that a period of more than seven years might be appropriate where the parties can demonstrate that this is necessary to guarantee an adequate return on the investment involved[15].

Where the parties seek an individual exemption for an R&D agreement, it should be noted that this can be given irrespective of prior notification where the 'sole object' of the agreement is joint research and development[16]. Such an agreement would be unlikely to infringe Article 81(1) anyway, but this procedural rule is helpful in that it means that it is not necessary to make a notification on a precautionary basis.

(C)   The block exemption for research and development agreements: Regulation 2659/00

Acting under powers conferred upon it by Council Regulation 2821/71[17], the Commission adopted a new block exemption for R&D agreements on 29 November 2000[18]. The Regulation entered into force on 1 January 2001 and will expire on 31 December 2010[19]. The new Regulation replaces Regulation

9   Ibid, para 62; on the block exemption, see pp 510-515 below.
10   Ibid, para 63.
11   Ibid, para 64.
12   Ibid, para 65.
13   Ibid, para 66.
14   For examples of individual exemptions being granted to R&D agreements, see *Asahi/St Gobain* OJ [1994] L 354/87; *Philips/Osram* OJ [1994] L 378/34, [1996] 4 CMLR 48.
15   *Guidelines*, para 73, final sentence.
16   Regulation 17/62, Article 4(3)(b): see further ch 4, p 137.
17   OJ [1971] L 285/46.
18   OJ [2000] L 304/7, [2001] 4 CMLR 808.
19   Regulation 2659/2000, Article 9.

418/85[20]. Article 8 provides transitional relief for agreements which were in force on 31 December 2000 and which satisfied the conditions for exemption in the old Regulation: they will be exempt until 30 June 2002. The new Regulation is without prejudice to Article 82[1].

The Regulation consists of 23 recitals and 9 Articles. Recital 2 refers specifically to Article 163(2) of the Treaty, which calls upon the Community to encourage undertakings, including small and medium-sized undertakings, in their R&D activities and to support efforts on their part to cooperate with one another. Article 1 confers block exemption upon certain R&D agreements. Article 2 defines key terms such as 'research and development', 'exploitation of the results' and 'competing undertaking'. Article 3 sets out conditions for application of the block exemption. Article 4 imposes a market share cap and deals with the duration of the exemption. Article 5 deals with agreements that are not covered by the block exemption because they contain 'hard-core' restrictions. Article 6 contains provisions on the application of the market share threshold. Article 7 provides for withdrawal of the block exemption. Articles 8 and 9 deal respectively with transitional matters and the period of validity of the Regulation. Regulation 2659/2000, like Regulation 2658/2000[2] and Regulation 2790/99[3], is a 'new-style' block exemption; it does not contain a detailed 'white list' of permitted restrictions, but instead confers block exemption upon a range of agreements up to a certain level of market power and specifies restrictions and clauses that must not be included[4].

(i) Article I: scope of the block exemption

Article 1(1) confers block exemption, pursuant to Article 81(3) of the Treaty, on three types of R&D agreements in relation to goods or services[5]:

'(a) joint research and development of products or processes and joint exploitation of the results of that research and development;

(b) joint exploitation of the results of research and development of products or processes jointly carried out pursuant to a prior agreement between the same parties; or

(c) joint research and development of products or processes excluding joint exploitation of the results'.

To benefit from the block exemption, the agreement must satisfy the conditions set out in Article 3[6]. Recital 3 of the Regulation states that agreements of the kind described in (c) would not normally fall within the scope of Article 81(1) at all; in case they do, however, they are included within the scope of the block exemption. Most agreements exempted by the Regulation will involve joint

---

20 OJ [1985] L 53/5, amended by Regulation 151/93 OJ [1993] L 21/8 and extended in force until 31 December 2001 by Regulation 2236/97, OJ [1997] L 306/12.

1   Regulation 2659/2000, Recital 20.

2   See pp 517-520 below.

3   See ch 16, pp 567-591.

4   Regulation 2659/2000, Recital 7.

5   Article 1 refers to research and development of 'products or processes'; products are defined in Article 2(5) to include 'a good and/or a service, including both intermediary goods and/or services and final goods and/or services'; processes are defined in Article 2(6) to mean 'a technology or process arising out of the joint research and development'.

6   See pp 512-513 below.

exploitation of the R&D. Recital 11 of the Regulation states that joint exploitation can be considered as the natural consequence of joint R&D, and can take various forms including manufacture, the exploitation of intellectual property rights or the marketing of new products. Definitions of 'research and development', 'exploitation of the results' and of what is meant by 'joint' exploitation are provided in Article 2. In particular, exploitation means the 'production or distribution of the contract products or the application of the contract processes or the assignment or licensing of intellectual property rights or the communication of know-how required for such manufacture or application'[7]; and R&D and exploitation are 'joint' where the work is carried out by a joint team, organisation or undertaking, is jointly entrusted to a third party or is allocated between the parties by way of specialisation in research, development, production or distribution[8].

Article 1(2) provides that the block exemption also applies to provisions in R&D agreements:

> 'which do not constitute the primary object of such agreements, but are directly related to and necessary for their implementation, such as an obligation not to carry out, independently or together with third parties, research and development in the field to which the agreement relates or in a closely connected field during the execution of the agreement'.

However Article 1(2) would not apply to provisions that have the same object as the hard-core restrictions set out in Article 5(1)[9].

(ii)   Article 2: definitions

Article 2 contains a series of definitions of expressions used in the Regulation including, as well as those already mentioned, terms such as 'contract process', 'contract product' and 'relevant market for the contract products'.

(iii)   Article 3: conditions for exemption

Article 3(1) provides that block exemption is available subject to the conditions set out in paragraphs 2 to 5 thereof; Article 3 should be read in conjunction with Recital 14. It should be stressed that these conditions are applicable only where an agreement infringes Article 81(1) so that the parties wish to avail themselves of the block exemption. If an agreement is not restrictive in the sense of Article 81(1), for example because it is not entered into between competitors, because it involves the outsourcing of R&D to a third party, or because it relates to 'pure' R&D, there is no need to comply with Article 3 of the Regulation.

Article 3(2) provides that all the parties must have access to the results of the joint R&D for the purposes of further research or exploitation[10]. However, the

---

7   Regulation 2659/2000, Article 2(8).
8   Ibid, Article 2(11).
9   Ibid, Article 1(2), second paragraph.
10   'Access' is not defined in the Regulation; it must mean more than merely a right to view the results of the R&D, since it is to be granted 'for the purposes of further research or exploitation'; Recital 14 refers to the idea that each party to the agreement should have 'the opportunity of exploiting any results that interest it'.

second sentence specifically provides that research institutes, academic bodies or undertakings which supply R&D as a commercial service but are not normally active in exploitation of the results, may agree to confine their use of the results to conducting further research. This means, for example, that a pharmaceutical company that enters into an R&D agreement with a research institute or a university can require its partner not to exploit the results commercially but to limit itself only to further research; if this restriction were not possible, the pharmaceutical company might refrain from beneficial joint R&D with the undertaking in question for fear that it would extend its activities beyond research into commercialisation.

Article 3(3) provides that, where an agreement provides only for joint R&D, each party must be free independently to exploit the results of it and of any pre-existing know-how necessary for the purposes of such exploitation. The second sentence of Article 3(3) provides that, where the parties were not competing undertakings at the time the agreement was entered into, the exploitation can be limited to one or more technical fields of development[11]. Article 3(3) will presumably apply only rarely, since most of the cases envisaged in this provision would not involve infringements of Article 81(1) anyway.

Article 3(4) provides that joint exploitation is permissible only where it relates to results of cooperation in R&D which are protected by intellectual property rights or are protected by know-how, which substantially contribute to technical or economic progress and where the results are decisive for the manufacture of the contract products or the application of the contract processes. The reason for this condition is that cooperation at the level of exploitation should be limited to those cases in which joint R&D has led to economic benefits; where this is not the case, the rationale for granting block exemption to joint exploitation is not satisfied.

Article 3(5) provides that undertakings charged with manufacture by way of specialisation in production must be required to fulfil orders for supplies from all the parties, except where the R&D also provides for joint distribution. The explanation for this is that where, for example, one party agrees to produce widgets and the other blodgets, each should have access to the products produced by the other and be able to compete in the relevant market; this is not necessary, however, where the parties carry out their distribution jointly.

(iv)   Article 4: the market share threshold and duration of exemption

Article 4 deals with the market share threshold and the duration of the exemption. Article 4(1) provides that, where the participating undertakings[12] are not competing undertakings[13], the exemption shall apply for the duration of the R&D and, where the results are jointly exploited, for seven years from the time the contract products are first put on the market within the common market; this is the case irrespective of the parties' market share, while the position stabilises and in order to guarantee a minimum period of return on the investments

---

11   Competing undertakings are defined in Article 2(12) to include both an 'actual competitor' that is active on the relevant market and a 'potential competitor' that could realistically enter the market in response to a small and permanent increase in relative prices: on the so-called 'SSNIP test', see generally ch 1, pp 27-28.

12   The expression 'participating undertakings' is defined in Article 2(2), and includes 'connected undertakings', defined in Article 2(3).

13   See n 11 above.

involved[14]. Article 4(3) provides that, at the end of the seven-year period, the exemption can continue as long as the parties' combined market share does not exceed 25%.

Article 4(2) deals with the position where the participating undertakings are competing undertakings. In that case the block exemption applies only if, at the time the parties entered into the agreement, their share of the market for the products capable of being improved or replaced by the contract products does not exceed 25%. Article 6 contains rules on how to apply the market share threshold; it contains specific rules to deal with the situation where the undertakings outgrow the market share cap[15].

(v)   Article 5: agreements not covered by the exemption

Article 5(1) prevents the block exemption from applying where agreements contain 'severe anti-competitive restraints'[16] which 'directly or indirectly, in isolation or in combination with other factors under the control of the parties, have as their object' any of the following:

(a)   a limitation on the freedom of the parties to carry out R&D in a field unconnected to the agreement;

(b)   certain prohibitions on the right to challenge intellectual property rights;

(c)   a limitation on output or sales;

(d)   the fixing of prices when selling the contract products to third parties;

(e)   a restriction of the customers that can be served after a period of 7 years from the time when the contract products are first put on the market within the common market;

(f)   a prohibition on passive sales in territories reserved for the other parties;

(g)   a prohibition on active sales in territories reserved for other parties after the end of 7 years from the time when the contract products are first put on the market within the common market;

(h)   a requirement not to grant licences to third parties where at least one of the parties is not allowed to or does not in fact exploit the results of the joint R&D;

(i)   a requirement to refuse to meet demand from users or resellers in their respective territories who would market them in other territories within the common market;

(j)   a requirement to make it difficult for users or resellers to obtain the contract products from other resellers within the common market.

The inclusion of any of these provisions excludes the entire agreement, not just the offensive provisions, from the block exemption[17]. However Article 5(2)(a) provides that the setting of production targets where the exploitation of the results includes joint production of the contract products is not caught by Article 5(1); while Article 5(2)(b) provides that sales targets and the fixing of prices to immediate customers are not caught where the exploitation includes the joint distribution of the contract products.

---

14   See Recital 16.
15   Regulation 2659/2000, Article 6(2)-(4).
16   Ibid, Recital 17.
17   *Guidelines*, para 37.

(vi)   Article 6: application of the market share threshold

Article 6 was referred to above in the context of the market share cap in Article 4[18].

(vii)   Article 7: withdrawal of the block exemption by the Commission

Article 7 enables the Commission to withdraw the benefit of the block exemption, in particular where the existence of the R&D agreement restricts the scope for third parties to carry out R&D because of the limited research capacity elsewhere[19]; where, because of the structure of supply, the existence of the R&D agreement substantially restricts the access of third parties to the market for the contract products[20]; where, without any objectively valid reason, the parties do not exploit the results of the R&D[1]; where the contract products are not subject to effective competition[2]; or where the existence of the R&D agreement would eliminate effective competition in R&D on a particular market[3].

(viii)   Article 8: transitional period

The transitional relief for agreements that benefit from the exemption provided for in Regulation 418/85 was explained above[4].

(ix)   Article 9: period of validity

The Regulation entered into force on 1 January 2001 and will expire on 31 December 2010.

6.   PRODUCTION AGREEMENTS, INCLUDING SPECIALISATION AGREEMENTS[5]

Chapter 3 of the *Guidelines*[6] deals with production agreements, including specialisation agreements. It notes that broadly speaking production agreements fall into three types: joint production, specialisation and sub-contracting agreements. Sub-contracting agreements between competitors are dealt with by the *Guidelines*[7]; sub-contracting agreements between non-competitors involving the transfer of know-how are dealt with by the Commission's *Notice on Sub-*

18   See p 514 above.
19   Regulation 2659/2000, Article 7(a).
20   Ibid, Article 7(b).
1   Ibid, Article 7(c).
2   Ibid, Article 7(d).
3   Ibid, Article 7(e).
4   See p 511 above.
5   See further *Faull and Nikpay* (p 498, n 5 above), paras 6.217-6.251; this does not cover the *Guidelines* nor the new block exemption for specialisation agreements, but nevertheless contains much useful material.
6   *Guidelines*, paras 78-114.
7   Ibid, paras 81 and 100.

contracting Agreements[8]. In determining whether Article 81(1) applies to production agreements, the relevant product and geographic markets must be defined; it may also be necessary to consider the possibility that there may be a 'spillover effect' in an upstream, downstream or neighbouring market, but only if cooperation in one market necessarily results in the coordination of competitive behaviour in a connected market and if the parties are in a strong position in the spillover market[9].

(A)   The application of Article 81(1) to production agreements

(i)   *Agreements that normally fall outside Article 81(1)*

Agreements between non-competitors are normally outside Article 81(1)[10], unless the agreement could have a foreclosure effect, for example because one party has a strong market position on an upstream market for a key component which could raise the costs of competitors in a downstream market[11]. Cooperation between firms that compete on markets closely related to the market directly concerned by the cooperation will not infringe Article 81(1) if cooperation is the only commercially possible way of entering a new market, to launch a new product or service or to carry out a specific project[12]. Article 81(1) is unlikely to be infringed where the cooperation does not lead to a high degree of commonality of costs; for example if the parties jointly produce an intermediate product which accounts for only a small proportion of the cost of the final product, competition is unlikely to be affected to a material extent[13].

(ii)   *Agreements that almost always fall within Article 81(1)*

Agreements to fix prices, limit output or to share markets or customer groups would be caught; but the parties can agree, for example, on the level of output of a joint venture and on the prices it will charge[14].

(iii)   *Agreements that may fall within Article 81(1)*

Paragraphs 91 to 101 deal with production agreements that may have the effect of restricting competition. As envisaged by the 'analytical framework' set out earlier in the *Guidelines*[15], both the market power of the parties and the structure of the market must be analysed. No market share figure is given for the application of Article 81(1), but the Commission points out that there is a safe haven in the block exemption for unilateral and bilateral specialisation where the parties' market share does not exceed 20%[16]. Where the parties have a market share in

8   OJ [1979] C 1/2; see ch 16, pp 593-594.
9   *Guidelines*, para 82.
10   Ibid, para 86.
11   Ibid, para 85.
12   Ibid, para 87.
13   Ibid, para 88.
14   Ibid, para 90.
15   See p 501ff above.
16   *Guidelines*, para 93; on the block exemption, see pp 517-520 below.

excess of 20%, the market concentration should also be considered[17]: the Commission refers at this point to HHI analysis, which was explained earlier[18]. The fact that parties to an agreement might have links with other competitors may be relevant to the competition analysis[19]; and in some cases cooperation between strong *potential* competitors may be caught[20]. Cooperation in an upstream market could be caught if it could give rise to a foreclosure or to a spillover effect[1]. Subcontracting agreements between competitors could be caught for the same reason[2]. Reciprocal specialisation agreements where the parties have a market share of more than 20%, the market share cap for application of the block exemption, would almost always fall within Article 81(1) and would have to be analysed carefully because of the risk of market partitioning before they could be exempted on an individual basis[3].

(B)   The application of Article 81(3) to production agreements

Paragraphs 102 to 105 discuss, but do not provide any particular guidance on, the criteria in Article 81(3) and their application to production agreements[4].

(C)   The block exemption for specialisation agreements: Regulation 2658/00

Acting under powers conferred upon it by Council Regulation 2821/71[5], the Commission adopted a new block exemption for specialisation agreements on 29 November 2000[6]. The Regulation entered into force on 1 January 2001 and will expire on 31 December 2010[7]. The new Regulation replaces Regulation 417/85[8]. Article 8 provides transitional relief for agreements which were in force on 31 December 2000 and which satisfied the conditions for exemption in the old Regulation: they will be exempt until 30 June 2002. The new Regulation is without prejudice to Article 82[9].

The Regulation consists of 19 recitals and 9 Articles. Article 1 confers block exemption upon certain specialisation agreements. Article 2 defines key terms such as 'competing undertaking', 'exclusive supply obligation' and 'exclusive purchase obligation'. Article 3 extends the block exemption to certain purchasing and marketing arrangements. Article 4 imposes a market share cap of 20%. Article 5 deals with agreements that are not covered by the block exemption

---

17 Ibid, para 96.
18 See pp 506-507 above.
19 *Guidelines*, para 97.
20 Ibid, para 98.
1   Ibid, para 99.
2   Ibid, para 100.
3   Ibid, para 101.
4   For examples of individual exemptions granted to production agreements, see eg *Fiat/ Hitachi* OJ [1993] L 20/10, [1994] 4 CMLR 571; *Ford/Volkswagen* OJ [1993] L 20/14, [1993] 5 CMLR 617; *Exxon/Mobil* OJ [1994] L 144/20: see XXIVth *Report on Competition Policy* (1994), pp 169-171; *Fujitsu/AMD* OJ [1994] L 341/66.
5   OJ [1971] L 285/46.
6   OJ [2000] L 304/3, [2001] 4 CMLR 800.
7   Regulation 2658/2000, Article 9.
8   OJ [1985] L 53/1, amended by Regulation 151/93 OJ [1993] L 21/8 and extended in force until 31 December 2001 by Regulation 2236/97, OJ [1997] L 306/12.
9   Regulation 2658/2000, Recital 18.

because they contain 'hard-core' restrictions. Article 6 contains provisions on the application of the market share threshold. Article 7 provides the Commission with the power to withdraw the benefit of the block exemption in certain circumstances. Articles 8 and 9 deal respectively with transitional matters and the period of validity of the Regulation. Regulation 2658/2000, like Regulation 2659/2000[10] and Regulation 2790/99[11], is a 'new-style' block exemption; it does not contain a detailed 'white list' of permitted restrictions, but instead confers block exemption upon a range of agreements up to a certain level of market power and specifies restrictions and clauses that must not be included[12].

(i)   Article 1: scope of the block exemption

Article 1(1) confers block exemption, pursuant to Article 81(3) of the Treaty, on three types of specialisation agreements in relation to goods or services[13]:

'(a) unilateral specialisation agreements, by virtue of which one party agrees to cease production of certain products or to refrain from producing those products and to purchase them from a competing undertaking, while the competing undertaking agrees to produce and supply those products; or

(b) reciprocal specialisation agreements, by virtue of which two or more parties on a reciprocal basis agree to cease or refrain from producing certain but different products and to purchase these products from the other parties, who agree to supply them; or

(c) joint production agreements, by virtue of which two or more parties agree to produce certain products jointly'.

Unilateral specialisation agreements are exempted only where the party that ceases or refrains from production agrees to purchase the products from a competing undertaking[14]. An agreement between non-competitors would be vertical, and could therefore benefit from Regulation 2790/99 on Vertical Agreements, subject to the 30% market share cap and the other terms of that Regulation[15]. This is why the block exemption in Regulation 2658/2000 is limited to agreements between competing undertakings[16]. In the case of both unilateral and reciprocal specialisation agreements, the party or parties that cease or refrain from production must agree to purchase the products from the other undertaking(s), who in turn must agree to supply them, so that there will continue to be competition in the market downstream from production: these supply and purchase

---

10 See pp 510-515 above.
11 See ch 16, pp 567-591.
12 Regulation 2658/2000, Recital 5.
13 Article 1 refers to specialisation in 'products', which are defined in Article 2(4) to include 'a good and/or a service, including both intermediary goods and/or services and final goods and/or services, with the exception of distribution and rental services'.
14 Competing undertakings are defined in Article 2(7) to include both an 'actual competitor' that is active on the relevant market and a 'potential competitor' that could realistically enter the market in response to a small and permanent increase in relative prices: on the so-called 'SSNIP test', see generally ch 1, pp 27-28.
15 See ch 16, pp 567-591.
16 Regulation 2658/2000, Recital 10.

obligations may, but do not have to be, exclusive[17]; if they are exclusive, they will benefit from block exemption under Article 3[18].

Article 1(2) provides that the block exemption also applies to provisions in specialisation agreements:

'which do not constitute the primary object of such agreements, but are directly related to and necessary for their implementation, such as those concerning the assignment or use of intellectual property rights'.

However Article 1(2) would not apply to provisions that have the same object as the hard-core restrictions set out in Article 5(1)[19].

(ii) Article 2: definitions

Article 2 contains a series of definitions of expressions used in the Regulation, including 'products'[20], 'competing undertaking'[1] and 'exclusive supply obligation' and 'exclusive purchase obligation'[2].

(iii) Article 3: block exemption for purchasing and marketing arrangements

Article 3 confers block exemption on two types of purchasing and marketing arrangements. Article 3(a) exempts exclusive supply and/or purchase obligations contained in any of the agreements exempted in Article 1. An exclusive supply obligation means an obligation not to supply a competing undertaking other than a party to the agreement with the product to which the specialisation agreement relates[3]. An exclusive purchase obligation means an obligation to purchase the product to which the specialisation relates only from the party which agrees to supply it[4]. Where the parties enter into a joint production agreement of the kind exempted by Article 1(1)(c) and do not themselves sell the products which are the subject of the specialisation independently, Article 3(b) exempts joint distribution, or the appointment, on an exclusive or non-exclusive basis, of a third party distributor, provided that it is not a competing undertaking.

(iv) Article 4: the market share threshold

Article 4 provides that the block exemption applies on condition that the combined market share cap of the participating undertakings does not exceed 20%. The expression 'participating undertakings' is defined in Article 2(2), and includes 'connected undertakings', defined in Article 2(3). Article 6 contains rules on how to apply the market share threshold; it contains specific rules to deal with the situation where the undertakings outgrow the market share cap[5].

---

17 Regulation 2658/2000, Recital 12.
18 See below.
19 Regulation 2658/2000, Article 1(2), second paragraph.
20 See n 13 above.
1   See n 14 above.
2   See nn 3 and 4 below.
3   Regulation 2658/2000, Article 2(8).
4   Ibid, Article 2(9).
5   Ibid, Article 6(2)-(4).

(v)   Article 5: agreements not covered by the exemption

Article 5(1) prevents the block exemption from applying where agreements contain the following 'severe anti-competitive restraints'[6], that is to say agreements which:

> 'directly or indirectly, in isolation or in combination with other factors under the control of the parties, have as their object:
> (a)   the fixing of prices when selling the products to third parties;
> (b)   the limitation of output or sales; or
> (c)   the allocation of markets or customers'.

The inclusion of any of these provisions excludes the entire agreement, not just the offensive provisions, from the block exemption[7]. However Article 5(2)(a) provides that provisions on the amount of products to be produced under a specialisation agreement are not caught by Article 5(1); while Article 5(2)(b) provides that sales targets given to a production joint venture, and the fixing of its prices to its immediate customers, are not caught.

(vi)   Article 6: application of the market share threshold

Article 6 was referred to above in the context of the market share cap in Article 3[8].

(vii)   Article 7: withdrawal of the block exemption by the Commission

Article 7 enables the Commission to withdraw the benefit of the block exemption, in particular where the agreement is not yielding significant results in terms of rationalisation[9], or where the products which are the subject of the specialisation are not subject to effective competition[10].

(viii)   Article 8: transitional period

The transitional relief for agreements that benefit from the exemption provided for in Regulation 417/85 was explained above[11].

(ix)   Article 9: period of validity

The Regulation entered into force on 1 January 2001 and will expire on 31 December 2010.

---

6   Ibid, Recital 14.
7   *Guidelines*, para 37.
8   See p 519 above.
9   Regulation 2658/2000, Article 7(a).
10   Ibid, Article 7(b).
11   See p 517 above.

7.   PURCHASING AGREEMENTS[12]

Chapter 4 of the *Guidelines*[13] deals with joint purchasing agreements. Surprisingly the *Guidelines* do not refer to the judgment of the ECJ on joint purchasing organisations in *Gøttrup-Klim Grovvareforeninger v Dansk Landburgs Grovvareselskab AmbA*[14]. The *Guidelines* point out that joint purchasing is often concluded by small and medium-sized undertakings to enable them to purchase in larger volumes and to obtain larger discounts similar to their bigger competitors[15]. The *Guidelines* consider the horizontal relationship between the members of the group purchasing organisation; the vertical relationships, between it and its suppliers and between it and its members, fall to be considered under the rules on vertical agreements[16]. Joint purchasing must be considered in the context of the relevant procurement market[17]; in some cases it may also be necessary to look at the selling market, if the parties to the joint purchasing agreement also actively compete in that market and if, for example, they jointly purchase a significant amount of what they sell[18].

(A)   Application of Article 81(1) to joint purchasing agreements

(i)   *Agreements that normally fall outside Article 81(1)*

Where competing purchasers are not active on the same relevant market further downstream, Article 81(1) is unlikely to be infringed: an example given is where retailers purchase products jointly, but themselves operate in different geographic markets from each other[19].

(ii)   *Agreements that almost always fall within Article 81(1)*

Purchasing agreements would be unlikely to have as their object the restriction of competition, unless they amounted to a disguised cartel[20].

---

12 See further *Faull and Nikpay* (p 498, n 5 above), paras 6.293-6.342; this was written prior to the adoption of the *Guidelines*, but contains much useful material, in particular on the phenomenon of buyer power; see also Dobson, Waterson and Chu *The Welfare Consequences of the Exercise of Buyer Power* (OFT Research Paper 16, 1998); Vogel 'Competition Law and Buying Power: the Case for a New Approach in Europe' (1998) 19 ECLR 4.
13 *Guidelines*, paras 115-138.
14 Case C-250/92 [1994] ECR I-5641, [1996] 4 CMLR 191; see also Cases C-399/93 etc *HG Oude Luttikhuis v Coberco* [1995] ECR I-4515, [1996] 5 CMLR 178.
15 *Guidelines*, para 116.
16 Ibid, paras 117-118; see ch 16, pp 573-574, on the application of Article 2(2) of Regulation 2790/99, the block exemption for vertical agreements, to agreements between associations of retailers and their suppliers and their members.
17 *Guidelines*, para 120; on procurement markets, see ch 1, p 35.
18 Ibid, para 122.
19 Ibid, para 123.
20 Ibid, para 124.

(iii)   Agreements that may fall within Article 81(1)

In determining whether joint purchasing could have the effect of restricting competition, the starting point is to determine the parties' buying power[1]. The *Guidelines* note that buying power is not always pro-competitive and may even, under certain circumstances, cause severe negative effects on competition[2]. This could be the case where the purchasers together have power on the selling market, since it would be unlikely in that case that lower costs would be passed on to consumers[3]; or where significant buyer power is used to foreclose competitors or to raise rivals' costs[4]. At paragraph 130, however, the Commission says that, in most cases, it is unlikely that market power exists if the parties to the agreement have a combined market share of below 15% on each of the purchasing and the selling markets. Other factors, such as the level of market concentration and the countervailing power of strong suppliers, would have to be considered where the market shares exceed 15%[5].

The application of Article 81 to 'B2B' joint purchasing, that is to say joint procurement through an electronic market place, was considered by the Commission in the case of *Covisint*, leading to the closure of the file by comfort letter[6].

(B)   Application of Article 81(3) to joint purchasing agreements[7]

Paragraphs 132 to 134 discuss Article 81(3) and joint purchasing agreements. Paragraph 133 notes that an obligation to purchase exclusively through the joint purchasing organisation may be regarded as indispensable to achieve the necessary volume for the realisation of economies of scale, but says that this must be assessed in the context of each case. In *Rennet*[8] the Commission considered that an exclusive purchasing requirement that members of a cooperative should purchase all their rennet from the cooperative was a restriction of competition and that it could not be exempted. Exemption is unavailable to agreements where there could be a substantial elimination of competition: paragraph 134 of the *Guidelines* states that, where the joint purchasing agreement could lead to dominance on either the buying or selling side of the market, the terms of Article 81(3) would be unlikely to be satisfied.

---

1   Ibid, para 126.
2   Ibid, para 127.
3   Ibid, para 128.
4   Ibid, para 129.
5   Ibid, para 131.
6   Commission Press Release IP/01/1155, 31 July 2001; see further Vollebregt 'E-Hubs, Syndication and Competition Concerns' (2000) 10 ECLR 437.
7   For examples of individual exemption granted to joint purchasing agreements, see *National Sulphuric Acid Association* OJ [1980] L 260/24, [1980] 3 CMLR 429; *National Sulphuric Acid Association (No 2)* OJ [1989] L 190/22, [1991] 4 CMLR 612; *ARD/MGM* OJ [1989] L 284/36, [1991] 4 CMLR 841; *Euoprean Broadcasting Union* OJ [1993] L 179/23, [1995] 4 CMLR 56, annulled on appeal Cases T-528/93 etc *Métropole Télévision SA v Commission* [1996] ECR II-649, [1996] 5 CMLR 386 and readopted as *Eurovision* OJ [2000] L 151/18, [2000] 5 CMLR 650; individual exemption was refused in the cases of *Rennet* OJ [1980] L 51/19, [1980] 2 CMLR 402, upheld on appeal, Case 61/80 *Coöperatieve Stremsel-en Kleurselfabriek v Commission* [1981] ECR 851, [1982] 1 CMLR 240; and *Screensport/EBU Members* OJ [1991] L 63/32, [1992] 5 CMLR 273.
8   See n 7 above.

8. COMMERCIALISATION AGREEMENTS

Chapter 5 of the *Guidelines*[9] deals with commercialisation agreements, that is to say cooperation between competitors in the selling, distribution or promotion of their products[10]. Distribution agreements generally are covered by the régime for vertical agreements[11]; however where competitors distribute one another's products, horizontal issues arise as well, and they should be analysed in accordance with the *Horizontal Guidelines*[12]. Where joint commercialisation is agreed upon pursuant to some other cooperation, for example on R&D or joint production, the agreement should be analysed under the corresponding chapter of the *Guidelines*[13].

(A)   The application of Article 81(1) to commercialisation agreements

(i)   Agreements that normally fall outside Article 81(1)

Commercialisation agreements between non-competitors do not create competition problems of a horizontal nature and will therefore not be caught by Article 81(1); this would include a consortium agreement between non-competing firms that jointly tender for a project that none of them could carry out individually[14].

(ii)   Agreements that almost always fall within Article 81(1)

The commercialisation agreements most likely to give rise to concern under Article 81(1) are those that give rise to price fixing. The Commission says that joint selling is likely to have as its object and effect the coordination of the pricing policy of competing manufacturers[15]. This may not be the case where the market power of the parties is particularly weak[16]; however there have been several examples of the Commission finding that joint sales agencies infringed Article 81(1)[17]. In some of these cases, individual exemption was granted[18].

(iii)   Agreements that may fall within Article 81(1)

Where joint commercialisation falls short of joint selling, the Commission expresses two possible concerns that might lead to a restrictive effect on competition: one is the exchange of commercially sensitive information, particularly on marketing strategy and pricing; the other is a possible high commonality of costs, which might affect the extent to which the parties can

9   *Guidelines*, paras 139-158.
10 Ibid, para 139; on joint brand advertising, see Vollebregt 'Joint Brand Advertising: Is It Allowed?' (1997) 18 ECLR 242.
11 See ch 16, pp 567-591.
12 *Guidelines*, para 140.
13 Ibid, para 141.
14 Ibid, para 143.
15 Ibid, paras 144-145; on joint selling, see *Faull and Nikpay* (p 498, n 5 above), paras 6.259-6.292.
16 See *SAFCO* OJ [1972] L 13/44.
17 See eg *Floral* OJ [1980] L 39/51, [1980] 2 CMLR 285; *UIP* OJ [1989] L 226/25, [1990] 4 CMLR 749; *Cekanan* OJ [1990] L 299/64, [1992] 4 CMLR 406; *Ansac* OJ [1991] L 152/54.
18 See p 524 below.

compete on price when they take their products to the market[19]. In the case of distribution agreements between competitors, the Commission is particularly concerned at the possibility of market partitioning[20]. Commercialisation agreements which do not extend to price fixing are unlikely to infringe Article 81(1) where the parties' market shares are below 15%; and would be likely to satisfy the terms of Article 81(3) even if they were caught by Article 81(1)[1]. Where the parties' market share exceeds 15%, market concentration would also have to be considered[2].

(B)   The application of Article 81(3) to commercialisation agreements

Paragraphs 151 to 155 discuss Article 81(3). Paragraph 151 states that price fixing can generally not be justified 'unless it is indispensable for the integration of other marketing functions, and this integration will generate substantial efficiencies'. Any efficiencies must result from the integration of economic activities[3], and must be clearly demonstrated[4]. The Commission gives two examples of commercialisation agreements that would satisfy Article 81(3). The first is an agreement between five small food producers, with a total market share of 10%, to combine their distribution facilities, to market under a common brand name and to sell products at a common price; their customers are large retail chains, and substantial multinational food groups dominate the market[5]. The second is where two producers of soft drinks are active on neighbouring markets, each having 20% of its home market; they agree on reciprocal distribution of each other's products, and in each market there is a dominant undertaking having a market share of 50%: the agreement would be exemptable[6].

The Commission has, on a few occasions, granted individual exemption to joint selling arrangements. In *Cekanan*[7] exemption was given to a joint venture that would enable the parties, based in Sweden and Germany, to enter new markets in the European Community with new types of packaging. In the case of *UIP*[8] exemption was given to a joint venture for the distribution and licensing of the films of Paramount, Universal Studios and MGM. An issue of particular interest in recent years has been the collective selling of broadcasting rights to sporting events[9].

---

19 *Guidelines*, para 146.
20 Ibid, para 147.
1   Ibid, para 149.
2   Ibid, para 150; see pp 506-507 above on the HHI Index.
3   Ibid, para 152.
4   Ibid, para 153.
5   Ibid, para 156
6   Ibid, para 158.
7   OJ [1990] L 299/64, [1992] 4 CMLR 406.
8   OJ [1989] L 226/25, [1990] 4 CMLR 749, renewed by comfort letter OJ [1999] C 205/6, [1999] 5 CMLR 732; see XXIXth *Report on Competition Policy* (1999), pp 148-149.
9   See eg Brinckman and Vollebregt 'The Marketing of Sport and its Relation to EC Competition Law' (1998) 19 ECLR 281; Fleming 'Exclusive Rights to Broadcast Sporting Events in Europe' (1999) 20 ECLR 143; Bishop and Oldale 'Sports Rights: the UK Premier League Football Case' (2000) 21 ECLR 185; and Nitsche 'Collective Marketing of Broadcasting by Sports Associations in Europe' (2000) 21 ECLR 208.

9. AGREEMENTS ON STANDARDS

Chapter 6 of the *Guidelines*[10] deals with agreements that have as their primary objective the definition of technical or quality requirements with which current or future products, production processes or methods may comply[11]. The *Guidelines* do not apply to professional rules[12]. Standardisation agreements may have effects in three markets, in the market for the product itself, in the service market for the setting of standards, and in the market for testing and certification[13].

(A) The application of Article 81(1) to standardisation agreements

(i) Agreements that normally fall outside Article 81(1)

Where participation in the setting of standards is unrestricted and transparent, standardisation agreements do not restrict competition. Standards adopted by recognised standards bodies based on non-discriminatory, open and transparent procedures would not be caught[14]. Nor would agreements having no appreciable effect on the market[15].

(ii) Agreements that almost always fall within Article 81(1)

Standardisation agreements aimed at excluding actual or potential competitors from the market would normally be caught, for example where a national association of manufacturers sets a standard and puts pressure on third parties not to market products that do not comply with the standard[16].

(iii) Agreements that may fall within Article 81(1)

Standardisation agreements may have the effect of restricting competition where they impinge upon the parties' freedom to develop alternative standards or products[17]. Standards that are not accessible to third parties may discriminate or foreclose the market, with the result that it is necessary to consider on a case-by-case basis the extent to which such barriers to entry are likely to be overcome[18]. In the specific context of the telecommunications market, the Commission investigated arrangements proposed by the European Telecommunications Standards Institute ('ETSI') to ensure that undertakings would not be unable to make use of a given standard because of the unavailability of necessary intellectual property rights: the Commission issued a 'negative clearance' comfort letter[19] after ETSI had introduced procedures intended to minimise this risk[20].

10 *Guidelines*, paras 159-178.
11 Ibid, para 159.
12 Ibid, para 160.
13 Ibid, para 161.
14 Ibid, para 163.
15 Ibid, para 164.
16 Ibid, para 165.
17 Ibid, para 167.
18 Ibid, para 168.
19 That is to say a comfort letter stating that Article 81(1) was not infringed: see ch 7, pp 217-218.
20 See OJ [1995] C 76/6, [1995] 5 CMLR 352; Commission's XXVth *Report on Competition Policy* (1995), pp 131-132.

(B)   The application of Article 81(3) to standardisation agreements

Paragraphs 169 to 175 deal with the application of Article 81(3). The Commission states at paragraph 169 that it generally takes a positive approach towards agreements that promote economic interpenetration in the common market or encourage the development of new markets and improved supply conditions. For the benefits of standardisation agreements to be realised, the necessary information to apply the standard must be available to those wishing to enter the market and an appreciable proportion of the industry must be involved in the setting of the standard in a transparent manner[1]. Standards must not limit innovation[2]. All competitors in the markets affected should have the possibility of being involved in discussions on the standards, unless it can be shown that this would give rise to important inefficiencies or unless there are recognised procedures for the collective representation of interests, as happens in the case of formal standards bodies[3]. As a general rule there should be a clear distinction between the setting of the standard and the parties' actual behaviour on the market[4]. Where the result of a standardisation agreement is the establishment of a *de facto* industry standard, access to the standard must be possible for third parties on fair, reasonable and non-discriminatory terms[5]; foreclosure of third parties must be avoided[6].

10.   ENVIRONMENTAL AGREEMENTS[7]

Chapter 7 of the *Guidelines*[8] deals with environmental agreements, which means agreements whereby the parties undertake to achieve pollution abatement or environmental objectives, in particular those set out in Article 174 EC (ex Article 130r)[9]. Environmental agreements may, for example, set out standards for environmental performance, or provide for recycling, emission reductions or the improvement of energy efficiency[10]. The *Guidelines* do not deal with the position of Member States' obligations under the Treaty, for example where they require or encourage environmental agreements[11], but only with the application of Article 81 to the agreements themselves[12].

---

1   Ibid, para 169.
2   Ibid, para 170.
3   Ibid, para 172.
4   Ibid, para 173.
5   Ibid, para 174.
6   Ibid, para 175; see eg *Canon/Kodak* XXVIIIth *Report on Competition Policy* (1998), p 147; *TÜV/Cenelec*, ibid, p 159.
7   See further the Commission's XXVIIIth *Report on Competition Policy* (1998), points 129-134 and pp 150-153 on *EUCAR, ACEA, EACEM and Valpak*; XXIXth *Report on Competition Policy* (1999), p 160 on *JAMA*.
8   *Guidelines*, paras 179-198.
9   Ibid, para 179.
10   Ibid, para 180.
11   On the position of Member States in relation to agreements entered into between undertakings see ch 6, pp 184-189.
12   *Guidelines*, para 183.

(A) Application of Article 81(1) to environmental agreements

(i) Agreements that normally fall outside Article 81(1)

Agreements that do not impose precise obligations on the parties but which loosely commit them to achieving environmental targets are unlikely to infringe Article 81(1)[13]; the same is true of agreements that have little effect on product diversity or on purchasing decisions[14]. Agreements that are innovative, for example by introducing new recycling arrangements, would not be caught[15].

(ii) Agreements that almost always fall within Article 81(1)

An environmental agreement that is really a disguised cartel would have as its object the restriction of competition and would therefore be caught by Article 81(1)[16].

(iii) Agreements that may fall within Article 81(1)

Other environmental agreements may have the effect of restricting competition, for example where they limit the parties' ability to decide what to produce or how to produce it[17]; this could happen where the parties allocate pollution quotas[18], or where they appoint an undertaking as exclusive provider of collection and/or recycling services[19].

(B) Application of Article 81(3) to environmental agreements

Paragraphs 192 to 197 discuss Article 81(3). The Commission states specifically that it takes a positive stance on the use of environmental agreements as a policy instrument to achieve the goals enshrined in Article 2 and Article 174 of the Treaty and in Community environmental action plans[20]. The benefits may be both individual and collective, but must outweigh the costs[1]. Cost-effectiveness will have to be proven[2]. In its decision in *CECED*[3] the Commission granted individual exemption to an agreement between manufacturers and importers of washing-machines that would result in the phasing-out of old models that were inefficient in terms of the use of water, detergent and electricity; the Commission was satisfied that both individual and collective benefits would result: cheaper fuel bills for individuals and less pollution for the community at large.

---

13 Ibid, para 185.
14 Ibid, para 186.
15 Ibid, para 187.
16 Ibid, para 188.
17 Ibid, para 189.
18 Ibid, para 190.
19 Ibid, para 191; see eg *Eco-Emballages* OJ [2000] C 227/6, [2000] 5 CMLR 745.
20 Ibid, para 192.
1 Ibid, para 193.
2 Ibid, para 196.
3 OJ [2000] L 187/47, [2000] 5 CMLR 635; see also *CEMEP* (Commission Press Release IP/00/58, 23 May 2000): clearance of agreement to reduce sales of motors with low energy efficiency.

I I.   OTHER CASES OF PERMISSIBLE HORIZONTAL COOPERATION

As the CFI stated in *Matra Hachette v Commission*[4], there is no type of agreement which, by its nature, is ineligible for exemption. For example, in the case of *REIMS II*[5] the Commission granted individual exemption to a price-fixing agreement 'with unusual characteristics' in the postal services sector. The fact that a horizontal cooperation agreement does not fit into one of the categories discussed in the *Guidelines* does not mean that it cannot satisfy the terms of Article 81(3). In each case, the question is whether the parties can demonstrate either that there is no restriction of competition or that the agreement will bring about efficiencies of the type envisaged in Article 81(3).

(A)   Restructuring agreements

There may be circumstances in which an industry faces severe problems – perhaps because of recession or because of over-capacity within it – where the competition authorities may be prepared to countenance some degree of cooperation to overcome this. As a general proposition, each operator on the market should make its own independent decision as to what and how much to produce. However making rational decisions about how to 'slim down' production in some economic sectors, perhaps where capital investment is high or where there is extensive vertical integration, may be difficult in the absence of an intelligent understanding of what competitors are going to do. There is a danger that each competitor may slim down so much that the market goes from a position of over-capacity to under-capacity; it may be difficult to put the process into reverse. A different consideration is that the restructuring of industry has a social cost involving loss of employment and harm to the fabric of local communities; there is therefore a political component as well as an economic one to this issue[6].

Restructuring agreements, whereby undertakings agree on their respective levels of output, are likely to infringe Article 81(1): output limitation has as its object the restriction of competition[7]. The fact that an industry faces a crisis does not mean that undertakings can enter into agreements that restrict competition and claim immunity from Article 81(1): rather the matter should be taken to the Commission for it to decide whether to grant exemption under Article 81(3); the fact that an industry is in crisis may help to mitigate the fine[8].

The Commission has on a few occasions allowed restructuring agreements under Article 81(3). It first did so in 1984, having indicated in its Annual Reports that it might be inclined to do so[9]. In *Synthetic Fibres*[10] the Commission permitted an agreement which was to last for three years and which would involve the closure of 18% of production capacity. The parties agreed to supply information to each other about their reductions of capacity, to consult one another in the event of important changes in the market, not to increase capacity and to

4   Case T-17/93 [1994] ECR II-595.
5   OJ [1999] L 275/17, [2000] 4 CMLR 704.
6   See ch 4, pp 125-128 for a discussion of the issues which can legitimately be taken into account under Article 81(3).
7   See ch 3, p 96.
8   See eg Case T-145/89 *Baustahlgewebe v Commission* [1995] ECR II-987, para 122.
9   See eg the XIIth *Report on Competition Policy* (1982), points 38–41; XIIIth *Report on Competition Policy* (1983), points 56–61; see also XXIIIth *Report on Competition Policy* (1993), points 82-89.
10   OJ [1984] L 207/17, [1985] 1 CMLR 787.

compensate each other if they failed to implement the reductions. The Commission held that this agreement would lead to improved production which would be slimmed down in a socially acceptable way; consumers would get a fair share of the resulting benefit as in due course they would be able to purchase from a healthier industry.

The Commission has permitted several restructuring agreements in the petrochemical and thermoplastics sectors. In *BPCL/ICI*[11] it allowed an agreement achieved by specialisation and the reciprocal sale of plant, assets and goodwill. A similar 'swap' deal was granted exemption in *ENI/Montedison*[12] and again in *Enichem/ICI*[13]. The decision in *BPCL/ICI* was followed by *Bayer/BP Chemicals*[14] in the same sector. Formal comfort letters were sent by the Commission in *Shell/AKZO*[15] and *EMC/DSM (LVM)*[16]. In *Stichting Baksteen*[17] the Commission granted individual exemption to plans for restructuring the Dutch brick industry, which involved agreed action to close plants and to cut capacity. A restructuring agreement that is indissolubly linked to a permitted state aid under Article 87 EC will not be prohibited under Article 81(1)[18].

(B) Insurance sector[19]

In the case of insurance the Commission has given individual exemption to a number of horizontal cooperation agreements, for example in *Nuovo CEGAM*[20], *Concordato Incendio*[1], *Teko*[2], *P&I Clubs*[3], *Assurpool*[4] and again in *P&I Clubs*[5].

In 1991 the Council conferred power on the Commission to adopt a block exemption in the insurance sector[6], and this duly happened at the end of 1992. Article 1 of Regulation 3932/92[7], which entered into force on 1 April 1993, grants exemption to agreements in the insurance sector which seek co-operation with respect to:

(a) the establishment of common risk-premium tariffs based on collectively ascertained statistics or on the number of claims;

11 OJ [1984] L 212/1, [1985] 2 CMLR 330.
12 OJ [1987] L 5/13, [1988] 4 CMLR 444.
13 OJ [1988] L 50/18, [1989] 4 CMLR 54.
14 OJ [1988] L 150/35, [1989] 4 CMLR 24; see subsequently *Bayer/BP Chemicals* OJ [1994] L 174/34.
15 XIVth *Report on Competition Policy* (1984), point 85.
16 OJ [1988] C 18/3.
17 OJ [1994] L 131/15, [1995] 4 CMLR 646; see XXIVth *Report on Competition Policy* (1994), pp 178-180.
18 Cases T-197/97 and T-198/97 *Weyl Beef Products v Commission* judgment of 31 January 2001.
19 See further Fitzsimmons *Insurance Competition Law* (Graham & Trotman, 1994); *Faull and Nikpay* (p 498 n 5 above), paras 9.88-9.155; Roth 'European Competition Policy for the Insurance Market' (2000) 21 ECLR 107.
20 OJ [1984] L 99/29, [1984] 2 CMLR 484.
1 OJ [1990] L 15/25, [1991] 4 CMLR 199.
2 OJ [1990] L 13/34, [1990] 4 CMLR 957.
3 OJ [1985] L 376/2, [1989] 4 CMLR 178.
4 OJ [1992] L 37/16, [1993] 4 CMLR 338.
5 OJ [1999] L 125/12, [1999] 5 CMLR 646; some other cases have been settled by comfort letter: see eg XXVIth *Report on Competition Policy* (1996), pp 131-132; XXVIIIth *Report on Competition Policy* (1998), points 111-115.
6 Regulation 1534/91, OJ [1991] L 143/1.
7 OJ [1992] L 398/7, [1993] 4 CMLR 90; see XXIIth *Report on Competition Policy*, points 274–288.

(b)   the establishment of standard policy conditions;
(c)   the common coverage of certain types of risks;
(d)   the establishment of common rules on the testing and acceptance of security devices.

Each of these four paragraphs is the subject of detailed rules in Titles II-V of the Regulation. Title VI contains miscellaneous provisions, including in Articles 18–20 transitional provisions. The Regulation will apply until 31 March 2003. The Commission has submitted a Report to the European Parliament and the Council on the operation of this Regulation[8].

(C)   Banking sector[9]

The Commission has dealt with many horizontal cooperation agreements in the banking sector. Such agreements might be found not to affect trade between Member States, as the ECJ concluded in *Bagnasco*[10] and the Commission in *Dutch Banks*[11]. The Commission has published a *Notice on Cross-border Credit Transfers*[12] on the extent to which cooperation between banks is permissible under the competition rules in order to improve cross-border credit transfers. In its decision in *Uniform Eurocheques*[13] the Commission permitted an agreement which fixed standard terms and conditions in relation to the cashing of Eurocheques. The Commission also permitted a second agreement relating to the production and finishing of the actual Eurocheques and cheque cards[14]. A 10-year individual exemption was granted in *Banque Nationale de Paris/Dresdner Bank*[15] to a cooperation agreement between two major banks operating in neighbouring Member States.

(D)   Transport

Many horizontal cooperation agreements have been allowed in the transport sector. Some of these are discussed in chapter 23[16].

---

8   This can be accessed at http://europa.eu.int/comm/competition/antitrust/others/; see also the Commission's XXIXth *Report on Competition Policy* (1999), points 112-118.
9   See *Faull and Nikpay* (p 498, n 5 above), paras 9.10-9.87; see also Balto 'The Problem of Interchange Fees: Costs without Benefits?' (2000) 21 ECLR 215.
10   Cases C-215/96 and 216/96 [1999] ECR I-135, [1999] 4 CMLR 624.
11   OJ [1999] L 271/28, [2000] 4 CMLR 137.
12   OJ [1995] C 251/3; see XXVth *Report on Competition Policy* (1995), points 45-48; XXVIth *Report on Competition Policy* (1996), point 109 and pp 128-130.
13   OJ [1985] L 35/43, [1985] 3 CMLR 434.
14   OJ [1989] L 36/16; most of this agreement was cleared under Article 81(1) rather than exempted under Article 81(3); for other exemptions on banking see *Belgian Banks* OJ [1986] L 7/27, [1989] 4 CMLR 141; *Associazione Bancaria Italiana* OJ [1986] L 43/51, [1989] 4 CMLR 238.
15   OJ [1996] L 188/37, [1996] 5 CMLR 582; XXVIth *Report on Competition Policy* (1996), point 108.
16   See ch 23, pp 859-866.

12.   THE APPLICATION OF THE CHAPTER I PROHIBITION IN THE UK COMPETITION ACT 1998 TO HORIZONTAL COOPERATION AGREEMENTS

(A)   Introduction

The general principles involved in the application of the Chapter I prohibition in the Competition Act 1998 have been described in chapter 9[17]; the procedural aspects of Chapter I were dealt with in chapter 10[18]. The Chapter I prohibition is applicable only to horizontal agreements; vertical agreements, with the exception of the imposition of minimum resale prices, are excluded from Chapter I[19], though they could amount to an abuse of a dominant position under the Chapter II prohibition[20].

(B)   Appreciable restrictions of competition under the Chapter I prohibition

As far as horizontal cooperation agreements are concerned, perhaps the most important point to stress is that the DGFT considers that agreements are not caught by the Chapter I prohibition where the parties have a market share of less than 25%, except in the case of agreements that directly or indirectly fix prices or share markets, agreements to impose minimum resale prices or networks of agreements having a cumulative effect on the market in question[1]. It follows that most of the agreements of the kind described in this chapter will not be subject to the Chapter I prohibition provided that the 25% market share cap is not exceeded. Guideline 401 adds, at paragraph 2.21, that even where the parties have a market share in excess of 25%, the Chapter I prohibition will not necessarily be infringed. Other factors, such as the structure of the market, barriers to entry and the conditions on the buyers' side of the market must also be considered: the Guideline on *Market Power*[2] provides further guidance on these matters.

(C)   Consistency with EC law and parallel exemption

Section 60(1) of the Competition Act requires consistency to be maintained with EC competition law, 'so far as is possible (having regard to any relevant differences ...)'[3]. The UK test of appreciability, at 25%, is 'relevantly different' from the current EC *de minimis* provision of 5% for horizontal agreements[4]; and will remain so even if, as is likely, the EC threshold is raised to 10%[5]. Other than this, however, the jurisprudence of the Community Courts will, in general, be applied in the UK; and regard will be had to relevant decisions and statements of

---

17   See ch 9, pp 291-314.
18   See ch 10, pp 343-348.
19   See ch 16, pp 595-598.
20   On the Chapter II prohibition see ch 9, pp 314-321.
1   OFT Guideline *The Chapter I prohibition* OFT 401, paras 2.18-2.20; see ch 9, pp 296-297.
2   OFT 415.
3   See ch 9, pp 329-333.
4   See ch 3, pp 107-110.
5   Ibid.

the Commission[6]. The Commission's *Guidelines on Horizontal Cooperation Agreements*[7] would undoubtedly be a 'relevant statement' for this purpose.

Agreements that benefit from block exemption under EC law enjoy parallel exemption under UK law[8]. However, given that Regulations 2658/00[9] and 2659/ 00[10] have market share caps of 20% and 25% respectively, and that the Chapter I prohibition does not apply to horizontal cooperation agreements where the parties' market share is below 25%, such agreements do not need to benefit from parallel exemption[11]. However, R&D agreements between non-competing undertakings enjoy the benefit of the block exemption conferred by Regulation 2659/00 irrespective of the parties' market share[12]; in so far as such an agreement did infringe the Chapter I prohibition, and is exempt under the EC block exemption, parallel exemption would apply.

(D)   Relevant DGFT Guidelines

The DGFT's Guidelines do not provide much guidance on the types of agreement dealt with in the European Commission's *Horizontal Guidelines*. An exception to this is the treatment of standards. The DGFT notes that an agreement on technical or design standards may lead to an improvement in production or raising quality; and that it may promote technical or economic progress by reducing waste and consumers' research costs[13]. However he continues that such agreements may restrict competition if producers are limited as to what they may produce or where they act as a barrier to entry. The DGFT also recognises that a trade association may play a rôle in the negotiation and promulgation of industry-wide standards[14]. The possibility of such standards being granted exemption is noted, however, since they may promote safety and protect consumers[15]. The possible restrictive effects of certification schemes are also noted[16].

(E)   The General Insurance Standards Council

The first decision adopted by the DGFT under the Competition Act was in the case of the *General Insurance Standards Council (GISC)*[17]. GISC had notified its

6   Competition Act 1998, s 60(3).
7   See p 501ff above.
8   Competition Act 1998, s 10; on parallel exemptions, see ch 9, pp 312-313.
9   See pp 517-520 above.
10   See pp 510-515 above.
11   For the same reason, agreements that are block exempted in the insurance sector under Regulation 3932/92 (see p 529, n 7 above) subject to market share caps of 10% or 15% would not require parallel exemption under UK law; parallel exemption would be available for maritime liner conferences that enjoy exemption under Regulation 823/2000 (see ch 23, p 861), since that Regulation does not have a market share cap; shipping consortia under Regulation 823/2000 (ch 23, pp 861-862) are subject to a 30% cap, so that there could – theoretically! – be parallel exemption for a consortium with a market share between 25% and 30%.
12   See Article 4(1) of Regulation 2659/00, which is considered at pp 513-514 above.
13   *Chapter I prohibition* OFT Guideline 401, para 3.26.
14   *Trade Associations, Professions and Self-Regulating Bodies* OFT Guideline 408, para 3.17.
15   Ibid, para 4.5.
16   Ibid, para 3.20.
17   Case CA98/1/2001, 24 January 2001; this decision can be accessed at http://www.oft.gov.uk/comp-act/case_register/decisions.html.

Rules to the DGFT, requesting that he should confirm that they did not infringe the Chapter I prohibition. The DGFT gave this confirmation.

GISC is a self-regulating body for the general insurance industry. The DGFT considered whether GISC's Rules would impose or increase barriers preventing entry into the industry; whether they would distort competition between insurers, between intermediaries, or between insurers and intermediaries; and whether they could result in the exchange of price or non-price information. He concluded that the Rules would have none of these effects. The DGFT's decision in this case has been appealed to the Competition Commission Appeal Tribunal by third parties that disagree with it.[17a]

(F) Block exemption for ticketing agreements

The Secretary of State has adopted a block exemption for public transport ticketing schemes.[18] This allows travel operators to adopt joint travel cards and through ticketing schemes. Conditions are imposed to ensure that operators cannot be excluded from the arrangements without objective, transparent and non-discriminatory reasons and to ensure that there will be no harm to consumers.

17a See Cases 1003/2/1/01 and 1004/2/1/01 *Institute of Independent Insurance Brokers v DGFT*, judgment expected on 28 August 2001.
18 Competition Act 1998 (Public Transport Ticketing Schemes Block Exemption) Order 2001, SI 2001/319.

CHAPTER 16

Vertical agreements

The previous three chapters have been concerned with horizontal relationships between firms. This chapter is concerned with the application of Article 81 EC to vertical agreements. The law on vertical agreements has undergone fundamental reform with the adoption by the European Commission of a new block exemption in 1999, which entered into force on 1 June 2000[1]; the Commission has also published the accompanying *Guidelines on Vertical Restraints*[2] ('the *Guidelines*'). In the UK vertical agreements, with the exception of agreements for the maintenance of minimum and fixed resale prices, are excluded from the Chapter I prohibition of the Competition Act 1998[3]; the application of the Competition Act 1998 and the Fair Trading Act 1973 to vertical agreements will be considered in the final section of this chapter. To the extent that vertical agreements might result in the abuse of a dominant position, contrary to Article 82 EC and the Chapter II prohibition in the Competition Act 1998, they are dealt with in chapters 17 and 18.

1.   THE DISTRIBUTION CHAIN

A producer of goods or a supplier of services will either require them for its own consumption or will want to supply them to the market. A firm wishing to sell its products must decide how to do so. There are various possibilities: it may carry out both the production and the sales and distribution functions itself: this may be referred to as vertical integration; it may use the services of a commercial agent to find customers; or it may supply its products to a distributor, whose function is to resell them to other undertakings, who may or may not be the final consumer. This chapter will consider how the law impacts upon each of these three situations, that is to say vertical integration, agency agreements and vertical agreements with third parties. It will also consider how the law applies to vertical sub-contracting agreements.

---

1   Regulation 2790/99 OJ [1999] L 336/21, [2000] 4 CMLR 398; see pp 567-591 below for detailed commentary on this Regulation.
2   OJ [2000] C 291/1, [2000] 5 CMLR 1074.
3   See pp 595-598 below.

For many products it is possible to depict a fairly simple distribution chain: for example a producer may sell goods to a retailer, who deals with the final consumer:

In other markets a wholesaler may carry out an important intermediate function, standing between the producer and the retailer:

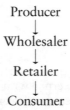

A vertically-integrated producer might deal directly with the consumer, for example by mail order, by establishing retail outlets or by selling through the Internet. An interesting example of vertical integration in the 'new' electronic economy is the merged Time-Warner/AOL[4], where the musical content of Time-Warner can be delivered direct to the personal computer of the consumer through the AOL on-line distribution system.

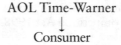

There can, of course, be many other configurations, in which quite different relationships are involved in the delivery of goods or services to their ultimate consumer. For example a brand owner in the food industry might sub-contract manufacture to a sub-contractor; the brand owner may negotiate sales directly with supermarkets, and engage a transport company to arrange for the physical distribution of the products from the sub-contractor to the supermarket, in which case the diagram would look quite different:

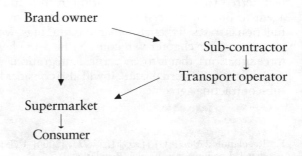

4   Case COMP/M.1845: see p 538 below.

It will be appreciated that many other vertical relationships are possible in the manufacture and supply of goods and services. This chapter will attempt to provide some guidance on how these vertical relationships are to be analysed in EC and UK law.

2. VERTICAL INTEGRATION

One option available for firms is vertical integration. This can be achieved internally by setting up retail outlets in the High Street or by establishing subsidiary companies to which the task of distribution is entrusted. Some firms may be able to sell their products through the Internet, thereby eliminating the need to appoint distributors: this process is known as disintermediation. Alternatively vertical integration may be achieved through external growth, by taking over distribution networks downstream in the market. Various considerations will influence a producer in its decision whether or not to integrate vertically[5]. On the one hand it may be costly to set up or take over one's own distribution channels; also it may be more efficient to appoint an independent undertaking with knowledge of and expertise in the distributive trade than to attempt to break into this area oneself. On the other hand vertical integration may mean that a high degree of efficiency and coordination can be achieved in a way that would not occur where products are distributed by third parties.

(A)   Non-application of Article 81 to agreements within a corporate group

One reason for achieving vertical integration might be that this will result in some immunity from competition law, since in general the internal affairs of companies or groups of companies are not subject to competition law. The ECJ confirmed in *Viho v Commission*[6] that Article 81(1) does not apply to parent-subsidiary agreements: this means that an intra-group agreement forbidding a subsidiary from exporting or selling at less than a certain price would not infringe Article 81(1)[7]. Vertical growth may not be the most efficient use of resources in terms of allocative efficiency and yet it may be the logical defensive response of firms fearful of anti-trust attack[8]. The agreements entered into between members of the group and third parties would themselves be capable of infringing Article 81(1), and would therefore be subject to the law on vertical agreements in the same way as any other.

(B)   Application of Article 82 to the behaviour of the group

Vertical integration may be regarded as a factor indicating dominance for the purpose of deciding whether a firm is in a dominant position within the meaning

---

5   See Coase 'The Nature of the Firm' 4 Economica 386 (1937); Williamson 'The Vertical Integration of Production; Market Failure Considerations' 61 Am Ec Rev 112 (1971); Lever and Neubauer 'Vertical Restraints, Their Motivation and Justification' (2000) 21 ECLR 7.
6   Case C-73/95 P [1996] ECR I-5457, [1997] 4 CMLR 419.
7   See ch 3, pp 72-74.
8   Warner AG warned of this danger in Case 30/78 *Distillers v Commission* [1980] ECR 2229, [1980] 3 CMLR 121.

of Article 82[9], and the group may be guilty of an abuse of a dominant position in the way in which it behaves on the market[10].

(C)   Application of the EC Merger Regulation to vertical integration

Vertical mergers are notifiable to the Commission under the EC Merger Regulation where the Community dimension thresholds are satisfied[11]. There have been several occasions on which the Commission has required modifications to, or even the abandonment of, vertical mergers[12]. An obvious example of this is *Time-Warner/AOL*[13], which required the approval of the Commission: this was granted subject to a severance of the structural links between AOL and Bertelsman, a competitor of Time-Warner.

3.   COMMERCIAL AGENTS

Some producers choose to sell through commercial agents. The function of the 'sales agent' is to negotiate business and to enter into contracts on the producer's behalf[14]. In this case the agent may be paid a commission for the business it transacts or it may be paid a salary. The essential point about its position is that it does not bear any risk itself (except that it may be required to provide *del credere* guarantees whereby it guarantees the creditworthiness of customers to the principal); no property passes to it under the agreement; and it does not directly share in the profits (or losses) of its principal's business. The agent's position is analogous to that of an employee.

(A)   Non-application of Article 81 to agency agreements

Where an agent is appointed which simply negotiates on behalf of a principal, it is treated by EC competition law as forming part of the business organisation of the principal, so that the agreement between the parties is an internal matter of that economic entity. The consequence is that the agreement will normally fall outside Article 81(1). Commercial agency is a more common feature of distribution in continental Europe than in the UK. The Council of Ministers has adopted a Directive on the treatment of commercial agents[15], which provides them with protection against wrongful dismissal and with compensation where this occurs.

---

9   See ch 5, p 159.
10   See *Interbrew* Commission's XXVIth *Report on Competition Policy* (1996), point 54 and pp 139-140.
11   See ch 21, pp 751-755 on these thresholds.
12   Ibid, p 776.
13   Case COMP/M.1845.
14   Agents are sometimes appointed simply to canvass potential customers or to introduce them to the producer rather than to negotiate contracts.
15   Council Directive on the Coordination of the Laws of Member States relating to Self-Employed Commercial Agents 86/653, OJ [1986] L 382/17; the Directive was implemented in the UK by the Commercial Agents (Council Directive) Regulations 1993, SI 1993/3053.

(B)   The application of the Commission's *Guidelines* to agency agreements

As early as 1962 the Commission published a Notice on agency agreements[16] stating that they were not subject to Article 81(1). It became necessary to amend this Notice, in particular since subsequent case law of the ECJ, for example in *Suiker Unie v Commission*[17] and *Vlaamse Reisbureaus*[18], made clear that it was not entirely reliable. The 1962 Notice was replaced by Section II (paragraphs 12 to 20) of the Commission's *Guidelines*[19]; paragraph 12 of the *Guidelines* specifically states that they replace the 1962 Notice.

Paragraph 12 defines agency agreements as those that cover a situation where one person negotiates and/or concludes contracts on behalf of another for the purchase or sale of goods or services, by or from the principal. Paragraph 13 states that, in the case of 'genuine' agency agreements, Article 81(1) does not apply to the obligations imposed on the agent; 'non-genuine' agency agreements may be caught: they must be analysed under the later sections of the *Guidelines* and the block exemption. Paragraph 13 provides that the determining factor in assessing whether Article 81(1) is applicable is 'the financial or commercial risk borne by the agent in relation to the activities for which he has been appointed as an agent by the principal'. Paragraphs 14 to 18 examine the meaning of risk for this purpose and the obligations that fall outside Article 81(1). Paragraphs 19 and 20 examine two circumstances in which provisions in an agency agreement could infringe Article 81(1).

(i)   The criterion of risk

Paragraph 14 states that there are two types of financial or commercial risk that are relevant in determining 'genuine' agency: first, those that are directly related to the contracts concluded and/or negotiated by the agent on behalf of the principal, such as the financing of stocks; secondly, those risks that are related to 'market-specific investments', meaning risks that the agent undertakes in order to be appointed. Paragraph 15 states that where the agent bears no or only insignificant risks in relation to either of these matters, the agency agreement falls outside Article 81(1): in such a case the selling or purchasing function forms an integral part of the principal's activities, despite the fact that the agent is, as a matter of law, a separate undertaking. Where the agent does accept risk which is more than insignificant, it is treated as an independent dealer, and the agreement with it is capable of infringing Article 81(1). Paragraph 16 states that the question of risk must be assessed on a case-by-case basis and with regard to economic reality rather than legal form. However, for the purpose of guidance, paragraph 16 continues by stating that Article 81(1) would not normally be applicable where the goods do not vest in the agent; nor where the agent does not supply services itself and is not involved in costs or risks in relation to various listed matters. The list in paragraph 16 contains seven indents setting

---

16 *Notice on exclusive dealing contracts with commercial agents of 1962*, OJ 139, 24.12.1962, p 2921.
17 Cases 40/73 etc [1975] ECR 1663, [1976] 1 CMLR 295.
18 Case 311/85 *Vereniging van Vlaamse Reisbureaus v Sociale Dienst van de Plaatselijke en Gewestelijke Overheidsdiensten* [1987] ECR 3801, [1989] 4 CMLR 213
19 OJ [2000] C 291/1, [2000] 5 CMLR 1074.

out factors that would be indicative of the agreement being a true agency agreement, for example that the agent does not contribute to the costs involved in the supply or purchase of the contract goods or services, or that it does not invest in sales promotion. Paragraph 17 provides that this list is not exhaustive, and that where the agent does incur one or more of the risks or costs listed, Article 81(1) may apply as it would do to any other vertical agreement. Paragraph 18 provides that, where an agency agreement does not fall within Article 81(1), all obligations on the agent will fall outside that provision, including limitations on the territory in which or the customers to which the agent may sell the goods or services and the prices and conditions at which the goods or services will be sold or purchased.

(ii)   Provisions in agency agreements that may infringe Article 81(1)

The *Guidelines* indicate, in paragraphs 19 and 20, two situations in which there could be an infringement of Article 81(1) in the case of a true agency agreement. The first is where the agreement contains exclusive agency or non-compete provisions. Since exclusive agency provisions concern only intra-brand competition[20], paragraph 19 says that they do not in general produce anti-competitive effects. However non-compete provisions may affect inter-brand competition[1] and could infringe Article 81(1) if they lead to foreclosure of the market: the Commission refers to the later provisions of the *Guidelines* in section VI.2.1 (paragraphs 138 to 160) on this. Paragraph 20 deals with the second situation in which Article 81(1) might be infringed, which is where the agency agreement facilitates an anti-competitive agreement or concerted practice: this could occur where a number of principals use the same agents whilst collectively excluding others from using these agents; or where they use agents for collusion on marketing strategy or to exchange sensitive market information between the principals.

4.   VERTICAL AGREEMENTS: COMPETITION POLICY CONSIDERATIONS

(A)   Introduction

In this section the competition policy considerations raised by vertical agreements will be examined, using the taxonomy adopted by the Commission in its *Guidelines*. Section 5 of this chapter will consider the application of Article 81(1) to vertical agreements in the light of the jurisprudence of the Community Courts and the Commission's *Guidelines*. Sections 6 and 7 will examine the path to reform of the old EC block exemptions for exclusive distribution, exclusive purchasing and franchising agreements and the very different treatment of vertical agreements under Regulation 2790/99. Section 8 will consider the possibility of obtaining individual exemption for vertical agreements under Article 81(3). Regulation 1475/95 on the distribution of motor cars will be considered briefly in section 9.

---

20 This expression is explained at p 541 below.
1   Ibid.

(B) Vertical agreements: possible detriments to competition

(i) Inter-brand and intra-brand competition

The application of Article 81 to vertical agreements has long been controversial. It is fairly obvious that horizontal agreements, for example to fix prices or to limit output, should be prohibited: in this situation, firms combine their market power to their own advantage[2]; vertical agreements do not involve a *combination* of market power[3]. Vertical agreements are likely to have an effect on competition only where the firm imposing a vertical restraint already has some degree of market power. Where this is the case, competition with other firms' products – 'inter-brand competition' – may be limited; as a result it may be desirable to ensure that there is competition between distributors and retailers in relation to the products of the firm with market power – so-called 'intra-brand competition'[4].

Suppose that A is the brand owner of Wonder Widgets and B is the brand owner of Beautiful Blodgets. A requires its retailers only to purchase Wonder Widgets and not to buy the competing products of M, N and O, a so-called 'single branding agreement'[5].

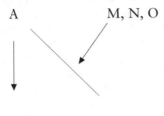

A   M, N, O

Retailers

There may be a restriction of inter-brand competition, since M, N and O cannot sell to retailers which have agreed to purchase only A's products.

The question in this case would be whether the single branding agreement has an effect on inter-brand competition, that is to say on competition between the brands of A and those of its competitors, M, N and O; this will depend on how much market power A has.

Suppose now that B requires its retailers X, Y and Z not to sell Beautiful Blodgets at less than the recommended price of EUR 100, and not to sell to customers who live in an area allotted to one of the other retailers.

B

X, Y and Z

There is a restriction of intra-brand competition between X, Y and Z in relation to sales of B's products.

The question in this case is whether the agreements have an effect on intra-brand competition between the three retailers X, Y and Z; it does not restrict competition between B and its competitors.

2   *Guidelines*, para 100.
3   Ibid.
4   Ibid, para 6.
5   See pp 553-555 below.

(ii)   Consten and Grundig v Commission

It was argued in *Consten and Grundig v Commission*[6] that Article 81(1) should not apply to vertical agreements at all, and that it was simply concerned with horizontal arrangements between independent firms. The ECJ rejected this argument[7] and proceeded to lay down that an exclusive agreement conferring absolute territorial protection upon a distributor was caught by Article 81(1) and could not be granted an exemption under Article 81(3)[8].

(iii)   The single market imperative and intra-brand competition

As a general proposition, competition law has less concern with restrictions of intra-brand competition than with restrictions of inter-brand competition: as already suggested, a restriction of intra-brand competition is likely to raise concerns only where inter-brand competition is weak. However, to this must be added a further concern of EC competition law, which has been mentioned several times in this book already: the integrity of the single market[9]. The Community Courts and the Commission have, from the earliest days, been concerned about vertical agreements that lead to a division of national markets, even where the restrictions relate to intra-brand rather than to inter-brand competition. The strict treatment of export bans, the determination to maintain parallel imports and the reluctance to allow distributors to enjoy absolute territorial protection are all issues affecting intra-brand rather than inter-brand competition. The law on vertical agreements in the Community therefore has a component – single market integration – that will not be found in other (domestic) systems of competition law[10].

(iv)   The commentary in the Guidelines on the negative effects of vertical restraints

Paragraph 107 of the Commission's *Guidelines* notes four possible negative effects arising from vertical restraints which EC competition law aims at preventing:
*   foreclosure of other suppliers or buyers by raising barriers to entry;
*   reduction of inter-brand competition, including the facilitation of both explicit and tacit collusion[11];
*   reduction of intra-brand competition between distributors of the same brand; and
*   the creation of obstacles to market integration.

There are many types of vertical agreement. The Commission, at paragraph 104 of the *Guidelines*, suggests that they can be grouped into four categories: a single branding group; a limited distribution group; a resale price maintenance group; and a market partitioning group. Each group, and the negative effects that may follow from agreements in that group, is discussed in the subsequent paragraphs of the *Guidelines*. It is important to become familiar with the

---

6   Cases 56/64 and 58/64 [1966] ECR 299, [1966] CMLR 418.
7   Ibid at 339, and 470 respectively; see further ch 3, pp 91-92.
8   Absolute territorial protection may be permitted in exceptional circumstances, as in Case 262/81 *Coditel II* [1982] ECR 3381, [1983] 1 CMLR 49: see ch 3, p 97.
9   See eg ch 1, p 19; ch 2, p 47.
10   *Guidelines*, para 7; for the position in the UK on vertical agreements, see pp 595-600 below.
11   On practices, including vertical agreements, that facilitate tacit collusion see ch 14, p 466.

terminology introduced in this part of the *Guidelines* in order to understand the law of vertical agreements.

(A) SINGLE BRANDING GROUP[12] .   The single branding group consists of agreements that have as their main element that the buyer is induced to concentrate its orders for a particular product on one supplier. An agreement not to purchase competing products, agreements which force or induce customers to purchase all or most of their products from one supplier and tie-in transactions fall within this group[13] . In the Commission's view, agreements in the single branding group may foreclose access to the market, facilitate collusion, restrict inter-brand competition within retail shops, and, in the case of tying, force the buyer to pay a higher price for tied products then would otherwise to be case. Each of these negative effects may lead to a reduction inter-brand competition[14] .

(B) LIMITED DISTRIBUTION GROUP[15] .   The limited distribution group consists of agreements which have as their main element that the manufacturer sells to only one or a limited of buyers. Exclusive distribution, exclusive customer allocation and selective distribution agreements fall within this group. In the Commission's view, agreements in the limited distribution group may lead to foreclosure at the buyer's level of the market, facilitate collusion and lead to a reduction, or even a total elimination of, intra-brand competition[16] .

(C) RESALE PRICE MAINTENANCE GROUP[17] .   This group consists of agreements which impose minimum, fixed, maximum or recommended resale prices[18] . The main negative effects are a reduction in intra-brand competition and increased transparency of prices, which may facilitate collusion[19] .

(D) MARKET PARTITIONING GROUP[20] .   This group consists of agreements the main element of which is that the buyer is restricted as to where it buys or resells a particular product[1] . The main negative effect is a reduction of intra-brand competition and a partitioning of the market, thereby hindering marketing integration; such agreements may also facilitate collusion[2] .

(C)   Vertical agreements: possible benefits to competition

Having set out the Commission's views as to the possible detriments to competition arising from vertical agreements, it is important to stress that there are also significant arguments in their favour. Some theorists argue that vertical restraints

12 *Guidelines*, paras 106-108; on the application of Article 81(1) to such agreements, see pp 553-55 and 563 below.
13 Ibid, para 106.
14 Ibid, para 107.
15 Ibid, paras 109-110; on the application of Article 81(1) to such agreements, see pp 555-563 below.
16 Ibid, para 110.
17 Ibid, paras 111-112; on the application of Article 81(1) to such agreements, see pp 563-564 below.
18 Ibid, para 111.
19 Ibid, para 112.
20 Ibid, paras 113-114; on the treatment of direct and indirect export bans under Article 81(1), see pp 550-553 below.
1   Ibid, para 113.
2   Ibid, para 114.

are not a suitable target for competition authorities at all[3]; a more realistic view is that they should be investigated only where a producer possesses power over the market[4]. Paragraph 115 of the Commission's *Guidelines* states that vertical restraints often have positive effects, in particular by promoting non-price competition and improved quality of service. Paragraph 116 sets out eight situations in which vertical restraints may help to realise efficiencies and the development of new markets; the Commission says that it does not claim that the list is complete or exhaustive.[5]

(i) The free-rider problem

One distributor may take a free ride on the investment of another. For example, a retailer may invest in a particular brand and create a demand for it: it has an obvious interest in preventing another retailer from making sales in circumstances where it made no contribution to the creation of that demand. The Commission states that free-riding between buyers can occur only on pre-sales services and not on after-sales services; it adds that free-riding is usually only a problem where the product is relatively new or complex and of reasonably high value. Exclusive distribution agreements may be used to prevent the problem of free-riding: for example if A appoints B as the exclusive distributor for France, this will provide some degree of immunity from intra-brand competition. The *Guidelines* do not say, but it is the case, that absolute territorial protection will not usually be countenanced in vertical agreements, because of the overriding goal of preventing the compartmentalisation of the single market. Community law permits exclusivity, but only a qualified exclusivity, in that parallel imports into the exclusive territory must be possible[6]. A free-rider issue can arise where a supplier invests in promotion at a retailer's premises which a competing supplier takes advantage of: a non-compete provision may be justified to prevent this type of free-riding.

(ii) Opening up and entering new markets

The second situation described in paragraph 116 is a 'special case of the free-rider problem'. This is where a manufacturer wants to enter a new geographic market and this requires its distributor to make 'first time investments'. It may be necessary to protect the distributor from competition so that it can recoup its investment by temporarily charging a higher price; this may mean that distributors in other markets should be restrained for a limited period from selling in the new market.

---

3 See eg Bork *The Antitrust Paradox* (Basic Books, 1978) chs 14 and 15.
4 See eg White 'Vertical Restraints in Antitrust law – a Coherent Model' (1981) 26 Antitrust Bulletin 327; Easterbrook 'Vertical Arrangements and the Rule of Reason' (1984) 53 Antitrust Law Journal 135; Bock 'An Economist Appraises Vertical Restraints' (1985) 30 Antitrust Bulletin 117; for criticism of the permissive view of vertical restraints adopted by many commentators in recent years see Comanor 'Vertical Price Fixing, Vertical Market Restrictions and the New Antitrust Policy' (1985) 98 Harv L Rev 983.
5 See further *Guidelines*, paras 117 and 118.
6 See further p 542 above and pp 583-585 below.

(iii)   The certification free-rider issue

The third situation discussed in paragraph 116 is that, in some sectors, certain retailers have a reputation for stocking only 'quality' products. In such a case a manufacturer must limit its sales to such retailers, since otherwise its products may be delisted. Restrictions from the 'limited distribution' group may be justified in these circumstances.

(iv)   The hold-up problem

This refers to a situation in which a supplier or buyer needs to make client-specific investments, and will not commit to these until supply agreements have been concluded. It may be that an undertaking making an investment will require a long-term supply agreement, so that it knows that it will recoup its costs. Where the supplier makes the investment, it may wish the buyer to agree to a non-compete, or to an analogous, provision; a buyer may seek the benefit of an exclusive distribution, customer allocation or exclusive supply provision.

(v)   The hold-up problem where know-how is transferred

Where know-how is supplied by one firm to another, it may be necessary to impose a non-compete provision on the recipient of the know-how to ensure that it is not used by competitors of the owner of it.

(vi)   Economies of scale in distribution

Economies of scale on the part of distributors may lead to lower retail prices. Various vertical agreements might contribute to this, including exclusive distribution and exclusive purchasing.

(vii)   Capital market imperfections

In some cases, banks may be unwilling to provide sufficient capital for the needs of the business of a supplier or a buyer. In such cases the supplier may lend to the buyer or *vice versa*. An obvious example is a brewer which makes a loan available to the operator of a public house or a café. A supplier in such a case may wish to impose a non-compete, or an analogous, provision; and a buyer may insist, for example, on exclusive supply.

(viii)   Uniformity and quality standardisation

Vertical restraints may help to promote the brand image of a product and increase its attractiveness to consumers by bringing about uniformity and quality standardisation. This is typical of selective distribution and franchising systems.

5.   VERTICAL AGREEMENTS: ARTICLE 81(1)

(A)   Introduction

This section will consider the application of Article 81(1) to vertical agreements. Given the breadth of the new block exemption for vertical agreements, in many cases it is not necessary, in practical terms, to decide whether an agreement infringes Article 81(1) in the first place: if an agreement is within the 'safe haven' of Regulation 2790/99 and therefore exempt under Article 81(3), the parties may have little interest in arguing, or even knowing, that the agreement did not infringe Article 81(1) anyway. Paragraph 120 of the Commission's *Guidelines* suggests, at indents (1) and (2), that there is no need to consider the application of Article 81(1) to agreements that are within the safe haven of the block exemption. This is a sensible and pragmatic point. However it would be intellectually incorrect to conclude that, *because* an agreement benefits from block exemption, it *therefore* infringes Article 81(1); and in some cases an agreement may not benefit from the block exemption, for example because the supplier's market share exceeds 30%[7], in which case the parties may wish to argue that Article 81(1) is not infringed.

(B)   The *de minimis* doctrine

Paragraphs 8 to 11 of the Commission's *Guidelines* point out that agreements of minor importance and agreements between small- and medium-sized undertakings usually fall outside Article 81(1) altogether. These paragraphs refer to the Commission's *Notice on Agreements of Minor Importance*[8], which has been described in chapter 3 of this book[9]. Vertical agreements entered into by undertakings with a market share of less than 10% are usually regarded as *de minimis*, although a 'hard-core' restriction such as an export ban might infringe Article 81(1) even below this threshold[10]. It is the intention of the Commission that the 10% threshold for vertical agreements under the *de minimis* doctrine will be raised to 15%: this may happen in the course of 2001[11].

(C)   The combined effect of the *de minimis* doctrine and the block exemption

The combined effect of the *de minimis* doctrine and the block exemption is that most vertical agreements where the supplier's market share is below 10% fall outside Article 81(1) altogether; and that most vertical agreements, even if they are caught by Article 81(1), will be block exempted under Regulation 2790/99, provided that the supplier's market share is below 30% and that the agreement does not contain any of the 'hard-core' black listed provisions in Article 4 of that Regulation[12]. As a consequence, a very large number of vertical agreements will enjoy the benefit of one of these two 'safe havens'. Individual examination of

---

7   Occasionally it is the buyer's market share that is relevant: see p 579 below.
8   OJ [1997] C 372/13, [1998] 4 CMLR 192.
9   See ch 3, pp 107-110.
10   See ch 3, p 109 and *Guidelines*, para 10.
11   See ch 3, p 107, n 15.
12   On the black list in Article 4, see pp 581-586 below.

vertical agreements will be necessary only where one of the safe havens is unavailable, for example because the supplier's market share exceeds 30% or because the parties wish to include a black listed provision in their agreement. Where the supplier's market share exceeds 30% it may be that it has a dominant position, in which case restrictions in its vertical agreements may amount to an abuse of a dominant position contrary to Article 82 EC: firms have been found to be dominant where they had a market share in the region of 40%, and they are presumed to be dominant at 50%[13]. Agreements containing black listed provisions are unlikely to be granted individual exemption, since these are hard-core restrictions to which the Commission generally takes exception. It follows that individual examination of vertical agreements under Article 81(1) and Article 81(3) is likely to be relatively rare: it is most likely to be necessary where the supplier has a market share in excess of 30% but does not have a dominant position in the sense of Article 82.

Market shares and vertical agreements

50%	An undertaking with a market share of more than 50% is presumed to be dominant
40%	An undertaking with a market share of more than 40% may be dominant
30%	An undertaking with a market share of more than 30% will not benefit from the block exemption
10%	Even if an agreement is caught by Article 81(1), it will benefit from block exemption if the market share is below 30% and the agreement does not contain Article 4 hard-core restrictions
0%	An undertaking with a market below 10% will usually benefit from the *de minimis* doctrine

(D)   The case law of the Community Courts on vertical agreements

The Community Courts have repeatedly made clear that, except in those cases where the *object*[14] of an agreement is plainly anti-competitive, for example because of the imposition of an export ban, the application of Article 81(1) to an agreement cannot be ascertained simply by taking into account its formal terms; rather it has to be assessed in its economic context in order to determine whether it could have an effect on competition in the relevant market. This case law is discussed in chapter 3 of this book[15]. Of particular importance in the context of vertical

13 See ch 5, pp 153-156.
14 See ch 3, pp 92-98.
15 See ch 3, pp 98-103.

agreements are the judgments in *Société Technique Minière v Maschinenbau Ulm*[16], *Brasserie de Haecht v Wilkin*[17], *Pronuptia de Paris v Schillgalis*[18] and *Delimitis v Henninger Bräu*[19], each of which makes clear that, in 'effect' rather than 'object' cases under Article 81(1), a detailed examination of all the relevant facts is required before a conclusion can be reached as to whether competition is restricted by a vertical agreement. Notwithstanding these important precedents, there has been a tendency on the part of the Commission over many years to adopt a formalistic approach to the application of Article 81(1) to vertical agreements, and a reluctance to follow the lead suggested by the Community Courts; the result has been that large numbers of vertical agreements have required exemption under Article 81(3) and, in particular, under the block exemptions adopted by the Commission. However it is clear from the *Guidelines* that the Commission is now more willing than it has been in the past to adopt a flexible and economics-oriented approach to the application of Article 81(1): this is an important part of the Commission's modernisation of its approach to the competition rules in the Treaty, and is a very welcome development. Paragraphs 120 to 133 of the *Guidelines* establish the methodology of analysis for determining whether vertical agreements infringe Article 81(1) and whether they might satisfy the terms of Article 81(3); there is regrettably little reference to the jurisprudence of the Community Courts in the *Guidelines*, but of course they must be read subject to the Courts' case law rather than the other way around.

(E)   The methodology for the analysis of vertical agreements in the Commission's *Guidelines*

(i)   The four steps involved in assessing vertical agreements under Article 81

Paragraph 120 of the *Guidelines* suggests that four steps should be taken when assessing vertical agreements under Article 81. First, the relevant market should be defined in order to determine the supplier's or the buyer's market share, depending on the type of vertical restraint involved; secondly, where the market share is below 30% the block exemption will usually be applicable, provided that there are no hard-core restrictions contrary to Article 4 of Regulation 2790/99[20]; the third step is that, where the market share of 30% is exceeded, it will be necessary to consider whether the agreement falls within Article 81(1); lastly, where Article 81(1) is infringed, it will be necessary to consider whether the agreement satisfies the terms of Article 81(3).

(ii)   Relevant factors for the assessment under Article 81(1)

Paragraphs 121 to 133 set out the factors that are relevant to the analysis of agreements under Article 81(1). Paragraph 121 refers to eight particular factors that are relevant to this assessment: the market position of the supplier; the market position of competitors; the position of the buyer; entry barriers; the

---

16   Case 56/65 [1966] ECR 235, [1966] CMLR 357.
17   Case 23/67 [1967] ECR 407, [1968] CMLR 26.
18   Case 161/84 [1986] ECR 353, [1986] 1 CMLR 414.
19   Case C-234/89 [1991] ECR I-935, [1992] 5 CMLR 210.
20   On Article 4, see pp 581-586 below.

maturity of the market; the level of trade affected by the agreement; the nature of the product; and 'other factors'. Each of these factors is expanded upon in the succeeding paragraphs. Paragraphs 126 to 129 are quite interesting on the issue of entry barriers, given that there is no Commission Notice on this particular issue; specific reference is made in paragraph 128 to the significance of sunk costs in determining how high the entry barriers are in a particular industry. Paragraph 133 deals with 'other factors' that may be relevant to the analysis: these include whether there is a 'cumulative effect' within the market of similar vertical agreements leading to a restriction of competition, the regulatory environment and the possibility of collusive behaviour arising from the operation of vertical agreements.

(iii)   Relevant factors for the assessment under Article 81(3)

Paragraphs 134 to 136 discuss the application of Article 81(3) to vertical agreements. Paragraph 135 states that, where an undertaking is dominant or becoming dominant as a consequence of the vertical agreement, a vertical restraint that has appreciable anti-competitive effects, in principle, cannot be exempted. Paragraph 136 says that, where there is no dominance, three questions arise: these correspond to the first three requirements of Article 81(3) itself[1]. The first is whether the agreement will lead to efficiencies of the kind discussed in paragraphs 115 to 118 of the *Guidelines*[2]; speculative claims will not be accepted. The second issue will be whether any benefits accrue to the advantage of consumers rather than the parties to the agreement: in general this will depend on the intensity of competition in the market. The third issue will be whether the restrictions in the agreement are disproportionate: the least anti-competitive restraint should be chosen to obtain the efficiency in question.

(iv)   Application of the methodology to particular types of agreement

Having set out this methodology, the Commission's *Guidelines* then proceed to consider the application of Article 81 to a series of particular types of vertical agreement, such as single branding and exclusive distribution: these are considered in section (G) below[3]. The *Guidelines* do not contain a specific section dealing with the application of Article 81(1) to direct and indirect export bans, other than the commentary on Article 4(b) of the block exemption[4]. However, there is a wealth of precedent on this subject and, as has been stressed throughout this book, the single market imperative is a dominant feature of Community competition law. For this reason section (F) below will consider the approach of the Community Courts and the Commission to direct and indirect export bans before the discussion in the *Guidelines* of other types of vertical agreement is considered in section (G).

---

1   See ch 4, pp 125-130.
2   See pp 543-545 above.
3   See pp 553-564 below.
4   See pp 583-585 below.

(F)   Direct and indirect export bans

(i)   Direct export bans

Export bans contained in vertical agreements will be held to infringe Article 81(1), and will not be permitted under Article 81(3) except in the most exceptional of circumstances. Such agreements will be found to have as their object the restriction of competition; anti-competitive effects do not need to be demonstrated[5]. Export bans are black listed by Article 4(b) of Regulation 2790/99, and their inclusion would therefore prevent the application of the block exemption to the agreement in question[6]. Examples of export bans which the Commission has objected to are legion, and the Community Courts have been equally opposed to them[7]. It is highly likely that the Commission will impose a fine where it discovers an export ban, although reluctant distributors which accepted the ban under duress may not themselves be fined[8]; alternatively it may be that the fine on unwilling participants will be reduced[9]. In a serious case the fine for imposing export bans could be very substantial indeed: in *VW*[10] the

---

5   For a recent statement to this effect by the CFI, see Cases T-175/95 and T-176/95 *BASF v Commission* [1999] ECR II-1581, [2000] 4 CMLR 33 and 67.

6   See pp 583-585 below.

7   See eg Case 19/77 *Miller International Schallplatten GmbH v Commission* [1978] ECR 131, [1978] 2 CMLR 334 (export ban regarded by ECJ as a *per se* infringement of Article 81); *William Teacher* OJ [1978] L 235/20, [1978] 3 CMLR 290; *Arthur Bell* OJ [1978] L 235/15, [1978] 3 CMLR 298; Cases 32/78 etc *BMW Belgium SA v Commission* [1979] ECR 2435, [1980] 1 CMLR 370 (subsidiary of BMW attempted to prevent exports into Germany, despite advice from the parent company not to do so); *Kawasaki* OJ [1979] L 16/9, [1979] 1 CMLR 448; *National Panasonic (UK) Ltd* OJ [1982] L 354/28, [1983] 1 CMLR 497; *Johnson and Johnson* OJ [1980] L 377/16, [1981] 2 CMLR 287 (formal ban dropped, but continued in practice); *Moët et Chandon (London) Ltd* OJ [1982] L 94/7, [1982] 2 CMLR 166 (circulating a price list for sales in UK held tantamount to an export ban); *Polistil SpA* OJ [1984] L 136/9, [1984] 2 CMLR 594; *John Deere* OJ [1985] L 35/58, [1985] 2 CMLR 554; *Tipp-ex* OJ [1987] L 222/1, [1989] 4 CMLR 425, upheld on appeal Case C–279/87 *Tipp-ex GmbH v Commission* [1990] ECR I-261; *Sandoz* OJ [1987] L 222/28, [1989] 4 CMLR 628, upheld on appeal Case–277/87 *Sandoz Prodotti Farmaceutici SpA v Commission* [1990] ECR I-45; *Fisher-Price/Quaker Oats Ltd-Toyco* OJ [1988] L 49/19, [1989] 4 CMLR 553; *Konica* OJ [1988] L 78/34, [1988] 4 CMLR 848; *Viho/Toshiba* OJ [1991] L 287/39, [1992] 5 CMLR 180 (see para 20: export ban a *per se* infringement of Article 81(1)); *Newitt/Dunlop Slazenger International* OJ [1992] L 131/32, [1993] 5 CMLR 352, paras 48–50, upheld on appeal Case T-43/92 *Dunlop Slazenger International v Commission* [1994] ECR II-441: the fine on one of the addressees of the Commission's decision was annulled in Case T–38/92 *All Weather Sports Benelux BV v Commission* [1994] ECR II-211, [1995] 4 CMLR 43; *Viho/Parker Pen* OJ [1992] L 233/27, [1993] 5 CMLR 382, paras 16–19, upheld on appeal Cases T-66/92 and T-77/92 *Herlitz v Commission* and *Parker Pen v Commission* [1994] ECR II-531, [1995] 5 CMLR 458 and [1994] ECR II-549, [1995] 5 CMLR 435 (fine reduced); *Ford Agricultural* OJ [1993] L 20/1, [1995] 5 CMLR 89, para 12; *Tretorn* OJ [1994] L 378/45, [1997] 4 CMLR 860, upheld on appeal Case T-49/95 *Van Megen Sports Group NV v Commission* [1996] ECR II-1799, [1997] 4 CMLR 843; *BASF Lacke+Farben AG and Accinauto SA* OJ [1995] L 272/16, [1996] 4 CMLR 811, upheld on appeal Cases T-175/95 and T-176/95 *BASF v Commission* [1999] ECR II-1581, [2000] 4 CMLR 33 and 67; *Organon*, Commission's XXVth *Report on Competition Policy* (1995), points 37-38 and pp 142-143; *Novalliance/Systemform* OJ [1997] L 47/11, [1997] 4 CMLR 876; *Lee Cooper* Commission's XXIXth *Report on Competition Policy* (1999) p 138.

8   See eg *Kawasaki* OJ [1979] L 16/9, [1979] 1 CMLR 448; *Johnson and Johnson* OJ [1980] L 377/16, [1981] 2 CMLR 287; *John Deere* OJ [1985] L 35/58, [1985] 2 CMLR 554.

9   See eg *BMW Belgium* OJ [1978] L 46/33, [1978] 2 CMLR 126; *Hasselblad* OJ [1982] L 161/18, [1982] 2 CMLR 233.

10   OJ [1998] L 124/60, [1998] 5 CMLR 33.

fine on Volkswagen amounted to EUR 102 million, the largest penalty to have been imposed by the Commission on one undertaking for infringing the competition rules; the fine was reduced to EUR 90 million on appeal[11].

It is perhaps surprising that, even though the law on export bans has been clearly established for many years, the Commission is still able to unearth new cases. For example in 2000 it imposed a fine of EUR 43 million on *Opel* for pursuing a strategy aimed at limiting sales of Opel cars from the Netherlands to other member states[12]; a fine of EUR 60,000 on *Nathan-Bricolux* for restricting parallel sales of educational materials within and outside distributors' exclusive territories and for fixing resale prices[13]; and a fine of EUR 39.6 million on *JC Bamford Group*[14] for restrictions on sales outside allotted territories and associated practices.

An important point to bear in mind is that the Commission will take a wide view of the term 'agreement' for the purpose of establishing whether an export ban infringes Article 81(1) and, in particular, that conduct that may appear to be unilateral may be characterised as sufficiently consensual to be caught by that provision[15]; however the Commission's decision to this effect in *Bayer AG/Adalat*[16] was annulled on appeal by the CFI[17]. A further point is that it may be relatively easy to establish a concerted practice between a supplier and its distributors to divide up the common market[18].

(ii) Indirect export bans

The Commission and the Community Courts will condemn indirect measures that might have the same effect as an export ban. Indirect export bans are black listed by Article 4(b) of Regulation 2790/99, and their inclusion in an agreement would prevent the application of the block exemption to the agreement in question[19]. An example of an indirect export ban would arise if a producer provides that its guarantees are available to consumers in a particular member state only if they buy the product from a distributor in that state; this obviously acts as a strong disincentive to purchase elsewhere. In *Zanussi*[20] the Commission condemned such an arrangement, and it has taken similar action on several occasions since[1]. As a general proposition, customer guarantees should be available for products no matter where they are marketed in the common market.

---

11 Case T-62/98 *Volkswagen AG v Commission* [2000] 5 CMLR 853; the case is on appeal to the ECJ, Case C-338/00 (judgment pending).
12 OJ [2001] L 59/1, [2001] 4 CMLR 1441, on appeal Case T-368/00 *Opel Nederland BV v Commission* (judgment pending).
13 OJ [2001] L 54/1.
14 IP(00)1526; on appeal Case T-67/01 *JCB Service v Commission* (judgment pending).
15 See ch 3, pp 86-89.
16 OJ [1996] L 201/1, [1996] 5 CMLR 416.
17 Case T-41/96 [2001] 4 CMLR 126; the case is on appeal to the ECJ, Case C-3/01 (judgment pending); see ch 3, pp 88-89.
18 See in particular Cases 100–103/80 *Musique Diffusion Française SA v Commission* [1983] ECR 1825, [1983] 3 CMLR 221.
19 See pp 583-585 below.
20 OJ [1978] L 322/26, [1979] 1 CMLR 81.
1 See *Matsushita Electrical Trading Company* XIIth *Report on Competition Policy* (1982), point 77; *Ford Garantie Deutschland* XIIIth *Report on Competition Policy* (1983), points 104–106; *Fiat* XIVth *Report on Competition Policy* (1984), point 70; XVIth *Report on Competition Policy* (1986), point 56; *Sony* XVIIth *Report on Competition Policy* (1987), point 67; *Saeco* Commission's *Competition Policy Newsletter*, October 2000, p 48.

The Commission's approach was endorsed by the ECJ in *ETA Fabriques d'Ebauches v DK Investments SA*[2], in which it held that the partitioning of national markets by denying the benefit of guarantees to imported goods infringed Article 81(1). However it may be legitimate to provide that the guarantee should extend only to services that a local representative is bound to provide in accordance with local safety and technical standards[3], and it is permissible to withhold the guarantee from products sold by a dealer who is not an authorised member of a selective distribution system[4].

Another way of indirectly affecting exports is through the use of monitoring clauses in contracts, whereby a producer requires information as to the destination of its products, and by the imposition on products of serial numbers which enable their movement from one territory to another to be traced. While these practices are not objectionable in themselves, they will be condemned where they are used by a producer in order to prevent or control parallel importing[5].

Exports may be impeded in numerous other ways. Price discrimination devised to prevent exports would be caught[6]; the withdrawal of discounts previously granted to a French dealer in so far as it exported the products in question to Italy attracted fines in *Gosmé/Martell*[7]. In *Konica*[8] Konica's policy of buying up supplies of its film imported from the UK into Germany in order to protect its German distributors from cheap imports was condemned under Article 81(1): this did not prevent parallel imports in itself, but it did deprive consumers in Germany of the possibility of buying cheaper film. Restrictions on cross-supplies between distributors would be caught, as they may prevent parallel imports between Member States[9]. A requirement that coffee beans be resold only in a roasted form could affect exports: the Commission required agreements to be amended so that the beans could also be sold in their raw form[10]. Reducing supplies to a distributor in a particular territory so that there are none available for export could be caught, provided that this is done by agreement[11]. In *Bayo-*

2   Case 31/85 [1985] ECR 3933, [1986] 2 CMLR 674.
3   See *Zanussi* (n 20 above) at para 14.
4   Case C-376/92 *Metro v Cartier* [1994] ECR I-15, [1994] 5 CMLR 331, paras 32-34.
5   See eg *Victor Hasselblad AB* OJ [1982] L 161/18, [1982] 2 CMLR 233: its cameras had serial numbers on them and the Commission considered that this afforded an opportunity to Hasselblad to discover whether there had been any parallel importing; *Sperry New Holland* OJ [1985] L 376/21, [1988] 4 CMLR 306; *Newitt/Dunlop Slazenger International* OJ [1992] L 131/32, [1993] 5 CMLR 352, paras 59–60.
6   See eg *Pittsburgh Corning Europe* JO [1972] L 272/35, [1973] CMLR D2; *Kodak* JO [1970] L 147/24, [1970] CMLR D19; Case 30/78 *Distillers v Commission* [1980] ECR 2229, [1980] 3 CMLR 121; the Commission declined to grant individual exemption to a dual pricing policy in *Glaxo SmithKline*: Commission Press Release IP(01)661, 8 May 2001.
7   OJ [1991] L 185/23, [1992] 5 CMLR 586; see similarly *Newitt/Dunlop Slazenger International* OJ [1992] L 131/32, [1993] 5 CMLR 352, paras 54–57; *Ford Agricultural* OJ [1993] L 20/1, [1995] 5 CMLR 89, paras 13–14 (discounts dependent on non-export and penalties for exporting infringed Article 81(1)).
8   OJ [1988] L 78/34, [1988] 4 CMLR 848; see similarly *Newitt/Dunlop Slazenger International* OJ [1992] L 131/32, [1993] 5 CMLR 352, para 58.
9   *German Spectacle Frames* [1985] 1 CMLR 574.
10   *Colombian Coffee* OJ [1982] L 360/31, [1983] 1 CMLR 703; see similarly the 'green banana' clause in Case 27/76 *United Brands Co v Commission* [1978] ECR 207, [1978] 1 CMLR 429.
11   *Sandoz* OJ [1987] L 222/28, [1989] 4 CMLR 628, para 30, upheld on appeal Case C-277/87 *Sandoz Prodotti Farmaceutici SpA v Commission* [1990] ECR I-45; the Commission's decision in *Bayer AG/ADALAT* (p 551, n 16 above) was annulled since the CFI disagreed with the Commission's view that the reduction of supplies to Bayer's wholesalers in France and Spain was effected pursuant to an agreement; see also *Chanelle Veterinary Ltd v Pfizer Ltd (No 2)* [1999] Eu LR 723 (Irish Supreme Court): delisting not attributable to an agreement.

n-ox[12] the supply of a product for a customer's own use was held to entail an export ban contrary to Article 81(1) and in *Bayer Dental*[13] the Commission condemned a clause forbidding the resale of Bayer's dental products in a repackaged form since it regarded this as an indirect ban on exports.

In *Zera/Montedison*[14] the Commission concluded that an agreement to differentiate agrochemical products between one national market and another, with the consequence that a German distributor enjoyed absolute territorial protection, infringed Article 81(1)[15].

(G) Application of Article 81(1) to other types of vertical agreements

Paragraphs 137 to 228 of the *Guidelines* provide guidance on the application of Article 81 to eight types of vertical agreements: single branding, exclusive distribution, exclusive customer allocation, selective distribution, franchising, exclusive supply, tying and recommended and maximum resale prices. Each of these categories will be examined in this section; relevant cross-references to Regulation 2790/99, the block exemption for vertical agreements, will be provided.

(i) Single branding agreements[16]

(A) POSSIBLE DETRIMENTS TO INTER-BRAND COMPETITION. The Commission's concern, expressed in paragraphs 106 to 108 of the *Guidelines*[17] and repeated at paragraph 138, is that single branding agreements, which cause a buyer to purchase all or most of its requirements of products on a particular market from one supplier, may restrict inter-brand competition; this could happen by foreclosing access on the part of other suppliers to the market, by facilitating collusion and by limiting in-store inter-brand competition. The Commission often refers to such agreements in the *Guidelines* as non-compete obligations, since they require or have the effect of reducing competition between the supplier and its competitors by preventing customers from buying competing products.

(B) APPLICATION OF THE BLOCK EXEMPTION TO SINGLE BRANDING AGREEMENTS. The block exemption for vertical agreements will apply to single branding agreements, provided that the supplier's market share is less than 30%[18] and provided that the duration of the non-compete obligation is limited to five years or less[19]. Where the block exemption applies, it will not be necessary to consider further whether Article 81(1) is infringed or whether the requirements of Article 81(3) are satisfied; however the *Guidelines* provide guidance for those cases in which individual assessment of agreements is necessary because the block exemption is not applicable[20].

12 OJ [1990] L 21/71, [1990] 4 CMLR 930, upheld on appeal to the CFI Case T–12/90 [1991] ECR II-219, [1993] 4 CMLR 30, and to the ECJ Case C–195/91 P *Bayer v Commission* [1994] ECR I-5619.
13 OJ [1990] L 351/46, [1992] 4 CMLR 61.
14 OJ [1993] L 272/28, [1995] 5 CMLR 320.
15 Ibid, paras 96-126.
16 Guidelines, paras 138-160.
17 See pp 542-543 above.
18 See pp 578-580 below.
19 See pp 586-587 below on Article 5(a) of Regulation 2790/99.
20 *Guidelines*, para 139.

(C)   FACTORS TO BE CONSIDERED IN DETERMINING WHETHER SINGLE BRANDING AGREEMENTS INFRINGE ARTICLE 81(1).   The Commission sets out the factors that are to be considered in determining whether Article 81(1) is infringed in paragraphs 140 to 152 of the *Guidelines*. The approach taken by the Commission is an economic one, and is consistent with the many judgments of the Community Courts (not referred to in the *Guidelines*) which have held that such agreements must be assessed in their economic context in order to determine whether they have an anti-competitive effect: agreements in the single branding group do not have the *object* of restricting competition. Judgments of particular note on this issue include *Brasserie de Haecht v Wilkin*[1], *Delimitis v Henninger Bräu*[2], *BPB Industries plc v Commission*[3], and *Neste Markkinointi Oy v Yötuuli*[4]. Decisions in which the Commission has concluded that single branding agreements infringed Article 81(1) and were ineligible for exemption under Article 81(3) include *Spices*[5], *Bloemenveilingen Aalsmeer*[6] and *Langnese/Schöller*[7].

As far as Article 81(1) is concerned the market position of the supplier must be considered[8], as must the duration of the agreement[9]. The higher the market share and the longer the duration, the more likely it is that there will be a significant foreclosure of the market[10]. Paragraph 141 states that agreements on the part of non-dominant undertakings of less than a year are unlikely to infringe Article 81(1)[11]; between one and five years they may do; and agreements of more than five years would normally be caught. Dominant undertakings would have to adduce an objective justification for any agreement that imposes a non-compete obligation on customers.

Where there are parallel networks of single branding agreements, the cumulative effect of them may be to foreclose access to the market[12]; this would be unlikely where the largest supplier in the market has a market share of less than 30% and the market share of the five largest suppliers is below 50%[13]. Other relevant factors are the level of entry barriers[14], countervailing power[15] and the level of trade affected[16].

1   Case 23/67 [1967] ECR 407, [1968] CMLR 26.
2   Case C–234/89 [1991] ECR I–935, [1992] 5 CMLR 210; see Lasok 'Assessing the Economic Consequences of Restrictive Agreements: A Comment on the Delimitis Case' (1991) 12 ECLR 194; Korah 'The Judgment in *Delimitis* – A Milestone Towards a Realistic Assessment of the Effects of an Agreement – or a Damp Squib' (1993) 8 Tulane European and Civil Law Forum 17; a shorter version is to be found at (1992) 5 EIPR 167.
3   Case T–65/89 [1993] ECR II-389, [1993] 5 CMLR 32, para 66.
4   Case C-214/99 [2001] 4 CMLR 993, [2001] All ER (EC) 76.
5   OJ [1978] L 53/20, [1978] 2 CMLR 116.
6   OJ [1988] L 262/27, [1989] 4 CMLR 500.
7   OJ [1993] L 183/19, [1994] 4 CMLR 51, substantially upheld on appeal Cases T-7/93 and T-9/93 *Langnese-Iglo GmbH etc v Commission* [1995] ECR II-1533, [1995] 5 CMLR 602 and [1995] ECR II-1611, [1995] 5 CMLR 659 and Case C-279/95 P [1998] ECR I-5609, [1998] 5 CMLR 933; see also the Commission's decision on Article 81 in *Van den Bergh Foods Ltd* OJ [1998] L 246/1, [1998] 5 CMLR 530, on appeal Case T-65/98 *Van den Bergh Foods Ltd v Commission* (judgment pending): the same dispute was the subject of the Article 234 reference in Case C-344/98 *Masterfoods Ltd v HB Ice Cream Ltd* [2001] 4 CMLR 449, [2001] All ER (EC) 130.
8   *Guidelines*, para 140.
9   Ibid, para 141.
10   Ibid.
11   See Case C-214/99 *Neste Markkinointi Oy v Yötuuli* [2000] 4 CMLR 993, [2001] All ER (EC) 76, where the ECJ concluded that exclusive purchasing agreements for petrol of not more than one year's duration did not infringe Article 81(1).
12   Ibid, para 142.
13   Ibid, para 143.
14   Ibid, para 144.
15   Ibid, para 145.
16   Ibid, paras 146-149.

(D) THE APPLICATION OF ARTICLE 81(3). Article 81(3) issues are discussed in paragraphs 153 to 158 of the *Guidelines*: this is considered below[17].

(ii) Exclusive distribution agreements[18]

(A) POSSIBLE DETRIMENTS TO INTRA-BRAND COMPETITION AND TO MARKET INTEGRATION. A supplier will often grant exclusive distribution rights to a distributor for a particular territory: for example it might appoint X as the exclusive distributor for France and Y as the exclusive distributor for Germany. The supplier may also agree that it will not sell its products directly into the territories granted to X and Y. The Commission's main concern in relation to exclusive distribution agreements, expressed in paragraphs 109 and 110 of the *Guidelines* and repeated at paragraph 161, is that intra-brand competition will be reduced and that the market will be partitioned. The Commission also notes that, when most or all suppliers in a particular market adopt exclusive distribution systems, this may facilitate collusion, both at the suppliers' and the distributors' level of the market; this would entail harm to inter-brand competition.

(B) APPLICATION OF THE BLOCK EXEMPTION TO EXCLUSIVE DISTRIBUTION AGREEMENTS. The block exemption for vertical agreements will apply to exclusive distribution agreements, provided that the supplier's market share is less than 30% and provided that there are no 'hard-core' restrictions contrary to Article 4 of the Regulation[19]. In particular, there should be no restrictions on passive sales[20] to other territories; where there is a combination of exclusive distribution and selective distribution, there must be no restrictions even of active sales by retailers to end users[1], and there must be no restrictions on sales between authorised distributors[2]. The *Guidelines* provide guidance for those cases in which individual assessment of agreements is necessary because the block exemption is not applicable[3].

(C) FACTORS TO BE CONSIDERED IN DETERMINING WHETHER EXCLUSIVE DISTRIBUTION AGREEMENTS INFRINGE ARTICLE 81(1). The Commission sets out the factors that are to be considered in determining whether Article 81(1) is infringed in paragraphs 163 to 170 of the *Guidelines*. There is no reference to the judgment of the ECJ in *Société Technique Minière v Maschinenbau Ulm*[4], where the Court held that an exclusive distribution agreement does not have as its object the restriction of competition, but must be considered in its market context to determine whether it has this effect. The reason that the ECJ took a stricter line in *Consten and Grundig v Commission*[5] was that in that case the distributor, Consten, was given absolute territorial protection against parallel imports[6]: because of the single market imperative in Community competition law, absolute territorial protection almost always infringes Article 81(1) and only rarely would benefit from Article

---

17 See pp 591-592 below.
18 *Guidelines*, paras 161-177.
19 On Article 4 of Regulation 2790/99, see pp 581-586 below.
20 Ibid, Article 4(b).
1   Ibid, Article 4(c).
2   Ibid, Article 4(d).
3   *Guidelines*, para 162.
4   Case 56/65 [1966] ECR 235, [1966] CMLR 357.
5   Cases 56/64 and 58/64 [1966] ECR 299, [1966] CMLR 418.
6   See ch 3, p 100; see also the discussion of the two US cases, *Schwinn* and *Sylvania* at p 97 n 1.

81(3)[7]. It is important however to bear in mind that an exclusive distribution agreement may not infringe Article 81(1) at all where there is not the additional element of absolute territorial protection.

As far as Article 81(1) is concerned the Commission states that the market position of the supplier and its competitors is of major importance, since the loss of intra-brand competition is problematic only if inter-brand competition is limited[8]. Where there are strong competitors, the restriction of intra-brand competition will be outweighed by inter-brand competition[9], although there may be a risk of collusion where the number of competitors is 'rather small'[10]. The *Guidelines* also discuss the possibility of exclusive distribution agreements having a foreclosure effect, which is considered unlikely unless the exclusive distributor has buyer power in the downstream market[11]; the *Guidelines* also discuss the relevance of the maturity of the market[12] and of the level of trade affected[13].

(D)   THE APPLICATION OF ARTICLE 81(3).   Article 81(3) issues are discussed in paragraphs 171 to 174 of the *Guidelines*; this is considered below[14].

(iii)   *Exclusive customer allocation agreements*[15]

Exclusive customer allocation, whereby a supplier agrees to sell its products to a distributor who will resell only to a particular class of customers, is discussed in paragraphs 178 to 183 of the *Guidelines*. Exclusive customer allocation is treated in much the same way as exclusive distribution, although the Commission makes a few specific comments on this particular type of vertical restraint[16]; in particular it says that exemption is unlikely where the market share of 30% is exceeded[17].

(iv)   *Selective distribution agreements*[18]

Selective distribution agreements are often deployed by producers of branded products. The producer establishes a system in which the products can be bought and resold only by officially appointed distributors and retailers. Non-appointed dealers will not be able to obtain the products, and the appointed dealers will be told that they can resell only to other members of the system or to the final consumer[19]. The *Guidelines* state that selective distribution systems may restrict intra-brand competition, may foreclose access to the market and may facilitate collusion between suppliers and buyers[20]. In determining the application of Article 81 to selective distribution agreements, a distinction must be made between a

---

7   See ch 3, p 97.
8   *Guidelines*, para 163.
9   Ibid, para 164.
10 Ibid.
11 Ibid, paras 165 and 166.
12 Ibid, para 168.
13 Ibid, paras 169 and 170.
14 See pp 591-592 below.
15 *Guidelines*, paras 178-183.
16 Ibid, paras 179-182.
17 Ibid, para 180.
18 *Guidelines*, paras 184-198.
19 Ibid, para 184.
20 Ibid, para 185.

'purely qualitative' system and a 'quantitative' system; a purely qualitative selective distribution system will not infringe Article 81(1) at all, even though, by its very nature, it may involve the restrictions just mentioned.

(A) PURELY QUALITATIVE SELECTIVE DISTRIBUTION SYSTEMS[1]. The ECJ held in *Metro v Commission (1)*[2] that:

'the Commission was justified in recognising that selective distribution systems constituted, together with others, an aspect of competition which accords with Article 81(1), provided that resellers are chosen on the basis of objective criteria of a qualitative nature relating to the technical qualifications of the reseller and its staff and the suitability of its trading premises and that such conditions are laid down uniformly for all potential resellers and are not applied in a discriminatory fashion. It is true that in such systems of distribution price competition is not generally emphasised either as an exclusive or indeed as a principal factor ... However, although price competition is so important that it can never be eliminated it does not constitute the only effective form of competition or that to which absolute priority must in all circumstances be afforded.'[3]

The judgment of the ECJ in *Metro* confirmed that the Commission's approach in earlier decisions had been correct[4] and provided the basis for subsequent cases. The ECJ has itself repeated the *Metro* test on several occasions[5], as has the CFI[6]; the Commission has adopted further decisions and issued comfort letters or otherwise refrained from taking action in reliance on the *Metro* doctrine[7].

1   Ibid.
2   Case 26/16 [1977] ECR 1875, [1978] 2 CMLR 44.
3   Ibid, para 21.
4   The Commission had granted negative clearance to various aspects of the selective distribution networks in *Kodak* JO [1970] L 147/24, [1970] CMLR D19 and *Omega Watches* JO [1970] L 242/22, [1970] CMLR D49; individual exemption was given to other terms.
5   See eg Case 99/79 *Lancôme SA v Etos BV* [1980] ECR 2511, [1981] 2 CMLR 164, paras 20–26; Case 31/80 *L'Oreal NV v de Nieuwe AMCK* [1980] ECR 3775, [1981] 2 CMLR 235, paras 15–21; Case 126/80 *Maria Salonia v Giorgio Poidomani* [1981] ECR 1563, [1982] 1 CMLR 64; Case 210/81 *Demo-Studio Schmidt v Commission* [1983] ECR 3045, [1984] 1 CMLR 63; Case 107/82 *AEG-Telefunken v Commission* [1983] ECR 3151, [1984] 2 CMLR 325; Case 75/84 *Metro v Commission (No 2)* [1986] ECR 3021, [1987] 1 CMLR 118.
6   Case T-19/91 *Vichy v Commission* [1992] ECR II-415; Case T-19/92 *Groupement d'Achat Édouard Leclerc v Commission* [1996] ECR II-1851, [1997] 4 CMLR 995; Case T-88/92 *Groupement d'Achat Édouard Leclerc v Commission* [1996] ECR II-1961, [1997] 4 CMLR 995.
7   See *Junghans* OJ [1977] L 30/10, [1977] 1 CMLR D82; *Murat* OJ [1983] L 348/20, [1984] 1 CMLR 219; *SABA (No 2)* OJ [1983] L 376/41, [1984] 1 CMLR 676; *IBM Personal Computers* OJ [1984] L 118/24, [1984] 2 CMLR 342; *Villeroy Boch* OJ [1985] L 376/15, [1988] 4 CMLR 461; *Grundig* OJ [1985] L 233/1, [1988] 4 CMLR 865; *Yves Saint Laurent Parfums SA* OJ [1992] L 12/24, [1993] 4 CMLR 120, mostly upheld on appeal Case T-19/92 *Groupement d'Achat Édouard Leclerc v Commission* [1996] ECR II-1851, [1997] 4 CMLR 995, and given further approval in 2001, Commission Press Release IP(01)713, 17 May 2001; *Parfums Givenchy System of Selective Distribution* OJ [1992] L 236/11, [1993] 5 CMLR 579, mostly upheld on appeal Case T-88/92 *Groupement d'Achat Édouard Leclerc v Commission* [1996] ECR II-1961, [1997] 4 CMLR 995; an application by Kruidvat challenging the Commission's decision in this case was found to be inadmissible in Case T-87/92 *BVBA Kruidvat v Commission* [1996] ECR II-1931, [1997] 4 CMLR 1046, upheld on appeal Case C-70/97 P *Kruidvat v Commission* [1998] ECR I-7183, [1999] 4 CMLR 68; *Kenwood Electronics Deutschland GmbH* OJ [1993] C 67/9, [1993] 4 CMLR 389; *Schott-Zwiesel-Glaswerke* OJ [1993] C 111/4, [1993] 5 CMLR 85; *Grundig* OJ [1994] L 20/15, [1995] 4 CMLR 658; *Sony España SA* OJ [1993] C 275/3, [1994] 4 CMLR 581.

Three criteria must be satisfied for a system to be treated as purely qualitative and therefore outside Article 81(1).

First, the product in question must be of a type that necessitates selective distribution. It is only in the case of such goods that the suppression of price competition inherent in selective distribution in favour of non-price competition is objectively justifiable. It is not only complex equipment such as cars and electronic equipment that have benefited from the *Metro* doctrine. From the judgments of the Community Courts and the decisions of the Commission it is possible to identify three categories of goods that may come within it, although it should be pointed out that this is not a formal classification that they themselves have adopted. The most obvious category consists of products that are technically complex, so that specialist sales staff and a suitable after-sales service are needed. In this category may be placed cars[8], cameras[9], electronic equipment such as hi-fis[10], consumer durables[11], clocks and watches[12], and computers[13]. The second category consists of products the brand image of which is particularly important, such as perfumes and luxury cosmetic products[14], ceramic tableware[15], and gold and silver jewellery[16]. A third category is newspapers, the special characteristic of which is their extremely short shelf-life which necessitates particularly careful distribution[17]. The Commission has doubted whether plumbing fittings qualify for such treatment[18].

The second requirement for the *Metro* doctrine to apply is that the criteria by which a producer may limit the retail outlets through which its products are resold must be purely qualitative in nature, laid down uniformly for all potential resellers and applied in a non-discriminatory manner[19]. Where this is the case,

---

8   *BMW* OJ [1975] L 29/1, [1975] 1 CMLR D44; note that there is a specific block exemption for the distribution of cars, Regulation 1475/95: see pp 592-593 below.
9   *Kodak* JO [1970] L 147/24, [1970] CMLR D19.
10   *Grundig* OJ [1985] L 223/1, [1988] 4 CMLR 865 and again OJ [1994] L 20/15, [1995] 4 CMLR 658.
11   Case 107/82 *AEG-Telefunken v Commission* [1983] ECR 3151, [1984] 3 CMLR 325; it was only when AEG's system was applied in a discriminatory way that it came within Article 81(1).
12   *Omega Watches* JO [1970] L 242/22, [1970] CMLR D49; *Junghans* OJ [1977] L 30/10, [1977] 1 CMLR D82; note however that the ECJ in Case 31/85 *ETA Fabriques d'Ebauches SA v DK Investment SA* [1985] ECR 3933, [1986] 2 CMLR 674 doubted that mass-produced Swatch watches would qualify for selective distribution under the *Metro* doctrine: ibid, para 16.
13   *IBM Personal Computers* OJ [1984] L 118/24, [1984] 2 CMLR 342.
14   Case 99/79 *Lancôme SA etc v Etos BV* [1980] ECR 2511, [1981] 2 CMLR 164; Case T-19/92 *Groupement d'Achat Édouard Leclerc v Commission* [1996] ECR II-1851, [1997] 4 CMLR 995, paras 113-123; Case T-88/92 *Groupement d'Achat Édouard Leclerc v Commission* [1996] ECR II-1961, [1997] 4 CMLR 995, paras 105-117.
15   *Villeroy Boch* OJ [1985] L 376/15, [1988] 4 CMLR 461.
16   *Murat* OJ [1983] L 348/20, [1984] 1 CMLR 219.
17   See eg Case 126/80 *Maria Salonia v Giorgio Poidomani* [1981] ECR 1563, [1982] 1 CMLR 64; Case 243/83 *Binon v Agence et Messageries de la Presse* [1985] ECR 2015, [1985] 3 CMLR 800; Commission's Notice *Agence et Messageries de la Presse* OJ [1987] C 164/2; Commission's XXIXth *Report on Competition Policy* (1999) pp 161-162.
18   *Grohe* OJ [1985] L 19/17, [1988] 4 CMLR 612; *Ideal Standard* OJ [1985] L 20/38, [1988] 4 CMLR 627.
19   For an example of the discriminatory application of a purely qualititative selective distribution system, see Case 107/82 *AEG-Telefunken v Commission* [1983] ECR 3151, [1984] 3 CMLR 325, in particular at para 39; where a producer refuses to supply to certain distributors or retailers, the problem arises of whether this refusal is attributable to an agreement or concerted practice, or whether it is a unilateral act and therefore outside Article 81(1): see ch 3, pp 86-89.

any dealer that can satisfy the qualitative criteria should be able to obtain the products in question: there is no direct, quantitative, restriction on the number of dealers in the system. A producer may require that its goods be sold only to retail outlets which employ suitably trained staff, have suitable premises in an appropriate area, use a suitable shop name consistent with the status of the brand, and that provide a proper after-sales service; also a restriction on sales to non-authorised distributors and retailers is permitted, as is a restriction not to advertise products at 'cash-and-carry prices'. A problem is that it is not always obvious whether a particular requirement is 'qualitative' or not. Criteria that do not relate to the technical proficiency of outlets but extend to such matters as the holding of minimum stocks, stocking the complete range of products, the achievement of a minimum turnover or a minimum percentage of turnover[20] in the products in question and the promotion of products have sometimes been treated as quantitative, although they have often been granted individual exemption[1].

In *Vichy*[2] the Commission decided that a restriction on the sale of Vichy products except to officially appointed pharmacists was quantitative rather than qualitative, thus bringing the selective distribution system within Article 81(1); the Commission withdrew the immunity from being fined that Vichy had enjoyed as a result of notifying its agreements[3]. In *Yves Saint Laurent*[4] the Commission concluded that provisions on admission to the producer's network, a minimum annual purchase figure and obligations on the carrying of stocks, stock rotation and co-operation in advertising and promotion infringed Article 81(1). The Commission is more comfortable with selective distribution systems which contain a formal procedure for determining whether a particular undertaking qualifies for admission[5].

Selective distribution systems that are within Article 81(1), for example because they contain quantitative as well as qualitative elements, may benefit from the block exemption provided by Regulation 2790/99 provided that its conditions are satisfied[6].

The third requirement of the *Metro* doctrine is that any restrictions that are imposed on appointed distributors and retailers must go no further than is objectively necessary to protect the quality of the product in question: this is a manifestation of the doctrine of proportionality. In *Hasselblad*[7] objection was taken by the Commission to provisions which enabled the producer to exercise supervision of the advertising indulged in by distributors and retailers, as this would mean that control could be exercised over advertisements indicating cuts in prices. In *AEG-Telefunken v Commission*[8] the ECJ made clear that restrictions would not be permitted simply in order to guarantee dealers a minimum profit

---

20 T-19/92 *Groupement d'Achat Édouard Leclerc v Commission* [1996] ECR II-1851, [1997] 4 CMLR 995, paras 148-155; Case T-88/92 *Groupement d'Achat Édouard Leclerc v Commission* [1996] ECR II-1961, [1997] 4 CMLR 995, paras 141-148.

1   See eg *Parfums Givenchy* OJ [1992] L 236/11, [1993] 5 CMLR 579; *Grundig* OJ [1994] L 20/15, [1995] 4 CMLR 658.

2   OJ [1991] L 75/57, upheld on appeal Case T–19/91 [1992] ECR II-415.

3   See ch 7, p 230 on notification and immunity from fines.

4   OJ [1992] L 12/24, [1993] 4 CMLR 120.

5   See eg *Sony Pan-European Dealer Agreement (PEDA)*, Commission's XXVth *Report on Competition Policy* (1995), pp 135-136.

6   See pp 560-561 below.

7   OJ [1982] L 161/18, [1982] 2 CMLR 233.

8   Case 107/82 [1983] ECR 3151, [1984] 3 CMLR 325, para 42.

margin. In *Grohe*[9] and *Ideal Standard*[10] restrictions were imposed on plumbing wholesalers not to resell to anyone but plumbing contractors. Sale and installation of plumbing fittings are separate functions and the laws of Member States require major plumbing work to be done by official plumbers. The Commission therefore decided that this provision did involve a restriction for the purposes of Article 81(1) as it was not necessary for producers to control the quality of plumbing work; the Commission also concluded that the agreements were ineligible for exemption under Article 81(3).

(B)   SELECTIVE DISTRIBUTION SYSTEMS THAT ARE NOT PURELY QUALITATIVE.   Where a selective distribution system is not purely qualitative in the sense of the *Metro* doctrine, it may be caught by Article 81(1), although it may also benefit from the block exemption conferred by Regulation 2790/99[11] or from individual exemption[12]. In determining whether Article 81(1) is infringed, the Commission will look at the market position of the supplier and its competitors, since the loss of intra-brand competition is problematic only where inter-brand competition is weak[13]. A further issue is whether, in a particular market, there is a number of selective distribution systems in operation: where this is the case, the Commission is anxious that there may be a lack of intra-brand competition, a foreclosure of certain types of distributors and retailers and that collusion may be facilitated[14]. In *Metro v Commission (No 2)*[15] the ECJ had warned that where, in a particular market, the existence of a number of selective distribution systems leaves no room for other methods of distribution or results in a rigidity in price structure which is not balanced by other types of competition, Article 81(1) may apply after all[16].

(C)   APPLICATION OF THE BLOCK EXEMPTION TO SELECTIVE DISTRIBUTION SYSTEMS.   Selective distribution agreements may benefit from the block exemption conferred by Regulation 2790/99. To do so, the producer's market share must be below 30%[17], and the requirements of Articles 4(a), 4(c), 4(d) and 5(c)[18] must be respected. Where a selective distribution system benefits from the block exemption, but there are minimal efficiency-enhancing effects, for example because the product is not suitable for this form of distribution, the Commission may withdraw the block exemption[19]. The Commission has indicated that it would consider withdrawing the benefit of the block exemption from selective distribution systems where there is a cumulative effect problem; however it says that such a problem is unlikely to arise when the share of the market covered by selective distribution is below 50%, or where this figure is exceeded but the aggregate market share of the five largest suppliers is below 50%[20]. An individual supplier with a market

9   OJ [1985] L 19/17, [1988] 4 CMLR 612.
10   OJ [1985] L 20/38, [1988] 4 CMLR 627.
11   See pp 567-591 below.
12   See pp 591-592 below.
13   *Guidelines*, para 187.
14   Ibid, para 188.
15   Case 75/84 [1986] ECR 3021, [1987] 1 CMLR 118.
16   Ibid, paras 41 and 42; a similar argument was considered, but rejected, in T-19/92 *Groupement d'Achat Édouard Leclerc v Commission* [1996] ECR II-1851, [1997] 4 CMLR 995, paras 178-192 and in Case T-88/92 *Groupement d'Achat Édouard Leclerc v Commission* [1996] ECR II-1961, [1997] 4 CMLR 995, paras 170-184.
17   See pp 578-580 below.
18   See *Guidelines*, para 192; these provisions are explained at pp 581-587 below.
19   *Guidelines*, para 186.
20   Ibid, para 189.

share of less than 5% is unlikely to be considered as making a contribution to the cumulative effect[1].

In some systems of domestic law a selective distribution system is binding on third parties, who can be sued for unfair competition if they obtain and attempt to sell the products; in German law there is a requirement on the producer which uses such a system to ensure that it is 'impervious', that is to say that its products are kept within the system; however the imperviousness ('lückenlosigkeit') of the system is not a requirement for its validity under EC law[2].

(v) Franchising agreements[3]

(A) *PRONUPTIA V SCHILLGALIS.* The application to franchising agreements of Article 81 was explored by the ECJ in *Pronuptia de Paris v Schillgalis*[4]. Mrs Schillgalis, the franchisee for Hamburg, Oldenburg and Hanover, was in dispute with Pronuptia, the franchisor, over her royalty payments and in the course of litigation pleaded that the agreement was void as it contravened Article 81. The ECJ identified the crux of a franchise system: that it enables a franchisee to operate as an independent business whilst using the name and know-how of the franchisor. The transfer of intellectual property rights from the franchisor to the franchisee is the feature of franchises that distinguishes them from more conventional distribution systems. In a franchise, the franchisee pays a fee to the franchisor for the right to use the know-how, trade marks, designs, logos and other intellectual property rights of the franchisor. In order for the franchise system to work effectively it is essential that each franchisee should conform with the uniform commercial methods laid down by the franchisor: from the public's point of view, it is important that all franchised outlets should achieve the same standard. Therefore it is essential that the franchisor should be able to impose common standards on all franchisees. Also, as the transfer of intellectual property rights is vital to the whole exercise, it is legitimate for the franchisor to impose terms on the franchisee to protect these rights. The ECJ concluded that restrictions in these two categories, that is to maintain common standards and to protect intellectual property rights, were not within Article 81(1) at all. However restrictions that could divide the market territorially or which imposed resale price maintenance would be within Article 81(1); the former might be granted exemption under Article 81(3), though not the latter.

(B) THE POSITION OF THE COMMISSION AFTER *PRONUPTIA.* The Commission published several individual decisions after this judgment in which it was able to expand upon the main principles laid down by the ECJ. These decisions granted individual exemption to territorial restrictions, and culminated in the publication of a block

---

1 Ibid, final sentence.
2 Case C-376/92 *Metro-SB-Großmärkte GmbH v Cartier* [1994] ECR I-15, [1994] 5 CMLR 331, para 28; see also Case C-41/96 *VAG-Händlerbeirat eV v SYD-Consult* [1997] ECR I-3123, [1997] 5 CMLR 537.
3 *Guidelines*, paras 199-201.
4 Case 161/84 [1986] ECR 353, [1986] 1 CMLR 414; see Dubois 'Franchising Under EC Competition Law: Implications of the *Pronuptia* Judgment and the Proposed Block Exemption' [1986] Fordham Corporate Law Institute ch 6; Waelbroeck 'The *Pronuptia* Judgment – A Critical Appraisal' [1986] Fordham Corporate Law Institute ch 9; Venit '*Pronuptia*: Ancillary Restraints or Unholy Alliances' (1986) 11 EL Rev 213.

exemption for franchise agreements in 1988[5]. In *Pronuptia*[6] and *Yves Rocher*[7] the franchisor selected or manufactured the goods sold by the franchisee. In *Computerland*[8] the franchisee was free to acquire microcomputers wherever it wished: the subject-matter of the franchise was the distribution method supplied by Computerland. In *ServiceMaster*[9] the Commission reached a decision on a service franchise for the supply of housekeeping, cleaning and maintenance services to both commercial and domestic customers. It considered that there were strong similarities between a service franchise and the franchises relating to the distribution of goods dealt with in earlier decisions[10] and granted an individual exemption. In *Charles Jourdan*[11] the Commission granted individual exemption to a franchise system for the sale of medium and top quality shoes.

(C)   THE COMMISSION'S GUIDELINES ON FRANCHISING.   The *Guidelines* discuss franchising at paragraphs 199 to 201. Paragraph 199 describes what franchising systems typically consist of and how they work. Paragraph 200 refers to paragraphs 23 to 45, which deal specifically with the meaning of vertical agreements in the block exemption and the extent to which the licensing of intellectual property rights, including franchise agreements, are covered by it[12]. Examples of franchise agreements are given in paragraph 201.

(vi)   Exclusive supply agreements[13]

An exclusive supply agreement, as defined in Article 1(c) of the block exemption[14], is one that causes a supplier to sell its products only to one buyer within the European Community for the purposes of a specific use or resale. As such, it is an 'extreme form of limited distribution' agreement[15]. Exclusive supply agreements may benefit from the block exemption, but in such cases it is the market share of the buyer rather than the seller that must be looked at when applying the 30% market share cap[16]. Paragraphs 204 to 210 discuss the application of Article 81(1) to exclusive supply agreements that are not covered by the block exemption; paragraphs 211 and 212 consider the application of Article 81(3)[17]. In considering whether Article 81(1) applies to such agreements, the buyer's market share in its downstream market will be of particular importance: the greater its market share there, the more likely there is to be an anti-competitive effect[18]; the duration of the supply obligation will also be of

5   Regulation 4087/88, OJ [1988] L 359/46.
6   OJ [1987] L 13/39, [1989] 4 CMLR 355.
7   OJ [1987] L 8/49, [1988] 4 CMLR 592.
8   OJ [1987] L 222/12, [1989] 4 CMLR 259.
9   OJ [1988] L 332/38, [1989] 4 CMLR 581.
10   Ibid, para 6.
11   OJ [1989] L 35/31, [1989] 4 CMLR 591.
12   See pp 574-577 below.
13   Guidelines, paras 202-214.
14   See pp 568-569 below.
15   *Guidelines*, para 202.
16   See Article 3(2) of Regulation 2790/99, p 579 below, and *Guidelines*, para 203.
17   See pp 591-592 below.
18   *Guidelines*, para 204.

relevance[19]. Other matters, such as entry barriers[20], the countervailing power of suppliers[1] and the level of trade affected[2], are also discussed.

(vii)   Tying agreements[3]

A tying agreement arises where a supplier makes the supply of one product (the 'tying product') conditional upon the buyer also buying a separate product (the 'tied product'). Tying may infringe Article 82 where the supplier has a dominant position[4]; however, a vertical agreement imposing a tie may also infringe Article 81(1) where it has a 'single branding' effect in relation to the tied product[5]. Tying agreements benefit from the block exemption when the market share of the supplier on the markets both for the tying and for the tied products is below the 30% cap in Article 3(1) of Regulation 2790/99[6]. Where the market share threshold is exceeded, paragraphs 219 to 221 discuss the application of Article 81(1) to tying agreements: the market position of the supplier is the most important issue[7]; the position of its competitors and the height of the entry barriers to the market for the tying product must also be considered[8]. Tying is less likely to be problematic where customers possess buying power[9]. Paragraphs 222 to 224 consider the possibility of tying practices benefiting from the provisions in Article 81(3)[10].

(viii)   Recommended and maximum resale prices[11]

The imposition upon distributors and retailers of minimum or fixed resale prices will be held to infringe Article 81(1): such agreements are considered to have as their object the restriction of competition[12]. Furthermore, this practice amounts to a hard-core restriction contrary to Article 4(a) of the block exemption[13]; paragraph 47 of the *Guidelines* considers a range of practices that might be considered as having as their 'direct or indirect object', to use the words of Article 4, the imposition of minimum or fixed resale prices[14]. It is highly unlikely that individual exemption would be granted to minimum or fixed resale price maintenance; an exceptional case is newspapers, where the publisher imposes a cover price which is, in effect, a fixed price: the Commission sent an Article

19   Ibid, para 205.
20   Ibid, para 207.
1   Ibid, para 208.
2   Ibid, para 209.
3   *Guidelines*, paras 215-224.
4   See ch 17, pp 605-611.
5   *Guidelines*, para 215.
6   Ibid, para 218.
7   Ibid, para 219.
8   Ibid, para 220.
9.   Ibid, para 221.
10   See pp 591-592 below.
11   *Guidelines*, paras 225-228.
12   See ch 3, pp 95-98; minimum and fixed resale prices will also infringe the Chapter I prohibition in the UK Competition Act 1998: see pp 595-598 below; in the US, the maintenance of minimum resale prices has been illegal *per se* since the Supreme Court decision in *Dr Miles Medical Co v John D Park & Sons Co* 220 US 373 (1911).
13   See pp 582-583 below; see generally Iacobucci 'The Case for Prohibiting Resale Price Maintenance' (1995) 19(2) World Competition 71.
14   See p 582 below on para 47 of the *Guidelines*.

81(3) comfort letter in 1999 to Agences et Messageries de la Presse permitting this practice[15]. The Commission has condemned resale price maintenance on various occasions[16]. In *Pronuptia de Paris v Schillgalis*[17] the ECJ held that resale price maintenance in the context of a franchising network infringed Article 81(1) and was not entitled to exemption under Article 81(3); however the Court did not object to recommended prices.

Paragraphs 225 to 228 of the *Guidelines* consider the extent to which it is lawful to recommend a resale price to a distributor or retailer or to impose a *maximum* rather than a minimum price[18]. Article 4(a) of the block exemption provides that these practices are not 'hard-core' restrictions, 'provided that they do not amount to a fixed or minimum sale price as a result of pressure from, or incentives offered by, any of the parties'. Agreements containing recommendations or maximum prices would therefore be exempt, provided that the market share cap of 30% is not exceeded[19]. Where the block exemption is not applicable, the Commission states at paragraph 226 of the *Guidelines* that it will wish to consider whether recommended or maximum prices might work 'as a focal point for the resellers and might be followed by most or all of them'[20]; it will also examine whether these practices could facilitate collusion between suppliers[1]. The market power of the supplier is the most important factor to be taken into consideration[2]; the next most important issue will be the structure of the market: in particular the Commission considers that, if it is oligopolistic, there is a greater likelihood of collusion[3].

6. THE PATH TO REFORM OF THE BLOCK EXEMPTIONS[4]

It was explained above that, despite jurisprudence of the Community Courts which stated that most vertical agreements should be analysed in their economic

---

15 See the Commission's XXIXth *Report on Competition Policy* (1999) pp 161-162; the Commission's Notice in *Agence et Messageries de la Presse* OJ [1987] C 164/2 had suggested that it might countenance resale price maintenance for newspapers and periodicals.

16 See eg *Deutsche Phillips* OJ [1973] L 293/40, [1973] CMLR D241; *Gerofabriek* OJ [1977] L 16/8, [1977] 1 CMLR D35; *Hennessey/Henkel* OJ [1980] L 383/11, [1981] 1 CMLR 601 where the Commission rejected the argument that setting resale prices was justified for the protection of the product's brand image; *Novalliance/Systemform* OJ [1997] L 47/11, [1997] 4 CMLR 876; *Nathan-Bricolux* OJ [2001] L 54/1; *Volkswagen AG*, Commission Press Release IP(01)760, 30 May 2001 (fine of EUR 30.96m for retail price maintenance in Germany).

17 Case 161/84, [1986] ECR 353, [1986] 1 CMLR 414.

18 In *Albrecht v Herald Co* 390 US 145 (1968) the US Supreme Court condemned *per se* the imposition of maximum resale prices; however it has since overruled itself in *State Oil v Khan*, substituting a rule of reason approach to this particular phenomenon: 118 US 275 (1997); see Steuer '*Khan* and the Issue of Dealer Power – Overview' (1997-98) 66 Antitrust Law Journal 531; Blair and Lopatka '*Albrecht* Overruled – At Last' ibid, 537; Gimes 'Making Sense of *State Oil Co v Khan*: Vertical Maximum Price Fixing under a Rule of Reason' ibid, 567.

19 *Guidelines*, para 225.

20 Ibid, para 226.

1 Ibid.

2 Ibid, para 227.

3 Ibid, para 228.

4 Part of the text that follows is based on the author's article 'Regulation 2790/99: the Commission's "New Style" Block Exemption for Vertical Agreements' (2000) 37 CML Rev 887; see also Schaub 'Vertical Restraints: Key Points and Issues under the New EC Block Exemption Regulation' [2000] Fordham Corporate Law Institute (ed Hawk, not yet published); Subiotto and Amato 'Preliminary Analysis of the Commission's Reform Concerning Vertical Restraints' (2000) 23(2) World Competition 5.

context to determine whether they have the effect of restricting competition, the Commission over many years tended to adopt a formalistic approach to the application of Article 81(1); as a result, it was necessary for many agreements to be brought within the 'safe haven' of one of the Commission's block exemptions. It adopted Regulation 1983/83 for exclusive distribution agreements[5], Regulation 1984/83 for exclusive purchasing agreements[6] and Regulation 4087/88 for franchise agreements[7]. However, these Regulations were themselves too formalistic (insufficiently economics-oriented) in their approach; and many vertical agreements were not covered at all. The criticism of the case law and the decisional practice of the Commission in relation to vertical agreements increased throughout the 1980s and 1990s, both as to its over-application of Article 81(1) and the content of the block exemptions. The drumbeat of the calls for reform became ever louder. An important contribution was made at the Fordham Corporate Law Institute in 1995, when a senior economist within DG COMP, David Deacon, acknowledged that it was necessary to rethink the application of Article 81 to vertical agreements[8]. Professor Barry Hawk wrote an article in which he described a systemic failure in the treatment of vertical agreements under Article 81 necessitating radical reform[9]. The Commission responded, first with its *Green Paper on Vertical Restraints in EC Competition Policy*[10] suggesting a range of possible options for reform. More concrete proposals were set out in the Commission's *Follow-up to the Green Paper on Vertical Restraints*[11]. In this document, the Commission concluded that a more economics-based approach to vertical agreements was required. One broad 'umbrella' block exemption would be adopted for all vertical agreements in both the goods and services sector (with the exception of the distribution of motor cars). A market-share test would be adopted; and there would be only a 'black-list' approach, to say what agreements were not block exempted, without a corresponding 'white-list' approach stating what could be block-exempted: this would avoid the 'strait-jacketing' effect of the old Regulations and simplify the rules. Proposals for two new Council Regulations that would have to be adopted to pave the way for the new régime were published in 1998[12].

The new Regulation was adopted on 22 December 1999[13] and entered fully into force on 1 June 2000. The *Guidelines* were approved by the Commission on 24 May 2000 and were published in the Official Journal in October[14]. A simplified version of the *Guidelines* will be produced for business in due course. The Commission's Press Release issued at the time of the approval of the *Guidelines* states that they will be revised after a period of four years[15]; this commitment was made pursuant to a recommendation of the European Parliament.

5   OJ [1983] L 173/1.
6   OJ [1983] L 173/5.
7   OJ [1988] L 359/46; Regulation 1475/95 (OJ [1995] L 145/25) on the distribution of motor cars is unaffected by Regulation 2790/99, and is the subject of a separate review: see pp 592-593 below.
8   Deacon 'Vertical Restraints under EU Competition Law: New Directions' [1995] Fordham Corporate Law Institute (ed Hawk) p 307.
9   'System Failure: Vertical Restraints and EC Competition Law' (1995) 32 CML Review 973.
10 COM(96) 721 final, [1997] 4 CMLR 519; see the Commission's XXVIth *Report on Competition Policy* (1996), points 46-50.
11 26 November 1998, OJ [1998] C 365/3, [1999] 4 CMLR 281; see the Commission's XXVIIIth *Report on Competition Policy* (1998), points 34-53.
12 COM(1998) 546 final, 30 September 1998; see pp 566-567 below.
13 OJ [1999] L 336/21, [2000] 4 CMLR 398.
14 *Guidelines on Vertical Restraints* OJ [2000] C 291/1, [2000] 5 CMLR 1074; see also the Commission's Press Release accompanying the *Guidelines*, IP/00/520, 24 May 2000.
15 Ibid.

In order to prepare for the new régime, significant changes to two old pieces of legislation were required. Council Regulations 1215/99[16] and 1216/99[17] amend Council Regulation 19/65 of 2 March 1965[18] and Council Regulation 17/62 of 6 February 1962[19]. The new Council Regulations entered into force on 13 June 1999.

(A)   Council Regulation 1215/99

This Regulation extends the legislative powers granted to the Commission by Regulation 19/65. That Regulation enabled the Commission to grant block exemption, *inter alia*, to bilateral exclusive supply and exclusive purchase agreements for the resale of goods. On the basis of the wider powers conferred on the Commission by the Council's amendment of Regulation 19/65, the Commission was enabled to adopt a much broader block exemption regulation covering all vertical agreements affecting finished or intermediate goods and services, including vertical agreements concluded by associations of retailers. Regulation 1215/99 also provided the *vires* for the Commission to omit a 'white-list' of permitted provisions from the new block exemption, and to adopt a regulation declaring that the block exemption will not apply to agreements where parallel networks cover more than 50% of a relevant market[20]; and for a Member State to withdraw the block exemption from agreements having detrimental effects in its territory[1].

(B)   Council Regulation 1216/99

The second Regulation makes an important procedural change in relation to the notification of agreements for individual exemption. As a general proposition an agreement can be granted an individual exemption only where it has been notified to the Commission pursuant to Article 4(1) of Regulation 17/62[2]. However, there has always been a narrow exception to this rule, for agreements of the kind described in Article 4(2) thereof. Fearful that the new Regulation might cause a spate of precautionary notifications, particularly because of the inclusion of a market share cap for application of the block exemption and the uncertainty that this might entail, the Commission proposed that the Council should broaden the scope of application of Article 4(2) of Regulation 17/62, exempting all vertical agreements from the requirement that they be notified prior to individual exemption; the Council obliged by adopting Regulation 1216/99. The practical advantage of this amendment is that the Commission will in future, even in the event of late notification or no notification at all, be able to adopt an exemption decision taking effect from the date on which the agreement was concluded,

---

16 Council Regulation (EC) No 1215/1999 amending Regulation no 19/65/EEC on the application of Article 81(3) of the Treaty to certain categories of agreements and concerted practices OJ [1999] L 148/1.
17 Council Regulation (EC) No 1216/1999 amending Regulation no 17: first Regulation implementing Articles 81 and 82 of the Treaty OJ [1999] L 148/5.
18 JO [1965] 533, OJ Sp Ed [1965-66] 35.
19 JO [1962] 204/62, [1962] OJ Sp Ed 87.
20 See Article 8 of Regulation 2790/99: pp 589-590 below.
1   See Article 7 of Regulation 2790/99: pp 587-588 below.
2   See ch 4, p 137.

rather than from the date it was notified. The Commission stresses the importance of this amendment at paragraphs 63 to 65 of its *Guidelines*. An important practical question that arises is whether Regulation 1216/99 is retrospective in effect. That is to say, does the right to seek individual exemption for a vertical agreement in the absence of notification apply only in relation to agreements entered into after Regulation 1216/99 entered into force, on 13 June 1999? Or does this right apply to any vertical agreement, whenever it was entered into? Regulation 1216/99 itself is silent on this point. There is a general principle of non-retroactivity in Community law[3], which would suggest that Regulation 1216/99 could not have retrospective effect. However, (a) the policy of the Regulation is to limit the number of notifications to the Commission; (b) it would be of immense benefit to the parties to any vertical agreement to be able to argue for exemption regardless of notification; except that (c) a party seeking to *avoid* a contractual obligation might seek to differ by arguing that it was unenforceable because of the failure to notify: but how meritorious is that person? There seems to be much to be said for retroactivity, and semantically this works: Regulation 1216/99 amends the words of Regulation 17/62 without any temporal adjustment, so that the amended Article 4(2) reads that the requirement to notify agreements set out in Article 4(1) does not apply to vertical agreements; Article 4(1) refers simply to the notification of agreements entered into after the entry into force of 'this Regulation', meaning Regulation 17/62. It is understood that the Commission's view is that Regulation 1216/99 has retroactive effect.

The effect of Regulation 1216/99 will be that a party to an agreement seeking to avoid a contractual obligation will not be able to argue that it is unenforceable solely on the ground that is was not notified. This is not to say that firms *cannot* notify, only that they *need not* notify in order to claim exemption. In the event that the proposals in the Commission's White Paper on Modernisation[4] are implemented, however, this part of the new system will cease to have effect, since notification for individual exemptions will be abandoned altogether.

7. VERTICAL AGREEMENTS: REGULATION 2790/99

The Commission adopted the block exemption on Vertical Agreements and Concerted Practices on 22 December 1999[5]. The Regulation entered into force on 1 January 2000, and the block exemption conferred by it applies with effect from 1 June 2000[6]. The existing block exemptions for exclusive distribution, exclusive purchasing and franchising agreements were prolonged until 31 May 2000 by virtue of Article 12(1) of the new Regulation: Article 12(1) was made effective from 1 January 2000[7]. Article 12(2) provides transitional relief for existing agreements which were in force on 31 May 2000 and which satisfy one of the three existing regulations but not the new one: they will be exempt until 31

---

3   See Hartley, *The Foundations of European Community Law* (Oxford, 4th ed, 1998), pp 143-5.
4   See ch 4, pp 146-147 and ch 7, pp 246-258.
5   Regulation 2790/99 OJ [1999] L 336/21, [2000] 4 CMLR 398; see the Commission's XXIXth *Report on Competition Policy* (1999) points 8-19.
6   Regulation 2790/99, Article 13.
7   Article 13, proviso to the second indent.

December 2001. The new Regulation is without prejudice to the application of Article 82[8].

The Regulation consists of 17 recitals and 13 articles. Article 1 defines certain key terms such as 'competing undertakings', 'non-compete obligation' and 'exclusive supply obligation'. The most important terms of all in the Regulation – 'vertical agreements' and 'vertical restraints' – are defined in Article 2. Article 2 is the provision that actually confers block exemption upon certain vertical agreements pursuant to Article 81(3) of the Treaty; Article 3 imposes a market share cap of 30%. Article 4 sets out the 'black list' of provisions that will prevent the block exemption from applying to an agreement. Article 5 sets out a list of obligations that will not be exempt if they are contained in an agreement: it is important to note however that the inclusion of Article 5 obligations does not prevent the block exemption from applying to the remainder of the agreement.

Articles 6 and 7 provide respectively for the possibility of the Commission or the competent authority of a Member State to withdraw the benefit of the block exemption in certain circumstances. Article 8 gives the power to the Commission by regulation to disapply the block exemption to vertical agreements containing specific restraints in a relevant market more than 50% of which is covered by parallel networks of similar vertical restraints. Articles 9 and 10 contain provisions on the calculation of market share and turnover. Article 11 brings 'connected undertakings' into account when applying the Regulation. Articles 12 and 13, as already noted, deal with entry into force of the Regulation and transitional matters.

(A)   Article 1: definitions

Article 1 contains important definitions. These will be explained below, in the specific context in which they are used in the Regulation. Two particular definitions merit a brief explanation at this stage. First, the term 'non-compete obligation'. It is important when applying Article 5, which limits the permissible maximum duration of such provisions[9]. Article 1(b) provides that 'non-compete obligation' means an obligation not to manufacture, purchase, sell or resell goods or services which compete with the contract goods or services: this is what most people would understand by this expression. However, Article 1(b) goes on to provide that the term also includes any obligation on the buyer to purchase from the supplier or from an undertaking designated by the supplier more than 80%[10] of the buyer's total purchases of the contract goods or services and their substitutes on the relevant market, calculated on the basis of the value of its purchases in the preceding year. The Commission's concern is not just that a 100% requirements contract could foreclose access to the market, but that lesser commitments of 'more than 80%' also might do so.

The second definition meriting a brief mention is 'exclusive supply obligation' in Article 1(c). This term is important when applying Article 3(2), which establishes a market share cap for application of the block exemption[11]. Normally, the

---

8   See Recital 16; on the relationship between Article 81(3) exemption and Article 82 abuse, see ch 4, pp 133-134.
9   See pp 586-587 below.
10   A literal interpretation would mean that an obligation to purchase 80% of the buyer's total purchases would not amount to a non-compete obligation, but that an obligation to purchase 81% would, since only the latter applies to 'more than 80%'.
11   See pp 578-580 below.

market share of the *supplier* is the measure to be used; however, where there is an exclusive supply obligation in the sense of Article 1(c), the market share is that of the buyer[12]. 'Exclusive supply obligation' means an obligation causing the supplier to sell the goods or services specified in the contract only to one buyer inside the Community for the purposes of a specific use or resale.

(B)   Article 2: scope of the block exemption

Article 2(1): block exemption for vertical agreements[13]

Article 2(1) confers block exemption on certain vertical agreements pursuant to Article 81(3) of the Treaty. It provides that, subject to the provisions of the Regulation, Article 81(1) shall not apply:

> 'to agreements or concerted practices entered into between two or more undertakings each of which operates, for the purposes of the agreement, at a different level of the production or distribution chain, and relating to the conditions under which the parties may purchase, sell or resell certain goods or services ("vertical agreements")[14].
>
>   This exemption shall apply to the extent that such agreements contain restrictions of competition falling within the scope of Article 81(1) ("vertical restraints")'.

Several points should be noted about Article 2(1).

(i)   Many vertical agreements do not infringe Article 81(1)

It is worth repeating that many vertical agreements do not infringe Article 81(1)[15]; where an agreement does not infringe Article 81(1), it follows that, no matter how generous and flexible the new Regulation is, it will not be necessary to bring the agreement in question within its terms. Despite this, however, many advisers will endeavour to satisfy the block exemption, which provides a 'safe haven' for many vertical agreements: as explained earlier, most firms will have no interest in knowing whether their agreement infringes Article 81(1) if they know that they benefit from exemption under Article 81(3) anyway[16]. The Commission itself, at paragraph 62 of the *Guidelines*, states that vertical agreements falling outside the block exemption will not be presumed to be illegal but may need individual examination, and that in such cases the burden would be on the Commission to show that the agreement violates Article 81(1); in the case of such a violation, the parties could argue that the conditions of Article 81(3) are satisfied. In the same paragraph the Commission encourages

---

12   The term 'buyer' is itself defined in Article 1(g) to include an undertaking which, under an agreement falling within Article 81(1), sells goods or services on behalf of another undertaking.

13   Guidelines, paras 23-25.

14   The UK has adopted a definition of 'vertical agreements' closely modelled on Articles 2(1) and 2(3) of the new Regulation in The Competition Act 1998 (Land and Vertical Restraints Exclusion) Order 2000 SI 2000/310, which excludes most vertical agreements from the Chapter I prohibition of the Competition Act 1998: see pp 595-598 below.

15   See pp 546-564 above.

16   See pp 546-547 above.

undertakings to do their own assessment of whether the agreement infringes Article 81(1) and/or satisfies Article 81(3) without notification: this is consistent with its White Paper proposals[17]. An example of a vertical agreement not infringing Article 81(1) would be a selective distribution system that satisfies the *Metro* doctrine[18]; only to the extent that it does not satisfy that doctrine – for example because the product is not of the type to which the doctrine applies[19] or because quantitative as well as qualitative criteria are applied[20] – is it necessary to have resort to the block exemption.

(ii)   If it is not forbidden, it is permitted

A second point to stress about the Regulation is that, in relation to a vertical agreement as defined in Article 2, if the Regulation does not prohibit something, it is permitted. This is the consequence of not having a 'white list', stating what must be included, but only a 'black list', stating what must not be in it, and is an essential feature of the 'new style' block exemption. For example, Regulation 1983/83 applied only to an agreement 'whereby one party agrees with the other to supply certain goods for resale within the whole or a defined area of the common market only to that other'[1]. Block exemption is available under the new Regulation to all vertical agreements, as defined, subject to Articles 2(2), 2(4) and (5) on agreements made by associations of retailers, agreements between competing undertakings and agreements subject to other block exemptions, Article 3 on market share, and to Articles 4 and 5 which deal with particular vertical restraints that the Commission has concerns about. It also follows from the fact that if something is not forbidden it is permitted, that there is no need for the new Regulation to exempt 'less restrictive provisions', as, for example, in the case of Article 2(3) of Regulation 240/96 on technology transfer agreements[2]. Any vertical restraint in the sense of Article 2(1) is exempt, subject to the provisions of Articles 2 to 5, without needing to be specifically authorised by a provision of that nature.

(iii)   The definition of a vertical agreement is taken from Regulation 1215/99

The definition of a vertical agreement is identical to Council Regulation 1215/99. As mentioned above, it was necessary to broaden the *vires* of the Commission in order to enable it to adopt the new Regulation, and specifically to enable agreements concerning intermediate (non-finished) goods and services to be included. Subject to Articles 2(2), 2(4) and (5), 3, 4 and 5, block exemption is conferred on all vertical agreements, whether or not they relate to the supply of goods or services, and irrespective of whether goods are supplied for resale or for use. This means that countless numbers of agreements that would never have been eligible for block exemption under the old Regulations can now benefit.

---

17   See p 567 above.
18   See pp 556-561 above.
19   See eg *Grohe* OJ [1985] L 19/17, [1988] 4 CMLR 612; note that, where it *is* necessary to apply the Regulation to a selective distribution system, the definition of this term in Article 1(d) does not bring into account the nature of the product; this consideration is relevant only to the question of whether the system falls outside Article 81(1) altogether.
20   See pp 558-559 above.
1   Regulation 1983/83, Article 1.
2   See ch 19, p 693.

The Regulation is much broader in scope than its predecessors, which applied only to exclusive distribution, exclusive purchasing or franchising agreements, as defined in the relevant block exemption.

(iv)   The exempted agreement may be multilateral

Article 2(1) confers block exemption on agreements between two *or more* undertakings: the old Regulations applied only to bilateral agreements. The position in Article 2(1) of the new Regulation is possible as a result of the extension of the Commission's *vires* by Council Regulation 1215/99. However, the Regulation applies only where each of the undertakings operates, for the purposes of the agreement, at a different level of the market. Some illustrations may help:

Agreement 1

Supplier

Exclusive wholesaler in UK   Exclusive wholesaler in France

(a) The agreement is trilateral
(b) The supplier supplies goods to each wholesaler
(c) It is agreed that neither wholesaler will sell into the other's territory
The agreement is not vertical, since there are two parties, the wholesalers, at the same level of the production and distribution chain.

Agreement 2

Supplier

Wholesaler

Retailer

(a) The agreement is trilateral
(b) The agreement sets out the mutual rights and obligations of each party
    The agreement is vertical, since each party operates at a different level of the production and distribution chain.
    Where the agreement is in the form of Agreement 2, both the supplier's and the wholesaler's market share would have to be considered for the purpose of the market share cap in Article 3(1)[3].

3   *Guidelines*, para 93.

(v)   'For the purposes of the agreement'

The definition of a vertical agreement refers to undertakings which operate, '*for the purposes of the agreement*, at a different level of the production or distribution chain' (emphasis added). It follows that the fact that two firms that are both manufacturers enter into an agreement does not in itself mean that the agreement is horizontal rather than vertical. If a manufacturer of a chemical were to supply the chemical to another chemical manufacturer, the relationship would still be vertical since, for the purposes of that agreement, each undertaking would be operating at a different level of the market. The expression 'for the purposes of the agreement' is essential to this analysis, since, without it, it would not be possible to say that the two chemical companies operate 'at a different level of the production or distribution chain'. However, Article 2(4) of the Regulation guards against the risk that vertical agreements as defined could be used as a cloak for horizontal restrictions by denying block exemption to certain agreements between actually or potentially competing undertakings[4].

(vi)   Agreements with final consumers would not normally be vertical agreements

Agreements entered into with final consumers would not normally be vertical agreements, since they would not be entered into 'between two or more undertakings': a final consumer in the sense of a member of the public buying goods or services would not be carrying on an economic activity[5]. For the same reason, however, such agreements would not infringe Article 81(1) in the first place, and therefore would not need to be exempted.

(vii)   'Relating to the conditions under which the parties may purchase, sell or resell certain goods or services'

To qualify as a vertical agreement, it must relate to the conditions under which the parties may purchase, sell or resell certain goods or services. It appears, therefore, that rental and leasing agreements would not be covered[6]; nor would bartering agreements. Provisions in vertical agreements which do not themselves relate to purchase, sale or resale would not be covered: an example would be a covenant not to compete in research and development[7].

(viii)   Interconnection agreements

In many industries, undertakings require access to an infrastructure owned by someone else in order to be able to operate on the market: for example in telecommunications, service providers may need access to the wires and cables of the main telecommunications company; in electricity, access will be needed

---

4   See pp 577-578 below.
5   *Guidelines*, para 24: on the meaning of the term 'undertaking' see ch 3, pp 66-71; however, the supplier would be an undertaking, and would infringe Article 82 if it acted in an abusive manner and if the other terms of that provision were satisfied: on Article 82 generally, see ch 5.
6   *Guidelines*, para 25.
7   *Guidelines*, para 20.

to the national grid. Where access is provided, there will be an 'interconnection agreement' between the owner of the infrastructure and the service provider. It would seem that such an agreement would be vertical in the sense of Article 2(1), since it would relate to the 'conditions under which the parties may purchase, sell or resell … services'[8]. However, in many (most?) such cases, the owner of the infrastructure would have a market share in excess of 30%, so that Article 3(1) of the Regulation would prevent the application of the block exemption[9].

(ix) Agency

Many agency agreements fall outside Article 81(1); paragraphs 12 to 20 of the *Guidelines* deal with this[10]. However, those paragraphs suggest that some agency agreements could fall within Article 81(1), if they are 'non-genuine', if they could foreclose access to the market or if they might facilitate explicit or tacit collusion. It is necessary to consider whether an agency agreement that does fall within Article 81(1) would be eligible for block exemption. In such a situation the agent is operating at a different level of the market from the principal in the sense of Article 2(1) of the Regulation. Therefore, to the extent that the agreement relates to the conditions under which the principal or the agent may purchase, sell or resell goods or services, the Regulation would apply. Paragraph 13 of the *Guidelines* specifically states that the Regulation is capable of application to 'non-genuine' agency agreements. In such cases, it will be necessary to avoid the hard-core restrictions listed in Article 4[11]; paragraph 48 of the *Guidelines* states that an obligation on a non-genuine agent preventing it from sharing its commission with its customers would be a 'hard-core' restriction under Article 4(a). Also it will be necessary to avoid non-compete provisions of the kind set out in Article 5[12].

Article 2(2): associations of retailers[13]

A common business phenomenon is that small retailers establish an association for the purchase of goods, which they then resell to final consumers[14]. This is necessary to enable the retailers to achieve some bargaining power in their dealings with large manufacturers and/or intermediaries. Consumers will benefit if the retailers are enabled to obtain lower prices which are transmitted on to them. Article 2(2) provides that *vertical* agreements entered into between such an association and (a) its suppliers or (b) its members[15] can benefit from block exemption, provided that all its members are retailers of goods and provided that no individual member of the association, together with its connected

---

8   Note however that the agreement would not be vertical in so far as it is a rental or leasing arrangement: see p 572 above.

9   Where the infrastructure is an essential facility, Article 82 may be applicable to issues of access and pricing: see ch 17, pp 611-624.

10 See pp 538-540 above.

11 On Article 4 generally, see pp 581-586 below.

12 On Article 5 generally, see pp 586-587 below.

13 *Guidelines*, paras 28 and 29.

14 See ch 15, pp 521-522.

15 In the case of an agreement between an association and its members, it is the association's market share that is relevant for the purpose of Article 3(1): *Guidelines*, para 89.

undertakings[16], has a total turnover in excess of EUR 50 million[17]. The Regulation does not define the term retailer, but paragraph 28 of the *Guidelines* says that '[r]etailers are distributors reselling goods to final consumers'[18]. The concluding words of Article 2(2) provide that the block exemption for such vertical agreements is without prejudice to the application of Article 81(1) to the horizontal agreement between the members of the association and to any recommendations of the trade association itself[19]. Paragraph 29 of the *Guidelines* states that it becomes relevant to assess the vertical agreements only if the assessment of the horizontal agreement is 'positive' (meaning presumably that it does not infringe Article 81(1)). There is no legal basis for this view in Article 2(2) of the Regulation.

Article 2(3): ancillary provisions in relation to intellectual property rights[20]

Article 2(3) deals with the important question of the extent to which vertical agreements which contain provisions on intellectual property rights can benefit from the new block exemption. The first sentence of Article 2(3) provides that the exemption shall apply to vertical agreements:

> 'containing provisions which relate to the assignment to the buyer or use by the buyer of intellectual property rights[1], provided that those provisions do not constitute the primary object of such agreements and are directly related to the use, sale or resale of goods or services by the buyer or its customers'.

Essentially, the policy is that Regulation 2790/99 will apply where any provisions relating to intellectual property rights are ancillary to the main purpose of the vertical agreement[2]; although the Regulation itself does not use the term, it is helpful to call such provisions 'IPR provisions'. The policy of Article 2(3) is simple to state; however the actual application of Article 2(3) is not without its difficulties. A number of points should be noted: the five headings used below are based upon paragraph 30 of the Commission's *Guidelines*.

---

16 Articles 10 and 11 deal with the calculation of turnover and with connected undertakings.
17 The final sentence of para 28 of the *Guidelines* states that where only a limited number of the members of the association have a turnover not significantly exceeding EUR 50 million, 'this will not normally change the assessment under Article 81'; the meaning of this is opaque: if this is intended to mean that the block exemption would still be applicable, it does not provide any legal justification for this view.
18 It presumably follows that if the association purchases for its own use, as for example a group of National Health hospitals in the UK, Article 2(2) would not be applicable since the group does not purchase in order to *sell* to final consumers.
19 On such agreements see ch 15, pp 521-522.
20 *Guidelines*, paras 30-44.
1   Intellectual property rights are defined in Article 1(e) to include 'industrial property rights, copyright and neighbouring rights'.
2   Although the term 'ancillary' does not feature in Article 2(3) itself, recital 3 states that the Regulation 'includes vertical agreements containing ancillary provisions on the assignment of intellectual property rights'.

(i)   Article 2(3) is applicable only where there is a vertical agreement

First, for Article 2(3) to apply to the IPR provisions – that is to say if they are to benefit from block exemption – there must be a vertical agreement; Article 2(1) defines this as an agreement relating to the conditions under which the parties may purchase, sell or resell goods or services. It follows that 'pure' licences – for example of know-how or of a trade mark – would not be covered, since they would not relate to the conditions under which the parties purchase, sell or resell of goods: rather, they would authorise the use of the know-how or of the trade mark. Pure know-how licences, however, would be able to benefit from Regulation 240/96[3] on transfer of technology agreements[4]. Paragraph 32 of the *Guidelines* gives five examples of agreements that would not benefit from block exemption: these are the provision of a recipe for the production of a drink under licence; the production and distribution of copies from a mould or master copy; a pure licence of a trade mark or sign for the purposes of merchandising; sponsorship contracts[5]; and copyright licensing such as broadcasting contracts concerning the right to record and/or the right to broadcast an event.

(ii)   The IPR provisions must be for the use of the buyer

Secondly, Article 2(3) applies only where the supplier supplies IPRs to the buyer; it does not apply where the buyer supplies IPRs to the supplier. It follows that a sub-contracting agreement, whereby one undertaking asks another to manufacture goods on its behalf, often with the use of the its IPRs, would not be covered by the block exemption[6], since the IPR is supplied by the buyer to the supplier, rather than the other way around. However, many sub-contracting agreements do not infringe Article 81(1) at all, so that block exemption is unnecessary[7]; and the *Guidelines* state that where the buyer simply provides specifications to the supplier as to the goods or services to be supplied, the block exemption remains applicable[8]: in that case, there are no IPR provisions, and Article 2(3) is irrelevant.

(iii)   The IPR provisions must not be the object of the agreement

Thirdly, for Article 2(3) to apply the IPR provisions must not be the 'primary' object of the agreement: in the language of the *Guidelines*, '[t]he primary object must be the purchase or distribution of goods or services and the IPR provisions must serve the implementation of the vertical agreement'[9].

---

3   OJ [1996] L 31/2.
4   See ch 19, pp 688-696.
5   On sponsorship contracts, see *Danish Tennis Federation Commission's* OJ [1996] C 138/6, [1996] 4 CMLR 885, Commission's XXVIIIth *Report on Competition Policy* (1998) p 160 (comfort letter issued).
6   *Guidelines*, para 33.
7   See the Commission's *Notice on Subcontracting Agreements* OJ [1979] C 1/2, discussed at pp 593-594 below.
8   *Guidelines*, para 33.
9   *Guidelines*, para 34.

(iv)   The IPR provisions must be directly related to the use, sale or resale of goods or services by the buyer or its customers

A trade mark licence to a distributor is generally necessary for and ancillary to the distribution of goods or services, so that an exclusive licence would benefit from the block exemption, provided that it satisfies the other rules in the Regulation[10]. A sale of hard copies of software, where the reseller does not acquire a licence to any rights over the software, is to be regarded as an agreement for the supply of goods for resale[11]. Paragraphs 42 to 44 of the *Guidelines* examine the application of the Regulation to franchise agreements. These were formerly afforded block exemption by Regulation 4087/88[12], but they are no longer subject to a separate régime: instead they are subject to the same rules as other vertical agreements. The Commission's view is that the Regulation is capable in principle of application to franchise agreements, other than industrial franchise agreements: the latter would be subject, if at all, to Regulation 240/96 on technology transfer agreements[13]. Paragraph 43 of the *Guidelines* states that most franchise agreements would be covered by Article 2(3), since the IPR provisions in them are directly related to the use, sale or resale of goods or services by the franchisee. It adds that, where a franchise agreement 'only or primarily concerns licensing of IPRs', it would not be covered by the block exemption, but 'it will be treated in a similar way'. This presumably means that the Commission's analysis would follow the principles of the block exemption, and that individual exemption could be presumed for the agreement where the franchisor's market share is less than 30%[14], provided that the agreement does not contain any 'black listed' provisions as set out in Article 4. Where the franchisor franchises a business method, it is the market share on the market where the business method is to be exploited that must be determined for the purpose of the market share cap in Article 3[15]. It should be noted that the relaxation of the rules on notification for individual exemption in Regulation 17/62 also applies to bilateral agreements involving only restrictions on the exercise of intellectual property rights[16].

Paragraph 44 of the *Guidelines* sets out a series of typical IPR-related obligations that are found in franchise agreements and which, if restrictive of competition, would be regarded as ancillary and therefore would benefit from block exemption. These are obligations on the franchisee:

(a)   not to engage, directly or indirectly, in any similar business;
(b)   not to acquire financial interests in competing undertakings;
(c)   not to disclose secret know-how to third parties;
(d)   to grant a non-exclusive licence to the franchisor of know-how obtained from exploitation of the franchise;
(e)   to assist the franchisor in action to protect the IPRs;
(f)   only to use the franchisor's know-how for the purpose of the franchise;
(g)   not to assign the rights and obligations under the franchise agreement without the consent of the franchisor.

10   *Guidelines*, para 38.
11   *Guidelines*, para 40; this would cover the sale of software subject to a 'shrink-wrap' licence, the conditions in which the end user accepts by opening the package.
12   OJ [1988] L 359/46.
13   The Commission notes the difference between industrial franchise and non-industrial franchise agreements at para 42 of the *Guidelines*; Regulation 240/96 is dealt with in ch 19, pp 688-696.
14   See pp 578-580 below on the market share cap in Article 3.
15   *Guidelines*, para 95.
16   Article 4(2) of Council Regulation 17/62, as amended.

(v) The IPR provisions must not have an illegitimate object or effect[17]

The final sentence of Article 2(3) provides that the IPR provisions will be exempt only in so far as they 'do not contain restrictions of competition having the same object or effect as vertical restraints which are not exempted under this Regulation'. Thus it is not possible to avoid the provisions of Articles 4 and 5 of the Regulation (see below) by attaching the vertical restraints which they seek to prevent to the IPR provisions rather than to the vertical agreement itself.

Article 2(3) should also be understood in conjunction with Article 2(5), which prevents the application of the new Regulation where another block exemption is applicable (below).

Article 2(4): agreements between competing undertakings[18]

Article 2(4) provides that the block exemption does not apply to vertical agreements entered into between competing undertakings; this applies to agreements at any level of the market: for example the undertakings may be competing as manufacturers, wholesalers or as retailers.

The definition of competing undertakings refers to 'actual or potential suppliers in the same product market'. Paragraph 26 of the *Guidelines* states that the definition applies irrespective of whether the undertakings are competitors on the same geographic market. The same paragraph goes on to consider what is meant by 'potential suppliers'. This refers to undertakings that could and would be likely to respond to a small and permanent increase in relative prices: such undertakings 'would be able and likely to undertake the necessary additional investments within one year' and so could enter the market. The Commission adds that this assessment must be 'realistic', not 'theoretical'[19]. The Guideline does *not* state that the potential suppliers' response must have been triggered by a price rise by 'competing undertakings', but presumably this is what the spirit of Article 1(a) is envisaging.

Non-reciprocal vertical agreements between competing undertakings are permitted subject to conditions. Article 2(4) allows a non-reciprocal vertical agreement between competing undertakings where:

- the buyer has a total annual turnover not exceeding EUR 100 million[20]; or
- the supplier is a manufacturer and a distributor of goods, whilst the buyer is a distributor not manufacturing goods competing with the contract goods[1]. In this case the manufacturer conducts its own distribution, but also appoints other distributors which are, according to the definition in Article 1(a), 'competing undertakings'. Paragraph 27 of the *Guidelines* describes this phenomenon as 'dual distribution'. There is no turnover restriction in this situation; or
- the supplier is a provider of services at several levels of trade, whilst the buyer does not provide competing services at the level of trade where it

17 *Guidelines*, para 36.
18 *Guidelines*, paras 26 and 27.
19 The Commission also refers in the *Guidelines* to paras 20-24 of its *Notice on Market Definition* (OJ [1997] C 372/5, [1998] 4 CMLR 177), to point 55 of its XIIIth *Report on Competition Policy* (1983) and to its decision in *Elopak/Metal Box-Odin* (OJ [1990] L 209/15); see further ch 3, pp 102-103 and ch 15, pp 501-502.
20 See Articles 10 and 11 on the calculation of turnover and on connected undertakings.
1 At para 27 of the *Guidelines*, the Commission states that an 'own-brand' retailer would not be treated as a manufacturer for this purpose.

purchases the contract services. This is the analogue of the previous situation, adjusted for the purposes of an agreement in the services sector. Again there is no turnover restriction.

Article 2(5): agreements within the scope of another block exemption[2]

Article 2(5) of the Regulation provides that 'This Regulation shall not apply to vertical agreements *the subject matter of which* falls within the scope of any other block exemption regulation' (emphasis added). The italicised words are important: Article 2(5) does not say that the Regulation shall not apply to an agreement which is exempt under another regulation; rather, it says that it does not apply to agreements which, generically, are of a kind covered by another regulation. Thus, car distribution agreements will be block exempted, if at all, by virtue of Regulation 1475/95[3]; technology transfer agreements by Regulation 240/96[4]; and the vertical aspects of specialisation and R&D agreements by Regulations 2658/00[5] and 2659/00[6] respectively. If an agreement fails to satisfy the criteria for exemption in any of these Regulations, Article 2(5) prevents the agreement from being exempted by Regulation 2790/99. Article 2(5) would also prevent Regulation 2790/99 from applying to any agreement within the scope of any future block exemption[7].

(C)   Article 3: the market share cap[8]

(i)   Why a market share test?

One of the key features of the Regulation is the inclusion of a market share cap: a manifestation of the 'economics-oriented approach' that the Commission wished to adopt in the new régime. At the time that Regulation 240/96 was adopted, the Commission proposed a market share cap, but the idea was widely criticised and eventually dropped. Concerns were expressed at the uncertainty that a market share test would entail, in particular because of the inherent difficulty in assessing how the relevant market should be defined. However, a market share test has now been included in the new Regulation. There are various explanations for this. First, the revolt against the over-application of Article 81(1) to vertical agreements stems, *inter alia*, from the proposition that such agreements are detrimental to competition only if the parties to them possess market power. If market power is at the heart of sensible analysis of such agreements (whether under Article 81(1) or 81(3)), the Commission can hardly be criticised for using a principled, economics-based approach in order to escape from the discredited and formalistic Regulations of the past. Secondly, understanding of market definition on the part of advisors and their clients has developed enormously in

---

2   *Guidelines*, para 45.
3   OJ [1995] L 145/25; see pp 592-593 below.
4   OJ [1997] L 31/2; see ch 19, pp 688-696.
5   OJ [2000] L 304/3, [2001] 4 CMLR 800; see ch 15, pp 517-520.
6   OJ [2000] L 304/7, [2001] 4 CMLR 803: see ch 15, pp 510-515.
7   The Commission specifically says this in para 45 of the *Guidelines*.
8   Section V of the *Guidelines* deals with market definition and market share calculation issues.

recent years[9]. The market share cap is now part of the law, and it is inconceivable that it will be jettisoned in the foreseeable future. This will mean that there will be cases in national courts where the application of the block exemption – and therefore the enforceability of an agreement – will turn on the particular market definition.

Recitals 8 and 9 of the Regulation discuss market share. Recital 8 says that it can be presumed that where the market share of the supplier or buyer[10] is below 30% an improvement in production of distribution will follow from which consumers will derive a fair share of the benefit, unless the agreement contains a severe anti-competitive restraint, in which case Article 4 would prevent the agreement from being block exempted; however Recital 9 states that the same presumption cannot be made where the market share exceeds 30%.

(ii)　What market share?

Of course it is possible to argue about what the market share cap should be. At one point the Commission suggested that certain restraints might be permitted where the market share was 40% or less, but that others, which could give rise to greater concern, only where the market share was below 20%. This proposal, which would have given rise to unnecessary complexity, was dropped in favour of a compromise market share cap of 30%. A market share cap of 40% would have come close to saying that only vertical restraints, other than the hard-core restrictions set out in Article 4, imposed by dominant undertakings are problematic: perhaps it is not surprising that the Commission was unwilling to diminish the rôle of Article 81 to this extent. The inclusion of a market share cap in the new Regulation means that many undertakings which benefited from block exemption under the old Regulations, and whose share of particular markets exceeds 30%, will be ineligible for block exemption under the new Regulation.

(iii)　Whose market share?

Article 3(1) provides that it is the market share of the supplier that is to be taken into account in determining whether an agreement benefits from block exemption. Article 3(2) provides the only exception to this: in the case of an exclusive supply obligation as defined in Article 1(c) of the Regulation, it is the buyer's market share that is relevant. The term 'exclusive supply' has been discussed above[11]: it covers only the situation where there is 'one supplier inside the Community for the purposes of a specific use or resale'. Therefore, where a US company appoints one distributor for the UK and Ireland and another for the rest of the Community, there is not an exclusive supply obligation, so that it is the US supplier's market share that is relevant. Where the supplier appoints one undertaking for the entire Community, it is the latter's. In that case, the market is determined from the buyer's perspective: that is to say, it is its share of the *purchase* market (goods or services purchased from suppliers) that is calculated; not the buyer's share of the market on which it sells[12].

9　On market definition generally see ch 1, pp 22-39.
10　See below on the relevance of the buyer's market share.
11　See pp 568-569.
12　*Guidelines*, para 82, following, eg, the Commission's decision under the EC Merger Regulation in Case No IV/M.1221 *Rewe/Meinl* OJ [1999] L 274/1, [2000] 5 CMLR 256.

(iv)   The Guidelines

Paragraph 21 of the *Guidelines* rehearses the provisions of Article 3. Paragraph 22 goes on to note that an agreement between a supplier and a buyer could have an effect on markets downstream of the buyer; however, the Commission says that this is unlikely where the market share of the supplier or buyer is less than 30%, and adds that the block exemption looks only at the market shares of the parties to the agreement itself: to look further downstream in the market would introduce a complexity into the Regulation which should be avoided. Paragraph 22 concludes by noting that, in the event that a vertical agreement causes problems in related markets, there is the possibility of withdrawing the benefit of the block exemption under Article 6[13]. Paragraph 65 of the *Guidelines* provides that, where undertakings do not notify an agreement because they assume in good faith that the market share threshold of the block exemption was not exceeded, the Commission will not impose fines. Paragraphs 68 and 69 of the *Guidelines* deal with the situation where a supplier supplies a portfolio of products, in relation to some of which the market share cap is exceeded and others it is not: the Commission states that the block exemption will not apply to the former but will apply to the latter; in relation to the latter, there is no presumption of illegality, and the Commission will consider whether any infringement of Article 81(1) could be resolved by alterations to the existing distribution system. If not, some other form of distribution will have to be adopted.

Section V of the *Guidelines* (paragraphs 88 to 99) discuss various issues concerning market share in more detail. Paragraph 91 examines issues concerning the supplier's market share and paragraph 92 the buyer's; paragraph 93 deals with the position where there are more than two parties to the agreement[14]. Paragraph 94 discusses the position of OEM suppliers; and paragraph 95 deals with market shares in the context of franchising agreements. Paragraph 96 considers market definition in the case of individual assessment of agreements rather than the application of the block exemption; and paragraphs 97 to 99 deal specifically with the calculation of market share under the Regulation.

(v)   Council Regulation 1216/99

There will, of course, be circumstances in which undertakings are unclear whether their agreement might be denied block exemption because of the market share cap. This is where Council Regulation 1216/99 is so important: to the extent that an individual exemption would be needed, it is not necessary to have notified the agreement to the Commission. The amendment to Article 4(2) of Council Regulation 17/62 means that the Commission can grant exemption retrospectively to a vertical agreement whether notified or not. In the absence of this amendment, there was a risk that the Commission might have been deluged with notifications: having experienced such a deluge in 1962, the Commission wisely acted to avoid a repeat inundation. Paragraphs 63 to 65 of the *Guidelines* specifically point out that, as a consequence of the amendment of Regulation 17/62, there is no need for firms to make precautionary notifications. The comfort provided by Regulation 1216/99 will, however, disappear if the Commission's White Paper proposals on the abolition of notifications are implemented[15].

---

13 See p 588 below.
14 See p 571 above.
15 See ch 4, pp 146-147 and ch 7, pp 246-258.

(vi) Article 8

It is worth noting in passing that the Regulation has a further market share test in Article 8, albeit one that will have only rare application. This provides that the Commission may withdraw the benefit of block exemption where 50% of a relevant market is covered by a network of similar vertical agreements. This is dealt with below[16].

(D) Article 4: hard-core restrictions[17]

Recital 10 of the Regulation states that vertical agreements 'containing certain types of severely anti-competitive restrictions such as minimum and resale prices, as well as certain types of territorial protection, should be excluded from the benefit of the block exemption'. Even hard-core restrictions might, as a matter of law, fall outside Article 81(1) where they could not have an appreciable effect on competition or on inter-state trade[18]. However the Commission's *Notice on Agreements of Minor Importance*[19] provides that, even below the 10% threshold, it cannot be ruled out that vertical agreements that have as their object or effect to fix resale prices or to confer territorial protection on the undertakings or third undertakings might infringe Article 81(1): the point is repeated in paragraph 10 of the *Guidelines*.

Article 4 contains the list of 'hard-core' restrictions which lead to the exclusion of the entire vertical agreement – not just the provision in question – from the block exemption. The Commission states specifically at paragraph 66 of the *Guidelines* that there is no severability for hard-core restrictions. Paragraph 46 of the *Guidelines* adds that individual exemption of vertical agreements containing such restrictions is unlikely. Article 4 is to be contrasted with Article 5, which denies block exemption to certain specific obligations, but which does not deprive the rest of the agreement of the benefit of the block exemption[20]. Each of the hard-core restrictions in Article 4 relates to a restriction of intra-brand competition, although the Commission's view is that in some cases restrictions of intra-brand competition can affect inter-brand competition by facilitating explicit or tacit collusion. Restrictions of inter-brand competition, or situations in which inter-brand competition is weak, are specifically dealt with in other parts of the Regulation, for example Article 2(4) (agreements between competing undertakings); Article 3 (market share cap); Article 5 (specific treatment of non-compete provisions); and Articles 6, 7 and 8 (withdrawal of the block exemption).

Article 4 provides that block exemption will not be available to agreements which 'directly or indirectly, in isolation or in combination with other factors under the control of the parties, have as their object' the matters dealt with below, such as resale price maintenance and excessive territorial protection. It is worth dwelling for a few moments on these opening words of Article 4 before looking at the specific hard-core restrictions themselves. Article 4 denies block exemption to agreements that have as their *object* one of the prohibited provisions: it might have said agreements that have as their object or *effect*, reflecting the wording of Article 81(1) of the Treaty, but it does not do so. The word 'object' in

---

16 See pp 589-590.
17 See *Guidelines*, paras 46-56.
18 Case 5/69 *Völk v Vervaecke* [1969] ECR 295, [1969] CMLR 273; Case C-306/96 *Javico v Yves Saint Laurent* [1998] ECR I-1983, [1998] 5 CMLR 172; see ch 3, p 109.
19 OJ [1997] C 372/13, [1998] 4 CMLR 192.
20 See pp 586-587 below.

Article 4 of the Regulation, and in Article 8(1) of the Treaty, does not refer to the subjective intention of the parties; rather to the aim of the agreement judged by objective standards[1]. The *Guidelines* are silent on this point. Notwithstanding that Article 4 applies only according to the object, and not the effect, of an agreement, it will prevent the block exemption from applying where the agreement 'directly or indirectly, in isolation or in combination with other factors', has one of the prohibited objects: in other words, even without the use of the word 'effect', the scope of the exclusion of the block exemption is quite extensive.

(i)   Article 4(a): resale price maintenance[2]

Block exemption will not be available where the object of the agreement is:

> '(a) the restriction of the buyer's ability to determine its sale price, without prejudice to the possibility of the supplier's imposing a maximum sale price or recommending a sale price, provided that they do not amount to a fixed or minimum sale price as a result of pressure from, or incentives offered by, any of the parties'.

This formulation explicitly recognises that the imposition of maximum[3] sale prices and the recommendation[4] of prices is permitted; this, however, is subject to the proviso that follows, which itself must be read in conjunction with the words 'directly or indirectly' in the opening part of Article 4. Paragraph 47 of the *Guidelines* picks up on the idea that the agreement may have the direct *or indirect* object of resale price maintenance. A contractual restriction establishing a minimum price would be a simple example of an agreement, the *direct* object of which is to fix prices. Paragraph 47 gives examples of price maintenance through indirect means: 'fixing the distribution margin, fixing the maximum level of discount the distributor can grant from a prescribed price level, making the grant of rebates or reimbursement of promotional costs by the supplier subject to the observance of a given price level, linking the prescribed resale price to the resale prices of competitors, threats, intimidation, warnings, penalties, delay or suspension of deliveries or contract terminations in relation to the observance of a certain price level'. Measures taken to identify price-cutting distributors might also amount to 'indirect pressure' to fix prices; paragraph 47 suggests that printing a recommended resale price or an obligation to apply a most favoured customer clause[5] would reduce the incentive to cut price and so could be within the mischief of Article 4. The paragraph acknowledges that the recommendation of prices is not, in itself, a hard-core restriction.

In the case of agency agreements, Article 81(1) would normally not be applicable[6]. However, where an agency agreement does fall within Article 81(1), paragraph 48 of the *Guidelines* states that a restriction on the agent preventing

1   See ch 3, pp 92-93.
2   See *Guidelines*, paras 47 and 48 and pp 563-564 above.
3   The ECJ has never ruled on the imposition of maximum prices; for the position in the US, see *State Oil v Khan* 118 US 275 (1997), p 564, n 18 above.
4   The ECJ held in Case 161/84 *Pronuptia de Paris v Pronuptia de Paris Irmgard Schillgalis* [1986] ECR 353, [1986] 1 CMLR 414 that the recommendation of prices would not, in itself, infringe Article 81(1).
5   A most-favoured customer clause is 'white-listed' in Article 2 of Regulation 240/96: see ch 19, p 693.
6   See pp 538-540 below.

or restricting the sharing of commission, whether fixed or variable, would amount to a hard-core restriction. The agent should be left free to lower the effective price paid by the customer without reducing the income for the principal[7].

(ii) Article 4(b): territorial and customer restrictions[8]

This important provision deals with the extent to which it is possible to grant territorial or customer exclusivity. To some extent it reflects Article 2(2)(c) of Regulation of 1983/83, which permitted a restriction on a reseller not to pursue an active sales policy outside its territory, but which did not permit a ban on passive sales. However, Article 4(b) is more complex than Article 2(2)(c), and the *Guidelines* on it are quite detailed; *inter alia* they deal with the active/ passive sales distinction in the case of e-commerce.

The opening words of Article 4(b) provide that the block exemption will not be available where the object of the agreement is:

'the restriction of the territory into which, or of the customers to whom, the buyer may sell the contract goods or services.'

Paragraph 49 of the *Guidelines* picks up on the 'direct/indirect object' dichotomy in the opening words of Article 4. Indirect measures to restrict the buyer could include 'refusal or reduction of bonuses or discounts, refusal to supply, reduction of supplied volumes or limitation of supplied volumes to the demand within the allocated territory or customer group, threat of contract termination or profit pass-over obligations.' The withholding of a guarantee service could also amount to indirect means. These practices would be more likely to be considered indirect measures to restrict the buyer's freedom when operated in conjunction with a monitoring system for detecting parallel imports and exports. Clearly this paragraph is based on the Commission's experience, upheld by the Community courts, in a series of decisions over many years[9].

Paragraph 49 of the *Guidelines* concludes by explaining two restrictions on buyers that would *not* be regarded as hard-core under Article 4(b): a prohibition on resale except to certain end users for which there is an objective justification, for example, on grounds of health or safety[10], and an obligation on the reseller relating to the display of the supplier's brand names[11].

Four exceptions to the basic prohibition in Article 4(b) are set out; the first is particularly important, since it deals with the distinction between active and passive sales.

Exception 1: it is permissible to have a restriction 'of active sales into the exclusive territory or to an exclusive customer group reserved to the supplier or allocated by the supplier to another buyer, where such a restriction does not limit sales by the customers of the buyer.'

---

7   See Case 311/85 *Vereniging van Vlaamse Reisbureaus v Sociale Dienst van de Plaatselijke en Gewestelijke Overheidsdiensten* [1987] ECR 3801, [1989] 4 CMLR 213.
8   *Guidelines*, paras 49-52.
9   See pp 550-553 above.
10 See eg *Kathon/Biocide* OJ [1984] C 59/6, [1984] 1 CMLR 476.
11 This is presumably based on Case 161/84 *Pronuptia de Paris v Pronuptia de Paris Irmgard Schillgalis* [1986] ECR 353, [1986] 1 CMLR 414.

The first point to note here is that a restriction of active sales to another group of customers is permitted: this was not exempted under Regulation 1983/83[12]. This is a welcome relaxation of the old law. The second point is that, although a restriction of active sales to other territories or customers is permitted, there must remain the possibility of passive sales to them. This is not stated specifically in the Regulation; it is stated explicitly, however, in paragraph 50 of the *Guidelines*. Thirdly, the restriction must be on active sales into the territory or customer group 'reserved to the supplier or allocated by the supplier to another buyer'. It seems, therefore, that the supplier *must* exclusively reserve a territory or customer group to itself or allocate it to another buyer in order to be able to impose an active sales ban: one can expect a reservation to the supplier or an allocation to another buyer to become a standard form clause for all distribution agreements[13]. It is apparently not possible to restrict active sales into an area reserved to a licensee of know-how or of a patent, although no explanation is given of why this should be so.

Paragraph 50 of the *Guidelines* deals with the distinction between active and passive sales. Active selling includes establishing a warehouse or distribution outlet in another's exclusive territory. As to passive selling, paragraph 50 says that 'General advertising or promotion in media or on the Internet' but which is a reasonable way to reach customers in other territories or customer groups would normally be regarded as passive rather than active selling. Paragraph 51 deals specifically with the Internet.[13a] It begins by stating that every distributor must be free to use the Internet to advertise or to sell products, and that in general Internet selling is not regarded as active selling, since it is a reasonable way to reach every customer. The paragraph specifically states that the language used on the website would not normally affect the view that sales made as a result of advertising on the Internet are 'passive' sales. An English producer advertising on its website in the German language is not regarded as actively seeking the business of German customers in Germany: intuition might suggest the opposite. The sending of unsolicited e-mails would be regarded as active selling. The supplier is allowed to impose quality standards on the reseller as to the content of the Internet site itself. Paragraph 51 concludes by stating that an outright ban on Internet selling would be possible only if there is an objective justification (no examples are given), and that the supplier cannot reserve to itself sales and/or advertising over the Internet.

Exception 2: it is permissible to have a restriction of sales – both active and passive – to end users by a buyer operating at the wholesale level of trade.

Exception 3: it is permissible to have a restriction on sales – both active and passive – to unauthorised distributors by members of a selective distribution system. This term is defined in Article 1(d) to mean a system where the supplier agrees to supply the contract goods or services only to distributors selected on the basis of specified criteria and those distributors agree not to sell to unauthorised distributors. It should be noted that this definition of a selective distribution system in the Regulation is not limited by reference to the nature of the goods or

---

12 Article 1 of Regulation 1983/83 exempted only agreements conferring exclusive territories, not customer groups.

13 Article 10(12) of Regulation 240/96 define the 'territory of the licensor' as 'territories in which the licensor has not granted any licences...', a negative formulation; the new Regulation requires a reservation or allocation.

13a See further on Internet sales *Yves Saint Laurent*, Commission Press Release IP(01)713, 17 May 2001; *Sammelrevers* Commission Press Release IP(01) 1035, 19 July 2001.

services in question; nor does it specify that the criteria should be qualitative rather than quantitative.

Exception 4: it is possible to restrict the buyer of components for use from selling them – both actively and passively – to a customer who would use them to manufacture goods that would compete with those of the supplier.

(iii) Article 4(c): the restriction of active or passive sales to end users by members of a selective distribution system operating at the retail level of trade[14]

As noted above, the third exception of Article 4(b) permits the restriction of sales by members of a selective distribution system to unauthorised distributors. However, Article 4(c) prevents the application of the block exception when there are restrictions on active or passive sales by selected distributors at the retail level of trade to end users. Paragraph 53 of the *Guidelines* says that the end users may be a professional buyer or a final consumer. However, there is a proviso to Article 4(c), which is that the distributor may be prohibited from operating out of an unauthorised place of establishment: without this proviso, the distributor would not be complying with the 'specified criteria' that make the system selective, and would effectively be operating as an unauthorised distributor[15].

Paragraph 53 of the *Guidelines* makes an important point which is not explicit in the Regulation itself: that selective distribution may be combined with exclusive distribution, provided that active or passive selling is not restricted. The supplier can commit to supply only one dealer or certain dealers in a given territory. The combination of selective and exclusive distribution was not possible under Regulation 1983/83[16]; uniquely it was permitted for cars by Regulation 1475/95[17]. However, under the new Regulation, as stated above[18], all vertical agreements are exempted unless the Regulation says otherwise. A selective distribution system that restricts the number of distributors that the supplier sells to, and which limits the authorised distributors by reference to specified criteria, is block exempted provided that:

- the agreement is a vertical agreement (Article 2(1));
- the supplier's market share is 30% or less (Article 3(1));
- resale prices are not fixed (Article 4(a));
- there are no restrictions on active or passive sales to end users (Article 4(c));
- there are no restrictions on cross-supplies between authorised distributors (Article 4(d)); and
- further, Article 5(c) prohibits group boycotts by members of a selective distribution system[19].

(iv) Article 4(d): restrictions on cross-supplies within a selective distribution system[20]

Article 4(d) prevents the application of the block exemption where there is a restriction of cross-supplies between distributors within a selective distribution

14 *Guidelines*, paras 53-54.
15 On this point, see para 54 of the *Guidelines*.
16 OJ [1983] L 173/1.
17 OJ [1983] L 173/5.
18 See p 570.
19 See pp 587-588 below.
20 *Guidelines*, para 55.

system, including distributors at different levels of the market. Thus it is not possible to require a selected retailer to purchase solely from one source: it must be able to buy from any approved distributor[1].

(v)   Article 4(e): restrictions on the supplier's ability to supply components to third parties[2]

Article 4(e) prevents the application of the block exemption where a restriction is agreed between a supplier and a buyer of components that the supplier will not sell the components as spare parts to end-users or to repairers or service-providers not entrusted by the buyer with the repair or servicing of its goods. End-users and independent services-providers should be free to obtain spare parts; but the buyer can insist that repairers and service-providers within its system should buy the spare-parts only from him[3].

(E)   Article 5: obligations in vertical agreements that are not exempt[4]

Recital 11 of the Regulation states that certain conditions are attached to the block exemption in order to ensure 'access to or to prevent collusion on the relevant market'. Where an agreement contains an obligation of the kind set out in Article 5, that obligation does not benefit from block exemption: this is true whether the supplier's market share is above or below the market share cap. However, as paragraph 57 of the *Guidelines* states, the block exemption continues to apply to the remaining parts of the vertical agreement if they are 'severable' from the non-exempted obligation. Neither the Regulation nor the *Guidelines* discuss the notion of 'severability' for the purpose of Article 5[5]. Paragraph 66 repeats that the benefit of the block exemption is lost only in relation to that part of the vertical agreement which does not comply with the conditions set out in Article 5.
  Article 5 contains three exclusions.

(i)   Article 5(a): non-compete obligations[6]

Article 5(a) excludes from the block exemption 'any direct or indirect non-compete obligation, the duration of which is indefinite or exceeds five years'. The definition of a non-compete obligation was discussed above[7]. An agreement which is 'tacitly renewable' is treated as having an indefinite duration. Paragraph 58 of the *Guidelines* states that an agreement which requires the explicit consent of both parties for renewal beyond five years is permissible; however there must be no obstacles that prevent the buyer from effectively terminating at the end of five years should it so wish. Longer periods are block exempted when the contract

---

1   Ibid.
2   *Guidelines*, para 56.
3   Ibid.
4   *Guidelines*, paras 57-61.
5   Whether a contractual obligation is 'severable' for the purpose of Article 81(2) is a matter for the applicable law of the contract: see ch 8, pp 268-269.
6   *Guidelines*, paras 58-59.
7   See p 568 above.

goods or services are sold from land and premises owned by the supplier or leased from third parties: paragraph 49 of the *Guidelines* states that 'artificial ownership constructions' to take advantage of this extension will not be permitted. These 'longer periods' mean that beer and petrol agreements in 'tied' houses and garages will be permissible for longer than five years; but the sector-specific rules in Titles II and III of Regulation 1984/83 are discontinued: such agreements are now dealt with under the new 'umbrella' Regulation[8].

There have been many cases in the English courts in which the validity of beer ties has been considered[9].

(ii) Article 5(b): post-term non-compete obligations[10]

Article 5(b) excludes from the block exemption obligations, after termination of the agreement, not to manufacture, purchase, sell or resell goods or services. However a limited derogation from this provision allows, for a period of not more than one year, a post-term ban on sales of competing goods or services from the point of sale at which the buyer operated during the contract period which is necessary to protect know-how transferred from the supplier to the buyer. Know-how for this purpose is defined in Article 1(f) of the Regulation, and must result from 'experience and testing by the supplier': this requirement is not included in the definition of know-how in Article 10(1) of Regulation 240/96.

(iii) Article 5(c): competing products in a selective distribution system[11]

Article 5(c) excludes from the block exemption an obligation causing the members of a selective distribution system not to sell the brands of particular competing suppliers. It is permissible, subject to Article 5(a), to require a selective distributor not to handle competing brands in general; however, Article 5(c) prevents the exemption from applying where there is a boycott of particular competing suppliers. As paragraph 51 of the *Guidelines* explains, this is to prevent the exclusion of 'a specific competitor or certain specific competitors'.

---

8   For individual exemptions granted by the Commission in recent years to beer-tie agreements, see *Whitbread* OJ [1999] L 88/26, [1999] 5 CMLR 118; *Bass* OJ [1999] L 186/1, [1999] 5 CMLR 782; *Scottish & Newcastle* OJ [1999] L 186/28, [1999] 5 CMLR 831, on appeal to the CFI, Case T-131/99 *Hamilton Shaw v Commission* (judgment pending); in *Roberts/ Greene King* the Commission concluded that the beer-supply agreements of Greene King did not contribute to the foreclosure of the UK market because of the weak position of Greene King in the market: Commission press release IP(98)967; the Commission's finding that Article 81(1) was not infringed was upheld in Case T-25/99 *Roberts v Commission* (judgment of 5 July 2001); negative clearance was also given to the standard agreements of The Grand Pub Company in *Inntrepreneur and Spring* OJ [2000] L 195/49.
9   See eg *Holleran v Thwaites* [1989] 2 CMLR 917; *Inntrepreneur Estates (GL) Ltd v Boyes* [1993] 2 EGLR 112; *Little v Courage Ltd* (1994) 70 P & CR 469; *Star Rider Ltd v Inntrepreneur Pub Co* [1998] 1 EGLR 53; *Greenall Management Ltd v Canavan (No 2)* [1998] Eu LR 507; *Gibbs Mew plc v Gemmell* [1998] Eu LR 588; *Trent Taverns Ltd v Sykes* [1998] Eu LR 492; *Passmore v Morland* [1999] Eu LR 501; *Crehan v Courage* [1999] Eu LR 409; the *Crehan* case has been referred to the ECJ under Article 234 EC Case C-453/99, and Advocate General Mischo delivered his opinion in this case of 22 March 2001.
10   *Guidelines*, para 60.
11   *Guidelines*, para 61.

(F)   Article 6: withdrawal of the block exemption by the Commission[12]

Recitals 12 and 13 of the Regulation introduce the idea that the Commission may in certain circumstances withdraw the benefit of the block exemption[13]. Recital 12 states that normally the market share cap in conjunction with the other provisions of the Regulation mean that most agreements to which it applies would not substantially eliminate competition; Recital 13 however provides that the Commission may withdraw the benefit of the Regulation, in particular where the buyer has significant market power in the relevant market in which it resells the goods or provides the services or where parallel networks of vertical agreements have similar effects which significantly restrict access to a relevant market or competition therein. The Recital notes that these cumulative effects may arise in particular in the case of selective distribution networks and non-compete obligations.

Article 6 provides that the Commission may withdraw the benefit of the block exemption where it finds in any particular case that vertical agreements to which the Regulation applies have effects which are incompatible with the conditions laid down in Article 81(3), 'and in particular where access to the relevant market or competition therein is significantly restricted by the cumulative effect[14] of parallel networks of similar vertical restraints implemented by competing suppliers or buyers'. Paragraph 73 of the *Guidelines* gives a further example of a situation where withdrawal might be considered: where the buyer has significant market power in a downstream market. Article 6 should be distinguished from Article 8 (below), where the block exemption may be withdrawn from all vertical agreements in a particular relevant market; under Article 6, the block exemption is withdrawn 'in any particular case ...' from the agreements having effects incompatible with Article 81(3). Paragraphs 71 to 75 of Part IV of the *Guidelines* deal with the withdrawal procedure under Article 6. Paragraph 71 says that the Commission may withdraw the benefit of the block exemption 'to establish an infringement of Article 81(1)'; at paragraph 81, which deals with the procedure in an Article 8 case, the Commission goes further and says that a withdrawal under Article 6 'implies the adoption of a decision establishing an infringement under Article 81 by an individual company'. Paragraph 72 states that the Commission would have the burden of proving that Article 81(1) is infringed and that the agreement does not fulfil the conditions of Article 81(3). Paragraph 75 states that a withdrawal can have only an *ex nunc* effect, so that exemption will persist until the time of the withdrawal.

(G)   Article 7: withdrawal of the block exemption by a Member State[15]

Recital 14 introduces the idea of the competent authorities of the Members States withdrawing the block exemption, made possible as a result of the amendment

---

12 *Guidelines*, paras 71-75.
13 See *Langnese* OJ [1993] L 183/19 where the Commission withdrew the benefit of Regulation 1984/83 from exclusive purchasing agreements in the German market for impulse ice-cream; the Commission's decision was upheld on appeal in Case T-7/93 *Langnese-Iglo v Commission* [1995] ECR II-1533, [1995] 5 CMLR 602; this is understood to be the only occasion on which the Commission has withdrawn the benefit of a block exemption.
14 Responsibility for such an effect can be attributed only to those undertakings which make an appreciable contribution to it: *Guidelines*, para 63, applying the ECJ's judgment in Case C-234/89 *Delimitis v Henninger Bräu* [1991] ECR I-935, [1992] 5 CMLR 210; see ch 3, pp 98-99 and 553-554 above.
15 *Guidelines*, paras 76-79.

to Regulation 19/65 effected by Regulation 1215/99[16]. Article 7 provides that this may be done where vertical agreements to which the Regulation applies have effects incompatible with the conditions laid down in Article 81(3) 'in the territory of a Member State, or in part thereof, which has all the characteristics of a distinct geographic market'[17]; Article 7 concludes that withdrawal may be made 'under the same conditions as provided in Article 6'[18]. It may be that a particular Member State will not provide powers to its competent authority to effect such a withdrawal, in which case paragraph 76 of the *Guidelines* provides that the Member States may ask the Commission to initiate proceedings to this effect[19]. Paragraph 77 provides that, where the geographic market is wider than a Member State, the Commission has the sole power to withdraw the block exemption. In other cases, the power is concurrent, and some cases will 'lend themselves to decentralised enforcement by national competition authorities'. However the Commission concludes the paragraph by saying that it reserves the right to take on cases that display a particular Community interest, for example because they raise a new point of law. National decisions will have effect only within the Member State concerned (paragraph 78) and must not prejudice the uniform application of Community competition law[20].

(H) Article 8: disapplication of the block exemption by Commission Regulation[1]

Recital 15 of the Regulation introduces the idea of the Commission disapplying the block exemption from agreements in a given market. Article 8(1) provides that, pursuant to the amended Article 1a of Regulation 19/65, the Commission may by regulation declare that, where parallel networks of similar vertical restraints cover more than 50% of a relevant market, the block exemption shall not apply to vertical agreements containing specific restraints in that market. Article 8(2) provides that such a regulation shall not become applicable earlier than six months following its adoption: as paragraph 86 of the *Guidelines* says, time may be needed for the undertakings concerned to adapt their agreements. Article 8 is a novel feature in Community block exemptions. The Commission discusses the 'disapplication' of the new Regulation in paragraphs 80 to 87 of Part IV of the *Guidelines*. As it explains in paragraph 80, a regulation under Article 8 removes the benefit of the block exemption and restores the full application of Article 81(1) and (3). It would have to decide how to proceed in relation to any individual agreements, and might take a decision in an individual case in order to provide guidance to undertakings in the market generally. The Commission may in some cases have a choice of whether it wishes to proceed

---

16 See p 566 above.
17 The wording is modelled upon Article 9(2) of the EC Merger Regulation, OJ [1990] L 257/13, as amended by Regulation 1310/97, OJ [1998] L 3/16.
18 The words 'under the same conditions' are opaque, and would perhaps be better understood as 'in the same circumstances set out in Article 6'.
19 There is no specific power in UK law enabling, for example, the Office of Fair Trading to withdraw the benefit of a block exemption; withdrawal of a 'parallel exemption' under section 10 of the Competition Act 1998 would not in itself withdraw the benefit of the EC block exemption; nor would an Order under Sch 8 of the Fair Trading Act 1973 following a monopoly or merger investigation allow the withdrawal of the EC exemption.
20 Case 14/68 *Walt Wilhelm v Bundeskartellamt* [1969] ECR 1, point 4; Case C-234/89 *Delimitis v Henninger Bräu* [1991] ECR I-935, [1992] 5 CMLR 210; also Recital 14 of the Regulation and para 78 of the *Guidelines*.
1 *Guidelines*, paras 80-87.

under Article 6 (against a particular undertaking or particular agreements) or under Article 8: paragraph 84 of the *Guidelines* says that, in making this choice, the Commission would consider the number of competing undertakings contributing to the cumulative effect or the number of geographic markets within the Community that are affected. Paragraph 84 of the *Guidelines* states that a regulation under Article 8 would not affect the exempted status of the agreements in question prior to its entry into force.

(I)   Articles 9 to 11: market share, turnover and connected undertakings

Article 9 deals with the calculation of market share. Article 9(1) provides that market share should be calculated by reference to market sales value; where market sales value data are not available, estimates based on other reliable market information, including sales volumes, may be used. Article 9(2)(a) provides that the market share data should be calculated by reference to the preceding calendar year[2]. Article 9(2)(c) to (e) provide some marginal relief for up to two years where the market share rises above 30% but not beyond 35%.

Article 10 explains how turnover is to be calculated for the purpose of the rules in Article 2(2) and 2(4). Article 11 contains rules extending the expressions 'undertaking', 'supplier' and 'buyer' to include connected undertakings.

(J)   Articles 12 and 13: transitional provisions and entry into force

As noted above[3], the Regulation entered into force on 1 January 2000 and the block exemption became available to agreements with effect from 1 June 2000. Transitional relief until the end of 2001 was provided for agreements already block exempted under the old Regulations. The new Regulation will expire on 31 May 2010.

The new Regulation is a radical departure from the block exemptions which it replaces. It is undoubtedly less formalistic and more economics-oriented. Many commentators will, no doubt, continue to press the case for 'more realistic assessment' of agreements under Article 81(1); but in the meantime the Regulation provides a more rational 'safe haven' for agreements under Article 81(3) than was the case previously. Firms with a market share above 30%, or which are uncertain on this point, have the benefit of Regulation 1216/99, so that individual exemption for agreements can be obtained even in the absence of a prior notification. This will not be possible if the Commission's White Paper proposals are implemented[4]. The new Regulation is complex, and there will be teething problems as its application to different types of vertical relationships is worked out; a particular area of interest will be how well it works in the growing world of e-commerce. Revised *Guidelines* will be essential as more is learnt of the practical operation of the Regulation, and these have been promised after a period of four years. The 'new style' Regulation is a considerable improvement

---

2   Under the EC Merger Regulation, turnover is calculated, according to Article 5(1), by reference to the 'preceding financial year'; there is no explanation of why the new Regulation proceeds on the basis of a calendar year rather than a financial year.

3   See p 567 above.

4   See ch 4, pp 146-147 and ch 7, pp 246-258.

on the system it replaces and is an important part of the Commission's modernisation of the Community competition rules.

8. INDIVIDUAL EXEMPTION

Vertical agreements which infringe Article 81(1) and which are ineligible for block exemption under Regulation 2790/99 may nevertheless satisfy the terms of Article 81(3). As the law currently stands, the Commission might be persuaded to grant an individual exemption to such an agreement; this can be granted retrospectively, since it is no longer necessary for vertical agreements to have been notified to qualify for a back-dated exemption[5]. If the Commission's White Paper proposals are put into effect there will no longer be individual exemptions, but national courts and national competition authorities will be able to apply the provisions of Article 81(3) to vertical (and any other) agreements[6].

As we have seen, Section VI of the Commission's *Guidelines* discuss at length the application of Article 81(1) to a series of different types of vertical agreement[7]. Guidance will also be found in Section VI on the application of Article 81(3) to vertical agreements where this is needed in individual cases because the block exemption is inapplicable. Possible efficiencies arising from vertical agreements are described in paragraph 116[8], and some general comments on the application of Article 81(3) will be found at paragraph 134[9]. It is unlikely that 'hard-core restrictions' of the kind set out in Article 4 of the block exemption would be found to satisfy Article 81(3); individual assessment of agreements is most likely to be necessary, therefore, where the 30% market share cap is exceeded[10].

Specific guidance is given on the application of Article 81(3) to single branding agreements at paragraphs 153 to 158. Where a 'client-specific investment' is made, a non-compete obligation of more than five years may be allowed under Article 81(3)[11]: this is consistent with the Commission's past practice where, for example, 15-year exclusive purchase agreements have been allowed where an investment is made in the building of new power stations[12]. Where a non-compete clause is included in an exclusive distribution agreement, this may be permitted for the duration of the agreement, even where this is for longer than the five years permitted by Article 5(a) of the block exemption[13]. The possible application of Article 81(3) to exclusive distribution agreements is considered at paragraphs 171 to 174 of the *Guidelines*. The point is repeated that a non-compete obligation of more than five years may be allowed when it is part of an exclusive distribution agreement[14]. The Commission specifically notes that exclusive distribution is most likely to have efficiency-enhancing effects where the products involved are new, complex or have qualities that are difficult to assess prior to consumption[15].

5   See pp 566-567 above on the changes effected to Regulation 17/62 by Regulation 1216/99.
6   See ch 4, pp 146-147 and ch 7, pp 246-258.
7   See p 540ff above.
8   See pp 543-545 above.
9   See pp 543-545 above.
10 See p 547 above.
11 *Guidelines*, para 155.
12 See eg *Isab Energy* [1996] 4 CMLR 889, Commission's XXVIth *Report on Competition Policy* (1996) pp 133-134; *REN/Turbogás* [1996] 4 CMLR 881, XXVIth *Report on Competition Policy* (1996), pp 134-135.
13 Ibid, para 158.
14 Ibid, para 171.
15 Ibid, para 174.

Paragraph 182 of the *Guidelines* considers the possible improvements in efficiency attributable to exclusive customer allocation. Article 81(3) and selective distribution agreements are considered at paragraphs 195 and 196; exclusive supply is dealt with at paragraphs 210 to 212 and tying at paragraphs 222 to 224.

9. REGULATION 1475/95 ON MOTOR VEHICLE DISTRIBUTION AND SERVICING AGREEMENTS[16]

The Commission has adopted Regulation 1475/95 to deal specifically with motor vehicle distribution and servicing agreements; it does not apply to agricultural machinery[17], nor to motor cycles[18]. The Regulation allows a combination of exclusive and selective distribution in relation to motor vehicles. It is not intended to provide a detailed examination of this Regulation here, not least since it will expire in 2002[19]; criticism of Regulation 1475/95 makes it likely that any future legislation will differ considerably from the existing block exemption[20]. The Commission has, over the years, had cause to examine numerous complaints about market partitioning in the market for motor cars, and has adopted several decisions finding infringements of Article 81(1)[1]. There have been many cases brought before the Community courts relating to Regulation 1475/95 and its predecessor, including *VAG France v Magne*[2], *BMW v ALD*[3], *Bundeskartellamt v Volkswagen AG*[4], *Grand Garage Albigeois*[5], *Nissan France*[6], *Fontaine*[7], VAG-

---

16 OJ [1995] L 145/25, [1996] 4 CMLR 69; Regulation 1475/95 replaced the earlier Regulation 123/85, OJ [1985] L 15/16.
17 Commission Press Release IP(90)917, 16 November 1990; see also *Ford Agricultural* OJ [1993] L 20/1, [1995] 5 CMLR 89, para 18.
18 Commission Press Release IP(92) 544, 3 July 1992.
19 For detailed treatment of Regulation 1475/95 see Taylor and Marks in *Butterworths Competition Law* (eds Freeman and Whish) paras [705]-[825]; Faull and Nikpay *The EC Law of Competition* (Oxford University Press, 1999) paras 7.293-7.335; Bellamy and Child *European Community Law of Competition* (Sweet & Maxwell, 5th ed, ed Roth, 2001), paras 7-108 to 7-129; see also Middleton 'The Legal Framework for Motor Vehicle Distribution – A New Model?' (2001) 22 ECLR 3.
20 See p 593 below.
1   See eg *BMW Belgium* OJ [1978] L 46/33, [1978] 2 CMLR 126, upheld on appeal Case 32/78 *BMW v Commission* [1979] ECR 2435, [1980] 1 CMLR 370; *Ford Werke* OJ [1983] L 327/31, [1984] 1 CMLR 596, upheld on appeal Cases 25 and 26/84 *Ford Werke AG v Commission* [1985] ECR 2725, [1985] 3 CMLR 528; *Fiat* XIVth *Report on Competition Policy* (1984), point 70; *Alfa Romeo* ibid, point 71; *BL* OJ [1984] L 207/11, [1984] 3 CMLR 92, upheld on appeal Case 226/84 *BL v Commission* [1986] ECR 3263, [1987] 1 CMLR 185; *Peugeot* OJ [1986] L 295/19, [1989] 4 CMLR 371; *Citroen* Commission Press Release IP(88)778, [1989] 4 CMLR 338; *Peugeot* OJ [1992] L 66/1, [1993] 4 CMLR 42, upheld on appeal Case T-9/92 *Peugeot v Commission* [1993] ECR II-493 and on appeal to the ECJ Case C-322/93 P [1994] ECR I-2727; *VW* OJ [1998] L 124/60, [1998] 5 CMLR 33, substantially upheld on appeal, Case T-62/98 *Volkswagen AG v Commission* [2000] 5 CMLR 853: the case is on appeal to the ECJ, Case C-338/00 (judgment pending); *Opel* OJ [2001] L 59/1, [2001] 4 CMLR 1441, on appeal Case T-368/00 *Opel Nederland BV v Commission* (judgment pending).
2   Case 10/86 [1986] ECR 4071, [1988] 4 CMLR 98.
3   Case C-70/93 [1995] ECR I-3439, [1996] 4 CMLR 478.
4   Case C-266/93 [1995] ECR I-3477, [1996] 4 CMLR 505.
5   Case C-226/94 [1996] ECR I-651, [1996] 4 CMLR 778.
6   Case C-309/94 [1996] ECR I-677, [1996] 4 CMLR 778.
7   Case C-128/95 [1997] ECR I-967, [1997] 5 CMLR 39.

Händlerbeirat eV v SYD-Consult[8] , and *Cabour SA v Automobiles Peugeot SA*[9] . The EFTA Court has also had to consider the block exemption under the EEA Agreement in *Jan and Kristia Jæger AS v Opel Norge AS*[10] . The UK courts have also considered cases under the block exemption for cars in *Cound v BMW*[11] and *Clover Leaf Cars v BMW*[12] .

The block exemption is due to expire on 30 September 2002. Its operation was criticised in the UK Competition Commission's report, *New Cars: A report on the supply of new motor cars within the UK*[13] , and the European Commission adopted an evaluation report on the block exemption in November 2000 which concluded that the aims of the Regulation have not been achieved, in particular given the high prices that consumers have to pay for cars in some Member States[14] . A public hearing was held in Brussels in February 2001 to discuss the evaluation report[15] . The Commission will produce proposals in due course for the future regulatory régime for motor vehicle distribution; it seems reasonable to expect that substantial changes are likely to be made.

10.   SUB-CONTRACTING AGREEMENTS

Sub-contracting agreements are a common feature of the commercial world. A contractor often entrusts another undertaking – the 'sub-contractor' – to manufacture goods, supply services or to perform work under the contractor's instructions. Where the sub-contractor simply supplies goods or services to the contractor, the agreement would be a vertical one and the agreement would be governed by the Commission's *Guidelines* and by the block exemption for vertical agreements[16] . Where a sub-contracting agreement is entered into between competing undertakings, it falls to be considered under the Commission's *Guidelines on Horizontal Cooperation Agreements*[17]. However in some cases the contractor transfers know-how to the sub-contractor in order for it to be able to perform the tasks entrusted to it. The Commission has adopted a *Notice on Sub-contracting Agreements* to explain the application of Article 81(1) to this situation[18] .

The Commission's view is that sub-contracting agreements of the kind just described do not infringe Article 81(1). Subject to the proviso explained below, clauses in such agreements which stipulate that any technology or equipment provided by the contractor to the sub-contractor may not be used except for the

8   Case C-41/96 [1997] ECR I-3123, [1997] 5 CMLR 537.
9   Case C-230/96 [1998] ECR I-2055, [1998] 5 CMLR 679.
10 Case E-3/97 [1999] 4 CMLR 147.
11 [1997] Eu LR 277.
12 [1997] Eu LR 535.
13 Cm 4660 (2000); on the position in the UK, see p 599 below.
14 The Report is available on the DG COMP's website at http://europa.eu.int/comm/competition/car_sector/.
15 See Commission Press Release, IP/01/204, 14 February 2001.
16 See the Commission's *Guidelines on Horizontal Cooperation Agreements* OJ [2001] C 3/2, [2001] 4 CMLR 819, para 80.
17 Ibid, paras 81, 89 and 100; on these *Guidelines* generally see ch 15, pp 501-508.
18 OJ [1979] C 1/2; for detailed commentary on this Notice, see Taylor and Marks in *Butterworths Competition Law* (eds Freeman and Whish) paras [1420]-[1447]; Bellamy and Child *European Community Law of Competition* (Sweet & Maxwell, 5th ed, ed Roth, 2001), paras 7-185 to 7-191; note also that in some cases an agreement might amount to a licence of intellectual property of the kind that benefit from block exemption under Regulation 240/96 on technology transfer agreements: on this Regulation, see ch 19, pp 688-696.

purpose of the agreement are outside Article 81(1); so too are restrictions on making that technology or equipment available to third parties and a requirement that goods, services or work arising from the use of the technology or equipment will be supplied only to the contractor. The proviso referred to is that the technology or equipment must be necessary to enable the sub-contractor to manufacture the goods, supply the services or carry out the work: where this is the case, the sub-contractor is not regarded as an independent supplier in the market. This proviso is satisfied where the sub-contractor makes use of intellectual property rights or know-how belonging to the contractor. However it would not be satisfied if the sub-contractor could have obtained access to the technology or equipment in question acting on its own.

The Notice sets out other permissible clauses. In particular the contractor can require the sub-contractor to pass on to it on a non-exclusive basis any technical improvements made during the agreement; an exclusive licence may be acceptable where any improvements or inventions on the part of the sub-contractor cannot be made without use of the contractor's intellectual property rights. The sub-contractor must be free, however, to dispose of the results of its own research and development.

II.   UK LAW

(A)   Vertical integration

It is unlikely that vertical integration through internal growth would be condemned in the UK, although theoretically it is possible to investigate a particular situation under the monopoly provisions of the Fair Trading Act. In *The Supply of Beer*[19] the former Monopolies and Mergers Commission recommended that the 'Big Six' brewers should not be permitted to own more than 2,000 retail outlets each: this would require them to divest themselves of 21,900 retail outlets. Radical changes to the UK beer industry were subsequently set in motion by the Supply of Beer (Loan Ties, Licensed Premises and Wholesale Prices) Order 1989[20] and the Supply of Beer (Tied Estate) Order 1989[1]. These orders will be amended in 2001[2].

It is possible for vertical mergers to be referred to the Competition Commission where assets worth more than £70 million are taken over[3].

(B)   Commercial agency agreements

There is no specific guidance in the UK on the treatment of commercial agency agreements under the Competition Act 1998. However, it can be assumed that the Chapter I prohibition does not apply to them for two reasons. The first is that, in so far as an agency agreement qualifies as a vertical agreement in the

---

19   Cm 651 (1989).
20   SI 1989/2258.
1   SI 1989/2390.
2   See DTI Press Release P/2000/805, 1 December 2000.
3   Fair Trading Act 1973, s 64(1)(b) as amended by the Merger References (Increase in Value of Assets) Order 1994, SI 1994/72; on vertical mergers under the FTA, see ch 22, p 824.

sense of Article 3 of the Exclusion Order[4], it is excluded from the Chapter I prohibition. The second is that, even if there were to be a suggestion that Chapter I might apply, section 60 would be likely to mean that paragraphs 12 to 20 of the European Commission's *Vertical Guidelines* would be followed, and they state that 'true agency agreements' are not caught by Article 81(1) EC[5].

A distribution system operated entirely through commercial agents could be investigated under the Fair Trading Act 1973. This would be likely to happen only where the principal possessed substantial market power so that competition was severely restricted, or where a number of operators on the supply side of the market conducted business in a similar way, thereby substantially limiting competition. In *Foreign Package Holidays*[6] the Commission concluded that the practice of tour operators prohibiting travel agents from supplying holidays at a price less than that in the operators' brochures was against the public interest. This had an effect similar to resale price maintenance in relation to goods and the Secretary of State made an Order making such conduct unlawful[7].

(C) Vertical agreements under the Competition Act 1998

For the Government in the UK, the question of how to treat vertical agreements under the Competition Act 1998 was complex. On the one hand, the 1998 Act involves the adoption in the UK of legislation incorporating the wording of Articles 81 and 82 EC, in order to achieve consistency with the position in the rest of the European Union. In addition, section 60 of the Act provides that, as a general proposition, the authorities in the UK should maintain consistency with the jurisprudence of the Community Courts and have regard to decisions of the European Commission[8]. On the other hand the application of Article 81 to vertical agreements has been strongly influenced by single market considerations, which are not an issue of concern *within* the UK. On a more pragmatic note, the DGFT in the UK is keen to avoid being inundated with notifications for exemption for agreements that may entail no restriction of competition at all. Having weighed up the various arguments, the Government committed itself to providing the Secretary of State with the power to exclude vertical agreements from the scope of the 1998 Act[9]; this was effected by the Competition Act 1998 (Land and Vertical Agreements Exclusion) Order 2000[10], which should be read in conjunction with the OFT's Guideline *Vertical Agreements and Restraints*[11] ('the *Vertical Guideline*').

---

4   See p 596 below.
5   See pp 538-540 above; on s 60 Competition Act see ch 9, pp 329-333.
6   Cmnd 9879 (1986).
7   Restriction on Agreements and Conduct (Tour Operators) Order 1987, SI 1987/1131.
8   See ch 9, pp 329-333.
9   It was difficult to exclude vertical agreements in the Act itself since the reform of EC law, including the definition in Regulation 1215/99 of a vertical agreement, had not been completed at the time that the Competition Act received the Royal Assent on 9 November 1998.
10 SI 2000/310; note that vertical agreements that comply with the EC block exemption would enjoy parallel exemption from the Chapter I prohibition under s 10 of the Competition Act (see ch 9, pp 312-313): however this is not in practice necessary, since vertical agreements are excluded from Chapter I anyway; paras 4.1-4.6 of the *Vertical Guideline* explain the relationship between EC and UK law on vertical agreements.
11 OFT 419, available at http://www.oft.gov.uk/html/comp-act/technical-guidelines/index.html.

The argument that the exclusion of vertical agreements from the Chapter I prohibition might be unduly lenient can be countered in at least three ways[12]. First, vertical agreements do not enjoy exclusion from the Chapter II prohibition; therefore a vertical agreement entered into by a firm or firms with a dominant position could be scrutinised under section 18 of the 1998 Act. Secondly, the complex monopoly provisions in the Fair Trading Act 1973 remain in force: where there is a competition problem in a particular sector because of the cumulative effect of the vertical agreements in operation – cars, perfumes or beer might be cited as examples – it would be open to the DGFT to refer the matter to the Competition Commission for investigation[13]. Finally, provision is made in section 50 for any order of the Secretary of State to contain a clawback provision, whereby the DGFT can withdraw the exclusion from any particular vertical agreement (but not from a category of agreements); the DGFT has been given this power in Article 7 of the Order[14].

(i)   The power to exclude vertical agreements

Section 50(1) provides that the Secretary of State may by order provide for any provision of Part I of the Competition Act 1998 to apply to vertical agreements with such modifications as may be prescribed. Section 50(2) states that such an order may provide for exclusions or exemptions, or otherwise provide for prescribed provisions not to apply in relation to such agreements. The Secretary of State is given power by section 50(3) to allow the DGFT to exercise a right of 'clawback' in relation to an individual agreement. Section 50(5) provides that the key expression – 'vertical agreement' – has such meaning as may be prescribed by order.

(ii)   The Exclusion Order

The Competition Act 1998 (Land and Vertical Agreements Exclusion) Order 2000 was enacted in March 2000[15]. It contains six main headings and deals with the exclusion of vertical agreements in the following way.

(A)   THE EXCLUSION.   Article 3 provides that:

> 'The Chapter I prohibition shall not apply to an agreement to the extent that it is a vertical agreement'.

It will be seen that the exclusion applies 'to the extent that' an agreement is a vertical agreement. The exclusion is limited, so that it may apply to some provisions of an agreement but not to others[16]. If the DGFT were called upon to consider the overall impact of an agreement, he would, by virtue of section 59(2) of the

---

12 See the discussion on this in the House of Lords, HL Report Stage, 9 February 1998, cols 901–903.
13 See ch 11 on the monopoly provisions in the Fair Trading Act 1973 generally, and pp 598-600 below for discussion of particular investigations of relevance to vertical agreements.
14 See p 598 below.
15 SI 2000/310; note that the Government has announced its intention to repeal the exclusion of vertical arrangements from the Chapter I prohibition: *A World Class Competition Régime* (July 2001), Cm 5233, paras 8.14-8.16.
16 *Vertical Guideline*, paras 3.4-3.5.

1998 Act, be entitled to take into account the excluded vertical agreement in making his assessment, even though that agreement is itself excluded.

(B)   DEFINITION OF A VERTICAL AGREEMENT . Article 2 defines a vertical agreement as:

'an agreement between undertakings, each of which operates for the purposes of the agreement, at a different level of the production or distribution chain, and relating to the conditions under which the parties may purchase, sell or resell certain goods or services and includes provisions contained in such agreements which relate to the assignment to the buyer or use by the buyer of intellectual property rights, provided that those provisions do not constitute the primary object of the agreement and are directly related to the use, sale or resale of goods or services by the buyer or its customers'.

This definition relies heavily on the definition of a vertical agreement in EC law[17], and is explained further at paragraphs 2.3 to 2.13 of the *Vertical Guideline*. By including the words 'for the purposes of the agreement' it provides for the exclusion of agreements between undertakings which are for other purposes competitors, because they operate at the same level of production and distribution. Unlike the EC block exemption, there is no specific provision covering agreements between competing undertakings[18].

(C)   PRICE-FIXING AGREEMENTS.   Fixed and minimum pricing is not excluded from the Chapter I prohibition, as Article 4 sets out:

'Article 3 shall not apply where the vertical agreement, directly or indirectly, in isolation or in combination with other factors under the control of the parties has the object or effect[19] of restricting the buyer's ability to determine its sale price, without prejudice to the possibility of the supplier imposing a maximum sale price or recommending a sale price, provided that these do not amount to a fixed or minimum sale price as a result of pressure from, or incentives offered by, any of the parties'.

The effect of the proviso in Article 3 is that the imposition of maximum resale prices and recommendations as to resale prices are excluded from the Chapter I prohibition, as long as these do not have the effect (through pressure or incentives) of fixed or minimum resale prices. The wording of Article 3 is taken from Article 4(a) of the EC block exemption[20], and is discussed at paragraphs 3.1 to 3.3 of the *Vertical Guideline*.

(D)   INTELLECTUAL PROPERTY RIGHTS.   The definition of a vertical agreement includes provisions relating to the assignment or licence to the buyer of intellectual property rights subject to certain limitations, and in particular that these provisions are not the primary object of the agreement. The meaning of these terms, taken from the EC block exemption, will be informed by the European Commission's *Guidelines*[1] and are considered at paragraphs 2.9 to 2.13 of the OFT's *Vertical Guideline*. Where the assignment or licence of intellectual property rights is the

---

17 See p 569 above.
18 See pp 577-578 above on Article 2(4) of Regulation 2790/99.
19 Note that Article 4 of Regulation 2790/99 refers only to agreements that have as their object, but not as their effect, the restrictions set out in paras (a)-(e): see pp 581-582 above.
20 See pp 582-583 above.
1 See pp 574-577 above.

primary object of the agreement the exclusion will not apply and such agreements will be considered under Chapter I; they would benefit from parallel exemption where they satisfy the terms of Regulation 240/96 on technology transfer agreements[2].

(E)   CLAWBACK.   Article 7 of the Order provides that the power to withdraw the benefit of the exclusions contained in Schedule 1 to the Act (in relation to mergers), applies equally to this exclusion[3]. The procedure to be followed in such cases is explained at paragraphs 5.1 to 5.6 of the *Vertical Guideline*. The power of clawback is likely to be applied only rarely[4]. Before exercising this power, the DGFT must consult the parties, and where he does so he will publish that fact in the public register[5]. Exercise of the clawback power does not in itself mean that the agreement infringes the Chapter I prohibition: that would require further assessment[6]. If the DGFT does find an infringement of the Chapter I prohibition, this finding can take effect only from the date of clawback, but not from an earlier date[7]. Even without the power of clawback under the Order, it should be remembered that a vertical agreement may amount to an abuse of dominant position under Chapter II; and it is also possible that an investigation under the Fair Trading Act 1973 might be launched[8].

(F)   AGREEMENTS TO LIKE EFFECT.   Article 8 prevents parties from concluding agreements to the like object or effect as an agreement from which the benefit of the exclusion has been withdrawn and claiming the benefit of the exclusion for the new agreements[9].

(iii)   Vertical agreements and the Chapter II prohibition

There is no exclusion for vertical agreements from the Chapter II prohibition[10].

(D)   Fair Trading Act 1973[11]

The retention of the powers in the Fair Trading Act 1973 ('the FTA') to investigate scale and complex monopolies is an important feature of UK competition law. Even though the Competition Act 1998 has been adopted, the 'safety net' of the FTA means that the Competition Commission can be asked to investigate sectors of the economy in which there appears to be a failure in the competitive market mechanism which the 1998 Act does not adequately address. The provisions of the FTA have been described in chapter 11. This chapter has explained that most vertical agreements are outside the Chapter I prohibition in the Competition Act[12]; however vertical agreements can still be investigated under the FTA, and

2   OJ [1996] L 31/2: see ch 19, pp 688-696.
3   See p 596 above.
4   *Vertical Guideline*, para 5.2.
5   Ibid, para 5.3.
6   Ibid, para 5.4.
7   Ibid, para 5.5.
8   See ch 11, pp 371-373.
9   Ibid, para 5.6.
10   Ibid, para 6.1; on the application of Chapter II to abusive practices, see ch 9, pp 314-321, ch 17, pp 627-632 and ch 18, pp 664-673.
11   See Pickering 'Competition Policy and Vertical Relationships: The Approach of the UK MMC' (1999) 20 ECLR 225.
12   See pp 595-598 above.

in particular under the complex monopoly provisions where there is a network of parallel vertical agreements in a particular sector leading to a restriction of competition.

The Competition Commission, and its predecessor the Monopolies and Mergers Commission, have conducted many investigations in which it was necessary to consider the effect of vertical agreements. The cases of *Beer* and *Foreign Package Holidays* have already been mentioned[13]. In *Petrol*[14] the Commission accepted that exclusive purchasing agreements with retail outlets were justifiable, but recommended that their duration be limited to five years. Undertakings were negotiated with the petrol suppliers after this report[15] which remained in effect until they were released in 2000[16]. The Commission was critical of exclusive purchasing provisions in its report on *Carbonated Soft Drinks*[17]. A DTI Press Release of 25 June 1992 indicated that undertakings to remedy the problem would be sought, and this was achieved in June 1993[18].

The Commission investigated the selective distribution of newspapers in *Newspapers and Periodicals*[19]. This is an industry in which selective distribution is commonly used, in particular because of the unique perishability of the product[20]. The Commission accepted that it was reasonable to limit the number of retail outlets selling newspapers as demand was stable and unlikely to increase. There were continuing complaints from excluded retailers, and a further reference to the Commission was made in 1992; this led to a report that was more critical than the earlier one[1]. Undertakings were agreed in 1994[2]. Retailers' complaints about the selective distribution systems of the manufacturers of perfumes led to a reference of 'fine fragrances' to the Commission in 1992, but it concluded that there were no public interest detriments[3].

The Commission reported in 1992 on Supply of New Motor Cars[4] and again, in 2000, in *New Cars*[5]. In the latter report, the Commission concluded that the selective and exclusive distribution agreements in operation in the UK in conjunction with the practice of publishing recommended resale prices led to higher prices to private customers, and operated against the public interest. As a result the *Supply of New Cars Order 2000* was adopted[6], effecting a number of changes to the vertical practices in the industry.

The reports on *Electrical Goods*[7] were critical of the practice of recommended resale prices, and led to this practice being made unlawful in relation to such products by the Restriction on Agreements and Conduct (Specified Domestic Electrical Goods) Order 1998[8]. The same fate befell recommended prices

13 See pp 594-595 above.
14 HCP (1965) 264.
15 For the full text, see *The Supply of Petrol* Cm 972 (1990) Appendix 2.2.
16 DTI Press Release P/2000/864, 21 December 2000.
17 Cm 1625 (1992).
18 DTI Press Release, 2 June 1993.
19 Cmnd 7214 (1978).
20 On EC law, see pp 558, n 17 above.
1   Cm 2422 (1993).
2   See the 1994 *Annual Report of the DGFT* p 40.
3   Cm 2380 (1993).
4   Cm 1808 (1992).
5   Cm 4660 (2000).
6   SI 2000/2088.
7   Cm 3675 and Cm 3676 (1997).
8   SI 1998/1271.

following a second investigation of Foreign Package Holidays[9], which found that this practice operated against the public interest and which led to the Foreign Package Holidays (Tour Operators and Travel Agents) Order 2000[10].

It is too early in the life of the new Competition Act in the UK to know how often, if at all, it will be necessary to investigate vertical agreements under the FTA. However it is useful that the possibility of an investigation has been retained for those cases that cannot be effectively controlled under the Chapter I or Chapter II prohibitions.

9   Cm 3813 (1997).
10 SI 2000/2110.

CHAPTER 17

Abuse of dominance (1): non-pricing practices

The previous five chapters have been concerned with the application of EC and UK competition law to horizontal and vertical agreements between undertakings. The focus of attention in this and the following chapter turns to a different issue: the extent to which the unilateral acts of dominant firms might infringe Article 82 EC and the Chapter II prohibition in the Competition Act 1998; these chapters will also consider briefly the extent to which such practices might be controlled in the UK under the Fair Trading Act 1973.

The main principles underlying Article 82 were discussed in chapter 5; the Chapter II prohibition was explained in chapter 9[1]. It may be helpful to recall that Article 82 has been applied to exploitative abuses, to anti-competitive practices and to actions that are detrimental to the single market[2]; that care must be taken in the application of Article 82 not to prevent dominant firms from being able to compete 'on the merits'[3]; that the dominant position, the abuse and the effects of the abuse may be in different markets[4]; and that the concepts of objective justification and proportionality may be invoked to distinguish between legitimate competition and conduct which is within the mischief of Article 82[5].

This chapter is concerned with non-pricing practices; abusive pricing practices are considered in chapter 18. This chapter will deal in turn with exclusive agreements; with tie-in agreements; with refusals to supply, including the so-called 'essential facilities' doctrine; with abusive practices that are harmful to the single market; and with miscellaneous other practices which might infringe Article 82. The application of Article 82 will be considered in sections 1 to 5; UK law in section 6.

1. EXCLUSIVE AGREEMENTS

The application of Article 81 to vertical agreements was considered in chapter 16, where the Commission's concerns with four groups of agreements – single

1   See ch 9, pp 314-321.
2   See ch 5, pp 168-180.
3   Ibid, pp 171-173.
4   Ibid, pp 173-175.
5   Ibid, pp 180-181.

branding, limited distribution, resale price maintenance and market partitioning – were discussed[6]. The same concerns apply in relation to the analysis of agreements under Article 82 only more so, given that competition is necessarily already weak where one firm has a dominant position in the market. The block exemption for vertical agreements confers block exemption on such agreements where the supplier has a market share of 30% or less[7], provided that the agreement contains no hard-core restrictions contrary to Article 4[8]; where the agreement is one for exclusive supply, the relevant market share is that of the buyer[9]. Article 5 of the block exemption limits the permissible duration of a non-compete clause to five years[10]. Where the market share exceeds 30%, an individual assessment of a vertical agreement is necessary to determine whether it infringes Article 81(1)[11] and whether it satisfies the terms of Article 81(3)[12].

A separate issue, however, is whether vertical agreements infringe Article 82. It is clear that this is possible. In this section, consideration will be given to the possibility that exclusive agreements might infringe Article 82; tie-in agreements will be discussed in the following section. In chapter 18, pricing practices having the same effect as such agreements will be considered[13]. A difference between the application of Article 81 and Article 82 to such agreements is that, where an agreement infringes Article 81, both (or all) of the parties to the agreement will have committed an infringement, since the offence lies in the fact of agreement. In the case of Article 82, however, it is the dominant firm that infringes the competition rules, since Article 82 applies to a dominant firm's *unilateral* behaviour; the conclusion of an anti-competitive agreement can be an abusive unilateral act.

(A)   The application of Article 82 to single-branding agreements

The most obvious vertical agreement that could infringe Article 82 is one whereby a customer is required to purchase a particular brand of goods or services only from a dominant supplier[14]. Various terminology can be used to describe such agreements – 'single branding', 'exclusive purchasing', 'requirements contracts' and 'non-compete obligations'. Each of these terms connotes the same idea: that the purchaser is prevented from purchasing competing products from anyone other than the dominant firm: the problem is the detriment that this might cause to inter-brand competition[15]. The Commission discusses single branding agreements at paragraphs 138 to 160 of the *Guidelines on Vertical Restraints*[16]. As far as Article 82 is concerned, the *Guidelines* state that a dominant firm may not impose a non-compete obligation[17] on buyers unless it can objectively justify

---

6   See ch 16, pp 542-543.
7   Regulation 2790/99, Article 3(1): see ch 16, p 579.
8   Ibid, pp 581-586.
9   Regulation 2790/99, Article 3(2): see ch 16, p 579.
10 See ch 16, pp 586-587.
11 Ibid, pp 546-564.
12 Ibid, pp 591-592.
13 See ch 18, pp 639-645.
14 For a helpful review of the treatment of such agreements under both Article 81 and 82 see Reinert 'Industrial Supply Contracts under EC Competition Law' (1996) 17 ECLR 6.
15 For discussion of this term see ch 16, p 541.
16 OJ [2000] C 291/1, [2000] 5 CMLR 398: see ch 16, pp 553-555.
17 This term is defined in Article 1(b) of Regulation 2790/99: see ch 16, p 568.

such a commercial practice[18]. The *Guidelines* state that Article 82 prevents dominant companies from applying so-called 'English clauses', which require the buyer to report any better offer that it receives and allow it to accept that offer only if the dominant supplier does not match it[19]: clauses such as this enable the dominant firm to exclude competitors, and they heighten the transparency of oligopolistic markets and thereby foster tacit collusion. The *Guidelines* also state that fidelity rebate schemes on the part of dominant firms are prohibited[20].

There is not a great deal of precedent on the application of Article 82 to single branding agreements; however it is clear that there is a strong possibility that Article 82 will be applied to such agreements when entered into by a firm in a dominant position. Once the ECJ had held in *Suiker Unie v Commission*[1] that it was contrary to Article 82 for a dominant firm to foreclose competition by offering loyalty rebates to customers that purchase only from it, it was inevitable that the same condemnation would apply to an exclusive purchasing commitment. This was confirmed in *Hoffmann-La Roche v Commission*[2]. The ECJ held that:

'An undertaking which is in a dominant position on a market and ties purchasers – even if it does so at their request – by an obligation or promise on their part to obtain all or most of their requirements exclusively from the said undertaking abuses its dominant position within the meaning of Article [82] of the Treaty, whether the obligation in question is stipulated without further qualification or whether it is undertaken in consideration of the grant of a rebate'[3].

This language suggests a *per se* approach on the part of the ECJ, that any exclusive purchasing agreement on the part of a dominant undertaking is abusive. This, however, is questionable: it is arguable that, to be abusive, the conduct must have the actual or potential effect of hindering the maintenance or development of competition[4]. In *BPB Industries v Commission*[5] the CFI held that exclusive purchasing cannot, as a matter of principle, be considered to infringe Article 81: it is necessary to examine the effects of such an agreement in its specific context[6]; however the Court went on to say that those considerations 'which apply in a normal competitive market situation, cannot be unreservedly accepted in the case of a market where, precisely because of the dominant position of one of the market operators, competition is already restricted'[7]. The CFI did not go so far as to say that there is a *per se* rule against exclusive purchasing agreements on the part of a dominant firm, but at the very least it suggests a very strict standard. An important point about the statement by the ECJ in

18 Ibid, para 141.
19 Ibid, para 152; this rule is based on Case 85/76 *Hoffmann-la Roche v Commission* [1979] ECR 461, [1979] 3 CMLR 211, paras 102-108.
20 Ibid; on loyalty rebates see ch 18, pp 639-644.
1   Cases 40/73 etc [1975] ECR 1663, [1976] 1 CMLR 295.
2   Case 85/76 [1979] ECR 461, [1979] 3 CMLR 211; see also Case T–65/89 *BPB Industries plc and British Gypsum v Commission* [1993] ECR II-389, [1993] 5 CMLR 32, paras 65–77, upheld on appeal Case C-310/93 P *BPB Industries plc and British Gypsum v Commission* [1995] ECR I-865, [1997] 4 CMLR 238.
3   Ibid, para 89.
4   See ch 5, p 172.
5   Case T-65/89 [1993] ECR II-389, [1993] 5 CMLR 32.
6   Ibid, para 66.
7   Ibid, para 67.

Hoffmann-la Roche quoted above is that it is no defence that the customer willingly entered into the agreement, or even that it requested exclusivity: the issue in these cases is not whether the agreement is oppressive to the customer, but whether it forecloses competition in the relevant market.

A requirement to purchase all of one's requirements from a dominant firm will be viewed less favourably than an obligation to purchase only a certain percentage: the block exemption for vertical agreements characterises a requirement to purchase more than 80% of one's requirements as a non-compete obligation[8]. The duration of the agreement will be a critical feature in determining whether it is abusive: the shorter it is, the less likely it is to infringe Article 82: these two factors – the extent and the duration of the exclusive obligation – should always be considered when analysing exclusive agreements under Article 82.

In *Istituto/IMC and Angus*[9] the Commission intervened in a case where the dominant supplier of a raw material was refusing to supply a customer except on terms which would have foreclosed competition from its competitors; it persuaded IMC and Angus to offer supply contracts that would last two years with automatic renewal for one year unless terminated by six months' notice. In the *Soda-ash* decisions[10] the Commission fined Solvay EUR 20 million and ICI EUR 10 million for requiring customers to enter into long-term indefinite requirements contracts and granting fidelity and top slice rebates designed to exclude competitors from the market. The Commission brought an end to exclusive contracts entered into by AC Nielsen for the procurement of data in relation to fast-moving consumer goods in 1997[11]. The Commission took action against Nordiron in respect of exclusive, long-term supply clauses for Molybdenum 99, a base product for radiopharmaceuticals used in nuclear medicine; following the receipt of a statement of objections Nordiron dropped the clauses[12]. The Commission required Frankfurt Airport to abandon long-term contracts covering periods from three to ten years which it had entered into with airlines for the provision of ramp-handling services[13]; the Commission had required the termination of Frankfurt Airport's monopoly of such services and, not surprisingly, was unwilling to see this replaced by long-term exclusive terms that would have the same effect in practice of excluding third parties. Agreement was reached with the Commission that the contracts would be for a period of one year only, automatically renewable but terminable on six months' notice[14].

In *Almelo*[15] the ECJ considered that an exclusive purchasing clause in a supply contract for electricity could infringe Article 82 if entered into by a dominant firm, even where the clause was requested by local distributors.

---

8   See Article 1(b) of Regulation 2790/99, discussed in ch 16, p 568.
9   XVIth *Report on Competition Policy* (1986), point 76.
10 *Soda-ash/Solvay* OJ [1991] L 152/21 and *Soda-ash/ICI* [1991] L 152/40; these decisions were annulled on procedural grounds by the CFI, Cases T-30/91 etc *Solvay SA v Commission* [1995] ECR II-1775, [1996] 5 CMLR 57, confirmed on appeal by the ECJ, Cases C-286/95 P [2000] 5 CMLR 413 and 454; however the Commission readopted the decisions in December 2000 Commission Press Release IP/00/1449, 13 December 2000.
11 XXVIIth *Report on Competition Policy* (1997), pp 144-148.
12 XXVIIIth *Report on Competition Policy* (1998), pp 169-170.
13 *Frankfurt Airport* OJ [1998] L 72/30, [1998] 4 CMLR 779.
14 IP/98/794, 8 September 1998.
15 Case C-393/92 [1994] ECR I-1477.

(B)   Article 82 applies to de facto as well as to contractual exclusivity

In *Van den Bergh Foods*[16] the Commission concluded that it was an abuse of a dominant position for Van den Bergh to provide freezer cabinets free of charge to retail outlets on condition that they were to be used exclusively for the storage of its ice-cream products[17]. The consequence of this practice was that, *de facto*, Van den Bergh achieved outlet exclusivity, since retailers were unlikely to, and in practice did not, maintain a second freezer in their shops; effectively, therefore, the retailers would purchase ice-cream exclusively from Van den Bergh. This decision, which is on appeal to the CFI[18], demonstrates that Article 82 can be applied to *de facto* as well as to contractual exclusivity.

(C)   Long-term agreements are not necessarily abusive

In some circumstances long-term supply agreements may be justifiable, for example where the supplier has to make a client-specific investment in order to be able to supply[19]. It was noted in chapter 16 that this may result in the terms of Article 81(3) being satisfied in relation to an agreement that infringes Article 81(1); in the case of Article 82, the same reasoning may result in a finding that an agreement is not abusive. In *Gas Natural/Endesa* the Commission required changes to a supply agreement for gas by Gas Natural, the dominant supplier in the Spanish gas market, to Endesa, the leader in electricity there: the agreement would have resulted in Endesa taking all its gas from Gas Natural, but this was changed so that Endesa could purchase a certain proportion of its requirements elsewhere; the duration of the agreement was limited to 12 years[20].

2.   TIE-IN AGREEMENTS[1]

Both Article 81(1)(e) and Article 82(2)(d) specifically state that tie-in agreements may amount to infringements. Although Article 81 may be applicable to tie-ins[2], particularly in the case of licences of intellectual property rights[3], most cases have been brought under Article 82. Article 82(2)(d) gives as an example of abuse:

> 'making the conclusion of contracts subject to acceptance by the other parties of supplementary obligations which, by their nature or according to commercial usage, have no connection with the nature of such contracts'.

---

16   OJ [1998] L 246/1, [1998] 5 CMLR 530.
17   Ibid, para 265.
18   Case T-65/98 *Van den Bergh Foods Ltd v Commission* (judgment pending).
19   See the Commission's *Guidelines on Vertical Restraints* (p 602, n 16 above), paras 116, sub-para 4 and 155.
20   Commission Press Release IP/00/297, 27 March 2000.
1   See Waelbroeck 'The Compatibility of Tying Agreements with Antitrust Rules: A Comparative Study of American and European Rules' (1987) Oxford Yearbook of European Law 39.
2   See the Commission's *Guidelines on Vertical Restraints* OJ [2000] C 291/1, [2000] 5 CMLR 1074, paras 215-224.
3   See ch 19, p 695, n 11.

(A)   The concept of a tie-in agreement

A tie-in agreement is one whereby a supplier causes, whether by contractual stipulation or by some other means, a buyer to purchase all or part of its requirements for a second (tied) product from the supplier of a first (tying) product. The competition policy objection to tying is that a firm that has market power in relation to the tying product uses that market power – or 'leverages' it – to induce the buyer also to buy the tied product. There is no objection to the supplier selling both widgets and blodgets to a customer; however there may be an objection where the two products are tied to one another. The offence of tying implies coercion on the part of the firm accused of infringing the competition rules which causes the customer to purchase the two products together.

Various examples can be given of tie-in agreements. A firm that manufactures photocopying machines might insist that its customers purchase ink and paper exclusively from it; a more modern example would be that of a producer of printers requiring customers only to purchase toner cartridges from it. This is perhaps the simplest form of a tie, where the customer is required to purchase accessories – or 'consumables' – necessary for the use of the tying product; the *Hilti* case is a classic example of this, where Hilti required users of its nail guns and nail cartridges to purchase nails exclusively from it[4]. A different example of a tie-in agreement would be where the supplier of a product insists that the customer should make use of its repair and maintenance service: this was the practice that was found to be unlawful in the *Kodak* case in the US[5]; a similar example would be where a supplier of sugar annexes to itself the ancillary market for the delivery of that sugar to its customers[6]. A further example of a tie-in agreement would be full-line forcing, which occurs where a buyer is required to purchase every item in a supplier's product range: in *Hoffmann-la Roche v Commission* 'across-the-board rebates' that induced customers to purchase the full range of Hoffmann-La Roche's vitamins were held to infringe Article 82[7]. It is also possible that a firm might attempt to tie supplies to one geographical market to sales in another one[8].

A tie-in may be achieved in a number of different ways. The most obvious is by express contractual stipulation, where the supplier insists that a customer must purchase the tied product as a condition of obtaining the tying product. However a tie-in may also be achieved by other means, such as a refusal to supply the tying product unless the customer purchases the tied product. Withdrawal of a guarantee unless a customer uses a supplier's components could have the effect of a tie-in agreement[9]. Pricing practices can also have a tying effect, for example where a customer is offered rebates or discounts if it purchases both the tying and the tied product; or where two products are 'bundled' together at a fixed and favourable price which leads the customer to purchase both: these practices are discussed in chapter 18[10].

---

4   See p 609 below; the *Tetra Pak* case is a further example of the same phenomenon: see p 610 below.
5   See p 607 below; see also, in the EC, the *Tetra Pak* case, p 610 below.
6   See p 610 below on the *Napier Brown-British Sugar* decision.
7   See ch 18, p 645.
8   This was one of the Commission's concerns in *IRI/Nielsen*, p 604, n 11 above.
9   The Commission required an end to this practice in *Novo Nordisk*: XXVIth *Report on Competition Policy* (1996), pp 142-143.
10   See ch 18, pp 644-645.

(B) Arguments for and against tying[11]

It is argued against tie-ins that they take away a purchaser's freedom of choice, as it cannot buy the tied product where it would wish; that they might foreclose competitors, deprived of outlets for their brand of the tied product; and that they enable the producer which imposes the tie to extend its monopoly power in respect of the tying product to the tied product. Of course the last proposition assumes that the firm possesses market power, but so impressed have the US courts been with the 'leverage theory' that they have sometimes condemned tying without a particularly critical assessment of this issue[12]. More recently the Supreme Court condemned a tie-in in the *Kodak*[13] case, where a manufacturer of photocopier and micrographic equipment tied repair services; the Court asked first, whether two separate products were involved; secondly, whether the defendant had required the tied product to be purchased with the tying product; thirdly, whether a substantial amount of inter-state commerce had been affected; and finally whether the defendant had market power in the tying product. This four-fold test was subsequently applied in the *Microsoft* case[14].

The condemnation of tie-ins has attracted criticism[15]. Apart from theoretical scepticism about the leverage theory, it is pointed out that tying may be used for reasonable purposes. One is to maintain the efficiency of the tying product: for example, a piece of equipment may function at its best only if a particular chemical or material is used which is available solely from the manufacturer, because it has a patent or relevant know-how. Another is to enable economies of scale to be achieved: a manufacturer of a photocopying machine which also supplies ink, paper and spare parts will be able to reduce costs if all these items are delivered to customers at the same time; tying all these products to one another may lead to lower prices. A third reason for tying is to enable a producer to discriminate between its customers: the manufacturer of a photocopying machine may wish to charge high-volume users more than low-volume ones; this it can do by tying-in photocopying paper: the customer which uses the machine the most will have to pay the most and the tie operates as a substitute for putting a meter onto the machine. Discrimination is not as obviously undesirable as might at first be thought[16], and anyway if the purpose of the tie is to discriminate it ought to be analysed as an issue of discrimination and not condemned simply as a tie-in.

(C) In what circumstances can products be said to be tied?

The notion of a tie-in agreement is, at first sight, simple enough; however, on closer inspection, it is clear that there is a difficulty in determining whether two or more products are so obviously part of a composite whole that it is a nonsense to consider that they are tied to one another. A car is sold with wheels and tyres:

11 For a helpful discussion of tie-ins see Bishop and Walker *The Economics of EC Competition Law* (Sweet & Maxwell, 1999), paras 5.13-5.22.
12 See eg *Northern Pacific Rly Co v United States* 336 US 1 (1958).
13 *Eastman Kodak Co v Image Technical Services Inc* 504 US 451 (1992).
14 See p 608 below.
15 See eg Bork *The Antitrust Paradox* (1978, Basic Books), ch 19; Bowman 'Tying Arrangements and the Leverage Problem' (1967) 67 Yale Law Journal 67; Turner 'The Validity of Tying Arrangements under the Antitrust Laws' (1958) 72 Harvard Law Review 73; for a review of the different arguments see Scherer & Ross *Industrial Market Structure and Economic Performance* (Houghton Mifflin, 3rd ed, 1990), pp 565–569.
16 See ch 18, pp 657-662 and 672-673.

clearly this does not involve a tie; there will also be a spare wheel: presumably this is not a tie; the car may be fitted with a radio: this perhaps does amount to a tie; if the purchaser is required to insure the car with an insurance company specified by the manufacturer or dealer, this presumably would be a tie. In the same way, a pair of shoes would not be regarded as a tie-in; nor would the sale of shoes with laces; but a requirement to purchase a particular brand of polish with the shoes presumably would be. It is necessary to determine at what point a case becomes one of tying; more importantly, it is also necessary to establish a legal rule that is capable of identifying that point. It is presumably the case that the burden of proving that two products are the subject of a tie-in is on the competition authority or the complainant; and that the burden of proving that a tie-in is objectively justified and proportionate is on the dominant firm.

In the *Microsoft*[17] case in the US Microsoft argued that its web browser and its operating software were a single, composite product, so that there was no tie-in[18]. However the court found that browsers and operating systems were 'distinguishable in the eyes of buyers'[19]. This was buttressed by the fact that the behaviour of other suppliers showed that the two products could be efficiently and separately provided. In the view of the court:

> '...Microsoft's decision to offer only the bundled – "integrated" – version of Windows and Internet Explorer derived not from technical necessity or business efficiencies; rather, it was the result of a deliberate and purposeful choice to quell incipient competition before it reached truly minatory proportions[20]'.

According to the formulation in Article 82(2)(d), products are tied when they have no connection either 'by their nature or according to commercial usage'. Thus two alternative criteria – the nature of the products and their commercial usage – are to be used in determining whether products are tied. The Commission's *Guidelines on Vertical Restraints*[1] state that, in determining whether two products are distinct, one should look at the demand of buyers and ask whether, from their perspective, in the absence of a tie-in, they would purchase the two products on different markets[2]. A problem with these criteria is that they do not assist with the question of whether *new* products are tied, when little is known about their nature and there is, so far, no commercial usage. This can pose a serious problem where highly complex products – for example in IT and multimedia markets – are being introduced to the market. In such cases it may be necessary

---

17 87 F Supp 2d 30 (DDC 2000); for a highly critical account of the Microsoft case, see McKenzie *Antitrust on Trial: How the Microsoft Case is Reframing the Rules of Competition* (Perseus Publishing, 2000); see also Auletta *World War 3.0: Microsoft and Its Enemies* (Random House, 2000), which includes interviews with the trial judge, Judge Jackson; and Heilemann *Pride Before the Fall: The Trials of Bill Gates and the End of the Microsoft Era* (HarperCollins, 2000) which looks at the case from the complainants' perspective; Beckner and Gustafson *Trial and Error: US v Microsoft* (Citizens for a Sound Economy Foundation, 2000); the case even inspired a film, *Antitrust*, starring Tim Robbins and released by MGM in 2000.

18 This is a frequent line of argument by defendants challenging alleged tie-ins in the US; see eg *Jefferson Parish Hospital District No 2 v Hyde* 466 US 2 (1984) at p 19; and *Eastman Kodak Co v Image Technical Services Inc* 504 US 451 (1992) at pp 466-67.

19 Findings of fact, paras 149-54, accessible at http://usvms.gpo.gov/ms-findings2.html.

20 http://usvms.gpo.gov/ms-conclusions.html p 14, II Part A; the US Court of Appeals remanded the finding of tying to the District Court on 28 June 2001, requiring that the matter be determined under the rule of reason, rather than a *per se* standard.

1   See p 605, n 2 above.

2   Ibid, para 216.

to concentrate on whether an apparent tie-in can be objectively justified rather than on whether it amounts to a tie-in in the first place; this, however, would appear to place the burden of proof on the dominant firm rather than on the competition authority or complainant opposing the practice[3].

Given that commercial usage is part of the test of what amounts to a tie-in, it must follow that what was once a tie-in may cease to be so because of changed consumer perceptions.

(D) Abuse

The fact that dominance, abuse and the effects of the abuse can be in different markets is particularly significant in analysing tie-ins, where an undertaking will be dominant in one market and impose a tie which has an effect in a neighbouring market[4]. The Commission has applied Article 82 to several tying transactions. In *IBM*[5] it brought an end to IBM's practices of 'memory bundling' and 'software bundling', accepting an undertaking that IBM would offer its System/370 central processing units without a main memory or with only sufficient memory as was needed for testing. In *Eurofix-Bauco v Hilti*[6] the Commission held that the requirement of Hilti that users of its patented nail cartridges should also acquire nails from it exploited customers and harmed competition and was an abuse of a dominant position; a fine of EUR 6 million was imposed for this and other infringements. Hilti appealed[7], *inter alia*, on the ground that the Commission had been wrong to find that the nail guns, the cartridge strips and the nails were three distinct product markets rather than forming one divisible whole, a 'powder actuated fastening system' comprising the nail guns and their consumables. The CFI held that there were three markets, and that independent producers should be free to manufacture consumables intended for use in equipment manufactured by others unless in so doing they would infringe intellectual property rights[8]. This was in line with earlier rulings about the separate nature of spare parts markets[9]. Hilti also argued that its behaviour was objectively justifiable as it was necessary to maintain safety standards, so that operators would not be injured by nail guns. The Commission had rejected this argument on the facts, concluding that Hilti's primary concern was the protection of its commercial position rather than a disinterested wish to protect users of its products. The CFI upheld this finding. It pointed out that in the UK, where the competitors were selling their nails, there were laws about product safety and authorities which enforced them. In those circumstances it was not the task of a dominant undertaking to take steps on its own initiative to eliminate products which, rightly or wrongly, it regarded as dangerous or inferior to its own products.

---

3 See p 608 above.
4 See ch 5, pp 173-175.
5 XIVth *Report on Competition Policy* (1984), points 94–95; see further on this matter XVIth *Report on Competition Policy* (1986), point 75 and XVIIth *Report on Competition Policy* (1987), point 85.
6 OJ [1988] L 65/19, [1989] 4 CMLR 677.
7 Case T–30/89 *Hilti AG v Commission* [1990] ECR II-163, [1992] 4 CMLR 16, upheld on appeal Case 53/92 P *Hilti AG v Commission* [1994] ECR I-667, [1994] 4 CMLR 614.
8 Case T–30/89 *Hilti AG v Commission* [1990] ECR II-163, [1992] 4 CMLR 16, para 68.
9 Case 22/78 *Hugin Kassaregister AB v EC Commission* [1979] ECR 1869, [1979] 3 CMLR 345; Case 53/87 *CICRA v Régie Nationale des Usines Renault* [1988] ECR 6039, [1990] 4 CMLR 265; Case 238/87 *Volvo (AB) v Erik Veng* [1988] ECR 6211, [1989] 4 CMLR 122.

Tying was one of the main issues in *Tetra Pak II*[10]. Tetra Pak required customers to whom it supplied liquid packaging machines to purchase cartons from it; it also insisted that only it should provide the services of repair and maintenance. Tetra Pak argued that it supplied an integrated distribution system for liquid and semi-liquid foods intended for human consumption and could not therefore be guilty of an abuse in tying the supply of its filling machines to the supply of its cartons. The Commission stated at paragraph 119 of its decision that it was not customary to tie cartons to machines. As in *Hilti*, the Commission held that the consumable cartons formed a separate market upon which the dominant firm was trying to eliminate competition. Tetra Pak was also indulging in discriminatory and predatory pricing and was fined a total of EUR 75 million. A particularly noteworthy feature of the judgment in *Tetra Pak* is that the ECJ stated that 'even where tied sales of two products are in accordance with commercial usage or there is a natural link between the two products in question, such sales may still constitute abuse within the meaning of Article [82] unless they are objectively justified'[11].

In *Centre Belge d'Etudes de Marché-Télémarketing v CLT*[12] the ECJ held that it was an abuse of a dominant position for the Luxembourg radio and television station, which had a statutory monopoly, to insist that advertisers should channel their advertising through its advertising manager or an agency appointed by it. This amounted to an extension of its monopoly power from one market into a neighbouring one, a kind of 'tie-in' that prevented other advertising agencies from competing with it and which limited the commercial freedom of users. In *Napier Brown-British Sugar*[13] the Commission applied this principle when condemning British Sugar's refusal to allow customers to collect sugar at ex-factory prices, thereby reserving to itself the distribution function in respect of this product. In *London European-Sabena*[14] the Commission held that an attempt by Sabena to stipulate that access to its computer reservation system on the part of London European should be conditional upon London European using Sabena's ground-handling services was an abuse under Article 82.

(E)   Objective justification and proportionality

A dominant undertaking may be able successfully to argue that a tie-in is objectively justified and proportionate: possible justifications for tie-ins were discussed above[15]. The burden of proof would be on the dominant firm[16]. An obvious example would be that the tie-in was going to enhance economic efficiency, for example by making the production or distribution of goods cheaper. It has already been noted that in *Hilti v Commission* the CFI agreed with the Commission that, where a public authority has the necessary powers to ensure

10 OJ [1992] L 72/1, [1992] 4 CMLR 551, upheld on appeal to the CFI Case T–83/91 *Tetra Pak International SA v Commission* [1994] ECR II-755, [1997] 4 CMLR 726 and on appeal to the ECJ Case C-333/94 P *Tetra Pak International SA v Commission* [1996] ECR I-5951, [1997] 4 CMLR 662; see Korah 'The Paucity of Economic Analysis in the EEC Decisions on Competition: Tetra Pak II' (1993) 46 Current Legal Problems 148, pp 156-172.
11 Case C-333/94 P *Tetra Pak International SA v Commission* [1996] ECR I-5951, [1997] 4 CMLR 662, para 37.
12 Case 311/84 [1985] ECR 3261, [1986] 2 CMLR 558.
13 OJ [1988] L 284/41, [1990] 4 CMLR 196.
14 OJ [1988] L 317/47, [1989] 4 CMLR 662.
15 See p 607 above.
16 See p 608 above.

product safety, it is not for the dominant undertaking to prevent third parties from selling consumable products that it considers might be unsafe.

3. REFUSAL TO SUPPLY

There are circumstances in which a refusal on the part of a dominant firm to supply goods or services or to grant access to a so-called 'essential facility' can amount to an abuse of a dominant position. Refusal to supply is a difficult and controversial topic in competition law. First, as a general proposition most legal systems in countries with a market economy adopt the view that firms should be allowed to contract with whomsoever they wish; compulsory dealing is not a normal part of the law of contract. Secondly, irrespective of whether the law should sometimes require that a dominant firm should be required to supply, there are many possible objective justifications for a refusal to do so: for example that a customer is a bad debtor, that there is a shortage of stocks, or that production has been disrupted. Thirdly, forcing a dominant undertaking to supply may not be conducive to economic welfare if it means that 'free riders' can expropriate the benefit of investments that have been made by other firms in the market: this will be discussed specifically in the context of the so-called 'essential facilities doctrine' below[17]. This section is concerned with the circumstances in which a refusal to supply might infringe Article 82.

(A) Refusals to supply a downstream competitor[18]

(i) The Commercial Solvents doctrine

Unilateral[19] refusals to supply are caught, if at all, under Article 82. The term 'refusal' in this context includes a constructive refusal, for example by charging unreasonable prices or by imposing unfair trading conditions for the supply in question or by treating a particular customer in a discriminatory manner. It was established by the ECJ in *Commercial Solvents v Commission*[20] that a refusal to supply could, in some circumstances, amount to an abuse of a dominant position. Zoja was an Italian producer of a drug used in the treatment of tuberculosis; it was dependent upon supplies of a raw material, amino-butanol, the dominant supplier of which was Commercial Solvents. When the latter refused to make amino-butanol available to Zoja, the Commission took action against it and ordered it to resume supplies. The Commission's decision, that Commercial Solvents had abused its dominant position, was upheld on appeal by the ECJ. In this case not only was Commercial Solvents a dominant supplier of amino-butanol in the 'upstream' market for the raw material; its refusal to supply Zoja coincided with the emergence of Commercial Solvent's own subsidiary, ICI, onto the 'downstream' market, for the anti-TB drug, on which Zoja was operating. The anti-competitive aspect of Commercial Solvents' behaviour was particularly clear where the refusal to supply would eliminate the only serious competitor that ICI would face in the downstream market. The *Commercial Solvents* doctrine

---

17 See pp 614-624 below.
18 For helpful discussion, see *Bishop and Walker* (p 607, n 11 above), paras 5.23-5.32.
19 Note the extent to which apparently 'unilateral' action may be held to be attributable to an agreement or concerted practice contrary to Article 81: ch 3, pp 86-89.
20 Cases 6/73 & 7/73 [1974] ECR 223, [1974] 1 CMLR 309.

states, therefore, that it is an infringement of Article 82 for an undertaking in a dominant position to refuse to supply a competitor in a downstream market where the effect of doing so would be to eliminate all competition in the downstream market[1]. The so-called 'essential facilities' doctrine, discussed below, is not an independent doctrine; it is the same principle as the one applied in *Commercial Solvents*, albeit with a different name.

(ii)   Subsequent cases

(A)   *HUGIN V COMMISSION*.   In *Hugin*[2] the Commission condemned that firm's decision to discontinue the supply of spare parts for Hugin's cash register machines to Liptons, a firm in the UK that serviced cash registers; Hugin's intention was itself to operate on the downstream market for servicing. On appeal[3] the ECJ annulled the Commission's decision, but only because of the failure on its part to show that trade between Member States would be affected: the ECJ did not depart from the Commission's view that the refusal to supply was abusive. The most controversial issue in *Hugin* was whether it was correct to define a separate product market for spare parts, or whether the Commission should have widened the market to include the original equipment itself. If it had done so, Hugin would not have been dominant in the wider market for cash registers and spare parts, so that there would not have been an abuse[4]. On a subsequent occasion the European considered that Kyocera was not in a dominant position in the toner cartridge market since it was subject to intense competition in the primary market for laser printers, which acted as a constraint on its behaviour in the aftermarket[5]; the Commission came to the opposite view in the later case of *Digital*[6]. Each case turns on its own facts, and it is an empirical question whether there is sufficient competitive constraint to allow a broader market definition than the spare part or consumable[7].

(B)   *MAGILL*.   In the *Magill* case[8] the Community Courts upheld the Commission's finding that the BBC, ITP and RTE, three television companies broadcasting programmes in the UK and Ireland, had each abused an individual dominant position by refusing to make available details of their television schedules to a television listings magazine containing details of all three broadcasters' programmes; no such publication existed at the time. The case was controversial, since it meant that the owners of intellectual property rights – the copyright in the TV schedules – were required to grant licences of those rights to third parties:

---

1   A variant on the *Commercial Solvents* doctrine is that there may sometimes be an obligation to supply a competitor in a horizontally-related market, rather than in a vertically-related downstream market: see the discussion of the *IBM* case at p 613 below.
2   OJ [1978] L 284/41, [1978] 1 CMLR D19.
3   Case 22/78 *Hugin Kassaregister v Commission* [1979] ECR 1869, [1979] 3 CMLR 345.
4   On this point see the judgment of the US Supreme Court in *Eastman Kodak Co v Image Technical Services Inc* 504 US 451 (1992) which held that there was a separate market for servicing photocopiers from the original market for the photocopiers themselves.
5   XXVth *Report on Competition Policy* (1995), p 87; see similarly *Info-Lab/Ricoh* XXIXth *Report on Competition Policy* (1999), pp 169-170.
6   XXVIIth *Report on Competition Policy* (1997), pp 153-154; see Andrews 'Aftermarket Power in the Computer Services Market: The Digital Undertaking' (1998) 19 ECLR 176.
7   The issue of market definition in such cases is discussed in ch 1, pp 22-39.
8   Cases T–69/89 etc *RTE v Commission* [1991] ECR II-485, [1991] 4 CMLR 586, upheld by the ECJ Cases 241/91 P etc *RTE and ITP v Commission* [1995] ECR I-743, [1995] 4 CMLR 718.

compulsory licensing is more naturally a matter for intellectual property law than competition law; the case will be considered in detail in chapter 19[9]. The relevance of *Magill* at this stage is that it is a further example of the *Commercial Solvents* doctrine: that it is an abuse of a dominant position to refuse to supply an upstream product that was necessary for a competitor to be able to compete in a downstream market for listings magazines: each of the broadcasters published their own magazines, listing only their own programmes. The *Magill* case was described by the ECJ in the *Oscar Bronner v Mediaprint* case as an exceptional one[10], and as a general proposition a refusal to supply intellectual property rights will not be abusive, as is shown by the cases on car parts, *Renault*[11] and *Volvo*[12], also discussed in chapter 19[13]. However in those cases the ECJ made clear that, although the car manufacturers did not have to grant licences of their intellectual property rights, it could be an abuse for them to refuse to supply the parts themselves to independent dealers who required them.

(C) THE PROVISION OF PROPRIETARY INFORMATION. The Commission has taken action on some occasions to require a dominant undertaking to provide proprietary information to a competitor. The best-known case is *IBM*, in which the Commission reached a settlement with IBM in 1984[14]. IBM was at that time the world's largest computer manufacturer. The Commission considered that IBM had a dominant position in the supply of two key products for its System/370 computers: the central processing unit and the operating system. Among the allegations of abuse was that IBM had failed to supply other manufacturers in sufficient time with the technical information needed to permit competitive products to be used with System/370. Without conceding that it was dominant or that it had acted abusively, IBM agreed, *inter alia*, to supply, in a timely manner, sufficient interface information to enable competing companies in the EC to attach both hardware and software products of their design to System/370. IBM would also disclose adequate and timely information to competitors to enable them to interconnect their systems or networks with IBM's System/370 Systems Network Architecture. For interfaces to hardware products, information would be made available by IBM within four months of the date of announcement of the product concerned or at the general availability of the product if earlier. For interfaces between software products the information would be made available as soon as the interface was reasonably stable, but no later than general availability. A notable feature of this case was that the relationship of IBM with its competitors was horizontal: manufacturers of computers that competed with IBM needed information from IBM in order to make their products compatible with it; the *Commercial Solvents* doctrine is usually applied where the dominant firm is vertically-integrated and supplies a vital input for the downstream market.

The Commission has taken action to ensure the provision of proprietary information on other occasions. In *Tetra Pak II*[15] it required, at Article 3(5) of its decision, that Tetra Pak should provide third parties with specifications that would enable them to produce cartons compatible with Tetra Pak's machines. In

9   See ch 19, pp 699-700.
10 See pp 619-620 below.
11 Case 53/87 *CICRA v Regie Nationale des Usines Renault* [1988] ECR 6039, [1990] 4 CMLR 265; see also the *Ladbroke* case, p below.
12 Case 238/87 *Volvo (AB) v Erik Veng* [1988] ECR 6211, [1989] 4 CMLR 122.
13 See ch 19, pp 698-699.
14 XIVth *Report on Competition Policy* 1984, points 94-95.
15 See p 610, n 10 above.

Decca Navigation System[16] Decca was the dominant manufacturer of electronic equipment for maritime navigation. It modified the electronic signals produced by its equipment, but did not inform manufacturers of competing equipment. The Commission adopted a decision finding that this was an abuse of a dominant position. In *ITT/Promedia/Belgacom*[17] the Commission considered that a refusal by Belgacom, the dominant telecommunications company in Belgium, to provide data about customers of telephone services to a new entrant in the telephone directories market, and the charging of discriminatory or excessive prices for providing that information, would amount to an abuse of a dominant position. A settlement was reached and the case was closed. In August 2000 the Commission commenced proceedings against Microsoft following a complaint from Sun Microsystems that Microsoft's refusal to disclose interface information about its personal computer operating systems prevented it from developing server operating systems[18].

(iii)   The Commercial Solvents doctrine can apply to existing and to new customers

In *Commercial Solvents* the abuse on the part of Commercial Solvents consisted of refusing to supply an existing customer, Zoja; the same was true in *Hugin*, where Hugin refused to continue to supply Liptons. However, it is important to appreciate that the *Commercial Solvents* doctrine can also apply to a refusal to supply a new customer: this is demonstrated, for example, by the *Magill* case. The essence of the cases under consideration in this section is not the protection of a customer who is dependent on supplies from a dominant supplier, but the maintenance of competition in the downstream market: for this reason, no distinction needs to be drawn between supply to existing customers and supply to new ones[19]. An example of an obligation to supply a new customer is *London European-Sabena*[20], where an airline's refusal to supply access to its computer reservation system to a new customer, London European, unless it agreed also to use Sabena's ground-handling services, was held to be an abuse.

(B)   The 'essential facilities' doctrine

(i)   Introduction

An issue that has been the subject of enormous attention in recent years is the so-called 'essential facilities' doctrine under Article 82. The expression 'essential facility' was not used in EC competition law until the Commission's decision in *Sealink/B&I – Holyhead*[1] in 1992. The essential facilities doctrine has its antecedents in US antitrust; the first case is considered to have been *United*

---

16   OJ [1989] L 43/27, [1990] 4 CMLR 627, paras 108-110.
17   Commission's XXVIIth *Report on Competition Policy* (1997), point 67 and pp 152-153.
18   Commission Press Release IP/00/906, 3 August 2000.
19   However, when withdrawing supplies from an existing customer, a dominant firm should do so in a reasonable manner; an abrupt cessation of supplies would be likely to be regarded as disproportionate: see eg p 625 below on the Commission's decision in *Boosey & Hawkes*.
20   OJ [1988] L 317/47, [1989] 4 CMLR 662.
1   [1992] 5 CMLR 255; see also, in relation to Holyhead Harbour, *Sea Containers v Stena Sealink – Interim Measures* OJ [1994] L 15/8, [1995] 4 CMLR 84.

States v Terminal RR Association[2], although the term was not used in that case. In the context of Article 82 the essential facilities doctrine is a natural consequence of the judgment in *Commercial Solvents*, that a refusal to supply a customer in a downstream market would amount to an abuse if the effect would be to eliminate all competition in that market. As has already been noted, there is no conceptual distinction between the *Commercial Solvents* doctrine and the essential facilities doctrine, and the judgment of the ECJ in the *Oscar Bronner* case was firmly based on the precedent of *Commercial Solvents*. As a matter of economics the point about these cases is that one firm controls an essential input which is necessary for a competitor to be able to compete in a downstream market. The expression 'essential facility' is a particularly apt one where an undertaking seeks access to a physical infrastructure such as a port, airport or pipeline: it is a fairly natural use of language to regard such infrastructures as 'facilities'; however the case law has demonstrated that there might also be an obligation to supply a raw material (*Commercial Solvents*), spare parts (*Hugin*), intellectual property rights (*Magill*), or proprietary information (*IBM*), where the expression 'essential facility' is less appropriate. The term essential facility will be used in the text that follows in deference to the weight of literature that deploys it, but the reader is urged to bear in mind that the controlling doctrine is the one that is derived from *Commercial Solvents*.

There is a vast amount of periodical literature on the essential facilities doctrine[3]. Put simply, the question is whether the owner of an essential facility, such as a port, an airport or a pipeline, can be required, as a matter of competition law, to make that facility available to other undertakings, in the same way that Zoja was able to insist on supplies of amino-butanol.

There is an obvious reason why this issue has aroused so much interest. From the 1980s onwards, the Commission developed a policy that favoured the demonopolisation and liberalisation of sectors that for much of the twentieth century were regarded as natural monopolies, or which were considered to be inappropriate for the market mechanism, and which, often, were under state control or in state ownership[4]. Exposing sectors such as telecommunications, energy markets and transport to competition was considered desirable. However, competition would be slow to emerge where service providers could compete only if they had access to important infrastructures such as telecommunication wires and cables, the electricity grid, gas and oil pipelines, ports, airports and railway lines owned and operated by dominant undertakings. In such cases, control of the infrastructure gives rise to what is often referred to as a 'bottleneck' problem: that competition is impossible where one firm, or a combination or firms, can prevent others from operating on the market by denying access to a facility which is essential and cannot be duplicated. In many Member States this problem was overcome by the establishment of specific regulatory régimes that

---

2   224 US 383 (1912).
3   The following articles would capture much of the writing on this subject: Areeda 'Essential Facilities: An Epithet in Need of Limiting Principles' 58 Antitrust Law Journal 841 (1990); Temple Lang 'Defining Legitimate Competition: Companies' Duties to Supply Competitors and Access to Essential Facilities' (1994) 18 Fordham International Law Journal 439; Ridyard 'Essential Facilities and the Obligation to Supply Competitors under UK and EC Competition Law' (1996) 17 ECLR 438; Lipsky and Sidak 'Essential Facilities' (1999) 51 Stanford Law Review 1187; Korah 'Access to Essential Facilities under the Commerce Act in the Light of Experience in Australia, the European Union and the United States' (2000) 31 Victoria University of Wellington Law Review 231.
4   See further ch 23, p 866ff.

mandate access to such infrastructures on reasonable, non-discriminatory terms[5]; and in some systems of competition law there are specific rules requiring undertakings in particular sectors to supply[6]. It may be sensible in principle that situations of natural or persistent monopoly should be dealt with by a system of *ex ante* regulation rather than by competition law: a competition authority is likely to be ill-equipped to deal with the persistent disputes in relation to access, and the appropriate price for access, that arise in relation to essential facilities. However the Commission, proceeding from the ECJ's judgment in *Commercial Solvents*, began to develop its practice under Article 82 in such a way that a refusal to allow access to an essential facility could be found to be an abuse of a dominant position. As a result of this, there are circumstances in which access can be achieved by invoking competition law[7].

(ii) The Commission's decision in Sealink/B&I – Holyhead

In *Sealink/B&I – Holyhead: Interim Measures*[8] the Commission dealt with a complaint against a company, Sealink, which owned and operated a port – Holyhead, in north Wales – out of which it provided a ferry service to and from Ireland. A rival ferry operator, B&I, claimed that Sealink organised the port's sailing schedules in a way which caused maximum disruption to its services and inconvenience to its passengers. The Commission held that there was *prima facie* a case of abuse and ordered interim measures. It stated that:

'A dominant undertaking which both owns or controls and itself uses an essential facility, ie a facility or infrastructure without access to which competitors cannot provide services to their customers, and which refuses its competitors access to that facility or grants access to competitors only on terms less favourable than those which it gives its own services, thereby placing the competitors at a competitive disadvantage, infringes Article [82], if the other conditions of that Article are met ... The owner of an essential facility which uses its power in one market in order to strengthen its position on another related market, in particular, by granting its competitor access to that related market on less favourable terms than those of its own services, infringes Article [82] where a competitive disadvantage is imposed upon its competitor without objective justification'.[9]

Sealink was ordered to change its schedules in order to avoid disruption during B&I's loading and unloading operations. This decision, even though it was only one for interim measures and was not taken on appeal to the CFI, was of considerable importance, since it demonstrated that the Commission was prepared

---

5   Ibid.
6   See para 53 of the Opinion of Advocate General Jacobs in Case C-7/97 *Oscar Bronner GmbH & Co. KG v Mediaprint Zeitungs-und Zeitschriftenverlag GmbH & Co KG* [1998] ECR I-7791, [1999] 4 CMLR 112; see also Part IIIA of the Australian Trade Practices Act 1974, inserted by the Competition Policy Reform Act 1995, and s 8(b) of the South African Competition Act 1998; on the provisions in Australian law, see Kench and Pengilley 'Part IIIA: Unleashing a Monster?' in *Trade Practices Act: A Twenty-Five Year Stocktake* (eds Hanks and Williams, The Federation Press, 2001).
7   See the comments on this in the Commission's XXIIIrd *Report on Competition Policy* (1993), points 40, 41 and 80.
8   See p 614, n 1 above.
9   Ibid, para 41.

to apply the *Commercial Solvents* doctrine to so-called essential facilities. In the years since the *Sealink* decision it has been necessary to determine quite how wide the essential facilities doctrine is, and what limitations need to be placed upon it. Recent case law of the CFI, in *Tiercé Ladbroke v Commission*[10] and in *European Night Services v Commission*[11], and of the ECJ in *Oscar Bronner GmbH & Co KG v Mediaprint Zeitungs-und Zeitschriftenverlag GmbH & Co KG*[12], have shed important light on these questions[13].

(iii)   The essential facilities doctrine must be applied with caution

It is understandable that the Commission was keen to apply Article 82 in such a way as to grant access to third parties to ports (as in *Sealink*) and other infrastructure such as airports and telecommunications and cables[14] in order to facilitate competition in downstream markets. Where infrastructures of this kind have been established by the state or with state-funding, or by undertakings to which monopoly rights have been granted by the state, a requirement that they should be shared with third parties may be considered to be a reasonable public policy choice. Undertakings controlling a bottleneck might be considered to be 'super-dominant', implying that they have a higher responsibility than the obligations attaching to 'merely' dominant firms[15]. However, it is important to recognise that there must be limits to the essential facilities doctrine. Demanding that a dominant firm should grant access to its facilities is a major intervention on the part of a competition authority; and an excessive application of the essential facilities doctrine can have harmful economic effects. This is not only because there is an element of expropriation in requiring one firm to grant access to its property to a competitor, but also because the prospect that third parties might be able to demand a 'free ride' on the fruits of another's investment might deter the latter from making the investment in the first place. It is clear, therefore, that there must be a sensible limit upon what is to be considered to be an essential facility, and that the circumstances in which access to it can be mandated under Article 82 should be determined with the need not to discourage investment in mind. In particular, where the infrastructure has been established by firms acting in the private sector, without recourse to public funds and without the benefit of monopoly rights conferred by the state, sensitivity to the free rider issue is important.

In *Oscar Bronner* Advocate General Jacobs set out the main features of the US doctrine of essential facilities at paragraph 47 of his Opinion, and in the following paragraph referred to the Commission's two decisions concerning Holyhead Harbour[16]. At paragraphs 56 to 58 of his Opinion, the Advocate General pointed out very clearly to the ECJ that allowing competitors to demand access to the essential facilities of dominant firms, which might seem to be pro-competitive by enabling claimants to enter the market in the short term, might ultimately be anti-competitive, if the consequence would be to discourage the necessary investment for the creation of the facility in the first place. At paragraph

10 Case T-504/93 [1997] ECR II-923, [1997] 5 CMLR 309.
11 Cases T-374/94 etc [1998] ECR II-3141, [1998] 5 CMLR 718.
12 Case C-7/97 [1998] ECR I-7791, [1999] 4 CMLR 112.
13 See pp 618-620 below.
14 See pp 622-623 below.
15 See ch 5, pp 162-163.
16 See p 614, n 1 above.

56 he pointed out that 'the right to choose one's trading partners and freely to dispose of one's property are generally recognised principles in the laws of the Member States' and that 'incursions on those rights require careful justification'. In the following paragraph the Advocate General states that in the long term it is generally pro-competitive to allow an undertaking to retain its facilities for its own use, since granting access to a third party may remove the incentive to invest in the establishment of efficient facilities. At paragraph 58 the Advocate General stressed the importance of the fact that the primary purpose of Article 82 is to prevent distortions of competition, and not to protect the position of particular competitors. While accepting that the case law did, in certain circumstances, impose a duty on dominant firms to supply, the Advocate General advised that the duty should be appropriately confined and should be invoked only where a clear detriment to competition would follow from a refusal.

(iv)   The case law of the Community Courts

(A)   *TIERCÉ LADBROKE v COMMISSION*.   In *Tiercé Ladbroke v Commission*[17] Ladbroke, a Belgian operator taking bets on horse races run abroad, wanted to be able to provide sound commentary of and to televise French races in its Belgian betting shops. Ladbroke claimed that a refusal by the French race-course operators (the 'société de courses') to provide it with the necessary sound and television pictures amounted to an abuse of a dominant position in the market for the transmission of French sound and pictures; it considered that the geographic market was the entire Community, or at least France, Germany and Belgium[18]. The Commission rejected Ladbroke's complaint, holding that the relevant market was the Belgian market for sound and pictures. Ladbroke appealed to the CFI, which upheld the Commission's decision. The CFI agreed that the market was the Belgian market for sound and pictures[19]. It held that, since the société de courses had not yet granted any licences for the Belgian territory, it was impossible for Ladbroke to argue that it had been discriminated against[20]. The CFI specifically refused to apply the precedent in *Magill*, 'since that decision is not in point'[1]. In *Magill*, the refusal to supply the TV listings prevented Magill from entering the downstream market for comprehensive television guides; in *Ladbroke*, Ladbroke was present in, and had the largest share of, the betting market in Belgium; the refusal to supply therefore did not result in any elimination of competition in the downstream market. At paragraph 131 of its judgment the CFI said that a refusal to supply could not fall within the prohibition of Article 82:

'unless it concerned a product or service which was either essential for the exercise of the activity in question, in that there was no real or potential substitute, or was a new product whose introduction might be prevented, despite specific, constant and regular potential demand on the part of consumers...'

17   Case T-504/93 [1997] ECR II-923, [1997] 5 CMLR 309; see Korah 'The Ladbroke Saga' (1998) 19 ECLR 169.
18   Ibid, paras 12 and 13.
19   Ibid, paras 81-89 (product market) and 102-108 (geographic market).
20   Ibid, paras 123-124.
1   Ibid, para 130.

On the facts of *Ladbroke*, the televised broadcasting of horse races, which would be an additional, indeed suitable, service for bettors, could not be regarded as in itself indispensable for the exercise of bookmakers' main activity, namely the taking of bets[2]. Furthermore, Ladbroke could not rely on the ECJ's judgments in the *Commercial Solvents v Commission* and the *Télémarketing*[3] cases since, in each of them, the dominant firm was present on the downstream market; the société de courses in *Ladbroke* had no presence on the Belgian betting markets.

(B)   *EUROPEAN NIGHT SERVICES v COMMISSION.*   In *European Night Services*[4] the Commission concluded that a joint venture, European Night Services, established by four rail operators to provide overnight rail services between the UK and the Continent through the Channel Tunnel, infringed Article 81(1); however it granted individual exemption under Article 81(3), subject to a condition that the parents of the joint venture should supply equivalent services – such as train paths, locomotives and train crews – to third parties to those that it supplied to European Night Services: in doing this, the Commission was treating these services as though they were essential facilities. On appeal to the CFI[5] the Court held that the Commission had failed to demonstrate that the agreement restricted competition contrary to Article 81(1), and annulled it for that reason[6]. However the CFI also held that, even if Article 81(1) was infringed, the condition that rail services should be supplied to third parties should be annulled[7]. Applying *Magill* and *Ladbroke*, the CFI said that 'a product or service cannot be considered necessary or essential unless there is no real or potential substitute'[8]. In the CFI's view the Commission had failed to prove that this was the case.

(C)   *OSCAR BRONNER v MEDIAPRINT.*   In *Oscar Bronner*[9], Bronner was a publisher of a daily newspaper, *Der Standard*, and wished to have access to the highly developed home-delivery distribution system of its much larger competitor, Mediaprint; Bronner complained that a refusal to allow such access amounted to an infringement of the Austrian equivalent of Article 82. The Austrian court sought the opinion of the ECJ under Article 234 EC whether such a refusal would infringe Article 82. The entire tone of the judgment is sceptical towards Bronner's case.

The ECJ stated that the first task for the national court would be to determine whether there was a separate market for the home-delivery of newspapers in Austria, and whether there was insufficient substitutability between Mediaprint's nationwide system and other, regional, schemes. If the market was the nationwide delivery of newspapers to homes, the national court would be bound to conclude that Mediaprint had a monopoly, and since this extended to the entire territory

---

2   Ibid, para 132.
3   Case 311/84 *Centre Belge d'Etudes de Marché-Télémarketing v CLT* [1985] ECR 3261, [1986] 2 CMLR 558.
4   OJ [1994] L 259/20, [1995] 5 CMLR 76.
5   Cases T-374/94 etc *European Night Services v Commission* [1998] ECR II-3141, [1998] 5 CMLR 718.
6   See ch 3, pp 102-103.
7   Ibid, paras 205-221.
8   Ibid, para 208.
9   Case C-7/97 [1998] ECR I-7791, [1999] 4 CMLR 112; see Treacy 'Essential Facilities – Is the Tide Turning?' (1998) 19 ECLR 501; Bergman 'The *Bronner* Case – A Turning Point for the Essential Facilities Doctrine?' (2000) 21 ECLR 59.

of Austria, that this monopoly would be held in a substantial part of the common market[10].

The ECJ then moved on to the question of abuse. It pointed out that in *Commercial Solvents* the effect of the refusal to supply the raw material on the part of the dominant firm was likely to eliminate all competition in the downstream market between its own subsidiary and anyone else[11]. The ECJ then referred to the *Magill* case, saying that the refusal by the owner of an intellectual property right to licence it to a third party could, 'in exceptional circumstances' involve an abuse[12]; in the Court's view, *Magill* was an exceptional case for four reasons. First, the information sought by Magill was indispensable to the publication of a comprehensive listings guide: without it Magill could not publish a magazine at all; secondly, there was a demonstrable potential consumer demand for the would-be product; thirdly, there were no objective justifications for the refusal to supply; and fourthly the refusal would eliminate all competition in the secondary market for TV guides[13]. The ECJ said, therefore, that, for there to be an abuse, it would have to be shown that refusal to grant access to the home-delivery service would be likely to eliminate all competition in the daily newspaper market (the downstream market) and that the home-delivery service was indispensable to carrying on business in the newspaper market[14]. In the ECJ's view, use of Mediaprint's home-delivery service was not indispensable, since there were other means of distributing daily newspapers, for example through shops, kiosks and by post[15]; furthermore, there were no technical, legal or economic obstacles that made it impossible for other publishers of daily newspapers to establish home-delivery systems of their own[16]. Specifically on the question of whether access to the distribution system could be considered indispensable the ECJ said that:

'45. It should be emphasised in that respect that, in order to demonstrate that the creation of such a system is not a realistic potential alternative and that access to the existing system is therefore indispensable, it is not enough to argue that it is not economically viable by reason of the small circulation of the daily newspaper or newspapers to be distributed.

46. For such access to be capable of being regarded as indispensable, it would be necessary at the very least to establish, as the Advocate General has pointed out at point 68 of his Opinion, that it is not economically viable to create a second home-delivery scheme for the distribution of daily newspapers with a circulation comparable to that of the daily newspapers distributed by the existing scheme'.

In the ECJ's view, the behaviour of Mediaprint did not amount to an abuse of a dominant position.

---

10 Ibid, paras 32-36.
11 Ibid, para 38.
12 Ibid, para 39.
13 Ibid, para 40.
14 Ibid, para 41.
15 Ibid, para 42.
16 Ibid, para 44.

(v)   The practical application of the essential facilities doctrine

Having reviewed the *Commercial Solvents* doctrine and the case law on essential facilities, it may be helpful to draw together the main points.

(A)   'ESSENTIALITY' AND INDISPENSABILITY.   The first issue to consider is what is meant by 'essentiality' or 'indispensability', the term used by the ECJ in *Oscar Bronner.* It is clear from the judgments just discussed that a narrow view should be taken of what amounts to an essential or indispensable product, service or facility. This was clearly the view of the CFI in *Ladbroke* and *European Night Services*; in *Oscar Bronner* the ECJ emphasised that it was not sufficient that it was economically impossible for a small publisher of newspapers such as Oscar Bronner to establish a nationwide home-delivery system: 'at the very least' it would be necessary to show that an undertaking with a circulation comparable to that of Mediaprint would not be able to do so.

Essentiality consists of two things. The first is that it is not possible for another undertaking to duplicate the facility in question: there must be 'no real or potential substitute' (*European Night Services*) or, to use the language of the Commission's *Notice on the Application of the Competition Rules to Access Agreements in the Telecommunications Sector*[17], the facility must be one 'which cannot be replicated by any reasonable means'[18]. This may be because of physical impossibility: examples of this would be that there are no other deep-sea ports available for the provision of ferry services, or that it is not possible to build a competing airport in the vicinity of Heathrow or a second railway line from London to Glasgow due to planning and environmental constraints. The impossibility may be legal, for example where an undertaking owns intellectual property rights, such as the copyright in *Magill.* More controversially, the impossibility may be economic, for example where a competitor cannot afford to establish a facility of its own; particular caution should be exercised in this situation not to grant access where this entails a 'free ride' on the risk and investment that another competitor has made. This is presumably why the ECJ confined the notion of economic indispensability in the way that it did in *Oscar Bronner.*

The second aspect of essentiality is the importance of access to competitors. It is clear that it is not sufficient that it would be convenient or 'suitable' for them to have access (*Ladbroke*); access to the facility must be indispensable (*Oscar Brönner*). In the Commission's *Notice on the Application of the Competition Rules to Access Agreements in the Telecommunications Sector*[19] it states that:

'It will not be sufficient that the position of the company requesting access would be more advantageous if access were granted – but refusal of access must lead to the proposed activities being made either impossible or seriously and unavoidably uneconomic'[20].

(B)   THE RELATIONSHIP BETWEEN MARKET DEFINITION AND THE ESSENTIALITY.   As in any investigation under Article 82, it is necessary to define the relevant market in an essential facilities case. The definition of the essential facility in the upstream market will inevitably be influenced by the downstream market: for example in

---

17   OJ [1998] C 265/2, [1998] 5 CMLR 821.
18   Ibid, para 68.
19   OJ [1998] C 265/2, [1998] 5 CMLR 821, para 91(a).
20   Ibid.

Sealink/B&I – Holyhead the Commission noted that there were three 'corridors' for short-sea routes between Great Britain and Ireland: the northern corridor, served, for example, by Stranraer in Scotland; the central corridor, served predominantly by Holyhead; and the southern corridor, served by Fishguard, Pembroke and Swansea in south and west Wales. The Commission defined the upstream market as the provision of port facilities for passenger and ferry services on the central corridor route; however, had it considered that the downstream market was all short-sea crossings between Great Britain and Ireland, it could not have defined the upstream market so narrowly; in this case, Holyhead harbour (or more precisely the services available there) would not have been found to be essential. This demonstrates that essential facility cases require an analysis of the downstream market, since without this it is not possible to define the upstream one.

The definition of the upstream market does not, in itself, determine the outcome of the case. It is possible for an undertaking to have a dominant position in the upstream market and yet for it not to have an obligation to grant access to the essential facility under its control. In *Oscar Bronner* the ECJ said that, even if Mediaprint was dominant in the market for the nationwide delivery of newspapers, it would not be an abuse to refuse to grant access to it if there were other ways of selling newspapers, for example through shops, kiosks and by post: defining the market and determining essentiality are not one and the same thing. Nor would there be an abuse unless the refusal to grant access would eliminate all competition in the downstream market, the key feature of the *Commercial Solvents* doctrine; and it is also possible that the refusal might have an objective justification.

(C) 'FACILITIES' TO WHICH THE DOCTRINE HAS BEEN APPLIED. As we have seen, the precedent of *Commercial Solvents* had been applied to raw materials, spare parts, intellectual property rights and proprietary information before the Commission specifically applied the 'essential facilities' doctrine in relation to the port of Holyhead[1]. The doctrine has been applied to other physical infrastructures. It was applied in the Commission's decision on the *Port of Rødby*[2]. In *Frankfurt Airport*[3] the Commission required that the airport authority should terminate its monopoly over ground-handling services and that it should grant access to third parties wishing to supply such services there[4]. Oil and gas pipelines are capable of being essential facilities[5]. So too are telecommunications wires

---

1 See pp 611-614 above.
2 OJ [1994] L 55/22, [1994] 5 CMLR 457; the Commission's interim measures in the case of *Irish Continental Group v CCI Morlaix*, reported in the Commission's XXVth *Report on Competition Policy* (1995), pp 120-121 and at [1995] 5 CMLR 177, was different from the Holyhead and Rødby cases, in that the port operator in this case was not active on the downstream ferry market; see also *Tariffs for Piloting in the Port of Genoa* OJ [1997] L 301/27.
3 OJ [1998] L 72/30, [1998] 4 CMLR 779; note that Council Directive 96/97/EC, OJ [1997] L 272/36 liberalises ground-handling at airports and prevents discriminatory fees.
4 See p 604 above on the termination of the long-term supply contracts.
5 See eg *Disma* XXIIIrd *Report on Competition Policy* (1993), pp 141-143 where the doctrine was applied to equipment for storing jet fuel and transferring it to supply points at Milan's Malpensa Airport; this case was brought under Article 81 rather than Article 82, since a number of undertakings owned the infrastructure in question.

and cables[6] and set-top boxes necessary, for example, for the provision of interactive television services[7].

The doctrine has also been applied to less obviously 'physical' facilities. For example, it may be unlawful to deny access to a computerised airline reservation system[8] or to a cross-border credit transfer system[9]. There may be circumstances in which access to the postal network may be granted under Article 82[10]. It may be unlawful to refuse to grant interlining facilities to a competing airline[11]. In the case of the Society for Worldwide International Financial Telecommunications (SWIFT) the Commission said, in a statement of objections initiating proceedings under Article 82, that SWIFT had abused a dominant position. SWIFT was the only operator on the international networks for transferring payment messages, and the only network to supply connections for banking establishments anywhere in the world. The Commission considered that the network constituted a 'basic infrastructure in its own right, since to refuse any entity access to such a network is tantamount to a *de facto* exclusion from the market for international transfers'[12]. The Commission's view was that it was a manifest abuse of a dominant position to lay down unjustified admission criteria and to apply them in a discriminatory manner[13]. SWIFT agreed to grant access to any entity meeting the criteria laid down by the European Monetary Institute for admission to domestic payment systems[14].

(D)   THE NATURE OF THE ABUSE.   The nature of the abuse in an essential facilities case was set out above in the discussion of the *Holyhead Harbour* case. A clear statement of what constitutes an abuse can also be found in the Commission's decision on the *Port of Rødby*[15]:

'[A]n undertaking that owns or manages and uses itself an essential facility, *ie* a facility or infrastructure without which its competitors are unable to offer their services to customers, and refuses to grant them access to such facility is abusing its dominant position'[16].

---

6   Commission *Notice on the Application of the Competition Rules to Access Agreements in the Telecommunications Sector* OJ [1998] C 265/2, [1998] 5 CMLR 821, paras 49-53 and 87-98; see Nikolinakos 'Access Agreements in the Telecommunications Sector – Refusal to Supply and the Essential Facilities Doctine under EC Competition Law' (1999) 20 ECLR 399.

7   See eg Case JV.37 *BSkyB/KirchPayTV* (under the EC Merger Regulation), Commission Press Release IP/00/279, 21 March 2000; *British Interactive Broadcasting* OJ [1999] L 312/1, [2000] 4 CMLR 901, paras 173-181 (under Article 81).

8   *London European-Sabena* OJ [1988] L 317/47, [1989] 4 CMLR 662; see also *Lufthansa* Commission Press Release IP/99/542, where the Commission imposed a fine of EUR 10,000 under Council Regulation 2299/89 on a code of conduct for computerised reservation systems.

9   Commission *Notice on the Application of the Competition Rules to Cross-border Credit Transfers* OJ [1995] C 251/3; see also the Commission's XXVIth *Report on Competition Policy* (1996), point 109, on the ECU Banking Association.

10   Commission *Notice on the Application of the Competition Rules to the Postal Sector* OJ [1998] C 39/9, [1998] 5 CMLR 108, paras 2.8 and 2.9.

11   *Aer Lingus/British Midland* OJ [1992] L 96/34.

12   Commission's XXVIIth *Report on Competition Policy* (1997), point 68.

13   Ibid.

14   For details of the settlement, see the Commission's XXVIIth *Report on Competition Policy* (1997), pp 143-145.

15   OJ [1994] L 55/22, [1994] 5 CMLR 457.

16   Ibid, para 12.

A constructive refusal to supply – for example by acting in a discriminatory manner, by delaying access in an unreasonable manner or by charging an excessive price for access – would also infringe Article 82. Where a firm controls an essential facility and operates on a downstream market, it would be sensible for it to operate the facility separately from the downstream activity and to maintain separate accounts for each business. If it operates the essential facility as an entirely separate business, without regard to its downstream activity, it is less likely to commit an abuse.

(E) OBJECTIVE JUSTIFICATION. The owner of an essential facility will not commit an abuse where it has an objective justification for a denial of access. Obvious justifications would be that the undertaking seeking access is not creditworthy or that it is technically incapable of using the facility in a proper manner. A particular issue that arises in the case of essential facilities is that there may be capacity constraints which make it impossible for access to be provided[17]. For example the owner of a port might already be using it to full capacity, in which case it would not be possible for it to grant access to a third party. If several competitors are already using the facility and are operating in the same downstream market, this would suggest that granting access to another undertaking would not be necessary to maintain competition there. If there is only capacity for one additional user, it might be appropriate to hold an auction and to grant access to the highest bidder. It is doubtful that the owner of the essential facility can be under a duty to increase capacity in order to enable a third party to have access.

If the dominant firm claims that all the capacity in the essential facility is being used, an investigation may be necessary to determine whether the claim is a genuine one or whether the argument is being deployed in order to deny access to the downstream competitor.

(F) ACCESS PRICING. The owner of an essential facility must charge reasonable, non-discriminatory fees for access. Determining what a reasonable fee should be is complex: this issue is discussed in chapter 18[18].

(C) Refusal to supply a distributor as a disciplining measure

A refusal to supply may be abusive where a dominant firm does so as a disciplinary measure against a distributor who handles competitors' products. This happened in *United Brands v Commission*[19], where United Brands was trying to prevent its distributor, which was not subject to an exclusive purchasing obligation, from taking part in a competitor's advertising campaign. The ECJ held that it was abusive to stop supplying a long-standing customer which abides by normal commercial practice, and that orders should be met which were in no way out of the ordinary. United Brand's objective was to prevent the distributor from selling competitors' products: in other words the practice was intended to achieve single branding. This was not a case in which the refusal to supply was intended to eliminate a competitor in a downstream market, as in the *Commercial Solvents* situation.

---

17 The Commission rejected the airport authority's arguments on capacity constraints in *Frankfurt Airports* OJ [1998] L 72/30, [1998] 4 CMLR 779, paras 74-88.
18 See ch 18, pp 637-638.
19 Case 27/76 [1978] ECR 207, [1978] 1 CMLR 429.

(D)   Refusal to supply a potential competitor in the supplier's market

It may be an abuse to refuse supplies as an exclusionary tactic against a customer trying to enter an upstream market in competition with the supplier. In *BBI/ Boosey & Hawkes: Interim Measures*[20] the Commission found that Boosey & Hawkes had abused a dominant position by refusing to supply brass band instruments to a distributor which was intending to commence the manufacture of such instruments in competition with it. The Commission said that the dominant firm was entitled to take reasonable steps to protect its commercial interest, but that such measures must be fair and proportional to the threat[1]; in its view it was not reasonable 'to withdraw all supplies immediately or to take reprisals against that customer'[2].

(E)   Refusal to supply at a time of shortage

The ECJ accepted in *BP v Commission*[3] that it is not an abuse if, in times of shortage, a supplier chooses to supply regular customers over more occasional ones. This case arose from the oil shortage that resulted from the activities of OPEC in the early 1970s. The ECJ said that it would be an abuse for a dominant firm to treat comparable customers in a discriminatory manner without objective justification.

(F)   Refusal to supply on the basis of nationality

Discrimination on grounds of nationality is contrary to Article 12 (ex Article 6) of the Treaty. In *GVL v Commission*[4] the ECJ held that it was abusive for a national copyright collecting society to refuse to admit to membership nationals of other Member States.

4.   ABUSES THAT ARE HARMFUL TO THE SINGLE MARKET

As noted in chapter 5, the Commission will condemn abusive practices that are harmful to the single market[5]. In *BL v Commission*[6] the ECJ upheld the decision of the Commission that BL had abused a dominant position by refusing to supply type-approval certificates for Metro cars imported from the Continent; this practice was part of a strategy of British Leyland aimed at discouraging parallel imports into the UK. In *United Brands v Commission*[7] one of the abuses committed by United Brands was to impose a restriction on its distributors against exporting green, unripened bananas: in practice this amounted to an export ban, since it would not be possible to export bananas that were already ripe. The Commission's

20   OJ [1987] L 286/36, [1988] 4 CMLR 67.
1   Ibid, para 19.
2   Ibid.
3   Case 77/77 [1978] ECR 1513, [1978] 3 CMLR 174.
4   Case 7/82 [1983] ECR 483, [1983] 3 CMLR 645.
5   See ch 5, pp 179-180; see also the XXVIIth *Report on Competition Policy* (1997) point 63.
6   Case 226/84 [1986] ECR 3263 [1987] 1 CMLR 185; see also Commission Press Release IP (87) 390 *Re Volvo Italia* [1988] 4 CMLR 423.
7   Case 27/76 [1978] ECR 207, [1978] 1 CMLR 429.

investigation of the ticketing arrangements in *Football World Cup 1998*[8] was prompted by the fact that they discriminated in favour of French residents. In *Amministrazione Autonoma dei Monopoli dello Stato*[9] the Commission concluded that AAMS, which had a dominant position on the Italian market for the wholesale distribution of cigarettes, had abused its dominant position by imposing distribution agreements on foreign producers which contained terms limiting the access of foreign cigarettes to the Italian market; a fine of EUR 6 million was imposed.

5.   MISCELLANEOUS CASES

Just as, at common law, it was once said that 'the categories of negligence are never closed'[10], so too the categories of abuse have yet to be exhausted. Numerous pricing practices have been held to be abusive, as the next chapter will demonstrate. Various other non-pricing abuses should be mentioned. Cabinet exclusivity in the Irish impulse ice-cream market has been discussed in chapter 5[11] and earlier in this chapter[12], as have abuses that are harmful to the competitive structure of the market[13]. An example of harming the structure of the market occurred in *Irish Sugar v Commission*[14], where the CFI upheld the decision of the Commission that it was an abuse of a dominant position for Irish Sugar, the dominant undertaking in the Irish sugar market, to purchase a competitor's sugar from a wholesaler and a retailer and to replace it with its own, a so-called 'product swap'[15].

It may be abusive for a dominant firm to resort to vexatious litigation. The Commission acknowledges that undertakings have a fundamental right of access to a judge, but considers that a dominant undertaking might be guilty of an abuse where litigation cannot reasonably be considered as an attempt to establish rights but instead serves to harass the other party and where it is conceived in the framework of a plan whose goal is to eliminate competition[16]. On appeal to the CFI the Court, without actually deciding whether the Commission's test of vexatiousness was correct[17], did nothing to cast doubt on the suggested test. The possibility that vexatious litigation could be abusive is a serious matter in industries in which intellectual property rights are of particular significance, such as pharmaceuticals and biotechnology, where infringement actions and the

---

8   OJ [2000] L 5/55, [2000] 4 CMLR 963; see Weatherill 'Fining the Organisers of the 1998 World Cup' (2000) 21 ECLR 275.
9   OJ [1998] L 252/47, on appeal Case T-139/98 *Amminstrazione Autonoma dei Monopoli dello Stato v Commission* (judgment pending).
10   Lord Atkin in *Donoghue v Stevenson* [1932] AC 562.
11   See ch 5, p 176, on the Commission's decision in *Van den Bergh Foods* OJ [1998] L 246/1, [1998] 5 CMLR 539, on appeal to the CFI Case T-65/98 *Ven den Bergh Foods Ltd v Commission* (judgment pending).
12   See p 605 above.
13   See ch 5, pp 175-176; note in particular the Commission's decision in *TACA* OJ [1999] L 95/1, [1999] 4 CMLR 1415, on appeal to the CFI Cases T-191/98 etc (judgment pending).
14   Case T-228/97 [1999] ECR II-2969, [1999] 5 CMLR 1300.
15   Ibid, paras 226-235.
16   Case T-111/96 *ITT Promedia NV v Commission* [1998] ECR II-2937, [1998] 5 CMLR 491, paras 29-30 and 54-62: see Preece '*ITT Promedia v Commission*: Establishing an Abuse of Predatory Litigation?' (1999) 20 ECLR 118; see also *Boosey & Hawkes* OJ [1987] L 286/36, [1988] 4 CMLR 67, para 9; on the position in the US, see *Professional Real Estate Investors v Columbia Pictures Industries* 508 US 49 (1993).
17   Ibid, para 58.

threat of such actions are commonplace. There may also be circumstances in which the conclusion of a contract or the acquisition of a contractual right might be abusive[18]; so also might a claim for performance of a contractual obligation where the claim exceeds what the party seeking to enforce the agreement could reasonably expect under it or where the circumstances applicable at the time of the contract have changed in the meantime[19]. In *Compagnie Maritime Belge Transports SA v Commission*[20] Cewal, a liner conference, had concluded an agreement with the Zaïrean Maritime Freight Management Office (the so-called 'Ogefrem agreement') granting Cewal exclusive rights to the freight trade between Zaïre and northern Europe. When Ogefrem allowed a third party, Grimaldi and Cobelfret, a small amount of the trade in question, Cewal repeatedly insisted that Ogefrem should strictly comply with the terms of the agreement. The ECJ upheld the finding of the Commission that it was abusive of Cewal to insist on its exclusive rights under the Ogefrem agreement in circumstances where the insistence was intended to remove its only competitor from the market and where Cewal had a discretion under the contract whether to insist on its performance or not[1].

The CFI upheld the Commission's rejection of a complaint that lobbying for the imposition of anti-dumping duties constituted an abuse of a dominant position in *Industrie des Poudres Sphériques v Commission*[2].

6. UK LAW

Abusive practices may be controlled in the UK both under the Chapter II prohibition in the Competition Act 1998 and under the monopoly provisions in the Fair Trading Act 1973 (the 'FTA'). Section 60 of the 1998 Act, requiring consistency between the application of EC and domestic competition law, will mean that Community law will be highly relevant in determining whether conduct will be considered to be abusive under Chapter II[3]. Each of the matters so far considered in this chapter, with the obvious exception of practices harmful to the single market which is unique to EC law, will now be reviewed under domestic law. Only brief consideration will be given to the FTA, since its use in the future will be relatively infrequent[4]. However, it would be unfortunate to overlook altogether the experience gained by the Competition Commission and its predecessor, the Monopolies and Mergers Commission, in its monopoly investigations. This institution will be referred to in the text that follows as 'the Commission', whatever its appellation may have been at the time of the investigation under consideration.

---

18 Ibid, para 139.
19 Ibid, para 140.
20 Cases C-395/96 P [2000] 4 CMLR 1076.
1   Ibid, paras 84-88.
2   Case T-5/97 [2001] 4 CMLR 1020.
3   See ch 9, pp 329-333.
4   See ch 11, pp 383-385.

(A)   Exclusive agreements

(i)   Competition Act 1998

Vertical restraints are excluded from the Chapter I prohibition[5]. However they remain subject to the Chapter II prohibition, with the result that requirements contracts and other exclusive dealing agreements may be held to be abusive under that provision. Section 6 of the DGFT's Guideline on *Assessment of Individual Agreements and Conduct*[6] considers the application of the Chapter II prohibition to vertical restraints. The main concerns are said to be that vertical restraints on the part of firms with market power may foreclose the market, raise rivals' costs and dampen competition[7]. Paragraphs 6.11 to 6.14 consider the extent to which vertical restraints may foreclose the market to manufacturers: exclusive purchasing and dealing, tie-in sales, full-line forcing, and fidelity discounts are cited as possible infringements[8]. In assessing whether such practices have a foreclosing effect, the DGFT will take into account the degree of competition between retailers, the scope for renegotiating contracts and the market power of the manufacturer[9]. Paragraphs 6.15 to 6.17 consider the possible foreclosure of retailers: exclusive and selective distribution, tie-in sales and full-line forcing are given as examples of possible problems[10]. The key issue in such cases is the market power of the manufacturer imposing the vertical restraint[11]; the DGFT will also examine whether there is an anti-competitive cumulative effect arising from a network of agreements[12]. A further issue will be the strength of a manufacturer's brands[13].

The *Guideline* states that the DGFT will assess the impact of a vertical restraint only if market power is present[14]. The scope and duration of the agreement and the degree of market power of the parties will be material to deciding whether the Chapter II prohibition has been contravened[15].

(ii)   Fair Trading Act 1973

Requirements contracts and similar practices have been investigated and brought under control under the FTA. For example in *Asbestos and Certain Asbestos Products*[16] the Commission criticised Turner and Newall's policy of requiring customers to buy exclusively from it and to sell only goods supplied by it. Various undertakings were taken from Turner and Newall, the last of which, to refrain from taking over competitors, was released in 1987. After *Metal Containers*[17] action was taken to weaken Metal Box's hold on the market and to facilitate

---

5   See ch 16, pp 595-598.
6   OFT 414.
7   Ibid, para 6.9.
8   Ibid, para 6.11.
9   Ibid, paras 6.12-6.14.
10   Ibid, para 6.15.
11   Ibid, para 6.16.
12   Ibid.
13   Ibid, para 6.17.
14   Ibid, para 6.29.
15   Ibid, para 6.30.
16   HCP (1972–73) 3.
17   HCP (1970) 6.

entry by other producers of containers[18]. In *Greyhound Racing*[19] the Commission recommended the modification of rule 174(i) of the rules of the National Greyhound Racing Club which prohibited anyone who ran greyhounds at NGRC stadia from participating in events at race courses elsewhere. In *Structural Warranty Services in Relation to New Homes*[20] the Commission recommended alterations to the rules of the National House Building Council which required that any builder registered with the NHBC had to apply to it for inspection of any house he intended to build, thereby incurring a fee; this discouraged NHBC registered builders from using competing warranty schemes. The rules also made it difficult for a member to cancel his NHBC membership in order to place homes with another scheme. The Commission praised the NHBC's rôle in improving building standards and protecting purchasers, but was concerned that unnecessarily restrictive rules prevented other schemes from providing a viable alternative. The Commission's findings were unsuccessfully challenged in *R v Commission, ex p NHBC*[1]. Various exclusive arrangements were investigated by the DGFT and brought under control under the Competition Act 1980: for example *British Railways Board/Brighton Taxis*[2] and *British Airports Authority*[3]. The practices of alignment and minimum exhibition periods in the distribution of films was found to operate against the public interest in the Commission's 1994 investigation of *Films*[4] leading to the Films (Exhibition Periods) Order 1996[5].

(B) Tie-ins

(i) Competition Act 1998

As in the case of Article 82(2)(d), section 18(2)(d) of the Competition Act 1998 specifically states that a tie-in agreement may constitute an abuse of a dominant position. Section 8 of the Guideline on *Assessment of Individual Agreements and Conduct*[6] explains the circumstances in which a firm which is dominant in one market may act abusively in relation to a neighbouring market, and gives as an example a tie-in[7]. The *Guideline* indicates that there are two principle ways in which an undertaking with a dominant position in one market may be able to act anti-competitively in a neighbouring market. A dominant undertaking may exploit its market power vertically, by virtue of its control of an essential input which is necessary for production downstream in that industry; or it may do so horizontally, through its production of complementary products[8]. This leveraging of market power may be achieved in a number of ways, including the use of

---

18 The Commission criticised several aspects of Metal Box's commercial practices including its discount policy (see ch 18, p 669) and its tie-in practices (see p 630 below) and contractual clauses which tied customers to it for an unduly long period.
19 Cmnd 9834 (1986); see also *RAC Motor Sports Association* (OFT Press Release, 11 June 1992: abandonment of restrictive rules).
20 Cm 1438 (1991).
1 Judgment of 1 October 1992 .
2 OFT, 24.11.82; 1983 *Annual Report of the DGFT*, pp 85–86.
3 OFT, 22.2.84; 1984 *Annual Report of the DGFT*, p 86.
4 Cm 2673 (1994).
5 SI 1996/3140.
6 OFT 414.
7 Ibid, para 8.3.
8 Ibid, para 8.2.

discounts, tie-ins or cross-subsidies[9]. The DGFT will determine the feasibility of an undertaking exercising market power on one market in order to influence another market by examining the proximity between them[10]; the more proximate the markets are, the greater the ability to leverage market power between them.

(ii)   Fair Trading Act 1973

Tie-ins and full-line forcing have been investigated under the FTA on a number of occasions[11]. In *Metal Containers*[12] the requirement that purchasers of cans also acquire can closing equipment from the supplier was condemned. In an investigation of *Films*[13] in 1967 the tying of a second film to the prime feature film was considered to operate against the public interest. In *Indirect Electrostatic Reprographic Equipment*[14] the Commission recommended that an undertaking should be negotiated with Rank Xerox that customers should be permitted to purchase toner for photocopying machines separately from the machines themselves. An undertaking was taken in due course, which was modified in 1983[15]; in 1991 the Commission concluded that the structure of the photocopier market had been transformed and was now highly competitive, so that the undertakings should be lifted[16].

When the Commission published a general report on tie-ins under section 78 FTA[17], it concluded in *Tie-in Sales and Full-Line Forcing*[18] that a blanket condemnation would not be justified. Apart from their justified use in distribution agreements, the Commission recognised that these practices could be used for other legitimate purposes.

(C)   Refusal to supply

(i)   Competition Act 1998

The DGFT discusses refusals to supply at paragraphs 4.47 to 4.49 of the *Guideline on the Chapter II prohibition*[19]. Paragraph 4.47 begins by referring to the judgment of the ECJ in *Commercial Solvents v Commission*[20] and stating that a refusal to supply without an objective justification could amount to an abuse; the *Guideline* does not point out that the abuse in that case did not consist merely of a refusal to supply, but a refusal that led to the elimination of a competitor on a downstream

---

9   Ibid, para 8.3.
10   Ibid, para 8.5.
11   Tie-ins may also be prohibited by specific legislation: see eg Courts and Legal Services Act 1990, ss 104–107 forbidding tie-ins between mortgages of residential properties and insurance policies.
12   HCP (1970) 6.
13   HCP (1966–67) 206; see also *Petrol* HCP (1964–65) 264 (tie-in of lubricants to petrol condemned) and *Colour Film* HCP (1966–67) 9 (processing of film tied to purchase of the film itself).
14   (1976–77) HCP 47.
15   1983 *Annual Report of the DGFT* pp 80–81.
16   *Indirect Electrostatic Photocopiers* Cm 1693 (1991).
17   On general reports under the FTA see ch 11, pp 388–389.
18   HCP (1980–81) 212.
19   OFT Guideline 402.
20   Cases 6/73 & 7/73 [1974] ECR 223, [1974] 1 CMLR 309.

market[1]. The *Guideline* suggests various objective justifications for a refusal to supply, such as poor creditworthiness and capacity constraints. Paragraph 4.48 states that a refusal to supply a new customer could, in limited circumstances, amount to an abuse: this is consistent with the position in EC law[2]. Paragraph 4.49 specifically refers to the essential facilities doctrine: a facility is viewed as essential 'if access to it is indispensable in order to compete on the market and duplication is impossible or extremely difficult owing to physical, geographic or legal constraints (or is highly undesirable for reasons of public policy)'; examples given are ports, bus stations, utility distribution networks and some telecommunications networks[3]. In the Guideline on *Assessment of Individual Agreements and Conduct*[4] the DGFT says that the question of whether a particular facility is essential 'has to be assessed on a case-by-case basis'[5]. If a facility is considered to be essential, the DGFT 'would expect competitors to have access at economically efficient prices in order to compete on a related market'[6]. Reference to the essential facilities doctrine will also be found in paragraphs 4.21 to 4.24 of the Guideline on *Competition Act: Application in the Water and Sewerage Sectors*[7] and in paragraphs 7.39 to 7.45 of the Guideline on *Competition Act 1998: The Application in the Telecommunications Sector*[8].

In *Network Multimedia Television Ltd v Jobserve Ltd*[9] the claimant claimed that the defendant had abused a dominant position contrary to the Chapter II prohibition of the Competition Act. The defendant operated a website on which IT recruitment agencies advertised job vacancies; it refused to accept advertisements from agencies that had an interest in a competing 'job board'. The court decided that there was a serious issue to be tried, and granted an injunction in the claimant's favour pending the trial of the action.

Problems of refusal to supply are sometimes settled informally following investigation by the DGFT[10].

(ii) Fair Trading Act 1973

A refusal to supply customers for an anti-competitive purpose could be investigated under the FTA. In its general report on *Refusal to Supply*[11] the Commission considered that a refusal to supply products where the market was dominated by a single producer might be a cause for concern, since it might hamper the ability of firms at a lower level in the market to compete effectively. In practice few such cases have arisen, although in *Certain Medical and Industrial Gases*[12] the Commission was critical of British Oxygen's refusal to supply some firms with gas storage apparatus. A refusal on the part of the leading manufacturer of fire alarm equipment designed for the needs of the elderly to supply spare parts to

1   See pp 611-612 above.
2   See p 614 above.
3   *Assessment of Individual Agreements and Conduct* OFT Guideline 414, paras 7.1-7.2.
4   OFT Guideline 414.
5   Ibid, para 7.3.
6   Ibid, para 7.5.
7   OFT Guideline 422.
8   OFT Guideline 417.
9   Judgment of 5 April 2001, Chancery Division.
10 See eg the 2000 *Annual Report of the Director General of Fair Trading*, p 46 (assurances by cement producers to supply bulk cement for resale).
11 Cmnd 4372 (1970).
12 HCP (1956–57) 13.

maintenance companies in the downstream service market was investigated by the DGFT in *Tunstall Telecom*, and was settled when Tunstall agreed to supply such companies[13]. A claim that non-solicitor estate agents in Scotland should be given access to an advertising system operated by solicitors who also conduct estate agency business was rejected by the Commission in *Solicitors' Estate Agency Services in Scotland*[14].

A specific régime has been proposed for access to payments systems in the banking sector[15].

(D)   Miscellaneous

The *Ice Cream* inquiry[16] of 1994 related to the ice cream market in which there was a scale monopolist, Birds Eye Walls, and a complex monopoly consisting of Birds Eye Walls, Mars and Nestlé. It was alleged that access to the market had become foreclosed through the use of exclusive freezer cabinet arrangements. The Commission disagreed, citing new entrants, greater consumer choice and lack of excessive prices or profits as evidence of the fact that competition was effective, notwithstanding the policy of freezer exclusivity. In 2000 the Commission published a further report on ice cream which was more critical than the previous one[17]. In April 2000 the Secretary of State accepted undertakings from Birds Eye Walls, Nestlé and Mars not to enter into or renew outlet exclusivity agreements with shops; further undertakings were accepted from Birds Eye Wall's that it would not reserve more than 50% of a retail outlet's freezer display space for its products and would not reserve any freezer storage space, that it would not grant retrospective bonuses, discounts or rebates and that it would not sell direct to retailers, except in the case of national buyers, but would instead sell only to the wholesale trade[18].

Following the Commission's report on *Electrical Contracting at Exhibition Halls in London*[19] an order was made prohibiting the owners of exhibition halls from imposing restrictions on who may provide electrical contracting services to exhibitors[20].

---

13 OFT Press Release 13/93, 25 February 1993; see similarly *Atis-Uher (UK) Ltd* 4/93, 26 January 1993.
14 Cm 3699 (1997).
15 *Competition in Payment Systems: A Consultation Document* HM Treasury, December 2000.
16 Cm 2524 (1994).
17 Cm 4510 (2000).
18 DTI Press Release P/2000/260, 7 April 2000; P/2000/430, 21 June 2000; and P/2000/509, 20 July 2000; prior to these undertakings, the Secretary of State accepted an interim undertaking from Bird's Eye Wall's in relation to supply to the wholesale trade: DTI Press Release P/2000/108, 16 February 2000.
19 Cm 995 (1995).
20 The Electrical Contracting (London Exhibition Halls) Order 1995, SI 1995/3299.

CHAPTER 18

Abuse of dominance (2): pricing practices

This chapter will consider abusive pricing practices under Article 82 EC and the Chapter II prohibition in the Competition Act 1998; it will also consider the extent to which these practices might be controlled under the Fair Trading Act 1973. The chapter will deal in turn with exploitative pricing practices; with practices that have an effect similar to exclusive or tie-in agreements; with practices intended to eliminate a competitor; with price discrimination; and with practices that are harmful to the single market. This taxonomy is over-schematic, in that in some cases the categories blur into one another: for example discrimination may be both exploitative and anti-competitive[1], and an excessively high price may in reality be a way of preventing parallel imports[2]; nevertheless this division provides helpful insights into the way in which the law is applied in practice. The application of Article 82 will be considered in sections 1 to 5; UK law in section 6.

The law on abusive pricing practices is complex and controversial. Dominant firms may infringe Article 82 where they raise their prices to unacceptably high levels; they may also be found to have abused their dominant position where they cut their prices, if such cuts can be characterised not as normal, competitive responses, but as strategic behaviour intended to eliminate competitors. Not unnaturally, a dominant firm, or one that is anxious that it will be held to be dominant, may feel itself to be on the horns of a dilemma where both a price rise and a price cut might be considered to be abusive; the dilemma might become a trilemma if leaving prices where they are might be considered to be evidence of a concerted practice with the other operators on the market, and if the word trilemma were to exist.

1. EXPLOITATIVE PRICING PRACTICES

Exploitative pricing raises interesting questions for competition law. To the extent that independent firms form a cartel in order artificially to restrict output, raise prices and take larger profits, EC and UK law both intervene: the price-fixing cartel is the most obvious target for any system of competition law; this has been

---

1   See pp 657-662 below.
2   See pp 635-639 below.

considered in chapter 13. The position is more complicated where oligopolists indulge in tacit collusion falling short of an agreement or concerted practice; this has been considered in chapter 14. Different problems are raised where a monopolist or dominant firm individually exploits its position by charging excessive (that is supra-competitive) prices. It might be thought obvious that direct action should be taken to control exploitative pricing, but the case for doing so is not as clear-cut as may at first appear.

(A) Arguments against direct control

There are arguments against direct control of prices under competition law. First, if normal market forces have their way, the fact that a monopolist is able to earn large profits should inevitably, in the absence of barriers to entry, attract new entrants to the market. In this case the extraction of monopoly profits will be self-defeating in the long run and can act as an important economic indicator to potential entrants to enter the market. If one accepts this view of the way that markets operate, one should accept with equanimity periods during which a firm earns a monopoly profit: the market will in due course correct itself, and intervention by the competition authorities will have the effect of undesirably distorting this process.

Secondly, there are formidable difficulties in telling whether a price really is exploitative: by what standards can this be assessed? To compare a monopolist's price with a hypothetical 'competitive' price is unscientific; alternatively to establish what would be a 'reasonable' price by adding an acceptable profit margin to the actual cost of producing goods or providing services is fraught with difficulties. One is that it is unclear what the relevant 'cost' of producing goods or services is: should one look at the historic costs involved in establishing a production line for goods or the cost that it would take to establish one at today's prices? Another problem is that it is difficult to apportion the costs of a multi-product firm between its different products in order to determine whether it is making an unreasonable profit in one particular market. Furthermore the fact that a firm is earning a large profit may be attributable to its superior efficiency over its rivals, rather than to its market power.

A third argument against price control is that a monopolist should be permitted to charge what the market will bear so that it will be able to earn sufficiently large profits to be able to carry out expensive and risky research and development[3]. Another view is that there is no objection to a monopolist increasing its personal wealth at consumers' expense since this involves only a transfer of wealth from one part of the economy to another, rather than a threat to the wealth of society generally. An argument against this view is that, even if one is prepared to tolerate the accretion of wealth by monopolists, there may be a loss to consumer welfare if the prospect of making monopoly profits entails a use of resources for that very purpose which might otherwise have been better used elsewhere in the economy[4].

A fourth problem is that even if it is accepted, despite these arguments, that exploitative pricing should be controlled, there is the difficulty of translating this policy into a sufficiently realistic legal test. A legal rule condemning exploitative pricing needs to be cast in sufficiently precise terms to enable a firm to know on

3   See eg Schumpeter *Capitalism, Socialism and Democracy* (1942); ch 1, p 4.
4   See Posner 'The Social Costs of Monopoly and Regulation' (1975) 83 Journal of Political Economy 807.

which side of legality it stands. A final point is that price regulation requires a competition authority to have a considerable amount of information about the market, which it may lack; it is even less easy for courts to determine what the correct level of prices should be.

Given these problems, it is not surprising that competition authorities prefer to deploy their resources by proceeding against anti-competitive abuses that exclude competitors from the market rather than establishing themselves as price regulators. Where there are natural monopolies there is much to be said for the establishment of a bespoke system of regulation, as in the UK in the form of OFTEL, the Gas and Electricity Markets Authority and OFWAT[5]. However, the fact that the Commission, in its prosecutorial discretion, has decided not to take direct control of prices[6] does not mean that Article 82 is inapplicable.

(B) Application of Article 82 to exploitative pricing prices

(i) Determining whether prices are excessive

Article 82(2)(a) gives as an illustration of abuse 'directly or indirectly imposing unfair purchase or selling prices or other unfair trading conditions'[7]. A practice which is harmful to consumers can be abusive, notwithstanding that it is not harmful to the structure of competition on the relevant market[8]; furthermore it is not necessary to show that the firm that is guilty of the abuse derives a commercial advantage from it[9].

(A) GENERAL MOTORS AND UNITED BRANDS. In *General Motors*[10] the Commission for the first time issued a decision condemning the excessive pricing of a dominant firm and imposing a fine for that practice. There had been earlier indications from the ECJ, in cases concerning the use of intellectual property rights, that such action could be taken under Article 82[11]. On appeal the decision in *General Motors* was quashed by the ECJ[12] because there was insufficient evidence to support it. In *United Brands*[13] the Commission imposed a fine for excessive pricing, but again its decision was quashed by the ECJ[14] because the Commission had failed to make out a clear case. However the ECJ did not say that excessive pricing could not be caught by Article 82. Rather it said that:

'charging a price which is excessive because it has no reasonable relation to the economic value of the product supplied is ... an abuse'[15].

5   See ch 23, p 866 on these regulatory bodies.
6   The Commission has often stated that it is not its rôle to become a price regulator: see eg the Vth *Report on Competition Policy* (1975), points 3-7 and 76; XXVIIth *Report on Competition Policy* (1997), point 77.
7   For an example of the imposition of unfair trading conditions, as opposed to unfair prices, see 1998 *Football World Cup* OJ [2000] L 5/55, [2000] 4 CMLR 963.
8   1998 *Football World Cup*, n 7 above, paras 99-100, citing Case 6/72 *Continental Can v Commission* [1973] ECR 215, [1973] CMLR 199, para 26.
9   1998 *Football World Cup*, n 7 above, paras 101-102.
10 OJ [1975] L 29/14, [1975] 1 CMLR D20.
11 Case 78/70 *Deutsche Grammophon GmbH v Metro-SB-Grossmärkte GmbH* [1971] ECR 487, [1971] CMLR 631; Case 40/70 *Sirena v Eda* [1971] ECR 69, [1971] CMLR 260.
12 Case 26/75 *General Motors v Commission* [1975] ECR 1367, [1976] 1 CMLR 95.
13 OJ [1976] L 95/1, [1976] 1 CMLR D28.
14 Case 27/76 *United Brands v Commission* [1978] ECR 207, [1978] 1 CMLR 429.
15 Ibid, para 250.

Clearly therefore excessive pricing can amount to an abuse of a dominant position. The difficulty is to know at what point a price is so high that it is abusive: the prohibitory nature of the EC system means that a legal test of excessiveness is necessary. The Commission in *United Brands* inferred that the price of bananas in Germany was too high by looking at the price charged in Ireland: it concluded that, since UBC could charge a low price in Ireland and still make a profit, it must follow that the higher price charged in Germany was excessive. The ECJ annulled the decision on the ground that it was improperly reasoned. In order to establish that a price was excessive the ECJ said, at paragraph 251, that the Commission had at least to 'require UBC to produce particulars of all the constituent elements of its production costs'. The burden was on the Commission to prove that UBC was charging unfair prices. Having undertaken a cost analysis, the ECJ said that the question to be asked is:

> 'whether the difference between the costs actually incurred and the price actually charged is excessive, and, if the answer to this question is in the affirmative, to consider whether a price has been charged which is either unfair in itself or when compared to other competing products'[16].

The ECJ accepted that it might be difficult to apportion costs to particular products, but concluded that there were no such difficulties in the case of the market for bananas.

(B)   YARDSTICK COMPETITION.   The ECJ suggested in *United Brands* that there might be other ways of proving that a price is excessive[17]. In an Article 234 reference from France, *Corinne Bodson v Pompes Funèbres*[18], one question before the ECJ was whether Pompes Funèbres, which had been given an exclusive concession to provide 'external services' for funerals in a particular French town, was guilty of charging excessive prices. The ECJ said that, given that more than 30,000 communes in France had not granted exclusive concessions such as that enjoyed by Pompes Funèbres, but instead had left the service unregulated or operated it themselves, it must be possible to make a comparison between the prices charged by undertakings with concessions and other undertakings:

> 'Such a comparison could provide a basis for assessing whether or not the prices charged by the concession holders are fair'[19].

This technique can be described as 'yardstick competition': comparing the performance of one undertaking with that of other ones. The idea in *Bodson* was repeated in *Lucazeau v SACEM*[20], which concerned the level of royalties charged for the playing of recorded music in discotheques; the ECJ again suggested that a comparison should be made with the level of fees charged in other Member States. Yardstick competition is only possible however where a suitable comparator can be found: it would be inappropriate to compare the prices charged in a high-price Member State against those in a low-price one.

---

16   Ibid, para 252; see similarly Case 226/84 *BL v Commission* [1986] ECR 3263, [1987] 1 CMLR 185, para 27; Case C-323/93 *Crespelle* [1994] ECR I-5077, para 25.
17   Case 27/76 *United Brands v Commission* [1978] ECR 207, [1978] 1 CMLR 429, para 253.
18   Case 30/87 [1988] ECR 2479, [1989] 4 CMLR 984.
19   Ibid, para 31.
20   Case 110/88 [1989] ECR 2811, [1991] 4 CMLR 248.

(C)   EXCESSIVE OR DISPROPORTIONATE COSTS SHOULD BE IGNORED.   In *Ministère Public v Tournier*[1], another case concerning the level of royalties charged to discotheques by a French performing rights society, the ECJ said that excessive or disproportionate costs should not be taken into account in determining the reasonableness of prices. The society in question had a *de facto* monopoly and the ECJ suggested that it was the very lack of competition which had led to high administrative costs: the society had no incentive to keep them down.

(ii)   Excessive pricing that impedes parallel imports and exports

In the *General Motors* case[2], and subsequently in *BL v Commission*[3], the reason for the Commission's intervention was not that it wished to establish itself as a regulator of the prices charged for the issuance of type-approval certificates for cars, but that the prices that the Commission regarded as excessive were imposed with the intention of impeding parallel imports and exports. Abuses that are harmful to the single market, including pricing abuses, are particularly likely to be condemned by the Commission[4].

(iii)   Excessive pricing that is anti-competitive

Quite apart from excessive prices being exploitative and/or detrimental to the single market, they may also be anti-competitive. The most obvious example would be the situation in which the owner of an essential facility charges an excessive (or discriminatory) price for granting access to it: this could be regarded as a constructive refusal to supply, and therefore as an abuse of a dominant position[5]. The Commission specifically states at paragraph 97 of the *Notice on the Application of the Competition Rules to Access Agreements in the Telecommunications Sector*[6] that excessive prices for access to essential facilities can be abusive[7]; the Commission summarises the case law set out above at paragraphs 105 to 109 of this *Notice*. In practice it is immensely complex to determine what the appropriate price for access to an essential facility should be[8]; a particular problem is that a firm that controls such a facility and makes use of it in a downstream market may not make an internal charge to itself for the service in question; this makes it particularly difficult to determine what price it should charge to a third party for access. For this reason the Commission

1   Case 395/87 [1989] ECR 2521, [1991] 4 CMLR 248.
2   See p 635 above.
3   Case 226/84 [1986] ECR 3263, [1987] 1 CMLR 185.
4   See pp 662-664 below.
5   See ch 17, pp 611-624 on the case law deriving from *Commercial Solvents v Commission* and the so-called essential facilities doctrine.
6   OJ [1998] C 265/2, [1998] 5 CMLR 821.
7   Ibid, para 97.
8   See Baumol, Ordover and Willig 'Parity Pricing and Its Critics: a Necessary Condition for Efficiency in the Provision of Bottleneck Services to Competition' (1997) Yale Journal of Regulation 14; Armstrong, Doyle and Vickers 'The Access Pricing Problem: A Synthesis' (1996) 44(2) Journal of Industrial Economics 131; OFTEL *The Pricing of Conditional Access and Access Control Services* (May 1999); see also *Telecom Corpn of New Zealand v Clear Communications* [1995] 1 NZLR 385, a case which reached the Privy Council in the UK on appeal from New Zealand, in relation to pricing for access to the telecommunications 'local loop' there: the case is discussed by Tollemache in (1994) 15 ECLR 43, (1994) 15 ECLR 236 and (1995) 16 ECLR 248.

has required, in the *Interconnection Directive* in the telecommunications industry, that separate accounting should be maintained for activities related to interconnection and for other activities[9].

Given the difficulties involved in access pricing, it is not surprising that the Commission would prefer not to become too involved in what may result in a large amount of detailed regulation: this activity is better carried out by a specific regulatory body, such as OFTEL in the UK in the case of telecommunications. However there have been some occasions on which the Commission has investigated access pricing issues. For example in 1997 it took action against Belgacom for charging excessive and discriminatory prices for access to data on its subscribers for voice telephony services[10]. Further examples of the Commission investigating the operation of essential facilities were given in chapter 17[11].

(iv)   Excessive pricing and spare parts

The ECJ has held that a car manufacturer may refuse to grant licences to third parties to produce spare parts for its cars; however if it charges excessive prices for the spares which it produces itself, this may amount to an abuse of its dominant position[12]. It may be that the market will solve this problem itself. Although such customers appear to be 'locked in' to the manufacturer's spare parts, the original car will eventually need to be replaced; excessive prices for spare parts will deter buyers of new cars from from buying from their existing manufacturer: this in turn may deter the manufacturer from an excessive pricing policy for parts in the first place.

(v)   Buyer power – excessively low prices

In *CICCE v Commission*[13] the ECJ rejected a complaint that the Commission had refused to condemn unfairly low prices paid by a monopsonist on the buying side of the market, as there was insufficient evidence to support the allegation. The complainant in this case was arguing that French television companies with a statutory monopoly were paying unfairly low fees for showing films. The ECJ agreed with the Commission that the complainant had to show that the price

---

9   Council Directive 97/33/EC, OJ [1997] L 199/32, Article 8(2); see also the Commission *Recommendation on Accounting Separation and Cost Accounting in Relation to Interconnection in a Liberalised Telecommunications Market* OJ [1998] L 141/6. Article 7(2) of the Interconnection Directive requires that certain telecommunications organisations having 'significant market power' should follow the principles of transparency and cost orientation for interconnection charges; see also the Commission Recommendation of January 8 1998 on *Interconnection Pricing in a Liberalised Telecommunications Market*, OJ [1998] L 73/42, and the Commission *Communication on Interconnection Pricing in a Liberalised Telecommunications Market* OJ [1998] C 84/3.

10   See the Commission's XXVIIth *Report on Competition Policy* (1997), point 67: the terms on which the case was settled are set out at pp 152-153 of the Report; see also point 77 of the same Report on the Commission's action against Deutsche Telecom for charging excessive prices for access to its infrastructures, and points 79-86 of the XXVIIIth *Report on Competition Policy* (1998) on further action in relation to excessive and discriminatory prices in the telecommunications sector.

11   See ch 17, pp 611-624.

12   Case 53/87 *CICRA v Renault* [1988] ECR 6039, [1990] 4 CMLR 265; Case 238/87 *AB Volvo v Erik Veng* [1988] ECR 6211, [1989] 4 CMLR 122.

13   Case 298/83 [1985] ECR 1105, [1986] 1 CMLR 486.

was low in relation to each individual film, and that it could not rely on average or undifferentiated figures. The interest of the case is that it demonstrates that, just as charging an excessively high price can be abusive, so too can the extraction of an unfairly low one demanded by an undertaking in a dominant position on the buying side of the market; on the facts of this case, however, the complainant failed.

2. PRICING PRACTICES HAVING EFFECTS SIMILAR TO EXCLUSIVE OR TIE-IN AGREEMENTS

In chapter 17 the application of Article 82 to exclusive agreements[14] and to tie-in agreements[15] was considered. The basic objection to each of these practices is that they may have a foreclosing effect on competitors of the dominant firm. Article 82 also applies to pricing practices that have the same effect as exclusive or tie-in agreements.

(A) Loyalty rebates and similar practices

(i) The basic rule

In *Hoffmann-La Roche v Commission*[16] the ECJ held that Hoffmann-la Roche had abused its dominant position both by entering into exclusive purchasing agreements with some of its customers and also by offering loyalty rebates. In relation to the latter it said that it was unlawful for a firm to tie a customer by an exclusive purchasing commitment and that:

> 'The same applies if the said undertaking, without tying the purchasers by a formal obligation, applies, either under the terms of the agreements concluded with these purchasers or unilaterally, a system of fidelity rebates, that is to say discounts conditional on the customer's obtaining all or most of its requirements – whether the quantity of its purchases be large or small – from the undertaking in a dominant position'[17].

This passage makes clear that the prohibition of loyalty rebates is directly related to the law that prohibits exclusive purchasing agreements: the cases on rebates follow closely the contours of those on exclusive purchasing. Behaviour becomes abusive when the inducement caused by the promise of loyalty rebates to a customer to purchase all or most of its requirements from the dominant firm is so great that it has the same effect that a contractual stipulation to purchase exclusively would have done. It may also be the case that a dominant firm infringes Article 82(2)(c) where its rebating policy has as its consequence that some customers are treated in a discriminatory manner compared with others[18].

14 See ch 17, pp 601-605.
15 Ibid, pp 605-611.
16 Case 85/76 [1979] ECR 461, [1979] 3 CMLR 211; see also Cases 43/73 etc *Suiker Unie* [1975] ECR 1663, [1976] 1 CMLR 295, paras 517-528.
17 Ibid, para 89; the ECJ also objected to the 'English clause' requiring the buyer to report any better offer it received to Hoffmann-la Roche and preventing it from accepting the offer unless Roche chose not to match it: see ch 17, p 603.
18 See pp 657-662 below on Article 82(2)(c).

The test set out in paragraph 89 of *Hoffmann-la Roche* is expressed in terms that suggest a *per se* standard; however, as has been pointed out in chapters 5[19] and 17[20] , it is arguable that the Commission should have to demonstrate that an alleged abuse would actually or potentially produce anti-competitive effects on the market. Rebates and similar pricing practices are a normal part of business life and are an important competitive tool, making them particularly unsuitable for *per se* prohibition. The ECJ has specifically stated in *AKZO v Commission*[1] that not all price competition is legitimate[2] ; however the law on pricing practices must ensure that all firms – including dominant ones – are able to compete on price: at its most simple, competition law is about delivering lower prices to consumers. While it may be appropriate that competition authorities should curb practices on the part of dominant firms that go beyond 'competition on the merits' and that are detrimental to the competitive process, the danger is that too intrusive an application of Article 82 might actually discourage price competition for fear that undercutting a rival or offering customers more favourable terms might be found to be unlawful. Not every loyalty rebate or discount is attributable to the sinister motive of destroying competition; the structure of any particular scheme must be carefully considered in order to determine whether it really could have the effect of inducing loyalty.

(ii)   Case law on loyalty rebates under Article 82

There have been many cases in which the Commission has condemned loyalty rebates and similar practices. In *BPB Industries*[3] the Commission held that British Gypsum Ltd and its parent, BPB Industries plc, had abused their dominant position by offering loyalty payments to builders' merchants in Great Britain who stocked only their plasterboard. This had the effect of excluding new competition from producers in France and Spain. BPB and British Gypsum claimed that the payments were made in order to assist merchants with the cost of promotion and advertising. The Commission held that, even if there was truth in this, the payments were also intended to induce loyalty on the part of merchants and so were abusive. A fine of EUR 3 million was imposed. The Commission's decision was substantially upheld on appeal[4] .

In the *Soda-ash* decisions[5] the Commission condemned the exclusionary practices and fidelity rebates of Solvay and ICI. One of the abuses was the granting of 'top-slice' rebates: customers for soda-ash tended to purchase some of their requirements from a source other than the dominant undertaking in their market; this was a way of reducing dependency on a supplier. The dominant undertaking in these circumstances would offer special rebates on such 'marginal tonnage' in order to secure that custom. The Commission found that this practice

19   Ch 5, pp 172-173.
20   Ch 17, pp 603-604.
1   Case C-62/86 [1991] ECR I-3359, [1993] 5 CMLR 215.
2   Ibid, para 70; see similarly the CFI in Case T-228/97 *Irish Sugar v Commission* [1999] ECR II-2969, [1999] 5 CMLR 1300, para 111: this case is on appeal to the ECJ, Case C-497/99 P (judgment pending); Advocate General Fennelly in Cases C-395/95 and 396/95 P *Compagnie Maritime Belge v Commission* [2000] 4 CMLR 1076, para 126.
3   OJ [1989] L 10/50, [1990] 4 CMLR 464.
4   Case T-65/89 *BPB Industries plc and British Gypsum v Commission* [1993] ECR II-389, [1993] 5 CMLR 32, upheld on appeal to the ECJ Case C-310/93 P [1995] ECR I-865, [1997] 4 CMLR 238.
5   *Soda-ash/Solvay* OJ [1991] L 152/21 and *Soda-ash/ICI* OJ [1991] L 152/40.

was abusive. In the Solvay decision it rejected Solvay's argument that the rebates were based on objective and predetermined thresholds[6]. The decisions were annulled on appeal for procedural reasons[7], but readopted by the Commission at the end of 2000[8].

In *Irish Sugar*[9] the Commission condemned fidelity and target rebates. On appeal the CFI upheld both of these findings in *Irish Sugar v Commission*[10]. As to the fidelity rebates, the CFI said that it was necessary to:

'appraise all the circumstances, and in particular the criteria and detailed rules for granting rebates, and determine whether there is any tendency, through an advantage not justified by any economic service, to remove or restrict the buyer's choice as to his sources of supply, to block competitors' access to the market, to apply dissimilar conditions to equivalent transactions with other trading parties, or to reinforce the dominant position by distorting competition'[11].

The CFI also upheld the finding that the target rebates infringed Article 82[12].

In *Compagnie Maritime Belge v Commission*[13] the ECJ upheld the decision of the Commission that the granting of loyalty rebates by members of a liner conference amounted to an abuse of a collective dominant position[14]; it was irrelevant to the finding of abuse under Article 82 that the rebates may have benefited from block exemption under Regulation 4056/86 on maritime transport[15].

In *Virgin/British Airways*[16] the Commission imposed a fine of EUR 6.8 million on British Airways ('BA') for operating a system of commission payments and other incentives with travel agents which, by rewarding loyalty and by discriminating between travel agents, had the object or effect of excluding BA's competitors from UK markets for air transport. The Commission looked at the commissions and incentives offered by BA for selling tickets for BA flights and considered first whether they fell foul of the law on exclusionary rebate schemes and secondly whether they infringed Article 82(2)(c)[17]. As to the former, the Commission reviewed the ECJ's judgments in *Hoffmann-la Roche*[18] and *Michelin v Commission*[19], and stated that these judgments establish a general principle:

'a dominant supplier can give discounts that relate to efficiencies, for example discounts for large orders that allow the supplier to produce large batches of product, but cannot give discounts or incentives to encourage

6   OJ [1991] L 152/40, para 54.
7   Cases T-30/91 etc *Solvay SA v Commission* [1995] ECR II-1775, [1996] 5 CMLR 57, upheld by the ECJ Cases C-286/95 P [2000] 5 CMLR 413 and 454.
8   Commission Press Release IP/00/1449, 13 December 2000.
9   OJ [1997] L 258/1, [1997] 5 CMLR 666.
10 Case T-228/97 [1999] ECR II-2969, [1999] 5 CMLR 1300.
11 Ibid, para 197.
12 Ibid, paras 203-225.
13 Cases 395/96 P etc [2000] 4 CMLR 1076.
14 Ibid, paras 129-137.
15 Ibid, para 130; on Regulation 4056/86, see ch 23, pp 861-863.
16 OJ [2000] L 30/1, [2000] 4 CMLR 999; on appeal Case T-219/99 *British Airways v Commission* (judgment pending).
17 See pp 657-662 below on Article 82(2)(c).
18 Case 85/76 [1979] ECR 461, [1979] 3 CMLR 211.
19 Case 322/81 [1983] ECR 3461, [1985] 1 CMLR 282.

loyalty, that is for avoiding purchases from a competitor of the dominant supplier'[20].

The Commission considered that BA's commission system related to loyalty rather than to efficiency, and that it was therefore abusive. A key point was that, where a travel agent exceeded the number of BA tickets that it had sold in the previous year, it became entitled to an additional payment on *all* the tickets it sold in the current year, not just on the *additional* ones. This would inevitably exert a strong influence on the travel agent to sell BA tickets; exceeding the previous year's figures would produce substantial additional income. The Commission's decision has been criticised: in an industry such as aviation, in which fixed costs are high, any revenue that can be earned and contribute to those costs is particularly desirable; BA's interest was to ensure that its aeroplanes were always full, in order to derive the maximum revenue possible. However the Commission's view was that BA had, by inducing loyalty, gone beyond legitimate competition for business. The Commission also considered that BA's commission system operated in a discriminatory manner contrary to Article 82(2)(c), since travel agents handling the same number of BA tickets received different commission rates, depending on their particular target; the Commission rejected the argument that there were objective justifications for this. The use of Article 82(2)(c) shows that the Commission has two weapons at its disposal in pricing cases such as these: the law on exclusionary rebates derived from *Hoffmann-la Roche* and Article 82(2)(c) itself; even if the Commission fails on one ground, it may succeed on the other.

Fidelity rebates were also found to be abusive in *Deutsche Post*[1]. The Commission stressed the distinction between quantity rebates exclusively linked to the volume of purchases from a supplier, fixed objectively and applied without discrimination, and fidelity rebates granted in return for fidelity;[2] it added that a rebate linked to quantity, but where the quantity was actually calculated by reference to the estimated capacity of absorption of the customer, would be treated as a fidelity rebate[3]. The policy of granting fidelity rebates was regarded as a serious infringement having as its object or effect the exclusion of private operators from the German parcel services market[4], and the Commission imposed a fine of EUR 24 million.

(iii)   'all or most of its requirements – whether the quantities be large or small ...'

Paragraph 89 of the judgment in *Hoffmann-la Roche* states that it is abusive to offer rebates 'conditional on the customer's obtaining all or most of its requirements – whether the quantity of its purchases be large or small – from the undertaking in a dominant position'[5]. As has been seen in chapter 16, the block exemption for vertical agreements defines a non-compete obligation as one which requires a customer to obtain 80% or more of its requirements of goods or services from the supplier[6]; it is reasonable to suppose that a similar threshold applies under

20   Ibid, para 101.
1   OJ [2001] L 125/27.
2   Ibid, para 33; see p 644 below on permissible rebates.
3   Ibid.
4   Ibid, para 50.
5   See p 639 above.
6   See ch 16, p 568.

Article 82 when determining what is meant by 'most' of a customer's requirements. The stipulation that loyalty rebates are unlawful even where the quantities involved are small imposes a strict standard: where the customer purchases small quantities, the foreclosure effect is likely to be insubstantial; however the ECJ's formulation indicates that there would still be an abuse.

(iv) Duration of the period by reference to which rebates are calculated

The condemnation of loyalty rebates under Article 82 is directly related to the rule that dominant firms may not enter into exclusive purchasing agreements that would foreclose access to the market[7]. It follows that, just as the duration of an exclusive purchasing agreement is relevant to the determination of whether it is abusive[8], so too the period by reference to which loyalty rebates are calculated must be considered. Rebates conditional upon loyal purchase over a period of five years would clearly be more likely to have a foreclosure effect than if the period was one year. In the case of *Coca-Cola/San Pelligrino* the Commission accepted that rebates awarded on the basis of performance over a period of not more than three months would not be abusive[9].

(v) Target rebates and transparency

In the case of *Michelin*[10] rebates were paid to dealers that achieved targets set by Michelin, individually and selectively for each dealer, in excess of their purchases in the preceding year. The dealers themselves were not informed in writing of the targets; these were communicated orally at the start of each year. The system put great pressure on the dealers to remain loyal, especially towards the end of the year, since a failure to meet the target would result in the loss of the rebates. The Commission objected to the duration of the reference period and to the lack of transparency, which intensified the tying effect of the rebates[11]. For the future it required that:

> 'with the exception of short term measures, no discount should be granted unless linked to a genuine cost reduction in the manufacturer's costs. The compensation paid to Michelin dealers must be commensurate with the tasks they perform and the services they actually provide, which reduce the manufacturer's burden. In addition the system of discounts and bonuses agreed upon must be clearly confirmed to each dealer when the sales contract is presented and concluded'[12].

The decision was upheld on appeal to the ECJ[13]. The case makes clear that a lack of transparency in a system of rebates is an exacerbating factor, making a finding of abuse more likely[14].

---

7   See p 639 above.
8   See ch 17, pp 602-604.
9   Commission's XIXth *Report on Competition Policy* (1989), point 50.
10 OJ [1981] L 353/33, [1982] 1 CMLR 643.
11 Ibid, paras 37-49.
12 Ibid, para 54.
13 Case 322/81 [1983] ECR 3461, [1985] 1 CMLR 282, paras 62-86.
14 Ibid, para 83; Michelin was fined again, this time a sum of EUR 19.76m, for offering loyalty-inducing rebates in June 2001: see Commission Press Release IP/01/873, 20 June 2001.

(vi)   Permissible rebates

As already noted, rebates and similar practices are a normal part of commercial life. Rebates should be condemned only where they could have a detrimental effect on competition, for example because they operate as a surrogate for an exclusive purchasing agreement. Where rebates can be objectively justified there will be no abuse; in the UK, the Guideline *Assessment of Individual Agreements and Conduct*[15] specifically acknowledges that the offering of discounts is a form of price competition and is therefore generally to be encouraged[16]. In *Hoffmann-la Roche v Commission* the ECJ accepted that not all discounts should be treated as abusive: for example it said that quantity discounts linked solely to the volume of purchases, fixed objectively and applicable to all purchasers, would be permissible[17]. Discounts granted for prompt payment would presumably also be regarded as objectively justifiable. Payments for services rendered by a customer, such as participation in a special promotion or for providing shelf-space in a supermarket, should also be permissible, provided that they are not, in fact, loyalty payments for exclusivity. In 1992 the Commission issued four Notices in the Official Journal indicating that it proposed to take a 'favourable view' of various rebating and pricing rebates in the plasterboard and related markets in the case of *British Gypsum*[18]: some of the rebates related to quantities purchased; others to sales promotion. In *Virgin/British Airways*[19] the Commission acknowledged that it was permissible to give discounts that relate to the achievement of economic efficiencies[20]. Objective justification for price differences is also relevant to charges of discrimination under Article 82(2)(c)[1].

(B)   Pricing practices that have the same effect as tie-in agreements

The application of Article 82 to tie-in agreements was considered in chapter 17[2]. It may be possible to achieve the same effect as a tie-in agreement through pricing practices.

(i)   Rebates and discounts having a tying effect

In *Eurofix-Bauco v Hilti*[3] the Commission held that it was an abuse of a dominant position to reduce discounts to customers for orders of nail cartridges without nails[4]; the Commission's decision was upheld on appeal[5]. In *Tetra Pak II*[6] the

---

15   OFT Guideline 414.
16   Ibid, para 5.1.
17   Case 85/76 [1979] ECR 461, [1979] 3 CMLR 211, para 90.
18   OJ [1992] C 321/9-C 321/12, [1993] 4 CMLR 143n.
19   OJ [2000] L 31/1, [2000] 4 CMLR 999.
20   Ibid, para 101.
1   See pp 657-662 below.
2   See ch 17, pp 605-611.
3   OJ [1988] L 65/19, [1989] 4 CMLR 677.
4   Ibid, para 75.
5   Case T–30/89 *Hilti AG v Commission* [1990] ECR II-163, [1992] 4 CMLR 16, upheld on appeal to the ECJ Case 53/92 P *Hilti AG v Commission* [1994] ECR I-667, [1994] 4 CMLR 614.
6   OJ [1992] L 72/1, [1992] 4 CMLR 551, upheld on appeal to the CFI, Case T–83/91 *Tetra Pak International v Commission* [1994] ECR II-755, [1997] 4 CMLR 726 and on appeal to the ECJ Case C-333/94 P *Tetra Pak International v Commission* [1996] ECR I-5951, [1997] 4 CMLR 662.

Commission held that Tetra Pak had adopted a pricing policy that was a means of persuading customers to use its maintenance services[7].

(ii) 'Across-the-board' rebates

In *Hoffmann-la Roche v Commission*[8] the ECJ condemned Hoffmann-la Roche's 'across-the-board' rebates, which were offered to customers which acquired the whole range of its vitamins; these rebates meant that customers were dissuaded from acquiring any particular vitamin from other suppliers[9]. The ECJ noted specifically that such rebates amounted to an unlawful tie-in, contrary to Article 82(2)(d)[10].

(iii) Delivered pricing as a tie-in

In *Napier Brown-British Sugar*[11] the Commission held that British Sugar's delivered pricing system constituted an abuse of a dominant position, although it did not impose a fine in respect of this offence as it was the first decision on this particular practice. Until 1986 British Sugar had refused to allow customers to collect sugar at an ex-factory price. The Commission, relying on the ECJ's judgment in *Centre Belge d'Etudes de Marche Télémarketing v CLT*[12], held that British Sugar had reserved to itself an ancillary market (the delivery of sugar) as part of its activity on a neighbouring but separate market (the sale of sugar). The Commission's view was that there was no objective necessity for this conduct on the part of British Sugar.

(iv) Bundling

A firm may sell two or more products together as a bundle and charge more attractive prices for the bundle than for the constituent parts of it. Bundling may have the same effect as a tie-in agreement. In *Digital* the Commission objected to the fact that Digital offered prices which were more attractive when the customer purchased software services in a package with hardware services than when purchasing software services alone[13].

3. PRICING PRACTICES INTENDED TO ELIMINATE COMPETITORS

The pricing practices considered in section 2 were condemned either because of their tendency to induce customers to purchase exclusively from the dominant firm or because they would cause them to purchase products that are tied together. In some cases pricing practices are condemned because they are considered to be

---

7   Ibid, paras 111-114; see also para 139.
8   Case 85/76 [1979] ECR 461, [1979] 3 CMLR 211.
9   Ibid, para 110.
10 Ibid, para 111.
11 OJ [1988] L 284/41, [1990] 4 CMLR 196.
12 Case 311/84 [1985] ECR 3261, [1986] 2 CMLR 558.
13 Commission's XXVIIth *Report on Competition Policy* (1997), pp 153-154; see similarly the Commission's action against AC Nielsen to prevent the charging of bundled prices: XXVIth *Report on Competition Policy* (1996), pp 144-148.

likely to eliminate competitors, albeit without this element of exclusivity or a tie-in. This section considers the extent to which predatory price-cutting (selling at a loss) and selective price-cutting to retain customers (but not at a loss) may amount to an abuse of a dominant position.

(A) Predatory price-cutting

(i) Introduction

The idea of predatory price-cutting is simple enough: that a dominant firm, replete with funds from the exploitation of its dominant position, reduces prices to a loss-making level when faced with competition from an existing competitor or a new entrant to the market; the existing competitor having been disciplined, or the new entrant having been fended off, the dominant firm then raises its prices again, accumulating further profits until the next wave of attacks. Attempts to eliminate an existing competitor may be more expensive and difficult to achieve than deterring a new one from entry, especially where the existing competitor is committed to remaining in the market. Where a dominant undertaking has a reputation for acting in a predatory manner, this in itself may deter new entrants: not only predatory pricing itself but also the reputation for predation may be a barrier to entry.

It is the essence of competition that firms should compete for custom by reducing prices. It has already been pointed out that rebates and similar practices are an essential component of the competitive process, and that the law should not condemn practices, even on the part of dominant firms, that are competitive; in particular a dominant firm should not be deterred from passing on its efficiency to customers in the form of lower prices[14]. The law on predatory price-cutting has to tread a fine line between not condemning competitive responses on the part of dominant firms on the one hand and prohibiting unreasonable exclusionary conduct on the other. It would be perverse if the effect of competition law were to be that dominant firms choose not to compete on price for fear that, by doing so, they would be found guilty of abusing a dominant position[15].

There is a considerable body of literature on predatory price-cutting[16]. There is some theoretical scepticism as to whether a monopolist would ever benefit from predatory price cutting[17]; if one agrees with this view, competition authorities

---

14 See p 640 above.
15 See eg the Supreme Court in the US in *Matsushita v Zenith Radio* 475 US 574 (1986): 'mistaken inferences in cases such as this chill the very conduct that antitrust laws are designed to protect'.
16 See eg Areeda and Turner 'Predatory Pricing and Related Practices under Section 2 of the Sherman Act: A Comment' (1975) 88 Harvard Law Review 697; Scherer 'Predatory Pricing and the Sherman Act: A Comment' (1976) 89 Harvard Law Review 869; Williamson 'Predatory Pricing: A Strategic and Welfare Analysis' (1977) 87 Yale Law Journal 284; Baumol 'Quasi-Permanence of Price Reductions: A Policy for Prevention of Predatory Pricing' (1979) 89 Yale Law Journal 1; Brodley and Hay 'Predatory Pricing: Competing Economic Theories and the Evolution of Legal Standards' (1981) 66 Cornell Law Review 738; Williamson *Antitrust Economics* (Blackwell, 1987), pp 328–338; Bishop and Walker *The Economics of EC Competition Law* (Sweet & Maxwell, 1999), paras 5.37-5.57; Mastromanolis 'Predatory Pricing Strategies in the European Union: a Case for Legal Reform' (1998) 19 ECLR 211.
17 See eg Bork *Antitrust Paradox* (Basic Books, 1976), pp 148–155; Bork argues that in practice predation is too expensive for the predator; that the predator will not earn monopoly profits

ought not to concern themselves at all with the issue. However there is no doubt that predatory price cutting can amount to an infringement of Article 82 and the Chapter II prohibition in the Competition Act 1998.

(ii) The Areeda and Turner test

Many attempts have been made to frame an economic test of when a price is predatory. Areeda and Turner[18] suggested that a price should be deemed predatory under US law where it was below a firm's short-run marginal cost ('SRMC') or average variable cost ('AVC'). A firm's AVC is calculated by dividing its variable costs, that is to say those costs which vary according to the amount of its output such as expenditure on raw materials, labour, fuel and maintenance, by its actual output. This calculation indicates the average cost of each extra unit of output. Since it is simpler to ascertain AVC than SRMC, the US courts have preferred the AVC standard. Areeda and Turner suggested that prices *above* SRMC or AVC should be presumed lawful.

The Areeda and Turner test relies exclusively on a cost/price analysis. Some commentators think that the test should be less strict, and that predation should be condemned only where it can also be demonstrated that a predator will be able to recoup any losses it has made through the exercise of its market power in the future: some US courts have required proof of recoupment as a key component of the offence of predation[19]. Others question whether the Areeda and Turner test is strict enough, arguing that pricing above AVC could be predatory in some circumstances, especially where there is evidence of an intention to discipline or deter competitors or where in practice it has this effect. However there are difficulties with a legal rule which requires specific proof of a predator's intention. In the ruthless process of competition, any competitor that enters a race wishes to win, so that by necessary implication it must also have 'intended' that its competitors should lose; in this sense a requirement of intention is hardly meaningful. In so far as a requirement of intention means that evidence of a 'smoking gun' should be adduced, for example in the form of written memoranda, minutes of meetings and e-mails documenting a settled policy of eliminating competitors, this may be difficult for a competition authority to find: well-advised companies will be perfectly aware that they should not generate incriminating documents of this kind and that they should destroy those that they do. A rule requiring evidence of intention to eliminate would make more sense where it has an objective quality based in economics, for example that a predator's conduct, by departing from short-term profit maximisation, makes commercial sense only

---

until some distant future time when the new firm has disappeared; and that if it is easy to drive firms out, it will be correspondingly easy for new firms to enter when the predator begins to reap a monopoly profit in the future; see also Koller 'The Myth of Predatory Pricing: An Empirical Study' (1971) 4 Antitrust L Ec Rev 105; Easterbrook 'Predatory Strategies and Counterstrategies' (1981) 48 University of Chicago Law Review 263.

18 See Areeda and Turner 'Predatory Pricing and Related Practices under Section 2 of the Sherman Act: A Comment' 88 Harvard Law Review 697 (1975).

19 See eg *Matsushita v Zenith Radio*, n 15 above; *AA Poultry Farms Inc v Rose Acre Farms Inc* 881 F 2d 1396 (1989); *Brooke Group v Brown & Williamson Tobacco* 509 US 209 (1993); on recoupment in US law, see Joskow and Klevorick 'A Framework for Analysing Predatory Pricing Policy' (1979) 89 Yale Law Journal 213; Elzinga and Mills 'Testing for Predation: Is Recoupment Feasible?' (1989) 34 Antitrust Bulletin 869; on recoupment in EC law, see pp 650-651 below; in UK law, see p 671 below.

as a way of eliminating a competitor; this variant of intention is very different from proving the subjective intention of the predator, but is extremely difficult to prove as a matter of economic analysis. This discussion demonstrates some of the problems involved in establishing a suitable test for cases on predatory price-cutting.

As we shall see, proving intention is sometimes relevant in the EC law on pricing abuses. The ECJ in *AKZO v Commission*[20] decided that pricing above AVC but below average total cost ('ATC') could be abusive where there was evidence of an intention on the part of the dominant firm to eliminate a competitor[1]. In *Compagnie Maritime Belge v Commission*[2] the ECJ held that a policy of selective price cutting to particular customers carried into effect with the intention of eliminating the dominant undertaking's only competitor was abusive in the particular circumstances of the market for the maritime transport of containerised cargo[3]. These judgments seem to be based on the 'smoking gun' variant of intention.

(iii)   The rule in AKZO v Commission

In *ECS/AKZO*[4] the Commission imposed a fine of EUR 10 million on AKZO for predatory price-cutting. ECS was a small UK firm producing benzoyl peroxide. Until 1979 it had sold this product to customers requiring it as a bleach in the treatment of flour in the UK and Eire. It then decided also to sell it to users in the polymer industry. AKZO, a Dutch company in a dominant position on the market, informed ECS that unless it withdrew from the polymer market it would reduce its prices, in particular in the flour additives market, in order to harm it. Subsequently AKZO did indeed reduce its prices. In holding that AKZO had abused its dominant position the Commission declined to adopt the Areeda and Turner test of predatory price cutting, according to which pricing above AVC should be presumed lawful[5]. While accepting that cost/price analysis is an element in deciding whether a price is predatory, the Commission considered that it was also relevant whether the dominant firm had adopted a strategy of eliminating competition, what the effects of its conduct would be likely to be, and what a competitor's likely reaction to the conduct of the dominant firm would be. At paragraph 79 of its decision the Commission suggested that even a price above ATC might be predatory when assessed in its particular market context[6]. A firm's ATC is the total of its variable and fixed costs divided by its output, the fixed costs being those that do not vary with an undertaking's output; a firm's ATC is obviously higher than its AVC.

---

20   Case C-62/86 *AKZO v Commission* [1991] ECR I-3359, [1993] 5 CMLR 215.
1   See p 649 below.
2   Cases C-395/96 P etc *Compagnie Maritime Belge v Commission* [2000] 4 CMLR 1076.
3   See pp 655-657 below.
4   OJ [1985] L 374/1, [1986] 3 CMLR 273; see Merkin 'Predatory Pricing or Competitive Pricing: Establishing the Truth in English and EC Law' (1987) 7 Oxford Journal of Legal Studies 182.
5   See pp 647-648 above.
6   See also the Commission's comments at point 82 of its XVth *Report on Competition Policy* (1985).

On appeal[7] the ECJ upheld the Commission's finding of predatory pricing, saying that not all price competition can be considered legitimate[8]. The ECJ held that where prices were below AVC predation had to be presumed, since every sale would generate a loss for the dominant firm[9]. The ECJ did not say that the presumption could never be rebutted, but in principle it would be wrong to have a *per se* rule that selling below AVC is always illegal: for example a dominant firm should be able to sell below cost where its competitors are doing the same; and the disposal of old stock at the end of the season at a price below cost would presumably not be unlawful[10].

The ECJ in *AKZO v Commission* went on to hold that where prices are above AVC but below ATC they will be regarded as abusive if they are determined as part of a plan which is aimed at eliminating a competitor[11]; such a pricing policy might mean that a dominant firm drives from the market undertakings that are as efficient as it but which, because of their smaller financial resources, are incapable of withstanding the competition waged against them. The ECJ therefore upheld the Commission's rejection of the Areeda/Turner test.

The rule in *AKZO v Commission* can be depicted as follows, where the dominant firm's prices range from 0 to 100:

100

> Where a dominant firm is charging prices above ATC, it is not guilty of predation under the rule in *AKZO v Commission*; however consideration must be given to the rule on selective price cutting in *Compagnie Maritime Belge v Commission* (see below)

ATC

> Where a dominant firm is selling at less than ATC, but above AVC, it is guilty of predation where this is done as part of a plan to eliminate a competitor

AVC

> Where a dominant firm is selling at less than AVC, it is presumed to be acting abusively; this presumption may be rebuttable where there is an objective justification for below-cost selling

0

(iv)   Tetra Pak v Commission

In *Tetra Pak II*[12] the Commission found Tetra Pak guilty of predatory pricing in relation to its non-asceptic cartons[13]; it considered that Tetra Pak was able to subsidise its losses from its substantial profits on the market for asceptic cartons,

---

7   Case C-62/86 *AKZO v Commission* [1991] ECR I-3359, [1993] 5 CMLR 215.
8   Ibid, para 70.
9   Ibid, para 71; the ECJ did not discuss the period of time over which the AVC should be calculated; in the UK, the Guideline on *Assessment of Individual Agreements and Conduct*, OFT Guideline 414, suggests, at para 4.6, that the timescale should be the period over which the alleged predatory prices prevailed; on predation in UK law, see pp 670-672 below.
10 The OFT Guideline 414 suggests, at para 4.8, various possible defences for prices below AVC: see p 670 below.
11 Case C-62/86 *AKZO v Commission* [1991] ECR I-3359, [1993] 5 CMLR 215, para 72.
12 OJ [1992] L 72/1 [1992] 4 CMLR 551.
13 Ibid, paras 147-153.

where it had virtually no competition. The Commission said that in seven Member States the non-asceptic cartons had been sold at a loss[14]. However the Commission concentrated on the position in Italy, where the cartons had been sold below AVC. The Commission did not merely rely on the *AKZO* presumption of predation where prices are below AVC, but said that it had 'gathered sufficiently clear and unequivocal data to be able to conclude that, in that country at least, sales at a loss were the result of a deliberate policy aimed at eliminating competition'[15]. The Commission continued by saying that, although it was difficult to believe that an efficient multi-national company could have indulged in behaviour so opposed to the logic of economic profitability through management error, it should be asked whether exceptional circumstances, independent of Tetra Pak's free will, forced it make losses. The Commission concluded that there were no such circumstances and that the prices were simply part of an 'eviction strategy'[16]. The ECJ upheld the Commission's finding of abuse; the judgment is of interest to the issue of recoupment, which is discussed in the following section[17].

(v)   Is it necessary to show the possibility of recoupment?

It was pointed out above that in US law some courts have required that an element of the offence of predatory price-cutting is that it can be shown that the predator has the ability to recoup any losses incurred. The ECJ has not yet adopted a requirement of recoupment under Article 82. In *AKZO v Commission* the Court acknowledged the significance of recoupment in paragraph 71 of its judgment, where it noted that a dominant firm has no interest in applying prices below average variable cost 'except that of eliminating competitors so as to enable it subsequently to raise its prices by taking advantage of its monopolistic position'. However it did not expressly incorporate the need to prove recoupment as part of the offence. In *Tetra Pak II* it was argued before the ECJ that the Commission should have to establish the possibility of recoupment as part of the offence of predation. The ECJ, upholding the finding that Tetra Pak was guilty of predatory pricing, remarked that 'it would not be appropriate, *in the circumstances of the present case,* to require in addition proof that Tetra Pak had a realistic chance of recouping its losses. It must be possible to penalise predatory pricing whenever there is a risk that competitors will be eliminated'[18] (emphasis added). The *Tetra Pak* case was one in which the anti-competitive intention of Tetra Pak, manifested in a series of abusive acts contrary to Article 82, was particularly clear; furthermore its market power was considerable, so that the case could be considered as one of 'super-dominance' rather than one of 'mere' dominance[19]. This may explain why the ECJ felt that 'in the circumstances of the present case' it was not necessary to require proof of recoupment; this clearly

---

14   Ibid, para 147.

15   Ibid.

16   Ibid, para 149.

17   Case C-333/94 P *Tetra Pak International SA v Commission* [1996] ECR I-5951, [1997] 4 CMLR 662; see Korah 'The Paucity of Economic Analysis in the EEC Decisions on Competition: Tetra Pak II' (1993) 46 Current Legal Problems 148, pp 172-181; Jones 'Distinguishing Predatory Prices from Competitive Ones' (1995) 17 EIPR 252.

18   Case C-333/94 P *Tetra Pak International SA v Commission* [1996] ECR I-5951, [1997] 4 CMLR 662, para 44; at paras 76-78 of his Opinion in this case Advocate General Ruiz-colomer considered that proof of recoupment was not necessary.

19   See ch 5, pp 162-163.

leaves open the possibility that in future cases, where the evidence of intention to eliminate competition is less clear-cut and where the predator is not super-dominant, the Court might require proof of the possibility of recoupment.

(vi) Are the standards of AVC and ATC always appropriate?

A complicating factor in applying cost-based rules to determine whether prices are predatory is that it may not always be appropriate to apply the standards of AVC or ATC. In some industries fixed costs are very high but variable costs are low. An obvious example is telecommunications, where it is likely to have been very expensive to establish the original infrastructure of wires and cables; once they have been laid, however, the actual cost of carrying telephone calls is low, and may be as low as zero. A further example of high fixed costs but low variable costs is the laying of oil and gas pipelines. In industries such as this, the AVC of telephone calls or the transmission of oil and gas is so low that there would hardly ever be predatory prices if the AVC standard were to be applied; and the ATC standard would require proof of the predator's intention to eliminate competition, following the rule in *AKZO v Commission*, with the difficulties that this entails. Similarly in some industries there are substantial economies of scale and scope, again with the result that variable costs are low, so that prices would hardly ever be predatory according to the AVC standard. Economies of scale arise where average costs decline as output increases; economies of scope occur where average costs are lower if two or more products are produced jointly: certain costs are common to a range of products[20]. Economies of scale and of scope are often present in the telecommunications industry, where the owner and operator of a network which also supplies a number of services using that network has a wide discretion when pricing its products to determine in which market to recover its costs. The same discretion over prices may be available to firms in similar (often regulated) industries such as postal services.

If the AVC and ATC standards in *AKZO v Commission* are inappropriate to determine whether prices are predatory in industries such as these, an alternative rule is needed. In the Commission's *Notice on the Application of the Competition Rules to Access Agreements*[1] it suggests that the *AKZO* standards are not appropriate in a network industry such as telecommunications[2] and that a standard based on long-run incremental cost might be preferable ('LRIC'). This standard is helpfully explained in the Guideline *Competition Act 1998: the Application in the Telecommunications Sector*[3] published by the OFT in the UK. LRIC takes into account the total long-run cost, both capital and operating, of supplying a specified additional unit of output such as a new service, referred to as 'the increment'[4]. If the price of a service covers the LRIC it will be profitable; as a result it would not be regarded as predatory.

---

20 See ch 1, pp 8-9.
1   OJ [1998] C 265/2, [1998] 5 CMLR 821.
2   Ibid, paras 113-115.
3   OFT Guideline 417; see also Baumol 'Predation Criteria in the Swedish Postal Zone Case' (2000) 21 ECLR 225.
4   OFT Guideline 417, paras 7.7-7.12; para 7.10 of the *Guideline* specifically cross-refers to the Commission's *Notice on Access Agreements* referred to in the text.

The Commission proceeded, for the first time in a formal decision, on the basis of incremental cost in *Deutsche Post*[5]. UPS complained that Deutsche Post was using revenue from its profitable letter-post monopoly to finance a strategy of below-cost selling in the commercial parcels market, which was open to competition. The Commission's view was that Deutsche Post, in the period from 1990 to 1995, had received revenue from this business which did not cover the incremental cost of providing it[6]. By remaining in the market without any foreseeable improvement in revenue, Deutsche Post was considered to have restricted the activities of competitors which were in a position to provide the service at a price that would cover their costs[7]. The Commission therefore concluded that Deutsche Post was guilty of predatory pricing; however it did not impose a fine for this infringement, since this was the first time that it had applied the incremental cost standard[8]. As a matter of remedy Deutsche Post agreed to create a separate legal entity ('Newco') for its commercial parcel service. The Commission required that at the end of each accounting year Deutsche Post would submit a statement of Newco's costs and revenue and would provide an itemised statement of the transfer prices for all goods and services procured by Newco from it[9].

(vii)   *Predatory price cutting and cross-subsidisation*[10]

An undertaking such as Deutsche Post, which enjoys a legal monopoly in relation to the basic letter service[11], is able to use the profits it makes there to support low prices in other markets where it faces competition: this was the essence of UPS's complaint[12]. Cross-subsidisation may facilitate abusive pricing practices such as predation and selective price cutting. This raises the interesting question of whether cross-subsidisation is an abuse of a dominant position in itself. There are no decisions of the Commission or judgments of the Community Courts finding that cross-subsidy is, in itself, an abuse of a dominant position, although the Commission in its *Notice on the Application of the Competition Rules to the Postal Sector*[13] suggests, at paragraph 3.3, that there could be circumstances in which it could be an abuse to subsidise activities open to competition by allocating their costs to those services in relation to which the postal operator enjoys a monopoly. Despite this statement, however, in principle it would appear that the existing rules on abusive pricing practices, described in this chapter, are sufficient to control the behaviour of dominant firms; the adoption of a rule forbidding cross-subsidy itself is unnecessary and would be fraught with difficulties.

5   OJ [2001] L 125/27.
6   Ibid, para 36; the Commission sets out the relevant cost concepts at paras 6 and 7 of the decision.
7   Ibid.
8   Ibid, para 47; a fine of EUR 24 million was imposed for the use of loyalty rebates: see p 642 above.
9   See Article 2 of the decision.
10   See Hancher and Buendia Sierra 'Cross-subsidisation and EC Law' (1998) 35 CML Rev 901; Abbamonte 'Cross-subsidsation and Community Competition Rules: Efficient Pricing Versus Equity?' (1998) 23 ELRev 414.
11   On the extent of the permissible monopoly in postal services under Community law see ch 23, p 872.
12   OJ [2001] L 125/27, para 5.
13   OJ [1998] C 39/2, [1998] 5 CMLR 108.

Where cross-subsidy is a problem, there are other ways of dealing with it. In the case of regulated industries, specific rules are often imposed to prevent the practice[14]. Useful remedies that the Commission can deploy in Article 82 cases include a requirement to establish different legal entities, the maintenance of separate accounts and full financial transparency of dominant firms' pricing practices.

(B)   Selective price cutting, but not below cost

(i)   Introduction

One of the most contentious issues under Article 82 is whether it can be unlawful for a dominant firm to cut its prices selectively, but not to below cost, to customers that might desert to a competitor, while leaving prices to other customers at a higher level. Such a policy might amount to unlawful discrimination contrary to Article 82(2)(c) where it involves the application of dissimilar conditions to equivalent transactions, thereby placing other trading parties at a competitive advantage[15]. The Commission has recently been applying Article 82(2)(c) with greater frequency[16], but a finding under that provision requires a number of elements to be established. In particular, Article 82(2)(c) appears to be directed to discrimination which distorts competition in the market downstream from the dominant firm, as a consequence of which the victim of the discrimination is unable to compete effectively with other undertakings at its level of the market; having said this, there is some doubt as to the significance of the reference to competitive disadvantage, particularly in the light of the *Corsica Ferries* case[17]. The specific issue under consideration in this section is whether selective price cutting could be held to be abusive irrespective of whether it infringes Article 82(2)(c) and, more specifically, where the undertaking harmed is a competitor operating at the same level of the market as the dominant firm rather than a trading party in a downstream market.

The position can be depicted as follows:

Article 82(2)(c) discrimination

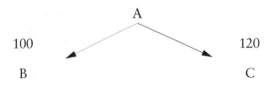

A charges B a price of 100 per widget, but charges C 120; B and C need widgets to manufacture blodgets, a market in which they compete. Clearly the discrimination puts C at a competitive disadvantage in the blodget market as against B. It may be, in a case such as this, that B is a subsidiary of A, or closely associated with it; this may help to explain why A practices discrimination in the first place. The detriment to competition occurs downstream from A's market;

---

14 See ch 23, p 866ff.
15 See pp 657-662 below.
16 See p 659 below.
17 See pp 661-662 below.

the harm to C is sometimes referred to as 'secondary line injury', to be compared with the 'primary line injury' that is suffered in the example that follows.

Selective price cutting as an abuse

In this example, A charges B 120 and C 100. B requires widgets for blodgets; C requires them for sprockets. Blodgets and sprockets do not compete, so that there is no harm to competition between B and C in the downstream market. The motivation for A's price cut to C is that A fears that it is going to lose C's business to X; X is able to supply a different input to C from which C could just as easily produce sprockets. The purpose of the selective price cut is to eliminate competition at A's level of the market: the case is one of primary line injury.

The question of whether selective price-cutting such as this is abusive is controversial. Provided that the dominant firm is not making a loss, it is not guilty of predatory price-cutting; if it has not offered loyalty rebates, it has not infringed the rule in *Hoffmann-la Roche*; and for the reasons just given it may not be infringing Article 82(2)(c). It would appear that, in making selective price cuts, the dominant firm is competing 'on the merits' with X, and that it has not acted abusively. The Community Courts have often stated that dominant firms are allowed to 'meet' competition, which is what A appears to have done[18]; and it is obviously in C's interest, and in the interest of C's customers, that it is the beneficiary of lower prices. Despite this, however, it is possible that selective price cuts of this nature may be held to be abusive, albeit only in narrowly defined circumstances.

(ii)   *Eurofix-Bauco v Hilti*

In *Eurofix-Bauco v Hilti*[19] the Commission imposed a fine of EUR 6 million on Hilti for abusing its dominant position in a number of ways. Hilti had taken action to prevent customers from purchasing nails from its competitors. Apart from entering into tie-in agreements with some customers[20], Hilti singled out competing firms' main customers and offered them particularly favourable conditions; it removed quantity discounts from long-standing customers who did buy from its competitors; and it classified certain customers as 'unsupported', which meant that they qualified for lower quantity discounts than 'supported' firms: it appeared to the Commission that the 'unsupported' firms were ones which had purchased nails and nail cartridges other than from Hilti. Hilti had

---

18   See eg the judgment of the CFI in Case T-228/97 *Irish Sugar v Commission* [1999] ECR II-2969, [1999] 5 CMLR 1300, para 112 and the judgments referred to in the footnote to that paragraph; for a general discussion of 'meeting' rather than beating competition, see Springer '"Meeting Competition": Justification of Price Discrimination under EC and US Antitrust Law' (1997) 18 ECLR 251.
19   OJ [1988] L 65/19, [1989] 4 CMLR 677.
20   See ch 17, p 609.

also given away some products free of charge. The Commission said that the pricing abuses in this case did not hinge on whether the prices were below cost, but on whether Hilti could rely on its dominance to offer discriminatory prices to its competitors' customers with a view to damaging the competitors' business; in other words the Commission proceeded not on the basis of predatory pricing contrary to *AKZO v Commission* nor on the basis of a detriment to competition in a downstream market contrary to Article 82(2)(c). The CFI, upholding the decision of the Commission, stated that Hilti's strategy was not a legitimate mode of competition on the part of an undertaking in a dominant position[1].

(iii) Irish Sugar v Commission

The Commission considered that Irish Sugar had abused its dominant position contrary to Article 82 by offering selective price cuts in *Irish Sugar*[2]. The CFI annulled the finding that Irish Sugar had applied selectively low prices to potential customers of a competitor, ASI, on factual grounds[3]; however it upheld the finding that Irish Sugar had been guilty of granting selective rebates to particular customers[4].

(iv) Compagnie Maritime Belge v Commission

In *Compagnie Maritime Belge v Commission*[5] the Commission investigated the policy of 'fighting ships', whereby members of a liner conference in the maritime transport sector, Cewal, reduced their charges to the level, or to below the level, of their one competitor, Grimaldi and Cobelfret; they also operated the fighting ships on the same route and at the same time as Grimaldi's. The Commission concluded that the policy was one of selective price cutting intended to eliminate the competitor and that Article 82 was infringed. The Commission's decision was upheld by the CFI[6]. The ECJ agreed that there was an infringement of Article 82, although the fines were annulled for technical reasons[7].

Advocate General Fennelly, urging that the application of Article 82 to selective price cutting should be approached with reserve, remarked that:

> 'Price competition is the essence of the free and open competition which it is the objective of Community policy to establish on the internal market. It favours more efficient firms and it is for the benefit of consumers both in the short and the long run. Dominant firms not only have the right but should be encouraged to compete on price.'[8]

In the Advocate General's view, non-discriminatory price cuts by a dominant undertaking which do not entail below-cost sales should not normally be regarded as being anti-competitive:

1   Case T–30/89 *Hilti AG v Commission* [1990] ECR II-163, [1992] 4 CMLR 16, para 100.
2   OJ [1997] L 258/1, [1997] 5 CMLR 666.
3   Case T-228/97 [1999] ECR II-2969, [1999] 5 CMLR 1300, paras 117-124.
4   Ibid, paras 215-225.
5   OJ [1993] L 34/20, [1995] 5 CMLR 198.
6   Cases T-24/93 etc [1996] ECR II-1201, [1997] 4 CMLR 273.
7   Cases C-395/96 P etc [2000] 4 CMLR 1076; for comment, see Preece '*Compagnie Maritime Belge*: Missing the Boat?' (2000) 21 ECLR 388.
8   Ibid, at para 117 of the Advocate General's Opinion.

'In the first place, even if they are only short lived, they benefit consumers and, secondly, if the dominant undertaking's competitors are equally or more efficient, they should be able to compete on the same terms. Community competition law should thus not offer less efficient undertakings a safe haven against vigorous competition even from dominant undertakings. Different considerations may, however, apply where an undertaking which enjoys a position of dominance approaching a monopoly, particularly on a market where price cuts can be implemented with relative autonomy from costs, implements a policy of selective price cutting with the demonstrable aim of eliminating all competition. In those circumstances, to accept that all selling above cost was automatically acceptable could enable the undertaking in question to eliminate all competition by pursuing a selective pricing policy which in the long run would permit it to increase prices and deter potential future entrants for fear of receiving the same targeted treatment'[9].

In its judgment the ECJ followed the Advocate General, holding that the selective price-cutting on the facts of this case was abusive[10]. After noting that the scope of the special responsibility of dominant undertakings must be considered in the light of the specific circumstances of each case[11], the ECJ noted that the maritime transport market is 'a very specialised sector'[12]; it declined to establish a general rule for selective price cutting on the part of liner conferences, but, upholding the Commission's finding of abuse, concluded that:

'It is sufficient to recall that the conduct at issue here is that of a conference having a share of over 90% of the market in question and only one competitor. The appellants have, moreover, never seriously disputed, and indeed admitted at the hearing, that the purpose of the conduct complained of was to eliminate [Grimaldi & Cobelfret] from the market'[13].

As a result of this judgment it is clear that selective price cutting is capable of being abusive in its own right. However it is important to point out a number of features of the *Compagnie Maritime Belge* case that restrict the scope of this precedent and which should therefore limit its application in the future. First, maritime transport is, as the ECJ remarked, an unusual sector in which an incumbent dominant firm is able to target its competitors and eliminate them by strategic behaviour with little regard to cost; secondly the conference had 90% or more of the market: it therefore was 'super-dominant', and subject to particularly close scrutiny under Article 82[14]; thirdly the conference had only one competitor, Grimaldi and Cobelfret; and fourthly there was a 'smoking gun', that is to say evidence of an intention on the part of the conference to eliminate Grimaldi from the market: indeed the smoke was seen by the judges of the ECJ, where the appellants admitted that they had this intention. The ECJ did not say, but may also have been influenced by the fact, that the liner conference itself was the product of a horizontal agreement amongst its members: there was effectively a horizontal collective boycott of Grimaldi, which would be a serious

9   Ibid, para 132.
10   See paras 112-121 of the ECJ's judgment.
11   Ibid, para 114.
12   Ibid, para 115.
13   Ibid, para 119.
14   See ch 5, pp 162-163.

offence under Article 81(1)[15]. The case should be read with these special features in mind; this makes it a less menacing precedent than it might otherwise appear to be, with the consequence that other dominant firms, operating in less unusual circumstances, should be free to respond to competition by price cuts that are not contrary to any of the other pricing abuses under Article 82 described in this chapter.

(C) Vertical price squeezing

A vertical price squeeze occurs where a firm supplies an intermediate product or service at a high price to its own downstream operation and also to a customer; it then sells the downstream product at a low price: the competitor in the downstream market will be unable to make a reasonable profit, and may even suffer a loss, because of the way in which the supplier of the intermediate product has 'squeezed' the price. This conduct can be unlawful when practised by a dominant undertaking. In *Napier Brown-British Sugar*[16] British Sugar was dominant both in the market for sugar beet and in the market for the derived product, sugar for retail. It reduced the price of retail sugar by more than the cost of transforming the raw material in order to drive sugar merchants such as Napier Brown from the retail level of the market; it also specifically undercut Napier Brown's prices in respect of certain customers. The Commission considered that this practice infringed Article 82. A fine of EUR 3 million was imposed for this (and other) abuses. It appears therefore that a dominant firm has an obligation to fix its prices at such a level that a reasonably efficient competitor on the derivatives market is able to survive[17]. The CFI upheld the Commission's rejection of a complaint about vertical price squeezing in *Industrie des Poudres Sphériques v Commission*[18].

4. PRICE DISCRIMINATION

(A) Article 82(2)(c) discrimination

Article 82(2)(c) specifically gives as an example of abuse:

> 'applying dissimilar conditions to equivalent transactions with other trading parties, thereby placing them at a competitive disadvantage'.

Clearly therefore price discrimination may infringe Article 82; so too could other types of discrimination, such as refusals to supply and preferential terms and conditions. Price discrimination may be exploitative of customers, for example where higher prices are charged to 'locked-in' customers unable to switch to alternative suppliers; it can also be harmful to the competitive process, where it leads to a distortion of competition in markets downstream of the dominant

---

15 See ch 13, pp 453-455.
16 OJ [1988] L 284/41, [1990] 4 CMLR 196.
17 See also *National Carbonising* OJ [1976] L 35/6 and the Commission's *Notice on the Application of the Competition Rules to Access Agreements in the Telecommunications Sector* (p 651, n 1 above), paras 117-119.
18 Case T-5/97 [2001] 4 CMLR 1020.

undertaking. As was explained above[19], Article 82(2)(c) appears on its face to be directed to discrimination which is detrimental to competition in downstream markets; however the ECJ and the Commission seem almost to have written the need for competitive disadvantage out of Article 82(2)(c)[20].

(B)   Meaning of price discrimination[1]

Price discrimination may be defined as the sale or purchase of different units of a good or service at prices not directly corresponding to differences in the cost of supplying them. There can be discrimination both where different, non-cost related prices are charged for the sale or purchase of goods or services of the same description and also where identical prices are charged in circumstances in which a difference in the cost of supplying them would justify their differentiation.

There are many costs involved in supplying goods or services which may result in the charging of differentiated yet non-discriminatory prices. For example, apart from the cost of transporting goods, a manufacturer may incur heavier costs where it has to handle a series of small orders from a particular customer rather than a single, annual one. Orders for large quantities of goods may mean that a producer can plan long production runs and achieve economies of scale which lead to lower unit costs. The incidence of different contractual terms and conditions, payment of local taxes and duties, the different costs involved in operating distributorship networks from one area to another, may all explain the charging of different prices. However it can be difficult to determine whether differences in the cost of supplying goods or services justify, objectively, the charging of differentiated prices; and even more difficult to calculate the justifiable differentiation.

It is important to appreciate that price discrimination can be positively beneficial in terms of allocative efficiency, since it may result in an *increase* in output[2]: a theatre might be able to sell 80% of its tickets to the public at £4 each, or alternatively 100% of its tickets by charging 70% of its customers £5 and the remaining 30% £1 each (for example to impoverished students). Through such discrimination more theatre tickets will have been sold than would otherwise have been the case: resources have been more efficiently allocated. A specific example of efficient price discrimination is so-called 'Ramsay pricing'. This occurs where a company supplies different products which share common costs. It may be that customers for product A are highly price sensitive, but that customers for product B are not; if customers for product A are charged high prices and customers for product B low ones – that is to say if prices are marked up in inverse proportion to customers' respective price sensitivities – output will be increased and economic efficiency will therefore be maximised. The principle of Ramsay pricing has been accepted by regulators and competition authorities in some sectors[3].

---

19   See p 653 above.
20   See pp 661-662 below.
1   For an economic analysis of price discrimination, see Scherer and Ross *Industrial Market Structure and Economic Performance* (Houghton Mifflin, 3rd ed, 1990) ch 13.
2   See eg Schmalensee 'Output and Welfare Implications of Third Degree Price Discrimination' (1981) 71 American Economic Review 242.
3   See Pflanz 'What Price is Right? Lessons from the UK Calls-to-Mobile Inquiry' (2000) 21 ECLR 147; the potential efficiency of price discrimination is explicitly recognised in the UK in the OFT's guideline on the domestic equivalent of Article 82(2)(c), OFT Guideline 414, paras 3.6-3.10; see pp 672-673 below.

In practice the allocative effects of discrimination will vary from one market situation to another: the question is ultimately an empirical rather than a theoretical one. There is no case for a *per se* prohibition of price discrimination, even on the part of a dominant firm. Furthermore it may be that preventing discrimination has the effect of redistributing income from poorer consumers to richer ones[4]. This can be illustrated by imagining what might happen if discrimination is prevented. A producer may charge £10 per widget in a prosperous area and £5 per widget in a poorer one. If this discrimination is prevented the producer may sell at a uniform price of, say, £7 in both areas. It is reasonable to assume that as a result fewer people in the poorer area will buy widgets, and that those that do will pay a higher proportion of their income than those in the prosperous one. The net effect therefore is to transfer wealth from poorer consumers with the result that more prosperous ones will be better off.

(C) The application of Article 82(2)(c) in practice

The Commission has applied Article 82(2)(c) on a number of occasions; in recent years this has happened with increasing frequency, in particular in relation to the operation of airports within the Community[5]. The ECJ upheld findings by the Commission that Article 82(2)(c) had been infringed in *Hoffmann-La Roche v Commission*[6] and in *United Brands v Commission*[7]. The Commission's decision in *Michelin*[8] that there had been an infringement of Article 82(2)(c) was annulled by the ECJ[9]. The ECJ upheld the Commission's finding of an Article 82(2)(c) abuse in *GVL v Commission*[10], where a copyright collecting society in Germany refused to provide its services to non-German residents, thereby placing them at a competitive disadvantage as against German residents.

The decision of the Commission in *Irish Sugar*[11] that there had been an infringement of Article 82(2)(c) was upheld by the CFI[12]. Irish Sugar granted 'sugar export rebates' to industrial customers in Ireland in relation to sugar exported to other Member States, to the disadvantage of customers selling in Ireland[13]. Irish Sugar also practised discrimination against sugar packers in Ireland, a practice which the CFI found to infringe Article 82(2)(c)[14]. In *Virgin/ British Airways*[15] the Commission concluded that BA was not only guilty of abuse by offering travel agents loyalty rebates; there was discrimination contrary to Article 82(2)(c), since travel agents in the same circumstances received different levels of rebates[16].

---

4 See eg Bishop 'Price Discrimination under Article [82]: Political Economy in the European Court' (1981) 44 MLR 282.
5 See pp 660-661 below.
6 Case 27/76 [1978] ECR 207, [1978] 1 CMLR 429.
7 Case 85/76 [1979] ECR 461, [1979l 3 CMLR 211.
8 OJ [1981] L 353/33, [1982] 1 CMLR 643.
9 Case 322/81 [1983] ECR 3461, [1985] 1 CMLR 282.
10 Case 7/82 [1983] ECR 483, [1983] 3 CMLR 645.
11 OJ [1997] L 258/1, [1997] 5 CMLR 666.
12 Case T-228/97 *Irish Sugar plc v Commission* [1999] ECR II-2969, [1999] 5 CMLR 1300.
13 Ibid, paras 125-149.
14 Ibid, paras 150-172.
15 OJ [2000] L 30/1, [2000] 4 CMLR 999, on appeal Case T-219/99 *British Airways v Commission* (judgment pending).
16 Ibid, paras 108-111.

(D)   The specific application of Article 82(2)(c) to airport operations

Article 82(2)(c) has been applied in recent years to discriminatory practices at a number of Community airports. In *Alpha Flight Services/Aéroports de Paris*[17] the Commission found that the operator of the two Paris airports (Orly and Charles de Gaulle) had abused its dominant position by imposing discriminatory commercial fees on suppliers or airlines providing ground-handling or self-handling services such as catering, cleaning and freight-handling. The Commission's decision was upheld on appeal to the CFI[18].

In *Portuguese Airports*[19] the Commission adopted a decision establishing that Portugal was in breach of Article 86 (ex Article 90) read in conjunction with Article 82 in respect of a system of discounts on landing charges at the airports of Lisbon, Oporto, Faro and the Azores. Discounts were offered to airlines according to the number of flights that landed at the Portuguese airports. For example, the second 50 flights would be charged at a discount of 7.2% from the price for the first 50; the third 50 at 14.6% and so on. As a result of this discounting structure TAP and Portugalia (Portuguese airlines) respectively enjoyed discounts of 30% and 22% on the total of their flights; the next beneficiary was Iberian Airlines (of Spain), which earned a discount of 8%. Airlines from beyond the Iberian peninsular received meagre discounts. At paragraph 27 of its decision the Commission cited the CFI's statement in *BPB Industries v Commission*[20] that business practices considered to be normal may constitute an abuse if carried out by an undertaking in a dominant position. In the next sentence the Commission said that:

'There must be an objective justification for any difference in treatment of its various clients by an undertaking in a dominant position'.

If the Commission intended this statement to be a reformulation of the CFI's in *BPB*, it is a *non-sequitur*; the CFI did not lay down such a broad principle, and it seems scarcely possible that, as a matter of law, a dominant undertaking must adduce an objective justification for '*any*' difference in treatment, irrespective of its impact on competition. It may be that the explanation for the Commission's excessively broad formulation was that the airports in question were natural monopolies, as the Commission goes on to say in the following sentence: in other words, this may have been a case of super-dominance, where particularly stringent standards applied to the undertaking under investigation[1]. The Commission dismissed the suggested justifications for the discount system. In so far as Madrid and Barcelona airports operated a similar system, the Commission was proceeding against them anyway, and a Member State cannot justify its infringement by arguing that another Member State was guilty of the same infringement[2]. Noting that there was no evidence of economies of scale – to the

---

17   OJ [1998] L 230/10.
18   Case T-128/98, [2001] 4 CMLR 1376.
19   OJ [1999] L 69/31, [1999] 5 CMLR 103, upheld on appeal, Case 163/99 *Portugal v Commission* judgment of 29 March 2001.
20   Case T-65/89 [1993] ECR II-389, [1993] 5 CMLR 32.
1   See ch 5, pp 162-163.
2   Case C-5/94 *R v MAFF, ex p Hedley Lomas (Ireland)* [1996] ECR I-2553, [1996] 2 CMLR 391; the Commission subsequently adopted a decision in relation to Spanish airports: see below.

airport authority the cost of an aeroplane landing was the same, whether it belonged to TAP which had landed many or to someone else which had landed few[3] – the Commission dismissed the argument that there was a cost justification. It also rejected the argument that the policy was necessary to promote tourism, since this objective could be achieved by non-discriminatory discounts accessible to all airlines operating services to and from the airports in mainland Portugal. A further aspect of the scheme, whereby domestic flights were given bigger discounts than international ones, was also condemned; the Commission applied the judgment of the ECJ in *Corsica Ferries II*[4], which unequivocally prohibited discrimination of this type.

On appeal the ECJ acknowledged that quantity discounts linked solely to the volume of purchases may be permissible, but said that the rules for calculating the discounts must not result in the application of dissimilar conditions to equivalent transactions in the sense of Article 82(2)(c)[5]. It went on to say that:

'where, as a result of the thresholds of the various discount bands, and the levels of discount offered, discounts (or additional discounts) are enjoyed by only some trading parties, giving them an economic advantage which is not justified by the volume of business they bring or by any economies of scale they allow the supplier to make compared with their competitors, a system of quantity discounts leads to the application of dissimilar conditions to equivalent transactions.

In the absence of any objective justification, having a high threshold in the system which can only be met by a few particularly large partners of the undertaking occupying a dominant position, or the absence of linear progression in the increase of the quantity discounts, may constitute evidence of such discriminatory treatment'[6].

The ECJ noted that the highest discount rate was enjoyed only by the two Portuguese airlines, that the discount rate was greatest for the highest band and that the airports concerned enjoyed a natural monopoly; it concluded that in these circumstances the discounts were discriminatory[7].

The Commission has also adopted decisions condemning similar discounts schemes under Article 82(2)(c) in *Zaventem*[8], *Finnish Airports*[9] and in *Spanish Airports*[10]. The Commission announced in May 2001 that it had completed its investigation into discrimination in the operation of Community airports[11].

(E)   The need for competitive disadvantage

The wording of Article 82(2)(c) specifically requires that one component of the abuse is the infliction of 'competitive disadvantage'. However it is noticeable

3   Any saving in the cost of invoicing one, large, customer was regarded as 'negligible'.
4   Case C-266/96 [1998] ECR I-3949.
5   Ibid, para 50.
6   Ibid, para 52 and 53.
7   Ibid, paras 54-57.
8   *Brussels National Airport (Zaventem)* OJ [1995] L 216/8, [1996] 4 CMLR 232.
9   *Ilmailulaitos/Luftfartsverket* OJ [1999] L 69/24, [1999] 5 CMLR 90.
10   OJ [2000] L 208/36.
11   Commission Press Release IP/01/673, 10 May 2001.

that in some cases little attention has been given to this issue. In *Corsica Ferries*[12] the ECJ said that Article 82(2)(c) applied to 'dissimilar conditions to equivalent transactions with trading partners', without mentioning the requirement of competitive disadvantage at all[13]. In its judgment, the Court said that if different tariffs were applied for compulsory piloting, according to whether a maritime transport undertaking was operating between Member States on the one hand or within one and the same Member Sate on the other, there would be an infringement of Article 82(2)(c); however there would be no competition between these two categories of undertakings, so that the Court seems to have written competitive disadvantage out of Article 82(2)(c) on this occasion. In his Opinion in this case Advocate General van Gerven remarked that the Court had not taken a restrictive approach to the requirement of competitive disadvantage; he specifically said at paragraph 34 of his Opinion that it was not necessary that the trading partners 'should suffer competitive disadvantage *as against each other or against the undertaking in the dominant position*' (his emphasis).

In the Commission's decisions on Community airports[14], scant attention was given to the need for competitive disadvantage. It may be that this element of the offence will be applied in a particularly liberal manner where, as in those decisions and as in *Corsica Ferries*, the discrimination is practised on national lines, to the detriment (though not the competitive disadvantage) of undertakings in other Member States.

In the Commission's *Notice on the Application of the Competition Rules to Access Agreements in the Telecommunications Sector*[15] it says that it could be abusive to charge discriminatory prices to customers in different downstream markets (for example in fixed and mobile telephony) where those markets are likely to converge in the future: the discrimination would be harmful to potential, if not existing, competition[16].

5.   PRICING PRACTICES THAT ARE HARMFUL TO THE SINGLE MARKET

The Commission will condemn pricing practices on the part of dominant firms that are harmful to the single market. High prices that are charged in order to prevent parallel imports will infringe Article 82.

(i)   Excessive pricing that impedes parallel imports and exports

In *BL*[17] the Commission condemned that firm for charging £150 to any importer of BL cars from the continent requiring a type-approval certificate to enable the cars to be driven in the UK. The interest of this case is that the purpose of the excessive pricing was not to exploit a monopoly situation by earning excessive profits, but to impede parallel imports into the UK: the Commission's action was motivated by single-market considerations, and not by a desire to establish itself as a price regulator; the circumstances in the *General Motors* case were the

---

12   Case C-18/93 *Corsica Ferries Italia v Corporazione dei Piloti del Porto di Genoa* [1994] ECR I-1783.
13   Ibid, para 43.
14   See pp 660-661 above.
15   OJ [1998] C 265/2, [1998] 5 CMLR 821.
16   Ibid, para 121.
17   OJ [1984] L 207/11, [1984] 3 CMLR 92.

same[18]. The Commission's decision in *BL* was upheld on appeal by the ECJ, which accepted that the price charged by BL was disproportionate to the value of the service provided[19].

(ii) Geographic price discrimination

In *United Brands v Commission*[20] the ECJ held that UBC had abused its dominant position by charging different prices for its bananas according to the Member State of their destination. It sold bananas to distributors/ripeners at Rotterdam and Bremerhaven, and charged the lowest price for bananas destined for Eire and the highest for those going to West Germany. The different prices were not based on differences in costs: in fact transport to Eire, for which UBC itself paid, cost more than to other countries so that, if anything, prices should have been higher there. UBC was also condemned for including clauses in contracts with distributors which had the effect of preventing parallel imports from one country to another by prohibiting the export of unripened bananas[1]. The ECJ reduced the fine on UBC from EUR 1 million to EUR 850,000 because the Commission had erred on the separate issue of excessive pricing[2].

The decision is curious[3]. UBC claimed that it was being required to achieve a common market by adopting a uniform pricing policy for all Member States and that this was an unreasonable requirement on the part of the Commission. The ECJ retorted that it was permissible for a supplier to charge whatever local conditions of supply and demand dictate, that is to say that there is no obligation to charge a uniform price throughout the EC. However it added that the equation of supply with demand could be taken into account only at the level of the market at which a supplier operates. In *United Brands* this would mean that only a retailer in a given Member State could consider what price the market could bear; UBC could not do so since it did not sell bananas at retail level in Member States: it supplied distributors/ripeners at Rotterdam and Bremerhaven. In the ECJ's view, therefore, it was entitled to take into account local market conditions only 'to a limited extent'. The reasoning has been questioned: supply and demand at retail level would inevitably exert a backward influence on UBC, and anyway it, rather than retailers, employed the staff who carried out market research and monitored the level of demand throughout the EC. A different criticism of the case is that the judgment could have undesirable redistributive effects. The logical response of UBC would be to charge a uniform price higher than that in Eire but lower than that in Germany; it would seem therefore that the judgment would benefit the Germans at the expense of the Irish. It is therefore arguable that the discrimination in *United Brands* should not have been condemned; the practice which was rightly found to be abusive was the prohibition on the export of unripened (green) bananas, since this is what had the effect of

---

18 OJ [1975] L 29/14, [1975] 1 CMLR D20, annulled on appeal for want of evidence Case 26/75 *General Motors v Commission* [1975] ECR 1367, [1976] 1 CMLR 95.
19 Case 226/84 [1986] ECR 3263, [1987] 1 CMLR 185.
20 Case 27/76 [1978] ECR 207, [1978] 1 CMLR 429.
1   See ch 17, p 625.
2   See p 636 above.
3   For criticism see Bishop 'Price Discrimination under Article [82]: Political Economy in the European Court' (1981) 44 MLR 282; Zanon 'Price Discrimination under Article [82] of the EC Treaty: the *United Brands* Case' (1982) 31 1CLQ 36.

harming the single market. In the absence of this practice, bananas could have moved from low- to high-priced parts of the Community.

The Commission also condemned geographical price discrimination in *Tetra Pak II*[4]. The Commission's view was that the relevant geographic market was the Community as a whole, and yet Tetra Pak had charged prices that varied considerably from one Member State to another. The Commission said that the price differences could not be explained in economic terms and lacked objective justification. They were possible because of Tetra Pak's policy of market compartmentalisation which it maintained by virtue of its other abusive practices, thereby enabling it to maximise its profits on the basis of discrimination and the elimination of competitors.

(iii) Rebates that impede imports and exports

The Commission will condemn rebates and similar practices which have the effect of impeding imports and exports. Pricing practices that were intended to dissuade customers from importing plasterboard from other Member States were held to be abusive in the *Plasterboard*[5] case. The Commission's decision in *Irish Sugar*[6] was prompted by single market considerations. Irish Sugar had a share of the Irish sugar market in excess of 90% and was found to have acted abusively by seeking to restrict competition from other Member States. In particular Irish Sugar was found to have offered selectively low prices to customers of an importer of French sugar and to have offered 'border rebates' to customers close to the border with Northern Ireland and who were therefore in a position to purchase cheaper sugar from the UK. On appeal to the CFI the Court annulled the former finding[7], but agreed that the border rebates were unlawful[8]. The CFI stressed the importance in Community competition law of the competitive influence on one national market from neighbouring markets, 'the very essence of a common market'[9].

6. UK LAW

Abusive pricing practices may infringe the Chapter II of the Competition Act 1998; they may also be investigated under the monopoly provisions in the Fair Trading Act 1973 (the 'FTA'), although the use of the FTA is likely to be relatively infrequent in the future[10]. There is also a provision in section 13 of the Competition Act 1980, which remains in force, whereby the Secretary of State may ask the DGFT to investigate prices 'of major public concern': only a factual report may be made under this section, which has never been used[11]. There are also systems

---

4   OJ [1992] L 72/1, [1992] 4 CMLR 551, paras 154, 155 and 160, upheld on appeal Case T–83/91 *Tetra Pak International SA v Commission* [1994] ECR II-755, upheld on appeal to ECJ Case C-333/94 P *Tetra Pak International SA v Commission* [1996] ECR I-5951, [1997] 4 CMLR 662.
5   Case T-65/89 *BPB Industries plc and British Gypsum v Commission* [1993] ECR II-389, [1993] 5 CMLR 32, paras 117-122.
6   OJ [1997] L 258/1, [1997] 5 CMLR 666.
7   Case T-228/97 *Irish Sugar v Commission* [1999] ECR II-2969, [1999] 5 CMLR 1300, paras 117-124.
8   Ibid, paras 173-193.
9   Ibid, para 185.
10 See ch 9, pp 383-385 and ch 17, p 627.
11 See 47 Halsbury's Laws of England, para 505, n 21.

of price regulation for the regulated industries such as telecommunications, gas and electricity[12].

(A)   Exploitative pricing practices

(i)   Competition Act 1998

The Chapter II prohibition could be applied to excessive prices. The Guideline *The Chapter II prohibition*[13] states that the key issue will be to determine what is meant by an excessive price; to be excessive the price must be higher than it would be in a competitive market[14]. After noting that there may be objective justifications for prices that appear to be excessive, the *Guideline* states that to be an abuse 'prices would have to be persistently excessive without stimulating new entry or innovation'.[15] Section 2 of the Guideline *Assessment of Individual Agreements and Conduct*[16] examines these issues in greater detail. Paragraph 2.6 states that prices can be regarded as excessive where they allow an undertaking to sustain profits higher than it could expect to earn in a competitive market, so-called 'supra-normal profits'. Methods of measuring supra-normal prices are discussed at paragraphs 2.14 to 2.19 of the *Guideline*; these build upon ideas contained in a Research Paper commissioned by the OFT and published in 1997[17]. The methods suggested go considerably beyond the case law and decisional practice under Article 82[18], which lack the sophistication of the OFT's analysis. The *Guideline* states that the DGFT would not normally be concerned with 'transiently high prices'[19].

Paragraphs 2.8 to 2.13 of the *Guideline* acknowledge that prices that appear to be excessive may not be abusive. Three situations are discussed: first, high prices leading to supra-normal profits may occur for short periods within competitive markets[20]; secondly, high prices may reflect superior efficiency[1]; and thirdly the prices may be high in markets where there is innovation leading to new and improved products and processes[2]: in this case high prices would be considered abusive only if the profits do not represent a 'fair return on the costs of the innovation itself and a fair reward for the risks faced in bringing that innovation to the market'[3]. However there would be concern about high prices in industries where there is no prospect of new entry or of innovation to replace existing monopolists[4]. The *Guideline* states that the DGFT 'will be mindful of the need not to interfere in natural market mechanisms where high prices will encourage new entry or innovation and thereby increase competition'[5].

---

12   See ch 23, p 866ff.
13   OFT Guideline 402.
14   Ibid, para 4.8.
15   Ibid, para 4.9.
16   OFT Guideline 414.
17   Graham and Steele 'The Assessment of Profitability by Competition Authorities', OFT Research Paper No 10, February 1997.
18   See pp 633-639 above.
19   OFT Guideline 414, para 2.19.
20   Ibid, para 2.8.
1   Ibid, para 2.9.
2   Ibid, paras 2.8-2.10.
3   Ibid, para 2.11.
4   Ibid, para 2.12.
5   Ibid, para 2.13 .

The *Guideline* states that the ability of a firm to charge excessive prices or to earn excessive profits may provide evidence that it possesses market power, one of the factors used in assessing whether an agreement appreciably restricts competition under the Chapter I prohibition or whether a firm is dominant under the Chapter II prohibition[6]. The *Guideline* also recognises the potential for excessive prices as a result of tacit collusion in oligopolistic markets[7]; this is dealt with in chapter 14.

In *Napp Pharmaceutical Holding Ltd*[8] the DGFT concluded that Napp had abused a dominant position contrary to the Chapter II prohibition by operating a discriminatory discount policy[9], by predatory price cutting[10] and by charging excessive prices. Napp supplied sustained release morphine (referred to by its trade name of MST) to hospitals and to patients in the community. The prices for sales to the community were typically more than ten times higher than to hospitals. Paragraphs 203 to 234 deal with excessive pricing. The DGFT considered that the margin between Napp's costs and its prices was excessive: he did this by comparing the profit margin Napp earned on community sales and comparing it with the margins it earned on sales of other products and on the sale of MST to other markets. He also compared the actual prices of MST and compared them with what a competitive price for it would be likely to be. A fine of £3.21 million was imposed for these infringements. Napp has appealed against the decision to the Competition Commission Appeal Tribunal[11].

At the end of 2000 the OFT was investigating the possibility that excessive prices were being charged for petrol in the Western Isles of Scotland[12]. The DGFT concluded in 2000 that motorway service stations were not charging excessive prices[13].

(ii)   Fair Trading Act 1973

A monopoly reference may require the Commission to consider whether prices charged or proposed to be charged operate or may be expected to operate against the public interest[14]. An order made pursuant to a monopoly investigation may limit the price at which goods or services may be sold[15]. The Secretary of State also has power following an adverse finding to order divestiture[16], so that control over excessive prices could be effected by the use of structural remedies; for example the Commission recommended in *Raw Cow's Milk*[17] that Milk Marque should be broken up, but this happened voluntarily before an Order was made[18].

---

6   Ibid, para 2.23.
7   OFT Guideline 414, paras 2.20-21.
8   CA98/2/2001, decision of 30 March 2001.
9   See p 669 below.
10 See pp 671-672 below.
11 Case 1000/1/1/01 (judgment pending).
12 See the 2000 *Annual Report of the Director General of Fair Trading* p 44.
13 Ibid, p 51.
14 FTA, s 49(3)(a).
15 Ibid, Sch 8, para 8.
16 Ibid, Sch 8, para 14.
17 Cm 4286 (1999).
18 See ch 11, p 382; the Commission also recommended divestiture in order to overcome the problem of excessive pricing by a monopolist in *Artificial Lower Limbs* Cm 594 (1989); again this was effected without an Order: see the 1989 *Annual Report of the DGFT*, pp 35-36.

There have been many reports concerned with the question of whether prices were excessive[19].

(A) DETERMINING WHETHER PRICES ARE EXCESSIVE. The Commission will investigate the profitability of a firm's business in the reference goods or services, since evidence of high profits may indicate excessive prices. Profitability, however, is often difficult to determine, particularly where fixed costs have to be allocated between reference and non-reference goods or services. It may be that a firm is found to be miscalculating its own costs, so that prices are higher than the firm's pricing policy itself requires[20]. The Commission's usual practice is to approach the determination of profits by considering the return on average capital employed (ROCE), but this may be inappropriate in markets where the capital employed is relatively low; where this is the case return on turnover may be used instead[1]. Sometimes the figures may be misleading, and in *Soluble Coffee*[2] the Commission accepted that Nestlé's high ROCE, of more than 100%, to some extent reflected the fact that some of the company's fixed assets had a book value of zero.

The Commission may also compare the prices of the reference goods or services with those of similar goods or services in the UK or with prices in other Member States of the Community. It did this in the 1992 and 2000 investigations of *New Motor Cars*[3] and *Cars*[4]. In the 2000 report the Commission used surveys carried out by the European Commission every six months since May 1993; these revealed that by May 1999 car prices in the UK were at least 20% higher than in the lowest-priced Member State.

(B) PRICE CONTROL AS A REMEDY. Some monopoly investigations have led to the imposition of price control. For example in its first report on *Contraceptive Sheaths*[5] the Commission recommended that LRC's prices should be reduced by 40%, although in the event much smaller reductions were negotiated[6]. A second investigation[7] again ended with an expression of concern about prices and renewed undertakings were given, calculated this time to reflect LRC's costs in order to spur it to greater efficiency[8]. In 1993 the DGFT referred the contraceptive sheaths market to the Commission for a third time, expressing anxiety that the restriction of LRC's prices may have deterred new entrants to the market[9]. In *Condoms*[10] the Commission recommended that price control should be lifted

---

19 See eg *Contraceptive Sheaths* Cmnd 8689 (1982); *Tampons* Cmnd 9470 (1985); *White Salt* Cmnd 9778 (1986); *Pest Control Services* Cm 302 (1988); *Gas* Cm 500 (1988); *The Supply of Beer* Cm 651 (1989); *Artificial Lower Limbs* Cm 594 (1989); *Opium Derivatives* Cm 630 (1989); *The Supply of Petrol* Cm 972 (1990); *Soluble Coffee* Cm 1459 (1991); *Supply of New Motor Cars* Cm 1808 (1992); *The Supply of Matches and Disposable Lighters* Cm 1854 (1992); *Contact Lens Solutions* Cm 2242 (1993); *Recorded Music* Cm 2599 (1994); *Private Medical Services* Cm 2452 (1994); *Video Games* Cm 2781 (1995); *Classified Directory Advertising Services* Cm 3171 (1996); *Foreign Package Holidays* Cm 3813 (1997); *The Supply of Raw Milk* Cm 4286 (1999); *New Cars* Cm 4660 (2000).
20 *Pest Control Services* Cm 302 (1988).
1   *Supply of Cinema Advertising Services* Cm 1080 (1990).
2   Cm 1459 (1991).
3   Cm 1808 (1992).
4   Cm 4660 (2000).
5   HCP (1974–75) 135.
6   See 1975 *Annual Report of the DGFT* p 80.
7   Cmnd 8689 (1982).
8   1983 *Annual Report of the DGFT*, p 79.
9   DTI Press Release, 1 May 1993.
10 Cm 2529 (1994).

from the dominant supplier, LRC Products, the manufacturer of Durex, in light of the fact that the retailing of condoms was becoming more competitive, particularly through retailers being prepared to change supplier and to engage in price wars. The undertaking was released in 1994[11].

In *White Salt*[12] the Commission concluded that British Salt's prices should be directly controlled. It had a market share of 50%, and ICI's was 45%. Over a long period their prices had remained about the same; they had risen faster than prices in the chemical industry in particular and manufacturing industry as a whole. There was no evidence that these duopolists had taken steps to exclude competitors, but natural barriers to entry were high (in particular economies of scale) and there was little chance of substantial import penetration. It was hard to see that new competition would emerge and customers did not have sufficient purchasing power to extract lower prices. In the circumstances the Commission concluded that British Salt should have its prices controlled: increases in its prices should be related only to rises in its costs. ICI's prices were not to be controlled as it was a less efficient producer: it would have either to increase its efficiency in order to meet the competition from British Salt, or lose its market share.

In the mobile phone sector the Director General of Telecommunications made a reference under section 13 of the Telecommunications Act 1984 of the charges made by Cellnet and Vodafone for the termination of calls from fixed-line telephones to their mobile networks[13]. He also asked the Commission to examine the charges made by BT for calls from its subscribers to the Cellnet and Vodafone networks[14]. The Commission found in both cases that the charges were clearly excessive and that they operated against the public interest, given the absence of effective competitive pressures; and that the appropriate remedy to reduce the rate charged for calls was price control[15].

Various other reports have also led to direct control over prices[16].

(C)   OTHER REMEDIES.   In *Pest Control Services*[17] the Commission came to the conclusion that many customers of Rentokil had had to pay prices higher than they would be in conditions of normal competition. On this occasion it recommended that the best remedy to deal with the problem was to require Rentokil to make more information available to customers. In particular, every quotation for pest control services should be accompanied by a written statement specifying the number of hours to be spent on the work, the hourly charging rate and similar information; furthermore customers should be given annual information about such matters. In *The Supply of Beer*[18] the Commission stressed the need for transparency of beer prices at the wholesaling level of the market. In

---

11   1994 *Annual Report of the DGFT*, p 36.
12   Cmnd 9778 (1986); undertakings were taken from British Salt in April 1988: 1988 *Annual Report of the DGFT*, pp 75–76; the undertakings were released in May 2001: DTI Press Release P/2001/293, 8 May 2001.
13   *Cellnet and Vodafone* 011 5154590 (1999).
14   *British Telecommunications plc* 0 11 515450 4 (1999).
15   For comment, see Pflanz 'What Price is Right? Lessons from the UK Calls-to-Mobile Inquiry' (2000) 21 ECLR 147.
16   See eg *Classified Directory Advertising Services* Cm 3171 (1996); undertakings were given which were revised in May 2001: DTI Press Release P/2001/307, 31 May 2001.
17   Cm 302 (1988).
18   Cm 651 (1989).

Gas[19] the Commission recommended that British Gas should be required to publish a schedule of its prices. In the case of *Contact Lens Solutions*[20] the Commission was critical of the prices charged both by Allergan, a scale monopolist at producer level, and by Boots, a retailer scale monopolist. Competition in the market was limited as a result of regulatory constraints, and the Minister decided that changes to the regulatory system would be a preferable remedy to direct price control[1].

(B) Pricing practices having effects similar to exclusive or tie-in agreements

(i) Competition Act 1998

The Guideline *Assessment of Individual Agreements and Conduct*[2] acknowledges that the offering of discounts is a form of price competition and is therefore generally to be encouraged[3]. Discounts would be abusive only if they were anti-competitive, for example because they are predatory or because they foreclose access to the market or have a tying effect; a specific example given is the use of fidelity rebates[4]. The *Guideline* discusses the foreclosure of manufacturers at paragraphs 6.11 to 6.14 and of retailers at paragraphs 6.15 to 6.17; these have been explained in chapter 17[5].

In *Napp Pharmaceutical Holding Ltd*[6] the DGFT held that Napp had abused its dominant position in the market for sustained release morphine by offering very large discounts to hospitals while charging excessive prices to patients in the community; more particularly Napp had targeted particular competitors, offering larger discounts to hospitals where it faced or anticipated competition and by granting higher discounts for specific products which were under competitive threat[7]. The DGFT considered that Napp's intention was to eliminate competitors, and rejected its argument that it was simply 'meeting competition'; its reaction to its competitors was held to be unreasonable and disproportionate[8]. Napp was fined £3.21 million, and has appealed to the Competition Commission Appeal Tribunal[9].

(ii) Fair Trading Act 1973

In *Metal Containers*[10] the Commission concluded that discounts which tended to tie customers to Metal Box and foreclose other competitors operated against the public interest. In *Tampons*[11] (actually an investigation under the old Competition Act 1980) the Commission concluded that discounts granted to retailers of

19 Cm 500 (1988).
20 Cm 2242 (1993).
1   DTI Press Release P/93/285, 27 May 1993.
2   OFT Guideline 414.
3   Ibid, para 5.1.
4   Ibid, para 5.2.
5   See ch 17, p 628.
6   CA98/2/2001, decision of 30 March 2001; see p 666 above.
7   Ibid, paras 144-202.
8   Ibid, paras 197-202.
9   See p 666, n 11 above.
10 HCP (1970) 6.
11 Cm 3168 (1996).

Tambrands' tampons on condition that a complete range of its products was stocked did not operate against the public interest; the practice did not restrict the availability of retail space and did not act as a barrier to entry to new entrants.

In *Foreign Package Holidays*[12] the Commission found complex monopoly situations in the markets for travel agents' and tour operators' services in relation to foreign package holidays. The Commission was critical of two particular practices: the tie-in of insurance and the use of 'most favoured customer' clauses. It recommended that the tying of travel insurance to the purchase of discounted holidays, which enabled travel agents to inflate the advertised discount on package holidays because of the large margins earned from the insurance business, and which therefore was misleading to consumers, should be prohibited. Secondly it objected to most favoured customer clauses; such clauses were agreed between a tour operator and a travel agent to the effect that the agent would offer the same discounts on that operator's foreign package holidays as on those of other operators: the effect was that discounting was inhibited, leading to higher prices. Each of these practices was prohibited by the Foreign Package Holidays (Tour Operators and Travel Agents) Order 1998[13].

(C)   Pricing practices intended to eliminate competitors

(i)   Competition Act 1998

Section 4 of the Guideline *Assessment of Individual Agreements and Conduct*[14] deals with predation. Section 4 is divided into four parts, dealing in turn with costs, intention, the feasibility of recouping losses and exclusions. The *Guideline* is more sophisticated than the case law of the ECJ[15]; it may therefore be that practice in the UK will diverge from the standards of EC law, although this could raise interesting questions under section 60 of the Competition Act[16].

(A)   COSTS.   The *Guideline* begins by referring to the judgment of the ECJ in *AKZO v Commission*[17] and to the rules on sales below average variable cost ('AVC') and below average total cost ('ATC'). The *Guideline* states that the timescale over which AVC should be calculated is the period for which the predatory prices prevailed or could reasonably be expected to prevail[18]. Prices below AVC will be considered to be abusive unless they can be objectively justified[19]. Possible justifications would be loss-leading; short run promotions; prices that match an inefficient entrant; mistakes in determining the correct market price; low prices that are attributable to network externalities; and that the undertaking is making an incremental profit[20]. The *Guideline* also explains that

---

12   Cm 3813 (1997).
13   SI 1998/1945.
14   OFT Guideline 414.
15   See pp 646-653 above.
16   See ch 9, pp 329-333.
17   OFT Guideline 414, para 4.3; on the *AKZO* case see pp 648-649 above.
18   OFT Guideline 414, paras 4.5 and 4.6.
19   Ibid, para 4.7.
20   Ibid, para 4.8.

the standards of AVC and ATC are not always appropriate and that alternative cost floors, such as avoidable costs, might be preferable[1].

(B) INTENTION. The *Guideline* notes that the rule in *AKZO v Commission* requires that, where an undertaking sells at more than AVC but below ATC, evidence of intention is needed for a finding of abuse[2]. Where the alleged predator appears to be making a loss, but in fact can demonstrate that its behaviour is incrementally profitable, this would suggest that there was no intention to predate. This is sometimes referred as the 'net revenue test'[3]. The example given in paragraph 4.16 of the *Guideline* is that of a shop that cuts the price of one product to less than cost, but which is incrementally profitable because that price cut leads to an increase in sales of complementary products. Paragraph 4.18 says that there may be other evidence of an intention to eliminate a competitor, for example the targeting of price cuts against a new entrant, the timing of the price cut and the use of 'dirty tricks'[4]. The DGFT may also inspect internal documents of undertakings in order to uncover the firm's 'true' intentions (the 'smoking gun')[5].

(C) FEASIBILITY OF RECOUPMENT OF LOSSES. Paragraphs 4.19 to 4.27 of the *Guideline* deal with the issue of the feasibility of recouping losses. It is not clear to what extent recoupment must be proved in EC law: the ECJ in *Tetra Pak* decided only that, on the facts of that case, there was no need to prove recoupment[6]. The *Guideline* says that the DGFT does not consider that he would necessarily be required to establish the feasibility of recoupment where the dominant firm abuses in the market in which it is dominant; however the issue would arise where the dominant firm cuts its prices in a neighbouring market in which it is not dominant[7]. Cross-subsidy may be relevant to the issue of feasibility; however it does not necessarily result in predation[8].

(D) EXCLUSIONS. The *Guideline* specifically notes that agreements and conduct benefit from an exclusion from the Competition Act in so far as they are necessary to comply with an obligation to provide services of general economic interest[9]. Where, for example, an undertaking is required to perform a universal service (for example the daily delivery of letters at a uniform price) there may be an element of cross-subsidy: urban users may subsidise rural users. Cross-subsidy of this kind would not infringe the Chapter II prohibition.

(E) THE *NAPP PHARMACEUTICALS* CASE. In *Napp Pharmaceutical Holding Ltd*[10] the DGFT held that Napp was guilty of charging predatory prices for sustained release morphine by selling some products to hospitals at less than direct cost,

1   Ibid, paras 4.9-4.11; on the application of the rules on predation in the regulated industries, see *Competition Act 1998: The Application in the Telecommunications Sector* OFT Guideline 417, paras 7.13-7.25; *Competition Act 1998: Application in the Water and Sewerage Sectors* OFT Guideline 422, paras 4.11-4.13.
2   OFT Guideline 414, paras 4.12-4.13.
3   Ibid, paras 4.15-4.17.
4   Ibid, para 4.18.
5   Ibid, para 4.18.
6   See pp 650-651 above.
7   OFT Guideline 414, para 4.21; in CA 98/5/2001 *Predation by Aberdeen Journals Ltd*, decision of 16 July 2001, the DGFT stated specifically that he did not need to address the possibility of recoupment in a predation test: ibid, para 113.
8   Ibid, para 4.26.
9   See ch 9, p 304.
10 CA98/2/2001, decision of 30 March 2001; see pp 666 and 669 above.

which he considered, on the facts of the case, to be a proxy for AVC[11]. The DGFT rejected Napp's argument that sales below cost to hospitals were objectively justified since Napp would be able to recover the full price from follow-on sales to patients in the community[12]; indeed the very reason that Napp was able to earn high margins on sales to the community was that it had been successful in stifling competition in relation to sales to hospitals[13].

(F)   THE *ABERDEEN JOURNALS* CASE   In *Predation by Aberdeen Journals Ltd*[13a] the DGFT imposed a penalty of £1,328,040 on Aberdeen Journals for predatory pricing by failing to cover its average variable costs from 1 March to 29 March 2000.

(ii)   Fair Trading Act 1973

The Commission has been critical of predatory practices in various reports. For example in *Bus Services in the North East of England*[14] the Commission concluded that Busways' actions in recruiting bus drivers from its main competitor, registering services on all its routes and running free services were 'predatory, deplorable and against the public interest'.

(D)   Price discrimination

(i)   Competition Act 1998

Section 3 of the Guideline on *Assessment of Individual Agreements and Conduct*[15] deals with the topic of price discrimination. Paragraph 3.2 states that price discrimination is only likely to be abusive where it leads to the imposition of excessive prices or where it can significantly reduce competition[16]. The exploitation of customers by excessive pricing might be an abuse, although the *Guideline* points out that it may also be welfare-enhancing, for example where off-peak travellers are able to travel at lower prices than commuters[17]. Competition might be significantly reduced where the discrimination involves predatory pricing[18] or where it is detrimental to competition in a downstream market[19]. Paragraph 3.3 notes that there can be discrimination both where different prices are charged for the same product and where the same price is charged even though the costs of supplying it are different. The *Guideline* says that there is no presumption that price discrimination by a dominant firm will constitute an abuse.

The DGFT distinguishes price discrimination from price differentiation. Price differentiation occurs where there are objective reasons for an undertaking charging different prices to different customers: different transport costs are an obvious

11   Ibid, paras 188-196.
12   Ibid, paras 192-195.
13   Ibid, para 195.
13a Case CA 98/5/2001, decision of 16 July 2001.
14   Cm 2933 (1995).
15   OFT Guideline 414.
16   See also para 3.11.
17   See below.
18   See pp 670-672 above on predatory pricing.
19   OFT Guideline 414, para 3.12.

example. Where such a justification exists, there will be no abuse[20]. The *Guideline* also notes that there may be a justification for price discrimination. For example a rail operator may charge commuters who travel at peak times more than off-peak travellers. This enables it to maximise its output (it sells more tickets) and its revenue, which it needs to recover the entire costs of its operation[1].

(ii)   Fair Trading Act 1973

In *Gas*[2] British Gas's policy of extensive discrimination in the prices of gas charged to industrial customers was strongly condemned by the Commission as an exploitation of a monopoly situation; so too was the refusal to supply particular types of gas to certain customers.

(E)   UK law: single market

This is not a concern in the UK. The competition authorities will not be bound by Community jurisprudence that is motivated by single market considerations[3].

---

20 Ibid, para 3.5.
1   Ibid, para 3.9.
2   Cm 500 (1988).
3   See ch 9, pp 329-333.

CHAPTER 19

The relationship between intellectual property rights and competition law

This chapter considers the relationship between intellectual property rights and competition law. After a brief introduction the chapter will deal with the application of Article 81 to licences of intellectual property rights including, in particular, the block exemption for technology transfer agreements. Horizontal agreements such as patent pools and trade mark delimitation agreements will then be considered, followed by a section on the possible application of Article 82 to undertakings that own intellectual property rights. The impact that the rules on the free movement of goods and services in the EC Treaty have had on intellectual property rights will be analysed in the penultimate section of this chapter, which will end with a look at the position in UK law.

I. INTRODUCTION

It is not possible to deal with the substantive law of intellectual property here in detail[1]. For present purposes the term 'intellectual property' includes patents, registered and unregistered designs, copyrights including computer software, trade marks and analogous rights such as plant breeders' rights. It should also be taken to include know-how, defined for the purpose of the block exemption on technology transfer agreements as 'a body of technical information that is secret, substantial and identified in any appropriate form'[2]; although not strictly speaking an intellectual property right[3], know-how may be extremely valuable and may be sold or 'licensed' for considerable amounts of money.

1 For a general account of the law see Torremans and Holyoak *Intellectual Property Law* (Butterworths, 2nd ed, 1998); Cornish *Intellectual Property: Patents, Copyright, Trade Marks and Allied Rights* (Sweet & Maxwell, 4th ed, 1999); for specific discussion of the relationship between intellectual property rights and Community competition law see Rothnie *Parallel Imports* (Sweet & Maxwell, 1993); Oliver *Free Movement of Goods* (Sweet & Maxwell, 3rd ed, 1995); Tritton *Intellectual Property in Europe* (Sweet & Maxwell, 1996); Govaere *The Use and Abuse of Intellectual Property Rights in EC Law* (Sweet & Maxwell, 1996); Anderman *EC Competition Law and Intellectual Property Rights: The Regulation of Innovation* (Clarendon Press Oxford, 1998); Maher 'Competition Law and Intellectual Property Rights: Evolving Formalism' in Craig and De Búrca (eds) *The Evolution of EU Law* (Oxford University Press, 1999).
2 Regulation 240/96, Article 10(1); the Regulation is considered at pp 688-696 below.
3 Know-how is protected by the law of obligations: see generally on confidential information *Cornish* ch 8.

Generally speaking intellectual property rights are the product of, and are protected by, national systems of law, although the growth of international commerce has resulted in an increasing measure of international cooperation[4]. The existence of different national laws on intellectual property presents particular difficulties in the European Community in so far as this may be detrimental to the goal of single market integration. Various harmonisation measures have been adopted to deal with this problem such as the Trade Mark Directive[5], implemented in the UK by the Trade Marks Act 1994. The adoption of the Community Trade Mark Regulation[6] takes a step further, by creating an intellectual property right that is itself a creature of Community rather than national law; there are plans for a Community Patent Regulation[7]. Much of this chapter is concerned with the problem that intellectual property rights may be used in a way that compartmentalises the single market.

The essential characteristic of intellectual property rights is that they confer upon their owners an exclusive right to behave in a particular way. For example the UK Patents Act 1977 grants the owner of a patent the right to prevent others from producing the patented goods or applying the patented process for a period of 20 years; patents may be granted where a product or process is technically innovative[8]. A patent does not necessarily make the patentee a monopolist in an economic sense: there may be other products that compete with the subject-matter of the patent; however the patent does afford a degree of immunity from the activities of rival firms. Because intellectual property rights confer exclusivity upon their owners, whereas competition law strives to keep markets open, there may be a conflict between these two areas of law, although this should not be over-stressed: competition law is as keen as intellectual property law to promote research and development and to encourage innovation[9]. It is a complex matter to determine how to balance the amount of protection that needs to be afforded to inventors, plant-breeders or artists to encourage them in their endeavours on the one hand against the desirability of maintaining an open and competitive market on the other[10].

---

4 See *Cornish* paras 1.29-1.34.
5 Council Directive 89/104, OJ [1989] L 40/1; see also the Directives on computer software, Directive 91/250, OJ [1991] L 122/42; on rental rights, Directive 92/100, OJ [1992] L 346/1; on the duration of copyright, Directive 93/98, OJ [1993] L 290/9; on satellite broadcasting and cable transmissions, Directive 93/83, OJ [1993] L 248/15; on databases, Directive 69/9, OJ [1996] L 77/20; on biotechnology, Directive 98/44, OJ [1998] L 213/3; and on designs, Directive 98/71, OJ [1998] L 289/28.
6 Regulation 40/94, OJ [1994] L 11/1.
7 COM(2000) 412 final, 1 August 2000.
8 On the law of patents see *Cornish*, chs 3-7.
9 See Tom and Newberg 'Antitrust and Intellectual Property: From Separate Spheres to Unified Field' (1997-98) 66 Antitrust Law Journal 167 on the 'marked reduction in antitrust hostility toward intellectual property' in the US in the last 50 years; see also Kobak 'Running the Gauntlet: Antitrust and Intellectual Pitfalls on the Two Sides of the Atlantic' (1995-96) 64 Antitrust Law Journal 341.
10 *Cornish* contains useful discussions of the economics of patents (paras 3.36-3.54), copyright (paras 9.45-9.54) and trade marks (paras 15.24-15.33); see also Barton 'The Balance Between Intellectual Property Rights and Competition: Paradigms in the Information Sector' (1997) 18 ECLR 440.

2.   LICENCES OF INTELLECTUAL PROPERTY RIGHTS: ARTICLE 81(1)

(A)   Introduction

A patentee may decide, instead of producing the patented goods or applying the patented process itself, to grant a licence to another firm enabling it to do so. The same may be true of any other intellectual property right. There are many reasons why a firm may choose to grant a licence. A patentee may lack the resources to produce in quantity; it may wish to limit its own production to a particular geographical area and to grant licences for other territories; or it may wish to apply a patented process for one purpose and to allow licensees to use it for others. A patentee may wish to impose various restrictions upon its licensees, for example as to the quantity or quality of goods that may be produced or the price at which they may be sold; these provisions relate to the patentee's own products and so can only be restrictive of intra-brand competition[11].

The argument for controlling restrictions of intra-brand competition in patent licences is weak. Given that a patentee has an exclusive right to produce and sell the patented goods, it is not obvious why it should not be able to impose whatever restrictions it chooses upon its licensees; the ability to do so is a manifestation of the right conferred by statute. Indeed the grant of a licence can be seen as increasing competition, by introducing a licensee onto the market which, without the licence, would not be there at all; even if the patentee imposes restrictions of intra-brand competition, these are likely to be compensated for by the stimulation of inter-brand competition[12]. However Article 81(1) has been applied to intra-brand restrictions in patent (and other) licences, in particular where they divide the single market: the 'single market imperative' is as influential in this area of EC competition law as it is elsewhere[13].

Some terms in patent licences may affect inter-brand competition: examples are tie-in clauses requiring a licensee to acquire particular goods solely from the patentee and non-competition clauses forbidding the licensee to compete or to handle goods which compete with the patentee's: provisions such as these may foreclose the opportunities of other producers. Objection might be taken to terms which are perceived to be an attempt to extend a patentee's monopoly power beyond the protection afforded to it by the law and/or which might be considered to be oppressive to a person in a weak bargaining position.

(B)   Typical terms in licences of intellectual property rights

It will facilitate an understanding of the law on licensing agreements to have some knowledge of typical clauses that may be found in them. In the absence of legal controls it would be a matter for the parties to the agreement to settle the terms of the licence through the bargaining process. It would be wrong to assume that it is always the patentee that is in the more powerful bargaining position: a patentee may be an individual inventor and his prospective licensee a powerful company, in which case the former's position may be weak.

---

11   For discussion of this expression see ch 16, p 541.
12   Ibid.
13   See ch 1, p 19 and ch 2, p 47.

(i)   Territorial exclusivity

In EC law territorial exclusivity is the most critical aspect of licensing agreements because of the overriding determination of the Commission and the Community Courts to prevent the isolation of national markets. A licensee may consider that the risk involved in exploitation of a patent or that the high level of capital investment required are so great that it would not be worth taking a licence at all unless it is given immunity from intra-brand competition from the licensor, other licensees and their customers: these issues have been discussed already in relation to vertical agreements[14]; a licensee will often be taking a greater risk than a 'mere' distributor, since it has to invest in production as well as distribution, and so may require more protection against free riders than a distributor needs. The extent of the exclusivity required will be a calculation for the licensee; the amount actually given, apart from any limiting legal constraints, will be a matter for bargaining between the licensor and licensee.

Often the licensor will grant to the licensee an exclusive right to manufacture and sell the goods in a particular territory and to refrain from granting similar rights to anyone else there; in this situation the licensor retains the right to produce the goods in the territory itself: this is known as a 'sole' licence. A sole licence may be distinguished from an 'exclusive' licence, where the licensor also agrees not to produce the goods in the licensee's territory itself; this of course gives the licensee more protection than in the case of a sole licence. The licensee's position may be further reinforced by the licensor agreeing to impose export bans on its other licensees preventing them, or requiring them to prevent their customers, from selling into the licensed territory. Apart from the imposition of export bans, there are indirect ways of achieving the same end: for example a maximum quantities clause can limit the amount that a licensee can produce to the anticipated level of demand on its domestic market. As we shall see, the mere grant of territorial exclusivity in a licence of an intellectual property right does not necessarily infringe Article 81(1); this will depend on the effect that this would have on the market. However, where a licensor grants a licensee absolute territorial protection against any form of intra-brand competition there will almost certainly be an infringement of Article 81(1) and it is unlikely that the terms of Article 81(3) will be satisfied.

(ii)   Royalties

A licensor will usually require the licensee to pay royalties for use of the patent. The licensee may be required to make lump-sum payments, and in some situations the parties may agree upon a profit-sharing scheme. The licensor may ask for a payment 'up-front' before production begins. A licensor may stipulate that the licensee must pay a minimum amount of royalties in a given period in order to encourage it to exploit the patented process. The agreement may provide that royalties should continue to be paid even after the patent in question has expired or that royalties shall be payable in respect of unpatented know-how as well as the subject-matter of the patent. In these situations competition authorities may take exception to what they perceive to be an attempt to extend the monopoly conferred by the patent beyond its intended range.

14   See ch 16, pp 543-545.

(iii)   Duration

A licensor will specify what the duration of the agreement should be. It may decide to grant only a limited licence which will expire before the patent itself, after which it can reconsider its position. On the other hand it may attempt to tie the licensee even after the patent has expired, for example by requiring it to continue to pay royalties or to take licences of newly discovered technology.

(iv)   Field of use restrictions

A common clause is a 'field-of-use' restriction whereby a licensor limits the licensee's authority to produce goods to a particular purpose: a chemical protected by a patent may be useful both medicinally and industrially and the licensee could be limited to production for one purpose only. Field of use clauses are normally seen as a reasonable exploitation of the patentee's position, although the Commission may object where the restriction appears to be motivated by an intention to divide markets.

(v)   Best endeavours and non-competition clauses

To ensure that the licensee does exploit the patent (and that the patentee receives adequate royalties) the licensee may be required to produce minimum quantities or to use its best endeavours to do so. A non-competition clause, whereby the licensee is forbidden to compete by using its own or rival technology, may encourage it to concentrate on producing the patented goods, although the tendency of such a clause to foreclose competitors might alarm the competition authorities.

(vi)   No-challenge clauses

The licensor may insist upon a no-challenge clause whereby the licensee agrees not to challenge the validity of the intellectual property right in question. A licensee with intimate knowledge of, say, a patented process may be in the best position to show that it lacks originality, and a licensor may be unwilling to grant a licence at all if it knows that the licensee might undermine its position by successfully applying for the patent to be revoked.

(vii)   Improvements

A licensor may be fearful that the licensee will build upon the knowledge that becomes available from using the patent and emerge as a strong competitor; it may therefore require the licensee to grant back to it any know-how or intellectual property rights acquired and not to grant licences to anyone else. Objection may be taken to this practice if the licensor requires the licensee to grant it exclusive access to such know-how, since this deprives the licensee of the opportunity to pass on the technology to third parties.

(viii)   Standards

The licensor will wish to ensure that the licensee does not debase standards or harm its brand-image in other ways; it may therefore impose requirements as to quality, marketing, labelling and so forth. A controversial question which may arise in this context is whether a licensor can require a licensee to purchase particular products from it as a condition of the licence. Such 'tie-in' provisions may be a vital element in quality control, although they may also be viewed as an attempt to extend the licensor's exclusive right to a non-patented product or to foreclose competitors.

(ix)   Prices, terms and conditions

The licensor may wish to fix the prices at which the licensee sells or the terms and conditions on which it does so. The Commission, however, takes the view that the licensee should be free to determine its own policy when it brings the patented products to the market.

(C)   The application of Article 81(1) to licences of intellectual property rights[15]

(i)   The Commission's evolving policy in relation to patent licences in the 1960s and 1970s

In the early 1960s the Commission took the view that most provisions in patent licences did not infringe Article 81(1) at all, since restrictions of intra-brand competition simply emanate from the exclusive right of the patentee. The Commission's *Notice on Patent Licensing Agreements*[16] of 1962 reflected this approach. However the Commission's abstentionist view began to alter towards the end of the decade; the change can be traced back to the judgment of the ECJ in *Consten and Grundig v Commission*[17]. There the ECJ established that vertical agreements could fall within Article 81(1) and, of particular importance in this context, that the use of intellectual property rights could contribute to an infringement where it enabled a distributor to enjoy absolute territorial protection in its allotted territory; in *Consten and Grundig* it was the assignment to Consten of the GINT trade mark for France that enabled Consten to repel parallel imports

---

15 On the position in the US see the *Antitrust Guidelines for the Licensing of Intellectual Property* of the Department of Justice and Federal Trade Commission of 6 April 1995, available at http://www.usdoj.gov/atr/public/guidelines/ipguide.htm; the *Guidelines* state at para 2.0 that there is no presumption that intellectual property creates market power and they also say that licences of intellectual property rights are generally pro-competitive; for comments on the EC system compared with that of the US see Fogt and Gotts 'US Technology Licensing Arrangements: Do New Enforcement Guidelines in the United States Mirror Developments in the European Community?' (1995) 16 ECLR 215 and the same authors 'A Tale of Two Continents: Block Exemption Takes Different Approach from US Counterpart Guidelines' (1996) 17 ECLR 327.

16 JO [1962] 2922; this Notice was withdrawn in 1984, OJ [1984] C 220/14.

17 Cases 56/84 and 58/64 [1966] ECR 299, [1966] CMLR 418; for discussion of this case see ch 3, p 100; on the Commission's change of policy see Anderman *EC Competition Law and Intellectual Property Rights: The Regulation of Innovation* (Clarendon Press Oxford, 1998) ch 5.

from other Member States[18]. The distinction drawn by the ECJ in this case – between the existence of an intellectual property right on the one hand and its improper exercise on the other – provided the foundation of much of the law in this area including, in particular, the exhaustion of rights doctrine[19].

In a series of decisions from the early 1970s the Commission applied Article 81(1) to various clauses found in patent licences, and in particular to territorial restrictions, although in some cases it was prepared to grant individual exemption under Article 81(3)[20]. Helpful guidance as to the Commission's thinking on the application of Article 81(1) to typical provisions in licences can be found in Article 2 of Regulation 240/96, the so-called 'white list', which contains a list of provisions which are considered not to infringe Article 81(1), but which are exempted where, on the facts of a particular case, they happen to do so[1]; and in Article 3, which 'black-lists' certain restrictions such as the imposition of minimum prices and non-competition clauses[2].

(ii) Territorial exclusivity and the Maize Seeds case

In many of the decisions referred to above the Commission held that manufacturing and sales licences granting territorial exclusivity to the licensee infringed Article 81(1); it also considered that export bans and provisions having similar effects such as maximum quantities clauses were caught[3]. Having concluded that many patent licences were caught by Article 81(1), the Commission proceeded to grant them block exemption in Regulation 2349/84[4]. However, as we have seen in chapter 3, Article 81(1) applies only to agreements 'which have as their object or effect the prevention, restriction or distortion of competition'[5]. It was explained there that the mere grant of exclusive territorial rights does not have as its object the restriction of competition[6]; such cases infringe Article

---

18 The exhaustion of rights doctrine in Community law (pp 703-714 below) had yet to be developed; this doctrine would now prevent an undertaking in the position of Consten from relying on the trade mark to keep parallel imports out of France if the goods had been put on the market in another Member State with the consent of the trade mark owner, which would have been the case in *Consten and Grundig*.

19 See pp 703-714 below.

20 In chronological order the Commission's decisions on patent licences are *Burroughs AG and Deplanque & Fils Agreement* OJ [1972] L 13/50, [1972] CMLR D67; *Burroughs AG and Geha-Werke GmbH Contract* OJ [1972] L 13/53, [1972] CMLR D72; *Davidson Rubber Co Agreements* OJ [1972] L 143/31, [1972] CMLR D52; *Raymond and Nagoya Rubber Ltd Agreement* OJ [1972] L 143/39, [1972] CMLR D45; *Kabelmetal/Luchaire* OJ [1975] L 222/34, [1975] 2 CMLR D40; *Zuid-Nederlandsche Bronbemaling en Grondboringen BV v Heidemaatschappij Beheer NV* OJ [1975] L 249/27, [1975] 2 CMLR D67; *AOIP v Beyrard* OJ [1976] L 6/8, [1976] 1 CMLR D14; *Vaessen BV v Moris* OJ [1979] L 19/32, [1979] 1 CMLR 511; *IMA AG Windsurfing International Inc* OJ [1983] L 229/1, [1984] 1 CMLR 1, upheld on appeal Case 193/83 *Windsurfing International Inc v Commission* [1986] ECR 611, [1986] 3 CMLR 489; *Velcro/Aplix* OJ [1985] L 233/22, [1989] 4 CMLR 157; the Commission has reached decisions on other types of licences in which it has applied similar principles: see pp 684-688 below.

1 The white-list is considered at pp 693-694 below.

2 See pp 694-695 below.

3 See now Article 3 of Regulation 240/96 which 'black-lists' provisions such as these: pp 694-695 below.

4 OJ [1984] L 219/15, OJ [1993] L 21/8; this Regulation has been replaced by Regulation 240/96.

5 See ch 3, p 92ff.

6 Ibid, p 100, in particular the discussion of Case 56/65 *Société Technique Minière v Maschinenbau Ulm* [1966] ECR 235, [1966] CMLR 357.

81(1), therefore, only where they can be shown to have appreciable effects on competition[7] and on trade between Member States[8]. The reason for the strict treatment of the agreement in *Consten and Grundig v Commission* was that it went beyond the mere grant of exclusive distribution rights in France by conferring upon Consten absolute territorial protection against parallel imports from other Member States. The application of Article 81(1) to territorial exclusivity in licence agreements follows the same contours.

The first case on the licensing of intellectual property rights to come before the ECJ was *Nungesser v Commission*[9] (often referred to as the *Maize Seeds* case). One issue for the ECJ was whether an exclusive licence of plant breeders' rights[10] by its very nature infringed Article 81(1): in other words, whether such agreements had as their object the restriction of competition[11]. The ECJ distinguished between an 'open exclusive licence', whereby a licensor agrees not to license anyone else in the licensee's territory, and not to compete there itself; and an exclusive licence which confers absolute territorial protection, so that all competition from third parties is eliminated[12]. This, of course, is the difference between the facts of *Société Technique Minière v Maschinenbau Ulm*[13] and *Consten and Grundig v Commission*. As to the open exclusive licence, the ECJ noted that a licensee of new technology might be deterred from accepting the risk of cultivating and marketing a new product unless it knew that it would not encounter competition from other licensees in its territory[14]. It followed that an open licence which does not affect the position of third parties such as parallel importers does not have as its object the restriction of competition; a detailed analysis would be required to determine the effects of the agreement[15]. Absolute territorial protection however would automatically be caught by Article 81(1)[16] and would not be eligible for exemption under Article 81(3)[17].

The *Maize Seeds* judgment meant that open exclusivity did not necessarily infringe Article 81(1); in particular where the licensee was accepting risk and marketing a new product the licence would not be caught. However in the years following the *Maize Seeds* judgment the Commission adopted a narrow approach to its application. For example in *Velcro/Aplix*[18] it held that although the doctrine may have applied to the licence in that case in its early years, when the technology in question was novel, this was no longer the case by the time of the decision. In *Tetra Pak I (BTG Licence)*[19] the Commission held that the doctrine was not applicable where an undertaking in a dominant position took over important technology: a dominant firm did not bear the same commercial and technical

---

7   On the *de minimis* doctrine see ch 3, pp 107-110.
8   On the requirement for an appreciable effect on trade between Member States see ch 3, pp 110-120.
9   Case 258/78 [1982] ECR 2015, [1983] 1 CMLR 278.
10 Plant breeders' rights are analogous to patents.
11 See ch 3, pp 95-98 for a discussion of agreements that have as their object the restriction of competition.
12 Case 258/78 [1982] ECR 2015, [1983] 1 CMLR 278, para 53.
13 Case 56/65 [1966] ECR 235, [1966] CMLR 357.
14 Case 258/78 [1982] ECR 2015, [1983] 1 CMLR 278, para 57.
15 Ibid, para 58.
16 Ibid, paras 60-63.
17 Ibid, paras 68-79; note that in the *Coditel* case even absolute territorial protection was found not to infringe Article 81(1) in the case of a performing copyright: see p 683 below.
18 OJ [1985] L 233/22, [1989] 4 CMLR 157, paras 43, 44 and 60.
19 OJ [1988] L 272/27, [1990] 4 CMLR 47, upheld on appeal Case T–51/89 *Tetra Pak Rausing SA v Commission* [1990] ECR II-309, [1991] 4 CMLR 334.

risks as a smaller undertaking and was not subject to strong inter-brand competition which might justify immunity from intra-brand competition. In *Delta Chemie/ DDD Ltd*[20], a decision on a licence of know-how rather than a patent, the Commission again concluded that the technology in question did not benefit from the *Maize Seeds* doctrine[1]. This reluctance on the part of the Commission to conclude that territorial exclusivity did not restrict competition was consistent with its formalistic approach towards vertical agreements[2]. The Commission did acknowledge the *Maize Seeds* doctrine in recital 10 of the block exemption on technology transfer agreements, but one suspects with no great enthusiasm; its preferred way of dealing with licences at the time was to exempt under Article 81(3) rather than to grant negative clearance under Article 81(1).

(iii) The case law of the Community Courts on territorial exclusivity after Maize Seeds

In chapter 3 we have seen that the ECJ has, in a number of judgments, refrained from concluding too readily that agreements containing contractual restrictions necessarily restrict competition: these two ideas should not be confused with one another[3]. Some agreements – for example to fix prices or to share markets – are so obviously reprehensible that they are considered to have as their object the restriction of competition[4]; other agreements, however, infringe Article 81(1) only where it can be demonstrated that they will produce appreciable anti-competitive effects on the market[5]. In various judgments since *Maize Seeds* the ECJ has concluded that provisions involving territorial exclusivity did not infringe Article 81(1). In *Coditel v Ciné Vog Films*[6] the ECJ acknowledged that, in the special circumstances of a performance copyright, a licensee may need absolute territorial protection from re-transmissions of films from neighbouring Member States. In *Louis Erauw-Jacquery Sprl v La Hesbignonne Société*[7] the ECJ held that a prohibition on the export of so-called 'basic seeds' did not infringe Article 81(1), but rather was an manifestation of Erauw-Jacquery's plant breeders' rights and necessary for their protection[8]. In *Pronuptia de Paris v Schillgalis*[9] the ECJ suggested that the grant of exclusive territorial rights to a franchisee for a particular territory might not infringe Article 81(1) where the business name or symbol of the franchise was not well-known[10].

Collectively these cases demonstrate that it is wrong to assume that all territorial exclusivity in licences of intellectual property rights infringe Article 81(1); a more nuanced approach is required than this, and even absolute territorial protection and export bans may be justified in particular circumstances.

---

20 OJ [1988] L 309/34, [1989] 4 CMLR 535, para 23.
1 See also *Knoll/Hille-Form* XIIIth *Report on Competition Policy* (1983), points 142–146.
2 For criticism of the Commission's position towards vertical agreements see ch 16, pp 564-565.
3 See ch 3, pp 99-100.
4 Ibid, pp 95-98.
5 Ibid, pp 98-103.
6 Case 262/81 [1982] ECR 3381, [1983] 1 CMLR 49.
7 Case 27/87 [1988] ECR 1919, [1988] 4 CMLR 576.
8 See pp 687 below.
9 Case 161/84 [1986] ECR 353, [1986] 1 CMLR 414.
10 Ibid, para 24.

(iv)   Non-territorial restrictions caught by Article 81(1)

The Commission's decisions have applied Article 81(1) to non-territorial restrictions in licences of intellectual property rights, as have some judgments of the Community Courts, in particular the judgment of the ECJ in *Windsurfing International Inc v Commission*[11]. The treatment of non-territorial restrictions will be considered below in the context of Articles 2 and 3 of Regulation 240/96[12].

(v)   Know-how licences

The Commission applied the principles that it had developed in its decisions on patent licences to licences of know-how[13]. This culminated in the adoption of Regulation 556/89[14] granting block exemption to know-how licences. As was noted at the beginning of this chapter, know-how is not an intellectual property right as such: it is protected by the law of obligations. An anxiety for the Commission was that spurious claims to exclusivity might be made for agreements that do not in practice have an enhancing effect on economic efficiency; this is why the Regulation stipulates that know-how must be secret and substantial[15]. In practice the licensing of know-how is as important and as common as patent licensing, so that the extension of the protection of block exemption to this category of agreements was important for industry.

(vi)   Copyright licences

There is not a great deal of authority specifically on the application of Article 81(1) or Article 81(3) to copyright licences. As we have seen, the ECJ held that absolute territorial protection was not contrary to Article 81(1) in the specific context of a performance copyright in *Coditel v Ciné Vog Films*[16].

The Commission has taken action in relation to copyright licences on a few occasions and in doing so it has applied the principles developed in relation to patent and know-how licences. In *Neilson-Hordell/Reichmark*[17] the Commission gave details of its objections to clauses in a licence of technical drawings and the products they represent; in particular it required the abandonment of a no-challenge clause, a royalties clause extending to products not protected by any copyright of the licensor, a non-competition clause which was to continue after the agreement and an exclusive grant-back to the licensor of the improvements. In *Ernest Benn*

11 Case 193/83 [1986] ECR 611, [1986] 3 CMLR 489.
12 See pp 693-695 below.
13 In chronological order the Commission's decisions on know-how licences are *Boussois/Interpane* OJ [1987] L 50/30, [1988] 4 CMLR 124; *Mitchell Cotts/Sofiltra* OJ [1987] L 41/31, [1988] 4 CMLR 111; *Rich Products/Jus-Rol* OJ [1988] L 69/21, [1988] 4 CMLR 527; *Delta Chemie/DDD Ltd* OJ [1988] L 309/34, [1989] 4 CMLR 535; see also *ICL/Fujitsu* XVIth *Report on Competition Policy* (1986), point 72 (case dealt with by comfort letter).
14 Corrected version at OJ [1990] L 257/15; this Regulation has been replaced by Regulation 240/96: see pp 688-696 below.
15 Regulation 240/96, Article 10(1).
16 Case 262/81 [1982] ECR 3381, [1983] 1 CMLR 49; see p 683 above.
17 XIIth *Annual Report on Competition Policy* (1982), points 88–89.

Ltd[18] the Commission took objection to a standard contractual term which prevented the export of books from the UK. In *Knoll/Hille-Form*[19] the Commission intervened in the case of an exclusive licence of a design right relating to furniture and closed its file after the parties agreed to remove export bans and to allow direct sales into each other's territories.

In *Film Purchases by German Television Stations*[20] the Commission investigated exclusive licence agreements entered into between MGM/UA, a major US film production and distribution company, and ARD, an association of public broadcasting organisations in Germany. The agreements granted ARD exclusive television rights to a large number of MGM/UA's feature films, including 14 James Bond films, in most cases for a period of 15 years. The Commission's view was that the agreements restricted competition, in particular because of the large number of the licensed rights and the duration of the exclusivity[1]. However the Commission granted an individual exemption following modifications to the agreements, for example so that ARD would license the films to third parties at certain periods known as 'windows'.

There is no specific block exemption for copyright licences, although it may be possible to take the benefit of Regulation 2790/99 on vertical agreements or of Regulation 240/96 on technology transfer agreements where the licensing of copyright is ancillary to an agreement covered by one of those Regulations[2].

(vii) Software licences[3]

In the case of *Sega and Nintendo*[4] the Commission required the deletion of clauses in licences of computer software with publishers of video games which, in the Commission's view, enabled Sega and Nintendo to control the market for video games; this intervention followed the Competition Commission's investigation of *Video Games* in the UK[5]. In the *Microsoft Internet Explorer*[6] case the Commission required Microsoft to remove clauses from its software licences providing for minimum distribution volumes for its Internet Explorer browser technology and imposing a prohibition on advertising competitors' browser technology. A minimum quantities clause is normally considered not to be restrictive of competition at all[7]; the Commission's concern here, however,

18 IXth *Annual Report on Competition Policy* (1979), points 118 and 119; see also *The Old Man and the Sea* VIth *Report on Competiton Policy* (1976), point 164; *STEMRA* XIth *Report on Competition Policy* (1981), point 98.
19 XIIIth *Report on Competition Policy* (1983), points 142–146.
20 OJ [1989] L 284/36, [1990] 4 CMLR 841; the decision is criticised by Rothnie 'Commission Re-runs Same Old Bill' (1990) 12 EIPR 72.
1 Ibid, paras 41-46.
2 See p 690 below.
3 See Forrester 'Software Licensing in the Light of Current EC Competition Law Considerations' (1992) 13 ECLR 5; Darbyshire 'Computer Programs and Competition Policy: A Block Exemption for Software Licensing?' (1994) 16 EIPR 374.
4 See the Commission's XXVIIth *Report on Competition Policy* (1997), point 80 and pp 148-149; see also on the similar *Sony* case the XXVIIIth *Report on Competition Policy* (1998), pp 159-160.
5 See p 717 below.
6 See the Commission's XXIXth *Report on Competition Policy* (1999), points 55 and 56 and p 162: details of Microsoft's notification in this case can be found at OJ [1998] C 175/3; for a separate investigation of Microsoft's licensing terms, following a complaint by Santa Cruz Operation in relation to the UNIX operating system, see the Commission's XXVIIth *Report on Competition Policy* (1997), point 79 and pp 140-141.
7 See p 693 below on Article 2(1)(9) of Regulation 240/96.

was that the two clauses in question could have a foreclosure effect on competitors. A comfort letter was sent after these amendments had been made; the Commission did not give a ruling on whether Microsoft's behaviour overall might amount to an abuse of a dominant position[8].

There are some typical clauses in software licences which have no analogies in the general law, for example prohibiting decompilation of a computer programme and restrictions on copying[9]; guidance on the application of Article 81 to such clauses would be helpful, especially given that notification for individual exemption is likely to be abolished under the Commission's modernisation proposals[10].

Block exemption would be available only to the extent that a software licence is ancillary to a vertical agreement under Regulation 240/96 or to a technology transfer agreement under Regulation 240/96[11].

(viii)   Trade mark licences[12]

The Commission has applied Article 81(1) to exclusive trade mark licences but granted individual exemption under Article 81(3) by applying principles derived from the block exemptions for vertical agreements. In *Davide Campari-Milano SpA Agreement*[13] the Commission granted an individual exemption to a standard form of agreement whereby firms were licensed to use the Campari trade mark and were given exclusive rights in their own territory to apply that mark and required not to pursue an active sales policy elsewhere.

In *Moosehead/Whitbread*[14] an exclusive licence of a trade mark with associated know-how was notified to the Commission. The licensee wished to manufacture and to promote the Moosehead brand, a popular Canadian beer, in the UK. The licence prohibited active selling outside the UK. The Commission concluded that the exclusive trade mark and the restriction on active sales infringed Article 81(1), as did a non-competition clause[15]. The know-how was considered by the Commission to be ancillary to the trade mark, so that the block exemption for know-how licensing in force at that time, Regulation 556/89, was not applicable[16]; presumably the same conclusion would be reached under Regulation 240/96[17]. However the Commission granted an individual exemption as consumers would have the advantage of another beer from which to choose[18]. The agreement contained a no-challenge clause in respect of the trade mark, but the Commission

---

8   Commission's XXIXth *Report on Competition Policy* (1999), point 56.
9   It may be arguable that, by analogy from the *Erauw-Jacquery* judgment on the propogation of seeds, a restriction on copying software is outside Article 81(1).
10   See ch 4, pp 146-147 and ch 7, pp 246-258.
11   See p 690 below.
12   See Joliet 'Territorial and Exclusive Trade Mark Licensing under the EC Law of Competition' [1984] IIC 21.
13   OJ [1978] L 70/69, [1978] 2 CMLR 397; see similarly *Goodyear Italiana SpA's Application* OJ [1975] L 38/10, [1975] 1 CMLR D31.
14   OJ [1990] L 100/32, [1991] 4 CMLR 391; see Subiotto '*Moosehead/Whitbread*: Industrial Franchises and No-challenge Clauses Relating to Licensed Trade Marks in the EEC' (1990) 11 ECLR 226.
15   OJ [1990] L 100/32, [1991] 4 CMLR 391, para 15(1).
16   Ibid, para 16(1); the corrected version of Regulation 556/89 will be found at OJ [1990] L 257/15.
17   See pp 688-696 below.
18   OJ [1990] L 100/32, [1991] 4 CMLR 391, para 15(2).

held this to be outside Article 81(1) because the mark was not well-known and its non-availability to competitors was not a barrier to entry[19].

Where a trade mark is ancillary to a vertical agreement or to a technology transfer agreement, it may benefit from the block exemption conferred by Regulation 2790/99 or Regulation 240/96[20].

(ix)   Licences of plant breeders' rights

As we have seen, in *Nungesser v Commission*[1] the ECJ held that an open exclusive licence to produce maize seeds did not infringe Article 81(1) where exclusivity was required to protect the investment of the licensee; the Court also considered that absolute territorial protection would infringe Article 81(1) and would be ineligible for exemption under Article 81(3). In *Louis Erauw-Jacquery Sprl v La Hesbignonne Société*[2] the ECJ was asked to rule on the application of Article 81(1) to two clauses in a licence for the propagation and sale of certain varieties of cereal seeds. Erauw-Jacquery had licensed La Hesbignonne to propagate 'basic seeds' and to sell seeds reproduced from them ('reproductive seeds'). Clause 2(f) of the licence prohibited the export of basic seeds; clause 2(i) required the licensee not to resell the reproductive seeds below minimum selling prices. The ECJ's view was that the export ban in relation to basic seeds did not infringe Article 81(1): a plant breeder is entitled to reserve the propagation of basic seeds to institutions approved by him and an export ban is objectively justifiable to protect this right[3]. Basic seeds are not intended for sale to farmers for sowing, but are intended solely for the purpose of propagation; it follows that an export ban of this kind arises from the existence of the plant breeders' rights and is not an improper exercise of it[4]. The ECJ concluded that the provision on minimum pricing had as its object and effect the restriction of competition[5] but that the national court must decide on the facts whether it had an effect on trade between Member States[6].

In *Sicasov*[7] the Commission applied the ECJ's judgment in the *Erauw-Jacquery* case to the standard licences of Sicasov, a French cooperative of plant breeders. The Commission explains in more detail than the judgment in *Erauw-Jacquery* the distinction between basic seeds, which are intended only for propagation, and 'certified' seeds, intended for sale to farmers for sowing[8]. The breeder is entitled to control the destination of basic seeds by virtue of its plant breeders' rights[9], but cannot control certified seeds that have been put onto the market with its consent[10]. It followed that obligations not to entrust basic seeds to a third party, not to export them and related provisions did not infringe Article 81(1)[11].

19   Ibid, para 15(4).
20   See p 690 below.
1   Case 258/78 [1982] ECR 2015, [1983] 1 CMLR 278.
2   Case 27/87 [1988] ECR 1919, [1988] 4 CMLR 576.
3   Ibid, para 10.
4   This was the view of Advocate General Mischo in this case, and of the Commission: ibid, para 9.
5   Ibid, para 15.
6   Ibid, para 19.
7   OJ [1999] L 4/27, [1999] 4 CMLR 192.
8   Ibid, paras 21-27.
9   Ibid, para 50, citing *Erauw-Jacquery*.
10   Ibid, para 51.
11   Ibid, paras 53-61.

However a restriction on the export of certified seeds did infringe Article 81(1)[12] but was exempted pursuant to Article 81(3)[13].

In *Roses*[14] the Commission condemned two clauses in a standard licence of plant breeders' rights. The first was an exclusive grant-back clause, which effectively removed the sub-licensee from the market for mutations which it discovered. The second was a no-challenge clause: the fact that plant breeders' rights are conferred only after a national authority's involvement does not mean that there might not have been an error of appreciation that could be challenged by a licensee.

(x)   Sub-contracting agreements

Sub-contracting agreements typically involve a licence from the principal to the sub-contractor. Horizontal sub-contracting agreements have been considered in chapter 15 and vertical ones on chapter 16[15].

3.   LICENCES OF INTELLECTUAL PROPERTY RIGHTS: REGULATION 240/96

Acting under powers conferred on it by Council Regulation 19/65[16] the Commission has adopted Regulation 240/96[17] conferring block exemption on certain technology transfer agreements pursuant to Article 81(3) of the Treaty. Prior to the adoption of this Regulation there had been separate regulations for licences of patents, Regulation 2349/84[18], and for licences of know-how, Regulation 556/89[19]; licences of each, and mixed licences, are now covered by a single regulation[20]. The Commission adopted Regulation 240/96 on 31 January 1996. It entered into force on 1 April 1996 and will apply until 31 March 2006[1]. The Regulation consists of 27 recitals and 13 Articles. Article 1 confers block exemption on bilateral licences of patents and know-how, including mixed licences. Article 2 contains the so-called 'white list' of provisions which normally do not infringe Article 81(1), but which are granted block exemption if they happen to do so. Article 3 sets out a 'black list' of provisions, the inclusion of

12 Ibid, paras 62-64.
13 Ibid, paras 73-77; note that Regulation 240/96 on technology transfer agreements did not apply since the standard licence did not correspond with any of the provisions listed in Article 1(1) thereof: ibid, para 72.
14 OJ [1985] L 369/9, [1988] 4 CMLR 193; see Harding 'Commission Decision on Breeders' Rights in Relation to Roses: Hard Line on Breeders' Rights Maintained' (1986) 9 EIPR 284.
15 See ch 15, pp 515-520 and ch 16, pp 593-594.
16 JO [1965] 533, OJ Sp Ed [1965-66] 87.
17 OJ [1996] L 31/2, [1996] 4 CMLR 405; for detailed commentary see *Butterworths Competition Law* (eds Freeman and Whish, 1991) Div V, paras [372]-[874]; Korah *Technology Transfer Agreements and the EC Competition Rules* (Clarendon Press Oxford, 1996); Gutterman *Innovation and Competition Policy: A Comparative Study of the Regulation of Patent Licensing and Collaborative Research & Development in the United States and the European Community* (Kluwer Law International, 1997); Kinsella *EU Technology Licensing* (Palladian Law Publishing, 1998); Anderman *EC Competition Law and Intellectual Property Rights: The Regulation of Innovation* (Clarendon Press Oxford, 1998) pp 81-89; on procedural issues under the block exemption see Kerse 'Block Exemptions under Article [81(3)]: The Technology Transfer Regulation – Procedural Issues' (1996) 17 ECLR 331.
18 OJ [1984] L 219/15, as amended by Regulation 151/93, OJ [1993] L 21/8.
19 Corrected version at OJ [1990] L 257/15, as amended by Regulation 151/93.
20 Regulation 240/96, recital 3.
1 Regulation 240/96, Article 13.

which will prevent the block exemption from applying to the licence. Article 4 provides an opposition procedure. Articles 5, 6 and 8 contain further provisions on the scope of application of the Regulation. Article 7 enables the Commission to withdraw the benefit of the block exemption in certain circumstances. Article 10 contains important definitions. As provided for in Article 12, the Commission has commenced a policy review which will lead to the publication of a report assessing whether any adaptation of the Regulation is desirable. The progress of this review can be followed on the Commission's website[2].

(A) Article 1: block exemption for technology transfer agreements

(i) Scope of the block exemption

Article 1 confers block exemption on pure patent licences, on pure know-how licences and on mixed patent and know-how licences to which only two undertakings are party[3] and which include one or more of the obligations set out in Article 1(1)(1)-(8).

(A) MEANING OF PATENTS. Recital 5 of Regulation 240/96 states it applies to national patents, to Community patents[4] and to European patents[5]; for the purpose of the Regulation the term 'patent' includes a number of analogous rights such as utility models, topographies of semiconductor products and plant breeders' rights[6]. The Regulation also applies to patent applications[7] and to licences that are automatically prolonged by the inclusion of new improvements, provided that the licensee has the right to refuse such improvements or that each party has the right to terminate the agreement at the expiry of the original term and at least every three years thereafter[8]. The Regulation also applies to sub-licences[9] and to assignments where the risk remains with the assignor[10].

(B) MEANING OF KNOW-HOW. 'Know-how' is defined in Article 10(1) of the Regulation to mean 'a body of technical information that is secret, substantial and identified in any form'; Articles 10(2)-(4) define the terms 'secret', 'substantial' and 'identified'[11]. It is necessary to have a definition of know-how within the

---

2 http://europa.eu.int/comm/competition/index_en.html.
3 Note that legal entities that form part of the same economic unit count as one undertaking for this purpose: Case 170/83 *Hydrotherm Gerätebau GmbH v Compact* [1984] ECR 2999, [1985] 3 CMLR 224, para 11 (decided under Regulation 67/67, an old block exemption for exclusive distribution agreements); Article 6(3) specifically states that licences are covered by the Regulation where the rights or obligations of the licensor or the licensee are assumed by undertakings connected with them, and the meaning of 'connected undertakings' for this purpose is defined in Article 10(14); on the concept of a single economic unit see ch 3, pp 72-74.
4 See the Community Patent Convention 1976, OJ [1976] L 17/1; it has not been ratified and is likely to be replaced by a Community Patent Regulation: see p 676, n 7 above.
5 See the European Patents Convention 1973.
6 Regulation 240/96, Article 8(1).
7 Ibid, Article 8(2).
8 Ibid, Article 8(3).
9 Ibid, Article 6(1); see recital 9.
10 Ibid, Article 6(2); see recital 9.
11 See also recital 4 of the Regulation which provides examples of what qualifies as know-how such as recipes, formulæ, designs and drawings.

Regulation since it is not an intellectual property right as such[12] and is not a term of art in national legal systems.

(C)   EXCLUSIONS FROM THE REGULATION[13].   Article 5 of the Regulation specifically excludes patent and know-how pools[14] unless the parties are free from territorial restraints within the common market[15]; licences between competitors having an interest in a joint venture, or between one of them and the joint venture, if the licence relates to the activities of a joint venture: however some licences between a parent and the joint venture are permitted subject to a market share test[16]; reciprocal licences between competitors[17]; licences of other intellectual property rights which are not ancillary[18]; and agreements entered into solely for the purpose of sale[19].

(ii)   Ancillary provisions

Regulation 240/96 grants block exemption to patent and know-how licences. Regulation 2790/99 exempts vertical agreements[20]. There are no block exemptions that relate specifically to other types of intellectual property such as trade marks or copyright. For example in *Moosehead/Whitbread*[1] the Commission granted individual exemption to a trade mark licence since no block exemption was applicable[2]. It is clear, therefore, that there are many licence agreements that do not enjoy the 'safe haven' of one of the existing block exemptions. However the block exemption in Regulation 240/96 does extend to licences of intellectual property rights other than patents 'when such additional licensing contributes to the achievement of the objects of the licensed technology and contains only ancillary provisions'[3]; this is given formal expression in a negative sense by Article 5(1)(4), which provides that the Regulation shall *not* apply to 'licensing agreements containing provisions relating to intellectual property rights other than patents which are not ancillary'.

It is also possible that ancillary provisions relating to intellectual property may benefit from the block exemption for vertical agreements where they contain 'provisions which relate to the assignment to the buyer or use by the buyer of intellectual property rights, provided that those provisions do not constitute the primary object of such agreements and are directly related to the use, sale or resale of goods or services by the buyer or its customers'. The practical consequences of Article 2(3) are explained in chapter 16[4].

---

12 See p 675, n 3 above.
13 See generally recital 8.
14 Ibid, Article 5(1)(1); on patent pools see pp 696-697 below.
15 Ibid, Article 5(2)(2).
16 Ibid, Article 5(2)(1) and (3).
17 Ibid, Article 5(1)(3); as in the case of Article 5(1)(1) this exclusion does not apply where the parties are free from territorial restraints within the common market: Article 5(2)(2).
18 Ibid, Article 5(1)(4): on ancillary agreements see below.
19 Ibid, Article 5(1)(4); a sales agreement should be analysed under Regulation 2790/99 on vertical agreements, as to which see ch 16, pp 567-591.
20 Ibid.
1   OJ [1990] L 100/32, [1991] 4 CMLR 391.
2   See p 686 above.
3   Regulation 240/96, recital 6; the expression 'ancillary provisions' is defined in Article 10(15).
4   See ch 16, pp 574-577.

(iii)   Article 1(1)(1)-(3): exclusivity between the licensor and the licensee

Article 1(1)(1)-(6) of Regulation 240/96 grants block exemption to territorial exclusivity in patent and know-how licences[5]. Article 1(1)(1)-(3) deals with exclusivity as between the licensor and the licensee; Article 1(1)(4)-(6) applies to exclusivity as between licensees. Article 10 contains definitions of key expressions in Article 1 such as 'licensed technology' and 'exploitation'; the latter term includes both manufacture and active and passive sales.

Article 1(1)(1) allows a restriction on the licensor not to licence other undertakings to exploit the licensed technology in the licensee's territory; Article 1(1)(2) permits an obligation on the licensor itself not to do so. Article 1(1)(3) allows an obligation to be imposed upon the licensee not to exploit the licensed technology in the licensor's territory. The permissible duration of these restrictions is dealt with in Articles 1(2)-1(4), which are explained below.

(iv)   Article 1(1)(4)-(6): exclusivity between licensees

Article 1(1)(4) permits an obligation on the licensee not to manufacture or use the licensed product, or to use the licensed process, in territories within the common market that are licensed to other licensees. Articles 1(1)(5) and (6) allow restrictions on sales. Article 1(1)(5) permits an obligation on the licensee not to pursue an active sales policy in territories which are licensed to other licensees and in particular not to engage in advertising specifically aimed at those territories or to maintain a branch or distribution depot there; this is consistent with the policy in Article 4(b) of Regulation 2790/99 on vertical agreements[6]. Article 1(1)(6) goes further than Regulation 2790/99, however, by allowing a prohibition of passive sales as well: the technology transfer régime permits greater exclusivity for licensees than Regulation 2790/99 does for distributors. However the permissible duration of the restrictions on active and passive sales is limited by Articles 1(2)-(4) (below), and the case law on the exhaustion of rights under Article 28 (ex Article 30) and Article 30 (ex Article 36) would apply to prevent any licensee from enjoying absolute territorial protection[7].

(v)   Article 1(1)(7): requirement to use the licensor's trade mark

Article 1(1)(7) permits an obligation on the licensee to use only the licensor's trade mark or get-up during the term of the agreement, but the licensee must be allowed to indicate that it is the manufacturer of the goods in question.

(vi)   Article 1(1)(8): limitation of production to the licensee's own requirements

Article 1(1)(8) permits an obligation on the licensee to limit its production to the quantities required for manufacturing its own products and to sell the licensed product only as an integral part of or a replacement part for its own products, provided that such quantities are freely determined by the licensee.

---

5   The fact that an agreement may contain obligations relating to third countries does not prevent the application of the block exemption: Regulation 240/96, recital 7.
6   See ch 16, pp 583-585.
7   Regulation 240/96, recital 11; on the exhaustion of rights doctrine, see pp 703-714 below.

(vii)   Permissible duration

Articles 1(2)-(4) deal with the permissible duration of licences under the block exemption. The block exemption itself applies until 31 March 2006[8]; however it is reasonable to expect that a new regulation will be put in place when Regulation 240/96 expires, and that transitional arrangements will be made for agreements that satisfy its terms[9]. It is necessary to consider pure patent licences, pure know-how licences and mixed licences in turn.

(A)   PURE PATENT LICENCES.   Pure patent licences are exempted to the extent that and for as long as the licensed product is protected by parallel patents[10]; however the prohibition on passive sales is granted only for a period of five years from the date when the licensed product is first put on the market within the common market by one of the licensees[11]. It follows that if a licensor granted a licence to X for France in 1999 and X put the products on the market there that year, a licence granted to Y for Germany in 2001 could restrict passive sales only for a period of three years until 2004; if the period were longer, it would exceed a period of five years from when the licensed products were first marketed by a licensee within the common market.

(B)   PURE KNOW-HOW LICENCES.   The basic rule is that pure know-how licences are exempted for a maximum of 10 years from the date when the licensed product is first put on the market within the common market by one of the licensees[12]; a prohibition on passive sales may not last for longer than five years[13]. Longer periods of protection require individual exemption[14]. The obligations in Article 1(1)(7) and (8) are exempted for the lifetime of the agreement for as long as the know-how remains secret and substantial[15].

(C)   MIXED PATENT AND KNOW-HOW LICENCES.   Mixed licences may be exempt for longer than the periods specified for pure know-how licences, provided that 'necessary patents' remain in force[16]; again the prohibition on passive sales may not exceed five years[17].

(viii)   Article 1(5): more limited scope

Article 1(5) provides that where an agreement contains obligations of a type referred to in Article 1(1), but which have a more limited scope, the block exemption is still applicable.

8   Regulation 240/96, Article 13.
9   See eg Article 11 of Regulation 240/96 in relation to agreements satisfying the old block exemptions for patent licences and know-how licences respectively.
10   Regulation 240/96, Article 1(2); 'parallel patents' are defined in Article 10(13) of the Regulation.
11   Ibid, Article 1(2), second sentence and recital 15.
12   Ibid, para 1(3), first indent: see also recital 13.
13   Regulation 240/96, Article 1(3), second indent.
14   Ibid, recital 14; in *Pasteur Mérieux-Merck* OJ [1994] L 309/1 a know-how licence was to last for more than 10 years and so was ineligible for block exemption (in that case under the old Regulation 556/89 for know-how licences); however the Commission granted individual exemption: ibid, paras 106-109.
15   Ibid, Article 1(3), third indent.
16   Ibid, Article 1(4) and recital 16; 'necessary patents' are defined in Article 10(5).
17   Ibid, Article 1(4), second indent.

(B)   Article 2: the 'white list'

Article 2(1) contains the so-called 'white list' of obligations which are commonly found in licences and which are normally not restrictive of competition; the list is not exhaustive[18]. If any of the white-listed obligations should happen to infringe Article 81(1), they will benefit from block exemption anyway[19]; so will any obligations having a more restricted scope than the obligations listed in Article 2(1)[20].

The following provisions are white-listed:

- An obligation not to divulge know-how communicated to the licensor, even after the agreement has expired[1] and an obligation not to grant sub-licences or to assign the licence[2].
- An obligation on the licensee not to exploit the licensed know-how or the patents after termination of the agreement in so far as the know-how is still secret or the patents are still in force[3].
- An obligation on the licensee to licence improvements to the licensor: in the case of non-severable improvements the licence must not be exclusive, and the licensor must undertake to grant a licence of its improvements to the licensee[4].
- An obligation on the licensee to observe minimum quality specifications or to procure goods or services from the licensor or from an undertaking designated by it for technical reasons or for maintaining quality[5].
- Obligations on the licensee to protect the know-how or patents[6].
- Obligations in relation to royalties[7].
- An obligation on the licensee to restrict its exploitation to one or more technical fields of use[8].
- An obligation to pay minimum royalties or to produce minimum quantities[9].
- An obligation on the licensor to grant the licensee any more favourable terms that it may grant to another undertaking after the agreement is entered into[10].
- An obligation on the licensee to mark the licensed product with an indication of the licensor's name or of the licensed patent[11].

18   Ibid, recital 18.
19   Ibid, Article 2(2).
20   Ibid, Article 2(3).
1   Ibid, Article 2(1)(1).
2   Ibid, Article 2(1)(2); a provision that a licence can be terminated in the event of a change in control of the licensee is analogous to a restriction on assignment or sub-licensing and does not infringe Article 81(1): *Vickers/Rolls Royce*, XXVIIIth *Report on Competition Policy* (1998), pp 168-169.
3   Regulation 240/96, Article 2(1)(3); see also recital 20 and Case 320/87 *Ottung v Klee and Weilbach A/S* [1989] ECR 1177, [1990] 4 CMLR 915, paras 17-20.
4   Regulation 240/96, Article 2(1)(4); see also recital 20 and Article 3(6), p 695 below.
5   Ibid, Article 2(1)(5); where an obligation is more restrictive than this provision envisages, Article 4(2)(a) of the opposition procedure may apply: see p 695 below.
6   Ibid, Article 2(1)(6).
7   Article 2(1)(7); see Case 320/87 *Ottung v Klee and Weilbach A/S* [1989] ECR 1177, [1990] 4 CMLR 915, paras 8-16.
8   Regulation 240/96, Article 2(1)(8); see also recitals 22 and 23 and Article 3(4).
9   Ibid, Article 2(1)(9); note that a minimum quantities clause could give rise to concern if it has a foreclosing effect on third parties: see Article 7(4) (pp 695-696 below) and the Commission's action against Microsoft in relation to its Internet Explorer (pp 685-686 above).
10   Regulation 240/96, Article 2(1)(10).
11   Ibid, Article 2(1)(11).

- An obligation on the licensee not to use the licensor's technology to construct facilities for third parties[12].
- An obligation on the licensee to supply only a limited quantity of the licensed product to a particular customer, where the licence was granted so that the customer might have a second source of supply inside the licensed territory[13].
- A reservation by the licensor of the right to exercise the rights conferred by a patent to oppose the exploitation of the technology by the licensee outside the territory[14].
- A reservation by the licensee to terminate the agreement if the licensee contests the secret or substantial nature of the licensed know-how or challenges the validity of the patent[15].
- A reservation by the licensor of the right to terminate the licence agreement if the licensee raises the claim that the patent is not necessary[16].
- An obligation on the licensee to use its best endeavours to manufacture and market the licensed product[17].
- A reservation by the licensor of the right to terminate the exclusivity granted to the licensee and to stop licensing improvements to it when the licensee enters into competition with the licensor or other undertakings within the common market[18].

(C)   Article 3: the 'black list'

Article 3 contains the so-called 'black list' of restrictions or provisions that may not be included in licences if they are to benefit from the block exemption or the opposition procedure; such restrictions can be allowed only on an individual basis[19].

The following provisions are black-listed:
- Restrictions on either party in relation to the determination of prices, components of prices or discounts for the licensed products[20]: the recommendation of prices is not mentioned and, by analogy with Article 4(a) of Regulation 2790/99[1], probably does not infringe Article 81(1) at all;
- A restriction on one party from competing within the common market with the other party or with other undertakings in respect of research and development, production, use or distribution of competing products; this is without prejudice to the right of the licensor, provided for in Article 2(1)(17) and (18), to impose a best endeavours clause or to terminate the agreement in the event that the licensee becomes a competitor[2].
- Requirements on the parties not to meet orders from users or resellers within their own territories which intend to resell them in other Members States and requirements to impede parallel imports within the Community[3].

12   Ibid, Article 2(1)(12).
13   Ibid, Article 2(1)(13).
14   Ibid, Article 2(1)(14).
15   Ibid, Article 2(1)(15).
16   Ibid, Article 2(1)(16).
17   Ibid, Article 2(1)(17).
18   Ibid, Article 2(1)(18).
19   Regulation 240/96, recital 19.
20   Ibid, Article 3(1); see also recital 24.
1   See ch 16, pp 582-583.
2   Regulation 240/96, Article 3(2).
3   Ibid, Article 3(3): see also recital 17; note that Article 7(3) gives power to withdraw the block exemption when parallel imports and exports are impeded, but not as a result of a *requirement* to that effect: see pp 695-696 below.

- Customer allocation as between licensor and licensee within the same technical field of use or within the same product market, where the parties were competing manufacturers before the grant of the licence[4]; this provision must be read subject to Article 1(1)(7) and Article 2(1)(13) above.
- Restrictions on the maximum quantities that the licensee can produce[5]; this provision must be read subject to Article 1(1)(8) and Article 2(1)(13) above.
- A requirement that the licensee must assign in whole or in part to the licensor rights to improvements to or new applications of the licensed technology[6]; this provision must be read subject to Article 2(1)(4) above.
- Longer periods of exclusivity than are provided for in Article 1[7].

(D) Article 4: the opposition procedure[8]

Article 4 contains an opposition procedure for licences containing restrictions which are not exempted under Articles 1 and/or 2 and which do not contain black-listed clauses contrary to Article 3; if the Commission does not object within four months of notification the block exemption will apply[9]; the Commission may be prepared to waive some of the informational requirements for the notification[10]. The Regulation suggests that the opposition procedure may in particular be invoked in the case of provisions relating to quality specifications or containing tie-in provisions[11] and for no-challenge clauses[12]. In practice the opposition procedure has hardly been used at all[13].

(E) Article 7: withdrawal of the block exemption

By Article 7 the Commission may withdraw the benefit of block exemption in certain cases[14]. Exemption could be withdrawn when an agreement forecloses the relevant market, especially where the licensee's market share exceeds 40%[15]; where a licensee refuses, without any objectively justified reason, to meet unsolicited orders from another territory: the latter provision is without prejudice to the prohibition on passive sales permitted by Article 1(1)(6)[16]; where the parties

---

4 Ibid, Article 3(4).
5 Ibid, Article 3(5); as to whether so-called 'site licences' should be treated as maximum quantities clauses, see Dolmans and Odriozola 'Site Licence, Right Licence? Site Licences under EC Competition Law' (1998) 19 ECLR 493, which describes the Commission's intervention in the *Arco/Repsol* case; see also Townsend 'The Case for Site Licences' (1999) 20 ECLR 169.
6 Article 3(6).
7 Article 3(7).
8 See ch 4, p 146.
9 Regulation 240/96, Article 4(1).
10 Ibid, recital 25.
11 Ibid, Article 4(2)(a).
12 Ibid, Article 4(2)(b); no-challenge clauses were found not to infringe Article 81(1) in Case 65/86 *Bayer v Süllhöfer* [1988] ECR 5249 (patent licence) and in *Moosehead/Whitbread* OJ [1990] L 100/32, [1991] 4 CMLR 391 (trade mark licence): see Subiotto '*Moosehead/Whitbread*: Industrial Franchises and No-challenge Clauses Relating to Licensed Trade Marks in the EEC' (1990) 11 ECLR 226.
13 See ch 4, p 146.
14 See Regulation 240/96, recital 26.
15 Regulation 240/96, Article 7(1).
16 Ibid, Article 7(2); on Article 1(1)(6) see p 691 above.

take steps to impede parallel imports and exports[17]; or where obligations on a licensee could have the effect of preventing it from using competing technology[18]. The Commission contemplated using the Article 7 procedure in *Tetra Pak I (BTG licence)*[19], but did not do so when Tetra renounced its claims to exclusivity under the patent licence in question[20].

4.   LICENCES OF INTELLECTUAL PROPERTY RIGHTS: INDIVIDUAL EXEMPTION

Licensing agreements which are not covered by Regulation 240/96 and which contain provisions which are not ancillary to an agreement covered by that Regulation or by Regulation 2790/99 on vertical agreements[1] may be notified to the Commission for individual exemption. In such a case the agreement should be drafted, in so far as it is possible, with the main principles of Regulation 240/96 in mind, as this will improve the chances of obtaining an exemption. Examples have already been given of individual exemptions for licences of intellectual property rights[2]. If the Commission's modernisation proposals are implemented there will no longer be the possibility of notifying licences for individual exemption[3], which will mean that the case law reviewed in this chapter and the terms of Regulation 240/96 will be particularly important when determining what provisions are likely to be acceptable in licence agreements.

5.   HORIZONTAL AGREEMENTS RELATING TO INTELLECTUAL PROPERTY RIGHTS

(A)   Pooling agreements

Horizontal agreements relating to intellectual property rights may infringe Article 81. For example if all the firms in an industry pool their patents and agree not to grant licences to third parties, at the same time fixing quotas and prices, they may earn supra-competitive profits and prevent entry into the market. The Commission condemned a patent pooling scheme in *Video Cassette Recorders Agreements*[4]. Article 5 of the block exemption on technology transfer agreements expressly excludes the cross-licensing and pooling of patents and know-how from the scope of the block exemption. Where pooling of patents and know-how could contribute to technical or economic progress, an exemption or comfort letter

---

17   Ibid, Article 7(3).
18   Ibid, Article 7(4); see p 693 above on the possibility that minimum quantities clauses could have an anti-competitive effect.
19   OJ [1988] L 272/27, [1990] 4 CMLR 47, upheld on appeal Case T–51/89 *Tetra Pak Rausing SA v Commission* [1990] ECR II-309, [1991] 4 CMLR 334.
20   OJ [1988] L 272/27, [1990] 4 CMLR 47 at para 61.
1   On ancillary provisions see p 690 above.
2   See eg *Film Purchases by German Television Stations* (copyright, p 685 above), *Davide Campari-Milano SpA Agreement* (trade mark, p 686, n 13 above), *Moosehead/Whitbread* (trade mark, p 686, n 14 above) and *Sicasov* (plant breeders' rights, p 687, n 7 above).
3   See ch 4, pp 146-147 and ch 7, pp 246-258.
4   OJ [1978] L 47/42, [1978] 2 CMLR 160; see also *Concast-Mannesman* Commission's XIth *Report on Competition Policy* (1981), point 93; *IGR Stereo Television* ibid, point 94 and XIVth *Report on Competition Policy* (1984), point 92.

might be forthcoming. An example of this is *MPEG-2*[5]. MPEG-2 is a technology that improves the quality of video signals. To apply the technology it is necessary to have access to a number of patents. These were pooled by their respective owners, who agreed that access to the pool would be permitted on a non-exclusive and non-discriminatory basis. This meant that the pool, far from foreclosing the market to third parties, would enable them to gain access to the technology with a beneficial effect on technical and economic progress. The Commission issued an Article 81(3) comfort letter.

Pooling agreements may be permitted where they are a necessary response to someone else's superior bargaining power. This point is exemplified by the phenomenon of collecting societies, to which individual artists assign their copyrights and which then negotiate royalties with the media from a position of strength. Where intellectual property rights are pooled for a legitimate reason such as this, Article 82 may be applied to prevent abusive behaviour on the part of the collecting society[6].

(B) Trade mark delimitation agreements

The Commission will carefully scrutinise trade mark delimitation agreements whereby owners of independent trade marks accept restrictions on the exercise and use of their respective marks[7]. This means that legal advisers must be careful when advising clients as to the terms on which they should settle a trade mark dispute, since it may be that the settlement itself will contravene Article 81(1)[8]. In *BAT v Commission*[9] the ECJ established that trade mark delimitation agreements are permissible and fall outside Article 81(1) where they serve to avoid confusion or conflict; however there must be a genuine dispute between the parties and the agreement must be no more restrictive than necessary to overcome the problem of confusion. In this case there was not a genuine dispute, the apparent intention of BAT being to prevent a Mr Segers from selling his tobacco on the German market; the trade mark in question had not been exploited in the past and was subject to cancellation under German law.

5   See OJ [1998] C 229/6 and the Commission's XXIXth *Report on Competiton* Policy (1999), points 55 and 56 and p 162; see similarly *Philips/Matsushita – D2B* OJ [1991] C 220/2, [1991] 4 CMLR 905; *Philips International – DCC* OJ [1992] C 333/8, [1993] 4 CMLR 286; see also *The European Telecommunications Standards Institute's Intellectual Property Rights Policy* OJ [1994] C 76/5, [1995] 5 CMLR 352.

6   See p 701 below.

7   See *Sirdar and Phildar Trade Marks* [1975] 1 CMLR D93 (a decision under Article 15(6) of Regulation 17/62); *Re Penney's Trade Mark* OJ [1978] L 60/19, [1978] 2 CMLR 100 (negative clearance to a trade mark agreement which was a genuine attempt to settle litigation and not an attempt to partition the market); *Syntex/Synthelabo* [1990] 4 CMLR 343 (Commission required modification of trade mark agreement that unjustifiably partitioned markets); *Toltecs and Dorcet Trade Marks* OJ [1982] L 379/19, [1983] 1 CMLR 412 (this decision was the subject of the appeal in *BAT v Commission* below); *Hershey/Herschi* XXth *Report on Competition Policy* (1990), point 111; *Chiquita/Fyffes plc* XXIInd *Report on Competition Policy* (1992), points 168-176 (agreement by Fyffes not to use the Fyffes trade mark in continental Europe contrary to Article 81; also an abuse of a dominant position under Article 82); see *Fyffes plc v Chiquita Brands International Inc* [1993] ECC 193 on the litigation in the English High Court in this case.

8   See generally Singleton 'IP Disputes: Settlement Agreements and Ancillary Licences' (1993) 15 EIPR 48.

9   Case 35/83 [1985] ECR 363, [1985] 2 CMLR 470; see Alexander (1985) 22 CML Rev 709.

(C)   Other horizontal agreements

It is possible that a concerted practice between the owners of intellectual property rights to litigate against parallel importers could infringe Article 81[10]. Where agreements lead to the splitting up of trade marks between different parties in different Member States this may lead to difficulties over rights which have a 'common origin'. This issue is considered later[11].

6.   ARTICLE 82 AND INTELLECTUAL PROPERTY RIGHTS

The law of intellectual property confers exclusive rights; Article 82 prohibits the abuse of a dominant position; the question arises of whether Article 82 can be applied in such a way as to limit the exclusive rights given by intellectual property law[12]. The ECJ has made clear that mere ownership of intellectual property rights cannot be attacked under Article 82; however Article 82 may apply to an improper exercise of the right in question[13].

(A)   Compulsory licences

A question that has been much debated is the extent to which the owner of an intellectual right can be compelled to grant a licence of it to a third party under Article 82. As a general proposition one would expect the issue of compulsory licensing to be addressed as a matter of intellectual property law, and not as a matter of competition law.

(i)   The Renault and Erik Veng judgments

In the *Renault* case[14] and in *Volvo v Erik Veng*[15] third parties wished to be granted licences of the car manufacturers' intellectual property rights in order to produce spare parts, and claimed that a refusal to grant such licences was an abuse of a dominant position under Article 82. The ECJ adopted an orthodox approach to the application of Article 82 to compulsory licensing and held that, in the absence of Community harmonisation of laws on designs and models, it

---

10   See *Glaxo Group Ltd v Dowelhurst Ltd* [2000] ECC 193, [2000] Eu LR 493.
11   See pp 712-713 below.
12   For further discussion of this subject see Tritton *Intellectual Property in Europe* (Sweet & Maxwell, 1996) ch 11; Govaere *The Use and Abuse of Intellectual Property Rights in EC Law* (Sweet & Maxwell, 1996) ch 5; Anderman *EC Competition Law and Intellectual Property Rights: The Regulation of Innovation* (Clarendon Press Oxford, 1998) chs 10-19.
13   See Case 24/67 *Parke, Davis & Co v Probel* [1968] ECR 55, [1968] CMLR 47 where the ECJ said that ownership of a patent is not an abuse in itself although 'the utilisation of the patent could degenerate into an improper exploitation of the protection'; the ownership of intellectual property is a factor to be taken into account in assessing whether a firm has a dominant position: see ch 5, pp 157-158.
14   Case 53/87 *Conzorzio Italiano della Componentistica di Ricambio per Autovericoli and Maxicar v Regie National des Usines Renault* [1988] ECR 6039, [1990] 4 CMLR 265.
15   Case 238/87 [1988] ECR 6211, [1989] 4 CMLR 122; see Korah 'No Duty to Licence Independent Repairers to Make Spare Parts: the *Renault, Volvo* and *Bayer* Cases' (1988) 12 EIPR 381; Groves 'The Use of Registered Designs to Protect Car Body Panels' (1989) 10 BLR 117.

was a matter for national law to determine the nature and extent of protection for such matters. In the *Volvo* case it stated at paragraph 8 that:

'the right of the proprietor of a protected design to prevent third parties from manufacturing and selling or importing, without its consent, products incorporating the design constitutes the very subject-matter of its exclusive rights. It follows that an obligation imposed upon the proprietor of a protected design to grant to third parties, even in return for a reasonable royalty, a licence for the supply of products incorporating the design would lead to the proprietor thereof being deprived of the substance of its exclusive right, and that a refusal to grant such a licence cannot in itself constitute an abuse of a dominant position.'

The ECJ added, however, that a car manufacturer might be guilty of abusing its dominant position where it refused to supply spare parts to independent repairers in an arbitrary manner, charged unfair prices for spare parts[16], or decided no longer to produce spare parts for models still in circulation.

(ii)   The Magill case

A less orthodox approach was taken by the Commission in *Magill TV Guide/ ITP, BBC and RTE*[17], variously known as the *Magill* case and the *TV Listings* case. Mr Magill wished to publish the listings of three television companies broadcasting in the UK and Ireland in a single weekly publication; at the time there was no publication which contained the details of all three companies' programmes for a week in advance; this information was available only in daily newspapers for the day in question, or on a Saturday for the weekend. There was an obvious public demand for listings magazines, which were widely available in continental countries. Copyright protection was available for TV listings under UK and Irish law, which is why Magill required a licence. The Commission concluded that the three television companies had abused their individual dominant positions in relation to their own TV listings by refusing to make them available to Magill and required that advance information be supplied in order to enable comprehensive weekly TV guides to be published. The Commission's decision was appealed to the CFI and the ECJ, each of which upheld it[18]. The ECJ stated that the abuse consisted of the refusal to provide basic information by relying on national copyright provisions, thereby preventing the appearance of a new product, a comprehensive guide to television programmes, which the television companies did not offer and for which there was a potential consumer demand[19]; the Court also noted that there was no objective justification for the

---

16 In Case T-198/98 *Micro Leader Business v Commission* [1999] ECR II-3989, [2000] 4 CMLR 886 the CFI held that the Commission, before rejecting a complaint against Microsoft concerning the exercise of its copyright protection, should have investigated whether its prices were discriminatory contrary to Article 82(2)(c): ibid, paras 49-59.

17 OJ [1989] L 78/43, [1989] 4 CMLR 757.

18 Cases T–69/89 etc *RTE v Commission* [1991] ECR II-485, [1991] 4 CMLR 586, upheld by the ECJ Cases C-241/91 P etc *RTE and ITP v Commission* [1995] ECR I-743, [1995] 4 CMLR 718.

19 Cases C-241/91 P etc *RTE and ITP v Commission* [1995] ECR I-743, [1995] 4 CMLR 718, para 54.

refusal[20] and that the result of the refusal was to reserve to the television companies the downstream market for television guides[1].

The case was immensely controversial and led to numerous comments and articles, mainly adverse[2]. It appeared to sit oddly with the earlier judgments of the ECJ in *Renault* and *Volvo v Erik Veng*; it meant that the possibility of compulsory licensing had been introduced under Article 82; and it could be seen to be an application of the so-called 'essential facilities doctrine' to intellectual property rights[3]. A particular anxiety was that the precedent might be applied to intellectual property rights that were the consequence of substantial risk-taking and investment – for example patents and computer software – as opposed to a mere list of television programmes.

(iii)   The aftermath of Magill

It is now clear that the Magill case was an exceptional one; as a precedent it has a narrow application. There is little doubt that the Commission and the Community Courts were influenced in Magill by the fact that information as prosaic as TV listings was entitled to copyright protection: most systems of law in the Member States would not have conferred intellectual property protection at all in such circumstances. However this was not an explicit part of the reasoning in the Commission's decision or the Courts' judgments. To understand the case it is necessary to recall the judgments of the ECJ in *Oscar Bronner v Mediaprint*[4] and of the CFI in *Tiercé Ladbroke v Commission*[5] and in *European Night Services v Commission*[6], which were discussed in some detail in chapter 17[7]. These judgments adopt a restrictive approach to the essential facilities doctrine[8]. In particular the ECJ in *Oscar Bronner* stressed the exceptional circumstances in Magill; it referred to four factors in particular: the information sought by Magill was indispensable to the publication of a comprehensive listings guide; there was a demonstrable potential consumer demand for the would-be product; there were no objective justifications for the refusal to supply; and the refusal would eliminate all competition in the secondary market for TV guides[9].

20   Ibid, para 55.
1   Ibid, para 56.
2   For comment on the ECJ's judgment see eg Pombo 'Intellectual Property and Intra-Community Trade' [1996] Fordham Corporate Law Institute (ed Hawk), 491-505; Crowther 'Compulsory Licensing of Intellectual Property Rights' (1995) 20 ELR 521; Anderman *EC Competition Law and Intellectual Property Rights: The Regulation of Innovation* (Clarendon Press Oxford, 1998) paras 14.3.1-14.4.
3   See ch 17, pp 611-624; see generally Cotter 'Intellectual Property and the Essential Facilities Doctrine' (1999) 44 Antitrust Bulletin 211 on the question of whether intellectual property rights can be regarded as essential facilities.
4   Case C-7/97 [1998] ECR I-7791, [1999] 4 CMLR 112.
5   Case T-504/93 [1997] ECR II-923, [1997] 5 CMLR 309; on *Ladbroke* see Fitzgerald '*Magill* Revisited' (1998) 20 EIPR 154.
6   Cases T-374/94 etc [1998] ECR II-3141, [1998] 5 CMLR 718.
7   See ch 17, pp 618-620.
8   The courts in the UK have applied *Magill* narrowly to cases involving intellectual property: see eg *Philips Electronics NV v Ingman Ltd* [1998] Eu LR 666; *Sandvik Aktiebolag v Pfiffner (UK) Ltd* [1999] Eu LR 755; *HMSO v Automobile Association Ltd* [2001] Eu LR 80; for other cases in the UK raising Article 82 issues in relation to intellectual property rights, see *Pitney Bowes v Francotyp-Postalia* [1991] FSR 72; *Chiron Corpn v Murex Diagnostics Ltd (No 2) Organon* [1994] 1 CMLR 410, CA; *Phonographic Performance Ltd v Grosvenor Leisure* [1984] FSR 24.
9   Perhaps the fifth, unarticulated, exceptional factor was that a mere list of television programmes enjoyed copyright protection: see above.

Despite the narrow interpretation of *Magill* in subsequent case law, it is not entirely defunct. In March 2001 the Commission announced that it had sent a statement of objections to IMS Health, the world leader in data collection on pharmaceutical sales and prescriptions, as a result of its refusal to grant a licence to competitors to enable them to have access to its regional sales data[10].

(B) Collecting societies

Article 82 may be applied to the activities of collecting societies. Article 82 has been invoked both by the Commission[11] and in private law actions in domestic courts, several of which have reached the ECJ under Article 234 EC (ex Article 177)[12].

The ECJ has indicated that there is nothing intrinsically objectionable about the establishment of collecting societies, which may be necessary in order that individual artists can obtain a reasonable return for their endeavours[13]. However the activities of a society may amount to a breach of Article 82 in various ways. Of particular significance in Community terms will be the tendency of national societies to discriminate against undertakings from other Member States[14]. Other aspects of collecting societies' activities have been condemned, such as clauses in the constitution which unreasonably restrict an author's right to act unilaterally and provisions which are unreasonable vis-à-vis the media or which attempt to extend the protection of copyright to non-copyrighted works[15]. In *Basset v SACEM*[16] the ECJ was asked whether SACEM was entitled to charge a 1.65% 'supplementary mechanical reproduction fee' above its normal royalty for performances at discotheques, on juke-boxes and radios, where the recordings in question were imported from other Member States in which no such fee was payable. The ECJ held that the extra charge was not in principle contrary to Articles 28, 30 and 82, as it amounted to a normal exploitation of copyright and was not an act of arbitrary discrimination nor a disguised restriction on inter-Member State trade.

---

10 Commission Press Release IP/01/365, 14 March 2001.
11 *GEMA* JO [1971] L 134/15, [1971] CMLR D35; *Interpar v GVL GmbH* OJ [1981] L 370/49, [1982] 1 CMLR 221; *GEMA Statutes* OJ [1982] L 94/12, [1982] 2 CMLR 482; *BIEM-FPI* XIIIth *Report on Competition Policy* (1983), points 147–150; *GEMA* XVth *Report on Competition Policy* (1985), point 81; *GVL* OJ [1981] L 370/49, upheld on appeal to the ECJ Case 7/82 *GVL v Commission* [1983] ECR 483, [1983] 3 CMLR 645; the Commission's decision not to proceed with complaints against SACEM, a French collecting society, was unsuccessfully challenged in Case T-114/92 *BEMIM v Commission* [1995] ECR II-147, [1996] 4 CMLR 305 and in Case T-5/93 *Roger Tremblay v Commission* [1995] ECR II-185, [1996] 4 CMLR 305, on appeal to the ECJ Case C-91/95 P [1996] ECR I-5547, [1997] 4 CMLR 211; for comment see Torremans and Stamatoudi 'Collecting Societies: Sorry, the Community is No Longer Interested!' (1997) 2 ELRev 352.
12 Case 127/73 *Belgische Radio en Televisie v SABAM* [1974] ECR 313, [1974] 2 CMLR 238; Case 22/79 *Greenwich Film Production v SACEM* [1979] ECR 3275, [1980] 1 CMLR 629; Case 402/85 *Basset v SACEM* [1987] ECR 1747, [1987] 3 CMLR 173; Case 395/87 *Ministère Public v Tournier* [1989] ECR 2521, [1991] 4 CMLR 248; Case 110/88 *Lucazeau v SACEM* [1989] ECR 2811, [1991] 4 CMLR 248.
13 See Case 127/73 *BRT v SABAM* [1974] ECR 313, [1974] 2 CMLR 238, paras 8–15.
14 *Re GEMA* JO [1971] L 134/15, [1971] CMLR D35; Case 7/82 *GVL v Commission* [1983] ECR 483, [1983] 3 CMLR 645.
15 The most thorough decision on these issues remains the Commission's decision in *Re GEMA* JO [1971] L 134/15, [1971] 1 CMLR D35.
16 Case 402/85 [1987] ECR 1747, [1987] 3 CMLR 173.

(C) Miscellaneous cases

In *Tetra Pak Rausing v Commission*[17] the CFI upheld the Commission's decision[18] that it was an abuse of Tetra Pak's dominant position in the market for cartons and machines for packaging milk to take over Liquipak and thereby acquire an exclusive licence relating to technology for a new method of sterilising cartons suitable for long-life milk. This finding was despite the fact that the licence complied with the provisions of the block exemption on patent licensing agreements[19]. It was interesting that the Commission chose to attack the acquisition of the licence rather than the merger itself, as it could have done at that time under Article 82[20]. There is no reason to suppose that the principle in the case would apply only to the acquisition of a licence rather than to a direct assignment, but the further issue is how far it could be applied to other ways in which a dominant undertaking acquires intellectual property rights, such as taking over a company with a strong R&D department. It should be noted that in *Tetra Pak Rausing* the undertaking already had a substantial technological lead over its competitors and that the licence related to a very significant development. The offence was to harm the competitive structure of the market[1].

In *Eurofix-Bauco v Hilti*[2] the Commission held that it was an abuse to demand an 'excessive' royalty with the sole object of blocking, or at any rate unreasonably delaying, a licence of right which was available under UK patent law. This was seen as part of Hilti's strategy of preventing competition in respect of its nail cartridges. In *BBI/Boosey and Hawkes: Interim Measures*[3] the Commission seems to have regarded it as an aspect of Boosey and Hawkes' abusive behaviour to have brought vexatious litigation against an undertaking for 'slavish imitation' of its products[4]. On one occasion the Commission intimated that it might be an abuse for a firm in a dominant position to register a trade mark knowing that a competitor already uses that mark[5]. In *Chiquita/Fyffes plc*[6] the Commission took the view that an agreement between Chiquita and Fyffes whereby Fyffes agreed not to use the Fyffes trade mark in continental Europe for a period of 20 years infringed both Articles 81 and 82. The Article 82 infringement lay in the fact that the inability of Fyffes to use that mark diminished its ability to compete vigorously with Chiquita in Europe. Following the Commission's intervention, Chiquita abandoned the agreement.

In the case of *Swedish Match Sverige AB/Skandinavisk Tobakskompagni A/S*[7] the Commission required substantial alterations to the relationship between two cigarette producers in Sweden and Denmark which it considered to amount to an abuse of a dominant position contrary to Article 82. Swedish Match, which was dominant in the Swedish cigarette market, had an exclusive licence to

---

17 Case T–51/89 [1990] ECR II-309, [1991] 4 CMLR 334.
18 *Tetra Pak I (BTG Licence)* OJ [1988] L 272/27, [1990] 4 CMLR 47.
19 See ch 4, pp 133-134.
20 See ch 21; mergers are now controlled primarily under Regulation 4064/89, although Article 82 may have some continuing vitality: ibid, pp 737-738 amd 757-758.
1   See ch 5, pp 175-176 .
2   OJ [1988] L 65/19, [1989] 4 CMLR 677, para 78, upheld on appeal Case T–30/89 *Hilti AG v Commission* [1991] ECR II-163, [1992] 4 CMLR 16, para 99; see also *Dvales System Deutschland*: fee payable for use of trademark an abuse of a dominant position (Competition Policy Newsletter, June 2001, pp 27-29).
3   OJ [1987] L 286/36, [1988] 4 CMLR 67, para 19.
4   See ch 18, p 625; on vexatious litigation see further ch 5, p 179.
5   *Osram/Airam*, XIth *Report on Competition Policy* (1981), point 97.
6   XXIInd *Report on Competition Policy* (1992), points 168-176.
7   See the Commission's XXVIIth *Report on Competition Policy* (1997), points 138-139.

manufacture and distribute the Danish company's Prince brand there; it had a strong position on the Swedish market, and Swedish Match was responsible for setting prices and brand management. The Commission permitted Swedish Match to continue to manufacture in Sweden and to take responsibility for the physical distribution of cigarettes; however Skandinavisk Tobakskompagni became solely responsible for sales, marketing and pricing of the Prince brand; by giving it control of the brand, while allowing it to take advantage of Swedish Match's manufacturing and distribution infrastructure, the Commission considered that effective competition would be introduced to the Swedish market.

7. INTELLECTUAL PROPERTY RIGHTS AND THE FREE MOVEMENT PROVISIONS OF THE TREATY OF ROME

The single market imperative has been emphasised throughout this book, and the application of Article 81(1) to territorial exclusivity in licence agreements was discussed earlier in this chapter[8]. The competition rules do not address all the situations in which national intellectual property rights can be used to reinforce national boundaries within the Community. The owner of an intellectual property right may be able, under national law, to prevent imports into one country of products that it has put onto the market in another one. This is not necessarily the case: national law may provide for so-called 'exhaustion' of the right in question, meaning that if the owner of the intellectual property right consented to the sale of its products – in whichever territory they were marketed – it thereby loses the right of further controlling their movement[9].

Where a national law does not contain a doctrine of exhaustion, the potential for hindrance to intra-Community trade is obvious. In a remarkable series of judgments beginning in the 1970s the ECJ developed a doctrine of exhaustion of intellectual property rights under Community law, in the interest of the overriding goal of single market integration. In doing so it relied on Article 28 EC (ex Article 30), which provides that 'quantitative restrictions on imports and all measures having equivalent effect shall ... be prohibited between Member States'; and on Article 30 EC (ex Article 36) which states that prohibitions and restrictions on the free movement of goods 'shall not, however, constitute a means of arbitrary discrimination or a disguised restriction on trade between Member States'[10]. The utility of these Articles had been thought to be limited, first, because Article 30 provides that the rules on the free movement of goods should not prejudice 'the protection of industrial and commercial property'; and second because of Article 295 (ex Article 222) which provides that the Treaty 'shall in no way prejudice the rules in Member States governing the system of property ownership'.

This section will describe briefly the Community doctrine of exhaustion. Although this is not competition law as such, it is necessary to understand what is meant by exhaustion since it is a relevant factor in determining how much territorial protection can be given to licensees of intellectual property rights. An export ban in a licence would normally be contrary to Article 81(1)[11]; however it would be possible to achieve exactly the same effect by assigning or licensing

---

8   See pp 681-688 above.
9   It is thought that the first application of the exhaustion principle occurred in the US Supreme Court judgment in *Adams v Burke* 84 US 453 (1873).
10 It has subsequently read a similar proviso into the Articles on free movement of services: see p 707 below.
11 See p 681ff above.

intellectual property rights to a licensee, enabling it to prevent parallel imports. Community law is opposed to absolute territorial protection, which is permitted only in exceptional circumstances. It is important to appreciate that the rules on the free movement of goods (and services) have a rôle to play in preventing absolute territorial protection as well as the competition rules. This chapter will also consider briefly some related case law on repackaging[12], on the position where a particular product has different trade marks in different Member States[13], and on the doctrine of 'common origin'[14]; all of this case law has implications for parallel imports within the Community.

(A) The doctrine of exhaustion[15]

This doctrine can be traced back to the ECJ's judgment in *Consten and Grundig v Commission*[16] where it indicated that a distinction could be drawn between a normal trade mark agreement, which would not fall within Article 81(1), and an agreement which amounted to an improper exercise of the trade mark. In *Parke, Davis & Co v Probel*[17] the ECJ intimated that a similar distinction might be drawn when considering the application of Articles 28 and 30 to intellectual property rights.

This possibility turned to reality in *Deutsche Grammophon GmbH v Metro-SB-Grossmarkte GmbH & Co KG*[18]. Deutsche Grammophon produced and sold records in Germany under the Polydor label. Metro obtained cheaper supplies of the same records in France, where they were sold by a subsidiary of Deutsche Grammophon. When Metro attempted to import them into Germany, Deutsche Grammophon claimed that this was an infringement of its rights under the German Copyright Act. A German court asked the ECJ to indicate whether the EC Treaty might affect the situation. The ECJ held that the derogation from the free movement of goods provisions afforded to industrial and commercial property was limited; in particular Article 30 permitted restrictions on the free movement of products only 'to the extent to which they are justified for the purpose of safeguarding rights which constitute the specific subject-matter of such property'[19]. Article 28 protected the existence but not the improper exercise of intellectual property rights[20]. Whether one approves of this distinction or not, it is too deeply rooted in the ECJ's jurisprudence now to be eradicated[1]. The ECJ held that it would be incompatible with the Treaty for Deutsche Grammophon, which had

12 See p 711 below.
13 See p 712 below.
14 See pp 712-714 below.
15 See further Tritton *Intellectual Property in Europe* (Sweet & Maxwell, 1996) ch 7; Govaere *The Use and Abuse of Intellectual Property Rights in EC Law* (Sweet & Maxwell, 1996) ch 4; Anderman *EC Competition Law and Intellectual Property Rights: The Regulation of Innovation* (Clarendon Press Oxford, 1998) ch 2.
16 Cases 56/84 and 58/84 [1966] ECR 299, [1966] CMLR 418.
17 Case 24/67 [1968] ECR 55, [1968] CMLR 47.
18 Case 78/70 [1971] ECR 487, [1971] CMLR 631.
19 Ibid, para 11.
20 Ibid.
1   It has often been pointed out that the distinction between the existence and the exercise of an intellectual property right is a tenuous one, since the way in which a property right is exercised is the practical expression of its existence: see eg Korah 'Dividing the Common Market through National Industrial Property Rights' (1972) 35 MLR 634 at 636 and Joliet 'Patented Articles and the Free Movement of Goods within the EEC' (1975) 28 Current Legal Problems 15 at 23–24.

consented to the marketing of the records in France, to rely upon its rights under German law to prevent their importation into Germany. By permitting the records to be sold abroad, it had exhausted its rights in respect of them so that its action must fail. The ECJ proceeded to apply its approach in *Deutsche Grammophon* in a series of important judgments.

(i) Patents

In *Centrafarm BV v Sterling Drug*[2] Centrafarm purchased a drug called Negram in the UK where prices were controlled by Government regulation and exported it to the Netherlands where prices were higher. Sterling Drug, which held the patents for the drug in both countries, brought an action against Centrafarm to prevent it from selling in the Netherlands. The Dutch Court referred various questions to the ECJ, including the compatibility of Sterling's rights with Articles 28 and 30. The ECJ repeated its position in *Deutsche Grammophon*, that Article 30 permitted derogations from the free movement of goods provision only to the extent necessary to protect the 'specific subject-matter' of any given intellectual property right. It then laid down its view of the specific subject-matter of a patent, which was:

> 'the exclusive right to use an invention with a view to manufacturing industrial products and putting them into circulation for the first time, either directly or by the grant of licences to third parties, as well as the right to oppose infringements'.

It also said that the *function* of patents (as opposed to their specific subject-matter) was to reward the creative effort of the inventor. The ECJ went on to say that it might be legitimate to invoke a patent right to prevent imports of a product from a Member State where it was not patentable and had been produced by a third party without the patentee's consent, or where separate patents existed for the same goods owned by separate undertakings. However a derogation from the free movement of goods provisions was not justified 'where the product has been put onto the market in a legal manner, by the patentee itself or with its consent, in the Member State from which it has been imported, in particular in the case of a proprietor of parallel patents'[3]. This meant that Sterling could not rely on its Dutch patent because the drug had been marketed in the UK with its consent by its licensee, a subsidiary company[4].

The effect of this judgment was that the patentee was entitled to earn a monopoly profit at the point at which the drugs were first put onto the market, but that after having done so it lost any right to control their further movement. The ECJ expressly stated that it was irrelevant that UK prices were low as a result of Government price control[5], although this obviously affected the profits

2 Case 15/74 [1974] ECR 1147, [1974] 2 CMLR 480; the case should be read in conjunction with Case 16/74 *Centrafarm BV v Winthrop BV* [1974] ECR 1183, [1974] 2 CMLR 480 which dealt with the position of trade marks (see p 708 below).
3 Case 15/74 [1974] ECR 1147, [1974] 2 CMLR 480, para 11.
4 Since Article 81(1) does not apply to an agreement between a parent and a subsidiary (see ch 3, pp 72-74) it was not possible to concluded that there was an agreement to divide markets contrary to the competition rules.
5 Case 15/74 [1974] ECR 1147, [1974] 2 CMLR 480, paras 22–25.

that Sterling could earn in the UK and – given the exhaustion principle – in the Netherlands. The ECJ also held that Sterling was not entitled to prevent parallel imports on grounds of quality control[6].

Where a parallel importer obtains goods in a Member State where the product is not patentable at all a patentee can prevent parallel imports from that territory if the goods were marketed there by a third party without its consent[7]. If however they were put into circulation with its consent it will have exhausted its rights and will be unable to restrict imports, notwithstanding that it had no opportunity to earn a monopoly profit in the Member State where it had no patent protection[8]; if the patentee chooses to sell or to allow sale where the product is unpatentable it must accept the consequences under Articles 28 and 30. Where goods are produced in a Member State in which a compulsory licence has been awarded because of the failure by the patentee to exploit its patent, there is no consent, and therefore no exhaustion, on the latter's part; this was decided by the ECJ in *Pharmon v Hoechst*[9]. There is no exhaustion where goods are marketed in a third country and then imported into the EC[10].

(ii) Copyright and analogous rights

The ECJ has applied the exhaustion principle to cases relating to 'non-performance' copyrights; 'performance' copyrights have been treated differently[11]. The right relied upon (unsuccessfully) to prevent parallel imports in *Deutsche Grammophon*[12] was analogous to copyright. In *Musik-Vertrieb Membran GmbH v GEMA*[13] the ECJ held that copyright in artistic works is within the term industrial and commercial property in Article 30 and is subject to the exhaustion doctrine, so that GEMA could not rely on its German rights to prevent parallel imports of records from the UK which had been put on the market there with its consent. The ECJ held that it was irrelevant that statute in the UK imposed a fixed royalty rate of 6¼% whereas GEMA in Germany charged 8½%. This difference would obviously affect GEMA's right to earn the profit it would have expected under German law. In *Dansk Supermarked A/S v Imerco A/S*[14] the ECJ held that the doctrine of exhaustion applied to the reproduction of goods from a copyright

---

6 Ibid, paras 26–30.
7 Case 24/67 *Parke, Davis & Co v Probel* [1968] ECR 55, [1968] CMLR 47.
8 See Case 187/80 *Merck & Co Inc v Stephar BV* [1981] ECR 2063, [1981] 3 CMLR 463; Cases C-267/95 and C-268/95 *Merck v Primecrown* [1996] ECR I-6285, [1997] 1 CMLR 83; the Opinion of Advocate General Fennelly in the latter case is of interest as he advised the ECJ that it should depart from the precedent in *Merck v Stephar* and allow Merck to prevent the parallel imports: the Court declined to do so; see further on *Merck v Primecrown* Reindle 'Intellectual Property and Intra-Community Trade' [1996] Fordham Corporate Law Institute (ed Hawk), pp 453-466; Kon and Schaeffer 'Parallel Imports of Pharmaceutical Products: A New Realism, or Back to Basics?' (1997) 18 ECLR 123, pp 132-139; Korah '*Merck v Primecrown*: The Exhaustion of Patents by Sale in a Member State Where a Monopoly Profit Could Not Be Earned' (1997) 18 ECLR 265.
9 Case 19/84 [1985] ECR 2281, [1985] 3 CMLR 775.
10 *Re Patented Bandaging Material* [1988] 2 CMLR 359 (Oberlandsgerichtshof); see further pp 709-710 below on the *Silhouette* judgment in relation to the international exhaustion of trade marks.
11 See p 707 below.
12 Case 78/70 [1971] ECR 487, [1971] CMLR 631.
13 Cases 55/80 and 57/80 [1981] ECR 147, [1981] 2 CMLR 44.
14 Case 58/80 [1981] ECR 181, [1981] 3 CMLR 590.

pattern and in *Keurkoop BV v Nancy Kean Gifts BV*[15] it confirmed that it could apply to industrial designs.

In *Warner Bros and Metronome Video v Christiansen*[16] video cassettes were sold by the copyright owner in the UK. At the time there was no right under UK copyright law to receive a royalty when the cassettes were hired out rather than sold; there was such a right in Denmark. A parallel importer bought copies of video cassettes in the UK and offered them for hire in Denmark. The ECJ was asked by the Danish court whether Warner Brothers, which had freely put the video on the market in the UK, could restrain parallel imports into Denmark which would undermine its rental rights there. The ECJ concluded that this was possible, even though there had been consent to the marketing in the UK: Warner was entitled to protect its lending rights in Denmark. The point arose again in *Metronome Musik GmbH v Musik Point Hokamp GmbH*[17], where a German court referred a similar issue to the ECJ in relation to the interpretation of the Directive on Rental Rights of 1992[18]. Hokamp argued that the Directive, by providing for an exclusive rental right, was itself contrary to Community law. The ECJ, relying on the *Warner Brothers* judgment, held that a law which provides specific protection of the right to hire out video-cassettes is clearly justified on grounds of the protection of industrial and commercial property pursuant to Article 30, and that such a law does not involve a breach of the principle of exhaustion of the distribution right.

In *Coditel SA v Ciné Vog Films*[19] the ECJ was asked to consider the compatibility of copyright in a film with the free movement provisions of the Treaty. Ciné Vog Films was the exclusive licensee in Belgium of the copyright in a French film. It brought an action to prevent a cable company, which had picked up a transmission of the film in Germany, from showing it in Belgium. According to the exhaustion principle the right could be said to have been exhausted, since the film had been shown in Germany with the copyright owner's consent. However the ECJ drew a distinction between cases which concerned the free circulation of goods, which would include artistic works such as books and records, and cases where the essence of the right was to control a series of performances. Films would obviously come into the latter category. The matter was not to be dealt with under Articles 28 and 30 on goods but rather under Articles 49 to 55 (ex Articles 59 to 66) which deal with the free movement of services. The ECJ held that an exhaustion principle also applied under these provisions, but that in certain situations a licensee could prevent transmission of broadcasts, even along national lines.

In *Micro Leader Business v Commission*[20] the CFI ruled that the marketing of Microsoft software in Canada would not exhaust its copyright in the EC: that would happen only if the software was put on the market in the Community with Microsoft's consent[1].

---

15 Case 144/81 [1982] ECR 2853, [1983] 2 CMLR 47.
16 Case 158/86 [1988] ECR 2605, [1990] 3 CMLR 684; see Defalque 'Copyright – Free Movement of Goods and Territoriality: Recent Developments' (1989) 11 EIPR 435.
17 Case C-200/96 [1998] ECR I-1953, [1998] 3 CMLR 919; see also Case C-61/97 *FDV acting for Egmont Films A/S v Laserdisken* [1998] ECR I-5171.
18 Council Directive 92/100, OJ [1992] L 346/1.
19 Case 62/79 [1980] ECR 881, [1981] 2 CMLR 362.
20 Case T-198/98 [1999] ECR II-3989, [2000] 4 CMLR 886.
1 Ibid, para 34.

(iii)   Trade marks[2]

In *Centrafarm BV v Winthrop BV*[3] the ECJ applied the exhaustion principle to trade marks. It said that the specific subject-matter of a trade mark is 'the guarantee that the owner of the trade mark has the exclusive right to use that trademark, for the purposes of putting products protected by the mark into circulation for the first time'. The ECJ held that Winthrop, a Dutch subsidiary of Sterling Drug, could not exercise its rights under its Dutch trade mark to prevent the import of drugs from the UK which had been marketed there by another company in the same group; in doing so the trade mark right had been exhausted. The principle of exhaustion has been incorporated in Article 7(1) of the Trade Mark Directive, which provides that:

> 'The trade mark shall not entitle the proprietor to prohibit its use in relation to goods which have been put on the market in the Community under that trade mark by the proprietor or with his consent'.

Article 7(2) provides an exception:

> 'where there exist legitimate reasons for the proprietor to oppose further commercialisation of the goods, especially where the condition of the goods is changed or impaired after they have been put on the market'[4].

In *Parfums Christian Dior SA v Evora BV*[5] the ECJ held that, if the right to put the goods on to the market had been exhausted, a parallel importer should also be able to make free use of the trade mark in order to bring to the public's attention the further commercialisation of those goods[6].

(iv)   Unfair competition

There are provisions in the domestic law of some Member States that enable producers to prevent unfair competition, for example where a rival has appropriated an idea belonging to someone else or has slavishly copied its goods. Even if the rights conferred by such laws do not qualify as intellectual property rights, their use would infringe Article 28 where they are necessary for the protection of consumers and for the fairness of commercial transactions[7]. It appears that an exhaustion principle exists in such cases, so that it would not be possible for a producer to prevent parallel imports from a Member State of goods which had been marketed there with the producer's consent[8].

---

2   See Walsh, Treacy and Feaster 'The Exhaustion and Unauthorised Exploitation of Trade Mark Rights in the European Union' (1999) 24 ELRev 259.
3   Case 16/74 [1974] ECR 1183, [1974] 2 CMLR 480, para 8.
4   See Urlesberger '"Legitimate Reasons" for the Proprietor of a Trade Mark to Oppose Further Dealings' (1999) 36 CML Rev 1195.
5   Case C-337/95 [1997] ECR I-6013, [1998] 1 CMLR 737.
6   Ibid, paras 32-38.
7   Case 6/81 *Industrie Diensten Groep v JA Beele Handelmaatschappij BV* [1982] ECR 707, [1982] 3 CMLR 102.
8   Ibid.

(v)   International exhaustion

An issue of considerable importance that has attracted much attention in recent years is whether the exhaustion of rights doctrine ought, as a matter of Community law, to extend to products voluntarily put onto the market outside the EC (or the EEA)[9]. Parallel importers may be able to buy cheap branded goods in a third country and try to import them into the Community. The question is whether a trade mark owner within the Community can bring an action under domestic law to prevent such imports, or whether Community law should extend the principles discussed in this section to sales by consent on markets outside the Community. From the consumer's point of view international exhaustion might lead to lower prices, perhaps considerably so.

(A)   THE *SILHOUETTE* CASE.   The issue came before the ECJ in *Silhouette International Schmied GmbH v Hartlauer Handelsgesellschaft mbH*[10]. Silhouette brought a trade mark action to prevent parallel imports into Austria of spectacle frames that it had sold in Bulgaria; the frames in question were by now 'out-of-fashion' in Austria. Under Austrian trade mark law Silhouette had exhausted its rights by placing them on the market voluntarily; Austrian law did not distinguish between sales within the Community and sales in third countries. Silhouette specifically told the buyer in Bulgaria that the frames were to be sold only in Bulgaria and the former USSR, but not elsewhere; however they were sold to Hartlauer, which offered them for sale in Austria. The ECJ was asked to consider whether Community law, in the form of Article 7(1) of the Trade Mark Directive[11], precluded national laws form providing for exhaustion in respect of products put on the market outside the Community. The ECJ, following the Opinion of Advocate General Jacobs, held that the purpose of the Directive was to harmonise national systems of trade mark law in order to promote the functioning of the single market. This would be impeded if individual Member States had a choice, exercisable independently, of determining whether there was an international exhaustion[12]; it followed that national rules providing for international exhaustion were contrary to Article 7(1)[13]. The judgment does not say how the Austrian court should proceed in these circumstances: obviously it could not apply the

9   There is no international agreement on exhaustion of rights; Article 6 of the GATT Agreement on Trade-Related Aspects of Intellectual Property Rights (the 'TRIPS Agreement') specifically leaves the issue of international exhaustion open.
10   Case C-355/96 [1998] ECR I-4799, [1998] 2 CMLR 953; for comment on *Silhouette* see Abbott and Feer Verkade 'The Silhouette of a Trojan Horse: Reflections on Advocate General Jacob's Opinion in *Silhouette v Hartlauer*' [1998] JBL 413; Carboni 'Cases About Spectacles and Torches: Now Can We See The Light?' (1998) 20 EIPR 472; Hays and Hansen '*Silhouette* Is Not the Proper Case to Decide the Parallel Importation Question' (1998) 20 EIPR 277; White 'Sunglasses: A Benefit to Health?' (1999) 21 EIPR 176; Kuilwijk 'Parallel Imports and WTO Law: Some Thoughts After *Silhouette*' (1999) 20 ECLR 292; Alexander 'Exhaustion of Trade Mark Rights in the European Economic Area' (1999) 24 ELRev 56; Gippini-Fournier (1999) 36 CML Rev 807; Norman 'Parallel Imports from Non-EEA Member States: The Vision Remains Unclear' (2000) 22 EIPR 159; Jones 'Does an Opportunity Still Exist for the Development of a Doctrine of International Exhaustion at a Community Level under Articles 28 and 30?' ibid, 171; see also Case C-352/95 *Phytheron International v Jean Bourdon* [1997] ECR I-1729; in *Mag Instrument v California Trading Co Norway* EFTA Court of Justice, E-2/97 [1998] 1 CMLR 331 the EFTA Court reached the conclusion that the EEA Agreement does provide for international exhaustion.
11   Council Directive 89/104, OJ [1989] L 40/1; see also Article 13 of the Community Trade Mark Regulation, OJ [1994] L 11/1.
12   Case C-355/96 [1998] ECR I-4799, [1998] 2 CMLR 953, paras 23-27.
13   Ibid, para 31.

Austrian rule of exhaustion, but nor does it say that the rule of non-exhaustion is directly effective so as to give Silhouette rights against Hartlauer.

Reactions to *Silhouette* were mixed: brand owners were naturally delighted that the ECJ had not adopted a rule of international exhaustion; parallel importers and consumer associations were outraged that the ECJ had apparently acted to the detriment of consumers by allowing cheap imports to be excluded from the Community.

(B)   THE *SEBAGO* CASE.   In *Sebago Inc v GB-Unic SA*[14] Sebago brought an action to prevent the parallel import of shoes imported from El Salvador. In an attempt to distinguish *Silhouette* GB-Unic argued that, since Sebago had put identical shoes on the market within the Community, it had exhausted its rights in relation to all such shoes, wherever they were marketed. The ECJ held that Article 7(1) of the Trade Mark Directive should be interpreted to the effect that the rights conferred by the trade mark are exhausted only if the products have been put on the market in the Community, and that such consent must relate to each individual item of the product in respect of which exhaustion is pleaded. The CFI applied *Silhouette* in a case concerned with Article 4(c) of the Directive on copyright harmonisation[15].

(C)   THE *DAVIDOFF* CASE.   In *Zino Davidoff SA v A & G Imports Ltd*[16] toiletries and cosmetic products that Davidoff had put on the market outside the Community were imported into the UK; the code numbers that would have indicated where the products were first marketed had been obliterated. Davidoff applied for summary judgment to prevent the parallel imports, arguing that it had not exhausted its trade mark rights by selling outside the Community, and that the obliteration of the code numbers would provide a good defence under Article 7(2) of the Trade Mark Directive even if it had given its consent. Laddie J interpreted the *Silhouette* judgment narrowly: in his view the ECJ was saying that the effect of the Trade Mark Directive was that a Member State cannot *impose* international exhaustion upon a trade mark owner; however if the proprietor of a trade mark agrees, either expressly or otherwise, to allow the entry of goods marketed in a third country into the Community, he cannot then use the trade mark to prevent this from happening. All the surrounding circumstances must be analysed to determine whether there was such agreement and in Laddie J's view Davidoff had so agreed. He also concluded that the obliteration of the codes did not provide a defence under Article 7(2) of the Directive. This was an important judgment indicating that it might be possible to avoid the apparent logic of *Silhouette* with the result that parallel imports form third countries might be allowed. The case was referred to the ECJ[17].

14   Case C-173/98 [1999] ECR I-4103, [1999] 2 CMLR 1317.
15   Case T-198/98 *Micro Leader Business v Commission* [1999] ECR II-3989, [2000] 4 CMLR 886, para 34.
16   [1999] 3 All ER 711, [1999] 2 CMLR 1056, see Carboni 'Zino Davidoff SA v A & G *Imports Ltd*: A Way Around *Silhouette*' (1999) EIPR 524; Hays 'The Burden of Proof in Parallel Import Cases' (2000) 22 EIPR 353; see also, on two Scottish judgments not following *Davidoff,* Swift '*Davidoff*: Scottish Court declines to follow English Ruling on Parallel Imports' (2000) 22 EIPR 376.
17   Case C-414/99 *Zino Davidoff SA v A & G Imports Ltd*; see also Cases C-415/99 and C-416/99 *Levi Strauss & Co v Tesco Stores* (judgment pending; the Opinion of Advocate General Stix-Hackl was given on 5 April 2001).

(D) INTERNATIONAL EXHAUSTION AND THE COMPETITION RULES. Notwithstanding the judgment in *Silhouette* on international exhaustion, it is important to recall the judgment of the ECJ in *Javico v Yves Saint Laurent*[18], which held that the enforcement of an export ban in a distribution agreement with a non-EU distributor restricting sales into the Community might be found to infringe Article 81(1)[19].

(B) Repackaging

Several cases have arisen where a parallel importer has obtained goods in one Member State and repackaged them in order to be able to sell them in another Member State. Such repackaging may be necessary, for example, where drugs must be sold in different sized packages from one Member State to another. The trade mark owner in such a case can argue that, even if it has exhausted its trade mark in relation to the goods in their original packaging, it has not done so in relation to the repackaged goods. On the other hand, the parallel importer can argue that the goods were put into circulation with the consent of the trade mark owner, so that it should not be able to impede their subsequent free circulation within the Community, notwithstanding the repackaging.

The matter came before the ECJ in *Hoffmann-la Roche v Centrafarm*[20]. Hoffmann-la Roche brought an action for infringement of its German trade mark when Centrafarm obtained drugs in the UK which it then repackaged (to comply with German packing requirements) before selling them there. Hoffmann-la Roche argued that it was legitimate in these circumstances to rely on its trade mark, since it had not applied the mark to the repackaged goods. The ECJ said that artifical partitioning of the market would not be allowed; it said that derogations from the rules on free movement of goods were justified only for the purpose of safeguarding rights which constitute the specific subject-matter of the trade mark; in determining this subject-matter regard must be had to the essential function of a trade mark, which is to guarantee the identity of the origin of the trade-marked product to the consumer or ultimate user. The ECJ held that, on the facts of that case, the parallel importer would be entitled to repackage the goods provided that the repackaging had no adverse effect on the original condition of the goods in question, that it should be stated that they had been repackaged and that the trade mark owner was notified of this fact[1].

---

18 Case C-306/96 [1998] ECR I-1983, [1998] 5 CMLR 172.
19 See ch 3, p 119.
20 Case 102/77 [1978] ECR 1139, [1978] 3 CMLR 217; the ECJ has since had to consider a number of subsequent cases on repackaging involving a range of different facts: see Case 1/81 *Pfizer Inc v Eurim-Pharm GmbH* [1981] ECR 2913, [1982] 1 CMLR 406; Cases C-71/94 etc *Eurim-Pharm Arzneimittel GmbH v Beiersdorf AG* [1996] ECR I-3603, [1997] 1 CMLR 1222; Cases C-427/93 etc *Bristol-Myers Squibb v Paranova A/S* [1996] ECR I-3457, [1997] 1 CMLR 1151; Cases C-232/94 *MPA Pharma v Rhône-Poulenc* [1997] ECR I-3671: on these three sets of proceedings see Kon and Schaeffer (p 706, n 8 above), pp 142-144; Seville (1997) 34 CML Rev 1039; Case C-349/95 *Loendersloot v Ballantine* [1997] ECR I-6227: see Clark 'Trade Marks and the Relabelling of Goods in the Single Market: Anti-counterfeiting Implications of *Loendersloot v Ballantine*' (1998) 20 EIPR 328; Case C-379/97 *Pharmacia and Upjohn v Paranova A/S* [1999] ECR I-6927, [2000] 1 CMLR 51: see Forrester 'The Repackaging of Trade Marked Pharmaceuticals in Europe: Recent Developments' (2000) 22 EIPR 512; in the UK courts see *Glaxo Group v Dowelhurst* [2000] 2 CMLR 571 (Patents Court).
1 When the case subsequently reached the German Supreme Court it was held that as there was no artificial partitioning of the market, Hoffmann-la Roche could rely on its trade mark: *Hoffmann-la Roche & Co AG v Centrafarm Vertriebsgesellschaft Pharmazeutischer Erzeugnisse mbH* [1984] 2 CMLR 561.

(C)   Products having different trade marks in different Member States

In *Centrafarm BV v American Home Products Corpn*[2] Centrafarm bought drugs marked 'Serenid' in the UK but sold them under the mark 'Seresta' in Holland. Each mark was owned by American Home Products. The question was whether Centrafarm could be prevented from applying the Seresta mark to the goods for sale in Holland. Normal principles of exhaustion could not determine this issue. The ECJ ruled that American Home Products could not rely on its Dutch trade mark to prevent parallel imports if it could be shown to be using several trade marks for an identical product in order to split up the common market artificially, thus causing a disguised restriction on trade between Member States.

(D)   The doctrine of common origin

Where identical (or, in the case of trade marks, confusingly similar) intellectual property rights are owned by different parties in different Member States the ECJ has accepted that the resulting barriers to trade are a natural consequence of the very existence of national rights[3]. However the position may be different where the rights were originally in common ownership.

If the ownership of the rights was split up by an assignment, that assignment may be caught as an agreement or concerted practice contrary to Article 81(1). In *Sirena Srl v Eda Srl*[4] the German and Italian trade marks 'Prep' had been separately assigned to different owners in 1937. When the Italian owner relied upon its trade mark in an infringement action, the ECJ indicated that the completed assignments in 1937 could qualify as agreements within the terms of Article 81(1) where their effect was to partition national markets. It resiled from this extreme view in *EMI Records Ltd v CBS UK Ltd*[5] where the relevant assignments had taken place in 1917. Here it indicated that for Article 81(1) to apply there would have to be some evidence of a continuing relationship between the parties from which an agreement or a concerted practice could be inferred.

Between 1974 and 1990 these problems over assignments were in abeyance, at least as far as trade marks were concerned, because of the 'common origin' doctrine which was established by the ECJ in *Van Zuylen Frères v Hag AG*, now known as *Hag I*[6]. A German company, Hag AG, owned the trade mark 'Hag' in Germany, Belgium and Luxembourg. After the second world war Hag's Belgian property was sequestrated and its trade mark assigned to Van Zuylen. The question for the ECJ was whether Van Zuylen could prevent Hag AG from importing coffee into Belgium. There was no agreement between the companies which could be attacked under Article 81, nor could meaningful use be made of exhaustion principles; it would make no sense to say that the coffee was sold in Belgium with Van Zuylen's consent. However the ECJ held that:

2   Case 3/78 [1978] ECR 1823, [1979] 1 CMLR 326; see also Case C-379/97 *Pharmacia and Upjohn v Paranova A/S* [1999] ECR I-6927, [2000] 1 CMLR 51.
3   See eg Case 119/75 *Terrapin (Overseas) Ltd v Terranova Industrie CA Kapferer & Co* [1976] ECR 1039, [1976] 2 CMLR 482.
4   Case 40/70 [1971] ECR 69, [1971] CMLR 260.
5   Case 51/75 [1976] ECR 811, [1976] 2 CMLR 235; see also *Warner-Lambert/Gillette* OJ [1993] L 116/21, paras 33–39: the geographical separation of marks between the Community and neighbouring markets held to infringe Article 81(1).
6   Case 192/73 [1974] ECR 731, [1974] 2 CMLR 127; but note that the common origin principle did not apply to *EMI v CBS* because the case concerned the importation of goods from outside the Community and not from one Member State to another.

'one cannot allow the holder of a trade mark to rely upon the exclusiveness of a trade mark right – which may have the consequence of the territorial limitation of national markets – with a view to prohibiting the marketing in a Member State of goods legally produced in another Member State under an identical trade mark having the same origin'.

Hag I was a controversial judgment in which the ECJ was clearly concerned at the tendency of national trade marks to inhibit single market integration. The exhaustion of rights principle[7] is founded on the idea of marketing *with consent*: consent was obviously lacking in *Hag I*. The decision had obvious implications for consumers, since goods from unrelated sources could bear the same mark. It was not clear from *Hag I* whether the common origin doctrine applied only to trade marks, or whether it could apply to other intellectual property rights. This was clarified with regard to patents in *Pharmon v Hoechst*[8] where the product had been placed on the market under a compulsory patent licence. The ECJ held that the patent holder could assert its right to prevent importation of the goods made under the compulsory licence; the patent holder had not exhausted its rights, because it had not consented to the licence and its acceptance of royalties did not affect this. In *Pharmon v Hoechst* it was the lack of consent, rather than the common origin, which was the crucial factor.

The ECJ had an opportunity to reconsider the common origin doctrine of *Hag I* in *SA CNL-Sucal v HAG GF AC*[9], known as *Hag II*. The 'Hag' mark was in issue again, but this time the Belgian owner was trying to export the coffee to Germany, so that the rôles of plaintiff and defendant were reversed. In *Hag II* the ECJ reviewed its previous judgment and said, at paragraph 15, that the decisive factor should be the absence of any element of consent. The ECJ's judgment shows how its attitude to trade marks had changed over the years since *Hag I*[10]. In *Hag 2* the ECJ said that trade marks 'constitute an essential element of the system of competition which the Treaty aims to establish and maintain': firms gain customers through the quality of their products and services and customers must be able to identify those products and services[11]. If a trade mark owner cannot prevent the importation of goods bearing the same mark consumers will be confused and goods for which the owner is in no way responsible (and which might be of inferior quality) could be attributed to it.

The further demise of the common origin doctrine can be seen in *IHT Internationale Heiztechnik v Ideal Standard*[12]. The America Standard Group ('ASG') had owned the trade mark 'Ideal Standard' in France and Germany for sanitary fittings and heating equipment; however the French trade mark ended up, as a result of a voluntary assignment, in the ownership of Compagnie

---

7 See pp 704-711 above.
8 Case 19/84 [1985] ECR 2281, [1985] 3 CMLR 775.
9 Case C–10/89 [1990] ECR I–3711, [1990] 3 CMLR 571: see Rothnie '*Hag II*: Putting the Common Origin Doctrine to Sleep' (1991) 13 EIPR 24; Oliver 'Of Split Trade Marks and Common Markets' (1991) 54 MLR 587; Gagliardi 'Trade Mark Assignments under EC Law' (1998) 20 EIPR 371.
10 See Case 102/77 *Hoffmann-la Roche v Centrafarm* [1978] ECR 1139, [1978] 3 CMLR 217; Case 3/78 *Centrafarm v American Home Products* [1978] ECR 1823, [1979] 1 CMLR 326.
11 [1990] ECR I-3711, [1990] 3 CMLR 571, para 13.
12 Case C-9/93 [1994] ECR I-2789, [1994] 3 CMLR 857; see Tritton 'Articles [28] and [30] and Intellectual Property: Is the Jurisprudence of the ECJ Now of an Ideal Standard?' (1994) 16 EIPR 422; Jarvis 'The *Ideal Standard* Standard in Court of Justice Case Law' (1995) 20 ELRev 200.

Internationale de Chauffage ('CICh'), which had no links with ASG. IHT, a subsidiary of CICh, began to market equipment in Germany using the Ideal Standard trade mark manufactured by CICh in France; ASG's German subsidiary brought an action for infringement in Germany. The ECJ stressed that the function of a trade mark was to enable consumers to identify the origin of the marked goods[13], and that therefore it was legitimate for the action in Germany to succeed[14].

8.   UK LAW

(A)   Licences of intellectual property rights: the Chapter I prohibition

(i)   Introduction

The Chapter I prohibition in the Competition Act 1998 applies to agreements that have as their object or effect the prevention, restriction or distortion of competition[15]. The Chapter I prohibition will not apply where the parties' market share is below 25%[16]; however this rule does not apply to price fixing, so that restrictions on a licensee's minimum prices or the fixing of prices may amount to an infringement; by analogy with the Competition Act 1998 (Land and Vertical Agreements Exclusion) Order 2000[17] the recommendation of prices or the imposition of maximum prices are unlikely to be caught. In applying the Chapter I prohibition consistency must be maintained with EC law, having regard to any relevant differences[18]. Much of Community law on the application of Article 81(1) to licences of intellectual property rights has been motivated by single market considerations, which may be relevantly different from the concerns of UK law[19]. It may therefore be that the treatment of intellectual property licences under UK law will diverge to some extent from the practice in Community law, at least in so far as territorial restrictions are concerned. It is likely that a Guideline on the application of the Competition Act to intellectual property rights will be adopted before the end of 2001.

(ii)   The exclusion of vertical agreements from the Chapter I prohibition

Vertical agreements, other than agreements fixing minimum and fixed resale prices, are excluded from the Chapter I prohibition by the *Competition Act 1998 (Land and Vertical Agreements Exclusion) Order 2000*[20]. However there is no exclusion for licences of intellectual property rights, except for:

> 'provisions contained in such agreements which relate to the assignment to the buyer or use by the buyer of intellectual property rights, provided that

13   Ibid, para 45.
14   Ibid, para 60.
15   For a general account of the Chapter I prohibition see ch 9, pp 291-314.
16   *The Chapter I prohibition*, OFT Guideline 401, para 2.19; see ch 9, pp 296-297.
17   SI 2000/310; see ch 16, pp 595-598.
18   See ch 9, pp 329-333 on s 60 of the Act.
19   Ibid, pp 330-331.
20   SI 2000/310; see ch 16, pp 595-598.

those provisions do not constitute the primary object of the agreement and are directly related to the use, sale or resale of goods or services by the buyer or its customers'[1].

This provision will presumably be interpreted in the same way as Article 2(3) of the Community block exemption on vertical agreements from which it is derived[2]; there is no 'single market' element to this idea of ancillarity. The Guideline *Vertical Agreements and Restrictions*[3] discusses ancillary provisions at paragraphs 2.9 to 2.13. Paragraph 2.11 states that an agreement under which a licence is given to a software buyer to reproduce the software in order to sell it may be ancillary; and paragraph 2.13 acknowledges that a trade mark licence granted to a distributor or franchisee could be so where it relates to the distribution of goods or services and forms part of the distribution arrangements.

(iii) Parallel exemption

Agreements that benefit from Regulation 240/96, including Article 4 which establishes an opposition procedure[4], would enjoy parallel exemption in the UK by virtue of section 10(1)[5]. Section 10(2) provides that this is also the case where the agreement has no effect on trade between Member States, but otherwise satisfies the terms of the Community block exemption[6].

(iv) Exclusion or block exemption

It would be possible for the Secretary of State to exclude licences of intellectual property rights by modifying the general exclusions in Schedule 3 of the Act or by granting block exemption under section 6; there are no plans to do so. A licence that infringes the Chapter I prohibition could be notified to the DGFT for individual exemption.

(v) Tie-ins

Section 70 of the Competition Act repealed sections 44 and 45 of the Patents Act 1977[7]; section 44 prohibited certain tie-in and non-competition clauses, while section 45 made it possible to terminate, on three months notice, patent licences or supply agreements for patented products after the expiry of the original patents. Given the broad ambit of the Competition Act 1998 it was considered that special treatment for these 'tie-in' and 'post-expiry' provisions was no longer necessary.

1   SI 2000/310, Article 2.
2   See ch 16, pp 574-577.
3   OFT Guideline 419.
4   On the opposition procedure, see p 695 above.
5   On parallel exemption see ch 9, pp 312-313.
6   Ibid.
7   See Heal 'Loosening the Ties' (1999) 21 EIPR 414.

(B) Horizontal agreements; the Chapter I prohibition

The Chapter I prohibition could apply to horizontal agreements relating to intellectual property rights. The provision in the DGFT's Guideline *The Chapter I prohibition* that the Act does not apply to agreements where the parties' market share is below 25% means that many agreements would not be caught[8]. Subject to this, the types of agreement considered under Article 81 earlier in this chapter such as patent pools could be caught[9], although the competition authorities in the UK would presumably not share the single market concerns of the Commission in relation to trade mark delimitation agreements[10].

(C)   Anti-monopoly control of intellectual property rights

The Chapter II prohibition could apply to abusive behaviour in relation to intellectual property rights; the decisional practice of the Commission and the judgments of the Community Courts would of course be relevant to the application of this prohibition[11]. The Fair Trading Act 1973 (the 'FTA') remains in force, and it is relevant therefore also to recall some investigations of the Competition Commission which have been concerned with the issues under consideration in this chapter[12].

(i)   Prices

Where a firm is investigated by the Commission under the FTA it is permitted to take into account the way in which it exploits its intellectual property rights. If the Commission comes to the conclusion that the public interest is being harmed, wide-ranging order-making powers are available to the Secretary of State. He could make an order reducing a patentee's prices or forbidding price discrimination, although he is not permitted to prevent the enforcement of a patent or patent licence[13]. The Secretary of State may apply to the Comptroller General of Patents for an order varying the conditions in a patent licence or making a licence available as of right[14].

The Commission has not frequently criticised the way in which firms exploit their patents, but it has done so on a few occasions. In *Indirect Electrostatic Reprographic Equipment*[15] it criticised Xerox's policy of acquiring patents and refusing to grant licences to third parties thereby foreclosing competition. In *Chlordiazepoxide and Diazepam*[16] the Commission considered that Roche's profits were excessive in relation to sales of librium and valium and recommended a drastic reduction in price. There was criticism of the Commission's recommendation, since the very purpose of patent protection is to give the incentive

---

8   See p 714 above.
9   See pp 696-698 above.
10   See p 697 above.
11   See pp 698-703 above.
12   See ch 11 on the operation of the FTA in relation to scale and complex monopolies.
13   FTA 1973, s 90(5).
14   Patents Act 1977, s 51.
15   HCP (1976–77) 47; it was not necessary for action to be taken because antitrust action in the US brought about a change in Xerox's policy.
16   HCP (1972–73) 197.

of monopoly profits to innovative firms that take risks and invest capital in research and development; research in pharmaceuticals is extremely expensive and necessitates a high-price policy in respect of those products that are a success to pay for failures and for future work. After the merger investigation of *BICC/Pyrotenax*[17] assurances were given that BICC would grant licences under any patents relating to mineral insulated cable to third parties if requested to do so by the Board of Trade.

In *Recorded Music*[18] the Commission investigated five UK subsidiaries of major record companies following complaints about the high prices of compact discs in the UK. The Commission found that these companies were complex monopolists[19], but that there were no detriments to the public interest; in particular it concluded that prices were not excessive. One concern was whether the record companies should be prevented from using their copyright to impede parallel imports of cheaper CDs from the US; the Commission rejected this idea, not least since removal of copyright protection would increase the risk of piracy. In the Commission's view much of the price differential between the US and the UK was attributable to different tax régimes.

In *Video Games*[20] the Commission investigated the terms contained in software licences between Sega and Nintendo on the one hand and publishers of video games on the other. These publishers competed with Sega and Nintendo in the market for video games, but needed licences from them to enable them to produce games that would be compatible with their games consoles. The licences restrained the number of games that they could publish, required prior approval of games and packaging, and provided that Sega and Nintendo would arrange manufacture of the cartridges. In the Commission's view these provisions raised the price of video games and it recommended that they should be removed from the licences. It also considered that the prices for cartridges were excessive.

(ii) Compulsory licences

The DGFT concluded in *Ford Spare Parts*[1] that Ford's refusal to grant licences to produce spare parts (which were protected under UK design copyright) was an anti-competitive practice. When the Commission was asked to investigate Ford's licensing policy it confirmed the finding of an anti-competitive practice and concluded that it operated against the public interest[2]. At that point a fatal weakness in the investigative system at that time became apparent: there was no power to order a firm to grant copyright licences in the way that a patent licence could be compelled under section 51(5) of the Patents Act 1977. A similar problem was revealed in *BBC and ITV/Publication of Programme Information*. The DGFT

17 HCP (1966–67) 490: see Appendix 5 of this report for BICC's assurances.
18 Cm 2599 (1994)
19 On the meaning of complex monopoly see ch 11, pp 368-370.
20 Cm 2781 (1995); for critical comment see Williams 'Sega, Nintendo and After-market Power: The MMC on Video Games' (1995) 16 ECLR 310; the 1996 *Annual Report of the DGFT* says, at p 37, that negotiations were continuing with Sega and Nintendo in relation to this investigation, but there is no mention in later Annual Reports of the eventual outcome; note that the European Commission conducted an investigation into Sega's and Nintendo's licence agreements following this report: see p 685 above.
1   OFT, 21.3.84; this investigation was actually conducted under the old Competition Act 1980.
2   Cmnd 9437 (1985).

concluded that the BBC and ITV were acting anti-competitively by refusing to make available their programme schedules, in respect of which they owned the copyright, to magazines such as Time Out which wished to publish a weekly publication containing details of all programmes[3]. The Commission agreed that the refusal to supply the information was an anti-competitive practice[4], but were split 3–3 as to whether there were detriments to the public interest. However, even if they had concluded that the public interest was being harmed, the same weakness revealed by the Ford case would have prevented action being taken: there was no provision for compulsory licences of copyrights.

The problem of a lack of remedy in these investigations was corrected by section 144(1) of the Copyright, Designs and Patents Act 1988. The Commission may conclude in a report under the FTA that conditions in a copyright licence restrict the use of a work by a licensee or that the rights of a copyright owner operate against the public interest; it may make the same finding in respect of a refusal to grant a copyright licence[5]. Where it makes such a finding, powers have been inserted into Schedule 8 of the FTA that can be exercised by the Secretary of State: he may cancel or modify the offensive conditions in a licence or provide that a licence shall be made available as of right. Section 144(3) provides that, when making such an order, the Secretary of State shall exercise these powers only where their use would not contravene any Convention to which the UK is party. By section 144(4) the terms of a licence shall, in default of agreement, be settled by the Copyright Tribunal, established under Chapter VIII of Part I of the Act. The specific issue of television listings raised by the *Magill* and the *BBC/ITV* cases was dealt with by section 176 of the Broadcasting Act 1990, which provides that programme providers must make information relating to the programmes available to any person who wishes to publish it in the UK. The terms of payment, if the parties cannot agree, are settled by an order of the Copyright Tribunal[6].

In *Historical On-line Database Services*[7] the Commission considered that the Financial Times Group's policy of refusing to provide access to historical on-line databases containing archival business and financial information other than to its own on-line supplier, FT Profile, did not operate against the public interest. Without using the term, the Commission did not regard the Financial Times' material as an essential facility. It acknowledged that competitors of FT Profile were disadvantaged by not having access to the FT's archives, but considered that the refusal of access was a legitimate competitive act on its part. The Commission considered that the market for the provision of on-line information was a competitive one and that new forms of competition were emerging as a result of technological change. The Commission also considered that the Financial Times Group was not charging excessively high prices or making excessive profits.

---

3   This investigation raised the same issues that were of concern to the European Commission in the *Magill* case: see pp 699–700 above.
4   Cmnd 9614 (1985); this was also an investigation under the old Competition Act 1980.
5   See similarly the Copyright, Designs and Patents Act, 1988, s 238 (unregistered designs) and s 270 (registered designs).
6   Broadcasting Act 1990, Sch 17; the Tribunal handed down a decision on payment on 16 March 1992: *News Group Newspapers Ltd v ITP Ltd* [1993] EMLR 1.
7   Cm 2554 (1994); see also *Exhaust Gas Analysers* Cm 2386 (1993), where there was a complaint that suppliers of exhaust gas analysers had refused to make computer software available to third parties, but the Commission did not consider that the complex monopoly operated against the public interest: see 1993 *Annual Report of the DGFT*, p 32.

(iii)   Collecting societies

Until 1988 the Commission had not been called upon to investigate collecting societies; however a general reference under section 78 FTA was made in that year, leading to the Commission's report on *Collective Licensing*[8]. The Commission was asked to report on the collective licensing of sound recordings for broadcasting and public performance and in particular on the practice of owners of copyright assigning their rights to collective licensing bodies and of these bodies stipulating royalties, common tariffs and restrictions on performance. The Commission concluded that collecting societies were the best available method for licensing sound recordings, provided that they could be restrained from abusing their monopoly power. It made several recommendations as to how Phonographic Performance Ltd, the only society found to fall within the terms of the reference, should conduct its affairs[9].

In *Performing Rights*[10] the Commission found that the Performing Rights Society ('the PRS') had a monopoly in the UK; there had been complaints about the way in which royalty income was distributed. The Commission highlighted a number of problems with the way in which the PRS conducted its affairs and made no fewer than 44 detailed recommendations in relation to a variety of matters including corporate structure, cost allocation, transparency and appeal procedures. The PRS agreed to implement the recommendations in full[11].

8   Cm 530 (1988); on s 78 FTA see ch 11, pp 374-375.
9   Ibid, ch 1 (summary) and ch 7 (conclusions).
10 Cm 3147 (1996).
11 See the 1996 *Annual Report of the DGFT*, p 36 and the 1997 *Annual Report of the DGFT*, p 39.

CHAPTER 20

Mergers (1) – introduction

1. INTRODUCTION

This chapter briefly introduces the subject of merger control. This book so far has been concerned essentially with two issues: anti-competitive agreements and abusive conduct. Merger control is an important third component of most, though not all, systems of competition law. The EC Merger Regulation ('the ECMR') will be described in chapter 21 and the merger provisions in the UK Fair Trading Act 1973 ('the FTA') in chapter 22. Before doing so it may be useful to make some brief preliminary observations about the subject of mergers generally and about systems of merger control in particular.

2. TERMINOLOGY

(A) The meaning of 'merger' and 'concentration'

A true merger involves two separate undertakings merging entirely into a new entity: a high-profile example of this was the fusion in 1996 of Ciba-Geigy and Sandoz to form the major pharmaceutical and chemical company Novartis[1]; a further example in 2000 was the creation of GlaxoSmithKlein as a result of the merger of Glaxo Wellcome and SmithKlein Beecham[2]. However it is important to understand that the expression 'merger' as used by company and competition lawyers includes a far broader range of corporate transactions than full mergers of this kind. Where A acquires all, or a majority of, the shares in B, this would be described as a merger if it results in A being able to control the affairs of B; even the acquisition of a minority shareholding may be sufficient, in particular circumstances, to qualify as a merger: under the ECMR the question is whether A will acquire 'the possibility of exercising decisive influence' over B[3]; under the FTA whether A would have 'material influence' over B[4]. The acquisition of assets – for example a well-known brand name – can amount to a merger. Two

1 Case No IV/M.737, OJ [1997] L 201/1.
2 Case No COMP/M.1846.
3 See ch 21, pp 745-748.
4 See ch 22, pp 805-806.

or more undertakings which merge part of their businesses into a joint venture company, 'Newco', may be found to be parties to a merger[5]. In each case the essential question is whether previously independent businesses have come or will come under common control. For the sake of convenience the term 'merger' will be used in this and the following chapters to encompass all these phenomena unless the context requires a different usage. When discussing the EC system an alternative expression, 'concentration', will also sometimes be used, since that is the word used in the ECMR itself.

(B)   The horizontal, vertical and conglomerate effects of mergers

It is helpful to draw attention to the distinction between the horizontal, vertical and conglomerate effects of mergers, while noting that the same transaction may produce some or all of these. Horizontal effects occur where a merger takes place between competitors in the same product market and at the same level of the production or distribution cycle. As a general proposition horizontal mergers present a greater danger to competition than vertical ones, in the same way that horizontal agreements are treated more strictly than vertical agreements[6]. Vertical effects may be experienced where a merger occurs between firms that operate at different levels of the market: a firm may acquire control of another firm further up or further down the distribution chain; the former is known as 'backward integration' and the latter as 'forward integration'. Vertical integration may have a harmful effect on competition, in particular if it gives rise to a risk of the market becoming foreclosed to third parties; an example of this would be where a firm downstream in the market acquires an upstream undertaking that has monopoly power in relation to an important raw material or input: there is an obvious concern here that competitors in the downstream market will be unable to obtain supplies of the raw material or input, or that they will be able to do so only on discriminatory terms, with the result that they will be unable to compete effectively. Vertical issues have arisen under the ECMR in a number of cases in the telecommunications/multimedia sector in particular[7].

A conglomerate merger is one that brings together firms which do not compete with each other in any product market and which does not entail vertical integration. Conglomerate mergers may be divided into three main types: product line extensions (where one firm, by acquiring another, adds related items to its existing products); market extensions (where the merged firms previously sold the same products in different geographical markets); and pure conglomerates (where there is no functional link whatever between the merged firms). Whether conglomerate mergers should be controlled at all is a matter of controversy: US law long ago abandoned any interest in the conglomerate effects of mergers[8]; however in recent years the European Commission has expressed concern about the 'portfolio' or 'range' effects of some mergers, most noticeably in the cases of

---

5   See in particular ch 21, pp 748-751 on the application of the ECMR to so-called 'full-function' joint ventures.
6   On horizontal mergers under the ECMR see ch 21, pp 774-776; for their treatment under UK law see ch 22, pp 819-823.
7   On vertical mergers under the ECMR see ch 21, p 776; for their treatment under UK law see ch 22, p 824.
8   See Scherer and Ross *Industrial Market Structure and Economic Performance* (Houghton Mifflin, 3rd ed, 1990), pp 188-190.

Grand Metropolitan/Guinness[9] and *General Electric/Honeywell International*[10].
This issue is discussed in chapter 21[11].

3. MERGER ACTIVITY

In the corporate world there are frequent bouts of 'merger mania' when the level
of merger activity is very high[12]; enormous fees are earned by financial and
legal (including competition law) advisers during these periods. For example,
there was a very high degree of merger activity in the second half of the 1980s[13],
and again in the mid-1990s[14]. From 1998 to 2000 there was a period of frenetic
merger activity, although this has since declined to some extent as the global
economy has slowed. In the European Commission's 1999 *Report on Competition
Policy* it reported that 292 mergers had been notified to it that year, an increase
of 24% from the previous year and of 70% since 1997[15]. In 2000 the number of
notifications increased to 345[16]. A notable feature of mergers in recent years has
been their increasing complexity, size and geographical reach. Very large mergers
have taken place in many sectors as companies have sought to restructure and
consolidate their place in the increasingly global market. For example in the
pharmaceuticals industry Glaxo Wellcome and SmithKline Beecham merged to
become the largest pharmaceutical company in the world[17]. Major mergers have
taken place in the car industry, for example between Daimler-Benz and Chrysler[18],
between Ford and Volvo[19], and between Renault and Nissan[20]. In the oil industry,
Exxon merged with Mobil to become the largest oil company in the world[1], and
BP Amoco merged with Arco[2]. Many other industries have seen a high degree of
merger activity, not least the legal profession. Several times in 1999 the Financial
Times announced 'the biggest deal in corporate history'. For example the merger
of America Online and Time-Warner[3], announced in January 1999, enjoyed
'biggest deal' status until the VodaphoneAirTouch/Mannesmann merger was
announced in February[4]; the latter case was also of interest in that it was the first
successful hostile bid for a German company.

4. THE PROLIFERATION OF SYSTEMS OF MERGER CONTROL

A particularly noticeable feature of competition policy in the final decade of the
twentieth century was the proliferation of systems of competition law around the

---

9   See Case No IV/M.938, OJ [1998] L 288/24.
10 See Case No COMP/M.2220.
11 See ch 21, pp 776-777.
12 See Scherer and Ross *Industrial Market Structure and Economic Performance* (Houghton
    Mifflin, 3rd ed, 1990), pp 153-159.
13 See eg the 1986 *Annual Report of the DGFT*, pp 27-28.
14 See eg the 1995 *Annual Report of the DGFT*, p 13.
15 XXIXth *Report on Competition Policy* (1999), point 147.
16 XXXth *Report on Competition Policy* (2000), point 231.
17 See p 721, n 2 above.
18 Case No IV/M.1204.
19 Case No IV/M.1452.
20 Case No IV/M.1519.
1   Case No IV/M.1383.
2   Case No IV/M.1532, [2001] 4 CMLR 774.
3   Case No COMP/M.1845.
4   Case No COMP/M.1795.

world. More than 80 countries now have competition law, and at least 50 of these laws include merger control[5]. The proliferation of laws on mergers has a greater impact on most firms than rules against cartels and abusive behaviour, not because these firms disregard the latter but because their transactions are often subject to mandatory pre-notification under the former. This means that any sizable transaction with an international dimension – of which there are many – may have to be notified to 10, 20 or even more competition authorities. Law firms advising on international transactions must be able to obtain access to all the relevant merger laws in order to determine where filings must be made[6]. Many competition lawyers in firms handling such cases will spend a substantial amount of time overseeing and coordinating a number of national filings; the initial enthusiasm of junior competition lawyers for such work often fades when it becomes apparent that the coordination of filings in Australia, Europe and the US entails an 18-hour working day or longer.

The problems that multiple notification can cause to the merging firms themselves – for example the cost of multiple filing, the workload involved in generating the data necessary for each filing, the delay involved in obtaining clearances from numerous jurisdictions, the differing procedural and substantive laws from one jurisdiction to another – are obvious. One of the major issues facing the 'world' of competition law – using this term both in its physical sense and to refer to the constituency of interested parties affected by merger control consisting of regulators, legal and business advisers, politicians, economists and the merging firms themselves – is to devise a sensible mechanism for investigating and adjudicating upon mergers having an international dimension in a way that minimises the administrative burden on business while at the same time ensuring that mergers do not escape scrutiny which could have detrimental effects upon competition. These issues are under active consideration: the subject of international cooperation has been discussed in chapter 12[7], while attempts in the European Community to avoid multiple filing in the Member States by introducing the idea of the 'one-stop shop' of notifying the European Commission will be discussed in chapter 21[8].

5.   WHY DO FIRMS MERGE?[9]

There are many reasons why firms merge, most of which are beneficial to, or at least not harmful to, the economy; there are others that are more problematic.

---

5   See Rowley and Campbell 'Multi-jurisdictional Merger Review – Is It Time for a Common Form Filing Treaty?' in *Policy Directions for Global Merger Review* (Global Competition Review, 1999).

6   Three particularly helpful sources are White & Case *2001 Survey of Worldwide Antitrust Merger Notification Requirements* which can be ordered on the Internet at http://www.whitecase.com; Rowley and Baker *Merger Control: The International Regulation of Mergers and Joint Ventures* (Sweet & Maxwell, 3rd ed, 2000); *Merger Control: The International Regulation of Mergers and Joint Ventures* (Global Competition Review, 2001).

7   See in particular ch 12, pp 409-414.

8   See ch 21, pp 756-758.

9   See further Scherer and Ross *Industrial Market Structure and Economic Performance* (Houghton Mifflin, 3rd ed, 1990), pp 159-167.

(A) Economies of scale and scope

An obvious explanation for some mergers is the achievement of economies of scale and scope[10]. A firm will produce goods at the lowest marginal cost where it is able to operate at the minimum efficient scale. If it operates on a smaller scale than this, marginal cost will increase and there will be a consequent loss of allocative efficiency. Economies of scale may be *product–specific*, where they enable a product to be produced more cheaply; *plant–specific*, where they mean that the overall use of a multi–product plant is made more rational; or *firm–specific*, where they result in lower overall costs. The globalisation of markets in recent years, as tariff and other barriers to trade have come down and as astonishingly rapid technological changes have altered the nature and structure of markets, has given opportunities to firms to grow into larger geographical markets. It may be that a firm can achieve economies of scale by internal growth; equally, however, it may be that this can most easily be achieved by external growth, that is by merging with other firms. Whether mergers actually lead to the achievement of the economies of scale expected of them is another matter: some commentators have argued that in practice the gains anticipated tend to prove illusory[11].

(B) Other efficiencies

Apart from economies of scale and scope, a merger may lead to efficiencies in other ways. For example it may be cheaper to take over a distributor than to set up a distribution network on a contractual basis; backward integration may guarantee supplies to a firm concerned about the availability of raw materials; a merger might mean that a firm will have improved access to loan and equity capital than it had when operating alone. A merger may result in a firm better able to carry out research and development and with access to a greater pool of industrial technology; quite often a merger is motivated by a desire to acquire the patents and know–how of a particular firm. Another possibility is that a merged firm may be able to make better use of the management skills of its constituent parts.

(C) National champions

Firms within one nation state – or within one political grouping such as the European Union – may wish to merge in order to become a 'national champion' (or a 'European champion'). Governments may positively encourage mergers that will create larger domestic firms more capable of competing on international markets, although 'national champions' free from the disciplining effect of competition on their domestic markets may lack the skills necessary to succeed in the wider world[12].

10 These concepts are discussed in ch 1, pp 8-9.
11 See Scherer and Ross *Industrial Market Structure and Economic Performance* (Houghton Mifflin, 3rd ed, 1990), pp 167-174; Meeks *Disappointing Marriage: A Study of the Gains from Merger* (Cambridge University Press, 1977).
12 See the discussion of industrial policy considerations under the ECMR and of *Aerospatiale-Alenia/de Havilland* and other cases in ch 21, pp 780-781.

(D)   Management efficiency and the market for corporate control

An explanation for some mergers is that one firm competes to run another; the threat of a successful takeover bid acts as an important influence upon the existing management of a firm to ensure that it functions as efficiently as possible. Where shareholders are satisfied with the current management's performance they will not sell their shares to another bidder, unless it is overbidding: the new régime would not be capable of generating greater profits than the existing one. If shareholders are dissatisfied, they may prefer to sell at the price offered and to reinvest the proceeds elsewhere; the result is likely to be that the old management will be replaced by the bidder. According to this argument the 'market for corporate control' is a crucial element in the promotion of economic efficiency[13]. It is particularly attractive if one agrees with the view that shareholders' influence over directors through the Annual General Meeting has been seriously diminished; at least the ability to sell to a bidder exercises some influence on the management of the company's affairs. If the threat of takeovers is considered to have this significant rôle, this has implications for merger policy: an interventionist approach to mergers in itself distorts the market for corporate control and thus weakens its disciplining effect on management.

(E)   Exiting an industry

Mergers present firms that wish to do so with an opportunity of exiting an industry. In a free market it is important to encourage entrepreneurs to invest their money and skills in setting up new businesses and in entering new markets. Just as it is desirable to prevent the erection of barriers to entry that prevent new firms from competing on the market, so too it is necessary to avoid barriers to exit that make it difficult to leave the market. The incentive to set up a firm, invest risk capital and develop new products may be diminished if it is not possible to sell the enterprise in question as a valuable going concern. It is quite common, for example, for firms to acquire small undertakings which possess useful know–how or intellectual property rights and, from the perspective of the innovator of such technology, the freedom to sell may be an important element in the reward for the risks taken. A strict approach to mergers could have an undesirable effect if it were to make exit unduly difficult.

(F)   Greed, vanity, fear and drugs

Having rehearsed some of the arguments in favour of mergers, and therefore against too strict a system of merger control, some opposing views should be mentioned. A sceptical view is that many mergers cannot be explained in the rational economic terms outlined above, but that instead they are fuelled by the

---

13   See eg Manne 'Mergers and the Market for Corporate Control' (1965) 73 Journal of Political Economy 110; Easterbrook and Fischel 'The Proper Rôle of a Target's Management in Responding to a Tender Offer' (1981) 94 Harvard Law Review 1161; Coffee 'Regulating the Market for Corporate Control: a Critical Assessment of the Tender Offer's Role in Corporate Governance' (1984) 84 Columbia Law Review 1145; Bradley 'Corporate Control: Markets and Rules' (1990) 53 MLR 170; Wright, Wong and Thompson 'The Market for Corporate Control: an Economic Perspective' in Miller (ed) *The Monopolies and Mergers Yearbook* (Blackwell Business, 1992) pp 32–42.

speculative greed of individuals or companies or the personal vanity of a particularly swashbuckling senior executive; it will not take a great deal of imagination to think of certain high-profile entrepreneurs that might answer this description. Some mergers seem to be motivated by simple fear: if every other undertaking in a particular sector appears to be involved in mergers, it may be considered important not to be left behind in the process of industry consolidation. For some individuals 'deal-making' has the same stimulating effect as mood-changing drugs, altogether more exciting than the mundane task of managing a firm well. Even if one shares these sceptical explanations of why firms merge, however, it does not follow that merger control is the appropriate tool to deal with the 'problem'.

(G)   Increasing market power

Of course it might be that the real reason why firms wish to merge is that this will eliminate competition between them, increase their market power and give them the ability to restrict output and raise price. It would be very foolish in today's world of vigorous merger control for merging firms to make such a claim for their merger, although it is sometimes surprising what firms do say in press releases, intended to impress shareholders, as to the expected economic benefits of a merger: for example a claim that a merger will 'eliminate wasteful capacity' and return an industry to greater profitability is unlikely to charm a competition authority into submission; even less charming is a press release that announces that 'this merger will create the dominant world player in the market for widgets'. The systems of merger control in place in the EC, the UK and elsewhere presumably inhibit the incidence of cases in which firms nakedly seek to achieve market power, but it is important to bear in mind that, in the absence of a system of merger control, firms would be able to do precisely this.

6.   WHAT IS THE PURPOSE OF MERGER CONTROL?[14]

This brings use to the central question: what is the purpose of merger control?

(A)   Merger control is not about the protection of shareholders' interests

Mergers may affect the interests of individual shareholders; however this is not the reason for merger control. Company law is concerned with issues such as the oppression of minority shareholders, and complex regulatory systems also exist to protect shareholders generally. Reference should be made to standard works on the laws and regulations that deal with these matters; in particular in the UK the City Code on Takeovers and Mergers provides an important system of

---

14   For useful discussion of mergers and the public interest, see Chiplin and Wright *The Logic of Mergers* (Hobart Paper 107, 1987); Fairburn and Kay (eds) *Mergers and Mergers Policy* (Oxford University Press, 1989); *Merger & Competition Policy in the European Community* (Blackwell 1990, ed Jacquemain); Bishop and Walker *The Economics of EC Competition Law* (Sweet & Maxwell, 1999) ch 6; Neven, Nuttall and Seabright *Mergers in Daylight: The Economics and Politics of European Merger Control* (CEPR, 1993).

protection[15]. The Panel on Takeovers and Mergers, a non–statutory organisation with no prerogative or common law powers, administers the rules in the Code; it is subject to judicial review, although interference by the courts is rare[16].

(B)   Merger control and the public interest

Merger control is carried out in the public interest rather than on behalf of shareholders. It is not inevitable that a system of competition law will include merger control. For example the first competition legislation in the UK, the Monopolies and Restrictive Practices (Inquiry and Control) Act 1948, had no application to mergers; merger control was not introduced in the UK until the Monopolies and Mergers Act 1965. The Treaty of Rome did not contain provisions on mergers; it was not until the adoption of the ECMR in 1989 that effective control could be exercised over concentrations by the European Commission; on the other hand the Treaty of Paris of 1951, establishing the European Coal and Steel Community, contained specific rules on mergers from the outset[17]. There are many other systems of competition law which contain rules forbidding cartels and abusive behaviour on the part of dominant firms but which do not contain provisions on mergers.

Merger control is an interference with the operation of the market in which shareholders buy and sell shares as they deem appropriate free from regulatory interference. As a general proposition merger decisions are best left to the informed judgments of the entrepreneurs and shareholders concerned. The important question is to determine whether, and if so on what grounds, it is appropriate to intervene and to prevent transactions, or to require alterations to them, because of possible detriments to the public interest. More specifically, should the only ground of interference be that a merger will be detrimental to competition, or should it be possible to intervene for other reasons as well? The test of whether a concentration should be allowed under the ECMR is based purely on the issue of competition[18]; in the UK the intention of the Labour Government is to repeal the 'public interest' test set out in section 84 of the FTA and to replace it with a competition test, albeit with the possibility in exceptional circumstances for the Secretary of State to intervene on narrowly-defined public interest grounds[19].

(C)   Merger control is concerned with market structure

It is important to understand that merger control is, above all, concerned with the maintenance of a competitive market structure. As was explained in chapter 1 competitive markets seem, on the whole, to deliver better outcomes than monopolistic ones[20]. Merger control is not, or not only, about preemptively preventing a merged entity from abusing its dominant position in the future; it is

---

15   See eg Weinberg and Blank (Sweet & Maxwell), Part 4; Gower's *Principles of Modern Company Law* (Sweet & Maxwell, 6th ed, 1997), ch 29; Farrar and Hannigan *Farrar's Company Law* (Butterworths, 4th ed, 1998), ch 36.
16   See eg *R v Panel on Takeovers and Mergers, ex p Datafin* [1987] QB 815, [1987] 1 All ER 564, CA; *R v Panel on Takeovers and Mergers, ex p Guinness plc* [1990] 1 QB 146, [1989] 1 All ER 509, CA.
17   See the ECSC Treaty, Article 66(1)-(6).
18   See ch 21, pp 772-781.
19   See ch 22, p 836.
20   See ch 1, pp 1-15.

also about maintaining a market structure that is capable of delivering the benefits that follow from competition: the influence of the 'structure-conduct-performance paradigm' on merger policy is a significant one[1]. An understanding of this point should be helpful to anyone who is puzzled by the following conundrum: since it is not unlawful under Article 82 (or under the Chapter II prohibition in the UK Competition Act 1998) to have a dominant position, but only to abuse it, how can it be possible to prevent the creation of a dominant position under the ECMR in the first place? The answer, of course, is that the ECMR is not an anticipatory Article 82; it is an instrument for the maintenance of a competitive market structure. There is a very useful paragraph in the judgment of the CFI in *Gencor v Commission*[2] which says precisely this:

> 'As regards the argument that the Community cannot claim to have jurisdiction in respect of a concentration on the basis of future and hypothetical behaviour, namely parallel conduct on the part of the undertakings operating in the relevant market where that conduct might or might not fall within the competence of the Community under the Treaty, it must be stated, as pointed out above in connection with the question whether the concentration has an immediate effect, that, while the elimination of the risk of future abuses may be a legitimate concern of any competent competition authority, the main objective in exercising control over concentrations at Community level is to ensure that the restructuring of undertakings does not result in the creation of positions of economic power which may significantly impede effective competition in the common market. Community jurisdiction is therefore founded, first and foremost, on the need to avoid the establishment of market structures which may create or strengthen a dominant position, and not on the need to control directly possible abuses of a dominant position'.

(D) Determining and applying the correct competition test

The point was made at the beginning of this chapter that mergers may have horizontal, vertical or conglomerate effects[3]. Most mergers are reviewed by competition authorities before they take place ('ex ante'), although in some cases they may be investigated after they have taken place (ex post')[4]. Merger control therefore is essentially about prediction: will the market be less competitive, and therefore be harmful to consumer welfare, if the merger is allowed to go ahead? This idea is a simple one; what is extremely difficult, however, is to devise techniques that enable competition authorities to predict accurately, and in a way which stands up to scrutiny, the likely effects of mergers. It must be possible to articulate a legal standard for intervention. Many systems permit the prohibition of a merger which will 'substantially lessen competition'[5]; the ECMR and some of its progeny in the Member States allow intervention where a merger will 'create or strengthen a dominant position as a result of which effective competition

---

1 See ch 1, p 12.
2 Case T-102/96 [1999] ECR II-753, [1999] 4 CMLR 971, para 106.
3 See pp 722-723 above.
4 See ch 22, pp 811-812 on the system in the UK where there is no mandatory pre-notification and where mergers sometimes have to be reversed after they have been completed.
5 See, eg, s 7 Clayton Act 1914 in the US; s 50 Trade Practices Act 1974 in Australia; s 92 Competition Act 1985 in Canada; s 12A Competition Act 1998 in South Africa.

would be significantly impeded'[6]. In the UK the current law is based on the possible detriments of a merger to the public interest, although in practice the overwhelming majority of cases are decided on competition grounds; the intention is to replace the public interest test with one based on substantial lessening of competition[7].

Having determined what substantive rule is appropriate, it is also necessary to provide guidance on how that rule will be applied in practice. Firms should be able to predict with reasonable certainty whether their mergers are likely to cause concern on the part of the competition authorities. The authorities themselves ought not to be given an unduly wide margin of appreciation in determining the outcome of cases. It is important therefore to give an objective meaning to expressions such as a 'substantial' lessening of competition or a 'significant' impediment to competition. The use of the Herfindahl-Hirschmann Index can provide some guidance on the likely effect of a merger on the structure of the market[8], as may concentration ratios[9]. However techniques such as these are not sufficient in themselves to predict the effect of a merger on the market, not least since they depend upon market definition which is far from being a precise science, if it is a science at all[10]. Some competition authorities have produced guidelines on merger analysis which set out relevant criteria. Of particular importance are the 1992 *Horizontal Merger Guidelines* in the US[11], which discuss the approach taken by the Department of Justice and the Federal Trade Commission to the 'coordinated effects'[12] and the 'unilateral effects'[13] of mergers. There are no such guidelines under the ECMR or the FTA. A specific problem in systems of merger control is whether a merger which reduces competition but which would lead to gains in efficiency should be permitted: the US Guidelines address this issue specifically in paragraph 4 and do, in certain circumstances, recognise efficiency arguments; the position under the ECMR and the FTA is not clear[14]. Another issue that sometimes arises is whether a merger should be allowed in order to save a 'failing firm', even though there will be less competition in the market after the merger than before. A failing firm defence does exist in US law[15], and has been applied under the ECMR[16]; it would probably be recognised also in an appropriate case under the FTA[17].

(E)   Other 'public interest' issues that might arise in relation to mergers

The previous two sections have briefly rehearsed the competition policy reasons why some mergers may be challenged. In practice mergers are often criticised

6   See ch 21, pp 772-781.
7   See ch 22, p 836.
8   See ch 15, pp 506-507.
9   Ibid.
10   See ch 1, pp 21-39 on market definition.
11   These are available at http://www.usdoj.gov/atr/public/guidelines/guidelin.htm; some information about the Australian Competition and Consumer Commission's Guidelines can be found at http://www.accc.gov.au/fs-search.htm.
12   Ibid, paras 2.1-2.12.
13   Ibid, paras 2.2-2.22.
14   See ch 21, pp 778-780 on the ECMR and ch 22, pp 825-826 on the FTA; on the position in Canada see *The Commissioner of Competition v Superior Propane Inc*, judgment of 4 April 2001.
15   See the *Horizontal Merger Guidelines*, paras 5.0-5.2.
16   See ch 21, pp 780.
17   See ch 22, pp 826.

on other grounds as well; some of these will be listed below. Systems of merger control may or may not allow intervention for these reasons; in so far as they do, the laws in question can hardly be called 'competition' laws; indeed prohibiting mergers on social grounds or for reasons of industrial policy may be directly antagonistic to the process of competition.

(i) Loss of efficiency and 'short–termism'

Some commentators would argue that mergers, far from promoting economic efficiency, have a disruptive effect upon the management of one or both of the merged firms and may be detrimental to their long-term prospects. This claim is made in particular of contested takeover bids, where it is possible that the management of the target company will either be removed by the new shareholders or will resign rather than stay on in the new conditions. Sceptics of the way in which the market for corporate control functions would argue that it is not inevitable that the decision of shareholders will produce the best result in the public interest, although it may yield the best financial deal for the shareholders themselves. In particular many would argue that a problem with takeovers is that they are motivated more by short-term profit-taking on the stock exchange than by serious analysis of the long-term prospects of companies. This may be particularly true of institutional investors in the market which are in the habit of regularly turning over their investments in pursuit of short-term gains.

(ii) Concentration of wealth

Mergers may be objected to on the ground that they lead to firms of such size and with such power as to be antithetical to a balanced distribution of wealth. This of course is a socio–political argument, but one which has become more widely accepted as aggregrate industrial concentration has increased. In the US the anti-merger laws were strengthened at a time when this problem was a dominant concern.

(iii) Unemployment and regional policy

Another objection to mergers is that they may lead to the closure of factories and result in serious unemployment. Mergers that savour of 'asset-stripping' and which appear to have no regard for the social problems that may follow attract particular opprobrium from sceptics of the free market. Similarly the market operating in its unfettered form may not attach much weight to the desirability of maintaining a balanced distribution of wealth and job opportunities throughout the UK; the market has no reason to be sentimental about such matters. Government can choose to adopt a regional policy, however, and it is possible to give expression to this issue in mergers policy as well as in laws on tax, planning and state aids.

(iv) Overseas control

Mergers may result in the control of indigenous firms passing to overseas companies, in which case any economic advantages of the merger may be thought to be outweighed by the desirability of maintaining the decision-making process and profits at home. Many UK firms have expanded abroad, in particular into the US, and this makes it somewhat difficult to argue that UK firms should themselves be shielded from hostile foreign takeover bids. However the case for intervention may be more compelling where there is a lack of reciprocity[18] between the laws of the two countries: if the law of country A *prevents* inward investment, whereas country B permits it, there may be a case for blocking a takeover by a firm from A of a firm in B.

(v)   Special sectors

Some sectors of the economy – for example the electronic and print media – are especially sensitive and this may mean that concentration of ownership within them requires special consideration. In the UK, as in several other countries, newspaper mergers are subject to special provisions[19] and mergers in industries such as oil, banking and defence may be particularly closely scrutinised; the UK also has a special régime for mergers in the water industry[20] and the Broadcasting Act 1990 contains special provisions on change of control[1]. Article 21(3) of the ECMR specifically recognises that Member States may have a 'legitimate interest' in investigating a merger other than on grounds of harm to competition[2].

7.   DESIGNING A SYSTEM OF MERGER CONTROL

Where a country decides, as a matter of policy, to adopt a system of merger control, a number of issues have to be addressed. In chapters 21 and 22 the EC and UK systems will be described; most cases would probably result in the same outcome, irrespective of which of these two laws is applied: the dominant consideration in each jurisdiction is the impact of a merger on competition, and the analysis will be conducted in much the same way in each of them. Despite this, however, it will be seen that the provisions themselves – for example on jurisdiction, notification and substantive analysis – are actually quite different.

The following are some of the issues that must be confronted in designing a system of merger control:

- Which transactions should be characterised as mergers? How should the acquisition of minority shareholdings and of assets be dealt with? Will joint ventures be considered as a matter of merger control or under the legal provisions that prohibit cartels?
- How should the jurisidictional test be framed for determining those mergers that can be investigated? Should the test be based on turnover, the value of assets acquired, market share or some other criterion?
- To what extent should a system of merger control apply to transactions consummated outside a country but which have effects within it?
- Should mergers be subject to a system of mandatory pre-notification, or should it be a matter for the parties to decide whether to notify? In the latter

---

18   Or, to put the matter more colloquially, where the 'playing fields' are not even.
19   See ch 22, pp 844-850.
20   See ch 22, pp 850-851.
1   Broadcasting Act 1990, ss 192–194.
2   See ch 21, pp 764-765.

case, in what circumstances and for how long after a merger has been completed should a competition authority be allowed to review a case?
- What should be the time period within which a merger investigation must be completed?
- What should be the substantive test for reviewing mergers? Should it be based solely on competition criteria, or should any or all of the other issues discussed above (for example unemployment, regional policy and overseas control) also be taken into account?
- How should the specific issues of (a) efficiency and (b) failing firms be dealt with?
- What mechanism should be put in place for the negotiation of remedies that would overcome any problems identified by the competition authority?
- Who should make decisions in merger cases? A Commission, in which case who should appoint the Commissioners? A court? A Minister in the Government?
- What system of judicial review or appeals should be put in place to test the findings of the decision-maker in merger cases? How quickly will any judicial review or appeal be completed?

These are just some of the many interesting and important issues that arise in relation to the control of mergers. With these preliminary observations in mind, this book will now describe the systems in force in the EC and UK.

CHAPTER 21

Mergers (2) – EC law

I. INTRODUCTION

The EC Treaty does not contain specific provisions on mergers or, to use an alternative term often used in the parlance of EC law, 'concentrations'; in this respect the EC Treaty differs from the earlier ECSC Treaty, Article 66(7) of which provides powers to prevent concentrations in the coal and steel industries[1]. Some attempt was made by the Commission and the ECJ to fill this lacuna by developing the law on Articles 81 and 82 to catch some concentrations. However these provisions were inadequate as a tool for merger control, and in 1989 the Council of Ministers adopted the European Community Merger Regulation[2] ('the ECMR'), which will be examined in this chapter. The ECMR was amended in important respects by Regulation 1310/97[3] with effect from 1 March 1998.

The advent of the ECMR has meant that the application of Articles 81 and 82 to concentrations is now predominantly, though not entirely, of historical interest.

(A)   Article 81

(i)   The 1966 Memorandum

In 1966 the Commission published a *Memorandum on the Concentration of Enterprises in the Common Market*[4] in which it said that Article 81 was not applicable to agreements 'whose purpose is the acquisition of total or partial

---

1   On the concentration provisions in the ECSC Treaty, see *Butterworths Competition Law* (eds Freeman and Whish) Div IX, paras [3028]-[3070]; note the alignment of procedures for the handling of concentrations in each Treaty: *Notice concerning the Alignment of Procedures for Processing Mergers under the ECSC and EC Treaties* OJ [1998] C 66/36. It can happen that the same transaction has to be investigated in part under the ECMR and in part under the ECSC Treaty: see eg Case No IV/M.1329 *Cockerill Sambre/Usinor*; for an example of an investigation conducted purely under Article 66 ECSC, see Case ECSC.1147 *Ruhrkohle Handel/Raad Karcher Kohle* OJ [1996] L 193/42 (unconditional authorisation).

2   Regulation 4064/89, OJ [1989] L 395/1, [1990] 4 CMLR 286, corrigendum OJ [1990] L 257/13.

3   OJ [1997] L 180/1, corrigendum OJ [1998] L 40/17.

4   EEC Competition Series Study No 3.

ownership of enterprises or the reorganisation of the ownership of enterprises'[5]. Structural changes in the market were to be controlled, if at all, under Article 82: Article 81 was concerned with agreements between undertakings that are, and remain, independent of one another.

(ii)   BAT v Commission

Notwithstanding the 1966 Memorandum, a difficult issue was presented by situations in which an undertaking acquired by agreement a minority shareholding in another, without assuming legal or *de facto* control of it. In this case, there would remain independent undertakings on the market, which in turn would mean that competition between them could be restricted. The possibility that Article 81(1) could be applicable in these circumstances was examined by the ECJ in *BAT and Reynolds v Commission*[6]. The ECJ held that the acquisition of a shareholding could in some circumstances restrict or distort competition in the sense of Article 81(1):

'37 Although the acquisition by one company of an equity interest in a competitor does not in itself constitute conduct restricting competition, such an acquisition may nevertheless serve as an instrument for influencing the commercial conduct of the companies in question so as to restrict or distort competition on the market on which they carry on business.

38   That will be true in particular where, by an acquisition of a shareholding … the investing company obtains legal or *de facto* control of the commercial conduct of the other company or where the agreement provides for commercial cooperation …

39   That may also be the case where the agreement gives the investing company the possibility of reinforcing its position at a later stage and taking effective control of the other company. Account must be taken not only of the immediate effects of the agreement but also of its potential effects and of the possibility that the agreement may be part of a long-term plan'.

The adoption of the ECMR has rendered the debate about the scope of the judgment in the *BAT* case largely otiose, since the acquisition of control would be regarded as a concentration under Article 3, and Article 22(1) of the Regulation effectively disapplies Article 81 in such cases by removing any powers that the Commission would otherwise have had in relation to them under Regulation 17/62[7]. However, the judgment in *BAT* is not entirely redundant. If A were to acquire shares in B which are not sufficient to 'confer the possibility of exercising

5   Ibid, para 58.
6   Cases 142/84 and 156/84 [1987] ECR 4487, [1988] 4 CMLR 24; see also *Warner-Lambert/ Gillette* OJ [1993] L 116/21, [1993] 5 CMLR 559, paras 33-39.
7   For a discussion of the difficulties raised by the *BAT* case, and its application prior to the entry into force of the ECMR, see Hawk and Huser 'Controlling the Shifting Sands: Minority Shareholdings under EEC Competition Law' [1993] Fordham Corporate Law Institute (ed Hawk), 373-407; see also, by the same authors, *European Community Merger Control: A Practitioner's Guide* (Kluwer Law International, 1996) pp 346-353.

decisive influence'[8], and yet which might lead to a coordination of the competitive behaviour of A and B, Article 81(1) may remain applicable. There have been a few occasions since the ECMR came into force in which such a situation has been examined by the Commission. The issue arose in *BT-MCI*[9], where BT acquired a 20% stake in MCI, could nominate representatives to its board, and could have access to its confidential information; however the Commission concluded that this investment in MCI did not, on the facts, infringe Article 81(1), partly since the investment agreement was drafted in a way to prevent BT seeking to control or influence MCI and partly because both corporate and antitrust law in the US would prevent the misuse by BT of any confidential information it might receive. In its decision on *BiB*[10] the Commission exempted a provision in a joint venture agreement preventing the parents from holding more than 20% in a competing company. In doing so, the Commission seems to have considered that such a shareholding, while not giving decisive influence in the sense of the ECMR, might nevertheless give some influence[11].

(iii) Article 81 and joint ventures

As a separate matter, it should be noted that Article 81 may be applicable where two or more parents create a joint venture company. In many cases the creation of the joint venture will itself amount to a concentration, with the result that it will be investigated under the ECMR if it has a Community dimension; in so far as such a joint venture could lead to a coordination of the parents' behaviour on the market, Article 2(4) of the Regulation subjects it to analysis akin to that found in Article 81 EC[12]. In so far as the joint venture is not a full-function joint venture, it would remain potentially subject to Article 81(1)[13].

(B) Article 82

The ECJ in *Continental Can v Commission*[14] established that Article 82 may be applicable to concentrations. Where an undertaking in a dominant position acquires a competitor, thereby substantially fettering competition, this may constitute an abuse; the dominant company does not have to have 'used' its dominance in order to bring about the concentration, for example by threatening to harm the target unless it agrees to be taken over[15]. The abuse lies in the fact of further limiting competition in a market which is already, *ex hypothesi*, dominated. This gave the Commission a limited control over concentrations, but it was always an imperfect tool. In particular Article 82 suffers from the defect that it can be applied only where an undertaking is already dominant: it does not catch the creation of dominance in the first place; an important feature of the ECMR is that it applies to both the creation and the strengthening of a

8   These words are taken from Article 3(3) of the ECMR, which defines 'control' for the purpose of determining whether there has been a concentration: see pp 745-748 below.
9   OJ [1994] L 223/36, [1995] 5 CMLR 285.
10   OJ [1999] L 312/1, [2000] 4 CMLR 901.
11   See Font Galarza *Competition Policy Newsletter* October 1999, pp 7-14, http://europa.eu.int/comm/competition/publications/cpn/.
12   See pp 781-783 below.
13   See pp 748-751 below.
14   Case 6/72 [1973] ECR 215, [1973] CMLR 199.
15   See ch 5, pp 170-171 on the issue of causation.

dominant position[16]. After *Continental Can* the Commission was able to use this precedent in order to exert some influence over concentrations, but only once subsequently did it formally prohibit a transaction under Article 82, in the case of *Warner–Lambert/Gillette*[17], which concerned a transaction that took place before the ECMR came into effect. Although mergers are now dealt with under the ECMR, the Commission considers that the *Continental Can* case is a continuing authority for the proposition that it can be an abuse under Article 82 to alter the competitive structure of a market where competition on that market is already weakened as a result of the very presence of the dominant undertaking on it[18].

An interesting theoretical question, which the ECJ may one day have to rule upon, is whether the adoption of the ECMR has deprived Articles 81 and 82 of direct effect in relation to concentrations[19].

2. EC MERGER REGULATION[20]

(A) Adoption of the ECMR

The Commission proposed, in 1973, that a specific regulation be adopted to deal with concentrations[1]. The issue was controversial, as opinions differed substantially between Member States on the extent to which concentrations should be controlled at the Community level, as opposed to domestically. However the determination in the late 1980s to achieve a single market by the end of 1992 made the need for an effective system of Community merger control all the more important. The Council of Ministers adopted the ECMR on 21 December 1989. At the time of the Regulation's adoption, policy and interpretative statements of the Commission and Council were entered in the minutes of the Council meeting; they shed useful light on its meaning[2].

(B) Subsequent developments

After the ECMR entered into force, on 21 September 1990, there followed a steep learning-curve for all involved, as a range of difficult and conceptually interesting issues arose. Procedures had to be developed that were workable both for Commission officials and for lawyers and their clients; numerous jurisdictional

---

16 See pp 772-781 below.
17 OJ [1993] L 116/21, [1993] 5 CMLR 559, paras 22–32.
18 See ch 5, pp 175-176.
19 See pp 757-758 below.
20 For detailed texts on the ECMR, readers are referred in particular to Brandenburger, Spearing and Swift in *Butterworths Competition Law* (eds Freeman and Whish) Div VII paras [731]–[876]; Hawk and Huser (n 7 above); Waelbroeck and Frignani *European Competition Law* (Transnational Publishers Inc, 1999) paras 900-932; Cook and Kerse *EC Merger Control* (Sweet & Maxwell, 3rd ed, 2000); Camesasca *European Merger Control: Getting the Efficiencies Rights* (Intersentia – Hart, 2000); and Levy 'The Control of Concentrations between Undertakings' in *Competition Law of the European Community* (Matthem Bender, 2000); Bellamy and Child *European Community Law of Competition* (Sweet & Maxwell, 5th edn, 2001, ed Roth) ch 6.
1 *Commission Proposal for a Regulation of the Council of Ministers on the Control of Concentrations between Undertakings* OJ [1973] C 92/1; for successive drafts, see OJ [1982] C 36/3; OJ [1984] C 51/8; OJ [1986] C 324/5; OJ [1988] C 130/4; as to mergers under the EEA Agreement, see ch 2, pp 52-53 and Broberg *The Delimitation of Jurisdiction with regard to Concentration Control under the EEA Agreement* (1995) 16 ECLR 30.
2 [1990] 4 CMLR 314.

matters had to be resolved; and the Commission had to develop the tools to enable it to determine when a concentration might be held to be 'incompatible with the common market', the test used in Article 2 of the ECMR, because of its detrimental effect on competition. In 1996 the Commission published a Green Paper on *Community Merger Control*[3] reviewing the operation of the ECMR since it came into effect, and presenting a series of possible amendments in relation to the level of the thresholds, the problem of multiple notification where a concentration was below the Community dimension thresholds, the treatment of joint ventures and procedural improvements, in particular concerning so-called 'Phase I commitments'. Following a period of consultation, the ECMR was amended in important respects by Council Regulation 1310/97[4], which entered into force on 1 March 1998. The text that follows incorporates these amendments[5].

(C) Supporting legislation and notices

The Commission has adopted Regulation 447/98 (replacing earlier legislation) which deals with the formalities of notifications, time limits and hearings under the ECMR[6]. In particular it specifies the information that must be provided when making a notification under the ECMR: such information is provided on 'Form CO', the equivalent of Form A/B for Articles 81 and 82[7].

The Commission has published several Notices which attempt to explain aspects of its decisional practice under the ECMR. The Regulation gives rise to immensely complex questions and it can be difficult, even for highly specialised practitioners who deal with the ECMR on a daily basis, to keep fully abreast of developments in the Commission's application of it. The Commission's practice of publishing Notices that summarise its approach to particular issues is therefore much to be welcomed. It is reasonable to point out that these Notices do not have binding legislative effect, that they must be interpreted with flexibility, and that, given that concentrations are so diverse in scope and effect, they may not have much bearing on the facts of any particular case. But these reservations do not undermine the fact that the Notices are of great utility. The Notices currently in force are as follows:

(i) Notice on restrictions directly related and necessary to concentrations[8]

The parties to a concentration will frequently agree to contractual restrictions as part of the transaction. The Notice provides guidance on those restrictions that the Commission regards as 'directly related and necessary to the implementation

3   COM(96)19 final.
4   OJ [1997] L 180/1, corrigendum OJ [1998] L 40/17; the amendments effected by Regulation 1310/97 are usefully summarised by Ahlborn and Turner 'Expanding Success: Reform of the ECMR' (1998) 19 ECLR 249; see also Broberg 'The EC Commission's Green Paper on the Review of the Merger Regulation' (1996) 17 ECLR 289; and the report of the House of Lords Select Committee on the European Communities *Review of the EC Merger Regulation* HL Paper 30, 1996.
5   A further report reviewing the operation of the ECMR was sent by the Commission to the Council on 28 June 2000; the possible changes that might follow from this review are discussed at p 791 below.
6   OJ [1998] L 61/1, [1998] 4 CMLR 542; the immediate predecessor to this Regulation was Regulation 3384/94, OJ [1994] L 377/1.
7   See ch 4, p 136ff.
8   OJ [2001] C 188/5; this Notice replaces the earlier Notice regarding restrictions ancillary to concentrations OJ [1990] C 203/5.

of the concentration'[9]. Disputes between the parties as to whether restrictions are ancillary fall under the jurisdiction of national courts[10].

(ii)   Notice on the concept of a concentration[11]

This Notice provides guidance on the most important issue of all under the ECMR: what is meant by the term 'concentration'[12].

(iii)   Notice on the concept of undertakings concerned[13]

The concept of 'undertakings concerned' is critical when determining jurisdiction under the ECMR, since Articles 1 and 5 provide that jurisdiction is determined according to the turnover of the undertakings concerned and affiliated undertakings[14].

(iv)   Notice on the calculation of turnover[15]

Jurisdiction under the ECMR is determined by reference to the turnover of the undertakings concerned. Although the calculation of turnover as a jurisdictional criterion is simpler than, for example, a market share test that would require a prior determination of the relevant market, nevertheless considerable difficulties can arise in calculating and in determining the geographical location of turnover[16].

(v)   Notice on the concept of full-function joint ventures[17]

A complex issue under the ECMR has been to determine whether joint ventures amount to concentrations or whether they fall to be considered, if at all, under Articles 81 and 82. This Notice provides guidance upon this issue: the position was simplified considerably by the entry into force of Regulation 1310/97, which amended the definition of a concentration in the case of joint ventures[18].

(vi)   Notice on simplified procedure for certain concentrations[19]

The Commission has adopted a simplified procedure in relation to concentrations that are unlikely to raise any competition concerns[20].

9   This expression is found in recital 25 and Articles 6(1)(b) and 8(2) of the ECMR.
10   See pp 783-784 below.
11   OJ [1998] C 66/5, [1998] 4 CMLR 586.
12   See pp 744-751 below.
13   OJ [1998] C 66/14, [1998] 4 CMLR 599.
14   See p 753 below.
15   OJ [1998] C 66/25, [1998] 4 CMLR 613.
16   See pp 751-756 below.
17   OJ [1998] C 66/1, [1998] 4 CMLR 581.
18   See pp 748-751 below.
19   OJ [2000] C 217/32, [2000] 5 CMLR 774.
20   See p 767 below.

(vii)   Notice on remedies[1]

In many cases, the Commission clears a concentration after the parties to the transaction agree to modifications to the transaction which allay concerns about potential detriments to competition. The Commission has published a Notice setting out its practice in relation to such commitments and providing guidance on the remedies that it might find acceptable[2].

The Commission has published a helpful booklet, *Merger Control Law in the European Union*, which contains the text of the original ECMR, the amending Regulation 1310/97, an unofficial but very useful consolidated text of the ECMR as amended, and most of the other materials described above. It is available, in all official languages of the Community, from the Office for Official Publications of the European Communities, L-2985 Luxembourg.

(D)   Institutional arrangements

The full College of Commissioners takes the most important decisions under the ECMR, for example to prohibit a concentration or to clear it subject to commitments at the end of a Phase II investigation. The fact that the full Commission is often involved in decisions that may be of considerable economic and political importance means there may be a degree of lobbying of all of the individual Commissioners, not just of the Commissioner for competition. A controversial issue is whether the Commission is the appropriate body to decide on concentration cases: a possibility would be to establish a separate Competition Tribunal to decide on competition issues[3]. Some influential figures have supported this idea, including Sir Sydney Lipworth, former Chairman of the UK Monopolies and Mergers Commission[4], Wolfgang Kartte, former head of the German Bundeskartellamt and Rolf Geberth, Director of the German Federal Ministry of Economics.

Some powers are delegated by the Commission to the Commissioner for competition: for example decisions at the end of a Phase I investigation can be taken by him. He in turn may delegate certain functions to the Director General of the Directorate General for Competition ('DG COMP'). A Directorate known as the Merger Task Force ('the MTF') within DG COMP is charged with the day-to-day responsibility of applying the ECMR. The MTF is divided into four operational units, each with a Head. Of the case–handlers in the MTF, about one third are officials seconded from national authorities. The total number of officials in the MTF is about 40, but additional resources have been promised.[4a]

The Advisory Committee on Concentrations[5] has an important rôle: this provides the Member States with the opportunity of input into the decision-making process. Appeals against decisions of the Commission are taken to the CFI or, where a Member State is the applicant, to the ECJ[6]. The first cases did

1   OJ [2001] C 68/3.
2   See pp 784-787 below.
3   See Goyder 'The Implementation of the ECMR' [1992] CLP 117, pp 141–143.
4   *The Independent* 29 September 1992.
4a   See the *XXXth Annual Report on Competition Policy* (2000), point 238
5   See p 789 below.
6   An example of an application to the ECJ is provided by Case C-68/94 *France v Commission* [1998] ECR I-1375, [1998] 4 CMLR 829.

not occur until more than two years after the ECMR came into force; since then, however, the number of cases has increased quite sharply[7].

(E)   Entry into force of the ECMR and the reporting of Commission decisions

As mentioned above, the ECMR entered into force on 21 September 1990. For many practitioners of competition law, application of the ECMR has become the core of their practice; the work is highly specialised, and detailed knowledge is required of the rapid development of the Commission's decisional practice and the evolving case law of the Community Courts. Many billable hours have been generated as a result of the extensive and detailed information required to be included in a Form CO and the discussions that take place before and after notification to the Commission. This chapter can provide only an introduction to the main provisions of the ECMR and the way in which it has been applied by the Commission and the Community Courts. The reader requiring a more detailed understanding of the ECMR in practice is referred to the detailed practitioners' works cited above[8].

The number of concentrations notified each year has risen considerably since 1990: the application of the ECMR in practice, including relevant statistics, is considered further below[9]. Each notification will be given a case number, which will normally be prefixed with an 'M' (as in Case No IV/M.1328 *KLM/Martinair*); however a full-function joint venture requiring examination under both the ECMR and Article 81, as imported into the Regulation by Article 2(4) thereof[10], will be prefixed with a 'JV' (as in Case No IV/JV.15 *BT/AT&T*)[11]. Since the appellation 'DG IV' was discontinued in 1999, cases are denominated 'Case No COMP' rather than 'Case No IV' (as in Case No COMP/M.1672 *Volvo/Scania*). Cases under the ECSC Treaty are referred to as 'Case No ECSC', as in the *Ruhrkohle* decision referred to in footnote 1 on page 735 above.

The decisions of the Commission on concentrations can be accessed in various ways. Phase I decisions – that is to say cases that do not require 'in-depth investigation'[12] – are not themselves published in the Official Journal, other than a brief statement of the outcome. Phase I decisions can however be obtained from the Office for Official Publications of the European Communities, the European Document Delivery Service, the home page of the Directorate General for Competition[13], CELEX, in the *EC Merger Control Reporter* published by Kluwer and on a CD Rom produced by Butterworths[14]. Phase I decisions are available only in the language in which the parties notified. A press release summarising the Commission's finding in each case will usually be published in English, French, German and in the language of the notification. The press release is normally issued at noon on the day following adoption of the decision. It can be obtained on the Rapid database of the Commission's website. Decisions

7   On judicial review under the ECMR, see p 790 below.
8   See p 738, n 20 above.
9   See pp 791-802.
10   See pp 781-783 below.
11   The complex topic of joint ventures under the ECMR is discussed at pp 748-751 below.
12   See pp 768-770 below.
13   http://europa.eu.int/comm/competition/index_en.html.
14   *Butterworths Competition Law Library*; this CD Rom is updated on a quarterly basis.

following an in-depth, Phase II investigation[15], are more widely available. Apart from the above sources, Phase II decisions are published in the 'L' series of the Official Journal; there may be a lengthy delay between the adoption of a decision and its appearance in the Official Journal while agreement is reached between the parties and the Commission as to what confidential information should be omitted from the published version and while the decision is translated into all the official Community languages. To reduce the delay, the Commission publishes on its website an advanced public version of the decision in its authentic language as soon as the confidential information has been omitted. Phase II decisions may also be published in the Common Market Law Reports. A press release will be published in relation to each Phase II decision. Where possible in this chapter, the law will be illustrated by reference to judgments of the Community Courts and Phase II decisions of the Commission, in particular because these materials will in general be easier to locate.

3. MAKING SENSE OF THE ECMR: OUTLINE OF THIS CHAPTER

In making sense of the ECMR, it is helpful to consider a series of matters in turn. The first is jurisdiction: what is meant by a concentration for the purpose of the ECMR, and in what circumstances does a concentration fall within the jurisdiction of the Commission? These matters are considered in section 4. The next issue is procedure: the ECMR makes it compulsory to notify concentrations having a Community dimension to the Commission prior to their execution, and strict time limits are imposed. Procedure is dealt with in section 5, including the powers of decision available to the Commission. Section 6 will consider the substantive appraisal of concentrations under the ECMR: assuming that a concentration falls within the jurisdiction of the Commission, what test will it apply in determining whether the concentration should be permitted, prohibited or authorised only subject to commitments? This section will also consider how the possibility of restrictions of competition between the parents of a joint venture and ancillary restraints are dealt with. Section 7 considers the possibility that commitments might be acceptable to the Commission as a condition of clearance. Section 8 will deal with the Commission's powers of investigation and enforcement. The international aspects of concentrations are briefly examined in section 9[16]. Section 10 will deal with judicial review of the Commission's decisions under the ECMR. Section 11 will consider possible changes to the ECMR in the future. The chapter will conclude with a review of the ECMR in practice, including tables setting out relevant statistics and listing those cases that have been taken to Phase II.

4. JURISDICTION

This section will deal in turn with the following matters:

(A) *Article 3: meaning of a concentration:* the ECMR applies to 'concentrations', a term defined in Article 3 and further explained in the case law of the Community Courts and the Commission's *Notice on the concept of a concentration*[17].

15 See pp 769-770 below.
16 International issues are dealt with in greater depth in ch 12.
17 See pp 744-751 below.

(B)   *Article 1: concentrations having a 'Community dimension'*: the ECMR applies to concentrations that have a 'Community dimension'. The meaning of this term is to be found in Article 1, and is determined by reference to the turnover of the 'undertakings concerned', including their affiliated undertakings.

(C)   *One–stop merger control*: as a general proposition, concentrations that have a Community dimension should be investigated only by the Commission and not by the Member States. This is the principle of so–called 'one–stop merger control'. Concentrations that do not have a Community dimension may be subject to the domestic merger control of Member States. This can mean that concentrations below the thresholds of the ECMR may have to be notified under numerous domestic systems of law: Article 1(3) of the ECMR as amended by Regulation 1310/97 makes a partial attempt to deal with this problem of 'multiple notification' by introducing an alternative category of concentrations to be treated as having a Community dimension[18].

(D)   *Article 9: referral to the competent authorities of the Member States – the 'German clause'*: in certain cases Article 9 provides a mechanism whereby concentrations that have a Community dimension can be reviewed under domestic law because of the harm they might cause to competition within a particular Member State.

(E)   *Article 22(3): referral by the competent authorities of the Member States to the Commission – the 'Dutch clause'*: in exceptional cases Article 22(3) provides a mechanism whereby concentrations that do not have a Community dimension can be investigated by the Commission at the request of a Member State or Member States.

(F)   *Article 21(3): legitimate interest clause*: Member States are not allowed to apply their domestic competition law to concentrations that have a Community dimension except in the circumstances in which Article 9 is applicable. However, provision is made by Article 21(3) for Member States to investigate a concentration having a Community dimension where it threatens to harm some 'legitimate interest' of the State other than the maintenance of competition.

(G)   *Defence*: Member States retain jurisdiction to examine the national security aspects of mergers under Article 296 (ex Article 223) of the Treaty.

(A)   Article 3: meaning of a concentration[19]

The first question to be asked in relation to any transaction is whether it would amount to a concentration. Article 3 of the ECMR defines this term; there has been some case law on it[20]; and the Commission's *Notice on the concept of a concentration*[1] is an important source of guidance on its practical application.

---

18   See p 752 below.
19   See *Butterworth's Competition Law* Div VII paras [731]-[777]; *Hawk and Huser* ch II; *Cook and Kerse* ch 2.
20   See p 746, n 12 below.
1   OJ [1998] C 66/5, [1998] 4 CMLR 586.

(i)   Article 3(1): basic definition[2]

Article 3(1) provides that a concentration shall be deemed to arise where:

> '(a)   two or more previously independent undertakings merge, or
> (b)   one or more persons already controlling at least one undertaking,
> or
> (c)   one or more undertakings
>
> acquire, whether by purchase of securities or assets, by contract or by any
> other means, direct or indirect control of the whole or parts of one or more
> other undertakings.'

Article 3(1)(a) applies to cases where there is a complete concentration between two or more undertakings, for example where two previously separate entities merge into a new one, where one acquires 100% of the shares in another or where undertakings combine their activities in a separate economic unit[3]. A good example of two undertakings merging into a single entity can be found in the *Ciba-Geigy/Sandoz* decision[4], where those two entities merged to establish Novartis.

Article 3(1)(b) deals with the more difficult (and more common) case of a change in the control of an undertaking falling short of a full concentration. To understand the application of Article 3(1)(b), it is necessary to take into account Article 3(3), which explains what is meant by control for this purpose.

(ii)   Article 3(3): control[5]

Article 3(3) provides that control:

> 'shall be constituted by rights, contracts or any other means which, either
> separately or in combination and having regard to the considerations of
> fact or law involved, confer the possibility of exercising decisive influence
> on an undertaking, in particular by:
> (a)   ownership or the right to use all or part of the assets of an undertaking;
> (b)   rights or contracts which confer decisive influence on the composition,
>   voting or decisions of the organs of an undertaking.'

It will be readily appreciated that this definition of control – which extends to a situation in which even the *possibility* of exercising decisive influence is caught – is a wide one, considerably wider than the definition in Article 5(4) when calculating the turnover of the 'undertakings concerned' in a concentration[6]. To

---

2   The application of the ECMR to joint ventures, and in particular the terms of Article 3(2), are dealt with separately in section (iii) below: see pp 748-751.

3   *Notice on the concept of a concentration*, paras 6 and 7.

4   Case No IV/M 737, OJ [1997] L 201/1, para 7; see similarly Case No IV/M.1069 *WorldCom/ MCI* OJ [1999] L 116/1, [1999] 5 CMLR 876.

5   Notice on the concept of a concentration, paras 8 et seq; note also Article 3(4) of the ECMR which provides that control may be acquired by the holders of the rights in question, and also by persons that do not hold the rights but have the power to exercise the rights deriving from them.

6   See pp 754-756 below; on the test of control in the UK, see ch 22, pp 805-807: the test of 'material' influence in the UK is wider than 'decisive' influence in the ECMR.

this should be added the possibility that the exercise of decisive influence may arise by operation of law or fact[7]; that it may not be the intention of the parties that such influence should be conferred[8]; and that a shareholding of less than 25% may be found to amount to control[9]. Bearing in mind that failure to notify a concentration having a Community dimension can attract a fine[10], and that implementation of an unnotified concentration can attract a larger one[11], great care must be taken to ensure that undertakings do not unwittingly enter into agreements that might amount to concentrations in the sense of the ECMR. There is little doubt that concentrations having a Community dimension have been consummated in breach of the ECMR, where the undertakings concerned failed to appreciate the possibility that the Regulation might apply. A number of cases have been brought before the Community Courts on the meaning of control in Article 3(3)[12].

It may be helpful to set out a series of situations in which there could be a change of control that amounts to a concentration.

(A)   ACQUISITION OF SOLE CONTROL[13].   Where one undertaking acquires more than 50% of the voting capital of another this would normally give rise to sole control, unless, for example, a shareholders' agreement gave the minority shareholder(s) joint control with the majority shareholder, for example through rights of veto[14]. A more difficult question is whether the acquisition of a minority shareholding may confer 'de facto' sole control. This is to be decided by reference to a combination of considerations both of law and of fact. As a matter of law, it may be that the shares that comprise the minority shareholding nevertheless carry a majority of the voting rights, in which case the minority shareholder could determine the strategic behaviour of the target company. The mere fact that an undertaking has an option to purchase a majority of the shares in a company does not give it control[15], although the position would be different if the option was to be exercised in the near future according to legally binding agreements[16]. As a matter of fact, a minority shareholding may be so large compared to all the others that it would be likely to achieve a majority in the shareholders' meeting: the Commission will look at the evidence of what has actually happened in recent shareholders' meetings. Examples of such a situation can be found in the Commission's decisions in *Société Générale de Belgique/Générale de Banque*[17], *Crown Cork & Seal/CarnaudMetalbox*[18] and in *Skanska/Scancem*[19]. In *Anglo American/Lonrho*[20] the Commission concluded that Anglo American's

7   *Notice on the concept of a concentration*, para 4.
8   Case No IV/M.157 *Air France/Sabena* [1994] 5 CMLR M1.
9   See p 747 below.
10   See p 788 below.
11   Ibid.
12   See Case T-2/93 *Air France v Commission* [1994] ECR II-323; Case T-221/95 *Endemol Entertainment Holdings BV v Commission* [1999] ECR II-1299, [1999] 5 CMLR 611, paras 159-164; Case T-102/96 *Gencor v Commission* [1999] ECR II-753, [1999] 4 CMLR 971, paras 167-194; Cases T-22/97 *Kesko Oy v Commission* [1999] ECR II-3775, [2000] 4 CMLR 335, paras 137-139; Cases T-125/97 etc *Coca-Cola v Commission* [2000] 5 CMLR 467, paras 107-109.
13   *Notice on the concept of a concentration*, paras 13-17.
14   See pp 747-748 below.
15   See Case T-2/93 *Air France v Commission* [1994] ECR II-323, paras 70-72.
16   *Notice on the concept of a concentration*, para 15.
17   Case No IV/M.343.
18   Case No IV/M.603, OJ [1996] L 75/38, para 6.
19   Case No IV/M.1157, OJ [1999] L 183/1, [1999] 4 CMLR 16, paras 14-20.
20   Case No IV/M.754, OJ [1998] L 149/21.

shareholding in Lonrho of 27.47% gave it control, and required a divestment of shares so that its stake would be reduced to 9.9%.

Control can be found to exist even where there is a shareholding of less than 25%: for example in *CCIE/GTE*[1] CCIE acquired 19% of the voting rights in EDIL and was found to have acquired control, the remaining shares being held by an independent investment bank whose approval was not needed for important decisions.

It is possible that an undertaking that acquires shares in another, but which does not acquire control in the sense of Article 3(3) of the ECMR, may nevertheless be party to an agreement that is restrictive of competition under Article 81[2].

(B)   ACQUISITION OF JOINT CONTROL[3].   As in the case of acquisition of sole control, the issue of joint control is determined by reference to considerations both of law and of fact. Paragraph 18 of the Commission's *Notice on the concept of a concentration* states that there will be joint control where 'the shareholders ... must reach agreement on major decisions concerning the controlled undertaking ...'. In a case of sole control, one undertaking is able to determine the strategic decisions of another; a case of joint control will exist where two or more undertakings must reach agreement in determining the commercial policy of the entity in question. A large percentage of cases involves the acquisition of joint control[4]. A change from joint control by three firms to two would also qualify as a concentration[5]. The Commission's Notice sets out a series of examples of situations in which there could be joint control:

• where two parent companies of a joint venture share equally the voting rights in a joint venture;
• where two parent companies have unequal rights, or where there are more than two parents, but the minority shareholder(s) are able to veto decisions which are essential for the strategic commercial behaviour of the joint venture ('negative control'): examples would be decisions related to the budget, the business plan, major investments or the appointment of senior management[6]; on the other hand veto rights simply to protect the financial interests of minority shareholders would not confer joint control[7];
• where there is a legally binding agreement between the shareholders on the common exercise of voting rights[8];

---

1   Case No IV/M.258.
2   See the discussion of *BAT and Reynolds v Commission* at pp 736-737 above.
3   *Notice on the concept of a concentration*, paras 18–38.
4   See the Commission's XXVIIIth *Annual Report on Competition Policy* p 80, where it provides a breakdown of cases for 1992-1998 and finds that 48% involved joint ventures or joint control.
5   Case No IV/M.993 *BertelsMann/Kirch/Premiere* OJ [1999] L 53/1, [1999] 4 CMLR 700.
6   Ibid, para 23; see eg Case T-221/95 *Endemol Entertainment Holding BV v Commission* [1999] ECR II-1299, [1999] 5 CMLR 611, paras 159 to 164, upholding the Commission's finding of joint control in Case No IV/M.553 *RTL/Veronica/Endemol* OJ [1996] L 134/32; see also Case T-102/96 *Gencor v Commission* [1999] ECR II-753, [1999] 4 CMLR 971, paras 169-194; Case No IV/M.774 *Saint Gobain/Wacker-Chemie/NOM* OJ [1997] L 247/1, where the shareholdings were 60%, 20% and 20%, but the Commission still found joint control.
7   *Notice on the concept of a concentration*, para 22.
8   Ibid, paras 30-31. In Case No IV/M.1479 *Thomson/Banco Zaragozano/Caja Madrid/Indra* the Commission found that a group with less than 25% of the shares, but with an agreement to coordinate their voting behaviour at the shareholders' meeting, were in joint control; in Case No IV/M.1366 *Paribas* the Commission found that there was neither joint nor sole control where there was no agreement between the shareholders on voting rights.

- (exceptionally) where the common interests of the shareholders are so strong that, *de facto*, they would not act against each other in exercising their rights in relation to the joint venture[9].

(C)   TRANSITION FROM JOINT TO SOLE CONTROL.   A transition from joint to sole control would qualify as a concentration. In *ICI/Tioxide*[10] ICI's acquisition of Cookson's 50% interest in Tioxide, in which ICI already had a 50% stake, qualified as a concentration. The Commission came to a similar decision was *ABB/BREL*[11]: ABB and Trafalgar House each had 40% holdings in BREL, thereby giving them joint control; when Trafalgar House sold its 40% holding to ABB this gave ABB sole as opposed to joint control and qualified as a concentration.

(D)   DIVISION OF A BUSINESS.   The division of a business can involve a concentration or concentrations. In *Solvay–Laporte/Interox*[12] Solvay and Laporte proposed to dissolve Interox, a joint venture company established in 1970; Solvay would take Interox's bulk chemical business and Laporte the speciality chemical business. As Solvay and Laporte would each acquire sole control of businesses in respect of which they had had joint control before, this entailed two concentrations. Only the Solvay bid had a Community dimension.

(E)   ACQUISITION OF ASSETS.   The acquisition of assets, such as branded products or licences, may amount to a concentration, provided the assets constitute a business to which a market turnover can be clearly attributed[13]. In *Blokker/Toys'R'Us*[14] the Commission, rejecting the contrary argument of the parties, concluded that the acquisition of assets coupled with a right to sell toys under a franchise agreement amounted to a concentration; the parties had argued that the case was one for consideration, if at all, under Article 81.

(iii)   Article 3(2): full-function joint ventures

The creation of a joint venture company may qualify as a concentration and be subject to the ECMR if it is a full-function joint venture; if not, it may be subject to Article 81. Article 3(2) of the ECMR addresses this issue.

(A)   ARTICLE 3(2) ECMR.   Article 3(2) of the ECMR was substantially amended by Regulation 1310/97, with effect from 1 March 1998. As amended it provides that:

> 'The creation of a joint venture performing on a lasting basis all the functions of an autonomous economic entity shall constitute a concentration within the meaning of paragraph 1(b)'.

---

9   *Notice on the concept of a concentration*, paras 32-35.
10   Case No IV/M.23, [1991] 4 CMLR 792.
11   Case No IV/M.221.
12   Case No IV/M.197; see also *CAMPSA* Case No IV/M.138.
13   *Notice on the concept of a concentration*, para 11.
14   Case No IV/M.890, OJ [1998] L 316/1, paras 12-16.

In the parlance of EC competition law, an operation that satisfies this test is known as a 'full-function joint venture'[15]. A full-function joint venture that has a Community dimension must be notified under the ECMR: its procedures, including its time limits, will apply. Under the ECMR as originally enacted, Article 3(2) provided that an operation, including the creation of a joint venture, which had as its object or effect the coordination of the competitive behaviour of undertakings which remain independent, would not constitute a concentration within the meaning of Article 3(1)(b). Such a joint venture might, however, be subject to Article 81. Thus the possibility that there might be coordination had a jurisdictional consequence, of determining whether a case had to be investigated under the procedures of the ECMR or Article 81. This caused immense complications. In general, as explained below, there are benefits to be derived from a transaction being classified as a concentration. Fortunately the amendment introduced by Regulation 1310/97 has eliminated this problem, since the issue of coordination of the parents' competitive behaviour is no longer relevant to the characterisation of the joint venture as a concentration or otherwise. The only question to be determined in deciding whether a joint venture is a concentration is whether it will be full function. This is an enormous improvement in the law. The possibility that there may be coordination of the behaviour of the parents of a joint venture still has relevance as a matter of substantive analysis under Article 2(4) of the revised ECMR: this is explained in section 6 below.

(B)   THE BENEFITS OF CHARACTERISATION AS A CONCENTRATION.   There were from the outset strong attractions in joint ventures being analysed under the ECMR rather than Article 81: under the ECMR there are strict time–limits for the Commission's investigation; joint ventures that qualify as concentrations but do not have a Community dimension cannot be challenged under EC law in accordance with the policy of 'one-stop merger control' except, theoretically, under Article 85 (ex Article 89) of the Treaty[16]; where a joint venture qualifies as a concentration and has a Community dimension there is a stronger likelihood that it will be permitted than under Article 81, given that the ECMR leads to a prohibition only where a dominant position would be created or strengthened, whereas under Article 81(1) the test is whether competition would be appreciably restricted; and a clearance under the ECMR is permanent. On the other hand analysis of joint ventures under Article 81 is normally less favourable: there are no formal time limits for investigations under Regulation 17/62; Article 81(1) may be infringed even though the firms would not be dominant on the market and the block exemptions may not be available; obtaining an individual exemption for an agreement is rare – most cases are settled by comfort letter; individual exemptions (and, by analogy, Article 81(3) comfort letters) are required to be limited in time. The effect of these differences was that legal advisers would often deliberately design joint ventures to fall on the concentrative side of the divide – an example of legal formalism affecting substance.

(C)   THE COMMISSION'S NOTICE ON FULL-FUNCTION JOINT VENTURES.   The amendments carried out by Regulation 1310/97 mean that more joint ventures than before are characterised as concentrations. The Commission's *Notice on the concept of*

15   The reader is strongly encouraged to abstain from using the expressions 'concentrative' and 'cooperative' joint ventures, which reflect the position under the original, unamended ECMR, and instead to distinguish between 'full-function' joint ventures on the one hand and 'non-full-function' or 'partial-function' joint ventures on the other.
16   See p 757 below.

full-function joint ventures[17] provides helpful guidance on this issue. For there to be a full-function joint venture, the first requirement is that there must be joint control of the entity in question: the Notice points out at paragraphs 9 and 10 that this issue is dealt with in paragraphs 18 to 39 of the *Notice on the concept of a concentration*[18]. The *Notice on the concept of full-function joint ventures* goes on to say that full-function joint ventures are ones that bring about a lasting change in the structure of the undertakings concerned. Paragraph 12 explains that:

> 'Essentially this means that a joint venture must operate on a market, performing the functions normally carried out by undertakings operating on the same market. In order to do so the joint venture must have a management dedicated to its day-to-day operations and access to sufficient resources including finance, staff, and assets (tangible and intangible) in order to conduct on a lasting basis its business activities within the area provided for in the joint venture agreement'.

Paragraph 13 says that a joint venture would not be full-function where it takes over only one function of its parents' activities, such as research and development or distribution or sales. Paragraph 14 deals with the situation in which the parents have a strong presence in a market upstream or downstream from the joint venture and there are substantial sales between the parents and the joint venture: this could suggest that it is not really full function, although sales for a start-up period only to enable the joint venture to establish itself or sales made on the basis of normal commercial conditions might be treated differently. Paragraph 15 deals with the question of whether the joint venture will operate 'on a lasting basis'. The fact that the parents devote the resources described in paragraph 12 of the Notice to the joint venture would normally indicate that they intend it to operate on a lasting basis. Where the agreement establishing the joint venture contains provisions for its dissolution in certain circumstances, this does not prevent it from being considered as operating on a lasting basis: terms such as this, for example in the event of fundamental disagreement between the parents, are normal in such cases. Where the joint venture is established for a finite period of time, the question will be whether the period is sufficiently long to bring about a lasting change in the structure of the undertakings concerned. Whether this is the case will depend on the facts of any particular case: a period as short as five years can be long enough to satisfy this test, as for example in *TKS/ITW Signode/Titan*[19].

It is presumably the case that, where there is a change of control in relation to a joint venture that is not full function, this is outside the scope of the ECMR, although this is not stated in any of the Commission's Notices.

(D)   METAMORPHOSIS OF A FORM CO INTO A FORM A/B.   Where it transpires that a joint venture notified as a concentration under the ECMR is not, in fact, full function, Article 5 of Regulation 447/98 provides that the notification can be treated as an application for individual exemption under Article 81(3). This has happened on numerous occasions[20].

---

17   OJ [1998] C 66/1, [1998] 4 CMLR 581.
18   OJ [1998] C 66/5, [1998] 4 CMLR 586.
19   Case No IV/M.970, para 10.
20   See eg *BT/MCI* OJ [1994] L 223/36, [1995] 5 CMLR 285.

(E) CONTRACTUAL ALLIANCES AS JOINT VENTURES. In the case of *KLM/Alitalia*[1] the Commission concluded that a contractual alliance between those two airlines amounted to a concentration between the parties, even though there was neither a merger in the conventional sense nor the creation of a joint venture company. The Commission's view was that the integration of the two businesses was sufficient to amount to a full-function joint venture. This was the first decision of its kind.

(F) PARTIAL-FUNCTION PRODUCTION JOINT VENTURES. The Commission's White Paper on Modernisation has suggested that, if the system of notification for exemption under Article 81(3) is abandoned, partial-function production joint ventures may be brought within the procedural framework of the ECMR[2].

(iv)   Article 3(5): certain operations not to be treated as concentrations

Article 3(5) provides that concentrations will not be held to arise where credit and other financial institutions, or insurance companies, hold securities for themselves or on behalf of others, provided that these holdings do not entitle them to influence the competitive behaviour of these companies[3]; the exemption applies to financial holding companies which do not use their votes for reasons other than maintaining the value of their investments[4]. Furthermore, control of companies acquired relating to their liquidation, or analogous proceedings, on account of the law of a Member State, are not concentrations[5].

(B)   Article 1: concentrations having a 'Community dimension'[6]

Having determined whether an operation amounts to a concentration in the sense of Article 3, it is necessary to consider whether that concentration has a Community dimension according to the provisions in Article 1. Article 1(1) provides that the ECMR shall apply to all concentrations having a Community dimension as defined in Article 1(2) or Article 1(3). The thresholds in Article 1(2) were those established by the ECMR as originally enacted. The Article 1(3) thresholds were introduced by Regulation 1310/97 with effect from 1 March 1998. The criteria set out in Article 1(2) and 1(3) of the ECMR are *alternative* grounds on which a concentration may have a Community dimension.

(i)   Article 1(2)

Article 1(2) provides that a concentration has a Community dimension where:

'(a) the combined aggregate worldwide turnover of all the undertakings concerned is more than EUR 5,000 million; and

---

1   Case No COMP/JV.19.
2   On the White Paper, see ch 4, pp 146-147 and ch 7, pp 246-258.
3   ECMR, Article 3(5)(a).
4   Ibid, Article 3(5)(b).
5   Ibid.
6   See *Butterworth's Competition Law* Div VII paras [778] to [818]; *Hawk and Huser* ch III; *Cook and Kerse* ch 3.

(b) the aggregate Community-wide turnover of each of at least two of the
     undertakings concerned is more than EUR 250 million,
unless each of the undertakings concerned achieves more than two–thirds
of its aggregate Community–wide turnover within one and the same
Member State.'

(ii)   Article 1(3)

Article 1(3) provides an alternative basis of jurisdiction to Article 1(2), that a
concentration that does not meet the Article 1(2) thresholds nevertheless has a
Community dimension where:

'(a) the combined aggregate worldwide turnover of all the undertakings
     concerned is more than EUR 2500 million; and
(b) in each of at least three Member States, the combined aggregate
     turnover of all the undertakings concerned is more than EUR 100
     million;
(c) in each of the three Member States included for the purpose of (b), the
     aggregate turnover of each of at least two of the undertakings concerned
     is more than EUR 25 million; and
(d) the aggregate Community-wide turnover of each of at least two of the
     undertakings concerned is more than EUR 100 million;
unless each of the undertakings concerned achieves more than two-thirds
of its aggregate Community-wide turnover within one and the same Member
State'.

This provision was inserted by Regulation 1310/97 as a result of the increasing
problem of multiple notification of concentrations within the Community.
Concentrations below the thresholds are subject to national law; as there has
been a proliferation of national systems of competition law, it follows that some
transactions might be subject to separate notification in numerous Member States,
obviously a serious regulatory burden for the parties to have to bear. The problem
was discussed in the Green Paper[7], and various ideas were floated for taking at
least some cases of multiple notification out of the domestic systems and giving
them to the Commission instead. Article 1(3) was the outcome of this process
and attempts to capture those concentrations where the undertakings concerned
are conducting reasonably substantial business in at least three Member States.
Since the amendment, 45 notifications had been made pursuant to Article 1(3)
by the end of 1999[8].

(iii)   Community dimension determined by reference to turnover thresholds

The definition of 'Community dimension' focuses on the size of the undertakings
concerned and *not* on their market power. The reason for this is that undertakings
should be enabled to determine with reasonable certainty whether they are under
an obligation to notify: if jurisdiction were to turn upon the parties' market
power (which would require a prior determination of the relevant market), this

7   See p 739 above.
8   *Report to the Council on the application of the Merger Regulation thresholds*, para 20.

would introduce considerable uncertainty. However, a consequence of making jurisdiction turn upon turnover alone is that many concentrations fall within the scope of the ECMR that do not have an adverse effect on competition[9]. Since pre-notification is mandatory[10], time and effort may have to be expended on preparing a Form CO in circumstances where a transaction will have no impact on competition at all.

(iv) 'Undertakings concerned'

The critical concept in determining whether a concentration has a Community dimension is that of 'undertakings concerned'. Having determined which are the undertakings concerned, it is then necessary to calculate their turnover, including the turnover of affiliated undertakings as defined in Article 5(4) of the ECMR[11]. Identification of the undertakings concerned can be complex. The Commission's *Notice on the concept of undertakings concerned*[12] is helpful in setting out its decisional practice in relation to this key concept. For example, in the case of acquisition of joint control of a pre-existing company, 'the undertakings concerned are each of the companies acquiring control on the one hand, and the pre-existing acquired company or business on the other'[13]. In the case of a change from joint control to sole control, 'the undertakings concerned are the remaining (acquiring) shareholder and the joint venture'[14].

(v) World wide turnover and Community turnover[15]

The reference in Articles 1(2) and 1(3) to world-wide turnover brings within the scope of the ECMR many non-EC undertakings; their concentrations may be notifiable, provided that (in the case of Article 1(2)) at least two of the undertakings concerned have an aggregate Community-wide turnover of more than EUR 250 million or (in the case of Article 1(3)) that at least two of the undertakings concerned have a Community turnover of at least EUR 100 million and that the other requirements are satisfied. The concentration may take place outside the Community, and the parties' turnover within the Community may be in relation to goods or services that have no connection with the transaction in question, and yet the arithmetic of Article 1 may result in there being a Community dimension. For example, the merger of the Royal Bank of Canada and the Bank of Montreal had to be notified, although the parties had only minor activities within the Community and a market share of less than 2%[16]. This raises the issue of the extraterritorial scope of the ECMR and of EC law generally, matters which are discussed further in chapter 12[17]. At this stage it is sufficient to note

9   For criticism of the ECMR's jurisdictional approach, see Kassamali 'From Fiction to Fallacy: Reviewing the EC Merger Regulation's Community-Dimension Thresholds in the Light of Economics and Experience in Merger Control' (1996) 21 EL Rev Checklist No 2 CC/89.
10   See p 766 below.
11   See section (vii) below.
12   OJ [1998] C 66/14, [1998] 4 CMLR 599.
13   *Notice on the concept of undertakings concerned*, para 22.
14   Ibid, para 31.
15   See Broberg 'The Geographical Allocation of Turnover under the Merger Regulation' (1997) 18 ECLR 103.
16   Case No IV/M.1138.
17   See ch 12, pp 398-403.

the practical point, that there is a simplified procedure for some cases that raise no competition concerns in the EC[18], and that, even where the simplified procedure does not apply, it may be possible to negotiate waivers with the case-handlers in the MTF to the effect that information that would ordinarily be required in a Form CO can be dispensed with[19].

(vi)   Turnover in one Member State

Where a concentration involves undertakings, each of which generates more than two thirds of its turnover in one and the same Member State, it does not have a Community dimension and (subject to Article 22(3))[20] can be investigated only by the domestic competition authorities. It can happen that concentrations between substantial undertakings fall outside the ECMR as a result of this rule, a good example being Lloyds Bank's bid for the Midland Bank in 1992. As each of these undertakings operated primarily within the UK, the proposed concentration did not have a Community dimension. The bid was referred to the UK Monopolies and Mergers Commission by the Secretary of State for Trade and Industry[1]; in the meantime a rival bid, which did have a Community dimension, was cleared by the Commission in *Hong Kong and Shanghai Banking Corp/Midland Bank*[2]. Thus rival bids for the same target fell under different régimes, the Lloyds bid faring less well under domestic law than the Hong Kong bid under EC law. The UK reference was set aside when Lloyds decided to withdraw.

(vii)   Calculation of turnover

Calculation of turnover is dealt with by Article 5 of the ECMR. The Commission has published a *Notice on calculation of turnover*[3]. Article 5(1) gives a basic definition of turnover: the amounts derived by the undertakings concerned in the preceding financial year from the sale of products and the provision of services falling within their normal activities. By way of derogation from Article 5(1), Article 5(2), first indent, provides that, where part of an undertaking is taken over, only the turnover of that part shall be taken into account[4]; however, as an anti–avoidance device, Article 5(2), second indent, provides that, where two or more transactions take place between the same parties within a two–year period, they should be treated as one and the same transaction, taking place on the date of the last one of them. Article 5(3) sets out special rules to determine the turnover of credit institutions, other financial institutions and insurance undertakings.

Article 5(4) is an important provision which states that, without prejudice to Article 5(2), the aggregate turnover of an undertaking concerned shall be calculated by adding together the respective turnover of the undertaking concerned

---

18   See p 767 below.
19   See pp 766-767 below.
20   See pp 761-763 below.
1   The UK could have asked the MTF to deal with the Lloyds' bid under Article 22(3) of the ECMR (see pp 761-763 below) but did not do so.
2   Case No IV/M.213.
3   OJ [1998] C 66/25, [1998] 4 CMLR 613.
4   See eg Case No IV/M.12 *Fiat Geotech/Ford New Holland*: Fiat acquired a subsidiary of Ford, Ford New Holland; only Fiat and FNH's turnover were taken into account.

and (to paraphrase) those undertakings that it legally controls, those undertakings that legally control it and other connected undertakings. Article 5(4) of the ECMR has a different notion of control from that found in Article 3(3). In Article 3(3), the issue is whether two or more businesses are coming under common control, and a wide notion of control is used, to include 'the possibility of exercising decisive influence'. In Article 5(4), turnover is being established for jurisdictional purposes, and a more certain test of legal control is applied. The intention of Article 5(4) is to ensure that the total volume of the economic resources being concentrated should be taken into account when determining whether a concentration has a Community dimension. It is often the inclusion of these additional undertakings' turnover that leads to the Community dimension thresholds being reached. The application of Article 5(4) is not without its difficulties. Some examples may help:

Example 1

A acquires B: A is the wholly-owned subsidiary of X

Undertakings concerned: A and B (Article 5(1))

Turnover to be taken into account: A and B (undertakings concerned) and X (X's turnover is included as a result of Article 5(4)(c)).

Example 2

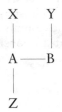

A acquires B, a division of Y; A is a part of X, and has a wholly-owned subsidiary, Z

Undertakings concerned: A and B (Article 5(1))

Turnover to be taken into account: A and B (undertakings concerned: disregard the turnover of Y, as A is acquiring B only, a part of Y); X (Article 5(4)(c)) and Z (Article 5(4)(b)).

Example 3

A acquires B. A is jointly controlled by X, Y and Z.

Undertakings concerned: A and B

Turnover to be taken into account: A and B (undertakings concerned); X, Y and Z (this is the interpretation in the third indent to paragraph 38 of the *Notice on the calculation of turnover*, and is based on the language of Article 5(4)(c) of the ECMR).

Example 4

A acquires B; A has joint control of X with Y

Undertakings concerned: A and B

Turnover to be taken into account: A and B (undertakings concerned); but is the turnover of X relevant? The answer to this question could determine whether the concentration has a Community dimension if A and B's combined turnover was below the Community dimension threshold. The Commission states at paragraph 40 of its *Notice on the calculation of turnover* that it would allocate a 50% share of the joint venture's turnover to A in these circumstances.

(viii)   Mandatory review

Article 1(4) and (5) provide for a review of the thresholds and criteria set out in Article 1(2) and (3) by 1 July 2000, whereupon the Council of Ministers may revise them, by a qualified majority in the case of Article 1(3). The Commission's Report to the Council of 28 June 2000 and the prospects for reform are considered in section 11 below[5].

(C)   One-stop merger control[6]

(i)   Article 21

It is undesirable from the business perspective if a particular concentration has to be investigated under two or more systems of law. Multiple investigation leads to delay, expense, uncertainty and the possibility of conflicting decisions. A central principle of the ECMR is that concentrations having a Community dimension should be investigated within the EU only by the Commission; the corollary is that concentrations below the relevant thresholds can be investigated under domestic law. This policy is given expression in Article 21. Article 21(1) provides that only the Commission may take decisions under the ECMR in respect of concentrations having a Community dimension; Article 21(2) adds that no

5   See p 791 below.
6   See *Butterworths Competition Law* Div VII paras [1114] to [1154]; *Hawk and Huser* ch IV; *Cook and Kerse* ch 1.9.

Member State shall apply its national competition legislation to such concentrations. The only situation in which a Member State could prohibit a concentration that has a Community dimension on competition grounds would be where the special provisions of Article 9, described below, apply.

(ii)   Residual rôle of Articles 81 and 82

As we have seen, prior to the adoption of the ECMR case law had established that both Articles 81 and 82 could apply to some concentrative activities[7]. An interesting question is the extent to which they remain applicable since the adoption of the ECMR[8]. Article 22(1) provides that Regulation 4064/89 alone shall apply to concentrations as defined in Article 3[9], and that Regulation 17/62 (and the implementing regulations in the transport sector) shall not apply, except in relation to joint ventures that do not have a Community dimension and that have as their object or effect the coordination of the competitive behaviour of undertakings that remain independent. This does not in itself mean that concentrations are not caught by Articles 81 and 82, only that the Commission cannot use the powers in those regulations to control them.

Two issues must be considered: first, the effect that Article 22 has on the Commission; second, the direct effect of Articles 81 and 82 in national courts.

(A)   THE COMMISSION.   Clearly the Commission has lost its powers under the general implementing regulations to oppose concentrations under Articles 81 and 82. However this leaves it with the general powers contained in Article 85 (ex Article 89) of the Treaty to investigate suspected infringements of Articles 81 and 82 and to authorise Member States to take measures to remedy the situation. It could therefore investigate a concentration that falls below the Community dimension thresholds. The Commission said at the time of the adoption of the ECMR that it would rarely take this step, but that it reserves the right to take action in accordance with the procedures laid down in the Treaty; it added that it did not intend to take action where the worldwide turnover of the parties is less than EUR 2 billion or their Community turnover level is below EUR 100 million or where the two-thirds threshold is exceeded[10]. To date the Commission has not made use of the Article 85 procedure in the case of a concentration, but the theoretical possibility of such an investigation remains.

(B)   NATIONAL COURTS.   The second issue raised by Article 22 of the ECMR is whether the disapplication of the implementing regulations can have taken away the direct effect of Articles 81 and 82. If the answer to this question is that Articles 81 and 82 remain directly effective, it follows that the possibility exists that an undertaking that objects to a concentration, for example a target company resisting a bid or a third party complainant, could bring an action in a domestic court. This would be a serious breach of the one-stop principle as it would mean that concentrations below the Community dimension threshold, in respect of which the Commission has no powers under the ECMR but only under Article 85

---

7   See pp 735-738 above.
8   See *Butterworths Competition Law* Div VII paras [1240] to [1244]; *Hawk and Huser* ch XII; *Cook and Kerse* ch 1.9.
9   Note that the reference to Article 3 is to all concentrations, *not* just to concentrations that have a Community dimension in the sense of Article 1.
10   Accompanying statements entered in the minutes of the Council [1990] 4 CMLR 314.

of the Treaty, could nonetheless be challenged under Articles 81 and 82; additionally the national authorities could apply their domestic law. The likely answer to this riddle is that Article 81 cannot be invoked in this manner as, in the absence of implementing regulations such as Regulation 17/62, it does not have direct effect: this would seem to follow from the judgment of the ECJ in *Ministère Public v Asjes*[11]. However the position under Article 82 is different: as there is no equivalent to Article 81(3), it has direct effect irrespective of implementing legislation. This was decided by the ECJ in *Ahmed Saeed*[12]. There must therefore be a real possibility of concentrations below the Community dimension threshold being challenged in domestic courts where objection is taken to a dominant undertaking merging with a competitor and thereby substantially fettering competition.

(D)   Article 9: referral to the competent authorities of the Member States – the 'German clause'[13]

(i)   Circumstances in which a referral may be made

At the time of the adoption of the ECMR, concern was expressed by Member States, particularly Germany, that some concentrations having a Community dimension might be regarded as innocuous by the Commission, considering them from a Community standpoint, and yet might be harmful to competition at a domestic level. Article 9 provides a mechanism whereby the Commission can, at the request of a Member State, refer a notified concentration back to the competent authorities in that State. Article 9(2) establishes two situations in which a Member State may make such a request. The first is where a concentration threatens to create or strengthen a dominant position as a result of which effective competition will be significantly impeded on a distinct market in that Member State[14]; the second is where a concentration affects competition on a distinct market within a Member State, which is not a substantial part of the common market[15]. The powers of the DGFT in the UK in relation to such cases are set out in a statutory instrument[16].

(ii)   Commission's response to a request from a Member State

Where the Commission receives a request from a Member State various possibilities are set out in Article 9(3), depending in part on whether it arises under Article 9(2)(a) or Article 9(2)(b).

11 Cases 209–213/84 [1986] ECR 1425, [1986] 3 CMLR 173; if the Commission's proposals on modernisation were to be implemented, the statement in the text would cease to be the position, since Article 81(3) would itself become directly effective: see ch 4, pp 146-147 and ch 7, pp 246-258.
12 Case 66/86 [1989] ECR 803, [1990] 4 CMLR 102.
13 See *Butterworth's Competition Law* Div VII, paras [1115] to [1135]; *Hawk and* pp 109-112; *Cook and Kerse* pp 233-238; Hirsbrunner 'Referral of Mergers in EC Merger Control' (1999) 20 ECLR 372; Morgan 'Subsidiarity and the Division of Jurisdiction in EU Merger Control' (2000) 45 Antitrust Bulletin 153; according to Sir Leon Brittan, the Commissioner responsible for competition policy at the time of the adoption of the ECMR, the German clause was the last one to be agreed upon when its terms were being negotiated: see 'The Law and Policy of Merger Control in the EEC' (1990) EL Rev 351 at 355.
14 ECMR, Article 9(2)(a).
15 Ibid, Article 9(2)(b); this provision was added by Regulation 1310/97 and, where it applies, the Commission must refer the case back, whereas it retains a discretion in an Article 9(2)(a) case: see further below.
16 EEC Merger Control (Distinct Market Investigations) Regulations 1990, SI 1990/1715.

(A)   ARTICLE 9(2)(A) CASES.   Where the Member State is proceeding under Article 9(2)(a) on the basis that there will be a creation or strengthening of dominance, Article 9(3)(a) provides that the Commission may decide, having regard to the market for the products or services concerned and the geographical reference market[17], that it should deal with the case itself. A second possibility is that it could decide in accordance with Article 9(3)(b) to refer 'the whole or part of' the case that affects competition in the Member State in question to be considered under that State's national competition law; obviously the words 'whole or part' mean that the Commission might decide to retain jurisdiction in relation to the case at a pan-European level while authorising a Member State (or two or more Member States) to review it locally. A further possibility is that the Commission will decide that there is no distinct market or any threat of the creation or strengthening of dominance, in which case it will adopt a decision to that effect and address it to the Member State. The Member State could appeal a decision to which it objected under Article 9 to the ECJ[18].

(B)   ARTICLE 9(2)(B) CASES.   Where the Member State is proceeding under Article 9(2)(b) on the basis that the concentration could affect competition in a distinct market which is not a substantial part of the common market, the Commission has no discretion in the matter, and is required under the final paragraph of Article 9(3)(b) to refer the matter once it has decided that competition will be affected in a distinct market.

(iii)   Time limits

The Member State making a request under Article 9(2) must do so within three weeks of the receipt of the copy of the notification. Where an Article 9 request is made, Article 10(1)(ii) extends the period within which the Commission must make a decision whether to proceed against the concentration from one month to six weeks. Further time limits are set out in Articles 9(4) to Article 9(6); for example Article 9(6) provides that a Member State must publish its report or announce its findings not more than four months after the Commission referred the matter to it.

(iv)   Article 9 in practice

In the early days of the ECMR, Article 9 requests were rare, and quite a number were unsuccessful. The first successful use of Article 9 was made by the UK in the case of *Steetly/Tarmac plc*[19] where the Commission allowed a concentration affecting the markets for bricks and clay tiles in the UK, which might lead to high market shares in the North East and South West of England, to be investigated under the Fair Trading Act 1973. The fact that Redland had also made a bid for Steetley and that this concentration fell *below* the ECMR's thresholds was also considered relevant in allowing a domestic review of the Tarmac bid, although it is not obvious what legal basis there is for considering this under Article 9. Tarmac's bid was referred to the UK Monopolies and Mergers Commission but Redland's was not, as it was able to give the Office of Fair Trading assurances about the effects its bid would have on competition. As a result the Redland bid was successful and the Tarmac/Steetley reference lapsed.

17   The meaning of this expression for this purpose is set out in Article 9(7) ECMR.
18   ECMR, Article 9(9).
19   Case No IV/M.180, [1992] 4 CMLR 343.

The number of Article 9 referrals has subsequently increased, which may be at least in part in recognition of the desirability of ensuring that decisions are taken at an appropriate level as between the Commission and the Member States. The fact that there remain many markets that are no wider than national and, in some cases, narrower than this, for example in the case of building materials, is another explanation. Even in such cases, however, the Commission may sometimes decide that it is the more appropriate body to investigate the case, and therefore decline to give jurisdiction back to a Member State. In some cases, the Commission has taken commitments in relation to those aspects of the concentration that it investigated, while referring other parts of it to a Member State: this happened, for example, in *Total/Petrofina*[20] and in *Carrefour/Promodes*[1]. The following table sets out the successful Article 9 claims that have been made since the ECMR came into effect, and indicates whether the referral back was total or partial.

Article 9 referrals

Case name and Member State to which referred	Case number	Year	Total or partial referral?
Steetley/Tarmac UK	Case No IV/M.180	1992	Partial
McCormick/CPC/ Rabobank/Ostman Germany	Case No IV/M.330	1993	Total
Holdercim/Cedest France	Case No IV/M.460	1994	Partial
RWE/Thyssengas Germany	Case No IV/M.713	1996	Total
Gehe/Lloyds Chemist UK	Case No IV/M.716	1996	Total
Bayernwerk/ Isarwerke Germany	Case No IV/M.808	1996	Total
Rheinmetall/British Aerospace/STN Atlas Germany	Case No IV/M.894	1997	Partial
Sehb/Viag/Pe-Bewag Germany	Case No IV/M.932	1997	Total
Promodès/Casino France	Case No IV/M.991	1997	Partial
Preussag/Hapag-Lloyd Germany	Case No IV/M.1001	1997	Partial
Preussag/Touristik Union International Germany	Case No IV/M.1019	1997	Partial
Compagnie Nationale De Navigation/Sogelfa France	Case No IV/ M.1021	1997	Partial
Lafarge/Redland France and the UK	Case No IV/M.1030	1997	Partial

20   Case No IV/M.1464.
1   Case No IV/M.1684.

Case name and Member State to which referred	Case number	Year	Total or partial referral?
Vendex/KBB Netherlands	Case No IV/M.1060	1998	Partial
Promodès/S21/ Gruppo GS Italy	Case No IV/M.1086	1998	Partial
Krauss-Maffei/ Wegmann Germany	Case No IV/M.1153	1998	Partial
Alliance Unichem/ Unifarma Italy	Case No IV/M.1220	1998	Total
Rabobank-Beeck/Homann Germany	Case No IV/M.1461	1999	Total
Total/Petrofina France	Case No IV/M.1464	1999	Partial
Totalfina/Elf Aquitaine France	Case No IV/M.1628	1999	Partial
CSME/MDPA/SCPA France	Case No IV/M.1522	1999	Total
Heineken/Cruzcampo Spain	Case No IV/M.1555	1999	Total
Anglo-American/Tarmac UK	Case No COMP/M.1779	2000	Total
Hanson/Pioneer UK	Case No COMP/M.1827	2000	Total
Carrefour/Promodès France and Spain	Case No COMP/M.1684	2000	Partial
Interbrew/Bass UK	Case No COMP/M.2044	2000	Partial
C3D/Rhône/Go-Ahead UK	Case No COMP/M.2154	2000	Partial
Enel/Infostrada Italy	Case No COMP/M.2216	2001	Partial
Metsäliitti/Vapo Finland	Case No COMP/M.2234	2001	Partial
Connex South Central/ Govia UK	Case No COMP/M.2446	2001	Whole

(E) Article 22(3): referral by the competent authorities of the Member States to the Commission – the 'Dutch clause'[2]

(i) Circumstances in which a referral may be made

A Member State, or two or more Member States acting jointly[3], may request that the Commission should investigate a concentration, even though it falls

---

2 See *Butterworths Competition Law* Div paras [817] to [818.1]; *Hawk and Huser* p 115; *Cook and Kerse* pp 245-8.
3 The possibility of a joint request was added by Regulation 1310/97: it had been unclear under the original version of the ECMR whether this was possible; there has never been a joint request.

below either of the Community thresholds, where it would create or strengthen a dominant position as a result of which effective competition would be significantly impeded within the territory of the Member State or States making the request. If the Commission considers this to be the case, it may take action against the concentration in so far as there is an effect on trade between Member States[4]. The Commission is not obliged to determine whether the body in the Member State making the request had competence to do so as a matter of internal law: the Commission's only obligation is to verify that *prima facie* the request comes from a Member State[5]. Once a Member State has referred a concentration to the Commission under Article 22(3), it cannot attempt to control the Commission's conduct of the investigation or define the scope of that investigation[6]. Article 22(4), as amended by Regulation 1310/97, provides for automatic suspension of the concentration on the date when the Commission informs the parties that a request has been made by a Member State, in so far as it has not already been implemented[7]. Prior to the amendment there was no automatic stay, so that technically the parties were free to proceed. If they did so, and the Commission were to decide to prohibit a particular concentration, then it would be necessary to order the parties to reverse the transaction in accordance with Article 8(4), as happened in *RTL/Veronica/Endemol*[8], *Blokker/Toys 'R' Us*[9] and *Kesko/Tuko*[10]. Article 22(5) provides that the Commission may only take the measures 'strictly necessary to maintain or restore effective competition within the territory of the Member State or States making the request'.

(ii)   Time limits

The Commission's time limit for commencing proceedings begins on the day following receipt of the request. The Member State(s) in (their) turn must make a request within one month of the time when the concentration was 'made known'[11] to them or of its being effected, whichever is earlier. What is not clear is whether a Member State, to which a concentration has been made known more than a month ago and which can no longer itself make an Article 22(3) request, can subsequently 'clamber aboard' a later request made by another Member State that is still within time: the wording of Article 22(4) can be interpreted to support each of these possibilities.

---

4   The CFI in Case T-22/97 *Kesko Oy v Commission* [1999] ECR II-3775, [2000] 4 CMLR 335 confirmed that the test for the effect on inter-state trade is the same under the ECMR as under Articles 81 and 82: see para 106.

5   Case T-22/97 *Kesko Oy v Commission* [1999] ECR II-3775, [2000] 4 CMLR 335, paras 81-93.

6   Case T-221/95 *Endemol Entertainment Holding BV v Commission* [1999] ECR II-1299, [1999] 5 CMLR 611, para 42.

7   Note there is no suspension of voting rights, under Article 7(2) ECMR, if the undertaking has already been acquired.

8   Case No IV/M.553, OJ [1996] L 134/32, upheld on appeal Case T-221/95 [1999] ECR II-1299, [1999] 5 CMLR 611.

9   Case No IV/M.890, OJ [1998] L 316/1.

10   Case No IV/M.784, OJ [1997] L 174/47.

11   The expression 'made known' is not defined: it is not clear whether it means simply that the Member State must have been informed of the fact of the transaction, or whether, where a Member State has a system of compulsory notification, the matter is made known when there is a complete notification; the latter interpretation could prolong the time in which a request could be made.

(iii)   Article 22(3) in practice

The purpose of the so-called 'Dutch clause' is to provide a mechanism for control in circumstances where effective review of concentrations at a domestic level is not possible, for example because the Member State lacks a system of concentration control or because there would be no effective remedy in domestic law. At the time of the adoption of the ECMR various Member States, including the Netherlands, had no system of merger control, and Article 22(3) was inserted as a precaution for transactions that might entirely escape scrutiny: this is how this provision came to be referred to as the 'Dutch clause'. Use of Article 22(3) by a single Member State in the future is likely to be rare, since all the Member States with the exception of Luxembourg now have a system of merger control. The most recent merger controls to be introduced were in the Netherlands with effect from 1 January 1998[12], in Finland with effect from 1 October 1998[13] and in Denmark with effect from 1 October 2000[14]. However Article 22(3) remains important for two reasons. First, a joint Member State request could be made to avoid multiple investigation in a number of jurisdictions; secondly, where a Member State would be unable to adopt a suitable remedy to deal with a merger taking place outside its jurisdiction, it could ask the Commission to conduct the investigation.

There have been four Article 22(3) requests:

Article 22(3) requests

Case name	Case number	Year	Conclusion
British Airways/Dan Air	Case No IV/M.278	1993	Unconditionally cleared
RTL/Veronica/ Endemol[15]	Case No IV/M.553	1996	Prohibited
Kesko/Tuko[16]	Case No IV/M.784	1996	Prohibited
Blokker/Toys 'R' Us	Case No IV/M.890	1997	Prohibited

The last three were referred because there was no domestic concentration control in the Netherlands (*RTL* and *Blokker*) and Finland (*Kesko*). There are now concentration control systems in both countries. The issue in *British Airways* related to remedy: Belgium would not have been able to prevent the merger of two UK undertakings under its own law and therefore asked the Commission to investigate, since it would have the power to do so. However the Commission concluded there was no creation or strengthening of dominance, so that no question of a prohibition arose. By contrast, *RTL* and *Kesko* were prohibited in their entirety; *Blokker* led to a substantial divestiture in order to restore effective competition.

12 See ch 2, p 54, n 16.
13 Ibid, n 10.
14 Ibid, n 17.
15 Upheld on appeal, Case T-221/95 *Endemol Entertainment Holding BV v Commission* [1999] ECR II-1299, [1999] 5 CMLR 611.
16 Upheld on appeal, Case T-22/97 *Kesko Oy v Commission* [1999] ECR II-3775, [2000] 4 CMLR 335.

(F)   Article 21(3): legitimate interest clause[17]

The prohibition on Member States applying their own competition law to concentrations having a Community dimension does not exhaust the possibilities of conflict between the Commission and domestic authorities. A Member State may wish to oppose a concentration for reasons other than its effect on competition; possible examples are concentrations which involve foreign take–over of important strategic industries, such as natural resources or energy, or which could be harmful to the free expression of opinion in the press.

Article 21(3) provides that Member States may take appropriate measures to protect legitimate interests other than those taken into consideration by the ECMR. Such measures must be compatible with the general provisions of Community law; for example a Member State could not take action against a concentration which would constitute arbitrary discrimination or a disguised restriction on trade between Member States[18] and any action taken would have to conform with the Community principle of proportionality. Public security[19], plurality of the media and prudential rules are specifically recognised in Article 21(3) as 'legitimate interests' for these purposes; any other legitimate interest claimed by a Member State must be notified to the Commission which, after investigating the claim in the light of Community law, must inform the Member State of its decision within one month. Curiously, no time limit is prescribed for the Member State to notify its legitimate interests to the Commission.

As Article 21(3) involves a derogation from the general principle of the ECMR, the Commission will apply it strictly. It has been invoked on a few occasions. In *Lyonnaise des Eaux SA/Northumbrian Water Group*[20] the Commission accepted that the UK was entitled to investigate the regulatory aspects of a transaction whereby Lyonnaise des Eaux acquired a UK water undertaking, while it considered the competition issues. The UK also investigated the *Independent Newspaper* case under the newspaper merger provisions of the Fair Trading Act 1973[1]. In the case of *Sun Alliance/Royal Insurance*[2] the Commission acknowledged in its decision that the UK would consider whether the merger would be in accordance with the Insurance Companies Act 1982, and that this would be done in close liaison with it. In *Electricité de France/London Electricity*[3] the UK requested a referral under Article 9(4) and claimed a legitimate interest under Article 21(3); the Commission did not accept either request: the regulatory concerns of the Director General of Electricity Supply were not with the concentration itself but with the conduct of the merged undertakings after it would have taken place, to which he could apply national regulatory provisions. In *Thomson-CSF/Racal*

---

17   See *Butterworth's Competition Law* Div VII, para [1136] to [1151]; *Hawk and Huser* p 112; *Cook and Kerse* pp 238-243.
18   This wording is the same as in Article 30(2) EC on the free movement of goods.
19   Note also Article 296 EC (ex Article 223), which reserves certain matters to Members States that relate to national security: see p 765 below.
20   Case No IV/M.567; the Monopolies and Mergers Commission, as it was then called, subsequently published a report *Lyonnaise des Eaux SA and Northumbrian Water Group plc* Cm 2936 (1995) identifying possible public interest detriments: see 1999 *Annual Report of the DGFT*, p 35.
1   Case No IV/M.423.
2   Case No IV/M.759, [1996] 5 CMLR 136.
3   See the Commission's XXIXth *Annual Report on Competition Policy* (1999), paras 193 and 197-198.

the UK investigated the public security aspects of the proposed transaction under the Fair Trading Act 1973[4].

In *Banco Santander Central Hispano/A.Champalimand*[5] a concentration in the financial services sector having a Community dimension was notified to the Commission. The Portugese Minister of Finance opposed the concentration, claiming to have anxieties about the prudential supervision of Mundial Confiança, an insurance undertaking, and also because he considered that the concentration would interfere with Portugese national interests; further it would prejudice an integral sector of the Portuguese economy and financial system. The concerns of the Minister were increased by the parties' procedural impropriety in failing to notify the Minister of Finance. The Commission rejected these arguments and required the Minister to suspend his opposition to the transaction[6].

(G) Defence[7]

Article 296(1)(b) EC (ex Article 223) provides that a Member State 'may take such measures as it considers necessary' in matters of security connected with its defence industry; such measures shall not adversely affect the conditions of competition in the common market regarding products which are not intended for specifically military purposes. This means that a Member State may investigate the military aspects of a concentration and the Commission the civilian aspects; this distinction in itself inevitably raises the problem of how to deal with products that have a 'dual-use', that is to say that can be used both for military and for civilian purposes. The UK government successfully invoked Article 296(1)(b) in relation to the proposed takeover of VSEL by British Aerospace[8], where both companies produced military equipment for the British defence forces; it required British Aerospace not to notify the military element of the takeover to the Commission. Subsequent to this, the *GEC/Thomson-CSF(II)*[9], *British Aerospace/Lagardère*[10] and *British Aerospace/GEC Marconi*[11] cases all involved the exercise of Article 296 by the UK. In the case of *GEC/Marconi* it was reported that the Competition Commissioner, Karel van Miert, was concerned that the Commission in the past had been too generous in allowing the UK to assert jurisdiction in defence matters: at the least he would wish to look at the civilian aspects of the case and might in future be more sceptical on how 'dual-use' products should be investigated. More recently it seems that the Commission has been taking a stricter view in relation to the application of Article 296; since late 1999, several mergers involving the defence industry in Europe have been fully notified to the Commission[12].

4   Commission Press Release IP(00)628 of 16 June 2000.
5   Case No IV/M.1616; see Mohamed 'National Interests Limiting EU Cross-border Mergers' (2000) 21 ECLR 248.
6   Commission decisions of 20 July 1999 and 20 October 2000: see the Commission's XXIXth *Annual Report on Competition Policy* (1999), paras 194-196.
7   See *Butterworth's Competition Law* Div VII, paras [1152] to [1154]; *Hawk and Huser* p 114; *Cook and Kerse*, p 233.
8   DTI Press Notice P/94/623 of 19 October 1994, Case No IV/M.528; see also Case No IV/M.529 *VSEL/GEC*.
9   Case No IV/M.724.
10 Case No IV/M.820.
11 Case No IV/M.1438.
12 See eg Case No M.1501 *GKN Westland/Agusta*; Case No M.1709 *Preussag/Babcock/Celsius*; Case No M.1745 *EADS*; Case No M.1797 *Saab/Celsius*; Case No M.1858 *Thomson-CSF/Racal*; Case No M.2021 *Snecma/Labinal*.

5.   NOTIFICATION, SUSPENSION OF CONCENTRATIONS, PROCEDURAL TIMETABLE AND POWERS OF DECISION[13]

This section will deal with the following matters:

(a)   *Notification:* concentrations that have a Community dimension are required by Article 4 to be notified on Form CO to the Commission.

(b)   *Suspension of concentrations:* Article 7 provides that concentrations that have a Community dimension are automatically suspended until they are declared compatible with the common market; this period may be waived in appropriate cases.

(c)   *Procedural timetables and powers of decision of the Commission:* strict time limits are imposed on the Commission's decision–making in order to disturb the operation of the market as little as possible; the Commission can make a range of decisions when reviewing concentrations.

(A)   Notification

Article 4(1) provides that concentrations with a Community dimension must be notified not more than one week after the conclusion of the agreement, the announcement of the public bid, or the acquisition of a controlling interest; the week begins when the first of these events occurs. Failure to notify within the specified time limit may attract a fine[14]. In some cases the parties to a transaction want to notify, in order to set the time limits of the ECMR running, but they may be unable to satisfy the MTF that a notifiable event has yet occurred. In particular, there can be a question of whether an agreement has been concluded that triggers the right and duty to notify. The meaning of 'agreement' in the context of Article 4(1) of the ECMR is relatively straightforward compared to Article 81[15]. In the case of the ECMR, the agreement must be enforceable, whether written or oral, such that it cannot be rescinded unilaterally by either party; it must be intended to create a legal relationship upon which each party can rely. The agreement may be subject to conditions – not least that satisfactory regulatory approval is forthcoming from the Commission under the ECMR – provided that the conditions do not allow one or more of the parties to withdraw from the agreement on a unilateral basis. In practice the MTF has been willing to extend the period for notification of one week and has refrained from imposing fines when, in a technical sense, a notification is late. The reality of the matter is that the staff of the MTF are severely overstretched, necessitating a pragmatic approach to the time limits. This is a matter that can usefully be discussed with the MTF at a pre-notification meeting.

Article 4(3) requires the MTF to publish the fact of notifications which it considers to fall within the scope of the ECMR. There are penalties for failure to comply with the obligation to notify, and for the furnishing of incorrect or misleading information[16]. The Commission may declare a notification to be incomplete – for example because it omits information which ought to have

---

13   On notification generally, see *Butterworth's Competition Law* Div VII [918] to [997]; *Hawk and Huser* ch X; *Cook and Kerse* ch 4.

14   See p 788 below.

15   See ch 3, pp 76-81.

16   See p 788 below.

been included – in which case the time-limits for reaching a decision will not have begun to run. There is little doubt that this has been happening more frequently recently than in the early days of the ECMR: often this happens in cases where there have been no pre-notification discussions with the MTF. Rejection of a notification may have very serious consequences for the undertakings concerned which, for a variety of reasons, may wish to conclude the transaction by a certain date. The European Competition Lawyers' Forum has, following discussion with the MTF, produced *Best Practice Guidelines*[17] which seek to minimise the possibility of this happening. The *Guidelines* suggest that even in the simplest of cases there should be pre-notification contact with the MTF; that a substantially complete draft Form CO should be submitted to the MTF prior to actual notification; that there should be an open discussion with the MTF about any potentially 'affected market'[18], even where there is disagreement between the parties and the Commission officials about how the market should be defined; and that, in the event of a meeting with the MTF to discuss the transaction, it is beneficial for business people to be present as well as the lawyers. It will be readily appreciated that substantial work is required in preparing for the submission of a Form CO, and much of the most important work in a merger case may have to be done prior to actual notification.

The Commission has adopted Regulation 447/98[19], which sets out the format in which a notification is to be made. This format is known as Form CO; an original and 23 copies must be submitted to the Commission. Form CO requires the notifying firms to provide substantial information; this is intended to enable the Commission to reach a decision within the tight time limits to which it is subject. As mentioned above, in practice firms and their legal advisers contact the MTF confidentially and prior to the time when the duty to notify arises. This is helpful to the parties, who obtain a preliminary sense of the MTF's thinking as well as guidance on the notification procedure itself; it is also helpful to the MTF, which may at this stage be able to advise the parties to dispense with supplying unnecessary information at the time of formal notification. It is often necessary to submit further information after notification and this will have to be done speedily if the time limits are to be complied with[20].

The Commission has introduced a simplified procedure for concentrations that can be expected not to give rise to competition concerns[1]; in such cases the Commission will adopt a 'short-form' decision. The procedure is available for joint ventures that have no, or negligible, activities in the EEA; for concentrations where the parties are not engaged in business activities in the same product and geographical markets; and for transactions where the parties' market shares are below 15% in the case of a horizontal concentration and 25% in a vertical one[2]. The simplified procedure became operative on 1 September 2000.

---

17 The Best Practice Guidelines can be accessed on the Commission's website: http://europa.eu.int/comm/competition/mergers/en/best_practice_gl.html.
18 See p 771 below on the meaning of 'affected markets'.
19 Regulation 447/98 OJ [1998] L 61/1; this Regulation replaces the earlier Regulation 3384/94, OJ [1994] L 377/1.
20 See pp 768-770 below on the time limits.
1 OJ [2000] C 217/32, [2000] 5 CMLR 774.
2 Ibid, para 4.

(B)   Suspension of concentrations

Article 7(1) requires automatic suspension of a concentration before notification and until it has been declared compatible with the common market[3]. Article 14 provides penalties for breach of this provision. In this situation the offence is far more serious than merely not notifying, and the fine imposed could be as much as 10% of the aggregate turnover of the undertakings concerned[4].

Article 7(4) provides that the MTF may grant a derogation from the provisions on suspension, subject to conditions where appropriate. A request for derogation from the automatic suspension must be reasoned, and the Commission will take into account *inter alia* the effects of the suspension on the undertakings concerned by a concentration or on a third party, and the threat to competition that the concentration poses.

(C)   Procedural timetable and powers of decision of the Commission

(i)   Phase I investigations

(A)   POSSIBLE DECISIONS AT THE END OF PHASE I.   The parties having notified a concentration in accordance with the ECMR, the Commission is required by Article 6 to examine it as soon as it is received. The Commission is required to make a decision either that the concentration:

- is outside the ECMR (Article 6(1)(a)); or
- is compatible with the common market (Article 6(1)(b)): this finding extends to any restrictions related and necessary to the concentration ('ancillary restraints')[5]; or
- as modified by the parties no longer raises serious doubts and so may be declared compatible with the common market: such a decision may be subject to conditions and obligations ('commitments'[6]) (Article 6(2)); or
- raises serious doubts[7] as to its compatibility with the common market (Article 6(1)(c)); in this situation the Commission must initiate a Phase II investigation.

A decision under Article 6(1)(a) or (b) can be revoked where it is based on incorrect information for which one of the undertakings is responsible or where it has been obtained by deceit[8] or where there has been a breach of an obligation attached to a decision[9].

3   Regulation 1310/97 amended Article 7(1) of the ECMR which, as originally enacted, suspended the concentration only for a period of 3 weeks; a decision on the part of the Commission was needed to continue the suspension, for example if the case was about to go into Phase II.
4   See p 788 below.
5   On ancillary restraints, see p 783 below.
6   See p 784 below.
7   It is arguable that this expression is inappropriate; during a Phase I investigation the MTF may have time only to decide that a more profound inquiry is necessary: it may not yet have been able to form a view as to whether there are serious doubts as to compatibility.
8   Article 6(3)(a): see Case No IV/M.1397 *Sanofi/Synthélabo* IP/99/255, [1999] 4 CMLR 1178 where the Commission revoked its decision as the notifying parties had failed to produce information about activities in a particular market; the Commission reopened its examination of the case, but allowed a partial exemption from the Article 7(4) suspension that would otherwise have automatically occurred, since the parties were preparing to offer suitable undertakings to overcome any competition concerns and because of the significant prejudice that a delay could have caused to the parties and their shareholders.
9   Article 6(3)(b): see Case No IV/M.1069 *World Com/MCI* OJ [1999] L 116/1, [1999] 5 CMLR 876.

(B)   TIMETABLE.   In general Phase I decisions must, in accordance with Article 10(1) of the ECMR, be made within one month at most of the day following notification[10]; if the notification is incomplete, the period begins on the day following receipt of complete information. It follows that concentrations that do not raise competition law problems should normally be held up for a maximum of one month; the Phase I period may, in accordance with the second sentence of Article 10(1), be extended to six weeks where either a Member State makes a request for a reference under Article 9, or commitments are offered in accordance with Article 6(2).

The Phase I timetable of one month can place great strain on all the relevant parties – the business people, the lawyers and the staff at the MTF – which is why pre-notification meetings are so important. The overwhelming majority of cases are dealt with within the Phase I time limit, a not inconsiderable achievement given the complexity and size of many of the transactions notified.

(ii)   Phase II investigations

(A)   POSSIBLE DECISIONS AT THE END OF PHASE II.   Where a concentration raises serious doubts about compatibility with the common market, the Commission will commence proceedings in accordance with Article 6(1)(c) of the ECMR. An Article 6(1)(c) decision inaugurates an in-depth Phase II investigation.

The decisions the Commission may make at the end of Phase II are set out in Article 8. It may decide that the concentration:

- is compatible with the common market, having regard to the provisions of Article 2(2) and, in some cases, Article 2(4)[11] (Article 8(2), first indent); or
- is compatible with the common market, subject to commitments to ensure compliance with modifications proposed by the parties (Article 8(2), second indent); or
- is incompatible with the common market (Article 8(3)); or
- in so far as it has already taken place must be reversed (Article 8(4)).

Further, the Commission may revoke a decision taken under Article 8(2) where it based its decision of compatibility on incorrect information or where the undertakings concerned have acted in breach of an obligation attached to the MTF's decision (Article 8(5)).

(B)   TIMETABLE.   Article 10 lays down the timetable within which the Commission must reach any of the decisions provided for in Article 8. The basic rule is that decisions under Article 8(2) or 8(3) must be taken within four months of the date on which proceedings were initiated. This period may, exceptionally, be extended where the MTF has had to obtain additional information owing to circumstances for which one of the undertakings involved is responsible[12]. Where the Commission fails to reach a decision within the prescribed time scale, whether in Phase I or Phase II, the concentration will be deemed to be compatible with the common market[13].

---

10   A decision cannot be adopted prior to the expiry of the three week deadline for Member States to make an Article 9 request: on Article 9, see pp 758-761 above.
11   See pp 781-783 below.
12   ECMR, Article 10(4).
13   Ibid, Article 10(6).

(C)   PHASE II PROCEDURE.   A Phase II investigation is usually an exhausting and exhaustive exercise for all concerned. The timetables are tight, given that the investigation is 'in depth'. During the four month period, there will normally[14] be a statement of objections sent by the Commission to the undertakings concerned; a period for them to reply; access for the parties to the files of the Commission[15]; an oral hearing which may last for one or two days; a meeting (or meetings) of the Advisory Committee on Concentrations; a period within which commitments can be discussed and an opportunity for interested third parties to comment on any such commitments[16]; the preparation of a draft decision for the College of Commissioners to consider; and the adoption by the full Commission of the final decision. Achieving all these steps within four months can be extremely difficult, especially since many of the cases that come to the Commission are immensely complex. A system whereby the parties could waive the time-limits in the ECMR to allow for a longer investigation might, in some cases, be to the benefit of all concerned.

6.   SUBSTANTIVE ANALYSIS

Once the Commission has jurisdiction in relation to a concentration, its task is to determine whether it is 'compatible with the common market'. The burden of proof is on the Commission. Article 2(1) sets out certain criteria which the Commission must take into account when making this appraisal: these criteria are described and explained below[17]. Compatibility with the common market turns on the issue of whether the concentration will create or strengthen a dominant position. Article 2(2) provides that:

'A concentration which does not create or strengthen a dominant position as a result of which effective competition would be significantly impeded in the common market or in a substantial part of it shall be declared compatible with the common market'.

Article 2(3) provides that:

'A concentration which creates or strengthens a dominant position as a result of which effective competition would be significantly impeded in the common market or in a substantial part of it shall be declared incompatible with the common market'.

The adoption in the ECMR of the expression 'dominant position' meant that the jurisprudence of the ECJ under Article 82 could be used by the Commission in developing its decisional practice under the Regulation. However it is important to stress that, whereas Article 82 applies only to the abuse of a pre-existing dominant position, the ECMR can be used to control *the creation*, as well as the strengthening, of a dominant position: this ability to prevent mergers that would

---

14   It is not inevitable that the full procedure will be followed; for example it may be that the parties offer suitable commitments during the beginning of the Phase II procedure, thereby obviating the need to complete the in-depth investigation.

15   On access to the file, see Case T-221/95 *Endemol Entertainment Holding BV v Commission* [1999] ECR II-1299, [1999] 5 CMLR 611, para 68.

16   See pp 784-787 below.

17   See pp 773-774 below.

bring about an undesirable market structure is a crucial feature of the ECMR. It is also of interest to note in passing that the substantive test for controlling concentrations in the ECMR is very different from that of the UK, which has a test based on detriments to 'the public interest'[18], and from the US, where the test is whether a merger will 'substantially lessen competition'[19]. Neither the UK nor the US system, therefore, requires the identification of a dominant position as an independent element of its substantive analysis. As a separate matter, EC law, in addition to determining whether a concentration is compatible with the common market in the terms of Article 2(2) and 2(3), requires that the Commission must also consider whether any coordinative aspects of a joint venture could be restrictive of competition in the sense of Article 2(4) of the ECMR[20]; furthermore it is necessary to determine which contractual restrictions are ancillary to the concentrations[1]. Each of these issues is dealt with separately below.

(A) Market definition

The concept of a dominant position is central to the working of the ECMR, which in turn means that market definition is also crucial. This issue, including the Commission's *Notice on market definition*[2], has been discussed in some detail in chapter one, to which the reader is referred. A few specific points about market definition under the ECMR follow.

(i) Form CO: 'affected markets'

Section 6 of Form CO, on which concentrations must be notified[3], requires the notifying parties to provide information in relation to 'affected markets'. Affected markets are defined to mean, in the case of horizontal relationships, relevant product markets where two or more parties to the concentration have a combined market share of 15% or more at the national or EU level; and, in the case of vertical relationships, where their individual or combined market share is more than 25%. The information required in relation to these affected markets is substantial, including an estimate of the total size of the market, the parties' market shares for each of the last three financial years, the structure of supply and demand and details of barriers to entry. The *quid pro quo* for the supply of such extensive information is that the Commission should be able to make a speedy assessment of the case. As noted earlier, the information contained in Form CO must be accurate and complete[4]; if it is not, the notification may be declared incomplete, in which case the time within which a decision must be made will not have begun to run. This is why extensive preparation in advance of notification, including contact with the MTF, is so crucial[5].

---

18 See ch 22, pp 816-817.
19 See ch 20, pp 729-730.
20 See pp 781-783 below.
1   See pp 783-784 below.
2   OJ [1997] C 372/5, [1998] 4 CMLR 177; see ch 1, p 26ff.
3   See p 767 above.
4   See pp 766-767 above.
5   See p 767 above.

(ii)   Commission decisions

In the period up to 30 June 2001, the Commission had adopted 1671 decisions under the ECMR, and these contain many useful insights into its likely definition of the relevant market. Practitioners therefore, quite apart from conducting SSNIP (and other) tests[6] to define the relevant market, will have recourse to the decisional practice of the Commission for guidance. How to access these decisions has been described above[7]; of particular interest for the purpose of market definition is that the Commission maintains on its website a classification of merger decisions by industry sector[8]. The point should perhaps be added that in many clearance decisions the Commission does not reach a finding on the market, since it is clear that to do so would not materially affect its assessment; the Commission will say that, however the market is defined, it is satisfied that the concentration would not be incompatible with the common market.

(iii)   Effect of decisions on market definition

In *Coca-Cola Co v Commission*[9] the CFI stated clearly that a market definition in an earlier decision of the Commission could not be binding in the case of a subsequent investigation, either by the Commission itself or a national court or competition authority: each case must turn on the particular facts and circumstances prevailing at the time.

(B)   Creation or strengthening of dominance

Having identified the affected markets, it is then necessary to consider whether the concentration would create or strengthen a dominant position as a result of which effective competition would be significantly impeded in the common market or a substantial part of it.

(i)   One test or two?

An important question is whether Article 2(2) and 2(3) contain one test or two when considering whether a concentration is compatible with the common market. They refer to the creation or strengthening of a dominant position as a result of which effective competition would be significantly impeded. It could be that the second idea is merely a statement of the consequences of the first, in which case it adds little. An alternative view is that the Commission has to satisfy both parts of Article 2(3) if it is to block a concentration. In this case a concentration that strengthens a dominant position, but only to a marginal extent, might escape prohibition: the second test would provide a *de minimis* exception, since the concentration would not have hindered competition significantly. Furthermore it could be that reference to impeding effective competition means that the Commission should take a dynamic view of the market and consider whether harm to competition is likely to be transitory or permanent: it should act only in

6   See ch 1, p 27ff.
7   See pp 742-743 above.
8   http://europa.eu.int/comm/competition/mergers/cases/index/by_nace.html.
9   Joined Cases T-125/97 and T-127/97 [2000] 5 CMLR 467.

the latter situation. This was the approach taken in *Aerospatiale-Alenia/de Havilland*[10] where the Commission, in blocking a concentration, said that the proposed concentration would create a dominant position and added that 'this dominant position is not merely temporary and will therefore significantly impede effective competition'[11].

(ii)   There must be a causal link between the concentration and the creation or strengthening of dominance

The judgment of the ECJ in *France v Commission*[12] established that there must be a causal link between the concentration and the deterioration of the competitive structure of the market for the ECMR to apply. In that case the ECJ was considering whether a 'failing firm' defence existed under the Regulation[13]. It held that a concentration should not be blocked where the firm would have failed anyway and its market share would have accrued to the acquiror, since the concentration did not cause the creation or strengthening of dominance.

(iii)   The assessment criteria

Article 2(1) of the ECMR sets out a list of 'appraisal criteria' which the Commission should take into account when investigating concentrations. However it is important to appreciate that the substantive test for determining whether a concentration is compatible with the common market is contained in Article 2(2) and (3): the creation or strengthening of a dominant position. The appraisal criteria are a checklist of factors that should guide the Commission towards its conclusion, but they do not in themselves determine the outcome of a case.
    Article 2(1) provides that:

'In making this appraisal, the Commission shall take into account:-
(a)   the need to preserve and develop effective competition within the common market in view of, among other things, the structure of all the markets concerned and the actual or potential competition from undertakings located either within or without the Community;
(b)   the market position of the undertakings concerned and their economic and financial power, the opportunities available to suppliers and users, their access to supplies or markets, any legal or other barriers to entry, supply and demand trends for the intermediate and ultimate consumers, and the development of technical and economic progress provided that it is to consumers' advantage and does not form an obstacle to competition'.

The information required in relation to affected markets by Form CO reflects the appraisal criteria set out in Article 2(1). The list of factors in Article 2(1) is presumably not exhaustive: the Commission must consider all matters relevant

10   Case No IV/M.53, OJ [1991] L 334/42, [1992] 4 CMLR M2.
11   Ibid, para 72.
12   Cases C-68/94 and C-30/95 [1998] ECR I-1375, [1998] 4 CMLR 829.
13   On the failing firm defence, see p 780 below.

to the assessment of dominance. Nor does Article 2(1) establish a hierarchy, giving greater weight to one assessment factor than another. The impact that the criteria have on the Commission's determination will vary enormously from case to case. In any particular case, some of these criteria will be more or less important. For example in *Enso/Stora*[14] countervailing power was important; the concentration of those two undertakings created the largest manufacturer of paper and board in the world; in liquid packaging board the merged entity would have a market share of more than 60%. However, the buying side of the market was very concentrated, Tetra Pak being responsible for 60%-80% of all demand. In these circumstances, a switch by Tetra Pak to other suppliers would have a serious effect on Enso/Stora, so that its buying power would be a constraint on the merged entity's ability to raise prices. The concentration was cleared, albeit subject to commitments that Enso/Stora would not raise prices to its other customers. In *ITS/Signode/Titan*[15] the Commission considered that the potential for new entrants to enter the plastic strapping sector provided an adequate safeguard to competition following the merger, given also that customers appeared to have at least some countervailing power.

(iv)   Single firm dominance

In determining whether a concentration is compatible with the common market, the Commission will consider both whether it would create or strengthen single firm dominance and whether it would lead to collective dominance. In cases of single firm dominance, the Commission will look both at the horizontal and the vertical effects of the transaction; it may also look for conglomerate effects.

(A)   HORIZONTAL EFFECTS.   Form CO requires the parties to a concentration to provide detailed information in relation to any affected market, that is to say, if the relationship of the parties is horizontal, where their market share exceeds 15%[16]. The mere fact that information must be provided where the market share exceeds 15% does not mean that any concentration above this figure is in jeopardy: Form CO is designed to provide the Commission with sufficient information to be able to make an assessment. In considering the compatibility of a horizontal concentration with the common market, the Commission is concerned with the 'unilateral effects' it might produce[17]. The 15th Recital of the ECMR, which does not have legal force but which gives a strong signal as to the way the Commission will proceed, states that where the combined market share of the undertakings concerned in a concentration does not exceed 25% in the common market or in a substantial part of it, this is an indication that the concentration is compatible with the common market. However, dominance can be established at relatively low market shares: for example, in *REWE/Meinl*[18] at 37%; in *Hutchinson/ECT/RMPM*[19] at 36% and in *Carrefour/Promodes*[20] at

---

14   Case IV/M.1225, OJ [1999] L 254/9, [2000] 4 CMLR 372.
15   Case No IV/M.970, OJ [1998] L 316/33.
16   See p 771 above.
17   See ch 20, p 730.
18   Case No IV/M.1221, OJ [1999] L 274/1, [2000] 5 CMLR 256.
19   Case No IV/M.1412.
20   Case No COMP/M.1684.

less than 30%. In *MCI WorldCom/Sprint*[1] the Commission found dominance where the merged entity would have a share in the market for top-level or universal Internet interconnectivity in the region of 40%-50%, three to four times larger than its nearest competitor[2]. An interesting question is whether the presumption of dominance in an Article 82 case at 50% or more[3] might be imported into analysis under the ECMR.

Each case necessarily turns on its own facts. The various appraisal criteria in Article 2(1) will impact differently upon the assessment according to the case under consideration. A very high market share may be tolerable where the merged entity will be subject to strong potential competition, strong buyer power[4], or where the introduction of public procurement directives will make the market substantially more competitive[5]. In other cases, however, even a small accretion of market share may lead to a prohibition; the most notable example of this is *Blokker/Toys'R'Us*[6], where an increase in market share of only 4% was sufficient to cause the Commission to block the concentration outright. The Commission will be concerned about accretion of market power on the buying as well as the selling side of the market. For example in *Rewe/Meinl*[7] the Commission required a substantial revision of the transaction to prevent the merged entity from having a dominant position on the Austrian food retail market and on nine regional procurement markets in Austria for daily consumer goods.

In determining whether a concentration might have adverse horizontal effects, the Commission will look predominantly at the increase in the combined entity's market share; however, it will not limit its consideration to 'numerology', but will also consider the extent to which other factors might lead to enhanced market power on the part of the merged entity. The first reason for this is that market share figures cannot provide any insight into the loss of potential competition that a concentration might entail[8]. For example, in *Telia/Telenor*[9] the Commission considered that the two incumbent national telephone operators in Sweden and Norway were the strongest potential entrants into each other's national markets. The second reason is that the Commission will also wish to examine whether a horizontal merger might strengthen the merged entity's market power other than by an accretion of market share. It will consider possible 'indirect effects'. For example in *Telia/Telenor*[10] the Commission was concerned that the merged entity would have an increased ability and incentive to eliminate actual and potential competition from third parties, to bundle products across a wider geographical area and to leverage sales. In *Air Liquide/BOC/Air Products*[11] the Commission was concerned that the merged entity would have an unparalleled distribution

1 Case No COMP/M.1741.
2 Ibid, para 196.
3 See ch 5, p 155.
4 See Case IV/M.1225 *Enso/Stora* OJ [1999] L 254/9, [2000] 4 CMLR 372, p 774 above; Case COMP/M.1882 *Pirelli/BICC*, paras 77-79.
5 See Case No IV/M.222 *Mannesmann/Hoesch* OJ [1993] L 114/34; Case COMP/M.1882 *Pirelli/BICC*, para 78.
6 Case No IV/M.890, OJ [1998] L 316/1; this case was an Article 22(3) reference from the Netherlands: see pp 761-763 above.
7 Case No IV/M.1221, OJ [1999] L 274/1, [2000] 5 CMLR 256, paras 71-117; see on this case the Commission's *XXIXth Annual Report on Competition Policy* (1999), para 169; the Commission cited OFT Research Paper 16 by Dobson, Waterson and Chu 'The Welfare Consequences of the Exercise of Buyer Power' (September 1998).
8 See ch 1, pp 39-40.
9 Case No COMP/M.1439, OJ [2001] L 40/1, [2001] 4 CMLR 1226, paras 148-154.
10 Ibid, paras 155-167.
11 Case No COMP/M.1630.

network in Europe, which would have given it additional power to deter others from market entry; the concentration would also have removed the most credible potential entrant to the UK market. Where the Commission investigates mergers in the 'new economy' it may wish to take commitments to overcome the possibility of 'transient dominance' while a new market becomes established and while existing barriers to entry are reduced. For example, in *VodafoneAirtouch/ Mannesmann*[12] commitments were accepted for a period of three years which, effectively, would give third parties access to the merged entity's pan-European mobile telephone network.

(B)   VERTICAL EFFECTS.   Form CO requires the parties to a concentration to provide information in relation to mergers where a party's market share in a market which is upstream or downstream of any market on which another party is present exceeds 25%[13]. The Commission will consider whether the vertical effects of concentrations could foreclose access to the market on the part of third parties. A clear example of the Commission's concerns with vertical effects is provided by *Skanska/Scancem*[14], where the merged entity would have been a powerful presence on the market for raw materials (cement and aggregates), the construction materials market (concrete and other construction products) and on the construction market itself. The Commission required Skanska to divest Scancem's cement business in Finland and to divest Skanska's entire shareholding in Scancem. A further example is *Nordic Satellite Distribution*[15], where the Commission prohibited a joint venture between Tele Danmark, Norsk Telecom and Kinnevik that would have created a vertically-integrated operation extending from the production of TV programmes through satellite operations and cable TV networks to retail distribution for TV and other encrypted channels. The Commission has had similar concerns about the vertical foreclosure effects in relation to several concentrations in the telecommunications and media industries, in particular where the technology in the sector is rapidly evolving and the possibility exists that one or a few firms will be able to control access to the market through their rôle as so-called 'gatekeepers': each resulted in an outright prohibition[16]. In the case of *Time-Warner/AOL*[17] the Commission investigated a merger between Time-Warner, one of the world's largest media and entertainment companies, and AOL, the only Internet access provider with a pan-European presence. Its particular concern was that the vertically-integrated merged entity would have dominated the emerging market for Internet music delivery on-line: AOL/Time-Warner would have been the 'gatekeeper' to this nascent market, dictating the conditions for the distribution of audio files over the Internet. The concentration was cleared after commitments were given to sever the links between AOL and Bertelsmann, another media and entertainment company.

12   Case No COMP/M.1795.
13   See p 771 above.
14   Case No IV/M.1157, OJ [1999] L 183/1, [2000] 5 CMLR 686.
15   Case No IV/M.490, OJ [1996] L 53/20, [1995] 5 CMLR 258.
16   See Case No IV/M.469 *MSG Media Service* OJ [1994] L 364/1; Case No IV/M.993 *BertelsMann/Kirch/Premiere* OJ [1999] L 53/1, [1999] 4 CMLR 700, on appeal Case T-121/ 98 *Taurus Beteiligungs GmbH v Commission* (judgment pending); Case No IV/M.1027 *Deutsche Telekom/BetaResearch* OJ [1999] L 53/51, [1999] 4 CMLR 700, on appeal, as in Case T-121/98 (judgment pending).
17   Case COMP/M.1845; see Abbamonte and Rabassa 'Foreclosure and Vertical Mergers: The Commission's Review of Vertical Effects in the Last Wave of Media and Internet Mergers' (2001) 22 ECLR 214.

(c) CONGLOMERATE EFFECTS.   Conglomerate mergers may be notifiable under the ECMR: the jurisdictional test in the Regulation is based on turnover, not on the impact of a concentration on competition, so that any transaction may be caught, whether it be horizontal, vertical or conglomerate. However, the question arises whether, as a matter of substantive analysis, a conglomerate merger could be held to create or strengthen a dominant position and so be declared incompatible with the ECMR. As noted in chapter 20, conglomeracy was once a ground for intervention in the US, but that doctrine was discredited a long time ago and is no longer applied[18]. In a few of its decisions, the Commission has expressed concerns about what it has termed 'portfolio power', a concept of uncertain scope but which may indicate an anxiety about conglomeracy.

In *Guinness/Grand Metropolitan*[19] the Commission conducted a Phase II investigation into the concentration of the spirits businesses of those two undertakings. Its view was that each spirit – whisky, vodka, gin etc. – was capable of forming a separate 'niche' product market[20]. The Commission looked to see what horizontal effects the concentration might have, and required commitments to deal with problems it had identified. However, the decision is of interest because the Commission looked in depth into the effect of the ownership of a wide portfolio of drinks which had been found to belong to different product markets: this would seem to amount to asking whether the market power derived from the concentration could exceed the sum of its parts. The Commission concluded that there were indeed portfolio effects in Greece, and required a commitment from the parties that the distribution agreement for Bacardi rum there should be terminated in order to abate its concerns. The decision is of importance since it was the first time that the Commission secured commitments in consequence of portfolio power[1]. What is unclear is what this theory consists of. If the portfolio effect means that the merged entity, with dominance in relation to one drink – for example whisky – might be able to use that dominance in order to effect sales of another one – perhaps gin – the theory is not novel: tying has always been a legitimate concern in antitrust analysis[2]. However, some of the Commission's language seems to suggest that it objects to the increased efficiency that possession of a portfolio of drinks might confer: at paragraph 40 of its decision in *Grand Metropolitan/Guinness* it refers to the ability of the holder of a portfolio 'to realise economies of scale and scope'. The development of a doctrine that the enhancement of efficiency could be a ground for intervention is controversial, and would considerably extend the Commission's ability to control concentrations[3]; whether this decision will inspire the Commission to develop a more generalised theory of conglomeracy remains to be seen.

---

18 See ch 20, pp 722-723.
19 Case No IV/M.938, OJ [1998] L 288/24, [1997] 5 CMLR 760.
20 Ibid, para 23 and, in the context of Greece, para 82; the Commission deals specifically with portfolio power at paras 38-46 and, in relation to Greece, at paras 91-103 and para 118; the commitment in relation to Bacardi rum in Greece is set out at para 183(v); in the US, portfolio effects were rejected in the analysis of the FTC.
1   The Commission had considered portfolio power in earlier decisions, without reaching a final conclusion on it: see eg Case No M.794 *Coca-Cola Enterprises/Amalgamated Beverages GB* OJ [1997] L 218/15; Case No IV/M.833 *Coca-Cola Carlsberg* OJ [1998] L 145/41, portfolio power was also an important issue in the *GE/Honeywell* prohibition, Case No COMP/M.2220.
2   See eg Whinston 'Tying, Foreclosure and Exclusion' (1990) 80 American Economic Review 837; on tie-in transactions under Article 82 EC, see ch 17, pp 605-611.
3   See pp 779-780 below.

(v) Collective dominance

As has been seen in chapter 14, the ECJ in *France v Commission*[4] and the CFI in *Gencor v Commission*[5] have confirmed that the ECMR applies to collective dominance as well as to single firm dominance[6]. It is particularly important that the Commission should be able to take action to prevent the creation of market structures which might be conducive to tacit collusion, given the difficulties of dealing with this phenomenon under Articles 81 and 82[7]. The Commission has investigated numerous cases in recent years in which collective dominance has been in issue. These are discussed in chapter 14[8].

(vi) Efficiency[9]

In the previous chapter, it was pointed out that one of the reasons why firms merge is to increase efficiency[10]. It was also explained that, in some narrowly defined circumstances, US law allows an 'efficiency defence' where the efficiency gains from a merger outweigh its detriment to competition. The treatment of efficiency under the ECMR is unclear.

(A) EFFICIENCY DEFENCE? The first question is whether the ECMR allows an efficiency defence. The test for prohibition is whether a dominant position will be created or strengthened as a result of which competition will be significantly impeded. Where a concentration will not create or strengthen a dominant position, it must be cleared, irrespective of efficiency considerations. However, where a dominant position will be created or strengthened, it is necessary to consider whether the firms can argue that their concentration should nevertheless be permitted because of the increased efficiency that will result. Article 2(1)(b) of the ECMR includes, as one of the appraisal criteria, 'the development of technical or economic progress'. This is suggestive of an 'efficiency defence', not dissimilar to the possibility of exemption being obtained for an agreement under Article 81(3) EC where it would contribute to an improvement in technical or economic progress, subject to the other terms of that provision. However, Article 2(1) of the ECMR goes on to add, significantly, 'provided that it [the technical or economic progress] is to consumers' advantage and does not form an obstacle to competition'. This seems to operate differently from Article 81(3): the latter can be used to 'trump' a restriction of competition, provided that the elimination of competition will not be substantial[11]. Article 2(1) of the ECMR however seems

---

4 Cases C-68/94 and 30/95 [1998] ECR I-1375, [1998] 4 CMLR 829.
5 Case T-102/96 [1999] ECR II-753, [1999] 4 CMLR 971.
6 See in particular ch 14, pp 484-488.
7 Ibid, pp 467-482.
8 See in particular ch 14 pp 489-492.
9 See further Griffin and Sharp 'Efficiency Issues in Competition Analysis in Australia, the European Union and the United States' (1995-96) 64 Antitrust Law Journal 649-700; Noël 'Efficiency Considerations in the Assessment of Horizontal Mergers under European and US Antitrust Law' (1997) 18 ECLR 498; Camasasca 'The Explicit Efficiency Defence in Merger Control: Does it Make the Difference'? (1999) 20 ECLR 14; Halliday 'The Recognition, Status and Form of the Efficiency Defence to a Merger' (1999) 22 World Competition 91-127; Camesasca European Merger Control: Getting the Efficiencies Rights (Intersentia–Hart, 2000).
10 See ch 20, pp 725-726.
11 See ch 4, pp 124-133.

to suggest that if competition would be affected at all, efficiency is not available as a trump card. Efficiency is therefore treated asymmetrically in Article 81(3) and the ECMR.

The Commission has yet to explain its view of how the somewhat tortuous provisions of Article 2(1) of the ECMR work in practice. In its decisions to date, it has normally either noted that a concentration would not create or strengthen a dominant position anyway, so that it has not needed to give an opinion on Article 2(1)(b); or it has disagreed with the parties' assessment that efficiency would be improved[12]; or it has found that there was no mechanism for ensuring that any efficiency benefits would be passed on to consumers[13], so that the terms of Article 2(1)(b) were not satisfied. The Commission has never concluded that, *despite the creation or strengthening of a dominant position*, it would clear a concentration because of the efficiency benefits that would follow from it. It is possible that the requirement in Article 2(1)(b) that there must be no obstacle to competition means, as a matter of law, that an efficiency defence is not available at all: in *Danish Crown/Vestjyske Slagterier*[14] the Commission said at paragraph 198 that, since the concentration in question would create a dominant position, 'the efficiency arguments of the parties cannot be taken into account'. It may be that, in practice, the fact that a concentration might yield reasonable efficiency benefits steers the Commission in the direction of finding that there will be no creation or strengthening of dominance at all, in which case there is no need to rule on the availability of an efficiency defence: the margin of discretion of the Commission in any particular case is sufficiently broad that efficiency considerations can exert an influence irrespective of the strict legal position .

Two postscripts may be added. First, where the Commission considers a full-function joint venture under the ECMR, it will apply the criteria of Article 2(4) to any coordinative aspects of the case[15]. It is possible that efficiency considerations might be relevant at that point also, in which case the 'trumping' potential of Article 81(3) would be available to that part of the assessment through Article 2(4) of the Regulation. Secondly, the enhanced efficiency of a concentration in an oligopolistic market might have the effect of destabilising the potential for tacit collusion, in which case there would seem to be greater reason for taking it into account. It remains to be seen whether either of these ideas will be reflected in the decisional practice of the Commission.

(B) EFFICIENCY ATTACK? A separate question is whether the Commission could argue that the very fact that a concentration would make the merged entity more efficient means that a dominant position would be created or strengthened, because of the advantage it would have over its competitors. The possibility of an 'efficiency attack' has been noted in the literature[16], and on some occasions the Commission does seem to have entertained this idea. Some of the language in *Grand Metropolitan/Guinness*[17] on portfolio power seems to come close to

---

12   See eg Case No IV/M.477 *Mercedes Benz/Kässbohrer* OJ [1995] L 211/1; Case No IV/M.53 *Aerospatiale-Alenia/de Havilland* OJ [1991] L 334/42, [1992] 4 CMLR 112 , para 65-68; *MSG/Media Service* OJ [1994] L 364/1, paras 100-101; *BertelsMann/Kirch/Premiere* OJ [1999] L 53/1, [1999] 4 CMLR 700, paras 119-122.
13   Case No IV/M.774 *Saint-Gobain/Wacker-Chemie/NOM* OJ [1997] L 247/1, [1997] 4 CMLR 25, paras 244-246.
14   Case IV/M.1313 OJ [2000] L 20/1, [2000] 5 CMLR 296.
15   See pp 781-783 below.
16   Jenny 'EEC Merger Control: Economies as an Antitrust Defence or an Antitrust Attack'? [1992] Fordham Corporate Law Institute 591; *Hawk and Huser*, pp 267-269.
17   Case No IV/M.938 OJ [1998] L 288/24, [1997] 5 CMLR 760.

suggesting that the added efficiency that would follow from the transaction was a reason for condemnation. Such a doctrine would be inimical to consumer welfare, and will hopefully be resisted.

(vii)   Failing firm defence

In some cases, a reason for a merger might be to prevent a firm from going out of business. As was explained in chapter 20[18], US law recognises, in limited circumstances, the availability of a 'failing firm' defence. Such a defence has been recognised in Community law in the judgment of the ECJ in *France v Commission*[19]. Kali und Salz intended to acquire MdK; the combined entity would have a 98% share of the German potash market. However the parties argued that the Commission should clear this part of the transaction, since MdK would not be able to survive on the market as an independent operator; the Commission agreed and cleared it. France and SCPA appealed to the ECJ, claiming that the Commission should not have permitted this acquisition. The ECJ therefore had to determine whether a failing firm defence was available under the ECMR and, if so, the conditions for its application. The ECJ considered this matter from the perspective of Article 2(2) of the ECMR, which provides that a concentration which does not create or strengthen a dominant position as a result of which effective competition would be significantly impeded shall be declared compatible with the common market. The ECJ pointed out that this language introduces a 'causal connection' between the concentration and the creation or strengthening of dominance. If the firm acquired would have failed anyway, the concentration cannot be said to have caused the deterioration of the competitive structure of the market. The ECJ said that a failing firm defence would be available where three conditions are satisfied: first, the acquired undertaking would in the near future be forced out of the market if not taken over by another undertaking; secondly the acquiring undertaking would gain the market share of the acquired undertaking if it were forced out of the market; and third there is no possibility of a less anti-competitive alternative purchase. On the facts, the ECJ was satisfied with the finding of the Commission. It is clear, therefore, that there is a failing firm defence under the ECMR; the defence has failed in several cases[20], but was successfully invoked in *BASF/Pantochem/Eurodial*[20a]. The burden is on the firms claiming the defence[21].

(viii)   Other considerations[22]

The 13th Recital of the ECMR states that, in considering the compatibility of a concentration with the common market, the Commission should bear in mind the fundamental objectives of the EC, including the strengthening of the

---

18 See ch 20, p 730.
19 Cases C-68/94 and 30/95 *France v Commission* [1998] ECR I-1375, [1998] 4 CMLR 829, paras 109-125; see Monti and Rousseva 'Failing Firms in the Framework of the EC Merger Regulation' (1999) 24 ELRev 38; on the position in UK law, see ch 22, p 826.
20 See eg Case No IV/M.774 *Saint-Gobain/Wacker-Chemie/NOM* OJ [1997] L 247/1, paras 247-259; Case No IV/M.1221 *Rewe/Meinl* OJ [1999] L 274/1, [2000] 5 CMLR 256, paras 63-69; *Blokker/Toys'R'Us* OJ [1998] L 316/1, paras 109-113.
20a Case No COMP/M.2314.
21 *Rewe/Meinl* (n 20 above), para 64.
22 See Banks 'Non-competition factors and their future relevance under European merger law' (1997) 18 ECLR 182.

Community's economic and social cohesion[1]. It is unclear to what extent this means that the Commission is entitled to take into account non-competition criteria when determining whether the concentration is compatible with the common market. The fact that the reference to economic and social cohesion appears in the recitals, rather than in the body of the ECMR itself, suggests that this issue will be only of marginal significance; and it is difficult to see how the recital can be squared with the clear test set out in Article 2(3) of the ECMR, which asks whether the concentration will create or strengthen a dominant position as a result of which competition will be significantly impeded.

From the beginning the Commission took a strong line that competition was the prime concern of the ECMR: 'the assessment criteria set out in Article 2 indicate clearly that concentration control is to be based on the principle of protecting free competition'[2]. In *Aerospatiale-Alenia/de Havilland*[3] the Commission was criticised in some quarters for blocking a concentration on competition grounds and for not considering industrial policy considerations: the concentration would have created the world's largest manufacturer of turbo propeller aircraft, and it would have been based in Europe. At a fairly late stage in the *Volvo/Scania* investigation, the Prime Minister of Sweden personally visited the Competition Commissioner in support of a concentration that would create a 'world player' in the market for trucks[4]; however the Commission prohibited the transaction[5]. On these occasions the competition considerations prevailed over industrial policy considerations. On the other hand, in *Mannesmann/Vallourec/Ilva*[6] a concentration was cleared in circumstances where there appeared to be a real possibility of serious harm to competition: the decision left the impression that the Commission had been influenced by political considerations when reaching its conclusion. Merger decisions at the end of Phase II are taken by the College of Commissioners: it is difficult to suppose that each time an individual Commissioner votes in a Phase II case he or she will be motivated purely by the competition test set out in Article 2(3) of the ECMR: in this sense it cannot be ruled out that 'other' considerations may have an influence in some cases, whether this can be reconciled with the legal test or not. The fact that the *cabinets* of some or all Commissioners, not just the Commissioner for Competition, are often contacted in the run-up to the decision itself is testament to this.

(C) Article 2(4)[7]

As was explained above[8], the ECMR as originally drafted provided that a joint venture that had as its object or effect the coordination of the competitive behaviour of independent undertakings was not treated as a concentration. It would fall to be analysed, if at all, under Article 81. Regulation 1310/97 deleted

---

1   See Case T-12/93 *Comité Central d'Enterprise de la Société Anonyme Vittel v Commission* [1995] ECR II-1247, paras 38-40.
2   Commission's XXth *Annual Report on Competition Policy* (1990), point 20.
3   Case No IV/M.53 OJ [1991] L 334/42, [1992] 4 CMLR M2; see p 800 below.
4   *Financial Times*, 17 February 2000.
5   Case No COMP/M.1672.
6   Case No IV/M.315, OJ [1994] L 102/15, [1994] 4 CMLR 529.
7   See further *Butterworth's Competition Law* Div VII, para [759]-[777.1]; *Cook and Kerse* pp 48-52; Zonnekeyn *The treatment of Joint Ventures under the Amended EC Merger Regulation* (1998) 19 ECLR 414; Faull and Nikpay *The EC Law of Competition* (Oxford University Press, 1999), paras 6.111-6.119.
8   See pp 748-751 above.

the coordination element of the test of what constituted a concentration: the only question now is whether the joint venture is full function. Full-function joint ventures having a Community dimension fall to be analysed within the procedural framework of the ECMR. However, the issue of coordination remains relevant when it comes to substantive analysis of the transaction. A full-function joint venture will be subjected to two forms of scrutiny: to the extent that it brings about a change in the structure of the market, it will be investigated in accordance with the provisions of Article 2(1) to (3) that have just been discussed. However, in so far as the joint venture could lead to a coordination of behaviour, this will be tested according to the provisions of Article 2(4), which is based upon Article 81 of the Treaty.

Article 2(4) provides that:

'To the extent that the creation of a joint venture constituting a concentration pursuant to Article 3 has as its object or effect the coordination of the competitive behaviour of undertakings that remain independent, such coordination shall be appraised in accordance with the criteria of Article 81(1) and (3) of the Treaty, with a view to establishing whether or not the operation is compatible with the common market'.

In making this appraisal, the Commission shall take into account in particular:
- whether two or more parent companies retain to a significant extent activities in the same market as the joint venture or in a market which is downstream or upstream from that of the joint venture or in a neighbouring market closely related to this market,
- whether the coordination which is the direct consequence of the creation of the joint venture affords the undertakings concerned the possibility of eliminating competition in respect of a substantial part of the products or services in question.'

The practical application of Article 2(4) is far from simple, and more than three years after it entered into force not much light has been shed on it. In principle, the intention behind the provision is clear. Suppose that two producers of widgets, A and B, decide to merge their widget production in a joint venture, 'Newco'. Suppose further that A and B each will continue to produce raw materials essential for the production of widgets, and that they will supply these raw materials to Newco. In this case, A and B will retain a presence in the 'upstream' market for raw materials. The concentration – that is to say the merger of the two widget businesses – will be tested according to the criteria in Article 2(1) to (3); however the possibility that there may be coordination of A and B's behaviour in the market for the raw materials will be analysed according to the standards of Article 2(4). The concentration is subject to a dominance test; the coordination to an Article 81 test.

Cases that may give rise to issues of coordination are generally dealt with by the sectoral units of DG COMP that apply Articles 81 and 82 rather than the MTF. Cases handled by these units are given 'JV' rather than 'M' numbers[9]. Decisions on both the concentrative and coordinative aspects of a case must be reached within the procedural framework of the ECMR[10]. In applying Article

9   See p 742 above.
10   See p 749 above.

2(4), the jurisprudence of the Community Courts and the decisional practice of the Commission under Article 81 will be followed. Some of the latter is set out in the Commission's 1994 old *Notice on the distinction between concentrative and cooperative joint ventures*[11]; the Commission's *Guidelines on horizontal cooperation agreements* are also important[12].

The first Phase II investigation where possible coordination effects were considered pursuant to Article 2(4) was in the case of the joint venture between the telecommunications operators BT and AT&T[13]. The Commission identified certain 'candidate markets' in which coordination was a possibility, and then considered, first, whether that coordination would happen as a result of the joint venture and, secondly, whether any restriction of competition would be appreciable. The joint venture was approved subject to commitments being offered by the parties to eliminate the risk of parental coordination, including a divestiture of ACC, a wholly-owned subsidiary of AT&T[14].

(D) 'Restrictions directly related and necessary to the concentration': ancillary restraints[15]

Recital 25 and Articles 6(1)(b) and 8(2) of the ECMR recognise that certain contractual restrictions may be necessary for the successful implementation of a concentration; an obvious example is that two undertakings that decide to merge their widget businesses into a joint venture 'Newco' will each agree not to compete with the widget business of Newco: to do so would undermine the very purpose of the transaction.

The question is whether a clause such as this falls outside Article 81 because it is essential to the success of the concentration. The Commission published a *Notice on ancillary restraints* in 1990[16] in which it provided guidance on those restrictions that it regarded as directly related and necessary to concentrations. This has been superseded by the Commission's *Notice on restrictions directly related and necessary to concentrations*[17]. The new *Notice* refers to an important alteration in the Commission's practice in relation to ancillary restraints; it no longer makes an assessment of them in its merger decisions, as it had previously

---

11 OJ [1994] C 385/1; this Notice is no longer relevant to the characterisation of joint ventures under the ECMR: in that respect it has been replaced by the *Notice on full-function joint ventures*.

12 OJ [2001] C 3/2; see ch 15, pp 501-508.

13 Case No JV.15 *BT/AT&T*; the first decision in Phase I was Case IV/JV.1 *Schibsted Multimedia AS/Telenor AS/Telia AB* [1999] 4 CMLR 216.

14 See the Commission's XXIXth *Annual Report on Competition Policy* (1999), para 185; paras 186-188 provide details of other cases in 1999 in which commitments were required to deal with perceived problems under Article 2(4) of the ECMR; for cases in 1998, see the Commission's XXVIIIth *Annual Report on Competition Policy* (1998), Insert 7, pp 77-78.

15 See further *Butterworth's Competition Law* Div VII, para [1039] to [1051]; *Hawk and Huser* ch IX; *Cook and Kerse* ch 6; Modrall 'Ancillary Restrictions in the Commission's Decisions under the Merger Regulation: Non-competition Clauses' (1995) 16 ECLR 40; González Diaz 'Some Reflections on the Notion of Ancillary Restraints under EC Competition Law' [1995] Fordham Corporate Law Institute (ed Hawk), pp 325-362.

16 OJ [1990] C 203/5.

17 OJ [2001] C 188/5; note the change in nomenclature from 'ancillary restraints' to the wording actually used in the ECMR.

done; rather the parties must assess whether the restrictions in question are directly related and necessary to the concentration, and disputes must be settled in national courts[17a]. Practitioners have been critical of this change, which they consider to be detrimental to legal certainty; however, the new procedure is consistent with the Commission's modernisation proposals, which will eliminate notification of agreements to the Commission in order to receive its imprimatur, and which will require undertakings instead to use their own judgment to determine whether Article 81 is infringed[17b].

Under the new *Notice* the Commission explains that agreements are necessary to the implementation of a concentration where, in the absence of those agreements, the concentration could not be implemented, or could only be implemented at substantially higher cost, over an appreciably longer period or with considerably higher difficulty[17c]. In determining whether a restriction is necessary one must consider its nature and its duration, subject-matter and geographical field of application[17d]. The *Notice* proceeds to consider the principles applicable to common clauses in cases of the acquisition of an undertaking[17e], the joint acquisition of an undertaking[17f] and the establishment of joint ventures[17g]. The Commission gives particular attention to non-competition clauses, to licence agreements and to purchase and supply obligations. Where an undertaking is acquired together with associated goodwill and know-how, the Commission considers that non-competition clauses are generally justified for periods of up to three years; where only goodwill is included, the normal justified period is two years[17h]. Longer periods can be justified only in a limited range of circumstances, for example if it can be shown that customer loyalty will persist for a longer period[17i]. Non-solicitation and confidentiality clauses are to be evaluated in the same way as non-competition clauses[17j]. Where a joint venture is established, the Commission considers that, as a general rule, non-competition clauses can be justified for periods of up to five years, although where the period is for longer than three years this will have to be justified; clauses that extend beyond the life-time of the joint venture will never be regarded as ancillary[17k].

Licences of intellectual property rights may be directly related and necessary to a concentration, even if they are exclusive[17l]; however territorial restrictions would normally not qualify[17m], nor licences between the parents of a joint venture[17n]. Licences that are not ancillary may, however, benefit from block exemption under Regulation 240/96[17p]. Purchase and supply obligations may be

17a   Ibid, paras 2 and 3.
17b   See ch 4, pp 146-147 an ch 7, pp 248-258.
17c   OJ [2001] C 188/5, para 8.
17d   Ibid, para 9.
17e   Ibid, paras 12-31.
17f   Ibid, paras 32-34.
17g   Ibid, paras 34-35.
17h   Ibid, para 15.
17i   Ibid.
17j   Ibid, para 20.
17k   Ibid, para 36.
17l   Ibid, paras 22 and 42.
17m   Ibid, para 22.
17n   Ibid, paras 22 and 44.
17p   See ch 19, pp 688-696.

directly related and necessary to a concentration, for example where they prevent disruption of a business that is transferred for a transitional period[17q]; however, obligations for unlimited quantities, or that confer preferred supplier or purchaser status, or that grant exclusivity, will be ancillary only in exceptional circumstances[17r]. Vertical agreements that are not ancillary may benefit from the block exemption conferred by Regulation 2790/99[17s]. Purchase and supply obligations between the parents of a joint venture and the joint venture itself are subject to the same principles[17t].

7. COMMITMENTS[18]

As has been explained above, various decisions are possible at the end of the Commission's investigation[19]. In particular, at the end of Phase I the Commission may clear a concentration unconditionally; clear it subject to commitments; or take it to a Phase II investigation. At the end of Phase II, the Commission may clear it conditionally or unconditionally; it may also prohibit it outright.

In practice, the majority of cases are cleared unconditionally, within Phase I; statistics to support this assertion will be found in section 12 below. This is not surprising: concentrations are notifiable not according to their impact on competition but the turnover of the undertakings concerned; it follows that many transactions are caught that give rise to no competition concerns: this is why the simplified procedure was introduced in 2000[19a]. At the other end of the spectrum, outright prohibitions are rare: by 31 July 2001, there have been only 15 since the ECMR entered into force. Having said this, the Commission does appear to have taken a tougher line recently than in the early years of the Regulation, and in several cases the parties have chosen to withdraw their notification in anticipation of an unfavourable outcome, so that the number of prohibitions could have been higher[20].

Between the unconditional clearance and the outright prohibition of concentrations there is another very important group of cases: those where the Commission grants clearance, but subject to commitments by the parties to modify their proposals in order to overcome problems identified by it. The negotiation of such commitments is an important feature of many merger cases, and has become more common.

17q   OJ [2001] C 188/5, paras 25-27.
17r   Ibid, paras 28-29.
17s   See ch 16, pp 567-591.
17t   OJ [2001] C 188/5, para 45.
18   See further *Butterworths Competition Law* Div VII paras [998]-[1002] and [1035]-[1038.1]; *Hawk and Huser* pp 318-326; *Cook and Kerse* pp 203-212; Drauz 'Remedies under the Merger Regulation' [1995] Fordham Corporate Law Institute (ed Hawk), pp 219-238; the Commission's XXXth Annual Report on Competition Policy (2000), points 268-278.
19   See pp 768-769 above.
19a   See p 767 above.
20   See further pp 791-792 below on the application of the ECMR in practice.

(A)   Legal basis

The legal basis for commitments to be accepted at the end of Phase I is to be found in Article 6(2) of the ECMR; prior to Regulation 1310/97 there had been no legal basis for such commitments, a significant omission remedied by that legislation[1]. Phase I commitments will be acceptable to the Commission in fairly straightforward cases: 'where the competition problem is readily identifiable and can easily be remedied', to use the language of recital 8 of Regulation 1310/97; more complex cases will usually require in-depth investigation in Phase II before the Commission will be prepared to consider a settlement. This said, there is an increasing number of cases in which Phase I commitments are given[2]. The legal basis for Phase II commitments is contained in Article 8(2) of the ECMR. In both Phase I and Phase II cases, breach of a commitment may lead to revocation of the decision[3] or to fines where there is a breach of an obligation attached to a decision[4]. On a few occasions the parties have offered commitments of which the Commission took notice, without accepting them as a condition to its approval[5].

(B)   Commitments may be structural or behavioural

The Commission prefers structural remedies to behavioural ones. That is to say, it would prefer a remedy whereby the structural problem – for example the accretion of market share – is directly addressed by the merged entity agreeing to divest itself of, for example, manufacturing capacity within a fixed period of time or of a controlling shareholding in a competing undertaking. A commitment to behave or not to behave in a particular way requires continual monitoring on the part of the already-overstretched staff of the MTF. However, it is clear that, as a matter of law, the Commission cannot refuse to accept behavioural commitments. In *Gencor v Commission*[6] the CFI ruled that the important question is not whether the commitment is structural or behavioural, but whether it would be sufficient to ensure that the concentration will not create or strengthen a dominant position. The Court accepted that, as a general proposition, there are great advantages in structural commitments, but nevertheless said that it is not possible automatically to rule out behavioural ones, such as agreeing not to use a trade mark, making production capacity available to third parties or agreeing

---

1   On the position prior to Regulation 1310/97, see Broberg 'Commitments in Phase I Merger Proceedings: the Commission's Power to Accept and Enforce Phase One Commitments' (1997) 34 CML Rev 845.
2   See the statistical Table at pp 791-792 below.
3   See Article 6(1)(b) and Article 8(5)(b) of the ECMR respectively.
4   Ibid, Article 14(2)(a).
5   See eg Case IV/M.794 *Coca-Cola/Amalgamated Beverages GB* OJ [1997] L 218/15, on appeal Cases T-125/97 and T-127/97 *Coca-Cola Co v Commission* [2000] 5 CMLR 467; Case No IV/M.1225 *Enso/Stora* OJ [1999] L 254/9, [2000] 4 CMLR 372; Case No COMP/M.1879 *Boeing/Hughes Electronics*, para 102.
6   Case T-102/96 [1999] ECR II-753, [1999] 4 CMLR 971, paras 313-330.

to grant access to essential facilities on non-discriminatory terms. This should be dealt with on a case-by-case basis.

Where the commitments offered are elaborate and require a complex mechanism to ensure compliance, the Commission will consider carefully whether an outright prohibition would not be more appropriate[7].

(C) Notice on remedies

The Commission published a *Notice on remedies* in 2000[8]. The Notice is divided into six parts. After an introduction, the Commission explains in Part II the general principles that are applicable to the negotiation and acceptance of remedies. Remedies, as a matter of law, may be structural or behavioural; however, the former are preferable, in particular since they do not require medium- or long-term monitoring measures.[8a] In Part III the Commission describes the types of remedy that may be acceptable, dealing in turn with divestiture and other remedies. As to the former, the Commission will require sale to a suitable purchaser within a specified deadline.[8b] Remedies other than divestiture may include the termination of exclusive agreements or a commitment to grant access to infrastructure or to technology.[8c] Part IV explains situations in which a remedy may be difficult, if not impossible. Part V provides details of specific requirements for the submission of remedies and Part VI discusses their practical implementation.

(D) Timetable

There are fixed timetables for the negotiation of commitments. Commitments will be 'market-tested' by the Commission to see if they are acceptable: recital 8 of Regulation 1310/97 states that 'transparency and effective consultation of Member States and interested third parties should be ensured in both phases of the procedure'[9]. In a Phase I case, commitments must be submitted to the Commission within not more than three weeks of the date of receipt of the notification[10]; no extension of time will be allowed. Phase II commitments must be submitted within not more than three months of the date on which proceedings were initiated: this period may be extended in exceptional circumstances[11]: this did happen, for example, in *Telia/ Telenor*[12]; the parties had let the MTF know in advance that they would be asking

---

7   XXIXth *AnnualReport on Competition Policy* (1999), para 180; Case No COMP/M.1741 *MCIWorldCom/Sprint* para 407.
8   OJ [2001] C 68/3.
8a   Ibid, para 9.
8b   Ibid, para 19.
8c   Ibid, para 27-28
9   On the rights of third parties to be heard, see the CFI's judgment in Case T-290/94 *Kayserberg SA v Commission* [1997] ECR II-2137, [1998] 4 CMLR 336, paras 98-123.
10   Regulation 447/98, Article 18(1).
11   Ibid, Article 18(2); see the Commission's XXIXth *Annual Report on Competition Policy* (1999), Box 8, p 71.
12   Case No COMP/M.1439, OJ [2000] L 40/1, [2001] 4 CMLR 1226, para 378.

for the extension. An extension of time was rejected in *Airtours/First Choice*[13], where the Commission considered that there were no exceptional circumstances. In practice, the tightness of the timetables under the ECMR means that the parties to a notification should consider whether, and if so what, commitments might be possible as early as possible in the procedure. A solution, albeit one that is less than ideal, where the time for offering commitments has elapsed or where there is difficulty in reaching final agreement with the Commission, is for the parties to withdraw the notification and begin the process again. In the case of *Time Warner/ EMI*[14] the parties withdrew their notification in circumstances where it seemed that there was insufficient time to finalise commitments suitable to the Commission within the existing procedure[15]. A preferable solution might be for the parties and the Commission, by agreement, to 'stop the clock': that is to say to suspend the ECMR's timetable while suitable commitments are negotiated; however there is no legal basis for this to happen under the current legislation.

(E)   Examples

The most obvious commitment in the case of a horizontal concentration that gives rise to concern is divestiture, for example of manufacturing capacity: the Commission will require any divestiture to be effected within a specified time, which may vary from one case to another; the purchaser will have to be an unconnected person; and prior to the sale the Commission will require the business to be divested to be held at arm's length and protected from sabotage. A reporting requirement will normally be imposed on the progress of the sale, and a trustee will be appointed to oversee the implementation of the commitment. The trustee typically will be an investment bank, an accountancy firm or a law firm of international standing. Examples of commitments to divest that conform with these characteristics can be found in *Siemens/Elektrowatt*[16] and in *Sanitec/ Sphinx*[17]. The *WorldCom/MCI*[18] concentration was cleared subject to a commitment to divest MCI's internet interests to a new entrant: this is understood to have been the largest divestiture in the world to have resulted from antitrust action, and was the subject of close cooperation between the Commission and the Department of Justice. Another substantial divestiture was the outcome of a Phase I proceeding in *Vodafone Airtouch/Mannesmann*[19] which led to the sale of the mobile telephone operator, Orange; the merged entity also gave a commitment to provide non-discriminatory access on the part of third parties to its pan-European integrated mobile network for a period of three years. In the case of

---

13   Case No IV/M. 1524, OJ [2000] L 93/1, [2000] 5 CMLR 494, para 193.
14   Case No COMP/M.1852.
15   *Financial Times*, 6 October 2000.
16   Case No IV/M.913, OJ [1999] L 88/1, [2000] 4 CMLR 1255, paras 121-132.
17   Case No IV/M.1578, OJ [2000] L 294/1, [2001] 4 CMLR 507, para 252; see the Commission's XXIXth *Annual Report on Competition Policy* (1999), para 178.
18   Case No IV/M.1069 OJ [1999] L 116/1, [1999] 5 CMLR 876.
19   Case No COMP/M.1795; the acquisition by France Telecom of Orange was itself notified to the Commission under the ECMR and the subject of commitments: see the Commission's *Competition Policy Newsletter* October 2000, p 71.

Totalfina/Elf Aquitaine[20] the Commission rejected the parties' list of proposed buyers of 70 French motorway petrol stations on the basis that none of them would provide sufficient competition to address its concerns[1]. This was the first occasion on which the Commission rejected a potential third party purchaser, and is indicative of a greater determination on its part to ensure that an effective competitive force will be the consequence of any divestiture[2]. In *Bosch/Rexroth*[2a] the Commission insisted, for the first time, that the parties must have entered into a binding agreement with an 'upfront buyer' for the sale of the business to be divested.

In *Anglo-American/Lonrho*[3] the Commission required the reduction of Anglo-American's shareholding in Lonrho from 27.5% to 9.99%. In other cases, different commitments have been given. For example, in *Boeing/McDonnell Douglas*[4] Boeing agreed not to enforce 20-year exclusivity clauses in its agreements with three American airlines; to keep the civil aircraft business of MDD a legally separate company for 10 years; not to leverage customer service and support between MDD and existing customers; and to licence and cross-licence certain patents; further, an annual report would be submitted to the Commission on R&D projects benefiting from public funding. In *Ciba-Geigy/Sandoz*[5] a commitment was given to license technology to third parties. An important commitment that was offered in the case of *Telia/Telenor* was the 'unbundling' of the local loop, which would introduce competition in the last link in telecommunications services between the local exchange and the consumer[6].

The Commission may exceptionally agree to the variation of a commitment where a change of circumstances is such that its concerns are no longer applicable[7]. Sometimes the divestiture itself entails a notifiable concentration: for example the notification of *BellSouth/E-Plus*[8] was a consequence of the commitment that was given in *Vodafone Airtouch/Mannesmann*[9].

20 Case No IV/M.1628.
1 *Financial Times*, 15 September 2000; see also the Commission's *XXXth Annual Report on Competition Policy* (2000), points 257-258.
2 See on this the speech of Mario Monti, Commissioner for Competition, at the EC Merger Control 10th Anniversary Conference, Brussels, 14-15 September 2000, http://europa.eu.int/comm/competition/speeches/.
2a Case No COMP M.2060.
3 Case No IV/M.754, OJ [1998] L 149/21.
4 Case No IV/M.877, OJ [1997] L 336/16.
5 Case No IV/M.737, OJ [1997] L 201/1, paras 275-280.
6 Case No IV/M.1439; see the Commission's XXIXth *Annual Report on Competition Policy*, paras 173-174.
7 See eg the Commission's amended decision in Case No IV/M.269 *Shell/Montecatini* OJ [1996] L 294/10, [1996] 4 CMLR 469.
8 Case No IV/M.1817.
9 Case No IV/M.1430; see also n 19 above on the sale of Orange to France Telecom.

8.   POWERS OF INVESTIGATION AND ENFORCEMENT

The Commission is given wide powers of investigation and the ability to impose fines for transgression of the ECMR similar to those granted to it by Regulation 17/62. To enable the Commission to carry out its functions, it is given powers to request information (Article 11), to carry out on–the–spot investigations (Article 13)[10] and to impose fines and periodic penalties (Articles 14 and 15) for breach of the Regulation's provisions. Article 11 requests for information are a standard feature of almost all investigations, and may be sent both to the notifying parties and to other undertakings – for example competitors, suppliers and customers – which might be able to supply the MTF with relevant information. Fines for failure to notify or for providing incorrect or misleading information are relatively small: from EUR 1,000 to EUR 50,000[11]. However fines for breaching obligations attached to certain decisions or for consummating a notifiable concentration without authorisation may be considerable: for example, undertakings that carry out a concentration without notifying it and which the Commission, upon investigation, considers to be incompatible with the common market could be fined as much as 10% of their aggregate group worldwide turnover in the preceding financial year. In determining the amount of a fine, the Commission is required by Article 14(3) to bear in mind the nature and gravity of the infringement. Clearly the possibility of a heavy fine, in association with the power under Article 8(4) to require the reversal of a concentration already effected, means that it is highly unwise to proceed without complying with the requirements of the ECMR. The Community Courts are given unlimited jurisdiction by Article 16 to review decisions imposing fines or periodic penalty payments.

The first fine (of EUR 33,000) under the ECMR, for failure to notify and for carrying out an operation without the prior approval of the Commission, was imposed in 1998 in the case of *Samsung*[12]. In the case of *A P Møller*[13] a larger fine, of EUR 219,000, was imposed for failure to notify and for putting into effect three concentrations which were discovered in the course of an investigation of a notified concentration. In setting the level of the fine, the Commission noted that the failure to notify was not intentional, but that there had been 'qualified negligence'. A P Møller was a large European undertaking that could be expected to have a good knowledge of the ECMR, and the concentrations had been operated for a considerable time before they were brought to the MTF's attention. A mitigating factor was that there had been no damage to the competitive process. Fines were also imposed for the provision of incorrect information in 1999 in the cases of *Sanofi/Synthélabo*, *KLM/Martinair* and *Deutsche Post*[14]. It can be expected that, in the future, the Commission will take a tougher line on failures to notify. In the case of *Mitsubishi*[15] the Commission for the first time imposed a fine on a third party, rather than the parties to the notified concentration;

---

10   See Case No IV/M.1157 *Skanska/Scancem* OJ [1999] L 183/1, [2000] 5 CMLR 686, para 11.
11   ECMR, Article 14(1).
12   Case No IV/M.920, OJ [1999] L 225/12, [1998] 4 CMLR 494.
13   Case No IV/M.969, OJ [1999] L 183/29, [1999] 4 CMLR 392.
14   See the Commission's XXIXth *Annual Report on Competition Policy* (1999), Box 9, pp 73-74; the *Deutsche Post* decision will be found at OJ [2001] L 97/1.
15   OJ [2001] L 4/31; see the Commission's *Competition Policy Newsletter*, October 2000, pp 62-63, http://europa.eu.int/comm/competition/publications/cpn/.

Mitsubishi had failed to provide information in response to requests from the Commission under Article 11(5) of the ECMR. The fines imposed in this case totalled EUR 950,000.

9. INTERNATIONAL COOPERATION

(A) Close and constant liaison with Member States

Article 10 of the EC Treaty establishes the principle of cooperation between Member States and the institutions of the EC. In the context of the ECMR, Article 19 sets out detailed provisions to establish liaison between the Commission and the Member States. Notifications under the ECMR must be transmitted to the competent authorities of Member States, which must be able to express their views on the Commission's treatment of cases; and the Advisory Committee on Concentrations must be consulted before important decisions – for example at the end of Phase II, or imposing fines – are taken. The Advisory Committee's opinion is not binding on the Commission, but considerable importance is attached to it. The CFI in *Kayserberg SA v Commission*[16] rejected a claim by a third party objecting to the Commission's clearance of the *Procter & Gamble/VP Schickedanz* transaction[17] that the Advisory Committee had not been properly consulted.

The Commission also cooperates with the EFTA Surveillance Authority pursuant to the provisions of the EEA Agreement[18]. Important examples of such cooperation are *Skanska/Scancem*[19], *Telia/Telenor*[20] and *Sanitec/Sphinx*[1]: this cooperation is provided for by Articles 57 and 58 of the EEA Agreement and Protocol 24.

(B) Relations with non-EC countries

(i) Reciprocity

Article 24 addresses the issue of reciprocity of treatment of concentrations by non-EC countries. Some systems of law make it difficult, if not impossible, for foreign firms to take over local ones. Not surprisingly resentment is felt where, for example, a British firm is prevented from taking over a Swiss one in circumstances in which, were the rôles reversed, there would be no obstacle to the concentration under UK law. Article 24(1) of the ECMR requires Member States to inform the Commission of any difficulties encountered by their undertakings in the case of concentrations in non-EC countries. Where it appears that a non-EC country is not affording reciprocal treatment to that granted by a Member State, the Commission may seek a mandate from the Council of Ministers to negotiate comparable treatment.

16   Case T-290/94 [1997] ECR II-2137, [1998] 4 CMLR 336, paras 80-97.
17   Case No IV/M.430 OJ [1994] L 354/32.
18   See ch 2, pp 52-53.
19   Case No IV/M.1157 OJ [1999] L 183/1, [2000] 5 CMLR 686.
20   Case No IV/ M.1439, OJ [2001] L 40/1, [2001] 4 CMLR 1226.
1   Case No IV/ M.1578, OJ [2000] L 294/1, [2001] 4 CMLR 507.

(ii) *The international dimension*

It is possible that a transaction might fall within the merger control systems of the EC, the US, Canada and many other countries. The problems associated with the international dimension – the burden on companies of multiple filings, the need for cooperation between competition authorities and the desirability of an expeditious and harmonious outcome – are considerable. These have been discussed in chapter 12, including the territorial reach of the ECMR and cooperation agreements between the EU, the US and Canada[2].

10. JUDICIAL REVIEW UNDER THE ECMR

Decisions of the Commission under the ECMR are subject to judicial review by the Community Courts. Quite a few judgments have been handed down. Some important points of law have been established in these cases, in particular on the meaning of control[3]; on the application of the ECMR to collective dominance[4]; on the nature of commitments under the Regulation[5]; and on the operation of the Dutch clause[6]. The Courts have also dealt with several procedural matters[7]. However judicial review by the Community judicature must take account of the discretionary margin implicit in provisions of an economic nature which form part of the rules on concentrations[8]; a result of this is that interference with the substantive analysis of the Commission will be infrequent. Given that the Commission is effectively the prosecutor, judge and jury in merger cases, some critics of the system consider that more effective judicial control should be exerted over its decisions. Furthermore, it is arguable that judicial review should be more speedily available than is currently the case: the House of Lords Select Committee on the European Union has remarked that the introduction of an expedited procedure for cases before the CFI might be appropriate for use in merger cases[9]. Several important cases were pending before the CFI on 31 July 2001, including applications for the annulment of the Commission's decisions in *BertelsMann/Kirch/Premiere*[10], *Deutsche Telekom/BetaResearch*[11], *Airtours/First Choice*[12], *BSkyB/KirchPay TV*[13] and *MCI WorldCom/Sprint*[14].

2   See ch 12, pp 402-403 and 411-413.
3   See pp 745-748 above.
4   See ch 14, pp 484-488.
5   See pp 784-787 above.
6   See p 761-763 above.
7   See eg Case T-12/93 *Comité Central d'Enterprise de la Société Anonyme Vittel v Commission* [1995] ECR II-1247; Case T-290/94 *Kayserberg SA v Commission* [1997] ECR II-2137, [1998] 4 CMLR 336.
8   Cases C-68/94 and 30/95 *France v Commission* [1998] ECR I-1375, [1998] 4 CMLR 829, paras 223 and 224; Case T-221/95 *Endemol Entertainment Holding BV v Commission* [1999] ECR II-1299, [1999] 5 CMLR 611, para 106.
9   *Strengthening the Rôle of the Hearing Officer in EC Competition Cases* HL Paper 125, paras 64-68 and 78.
10   Case No IV/M.993 OJ [1999] L 53/1, [1999] 4 CMLR 700, on appeal Case T-121/98 *Taurus Beteiligungs GmbH v Commission* (judgment pending).
11   Case No IV/M.1027 OJ [1999] L 53/51, [1999] 4 CMLR 700, on appeal, as in Case T-121/98 (judgment pending).
12   Case No IV/M.1524 OJ [2000] L 93/1, [2000] 5 CMLR 494, on appeal Case T-342/99 (judgment pending).
13   Case No No IV/M.1524, on appeal Case T-158/00 (judgment pending).
14   Case No COMP/M.1741, on appeal Case T-310/00 *WorldCom v Commission* (judgment pending).

11. MANDATORY REVIEW AND PROPOSALS FOR REFORM

Article 1(4) of the ECMR required the Commission to report to the Council before 1 July 2000 on the operation of the thresholds and the criteria for determining whether a concentration has a Community dimension. The Council may amend the thresholds should it consider it to be appropriate to do so, in the case of Article 1(3) by a qualified majority. The Commission sent out questionnaires in 1999 as part of the review process, and submitted a Report to the Council on 28 June 2000. The Commission's conclusion was that the criteria in Articles 1(2) and 1(3) have as their consequence that an important number of transactions with significant cross-border effects, which therefore have a Community interest, remain outside the scope of the ECMR; and further that the business community considers this to be problematic. The Commission suggested that an in-depth analysis should be conducted into the appropriate mechanism for establishing Community jurisdiction in merger cases. It considered that other procedural and substantive matters should be investigated at the same time; these were listed in the Annex to the Report, and include, for example, the referral systems in Articles 9 and 22, the rôle of the Advisory Committee in cases where commitments are offered to remedy competition concerns, fines, the meaning of various expressions in Article 4, such as 'agreement' and 'acquisition of control'; resources; and the appellate process to the CFI. The Council has asked the Commission to proceed with a detailed review of these matters.

12. THE ECMR IN PRACTICE

(A) Statistics

From 21 September 1990, when the ECMR entered into force, until 30 June 2001, the number of notifications and the decisions reached by the Commission were as follows:

I.) Notifications

	90	91	92	93	94	95	96	97	98	99	00	01	Total
Number of notified cases	12	63	60	58	95	110	131	172	235	292	345	183	1756
Cases withdrawn - Phase 1			3	1	6	4	5	9	5	7	8	8	56
Cases withdrawn - Phase 2				1			1		4	5	6	0	17

II.) Final decisions

Article, kind of decision	90	91	92	93	94	95	96	97	98	99	00	01	Total
6.1 (a) out of scope Merger													
Reg.	2	5	9	4	5	9	6	4	6	1	1	0	52
6.1 (b) compatible	5	47	43	49	78	90	109	118	207	236	293	151	1426
6.1 (b) comp.w.commit-													
ments(6.2)		3	4		2	3		2	12	19	28	7	80
Total 6.1 (b) + 6.2	5	50	47	49	80	93	109	120	219	255	321	158	1506
9.3 partial referral to M.S.													
(ph.I)			1		1			6	3	1	4	2	18
9.3 full referral to Member													
States				1			3	1	1	3	2	0	11
Total 9.3 (ph.I)			1	1	1		3	7	4	4	6	2	29
Phase I	7	55	57	54	86	102	118	131	229	260	328	160	1587

Article, kind of decision	90	91	92	93	94	95	96	97	98	99	00	01	Total
9.3 partial referral to M.S. (ph.II)										1		0	1
8.2 compatible		1	1	1	2	2	1	1	3	0	3	1	16
8.2 compatible with commitments		3	3	2	2	3	3	7	4	8	12	4	51
8.3 prohibition		1			1	2	3	1	2	1	2	1	14
8.4 restore effective competition							2					0	2
Total 8		5	4	3	5	7	7	11	9	9	17	6	83
Phase II		5	4	3	5	7	7	11	9	10	17	6	84
Total final decisions	7	60	61	57	91	109	125	142	238	270	345	166	1671

III.) Phase II Proceedings initiated

Article, kind of decision	90	91	92	93	94	95	96	97	98	99	00	01	Total
6.1 (c)		6	4	4	6	7	6	11	12	20	19	11	106

IV.) Other decisions

Article, kind of decision	90	91	92	93	94	95	96	97	98	99	00	01	Total
6.3 (a) decision revoked										1		0	1
8.5 (a) decision revoked												0	0
14 decision imposing fines								1	4	1		0	6
22. 3				1		1	1	1				0	4
9 request rejected by decision		1								1		0	2
7.4 derogation from suspension	1	1	2	3	1	2	3	5	13	7	4	1	43

(B)   Table of Phase II investigations

The following Table contains a list of all cases in which a Phase II investigation was initiated, and completed by 31 July 2001.

Case and references	Cleared	Cleared subject to conditions	Prohibited outright
Case No IV/M.12 *Varta/Bosch* OJ [1991] L 320/26, [1992] 5 CMLR M1		YES	
Case No IV/M.42 *Alcatel/Telettra* OJ [1991] L 122/48		YES	
Case No IV/M.43 *Magneti Marelli/CEAc* OJ [1991] L 222/38, [1992] 4 CMLR M61		YES	
Case No IV/M.53 *Aerospatiale-Alenia/de Havilland* OJ [1991] L 334/42, [1992] 4 CMLR M2			YES

Case and references	Cleared	Cleared subject to conditions	Prohibited outright
Case No IV/M.68 *Tetra Pak/Alfa-Laval* OJ [1991] L 290/35, [1992] 4 CMLR M81	YES		
Case No IV/M.126 *Accor/Wagons-Lits* OJ [1992] L 204/1, [1993] 5 CMLR M13		YES	
Case No IV/M.190 *Nestlé/Perrier* OJ [1992] L 356/1, [1993] 4 CMLR M17		YES	
Case No IV/M.214 *Du Pont/ICI* OJ [1993] L 7/13, [1993] 5 CMLR M41		YES	
Case No IV/M.222 *Mannesmann/Hoesch* OJ [1993] L 114/34	YES		
Case No IV/M.238 *Siemens/Philips* **NB: abandoned by the parties**			
Case No IV/M.269 *Shell/Montecatini* OJ [1994] L 332/48		YES	
Case No IV/M.291 *KNP/BT/VRG* OJ [1993] L 217/35		YES	

Case No IV/M.308
Kali + Salz/MdK/Treuhand
OJ [1994] L 186/38 (annulled on appeal
   Cases C-68/94 and 30/95 *France v*
   Commission [1998] ECR I-1375,
   [1998] 4 CMLR 829)
		YES	

Case No IV/M.315 *Mannesmann/Vallourec/Ilva* OJ [1994] L 102/15	YES		
Case No IV/M.358 *Pilkington-Techint/SIV* OJ [1994] L 158/24	YES		
CCase No IV/M.430 *Procter & Gamble/VP Schickedanz (II)* OJ [1994] L 354/32		YES	

Case and references	Cleared	Cleared subject to conditions	Prohibited outright
(unsuccessfully challenged on appeal Case T-290/94 *Kayserberg v Commission* [1997] ECR II-2137, [1998] 4 CMLR 336)			
Case No IV/M.468 *Siemens/Italtel* OJ [1995] L 161/27	YES		
Case No IV/M.469 *MSG Media Service* OJ [1994] L 364/1			YES
Case No IV/M.477 *Mercedes-Benz/Kässbohrer* OJ [1995] L 211/1	YES		
Case No IV/M.484 *Krupp/Thyssen/Riva/Falck/Tadfin/AST* OJ [1995] L 251/18	YES		
Case No IV/M.490 *Nordic Satellite Distribution* OJ [1996] L 53/20			YES
Case No IV/M.553 *RTL/Veronica/Endemol* OJ [1996] L 134/32 (upheld on appeal Case T-221/95 *Endemol v Commission* [1999] ECR II-1299, [1999] 5 CMLR 611)			YES
Case No IV/M.580 *ABB/Daimler-Benz* OJ [1997] L 11/1		YES	
Case No IV/M.582 *Orkla/Volvo* OJ [1996] L 66/17		YES	
Case No IV/M.603 *Crown Cork & Seal/Carnaud Metalbox* OJ [1996] L 75/38		YES	
Case No IV/M.619 *Gencor/Lonrho* OJ [1997] L 11/30, [2000] 4 CMLR 1076 (upheld on appeal *Gencor v Commission* [1999] ECR II-753, [1999] 4 CMLR 971)			YES
Case No IV/M.623 *Kimberly-Clark/Scott* OJ [1996] L 183/1		YES	

Case and references	Cleared	Cleared subject to conditions	Prohibited outright
Case No IV/M.709 *Telefonica/Sogecable/Cablevision* **NB: Abandoned by the parties**			
Case No IV/M.737 *Ciba-Geigy/Sandoz* OJ [1997] L 201/1		YES	
Case No IV/M.754 *Anglo American Corporation/Lonrho* OJ [1998] L 149/21		YES	
Case No IV/M.774 *Saint-Gobain/Wacker-Chemie/NOM* OJ [1997] L 247/1			YES

Case No IV/M.784
Kesko/Tuko
OJ [1997] L 110/53 (upheld on appeal
    Case T-22/97 *Kesko v Commission*
    [1999] ECR II-3775, [2000] 4 CMLR 335)
			YES

Case No IV/M.794
Coca-Cola/Amalgamated Beverages GB
OJ [1997] L 218/15, [1997] 4 CMLR 368
    (there was an appeal in this case:
    Cases T-125/97 and T-127/97
    Coca-Cola Company
    [2000] 5 CMLR 467)
	YES		

Case No IV/M.833 *Coca-Cola Company/Carlsberg AS* OJ [1998] L 145/41, [1997] 5 CMLR 564		YES	
Case No IV/M.856 *British Telecom/MCI (II)* OJ [1997] L 336/1		YES	
Case No IV/M.877 *Boeing/McDonnell Douglas* OJ [1997] L 336/16		YES	
Case No IV/M.890 *Blokker/Toys 'R' Us (II)* OJ [1998] L 316/1			YES
Case No IV/M.913 *Siemens/Elektrowatt* OJ [1999] L 88/1, [2000] 4 CMLR 1255		YES	

Case and references	Cleared	Cleared subject to conditions	Prohibited outright
Case No IV/M.938 *Guinness/Grand Metropolitan* OJ [1998] L 288/24		YES	
Case No IV/M.942 *VEBA/Degussa* OJ [1998] L 201/102		YES	
Case No IV/M.950 *Hoffmann-La Roche/Boehringer Mannheim* OJ [1998] L 234/14, [2000] 4 CMLR 735		YES	
Case No IV/M.970 *TKS/ITW Signode/Titan* OJ [1998] L 316/33	YES		
Case No IV/M.986 *AGFA-Gevaert/Du Pont* OJ [1998] L 211/22		YES	

Case No IV/M.993
BertelsMann/Kirch/Premiere
OJ [1999] L 53/1, [1999] 4 CMLR 700
    (on appeal Case T-121/98 *Taurus*
    Beteiligungs GmbH v Commission,
    judgment pending)
			YES

Case No IV/M.1016 *Price Waterhouse/Coopers & Lybrand* OJ [1999] L 50/27, [1999] 4 CMLR 665	YES		
Case No IV/M.1027 *Deutsche Telekom/BetaResearch* OJ [1999] L 53/31, [1999] 4 CMLR 700 (on appeal, as in Case T-121/98, above)			YES
Case No IV/M.1040 *Wolters Kluwer/Reed Elsevier* **NB: abandoned by the parties**			
Case No IV/M.1044 *KPMG/Ernst & Young* **NB: abandoned by the parties**			
Case No IV/M. 1047 *Wienerberger/Cremer & Breuer* **NB: abandoned by the parties**			
Case No IV/JV.15 *BT/AT&T*		YES	

Case and references	Cleared	Cleared subject to conditions	Prohibited outright
Case No IV/M.1069 *WorldCom/MCI (II)* OJ [1999] L 116/1, [1999] 5 CMLR 876		YES	
Case No IV/M.1157 *Skanska/Scancem* OJ [1999] L 183/1, [2000] 5 CMLR 686		YES	
Case No IV/M.1221 *REWE/Meinl* OJ [1999] L 274/1, [2000] 5 CMLR 256		YES	
Case No IV/M.1225 *Enso/Stora* OJ [1999] L 254/9, [2000] 4 CMLR 372	YES		
Case No IV/M.1246 *LHZ/Carl Zeiss* **NB: abandoned by the parties**			
Case No IV/M.1313 *Danish Crown/Vestjyske Slagterier* OJ [2000] L 20/1, [2000] 5 CMLR 296		YES	
Case No IV/M.1328 *KLM/Martinair* **NB: abandoned by the parties**			
Case No IV/M.1383 *Exxon/Mobil*		YES	
Case No IV/M.1412 *Hutchison Port Holdings/Whampoa/RMPM/* ECT **NB: abandoned by the parties**			
Case No IV/M.1431 *Kvaerner/Ahlström* **NB: abandoned by the parties**			
Case No IV/M.1439 *Telia/Telenor* OJ [2001] L 40/1, [2001] 4 CMLR 1226		YES	
Case No IV/M.1447 *Deutsche Post/trans-o-flex* **NB: abandoned by the parties**			
Case No IV/M.1524 *Airtours/First Choice* OJ [2000] L 93/1, [2000] 5 CMLR 494			

Case and references	Cleared	Cleared subject to conditions	Prohibited outright
(on appeal, Case T-342/99 *Airtours v Commission* (judgment pending)			YES
Case No IV/M.1532 *BP Amoco/Arco* OJ [2001] L 18/1, [2001] 4 CMLR 774		YES	
Case No IV/M.1578 *Sanitec/Sphinx* OJ [2000] L 294/1, [2001] 4 CMLR 507		YES	
Case No IV/M.1601 *Allied-Signal/Honeywell* Case COMP/M.1628 *Totalfina/Elf Aquitaine*		YES YES	
Case No IV/M.1630 *Air Liquide/BOC*		YES	
Case No COMP/M.1636 *MMS/DASA/Astrium*		YES	
Case No IV/M.1641 *Linde/Aga*		YES	
Case No COMP/M.1646 *CGD/Partest/BCP/SAirGroup/Portugália* **NB: abandoned by the parties**			
Case No COMP/M.1663 *Alcan/Alusuisse*		YES	
Case No COMP/M.1671 *Dow Chemical/Union Carbide*		YES	
Case No COMP/M.1672 *Volvo/Scania*			YES
Case No COMP/M.1673 *VEBA/VIAG*		YES	
Case No COMP/M.1693 *Alcoa/Reynolds*		YES	
Case No COMP/M.1715 *Alcan/Pechiney* **NB: abandoned by the parties**			
Case No COMP/M.1741 *MCI WorldCom/Sprint* (on appeal, Case T-310/00 *WorldCom v Commission* (judgment pending)			YES

Case and references	Cleared	Cleared subject to conditions	Prohibited outright
Case No COMP/JV.27 *Microsoft/Liberty Media/Telewest* **NB: abandoned by the parties**			
Case No COMP/M.1806 *Astra Zeneca/Novartis*		YES	
Case No COMP/M.1813 *Industri Kapital (Nordkem)/Dyno*		YES	
Case No COMP/M.1845 *AOL/Time Warner*		YES	
Case No COMP/M.1852 *Time Warner/EMI* **NB: abandoned by the parties**			
Case No COMP/M.1853 *EDF/ENBW*		YES	
Case No COMP/M.1879 *Boeing/Hughes*	YES		
Case No COMP/M.1882 *Pirelli/BICC*	YES		
Case No COMP/M.1915 *Post Office/TPG/SPPL*		YES	
Case No COMP/M.1940 *Framatone/Siemens/Cogema/JV*	YES		
Case No COMP/M.1963 *Industri Kapital/Perstorp* **NB: abandoned by the parties**			
Case No COMP/M.2033 *Metso/Svedala*		YES	
Case No COMP/M.2060 *Bosch/Rexroth*		YES	
Case No COMP/M.2097 *SCA/Metsä Tissue*			YES
Case No COMP/M.2117 *Aker Maritime/Kværner* **NB: abandoned by the parties**			
Case No COMP/M.2139 *Bombardier/ADtranz*		YES	

Case and references	Cleared	Cleared subject to conditions	Prohibited outright
Case No COMP/M.2220 *General Electric/Honeywell*			YES
Case No COMP/M.2314 *BASF/Pantochim/Eurodial*	YES		
Case No COMP/M.2333 *De Beers/LVMH*	YES		

(C)   Comment

(i)   Outright prohibitions

Outright prohibitions are rare: by 30 June 2001 there had been only 14 examples[15]; the Commission prohibited the *General Electric/Honeywell* concentration in early July 2001.[15a] The first concentration to be blocked, in 1991, was *Aerospatiale-Alenia/De Havilland*[16]. Aerospatiale and Alenia intended to purchase the De Havilland division of Boeing. The Commission defined three relevant product markets: regional turbo–prop aircraft, excluding regional jet aircraft and jet aircraft of around 100 seats developed for short-haul and medium-haul flights, with 20 to 39 seats, 40 to 59 seats and 60 seats and over. It defined the geographical market as the world excluding China and Eastern Europe. The Commission concluded that the concentration would create a dominant position in the 40 to 59 seat and the 60 plus seat market, in which its market shares would be 63% or more; also the takeover of De Havilland would remove Aerospatiale/Alenia's most effective competitor and would give the latter complete coverage of the market and significantly broaden its customer base. The Commission also considered that new entry into the market was unlikely and decided to block the concentration. Its decision was not unanimous, and the Advisory Committee on Concentrations was also divided[17]. The Commissioner responsible for Industry disagreed violently over the decision with Sir Leon Brittan, the Competition Commissioner, in particular as industrial policy considerations were not taken on board. However the language of Article 2(3) of the ECMR does not provide for industrial policy to be taken into account, and the decision set an important precedent in demonstrating that the test of the compatibility of a concentration with the common market was its impact on competition[18].

The second concentration to be blocked, in 1994, was *MSG Media Service*[19]. Three companies intended to establish a German pay-television joint venture, MSG. In the Commission's view, the joint venture would give MSG a lasting dominant position on the pay-TV market for administrative and technical services; it would give Bertelsmann and Kirch a dominant position on the German-speaking pay-TV market; and it would protect and strengthen the dominant position of Deutsche Telekom for cable infrastructure. It is of interest that this was the first

---

15 See p 792 above.
15a Case No COMP/M.2220; see Commission Press Release IP/01/939, 3 July 2001.
16 Case No IV/M.53 OJ [1991] L 334/42, [1992] 4 CMLR M2.
17 See OJ [1991] C 314/7.
18 Fox 'Merger Control in the EEC – towards a European Merger Jurisprudence' [1991] Fordham Corporate Law Institute, 738-9.
19 Case No IV/M.469 OJ [1994] L 364/1.

of several concentrations in the media sector to be prohibited outright: the very rapid changes in technology in this sector, and the possibility that concentrations could have serious foreclosure effects on third parties, particularly through vertical integration, help to explain the Commission's cautious approach[20].

Three of the outright prohibitions – *RTL/Veronica/Endemol*[1], *Kesko/Tuko*[2] and *Blokker/Toys'R'Us*[3] – were requests from Member States under Article 22(3) of the ECMR. That these requests led to prohibitions is perhaps not surprising: the Member States making the request must already have concluded that there was a very serious threat to competition, so that the cases were always likely, at the very least, to raise serious doubts; of the Article 22(3) requests, only *BA/Dan Air*[4] was cleared in Phase I.

Of the other outright prohibitions, two, *Gencor/Lonrho*[5] and *Airtours/First Choice*[6] were cases on collective dominance[7]. In *Saint-Gobain/Wacker-Chemie/ NOM*[8] the Commission found that the merged entity would enjoy very high market shares in relation to silicon carbide, substantially higher than its competitors, that potential competition and countervailing power were weak, and that the case could not be 'saved' by an efficiency or a failing firm defence. In *Volvo/Scania*[9] the Commission prohibited a merger that would lead to high market shares for buses and tracks in a series of national markets, Sweden, Finland, Denmark, Norway and Ireland: the delimitation of national markets, rather than a European-wide one, was a crucial feature of this case. In *MCI WorldCom/Sprint*[10] the Commission was concerned that the merger would create a dominant firm in the market for top-level Internet interconnectivity. The concentration in *SCA/Metsä Tissue*[10a] was prohibited as it would have led to very high market shares in hygienic tissue products in Scandanavia and Finland; while *GE/Honeywell*[10b] was blocked in July 2001 on the basis of 'portfolio power'.[10c]

(ii) Unconditional clearance

Unconditional clearances at the end of Phase II are rare: by 31 December 2000 there had been only 16 examples[11]. It is perhaps not surprising that, if the case raised serious doubts in Phase I, the Commission goes on to conclude at the end

20 See also Case No IV/M.490 *Nordic Satellite Distribution* OJ [1996] L 53/20; Case No IV/ M.553 *RTL/Veronica/Endemol* OJ [1996] L 134/32 (this concentration was subsequently cleared in an amended form: OJ [1996] L 294/14); Case No IV/M.993 *BertelsMann/Kirch/ Premiere* OJ [1999] L 53/1 [1999] 4 CMLR 700; Case No IV/M.1027 *Deutsche Telecom/ BetaResearch* OJ [1999] L53/31.
1 Case No IV/M.553 *RTL/Veronica/Endemol* OJ [1996] L 134/32, upheld on appeal Case T-221/95 *Endemol Entertainment Holding BV v Commission* [1999] ECR II-1299, [1999] 5 CMLR 611.
2 Case No IV/M.784 *Kesko/Tuko* OJ [1997] L 174/47, upheld on appeal Case T-22/97 [1999] ECR II-3775, [2000] 4 CMLR 335.
3 *Blokker/Toys'R'Us* OJ [1998] L 316/1.
4 Case No IV/M.278, [1993] 5 CMLR M61.
5 Case T-102/96 *Gencor v Commission* [1999] ECR II-753, [1999] 4 CMLR 971.
6 Case No IV/M.1524 *Airtours/First Choice* OJ [2000] L 93/1, [2000] 5 CMLR 494, on appeal to the CFI: Case T-342/99, *Airtours v Commission* (judgment pending).
7 See ch 14, pp 482-492.
8 Case No IV/M.774 OJ [1997] L 247/1, [1997] 4 CMLR 25.
9 Case No COMP/M.1672.
10 Case No COMP/M.1741; see the Commission's XXXth Annual Report on Competition Policy (2000), point 249 and Box 6.
10a Case No COMP/M.2097.
10b Case No COMP/M.2220.
10c See p 777 above.
11 See p 792 above.

of Phase II that the concentration will create or strengthen a dominant position. A reform that is sometimes suggested is that a different team of officials should examine the case in Phase II, since 'fresh eyes' might see the arguments in a new light: this would reflect, to some extent, the position in the UK, where the DGFT effectively carries out a Phase I analysis before serious cases are referred by the Secretary of State to the Competition Commission for a Phase II investigation[12]. It is noticeable that unconditional clearances happened more frequently in the early years of the ECMR when the Commission was feeling its way; there have been few unconditional clearances in recent years. The message is clear: a case that goes to Phase II is in danger of outright prohibition, and at the least is likely to be cleared only if satisfactory commitments can be offered to the Commission. There are exceptions to this: for example in 2000 both *Boeing/Hughes Electronics*[13] and *Pirelli/BICC*[14] were cleared outright.

(iii)   Clearance subject to commitments[15]

A notable feature of the ECMR is a majority of Phase II decisions have resulted in clearances subject to commitments. This is shown both in the statistical Table and in the Table of Phase II investigations above.

(iv)   Increased incidence of findings of collective dominance

The increased incidence of findings of collective dominance in recent years is another notable feature of the Commission's decisions. These are analysed in chapter 14[16].

(v)   Withdrawal of notifications

It is of interest that there have been several cases in which the parties to a concentration subject to a Phase II investigation, faced with the possibility that there might be a total prohibition, have chosen to withdraw the notification. These cases are noted in the Table of Phase II investigations. A dramatic example of this practice occurred in *Alcan/Pechiney*[17] when the parties abandoned the deal hours before an imminent prohibition. Where this happens, the Commission will not adopt a decision prohibiting the concentration unless it considers that the parties have not truly abandoned the agreement in question, as in the case of *MCI WorldCom/Sprint*[18]. Where it has this belief, it will adopt a decision notwithstanding the withdrawal of the notification. In other cases, the Commission may decide to publish a fairly detailed press release indicating why it was inclined to prohibit the concentration. It did so in the case of *Alcan/Pechiney*[19]. In its Annual Report for 1999, the Commission explained the concerns it had in relation to the Phase II cases that were abandoned prior to the adoption of a decision[20].

12   See ch 22, pp 809-813.
13   Case No COMP/M.1879.
14   Case No COMP/M.1882.
15   On a few occasions the Commission has accepted 'non-binding' commitments when clearing a concentration: see p 785, n 5 above; see eg Case No IV/M.1225 *Enso/Stora* OJ [1999] L 254/9, [2000] 4 CMLR 372.
16   See ch 14, pp 482-492.
17   Case No COMP/M.1663.
18   Case No COMP/M.1741, para 12.
19   Commission Press Release 14 March 2000, IP/00/258.
20   XXIXth *Annual Report on Competition Policy* (1999), paras 163-167.

CHAPTER 22

Mergers (3) – UK law

There was no provision in the UK for the control of mergers until the Monopolies and Mergers Act 1965. This Act was modelled upon the investigative system that had been in operation for the investigation of scale and complex monopolies since 1948[1], with the exception that newspaper mergers were subjected to a stricter régime. The 1965 Act was replaced by the Fair Trading Act 1973 ('the FTA') which as amended, in particular by the Companies Act 1989 and the Contracting Out and Deregulation Act 1994, is the relevant legislation today; there are proposals for substantial reform[2]. This chapter will begin with the general rules applicable to the majority of mergers; thereafter the special rules for newspaper mergers and for mergers between water companies will be briefly described[3].

I. GENERAL RULES: INTRODUCTION[4]

The provisions of the FTA 1973 enable the Secretary of State to refer a merger to the Competition Commission ('the Commission') where he considers it appropriate to do so. In making this decision, the Secretary of State is advised by the Director General of Fair Trading ('the DGFT'). The Secretary of State is not bound to follow this advice, and has sometimes departed from it; however, in October 2000 he announced that he would in future accept the advice of the DGFT 'save in exceptional circumstances'[5]. Only a small proportion of mergers qualifying for investigation under the Act is referred to the Commission[6], and a merger

---

1 See ch 11.
2 See p 836 below.
3 See pp 844-850 below on newspaper mergers and pp 850-851 below on water mergers.
4 See generally the OFT's Guide *Mergers: a Guide to the Procedures under the FTA 1973* (OFT 036, Edition 01/01); the DTI's *Guidance on DTI procedures for handling merger references and reports*: this can be accessed at http://www2.dti.gov.uk/CACP/cp/merger.htm; for practitioners' guides to the legislation, see Spearing, Brandenburger and Swift in *Butterworths Competition Law* (eds Freeman and Whish) Div VII paras [4]–[521]; Finbow and Parr *UK Merger Control: Law and Practice* (Sweet & Maxwell, 1995); Livingstone *Competition Law and Practice* (Pearson Professional Ltd, 1995) ch 33.
5 DTI Press Notice P/2000/705, 26 October 2000; see p 813 below.
6 See p 837 below.

may be prohibited only if at least a two-thirds majority of the Commission panel investigating the case considers that it operates or may be expected to operate against the public interest; even at that stage the Secretary of State has a discretion not to prohibit the merger or to impose some other remedy, despite the Commission's finding[7]. Where the Secretary of State does decide to act upon an adverse report of the Commission, the DGFT will usually negotiate with the parties in order to obtain suitable undertakings[8]. The undertakings themselves are given to the Secretary of State. In the event that appropriate undertakings are not forthcoming, the Secretary of State has power to prohibit the merger outright. As a general proposition, the Competition Act 1998 has no application to mergers qualifying for investigation[9].

There is no legal duty to pre-notify mergers in the UK, although in practice many are brought to the attention of the DGFT on a voluntary basis[10] and the Companies Act 1989 introduced a statutory voluntary system of notification[11]. There are no penalties under domestic law for consummating a non-notified merger, as under the European Community Merger regulation ('the ECMR')[12]. However, power exists to require a merger to be reversed where it operates or may be expected to operate against the public interest, and this power has been exercised on some occasions[13]. As a general proposition a merger that has a 'Community dimension' under the ECMR cannot be investigated under domestic law[14], although exceptions to this are to be found in Article 9[15] and in Article 21(3)[16] of that Regulation. A Consultation Document on the rôle of the Secretary of State and the procedural framework of the UK merger control process was published in 1999[17]; a further Response to the Consultation was published in October 2000[18]. It is likely that these publications will lead to significant changes in the domestic system; however these are unlikely to be effected before 2002 at the earliest[19].

2.   JURISDICTION

In the case of the ECMR, the first issue to consider is jurisdiction: what is meant by a concentration and which concentrations have a Community dimension? In the same way, in the case of the FTA, it is necessary to ask what is meant by a merger and which mergers qualify for investigation.

7   See p 834 below.
8   See pp 831-834 below.
9   See ch 9, pp 299-302.
10   See pp 811-812 below.
11   See pp 812 below.
12   See ch 21, p 788.
13   See p 831 below.
14   See chapter 21, pp 756-758 above on the principle of 'one–stop control' of mergers.
15   See ch 21, pp 758-761.
16   See ch 21, pp 764-765.
17   DTI/Pub 4308.
18   URN 00/805.
19   See p 836 below.

(A) Definition of a merger

(i) Enterprises 'ceasing to be distinct'

Section 64 of the FTA provides that a merger occurs where two or more enterprises have 'ceased to be distinct'. In this context, enterprise means 'the activities, or part of the activities, of a business'[20]. Three points should be noted about this definition. The first is that the legislation is drafted in terms of mergers that have taken place. However, mergers that are in contemplation can also be investigated due to the provisions in section 75, and the reality is that many investigations are conducted *ex ante* rather than *ex post*[1]. Secondly, the acquisition of assets alone will not normally give rise to a merger qualifying for investigation, because no *activities* are transferred. However a sale of assets combined with goodwill and the benefit of contracts does involve the transfer of activities, and the Commission will determine this issue by reference to substance rather than form; the mere fact that a company has ceased to trade does not mean that there are no activities capable of transfer[2]. The acquisition of a brand or brands could amount to a merger where a clear turnover can be attributed to those brands. The third point is that the reference to 'part of the activities' means that the sale of a division of a company may be investigated, provided that the other requirements about to be described are satisfied.

(ii) The circumstances in which enterprises cease to be distinct

Section 65 elaborates upon the circumstances in which enterprises cease to be distinct. If the enterprises in question agree between themselves that one should cease production in order to prevent competition between them, this constitutes a merger[3]. If the enterprises come under common ownership, they cease to be distinct[4]. They will also do so where they come under common control[5], a term which is given a wide meaning[6]. Three levels of control are identified: there can be a merger in the sense of the Act without one firm acquiring legal control of another. First, two enterprises are to be regarded as coming under common control where the same person has actual control of them in company law terms: this is referred to as '*de jure*' or 'legal' control[7]. Secondly, a person may be treated as having control if he is able, directly or indirectly, to control the policy of the company: this is referred to as '*de facto*' control[8]; the Commission has a discretion whether to regard such cases as amounting to control, a conclusion which it did not reach in the case of *Mid Kent Holdings plc/General Utilities plc/ SAUR Water Services*[9]. Thirdly, a person is deemed to be in control if he is in a

---

20 FTA 1973, s 63(2).
1   See p 809 below.
2   *AAH Holdings plc/Medicopharma NV* Cm 1950 (1992) paras 6.101-6.102; see also *William Cook Acquisitions* Cm 1196 (1990) paras 6.5–6.6; *Stagecoach Holdings plc/Lancaster City Transport Ltd* Cm 2423 (1993) para 6.21.
3   FTA 1973, s 65(1)(b).
4   Ibid, s 65(1)(a).
5   Ibid.
6   Ibid, s 65(2).
7   Ibid, s 65(2) and s 137(5) as amended by the Companies Consolidation (Consequential Provisions) Act 1985, s 30, Sch 2.
8   FTA s 65(3) refers to 'a person ... able ... to control the policy of a body corporate'.
9   Cm 3514 (1997).

position, directly or indirectly, materially to influence the policy of the other company[10]. The expression 'material' influence would seem to import a test that is wider than 'decisive' influence in Article 3(3) of the ECMR, with the result that some transactions would not amount to mergers in Community law but would in the UK[11].

(iii)   Low threshold for 'material influence'

The effect of the provisions in section 65 of the FTA is that a person who acquires a shareholding in a company of much less than 51% may have control for the purpose of UK merger control. There can be material influence even where the shareholding is less than 25%, and the OFT has said that it will look at any shareholding greater than 15% to determine whether this is the case[12]. In *Pleasurama/Trident/Grand Metropolitan*[13] the Commission considered that Grand Metropolitan would be in a position materially to influence the policy of Pleasurama even if its stake was reduced from 29% to 20.02%, given the fragmented nature of the other shareholdings. In *Peninsular and Oriental Steam Navigation Co/European Ferries Group plc*[14] the Commission concluded that a shareholding of 16.1% of the voting rights of European Ferries was sufficient to put P&O in a position materially to influence its policy. Relevant factors in reaching this conclusion were specific examples of past influence by P&O over the affairs of European Ferries, the particularly fragmented nature of the other shareholdings[15], and the fact that P&O itself was on good terms with many of the institutional shareholders. Material influence may be obtained not only by the acquisition of shares; for example contractual arrangements and rights attaching to securities may suffice[16].

In 1999 and 2000, broadcasters began to acquire shares in certain football clubs that had been publicly floated on the Stock Exchange. In the case of BSkyB's acquisition of 9.08% of the shares in Leeds United, the OFT concluded that this did not give it material influence; however, it added that each case would be treated on its own merits and that other cases were being investigated[17]. The latter point indicates that there could be control even with a shareholding of less than 15% on the facts of a particular case.

The OFT has stated that, since a shareholding of 25% or more generally enables the holder to block special resolutions, this proportion is likely to be seen as automatically conferring the ability materially to influence policy[18]. It is possible that one person may have the ability materially to influence the policy of a company even though another has a controlling interest[19].

---

10   FTA 1973, s 65(3): ' a person ... able ... materially to influence the policy of a body corporate'.
11   On Article 3(3) of the ECMR, see ch 21 pp 745-748.
12   *Mergers Guide* para 2.6.
13   Cmnd 9108 (1983).
14   Cm 31 (1986); see also *Government of Kuwait/BP* Cm 477 (1988); *British Airways/Sabena* Cm 1155 (1990).
15   There were far more individual shareholders in European Ferries than in most public companies as shareholders benefited from valuable concessions in the use of cross–channel ferries.
16   See eg *Stora Koppabergs Bergslags AB/Swedish Match NV* Cm 1473 (1991).
17   OFT Press Release PN 8/00, 3 February 2000.
18   *Mergers Guide*, para 2.6.
19   Ibid; this situation might be characterised, under the ECMR, as one of joint control: see ch 21, pp 748-751.

(iv)   Moving from one level of control to another

The Act provides that moving up from one level of control to another amounts to a merger. For example, if a person with the ability materially to influence the policy of a company increases his shareholding so that it can actually control it (*de jure* or *de facto*), that constitutes a merger[20]. This happened in *Amalgamated Industries (AI)/Herbert Morris*[1]: no reference was made when AI first acquired material influence over Morris, but the matter was referred to the Commission when it became able to control its policy. Similarly, in *Lonrho/House of Fraser*[2] Lonrho already held 27.99% of the shares in House of Fraser, but then attempted to elect 12 directors to the Board: the question was whether this 'cashless takeover' meant that Lonrho could now control Fraser's policy. The Commission concluded that there was a merger in these circumstances, but that it would not operate against the public interest. In the meantime a rival bid from the Al Fayed brothers was successful, which led to protracted litigation[3]. In *British Electric Traction Co plc/Initial plc*[4] the Commission came to the conclusion that for BET to go from a position in which it could influence the behaviour of Initial to being in full control could not be expected to operate against the public interest, as any harm to competition had already occurred.

(B)   Mergers qualifying for investigation

(i)   The 'share of supply' and 'assets' tests

Only mergers 'qualifying for investigation' may be referred to the Commission. Section 64 of the FTA provides that the Secretary of State may refer a merger which may[5] *either* result in the merged entity supplying or acquiring 25% or more of the goods[6] or services[7] of a particular description in the UK or a substantial part of it *or* result in the acquisition of assets with a balance sheet value of £70 million or more[8]. The OFT refers to the former criterion as the 'share of supply test' and the latter as the 'assets test'[9]. The share of supply test requires an *increment* in the market share[10]. Section 67 of the FTA deals with the valuation of assets for this purpose. The gross book value of all assets (not just assets held in the UK) is to be taken, less depreciation, renewals or diminution in value but without deducting liabilities of any kind. The assets test means that many vertical and conglomerate mergers qualify for investigation. It would be difficult to argue that a vertical or conglomerate merger *results* in a monopoly situation (even if

---

20   FTA 1973, s 65(4).
1   HCP (1975–76) 434.
2   Cm 9458 (1985).
3   See p 835 below.
4   Cmnd 9444 (1985).
5   It is for the Commission to decide whether the merger actually will have this effect.
6   FTA 1973, s 64(1)(a) and s 64(2).
7   Ibid, s 64(1)(a) and s 64(3).
8   Ibid, s 64(1)(b); the relevant figure can be varied by statutory instrument (see s 64(7)): it was raised from £30m to £70m by the Merger References (Increase in Value of Assets) Order 1994, SI 1994/72.
9   *Mergers Guide*, paras 2.11-2.17; the 'share of supply test' is not based on market share, in an economic sense, and therefore the FTA does not formally require a market definition approach: see ch 11, p 367 .
10   *Mergers Guide* para 2.12; for argument to the contrary, see Black 'The Fair Trading Act's Market Share Test: A Heresy' (1996) 17 ECLR 414.

the foreclosure of competitors might eventually have this effect); however such mergers could obviously qualify for investigation on an assets basis. The Government proposed in October 2000 that the assets test should be replaced by a turnover test, and that the share of supply test might be altered to apply to mergers in linked markets where there is no increment in market share in either[11].

(ii) Meaning of 'a substantial part of the UK'

Where a reference is made on a share-of-supply basis, the supply must be in the UK or 'a substantial part of it'. Some mergers have an impact only on local markets: the most obvious example of this has been in the bus sector. The Commission and the courts on judicial review – up to the House of Lords – have had to grapple with the meaning of this expression. In *South Yorkshire Transport Ltd Acquisitions*[12] the Commission concluded that an area comprising South Yorkshire and parts of Derbyshire and Nottinghamshire was sufficiently substantial to qualify under section 64; it went on to conclude that a bus merger in that area could be expected to operate against the public interest. The Secretary of State accepted the recommendation, whereupon South Yorkshire Transport sought judicial review on the ground that the area in question could not be considered to be a substantial part of the UK, with the consequence that the Commission had no jurisdiction to investigate and that its report was a nullity. In *R v Monopolies and Mergers Commission, ex p South Yorkshire Transport Ltd* this argument prevailed in the Divisional Court[13] and in the Court of Appeal[14], but failed in the House of Lords[15]. Lord Mustill, in whose speech the other Law Lords concurred, endorsed the dissenting judgment of Nourse LJ in the Court of Appeal, who had said that the part must be of such size, character and importance as to make it worth consideration by the Commission. According to the OFT, among the factors taken into account in deciding whether the merger is 'worth' consideration and can therefore be referred are the size of the specified area, its population, its social, political, economic, financial and geographic significance, and whether it has any particular characteristics that might render it special or signficant[16].

(iii) Territorial scope

A merger may be referred to the Commission only where at least one of the enterprises in question is carried on in the UK or by or under the control of a company incorporated in the UK[17]. It follows that a merger between two foreign companies may qualify for investigation, provided that at least one of them controls, directly or indirectly, an enterprise which is carried on in the UK. It is also possible for a takeover by a UK firm of a foreign operator to be investigated;

---

11 *Mergers: The Response to the Consultation on Proposals for Reform* URN/00/805, paras 6.12-6.25.
12 Cm 1166 (1990).
13 [1991] BCC 347.
14 [1992] 1 All ER 257, [1992] 1 WLR 291, CA.
15 [1993] 1 All ER 289, [1993] 1 WLR 23, HL; see also *Stagecoach Holdings v Secretary of State and Trade and Industry* 1997 SLT 940, OH.
16 *Mergers Guide*, para 2.14.
17 FTA 1973, s 64(1).

such a merger would not normally be referred, although in the case of *British Telecommunications plc/Mitel Corpn*[18] the Commission concluded that a takeover by BT of Mitel of Canada could be expected to operate against the public interest.

(iv) Ex ante and ex post investigations

Merger references may be made both before (*ex ante*) and after (*ex post*) a merger has taken place. Sections 64 to 73 deal with references after a merger has taken place. Section 75 provides that a reference may be made in anticipation of a merger and makes the necessary grammatical amendments for this purpose to the preceding sections. There is no legal duty to pre–notify mergers; however, most mergers are brought to the attention of the DGFT on a voluntary basis before they take place[19]. If this were not done, the merger could be referred after the event and the Commission might conclude that it may be expected to operate against the public interest and recommend that it should be reversed; this is a risk that the merging parties are not normally prepared to take.

In the case of *ex post* investigations, a merger can be referred within four months of its having taken place[20], unless it took place without the knowledge of the Secretary of State or the DGFT, in which case it can be referred within four months of one of them obtaining that knowledge or being made public[1]. A special provision deals with creeping mergers, designed to enable a progression of events over time to be investigated by the Commission[2].

3. REFERENCE PROCEDURE

(A) The rôle of the DGFT and the Mergers Panel

(i) Statutory duties

The Act reposes the most important functions in the control of mergers in the Secretary of State, who makes references and who decides how to proceed following the Commission's report, although it is the Commission which considers the compatibility of the merger with the public interest. In practice, however, the DGFT is of central importance in the administration of mergers policy. Within the OFT there is a Mergers Branch (formerly called the Mergers Secretariat) which is responsible for the evaluation of mergers. When a submission in a particular case is received by the OFT, a case officer will be nominated who will have primary responsibility for it; an economist will also be nominated. The Director of the Mergers Branch will oversee and coordinate the work of the individual case officers[3]. The Mergers Branch reports, through the Director of Competition Policy, to the DGFT, who in turn advises the Secretary of State whether or not to refer a merger to the Commission. Part Two of the OFT Weekly Gazette provides details of cases being dealt with under the merger provisions of

18 Cmnd 9715 (1986).
19 See below.
20 FTA 1973, s 64(1) and s 64(4)(a), as amended by the Deregulation (Fair Trading Act 1973)(Amendment)(Merger Reference Time Limits) Order 1996, SI 1996/345.
1 Ibid, s 64(1) and s 64(4)(b) as amended by SI 1996/345.
2 Ibid, s 66 and 66A (added by the Companies Act 1989, s 150(1)).
3 *Mergers Guide* para 5.3.

the FTA[4]. The OFT website has a section enabling the progress of a merger, from the initial invitation to comment to the final decision, to be tracked[5].

In carrying out his tasks, the DGFT is assisted by a non–statutory Inter–Departmental Committee, known as the Mergers Panel, which has a Secretariat within the OFT. A meeting of the Panel is usually called where the OFT's assessment concludes that a merger raises significant competition or other issues.

The DGFT is required by the Act to keep himself informed about actual and prospective mergers which may be within the terms of the Act[6] and to make appropriate recommendations to the Secretary of State about any action which it would be expedient to take[7]. Since it is possible for divestiture to be ordered after a merger has taken place, the practice arose of notifying proposed mergers on a voluntary basis to the DGFT in order to ascertain the likelihood of a reference; since the Companies Act 1989 there is a statutory basis for this practice[8]. The DGFT has described some of the issues which are relevant when deciding whether to recommend a reference and the procedure that will be adopted by the OFT[9]. In practice the issues that the Commission has itself considered in its reports over the years are influential, both when the DGFT decides whether to recommend to the Secretary of State a reference to the Commission and when the Secretary of State actually makes his decision whether to refer. Although there is nothing in the legislation requiring the DGFT or the Secretary of State to take into account section 84 of the FTA on the meaning of the public interest when exercising their functions, it undoubtedly exerts an influence over them[10]. The DGFT will inform the Secretary of State of any non-competition issues that are drawn to his attention, although he would not make any recommendations upon them, since they fall outside his area of expertise.

(ii)   Informal advice: 'fireside chats'

It is possible to approach the Mergers Branch for informal advice on the possibility of a merger being referred to the Commission[11]. This is a confidential process, and is subject to the same confidentiality restrictions that apply where confidential guidance is sought[12]. Informal advice is given purely by the Mergers Branch, and does not commit the DGFT or the Secretary of State in any way. The advice will be rendered on the basis of the information provided to the Mergers Branch by the parties; there is no third-party involvement. The advice is given orally, and the process is often referred to as a 'fireside chat'.

---

4   http://www.oft.gov.uk/html/comp-act/case_register/weekly-gazette.html.
5   http://www.oft.gov.uk/html/mergers/mergers-listings.htm.
6   FTA 1973, s 76(1)(a); the DGFT's Annual Reports analyse in some detail merger activity during the year to which they relate: see eg 1998 *Annual Report of the DGFT*, pp 36–42; 1999 *Annual Report of the DGFT* pp 51-58; 2000 *Annual Report of the DGFT*, pp 112-114.
7   FTA 1973, s 76(2)(b); in exercising these duties the DGFT must take into account representations made to him by interested persons or their representative bodies: s 76(2) (added by the Companies Act 1989, s 153).
8   See p 812 below.
9   *Mergers Guide*, paras 4.1-4.7 and 6.1-6.25.
10   *Mergers Guide*, para 3.2.
11   *Mergers Guide*, para 5.15.
12   See below.

(iii)   Confidential guidance

Firms may apply to the DGFT at an early stage for 'confidential guidance' as to the likelihood of the Secretary of State making a reference[13]. The OFT and the DTI have adopted an administrative, non-binding, timetable which ensures that confidential guidance can normally be given within 25 working days of a request. Firms seeking confidential guidance will have to provide information to the OFT, which will then give advice to the Secretary of State. The OFT will inform the parties of the decision of the Secretary of State. This may be that, on the basis of the information in his possession, a reference is unlikely; or that he has insufficient information to be able to make a decision; or that a reference is possible but could be avoided by offering suitable undertakings; or that a reference is highly likely. Since this procedure is confidential, it follows that third parties will have no involvement; there is always a danger that, when knowledge of the transaction enters the public domain, representations might be made to the OFT and Secretary of State that cause them to change their minds[14]; confidential guidance, therefore, cannot be absolutely binding. Nevertheless the procedure is a helpful one, as the statistics demonstrate: in 1998, the OFT considered 61 requests for confidential guidance[15]; in 1999 the corresponding figure was 50[16]. An important feature of the confidential guidance procedure is that not only will the OFT and DTI respect the confidentiality of the information they receive: the OFT also insists on reciprocity, so that the firms that seek guidance must themselves respect the confidentiality of the procedure[17]. A firm that makes public the fact that it had sought and received confidential guidance, let alone the content of the guidance, would probably not be allowed to avail itself of the procedure on a subsequent occasion.

(iv)   Voluntary notification

Once a merger proposal has been announced it may be notified to the OFT. There is no compulsory system of pre–notification in the UK[18], but voluntary notification is common.

(A)   INFORMAL VOLUNTARY NOTIFICATION.   Voluntary notification has happened informally for many years; the parties may make an informal written submission, or they may use a common notification form, published by the competition authorities in the UK, France and Germany. The common notification form and guidance notes are available from the OFT by post or from the Internet[19]. The OFT will require, *inter alia,* information about the relevant product and geographic markets[20], the possible horizontal and vertical effects of the merger, any buyer power that there may be[1] and details of barriers to entry[2]. The OFT

---

13   *Mergers Guide*, paras 5.10-5.14.
14   See p 820 below on the *Ladbroke Group plc/Coral Betting Business* investigation.
15   1998 *Annual Report of the DGFT*, p 37.
16   1999 *Annual Report of the DGFT*, p 51.
17   *Mergers Guide*, para 5.14.
18   Compare Article 4 of the ECMR, requires pre–notification of mergers that have a Community dimension: see ch 21, pp 766-767.
19   http://www.oft.gov.uk/html/rsearch/intmerg.htm.
20   See OFT Guideline 403 *Market definition*.
1   See OFT Research Paper 16 *The Welfare Consequences of the Exercise of Buyer Power* OFT 239 (Dobson, Waterson and Chu, September 1998).
2   See OFT Guideline 415 *Assessment of market power*, paras 5.1-5.29.

also asks for information about any ancillary restraints and for an explanation of why they should be regarded as ancillary in the terms of the OFT's Guideline *Exclusion for mergers and ancillary restrictions*[3]. Once the information is provided, a decision is normally made within 45 working days[4].

(B)   STATUTORY VOLUNTARY NOTIFICATION.   An alternative for the parties is to make a 'statutory voluntary' notification. The legal basis for this is to be found in sections 75A to 75F of the FTA, and is available only for mergers in contemplation, not for completed ones[5]. There is no requirement that firms should make use of the statutory procedure, and in the majority of cases it is not used. However there are sometimes advantages in doing so; in particular the Secretary of State must decide within 20 working days of a statutory notification whether to refer[6]: this period can be extended by a maximum of 15 further days. If the Secretary of State fails to make a decision within the statutory period, the merger is automatically cleared[7]. A prescribed form of merger notice must be used when invoking the statutory procedure[8]. Statutory notification is permissible only where the merger proposal has been made public: the OFT will wish to consult third parties and so the procedure is not available where confidential guidance is required in respect of a proposal not yet publicly known. At one time, the statutory procedure was used only rarely. However it is now used more often, because of the benefits to the parties of having fixed time limits within which it will be known whether a reference to the Commission will be made: this can be particularly important in cases affected by the City Code on Takeovers. In 1999, for example, 69 statutory pre–notifications were received by the OFT, of which 38 were decided within the initial consideration period of 20 working days[9]. Some practitioners are understood to use the statutory procedure in all cases.

(v)   DGFT's advice

Once the DGFT knows of a merger or a proposed merger, whether as a result of voluntary pre–notification, the intervention of third parties or his own research, the OFT will gather relevant information about it, from the parties themselves and from other interested persons, including competitors and customers. In the case of a contested takeover, the OFT will usually see the parties separately. Having gathered this information, the OFT will make an assessment of the merger and submit it to the Secretary of State who will make the actual decision whether to refer or not. Any merger in relation to which there is a prima facie case for reference will be brought to the attention of the Mergers Panel, which may be chaired by the deputy DGFT or the Director of Competition Policy and is attended by representatives of various Whitehall departments. Where a case is discussed by the Mergers Panel, the DGFT or his deputy will submit a full

---

3   OFT Guideline 416.
4   *Mergers Guide*, para 5.7.
5   FTA 1973, s 75A(1).
6   FTA 1973, s 75B(2).
7   Ibid, s 75B(3), as amended by the Fair Trading Act (Amendment)(Mergers Pre-notification) Regulations 1994, SI 1994/1934.
8   Ibid, s 75A(2): see the Merger (Pre-notification) Regulations 1990, SI 1990/501; the form can be obtained from the Mergers Branch of the OFT, Fleetbank House, 2-6 Salisbury Square, London EC4Y 8JX.
9   1999 *Annual Report of the DGFT*, p 52.

assessment of the case to the Secretary of State and make a recommendation as to whether a reference should be made.

The Secretary of State relies heavily on the advice he is given by the DGFT when exercising his discretion whether to refer a merger. An important innovation made in the summer of 2000 was the decision of the DGFT to make public the advice he gives to the Secretary of State. This information is available on the OFT's website[10]. In the majority of cases the Secretary of State follows the recommendation of the DGFT, and in October 2000 he announced that in future he would accept the DGFT's advice except in exceptional cases[11]. He might intervene, for example, where a merger raises national security issues or where there are other unusual circumstances, such as a material change after submission of the DGFT's advice or where the advice of the DGFT conflicts with the views of sectoral regulators[12].

(vi) *Departure by the Secretary of State from the advice of the DGFT*

In the past, Secretaries of State have sometimes departed from the advice of the DGFT, often attracting a furore in the media. For example, in 1997 Margaret Beckett made references on three occasions in cases where the DGFT had recommended clearance or clearance subject to conditions: *Pacifiorp/Energy Group*[13], *National Express/ScotRail*[14] and *National Express/Central Trains*[15]. The Commission in each case found no detriment to the public interest. In its Annual Report for 1997, the Commission pointed out that the cost of these investigations was £406,000 in the case of Energy Group and £478,000 in the case of the two National Express investigations. A further controversial example of a reference despite a contrary recommendation occurred in the case of *NTL/ Cable & Wireless Communications*[16], where the DGFT advised against a reference but Stephen Byers did refer it[17]. However the change initiated by the Secretary of State in October 2000, referred to in the previous paragraph, should mean that cases such as these do not arise in the future.

(B) The rôle of the Secretary of State[18]

(i) *Most references are made on the basis of a possible detriment to competition*

It is the Secretary of State who actually refers mergers to the Commission. The FTA provides the Secretary of State with an extremely wide discretion, but in practice the overwhelming majority of mergers are referred because of a possible detriment to competition. In 1984 the Secretary of State, Norman Tebbit, stated in a House of Commons written answer that this was the case; the so–called

10 See http://www.oft.gov.uk/html/mergers/mergers-advice.htm.
11 DTI Press Notice P/2000/705, 26 October 2000; see further p 836 below on the proposals for legislative changes to the system of merger control in the UK.
12 DTI Press Notice P/2000/705, 26 October 2000.
13 Cm 3816 (1997).
14 Cm 3773 (1997).
15 Cm 3774 (1997).
16 Cm 4666 (2000).
17 DTI Press Release P/99/921, 12 November 99.
18 On the rôle of the Secretary of State and the DTI, see the DTI's *Guidance on DTI Procedures for Handling Merger References and Reports* (revised ed, November 1999).

'Tebbit guidelines' have been reasserted by ministers several times since. The first Secretary of State in the Labour Government elected in May 1997, Margaret Beckett, restated that competition was the primary ground for referring mergers in her first speech on the subject, on 4 June 1997. Stephen Byers said the same thing in October 2000[19]. However, the broad discretion of the Secretary of State under the FTA remains intact, so that as a matter of law references may continue to be made on other grounds. The former Conservative Government decided in 1990 that it would look carefully at mergers where the acquiring company was foreign and state–owned or controlled. The so–called 'Lilley doctrine'[20] resulted in five references to the Commission[1], four of them involving acquisitions of UK companies by French state–owned undertakings. The Commission identified public interest concerns in only one of them[2], in a case in which the merger would lead to high market shares so that it could have caused concern under the traditional Tebbit guidelines anyway. The suspicion that the UK Government was operating a policy aimed specifically at repelling French state–owned undertakings investing in the UK led Credit Lyonnais to file a formal complaint with the European Commission; following an exchange of letters between the Commission and the UK Government, the Government retreated from the Lilley doctrine, saying that state ownership would not in future *per se* justify a reference.

(ii)   Announcement of the reference

The Secretary of State's decision to refer or clear a merger, or to accept undertakings in lieu of a reference, is announced by means of a DTI Press Notice. These can be accessed on the DTI's website[3]. The parties are informed five minutes beforehand that the Press Notice is about to be issued, though they are not told of its content; the Stock Exchange is informed contemporaneously. The Press Notice will state whether the Secretary of State's decision is in accordance with the DGFT's advice. In all cases the Secretary of State, when deciding whether to make a merger reference, is enjoined to make a decision as soon as is reasonably practicable with a view to preventing or removing uncertainty[4].

(iii)   Competing bids

It sometimes happens that there are two suitors for the same target company. In this situation it is possible for both mergers to be referred to the Commission[5], although there is no legal compulsion on the Secretary of State to do so. He must exercise his discretion in respect of each individual merger and he may decide

19 DTI Press Notice P/2000/705, 26 October 2000.
20 The doctrine was espoused by Peter Lilley, the Secretary of State at the time, in a reply to a Parliamentary question on 26 July 1990.
1 *Crédit Lyonnais/Woodchester* Cm 1404 (1991); *Kemira Oy/ICI* Cm 1406 (1991); *BAe/ Thomson-SF* Cm 1416 (1991); *Sligos/Signet* Cm 1450 (1991); *Amoco Corp/Société Nationale Elf Acquitaine* Cm 1521 (1991).
2 *Kemira Oy/ICI* Cm 1406 (1991).
3 http://www.dti.gov.uk.
4 FTA 1973, s 64(5); this reflects the importance of decisions being made speedily in merger cases.
5 See eg *Strong & Fisher (Holdings) plc/Pittard Garnar plc* Cm 663 (1989) and *Hillsdown Holdings plc/Pittard Garnar plc* Cm 665 (1989) (the Commission found no detriments to the public interest in either report).

that a bid by A for X raises competition problems whereas a rival bid from B does not. It can also happen that one competing bid is subject to UK law and the other is within the scope of the ECMR, meaning that different procedures and substantive standards might apply[6]; it might be that in such a situation there would be a case for seeking a reference back to the UK under Article 9 of the ECMR of the merger having a Community dimension[7].

(iv) The framing of the reference

A merger reference may be limited in various ways. The Commission may be acquitted of the responsibility, which it would otherwise have, of deciding whether a merger satisfies both the share of supply and assets criteria[8]; it may be directed to confine its investigation to a specified part only of the UK[9]; and it may be restricted in its public interest investigation to particular effects of the merger[10]. A merger reference may be varied[11]. The Secretary of State can consent to a reference of a merger in contemplation being set aside where the merger is abandoned[12]; however this cannot be done where the Commission is asked to investigate a merger that has already, or may have already, been consummated[13]. All merger references must set the Commission a time limit, which may be extended for special reasons; if the report is not made within the prescribed period, no further action can be taken[14]. Under Rule 12 of the City Code on Takeovers and Mergers a public bid for the acquisition of a company lapses when a merger reference is made[15].

(C) Undertakings in lieu of a reference ('fix-it-first')

A practice grew over a number of years of companies negotiating undertakings with the DGFT to remedy any possible detriments to the public interest, in consequence of which a recommendation would be made to the Secretary of State to refrain from referring the merger to the Commission. This 'plea-bargaining' or 'fix-it-first' approach to merger control had no statutory basis, but this was provided by sections 75G to K of the FTA, introduced by section 147 of the Companies Act 1989 and amended by section 9 of the Deregulation and Contracting Out Act 1994[16]. These provisions enable the Secretary of State to accept binding undertakings in lieu of making a reference to the Commission. The Companies Act 1989 provides for the possibility of structural undertakings, and the 1994 Act for behavioural ones. Undertakings in lieu of a reference can

---

6   This happened in 1992 in the case of the competing bids for Midland Bank Ltd by Lloyds Bank and the Hong Kong and Shanghai Bank: see ch 21, p 754.
7   On Article 9 of the ECMR, see ch 21, pp 758-761.
8   Ibid, s 69(2).
9   Ibid, s 69(3).
10 Ibid, s 69(4).
11 Ibid, s 71(1) (amended by the Companies Act 1989, ss 153 and 212); this happened, for example, in the case of *Air Canada/Canadian Airlines* Cm 4838 (2000).
12 Ibid, s 75(5); see eg the setting aside of the *Myson Pumps/Grundfos* merger inquiry: http://www.competition-commission.gov.uk/58-00.htm.
13 See *NTL Communications Corp/ Newcastle United plc* Cm 4411 (1999).
14 FTA 1973, s 70.
15 See Gower's *Principles of Modern Company Law* (6th ed, 1997) p 793.
16 See *Mergers Guide* paras 7.1-7.11.

be used only where the DGFT has recommended that a merger should be referred to the Commission, and only to remedy or prevent the adverse effects that he has identified. The Secretary of State is not bound by any advice that he may have been given by the DGFT. Where undertakings might be acceptable, the Secretary of State will ask the DGFT to negotiate them. They are sometimes quite detailed. In 1996, four cases were settled in this way[17]; one in 1997[18]; three in 1998[19] and seven in 1999[20] and eight in 2000[20a]. The Secretary of State retains the power to make a reference until suitable undertakings have been secured.

(D)   Fees

Section 152 of the Companies Act 1989 enables the Secretary of State to make regulations on fees in respect of his own expenses and those of the DGFT and the Commission in connection with certain mergers qualifying for investigation[1]. In respect of mergers notified under the statutory scheme in sections 75A to 75F, the fee is payable upon notification[2]; otherwise it is payable when a merger is referred to the Commission or, where there is no reference, upon the announcement of the decision not to refer[3]. The amount of the fee varies according to the value of the assets taken over; the maximum fee payable is £15,000. Fees are payable in respect of any merger which *qualifies* for investigation, even where it is entirely innocuous in terms of competition or any other public interest concerns. Receipt of an invoice for £15,000 in relation to a case that no rational competition authority could possibly have considered to be of concern sometimes comes as something of a shock. The fees may be changed periodically. A Consultative Document was published in October 2000 on the possibility of exempting small and medium-sized enterprises from paying merger fees[4]; this proposal was implemented with effect from 1 June 2001.[4a] Fees are also payable in respect of newspaper and water mergers.

4.   THE COMMISSION'S INVESTIGATION

(A)   The 'public interest' test

The principle function of the Commission is to consider whether the merger operates or may be expected to operate against the public interest. This is the same test that is used in the case of scale and complex monopoly investigations and is set out in section 84 of the FTA: this section is reproduced in full in chapter 11[5]. At this stage it is simply necessary to emphasise that the section enables the Commission to consider 'all matters which appear to them in the particular circumstances to be relevant'; and that the non–exclusive matters which are then specified mention both the desirability of competition and other aims such as the

17   1996 *Annual Report of the DGFT*, pp 40-41.
18   1997 *Annual Report of the DGFT*, pp 42-43.
19   1998 *Annual Report of the DGFT*, pp 39-40.
20   1999 *Annual Report of the DGFT*, pp 54-55.
20a 2000 *Annual Report of the DGFT*, p 81.
1   See the Merger (Fees) Regulations 1990, SI 1990/1660.
2   Ibid, reg 7(2).
3   Ibid, reg 7(3).
4   URN 00/895.
4a   See the Merger (Fees) (Amendment) Regulations 2001, SI 2001/1199.
5   See ch 11, pp 374-375.

balanced distribution of wealth within the UK, which are not necessarily compatible with free competition. In practice, the main consideration of the Commission will be given to competition, although in particular circumstances other matters – for example regulatory concerns or issues of public security – might have an influence on the overall assessment[6].

Once a reference has been made, the Commission is required to report, within the stipulated period, upon the questions referred to it. It must decide whether the merger qualifies for investigation[7] and whether it operates, or may be expected to operate, against the public interest[8]. Where a panel of the Commission is divided in a particular case, the Chairman has a casting vote[9]. In *British Sugar/ Berisford*[10] the Commission made clear that it considers that it has a duty, not simply to identify some possible detriment, but to see whether the evidence raises a real expectation that the merger will operate against the public interest in some way. The presumption is therefore in favour of the merger. The Commission must come to definite conclusions and give such an account of the general position with respect to the subject–matter of the reference as it considers expedient for facilitating a proper understanding of the questions and conclusions[11]. If the Commission concludes that the merger may operate or be expected to operate against the public interest, the report must state which particular effects of the merger do so or may be expected to do so and must recommend any action which the Commission considers may remedy or prevent the adverse effects referred to[12].

(B) Conduct of the investigation

The Commission's investigation is carried out in much the same way as monopoly investigations[13] except that it has less time in which to act because of the limits that are imposed by statute and by the Secretary of State, and it has the same powers to obtain information and to summon witnesses. Under the FTA the Secretary of State can impose a time limit on the Commission of not more than six months, which can be extended once to nine months[14]. In most cases the Commission is actually given three months in which to report, but an extension may be given where, for example, there are an unusually large number of third party submissions and where they are particularly extensive[15]. It is easy to track the progress of investigations by accessing the Competition Commission's website, which will disclose, for example, the terms of reference, the members of the Commission conducting the inquiry in question and the timetable of the inquiry; it will also contain a summary of the issues and remedies statements once they have been formulated[16]. Liaison takes place between the OFT and the Commission in relation to merger references in order to avoid unnecessary duplication of

6   See pp 818-830 below.
7   FTA 1973, s 69(1)(a).
8   Ibid, s 69(1)(b).
9   See eg *Strong and Fisher (Holdings) plc/Pittard/Garnar plc* Cm 663 (1989), para 1.83.
10 HCP (1980–81) 241, para 9.40.
11 FTA 1973, s 72(1).
12 Ibid, s 72(2).
13 See ch 11, pp 376-378.
14 FTA 1973, s 70.
15 An example of this occurred in 1998, when the *Ladbroke/Coral* investigation, launched on 31 March and due to be completed by 7 July, was extended until 31 July: DTI Press Notice P/98/526, 1 July 1998; *Ladbroke Group/Coral* Cm 4030 (1998).
16 See http://www.competition-commission.gov.uk/ref.htm.

work: the Commission receives a copy of the OFT's assessment of the merger and attends the Mergers Panel discussing the case; officials from the Commission examine the OFT's files once a reference has been made; the Commission's questionnaires are designed so that companies may be able simply to refer to material already supplied to the OFT; and the Commissioners conducting an inquiry meet with officials from the OFT who will give a presentation setting out their thinking and answer any questions[17]. The report of the Commission is sent to the Secretary of State and a copy is sent to the DGFT[18].

(C)   Interim orders during the Commission's investigation

Pursuant to section 74 of the FTA the Secretary of State has the power to make an interim order while the Commission is carrying out its investigation in order to prevent anything being done which could prejudice the implementation of its recommendations. Section 75(4A) of the FTA, inserted by the Companies Act 1989, imposes an automatic prohibition on the parties or their subsidiaries acquiring shares in each other, except with the consent of the Secretary of State, from the time that a contemplated merger is referred until, at the latest, 40 days after the report on the merger is laid before Parliament. The Secretary of State may give general or specific consents exempting undertakings from the prohibition in section 75(4A). The Secretary of State has issued a general consent exempting from this prohibition transactions between members of the same group. Application may be made for special consent on an individual basis, but the Secretary of State would not normally allow an acquiring party to acquire a holding of more than 15% in the target company[19]. A specific consent, subject to conditions, was given in the case of Nutreco's acquisition of the non-UK businesses of Hydro Seafood in November 2000[20]. Section 75(4A) does not apply to the acquisition of assets as distinct from shares: if it is deemed necessary to prevent the acquisition of assets, the Secretary of State would have to use the interim procedure in section 74 of the Act; this was done, for example, in the case of *Medicopharma NV/AAH Holdings plc*[1].

5.   SUBSTANTIVE ANALYSIS

As noted above, the public interest test in section 84 of the Act is a broad one; in practice, however, competition is the key issue in most investigations, although other issues are sometimes influential. This section considers some of the key features of the Commission's substantive analysis in its inquiries. The proposals of the Government to make competition the main test in merger cases are considered in section 8[2].

---

17 See Annex F of *Mergers: The Response to the Consultation on Proposals for Reform* URN 00/805.
18 FTA 1973, s 86(1).
19 *Mergers Guide*, para 8.3.
20 DTI Press Notice P/2000/764, 15 November 2000; see also DTI press Notice P/2001/140, 8 March 2001, giving consent to Lloyd's TSB and Abbey National plc to acquire shares in each other during the merger investigation.
1   Merger Reference (Medicopharma NV and AAH Holdings plc) Order 1991, SI 1991/2648, amended by SI 1991/2702; see also Merger Reference (InterbrewSA/Bass plc)(Interim Provisions) Order 2000, SI 2000/2566.
2   See p 836 below.

(A) Competition: horizontal effects

As one would expect, most of the Commission's investigations have been concerned with the horizontal effects of mergers. Due to constraints of space, it is sensible to focus here on some of the Commission's investigations of horizontal mergers in recent years, rather than to look to earlier reports. Readers wishing to find an account of the Commission's investigations over a longer time frame are referred to specialist practitioner's works[3] and to the Annual Reports of the DGFT and the Competition Commission.

(i) Reports published in 1997

In 1997 the Commission concluded in several investigations that public interest detriments could follow from horizontal mergers: *FirstBus plc/SB Holdings Ltd*[4]; *Bass plc/Carlsberg A/S/Carlsberg-Tetley plc*[5]; *London Clubs International plc/ Capital Corpn plc*[6]; *The Littlewoods Organisation plc/Freemans plc*[7]; *The Peninsular and Oriental Steam Navigation Co/Stena Line AB*[8]; and *National Express Group plc/ScotRail Railways Ltd*[9]. Of these cases, the mergers in *Bass*, *London Clubs International* and *The Littlewoods Organisation* were prohibited in their entirety[10]; the others were permitted subject to various undertakings[11].

In the Commission's reports on *Technicolor Ltd/Metrocolor London Ltd*[12] and *Klaus J Jacobs Holding AG/Société Centrale d'Investissements et Associés*[13] it found no public interest detriments, notwithstanding horizontal overlaps. In the former investigation, it concluded that the merged entity would have a share of up to 41.6% of the market for processing services required by the motion picture industry. However, the Commission considered that other processing laboratories provided a competitive constraint, including those in mainland Europe; that, for the most part, barriers to entry were low; and that the major customers for film processing services had considerable buying power. In the latter investigation, the Commission noted that the merging enterprises, historically, had represented the main competitive constraint on each other in the UK market for industrial chocolate; however, the market had recently been changing rapidly; there had been entry by new suppliers in recent years; independent producers could offer strong competition; barriers to entry were low; and some of the main customers enjoyed significant bargaining power. The Commission also found that European producers did not have significant shares of the UK market, and evidence showed that they were willing to penetrate the market[14].

---

3   See eg *Finbow and Parr*, p 803, n 4 above, ch 6, and in particular paras 6-019-6.043; *Livingstone* (ibid) pp 856-859
4   Cm 3531 (1997).
5   Cm 3662 (1997).
6   Cm 3721 (1997).
7   Cm 3761 (1997).
8   Cm 3664 (1997).
9   Cm 3773 (1997).
10 1998 *Annual Report of the DGFT*, p 42.
11 Ibid, pp 41-42.
12 Cm 3720 (1997).
13 Cm 3663 (1997).
14 Cm 3720 (1997) paras 2.42-2.87.

(ii)   Reports published in 1998

In 1998 the Commission concluded in several investigations that public interest detriments could follow from horizontal mergers: *Capital Radio plc/Virgin Radio Holdings Ltd*[15] : this merger was abandoned anyway; *Fresenius AG/Caremark Ltd*[16] ; *Ladbroke Group plc/Coral Betting Business*[17] , *Tomkins plc/Kerry Group plc*[18] and *ARRIVA plc/Lutonian Buses Ltd*[19] . The Commission concluded that the merger in *Ladbroke Group plc/Coral Betting Business*[20] was against the public interest. Ladbroke had already acquired the Coral betting shops from Bass. When the merger became publicly known, there were adverse comments and the Secretary of State referred it to the Commission. The Commission concluded that there would be a weakening of price competition at the national level to the detriment of punters, and that the merger would lead to a dampening of innovation and reduce punters' choice. Ladbroke was required to divest itself of the 833 Coral shops it had acquired within six months. The *Fresenius AG/Caremark Ltd* led to an outright prohibition[1] . The Commission's investigation of *Tomkins plc/Kerry Group plc* led to an undertaking for the divestiture of four flour mills at Avonmouth, Liverpool, Newcastle and Tilbury[2] . In the case of *ARRIVA plc/Lutonian Buses Ltd*, ARRIVA was requested to divest itself of Lutonian Buses and to give behavioural undertakings in relation to its future conduct towards the divested business[3] .

(iii)   Reports published in 1999

In 1999, there were several more investigations in which the Commission identified horizontal problems: *Cendant Corp/RAC Holdings Ltd*[4] ; *IMS Health Inc/Pharmaceutical Marketing Services Inc*[5] ; *Rockwool/Owens-Corning Building Products (UK) Ltd*[6] and *British Airways plc/CityFlyer Express Ltd*[7] . In the case of *Cendant Corp/RAC Holdings Ltd* an undertaking was given that, before acquiring the RAC, Cendant should first divest itself of Green Flag, the third independent force in the supply of insurers' breakdown services for light vehicles[8] . In the case of *IMS Health Inc/Pharmaceutical Marketing Services Inc*[9] undertakings were given of both a structural and behavioural nature to overcome a loss of actual and potential competition in the supply of specialist pharmaceutical information services[10] . The importance of sustaining competition to achieve lower costs and retain lower prices was emphasised by the Commission in *Rockwool/*

---

15 Cm 3817 (1998).
16 Cm 3925 (1998).
17 Cm 4030 (1998).
18 Cm 4031 (1998).
19 Cm 4074 (1998).
20 Cm 4030 (1998)
1   DTI Press Notice P/99/361, 30 April 1999.
2   DTI Press Notice P/99/51, 21 January 1999.
3   DTI Press Notice P/2000/79, 7 February 2000.
4   Cm 4196 (1999).
5   Cm 4261 (1999).
6   Cm 4330 (1999).
7   Cm 4346 (1999).
8   DTI Press Notice P/99/950, 23 November 1999.
9   Cm 4261 (1999).
10 DTI Press Notice P/99/876, 29 October 1999.

Owens-Corning Building Products[11]. The Commission concluded that a horizontal merger whereby Rockwool, with a market share in stone wool manufacturing of 78%, would acquire OCBP, with a market share of 18%, would operate against the public interest as prices for stone wool would be higher than otherwise, costs incurred by customers would be increased and there would be a decrease in competition in the distribution and fabrication sectors. The Commission considered that no suitable remedy could be found, so that the merger should be prohibited. An undertaking to this effect was given in May 1999[12].

In the case of *British Airways plc/CityFlyer Express Ltd* the Commission considered that the benefits and detriments of the proposed merger were finely balanced. It did not consider that there would be much harm to competition on those routes already served by both airlines – the so-called 'overlap routes' – since there was a fair degree of competition on them anyway. However the Commission was concerned at the effect on competition of BA, through the acquisition of CityFlyer, acquiring the latter's takeoff and landing slots at Gatwick Airport: this would deprive potential competitors of the possibility of acquiring those slots. The Commission could see that there might be certain benefits from the merger, but concluded, on balance, that it could be expected to operate against the public interest. The Secretary of State cleared the merger, subject to an undertaking on the part of BA, following protracted negotiations, to limit the number of its slots at Gatwick[13].

In *Universal Foods Corp/Pointing Holdings Ltd*[14] the Commission investigated a merger that had already taken place and where there were competition concerns in the market for food colourings. The Commission considered that synthetic and natural food colourings were in separate product markets, and that the geographical market was the UK. It concluded that the merger could not be expected to operate against the public interest, partly on the basis that there were two Indian-based manufacturers which enjoyed lower production costs and prices and which had UK-based supply partners; although the Indian manufacturers suffered a 'reputational hurdle' as to quality, nevertheless they did exercise a competitive constraint on the merged entity. One of the four Commissioners entered a dissenting opinion in this case.

(iv) Reports published in 2000

In 2000, Commission reports dealing with horizontal mergers were published in several cases: *Alanod Aluminium-Verdlung GmbH & Co/Metalloxyd Ano-Coil Ltd*[15]; *CHC Helicopter/Helicopter Services Group*[16]; *Carlton Communications plc/United News & Media/Granada Group*[17]; *Air Canada/Canadian Airlines*[18]; and *Sylvan International Ltd/Locker Group*[19]. In the case of *Alanod Aluminium-Veredlung GmbH & Co/Metalloxyd Ano-Coil Ltd* the Commission considered that a merger that had already been completed operated against the public interest where Alanod's market share of the market in the UK for anodised aluminium

11 Cm 4330 (1999).
12 DTI Press Notice P/99/380, 7 May 1999.
13 DTI Press Notice P/99/624, 20 July 1999; see also the 1999 *Annual Report of the DGFT* p 54.
14 Cm 4544 (1999).
15 Cm 4545 (2000).
16 Cm 4556 (2000).
17 Cm 4781 (2000).
18 Cm 4838 (2000).
19 Cm 4883 (2000).

coil had increased from about 35% to about 75%. The merged entity had both the incentive and the means to exploit its market power by charging higher prices; it would have an increased opportunity to practice price discrimination; and there would be greater potential for tying the sale of other products to anodised coil. The Commission could not find a suitable structural remedy, and therefore recommended that a range of behavioural remedies should be sought. Undertakings were accepted in August 2000, including a price cap; the individual price list to each customer was made part of the undertaking, the list to be available only to the relevant customer from the DGFT[20].

An interesting investigation was *CHC Helicopter/Helicopter Services Group*. The Commission concluded that the acquisition by CHC of HSG, two of the three main suppliers of helicopter services to oil and gas installations on the UK Continental Shelf, would not operate against the public interest. Although the market would be left with only two players, the Commission considered that barriers to entry, including regulatory barriers, were low, and that the market was 'contestable'[1]. The Commission also noted that the customers for helicopter services were large oil companies, which were commercially stronger than their suppliers, and which would encourage new entrants to tender for services if they were dissatisfied with the prices of the two remaining competitors.

In *Carlton Communications plc/United News & Media/Granada Group* the Commission concluded that a merger between Carlton and United News could give rise to a distortion of competition in the market for television advertising, and that only a structural remedy, the divestment of one of the ITV regional licences, would suffice[2]. The Commission was not concerned about the mergers between Carlton and Granada or between United News and Granada, in particular since obligatory divestments would have to be made anyway to satisfy the rules in the Broadcasting Act 1990, which provide that that no company should have a share of the TV audience of more than 15%. In its investigation of *Air Canada/Canadian Airlines* the Commission noted that there was a lack of competition on various routes between the UK and Canada; however there was a real risk that, in the absence of the merger, Canadian Airlines would fail. As a result, the Commission concluded that reduced competition in the future would not be a consequence of the merger itself.

In the case of *Sylvan International Ltd/Locker Group*[3] the Minister decided that a joint venture in which those two companies had merged their cable drums businesses, and which had a market share in excess of 80%, should be wound up and that the businesses should be returned to the separate ownership of Sylvan and Locker respectively. The majority of the group that investigated this case at the Competition Commission considered that lesser, behavioural, remedies would have been adequate, but the Minister accepted the advice of the minority member of the group and the DGFT that the more drastic, structural, remedy was appropriate[4].

In the case of *British United Provident Association Ltd/Community Hospitals Group*[5] the Commission concluded that the proposed merger of BUPA with CHG, and associated mergers involving Salomons, could be expected to operate against the public interest, reducing competition in the market for private medical services and causing prices to be higher in both that market and the market for private

---

20   DTI Press Notice P/2000/588, 24 August 2000.
1   See ch 1, pp 13-14.
2   Carlton declined to proceed on this basis: see the *Annual Report of the DGFT* p 56.
3   Cm 4883 (2000).
4   DTI Press Notice P/2000/729, 2 November 2000; the advice of the DGFT is included in the Press Notice.
5   Cm 5003 (2000).

medical insurance. The Secretary of State blocked the proposed merger and required that the Salomons' shareholding in CHG should be disposed of[6].

The horizontal merger in *Nutricia Holding NV/Hydro Seafood GSP Ltd*[7] was prohibited outright: it would have reduced competition in the market for salmon feed and raised prices: the Competition Commission could not find behavioural remedies or divestments that could have overcome this[7a].

(v) Reports published in 2001

A particularly interesting case was *Interbrew/Bass plc*[8]. Interbrew, the owner, inter alia, of the lager Stella Artois, had acquired Bass, the owner of Carling: it would therefore own two of the top three lager brands in the UK; the acquisition was not made conditional on approval by the UK competition authorities. The merger was notified under the ECMR, but the UK successfully asked for it to be referred back to it under Article 9 of the ECMR. The Competition Commission recommended that the merger should be reversed, and this was accepted by the Secretary of State[9]. The Commission's concern was that the merger would have created a duopoly, of the merged business and Scottish and Newcastle, in the UK, that would have led to higher prices for end consumers and reduced choice. Interbrew sought a judicial review in this case which, though largely unsuccessful, necessitated further consultation as to the appropriate remedy.[9a] In *SCR-Sibelco/ Fife Silicon Sands Ltd*[9b] the Secretary of State required a horizontal merger to be reversed following an adverse report from the Commission[9c], and the merger in *Lloyds TSB Group/Abbey National plc*[9d] was prohibited outright[9e].

(vi) The particular case of buses

The Commission has been asked to investigate a number of mergers in the bus industry following deregulation. For example, in *Badgerline Holdings Ltd/ Midland Red West Holdings Ltd*[10] it concluded that the merger could lead to a serious loss of competition in bus services subsidised by local authorities in the County of Avon. The Commission also considered that the mergers in *Stagecoach (Holdings) Ltd/Portsmouth Citybus Ltd*[11], *South Yorkshire Transport Ltd Acquisitions*[12], *Stagecoach (Holdings) Ltd/Formia Ltd*[13] and *Caldaire Holdings Ltd/Bluebird Securities Ltd*[14] could be expected to operate against the public interest. It will be seen from the Table of Merger Investigations since 1994 that there continued to be many such investigations up to 1998, in several of which the Commission identified public interest detriments[15].

6   DTI Press Notice P/2000/825, 7 December 2000.
7   Cm 5004 (2000).
7a DTI Press Release P/2000/867, 22 December 2000.
8   Cm 5014 (2001).
9   DTI Press Notice P/2001/11.
9a See Competition Commission Press Release 20/01, 23 May 2001.
9b Cm 5139 (2001).
9c DTI Press Release P/2001/347, 4 July 2001.
9d Cm 5208 (2001).
9e DTI Press Release P/2001/362, 10 July 2001.
10 Cm 595 (1989).
11 Cm 1130 (1990).
12 Cm 1166 (1990); after the House of Lords' ruling in the *South Yorkshire* case (see p above), the Secretary of State asked the DGFT to seek remedies in respect of this report and the next two reports: DTI Press Notices 292–294 of 28 May 1993.
13 Cm 1382 (1990).
14 Cm 1403 (1991).
15 See pp 837–844 below.

(B)   Competition: vertical effects[16]

The Commission has expressed concern about the effects upon competition of vertical mergers. In *British Sugar/Berisford*[17] it recommended that Berisford should be permitted to take over its supplier, British Sugar, only if it ceased to deal in sugar produced by the only other UK supplier, Tate and Lyle. Unless it did so, competition at the wholesale stage would be seriously impaired. Appropriate undertakings were given[18]. In *British Telecommunications plc/Mitel*[19] the Commission concluded that a vertical merger could be expected to harm the public interest, although it suggested various ways in which this could be avoided short of an outright prohibition; undertakings were given in 1986[20]. In *Scottish Milk Marketing Board/Cooperative Wholesale Society Ltd*[1] the Commission recommended that the transaction be blocked unless safeguards could be put in place to prevent adverse vertical effects. The Commission had worries about the vertical effects of the merger between *Fresenius AG/Caremark Ltd*[2] since Fresenius, a large, fast-growing German healthcare company, would be able to sell its products to Caremark, which provided services to patients suffering serious medical conditions but who were treated at home; purchasers' freedom to choose the products and services they wanted would thereby be reduced. There were also horizontal concerns in this case, and the merger was prohibited[3].

A striking case on vertical effects was *British Sky Broadcasting Group plc/ Manchester United plc*[4]. The inquiry concerned the proposed acquisition by BSkyB of Manchester United. The Commission considered that the relevant football market was no wider than the matches of Premier League clubs and that the relevant broadcasting market was the market for sports premium TV channels. The Commission considered that BSkyB enjoyed market power in the latter market. In its view, whether the selling of Premier League rights continued to be collective, or whether it were in the future to be effected by individual clubs[5], the vertical relationship between BSkyB and Manchester United would enhance the position of BSkyB and restrict entry into the sports premium channel market, causing its prices to be higher and choice and innovation to be less than they would otherwise be. The Commission also considered that the merger could be harmful to British football, by further weakening smaller clubs and giving BSkyB additional influence over football matters which might not be in the long-term interest of the game. The Commission considered that there were no undertakings that could be given to overcome the detriments to the public interest that it identified and recommended that the merger should be prohibited. The Secretary of State accepted the recommendation of the Commission[6].

16   See further *Finbow and Parr*, p 803, n 4 above, paras 6.044-6.046; *Livingstone* (ibid), pp 859-862.
17   HCP (1980–81) 241.
18   See the 1981 *Annual Report of the DGFT*, pp 105–106.
19   Cm 9715 (1986).
20   1986 *Annual Report of the DGFT*, pp 66–67; they were released in 1992 following British Telecom's sale of Mitel: DTI Press Notice, 11 August 1992.
1   Cm 2120 (1992).
2   Cm 3925 (1998).
3   See p 820 above.
4   Cm 4305 (1999).
5   In separate, but contemporaneous, proceedings, under the now repealed Restrictive Trade Practices Act 1976, the Restrictive Practices Court subsequently decided that the collective and exclusive selling of Premier League rights did not operate against the public interest: judgment of 28 July 1999.
6   DTI Press Notice P/99/309, 9 April 1999.

(C) Conglomerate effects[7]

A fairly large percentage of mergers qualifying for investigation each year are conglomerate. However, normally a conglomerate merger would not be referred to the Commission unless it could be expected to have a harmful effect on competition, and conglomeracy has not figured as an issue in any recent reports. Some arguments against conglomerate mergers were rehearsed by the Commission in its 'general observations' which it appended to its report on *Rank Organization/ de la Rue*[8]. In the early 1980s the Commission was sometimes critical of conglomerate mergers, for example because of the incompatibility of management teams[9] or because of the implications of the merger for regional policy[10]; it seems unlikely that the Commission would reach a similar conclusion today. In *Blue Circle/Armitage Shanks*[11] the Commission expressed concern that it was difficult to tell from the accounts of a diversified company how well or badly it was performing on the market, but nothing has been done to increase the transparency of such information.

(D) Efficiency[12]

Parties to mergers often argue before the Commission that their transaction will enhance efficiency. The Commission will, of course, listen to such representations, and will sometimes acknowledge that efficiencies will be achieved. However, it has been reluctant to accept that an improvement in efficiency should be a reason for allowing a merger that would otherwise be detrimental to competition. For example, in *Rockwool Ltd/Owens-Corning Building Products (UK) Ltd*[13] the Commission noted that the proposed merger between those two firms would lead to an improvement in the efficiency of production and distribution of stone wool in the UK, but did not expect the benefits to be passed on to consumers. It did not believe that price control or any other remedy could overcome the adverse effects of this horizontal merger, which were that Rockwool would be able to raise its prices in relation to a significant minority of its sales. The Commission recommended that the merger should be prohibited, and the Secretary of State accepted this recommendation[14]. In *Alanod Aluminium-Veredlung GmbH & Co/Metalloxyd Ano-Coil Ltd*[15] the Commission accepted that the merger had created opportunities for cost savings and that it had contributed to the security of production and employment in Milton Keynes, but did not believe that these benefits were sufficient to balance the detriments to competition. The merger was permitted subject to behavioural remedies, including a price cap[16].

---

7   See *Livingstone* (p 803, n 4 above) pp 862-863.
8   HCP (1968–69) 298.
9   See eg *Rank Organization/de la Rue* HCP (1968–69) 298; *Lonrho/House of Fraser* HCP (1981–82) 73.
10 *Charter Consolidated Ltd/Anderson Strathclyde* Cmnd 8771 (1982).
11 Cmnd 8039 (1980).
12 See further *Finbow and Parr*, paras 6.051-6.054.
13 Cm 4330 (1999).
14 See pp 820-821 above; see similarly *Elders IXL Ltd/Grand Metropolitan plc* Cm 1227 (1990), paras 8.66-8.69; *Scottish Milk Marketing Board/Co-operative Wholesale Society Ltd* Cm 2120 (1992), paras 7.108-7.119.
15 Cm 4545 (2000).
16 See pp 821-822 above.

A reduction in efficiency was considered by the Commission in *IMS Health Inc/ Pharmaceutical Marketing Inc*[17] as one of the reasons for concluding that this proposed merger could operate against the public interest. The merger was in the pharmaceutical business information market, in which IMS was already dominant. The Commission believed that the merger would have an adverse effect on the efficiency, effectiveness and costs of the management and marketing of the companies. Structural and behavioural remedies were required[18].

An exceptional case was *Prosper De Mulder Ltd/Croda International plc*[19], where the Commission was persuaded that a merger which would have an adverse effect on competition nevertheless could not be expected to operate against the public interest, since it would lead to wider public health and environmental benefits[20].

(E)   Failing company defence[1]

It may be possible to argue that a merger should be permitted to save a failing firm from extinction, although the Commission has taken a sceptical line on this defence[2]. In *Robert Wiseman Dairies plc/Scottish Pride Holdings plc*[3] the Commission considered that the proposed merger could be expected to operate against the public interest, but decided not to recommend outright prohibition since it did not believe that Scottish Pride could continue as an independent company. It therefore proposed behavioural remedies instead[4]. In *Air Canada/ Canadian Airlines*[5] the Commission concluded that reduced competition on routes between the UK and Canada in the future would be the result not of the merger under investigation but of the fact that, without the merger, Canadian Airlines would fail and be broken up. There was little or no evidence that other operators would take over the routes serviced by Canadian Airlines, and the Commission therefore concluded that the merger could not be expected to operate against the public interest.

(F)   Other considerations

(i)   The balance of payments

In its early reports, the Commission frequently considered the impact that a merger would have upon the balance of payments, and considered that there would be public interest detriments because of the adverse effect they would have; this happened, for example, in *Enserch/Davy International*[6], *Dentsply*

---

17   Cm 4261 (1999).
18   See p 820 above.
19   Cm 1611 (1991).
20   Ibid, paras 6.68-6.81.
1   See further *Finbow and Parr* paras 6.056-6.059; on the position under the ECMR, see ch 21, p 780.
2   See *Avenir Havas Media SA/Brunton Curtis Outdoor Advertising Ltd* Cm 1737 (1991); *AAH Holdings plc/Medicopharma NV* Cm 1950 (1992).
3   Cm 3504 (1996).
4   1997 *Annual Report of the DGFT*, pp 43-44.
5   Cm 4838 (2000).
6   Cmnd 8360 (1981).

International/AD International[7], *Weidmann/Whiteley*[8], *Hiram Walker/Highland Distilleries*[9], *Hepworth Ceramic Holdings plc/Streetly plc*[10], *GKN/AE*[11] and *Swedish Match AB/Allegheny International plc*[12]. However this is not a factor that has been relevant in recent reports, no doubt in part because of the much greater health of the UK economy and because of the corresponding weakening of the former obsession with the balance of payments deficit.

(ii)　Mergers with overseas companies; the 'national interest'

In some early reports the Commission appeared to indicate that it was keen to prevent takeovers of UK companies by overseas ones. For example, in its first merger report, *BMC/Pressed Steel*[13], it did not condemn the backward integration of BMC *inter alia* since the alternative might have been a foreign take–over of Pressed Steel. Later reports, however, suggested a change in the Commission's stance on this issue, as in *Weidmann/Whiteley*[14]: there the Commission saw no objection to a foreign takeover: indeed it could see positive advantages in the merger. In *Alfred Taubman/Sotheby Parke Bernet Group*[15] the Commission stated that it was not concerned at the prospect of control of a UK company passing overseas as a matter of general principle, although there might be particular sectors where this would be a relevant issue.

In *Hong Kong and Shanghai Banking Corpn/Royal Bank of Scotland*[16] the Commission found a public interest detriment, *inter alia*, where the merger would mean that responsibility for an important part of the banking sector would pass out of UK control. In *The Government of Kuwait/British Petroleum*[17] the Commission concluded that a merger would operate against the public interest which would involve the Government of Kuwait obtaining control of BP. In both *Hong Kong and Shanghai* and *Kuwait* the industries concerned, banking and oil respectively, were of particular strategic importance, and it was not surprising that the Commission was prepared to recognise a 'national' interest meriting protection. However in the case of a bid by Nestlé for Rowntree the view taken by the Secretary of State in deciding not to refer the bid was that, as a general proposition, there is nothing objectionable about inward investment into the UK by overseas firms: chocolate does not have quite the same strategic significance as oil.

When the Minorco bid for Consolidated Gold was referred in November 1988, the Secretary of State claimed that this reference was made because of concern about competition and not because this was a bid by a South African company for a British one. The Commission cleared the merger[18], saying that the South

---

7　HCP (1974–75) 394.
8　Cmnd 6208 (1975).
9　HCP (1979–80) 743.
10　Cmnd 9164 (1984).
11　Cm 9199 (1984).
12　Cm 227 (1987).
13　HCP (1965–66) 46.
14　Cmnd 6208 (1975).
15　Cmnd 9046 (1983).
16　Cmnd 8472 (1982).
17　Cm 477 (1988).
18　Cm 587 (1989).

African connection was not a matter of concern for it. This bid eventually failed following intervention by the US authorities[19].

(iii)   Regulatory concerns

On some occasions the Commission has been asked to investigate mergers that could give rise to regulatory concerns other than the conventional one of protecting competition. For example in the water industry, where competition is extremely limited, it is important that there should be sufficient independent water companies to enable the Director General of Water Services to compare their performance in order to determine appropriate regulatory standards: this phenomenon is known as 'yardstick' competition. Four references have been made in the water sector where this was a concern: *Lyonnaise des Eaux SA/Northumbrian Water Group plc*[20]; *Severn Trent plc/South West Water plc*[1]; *Wessex Water plc/South West Water plc*[2]; and *Mid Kent Holdings plc/General Utilities plc/SAUR Water Services*[3]. The *Lyonnaise des Eaux* merger was authorised, subject to undertakings[4]; the other three were prohibited outright[5].

In the electricity sector *National Power plc/Southern Electricity plc*[6] and *PowerGen plc/Midlands Electricity plc*[7] were both prohibited, partly due to regulatory concerns[8]. In the cases of *Northern Electric/CalEnergy, East Midlands/Dominion* and *London Electricity/Entergy* mergers in the electricity sector were allowed, subject to informal assurances given to the Secretary of State as to financial and management resources, provision of financial information to the regulator, maintenance of financial separation between the generation and distribution arms of the electricity businesses and certain licence amendments[9].

(iv)   Employment

The Commission is entitled, because of the breadth of section 84, to consider any matter which might be relevant in the circumstances. For example, it may consider what implications a merger might have on the level of unemployment. A merger which would increase employment without seriously impairing competition would have a good chance of being permitted[10]. The Commission has never condemned a merger solely because it would raise unemployment; what is more common is that it refers to unemployment as an incidental adverse effect of a merger which

19 See *Consolidated Gold Fields v Minorco*, US Court of Appeals (2nd Circ), docket 88–7932, 7934.
20 Cm 2936 (1995).
1   Cm 3429 (1996).
2   Cm 3430 (1996).
3   Cm 3514 (1997).
4   1995 *Annual Report of the DGFT*, p 35.
5   1996 *Annual Report of the DGFT*, p 40; 1998 *Annual Report of the DGFT*, p 41-42.
6   Cm 3230 (1996).
7   Cm 3231 (1996).
8   1996 *Annual Report of the DGFT*, pp 39-40.
9   See DTI Press Notices P/96/932, 13 December 1996; P/96/952, 18 December 1996; and P/97/106, 3 February 1997.
10 See eg *Weidmann/Whiteley* Cm 6208 (1975) and *Swedish Match AB/Allegheny International Inc* Cm 227 (1987).

it condemns predominantly on other grounds[11]. An unusual case was *Swedish Match AB/Allegheny International Inc*[12] where, although the merger would lead to a high degree of concentration in the match industry, the Commission chose not to condemn it as, *inter alia*, it would mean that a factory in Liverpool in an area of high unemployment would be kept open which might otherwise shut; that without the merger there might be an increase in imports; that there was strong purchasing power on the market which would have a constraining effect on the merged enterprise; and because an undertaking was offered as to price rises that would be allowed. In *Ladbroke Group plc/Coral Betting Business*[13] the loss of about 200 jobs was presented to the Commission as an efficiency gain; however this was considered to be unlikely to benefit the consumer and therefore to amount to a disadvantage of the merger[14].

(v) Public security and defence

Issues of public security can, of course, be considered under the public interest test[15]. In the case of *Thomson CSF/Racal Electronics*[16] the Secretary of State announced that he had accepted undertakings on a 'fix-it-first' basis[17] to remedy or prevent any adverse public security concerns about the merger without it having been referred to the Commission. Similarly, undertakings were announced in the case of *BAE Systems/Marconi Electronic Systems*[18].

(vi) Other matters

The Commission may take other matters into account. One example is regional policy: in three reports in the early 1980s it condemned mergers that would have resulted in the removal of decision–making and career opportunities from Scotland[19]. Another could be environmental concerns: in *Prosper de Mulder Ltd/Croda International plc*[20] the Commission took into account environmental advantages that would follow from a merger in the animal waste market. An issue considered by the Commission in *Elders IXL/Allied Lyons*[1] was the method whereby Elders' bid for Allied Lyons was to be financed. The Commission's view was that the making of leveraged bids was not an issue on which it could

---

11 See eg *Guest, Keen and Nettlefold/AE* Cm 9199 (1984); *Davy International/Enserch* Cm 8360 (1981); *GKN/AE* Cm 9199 (1984).

12 Cm 227 (1987); the match industry was subsequently the subject of a monopoly investigation under the FTA in which the Commission found detriments to the public interest: see *The Supply of Matches and Disposable Lighters* Cm 1854 (1992).

13 Cm 4030 (1998).

14 Ibid, para 2.183.

15 Note that Article 21(3) provides that a Member State can protect its legitimate interests, including its public security, in relation to concentrations having a Community dimension: ch 21, pp 764-765; defence issues are outside the ECMR, and indeed the EC Treaty, altogether: ibid, p 765.

16 DTI Press Notice P/2000/678, 11 October 2000.

17 See pp 815-16 above.

18 DTI Press Notice P/2000/220, 28 March 2000.

19 See *Charter Consolidated/Anderson Strathclyde* Cm 8771 (1982); *Royal Bank of Scotland/ Shanghai Bank* Cm 8472 (1982); *Hiram Walker/Highland Distilleries* HCP (1979–80) 743; see MacQueen 'The Monopolies Commission and the Scottish Factor' [1982] JBL 316.

20 Cm 1611 (1991).

1 Cm 9892 (1986).

adjudicate, but rather that it should be a matter for the Bank of England[2]. In *Pacificorp/Energy Group plc*[3] the Commission was mainly concerned with the financial arrangements for the acquisition of the Energy Group. It believed that there was a significant risk of financial pressure on the holding company of the acquired entity, thereby putting service standards and investment at risk; however the Commission concluded that the regulatory system contained in the Electricity Act 1989, together with licence amendments agreed between Pacificorp and the Director General of Electricity Supply (now the Gas and Electricity Markets Authority), would be sufficient to contain these risks and that the merger could not be expected to operate against the public interest.

While it is always open to the parties, given the breadth of the public interest in section 84, to raise these – and other – issues in merger investigations, the reality of the matter is that in the great majority of cases the predominant issue will always be competition.

6.   POSSIBLE OUTCOMES AND REMEDIES

(A)   Merger not expected to operate against the public interest

If the Commission concludes that a merger may not be expected to operate against the public interest, the Secretary of State has no power to block it under the FTA. In this sense, the Commission's report is more than merely advisory: without an adverse finding, the Secretary of State is powerless; to put the point another way, the Commission effectively authorises a merger in those cases where it finds no public interest detriments. However, it may be that, even where there is no adverse public interest finding, the parties themselves will have a change of mind and decide not to go ahead, or that a target company will in the interim have prepared further defences so that it can fend off the bidder itself.

(B)   Merger expected to operate against the public interest

(i)   The power to make orders

If the Commission reports that a merger operates or may be expected to operate against the public interest then, provided that this decision was reached by a majority of at least two thirds of the group that carried out the investigation[4], the Secretary of State has the power to make an order preventing the merger, attaching conditions to it, or even unscrambling a merger that has already taken place[5]. The order-making powers will not be used in cases that can be settled on the basis of undertakings.

2   It had also considered the financing arrangements in the *Lonrho plc/House of Fraser plc* bid, but concluded that there was no cause for concern: Cmd 9458 (1985).
3   Cm 3861 (1997).
4   Competition Act 1998, Sch 7, para 20(2); note that in *Barclays Bank/Lloyds Bank/Martins Bank* HCP (1967–68) 319 and in *Illingworth Morris/Alan Lewis Enterprises* Cmnd 9012 (1983) there were majorities, but not 2/3 majorities, against the mergers.
5   FTA 1973, s 73(2), and Sch 8; the powers available under Sch 8 are described in ch 11, p 380; also note the power in s 89 to make an interim order after an investigation: see eg the Merger Situation (Medicopharma NV and AAH Holdings plc) (Interim Provision Order) 1992, SI 1992/1115, revoked by SI 1992/2619; Merger Report (Interbrew SA and Bass plc) (Interim Provision) Order 2001, 2001/318.

(ii)   Reversals of completed mergers

Cases are relatively rare where a reversal of a merger that has already been completed is required, although quite a few examples can be found. In *MiTeK Industries Inc/Gang-Nail Systems Inc*[6] the Commission concluded that a merger that had taken place would reduce competition and customer choice and lead to higher prices and a worse standard of service and recommended that MiTeK should divest itself of Gang-Nail Systems. In *The Government of Kuwait/The British Petroleum Co plc*[7] the Commission recommended that the Government of Kuwait should reduce its shareholding in BP to 9.9% as the merger that had occurred could be expected to operate against the public interest and in *Sara Lee Corpn/Reckitt & Colman plc*[8] the Commission recommended the divestiture of a particular brand of shoe polish if the merger were to be allowed to go ahead. Several further examples of divestitures following merger investigations were given in the discussion above of horizontal mergers[9]. The Table of Merger Investigations towards the end of this chapter indicates which cases since 1994 have resulted in divestitures[10].

Although divestiture may be viewed as the ultimate remedy to reverse the ill-effects of a merger, the effectiveness of this measure may be thwarted by the actions of the parties. In *Tomkins/Kerry Group*[11], Tomkins bought from Kerry its flour-milling business (Spillers Milling Mills), a competitor to Tomkins, which consisted of a certain number of mills. After the merger, Tomkins cut back staff and research facilities at Spillers; Spillers also lost some of its customer base. In its report, the Commission concluded that the merger would operate against the public interest and that complete divestiture would have been recommended. However, since Spillers had restructured since the merger, complete divestiture would not restore it to its former position as a competitor to Tomkins. As a result, only partial divestiture was recommended to reduce Tomkins' market power.

(iii)   Outright prohibitions

Outright prohibitions are relatively rare, but not unknown. As will be seen from the Table of Merger Investigations, there were three outright prohibitions in 1999 and one in 2000[12].

(iv)   Settlement by undertakings

In practice the formal powers in the FTA to make orders are rarely exercised. What is more usual in cases that give rise to concern is that a solution short of outright prohibition will be found and undertakings will be given. The Commission, and the DGFT, will normally make recommendations as to possible remedies. The Secretary of State, if he decides to accept the recommendations of

6   Cm 429 (1988).
7   Cm 477 (1988).
8   Cm 2040 (1992).
9   See pp 819-823 above.
10   See pp 837-844 below.
11   Cm 4031 (1998).
12   See pp 837-844 below.

the Commission, will ask the DGFT to enter into negotiations with the companies concerned to secure appropriate undertakings. The Secretary of State (and his Ministers) will not agree to meetings with the parties during the period in which undertakings are being negotiated with the DGFT[13]. The undertakings will be given to the Secretary of State, although it will be the DGFT who monitors them. The undertakings may be structural or behavioural.

(v)   Structural undertakings

As in the case of the ECMR, there is a preference in the UK for a structural solution where a merger is expected to operate against the public interest[14]. A standard remedy therefore is that a condition will be attached to the clearance of a merger, requiring the merging parties to divest that part of the business that would give rise to a serious reduction in competition. Numerous examples can be found of such divestitures. Recent cases in which divestiture was required are noted in the Table of Merger Investigations[15].

(vi)   Behavioural undertakings

Behavioural undertakings are also accepted in appropriate circumstances. Practice in the UK seems to be more favourable to behavioural undertakings than under the ECMR. A partial explanation is that in some cases in the UK the merger has already taken place, and it can be difficult to unscramble the transaction; under the ECMR, it is unlawful to proceed with the merger until clearance has been obtained[16]. In particular, in quite a few cases in the UK some form of price control has been accepted as a remedy; it is highly unlikely that the European Commission would settle a case on such a basis. For example in *Robert Wiseman Dairies/Scottish Pride Holdings*[17] it was agreed that Robert Wiseman would submit to regular audited reports on its prices to certain customers; also that it would make that information publicly available: as Scottish Pride went out of business anyway, it proved unnecessary for this undertaking to be given. In *Nutricia Holdings Ltd/Valio International UK Ltd*[18], where there was little competition in the market for gluten-free and low-protein products, the Commission recommended an RPI-X price cap, which the Secretary of State accepted[19]. Another example occurred in *National Express Group plc/Midland Main Line Ltd*[20], where NEG agreed not to increase fares above the retail price index, not to reduce levels of service on certain coach routes, to maintain the quality of service at levels at least equal to the standards on other parts of its network and to provide the DGFT with such information as he might require to ensure that the undertakings were being carried out[1]. Price control was also recommended in the case of *National Express Group plc/ScotRail Railways*

---

13   DTI *Guidance on DTI Procedures for Handling Merger References and Reports* p 13 URN/ 98/702 and see further at http://www.dti.gov.uk/CACP/cp/merger.htm.
14   See ch 21, pp 784-786.
15   See pp 837-844 below.
16   See ch 21, p 768.
17   Cm 3504 (1996).
18   Cm 3064 (1995).
19   1997 *Annual Report of the DGFT*, p 43.
20   Cm 3495 (1996).
1   DTI Press Notice P/97/844, 16 December 1997.

Ltd[2]. A price cap was imposed in the case of *The Peninsular and Oriental Steam Navigation Co/Stena Line AB*[3], although the cap was to be imposed only if a duopoly between the merged entity and Eurotunnel should develop after the abolition of duty free sales within the Community in 1999[4]. A price cap was also imposed in the case of *Alanod Aluminium-Verdlung GmbH & Co/Metalloxyd Ano-Coil Ltd*[5].

As a general proposition, price regulation is an unusual remedy outside the regulated industries: if price control is perceived to be necessary, this is the strongest possible indication that the merger should not be allowed in the first place. A more natural analysis is that in the case of *Belfast International Airport Ltd/Belfast City Airport Ltd*[6]: the Commission's view was that a merger that would increase BIA's share of airport services in Northern Ireland from 63% to 89% should be prohibited outright, a recommendation accepted by the Secretary of State. BIA offered to submit to price regulation, but the Commission's view was that as a general proposition in a 'competition versus regulation' fight the former wins.

In the case of buses, a remedy against predatory price cutting has been to require that, in the event of reducing prices to below those of a competitor, fares should be kept at that level in real terms for a period of three years[7]. Other behavioural undertakings have included, for example, an agreement to licence and supply pharmaceutical data to third parties[8].

(vii) Change of circumstances

Where there is a change of circumstances after the Commission's report on a merger, it is possible for there to be a variation in the order of, or the undertakings given to, the Secretary of State. This occurred for example in the case of *The General Electric Co plc/Siemens AG/The Plessey Co plc*[9]: some (not all) of the undertakings were released in 1997[10]. Another example is *FirstBus plc/ SBHoldings Ltd*[11]: the Commission had concluded that the merger would adversely affect future competition in the Glasgow bus market; the Minister for Corporate and Consumer Affairs required First Group to divest itself of one of its subsidiaries (Midland Bluebird). However circumstances changed after the merger when another competitor (Stagecoach) announced its intention to enter the market. On this basis the previous decision was reviewed and the Secretary of State decided, against the DGFT's advice, to require behavioural undertakings from

---

2   Cm 3773 (1997); 1998 *Annual Report of the DGFT*, p 42.
3   Cm 3664 (1997).
4   DTI Press Notice P/97/757, 19 November 1997.
5   Cm 4545 (2000); see DTI Press Notice P/2000/588, 24 August 2000.
6   Cm 3068 (1996); see also *SCR-Sibelco/Fife Silica Sands Ltd* Cm 5139 (2001).
7   See eg DTI Press Notice P/96/423, 7 June 1996 on *Stagecoach Holdings plc/Lancaster City Transport Ltd* Cm 2423 (1993); see similarly *Stagecoach Holdings plc/Ayreshire Bus Owners (AI Service) Ltd* Cm 3032 (1995), 1997 *Annual Report of the DGFT*, p 44; *FirstBus plc/SB Holdings* Cm 3531 (1997), 1998 *Annual Report of the DGFT*, pp 41-42.
8   *IMS Health Inc/Pharmaceutical Marketing Services Inc* Cm 4261 (1999); DTI Press Notice P/99/876, 29 October 1999.
9   Cm 676 (1989).
10 DTI Press Notice P/97/463, 11 July 1997.
11 Cm 3531 (1997).

First Group rather than divestiture of Midland Bluebird[12]. Numerous further examples can be found of the variation of undertakings[13].

(viii)   Consequences of breaching an undertaking

If an undertaking were broken the Secretary of State could make an order and any person harmed may bring civil proceedings against the person responsible, although this does not necessarily mean that damages are available[14]; the system operates in the same way as in the case of monopoly references[15].

(ix)   The discretion of the Secretary of State

The Secretary of State is entitled to depart from the conclusions of the Commission where he considers it appropriate to do so. The Secretary of State cannot block a merger if the Commission does not conclude that it may be expected to operate against the public interest; however he is under no duty to block it if it concludes that it may be. The system of merger control is essentially discretionary and ultimately both the decision to refer and the decision to block must be taken by the Minister. This was illustrated after *Charter Consolidated Ltd/Anderson Strathclyde Ltd*[16]. The Commission had concluded by a 4 to 2 vote (one of the dissentients being the Chairman) that the merger would operate against the public interest. The Secretary of State decided to allow the bid to go ahead. The target company applied for judicial review of his decision on the basis *inter alia* that the Secretary of State had erred in law in not accepting the Commission's recommendations. This was emphatically rejected by the Divisional Court, which concluded that Parliament had clearly intended that the final decision in a merger case should be that of the Minister; the Commission's rôle is simply advisory[17]. In the case of *The General Electric Co plc/VSEL plc*[18] the Commission considered that the bid by GEC for VSEL should be prohibited, but the Secretary of State (who had referred the bid in the first place) decided that it should be permitted[19]. In October 2000, the Secretary of State announced that he would review, in the autumn of 2001, his position in relation to the taking of decisions following advice from the Competition Commission[20].

12 *Review of FirstGroup Undertakings*, DTI Press Notice, P/98/617, 31 July 1998.
13 See for example DTI Press Notice P/96/86, 2 February 1996 on *Badgerline/Midland Red West* Cm 595 (1989); DTI Press Notice P/97/607, 26 September 1997 on *General Utilities/ The Mid Kent Water Company* Cm 1125 (1990).
14 FTA 1973, s 93A (added by the Companies Act 1989, s 148).
15 See ch 11, pp 380 and 383, and in particular the action brought following the *Mid Kent* case.
16 Cmnd 8771 (1982).
17 *R v Secretary of State for Trade, ex p Anderson Strathclyde plc* [1983] 2 All ER 233, DC; see pp 835-836 below on judicial review under the merger provisions of the FTA.
18 Cm 2852 (1995).
19 1995 *Annual Report of the DGFT* p 35.
20 DTI Press Notice P/2000/705, 26 October 2000.

7. JUDICIAL REVIEW[1]

There have been several claims for judicial review when firms have been dissatisfied with the operation of the merger provisions. The FTA, which establishes a flexible system of control and invests wide discretionary powers in the Secretary of State, is not a promising statute for judicial review, except in so far as a pure point of law is concerned[2]. The decision of the Secretary of State not to refer the bid of the Al Fayed brothers for the House of Fraser was challenged, but in *Lonrho plc v Secretary of State for Trade and Industry*[3] the House of Lords refused to interfere with the exercise of his discretion; in *Lonrho plc v Tebbit*[4], however, the Court of Appeal refused to strike out a claim by Lonrho alleging negligence against the Secretary of State in failing to release Lonrho from an earlier undertaking not to increase its shareholding in the House of Fraser above 30%; the failure to do this meant that the Al Fayeds were able to acquire the House of Fraser without opposition from Lonrho.

The fairness of the Commission's procedures is subject to judicial review, but the courts have not wanted to impose a procedural straitjacket upon it. In *R v Monopolies and Mergers Commission, ex p Argyll Group plc*[5], *R v Monopolies and Mergers Commission, ex p Elders IXL Ltd*[6] and *R v Monopolies and Mergers Commission, ex p Matthew Brown plc*[7] complaints were rejected about the way in which the Commission had conducted its investigations[8]. A similar case was dismissed by the Divisional Court in *R v Monopolies and Mergers Commission, ex p Air Europe*[9]. In *R v Monopolies and Mergers Commission, ex p Stagecoach Holdings plc*[10] Collins J explained that the test to be applied, in considering the procedural fairness of the Commission's proceedings, was the normal one in cases on natural justice, and not the more stringent test of *Wednesbury* unreasonableness, as the Court of Appeal had suggested for proceedings of the Panel on Take-overs and Mergers[11]. In *R v Secretary of State for Trade, ex p Anderson Strathclyde*[12] the Secretary of State's decision not to block a merger following an adverse report of the Commission was unsuccessfully challenged. These decisions suggest that the courts do not want to be brought into the feverish

1   See further *Finbow and Parr*, p 803, n 4 above, ch 9; Wade and Forsyth *Administrative Law* (Clarendon Press, 8th ed, 2000) Parts V and VI, Smith *Competition Law: Enforcement and Procedure* (Butterworths, 2001), ch 16. .

2   As in *South Yorkshire Transport Ltd v Monopolies and Mergers Commission* [1993] 1 All ER 289, [1993] 1 WLR 23: see p 808, n 15 above.

3   [1989] 2 All ER 609, HL; Lonrho also sued the Al Fayeds, claiming that they had acted tortiously in giving misleading information to the Secretary of State which influenced his decision not to make a reference: see *Lonrho plc v Fayed* [1992] 1 AC 448, [1991] 3 All ER 303; the provision of misleading information was subsequently made a criminal offence by s 151 Companies Act 1989, inserting a new s 93B into the FTA.

4   [1992] 4 All ER 280, CA.

5   [1986] 2 All ER 257, [1986] 1 WLR 763, CA.

6   [1987] 1 All ER 451, [1987] 1 WLR 1221.

7   [1987] 1 All ER 463, [1987] 1 WLR 1235.

8   In the *Argyll* case the Court agreed that there had been a technical irregularity on the part of the Chairman of the Commission in choosing to lay aside an investigation; this matter was dealt with by the Monopolies and Mergers Commission (Performance of Functions) Order 1989, SI 1989/122; see now Competition Act 1998, Sch 7, para 15(7)(b).

9   (1988) 4 BCC 182.

10 (1996) Times, 23 July.

11 See *R v Panel on Take-overs and Mergers, ex p Guinness plc* [1990] 1 QB 146, [1989] 1 All ER 509.

12 [1983] 2 All ER 233, DC.

controversies that frequently surround mergers and, in particular, contested takeovers, preferring to defer to the specialist agencies established for these purposes.

8.   THE 1999 AND 2000 CONSULTATION DOCUMENTS

In August 1999 the Secretary of State published a Consultation Document[13] proposing a number of changes to the system of merger control in the UK; a further publication in October 2000 developed these proposals further[14]. The intention of the Government is to introduce fundamental changes to the system of merger control in the UK when legislative time is available. As an interim measure, the Secretary of State announced that in future he would always follow the advice of the DGFT whether to refer a merger to the Competition Commission, except in exceptional circumstances[15]. This did not require an alteration of the legislation, and was introduced with immediate effect.

As to the proposed legislative changes, the intention is that responsibility for making decisions in merger cases should be given to the independent competition authorities; the Secretary of State should become involved only in the small minority of cases which raise defined exceptional public interest issues[16]. The decisions to be adopted by the independent competition authorities would be made against a competition-based test rather than the public interest test set out in section 84 of the FTA. The substantive test proposed will be whether the merger would lead to a substantial lessening of competition, rather than the creation or strengthening of a dominant position, as it is under the ECMR[17]. Where a merger may be harmful to competition, it may be possible to take into account offsetting benefits to consumers at the remedies stage of the process[18].

The division of responsibility between the OFT and the Competition Commission will remain as it is now: the OFT will conduct the first-stage, preliminary investigation into a merger, and the Commission will carry out a second-stage, in-depth inquiry if merited[19]. Notification will remain voluntary[20]. Timetables for investigations will be tightened[1]. Some alterations are proposed to the reference criteria, in particular the replacement of the assets test by a turnover test[2]. Various options are proposed as to the way in which remedies will be decided upon and the timetable for agreeing them[3]. It is likely that an Enterprise Bill will be presented to Parliament in the Spring of 2002 to carry these proposals into effect.

---

13 *Mergers: A Consultation Document on Proposals for Reform* DTI/Pub 4308; for critical comment on this proposal, see Rodger *UK Merger Control: Politics, the Public Interest and Reform* (2000) 21 ECLR 24.
14 *Mergers: The Response to the Consultation on Proposals for Reform* URN 00/805, October 2000; see also DTI Press Notice P/2000/705, 26 October 2000; also, published at the same time, *Exempting Small and Medium Sized Enterprises from Paying Merger Fees* URN 00/895, as to which see p 816, n 4a above; see further *A World Class Competition Régime* (July 2001), Cm 5233, ch 5.
15 DTI Press Notice P/2000/705, 26 October 2000; see p 813 above.
16 *Mergers: The Response to the Consultation on Proposals for Reform* URN 00/805, October 2000, paras 4.10-4.12.
17 Ibid, paras 2.16-2.21.
18 Ibid, paras 2.22-2.26.
19 Ibid, paras 3.10-3.12.
20 Ibid, paras 5.14-5.17.
1   Ibid, paras 5.18-5.37.
2   Ibid, paras 6.12-6.28.
3   Ibid, paras 7.1-7.10.

9. THE MERGER PROVISIONS IN PRACTICE

The Annual Report of the DGFT provides a statistical analysis of merger activity. The 1999 Report, at pages 96 to 98, analyses the number of mergers falling within the general provisions of the FTA during that year: mergers handled under the ECMR and the newspaper provisions are excluded. Table G.2 shows a total of 254 mergers falling within the FTA, representing assets bid for of £116,618 million. Of these, Table G.5 shows that a total of 10 were referred to the Commission. The DGFT was asked to examine a total of 415 cases in the course of 1999. The number of qualifying cases in 2000 fell to 192.[3a]

The following Table provides details of merger investigations completed, other than newspaper mergers, since the last edition of this book, that is to say from 1994 to the end of July 2001.

Table of merger investigations

Title	Command number	Date published	Merger expected to operate against the public interest?
1994			
National Express Group plc and Saltire Holdings Ltd	Cm 2468	17.2.94	No
Alcatel Cable SA and STC Ltd	Cm 2477	24.2.94	No
1995			
Stagecoach Holdings plc and Mainline Partnership Ltd	Cm 2782	9.3.95	Yes Note: divestiture required
Thomas Cook Group Ltd and Interpayment Services Ltd	Cm 2789	23.3.95	Yes
S B Holdings Ltd and Kelvin Central Buses Ltd	Cm 2829	27.4.95	No
Stagecoach Holdings plc and S B Holdings Ltd	Cm 2845	27.4.95	Yes Note: divestiture required

3a   *2000 Annual Report of the DGFT*, pp 112-114.

Title	Command number	Date published	Merger expected to operate against the public interest?
1994			
British Aerospace plc and VSEL plc	Cm 2851	23.5.95	No
The General Electricity Co plc and VSEL plc	Cm 2852	23.5.95	Yes Note: the Secretary of State cleared this bid
Service Corpn International and Plantsbrook Group plc	Cm 2880	25.5.95	Yes Note: divestiture required
Lyonnaise des Eaux SA and Northumbrian Water Group plc	Cm 2936	28.7.95	Yes
Stagecoach Holdings plc/Ayrshire Bus Owners (A1 Service) Ltd	Cm 3032	3.11.95	Yes Note: undertakings included price control
Nutricia Holdings Ltd and Valio International UK Ltd	Cm 3064	21.12.95	Yes Note: undertakings included price control
1996			
Belfast International Airport Ltd and Belfast City Airport Ltd	Cm 3068	9.1.96	Yes Note: outright prohibition
Stagecoach Holdings plc and Chesterfield Transport (1989) Ltd	Cm 3086	18.1.96	No
The Go-Ahead Group plc and OK Motor Services Ltd	Cm 3150	2.2.96	No

Title	Command number	Date published	Merger expected to operate against the public interest?
British Bus Plc and Arrowline (Travel) Ltd	Cm 2383	8.3.96	No
National Power plc and Southern Electric plc	Cm 3230	25.4.96	Yes Note: outright prohibition
PowerGen Plc and Midlands Electricity plc	Cm 3231	25.4.96	Yes Note: outright prohibition
UniChem plc/Lloyds Chemists plc and GEHE AG/Lloyds Chemists plc	Cm 3344	19.7.96	Yes Note: divestiture required
NV Verenigde Bedrijven Nutricia and enterprises belonging to Milupa AG	Cm 3356	9.8.96	No
Severn Trent plc and South West Water plc	Cm 3429	25.10.96	Yes Note: outright prohibition
Wessex Water plc and South West Water plc	Cm 3430	25.10.96	Yes Note: outright prohibition
National Express Group plc and Midland Main Line Ltd	Cm 3495	20.12.96	Yes Note: undertakings included price control
Robert Wiseman Dairies plc and Scottish Pride Holdings plc	Cm 3504	24.12.96	Yes
1997			
Mid Kent Holdings plc and General Utilities plc and SAUR Water Services plc	Cm 3514	21.1.97	Yes Note: outright prohibition

Title	Command number	Date published	Merger expected to operate against the public interest?
FirstBus plc and SB Holdings Ltd	Cm 3531	24.1.97	Yes Note: divestiture required; also price control
Cowie Group plc and British Bus Group Ltd	Cm 3578	18.3.97	No
Bass plc, Carlsberg A/S and Carlsberg-Tetley plc	Cm 3662	27.6.97	Yes Note: outright prohibition
Klaus J Jacobs Holding AG and Societé Centrale d'Investissements et Associés	Cm 3663	13.6.97	No
The Peninsular and Oriental Steam Navigation Co and Stena Line AB	Cm 3664	19.11.97	Yes Note: price control
Technicolor Ltd and Metrocolor London Ltd	Cm 3720	24.7.97	No
London Clubs International plc and Capital Corpn plc	Cm 3721	05.8.97	Yes Note: outright prohibition
The Littlewoods Organisation plc and Freemans plc (a subsidiary of Sears plc)	Cm 3761	18.11.97	Yes Note: outright prohibition
National Express Group plc and ScotRail Railways Ltd	Cm 3773	16.12.97	Yes

Title	Command number	Date published	Merger expected to operate against the public interest?
National Express Group plc and Central Trains Ltd	Cm 3774	16.12.97	No
Pacificorp/ Energy Group plc	Cm 3816	19.12.97	No
1998			
Capital Radio plc and Virgin Radio Holdings Ltd	Cm 3817	13.01.98	Yes Note: abandoned
Fresenius AG and Caremark Ltd	Cm 3925	30.04.98	Yes Note: outright prohibition
Ladbroke Group plc and the Coral Betting Business	Cm 4030	24.09.98	Yes Note: divestiture required
Tomkins plc and Kerry Group plc	Cm 4031	25.09.98	Yes Note: divestiture required
ARRIVA plc and Lutonian Buses Ltd	Cm 4074	18.11.98	Yes Note: divestiture required
1999			
Cendant Corpn and RAC Holdings Ltd	Cm 4196	4.02.99	Yes Note: conditional prohibition
IMS Health Inc and Pharmaceutical Marketing Services Inc	Cm 4261	25.02.99	Yes Note: divestiture required
British Sky Broadcasting Group plc and Manchester United plc	Cm 4305	09.04.99	Yes Note: outright prohibition

Title	Command number	Date published	Merger expected to operate against the public interest?
Rockwool Ltd and Owens-Corning Building Products (UK) Ltd	Cm 4330	07.05.99	Yes Note: outright prohibition
British Airways plc/CityFlyer Express Ltd	Cm 4346	20.07.99	Yes
NTL Communications Corp/Newcastle United plc	Cm 4411	27.07.99	No
Universal Foods Corpn and Pointings Holdings Ltd	Cm 4544	21.12.99	No
2000			
Alanod Aluminium-Veredlung GmbH & Co and Metalloxyd Ano-Coil Ltd	Cm 4545	19.01.00	Yes Note: undertaking as to price control
CHC Helicopter Corpn and Helicopter Services Group ASA	Cm 4556	28.01.00	No
NTL Incorporated and Cable & Wireless Communications plc	Cm 4666	22.03.00	No
Vivendi SA & British Sky Broadcasting Group plc	Cm 4691	18.04.00	No

Title	Command number	Date published	Merger expected to operate against the public interest?
Carlton Communications plc/United News & Media/Granada Group	Cm 4781	14.07.00	Yes, in the case of Carlton/United News & Media; no, in the cases of Carlton/ Granada and Granada/United News & Media Note: divestiture required
Air Canada/ Canadian Airlines	Cm 4838	31.8.00	No
Sylvan International Ltd/Locker Group plc	Cm 4883	2.11.00	Yes Note: outright prohibition
BUPA/Comm-unity Hospitals Group	Cm 5003	7.12.00	Yes Note: outright prohibition
BUPA/Salomon International LLC/Comm-unity Hospitals Group	Cm 5003	7.12.00	Yes Note: divestiture required
Interbrew/Bass	Cm 5014	3.1.01	Yes Note: outright prohibition and divestiture required; final outcome to be decided following judicial review
Nutreco Holding BV/Norsk Hydro ASA	Cm 5004	22.12.00	Yes Note: outright prohibition
Icopal Holding A/S/Icopal Holding A/S and Icopal a/s	Cm 5089	10.4.01	No

Title	Command number	Date published	Merger expected to operate against the public interest?
BASF AG/Takeda Chemical Industries Ltd	Cm 5209	4.7.01	No
SCR-Sibelco SA/Fife Silica Sands Ltd	Cm 5139	4.7.01	Yes. Note: divestiture required
Reed Elsevier/ Harcourt General	Cm 5186	5.7.01	No
Lloyds TSB/Abbey National plc	Cm 5208	10.7.01	Yes. Note: outright prohibition

10.   CONTROL OF NEWSPAPER MERGERS[4]

Newspaper mergers are subject to a stricter form of control than other mergers. The reason is that control of the media is a matter of particular political sensitivity, and that the concentration of the press in too few hands could stifle the expression of opinion and argument and distort the presentation of news[5]. As the DGFT said at page 42 of his Annual Report for 1979:

'Transfers or closures of newspapers may raise issues which cannot be judged solely by economic criteria, since they could affect accurate presentation of news and free expression of opinion.'

The relevant provisions are contained in sections 57 to 62 of the FTA. Newspaper mergers caught by these provisions can be effected only with the consent of the Secretary of State; normally this consent can be given only after the Commission has investigated the merger in order to consider its impact upon the public interest. The DGFT has no involvement in cases that fall under the special newspaper provisions. Any purported newspaper merger for which such consent is not given is unlawful and void[6] and penalties can be imposed upon

4   On newspaper mergers, see further *Finbow and Parr*, p 803, n 4 above, Appendix 1; *Butterworths Competition Law* (eds Freeman and Whish) Div VII, paras [562]-[624]; Livingstone *Competition Law and Practice* (Pearson Professional Ltd, 1995) pp 870-885.

5   The Royal Commission on the Press (Cmnd 1811, 1961–62) had recommended that newspaper mergers should be dealt with by a special court; this was rejected as a court was not considered a suitable forum.

6   FTA 1973, s 58(1); since the transfer is void there is no need to provide interim powers to prevent the merger, nor to provide for post hoc investigations, as in the case of other mergers.

anyone knowingly concerned in, or privy to, any such purported transfer[7]. Because these provisions may result in the commission of offences, they are drawn with more precision than those dealing with 'other' mergers, where the leniency of the system is such that the Act could be drafted in broad terms.

(A)   Definition of a newspaper merger

A newspaper merger is one whereby a newspaper or newspaper assets are transferred to a newspaper proprietor whose newspapers, including that taken over, have an average circulation, per day of publication, of 500,000 or more[8]. This definition means that only *concentrations* of press ownership qualify under these provisions. A takeover of a newspaper by a non–newspaper proprietor could be investigated only under the general provisions on mergers. A newspaper for these purposes does not include trade journals, magazines and periodicals[9].

Section 57(1)(b) of the FTA, as amended by section 8 of the Deregulation and Contracting Out Act 1994, defines who constitutes a newspaper proprietor for these purposes. The actual owner of a newspaper obviously qualifies, as does any member of a group of persons of which another member is an actual proprietor of a newspaper. Section 57(2) of the FTA, as amended, defines what is meant by a transfer for these purposes. It includes any transaction by virtue of which a person would become, or would be entitled to become, an actual newspaper proprietor, or a person with a primary or secondary controlling interest in an actual newspaper proprietor[10]; any transfer of assets necessary to the continuation of the newspaper as a separate newspaper[11]; and any transfer of plant or premises used in the publication of a newspaper, unless the transfer will not effect a change of ownership of the newspaper or will not result in the newspaper's closure[12].

(B)   The consent of the Secretary of State

Newspaper mergers as defined above require the Secretary of State's consent. When giving his consent he is permitted to do so conditionally or unconditionally[13]; a breach of any condition imposed is a punishable offence[14]. Such conditions may be imposed whether the case is one which has been referred

7   FTA 1973, s 62; no penalties have ever been imposed but see *West Somerset Free Press/Bristol United Press* (1979–80) HCP 546 where an unlawful transfer was discovered.
8   FTA 1973, s 58(1); s 57(3) deals with the method by which the average circulation of a newspaper is to be calculated; the figure of 500,000 can be varied by the Secretary of State: s 58(5); as to the newspapers of a newspaper proprietor, see FTA, s 57(1A), inserted by Deregulation and Contracting Out Act 1994, s 8.
9   FTA 1973, s 57(1)(a) defines a newspaper as a daily, Sunday or local newspaper circulating mainly or wholly in the UK or a part thereof.
10 Ibid, s 57(2)(a): the subjunctive is used because the transfer is unlawful and void without the consent of the Secretary of State; as to the terms 'primary' and 'secondary' controlling interests, see s 58(4) and (5).
11 Ibid, s 57(2)(b).
12 Ibid, s 57(2)(c).
13 Ibid, s 58(1); s 58(3) requires the consent to be unconditional where the Secretary of State is satisfied that it is not intended to continue the newspaper as a separate newspaper.
14 Ibid, s 62(2); the penalties are the same as for unlawful transfers: an unlimited fine or up to two years' imprisonment on conviction on indictment.

to the Commission or not. The basic position is that the Secretary of State can give his consent only after the case has been referred to the Commission; such reference must be made within one month of his having received an application from those concerned[15]. However in certain cases the Secretary of State may, and in one case he must, give his consent to the transfer without referring the matter to the Commission. He may do so in three situations: first, where the newspaper is not economic as a going concern and he is satisfied that the case is one of urgency if it is to continue as a separate newspaper[16]; secondly, where the newspaper being transferred has an average circulation of 50,000 or less per day of publication[17]; and thirdly, where the Commission has failed to make its report within the appointed time limit[18]. He must do so where he is satisfied that the newspaper is not economic as a going concern and that there is no intention to continue it as a separate newspaper[19].

(C)   Investigation by the Commission

Where a newspaper reference is made to the Commission, it will be instructed to report within a maximum of three months[20]; the usual period given is two months. This period may be extended for special reasons[1]. There is a panel of persons from which additional members may be appointed to the Commission for the purpose of newspaper references[2]; the Secretary of State is responsible for it and details of its composition may be found on the Commission's website[3]. At the end of March 2001, this panel had ten members. In its investigations the Commission is required to consider whether the merger may be expected to operate against the public interest[4]; in its report it must reach definite conclusions on the questions referred to it and give such an account of its reasons and the position generally as will facilitate a proper understanding of them[5]. If it concludes that the merger could be expected to operate against the public interest, it must consider whether any, and if so what, conditions might be required to prevent this effect[6]. It is important to note that, in its consideration of the public interest in newspaper references, the Commission is required to report whether the merger may be expected to operate against the public interest, taking into account:

> 'all matters which appear in the circumstances to be relevant and, in particular, the need for accurate presentation of news and free expression of opinion'[7].

15 Ibid, s 59(1).
16 Ibid, s 58(3)(a) and s 59(2)(b).
17 Ibid, s 58(4), as amended by the Fair Trading Act (Amendment)(Newspaper Mergers) Order 1995, SI 1995/1351, and s 59(2)(b).
18 Ibid, s 60(3).
19 Ibid, s 58(3)(b) and s 59(2)(a).
20 Ibid, s 60(1).
1   Ibid, s 60(2).
2   Competition Act 1998, Sch 7, para 22.
3   http://www.competition-commission.gov.uk/role2.htm#newsr.
4   FTA 1973, s 59(3).
5   Ibid, s 61(1).
6   Ibid, s 61(2).
7   Ibid, s 59(3).

The Commission does not apply the test of the public interest in section 84 when conducting an investigation into a newspaper merger[8].

(D) Action by the Secretary of State after a newspaper reference

Having received a report from the Commission, it is for the Secretary of State to decide, in his discretion, whether or not he should give his consent and whether any conditions should be imposed upon the transfer[9]. He is not bound in a formal sense by the findings of the Commission, although he will normally be guided by them. He could withhold consent to the merger where the Commission is of the opinion that it would operate against the public interest. It would seem that he could do so even if the Commission makes no adverse comment on the merger at all: nothing in the legislation specifically says that he can withhold consent only after an adverse report[10]. There are no provisions enabling the Secretary of State to make an interim order preventing a newspaper merger or ordering one to be unscrambled, since section 58 of the FTA 1973 provides that transfers without consent are unlawful and void anyway. The DGFT is not involved in the investigation of newspaper mergers at any stage; any undertakings are given to and monitored by the Secretary of State. However details of newspaper mergers, whether referred to the Commission or not, are given in the DGFT's Annual Report[11].

(E) The newspaper merger provisions in practice

Since the provisions were introduced there have been many references to the Commission[12]: the overwhelming majority of cases involved local newspapers, but in two the Commission dealt with national titles.

(i) Local newspaper mergers

In the majority of cases takeovers of local newspapers were involved and in its early reports the Commission normally concluded that the merger would not operate against the public interest and the transfer was allowed to go ahead. However it did from time to time express concern about the increasing concentration that was taking place in the ownership of the local press[13], and in 1977 a Royal Commission drew attention to the same problem[14]. The report on *West Somerset Free Press/Bristol United Press Ltd*[15] saw this concern turn to conviction when, for the first time, the Commission concluded that a merger would operate against the public interest; it also considered that there were no

8   Ibid, s 84(2).
9   Ibid.
10 Compare the position with the general mergers provisions, under which a merger can be blocked only after an adverse report: see p 830 above.
11 See eg the 1999 *Annual Report of the DGFT* p 63-64.
12 These are listed in *Butterworths Competition Law* (eds Freeman and Whish) Div VII, para [3.1].
13 See eg *George Outram/Hamilton Advertiser* HCP (1969–70) 76; *Guardian and Manchester Evening News/Surrey Advertiser Newspaper Holdings* HCP (1979) 100.
14 Cm 6810.
15 HCP (1979–80) 546.

conditions which could prevent this. The Commission's view was that it was desirable to prevent greater regional concentration of ownership of the press and it was concerned that the merger would result in less competition in the west of England than if the Free Press remained in the hands of its existing owners. In reaching its conclusion it stressed that it did not wish to imply any criticism of either Bristol United Press or its parent company Associated Newspapers, which was itself a newspaper proprietor within the terms of the FTA 1973, s 57(1)(b). Consent to the transfer was refused.

In *Reed International Ltd/News International Ltd*[16] the Secretary of State at first refused his consent to the transfer. Subsequently consent was given upon assurances by Reed that it would endeavour to divest itself of its ownership of West of England Newspapers and that, during any interim dual ownership of both groups of newspapers, there would be no consultation or co–operation on trading matters between them[17]. In *TR Beckett Ltd/EMAP plc*[18] the Commission considered that a newspaper merger would operate against the public interest where it would lead to a concentration of press ownership in part of Sussex, although the Commission was prepared to allow it to go ahead on certain conditions; the Secretary of State took this advice and the transaction was permitted subject to conditions modelled upon the Commission's recommendation[19]. In *Century Newspapers Ltd/Thomson Regional Newspapers Ltd*[20] the Commission concluded that the takeover by Thomsons of regional daily newspapers in Northern Ireland should be blocked, in particular as it would have affected the balance of the expression of opinion in Northern Ireland. The Secretary of State refused consent[1]. In *Mr David Sullivan/The Bristol Evening Post plc*[2] the Commission concluded that the transfer to David Sullivan of a controlling interest in Bristol Evening Post plc could be expected to operate against the public interest. Sullivan was the proprietor of the *Sport on Sunday*, the external appearance of which resembles a newspaper but the contents of which verge on pornography. The Commission considered that if he were to gain control of the titles owned by Bristol Evening Post plc, this would have an adverse effect on their character and content; also Sullivan could be expected to influence editorial policy and this could harm the accurate presentation of news and the free expression of opinion. Conditions were attached to the clearance of the acquisition by the *Daily Mail* of the *Nottingham Evening Post*, following the Commission's report in *Daily Mail & General Trust plc/T Bailey Forman Ltd*[3] in which it expressed concern as to the risk to diversity of opinion in the area. The Secretary of State was concerned, in the case of *Trinity plc/Regional Independent Media Holdings Ltd*[4], that the merger could be detrimental to the expression of opinion in Northern Ireland, and gave consent to the acquisition on condition that certain titles there were disposed of[5]. In *Independent News & Media plc/Trinity Mirror plc*[6] the Commission concluded that the transfer of various titles in Northern Ireland,

---

16   Cm 8337 (1981).
17   See the 1981 *Annual Report of the DGFT*, pp 125–126.
18   Cm 623 (1989).
19   1989 *Annual Report of the DGFT*, p 103.
20   Cm 677 (1989).
1   1989 *Annual Report of the DGFT*, p 103.
2   Cm 1083 (1990).
3   Cm 2693 (1994); see DTI Press Notice P/94/730, 5 December 1994.
4   Cm 4393 (1999).
5   1999 *Annual Report of the DGFT*, pp 63-64.
6   Cm 4770 (2000).

including the *Belfast Telegraph*, to Independent News & Media plc would not be expected to operate against the public interest.

(ii) National newspaper mergers

On two occasions the Commission has considered mergers involving major national newspapers. Its first report was upon the proposed transfer of *The Times* to the Thomson Organisation, which already owned the *Sunday Times*[7]. There were several arguments raised against the takeover: that the two papers would cease to be distinct, that they would be subject to editorial control by Thomson, that there would be an undesirable concentration of press ownership in the Thomson Organisation and that the special status of *The Times* would go. However the Commission concluded that the transfer would not operate against the public interest. It accepted that *The Times* was in a poor financial condition (faced with competition from other quality papers its revenue had declined considerably), and that it would benefit from being part of a larger concern with proven managerial ability in the field. Lord Thomson had given the Commission various assurances on matters such as editorial independence and it was therefore of the opinion that the takeover should not be prevented. When similar assurances were given to the President of the Board of Trade (the predecessor of the Secretary of State) the transfer was given unconditional consent. In 1980 the Thomson Organisation sold both newspapers to News International. The Secretary of State, in the exercise of his discretion, chose not to refer this newspaper merger to the Commission, although certain conditions were imposed upon the purchaser[8].

In 1981 the proposed transfer of *The Observer* from Atlantic Richfield to George Outram (itself a part of the Lonrho organisation) was considered by the Commission which concluded that it would not be against the public interest, provided that the transfer was made subject to certain conditions[9]; these conditions should ensure that the editorial independence of *The Observer* would be safeguarded against a potential conflict of interest arising from Lonrho's extensive commercial interests. The transfer was permitted by the Secretary of State subject to conditions similar to those imposed when the Thomson Organisation transferred *The Times* and *Sunday Times* to News International in 1980. A subsequent transfer of the *Observer* to Guardian Newspapers Ltd was cleared without a reference as the *Observer* was considered not to be economic as a going concern[10].

(iii) Newspaper mergers permitted without a reference to the Commission

Although the basic structure of the Act is that newspaper mergers should be referred to the Commission, many transfers have been permitted without reference to the Commission under the terms of section 58. The Annual Reports of the DGFT contain brief details of mergers not referred and the reasons why. For example, in 1999 there were three transfers not referred to the Commission[11].

Some of the instances where the Secretary of State refrained from making a reference to the Commission have led to heated political argument. In 1980 the

7   HCP (1966–67) 273.
8   See p 850 below.
9   HCP (1980–81) 378; one member of the Commission was opposed to the transfer.
10 DTI Press Release, 27 May 1993.
11 1999 *Annual Report of the DGFT*, p 64

transfer of *The Times* and *Sunday Times* to News International, the publisher of *The Sun* and *The News of the World* (which for the purpose of the FTA qualify as newspapers) was permitted without a reference to the Commission, on the ground that the papers were not economic as going concerns and that the case was one of urgency. The decision not to refer was the subject of criticism, in particular as it was far from clear that *The Times* and *Sunday Times* were not economic as going concerns. The Secretary of State allowed the merger, subject to conditions. In particular News International Ltd was required to amend the Articles of Association of Times Newspapers Ltd in such a way that the editorial independence of the newspapers' editors would be assured and their exclusive right to give instructions to journalists would be respected. Removal of the editors was not to be carried out unless approved by a majority of the six 'independent national directors' who would be appointed by the Secretary of State. Also it was required that *The Times* and the *Sunday Times* should continue to be published as separate newspapers. The success of these conditions came into question when the editor of *The Times*, Harold Evans, resigned in acrimonious circumstances.

Against this background there followed further controversy when News International acquired another national daily, *Today*, to add to its portfolio of *The Sun, The News of the World, The Times* and the *Sunday Times*. A better example of the concentration of press ownership it would be hard to imagine; with this acquisition News International added a 'middle–market' paper to its 'popular' and 'quality' titles. Yet again no reference to the Commission was made as the Secretary of State was satisfied that *Today* was not economic as a going concern[12]; it has since ceased publication anyway.

In 1988 News International acquired a stake of just over 20% in Pearson, which owns the *Financial Times*. This stake was too low to trigger the newspaper merger provisions. The Secretary of State also declined to make a reference under the general provisions on mergers, as he was advised by the DGFT that there was no common control for the purposes of the legislation[13].

11.   MERGERS IN THE WATER INDUSTRY[14]

Under the Water Industry Act 1991 the Secretary of State has a duty to refer to the Commission mergers or proposed mergers involving two or more 'water enterprises' when the value of the gross assets taken over and those of the acquirer each exceed £30 million[15]; other mergers involving water enterprises may fall within the 'ordinary' merger provisions described above. When investigating such mergers the Commission must have regard to the principle that the number of water enterprises under independent control should not be reduced so as to prejudice the ability of the Director General of Water Supply to make comparisons between different water enterprises in order to determine their efficiency. By 31 July 2001 there had been six reports by the Commission on mergers under this

---

12   1987 *Annual Report of the DGFT*, p 81.
13   *Financial Times*, 13 July 1988.
14   See further Hurdley and Price in *Butterworths Competition Law* (eds Freeman and Whish) Div IX paras [1420]-[1463.7]; Livingstone *Competition Law and Practice* (Pearson Professional Ltd, 1995), pp 885-889; Weir 'Comparative Competition and the Regulation of Mergers in the Water Industry of England and Wales' (2000) XLV Antitrust Bulletin 811.
15   The figure remains £30 million, even though it is £70 million under the general rules: Water Enterprises (Merger)(Modification) Regulations 1994, SI 1994/73.

Act[16], of which three were prohibited outright, *Wessex Water plc/South West Water*[17], *Severn Trent plc/South West Water*[18] and *Mid Kent Holdings and General Utilities/SAUR Water Services*[19].

Where the merger does not involve one water company acquiring another, it will be subject to the general rules. In such a case, the DGFT will look to the Director General of Water Services for advice on those aspects of the offer which will impact upon his ability to regulate the appointees or which might impact upon his wider ability to regulate other licensed providers of water and sewerage services[20].

16 *General Utilities plc/Colne Valley Water Company/Rickmansworth Water Co* Cm 1929 (1990); *General Utilities plc/Mid Kent Water Co* Cm 1125 (1990); *Southern Water plc/Mid Sussex Water Co* Cm 1126 (1990); *Wessex Water plc/South West Water* Cm 3430 (1996); *Severn Trent plc/South West Water* Cm 3429 (1996); *Mid Kent Holdings and General Utilities/SAUR Water Services* Cm 3514 (1997).
17 Cm 3429 (1996).
18 Cm 3430 (1996).
19 Cm 3514 (1997).
20 For an example, see OFWAT Press Release 32/98, 27 July 1998 in relation to Enron's bid for Wessex Water.

CHAPTER 23

Particular sectors

The final chapter of this book will deal with three issues. First it will examine those sectors of the economy that are wholly or partly excluded from the competition rules in the EC Treaty, namely coal and steel, nuclear energy, military equipment and agriculture. Secondly it will describe how the EC competition rules apply to the transport sector, which is subject to different procedural rules from those contained in Regulation 17/62. Finally the chapter will look at the specific circumstances of so-called 'regulated industries' such as telecommunications, post and energy markets and the way in which EC and UK competition law apply to them. Constraints of space mean that these matters can be described only in outline; references to specialised literature on the application of competition law to particular sectors will be provided where appropriate.

I. COAL AND STEEL[1]

Coal and steel are dealt with by the Treaty of Paris of 1951 establishing the European Coal and Steel Community. The ECSC Treaty contains rules on competition that are similar in many respects to Articles 81 and 82 of the EC Treaty, although there are some material differences. Agreements that are restrictive of competition between undertakings[2] engaged in the production of coal or steel, or in the distribution of these products other than to domestic consumers or small craft industries, are prohibited by Article 65(1). By Article 65(2) the Commission may authorise certain cooperation agreements. The Commission has condemned cartels in the steel sector under Article 65 in *Steel Beams*[3], in which it imposed fines of EUR 104.36 million, and in *Alloy Surcharge*[4], where the fines amounted to EUR 27.3 million. The Commission

---

1   For detailed discussion of the competition rules in the ECSC Treaty see Lewis in ch 10 of Div IX of *Butterworths Competition Law* (eds Freeman and Whish); Kapteyn and VerLoren van Themaat *Introduction to the Law of the European Communities* (Kluwer Law International, 3rd ed, 1998, ed Gormley) pp 1207-1217; Bellamy and Child *European Community Law of Competition* (Sweet & Maxwell, 5th ed, 2001, ed Roth) ch 17.
2   Undertakings for this purpose are defined in Article 80 ECSC.
3   OJ [1994] L 116/1, [1994] 5 CMLR 353, upheld on appeal Cases T-141/94 etc *Thyssen Stahl v Commission* [1999] ECR II-347, [1999] 4 CMLR 810; the case has been appealed further to the ECJ, Cases C-176/99 P etc *ARBED v Commission* (judgment pending).
4   OJ [1998] L 100/55, [1998] 4 CMLR 973.

has also held that a system for the exchange of sensitive, recent and individualised information on quantities of steel products sold and on the parties' market shares infringed Article 65(1) in *Wirtschaftsvereingung Stahl*[5], although no fines were imposed in this case as the agreement had been notified. Article 66(7) ECSC prohibits the abuse of a dominant position, while Articles 4(b), 60 and 63 contain specific provisions to prevent discrimination. The ECJ has held, in *HJ Banks & Co v British Coal Corpn*[6], that Articles 65 and 66(7) do not have direct effect; in *Hopkins v National Power*[7] it held that Article 4(b) does not have direct effect[8], although recommendations under Article 63 may do[9]. Articles 81 and 82 of the EC Treaty do not apply to agreements and abusive behaviour to the extent that the ECSC Treaty does[10]; the fine in *Seamless Steel Tubes*[11] of EUR 99 million was imposed under Article 81 EC rather than Article 65 ECSC, since steel tubes qualify as 'Rome products' rather than 'Paris products'. Article 66(1) ECSC contains specific rules on mergers (or 'concentrations' in the language of the Treaty) which, in certain circumstances, require prior authorisation from the Commission. Article 66(1) operates to the exclusion of the EC Merger Regulation ('the ECMR'), although in practice cases are dealt with in the same way under each of these legal instruments[12]. The ECSC Treaty will cease to have effect at the end of 2002.

2. NUCLEAR ENERGY[13]

The Euratom Treaty, which was entered into on the same day as the EC Treaty, deals with agreements regulating the supply and price of various nuclear materials. Article 305(2) of the EC Treaty (ex Article 232(2)) provides that nothing in it shall derogate from the provisions of the Euratom Treaty. Articles 81 and 82 are capable of application to agreements and to the abuse of a dominant position to the extent that the Euratom Treaty is not applicable. In its decisions under Article 81(3) EC the Commission has tended to adopt a sympathetic attitude towards cooperation agreements in the nuclear industry[14].

5   OJ [1998] L 1/10, [1998] 4 CMLR 450.
6   Case C-128/92 [1994] ECR I-1209, [1994] 5 CMLR 30; see ch 8, pp 278-279 on the various cases brought in the English courts, of which *Banks* is one, under the competition rules in the ECSC Treaty.
7   Case C-18/94 [1996] ECR I-2281, [1996] 4 CMLR 745; see further Case T-89/98 *National Association of Licensed Opencast Operators v Commission* [2001] 4 CMLR 1189.
8   Ibid, para 26.
9   Ibid, para 28.
10   See EC Treaty, Article 305(1) (ex Article 232(1)).
11   See the Commission's XXIXth *Annual Report on Competition Policy* (1999), p 137, on appeal Cases T-78/00 etc *Sumitomo v Commission* (judgment pending).
12   See ch 21, p 735.
13   See further Kapteyn and VerLoren van Themaat *Introduction to the Law of the European Communities* (Kluwer Law International, 3rd ed, 1998, ed Gormley) pp 1217-1230; Faull and Nikpay *The EC Law of Competition* (Oxford University Press, 1999), paras 10.152-10.161; *Bellamy and Child* ch 16, Part 3.
14   See eg *United Reprocessors GmbH* OJ [1976] L 51/7, [1976] 2 CMLR D1; *KEWA* OJ [1976] L 51/15, [1976] 2 CMLR D15; *GEC/Weir* OJ [1977] L 327/26, [1978] 1 CMLR D42; *Amersham International and Buchler GmbH Venture* OJ [1982] L 314/34, [1983] 1 CMLR 619; *European Nuclear Assistance Consortium* OJ [1993] C 175/12, [1993] 5 CMLR 513; *European Fuel Cycle Consortium* OJ [1993] C 351/6, [1994] 4 CMLR 589; *Nuclear Electric/ British Nuclear Fuels* OJ [1996] C 89/4, [1996] 4 CMLR 716; *Scottish Nuclear/British Nuclear Fuels* OJ [1996] C 89/6, [1996] 4 CMLR 718.

3. MILITARY EQUIPMENT[15]

Article 296(1)(b) of the EC Treaty (ex Article 223(1)(b)) provides that a Member State may take such measures as it thinks necessary for the protection of the essential interests of its security which are connected with the production of or trade in arms, ammunitions and war materials; however these measures must not adversely affect the conditions of competition in the common market regarding products which are not intended for specifically military purposes. The Council of Ministers has drawn up a list of the products to which Article 296(1) applies, although it has not been published; Article 296(2) provides that the Council may, acting unanimously on a proposal from the Commission, amend this list. There have been some concentrations in which the Commission's jurisdiction to apply the ECMR was limited as a result of the operation of Article 296[16].

4. AGRICULTURE[17]

Articles 32 to 38 of the EC Treaty (ex Articles 38 to 46) subject agriculture to a special régime with its own philosophy[18]. Article 36 provides that 'the rules on competition shall apply to production of and trade in agricultural products only to the extent determined by the Council ...'

(A) Council Regulation 26/62

Article 1 of Council Regulation 26/62[19] provides that Articles 81 and 82 shall apply to the production of or trade in the products listed in Annex II to the Treaty, subject to the derogations set out in Article 2(1). Article 2(1) of Regulation 26/62 provides that Article 81(1) shall *not* apply in two situations: first, to agreements which form an integral part of a national market organisation; and, secondly, to agreements which are necessary for the attainment of the objectives set out in Article 33 of the Treaty (ex Article 39)[20]. These derogations from the

---

15 See further *Bellamy and Child*, ch 13, Part 4.
16 See ch 21, p 765.
17 See further Freeman in ch 2 of Div IX of *Butterworths Competition Law* (eds Freeman and Whish); *Bellamy and Child*, ch 18.
18 On agricultural policy in the EC see Lasok *Law of the Economy in the European Communities* (Butterworths, 1980) ch 12; Snyder *Law of the Common Agricultural Policy* (Sweet & Maxwell, 1985); Vaughan *The Law of the European Communities* (Butterworths, 1985) ch 13; Usher *Legal Aspects of Agriculture in the European Community* (Clarendon Press Oxford, 1988); Kapteyn and VerLoren van Themaat *Introduction to the Law of the European Communities* (Kluwer Law International, 3rd ed, 1998, ed Gormley) pp 1128-1171; *Agricultural Law of the European Union* (Academy of European Law, Trier and Irish Centre for European Law, Trinity College Dublin, 1999, eds Heusel and Collins); McMahon *Law of the Common Agricultural Policy* (Longman, 2000).
19 JO [1962] p 993, OJ [1959–62] p 129.
20 On Article 33, see pp 857-858 below. Article 2(1) contains a sentence dealing with the activities of farmers' associations; this, however, is not a further exception, but rather an embellishment of the policy expressed in that provision: see *Milchförderungsfonds* OJ [1985] L 35/35, [1985] 3 CMLR 101; *Bloemenveilingen Aalsmeer* OJ [1988] L 262/27, [1989] 4 CMLR 500, paras 150–152.

application of Article 81(1) must be strictly construed, and the Commission must give adequate reasons in the event that it allows such a derogation[1].

The derogations provided for in Article 2(1) of Regulation 26/62 relate only to the application of Article 81; there is no derogation from the application of Article 82 to the agricultural sector. The monopoly powers of the Milk Marketing Board in the UK were the subject of various proceedings under Article 82[2]; in September 1999 Milk Marque, a successor to some of the Board's assets, was broken up of its own volition[3]. A reference has been made to the ECJ from the High Court in the UK on the relationship between the monopoly provisions in the Fair Trading Act 1973 and the rules of the common agricultural policy[4].

(B)   Annex II products

If a product is *not* mentioned in Annex II, it cannot benefit from the derogations provided by Article 2(1) of Regulation 26/62. In *Cöoperative Stremsel-en Kleurselfabriek v Commission*[5] the ECJ held that, as rennet was not specifically mentioned in Annex II, it was fully subject to the competition rules; the fact that rennet was used in the production of cheese, which is itself listed in the Annex, did not provide it with immunity from the application of Article 81(1). In *Pabst and Richarz/BNIA*[6] the Commission applied Article 81 to the French trade association responsible for armagnac, pointing out that, as this product did not appear in Annex II, it was to be treated as an industrial product. In *BNIC v Clair*[7] the ECJ held, for the same reason, that cognac was an industrial product and rejected an argument that it should be treated in a special way because of its importance to the economic welfare of a particular region of France. In *BNIC v Yves Aubert*[8] the ECJ had to deal with the application of the competition rules to a demand by BNIC for a levy claimed against a wine grower for having exceeded a marketing quota. One issue was whether the competition rules could be applied to brandy. The ECJ, having observed that brandies are not listed in Annex II and so are industrial rather than agricultural products, added that the fact that some of the proceeds of levies raised by BNIC were intended for measures on wine and must, which do appear in Annex II, did not affect the application of Article 81(1). In *Dansk Pelsdyravlerforening v Commission*[9] the CFI rejected a claim that animal furs should be treated as an agricultural product, and in *Gøttrup-Klim Grovvareforeninger v Dansk Landburgs Grovvareselskab AmbA*[10] the ECJ

---

1   See Cases T-70/92 and T-71/92 *Florimex v Commission* [1997] ECR II-697, [1997] 5 CMLR 769, upheld on appeal Case C-265/97 P *VBA and Florimex v Commission* (judgment of 30 March 2000); see also Case T-77/94 *Vereniging van Groothandelaren v Commission* [1997] ECR II-759, [1997] 5 CMLR 812, upheld on appeal Case C-266/97 P *VBA and Florimex v Commission* (judgment of 30 March 2000).

2   See *Garden Cottage Foods v Milk Marketing Board* [1984] AC 130, [1983] 2 All ER 770, HL; *An Bord Bainne Cooperative Ltd v Milk Marketing Board* [1984] 1 CMLR 519; affd [1984] 2 CMLR 584, CA.

3   See ch 11, p 382.

4   Case C-137/00 *R v Monopolies and Mergers Commission and the Secretary of State for Trade and Industry, ex p Milk Marque Ltd* (judgment pending).

5   Case 61/80 [1981] ECR 851, [1982] 1 CMLR 240.

6   OJ [1976] L 231/24, [1976] 2 CMLR D63.

7   Case 123/83 [1985] ECR 391, [1985] 2 CMLR 430.

8   Case 136/86 [1987] ECR 4789, [1988] 4 CMLR 331.

9   Case T–61/89 [1992] ECR II-1931.

10   Case C-250/92 [1994] ECR I-5641, [1996] 4 CMLR 191, paras 21-27 .

held that fertiliser and plant protection products were not agricultural products. In *Sicasov* the Commission acknowledged that seeds fell within Annex II, but concluded that neither of the derogations in Regulation 26/62 was applicable[11].

(C) The first derogation: national market organisations

Article 2(1) of Regulation 26/62 provides that Article 81 shall not apply to agreements which form an integral part of a national market organisation. The Council of Ministers had established common organisations for most agricultural products by 1967, so that the majority of national marketing organisations have ceased to exist. The Commission has construed this derogation from the application of Article 81(1) strictly[12]. In *FRUBO v Commission*[13] the ECJ upheld the Commission's decision[14] that a Dutch fruit marketing organisation did not benefit from the immunity contained in Article 2(1) since it was not a national marketing organisation. In *Scottish Salmon Board*[15] the Commission found that, as there was a common organisation of the market in fishery products[16], the Scottish Salmon Board could not rely on the national market organisation defence.

In *New Potatoes*[17] rules were laid down by seven economic committees in France, acting under a French law of 1962, to organise and regulate the production and marketing of new potatoes. The rules were intended to deal with the problem of a slump in the market at a time of over–production. The Commission was asked to grant the rules negative clearance under Article 81(1): as there was no common organisation of the market in question, the Commission had to decide whether the system qualified as a national market organisation. It held that this term must be defined in a way that would be consistent with the objectives of a common organisation under the second exception of Article 2(1) of Regulation 26/62: thus the objectives of the common agricultural policy, contained in Article 33 EC and referred to below, were read into the first exception of Article 2(1). The Commission went on to hold that the decisions and agreements of various producer groups did form an integral part of the national market organisation in question and negative clearance was granted.

(D) The second derogation: common market organisations

Article 2(1) of Regulation 26/62 also permits agreements which are necessary for the attainment of the objectives of the common agricultural policy. Article 33 sets out these objectives: they are listed under five heads, and are to increase agricultural productivity, to ensure a fair standard of living for the agricultural community, to stabilise markets, to ensure the availability of supplies, and to ensure supplies to consumers at reasonable prices. Article 33(2) provides that, in

11 OJ [1999] L 14/27, [1999] 4 CMLR 192, paras 65-69.
12 As well as the decisions mentioned in the text, see *Cauliflowers* OJ [1978] L 21/23, [1978] 1 CMLR D66; *Bloemenveilingen Aalsmeer* OJ [1988] L 262/27, [1989] 4 CMLR 500; *Sugar Beet* OJ [1990] L 31/32, [1991] 4 CMLR 629; *Sicasov* OJ [1999] L 14/27, [1999] 4 CMLR 192; *British Sugar* OJ [1999] L 76/1, [1999] 4 CMLR 1316, paras 185-188, on appeal Cases T-202/98 etc *Tate & Lyle v Commission* (judgment pending).
13 Case 71/74 [1975] ECR 563, [1975] 2 CMLR 123.
14 *Geeves and Zonen v FRUBO* OJ [1974] L 237/16, [1974] 2 CMLR D89.
15 OJ [1992] L 246/37, [1993] 5 CMLR 602, para 22.
16 See Council Regulation 3796/81.
17 OJ [1988] L 59/25, [1988] 4 CMLR 790.

implementing the common agricultural policy, account shall be taken, *inter alia*, of 'the particular nature of agricultural activity, which results from the social structure of agriculture and from structural and natural disparities between the various agricultural regions'. The aims expressed in Article 33 are not necessarily consistent with the normal forces of competition.

In *FRUBO v Commission*[18] the ECJ rejected a defence based on the second derogation in Article 2(1) of Regulation 26/62. A noticeable feature of the judgment is that, although some of the heads of Article 33 may have been satisfied, not all of them were: to put the matter another way, in order to come within this derogation it is necessary to satisfy all five heads of Article 33. In practice it is likely that the Commission and the Community Courts will hold that the objectives of Article 33 are expressly or impliedly advanced by the provisions of any particular regulation establishing a common organisation of an agricultural sector, with the result that there is no remaining latitude for the parties to an agreement to argue that their agreement will have this effect[19]. In *Bloemenveilingen Aalsmeer*[20] the Commission rejected an argument that exclusive dealing agreements between auctioneers and flower traders in respect of live plants and floricultural products could advance the objectives of Article 33. It published a decision to this effect, not only as the rules in question were the subject of litigation in the Dutch courts, but also as similar rules were being applied by other auction houses[1]. In *Scottish Salmon Board*[2] the Commission rejected an argument that the Board's conduct was permissible as the industry was in economic difficulties; the Commission's view was that, if this was so, Community initiatives should be taken to deal with the problem: it was not for the parties themselves to take action which was unlawful under Article 81. In *Sicasov*[3] the Commission held that an agreement for the licensing of seeds was not necessary for the attainment of the objectives in Article 33[4].

(E)   Procedure

Article 2(2) of Regulation 26/62 confers sole power on the Commission to determine the applicability of Article 2(1), subject to review by the Community Courts. However the ECJ has held in the *Dijkstra* cases[5], and in *Oude Luttikhuis v Coberco*[6], that it is possible for a national court to apply Article 81(1) to agreements where it is satisfied that the Commission would not permit a derogation pursuant to Regulation 26/62. Agreements which may fall within the derogations from the application of Article 81(1) provided for in Article 2(1) of Regulation 26/62 do not enjoy the benefit of provisional validity[7].

---

18   Case 71/74 [1975] ECR 563, [1975] 2 CMLR 123.
19   See eg *Cauliflowers* OJ [1978] L 21/23, [1978] 1 CMLR D66; *Milchförderungsfonds* OJ [1985] L 35/35, [1985] 3 CMLR 101.
20   OJ [1988] L 262/27, [1989] 4 CMLR 500.
1   Ibid, para 168.
2   OJ [1992] L 246/37, [1993] 5 CMLR 602, para 22.
3   OJ [1999] L 14/27, [1999] 4 CMLR 192.
4   Ibid, para 68.
5   Cases C-319/93 etc *Dijkstra v Friesland Coöperatie* [1995] ECR I-4471, [1996] 5 CMLR 178, paras 25-36.
6   Case C-399/93 [1995] ECR I-4515, [1996] 5 CMLR 178, para 30.
7   Cases C-319/93 etc *Dijkstra v Friesland Coöperatie* [1995] ECR I-4471, [1996] 5 CMLR 178, paras 21-24; on provisional validity see ch 8, pp 262-263.

5. TRANSPORT[8]

The EC Treaty contains special provisions on transport in Articles 70 to 80 (ex Articles 74 to 84). Article 80(1) provides that these provisions are applicable to road, rail and inland waterway transport; Article 80(2) provides that the Council of Ministers may decide on appropriate measures for the sea and air transport sectors. Thus the Treaty itself recognises a distinction between these two categories, the difficulty being that the latter are subject to numerous international arrangements and are of particular political sensitivity. Articles 81 and 82 do apply to the transport sector (including air transport[9]), but Council Regulation 141/62[10] provided that Regulation 17/62, which gave the Commission the necessary powers to implement the competition rules, did not apply to transport. Since then the procedural lacuna left by Regulation 141/62 has been filled in three stages: first, Council Regulation 1017/68[11] adopted specific provisions on the application of the competition rules to transport by road, rail and inland waterway; secondly, Council Regulation 4056/86[12] provided the Commission with powers in the maritime transport sector; lastly came Council Regulation 3975/87[13] to deal with air transport. Notifications in all transport sectors must be made in the form prescribed by Commission Regulation 2843/98[14].

(A) Road, rail and inland waterways[15]

(i) Legislative régime

Council Regulation 1017/68 contains detailed provisions, both substantive and procedural, on the application of the competition rules in this sector. After lengthy recitals which express the Council's policy, the Regulation deals with prohibitions, exemptions, the abuse of a dominant position and with procedural matters such as the gathering of information, professional secrecy and the imposition of fines. A series of Council Directives have been published to open up the rail sector to competition[16], although the development of a single market in rail transport has been slow to develop[17]. The rail sector is subject to a complex regulatory régime

---

8   On the common transport policy of the Community generally see Kapteyn and VerLoren van Themaat *Introduction to the Law of the European Communities* (Kluwer Law International, 3rd ed, 1998, ed Gormley) pp 1172-1207.
9   See Cases 209/84 etc *Ministère Public v Asjes* [1986] ECR 1425, [1986] 3 CMLR 173.
10 OJ (Sp edn, 1959-62) 291.
11 OJ (Sp edn, 1968) 302.
12 OJ [1986] L 378/4, [1989] 4 CMLR 461.
13 OJ [1987] L 374/1, [1988] 4 CMLR 222.
14 OJ [1998] L 334/22, [1999] 4 CMLR 236; see ch 4, pp 138-139.
15 See further Maltby, Soames and Farquharson in ch 3 of Div IX of *Butterworths Competition Law* (eds Freeman and Whish), Parts D, E and F; *Bellamy and Child* ch 15, Part 2.
16 Council Directive 91/440/EEC on *Development of the Community's Railways*, OJ [1991] L 237/25; Council Directive 95/18/EC on *Licensing of Railway Undertakings*, OJ [1995] L 143/70; Council Directive 95/19 EC on *Allocation of Railway Infrastructure Capacity and the Charging of Infrastructure Fees*, OJ [1995] L 143/75.
17 See the Commission's XXXth *Annual Report on Competition Policy* (2000), points 198-199.

under UK law[18], and the Rail Regulator enjoys concurrent powers to apply the provisions of the Competition Act 1998 to this sector[19].

(ii)   Practical application of Regulation 1017/68

The Commission has adopted several decisions under Regulation 1017/68. In *EATE Levy*[20] it condemned an agreement between French waterway carriers and French forwarding agents imposing a levy of 10% on freight charges for boat charters to destinations outside France, as it discriminated in favour of French carriers. For this reason the agreement was also denied an exemption. The ECJ upheld the Commission on appeal[1]. In *Distribution of Railway Tickets by Travel Agents*[2] the Commission concluded that a circular of the Union des Chemins de Fer relating to railway tickets was not directly concerned with the provision of transport services, with the result that Regulation 17/62, rather than Regulation 1017/68, was the applicable procedural instrument[3]. However the CFI annulled the Commission's decision on the basis that it was wrong, and that the decision should have been adopted under Regulation 1017/68[4]. In *Tariff Structures in the Combined Transport of Goods*[5] the Commission granted exemption under Regulation 1017/68 to a tariff structure agreement between the rail companies of the EC on the sale of rail haulage in the international combined transport of goods. In *ACI*[6] the Commission granted exemption, subject to conditions, to the creation by British Railways Board, SNCF of France and Intercontainer CV of a joint venture company, Allied Continental Intermodal Services, to market intermodal rail services through the Channel Tunnel.

In *European Night Services*[7] the Commission granted individual exemption to a joint venture established by five rail operators to provide night sleeper services through the Channel Tunnel between a variety of cities in the UK and continental Europe. The exemption was granted subject to conditions and obligations to which the parents of the joint venture objected and for a period of time, 10 years, which they considered to be too short, given the level of risk that they were undertaking. In *European Night Services v Commission*[8] the CFI held

---

18   See Maltby, Soames and Farquharson in ch 3 of Div IX of *Butterworths Competition Law* (eds Freeman and Whish), paras [804]-[838].

19   On concurrency under the Competition Act 1998 see ch 10, p 357; see also the draft Guideline *The Competition Act 1998: The Application of the Competition Act to Railway Services* (OFT 430).

20   OJ [1985] L 219/35, [1988] 4 CMLR 698.

1   Case 272/85 *ANTIB v Commission* [1987] ECR 2201, [1988] 4 CMLR 677.

2   OJ [1992] L 366/47.

3   Ibid, paras 47–59.

4   Case T-14/93 *Union Internationale des Chemins de Fer v Commission* [1995] ECR II-1503, [1996] 5 CMLR 40; the Commission's appeal against this judgment was rejected in Case C-264/95 P *Commission v Union Internationale des Chemins de Fer* [1997] ECR I-1287, [1997] 5 CMLR 49.

5   OJ [1993] L 73/38.

6   OJ [1994] L 224/28.

7   OJ [1994] L 259/21, [1995] 5 CMLR 76.

8   Cases T-374/94 etc [1998] ECR II-3141, [1998] 5 CMLR 718; see similarly the Commission's decision in *Eurotunnel* OJ [1994] L 354/66, [1995] 4 CMLR 801: the Commission had granted exemption to the operating agreement for the Tunnel, but its decision was annulled on appeal by the CFI in Cases T-79/95 and T-80/95 *SNCF v Commission* [1996] ECR II-1491, [1997] 4 CMLR 334 since the Commission had failed to demonstrate that the agreement would be restrictive of competition; for the eventual outcome of this case, see the Commission's XXIXth *Annual Report on Competition Policy* (1999), p 163.

that the Commission had abjectly failed to demonstrate that the agreement between the rail operators had the effect of restricting actual and/or potential competition, with the consequence that its decision should be annulled; the CFI went further, holding that, even if there was an appreciable effect on competition, the Commission had failed to demonstrate that the exemption should be subject to the conditions and obligations imposed or should be granted for such a short period[9].

In *HOV SVZ/MCN*[10] the Commission imposed a fine on Deutsche Bahn of EUR 11 million for imposing discriminatory rail transport tariffs for the inland carriage of sea-borne containers to and from Germany, depending on whether they were shipped through German ports on the one hand or Belgian and Dutch ones on the other. The decision was upheld on appeal to the CFI[11], and the ECJ ruled that Deutsche Bahn's appeal to it was inadmissible[12].

(B) Maritime transport[13]

(i) Legislative régime

Council Regulation 4056/86[14] contains detailed provisions, both substantive and procedural, on the application of the competition rules to the maritime transport sector. Article 1(2) provides that the Regulation shall apply only to international maritime transport services from or to one or more Community ports, other than tramp vessel services; the latter are defined in Article 1(3). The jurisdictional reach of Regulation 4056/86 is interesting: in air transport, the relevant implementing Regulation applies only to transport *between* Community airports, although it includes flights *within* a single Member State[15]; the maritime transport Regulation applies to services from or to a Community port, but would not apply to services within a Member State as they would not be international.

Article 2 provides that agreements that are purely technical do not infringe Article 81(1); the Commission has consistently construed this provision narrowly[16]. Articles 3 and 4 provide block exemption, subject to conditions, for 'liner conferences', that is to say agreements between carriers concerning the operation of scheduled maritime transport services; uniquely, this block exemption permits horizontal price fixing. An unusual feature of Regulation 4056/86 is that the block exemption is conferred by a Council Regulation: all other block exemptions have been granted by the Commission acting under powers conferred upon it by the Council[17].

The Commission was given power by Council Regulation 479/92[18] to grant block exemption to some shipping consortia; in 1995 it adopted Regulation 870/

9   For further comment on this case see ch 3, pp 94-95 and 103.
10   OJ [1994] L 104/34.
11   Case T-229/94 *Deutsche Bahn AG v Commission* [1997] ECR II-1689, [1998] 4 CMLR 220.
12   Case C-436/97 [1999] ECR I-2387, [1999] 5 CMLR 776.
13   See further Maltby, Soames and Farquharson in ch 3 of Div IX of *Butterworths Competition Law* (eds Whish and Freeman, 1991), Part C; Ortiz Blanco and van Houtte *EC Competition Law in the Transport Sector* (Clarendon Press Oxford, 1996) ch 4; Power *EC Shipping Law* (LLP, 2nd ed, 1998) chs 9-12; *Bellamy and Child* ch 15, Part 3.
14   OJ [1986] L 378/4, [1989] 4 CMLR 461.
15   See pp 864-865 below.
16   See eg *French-West African Shipowners' Committees* OJ [1992] L 134/1, [1993] 5 CMLR 446.
17   See ch 4, pp 141-144.
18   OJ [1992] L 55/3, [1994] 5 CMLR 192.

95[19], which was replaced in 2000, following the publication of a report on its operation[20], by Regulation 823/2000[1].

(ii)   Practical application of Regulation 4056/86

The relationship between the Commission and certain operators in the maritime transport sector has not been particularly harmonious. In the relatively short period that Regulation 4056/86 has been in effect there have been a number of decisions in which the Commission has found infringements of Articles 81 and 82, and in *Trans-Atlantic Conference Agreement* it imposed the largest fine in a single decision to date[2]. The first fine in this sector was imposed in *Secrétama*[3], for supplying incorrect information in response to a request for information by the Commission under Article 16(3) of Regulation 4056/86. The Commission also imposed fines of EUR 5,000 on *Ukwal*[4] and EUR 4,000 on *Mewac*[5] for failing to submit to investigations under Article 18 of Regulation 4056/86.

The first decision of the Commission imposing a fine for a substantive infringement of Articles 81 and 82 in the maritime transport sector was *French-West African Shipowners' Committees*[6]. The Commission considered that the Committees had cartelised the entire trade in liner cargo between France and various West African ports; quotas had been established and procedures established to ensure compliance. The offences arose both under Article 81 and under the concept of collective dominance in Article 82. The result of the practices was to exclude third parties from the trade. Various defences (for example that the agreements were 'technical' under Article 2 of Regulation 4056/86, that the block exemption under Article 3 was applicable and that the Committees were subject to 'state compulsion'[7]), were rejected. In fixing the level of the fines, which exceeded EUR 15 million, the Commission noted that usually when it applies the competition rules in new circumstances it proceeds with moderation; on this occasion however it saw no reason for moderation, since the parties were well aware of the illegality of their conduct and that the block exemption in Regulation 4056/86 was unavailable[8]. In *Cewal*[9] the Commission imposed fines totalling EUR 10.1 million on members of a liner conference, Cewal, for abusing their collective dominant position by taking action designed to eliminate their principal independent competitors, for example by offering lower freight rates and by offering loyalty rebates. The Commission's finding of collective dominance and its condemnation of the abusive practices was upheld both by the CFI[10] and

---

19   OJ [1995] L 89/7, [1995] 5 CMLR 107.
20   Working Paper of DG IV, 28 January 1999, available at http://europa.eu.int/comm/ competition/antitrust/others/.
1   OJ [2000] L 100/24, [2000] 5 CMLR 92; see the Commission's XXXth *Annual Report on Competition Policy* (2000), points 192-196.
2   See p 863 below.
3   OJ [1991] L 35/23, [1992] 5 CMLR 76.
4   OJ [1992] L 121/45, [1993] 5 CMLR 632.
5   OJ [1993] L 20/6, [1994] 5 CMLR 275.
6   OJ [1992] L 134/1, [1993] 5 CMLR 446.
7   See ch 3, pp 104-105.
8   OJ [1992] L 134/1, [1993] 5 CMLR 446, para 74(g).
9   OJ [1993] L 34/20, [1995] 5 CMLR 198; the treatment of collective dominance in this case is discussed in ch 14, pp 478-479, and the condemnation of the lower freight rates is discussed in ch 18, pp 655-657.
10   Cases T–24/93 *Compagnie Maritime Belge NV v Commission* [1996] ECR II-1201, [1997] 4 CMLR 273.

the ECJ[11], although the fines on the appellants were annulled by the ECJ for procedural reasons.

In *TAA*[12] and in *FEFC*[13] the Commission prohibited price fixing in relation to the land-leg of combined transport operations; even though Council Regulation 4056/86 confers block exemption on price fixing in relation to the maritime element of the transportation of containers, the Commission does not consider that this should extend to the non-maritime part of a journey. The Commission imposed a fine in *Ferry Operators*[14] on five ferry operators who colluded with one another in order to overcome difficulties experienced in currency fluctuations following the devaluation of the pound sterling in September 1992. In *Europe Asia Trades Agreement*[15] the Commission held that agreements not to use capacity and to exchange information infringed Article 81(1) and were ineligible for exemption under Article 81(3). In *Trans-Atlantic Conference Agreement*[16] the Commission imposed fines totalling EUR 273 million for abusing a collective dominant position contrary to Article 82 by altering the competitive structure of the market and by placing restrictions on the availability and contents of service contracts. In *Greek Ferries*[17] the Commission imposed fines of EUR 9.12 for fixing ferry prices between Italy and Greece. In *Far East Trade and Tariff and Surcharges Agreement*[18] it imposed fines totalling EUR 6.932 million where the parties to the agreement in question had agreed not to discount from their published tariffs.

On a less hostile note, in *P&O Stena Line*[19] the Commission granted an exemption for three years to a joint venture to provide short cross-channel ferry services between the UK and France and Belgium. In 2001 the Commission renewed this exemption for a period of six years[20]. The Commission was aware that there were some anxieties about price rises, but considered that they were understandable as the market adjusted to more normal competitive conditions following the abolition of duty-free sales on ferry crossings, as new capacity was absorbed and as fuel prices rose.

11 Cases C-395/96 and C-396/96 P, [2000] 4 CMLR 1076.
12 OJ [1994] L 376/1, on appeal to the CFI Cases T-395/94 etc *Atlantic Container Line* (judgment pending).
13 OJ [1994] L 378/17, on appeal to the CFI Case T-86/95 etc *Compagnie Générale Maritime v Commission* (judgment pending).
14 OJ [1997] L 26/23, [1997] 4 CMLR 798.
15 OJ [1999] L 193/23, [1999] 5 CMLR 1380.
16 OJ [1999] L 95/1, [1999] 4 CMLR 1415, on appeal to the CFI Case T-191/98 *Atlantic Container Line v Commission* (judgment pending).
17 OJ [1999] L 109/24, [1999] 5 CMLR 47, on appeal to the CFI Cases T-56/99 etc *Marlines v Commission* (judgment pending).
18 OJ [2000] L 268/1, [2000] 5 CMLR 1011, on appeal to the CFI Case T-213/00 *CMA v Commission* (judgment pending).
19 OJ [1999] L 163/61, [1999] 5 CMLR 682; see further the table at para [574] of ch 3 of Div IX of *Butterworths Competition Law* for details of several other cooperation agreements in the maritime transport sector to which the Commission has given its approval; see also the Commission's XXVIth *Report on Competition Policy* (1996), points 84-87; and the XXVIIth *Report on Competition Policy* (1997), points 81-84 and pp 134-138.
20 Commission Press Release IP/01/806, 7 June 2001.

(C)   Air transport[1]

(i)   Legislative régime

A number of measures have been adopted in order to liberalise air transport in the Community. In the first liberalisation package of 1987 the Council of Ministers adopted a Directive on fares for scheduled air services between Member States[2] and a Decision on the sharing of passenger capacity between Member States[3]. The 1987 package[4] was regarded as a first step towards the completion of the internal market in air transport. In 1990 Regulation 2343/90[5] on access for air carriers to scheduled intra-Community routes was adopted. In 1991 the Council adopted Regulation 249/91[6] on air cargo services between Member States and Regulation 295/91 on compensation to passengers denied boarding ('bumped off') in air transport. In 1992 a further liberalisation package was adopted. Regulation 2407/92[7] dealt with the licensing of air carriers. Regulation 2408/92[8] provides that all Community carriers should have access to intra-Community routes (cabotage). Regulation 2409/92[9], which replaced Regulation 2342/90, provides that Community air carriers shall freely set their own fares. Regulation 95/93[10] establishes common rules for the allocation of slots at Community airports in order to ensure that they are made available on a neutral, transparent and non-discriminatory basis. Council Regulation 2299/89/EEC established a *Code of Conduct for Computerised Reservation Systems*[11]. The ground-handling sector was liberalised to allow greater access to the market by Directive 96/97[12]. Despite the liberalisation measures so far adopted, there remain serious impediments to free competition in air transport markets. The lack of slots at premier airports itself distorts the market, as do the bilateral agreements that still exist between individual Member States and third countries governing access to air space. Further measures are needed before the sector can be fully competitive, and proposals are under consideration for the establishment of a 'Single European Sky'[13] and for a Transatlantic Common Aviation Area.

---

1   See further Maltby, Soames and Farquharson in ch 3 of Div IX of *Butterworths Competition Law* (eds Whish and Freeman, 1991), Part B; Adkins *Air Transport and EC Competition Law* (Sweet & Maxwell, 1994); Balfour *European Community Air Law* (Butterworths, 1995) chs 16-21; Ortiz Blanco and van Houtte *EC Competition Law in the Transport Sector* (Clarendon Press Oxford, 1996) ch 5; Goh *European Air Transport Law and Competition* (John Wiley & Sons, 1997); *Bellamy and Child* ch 15, Part 4.
2   Council Directive 87/601/EEC, OJ [1987] L 374/12.
3   Council Decision 87/602/EEC, OJ [1987] L 374/19.
4   The package is helpfully summarised in the Commission's XVIIth *Annual Report on Competition Policy* (1987), points 43–45.
5   OJ [1990] L 217/8.
6   OJ [1991] L 36/1, as amended by Regulation 2408/92/EEC.
7   OJ [1992] L 240/1.
8   OJ [1992] L 240/8; on the application of Regulation 2408/92 see Case T-260/94 *Air Inter v Commission* [1997] ECR II-997, [1997] 5 CMLR 851.
9   OJ [1992] L 240/15.
10   OJ [1993] L 14/1.
11   OJ [1989] L 220/1, as amended by Council Regulations 3089/93/EEC, OJ [1993] L 278/1, and 323/99/EC; a fine of EUR 10,000 was imposed under this Regulation in the case of *Lufthansa*: Commission Press Release IP/99/542, 20 July 1999.
12   OJ [1996] L 272/56.
13   See the final report of the so-called High-Level Group, http://europa.eu.int/comm/transport/library/hlg-final-report-en.pdf.

Council Regulation 3975/87[14] confers power on the Commission to enforce the competition rules in the air transport sector. Article 1(2), as amended by Regulation 2410/92[15], provides that the Regulation applies to air transport services between Community airports. Air transport between Community airports and third countries is not covered by Regulation 3975/87, and can therefore be investigated only under the procedure provided for in Articles 84 and 85 (ex Articles 88 and 89) of the EC Treaty[16]. The Commission's investigation of the proposed alliance between British Airways and American Airlines was conducted under Articles 84 and 85, since it was concerned predominantly with air transport between the UK and the US, and the Commission has investigated several other alliances on the basis of these provisions rather than under the procedures established by Regulation 3975/87[17]. Regulation 1284/91[18] introduced a 'fast-track' procedure for the grant of interim measures in the air transport sector[19].

Council Regulation 3976/87[20] gave the Commission power to publish block exemptions in respect of certain types of agreement; Regulation 2411/92[1] amended Regulation 3976/87 to confer wider powers on the Commission to adopt block exemptions. There is one block exemption in force in the air transport sector, for passenger transit consultations and slot allocation[2]; it has been extended in force until 30 June 2002[3].

(ii)   Practical application of Regulation 3975/87

The Commission has applied Regulation 3975/87 to some cooperation agreements in the air transport sector, for example in the case of *Lufthansa/SAS*[4] and *Finnair/Maersk*[5]; however investigations of airline alliances involving routes to airports outside the Community have to be conducted under Articles 84 and 85 EC for the reasons explained above. The proposed joint venture in *Alitalia/KLM*[6] was regarded by the Commission as a full-function joint venture, even though the parties did not create a corporate vehicle for the cooperation, and was therefore dealt with under the ECMR[7]. The Commission has cleared several concentrations

---

14   OJ [1987] L 374/1, [1988] 4 CMLR 222; as to whether the Commission should proceed under Regulation 17/62 or Regulation 3975/87 see Case T-128/98 *Aéroports de Paris v Commission* [2001] 4 CMLR 1376, paras 34-58.

15   OJ [1992] L 240/18.

16   See further ch 7, pp 216-217; for the use of these provisions specifically in relation to air transport prior to the adoption of Regulation 3975/87, see Cases 209/84 etc *Ministère Public v Asjes* [1986] ECR 1425, [1986] 3 CMLR 173; Case 66/86 *Ahmed Saeed Flugreisen v Zentrale zur Bekämpfung Unlauteren Wettbewerbs* [1989] ECR 803, [1990] 4 CMLR 102.

17   See the Commission's *Annual Report on Competition Policy* (1996), points 99-101; XXVIIth *Annual Report on Competition Policy* (1997), points 86-92; and the XXVIIIth *Annual Report on Competition Policy* (1998), points 101-104.

18   OJ [1991] L 122/2.

19   See ch 7, p 229.

20   OJ [1988] L 374/9, [1988] 4 CMLR 235; this Regulation was slightly amended by Regulation 2344/90, OJ [1990] L 217/15.

1   OJ [1992] L 240/19.

2   Regulation 1617/93, OJ [1993] L 155/18, as amended by Regulations 1523/96/EC and 1083/99/EC: see ch 4, pp 143.

3   Commission Regulation 1324/2000, OJ [2001] L 177/56.

4   OJ [1996] L 54/28, [1996] 4 CMLR 845; see Crocioni 'The *Lufthansa/SAS* Case: Did the Commission Get the Economics Right?' (1998) 19 ECLR 116.

5   See the Commission's XXVIIIth *Annual Report on Competition Policy* (1998), pp 146-147.

6   Case No COMP/JV.19.

7   See ch 21, p 751.

under the ECMR[8]. The Commission sent a warning letter to Swissair, Sabena, TAP, AOM and Crossair in 2000 in relation to suspected coordination of fares; as the parties discontinued the practices to which the Commission objected, formal proceedings were not initiated[9].

6. REGULATED INDUSTRIES

(A)   Demonopolisation, liberalisation and privatisation

One of the most dramatic economic developments in the final two decades of the twentieth century was the demonopolisation and liberalisation of industries which for many years had been the preserve of state-owned monopolies; in many cases this process was coupled with privatisation or partial privatisation of state-owned undertakings[10]. Obvious examples are the so-called 'utilities' such as telecommunications, gas, electricity and water. The problems for competition policy that arise where former monopolists are 'released' into the free market are obvious: in so far as there is no effective competition, which is particularly likely to be the case in the early years, they may be able to charge excessive prices; and they may also be able to adopt tactics intended to preclude new competitors from entering the market. At the same time it is necessary to ensure that former monopolists provide adequate services of an appropriate standard. A complicating factor is that utilities are often subject to a requirement that they comply with a 'universal service obligation', for example a duty to undertake the daily delivery of letters or to maintain an electricity or water supply to business and residential premises. Undertakings that are subject to a universal service obligation of this kind may need some immunity from competition so that they can make sufficient profits to enable them to perform it, which is why, for example, postal operators such as Consignia in the UK (formerly the Post Office) are given a legal monopoly over the delivery of letters of less than a certain weight and size[11].

(B)   Regulatory systems in the UK for utilities

In the UK detailed regulatory régimes have been established for the industries that were privatised in the 1980s and 1990s, namely telecommunications, gas, electricity, water and the rail transport sector; these régimes provide, *inter alia*, for price control where persistent market power means that the normal process of competition will not deliver competitive prices to consumers[12]. The regulators – the Director General of Telecommunications, the Gas and Electricity Markets Authority, the Director General of Water Services and the Rail Regulator – act

---

8   See eg Case No COMP/M.2041 *United Airlines/US Airways*, 12 January 2001, where the Commission required the divestiture of some slots at Frankfurt and Munich airports as a condition of clearance.

9   See the Commission's XXXth *Annual Report on Competition Policy* (2000), point 180.

10   On privatisation see Vickers and Yarrow *Privatisation and Economic Analysis* (MIT Press, 1987); Veljanowski *Selling the State – Privatisation in Britain* (Weidenfeld and Nicolson, 1987); *Privatisation and Competition: A Market Prospectus* (Hobart Paperback 28, 1988, ed Veljanowski); Graham and Prosser *Privatising Public Enterprises* (Oxford University Press, 1991).

11   On the permitted 'reserved area' for letters under EC law, see pp below.

12   See generally Armstrong, Cowan and Vickers *Regulatory Reform: Economic Analysis and British Experience* (MIT Press, 1994); *Competition in Regulation Industries* (Oxford University

as a surrogate for competition, at least until effective competition develops, by imposing constraints on what the regulated undertakings can do; the regulators are charged with the responsibility of protecting consumers, promoting competition where possible and controlling prices. In a sense, regulators 'hold the fort' until competition arrives. Regulated undertakings operate subject to licences that impose obligations upon them and that attempt to prevent conduct, *inter alia*, that will be anti-competitive, discriminatory or exploitative. The regulators monitor these licences and have powers to enforce compliance with them; in the event of disputes with regulated undertakings as to the appropriate terms for inclusion in a licence, the regulators can make a so-called 'modification reference' to the reporting side of the Competition Commission[13]. The regulators also have concurrent powers, with the Director General of Fair Trading, to apply the Chapter I and Chapter II prohibitions in the Competition Act 1998 in the sectors for which they are responsible[14].

(C) Price caps

A particular problem in the regulated industries is the control of prices. A central proposition of competition policy is that price should be determined by the market, and not by the state or an agency of the state. Competition authorities take action against excessive prices only rarely[15]. However where there is monopoly or near-monopoly, in particular in relation to essential services such as voice telephony or the supply of electricity, price control may be necessary; where this is the case, various techniques can be deployed to determine what the price should be. One method of capping prices is to fix an upper limit on the rate of return permissible on the capital invested in an industry: this, however, may encourage regulated bodies to over–invest, in order to expand the base on which profit can be earned; furthermore this technique does nothing to encourage efficiency. In the UK, the price control function has therefore been exercised through the 'RPI minus X' formula: regulated undertakings are allowed to increase their prices only by the increase in the Resale Prices Index *less* a particular percentage as fixed by the relevant regulator[16]. Over a period of time this formula leads to a reduction in prices in real terms, thereby benefiting the consumer and forcing the privatised industries to increase efficiency in order to continue in profit. The 'RPI minus X' formula encourages firms to become more efficient since, if they can cut their costs, they will make a higher profit. A further benefit of the 'RPI minus X' formula is that it is relatively simple to apply: the regulator simply sets the figure, after which all that is necessary is to check that the price is not being exceeded. When deciding the value of X for the purpose of 'RPI minus X', the industry regulator is asked, in effect, to determine the extent to which added efficiency is possible within the industry in question.

Press, 1998, eds Helm and Jenkinson); Baldwin and Cave *Understanding Regulation: Theory, Strategy and Practice* (Oxford University Press, 1999), in particular chs 14-18.
13 For recent examples of modification references see *Cellnet and Vodafone* 011 5154590 and *British Telecommunications* 011 5154504 (21 January 1999); *AES and British Energy* CC No 453 (31 January 2001); summaries of these reports can be found at http://www.competition-commission.gov.uk/.
14 On concurrency under the Competition Act 1998 see ch 10, p 357.
15 See ch 18, pp 633-639.
16 See generally *Incentive Regulation: Reviewing RPI-X and Promoting Competition* (Centre for the Study of Regulated Industries, 1992); Spring 'An Investigation of RPI–X Price Cap Regulation using British Gas as a Case–study' (CRI 1992); Cave and Mill 'Cost Allocation in Regulated Industries' (CRI 1992).

(D)   EC law and the liberalisation of markets

In the EC considerable steps have been taken towards the liberalisation of utilities and the development of a single market, albeit with greater success in some sectors than in others. Directives have been adopted in the case of telecommunications, post and energy markets with a view to creating conditions in which competitive markets develop. At the same time the European Commission has been adapting the principles of competition law and applying them to these sectors; in particular the so-called 'essential facilities doctrine' may play an important rôle in enabling third parties to gain access to physical infrastructures where this is necessary for the provision of competitive services[17].

In the text that follows relevant provisions of EC and UK law will be briefly discussed, so that the reader has an idea of the regulatory environment of the telecommunications, post, energy and water markets and of the possible application of competition law to them. However the text is intended as a mere introduction to subject-matter that is substantial and complex; references to more detailed literature will be provided where appropriate.

7.   TELECOMMUNICATIONS[18]

(A)   EC law

(i)   Legislation

There are two 'streams' of Directives of relevance to the telecommunications sector. The first consists of Directives adopted by the Council of Ministers and the European Parliament under Article 95 EC (ex Article 100a) to bring about harmonisation necessary for the establishment of an internal market[19]. The Commission has also published a Recommendation in relation to interconnection

---

17 See ch 17, pp 611-624 on the essential facilities doctrine, noting the need, discussed there, to impose constraints upon it; these constraints are not so important where a facility was developed by a state-owned monopolist as opposed to an undertaking operating in the private sector.

18 See further Crowther in ch 8 of Div IX of *Butterworths Competition Law* (eds Freeman and Whish); Ungerer 'EU Competition Law in the Telecommunications, Media and Information Technology Sectors' [1995] Fordham Corporate Law Institute (ed Hawk), ch 24; Long *Telecommunications Law and Practice* (Sweet & Maxwell, 2nd ed, 1995); Gillies and Marshall *Telecommunications Law* (Butterworths, 1997) ch 10; Faull and Nikpay *The EC Law of Competition* (Oxford University Press, 1999) ch 11; Larouche *Competition Law and Regulation in European Telecommunications* (Hart Publishing, 2000); Garzaniti *Telecommunications, Broadcasting and the Internet: EU Competition Law and Regulation* (Sweet & Maxwell, 2000); Bellamy and Child, ch 14; Ungerer 'Use of Competition Rules in the Liberalisation of the European Union's Telecommunications Sector: Assessment of Past Experience and Some Conclusions' Commission's Competition Policy Newsletter, June 2001, p 16; for a review of telecommunications laws in the EC and also in each Member State, as well as in some non-Member States, see Baker & McKenzie's *Telecommunications Laws in Europe* (Butterworths, 4th ed, 1998, ed Scherer).

19 See the *ONP Framework Directive*, Directive 90/387/EEC, OJ [1990] L 192/9, amended by Directive 97/51/EC, OJ [1997] L 295/23; the *Leased Lines Directive*, Directive 92/44/EEC, OJ [1992] L 165/27, amended by Directive 97/51/EC, OJ [1997] L 295/23; the *ONP Directive*, Directive 95/62/EC, OJ [1995] L 321/6, amended by Directive 98/10 EC, OJ [1998] L 101/24; the *Licensing Directive*, Directive 97/13/EC, OJ [1997] L 117/15; the *Interconnection Directive*, Directive 97/33/EC, OJ [1997] L 199/32; and the *Number Portability and Carrier Pre-selection Directive*, Directive 98/61/EC, OJ [1998] L 268/37.

issues, Part 1 of which deals with *Interconnection Pricing*[20] and Part 2 with *Accounting Separation and Cost Accounting*[1]. In 2000 the Council and Parliament adopted a Regulation on *Unbundled Access to the Local Loop*[2]. The Commission reports each year to the Council, the Parliament, ECOSOC and the Committee of the Regions on progress achieved in implementing the Community's telecommunications policy[3]. In March 2001 the Commission produced a Working Document on a *Proposed New Regulatory Framework for Electronic Communications Networks and Services*, together with draft guidelines on *Market Analysis and the Calculation of Significant Market Power*[4].

The second stream consists of Directives adopted by the Commission pursuant to Article 86(3) EC (ex Article 90(3))[5]. The first of these was the *Telecommunications Terminal Equipment Directive* of 1988[6], which required Member States to withdraw special or exclusive rights granted to undertakings with respect to the importation, marketing, connection and bringing into service of telecommunications terminal equipment and the maintenance of such equipment. The Commission subsequently adopted the *Telecommunications Services Directive* of 1990[7], which began the process of opening up telecommunications markets themselves to competition. The Services Directive has been amended several times in order to expand its scope; it was successively extended to apply to the satellite[8], cable[9] and mobile telephony[10] sectors, and ultimately required full competition in telecommunications markets[11]. The Commission has also amended the original *Services Directive* to require that, where a single operator owns both a telecommunications and a cable network, they must be established as separate legal entities[12].

(ii) Application of EC competition law

The Commission has been active in applying the competition rules to the telecommunications sector for many years. In 1991 it published *Guidelines on*

20 OJ [1998] L 73/42; see also the Commission's *Communication on Interconnection Pricing in a Liberalised Telecommunications Market* OJ [1998] C 84/3.
1 OJ [1998] L 141/6.
2 Regulation 2887/2000/EC, OJ [2000] L 336/00; on the issue of the local loop, see Nikolinakos 'Promoting Competition in the Local Access Network: Local Loop Unbundling' (2001) 22 ECLR 266.
3 See eg the Sixth Report, COM(2000) 814, 7 December 2000; the Commission's *Annual Report on Competition Policy* also discusses progress in liberalising telecommunications markets: see eg the XXVIIIth Report (1998), points 75-78; the XXIXth Report (1999), points 65-72; and the XXXth Report (2000), points 144-154.
4 COM(2001) 175, 28 March 2001; these can be accessed at http://europa.eu.int/comm/competition/liberalization/legislation/#telecom_guidelines.
5 On the Commission's powers to adopt directives under Article 86(3) see ch 6, pp 208-210.
6 Commission Directive 88/301/EEC, OJ [1988] L 131/73, [1991] 4 CMLR 922; on the (mostly unsuccessful) challenge to this Directive, see Case C-202/88 *France v Commission* [1991] ECR I-1223, [1992] 5 CMLR 552, and for comment see Naftel 'The Natural Death of a Natural Monopoly' (1993) 14 ECLR 105; on France's failure to implement the Directive correctly see Case C-91/94 *Tranchant v Telephone Store* [1995] ECR I-3911, [1997] 4 CMLR 74.
7 Commission Directive 90/388/EEC, OJ [1990] L 192/10, [1991] 4 CMLR 932; this Directive was unsuccessfully challenged in Cases C–271/90 etc *Spain, Belgium and Italy v Commission* [1992] ECR I-5833, [1993] 4 CMLR 110.
8 Commission Directive 94/46/EC, OJ [1994] L 268/15.
9 Commission Directive 95/51/EC, OJ [1995] L 256/49.
10 Commission Directive 92/1/EC, OJ [1996] L 20/59.
11 Commission Directive 96/19/EC, OJ [1996] L 74/13.
12 Commission Directive 99/64/EC, [1999] L 175/39.

the Application of EEC Competition Rules in the Telecommunications Sector[13], and in 1998 it adopted the *Notice on the Application of the Competition Rules to Access Agreements in the Telecommunications Sector*[14]. The latter of these two instruments is of particular interest. Part I is entitled 'Framework', and discusses the relationship between the competition rules and sector-specific regulation. Part II deals with market definition, and Part III provides detailed analysis of the application of the principles of competition law to access agreements; the most extensive discussion is of the essential facilities doctrine under Article 82, but the Notice also contains useful guidance on issues such as network configuration, tying, excessive pricing, predation, vertical price squeezing and discrimination.

The Commission has adopted numerous decisions such as *BT/MCI*[15], *Atlas*[16], *Iridium*[17], *Phoenix/GlobalOne*[18], *Uniworld*[19], *Unisource*[20], *Cégétel*[1] and *Télécom Developpement*[2] granting clearance and/or individual exemption under Article 81(3) to strategic alliances in the telecommunications sector. It has also approved the *GSM MoU Standard International Roaming Agreement*, which enables GSM mobile telephone users in one country to use the network in another country[3]. Acting under Article 82 in conjunction with Article 86, the Commission took action against Italy and Spain as a result of their discriminatory treatment of the second operators of mobile telephony in those countries[4]; and in 1998 it initiated action in relation to possible excessive or discriminatory prices for calls to mobile telephones[5]. In 1999 the Commission launched an inquiry under Article 12 of Regulation 17/62 into three issues, leased lines, mobile roaming services and the local loop: this was only the third occasion on which the Commission has initiated an investigation under this provision[6].

The Commission has investigated many concentrations in the telecommunications sector under the ECMR. Of particular interest was *Telia/Telenor*[7], where the Commission granted conditional clearance, following a Phase II investigation, to a proposed concentration between the public telecommunications operators of Sweden and Norway; having received the clearance, the parties decided not to proceed with the transaction. The Commission also granted conditional clearance, following a Phase II investigation, to *WorldCom/MCI*[8]; in 2000, however, it prohibited the proposed concentration in *MCI WorldCom/Sprint*[9] which, in its view, would either have created a dominant position for the merged entity or would have reinforced the dominant

13   OJ [1991] C 233/2, [1991] 4 CMLR 946.
14   OJ [1998] C 265/2, [1998] 5 CMLR 821.
15   OJ [1994] L 223/36, [1995] 5 CMLR 285.
16   OJ [1996] L 239/29, [1997] 4 CMLR 89.
17   OJ [1997] L 16/87, [1997] 4 CMLR 1065.
18   OJ [1996] L 239/57, [1997] 4 CMLR 147.
19   OJ [1997] L 318/24, [1998] 4 CMLR 145.
20   OJ [1997] L 318/1, [1998] 4 CMLR 105; this decision was subsequently repealed due to changes in the market: Commission Press Release IP/01/1, 3 January 2001.
1   OJ [1999] L 218/14, [2000] 4 CMLR 106.
2   OJ [1999] L 218/24, [2000] 4 CMLR 124.
3   See the Commission's XXVIIth *Annual Report on Competition Policy* (1997), point 75 and pp 139-140.
4   See *Second Operator of GSM Radiotelephony in Italy* OJ [1995] L 280/49, [1996] 4 CMLR 700; *Second Operator of GSM Radiotelephony in Spain* OJ [1997] L 76/19.
5   See the Commission's XXVIIIth *Annual Report on Competition Policy* (1998), points 79-81.
6   See the Commission's XXIXth *Annual Report on Competition Policy* (1999), points 74-76; see further the XXXth Report (2000), points 157-160.
7   Case No IV/M.1439 OJ [2001] L 40/1, [2001] 4 CMLR 1226.
8   Case IV/M.1069, OJ [1999] L 116/1, [1999] 5 CMLR 876.
9   Case COMP/M.1741, on appeal Case T-310/00 *WorldCom v Commission* (judgment pending).

position of MCI WorldCom in the provision of 'top-level' or universal interconnectivity on the Internet.

(B) UK law

The Telecommunications Act 1984 established the office of Director General of Telecommunications and the regulatory framework for the telecommunications sector[9a]. The Director General of Telecommunications has concurrent powers with the Director General of Fair Trading to apply the Chapter I and Chapter II prohibitions in the Competition Act 1998. A Guideline has been adopted under the Act, *Competition Act 1998: The Application in the Telecommunications Sector*[10]. The *Guideline* is divided into seven parts. After an introduction and an explanation of the major provisions of the Act, the *Guideline* goes on to consider the relationship between the Competition Act and EC law. Part 4 of the *Guideline* discusses the relationship between the Competition Act and the Telecommunications Act and the Fair Trading Act 1973. Market definition and the assessment of market power are then considered. The *Guideline* concludes with a detailed discussion of how agreements and conduct in the telecommunications sector will be dealt with under the Competition Act; in particular it explains the approach that will be taken to determining costs in a network industry such as telecommunications[11]. The *Guideline* looks in detail at different pricing practices such as predation, price squeezing and discrimination[12], and it also deals with other types of abuse such as refusal to supply and bundling[13]. The Director General of Telecommunications adopted a decision in March 2001 that Avaya ECS Ltd had not infringed the Competition Act by failing to make interface information available about its telecommunications equipment[14]; and he concluded in May 2001 that BT's pricing for off-peak access to the Internet was not abusive[15].

8.   POST[16]

(A)   EC law

(i)   Legislation

Development of Community law and policy in the postal sector has come about partly through initiatives of the Community institutions, in particular the

---

9a A Bill will be introduced to allow the establishment of OFCOM (the Office of Communications), a single regulator for the media and communications industries: DTI Press Release P/2001/373, 13 July 2001.

10 OFT 417.

11 Ibid, paras 7.5-7.12.

12 Ibid, paras 7.13-7.37.

13 Ibid, paras 7.38-7.57.

14 See *Swan Solutions Ltd/Avaya ECS Ltd* (6 April 2001), available at http://www.oft.gov.uk/html/comp-act/case_register/swan.html.

15 See *BT Surf* (4 May 2001), available at http://www.oft.gov.uk/html/comp-act/case_register/bt.html.

16 On regulation and competition in the postal sector, see *Competition and Innovation in Postal Services* (Kluwer Academic Publishers, 1991, eds Crew and Kleindorfer); *Managing Change in the Postal and Delivery Industries* (Kluwer Academic Publishers, 1997, eds Crew and Kleindorfer); Griffiths 'Failing to Install Effective Competition in Postal Services – The Limited Impact of EC Law' (2000) 21 ECLR 399; see also the Commission's XXXth *Annual Report on Competition Policy* (2000), points 170-178.

Commission, and partly as a result of the very important judgment of the ECJ in the *Corbeau* case[17]. The Commission first began to take an interest in the postal sector, and the possibility of applying the competition rules to it, in the late 1980s. This culminated in the adoption of the Commission's Green Paper on *The Development of the Single Market for Postal Services* which was published on 13 May 1992. It proposed that all postal services, except ordinary internal letter deliveries, should be liberalised. In 1993 the Commission issued a communication setting out *Guidelines for the Development of Community Postal Services*[18]. The Council of Ministers asked the Commission to draft a proposal for a legislative framework; there are now two legislative instruments, the Directive of the European Parliament and of the Council on *Common Rules for the Development of the Internal Market of Community Postal Services and the Improvement of Quality of Service*[19] and the Commission *Notice on the Application of the Competition Rules to the Postal Sector*[20]. The Directive was adopted on 1 December 1997 and entered into force on 10 February 1998[1]. The Notice was adopted by the Commission on 17 December 1997. These two measures should be seen as part of a single package, the Directive intended to liberalise access to certain postal activities in the Community and the Notice to ensure that it is understood how the competition rules impact upon the sector.

The Directive establishes common rules throughout the Community on six matters: the provision of a universal service; the extent of the permissible monopoly and the conditions governing the provision of non-monopolised services; tariff principles and transparency of accounts for universal service provision; the setting of quality standards for universal service provision; the harmonisation of technical standards; and the creation of independent national regulatory authorities. As regards the first two matters, the Directive establishes *minimum* standards as to the universal standards and *maximum* limits to the permissible monopoly. Member States are entitled to confer lesser, but not broader, monopoly rights than those set out in the Directive. Article 7(1) provides essentially that the services 'which may be reserved' (that is which may remain a monopoly) shall be 'the clearance, sorting, transport and delivery of items of domestic correspondence ... provided they weigh less than 350 grams'. In June 2001 the Commission published in the Official Journal its *Amended Proposal for a Directive to Amend Directive 97/96*[2], which would reduce the monopoly to letters weighing less than 50 grams.

(ii)   Application of EC competition law

(A)   THE *CORBEAU* CASE AND THE UNIVERSAL SERVICE OBLIGATION[2a].   There is general agreement among Member States that there are societal benefits in the maintenance of a universal postal service, that is to say a right of access to a minimum range of postal services, of a specified quality, which must be provided in all Member States at affordable prices for the benefit of all users, irrespective of their geographical location. People living in remote rural areas should have

---

17   Case C–320/91 *Corbeau* [1993] ECR I-2533, [1995] 4 CMLR 621: see below
18   COM(93)247.
19   Directive 97/67/EC, OJ [1998] L 15/14.
20   OJ [1998] C 39/2, [1998] 5 CMLR 108.
1   The Directive was implemented in the UK by *The Postal Services Regulations 1999* SI 1999/2107.
2   OJ [2000] C 180 E/27, [2001] 4 CMLR 16.
2a   See also Case C-340/99 *TNT Traco SpA v Poste Italiane SpA* (judgment of 17 May 2001).

access to these services on no less favourable terms than those living in major conurbations; there is an obvious benefit, in terms of social cohesion, if all members of society can communicate with one another through the postal system, no matter where they live. A complex policy issue is to determine whether, and if so how extensive, a legal monopoly needs to be granted to the undertaking charged with performing this universal service in order to enable it to perform its duties; this question turns in part on how costly the universal service obligation is to the undertaking that has to perform it. Clearly the maintenance of a universal service is likely to be expensive, and the relevant provider will need to be assured of sufficient profits to pay for it; competitors should not be able to 'pick the cherries' and earn profits from lucrative services, while leaving the unprofitable services to the undertaking charged with the universal service obligation.

These issues came before the ECJ in the *Corbeau* case[3]. Corbeau had been charged with infringing a Belgian criminal law which conferred a monopoly on the Régie des Postes to collect, carry and distribute post in Belgium. Corbeau offered local courier services, but not a basic postal service. The Belgian court sought the opinion of the ECJ on the compatibility of the monopoly conferred by Belgian law with Articles 82 and 86 of the Treaty. The task for the ECJ was to determine whether Belgium was in breach of Article 86(1) in maintaining in force a measure contrary to Article 82, or whether the rights conferred on Régie des Postes satisfied the terms of Article 86(2). This provision does permit a restriction of competition – or even the elimination of all competition – where this is necessary to enable an undertaking to carry on the task entrusted to it[4]. At paragraph 15 of its judgment the ECJ noted that it could not be disputed that Régie des Postes was entrusted with a service of general economic interest[5]; the question was the extent to which a restriction of competition was necessary to enable it to carry on that function[6]. The Court continued at paragraph 17:

'The starting point of such an examination must be the premise that the obligation on the part of the undertaking entrusted with that task to perform its services in conditions of economic equilibrium presupposes that it will be possible to offset less profitable sectors against the profitable sectors and hence justifies a restriction of competition from individual undertakings where the economically profitable sectors are concerned'.

In the following paragraph the ECJ notes that, in the absence of a monopoly, it would be possible for individual undertakings 'to concentrate on the economically profitable operations' (in other words, to 'cherry pick'). But the ECJ went on, at paragraph 19:

'However, the exclusion of competition is not justified as regards specific services dissociable from the service of general interest which meet special needs of economic operators and which call for certain additional services not offered by the traditional postal service, such as collection from the senders' address, greater speed or reliability of distribution or the possibility of changing the destination in the course of transit in so far as such specific services, by their nature and the conditions in which they are offered, such as the geographical area in which they are provided, do not compromise

3   See n 17 above.
4   See ch 6, pp 202-208.
5   *Corbeau*, at para 15.
6   Ibid, at para 16.

the economic equilibrium of the service of general economic interest performed by the holder of the exclusive right'.

At paragraph 20, the ECJ said that the application of the foregoing tests would be a task for the national court dealing with the case.

The importance of this delicately crafted judgment is clear: postal monopolies may be consistent with Community competition law, but subject to the important tests set out in paragraph 19. That paragraph makes clear that it is possible, as a matter of law, that a Member State may have conferred a monopoly that is wider than is legitimate for the purpose of maintaining the universal service, and that, where this is the case, the monopoly rights in question may be unenforceable. The first package of measures in the postal sector attempts on the one hand, in the Directive, to determine the permissible limits of the legal monopoly and on the other, in the Notice, to explain the circumstances in which a legitimate monopolist might nonetheless be found guilty of infringing the competition rules. The Commission has itself taken action to strike down monopolies that go beyond what is justifiable under the *Corbeau* judgment[7].

(B)   THE COMMISSION'S NOTICE ON COMPETITION IN THE POSTAL SECTOR[8].   This Notice sets out in some detail how the Commission expects to apply the competition rules in the postal sector. It is divided into nine parts. After a preface and a discussion of terminology, the Notice considers market definition in the postal sector. Part 3 considers the issue of cross-subsidisation in some detail; the position of public undertakings and the freedom to provide services are then looked at, followed by state measures and state aid. Part 8 discusses what are meant by services of general economic interest in Article 86(2) EC, and the Notice concludes with a commitment by the Commission to undertake a review of the application of the competition rules to this sector in due course.

(C)   CASES AND DECISIONS.   In *Spanish International Courier Services*[9] the Commission held that it was unlawful for Spain to reserve to the Spanish Post Office, which already had a monopoly of the basic postal service, the ancillary activity of international courier services. In practice the Spanish Post Office was unable to meet the demand for international courier services (for example it did not cover the whole territory of Spain, nor did it extend to all countries in the world), so that there was a limitation of supply and technical development in the sense of Article 82(2)(b) EC. A similar decision in *Dutch Express Delivery Services*[10] was annulled on appeal by the ECJ as the Commission had not followed the correct procedure in adopting its decision[11]. In *Deutsche Post AG*[12] the Commission imposed a fine of EUR 24m on Deutsche Post for offering loyalty rebates to customers of its business parcels service, and it also concluded that it was guilty of predatory pricing[13]. In *New Postal Services with a Guaranteed Day- or Time-Certain Delivery in Italy*[14] the Commission concluded that an

---

7   On the Commission's infringement proceedings, see below.
8   OJ [1998] C 39/2, [1998] 5 CMLR 108.
9   OJ [1990] L 233/19, [1991] 4 CMLR 560.
10   OJ [1990] L 10/47, [1990] 4 CMLR 947.
11   Cases C-48/90 & 66/90 *Netherlands v Commission* [1992] ECR I-565, [1993] 5 CMLR 316.
12   OJ [2001] L 125/27; see also Commission Press Release IP/01/1068 (25 July 2001) for details of a 'symbolic' fine of EUR 1000 on Deutsche Post for abusing its dominant position in relation to so-called A-B-A remail.
13   For discussion of the Commission's approach to predatory pricing in this case see ch 18, p 652.
14   OJ [2001] L 63/59; on appeal Case C-102/01 *Italy v Commission* (judgment pending).

Italian Decree excluding competition for a specific type of hybridised electronic mail service was contrary to Article 86(1) in conjunction with Article 82. In *Reims II*[15] the Commission granted individual exemption to an agreement between the postal operators of the EC as to the amount that one operator would pay to another when a letter posted in the former's country had to be delivered in the territory of the latter, so-called 'terminal dues'. A long-running battle between the Union Française de l'Express, La Poste of France and the Commission, in relation to international express mail, remains unresolved[16].

A number of concentrations have been notified to the Commission under the ECMR. In the first case, *TNT/Canada Post*[17], the establishment of a joint venture between TNT and five postal administrations for the purpose of offering worldwide international express delivery services was cleared, subject to the offering of commitments by the four European postal administrations concerned that they would not discriminate in favour of the joint venture (the Canadian Post Office was not asked to give such a commitment). Similar commitments have been offered in subsequent cases[18]. The Commission granted conditional clearance to a joint venture in *Post Office/TPG/SPPL*[19].

(B) UK law

The Postal Services Act 2000 established the Postal Services Commission and the regulatory framework for the postal sector. The Commission does not have concurrent powers to apply the Chapter I and Chapter II prohibitions in the Competition Act; the Director General of Fair Trading alone can exercise these powers. In June 2001 he decided that Consignia had not abused its dominant position in the postal services market by refusing to licence its Royal Mail trade mark to an operator in the market for consumer lifestyle surveys[20].

9.   GAS[1]

(A) EC law

(i) Legislation

The Council of Ministers has adopted three Directives in the gas sector. The first establishes a procedure to improve the transparency of prices for gas in the EC[2].

---

15 OJ [1999] L 275/17, [2000] 4 CMLR 704; see Reeves 'Terminal Problems in the Postal Sector' (2000) 21 ECLR 283; see also Cases C-147/97 and C-148/97 *Deutsche Post v GZS* [2000] 4 CMLR 838, dealing with the right of Deutsche Post to impose charges for cross-border mail prior to the agreement on terminal dues.
16 The latest judgment in this dispute was handed down by the CFI in Case T-77/95 *Union Française de l'Express v Commission* [2001] 4 CMLR 1210.
17 Case No IV/M.102.
18 See eg Case No IV/M.787 *PTT Post/TNT-GD Net* Case No IV/M.1168 *DHL/Deutsche Post*.
19 Case No COMP/M.1915.
20 See *Consignia/Postal Preference Service Ltd* (15 June 2001), available at http://www.oft.gov.uk/html/comp-act/case_register/consignia.html
1 See further Weitzman and Charlton in ch 6 of Div IX of *Butterworths Competition Law* (eds Freeman and Whish); Faull and Nikpay *The EC Law of Competition* (Oxford University Press, 1999), paras 10.201-10.225; *Bellamy and Child*, ch 16, Part 4; see also the Commission's XXXth *Annual Report on Competition Policy* (2000), points 122-136.
2 Council Directive 90/377/EEC OJ [1990] L 185/16.

The second Directive requires Member States to take steps to ensure the possibility of transit of gas between Member States[3]. The third Directive establishes common rules for the storage, transmission and distribution of natural gas[4].

(ii)   Application of EC competition law

The Commission gave its approval in 1995 to a joint venture established by nine gas companies to construct and operate a gas interconnector between the UK and Belgium[5]. In 1996 it approved a long-term take-or-pay agreement for the supply of natural gas from Algeria to Portugal in *Transgás/Turbogás*[6] and the arrangements for use of the gas transport network in the UK in *British Gas Network Code*[7].

(B)   UK law

The Gas Act 1986 established a regulatory régime for the gas sector. Section 1 of the Act created the post of Director General of Gas Supply, who headed the former Office of Gas Supply (OFGAS). The powers of the Director General of Gas Supply were transferred to the Gas and Electricity Markets Authority by the Utilities Act 2000. The Gas and Electricity Markets Authority has concurrent powers with the Director General of Fair Trading to apply the Chapter I and Chapter II prohibitions in the Competition Act 1998. A *Guideline* has been adopted under the Act, *Competition Act 1998: The Application in the Energy Sector*[8].

10.   ELECTRICITY[9]

(A)   EC law

(i)   Legislation

The Council of Ministers has adopted three Directives in the electricity sector. The first establishes a procedure to improve the transparency of prices for electricity

---

3   Council Directive 91/296/EEC OJ [1991] L 147/37, as amended by Council Directive 95/49/EC, OJ [1995] L 233/86.
4   Council Directive 98/30/EC, OJ [1998] L 204/1, as amended by Corrigendum OJ [1998] L 245/43.
5   See the Commission's XXVth *Annual Report on Competition Policy* (1995), point 82.
6   See the Commission's XXVIth *Annual Report on Competition Policy* (1996), p 135.
7   See the Commission's XXVIth *Annual Report on Competition Policy* (1996), pp 136-137.
8   OFT 428.
9   See further Marks and Eccles in ch 7 of Div IX of *Butterworths Competition Law* (eds Freeman and Whish); Hancher *EC Electricity Law* (Chancery Law Publishing, 1992); Pfrang *Towards Liberalisation of the European Electricity Markets* (Peter Lang, 1999); Faull and Nikpay *The EC Law of Competition* (Oxford University Press, 1999), paras 10.167-10.200; *Bellamy and Child* ch 16, Part 2; see also the Commission's XXVIIIth *Annual Report on Competition Policy* (1998), points 121-125; XXIXth *Annual Report on Competition Policy* (1999), points 120-122; and the XXXth *Annual Report on Competition Policy* (2000), point 137.

in the EC[10]. The second Directive requires Member States to take steps to ensure the possibility of transit of electricity between Member States[11]. The third Directive establishes common rules for the internal market in electricity[12].

(ii) Application of EC competition law

The Commission has investigated a number of agreements in the electricity sector, several of which have been cleared, some of which received individual exemptions and some of which were dealt with by comfort letter. The privatisation of the electricity industry in Great Britain led to an individual exemption in *Scottish Nuclear, Nuclear Energy Agreement*[13] and to two notices in the Official Journal dealing with numerous agreements[14]. In *Northern Irish Electricity*[15] the Commission proposed to take no action as there was no trade between Northern Ireland and any other Member State of the EC. A joint venture to develop independent generators of electricity was the subject of a favourable notice in the Official Journal in 1992[16]. In *IJsselcentrale*[17] the Commission held that an agreement between all the generators of electricity in the Netherlands and a joint subsidiary that only the latter could import and export electricity to and from that country entailed a restriction of competition that infringed Article 81(1). In *REN/Turbogás*[18] and in *ISAB Energy*[19] the Commission approved long-term agreements for the supply of electricity. The Commission granted conditional clearances to concentrations in the electricity industry following Phase II investigations in *VEBA/Viag*[20] and in *EDF/EnBW*[1].

(B) UK law

The Electricity Act 1989 established a regulatory régime for the electricity sector. The powers of the Director General of Electricity Supply have been transferred by the Utilities Act 2000 to the Gas and Electricity Markets Authority, which has concurrent powers to apply the Competition Act 1998 with the Director General of Fair Trading[2]. There is a *Guideline* on the application of the Act to the energy sector[3], and a draft *Guideline* on its application in Northern Ireland[4].

10 Council Directive 90/377/EEC, OJ [1990] L 185/16.
11 Council Directive 90/547/EEC, OJ [1990] L 313/30.
12 Council Directive 96/92/EC, OJ [1997] L 27/20.
13 OJ [1991] L 178/31.
14 See OJ [1990] C 191/9 (dealing with ten notifications) and OJ [1990] C 245/9 (dealing with eight notifications).
15 OJ [1992] C 92/5.
16 OJ [1992] C 92/4.
17 OJ [1991] L 28/32, [1992] 5 CMLR 154; the decision was (eventually) partly annulled on appeal in Case T-16/91 RV *Rendo v Commission* [1996] ECR II-1827, [1997] 4 CMLR 453.
18 OJ [1996] C 118/7, [1996] 4 CMLR 881.
19 OJ [1996] C 138/3, [1996] 4 CMLR 889.
20 Case No COMP/M.1673.
1   Case No COMP/M.1853.
2   See p 876 above.
3   OFT 428.
4   OFT 437.

11. WATER[5]

The Water Act 1989 (now the Water Industry Act 1991) established the office of Director General of Water Supply. The Act empowered the Director General to establish the Office of Water Supply (OFWAT). The Director General of Water Supply has concurrent powers to apply the Chapter I and Chapter II prohibitions in the Competition Act 1998. A *Guideline* has been adopted under the Act, *Competition Act 1998: Application in the Water and Sewerage Sectors*[6]. There are special rules requiring mergers between water companies to be referred to the Competition Commission[7].

---

5   See further Hurdley and Price in ch 5 of Div IX of *Butterworths Competition Law* (eds Freeman and Whish).
6   OFT 422.
7   See ch 22, pp 850-851.

Bibliography

There is a considerable body of literature on competition law. The following books are particularly recommended.

UK and EC competition law combined

Butterworths Competition Law (editors Freeman and Whish)

Furse *Competition Law of the UK and EC* (Blackstone Press Limited, 2nd edn, 2000)

Green and Robertson *Commercial Agreements and Competition Law* (Kluwer Law International, 2nd edn, 1997)

Livingstone *Competition Law and Practice* (Pearson Professional, 1995)

Rodger and MacCulloch *Competition Law and Policy* (Cavendish Publishing Ltd, 2nd edn, 2001)

Smith *Competition Law: Enforcement and Procedure* (Butterworths, 2001)

Taylor *EC and UK Competition Law and Compliance* (Sweet and Maxwell, 1999)

EC competition law

Bellamy and Child *European Community Law of Competition* (Sweet and Maxwell, 5th edn, 2001, ed Roth)

Bishop and Walker *The Economics of EC Competition Law: Concepts, Application and Measurement* (Sweet and Maxwell, 1999)

Buendia Sierra *Exclusive Rights and State Monopolies under EC Law* (Oxford University Press, 1999)

Cini and McGowan *Competition Policy in the European Union* (Macmillan, 1998)

Faull and Nikpay *The EC Law of Competition* (Oxford University Press, 1999)

Garzaniti *Telecommunications, Broadcasting and the Internet: EU Competition Law and Regulation* (Sweet and Maxwell, 2000)

D Goyder *EC Competition Law* (Oxford University Press, 3rd edn, 1998)

J Goyder *EU Distribution Law* (Palladian Law Publishing, 3rd edn, 2000)

Jones and van der Woude *EC Competition Law Handbook* (Sweet & Maxwell, 1999/2000 edition)

Jones and Sufrin *EC Competition Law: Text, Cases and Materials* (Oxford University Press, 2001)

Kerse *EC Antitrust Procedure* (Sweet and Maxwell, 4th edn, 1998)

Korah *An Introductory Guide to EC Competition Law and Practice* (Hart Publishing, 7th edn, 2000)

Korah *Cases and Materials on EC Competition Law* (Hart Publishing, 1997; second edition due September 2001)

Korah *Vertical Agreements: Distribution under the EC Competition Rules* (Hart Publishing, 2001)

Lane *EC Competition Law* (Longman, 2000)

Larouche *Competition Law and Regulation in European Telecommunications* (Hart Publishing, 2000)

Lugard *Vertical Restraints under EC Competition Law* (Hart Publishing, 2001)

Neven, Papandropoulos and Seabright *Trawling for Minnows: European Competition Policy and Agreements Between Firms* (CEPR, 1998)

Ortiz Blanco and van Houtte *EC Competition Law in the Transport Sector* (Oxford University Press, 1996)

Ortiz Blanco *EC Competition Procedure* (Oxford University Press, 1996)

Ritter, Braun and Rawlinson *European Competition Law: A Practitioner's Guide* (Kluwer Law International, 2nd edn, 2000)

Sauter *Competition Law and Industrial Policy in the EU* (Clarendon Press Oxford, 1997)

Singleton *EC Competition Law and Telecommunications* (Monitor Press, 2nd edn, 1999)

Taylor *Vertical Agreements: The New Regulation in Context* (Monitor Press, 2000)

Van Bael and Bellis *Competition Law of the European Community* (CCH Europe, 3rd edn, 1994)

Waelbroeck and Frignani *European Competition Law* (Transnational Publishers Inc, 1999)

Wesseling *The Modernisation of EC Antitrust Law* (Hart Publishing, 2000)

Mergers and concentrations

Camesasca *European Merger Control: Getting the Efficiencies Rights* (Intersentia – Hart, 2000)

Cook and Kerse *EC Merger Control* (Sweet and Maxwell, 3rd edn, 2000)

Finbow and Parr *UK Merger Control: Law and Practice* (Sweet and Maxwell, 1995)

Hawk and Huser *European Community Merger Control: A Practitioner's Guide* (Kluwer Law International, 1996)

Levy 'The Control of Concentrations between Undertakings' in *Competition Law of the European Community* (Matthew Bender, 2000)

Neven, Nuttall and Seabright *Merger in Daylight: the Economics and Politics of European Merger Control* (CEPR, 1993)

Rowley and Baker *Merger Control: The International Regulation of Mergers and Joint Ventures* (Sweet & Maxwell, 3rd edn, 2000)

Intellectual property

Anderman *EC Competition Law and Intellectual Property Rights: The Regulation of Innovation* (Clarendon Press Oxford, 1998)

Cornish *Intellectual Property: Patents, Copyright, Trade Marks and Allied Rights* (Sweet and Maxwell, 4th edn, 1999)

Kinsella *EU Technology Licensing* (Palladian Law Publishing Ltd, 1998)

Korah *Technology Transfer Agreements and the EC Competition Rules* (Clarendon Press Oxford, 1996)

UK Competition Act 1998

Coleman and Grenfell *The Competition Act 1998* (Oxford University Press, 1999)

Flynn and Stratford *Competition: Understanding the 1998 Act* (Palladian Law Publishing, 1999)

Frazer and Hornsby *The Competition Act 1998: a Practical Guide* (Jordans, 1999)

Freeman and Whish *A Guide to the Competition Act 1998* (Butterworths, 1999)

Kellaway and Rose *Tolley's Competition Act 1998: A Practical Guide* (Tolley's, 1999)

Latham *A Practitioner's Guide to the Competition Act 1998* (Sweet and Maxwell, 2000)

Livingstone *The Competition Act 1998: A Practical Guide* (Sweet and Maxwell, 2001)

Singleton *Blackstone's Guide to the Competition Act 1998* (Blackstone Press, 1999)

SJ Berwin and Co *Competition Law of the UK* (Juris Publishing, Inc, 2000)

Willis *The Competition Act 1998: A Guide for Businesses* (Monitor Press Ltd, 2nd edn, 2000)

The UK Competition Act: A New Era for UK Competition Law (Hart Publishing, 2000, eds Rodger and MacCulloch)

Economics

Black *Oxford Dictionary of Economics* (Oxford University Press, 1997)

Scherer and Ross *Industrial Market Structure and Economic Performance* (Houghton Mifflin, 3rd edn, 1990)

Tirole *The Theory of Industrial Organization* (MIT Press, 1988)

Miscellaneous

Amato *Antitrust and the Bounds of Power: The Dilemma of Liberal Democracy in the History of the Market* (Hart Publishing, 1997)

Bork *The Antitrust Paradox* (Basic Books, 1995)

Gerber *Law and Competition in Twentieth Century Europe* (Oxford University Press, 1998)

Jones *Private Enforcement of Antitrust Law in the EU, UK and USA* (Oxford University Press, 1999)

Wilks *In the Public Interest: Competition Policy and the Monopolies and Mergers Commission* (Manchester University Press, 1999)

Statutes, treaties, Community Regulations etc

Butterworths Competition Law Handbook (Butterworths, 7th edn, 2001)

Middleton *Statutes on Competition Law* (Blackstones, 2000)

Important websites

Competition Commission	http://www.competition-commission.gov.uk/
Department of Justice	http://www.usdoj.gov
DTI Competition Policy Division	http://wwws.dti.gov.uk/cacp/cp/default.htm
European Commission, DG COMP	http://europa.eu.int/comm/competition/
European Court of Justice	http://www.curia.eu.int
Federal Trade Commission	http://www/ftc/gov
Office of Fair Trading	http//www.open.gov.uk/oft/ofthome/htm

Index